International Handbook of Political Science

International Handbook of Political Science

Edited by William G. Andrews

GREENWOOD PRESS
WESTPORT, CONNECTICUT • LONDON, ENGLAND

Library of Congress Cataloging in Publication Data
Main entry under title:

International handbook of political science.

   Bibliography: p.
   Includes index.
   1. Political science. 2. Political science—Research.
3. Political science—Study and teaching (Higher)
I. Andrews, William George, 1930-   .
JA71.I57   320′.09045   81-6245
ISBN 0-313-22889-2 (lib. bdg.)   AACR2

Copyright © 1982 by William G. Andrews

All rights reserved. No portion of this book may be reproduced, by any process or technique, without the express written consent of the publisher.

Library of Congress Catalog Card Number: 81-6245
ISBN: 0-313-22889-2

First published in 1982

Greenwood Press
A division of Congressional Information Service, Inc.
88 Post Road West
Westport, Connecticut 06881

Printed in the United States of America

Distributed in the United Kingdom and Europe
by Aldwych Press, Ltd., London

10 9 8 7 6 5 4 3 2 1

TO MONIKA

CONTENTS

Tables and Figures ix

Preface xi

Introduction: Freaks, Rainbows, and Pots of Gold 1
 by William G. Andrews

Part I
International Political Science 7

1. Intellectual Development 9
   Karl W. Deutsch

2. Institutional Development 34
   John E. Trent

3. Position in the Social Sciences 47
   André Philippart

4. Developing Countries: Teaching Political Science 56
   Raul Bejar Navarro, Francisco Casanova Alvarez, and Lian Karp S.

Part II
Political Science in Individual Countries 63

5. Argentina 65
   Segundo V. Linares Quintana and Associates

6. Australia 74
   Colin Tatz and Graeme Starr

7. Austria 85
   Peter Gerlich, Emmerich Talos, and Karl Ucakar

8. Belgium 93
   André Philippart

9. Brazil 100
   Themistocles Brandão Cavalcanti, assisted by Lidice Aparecida Pontes Maduro

10. Canada 111
    Michael Stein and John E. Trent

11. Denmark 132
    Peter Nannestad and Øystein Gaasholt

12. Finland 144
    Erik Allardt

13. France 154
    Pierre Favre

14. Germany, Federal Republic of 169
    Klaus von Beyme

15. German Democratic Republic 177
    Karl-Heinz Röder and Jörg Franke

16. Iceland 185
    Ólafur Ragnar Grimsson

17. India 194
    Iqbal Narain and P. C. Mathur

18. Japan 207
    Takashi Inoguchi

19. Korea 219
    Ke Soo Kim

20. The Netherlands 227
    Andries Hoogerwerf

21. New Zealand 246
    Ray Goldstein and John Halligan

22. Norway 256
    Stein Kuhnle

23. Pakistan 275
    A. Saleem Khan

24. Poland 291
    Kazimierz Opałek

25. Sweden
    Research, *Olof Ruin* — 299
    Teaching and Associational Activities, *Nils Elvander* — 320

26. Switzerland — 327
    Monica Wemegah with the collaboration of Daniel Frei

27. Union of Soviet Socialist Republics
    Socialist Political Science, *V. E. Chirkin* — 336
    Tasks of Social Science Departments, *V. Eliutin* — 340
    The Soviet Political Science Association, *William Smirnov* — 351

28. United Kingdom — 355
    Jack Hayward

29. United States of America — 364
    Evron M. Kirkpatrick and William G. Andrews

30. Yugoslavia — 383
    Adolf Bibič

Appendixes

APPENDIX 1 — 413
Political Science in Selected Countries

APPENDIX 2 — 414
International Political Science Association Congresses

APPENDIX 3 — 416
International Political Science Association Financial Reports, 1955–1980

APPENDIX 4 — 417
General Secretaries of the International Political Science Association

APPENDIX 5 — 418
Information on International Political Science Associations

Bibliography of Works on Political Science in Countries Not Included in This Volume — 426

Index — 431

Contributors — 463

TABLES AND FIGURES

TABLES

International Political Science Association

2.1. Participation in Round Tables and Seminars Organized or Sponsored by the IPSA 1950-1977 — 37

2.2. Representation in the Governing Organs of the IPSA 1952-1980 — 38

2.3. Location of Executive Committee Meetings and World Congresses: IPSA 1949-1977 — 38

2.4. World Congress Participation: IPSA 1950-1982 — 39

2.5. Participation in the IPSA Academic Meetings and Membership by World Groups 1953-1977 — 39

Australia

6.1. Political Science Departments in Universities and Colleges — 77

6.2. Political Scientists in University Political Science, Politics and Government Departments — 77

6.3. Teachers of Political Science: Sources of Qualification — 78

6.4. Students Enrolled in University Political Science Courses — 78

6.5. Professional Interests of Members of the Australasian Political Science Association — 82

Germany, Federal Republic of

14.1. Subjects Taught in German Universities — 172

Iceland

16.1. Social Science Graduates from the University of Iceland: 1973-1976 — 187

Korea

19.1. Korean Journals — 226

The Netherlands

20.1. Positions Held by Dutch Political Science Graduates — 238

Norway

22.1. Number of Graduates in Political Science 1950-1975, by Sex — 257

22.2. Magazine Articles and Candidates' Political Theses by Field 1960-1975 — 258

Sweden

25.1. Undergraduate Students at Swedish Universities and Branches 1963-1975: First-Time Registration for First-Term Studies in Political Science — 321

25.2. Department Staffs in Political Science at Swedish Universities 1960-1975 — 322

25.3. Graduate Students at Swedish Universities 1963-1975 — 322

25.4. Graduate Examination in Political Science 1960-1975 — 323

25.5. Topics of Dissertations in Political Science 1950-1973: Divided into Examination Categories — 323

25.6. Main Occupations of Graduated Political Scientists Divided into Time Periods of Examination 1950-1973 — 324

25.7. Occupations of Graduated Political Scientists Divided into Type of Examination — 325

FIGURES

10.1. Canada — 112

26.1. Switzerland — 332

PREFACE

This book has been designed to be a professional reference work. Its original plan called for chapters on the development of political science since 1945 in each of as many different countries as possible. Also, one part of the volume was reserved for discussions of international political science.

A review of existing literature disclosed that no similar book had been published. The closest counterpart was the UNESCO volume *Contemporary Political Science,* of 1950, issued when international political science was in its infancy. An international survey of the current discipline seemed long overdue.

Using the directories of national political science associations published in *Participation* of the International Political Science Association (IPSA) and *PS* of the American Political Science Association, the editor invited leading political scientists in each country that had an organized discipline to contribute a chapter. The response was gratifying. Thirty-four countries appeared on the original list. Twenty-seven are represented by chapters in this book. Despite repeated attempts, no authors could be found to write chapters on the political science of several countries. In three cases (India, Soviet Union, Sweden) suitable existing studies were located and have been included. In other cases, no appropriate substitutions were available and some countries with important political science professions had to be omitted. Although the coverage attained 80 percent of the goal, the gaps are disappointing. In addition to the chapters on individual countries, the completed book includes four chapters on international political science, one of them written by three political scientists from a country not represented in Part 2.

In an effort to produce greater uniformity among the chapters and, therefore, to facilitate comparisons, a model outline was proposed to the authors. However, the authors were encouraged to make whatever adjustments might seem appropriate to reflect the character of the political science profession in their respective countries. The main points on the outline were:

I. Introduction

II. The state of political science in 1945

III. The evolution of political science in 1945
  A. The intellectual structure of the discipline
  B. The teaching of political science
  C. Research in political science
  D. Associational activities
  E. Political science and the world of politics

IV. The present state and future prospects of political science

Also, each author was asked to provide a short bibliography.

The authors' contributions were edited for style and to ensure maximum conformity to the common outline. The authors' preferences on substance were carefully respected. The editor did not attempt to overrule the authors in deciding what material was appropriate for inclusion in each section of the outline, because this book is supposed to *reflect* the political science of the various countries as well as *describe* it. Each chapter should provide an understanding of how political science in that country is perceived by one or more of its own practitioners.

A careful reading of the following pages will make clear that the level of development of political science throughout the world remains uneven, indeed, rudimentary in some countries. This may be partly the result of poor communications among the professions of the various countries. The International Political Science Association has accomplished much in improving that communication, but much remains to be done. Perhaps this volume will assist that effort in some small way.

This project was proposed by Greenwood Press. I am

grateful for the encouragement and patience of Marilyn Brownstein, Cynthia Harris, and Anne Kugielsky. Also, Professor John E. Trent, General Secretary of IPSA, offered welcome support and help. Victor Rojas, Luis Oyarzun, and Paula Lieberman gave valuable assistance with translations into English. Shirley Schuff, Patricia Felter, Janice Freeman, and Fely Cieza bore the main burden of the secretarial tasks required by a project whose collaborators were so widely dispersed. However, I owe my greatest debt to the authors of this book who found time in their busy schedules to make contributions that might not have been obtainable otherwise, especially as they agreed that the authors' share of the royalties be donated to the International Political Science Association. Finally, I must add that, without the pleasant distractions of my wife, Monika, this book would have been finished much sooner.

William G. Andrews

Brockport, New York

International Handbook of Political Science

Introduction: Freaks, Rainbows, and Pots of Gold

WILLIAM G. ANDREWS

"The term 'political science' is greatly in need of definition."

So reads the first sentence of the first issue of the first professional political science journal in 1886.[1]

What is Political Science?

So reads the 1888 title of the inaugural lecture by W. J. Ashley, Canada's first full-time professional political scientist.[2]

The birth pangs of a new discipline?

Perhaps, but evidence from the following chapters and elsewhere suggests that the initial questions have not yet been answered. Political science is unusual—unique?—among academic disciplines in suffering the affliction of a chronic identity crisis. What other field has had such difficulty defining its character, purposes, even language, as has political science? Though this problem may lie in the consciousness of most political scientists, it comes to the forefront only rarely. Yet, the chapters that follow show that such uncertainty is one of the most widespread and pervasive features of contemporary political science. Perhaps this is most true of countries where political scientists claim most insistently to have set that issue at rest, for each of them has made different conclusive findings. The careful reader is led inevitably to the conclusion that the discipline is so variegated and disparate internationally that its character and identity cannot be defined simply and easily—if at all. To see that more clearly, it may be helpful to consider the symptoms, causes, and prognosis of that condition.

Symptoms

The best evidence that political science continues to suffer from its congenital ailment is the persisting complaints of its practitioners. Political science is "a discipline in search of its identity," says one of the profession's stars in the leading encyclopedia article on the topic.[3] "Its definition is as open to dispute as are its methods and fields," says one of Europe's leading political scientists in another encyclopedia.[4] Another European opens a book-length essay on the discipline with the very question that Professor Ashley had posed 84 years earlier.[5] One president of the American Political Science Association proclaimed the arrival of the postbehavioral era,[6] yet one of his successors called the discipline prebehavioral.[7]

The pages of the present volume offer ample evidence of the continuing perplexity over the identity of political science. One author comments that "we are not a discipline but a problem-area parasitic upon other disciplines."[8] Another cites an official governmental report declaring that "objections to a new, independent political science are justified."[9] Almost every chapter deals with this identity crisis in one way or another, directly or indirectly.

This confusion extends even to the name of the discipline. "Political science" has been the most widely accepted designation from the outset. Also, the largest associations—American and international—use that term in their names. So did UNESCO in its important 1948 conference on the discipline.[10]

However, neither "political science" nor any other designation has been adopted universally, or even by consensus, throughout the discipline. The first four academic departments with which the author was associated bore the name "government." Among American Ivy League universities, for example, Harvard and Cornell say "government," Princeton uses "politics," and Columbia had, until recently, "public law and government."

The pages below provide many other examples. The association and official journal of the discipline in the United Kingdom engage in "political studies" and their representative in this volume calls his colleagues "politists." His French counterparts belong to a "political science" association, but their official research arm is a foundation of "political sciences" and most of them teach in institutes of "political studies." Australians debate "over what to call the beast: Political Science, Politics, or Government." Even the coauthors of the chapter on Australia in this volume disagree between themselves.[11]

Many other names appear in the various chapters. They include politology, theory of politics, public law, politicological studies, state science (*Staatswissenschaft*), politicology, political and international relations, social administration (or management), science of politics, science of the state, theory of state and law, science of politics, science of constitutional law. The Soviet Union has an academic "political science" association that hosted the 1979 Congress of the International Political Science Association and provided 260 of its participants, the largest national delegation.[12] Yet, apparently none of them teaches political science.[13] This rich array of names is not the result of idle academic minds spinning pointlessly but, rather, the reflection of the basic character of the discipline.

Causes

The causes of the confusion are nearly as numerous and varied as their effects. They lie in the origins of the discipline, its youth, its manner of development, its image in society, its relationship to cultures, and its voracious eclecticism. Some of those causes are interrelated and indistinctly separate, yet all are identifiable and warrant discussion.

Multiple paternity. The roots of political science internationally lie deep in a variety of soils. The discipline has sprung from law and history more often than from any other sources. However, many other academic fields have substantial claims to paternity. For instance, the founders of American political science at Johns Hopkins and Columbia had been trained in German state science (*Staatswissenschaft*). The corresponding disciplines in the Soviet Union, Poland, East Germany, and Yugoslavia are products of Marxist-Leninist ideology. Marxism has produced important currents in the political science of certain other countries as well: Denmark, France, West Germany, and the United States. Many other disciplinary antecedents are mentioned in the following chapters. They include political law, political economy, philosophy, theology, public administration, economics, commerce, legal studies or science, administrative science, fiscal science, sociology, geography, psychology (especially social), linguistics, statistics, journalism, foreign language study, theory of the state, rhetoric, and constitutional law.

Despite its length, this list is almost certainly incomplete. It enumerates the derivations of major currents in the discipline. However, it surely omits other disciplines that have been the source of inspiration—even the disciplines of origin—for many individual political scientists. Perhaps the only country where political science did not grow, at least largely, out of other academic disciplines is Iceland, where political science arrived intact from abroad like "the landing of the first astronauts on the moon."[14] Everywhere else, political science "plucks the feathers from other disciplines and adorns itself with them."[15] It should not be surprising that, with such a background, political science itself might wonder about the identity of the creature beneath all the finery.

Youth. The chronic identity crisis of the discipline may be accentuated by youthfulness. Of course, politics has been studied as long as it has been practised and as long as men have been scholars. Indeed, the ancient Greeks held the study of politics in especially high regard and gave it a prominent and important place in their range of interests. Furthermore, politics has drawn the attention of great thinkers throughout history, under the cover of other disciplines, such as philosophy.

However, political science emerged late as a modern academic discipline. It may be called the last of the social sciences, perhaps the last of the liberal arts. A key indicator of the emergence of a modern academic discipline is the founding of its professional society in the United States. By that measure, geography appeared in 1852, history in 1884, economics in 1885, psychology in 1892, and anthropology in 1902. Sociologists were the principal founders of the American Social Science Association in 1865 but waited until 1906 to form the American Sociological Association. The American Political Science Association was founded in 1903.

Political science emerged even more slowly elsewhere. Only five other national associations existed when the International Political Science Association was formed under UNESCO auspices in 1950. The oldest of them, in Canada, was twenty-three years younger than the APSA.[16] Thus, political science did not become a significant international discipline until the present generation. If it has identity problems, they may be those typical of adolescence.

Retarded Development. International political science has not really overcome the effects of its tardy birth. Thirty years after the founding of the International Political Science Association, the discipline continues to lead a spotty global existence. Only thirty-nine national associations belong to the IPSA (compared to 151 members of the UN) and some of them appear to exist on paper only.[17] All of Africa forms a single regional association, Morocco being the only African country with its own association. Only three South American countries and none in Central America or the Caribbean are IPSA members. China (both mainland and Taiwan), Afghanistan, Iran, and all of Southeast Asia are absent. The Middle East has only Turkey, Israel, and Lebanon. Only in Europe (except Eire, Luxemburg, and Portugal)[18] and North America does the coverage approach comprehensiveness. Even so, some of the political science associations of Eastern Europe are suspiciously artificial.

The distribution of political scientists is still more uneven than that of their associations. The United States, with 15,000 or 16,000 political scientists, has 75 or 80 percent of the world's supply. No other country approaches 1,000 and only two or three have more than 500. All of Western Europe has fewer than 2,500, scattered among seventeen countries.[19] Even that distribution is a very recent phenomenon. Ten years ago, the imbalance was still greater.

University teaching of political science developed almost as late and spottily as did the professional organization and research. For the most part, the countries included in this volume have the most fully developed political science professions. Yet, in more than half of them, political science was not taught as a university program until after World War II. In some cases, the discipline arrived on American or Soviet bayonets.

The tardy emergence of political science received official notice when UNESCO undertook a review of the social sciences soon after World War II. It selected political science for its first study, largely because it saw a "need to raise political science as quickly as possible to the same level as other studies," especially in the social sciences, and because "the development of political science has been uneven in different parts of the world."[20] That assessment led to a special UNESCO conference in September 1948 and to the production of a set of papers of somewhat the same type as the chapters in this volume. They assessed the state of political science in twenty-eight different countries.[21] That scholars in at least twenty-eight countries could report on the status of the discipline in them in 1950 and that thirty years later IPSA would have only thirty-nine national association members suggests the slow pace of the development of political science.

That situation is not likely to change very substantially. The following studies indicate that political science reached a peak in enrollments in the early 1970s in most countries and has stabilized or declined since then. This seems to coincide with the worldwide economic slowdown, the end of the post–World War II baby-boom effects, and the accompanying stagnation in the growth of higher education. Conditions are not ripe, then, for political science to overcome its spottiness and retardation. That, in turn, may delay further the emergence of a clear sense of identity and purpose.

Image. Those internal problems are reflected and exacerbated by certain widespread attitudes toward political science in the general public, in other parts of the academic profession, and among practical politicians. Perhaps no other academic discipline has had such difficulty winning acceptance by those groups. What chemist, for instance, or historian or philosopher is ever asked if those disciplines *really* exist? Yet, what political scientist has escaped similar questions?

When posed by a layman, the question may reflect an attitude that lumps politics together with war and sex as one of those activities that are performed better by amateurs than professionals. For instance, few citizens will defer to the judgment of professional political scientists in evaluating incumbent politicians. Most practicing politicians share that skepticism. They tend to be among the most practical of people and have little use for the theorizing that they associate with political science. In any case, they usually see politics as much more art than science. They tend to share the opinion of that preeminently practical theorist, Edmund Burke, that "no reasonable man ever did govern himself by abstracts and universals."[22] Yet, abstracts and universals are the lifeblood of academic disciplines. Political scientists as technical experts have become somewhat more marketable in the world of practical politics in recent years, but they remain outsiders, for the most part. Occasionally, a Richard Crossman or Henry Kissinger crosses the Great Divide, but they seem more like alien intruders than pioneers.

The suspicion of our academic neighbors is the other side of the same coin. They tend to see politics as a subject too unscientific and unscholarly—too few abstracts and universals—for academic legitimacy. They suspect that the study of politics and government should be confined to the world of journalism and smoke-filled rooms. That attitude may not always be wholly devoid of selfish interest. After all, political science can accede to its place in the academic firmament only by overlapping or ingesting a bit of history here, a bit of philosophy there, and so forth. Few academic disciplines acquiesce willing to being overlaid or devoured. Some leading political scientists bear water to that mill. One of them tells his students: "Even if we were to drop the whole profession ... of political scientists into the ocean, ... the study of politics would go on."[23]

In the present condition of the discipline, political scientists are bound to lose both sides of the argument. The profession is not sufficiently "practical" to succeed in politics, though its brains may be picked for technical expertise by those who are politicians. Nor is it "pure" enough to pass unchallenged as a legitimate field of academic inquiry. Except that the enormous expansion of higher education after World War II eased the pressures of academic jealousy, political science might still be fighting to get through the gates.

Culture-bound. The academic criticism acquires a measure of credence from examination of the chapters that follow. Nothing emerges so strikingly from those studies as the sensitivity of political science to its national and cultural environments. So readily does it assume the coloration of its surroundings that it might be nicknamed the "chameleon science." Can a discipline that varies so greatly, depending on its location, be taken seriously as a science?

The classification of national political science professions might well follow the same terms as are used to classify the countries themselves. Almost invariably, the least developed countries in economic terms have the least developed political science disciplines. Most of them "do not have enough political science to write about" and do not appear in this volume. Generally speaking, those Third World countries that are represented exhibit rather rudimentary political science development. Then, too, the East–West split is clearly evident in political science. The East is Marxist-Leninist; the West is pluralist. On each side of that equation, further distinctions are reflected also. For instance, the different political structures of the Soviet Union and Yugoslavia have affected the character of political science in the two countries.

Equally suggestive is the way political science currents follow the flow of culture, language, and ethnicity. Canadian political science is split organizationally, in intellectual approach, and in general character along the boundary between Quebec and Ontario. Similar phenomena appear in Belgium and Switzerland. The historic bonds of Austria and Finland with Germany have influenced their political science professions. The countries where American military forces were most evident after World War II (West Germany, Japan, Korea) are among those with the most "Americanized" political science. Islamic Pakistan's political science is deeply touched by that religious presence. The hand of law is heavier on political science in countries where the political branches of government deal with codified legal systems than in common-law countries like Great Britain and the United States. Swedish political science shows the marks of that country's historical political neutrality.

In short, to a remarkable extent, political science follows the flag, the bloodlines, and the dictionary.

The Rainbow Science. All the factors discussed above—and others—have produced a highly eclectic discipline. The multiple paternity has spawned in streams of influence from other disciplines. In youthful exuberance, political science feeds its ravenous appetite wherever intellectual sustenance can be found. Its uneven development leaves the great variety of approaches unintegrated. The unresolved dilemma of practicality and theory pulls it in both directions. The force of cultural impact produces a myriad of centrifugal effects.

The impact of those factors is reinforced by the character of the subject matter of political science. It may be studied by a wide variety of investigative methods, most of which have been taken from older disciplines. An arm from psychology, a leg from history, an ear from sociology, hair from philosophy.... Some unkind soul might allege that the product of such an operation would be a freak or monster—political science: The *Freak Science* or the *Monster Science*. Alternatively, it may be compared to a Rube Goldberg invention: a contraption assembled from disparate parts and operating in a needlessly complicated manner to perform simple tasks.

Put another way, almost every political scientist and almost every work (or portion thereof) in political science may be identified with another discipline on the basis of the method of inquiry used.

> I use behavioral theory, color me psychologist.
>
> I use the written record of mankind, color me historian.
>
> I examine social context, color me sociologist.
>
> I examine cultural context, color me anthropologist.
>
> I examine the terrestrial context, color me geographer.
>
> I rely on ethnic factors, color me ethnologist.
>
> I count, color me statistician.
>
> "Man does not live by bread alone," color me philosopher.
>
> "Man does live by bread alone," color me economist.
>
> "Man lives by modes of production," color me Marxist.
>
> I combine all these approaches and many others, color me the Rainbow Science.

All roads lead to political science. One of the most striking impressions generated by the studies in this volume is that our sister disciplines have used those roads to bring an immensely rich intellectual cargo to political science. This is why, to paraphrase André Philippart, political science is a crossroads discipline *and* a synthetic discipline *and* a residual discipline.[24] This is what makes it interdisciplinary. This is why it has become the Rainbow

Science. In short, then, the very qualities that produce such perplexity over the identity of political science contribute much to its richness and strength.

Cures

Much of the cure, then, lies in recognizing that the problem of political science is also a large part of the solution. What seem to be difficulties in molding a cohesive discipline are, in fact, opportunities to enrich it. Of course, that is by no means the whole story.

ECPR. Another part of the story may lie in the kind of effort that has been made through the European Consortium for Political Research. The ECPR was formed in 1970 under the leadership of the late Stein Rokkan of Bergen, Norway, and was modeled somewhat on the Interuniversity Consortium for Political and Social Research at the University of Michigan.[25] Among Rokkan's early collaborators on this project were Jean Blondel of Essex, England; Jean Touchard and Serge Hurtig of Paris; Sir Norman Chester of Oxford; Rudolf Wildenmann of Mannheim, West Germany; and Hans Daalder of Leyden, the Netherlands. Financial assistance was provided by the Ford Foundation. By 1980, the nine founding institutions had become ninety-six, distributed as follows: Great Britain 25, West Germany 13, France 11, Netherlands 9, Italy 7, Belgium 5, Sweden 5, Switzerland 4, Denmark 4, Norway 4, Finland 3, Spain 3, Eire 2, Iceland 1.

The ECPR has contributed to the development of political science in Western Europe in a variety of ways. Most notable are its annual conferences, when some 300 political scientists join in twenty workshops on a broad range of topics. Also, it holds triennial congresses; organizes team research projects; sponsors summer institutes and doctoral seminars; and publishes monographs, the *European Journal of Political Research*, brochures, and a newsletter. According to Jean Blondel, executive director of the consortium, as a result of those efforts, "reciprocal understanding has developed to an astonishing extent and a veritable European community of political science is forming." He sees this community as a "counterweight to the mass of American universities" and believes that it "diminishes the risks of cultural dependence that are noted sometimes."

Somewhat similar, though less extensive in its activities, is the regional African Political Science Association. It publishes a newsletter and has held four biennial conferences. Perhaps the emergence of other regional organizations would foster the same sense of international political science community that the ECPR reports. Of course, the IPSA has been working toward such an end since its founding. Eventually, such efforts may help political science to overcome its weak sense of identity.

The Pot of Gold. Perhaps the most important part of the solution is recognition that the identity and character of political science are not formed by the methods it begs, borrows, or steals nor by the national cultural manifestations it displays. Neither its youth nor its retardation nor its split personality give political science its fundamental character.

None of these qualities gave rise to Aristotle's opinion that the study of politics was the "master science" or "sovereign science."[26] None inspired Jean Bodin to call it the "princess among sciences" or Abu Nasr al-Farabi to describe it as "the royal and political art assigned the task of directing Man to happiness."[27] To the extent that political science deserves those compliments, it has earned them, not by its methods—however rich they may be—but by the object of its attention.

Political science may be distinguished among academic disciplines, not only for its eclecticism, but also by its focus on power and on the political and governmental institutions and personnel that wield that power. Virtually all modern definitions of political science emphasize its concern with the allocation and exercise of political power. To seek a better understanding of politics and government is to work to give mankind the possibility of mobilizing its capacity for benevolence to the maximum extent. Political science provides an understanding of why the community can achieve more collectively than can its members individually. It explains why the whole may be greater than the sum of its parts. That opportunity is the Pot of Gold at the end of the Rainbow Science. Recognition that the importance of the object exceeds the importance of the methods suggests an obvious solution to the identity problems of political science. The discipline is defined properly by its object. Any method of inquiry that will produce plausible results should be appropriate for political science, regardless of its disciplinary origins. Using that approach, political science finally may be defined and a generally acceptable answer given to the question of what it is.

Notes

1. Edward Munroe Smith, "The Domain of Political Science," *Political Science Quarterly* 1, no. 1 (1886): 1-8.
2. See below, p. 116.
3. David Easton, "Political Science," in David L. Sills, ed., *International Encyclopedia of the Social Sciences*, 17 vols. (New York: Macmillan, 1968), 12: 282-98.

4. Klaus von Beyme, "Political Science," in C. D. Kernig, ed., *Marxism, Communism, and Western Society: A Comparative Encyclopedia,* 8 vols. (New York: Herder and Herder, 1973), 6: 361-76.

5. Alfred Grosser, *L'explication politique* (Paris: Fondation nationale des sciences politiques, 1972), p. 144.

6. David Easton, "The New Revolution in Political Science," *American Political Science Review* (December 1969): 1051.

7. John C. Wahlke, "Pre-Behavioralism in Political Science," *American Political Science Review* (March 1979): 30.

8. See below, p. 357.

9. See below, p. 338.

10. *Contemporary Political Science* (Paris: UNESCO, 1950), p. 4.

11. See below, p. 74.

12. John E. Trent, "Report on the 1979 Moscow World Congress of the International Political Science Association," *Participation* (IPSA newsletter) (January 1980): 13.

13. For instance, the volume, *The National Economy of the USSR, 1922-1972,* does not include political science or any comparable term among its branches of science. See *Soviet Education* (October 1974): 79-137. Also, none of the articles on the Soviet Union in this volume mentions courses or programs in political science. Mareen Gapotchka and Stanislav Smirnov, "The Social Sciences in the USSR: Status, Policy, Structures and Achievements," *International Social Science Journal* 28, no. 1 (1976): 65-98. See also Rolf H. W. Theen, "Political Science in the USSR," *Problems of Communism* (May-June 1972): 64-70; Theen, "Political Science in the USSR: To Be or Not To Be," *World Politics* (July 1971): 684-703; and David E. Powell and Paul Shoup, "The Emergence of Political Science in Communist Countries," *American Political Science Review* (June 1970): 572-88.

14. See below, p. 185.

15. See below, p. 169.

16. The others were Finland, 1935; India, 1938; Japan, 1948; France, 1949.

17. The president of one of the associations told the author: "At a meeting of our association, we decided that there wasn't enough political science in our country to write about." That association sent fifty members to the 1979 IPSA Congress. On the other hand, Iceland has enough political science to produce a chapter for this book with only five political scientists in the whole country.

18. Austria has an association, but has withdrawn from IPSA.

19. The *Directory of European Political Scientists* (New York: Holmes and Meier, 1979) lists 2,153 "academics working on a permanent or semi-permanent basis in Europe," including the following approximate numbers by country: United Kingdom 587, Federal Republic of Germany 390, France 306, Netherlands 164, Italy 112, Belgium 92, Denmark 83, Switzerland 81, Sweden 80, Austria 68, Norway 54, Finland 51, Spain 26, Eire 21, Portugal 4, Greece 2, Iceland 1.

20. *Contemporary Political Science,* p. 1.

21. Ibid., pp. 658-62. The UNESCO report included the countries covered in this book (except Denmark, Finland, the two Germanies, Iceland, Korea, and Pakistan) plus China, Czechoslovakia, Egypt, Israel, Italy, Lebanon, Mexico, Spain, and Uruguay. Most of the papers were published in ibid., although Czechoslovakia, Egypt, Israel, Lebanon, New Zealand, Norway, and Yugoslavia were omitted. The same project led to the founding of IPSA. See below, p. 35.

22. Quoted by D. W. Brogan in "The Study of Politics," in Preston King, ed., *The Study of Politics* (London: Cass, 1977), p. 35.

23. Heinz Eulau in "Conference Discussion on Scope," in James C. Charlesworth, ed., *A Design for Political Science: Scope, Objectives, and Methods* (Philadelphia: American Academy of Political and Social Science, 1966), p. 60.

24. See below, p. 197.

25. For information on ECPR, see the *Directory* mentioned in note 19 and *Le Monde,* 4 March 1980.

26. See below, pp. 65-66.

27. See below, p. 275.

Part I
INTERNATIONAL POLITICAL SCIENCE

Intellectual Development*

KARL W. DEUTSCH

During the past quarter century, political science has grown a great deal, as have most of the social sciences. It has grown in its number of university chairs and professional personnel, full-time students and courses of study, learned journals and scholarly books, case studies and empirical data, case studies and comparisons within and across nations. Its subject matter has increased. Today there are about twice as many legally sovereign states in the world, and in most of them governments are trying to regulate and govern much larger sections of the lives of their inhabitants. There have been many changes of public policies, of governments, of political regimes, and in several countries of the entire social order.

What have we learned from this large expansion of our tasks and resources? Or at least, to what extent and in what directions have our preoccupations changed?

The first answers to these questions may be sought best in the substance of our concerns, that is, in the main focus and key problems of our professional concerns. In the work of actual political analysts, several of these concerns of course will tend to overlap. In what follows, I can list each scholar only provisionally under that one of his several concerns which appears to me the strongest.

Five Traditional Foci of Political Enquiry

Justice. From the days of Solon, Plato, and Aristotle through the times of Saint Augustine, John of Salisbury, Jean Jacques Rousseau, John Locke and to the present-day concerns of John Rawls, political thinkers have tended to make *rational justice* the main target of their search.[1] By this, they meant either distributive justice, that is giving to each person his or her due, or else what we may call functional justice, that is, allocating to each member of society whatever would be conducive to some commonly accepted overriding goal.

What was to be a person's due might, of course, change from thinker to thinker and age to age—from Aristotle's justification of inequality between "natural-born" freemen and "natural-born" slaves to the assertions of equal natural rights by John Locke and Thomas Jefferson.

Overriding goals proved no less changeable. For Plato's *Republic,* the goal was stability and the support of philosophic studies. For Rousseau, it was obedience to the enlightened general will in response to the logic of things—*la logique des choses;* for Lenin it was the pursuit of the revolutionary transformation of society in accordance with the way in which he had understood and developed the doctrines of Karl Marx.

Despite the difference of these notions of justice, they were all intended to be rational. They were rational in a formal sense, in that the arguments by which they were proposed were meant to be retraceable, step by step, by every educated and capable reader, who thus should be able to check them for their logic and consistency. And they were to be also substantively rational, in the sense that they were supposed to work when applied in practice under the conditions of time and place which their authors observed or imagined.

Power. Though justice has continued as a significant concern of political science, it yielded pride of place to the concerns for power and interest, particularly from the sixteenth century onward, from Nicolò Machiavelli, Thomas Hobbes, and Alexander Hamilton to Frederick Schuman, Hans Morgenthau, Klaus Knorr, Herman Kahn, Henry Kissinger, Bertrand de Jouvenel, and Gerhart Ritter. These concerns have played an important part in political thought.[2] Power, more precisely defined as the weight of power, is the capacity of an actor to shift the probability of outcomes in a predictable direction. Traditionally it has been assumed that this direction is

---

*This chapter was presented originally to the twenty-fifth anniversary round table of IPSA.

predictable by the actor himself, and that it will coincide with what he conceives to be his interest, that is, some outcome he prefers. "Interest" usually means both a subjective concentration of attention and an objective probability of reward or value gain—for that actor. The two, attention and reward, are held to coincide normally by many power theorists, although they have often failed to coincide—the supposed "interests" often have turned out to be erroneous—from the days of Machiavelli to the rulers who started World War II.[3]

Legitimacy and Stability. The stability of a potential system means the probability that, after having been disturbed in some relevant characteristic, it will soon return to its state before the disturbance. Legitimacy means that its predominant values have been psychologically internalized by its citizens, and that they can be pursued without intolerable damage to other major values held by them.

A third traditional concern of political scientists has been with the legitimacy and stability of states and governments. Bodin's notion of France as a community of families pointed in this direction; so did Edmund Burke's conservatism and, with a different approach, Friedrich Meinecke's treatment of the "Reasons of State."[4] After 1952, some of the work of Seymour Martin Lipset and of Samuel P. Huntington continued and deepened this concern for the legitimacy and stability of governments and political regimes and for the social conditions favoring these characteristics.[5]

Institutions and Procedures. Related to this general interest in questions of political legitimacy and stability is the traditional interest of political scientists in the descriptive, historical and analytical study of particular *institutions and procedures*: from Edmund Burke, James Madison, John Stuart Mill, and Woodrow Wilson to the sophisticated reformulations of institutional approaches by Arnold Brecht, Carl J. Friedrich, Zbigniew Brzezinski, and Samuel P. Huntington.[6]

Large-Scale Trends. A fifth traditional interest of political philosophy and political science has been the identification of large-scale trends in history and social development and the alignment of political action in accordance with them. History, in this view, has a recognizable direction, and in the long run politics will have to move along with it. Forerunners of this tradition include Vico, Lessing, and Condorcet. Explicit formulations were developed by Kant, Hegel, Marx, Lenin, Stalin, and Mao Tse-Tung. All these writers believe that they have foreseen at least a part of mankind's future and that they know at least some of the political steps that are to lead to it.[7]

Other writers take their trends less from history than from what they believe to be biology—and what in fact turns out to be abstracted versions of much of nineteenth-century market competition, imperial power politics, and arguments in favor of the ruthless exploitation of the weak and poor. Thus, Darwin's work was distorted into social Darwinism, and the pitiless nineteenth-century tradition stretches from the competition of individuals and families in the thought of Herbert Spencer to the supposed competition of peoples and races in the murderous ideas and actions of Hitler and Mussolini.[8]

More complex and sophisticated images of historic trends, based on culture rather than on simplified biology, were developed in the first half of the twentieth century by Vilfredo Pareto, Oswald Spengler, and in a far richer and more humane mood by Max Weber and Arnold Toynbee.[9]

After 1950 somewhat more limited efforts at analyzing large historic trends were made by Schmuel Eisenstadt, Adda Bozeman, and Stein Rokkan.[10] Modified versions of social Darwinist ideas were revived in terms of selected animal observations by Konrad Lorenz—and strongly criticized by Nicolaas Tinbergen.[11] Popularized versions of the social Darwinist tradition were offered by such writers as Robert Ardrey and Lionel Tiger, and notions of the inherited superiority or inferiority of particular peoples and races were revived by Arthur Jensen and a few others.[12]

During the same period, however, the ideas of biologists about the nature of evolution had become much more sophisticated. Already Gregor Mendel had shown evolution to be a combinational process. De Vries had shown the occurrence of step-wise mutations; and between 1930 and 1950, J. B. S. Haldane and Julian Huxley offered richer, more accurate and in part more calculable versions of the evolutionary process than the social Darwinists had ever been able to do.[13] After World War II this movement toward a more modern biology, exemplified by C. H. Waddington, John R. Platt, Carl Sagan, Rupert Riedl and others, was to go much farther in this direction.[14]

Three New Centers of Attention: Cognition; Policy Research; System Performance and the Interplay between Innovative System Transformation and Identity

The many new concerns of the much larger number of political scientists who have been active during the past quarter-century may be grouped conveniently under the three headings of cognition, system characteristics and performance, and the interplay between the processes that tend to transform a system or to preserve some important part of its identity.

COGNITION

The operation of cognition consists in a double process of attempted matching. First is the operation of recognition, that is, the matching of information derived from an incoming message with some information recalled by the receiving system from its memory, with the result of forming a perception. Second is the operation of verification, that is, the matching of this perception against some further information, derived from the actual or potential object or relationship in the outside world to which the original message and the resulting percept are supposed to refer.[15]

Hermeneutics. An old aspect of cognition, hermeneutics or the science of the interpretation and understanding of messages, has received a good deal of new attention. Hermeneutics deals with such questions as these: What did the actor or writer mean by his actions or his words? Meaning is context. Hence, to what context of his own memories, feelings, and intentions—that is, his then-accepted but still unexpected program for further action—did they refer? From these questions, other questions can be developed: What did the actor's or writer's deeds or words mean to his contemporaries (who might have understood him differently from the way which he had intended)? And what could those acts or words mean to us with our different memories, feelings, and intentions today?

Already in the nineteenth century, important work in this area was carried on in the French tradition of *explication des textes* and in Germany by Wilhelm Dilthey. Among those influenced by Dilthey were Max Weber, Alfred Schütz, and the entire tradition of *verstehende Soziologie*—that is, a sociology that aimed at reconstructing and reproducing, at least vicariously, the rational and emotional context of each actor or writer under study.[16] This interest was developed in American political science by Herbert Marcuse, Leo Strauss, and Richard Cox, in Britain by Peter Laslett, James Weldon, and Michael Oakeshott, in France by Raymond Polin and Robert Derathé, and in West Germany by Iring Fetscher.[17]

Another aspect of hermeneutics is the problem of how two contemporaries can come to understand each other, despite their different original cognitive backgrounds. Here political science received important impulses from the work of Jürgen Habermas in West Germany, which is now beginning to have a wider international effect through its English translations.[18]

Critical Cognition of Reality. It is not only messages from other persons that we are likely to misunderstand. Even in looking at the world around us, we are quite capable of deceiving ourselves. A long line of thinkers has pointed to this human talent for misperception and self-deception, among them such major figures as Hume, Rousseau, Kant, Burke, and John Stuart Mill. While many other political scientists and thinkers naively accepted the notions of interest and power, these men asked insistently about the capacity of individuals and governments to know the true conditions and directions of their own interests and the real sources and limits of their power.

Since the early 1950s, these critical questions for the first time have moved closer to the center of attention, and critical epistemology—the study of the process of knowing and of its conditions and limits at each particular time and place—became a major part of political analysis. One group took up the old topics of conflict, special interests, and class bias as sources of cognitive distortion, as such writers as Marx, Engels, Lenin, Georg Lukàcz, Karl Mannheim, Max Horkheimer, Charles Beard, and Gunnar Myrdal had done well before the 1950s.[19] In the original view of adherents of this point of view, the members of the propertied and privileged classes are most likely to deceive themselves about reality, for their social and economic situations and subculture would reward and reinforce them for a long time in their errors before some eventual catastrophe. Only the common people, or even only the factory workers—the proletariat—have a chance, according to this view, to shed their illusions and to learn to recognize the shape of reality and their own true interests.

Many of these notions have been revived in various forms by writers of a "New Left," who insisted even more strongly that most of the accepted views of politics were class-bound and hence invalid, but who seemed much less confident that the working class would develop a more concrete and realistic conception of politics, and who remained much more vague in regard to their own positive images of political reality. Nonetheless, some new traits are discernible in these recent writings. Though they clearly owe something to Marxist, and sometimes Leninist, traditions, they go beyond them in several respects. They put much less emphasis on objective processes of social development and far more stress on subjective factors, such as consciousness and will. They expect much less from organized workers and more from intellectuals, students, paupers, and marginal minorities. They are less concerned with the production of social wealth than with its distribution and less with socialist order and discipline than with spontaneity and an element of anarchism: if domination can be defined with Max Weber as the chance or probability of being obeyed, then they seek for a future society in which all or most of such domination should be absent.

So long as highly developed industrial societies become increasingly bureaucratized, anarchistic ideas are likely to increase at least somewhat in allure. Here the criticism of allegedly class-bound political perceptions meets with the age-old human longing for a society of free and equal persons, with the least possible amounts of domination, coercion, and conformity. These longings aroused new interests in recent decades but as yet with few substantial contributions to political thought.

Very similar epistemological criticisms, however, could be brought to bear against the decisions of governments, states, and would-be reformers. They, too, could err; and such writers as Karl Popper, Friedrich von Hayek, Milton Friedman, Gordon Tullock, and W. Roepke insisted that the automatic wisdom of competition and free markets deserved more trust than the all-too-fallible decisions of individuals and groups acting through the political machinery of a welfare state.[20]

Some writers, finally, found both private and public decision makers fallible. Early champions of such an enlightened skepticism included Vilfredo Pareto, Gaetano Mosca, and Joseph Schumpeter.[21] By contrast, the rationality of political actors in the large was defended after 1950 by V. O. Key's thesis of the rational electorate and by the efforts of such writers as Anthony Downs, Mançur Olson, and others to construct a theory of politics more or less analogous to economic theory.[22]

The Impact of Psychology, Psychiatry, and Anthropology. Instead of debating in general terms, however, whether political actors are rational or not in perceiving their own interests and in pursuing them, an increasing number of investigators began to ask in a more discriminating manner about the psychological sources of perception and motivation, of insight and error, at the heart of political action. In this effort, they drew upon the work of psychologists and psychiatrists, reaching back to the pre-1950 contributions of such pioneers as Sigmund Freud, Alfred Adler, and C. G. Jung and the path-breaking 1934 study by Harold Lasswell, *Psychopathology and Politics.*[23]

During the same period in the late 1930s and the 1940s, some anthropologists also had turned to the psychiatrists and psychologists for evidence of the interplay of culture and personality and of the distributions of particular character structures among a population, from which its "national character" might be derived.[24]

In the 1950s and thereafter, the trickle became a stream. Psychiatrists such as Erik H. Erikson and Robert Lifton concerned themselves with political problems. Margaret Mead, Geoffrey Gorer, and Daniel Levinson wrote extensively on national character. The political philosopher T. W. Adorno collaborated with two social psychologists and a psychiatrist in an important study of *The Authoritarian Personality.* The political economist Kenneth Boulding proposed a new science of eiconics, the formation and role of images underlying and guiding human attitudes and actions. Some of these concerns were continued, albeit with a different vocabulary, in a volume edited by Herbert Kelman, *International Behavior.* In the United States, Leon Festinger and later Robert Abelson developed important studies of cognitive dissonance; the mathematical psychologist Anatol Rapoport explored patterns of conflict and conflict behavior through fertile combinations of game theory, mathematical analysis, and a large array of laboratory experiments. In France, the anthropologist Claude Lévi-Strauss developed a theoretical approach of structuralism which then was elaborated by the French-Swiss psychologist Jean Piaget, with implications for several social sciences, including political science.[25] Other French thinkers who have posed new challenges to social science and political thought include Michel Foucault and Jacques Lacan.[26]

Thus far, only a few of these theoretical approaches have led to empirical work, most often in the United States. The *Authoritarian Personality* did so. Robert E. Lane tested the psychological theories of John Dollard and others in a series of careful and influential studies. Fred Greenstein, who was familiar with Lane's approach opened up with other researchers the field of the political socialization of adolescents to systematic research.[27]

POLICY RESEARCH

Logical and Empirical Approaches. Political scientists did not rest content with the criticism of errors. They wanted to put political knowledge on a reproducible basis, in the hope that such an achievement of formal rationality eventually would lead also to substantive rationality, to the successful functioning of their theories and predictions in practice.

The first approach to reproducibility was through a search for more rigorous logic. Already such philosophic and scientific forerunners as Ernst Mach, Bertrand Russell, Percy W. Bridgman, Philipp Frank, Hans Kelsen, Charles W. Morris, Ernest Nagel and others had pointed the way toward a unity of science that was to join the natural and social sciences and in which the logical connections between empirical data were to play a major role.[28] Robert Dahl's *Preface to Democratic Theory* showed the potential power of this approach by using the methods of symbolic logic to reveal the structure of

James Madison's ambiguous Tenth Federalist Letter and of other examples of political theorizing.[29] Other writers, some of them already mentioned above, used logic as a major tool in their efforts to show the possibility of rationality in politics: John Rawls, Anthony Downs, Mançur Olson, Richard Zeckhauser, Hermann Lübbe, and Niklas Luhmann among others.[30]

Even more numerous investigators sought the reproducibility of their findings by basing them on empirical evidence which itself could be reproduced through suitably standardized operational methods. Here scientific substance was to be attained through the substantial development of old and new methods. Results were often impressive. Again, many early contributions came from neighboring fields of social science: Paul Lazarsfeld's and Samuel Stouffer's four-volume work *The American Soldier;* such voting studies as Lazarsfeld's *The People's Choice,* Hazel Gaudet's and Bernard Berelson's *Voting,* the survey research by Jean Stoetzel, Elisabeth Noelle-Neumann, Klaus Liepelt, Viggo Count Blücher, Max Kaase and many others. Soon professional political scientists appeared on the research teams: Campbell, Converse, Miller, and Stokes began their series of studies of *The American Voter* at the University of Michigan; David Butler and Donald Stokes produced a major study of the British electorate; Sidney Verba and Norman Nie advanced the field with their studies of *Participation in America,* and soon thereafter with *The New American Voter.* At the same time, Rudolf Wildenmann and Max Kaase in 1968 compared the attitudes of West German university students with those of their nonacademic age-mates, and with those of the general electorate.[31]

The boundaries between political science and political sociology were transcended freely. Stein Rokkan, Robert Merton, Seymour Martin Lipset, Alex Inkeles, Daniel Lerner, Erwin Scheuch, Erik Allardt, and Pertti Pesonen all made contributions on both sides of the formal dividing line between the professions.[32]

Side by side with the use of empirical data from survey research came the use of reproducible data from content analysis. Its methods were elucidated by Bernard Berelson, Ole Holsti, Ithiel Pool, and Alexander George; its substantive application to political questions was pioneered by Harold Lasswell, Ithiel Pool, Richard Merritt, and others.[33]

At the same time the use of aggregate data in political research reached new levels of magnitude and later also of thoroughness. Such data are those which public or private organizations collect for their own purposes, such as trade statistics, census data, voting statistics, budgets and the like, but which then can be reanalyzed for purposes of political research. Arthur Banks, Robert Textor, Karl Deutsch, Bruce Russett, and Hayward L. Alker, Jr., were among the early workers. Charles L. Taylor and Michael Hudson, Wolfgang Zapf, and Peter Flora later made important additions.[34]

Finally, there were reproducible data from standardized operations of observation and experiment. James D. Barber observed the behavior of municipal finance committees through a one-way glass; Sidney Verba surveyed the evidence from a variety of studies of small group behavior; and Jean Laponce edited a volume on the role of experimentation in political research.[35]

The Behavioral Approach. The use of any or all of these kinds of reproducible evidence may be summarized under the heading of behavioral research. Behavior, in this view, consists of those aspects of human life that can be observed from the outside and on which, therefore, several qualified observers could agree. The intentions of a person are not behavior, but they could be inferred, more or less fallibly, from what he or she has been doing. Something similar applies to groups: their behavior can be observed, but the inner predispositions of its members, or possibly those of the group acting as a whole, can only be inferred from whatever observable and reproducible evidence can be obtained.

The behavioral approach does not mean, therefore, a mindless refusal to consider anything in political and social life that is not directly and externally observable. It does mean, however, a consistent effort to distinguish between knowledge that can be shared and verified in common through simultaneous or repeated observation, or that can be inferred through reproducible procedures from observable physical traces, on the one hand, and on the other hand, that different and far less readily reproducible knowledge of other persons that we must infer from our own introspection, speculations, or particular experience.[36]

From this point of view it seems unlikely that the use of behavioral evidence will soon disappear like a fashion whose day is past. Once chemists learned about two hundred years ago, to weigh all ingredients before and after a chemical reaction, the transition from alchemy to quantitative chemistry became irreversible, and chemists have not stopped taking into account the weights of the materials in their experiments. But the development of chemistry has not stopped with weighing; other and in part more subtle aspects of chemical processes are now also taken into consideration. Perhaps political research similarly will continue to make major use of behavioral data for a long time, but it may not stop with them but rather add to them a more sophisticated concern for the intentions, memories, preference structures, emotions, and mental processes of political actors.

The succession of research topics and methods therefore seems unlikely to show us a sequence of displacements and more likely to reveal a sequence of additions. There will hardly soon be a postbehavioral evidence epoch in political science,[37] in the sense that interest in behavioral evidence will cease, any more than there has been any postquantitative chemistry or any postmathematical physics or biology. What seems more likely to happen is that other considerations will be added, going well beyond what was observed in each case, but aiding significantly toward its deeper understanding.

Three such approaches toward reaching beyond the immediately observable were developed during the past quarter-century. One was the development of probabilistic and mathematical reasoning and model construction. A second was the development of systems analysis and systems theory; and a third was a concern with political innovation and the self-transformation of a political system with the simultaneous preservation of major elements.

Probabilistic and Mathematical Model Building. One major change in the substance of political thought, not merely in method, has been the gradual entry of probabilistic and combinatorial points of view. This change is by no means complete, but is continuing and seems likely to prove irreversible. These viewpoints had triumphed several decades earlier in the natural sciences; only in the lagging social sciences had scholars still been confronted with an unhappy choice between deterministic one-way causation on the one hand, and more or less poetic intuition on the other.[38]

Blaise Pascal and Baron von Leibnitz were among the pioneers of the probabilistic approach, but the physicist Willard Gibbs was among the first to propose a consistently probabilistic point of view. Every event that occurred, he taught, had to be understood in terms of its position within the ensemble of possible events that could have occurred in that particular situation. This new viewpoint provided an intellectual foundation for the new theories of information, communication, and control, developed by Claude Shannon and Norbert Wiener, and it proved fruitful in many fields. It had been difficult to treat probabilistic situations as special cases within a causally determined world, but it turned out to be easy to treat strongly determined situations as special cases of very high probability within a probabilistic universe.[39] Applications to political science followed.[40]

Other probabilistic approaches to social and political problems were developed by Raymond Boudon and by Harrison White.[41] Generally, the new mathematical techniques such as stochastic processes, waiting-line theory, matrix analysis, and vacancy chain analysis are likely to become a lasting resource of political science—provided that they are applied with a critical sense of the substance of each problem and of their relevance to it.[42]

If applied with such a sense of relevance and substance, and with a sound background of historical and empirical knowledge, the new methods in their ensemble offer the possibility of a widening of the horizons of political research. In addition to the study of what did happen, they offer the chance of modelling what else could have happened in the past, or could happen now, or might yet happen in the future with various degrees of contingency and probability.

Another new avenue is opened up by the techniques for more clearly keeping track of the complex interactions of various actors and sectors of social and political reality. It is here that the theory of communication and control—that is, cybernetics, is merging with the theory of systems.

SYSTEM CHARACTERISTICS

Coherence, Governability, Legitimacy and Governing Capacity. A system is a set of recognizable units with a markedly higher degree of interdependence with each other than with their environment, such that a change in one element within the system will be followed by, or associated with, a predictable change in some other element within the same system. Since this interdependence of results—and often also the frequency of interactions—is markedly higher within the system, it follows that every system is bounded, in the sense that interdependence and interactions will decline in some respects faster across the boundary than they do within the system, and/or that at the boundary they will decline below some critical threshold.

Social and political systems may be conspicuously bounded, or else they may be at first more difficult to identify. In the latter case, it is a task of systems analysis to trace through the entire set of transactions or interactions that are critically relevant for the particular problem the investigator is interested in.[43]

In the political science of recent decades, the identity and characteristics of large political systems, such as nation-states, have attracted increasing interest. Since 1914 over 100 new states have come into existence, most of them through secession from former empires, and only a very few states have disappeared through voluntary mergers or military occupation or some combination of the two. Thus, during those years cases of secession have been perhaps more than ten times as frequent as cases of union, but at the same time major projects of union, such as that of Western Europe, have been proposed, promoted, and in some limited respects approached.[44] During the same decades, and particularly after World War II, policies of nation-building in many newly emerged states have raised to some extent comparable questions of national political integration and cohesion.[45]

Related to the question of whether a cohesive political system exists at all in a particular country, there arises the question as to who participates there in politics with what activity, which groups and strata are relevant in politics, and who gets what shares of benefits or burdens out of the political process.[46]

Along with the widening circle of political claimants and participants is the changing size and scope of the political system, and perhaps a changing set of major tasks confronting it, ranging from internal pressures from newly active groups or classes to new challenges from world economics, world politics, and the physical and biological environment.[47]

To cope with these changing tasks and rising needs and claims, the governing capacity of political systems, their ruling institutions and personnel all are being put to increasingly severe tests. Research on the capabilities of governments has increased accordingly. Work on governmental decision-making, legislation, and implementation has increased in quantity and quality.[48] How are elites recruited and how do they change?[49] What are the cybernetic characteristics—the steering capabilities—of political systems?

In this last respect, our perspective on government may have been shifting. We are no longer thinking of governments mainly as engines of enforcement or even as distributors of welfare or other benefits, or as manipulators of symbols and of popular emotions.[50] Rather, we think increasingly of governments as having difficulties in deciding what they want, how to get it, what price they can afford to pay for it, how to deploy their own resources, and how to foresee what consequences will follow. In short, the limited steering capacities and learning capacities of governments now command a growing part of our attention.[51]

From the governing capabilities of a political system one progresses logically to the question of its actual performance. What services and values can it deliver to its population? In what amounts and kinds, with what security, and with what opportunities for spontaneity and choice, and hence for freedom? To what extent is this population aware of this performance, perhaps satisfied with it and proud of it? Comprehensive answers to such questions are hard to find, but partial information has become available through the movement toward the collection of aggregate data and of political and social indicators, as well as through the development of more systematic methods for political comparisons.[52]

Out of the performance of the system, in turn, come impulses toward an increase or decrease in the initial legitimacy of a state, a regime and a government in the eyes of their population, and hence in the loyalty they may be feeling toward it and in their greater or lesser readiness to support and defend it in case of need. Here comparative survey studies, such as Almond's and Verba's *The Civic Culture*, have contributed important information.[53]

Against this background, as well as out of the experiences of World War II and the dictatorships that preceded it, has developed a new interest in the theory of democracy that seems likely to endure. In many ways, it represents a combination of several of the strands mentioned earlier. Lipset's view of the social preconditions for democracy and Rokkan's interest in particular historic sequences meet here with Dahl's interest in pluralism and polyarchy and with Huntington's stress on the importance of the early and adequate development of political institutions. The preferences of these scholars vary. They range from Huntington's concern for order and stability to Dahl's interest in the functioning of organized opposition groups to W. D. Narr's search for a society as free as possible from domination. An interesting sketch of a complex theory of democracy has been developed by Fritz Scharpf, as an effort to combine several major goals of democracy with several institutions and procedures, including equal mass voting, pluralistic group participation, capacity for innovation, improved information processing, progress toward greater equality, and care for poorly organized or otherwise weak groups through the top leadership of the system and through an active public of concerned persons.[54]

A similar concern has arisen on the international level. Proposals to organize the world community by methods of empire-building have become discredited and have almost disappeared[55] and so have proposals for complete national autarchy and isolation. Notions of regional or worldwide federations have become more popular but an increasing body of research, as well as a good deal of political experience, have shown that the way to their popular acceptance will at the very least be long and difficult. In the work of such writers as Joseph B. Nye, Ernst Haas, Dieter Senghaas, and J. David Singer among others, the old visions of world government have largely been replaced by more specific questions: What links among which states should be strengthened or weakened? What inequalities and inequities should be attacked first and by what means? In what regard is national sovereignty likely to remain important? In which states can sovereignty be modified or replaced by arrangements for common action? On the national level, it has become widely accepted that democracy requires a good deal of social welfare policy, a limitation of economic and social inequalities, and a reasonable preservation of the national habitat and resource base. On the international level, analogous insights are accepted at most among some scholars and a few other special groups, but hardly at all among the bulk of national interest groups, electorates, and governments. The extent and speed of any future change in this state of affairs may itself become a significant topic of political research.[56]

These questions lead to the last of the new major areas of interest: the capacity of political systems to change their goals and to transform themselves, while preserving some essential elements of their own identity.

Innovation, Self-Transformation and Identity. The first area of concern about the innovative change of political systems arose in the field of political development. How to move from colonial and directly, politically dependent status to legal sovereignty and substantial political independence, as well as moving from a traditional and locally dispersed native political system to a more modern and centrally coordinated one—that has been a key problem for about one hundred new states; and political scientists have responded to the new experiences, and to the new opportunities for research support, with a flood of studies.

Many of these studies were of high quality. Daniel Lerner's *The Passing of Traditional Society* was an early and important contribution. Gabriel Almond's *The Politics of Developing Areas* was a major study which was followed by a series of further volumes by Ithiel Pool, Lucien Pye, Joseph La Palombara, Dankwart Rustow, and Robert Ward among others. Seymour Martin Lipset applied some of the lessons of these modern studies of political development to the early years of "the first new nation"—the United States—with uncommonly interesting results. Alex Inkeles and David Smith, in their comparative six-country study of the social, psychological, and potentially political effects of factory work, *Becoming Modern,* set new research standards in substance and method. Interesting ideas are also found in the volume edited by Georges Balandier, *Sociologie des mutations,* and in Werner Ruf's study of the Tunisian leader Habib Bourguiba.[57]

Practically all these studies, however, were written by Western scholars, even though most of these had spent significant amounts of time in the countries whose transformation they described. A good deal of the writing in this area by scholars from Third World countries, such as Frantz Fanon, Anouar Abd el Malek, Samir Amin, and Osvaldo Sunkel, pose significant challenges to accepted Western notions but still leave something to be desired in terms of relevant and conclusive evidence that can be reproduced and verified.[58]

From only a few countries have there emerged some scholars working at world standards of originality and care for evidence, such as Masao Maruyama, Junichi Kyogoku, Kinhide Mushakoji, and others in Japan, or V. M. Sirsikar, A. H. Somjee, R. K. Mukherjee, Rajni Kothari, Gopal Krishna and others in India, Julio Cotler in Peru, José De Imáz in Argentina, and Helio Jaguaribe, Candido Mendes de Almeida, Simon Schwartzman, Glaucio Soares, Celso Lafer, and others in Brazil.[59]

Both in developing and in more highly industrialized countries in the 1960s and 1970s, the propensity toward the study of political inventions and innovations has been small. The Swedish innovation of the ombudsman, the new party finance laws in a number of Western countries, the "constructive vote of no-confidence" and the "five-percent barrier" against splinter parties in the Basic Law of the Federal Republic of Germany and the variety of national health plans in Britain, Scandinavia, West Germany, Austria and elsewhere all could stand a good deal more study.[60]

Something similar applies to the capacity of political systems to change some of their major goals, such as in the loss of colonies by former imperial powers during the three decades after World War II. Arend Lijphart's pathbreaking study of the politics of the Netherlands, *The Trauma of Decolonization,* has as yet found few, if any, parallels.[61] Studies of earlier goal changes, such as those of England and Switzerland, both in the sixteenth century, or Sweden in the eighteenth century, seem to have remained equally rare.

Cases of system transformation that have been studied somewhat better are those of the major revolutions. Much of this work, however, had been done by historians, and in any case it had been done before 1950. The volume *Revolutions,* edited by Carl J. Friedrich, is a creditable exception.[62] Only the Chinese Revolution, 1911–1949, has given rise to a substantial literature.[63] Yet in all the major revolutions—the English in the days of Cromwell, the American, the French, the Mexican, the Russian, the Turkish and the Chinese—great political, social, and cultural changes have been associated with striking elements of continuity. Each of the six peoples have remained unmistakably what they had been—English, American, French, Mexican, Russian, Turkish, and Chinese. Identity may be defined for individuals, groups, and peoples as the continuing applicability of memory. Throughout each of these revolutions, a great deal of such identity has been preserved—as it was preserved at other times and places among many peoples who underwent religious conversion, reformation, or counterreformation. Such combinations of radical change in some aspects of life and politics with continuing identity of the whole are as yet not well understood, and here again might be a worthwhile field for political research.

Changes in Regard to Methods

The preceding discussion of changes in the substance and emphasis of political research has already pointed to the influence of new methods. Only a summary needs to be attempted here.

The development of the science of sampling freed the gathering of opinions and of other evidence from much of its accidental character—though not from all of it, since opinions may change, sometimes quickly, with changes in time, place, or circumstances. Together with improved techniques of interviews and of cross-checking the effects of particular interviewers, the wording of questions and other conditions under which interviews take place, survey research was developed as a powerful new instrument, both in the form of long, depth interviews with relatively limited numbers of respondents, and of broad surveys where brief questions can be put to much larger numbers of people. Still larger numbers of usable responses can be obtained by the "Simulmatic" method, as developed by Pool, Abelson, and Popkin, where identical questions from several surveys, made in different months or years but still under comparable conditions, are combined into a single pool of up to 100,000 responses, so as to permit the singling out of a much larger number of particular subgroups within a general population or electorate.[64]

Altogether, using the results of survey research and interviewing—of voters, elite members, age groups or other political actors—became a new key experience for many political scientists and hence something like a new paradigm, similar to one of the senses in which Thomas Kuhn has used the word.[65] If we remember once more that Plato called the philosophers the physicians of society, then survey research made the work of the political scientist less like that of a veterinary whose patients are mute, and more like that of a physician whose patients can talk.

Another new technique in political research was content analysis, originally developed by literary scholars, later applied by Harold Lasswell and his associates during and after World War II. Here, too, was room for the application of sampling theory; and from the 1960s onward the old "hand methods" of content analysis were supplemented by computer methods.[66]

Computers also greatly facilitated the tabulation, cross-tabulation, and other processing of aggregate data. In addition to samples, computers often could process complete or near-complete inventories, such as those of countries, provinces, or districts; and they could produce large arrays of derived data, such as ratios, configurations, or dynamic rates of change. As a result, the data available to political scientists now have increased tenfold or more.[67]

Computers can assist thought but not replace it. As mentioned earlier, mathematical thought produced new ideas and techniques, such as game theory and coalition theory, scaling, latent structure analysis, matrix analysis, and a succession of increasingly sophisticated models of social and political structures and processes. Such models were developed for different system levels, ranging from models of small groups or committees to models of national economic or political systems and to the world models sponsored by the Club of Rome and other organizations.[68] The extension of these models, most often developed in economics, demography, and ecology, to include political aspects will be a significant task for political scientists in the years to come.[69] Some of them are moving toward it with pleasure. Stuart Bremer's recent book on political simulation is a good example—and there will be more to follow.[70]

Conclusions

To sum up: political science has undergone something like a revolution, and it has gone through this major change while preserving its identity. Carl J. Friedrich's masterful summary of 1963, *Man and His Government,* and the republication in 1965 of Quincy Wrights's *A Study of War,* first published in 1942, testify to the continuing vitality of our great tradition.[71]

The changes, however, must not be underestimated. Major new foci of interest in political communication and control have arisen, including the limited capacities and considerable error rates of governments; in the processes of political socialization and alienation; in the forms and conditions of political participation and activity; in elite recruitment and behavior; in political culture and the politics of different social orders; in political development; in political integration and secession; and in conflict theory and peace research.[72]

In addition, there is a perhaps new critical normativeness, a politics of conscience. It is explicit in the work of such writers as Sheldon Wolin, Christian Bay, Richard Falk, Saul Mendlovitz, Anatol Rapoport, and many Europeans.[73] And it is implicit in the work of many more, including those 80 percent of respondents to a sample survey of American political scientists in 1969-1970 who designated the United States' involvement in Vietnam as a mistake, regardless of whether political or moral.[74]

These developments add up to a striking process of intellectual expansion. The total of fields and subfields of active research concern has doubled. The geographic and cultural areas of political concern have more than doubled, and the number of states in the world has tripled. Outside Europe and North America, the scope of government and the size of the public sectors in the national economy of most countries have more than doubled, similar to what had happened earlier in most of Europe and North America during the first quarter of the present century. This means a more than eightfold increase in matters to be covered by political scientists.

But, at the same time, there also has been more than a doubling of research methods available to students of political science; papers and journal articles in political science have grown by a factor of four; the volume of politically relevant aggregate data, published by the world's national governments and by the United Nations and its agencies has grown by a factor of ten; and so has the volume of survey data that are now coming in from many countries. The grand total today, conservatively estimated, amounts to eight times the subject matters of twenty-five years ago, twice the methods and perhaps up to twenty times the data.

In contrast to this, the amount of published research in political science has only about quadrupled during that period and so, one may estimate, has the number of professional political scientists. This leads to a startling thought. On the average, the political scientists of today are spread out about four times as thinly over the sources of evidence, research methods, and subject matters which they are supposed to cover, than were their predecessors of twenty-five years ago. It is thought that this might suffice to give nightmares to doctoral candidates on the eve of their examination, and an uneasy conscience to their teachers.

How have political scientists tried to defend themselves against this threat of creeping superficiality? Some of us have tried to deal with it by overspecialization, risking falling into the old trap of learning more and more about less and less. Others have sought to retreat into a new parochialism, confining themselves to the study of only one state or geographic area, either their own as nationalists or some other as area experts. The latter strategy was less confining but it, too, made it hard for them to use comparisons as tools of discovery.

Still others escaped into some strongly held ideology of one kind or another, rejecting all views that did not tally with their own. More tolerant souls simply would retreat from the attempt to test the truth of a proposition about politics and would rather respond to it by a vague expression of ethical or philosophic preference.

But enough men and women have remained to continue the study of politics by the methods of scholarship and social science.

The cognitive tasks before our profession will continue to increase. They will require major efforts in professional training and even retraining for those of us still lively enough to want it. At the same time, the tasks of governments and the size of public sectors are expanding everywhere; and the potential scarcities of food, energy, and resources, together with the increasing numbers of people and weapons make the steering performance of governments an even more critical factor of long-term human survival.

We have more problems, more data, more tools, more work—and we have not a single received doctrine but a plurality of paradigms. Our best common ground in matters of cognition might be to search for an increasing cumulative truth content of our theories, that is, for an increasing number of statements of the type "there is...." and "if... then...," which have been confirmed by a widening array of different operations of verification. And in matters of value, we might do best to accept the complex plurality of values by which each of us must live but to agree to hold in common the value and protection of human life in its fullness and its unfinished possibilities.

Notes

1. John Rawls, *A Theory of Justice* (Cambridge, Mass.: Harvard University Press, 1971). Cf. also Robert Nozick, *Anarchy, State and Utopia* (New York: Basic Books, 1974).

2. Frederick L. Schuman, *International Politics: Anarchy and Order in the World Society,* 7th ed. (New York: McGraw-Hill, 1969); Hans Morgenthau, *Politics Among Nations* (New York: Alfred A. Knopf, 1948); Klaus Knorr, *The War Potential of Nations* (Princeton: Princeton University Press, 1956); idem., *The Power of Nations* (New York: Basic Books, 1975); Herman Kahn, *Thinking About the Unthinkable* (New York: Avon Books, 1964); Henry Kissinger, *The Necessity for Choice* (New York: Harper & Row, 1961); Gerhard Ritter, *Die Dämonie der Macht* (Stuttgart: Hannsmann, 1947); Bertrand de Jouvenel, *The Pure Theory of Politics* (Cambridge: At the University Press, 1963) and *On Power: Its Nature and the History of its Growth,* trans. J. Huntington (New York: Viking Press, 1949). For more critical approaches, see also: Robert A. Dahl, "The Concept of Power," *Behavioral Science* 2 (1957): 201-15; *Who Governs? Democracy and Power in an American City* (New Haven: Yale University Press, 1961); and "Power," in *International Encyclopedia of the Social Sciences*

(New York: Crowell-Collier and Macmillan, 1968), 12: 405–15.

3. Harold D. Lasswell and Abraham Kaplan, *Power and Society: A Framework for Political Inquiry* (New Haven: Yale University Press, 1950); Charles Merriam, *Political Power* (New York: Macmillan Co., 1964).

4. Friedrich Meinecke, *Cosmopolitanism and the National State*, trans. Robert Kimber (Princeton: Princeton University Press, 1970); and *Reasons of State* (first published as *Die Idee der Staatsräson in der neueren Geschichte*) (Munich and Berlin: Oldenbourg, 1924).

5. Seymour Martin Lipset, *Political Man* (New York: Doubleday & Co., 1959), and *Revolution and Counterrevolution: Change and Persistence in Social Structures* (New York: Heinemann, 1969), and "Some Social Requisites of Democracy: Economic Development and Political Legitimacy," *American Political Science Review* 53, no. 1 (March 1959): 69–105; Samuel P. Huntington, *Political Order in Changing Societies* (New Haven: Yale University Press, 1968).

6. Arnold Brecht, *Political Theory: The Foundations of Twentieth Century Political Thought* (Princeton: Princeton University Press, 1959); Carl J. Friedrich, *Man and his Government* (New York: McGraw-Hill, 1963), and *Totalitarianism* (New York: Universal Library, 1964); Zbigniew Brzezinski and Samuel P. Huntington, *Political Power: USA/USSR* (New York: Viking Press, 1963).

7. Giambattista Vico, *On the Study Methods of Our Time* (New York: Bobbs-Merrill, 1965); Gotthold E. Lessing, *Erziehung des Menschengeschlechts* (Hamburg: Hamburger Kulturverlag, 1948); Jean Condorcet, *Esquisse d'un tableau historique des progrès de l'ésprit humain* (Paris: Librairie de la Bibliotheque nationale, 1878–1879); Immanuel Kant, *On History* (New York: Bobbs-Merrill, 1963); George W. Hegel, "On History," in Carl J. Friedrich, ed., *The Philosophy of Hegel* (New York: Modern Library, 1953); Karl Marx and Friedrich Engels, *Writings on the Paris Commune* (New York: Monthly Review Press, 1971), and *The Communist Manifesto* (New York: Penguin Books, 1968); Karl Marx, *Critique of the Gotha Program* (New York: International Publishing Co., 1938); Vladimir I. Lenin, *State and Revolution* (New York: International Publishing Co., 1932); Joseph Stalin, *Marxism and the National-Colonial Question* (San Francisco: Proletarian Publishers, 1975); Mao Tse-Tung, "Where Things Come From and Where They Go," in *Selected Works of Mao Tse-Tung* (Hazelwood, Mo.: Great Wall Press, 1972).

8. For social Darwinism see Ludwig Gumplowicz, *Der Rassenkampf* (Innsbruck: Neudr. d. Ausg., 1926); Adolf Hitler, *Mein Kampf*, trans. R. Manheim (Boston: Houghton Mifflin, 1943); Benito Mussolini, *Fascism: Doctrine and Institutions* (New York: Fertig-Howard, 1935). For critical discussion, see Richard Hofstadter, *Social Darwinism in American Thought* (Boston: Beacon Press, 1955; rev. ed., New York: George Braziller, 1959); Julian Huxley, *Evolution: The Modern Synthesis*, 3d ed. (New York: Hafner Press, 1975); and George W. Shepard and Tilden L. Lemelle, eds., *Race Among Nations: A Conceptual Approach* (Boston: D. C. Heath & Co., 1970).

9. Vilfredo Pareto, *The Mind and Society: A Treatise on General Sociology* (New York: Dover Publications, 1963); Oswald Spengler, *Die Untergang des Abendlandes (The Decline of the West)* (Munich: Beck, 1920); Max Weber, *Wirtschaftsgeschichte* (Munich and Leipzig: Dunsker and Humbolt, 1924); Arnold Toynbee, *A Study of History*, 12 vols. (Oxford: Oxford University Press, 1947–1961).

10. Schmuel Eisenstadt, *Modernization: Protest and Change* (Englewood Cliffs, N.J.: Prentice-Hall, 1966), and *The Protestant Ethic and Modernization: A Comparative View* (New York: Basic Books, 1968); Adda B. Bozeman, *Politics and Culture in International History* (Princeton: Princeton University Press, 1960); Stein Rokkan, et al., *Citizens, Elections and Parties: Approaches to the Comparative Study of the Processes of Development* (New York: David McKay, 1970), and *Comparative Research Across Cultures and Nations* (Atlantic Highlands, N.J.: Humanities, 1968).

11. Konrad Lorenz, *On Aggression*, trans. Marjorie Wilson (New York: Harcourt Brace Jovanovich, 1966); Nikolaas Tinbergen, *Study of Instinct* (Folcroft, Pa.: Folcroft Library Editions, 1951), and *The Animal in Its World*, 2 vols. (Cambridge, Mass.: Harvard University Press, 1975).

12. Robert Ardrey, *The Territorial Imperative* (New York: Atheneum, 1966); Desmond Morris, *The Naked Ape* (New York: McGraw-Hill, 1968); Lionel Tiger and Robin Fox, *The Imperial Animal* (New York: Dell Publishing Co., 1972).

13. J. B. S. Haldane, *The Inequality of Man and Other Essays* (Philadelphia: R. West, 1932); Julian S. Huxley, *Man Stands Alone* (Plainview, N.Y.: Books for Libraries, 1941).

14. C. H. Waddington, ed., *Towards a Theoretical Biology* (Edinburgh: Edinburgh University Press, 1968); John R. Platt, *The Step to Man* (New York: John Wiley & Sons, 1966); Carl Sagan, *The Cosmic Connection: An Extraterrestrial Perspective* (New York: Doubleday & Co., 1973), and *Dragons of Eden* (New York: Random House, 1977); and Rupert Riedl, *Die Strategie der Genesis* (Munich and Zurich: Piper, 1976).

15. Peter B. Neiman, Bachelor's thesis, "The Organizational Significance of Recognition," MIT, 1949.

16. Wilhelm Dilthey, *Der Aufbau der geschichtlichen Welt in den Geisteswissenschaften* (Frankfurt a.M.: Suhrkamp, 1970), *The Pattern and Meaning in History* (New York: Harper & Row, 1962), and *Gesammelte Schriften*, 18 vols. (Göttingen: Vandenhoeck und Ruprecht/Teubner, 1966–1977); Joachim Wach, *Das Verstehen*, 3 vols. (Tübingen: Mohr, 1926–1933); *From Max Weber: Essays in Sociology*, trans. Hans Gerth and C. Wright Mills (Oxford: Oxford University Press, 1946); Alfred Schutz, *The Problem of Social Reality*, Collected Papers, ed. Maurice Natanson (Atlantic Highlands, N.J.: Humanities Press, 1962–1966), vol. 1; Herbert Hodges, *The Philosophy of Wilhelm Dilthey* (Westport, Conn.: Greenwood Press, 1974).

17. Herbert Marcuse, *Reason and Revolution: Hegel and the Rise of Social Theory* (Boston: Beacon Press, 1960), *Eros and Civilization* (Boston: Beacon Press, 1955), and *One Dimensional Man* (Boston: Beacon Press, 1964); Leo Strauss, *The Political Philosophy of Hobbes: Its Basis and Its Genesis*, trans. Elsa Sinclair (Chicago: University of Chicago Press,

1952), and *Political Philosophy: Six Essays,* ed. Hilail Gilden (Indianapolis: Pegasus, 1975); Richard H. Cox, *Locke on War and Peace* (Oxford: Clarendon Press, 1960); Peter Laslett, ed., *John Locke: Two Treatises on Government* (Cambridge: At the University Press, 1960), and *The World We Have Lost* (London: Methuen, 1971); Michael Oakeshott, *Rationalism in Politics and Other Essays* (London: Methuen, 1962); Raymond Polin, *La Politique de la Solitude: Essai sur la philosophie politique de Jean-Jacques Rousseau* (Paris: Sirey, 1971); Robert Derathé, *Jean-Jacques Rousseau et la science politique de son temps* (Paris: Vrin, 1970); Iring Fetscher, *Marx and Marxism* (New York: Seabury Press, 1971), and *Der Marxismus* (Munich and Zurich: R. Piper and Co. Verlag, 1976), and *Rousseau's politische Philosophie* (Neuwied a. Rhein and Berlin: Luchterhand, 1968).

18. Jürgen Habermas, *Knowledge and Human Interests* (Boston: Beacon Press, 1971), *The Legitimation Crisis* (Boston: Beacon Press, 1975), and *Theory and Practice* (Boston: Beacon Press, 1974).

19. Georg Lukacz, *History and Class Consciousness* (Cambridge, Mass.: MIT Press, 1971); Karl Mannheim, *Man and Society in an Age of Reconstruction* (New York: Harcourt Brace Jovanovich, 1967), *Ideology and Utopia: An Introduction to the Sociology of Knowledge* (New York: Harcourt Brace Jovanovich, 1955), and *Essays on the Sociology of Knowledge* (London: Routledge and Kegan Paul, 1952); Max Horkheimer and Theodor W. Adorno, *The Dialectic of Enlightenment* (New York: Seabury Press, 1975); Charles A. Beard, *An Economic Interpretation of the Constitution of the United States* (New York: Free Press, 1935); Gunnar Myrdal, *Against the Stream: Critical Essays on Economics* (New York: Pantheon, 1973) and *The Political Element in the Development of Economic Theory* (New York: Simon and Schuster, 1969).

20. Karl R. Popper, *The Open Society and Its Enemies,* 5th rev. ed., 2 vols. (Princeton: Princeton University Press, 1966); Friedrich A. Hayek, *Individualism and Economic Order* (Chicago: Henry Regnery Co., 1972); Milton Friedman, *Capitalism and Freedom* (Chicago: University of Chicago Press, 1962), and *Essays in Positive Economics* (Chicago: University of Chicago Press, 1953); James M. Buchanan and Gordon Tullock, *Calculus of Consent: Logical Foundations of Constitutional Democracy* (Ann Arbor: University of Michigan Press, 1962); W. Roepke, *International Order and Economic Integration* (Hingham, Mass.: Reidel Publishers, 1960). For a recent critical view, see Amitai Etzioni, "Societal Overload: Sources, Components and Corrections," *Political Science Quarterly* 92, no. 4 (Winter 1977-1978): 607-31.

21. See note 9 above. See also Gaetano Mosca, *The Ruling Class* (New York: McGraw-Hill, 1939); Joseph Schumpeter, *Capitalism, Socialism and Democracy* (New York: Harper & Row, 1947), and *Imperialism and Social Classes* (New York: New American Library, 1955).

22. V. O. Key, *The Responsible Electorate: Rationality in Presidential Voting, 1936-1960* (Cambridge, Mass.: Harvard University Press, 1966); Anthony Downs, *An Economic Theory of Democracy* (New York: Harper & Row, 1957); Mancur Olson, *The Logic of Collective Action: Public Goods and the Theory of Groups,* rev. ed. (Cambridge, Mass.: Harvard University Press, 1971). See also Bruce Russett, ed., *Economic Theories of International Politics* (Chicago: Markham, 1968).

23. Harold D. Lasswell, *Psychopathology and Politics* (New York: Viking Press, 1960).

24. Ruth Benedict, *Patterns of Culture* (Boston: Houghton Mifflin, 1961), *Race, Science and Politics* (New York: Modern Age Books, 1940), and *The Chrysanthemum and the Sword* (New York: New American Library, 1967); Margaret Mead, *And Keep Your Powder Dry: An Anthropologist Looks at America* (Plainview, N.Y.: Books for Libraries, 1942); Jean Stoetzel, *Without the Chrysanthemum and the Sword* (Westport, Conn.: Greenwood Press, 1976).

25. Erik H. Erikson, *Gandhi's Truth: On the Origins of Militant Nonviolence* (New York: W. W. Norton, 1969); Robert J. Lifton, *America and the Asian Revolutions,* 2d ed. (New Brunswick, N.J.: Transaction Books, 1973); Alex Inkeles and Daniel Levinson, "Modal Personality," in Gardner Lindzey and E. Aronson, eds., *Handbook of Social Psychology,* 2d ed. 5 vols. (Reading, Mass.: Addison-Wesley Publishing Co., 1968), vol. 4: *Group Psychology and Phenomena of Interaction*; Margaret Mead, "National Character," in Alfred L. Kroeber, ed., *Anthropology Today* (Chicago: University of Chicago Press, 1952); Geoffrey Gorer, *The American People: A Study in National Character* (New York: W. W. Norton, 1964), and *Exploring English Character* (New York: Criterion Books, 1955), and with John Rickman, *The People of Great Russia: A Psychological Study* (New York: W. W. Norton, 1962); T. W. Adorno, E. Frankel Brunswick, Daniel Levinson, and Nevy Savaford, *The Authoritarian Personality* (New York: Harper & Row, 1950); Richard Cristie and Marie Johoda, eds., *Studies in the Scope and Method of "The Authoritarian Personality"* (Glencoe, Ill.: Free Press, 1954); Kenneth E. Boulding, *Image: Knowledge in Life and Society* (Ann Arbor: University of Michigan Press, 1956); Herbert Kelman, *International Behavior: A Social Psychological Analysis* (New York: Irvington Publishers, 1965); L. Festinger, *A Theory of Cognitive Dissonance* (Stanford: Stanford University Press, 1962); Robert Abelson, *Theories of Cognitive Consistency* (Chicago: Rand McNally and Co., 1968); Robert Axelrod, ed., *Structure of Decision: The Cognitive Maps of Political Elites* (Princeton: Princeton University Press, 1976); Anatol Rapoport, *Fights, Games, Debates* (Ann Arbor: University of Michigan Press, 1960); Claude Levi-Strauss, *Structural Anthropology,* 2 vols. (New York: Basic Books, 1963, 1976); and Jean Piaget, *Structuralism* (New York: Basic Books, 1970).

26. Michel Foucault, *The Archeology of Knowledge* (New York: Harper & Row, 1976), *Discipline and Punish: The Birth of the Prison* (New York: Pantheon, 1977), *Mental Illness and Psychology* (New York: Harper & Row, 1976), *The Order of Things: An Archeology of the Human Sciences* (New York: Pantheon, 1970); Jacques Lacan, *Ecrits* (New York: W. W. Norton, 1975), *The Language of the Self* (New York: Dell Publishing Co., 1975).

27. Robert E. Lane, *Political Ideology* (New York: Free Press, 1967); Fred Greenstein, *Personality and Politics* (Chicago: Markham, 1969).

28. Percy W. Bridgman, *The Logic of Modern Physics*

(New York: Macmillan Co., 1960), *The Way Things Are* (Cambridge, Mass.: Harvard University Press, 1959); Philipp Frank, *Foundations of Physics* (Chicago: University of Chicago Press, 1946); Hans Kelsen, *The Pure Theory of Law*, 2d ed. rev. and enl. (Berkeley: University of California Press, 1967); Charles W. Morris, "Foundations of the Theory of Signs," in *Foundations of the Unity of Science Series* (Chicago: University of Chicago Press, 1938), 1, no. 2; Ernest Nagel, *Structure of Science: Problems in the Logic of Scientific Explanation* (New York: Harcourt Brace Jovanovich, 1961).

29. Robert Dahl, *Preface to Democratic Theory* (Chicago: University of Chicago Press, 1956).

30. Wissenschaftszentrum Berlin, *Interaktion von Wissenschaft und Politik* (Frankfurt, N.Y.: Campus Verlag, 1977); Hermann Lübbe, *Wissenschaftspolitik: Planung, Politizierung, Relevanz* (Zurich: Interfromm, 1977); and Rainer M. Lepsius, "Heraus-forderung und Förderung der Sozialwissenschaftlicher Forschung," in *Mitteilungen der Deutscher Forschungsgemeinschaft* 3 (1973): 31-46.

31. Paul Lazarsfeld and Samuel Stouffer et al., *The American Soldier*, 4 vols. (Princeton: Princeton University Press, 1950); Paul Lazarsfeld, B. Berelson, and H. Gaudet, *Wahlen und Wähler* (first published as *The People's Choice*) (Neuwied and Berlin: Luchterhand, 1968); Bernard Berelson, *Voting: A Study of Opinion Formation in a Presidential Campaign* (Chicago: University of Chicago Press, 1954); Elisabeth Noelle-Neumann, *Umfragen in der Massengesellschaft: Einfuhrung in die Methoden der Demoskopie* (Reinbek b. Hamburg: Rowohlt, 1963); Klaus Liepelt und Christoph Loew, *Menschen an der Saar* (Frankfurt/M.: Europe. Verl. Anst., 1962); David Butler and Donald Stokes, *Political Change in Britain: Forces Shaping Electoral Choice* (London: Macmillan & Co., 1970); Sidney Verba and N. H. Nie, *Participation in America: Political Democracy and Social Equality* (New York: Harper & Row, 1972), and *The Changing American Voter* (Cambridge, Mass.: Harvard University Press, 1976); Rudolf Wildenmann, *Gutachten zur Frage der Subventionierung politischer Parteien aus öffentlichen Mitteln* (Meisenheim am Glan: Hain, 1968), and with Max Kaase, *Die Unruhige Generation* (Mannheim: Working Paper, 1968); and Erik Allardt and Stein Rokkan, *Mass Politics* (New York: Free Press, 1970).

32. S. M. Lipset and Stein Rokkan, eds., *Party Systems and Voter Alignments* (New York: Free Press, 1967); Robert K. Merton, *The Sociology of Science* (Chicago: University of Chicago Press, 1973), and *Sociology Today: Problems and Prospects*, 2 vols. (New York: Harper & Row, 1959); Robert Scalapino, *Elites in the People's Republic of China* (Seattle: University of Washington Press, 1972); Daniel Lerner et al., *The Nazi Elite* (Stanford: Stanford University Press, 1951); Alex Inkeles, *Social Change in Russia* (New York: Simon and Schuster, 1971), and *Public Opinion in Soviet Russia: A Study in Mass Persuasion* (Cambridge, Mass.: Harvard University Press, 1950); Wolfgang Zapf, *Wandlungen der deutschen Elite: Ein Zirkulationsmodell deutscher Fuhrungsgruppen 1919-1961* (Munich: Piper, 1965); Erik Allardt and Yrjö Littunen, eds., *Cleavages, Ideologies and Party Systems* (Helsinki: Westermarck Society, 1964); Allardt, "Implications of Within-Nation Variations and Regional Imbalances for Cross-National Research," in Richard L. Merritt and Stein Rokkan, eds., *Comparing Nations: The Use of Quantitative Data in Cross-National Research* (New Haven: Yale University Press, 1966); Pertti A. Pesonen, *Valitsijamiesvaalien Ylioppilas Äänestäjät* (Helsinki, 1958), and *Protestivaalit, Nuorisovaalit* (Helsinki, 1972).

33. Harold Lasswell et al., *Language of Politics: Studies in Quantitative Semantics* (Cambridge, Mass.: MIT Press, 1965); Ithiel de Sola Pool, with Harold Lasswell, Daniel Lerner et al., *The "Prestige Papers": A Survey of Their Editorials* (Stanford: Stanford University Press, 1952); Richard L. Merritt, *Symbols of American Community, 1735-1775* (Westport, Conn.: Greenwood Press, 1976); Bernard R. Berelson, *Content Analysis in Communications Research* (New York: Hafner, 1971); Robert C. North et al., *Content Analysis: A Handbook with Applications for the Study of International Crisis* (Evanston, Ill.: Northwestern University Press, 1963); Ole R. Holsti, *Content Analysis for the Social Sciences and Humanities* (Reading, Mass.: Addison-Wesley, 1969).

34. Arthur S. Banks and Robert Textor, *A Cross-Polity Survey* (Cambridge, Mass.: MIT Press, 1963); Bruce M. Russett, Karl W. Deutsch, Hayward Alker and Harold D. Lasswell, *World Handbook of Political and Social Indicators* (New Haven: Yale University Press, 1964); Charles Taylor and Michael C. Hudson, *World Handbook of Political and Social Indicators*, 2d ed. (New Haven: Yale University Press, 1972); Hayward Alker and Bruce Russett, *World Politics in the General Assembly* (New Haven: Yale University Press, 1965); Karl W. Deutsch, "On Methodological Problems of Quantitative Research," in Mattei Dogan and Stein Rokkan, eds., *Quantitative Ecological Analysis in the Social Sciences* (Cambridge, Mass.: MIT Press, 1969), pp. 19-39, and "The Impact of Complex Data Bases on the Social Sciences," in Ralph Bisco, ed., *Data Bases, Computers and the Social Sciences* (New York: John Wiley & Sons, 1970), pp. 19-41 and with H. R. Alker and Antoine Stoetzel, eds. *Mathematical Approaches to Politics* (Amsterdam, New York: Elsevier, 1973); Douglas A. Hibbs, Jr., *Mass Political Violence: A Cross-National Causal Analysis* (New York: John Wiley & Sons, 1973); OECD, *Measuring Social Well-Being: A Progress Report on the Development of Social Indicators* (Paris: OECD, 1976), and *1976 Progress Report on Phase II—Plan for Future Activities* (Paris: OECD, 1977); Peter Flora, "Historical Processes of Social Mobilization, Urbanization and Literacy, 1850-1965," and with Wolfgang Zapf, "Differences in Path Development: An Analysis for 10 Countries," in S. N. Eisenstadt and Stein Rokkan, eds., *Building States and Nations: Models and Data Resources* (Beverly Hills, Calif.: Sage, 1973), and with Zapf, "Some Problems of Time Series Analysis in Research on Modernization," *Social Science Information* 10 (1971): 53-102.

35. James D. Barber, *Power in Committees: An Experiment in the Governmental Process* (Chicago: Rand McNally and Co., 1966); Sidney Verba, *Small Groups and Political Behavior: A Study of Leadership* (Princeton: Princeton University Press, 1961); and Jean Laponce and Paul Smoker, eds., *Experimentation and Simulation in Political Science* (Toronto: University of Toronto Press, 1972).

36. For early discussions of what would prove transitory and what would remain more durable in this approach, see Robert Dahl, "The Behavioral Approach," *American Political Science Review* 55, no. 4 (December 1961): 763-72; David Easton, "The New Revolution in Political Science," *American Political Science Review* 63, no. 4 (December 1959): 1051-61; Karl W. Deutsch, "On Political Theory and Political Action," *American Political Science Review* 65, no. 1 (March 1971): 11-27.

37. See Easton's article referred to in note 36.

38. For an effort to overcome this dilemma, see Robert M. MacIver, *Social Causation* (Boston: Ginn and Co., 1942); cf. also his *The Web of Government* (New York: Macmillan Co., 1947).

39. See Claude E. Shannon and Warren Weaver, *The Mathematical Theory of Communication* (Urbana: University of Illinois Press, 1949); Norbert Wiener, *The Human Use of Human Beings* (Boston: Houghton Mifflin Co., 1950), and his *Cybernetics*, 2d rev. ed. (Cambridge, Mass.: MIT Press, 1962); Colin Cherry, *On Human Communication*, 2d ed. (Cambridge, Mass.: MIT Press, 1966); W. Ross Ashby, *Introduction to Cybernetics* (New York: Barnes and Noble, 1968) and *Design for a Brain: The Origin of Adaptive Behavior*, 2d ed. (New York: Halsted Press, 1960); Warren S. McCulloch, *Embodiments of Mind* (Cambridge, Mass.: MIT Press, 1965). For applications to biology, see James Watson, *The Double Helix* (New York: Atheneum, 1968), and J. G. Miller, *Living Systems* (New York: John Wiley & Sons, 1977).

40. See K. W. Deutsch, *Nationalism and Social Communication*, 2d rev. ed. (Cambridge, Mass.: MIT Press, 1966), and *The Nerves of Government*, 2d ed. (New York: Free Press, 1966); John Steinbruner, *The Cybernetic Theory of Decision: New Dimensions of Political Analysis* (Princeton: Princeton University Press, 1976).

41. Raymond Boudon, *Education, Opportunity and Social Inequality: Changing Prospects in Western Society* (New York: John Wiley & Sons, 1974); Harrison C. White, *Chains of Opportunity: System Models of Mobility in Organizations* (Cambridge, Mass.: Harvard University Press, 1970), and his "Life in Stochastic Networks," in Alker, Deutsch, and Stoetzel, eds., *Mathematical Approaches*, pp. 287-300, "Cause and Effect in Social Mobility Tables," *Behavioral Science* (January 1963): 2-63, and "Uses of Mathematics in Sociology, Mathematics and the Social Sciences," *Annals of the American Academy of Political and Social Science* (June 1963): 77-94.

42. Alker, Deutsch and Stoetzel, *Mathematical Approaches;* K. W. Deutsch and Rudolf Wildenmann, eds., *Mathematical Political Analysis* (Munich and Wien: Gunter Olzog Verlag, 1976).

43. Cf., e.g., Mihajlo Mesarovic and Yasuhiko Takahara, *General Systems Theory: Mathematical Foundations* (New York: Academic Press, 1975); Niklas Luhmann, "Theoretische und Praktische Probleme der Anwendungsbezogenen Sozialwissenschaften," in Wissenschaftszentrum Berlin (see note 30); Ludwig von Bertalanffy, *General System Theory* (New York: George Braziller, 1968); Deutsch, *Nerves of Government;* David Easton, *The Political System* (New York: Alfred A. Knopf, 1953), *Framework for Political Analysis* (Englewood Cliffs, N.J.: Prentice-Hall, 1965), and *Systems Analysis of Political Life* (New York: John Wiley & Sons, 1965); Talcott Parsons, *The Social System* (Glencoe, Ill.: Free Press, 1951), and *Societies: Evolutionary and Comparative Perspectives* (Englewood Cliffs, N.J.: Prentice-Hall, 1966); and Oran R. Young, *Systems of Political Science* (Englewood Cliffs, N.J.: Prentice-Hall, 1968). For applications to politics, see note 50.

44. For data on the emergence of states, see Taylor and Hudson, *World Handbook,* pp. 26-29, table 2.1. On problems of mergers and secessions among states, see Robert R. Bowie and Carl J. Friedrich, eds., *Studies in Federalism* (Boston: Little, Brown & Co., 1954); Carl J. Friedrich, *Europe: An Emergent Nation?* (New York: Harper & Row, 1970); K. W. Deutsch, *Political Community at the International Level* (New York: Doubleday-Random House, 1954); K. W. Deutsch, Sidney A. Burrell et al., *Political Community and the North Atlantic Area* (Princeton: Princeton University Press, 1957); K. W. Deutsch, L. J. Edinger, R. C. Macridis and R. L. Merritt, *France, Germany and the Western Alliance* (New York: Charles Scribner's Sons, 1967); Ernst B. Haas, *The Uniting of Europe* (Stanford: Stanford University Press, 1956); Bruce M. Russett, *Community and Contention: Britain and the United States in the Twentieth Century* (Cambridge, Mass.: MIT Press, 1962); Merritt, *Symbols of American Community;* Michael C. Hudson, *The Precarious Republic: Political Modernization in Lebanon* (Philadelphia: Philadelphia Book Co., 1968); and Peter Katzenstein, *Disjointed Partners: Austria and Germany Since 1815* (Berkeley, Calif.: University of California Press, 1976).

45. Karl W. Deutsch and William J. Foltz, *Nation-Building* (New York: Atherton Press, 1963).

46. Cf., e.g., Verba and Nie, *Participation in America;* Sidney Verba, Bashiruddin Ahmed, and Anil Bhatt, *Caste, Race and Politics: A Comparative Study of India and the United States* (Beverly Hills and London: Sage, 1971).

47. Frederick L. Pryor, *Public Expenditure in Communist and Capitalist Nations* (Homewood, Ill.: Irwin, 1968); Francis Bator, *The Question of Public Spending: Public Needs and Private Wants* (New York: Macmillan Co., 1962). For discussion of public spending as an indicator of the expanding tasks of government, see Jerome Monod and Ph. De Castelbajac, *L'amenagement du territoire* (Paris: Presses Universitaires de France, 1971).

48. See, e.g., R. C. Snyder et al., *Decision-Making in Foreign Policy* (New York: Free Press, 1962); Eric Redman, *The Dance of Legislation* (New York: Simon and Schuster, 1973); Richard F. Fenno, *Congressmen in Committees* (Boston: Little, Brown & Co., 1973); Daniel P. Moynihan, *The Politics of a Guaranteed Income: The Nixon Administration and the Family Assistance Plan* (New York: Random House, 1973); Jeffrey L. Pressman and Aaron B. Wildavsky, *Implementation* (Berkeley: University of California Press, 1973); Bruce M. Russett, *What Price Vigilance? The Burdens of National Defense* (New Haven: Yale University Press, 1970); L. N. Rieselbach, *Congressional Politics* (New York: McGraw-Hill, 1973); and T. R. Dye, *The Measurement of Policy Impact* (Tallahassee, Fla.: Florida State University, 1971).

49. See references in note 32.

50. The first view has been common to the laissez-faire liberals since Adam Smith and to the Marxist tradition. On some problems of the second, see Gunnar Myrdal, *Beyond the Welfare State* (New Haven: Yale University Press, 1970). For two examples of the third tradition, see José Ortega y Gasset, *The Revolt of the Masses* (New York: W. W. Norton, 1957); and Charles Merriam, *Systematic Politics*, 2d ed. (Chicago: University of Chicago Press, 1945, 1966).

51. See references in note 32. See also Michel Crozier, *The Bureaucratic Phenomenon* (Chicago: University of Chicago Press, 1964); C. Northcote Parkinson, *Parkinson's Law* (Boston: Houghton Mifflin, 1962); Easton, *Political System;* Hayward R. Alker, Jr., "Le comportement directeur," *Revue Française de Sociologie* (1971); Hugh Heclo, *Modern Social Politics in Britain and Sweden: From Relief to Income Maintenance* (New Haven: Yale University Press, 1974); K. W. Deutsch, *Politics and Government*, 2d rev. ed. (Boston: Houghton Mifflin, 1974); Wolf-Dieter Narr, *Theoriebegriffe und Systemtheorie* (Stuttgart: Kohlhammer, 1969); Frieder Naschold, *Systemsteuerung* (Stuttgart: Kohlhammer, 1969); W. D. Narr and F. Naschold, *Theorie der Demokratie* (Stuttgart: Kohlhammer, 1971); Gebhard L. Schweigler, *National Consciousness in Divided Germany* (Beverly Hills, Calif., and London: Sage, 1975); Harold L. Wilensky, *Organizational Intelligence: Knowledge and Policy in Government and Industry* (New York: Basic Books, 1969).

52. See references in note 32. See also Merritt and Rokkan, *Comparing Nations,* Richard L. Merritt, *The Systematic Study of Comparative Politics* (Chicago: Rand McNally and Co., 1970). Cf. Samuel H. Beer and Adam Ulam, *Patterns of Government*, 2d ed. (New York: Random House, 1962) and Roy C. Macridis and Robert E. Ward, *Modern Political Systems*, 3d ed. (Englewood Cliffs, N.J.: Prentice-Hall, 1972), vol. 1, *Europe*, vol. 2, *Asia*. For an outstanding study of the performance of one particular country, see Alfred Grosser, *Die Bonner Demokratie* (Düsseldorf: Rauch, 1960).

53. Gabriel Almond and Sidney Verba, *The Civic Culture: Political Attitudes and Democracy in Five Nations* (Princeton: Princeton University Press, 1963); compare this work with that of Charles E. Osgood, William H. May, and Murray S. Miron, *Cross-Cultural Universals of Affective Meaning* (Urbana: University of Illinois Press, 1975).

54. See Fritz W. Scharpf, *Demokratie theorie zwischen Utopie und Anpassung* (Konstanz: Konstanz University, 1970); and the works by Wolf-Dieter Narr and Frieder Naschold cited in note 51.

55. See, however, Sir Alan Burns, *In Defense of Colonies: British Colonial Territories in International Affairs* (London: Allen & Unwin, 1957), and George Liska, *Imperial America: The International Politics of Primacy* (Baltimore: Johns Hopkins University Press, 1967). Hegemony and the striving for it, were still laudable notions in Heinrich Triepel's *Die Hegemonie: Ein Buch von führenden Staaten* (Stuttgart: Kohlhammer, 1943), but now most often they have become terms of reproach leveled by writers in one nation against the government of another.

56. Joseph S. Nye, *Peace in Parts: Integration and Conflict in Regional Organization* (Boston: Little, Brown & Co., 1971); Joseph Nye and Robert Keohane, *Transnational Relations and World Politics* (Cambridge, Mass.: Harvard University Press, 1972); Ernst B. Haas, *Tangle of Hopes* (Englewood Cliffs, N.J.: Prentice-Hall, 1969); Dieter Senghaas, *Friedensforschung und Gesellschaftskritik, 1970-1973,* and *Gewalt-Konflikt-Frieden: Essays zur Friedensforschung* (Hamburg: Hoffman und Campe, 1974); Senghaas and Karl W. Deutsch, "The Steps to War: A Survey of System Levels, Decision Stages and Research Findings," in Patrick J. McGowan, ed., *Sage International Yearbook of Foreign Policy Studies* (Beverly Hills, Calif.: Sage Publications, 1973), 1: 275-329; J. David Singer, *Financing International Organizations* (The Hague: Nijhoff, 1961).

57. Daniel Lerner, *The Passing of Traditional Society* (Glencoe, Ill.: Free Press, 1958); Gabriel Almond and James S. Coleman, eds., *The Politics of the Developing Areas,* in Studies in Political Development Series, vol. 1 (Princeton: Princeton University Press, 1960); Joseph La Palombara, ed., *Bureaucracy and Political Development,* vol. 2; Robert E. Ward and Dankwart Rustow, eds., *Political Modernization in Japan and Turkey,* vol. 3, 1964; Lucien Pye and Sidney Verba, eds., *Political Culture and Political Development* in ibid., vol. 5, 1965; M. Weiner, *Political Parties and Political Development,* vol. 6, 1966; Seymour Martin Lipset, *The First New Nation: The US in Historical and Comparative Perspective* (New York: Basic Books, 1963); Alex Inkeles and David Smith, *Becoming Modern: Individual Change in Six Developing Countries* (Cambridge, Mass.: Harvard University Press, 1974); Georges Balandier, *Sociologie des mutations* (Paris: Anthropos, 1970); Werner K. Ruf, *Der Burgibismus und die Aussenpolitik des unabhängigen Tunesien* (Bielefeld: Bertelsmann University Verlag, 1969); and Michael Brecher, *India and World Politics: Krishna Menon's View of the World* (London: Oxford University Press, 1968).

58. Frantz Fanon, *The Wretched of the Earth* (New York: Grove Press, 1963); Anouar Abdel-Malek, *Sociologie de l'Impérialisme* (Paris: Editions Anthropos, 1971); Samir Amin, *Le Développement Inégal: Essai sur les formations sociales du capitalisme périphérique* (Paris: Les Editions de Minuit, 1973), *Accumulation on a World Scale: A Critique of the Theory of Underdevelopment,* 2 vols. (New York: Monthly Review, 1974), and *Neocolonialism in West Africa* (New York: Monthly Review, 1975); Osvaldo Sunkel, "Integration capitaliste transnationale et désintégration nationale en Amérique latine," *Politique étrangère,* no. 6 (1970) and with Pedro Paz, *El subdesarrollo latinoamericano y la teoria del desarrollo* (I.L.P.E.S., 1970).

59. Masao Maruyama, *Thought and Behavior in Modern Japanese Politics* (London: Oxford University Press, 1963); Junichi Kyogoku, *Gendai minshusei to seijigaku* (Tokyo: Iwanami Shoten, 1969) and *Seiji ishiki no bunseki* (Tokyo: Tokyo Daigaku Shuppan-kai, 1968); Kinhide Mushakoji and Morton A. Kaplan, *Japan, America and the Future World Order* (New York: Free Press, 1976); Kazuo Kawai, *Japan's American Interlude* (Chicago: University of Chicago Press, 1960); Chitoshi Yanaga, *Japanese People and Politics* (New York: John Wiley & Sons, 1956); Nobutaka Ike, *Japanese*

Politics: An Introductory Survey (New York: Alfred A. Knopf, 1957) and *The Beginnings of Political Democracy in Japan* (Baltimore: Johns Hopkins University Press, 1950); V. M. Sirsikar, *The Rural Elite in a Developing Society: A Study in Political Sociology* (Port Washington, N.Y.: Kennikat, 1970); A. H. Somjee, *Democracy and Political Change in Village India: A Case Study* (Port Washington, N.Y.: Kennikat, 1971); R. K. Mukherjee, *Social Indicators* (Delhi: Macmillan Co. of India, 1975); Rajni Kothari, *Caste in Indian Politics* (Atlantic Highlands, N.J.: Humanities Press, 1972), and *The Democratic Polity and Social Change in India: Crisis and Opportunities* (Columbia, Mo.: South Asia Books, 1976); Gopal Krishna and Reginald Green, *Economic Cooperation in Africa: Retrospect and Prospect* (London: Oxford University Press, 1967); Julio Cotler and Richard Fagen, eds., *Latin America and the United States: The Changing Political Realities* (Stanford: Stanford University Press, 1974), and Cotler, "Actuales pautas de cambio en la sociedad rural del Perú," in José Matos Mar, ed., *Dominación y cambios en el Perú rural: la microregion del Valle de Chancay* (Lima: Instituto de Estudios Peruanos, 1969); José L. De Imáz, *Los Que Mandan* (Albany, N.Y.: State University of New York Press, 1970); Helio Jaguaribe, *Economic and Political Development: A Brazilian Case Study* (Cambridge, Mass.: Harvard University Press, 1968), and *Political Development: A General Theory and a Latin American Case Study* (New York: Harper & Row, 1973); Candido Mendes de Almeida, ed., *Le Mythe du développement* (Paris: Editions du Seuil, 1977); Simon Schwartzman, "Twenty Years of Representative Democracy in Brazil, 1945-1964," in Alker, *Mathematical Approaches to Politics*, pp. 137-62; Glaucio Ary Dillon Soares, "Densenvolvimento economico e radicalismo politico: o teste de uma hypotese" (Rio de Janeiro: *CLAPCS/AL* 5, no. 3, July-September 1962): 65-83, "Classes sociais, strata sociais e as eleicoes presidencias de 1960" (Sao Paulo: *FESPSP/S* 23, no. 3, September 1961): 217-38, and "Urbanizacao e dispersao eleitoral" (Rio de Janeiro: *FGU/RDP* 3, no. 2, July-December 1960): 258-70; Celso Lafer and Félix Pena, *Argentina y Brasil en el sistema de relaciones internacionales* (Buenos Aires: Ediciones Nueva Vision, 1973), and Lafer, "El planeamiento en el Brasil: observaciones sobre El Plan de Metas, 1956-1961" (Buenos Aires: *IDES/DE* 10, nos. 39/40, October-December 1970 and January-March 1971): 309-30 and tables, and "Una interpretación del sistema de los relaciones internacionales del Brasil" (Mexico City: *CM/FI*, 9, no. 3, January-March 1969): 298-318. For Brazilian works, see also the periodical *Dados*, a publication of the Instituto Universitario de Pesquisas do Rio de Janeiro.

60. Herbert Alexander and Richard Lampert, *Political Finance: Reform and Reality* (Philadelphia: American Academy of Political and Social Science, 1976); Delmer Dunn, *Financing Presidential Campaigns* (Washington, D.C.: Brookings Institute, 1972); David Nichols, *Financing Elections: The Politics of an American Ruling Class* (New York: Watts, 1973); and D. W. Adamany, *Campaign Finance in America* (North Scituate, Mass.: Duxbury Press, 1972).

61. Arend Lijphart, *The Trauma of Decolonization: The Dutch and West New Guinea* (New Haven: Yale University Press, 1966).

62. Carl J. Friedrich, ed., *Revolutions* (New York: Lieber-Atherton, 1966). Three important earlier works in this area were Eure Rosenstock, *Out of Revolution* (Philadelphia: William Morrow and Co., 1938); Crane Brinton, *A Decade of Revolution: 1789-1799* (New York: Harper & Row, 1935); and George S. Pettee, *The Process of Revolution* (New York: Harper & Brothers, 1938).

63. Chalmers Johnson, *Peasant Nationalism and Communist Power: The Emergence of Revolutionary China, 1937-1945* (Stanford: Stanford University Press, 1962), and his *Revolutionary Change* (Boston: Little, Brown & Co., 1966); Franz Schurmann, *Ideology and Organization in Communist China*, 2d ed. (Berkeley: University of California Press, 1968).

64. Ithiel de Sola Pool et al., *Candidates, Issues and Strategies: A Computer Simulation of the 1960 and 1964 Presidential Elections*, 2d rev. ed. (Cambridge, Mass.: MIT Press, 1965).

65. Thomas S. Kuhn, *The Structure of Scientific Revolutions* (Chicago: University of Chicago Press, 1963).

66. Philip J. Stone et al., *General Inquirer: A Computer Approach to Content Analysis* (Cambridge, Mass.: MIT Press, 1966).

67. Charles L. Taylor, ed., *Aggregate Data Analysis: Political and Social Indicators in Cross-National Research* (Atlantic Highlands, N.J.: Humanities Press, 1968).

68. Dennis Meadows et al., *The Limits to Growth* (Washington, D.C.: Potomac Associates, 1972); Mihajlo Mesarovic and Eduard Pestel, *Mankind at the Turning Point* (New York: E. P. Dutton, 1974). For a critical approach, see H. S. D. Cole et al., *Models of Doom* (New York: Universe Books, 1973); Bruno Fritsch, *Growth Limitation and Political Power* (Cambridge, Mass.: Ballinger Publishing Co., 1976); and Fred Hirsch, *Social Limits to Growth* (Cambridge, Mass.: Harvard University Press, 1976).

69. Karl W. Deutsch, Bruno Fritsch, Helio Jaguaribe and Andrei Markovits, eds., *Problems of World Modeling: Political and Social Implications* (Cambridge, Mass.: Ballinger Publishing Co., 1977).

70. Stuart Bremer, *Simulated Worlds: A Computer Model of Decision-Making* (Princeton: Princeton University Press, 1977).

71. See the reference to Friedrich's work in note 6; and Quincy Wright, *A Study of War*, 2d ed. (Chicago: University of Chicago Press, 1965).

72. On political communication, see Philip Davidson, *Propaganda and the American Revolution, 1763-1789* (Chapel Hill: University of North Carolina Press, 1941); Richard L. Merritt, ed., *Communication in International Politics* (Urbana: University of Illinois Press, 1972); Karl W. Deutsch, *Politics and Government: How People Decide Their Fate*, 2d ed. (Boston: Houghton Mifflin, 1974); Naschold, *Systemsteuerung;* Greenstein, *Personality and Politics;* B. Ollman, *Alienation: Studies in the History and Theory of Politics*, 2d ed. (Cambridge: At the University Press, 1976); Verba and Nie, *Participation in America;* Suzanne Keller, *Beyond the Ruling Class:*

Strategic Elites in Modern Society (New York: Random House, 1963); Robert Putnam, *The Beliefs of Politicians* (New Haven: Yale University Press, 1973); and Ronald Inglehart, *The Silent Revolution* (Princeton: Princeton University Press, 1977).

73. Sheldon Wolin, *Politics and Vision: Continuity and Innovation in Western Political Thought* (Boston: Little, Brown & Co., 1960); Christian Bay, *The Structure of Freedom*, rev. ed. (Stanford: Stanford University Press, 1970); Richard A. Falk, *A Study of Future Worlds* (New York: Free Press, 1975), *This Endangered Planet: Prospects and Proposals for Human Survival* (New York: Random House, 1972), and *A Global Approach to National Policy* (Cambridge, Mass.: Harvard University Press, 1975); Saul Mendlovitz, *On the Creation of a Just World Order: Preferred Worlds for the 1990's* (New York: Free Press, 1975); Anatol Rapoport, *Strategy and Conscience* (New York: Harper & Row, 1964), and his *Science and the Goals of Man: A Study in Semantic Orientation* (Westport, Conn.: Greenwood Press, 1971).

74. A 1970 survey conducted by the Columbia University Bureau of Applied Social Research for the American Political Science Association.

Bibliography

Abdel Malek, Naouar. *Sociologie de l'Imperialisme*. Paris: Editions Anthropos, 1971.

Abelson, Robert. *Theories of Cognitive Consistency*. Chicago: Rand McNally, 1968.

Adamany, D. W. *Campaign Finance in America*. North Scituate, Mass.: Duxbury Press, 1972.

Adamson, Walter L. *Hegemony and Revolution*. Berkeley: University of California Press, 1981.

Adorno, T. W., Brunswick, E. Frankel; Levinson, Daniel; and Savaford, Nevy. *The Authoritarian Personality*. New York: Harper and Row, 1950.

Alexander, Herbert, and Lampert, Richard. *Political Finance: Reform and Reality*. Philadelphia: American Academy of Political and Social Science, 1976.

Alker, Howard R., Jr. "Le comportement directeur [Directive Behavior]." *Revue française de Sociologie* (1971).

———; Deutsch, K. W.; and Stoetzel, Antoine H. *Mathematical Approaches to Politics*. San Francisco: Jossey-Bass, 1973.

———, and Russett, Bruce. *World Politics in the General Assembly*. New Haven: Yale University Press, 1965.

Allardt, Erik. "Implications of Within-Nation Variations and Regional Imbalances for Cross-National Research," in Richard L. Merritt and Stein Rokkan, eds. *Comparing Nations: The Use of Quantitative Data in Cross-National Research*. New Haven: Yale University Press, 1966.

———, and Littunen, Yrjo, eds. *Cleavages, Ideologies and Party Systems*. Helsinki: Westermarck Society, 1964.

———, and Rokkan, Stein. *Mass Politics*. New York: Free Press, 1970.

Almond, Gabriel, and Coleman, James S., eds. *The Politics of Developing Areas*. Princeton: Princeton University Press, 1960.

———, and Verba, Sidney. *The Civic Culture: Political Attitudes and Democracy in Five Nations*. Princeton: Princeton University Press, 1963.

———. *The Civic Revisited*. Boston: Little, Brown and Company, 1980.

Amin, Samir. *Accumulation on World Scale: A Critique of the Theory of Underdevelopment*. 2 vols. New York: Monthly Review, 1974.

———. *Le Développement Inégal: Essai sur les formations sociales du capitalisme périphérique*. Paris: Editions de Minuit, 1973.

———. *Neocolonialism in West Africa*. New York: Monthly Review, 1975.

Ardrey, Robert. *The Territorial Imperative*. New York: Atheneum, 1966.

Ashby, W. Ross. *Design for a Brain: The Origin of Adaptive Behavior*. 2d ed. New York: Halsted Press, 1960.

———. *Introduction to Cybernetics*. New York: Barnes and Noble, 1968.

Ashford, Douglas E. *Policy and Politics in Britain*. Philadelphia: Temple University Press, 1981.

Axelrod, Robert, ed. *Structure of Decision: The Cognitive Maps of Political Elites*. Princeton: Princeton University Press, 1976.

Balandier, Georges. *Sociologie des mutations*. Paris: Anthropos, 1970.

Banks, Arthur S., and Textor, Robert. *A Cross-Polity Survey*. Cambridge: MIT Press, 1963.

Barber, James D. *Power in Committee: An Experiment in the Governmental Process*. Chicago: Rand McNally, 1966.

Barnes, Samuel H., and Kaase, Max. *Political Action: Mass Participation in Five Western Democracies*. Beverly Hills: Sage Publications, 1979.

Bator, Francis. *The Question of Public Spending: Public Needs and Private Wants*. New York: Macmillan, 1962.

Baxter, Sandra, and Lansing, Marjorie. *Women and Politics: The Invisible Majority*. Ann Arbor: University of Michigan Press, 1981.

Bay, Christian. *The Structure of Freedom*. Rev. ed. Stanford: Stanford University Press, 1970.

Beer, Samuel H., and Ulam, Adam, eds. *Patterns of Government*. 2d ed. New York: Random House, 1962.

Benedict, Ruth. *The Chrysanthemum and the Sword*. New York: New American Library, 1967.

———. *Patterns of Culture*. Boston: Houghton Mifflin, 1961.

———. *Race, Science and Politics*. New York: Modern Age Books, 1940.

Berelson, Bernard R. *Voting: A Study of Opinion Formation in a Presidential Campaign*. Chicago: University of Chicago Press, 1954.

Bialer, Seweryn. *Stalin's Successors: Leadership, Stability and Change in the Soviet Union*. New York: Cambridge University Press, 1980.

Bone, Hugh A. and Ranney, Austin. *Politics and Voters*. 5th ed. New York: McGraw Hill, 1981.

Boudon, Raymond. *Education, Opportunity and Social Inequality: Changing Prospects in Western Society.* New York: Wiley, 1974.

Boulding, Kenneth E. *Image: Knowledge in Life and Society.* Ann Arbor: University of Michigan Press, 1956.

Bowie, Robert R., and Friedrich, Carl J., eds. *Studies in Federalism.* Boston: Little, Brown, 1954.

Bozeman, Alda B. *Politics and Culture in International History.* Princeton: Princeton University Press, 1960.

Brecher, Michael. *India and World Politics: Krishna Menon's View of the World.* London: Oxford University Press, 1968.

Brecht, Arnold. *Political Theory: The Foundations of Twentieth Century Political Thought.* Princeton: Princeton University Press, 1959.

Bremer, Stuart. *Simulated Worlds: A Computer Model of Decision Making.* Princeton: Princeton University Press, 1977.

Brzezinski, Zbigniew, and Huntington, Samuel P. *Political Power: USA/USSR.* New York: Viking Press, 1963.

Bridgman, Percy W. *The Logic of Modern Physics.* New York: Macmillan, 1960.

———. *The Way Things Are.* Cambridge, Mass.: Harvard University Press, 1959.

Brinton, Crane. *A Decade of Revolution: 1789-1799.* New York: Harper and Row, 1935.

Buchanan, James M., and Tullock, Gordon. *Calculus of Consent: Logical Foundations of Constitutional Democracy.* Ann Arbor: University of Michigan Press, 1962.

Burger, Edward J. Jr. *Science at the White House: A Political Liability.* Baltimore: Johns Hopkins University Press, 1981.

Burns, Sir Alan. *In Defense of Colonies: British Colonial Territories in International Affairs.* London: Allen and Unwin, 1957.

Butler, David, and Stokes, Donald. *Political Change in Britain: Forces Shaping Electoral Choice.* London: Macmillan, 1970.

Campbell, Donald T. *Experimental and Quasi-Experimental Designs for Research.* Boston: Houghton Mifflin, 1981.

Cherry, Colin. *On Human Communication.* Cambridge: MIT Press, 1962.

Cole, H.S.D., et al. *Models of Doom.* New York: Universe Books, 1973.

Condorect, Jean. *Esquisse d'un tableau historique des progrès de l'esprit humain.* Paris: Librairie de la Bibliothèque nationale, 1878-1879.

Cotler, Julio, "Actuales puatas en cambio en la sociedad rural del Peru," in José Matos Mar, ed. *Dominación y cambios en el Peru rural: la micro-region de la Valle de Chancey.* Lima: Instituto de Estudios Peruanos, 1969.

Cotler, Julio and Fagen, Richard, eds. *Latin America and the United States: The Changing Political Realities.* Stanford: Stanford University Press, 1974.

Cox, Richard H. *Locke on War and Peace.* Oxford: Clarendon Press, 1960.

Cristie, Richard, and Johoda, Marie, eds. *Studies in the Scope and Method of "The Authoritarian Personality."* Glencoe, Ill.: Free Press, 1954.

Crozier, Michel. *The Bureaucratic Phenomenon.* Chicago: University of Chicago, 1964.

Dahl, Robert. "The Behavioral Approach." *The American Political Science Review* 55, no. 4 (December 1961), pp. 763-72.

———. "The Concept of Power." *Behavioral Science* no. 2 (1957), pp. 201-15.

———. "Power." *International Encyclopedia of the Social Sciences.* Vol. 12. London: Crowell Collier and Macmillan, 1968, pp. 405-15.

———. *Preface to Democratic Theory.* Chicago: University of Chicago Press, 1956.

———. *Who Governs? Democracy and Power in an American City.* New Haven: Yale University Press, 1961.

Davidson, Philip. *Propaganda and the American Revolution, 1763-1789.* Chapel Hill: University of North Carolina Press, 1941.

De Imaz, José L. *Los Qué Mandan [Those Who Rule].* Albany: State University of New York Press, 1970.

Derathé, Robert. *Jean-Jacques Rousseau et la science politique de son temps.* Paris: Vrin, 1970.

Deutsch, Karl W. "The Impact of Complex Data Bases on the Social Sciences," in Ralph Bisco, ed. *Data Bases: Computers and the Social Sciences.* New York: John Wiley, 1970, pp. 19-41.

———. "On Methodological Problems of Quantitative Research," in Mattei Dogan and Stein Rokkan, eds. *Quantitative Ecological Analysis in the Social Sciences.* Cambridge: MIT Press, 1969, pp. 19-39.

———. *Nationalism and Social Communication.* 2d rev. ed. Cambridge: MIT Press, 1966.

———. *The Nerves of Government.* 2d ed. New York: Free Press, 1966.

———. *Political Community at the International Level.* New York: Doubleday-Random House, 1954.

———. "On Political Theory and Political Action." *The American Political Science Review* 65, no. 1 (March 1971), pp. 11-27.

———. *Politics and Government: How People Decide Their Fate.* Boston: Houghton Mifflin, 1981.

———; Alker, Howard R.; and Stoetzel, Jean, eds. *Mathematical Approaches to Politics.* Amsterdam and New York: Elsevier, 1973.

———; Burrell, Sidney A., et al. *Political Community and the North Atlantic Area.* Princeton: Princeton University Press, 1957.

———; Dominguez, Jorge I.; and Heclo, Hugh. *Comparative Government: Politics of Industrialized and Developing Nations.* Boston: Houghton Mifflin, 1981.

———; Edinger, L. J.; Macridis, R. C.; and Merritt, R. L. *France, Germany and the Western Alliance.* New York: Charles Scribner's Sons, 1967.

———, and Foltz, William J. *Nation Building.* New York: Atherton Press, 1963.

———; Fritsch, Bruno; Jaguaribe, Helio; and Markovitz, André, eds. *Problems of World Modeling: Political and*

Social Implications. Cambridge, Mass.: Ballinger, 1977.

Dilthey, Wilhelm. *Der Aufbau der geschichtlichen Welt in den Geistewissenschaften.* Frankfurt: Suhrkamp, 1970.

―――. *Gesammelte Schriften.* 18 vols. Göttingen: Vanderhoeck und Ruprecht/Teubner, 1966-1977.

―――. *The Pattern and Meaning in History.* New York: Harper and Row, 1962.

Dominguez, Jorge I. *Insurrection or Loyalty: The Breakdown of the Spanish American Empire.* Cambridge, Mass.: Harvard University Press, 1981.

Downs, Anthony. *An Economic Theory of Democracy.* New York: Harper and Row, 1957.

Dunn, Delmer. *Financing Presidential Campaigns.* Washington: Brookings, 1972.

Dye, T. R. *The Measurement of Political Impact.* Tallahassee: Florida State University, 1971.

Easton, David. *Framework for Political Analysis.* Englewood Cliffs, N.J.: Prentice-Hall, 1965.

―――. *The Political System: An Inquiry into the State of Political Science.* 2d ed. Chicago: University of Chicago Press, 1981.

―――. *Systems Analysis of Political Life.* New York: John Wiley, 1965.

―――. "The New Revolution in Political Science." *The American Political Science Review* 63, no. 4 (December 1959), pp. 1051-61.

Eisenstadt, Schmuel. *Modernization: Protest and Change.* Englewood Cliffs, N.J.: Prentice-Hall, 1966.

―――. *The Protestant Ethic and Modernization: A Comparative View.* New York: Basic Books, 1968.

Erikson, Erik H. *Gandhi's Truth: On the Origins of Militant Non-Violence.* New York: Norton, 1969.

Etzioni, Amitai. "Societal Overload: Sources, Components, and Corrections." *Political Science Quarterly* 92, no. 4 (Winter 1977-1978), pp. 607-31.

Falk, Richard A. *A Global Approach to National Policy.* Cambridge: Harvard University Press, 1975.

―――. *This Endangered Planet: Prospects and Proposals for Human Survival.* New York: Random House, 1972.

―――. *A Study of Future Worlds.* New York: Free Press, 1975.

Fanon, Frantz. *The Wretched of the Earth.* New York: Grove Press, 1963.

Fenno, Richard F. *Congressmen in Committees.* Boston: Little, Brown, 1973.

Festinger, L. *A Theory of Cognitive Dissonance.* Chicago: Rand McNally, 1968.

Fetscher, Irving. *Marx and Marxism.* New York: Seabury Press, 1971.

―――. *Der Marxismus.* Munich and Zurich: R. Piper and Co., 1976.

―――. *Rousseaus Politische Philosophie.* Neuwied a. Rhein and Berlin: Luchterhand, 1968.

Flora, Peter. "Historical Processes of Social Mobilization, Urbanization, and Literacy," in S. N. Eisenstadt and Stein Rokkan, eds. *Building States and Nations: Models and Data Resources.* Beverly Hills, Sage, 1973.

―――, and Zapf, Wolfgang. "Differences in Path Development: An Analysis for Ten Countries," in S. N. Eisenstadt and Stein Rokkan, eds. *Building States and Nations: Models and Data Resources.* Beverly Hills: Sage, 1973.

―――. "Some Problems of Time Series Analysis in Research on Modernization." *Social Science Information* 10 (1971), pp. 53-102.

Foucault, Michael. *The Archeology of Knowledge.* New York: Harper and Row, 1976.

―――. *Discipline and Punish: The Birth of the Prison.* New York: Pantheon, 1977.

―――. *Mental Illness and Psychology.* New York: Harper and Row, 1976.

―――. *The Order of Things: An Archeology of the Human Sciences.* New York: Pantheon, 1970.

Frank, Philip. *Foundations of Physics.* Chicago: University of Chicago Press, 1946.

Frederickson, George M. *White Supremacy: A Comparative Study In American and South African History.* New York: Oxford Press, 1981.

Friedman, George. *The Political Philosophy of the Frankfurt School.* Ithaca: Cornell University Press, 1980.

Friedman, Milton. *Capitalism and Freedom.* Chicago: University of Chicago Press, 1962.

―――. *Essays in Positive Economics.* Chicago: University of Chicago Press, 1953.

Friedrich, Carl J. *Europe: An Emergent Nation?* New York: Harper and Row, 1970.

―――. *Man and His Government.* New York: McGraw-Hill, 1963.

―――. *Revolutions.* New York: Lieber-Atherton, 1966.

―――. *Totalitarianism.* New York: Universal Library, 1964.

Fritsch, Bruno. *Growth Limitation and Political Power.* Cambridge, Mass.: Ballinger, 1976.

Gover, Geoffrey. *The American People: A Study in National Character.* New York: Norton, 1964.

―――. *Exploring English Character.* New York: Criterion, 1955.

Gourevitch, Peter Alexis. *Paris and the Provinces.* Berkeley: University of California Press, 1981.

Greenstein, Fred. *Personality and Politics.* Chicago: Markham, 1966.

Grosser, Alfred. *Die Bonner Demokratie.* Düsseldorf: Rauch, 1960.

Gumplowicz, Ludwig. *Der Rassenkampf.* Innsbruck: Neudr. d. Ausg., 1926.

Haas, Ernst B. *Tangle of Hopes.* Englewood Cliffs, N.J.: Prentice-Hall, 1969.

―――. *The Uniting of Europe.* Stanford: Stanford University Press, 1956.

Habermas, Jürgen. *Knowledge and Human Interests.* Boston: Beacon Press, 1971.

―――. *The Legislation Crisis.* Boston: Beacon Press, 1975.

―――. *Theory and Practice.* Boston: Beacon Press, 1974.

Haldane, J.B.S. *The Inequality of Man and Other Essays.* Philadelphia: R. West, 1932.

Hayek, Friedrick A. *Individualism and Economic Order*. Chicago: Regnery, 1972.

Heclo, Hugh. *Modern Social Policies in Britain and Sweden: From Relief to Income Maintenance*. New Haven: Yale University Press, 1974.

Hibbs, Douglas A., Jr. *Mass Political Violence: A Cross-National Causal Analysis*. New York: Wiley, 1973.

Hinckley, Barbara. *Coalitions and Politics*. New York: Harcourt Brace Jovanovich, 1981.

Hirsch, Fred. *Social Limits to Growth*. Cambridge: Harvard University Press, 1976.

Hitler, Adolph. *Mein Kampf*. Translated by R. Manheim. Boston: Houghton Mifflin, 1943.

Hodges, Herbert. *The Philosophy of Wilhelm Dilthey*. Westport, Conn: Greenwood Press, 1974.

Hofstadter, Richard. *Social Darwinism in American Thought*. Boston: Beacon Press, 1955. Rev. ed. New York: Braziller, 1959.

Holsti, Ole R. *Content Analysis for the Social Sciences and Humanities*. Reading, Mass.: Addison-Wesley, 1969.

Horkheimer, Max, and Adorno, Theodor W. *The Dialectic of Enlightenment*. New York: Seabury Press, 1975.

Hudson, Michael C. *The Precarious Republic: Political Modernization in Lebanon*. Philadelphia: Philadelphia Book Co., 1968.

Huntington, Samuel P. *Political Order in Changing Societies*. New Haven: Yale University Press, 1968.

Huxley, Julian. *Evolution: The Modern Synthesis*. 3d ed. New York: Hafner Press, 1975.

———. *Man Stands Alone*. Plainview, New York: Books for Libraries, 1941.

Ike, Nobutaka. *The Beginnings of Political Democracy in Japan*. Baltimore: Johns Hopkins University Press, 1950.

———. *Japanese Politics: An Introductory Survey*. New York: Knopf, 1957.

Inglehart, Ronald. *The Silent Revolution: Changing Values and Political Styles Among Western Republics*. Princeton: Princeton University Press, 1977.

Inkeles, Alex. *Public Opinion in Soviet Russia: A Study in Mass Persuasion*. Cambridge: Harvard University Press, 1950.

———. *Social Change in Russia*. New York: Simon and Schuster, 1971.

———, and Levinson, Daniel. "Model Personality," in Gardner Lindzey and E. Aronson, eds. *Handbook of Social Psychology*. 5 vols. 2d ed. Vol. 4, *Group Psychology and Phenomena of Interaction*. Reading, Mass.: Addison-Wesley, 1968.

———, and Smith, David. *Becoming Modern: Individual Change in Six Developing Countries*. Cambridge: Harvard University Press, 1974.

Iriye, Akira. *Power and Culture: The Japanese-American War, 1941–1945*. Cambridge: Harvard University Press, 1981.

Jaguaribe, Helio. *Economic and Political Development: A Brazilian Case Study*. Cambridge: Harvard University Press, 1968.

———. *Political Development: A General Theory and a Latin American Case Study*. New York: Harper and Row, 1973.

Janowitz, Morris and Hirsch, Paul. *Reader in Public Opinion and Mass Communication*. 3d ed. Riverside, N.J.: Free Press, 1981.

Johansen, Robert. *The National Interest and the Human Interest: An Analysis of U.S. Foreign Policy*. Princeton: Princeton University Press, 1980.

Johnson, Chalmers. *Peasant Nationalism and Communist Power: The Emergence of Revolutionary China; 1937–1945*. Stanford: Stanford University Press, 1962.

———. *Revolutionary Change*. Boston: Little, Brown, 1966.

Jouvenel, Bertrand de. *On Power: Its Nature and the History of its Growth*. Translated by J. Huntington. New York: Viking Press, 1949.

———. *The Pure Theory of Politics*. Translated by J. Huntington. Cambridge: Cambridge University Press, 1963.

Kahn, Herman. *Thinking about the Unthinkable*. New York: Avon Books, 1964.

Katzenstein, Peter J. *Disjoined Partners: Austria and Germany Since 1815*. Berkeley: University of California Press, 1976.

———, ed. *Between Power and Plenty*. Madison: Wisconsin University Press, 1978.

Kawai, Kazuo. *Japan's American Interlude*. Chicago: University of Chicago Press, 1960.

Keller, Suzanne. *Beyond the Ruling Class: Strategic Elites in Modern Society*. New York: Random House, 1963.

Kelman, Herbert. *International Behavior: A Social Psychological Analysis*. New York: Irvington Publishers, 1965.

Kelsen, Hans. *The Pure Theory of Law*. 2d rev. ed. Berkeley: University of California Press, 1967.

Key, V. O. *The Responsible Electorate: Rationality in Presidential Voting 1936–1960*. Cambridge: Harvard University Press, 1966.

Kissinger, Henry. *The Necessity for Choice*. New York: Harper and Row, 1961.

Knorr, Klaus. *The Power of Nations*. New York: Basic Books, 1975.

———. *The War Potential of Nations*. Princeton: Princeton University Press, 1956.

Kothari, Raji. *Caste in Indian Politics*. Atlantic Highlands, N.J.: Humanities Press, 1972.

———. *The Democratic Policy and Social Change in India: Crisis and Opportunities*. Columbia, Mo.: South Asia Books, 1976.

Krejci, Jaroslav, and Velinsky, V. *Ethnic and Political Nations in Europe*. New York: St. Martin's Press, 1981.

Krishna, Gopal, and Green, Reginald. *Economic Cooperation in Africa: Retrospect and Prospect*. London: Oxford University Press, 1967.

Kuhn, Thomas S. *The Structure of Scientific Revolutions*. Chicago: University of Chicago Press, 1963.

Kyogoku Junichi. *Gendia minshusei to seyigaku*. Tokyo: Iwanami Shoten, 1969.

———. *Seyi ishiki no bunseki*. Tokyo: Tokygo Daigaku Shuppan-kai, 1968.

Lacan, Jacques, *Ecrits*. New York: Norton, 1975.

———. *The Language of the Self*. New York: Dell, 1975.

Lafer, Celso, and Pena, Félix. *Argentina y Brasil en el sistema de relaciones internacionales*. Buenos Aires: Ediciones Nueva Vision, 1973.

Lane, Robert E. *Political Ideology*. New York: Free Press, 1967.

La Palombara, Joseph, ed. *Bureaucracy and Political Development*. Princeton: Princeton University Press, 1964.

Laponce, Jean, and Smoker, Paul, eds. *Experimentation and Simulation in Political Science*. Toronto: University of Toronto Press, 1972.

Laslett, Peter. *The World We Have Lost*. London: Methuen, 1971.

———, ed. *John Locke: Two Treatises on Government*. Cambridge: Cambridge University Press, 1960.

Lasswell, Harold D. *Psychopathology and Politics*. New York: Viking, 1960.

———, and Kaplan, Abraham. *Power and Society: A Framework for Political Inquiry*. New Haven: Yale University Press, 1950.

———, et al. *The Language of Politics: Studies in Quantitative Semantics*. Cambridge: MIT Press, 1965.

Lazarsfeld, Paul; Berelson, Bernard; and Gaudet, H. *Wahlen und Wähler*. Neuwied and Berlin: Luchterhand, 1968. First published as *The People's Choice*.

———; Stouffer, Samuel; et al. *The American Soldier*. 4 vols. Princeton: Princeton University Press, 1950.

Lenin, Vladimir I. *State and Revolution*. New York: International Publishing Co., 1932.

Lepsius, Rainer M. "Heraus-födering und Förderung der Sozialwissenschaftlicher Forschung." *Mitteilungen der Deutscher Forschungsgemeinschaft* 3 (1973), pp. 31-46.

Lerner, Daniel. *The Passing of Traditional Society*. Glencoe, Ill.: Free Press, 1958.

———, et al. *The Nazi Elite*. Stanford: Stanford University Press, 1951.

Lessing, Gotthold E. *Erziehung des Menschen geschlechts* (Hamburg: Hamburger Kulturverlag, 1948).

Lévi-Strauss, Claude. *Structural Anthropology*. 2 vols. New York: Basic Books, 1963. Rev. ed., 1976.

Lifton, Robert Jay. *America and the Asian Revolutions*. 2nd ed. New Brunswick, N.J.: Transaction Books, 1973.

———. *The Broken Connection: On Death and the Continuity of Life*. New York: Simon and Schuster, 1979.

Lijphart, Arend. *The Trauma of Decolonization: The Dutch and West New Guinea*. New Haven: Yale University Press, 1966.

Lindblom, Charles E. *Politics and Markets: The World's Political-Economic Systems*. New York: Basic Books, 1977.

Lipset, Seymour Martin. *The First New Nation: The US in Historical and Comparative Perspective*. New York: Basic Books, 1963.

———. *Political Man*. New York: Doubleday, 1959.

———. *Revolution and Counterrevolution: Change and Persistence in Social Structures*. New York: Heinemann, 1969.

———. "Some Social Requisites of Democracy: Economic Development and Political Legitimacy." *American Political Science Review* 53, no. 1 (March 1959), pp. 69-105.

———, and Rokkan, Stein, eds. *Party Systems and Voter Alignments*. New York: Free Press, 1967.

Liska, George. *Imperial America: The International Politics of Primacy*. Baltimore: Johns Hopkins University Press, 1967.

Lorenz, Konrad. *On Aggression*. Translated by Marjorie Wilson. New York: Harcourt, Brace, Jovanovich, 1966.

Lübbe, Hermann. *Wissenschaftspolitik: Planung, Politiziering, Relevanz*. Zurich: Interfromm, 1977.

Luhmann, Niklas. "Theoretische und Praktische Probleme der Anwendungsbezogenen Sozialwissenschaften," in *Wissenschaftszentrum Berlin Interaktion von Wissenschaft und Politik*. Frankfurt and New York: Campus Verlag, 1977.

Lukacz, Georg. *History and Class Consciousness*. Cambridge: MIT Press, 1971.

MacIver, Robert M. *Social Causation*. Boston: Ginn, 1942.

———. *The Web of Government*. New York: Macmillan, 1947.

Macridis, Roy C., and Ward, Robert E. *Modern Political Systems*. 2 vols. 3d ed. Englewood Cliffs, N.J.: Prentice-Hall, 1972.

Mannheim, Karl. *Essays on the Sociology of Knowledge*. London: Routledge and Kegan Paul, 1952.

———. *Ideology and Utopia: An Introduction to the Sociology of Knowledge*. New York: Harcourt, Brace, Jovanovich, 1955.

———. *Man and Society in an Age of Reconstruction*. New York: Harcourt, Brace, Jovanovich, 1967.

Mao Tse-Tung. "Where Things Come From and Where They Go." in *Selected Works of Mao Tse-Tung*. Hazelwood, Mo.: Great Wall Press, 1972.

Marcuse, Herbert. *Eros and Civilization*. Boston: Beacon Press, 1955.

———. *One Dimensional Man*. Boston: Beacon Press, 1964.

———. *Reason and Revolution: Hegel and the Rise of Social Theory*. Boston: Beacon Press, 1960.

Marx, Karl. *Critique of the Gotha Program*. New York: International Publishing Co., 1938.

———, and Engels, Friedrich. *The Communist Manifesto*. New York: Penguin, 1968.

———. *Writings on the Paris Commune*. New York: Monthly Review Press, 1971.

Maruyama, Masao. *Thought and Behavior in Modern Japanese Politics*. London: Oxford University Press, 1963.

McCulloch, Warren S. *Embodiments of Mind*. Cambridge: MIT Press, 1965.

Mead, Margaret. *And Keep Your Powder Dry: An Anthropologist Looks at America*. Plainview, N.Y.: Books for Libraries, 1942.

———. "National Character," in Alfred L. Kroeber, ed. *Anthropology Today*. Chicago: University of Chicago Press, 1952.

Meadows, Dennis, et al. *The Limits to Growth*. Washington: Potomac Associates, 1972.

Meinecke, Friedrich. *Cosmopolitanism and the National State*. Translated by Robert Kimber. Princeton: Princeton University Press, 1970.

———. *Machiavellism: The Doctrine of Reason of State and Its Place in Modern History*. Translated by Douglas Scott. New Haven: Yale University Press 1957. First published as *Die Idee der Staatsräson in der neueren Geschichte*. Munich and Berlin: Oldenbourg, 1924.

Mendes de Almeida, Candido, ed. *Le Mythe du déveloippement*. Paris: Editions du Seuil, 1977.

Mendlovitz, Saul. *On the Creation of a Just World Order: Preferred Worlds for the 1990's*. New York: Free Press, 1975.

Merriam, Charles. *Political Power*. New York: Macmillan, 1964.

———. *Systematic Politics*. 2d ed. Chicago: University of Chicago Press, 1966.

Merritt, Richard L. *Communication in International Politics*. Urbana: University of Illinois Press, 1972.

———. *Symbols of American Community, 1735-1775*. Westport, Conn.: Greenwood Press, 1976.

———. *The Systematic Study of Comparative Politics*. Chicago: Rand McNally, 1970.

———, and Rokkan, Stein, eds. *Comparing Nations*. New Haven: Yale University Press, 1966.

Merton, Robert K. *The Sociology of Science*. Chicago: University of Chicago Press, 1973.

———. *Sociology Today: Problems and Prospects*. 2 vols. New York: Harper and Row, 1959.

Mesarovic, Mihajlo, and Takahara, Yasuhiko. *General Systems Theory: Mathematical Foundations*. New York: Academic Press, 1975.

———, and Pestel, Eduard. *Mankind at the Turning Point*. New York: Dutton, 1974.

Mickiewicz, Ellen Propper. *Media and the Russian Republic*. New York: Praeger, 1980.

Miller, J. G. *Living Systems*. New York: Wiley, 1977.

Monod, Jerome, and de Castelbajac, Ph. *L'Aménagement du territoire*. Paris: Presses Universitaires de France, 1971.

Moore, Barrington, Jr. *Injustice: The Social Bases of Obedience and Revolt*. White Plains, N.Y.: M. E. Sharpe, 1978.

Morgenthau, Hans. *Politics Among Nations*. New York: Knopf, 1948.

Morris, Charles W. "Foundations of the Theory of Signs," in *Foundations of the Unity of Science Series*. Vol. 1, no. 2. Chicago: University of Chicago Press, 1938.

Morris, Desmond. *The Naked Ape*. New York: McGraw-Hill, 1968.

Mosca, Gaetano. *The Ruling Class*. New York: McGraw-Hill, 1939.

Moynihan, Daniel P. *The Politics of a Guaranteed Income: The Nixon Administration and the Family Assistance Plan*. New York: Random House, 1973.

Mukherjee, R. K. *Social Indicators*. Delhi: Macmillan, 1975.

Murdoch, William W. *The Poverty of Nations: The Political Economy of Hunger and Population*. Baltimore: Johns Hopkins University Press, 1981.

Mushakoji, Kinhide, and Kaplan, Morton A. *Japan, America and the Future World Order*. New York: Free Press, 1976.

Mussolini, Benito. *Fascism: Doctrine and Institutions*. New York: Fertig-Howard, 1935.

Myrdal, Gunnar. *Against the Stream: Critical Essays on Economics*. New York: Pantheon, 1973.

———. *Beyond the Welfare State*. New Haven: Yale University Press, 1970.

———. *The Political Element in the Development of Economic Theory*. New York: Simon and Schuster, 1969.

Nagel, Ernest. *Structure of Science: Problems in the Logic of Scientific Explanation*. New York: Harcourt, Brace, Jovanovich, 1961.

Narr, Wolf-Dieter. *Theoriebegriffe und Systemtheorie*. Stuttgart: Kohlhammer, 1969.

———, and Naschold, Frieder. *Theorie der Demokratie*. Stuttgart: Kohlhammer, 1971.

Naschold, Frieder. *Systemteuerung*. Stuttgart: Kohlhammer, 1969.

Neiman, Peter B. "The Organizational Significance of Recognition." Bachelor's thesis, MIT, 1949.

Nichols, David. *Financing Elections: The Politics of an American Ruling Class*. New York: Watts, 1973.

Noelle-Neumann, Elizabeth. *Umfragen in der Massengesellschaft: Einfuhrung in die Methoden der Demoskopie*. Reinbeck b. Hamburg: Rowalt, 1963.

North, Robert C., et al. *Content Analysis: A Handbook with Applications for the Study of International Crisis*. Evanston: Northwestern University Press, 1963.

Nozick, Robert. *Anarchy, State and Utopia*. New York: Basic Books, 1974.

Nye, Joseph S. *Peace in Parts: Integration and Conflict in Regional Organization*. Boston: Little, Brown, 1971.

———, and Keohane, Robert. *Transnational Relations and World Politics*. Cambridge: Harvard University Press, 1972.

OECD. *Measuring Social Well-Being: A Progress Report on the Development of Social Indicators*. Paris: OECD, 1976.

———. *1976 Progress Report on Phase II—Plan for Future Activities*. Paris: OECD, 1977.

Oakeshott, Michael. *Rationalism in Politics and Other Essays*. London: Methuen, 1962.

Ollman, B. *Alienation: Studies in the History and Theory of Politics*. 2d ed. Cambridge: Harvard University Press, 1976.

Olson, Mancur. *The Logic of Collective Action: Public Goods and the Theory of Groups*. Rev. ed. Cambridge: Harvard University Press, 1971.

Ortega y Gasset, José. *The Revolt of the Masses*. New York: Norton, 1957.

Osgood, Charles; May, William H.; and Miron, Murray S. *Cross-Cultural Universals of Affective Meaning*. Urbana: University of Illinois Press, 1975.
Pareto, Vilfredo. *The Mind and Society: A Treatise on General Sociology*. New York: Dover, 1963.
Parkes, D. N., and Thrift, N. J. *Times, Spaces and Places: A Chronogeographic Perspective*. New York: Wiley and Sons, 1980.
Parkinson, C. Northcote. *Parkinson's Law*. Boston: Houghton Mifflin, 1962.
Parsons, Talcott. *The Social System*. Glencoe, Ill.: Free Press, 1951.
———. *Societies: Evolutionary and Comparative Perspectives*. Englewood Cliffs, N.J.: Prentice-Hall, 1966.
Paz, Pedro. *El subdesarrollo latino americano y la teoria del desarrollo*. n. p.: ILPES, 1970.
Pesonen, Pertti A. *Valitsijamiesvaalien Ylioppilas Aanestäjät* [Students as Voters in Presidential Elections]. Helsinki: n.p., 1958.
———. *Protestivaalit Nuorisovaalit* [Protest Elections, Youth Elections]. Helsinki-Tampere: Poliitiikan tutkimuksia, 1972.
Pettee, George S. *The Process of Revolution*. New York: Harper, 1938.
Piaget, Jean. *Structuralism*. New York: Basic Books, 1970.
Platt, John R. *The Step to Man*. New York: Wiley, 1960.
Polin, Raymond. *La Politique de la Solitude: Essai sur la philosophie politique de Jean-Jacques Rousseau*. Paris: Sirey, 1971.
Popkin, Samuel. *The Rational Peasant: The Political Economy of Rural Society in Vietnam*. Berkeley: University of California Press, 1980.
Popper, Karl R. *The Open Society and Its Enemies*. 2 vols. 5th rev. ed. Princeton: Princeton University Press, 1966.
Pressman, Jeffrey L., and Wildavsky, Aaron B. *Implementation*. Berkeley: University of California Press, 1973.
Pryor, Frederick L. *Public Expenditure in Communist and Capitalist Nations*. Homewood, Ill.: Irwin, 1968.
Putnam, Robert. *The Beliefs of Politicians*. New Haven: Yale University Press, 1973.
Pye, Lucien, and Verba, Sidney, eds. *Political Culture and Political Development*. Princeton: Princeton University Press, 1965.
Rapoport, Anatol. *Fights, Games, Debates*. Ann Arbor: University of Michigan Press, 1960.
———. *Science and the Goals of Man: A Study in Semantic Orientation*. Westport, Conn.: Greenwood Press, 1971.
———. *Strategy and Conscience*. New York: Harper, 1964.
Rawls, John. *A Theory of Justice*. Cambridge: Harvard University Press, 1971.
Redman, Eric. *The Dance of Legislation*. New York: Simon and Schuster, 1973.
Rickman, John. *The People of Great Russia: A Psychological Study*. New York: Norton, 1962.
Riedl, Ruper. *Die Strategie der Genesis*. Munich and Zurich: R. Piper, 1976.
Rieselbach, L. N. *Congressional Politics*. New York: McGraw-Hill, 1973.
Ritter, Gerhard. *Die Dämonie der Macht*. Stuttgart: Hannsmann, 1947.
Roepke, W. *International Order and Economic Integration*. Hingham, Mass.: Reidel Publishers, 1960.
Rokkan, Stein, et al. *Citizens, Elections and Parties: Approaches to the Comparative Study of the Processes of Development*. New York: David McKay, 1970.
Rose, Richard. *Do Parties Make a Difference?* Chatham, N.J.: Chatham House, 1980.
Rosenstock, Eure. *Out of Revolution*. Philadelphia: Morrow, 1938.
Ruf, Werner K. *Der Burgibismus und die Aussenpolitik des unabhängigen Tunesien*. Bielefeld: Bertelsmann University Verlag, 1969.
Russett, Bruce M. *Community and Contention: Britain and the United States in the Twentieth Century*. Cambridge: MIT Press, 1962.
———. *What Price Vigilance? The Burdens of National Defense*. New Haven: Yale University Press, 1970.
———, ed. *Economic Theories of International Politics*. Chicago: Markham. 1968.
———; Deutsch, Karl W.; Alker, Hayward; and Lasswell, Harold D. *World Handbook of Political and Social Indicators*. New Haven: Yale University Press, 1964.
———, and Starr, Harvey. *World Politics: The Menu for Choice*. San Francisco: W. H. Freeman, 1981.
Sagan, Carl. *The Cosmic Connection: An Extraterrestrial Perspective*. New York: Doubleday, 1973.
———. *Dragons of Eden*. New York: Random House, 1977.
Scalapino, Robert. *Elites in the People's Republic of China*. Seattle: University of Washington Press, 1972.
Scharpf, Fritz W. *Demokratie-theorie zwischen Utopie und Anpassung*. Konstanz: Konstanz University Press, 1970.
Schlozman, Kay Leham, and Verba, Sidney. *Injury to Insult: Unemployment, Class, and Political Response*. Cambridge: Harvard University Press, 1979.
Schuman, Frederick L. *International Politics: Anarchy and Order in the World Society*. 7th ed. New York: McGraw-Hill, 1969.
Schumpeter, Joseph. *Capitalism, Socialism and Democracy*. New York: Harper and Row, 1947.
———. *Imperialism and Social Classes*. New York: New American Library, 1955.
Schutz, Alfred. *The Problem of Social Reality*. Collected Papers, vol. 1. Series editor Maurice Natanson. Atlantic Highlands, N.J.: Humanities Press, 1962-1966.
Schurmann, Franz. *Ideology and Organization in Communist China*. 2d ed. Berkeley: University of California Press, 1968.
Schwartzman, Simon. "Twenty Years of Representative Democracy in Brazil, 1945-1964," in Howard Alker and Antoine Stoetzel, eds. *Mathematical Approaches to Politics*. Amsterdam and New York: Elsevier, 1973.
Schweigler, Gebhard L. *National Consciousness in Divided Germany*. Beverly Hills, Calif.: Sage, 1975.
Senghaas, Dieter. *Friedenforschung und Gesellschaftskritik, 1970-1973: Gewalt-Konflikt-Frieden: Essays zur*

Friedens-Forschung. Hamburg: Hoffman und Campe, 1974.

———, and Deutsch, Karl. "The Steps to War: A Survey of System Levels, Decision Stages and Research Findings," in Patrick J. McGowen, ed. *Sage International Yearbook of Foreign Policy Studies.* Vol. 1. Beverly Hills, Calif.: Sage, 1973.

Shannon, Claude E., and Weaver, Warren. *The Mathematical Theory of Communication.* Urbana: University of Illinois, 1949.

Shatz, Marshall S. *Soviet Dissent in Historical Perspective.* New York: Cambridge University Press, 1980.

Shue, Henry. *Basic Rights: Subsistence, Affluence, and U.S. Foreign Policy.* Princeton: Princeton University Press, 1980.

Shepard, George W., and Lemelle, Tilden L., eds. *Race Among Nations: A Conceptual Approach.* Boston: D.C. Heath, 1970.

Sigmund, Paul E. *Multinationals in Latin America: The Politics of Nationalization.* Madison: University of Wisconsin Press, 1980.

Singer, J. David. *Explaining War: Selected Papers from the Correlates of War.* New York: Free Press, 1980.

———. *Financing International Organization.* The Hague: Nijhoff, 1961.

———, ed. *The Correlates of War*, Vol. 1, *Research Origins and Rationale.* Vol. 2, *Testing Some Real Political Models.* New York: Free Press, 1979, 1980.

———, and LaBarr, Dorothy F. *The Study of International Politics.* Oxford, England: Clio Books, 1976.

Sirsikar, V. M. *The Rural Elite in a Developing Society: A Study in Political Sociology.* Port Washington, New York: Kennikat, 1970.

Smith, Geoffrey, and Polsby, Nelson W. *British Government and its Discontents.* New York: Basic Books, 1981.

Snyder, R. C., et al. *Decision Making in Foreign Policy.* New York: Free Press, 1962.

Soares, Glaucio Ary Dillon. "Classes socias, strata sociaise as eleicoes presidencias de 1960." Sao Paulo: FESPSP/S, 23:3, Sept., 1961, pp. 217–38.

———. "Desenvolvimento economico e radicalismo politico: o testo de uma hypotese." Rio de Janeiro: CLAPCS/AL, 5:3, July/September 1962, pp. 65–83.

———. "Urbanizacao e dispersao eleitoral." Rio de Janeiro: FGU/RDP, 3:2, July–December 1960, pp. 258–70.

Sola Pool, Ithiel de. *Candidates, Issues and Strategies: A Computer Simulation of the 1960 and 1964 Presidential Elections.* 2d rev. ed. Cambridge: MIT Press, 1965.

———; with Lasswell, Harold; Lerner, Daniel; et al. *The "Prestige Papers": A Survey of Their Editorials.* Stanford: Stanford University Press, 1952.

Somjee, A. H., *Democracy and Political Change in Village India: A Case Study.* Port Washington, N.Y.: Kennikat, 1971.

Spengler, Oswald. *Die Untergang des Abendlandes* [*The Decline of the West*]. Munich: Beck, 1920.

Stalin, Joseph. *Marxism and the National-Colonial Question.* San Francisco: Proletarian Publishers, 1975.

Steinbruner, John. *The Cybernetic Theory of Decision: New Dimensions of Political Analysis.* Princeton: Princeton University Press, 1976.

Steinfels, Peter. *The Neoconservatives: The Men Who Are Changing America's Politics.* New York: Simon and Schuster, 1980.

Stoetzel, Jean. *Without the Chrysanthemum and the Sword.* 1955. Reprinted, Westport, Conn.: Greenwood Press, 1976.

Stone, Philip J., et al. *General Inquirer: A Computer Approach to Content Analysis.* Cambridge: MIT, 1966.

Strauss, Leo. *The Political Philosophy of Hobbes: Its Basis and Its Genesis.* Translated by Elsa Sinclair. Chicago: University of Chicago Press, 1952.

———. *Political Philosophy: Six Essays.* Edited by Hilail Gilden. Indianapolis: Pegasus, 1975.

Sunkel, Osvaldo. "Integration capitaliste transnationale et desintegration nationale en Amérique latine." *Politique étrangère,* no. 6 1970.

———, and Paz, Pedro. *El subdesarrollo latino-americano y la teoria del desarrollo.* N. p.: ILPES, 1970.

Taylor, Charles L., ed. *Aggregate Data Analysis: Political and Social Indicators in Cross-National Research.* Atlantic Highlands, N.J.: The Humanities Press, 1968.

———, and Hudson, Michael C. *World Handbook of Political and Social Indicators.* 2d ed. New Haven: Yale University Press, 1972.

Thies, Wallace J. *When Governments Collide: Coercion and Diplomacy in the Vietnam Conflict, 1964–1968.* Berkeley: University of California Press, 1980.

Thompson, Kenneth W. *Masters of International Thought.* Baton Rouge: Louisiana State University Press, 1981.

Tiger, Lionel, and Fox, Robin. *The Imperial Animal.* New York: Dell, 1972.

Tinbergen, Nikolaas. *The Animal in Its World.* 2 vols. Cambridge: Harvard University Press, 1975.

———. *Study of Instinct.* Folcroft, Pa.: Folcroft Library Editions, 1951.

Toynbee, Arnold. *A Study of History.* 12 vols. Oxford: Oxford University Press, 1947–1961.

Triepel, Heinrich. *Die Hegemonie: Ein Buch von führenden Staaten.* Stuttgart: Kohlhammer, 1943.

Verba, Sidney. *Small Groups and Political Behavior: A Study of Leadership.* Princeton: Princeton University Press, 1961.

———, Ahmed, Bashirudden; and Bhatt, A. *Caste, Race and Politics: A Comparative Study of India and the United States.* Beverly Hills, Calif.: Sage, 1971.

———, and Nie, N. H. *The Changing American Voter.* Cambridge: Harvard University Press, 1976.

———. *Participation in America: Political Democracy and Social Equality.* New York: Harper and Row, 1972.

Wach, Joachim. *Das Verstehen.* 3 vols. Tubingen: Mohr, 1926–1933.

Waddington, C. H., ed. *Towards a Theoretical Biology.* Edinburgh: Edinburgh University Press, 1968.

Ward, Robert E., and Rustow, Dankwart, eds. *Political

Modernization in Japan and Turkey. Princeton: Princeton University Press, 1964.

Watson, James. *The Double Helix*. New York: Atheneum, 1968.

Weber, Max. *From Max Weber: Essays in Sociology*. Translated by Hans Gerth and C. Wright Mills. Oxford: Oxford University Press, 1946.

———. *Wirtschaftsgeschichte*. Munich and Leipzig: Dimsker and Humboldt, 1924.

Weiner, M. *Political Parties and Political Development*. Princeton: Princeton University Press, 1966.

Weiner, Norbert. *Cybernetics*. 2d rev. ed. Cambridge: MIT Press, 1962.

———. *The Human Use of Human Beings*. Boston: Houghton Mifflin, 1950.

White, Harrison C. "Cause and Effect in Social Mobility Tables." *Behavioral Science* (January 1963), pp. 2–63.

———. *Chains of Opportunity: System Models of Mobility in Organizations*. Cambridge: Harvard University Press, 1970.

———. "Life in Stochastic Networks," in Howard Alker, *et al.*, eds. *Mathematical Approaches to Politics*. San Francisco: Jossey-Bass, 1973, pp. 287–300.

———. "Uses of Mathematics in Sociology, Mathematics and the Social Sciences." *Annals of the American Academy of Political and Social Science* (June 1963), pp. 77–94.

Wildenmann, Rudolf. *Gurachten zur Frage der Subentionierung. Politischer Parteien aus Offentlichen Mitteln*. Meisenheim am Glan: Hain, 1968.

———, and Kaase, Max. *Die Unruhige Generation*. Mannheim: Working Paper, 1968.

Wilensky, Harold L. *Organizational Intelligence: Knowledge and Policy in Government and Industry*. New York: Basic Books, 1969.

Wilson, James, ed. *The Politics of Regulation*. New York: Basic Books, 1980.

Wissenschaftszentrum Berlin Interaktion von Wissenschaft und Politik. Frankfurt and New York: Campus Verlag, 1977.

Wolin, Sheldon. *Politics and Vision: Continuity and Innovation in Western Political Thought*. Boston: Little, Brown, 1960.

Wright, Quincy. *A Study of War*. 2d ed. Chicago: University of Chicago Press, 1965.

Yanaga, Chitoshi. *Japanese People and Politics*. New York: Wiley, 1956.

Young, Oran R. *Systems of Political Science*. Englewood Cliffs, N.J.: Prentice-Hall, 1968.

Zapf, Wolfgang. *Wandlungen der Deutschen Elite: Ein Zirculationsmodell deutscher Fuhrungsgruppen 1919–1961*. Munich: R. Piper, 1965.

Zuzanek, Jiri. *Work and Leisure in the Soviet Union: A Time-Budget Analysis*. New York: Praeger, 1980.

Institutional Development*

JOHN E. TRENT

Introduction

Even more perhaps than within countries, the international development of a discipline depends on an increasing scale of direct contacts among scholars. The days of the single, itinerant social science genius, à la Tocqueville, are, it would seem, long gone.[1] If we are to analyze the conditions and dimensions of the internationalization of disciplines and the potential for their universalization, it is useful to concentrate on the contacts among scholars and the infrastructure which underlies these contacts. In this sense, this chapter is a complement to the preceding one by Karl Deutsch, which studies the internationalization of the discipline of political science during the past quarter-century. Here, we look at the institutions, the networks, the cooperation, the exchanges which underlie the growth of cross-national research, theorizing, and comparative studies in political science.

The rapid and quite massive internationalization of the social sciences since the 1950s is not an isolated phenomenon. It parallels the growing interdependence of economic and political systems, the increasing surplus wealth of industrialized societies, the need for knowledge of centralized governments. Even more perhaps, it is a response to the increased recognition of the ethnocentric or state-centered bias of much research, the criticism of the linearity of previous theories, and the availability both of new social science techniques and the technology and hardware to apply them.[2] Obviously, the availability of high speed, relatively low cost transportation and communications has also had an impact on the willingness and the ability of researchers to cooperate over long distances. One might even wonder if such mundane factors as the increase in international tourism and new, inexpensive means of reproduction of papers have not had quite an influence on the possibility of social scientists to participate in international meetings.

Be this as it may, it is both more interesting and more useful to analyze not the general trend toward international organization but its limitations, its sporadicalness, and its uneven distribution in different regions and countries of the world. To probe the potential for further growth in international cooperation, we must first analyze the current levels and intensity of participation by different countries and various scholars. This paper is a first, sometimes impressionistic, attempt to study the growth in contacts between political scientists and the institutional infrastructure for such contacts, followed by some tentative explanations of the current situation and possible ways for improving it.[3]

The International Political Science Association and Scholarly Contacts

Political science is a relatively young, specialized, university discipline. Certainly its international development is a post–World War II phenomenon. Aside from the general trends affecting the social sciences mentioned above, this international development owes much not only to the globalization of world politics and the almost universal influence of American and Marxist analytical paradigms, but also, to the early initiatives of UNESCO and the continuing impact of the International Political Science Association (IPSA).

The youthfulness of political science as a specialized discipline is reflected in the fact that very few national political science associations, such as those in the United States (1903), Canada (1913), Finland (1935), India (1938) and France existed prior to the Second World War. In fact, most were organized only in the 1950s

---

*This chapter is a revision of a paper presented to the twenty-fifth anniversary round table of IPSA.

(e.g., Israel, Belgium, West Germany, The Netherlands, Argentina, Switzerland, Australia, Great Britain) and the 1960s (e.g., Denmark, Philippines).[4] The lack of political science associations in the 1940s and even the 1950s mirrored the small number of political scientists, except in the United States where there were already 5,100 members of the APSA by 1950. For instance, Great Britain, a country recognized for its contributions to political studies over the centuries, had approximately only 50 political science teachers at the time of the founding of the association in 1950 but more than 450 by the early 1970s.[5] Similar figures for Belgium are 37 and 225, for Canada 30 and 650, Netherlands 10 and 375, Switzerland 2 and 25, Japan 250 and 750. There was a similar expansion in the number of departments of political science and a somewhat smaller increase in the number of political science journals.[6]

One would presume that the political science discipline after the war was following not only the American example but a general modernizing trend toward functional differentiation. In the Canadian case, for instance, the approximately 30 political scientists of the 1950s shared the Canadian Political Science Association and the *Canadian Journal of Economics and Political Science* with economists, sociologists, and anthropologists. Not until the mid-1960s did the latter two groups take their leave prior to the political scientists and economists each forming their own journals and associations in 1968, by which time more than 300 political scientists were teaching in Canada. Similarly, in Poland and Yugoslavia, the political science associations found their origins in the associations of jurists.

The development of relationships among political scientists at the international level since 1950 (and the relative lack of relationships prior to that date) would seem to be closely related to this massive increase in the number of political scientists and the improved national, institutional infrastructures of independent political science departments, associations, journals, and funding. This general trend of development, however, was given a boost by UNESCO, first, and later by the IPSA. The Second General Conference of UNESCO agreed that a comparative survey should be made of political science. This led to a small meeting of political scientists in Paris in 1948 which not only issued a statement about the aims, method, and scope of political science but also decided it was desirable to create an International Political Science Association.[7] At the Third General Conference of UNESCO in 1948, the director general was instructed to assist in the establishment of international associations in the social sciences and the Fourth General Conference in 1949 passed resolution 4.11 authorizing the sponsorship of associations and their financial support. Subsequently, the IPSA was founded at an international conference on political science held under the auspices of UNESCO in September 1949.

The new international association, however, was to be primarily a collection of national bodies. All basic powers were invested in a council to be composed of Collective Members (national associations plus regional associations composed of countries in the same geographical region) recognized as being representative of political science in their country. This requirement led directly to the founding of national associations. Of the twelve associations included in the council in 1952 only four had existed prior to 1950 (United States, Canada, India, and France). In the case of Great Britain, the invitation to attend the UNESCO conference in 1949 led to a movement to form the Political Studies Association in 1950.[8] The Belgium Association was given a direct grant from UNESCO to commence its operations.[9] Similar processes were sparked in other countries by the desire of political scientists to be represented in the IPSA or the desire of the latter to have wider geographical representation.

UNESCO has contributed in at least three other ways to the development of political science organizations both at the national and international levels. First, because the IPSA has consultative status with UNESCO (and with the Economic and Social Council of the United Nations) it is easier to gain access to all countries of the world and to gain funding from foundations and governments. Second, UNESCO itself has provided a small but regular base of funding for "administration, publications, research and meetings" which has helped keep the chronically underfunded international social science associations alive.[10] Third, UNESCO has made available limited funding for Third World travel to the World Congresses and, from time to time, has provided financing for international round tables of the association and some of its research committees. The regular meetings of the Committee on Political Sociology in the 1960s, for instance, were usually made possible by a grant from UNESCO.

Nevertheless, in comparison with its original contribution to international organization of the social sciences, the present level of UNESCO support is disappointing. A former IPSA president has written, "One should note the little contribution that UNESCO has made after the initial impetus. Most of the UNESCO officers with whom I have dealt have been helpful as persons but without much financial or institutional backing." This point is of extraordinary importance for the international development of the social sciences in the foreseeable future—and this for several reasons. Actual face-to-face contacts between social scientists of different countries, on a sustained, regular basis, are a sine qua non of development at the international level for progress beyond the minimal accomplishments of random, unrelated meetings at sporadic round tables and congresses. At one level, scholars who are dealing with one another over great distances and across political and ideological boundaries must get to know each other to be able to exchange ideas and research findings and have the confidence necessary to compare and contrast their work. At another level, continuity is necessary if the scholars are to plan their activity, on either a regional or intercontinental basis, in such a way that serious comparative theory and research will result.[11] However, international activity is always competing against both the relative ease of intrasocietal research (fewer impediments of language, culture, ideology, distance, finance, publishing) and the greater constraints on international research (national societies set research objectives, methods, and budgets). At the present time, for instance, less and less money is available for international travel, meetings and projects. Of the eleven national associations reporting, two replied there is no money and seven said it is more difficult now than five years ago to obtain financing for international research and meetings. This is particularly true of the United States, the traditional source of much international funding, where many universities are restricting use of their travel funds to travel in the United States and in some cases to meetings within the state. Finally, many social scientists believe that when they turn to UNESCO for support they have to compete with the organization's own program objectives—which leaves proportionately decreasing sums for the support of independent research activity.

For all these reasons, we must call on UNESCO at this time to reinforce its policies for the development of the social sciences and to take up the slack caused by the much reduced national support for international social science activity. Joseph Ben-David has summed up the general case very succinctly.

But these formal (statistical methods and mathematical models) aspects of social science can contribute little to the field in general without systematic comparative research. This is because there are so few possibilities for social experimentation that comparative research is usually the only way to test the validity of a generalization....

In the organization and support of comparative studies there has been actually a retrogression since the 1950's.... Comparative studies can advance only when competent workers with genuinely common interests can coordinate research in different countries.... In the 1950's, when the social sciences, for the first time in their history, became genuinely international ... their work received some small but effective support both from UNESCO and from foundations. The UNESCO funds involved were small, but permanently available. They were allocated rather informally.... Their criterion for allocating funds to a research committee was that it consist of a strong international group which could be expected to produce good research....

The disappearance of this framework (for the informal coordination of research) combined with the new tendency to pressure social, as well as other, scientists to do socially relevant research has weakened comparative research considerably. Since practical social policy is made on a national level, the pressure for social relevance usually implies a devaluation of comparative work.

As a result of these developments, a new parochialism has arisen in social research.... This trend ought to be, and probably could be reversed by relatively modest support for comparative research.[12]

After the original stimulus given by UNESCO, the International Political Science Association took off with its own program to develop political science at the international level. During the past quarter-century, it has grown from an association with 4 original Collective Members and a number of individual members to a worldwide organization with 39 Collective Members on every continent, representing Western, socialist, and Third World regimes.[13] Its 52 individual members in 1952 now number more than 1,000 and the 8 associate members (libraries, research centers) have grown to 114. There were 80 participants at the first World Congress held in Zurich in 1950 and 1,466 at the eleventh congress in Moscow in 1979. In addition, the association sponsors 21 research committees, 7 study groups and supports three periodicals, the *International Political Science Abstracts*, *Participation* (the IPSA newsletter), and the *International Political Science Review*. Also, it initiated the *International Bibliography of Political Science*. The association and its research committees have been responsible for more than 54 books, reports, and special issues of journals and for microfiche sets of congress and round-table papers.[14] In 1980 it established a book series to be published by Sage.

From its origin, the IPSA had had a double mandate. One was the advancement of political science throughout the world by promoting research and communications and contacts among political scientists. The second was encouraging the establishment and development of national political science associations. In his 1976 report to the association, the secretary-general, André Philippart, was able to report that the IPSA had played a fundamental role in the establishment of 27 national associations and in the introduction of political science as an autonomous discipline in these countries.

This continuing process was carried out in a number of ways. Promotional round tables and seminars have been

Table 2.1 Participation in Round Tables and Seminars Organized or Sponsored by the International Political Science Association 1950–1977

YEAR	MEMBER	TOTAL	Western Europe, North America, Israel, Australasia	Socialist countries in Eastern Europe	Middle East, Africa, Asia, Latin America
1953	France	38	31		7
	France	20	18	2	0
1954	Italy	46	43	0	3
1956	Switzerland	33	29	2	2
1957	USA	38	32	2	4
1959	Yugoslavia	41	29	9	3
1960	USA	41	37	2	2
1962	Germany	—	—	—	—
1963	UK	—	—	—	—
1964	India	31	12	0	19
1964	Uganda (seminar)	24	5		19
1965	France	36	24	5	7
1966	Poland	59	23	31	5
1967	India (seminar)	32	1		31
1967	Turkey	24	13	2	9
1968	Austria	40	28	9	3
1969	Italy	44	33	8	3
1969	Czechoslovakia	58	11	42	5
1970	Brazil	26	6	0	20
1971	Belgium	57	46	3	8
1972	Romania	53	19	29	5
1973	Italy	17	17	0	0
1974	Brazil	12	6	0	6
1974	Israel	28	25	2	1
1974	Belgium	22	17	3	2
1975	Paris	20	19	1	0
1975	Paris	22	17	3	2
1975	Malaysia	20	—	—	—
1975	Canada	20	20	0	0
1975	Luxemburg	8	8	0	0
1975	Poland	17	7	8	2
1975	Yugoslavia	31	18	9	4
1975	Poland	17	4	11	2
1977	Poland	35	16	14	5
	Total	1010	614	197	179

SOURCE: IPSA records, 1978.

sponsored by the IPSA in various countries of Asia, Africa, Latin America, and Eastern Europe since 1959 (see table 2.1). Individual political scientists from countries without associations are named by the president to the association's council which then makes them eligible for election to the executive committee. Special travel grants are provided to bring Third World scholars to the congresses and round tables. The president, vice-presidents, and secretary-general attend local meetings and develop contacts with individual scholars, academies, and various centers and institutes. In some cases, regional-continental associations (e.g., in Africa) are formed, so that the relatively small number of political scientists may lend each other mutual cooperation and support. IPSA individual and associate memberships have also had a limited effect in bringing information to a few scholars in the Third World. In these ways, the IPSA has built up its official representation from around the world to a reasonable degree—given the fact that political science scholarship just does not exist yet, or is not tolerated, in many countries.

Table 2.2 shows us that in 1980 Western Europeans and European-settled countries were balanced in the IPSA by socialist and Third World countries as far as the number of Collective Members and membership on the council and executive committee were concerned. While

Table 2.2 Representation in the Governing Organs of the International Political Science Association 1952–1980

YEAR	MEMBERSHIP	TOTAL	Western Europe, North America, Israel, Australasia	Socialist countries in Eastern Europe	Middle East, Africa, Asia, Latin America
1980	Collective members	40	19	8	13
1952–1976	Council members	403	228	67	108
1952	Council members	33	27	2	4
1976	Council members	57	29	12	16
1949–1977	Executive Committee members	82	47	14	21
1949	Executive Committee members	11	7	1	3
1980	Executive Committee members	18	9	4	5
1953–1977	Location of round tables	34	19	8	7

SOURCE: IPSA membership records, 1980.

this balance does not, of course, reflect the real number of countries in the world in each category, or the world population, it is a considerable improvement on the early 1950s and more than reflects the distribution of the equally real activity of political scientists (as we shall see below). We also note that through the years there has been the same rough balance between the three groupings of countries in membership on the council and in the location of round tables. Such a situation is much more a result of recognition within the IPSA that part of its vocation is as a representative, international organization than it is a result of natural forces within the discipline.

The same conclusion of movement toward a better regional distribution of activity can be drawn from an analysis of the location of IPSA executive committee meetings and world congresses.

Tables 2.3 and 2.4 read together indicate a slow but steady decentralization of IPSA official activities. Between 1949 and 1970, all world congresses and 21 of 25 executive committee meetings were held in Western Europe. But from 1970 to 1977 more than half of the executive committee meetings were held outside this area and of the four congresses held between 1970 and 1982, only one was within Europe (see table 2.3). Underneath the figures lies the highly significant fact that non-Western countries are beginning to be willing to host and finance world congresses and executive meetings of political scientists (see table 2.4). There will be, therefore, greater prospects for contacts between these scholars from different political systems.

Aside from the greater regional distribution in the official activities of the IPSA, tables 2.1 and 2.4 also point out the rapid increase in both the number of activities and the number of participants. While only 8 papers were presented at the first congress in 1950, some 327 papers were presented at the tenth congress in 1976. Again, during the first 20 years of the association, there were 18 round tables but the rhythm of activity had increased to 16 round tables in 1970–1977. However, the quickening rhythm of activity and the greater and somewhat more diversified participation should be considered in the context of even greater activity within countries. More than 2,000 Americans come together at the annual meetings of their association and between 300 and 500 political scientists attend the annual meetings within countries such as Germany, the United Kingdom, Japan, India and Canada, whereas only 1,000–1,500 attend the international congresses once every three years. Clearly, only a small proportion of political scientists are active at the international level. We may now turn to the question of

Table 2.3 Location of Executive Committee Meetings and World Congresses: IPSA 1949–1977

YEAR	LOCATION	TOTAL	Western Europe, North America, Israel, Australasia	Socialist countries in Eastern Europe	Middle East, Africa, Asia, Latin America
1949–1969	Executive Committee meeting	25	21 + 2 USA	2	0
1970–1977	Executive Committee meeting	12	5 + 2 Canada + 1 Israel	3	1
1950–1970	World Congresses	8	8	0	0
1973–1982	World Congresses	4	1 + 1 Canada	1	1

SOURCE: IPSA records, 1981.

Table 2.4 World Congress Participation: IPSA 1950–1982

YEAR	LOCATION	PARTICIPANTS	COUNTRIES	PAPERS	TOPICS
1950	Zurich	80	23	8	3
1952	The Hague	220	31	57	4
1955	Stockholm	275	36	25	6
1958	Rome	320	31	77	6
1961	Paris	425	46	59	5
1964	Geneva	494	43	94	6 + 6 SM*
1967	Brussels	745	56	146	9 + 10 SM*
1970	Munich	894	46	259	4 + 15 SM*
1973	Montreal	1144	46	324	20 + 7 RC** + 12 SM*
1976	Edinburgh	1081	56	327	22 + 10 RC** + 32 SM*
1979	Moscow	1466	53	...	27 + 14 RC** + 50 SM*
1982	Rio de Janeiro	...	...	...	...

SOURCE: IPSA records, 1981.
NOTES: *SM: Special meeting
**RC: Research committee

who these people are. Who participates in IPSA academic meetings and what do they discuss?

Tables 2.4 and 2.5 indicate that while activity was being rapidly increased and slowly redistributed on a world scale, the actual participation in IPSA academic events is still very lop-sided. Table 2.5 confirms that the political scientists who are able to participate actively on a continuing basis in IPSA scientific activities and benefit from the membership services of the association are for the most part of Western European extraction. Not more than 20% of the members of the research committees and of the association, or of the participants in the 1973 and 1976 congresses, have come from the socialist and Third World countries combined, although the percentage passed 50 for the Moscow Congress. The conclusion is clear that at the research end of things the IPSA is still a place where political scientists from similar regimes and similar cultures are able to work together. Once again, this conclusion must not be considered out of context. The fact is that the vast majority of the world's political scientists live in Western Europe and North America and meetings and research are likely to correspond to their interests and locale. Both these factors must be taken into account. Without common interests cooperation cannot be sustained. But, at the same time, table 2.1 shows that when the locale of a meeting changes so does the structure of participation. Particularly disturbing, however, is the relative absence of Third World and socialist country political scientists from the research committees because these committees "are carrying out many more functions than originally assumed and are, in effect, responsible for the continuing academic activity of the Association."[15]

One final point needs to be made about participation—a point which does not show up in the quantitative data. Over the years, the IPSA has been driven along, oriented, and maintained by a small group of men.[16] These include the presidents and secretaries-general, of course, but they also include, during the past ten years of rapid growth, many of the members of the

Table 2.5 Participation in the IPSA Academic Meetings and Membership by World Groups 1953–1977

YEAR	MEMBERSHIP	TOTAL NO.	Western Europe, North America, Israel, Australasia	Socialist countries in Eastern Europe	Middle East, Africa, Asia, Latin America
1953–77	Participants in round tables	1010	614	197	179
1973	World Congress participants	1181	1103	24	54
1976	World Congress participants	1081	885	91	105
1979	World Congress participants	1466	662	610	194
1977	Research Committee members	388	315	35	38
1977	Individual IPSA members	600	530	8	62
1977	Associate members of IPSA	150	120	3	27

SOURCE: IPSA records, 1979.

executive committee and individuals who started up and operated the research committees. Often, they were one and the same.

But, participation for what? What topics have attracted the attention of political scientists working in the IPSA? The following list gives a rather rough categorization of the research interests as indicated by the main topics and special group sessions at world congresses and by topics of the round tables of the IPSA from 1950 to 1977:

Topic Area	Number of Meetings
1. Political behavior and attitudes (including leadership, violence, recruitment, opinion, generations, consciousness, communications, women, youth, political support, protest and opposition)	26
Parties and elections	10 } 44
Interest groups	5
Elites and stratification	3
2. Institutional structures and processes (including legislatures, executives, military decision-making, policy analysis, decentralization, and ungovernability)	11
Public administration	8 } 39
Local government, and politics	6
Finance, corruption, and politics	4
Science and politics	4
Church as a political institution	3
The courts, laws, and the constitution	3
3. Political science and theory (including research, teaching, experimentation, quantitative and mathematical methods, models, comparative, surveys, and theory)	34
4. Interdisciplinary studies (including politics and psychology, biology, economics, geography, history, culture, environment)	34
5. International relations (including foreign policy, peace and conflict studies, international organizations)	25
6. Political development and modernization	13 } 19
Political change (including futurology, planning, cycles, alternate models)	6
7. The study of segmented societies and integration (including federalism, ethnic and linguistic politics, regionalism, pluralism, European integration, minimum conditions)	17
8. Ideologies	4
History of political thought	3 } 8
Political philosophy	1
9. Area studies	6
TOTAL	226

NOTE: Some of the topics had to be included under two headings. Also, the categories are a little more numerous and detailed than those used in some bibliographic materials (such as the *International Political Science Abstracts*) so the reader may obtain a better impression of the substance of the meetings.

The following list of the IPSA research committees and study groups in 1981 reinforces the categorization of the subject matters handled by the association:

Research Committees
1. Conceptual and terminological analysis
2. Political elites
3. European unification
4. Latin American politics
5. Comparative studies on local government and politics
6. Political sociology
7. Quantitative and mathematical approaches to politics
8. Legislative specialists
9. Comparative judicial studies
10. Peace and conflict studies
11. Science and politics
12. Biology and politics
13. Development and political systems
14. Politics and ethnicity
15. Political geography
16. Sociopolitical problems of pluralism
17. The emerging international economic order
18. Asian political studies
19. Sex roles and politics
20. Political finance and political corruption
21. Political education

Study Groups
1. Politics and law
2. Comparative political ideas
3. Political support and alienation
4. Human rights
5. Global communication
6. Technology and development
7. Armed forces and society
8. Political science in developing countries
9. Marxist political thought
10. Constitution-making as a political process
11. Psychopolitics
12. Analytical political philosophy

The topics are broad and numerous and indicate a reasonable balance of interest between process and structure, a firm commitment to interdisciplinary work, and a tradition of interest in political development. The subject matter is usually field rather than issue oriented and only rarely concentrates on specific geographical problem areas or conflicts. The approach is heavily behavioral and even many of the institutional topics could be included under this heading—thus reflecting American political science. As one would expect in an international association, international relations is a subject rating high in importance. There also seems to be a bias toward the study of the maintenance of political systems, especially pluralistic ones. Although not categorized as such, much of the analysis in the round tables and research committees is comparative. Finally, one must note that political philosophy, political ideas, and the history of political thought play a small role in the interests of the association; they are, in fact, almost completely absent.

Non-IPSA Contacts Among Political Scientists

Of course, not all the international contacts between political scientists are made within the framework of the International Political Science Association. Many contacts between scholars result from the international movement of individuals—through migration, foreign scholarships, guest professorships, internationally coordinated research projects, and editorial boards for publications.

Many of these individual contacts stemmed from the predominant position of American social sciences in the third quarter of the twentieth century. While this chapter is mainly concerned with bilateral and multilateral international contacts, it would be incomplete without reference to the profound impact of the United States on social scientists around the world. The United States was both the social science Mecca and the home of the evangelizing prophets.

American scholarships brought in political science students and sent abroad American graduate students in hundreds. One prominent political scientist wrote that almost all his sustained, international contacts were with the colleagues from around the world he had met as a graduate student at Yale. American foundations not only funded most of the major international research projects (usually designed and built in the U.S.) but sent out ambassadors-at-large for American political science in the Third World. A leading American political scientist has written, "What lay behind my own efforts during these years, and those of many others, was the conviction that the uneven development of the social sciences and their practical monopoly by the U.S. imposed an obligation to encourage social science development in other parts of the world." American foundations also financed many foreign scholars from their regional offices throughout the world. American graduate schools (Harvard, Yale, Princeton, Stanford, Berkeley, Duke, and M.I.T. to mention a few) and specialized institutes such as the Survey Research Center at Michigan, the School of Advanced International Studies of Johns Hopkins and its Bologna Center, and the Center for Advanced Research at Stanford, were growth centers which brought people together from many countries and sparked the international development of the discipline. Also, major projects such as the SSRC Committee on Comparative Politics included scholars from many countries. Foreign political scientists published in American publications and American political scientists created informal networks for research and communication. For instance, of the fifteen research committees of the IPSA in 1980, the chairman or secretary of ten was located in the United States.

However, we are probably already facing a changing situation. As one correspondent has commented, "Clearly, the 1970's/80's is likely to be polycentric. It remains to be seen whether the same sort of international network will operate from a variety of nodes, as it did with America as a central clearing house." This polycentric international development of political science, often in tandem with other social sciences, is taking several forms outside the IPSA including financing, regional activity, and subdisciplinary contacts.

Research and conference funding is now becoming available from multiple sources including international and regional organizations such as the Common Market and OPEC, and such countries as Japan, Germany, Sweden, Brazil, and Canada. At the same time that we hear complaints from Americans about their growing difficulties in obtaining financial support for comparative research and international activity, we hear increasingly of support from European, Latin American, and Japanese foundations. Also, new, experimental, thoroughly internationalized agencies have appeared, such as the International Development Research Center based in Canada.

The past ten years have seen a striking increase in regional cooperation among political scientists. One can note, for instance, the role of the European Consortium for Political Research and the Nordic Cooperation Committee on International Politics, the increasing activity of the African Political Science Association and the importance of FLACSO and CLACSO for maintaining the social sciences in Latin America. The Eastern European political science associations have also held their first joint meetings. Another new development is interregional contact in the form of the Twinned Workshops of the European Consortium and the Canadian Political Science Association, initiated in 1976.

Some of the activity within the regions is concentrated around specific institutes which are becoming poles of attraction and centers of contact. Usually, these institutes and research centers are wedded to particular subdisciplinary topics. For instance, the Wiessenschaft Zentrum in Berlin and the Rio Research Center are delving heavily into the political and social aspects of world modelling. Many countries have peace research institutes which attract foreign scholars and which meet together in regular world conferences. The same is true of strategic studies and foreign affairs institutes which cooperate both bilaterally and internationally. The International Studies Association (USA) has, for some time, been the place of meeting for international relations specialists and comparativists from numerous countries. The Vienna Center for the Coordination of Research and Documentation in the Social Sciences has played a widely recognized role in stimulating East-West research cooperation. In addition, there is a growing number of institutes, conferences, and summer training schools for the study of comparative politics, futurology, survey methods, data-banking and coordination, political development, political integration, and area studies. There is also a whole panoply of area studies associations in which political scientists are active.

One general category of scholars which is rather remarkable for its absence from both the mainstream political groups and from the IPSA are political philosophers, in general, and Western Marxist-oriented scholars, Neo-Marxists and representatives from the various critical, radical schools of political theory, in particular. Various individuals from these groups appear on IPSA programs from time to time but, as representatives of a political science approach, they have little impact on IPSA activities—witness the composition of the executive, the congresses, and the research committees. One reason for this is that many have little attraction for what they perceive as the American scientific-behavioralist approach which holds sway in the IPSA. A second reason is that few of them consider political science to be their discipline.[17] Most, at least in Europe, are in the neighboring disciplines of history, philosophy, sociology, and economics.

These disciplines provide some institutional networks, such as the International Sociological Association and the Association de sociologues de langue française, for the Marxists (a generic term, probably incorrect, to denote Marxist theorists, students of Marxism-Leninism, those using a Marxist approach, Communists, Socialists and Leftists). Also, new groupings such as the recently formed "Centre international de coordination des recherches sur l'autogestion" have resulted from the two International Conferences on Participation, Workers' Control and Self-Management held in Dubrovnik (1972) and in Paris (1977). In North America, there is also the Association for Economic Democracy, formerly People for Self-Management. There is also a European committee doing comparative studies of workers' participation in the various European economies.

However, the main networks of contact between these scholars are more individually based. They arise from a number of sources. Major philosophers and theorists often create schools transcending state boundaries. Some scholars work through the semiofficial channels of meetings and conferences organized by agencies and parties, especially in Eastern Europe. But the majority of contacts are personal and individual, including visiting lectureships, relations with former students and colleagues, and often following the path traced by former colonial ties. These individual contacts are reinforced by relationships formed around certain institutes and centers (such as the International Institute for Social History in Amsterdam, the Feltrinelli Institute of Milan, the Max Planck Institute in Starnberg, and the Centre d'études et de recherches Marxistes), and also certain journals and publishing houses of the Left (including *Telos, New Left Review, Monthly Review, Science and Society,* and publishers like Anthropos and Maspero). Personal contacts are often developed into informal, individually sponsored circles of scholars working over long periods of time on specific theoretical or research problems that are of common interest.

Why the Western Marxists and other critical theorists are not active in the mainstream of international political science institutions is another question. One may hazard a number of hypotheses. One is that they do not perceive a hospitable climate in the international institutions, that is, they do not find program items that interest them or they do not know people active in the groups. Secondly, some are active in national class struggles and have few international dimensions or contacts in their work. A third is that there is not, as yet, a clear relationship between the presence of representatives of socialist countries in international associations and their reactions to Western radical scholars. Fourth, many Marxists reject the division of labor and theorizing implicit in a separate discipline of political science and prefer to work in interdisciplinary groups or publications which they believe capture better the dynamism and interaction of the elements of the societies they are studying. Finally, the lack of contact between the Marxist and non-Marxist approaches at the international level may simply reflect a similar state of affairs in universities where many political scientists, even well-disposed ones, find Left-sponsored meetings to be a curious mixture of scientists, party hacks, and polemicists.

Some slight signs indicate that this rather unproductive, ideological isolation is slowly being bridged. One notes an (unquantified) tendency to more eclectic references in bibliographies. A growing number of self-proclaimed, Marxist-oriented scholars are in North American departments of political science. In the United States, the Caucus for a New Political Science and in Canada, the Political Economy Network, bring together all strains of normative-critical approaches. At another level, there is even a growing communication between political scientists in the East and West with Western Europeans perhaps providing the bridge both through the exchange of professors and through such organizations as the Vienna Center.[18] IPSA itself has held round tables in Rumania, Yugoslavia, and Poland in recent years and the eleventh World Congress met in Moscow in 1979. Also, a growing number of social scientists in the USSR,

Poland, and Yugoslavia refer to staple Western political science literature, both favorably and unfavorably.[19]

Conclusion

On the occasion of the twenty-fifth anniversary of the International Social Science Council, Stein Rokkan asked, how much farther have we moved toward a genuine, a lasting internationalization of the pursuit, the production, and the application of knowledge about human societies? This chapter has demonstrated that there has, in fact, been a continuing and growing trend toward the internationalization of contacts, communications, and cooperation among political scientists since 1952—a trend which is beginning to show signs of being reversed if current tendencies toward parochial interests and funding in a number of countries continue. We have seen an explosion in the number of meetings, in the amount of material produced, and in the diversity of channels of contact among political scientists at the international level. We also note that, at least at the official or organizational level within IPSA, there has been a considerable effort to augment the flow of contacts with scholars from Socialist and Third World countries. This has borne fruit in the form of a more balanced regional representation in the councils of the IPSA and also in an increase in contacts among political scientists from the East and the West.

However, our findings make it equally clear a number of major impediments to the internationalization of the pursuit of political knowledge remain. First, political science at the international level is still pretty much a Western rather than global discipline. Scholars from Third World and Socialist countries are only present in very limited numbers at conferences and in the various working groups. There are ideological, regional, political, and financial barriers to the development of the geographical reach of the discipline. Second, there is little contact between political philosophy and political science, even if the latter has been tending toward a more interdisciplinary approach. Third, there is a clear rupture in relations at the international level between what one might loosely call the American behavioral approach and the Marxist-oriented or critical school. Fourth, there are some indications we may be into a down-cycle of internationalism tied in part to criticism of the American monopoly in the discipline and in part to national demands for relevance in political research and a consonant disinclination to fund comparative and international undertakings. This tendency may be offset, at least in part, by the polycentric dimension of political science activity and funding. Fifth, international organization of the discipline continually runs the risk of being dominated by a small number of prominent, internationally recognized scholars, which may hamper a more balanced representation of all levels of personnel in the discipline.

Natural tendencies within the discipline will not be sufficient to overcome these impediments to a balanced and global internationalization. All internationally active political scientists agree that the sustained, systematic, cross-national pursuit of knowledge in the discipline takes place only when scholars share common interests and have trust and confidence in each other. The very subject matter of political science, touching as it does the nerve ends of national security and the philosophical fundamentals of societies, is bound to hamper this process. In addition, as W. J. M. Mackenzie has noted,

Political science cannot develop except in certain limited intellectual and social conditions; there must be an established practice of debate based on analysis and observation, and it must be accepted that there exist political questions open to settlement by argument rather than by tradition or by authority. In this sense, political science is conditioned by political society.[20]

We should not be surprised, then, if political science development is very much conditioned and limited by the real world of politics. There will be no magic or immediate paths to internationalization.

It may be argued though, that slow but persistent efforts by the International Political Science Association, the one body specifically created for this purpose, can do much to maximize the process of cooperation among political scientists. The association, being aware of the specific areas in which internationalization is weakest, may take steps to create the conditions which will permit scholars to discover their mutual interests and develop mutual confidence. Clearly, this is a necessary activity because as Mackenzie has also pointed out,

For the Greeks and the Romans, as for us, all political science was in a sense comparative politics. Political science has its beginning when an observer notes that another people is not governed as we are. Why? What is better?[21]

Bringing political scientists together from different countries will provide better answers to these questions. But the best strategy for universalization depends on keeping in mind what is possible *now*. This means building contacts and communication first with the expectation (justified by IPSA experience) that this will lead to common research later. The task, then, of international associations would seem to be to develop contacts, to diversify the location of meetings, and to create conditions that will both permit and attract participation by all elements of the discipline.

Notes

1. For the explanation of this process, see Stein Rokkan, "Introduction: International Cooperation in Political Sociology," in Erik Allardt and Stein Rokkan, *Mass Politics: Studies in Political Sociology* (New York: Free Press, 1970).

2. Allardt and Rokkan, *Mass Politics,* makes hypotheses along some of these lines. Almond explicitly recognized these influences on his comparative, international study of the "Civic Culture." See his "The Intellectual History of the Political Culture Concept, Round Table on Political Culture," Cracow, Poland, IPSA, 1977.

3. A more documented follow-up is being prepared. Commentary and suggestions are, therefore, welcome. In the meantime, I would like to thank all those who have offered me, orally or in written communication, the benefit of their knowledge of this period in the development of political science.

4. IPSA data from questionnaires sent to national political science associations, June 1977.

5. Norman Chester, "Political Studies in Great Britain: Recollections and Comments," *Political Studies* (1975): 161.

6. Maurice Line and Stephen Roberts, "The Size, Growth and Composition of Social Science Literature," *International Social Science Journal* 28, no. 1 (1976). The authors show that while 150 political science periodicals existed in 1950, the number was almost double (270) in 1970. But this was a fairly average growth rate for all the social sciences.

7. Chester, "Political Studies," recapitulates the story. The Preparatory Committee appointed to prepare a draft constitution for the Association consisted of Professor Walter Sharp (USA), chairman; John Goormaghtigh (Belgium), secretary; Raymond Aron (France); William Robson (UK); and Professors Appadorai (India) and M. Bridel (Switzerland). See also William Ebenstein, "Toward International Collaboration in Political Science," *American Political Science Review* 42 (December 1948): 1181–89.

8. Chester, "Political Studies," pp. 152 and 161.

9. André Philippart and Michèle Scohy-Goethals, "Les 20 ans de l'Institut belge de Science politique," *Res Publica* 13, nos. 3-4 (1971): 582.

10. In 1977 the UNESCO grant amounted to $15,000 plus a further $5,000 for a contract grant for round tables on development.

11. Not without cause, some of the best-known political researchers internationally are the ones who have served together during the past fifteen years in the IPSA and/or the Research Committee on Political Sociology (e.g., Stein Rokkan, S. M. Lipset, Juan Linz, Richard Rose, Erik Allardt, Giovanni Sartori, Jerzy Wiatr, Schmuel Eisenstadt, Mattei Dogan, Jean Laponce, Sammy Finer, Karl Deutsch, Ali Mazrui, Raymond Aron, Morris Janowitz, R. T. McKenzie, Dwaine Marvick, Otto Stammer, Erwin Scheuch, Carl J. Friedrich, Klaus von Beyme, Marcel Merle, John Meisel, Candido Mendes, Anthony Birch. Also, almost all the key members of the American SSRC Committee on Comparative Politics interacted with the IPSA/ISA Committee on Political Sociology.

12. "How to Organize Research in the Social Sciences," *Daedalus* (Spring 1973).

13. The political science associations of the following countries and world regions were Collective Members of the IPSA in 1980: Africa, Argentina, Australasia, Belgium, Bulgaria, Brazil, Canada, Denmark, Czechoslovakia, Finland, France, German Democratic Republic, German Federal Republic, Greece, Hungary, India, Israel, Italy, Japan, Korea, Lebanon, Morocco, Mexico, Netherlands, New Zealand, Norway, Pakistan, Philippines, Poland, Rumania, Spain, Sweden, Switzerland, Turkey, United Kingdom, USSR, USA, Venezuela, Yugoslavia.

14. Much of the data in this section of this chapter are based on the current records of the IPSA and on André Philippart, *Synthesis Report on the IPSA—20 Years' Activities,* IPSA, Paris, 1969, and Supplement 1970-76 by Michèle Scohy.

15. John Trent, "International Research Committees and Political Science," *Participation* (newsletter of the International Political Science Association, Ottawa) 2, no. 1 (January 1978).

16. One can also take this word in the literal sense. No woman has had an opportunity to play a dominant role in the IPSA and very few have been on the council, executive, or research committees.

17. Von Beyme, for instance, makes this point about critical theorists in Germany. Klaus von Beyme, "Bibliographical Essay on the State of Research in Political Science in the Federal Republic of Germany," *German Political Studies* 1 (1974).

18. The European Center for Coordination of Research and Documentation in Social Sciences. Many of my correspondents noted the significance of the Vienna Center. R. Petrella and A. Schaff have written about it in *An European Experiment in Cooperation in the Social Sciences* (Vienna: European Coordination Center, 1974).

19. See, for example, Jerzy Wiatr, "The Civic Culture: A Marxist Reassessment," Round Table on Political Culture, Cracow, Poland, IPSA, Ottawa, 1977, and D. E. Powell and P. Shoup, "The Emergence of Political Science in Communist Countries," *American Political Science Review* 64, no. 2 (January 1970): 572-88.

20. "The Political Science of Political Science," *Government and Opposition* 6, no. 3 (Summer 1971): 277-302.

21. Ibid., p. 293.

Bibliography

Almond, G. "The Intellectual History of the Political Culture Concept." Round Table on Political Culture, Cracow, Poland, IPSA, Ottawa, 1977.

Aron, R. "Réflexions sur la politique et la science politique français." *Revue française de science politique* 5, no. 1 (January–March 1955): 5–22.

Asirvatham, E. "Study of Political Science in India." *Indian Journal of Political Science* 16, no. 1 (January–March 1955): 1–22.

Bains, J. S. "State of Political Science in India." *Indian Journal of Political Science* 32, no. 4 (October–December 1971): 393-444.

Barents, J. *Political Science in Western Europe.* London: Stevens and Sons, 1961.

Ben-David, J. "How to Organize Research in the Social Sciences." *Daedalus* (Spring 1973).

Bociurkiw, B. R. "The Post-Stalin 'Thaw' and Soviet Political Science." *Canadian Journal of Economics and Political Science* 30, no. 1 (February 1964): 22-48.

Bonenfant, J. C. "Les études politiques (au Québec)." *Recherches socio-graphiques* 3, nos. 1-2 (January-August 1962): 75-83.

Broadhead, R. S., and Rist, R. C. "Gatekeepers and the Social Control of Social Research." *Social Problems* 23, no. 3 (February 1976): 325-36.

Cairns, A. C. "Political Science in Canada and the Americanization Issue." *Canadian Journal of Political Science* 8, no. 2 (June 1975): 191-234.

Charlesworth, J. C., ed. *A Design for Political Science.* Philadelphia: American Academy of Political Science, 1966.

Chester, N. "Political Studies in Great Britain: Recollections and Comments." *Political Studies* (1975): 151-64.

Churdrisard, L. G. "Towards a Soviet Political Science." *Australian Journal of Politics and History* 12, no. 1 (April 1966): 66-75.

Committee on Comparative Politics. *A Report on the Activities of the Committee 1954-1970.* New York: Social Science Research Council, 1971.

Dahlstrom, E. "Development Direction and Societal Rationality: The Organization of Social Knowledge Creation." *Acta Sociologica* 19, no. 1 (1976): 3-22.

Dion, L. "Politique et science politique." *Revue canadienne de science politique* 8, no. 3 (September 1975): 367-80.

Easton, D. *The Political System: An Inquiry into the State of Political Science.* New York: Alfred A. Knopf, 1953.

Gapotchka, M., and Smirnov, S. "The Social Sciences in the USSR: Status, Policy, Structures and Achievements." *International Social Science Journal* 28, no. 1 (1976): 65-98.

Goguel, F. "Situation de la science politique en France." *Annuaire suisse de science politique* 8 (1968): 19-30.

Hajjar, S. G; Bowman, J.S.; Richard, J. B. "A Portrait of the Discipline: The Professional Literature of Political Science in the '70's." *Political Science Reviewer* 5 (Fall 1975): 361-82.

Harrison, W. "The Early Days of Political Studies." *Political Studies* 23, nos. 2-3 (June-September 1975): 183-92.

Hull, W. H. N. "The 1971 Survey of the Profession." *Canadian Journal of Political Science* 6, no. 1 (March 1973): 88-94.

Irish, M. D. "Introduction: Advance of the Discipline." *Journal of Politics* 30, no. 2 (May 1968): 291-310.

———, ed. *Political Science: Advance of the Discipline.* Englewood Cliffs, N.J.: Prentice-Hall, 1968.

Kariel, H. S. *Saving Appearance: The Re-establishment of Political Science.* North Scituate, Mass.: Duxbury Press, 1972.

Klassen, D. M. C. "The Students' Image of Politics and Political Science." *Teaching Political Science* no. 1 (October 1973): 35-46.

Kuhnle, S., and Rokkan, S. "Political Research in Norway 1960-1975: An Overview," pp. 127-56. In *Scandinavian Political Studies* 12 (1977).

Ladd, E. C., Jr. and Lipset, S. M. "Portrait of a Discipline: The American Political Science Community." *Teaching Political Science* 2, no. 1 (October 1974): 3-39 and 2, no. 2 (January 1975): 144-71.

Lane, R. E. "To Nurture a Discipline." *American Political Science Review* 66, no. 1 (March 1972): 164-82.

Lasswell, H. *The Future of Political Science.* Atherton, New York, 1963.

Line, Maurice, and Roberts, Stephen. "The Size, Growth and Composition of Social Science Literature." *International Social Science Journal* 28, no. 1 (1976).

Lipset, S. M., ed. *Politics and the Social Sciences.* New York: Oxford University Press, 1969.

Lowi, T. J. "The Politicization of Political Science." *American Political Quarterly* 1, no. 1 (January 1973): 43-71.

Lucas Verdu, P. "Situation de la science politique en Espagne depuis 1945." *Social Science Information* 4, no. 4 (December 1965): 79-96.

McCloskey, R. G., and Ranney, A. "Political Science: The State of the Profession." *Political Science Quarterly* 80, no. 2 (June 1965): 277-87.

Mackenzie, W. J. M. "The Political Science of Political Science." *Government and Opposition* 6, no. 3 (Summer 1971): 277-302.

Macovescu, G. "La science politique en Roumanie." *Res Publica* 13, no. 5 (1971): 699-705.

Macpherson, C. B. "World Trends in Political Science Research." *APSR* 48 (June 1954): 427-49.

March, R. R., and Jackson, R. J. "Aspects of the State of Political Science in Canada." *Midwest Journal of Political Science* 2, no. 4 (November 1967): 433-50.

Meynaud, J. "International Cooperation in the Field of the Social Sciences: A Tentative Balance Sheet." *Reports and Papers in the Social Sciences.* UNESCO, 1961.

———, and Reynolds, P. A. "Third Congress of the IPSA." *International Social Science Bulletin* 8, no. 1 (1956): 191-97.

Morgenthau, H. J. "Reflections on the State of Political Science." *Review of Politics* 17, no. 4 (October 1955): 431-60.

Mujaju, A. B. "Political Science and Political Science Research in Africa." *African Review* 4, no. 3 (1974): 339-58.

Petrella, R., and Schaff, A. *An European Experiment in Cooperation in the Social Sciences.* Vienna: European Coordination Center, 1974.

Pfotenhauer, D. "Conceptions of Political Science in West Germany and the US: 1960-1969." *Journal of Politics* 34, no. 2 (May 1972): 554-91.

Philippart, A. "La situation de la science politique en Belgique." *Annuaire suisse de science politique* 8 (1968): 45-58.

———. *Synthesis Report on the IPSA—20 Years' Activities.*

Paris: International Political Science Association, 1969, and *Supplement 1970-1976* by Michèle Scohy.

———, and Scohy-Goethals, M. "Les 20 ans de l'Institut belge de Science politique." *Res Publica* 13, nos. 3-4 (1971): 581-646.

Pollock, J. K. "La science politique à l'ère nucléaire." *Revue française de science politique* 8, no. 4 (December 1958): 1003-10.

Powell, D. E., and Shoup, P. "The Emergence of Political Science in Communist Countries." *American Political Science Review* 64, no. 2 (January 1970): 572-88.

Revue d'enseignement supérieur, Numéro special sur différents aspects de la science politique en France no. 4 (1965).

Robson, W. A. *The University Teaching: Political Science.* UNESCO, 1954.

Rokkan, S. "Cross-Cultural, Cross-Societal and Cross-National Research in Main Trends," chapter 10. In *Main Trends of Research in the Human and the Social Sciences.* Paris: UNESCO, 1970.

———. "Introduction: International Cooperation in Political Sociology: Current Efforts and Future Possibilities." In *Mass Politics: Studies in Political Sociology,* edited by E. Allardt and S. Rokkan. New York: Free Press, 1970.

Rose, R. Introduction to *Electoral Behavior: A Comparative Handbook.* Edited by R. Rose. New York: Free Press, 1973.

Ruffieux, R. "La science politique en Suisse." *Annuaire suisse de science politique* 8 (1968): 73-88.

Ruin, O. "Political Science in Sweden in the Post-War Period." *Scandinavian Political Studies* 4 (1969): 171-82.

Sidjanski, D. "Dimensions européennes de la science politique." Paris: Librairie générale de droit et de jurisprudence, 1963.

Somit, A., and Tanenhaus, J. *American Political Science.* New York: Atherton Press, 1964.

———. *The Development of Political Science.* Boston: Allyn and Bacon, 1967.

Spadaro, R. N., et al. *The Policy Vacuum: Toward a More Professional Political Science.* Toronto: Lexington Books, 1975.

Spann, R. N. "Political Science in Australia." *Australian Journal of Politics and History* 1, no. 1 (November 1955): 86-97.

Surkin, M., and Wolfe, A., eds. *An End to Political Science.* New York: Basic Books, 1970.

Szalai, A., et al. "Introduction." *Cross-National Comparative Survey Research: Theory and Practice.* Mouton: The Hague, 1975.

Thakurdas, F. "The Expanding Frontier of Political Science." *Indian Journal of Political Science* 34, no. 4 (October-December 1973): 397-404.

Theen, R. H. W. "Political Science in the USSR." *World Politics* 23, no. 4 (July 1971): 684-703.

Thormann, M. "La renaissance de la science politique en Allemagne." *Politique* 6, nos. 21-24 (1963): 285-300.

Trent, J. E. "International Research Committees and Political Science." In *Participation* (newsletter of the International Political Science Association, Ottawa) 2, no. 1 (January 1978).

———. IPSA World Congress Reports. *PS* (Fall 1973 and Fall 1976).

UNESCO. *Contemporary Political Science.* Paris: UNESCO, 1950.

———. *Social Science Organization and Policy.* 1st ser.: Belgium, Chile, Egypt, Hungary, Nigeria, Sri Lanka. With an introduction by A. B. Cherns. The Hague: Mouton, 1974.

———. *The Social Sciences: Problems and Orientations.* The Hague: Mouton; Paris: UNESCO, 1968.

von Beyme, K. "Bibliographical Essay on the State of Research in Political Science in the Federal Republic of Germany." *German Political Studies* 1 (1974).

Waldo, D. Introduction to *Handbook of Political Science.* Edited by N. Polsby and F. Greenstein. New York: Addison-Wesley, 1975.

White, L. "Political Science, Mid-Century." *Journal of Politics* 12, no. 1 (February 1950): 13-19.

Wiatr, J. J. "The Civic Culture: A Marxist Reassessment." Round Table on Political Culture. Cracow, Poland: IPSA, Ottawa, 1977.

———. "Les sciences politiques en Pologne." *Social Science Information* 5, no. 1 (March 1966): 66-77.

Wright, Q. "The Significance of the International Political Science Association." *International Social Science Bulletin* 3, no. 2 (1951): 275-80.

Position in the Social Sciences* 3

ANDRÉ PHILIPPART

About the Concept and the Outlines

Marcel Proust wrote that "the state of mind when one invents is superior to the state of mind when one recounts." An analysis of the evolution of political science relies more on invention than narration, and to situate it among the social sciences is a delicate task that many specialists have abandoned. Nevertheless, political science functions. Over the last thirty years it has expanded considerably—allowing the belief that it has secured its place among the disciplines of the human sciences. Even so, after thirty years, specialists do not agree on the epistemology of political science.

In its uniqueness, the concept simultaneously represents contexts that vary from one generation to another and hermetic languages among specialists of different political regimes and of varying levels of economic development. Nevertheless, it helps in becoming oriented, *a contrario* sometimes, to become a *politiste, politicologue*, a political scientist by rejecting other disciplines.

The basis of political science is always a model of society to be defended or extolled. What could be more natural, it will be said: does not medicine have the safekeeping of the individual as its objective? And other sciences, do they not tend invariably toward a model of improved conditions?

It would be reckless to affirm that political science is a science in the sense that it covers a coherent body of knowledge of a precise subject obtained by methods proved by experimentation whose objective relationships can be submitted to observation constantly.

Political science is a discipline of observation where the subject for study—*political power*—is only described. From the moment its followers make models and try to quantify it, they go astray in formulating doctrines of the self-regulation of societies, revolutionary ideology, political morality, the psychology of groups.

Political science has frontiers of great elasticity and an extensive capacity for appropriation. In other words, there has been a latent conflict for 25 years between those who see political science as a *crossroads science* and those who see it as a *synthetic science*. We are not going to resolve this conflict, since we are close to François Bourricaud: "There is nothing more vain than quarrels about boundaries. But there is nothing worse than 'interdisciplinary' integrations that mix everything up in a magma of generalities and good intentions."[1]

No specialist any longer waits to resolve that conflict after the great period of the masters in the 1950s, from Georges Burdeau to Raymond Aron including J. J. Chevallier, C. A. Colliard, F. Goguel and many others like Bertrand de Jouvenel.

Alongside the French school that sprang from the long tradition of Emile Boutmy, the founder of the *Ecole libre des Sciences politiques* in 1872 which became the *Fondation nationale des Sciences politiques* in 1945, the English-speaking school was developing—American more than anything—less preoccupied than its sister in resolving an epistemological question but more inclined to give concrete significance to the mechanisms of power.

The Main Orientations of the Discipline

Jean Meynaud had been nurtured at the springs of the French school (he was, moreover, the general secretary of the *Fondation nationale des Sciences politiques* until July 1954). But his intellectual penchant induced him to examine himself in the manner of his English-speaking

---

*Report prepared in August 1978 for the colloquium organized by CRISP on September 27, 28, 29, 1978, on the theme: "Jean Meynaud: Le système de la décision politique."

colleagues. His *Introduction à la science politique* is one of the great contemporary works of political science.[2]

It provides a very complete discussion of current questions about the discipline, without aspiring to be a treatise:

— theoretical models of analysis
— the object of political science
— the selection and processing of data
— the influence of law, sociology, history, and economics on the discipline
— the attractiveness of quantification techniques and their transposition in political science
— the place of political science among the social sciences
— terminological deficiencies
— ideological pluralism
— the conditions of the development of the discipline

At the time that he concluded his work with a statement of conditions proper to all science (requirement for exactness, refusal of moralism, freedom of expression and autonomy), a committee of the American Political Science Association proposed that it prepare specialists at "teaching good citizenship."[3] This was the object of recriminations by many colleagues.

This dilemma continues, with the amount of constraint varying by political regimes. And, if political science is the emanation of political power, of whatever the ideological foundation, it tends invariably to remain aloof from the regime that represents power, including Marxist regimes. But is this a sufficient reason to place political science among the sciences?

The question has not been resolved. Perhaps several more generations will be necessary for our discipline to acquire the characteristics of a science, of becoming as J. Meynaud said: "a discipline capable of attaining results that only the blind or partisans could contest."[4]

Evolution: The First-Generation *Politistes*

The evolution of international political science began in 1949 with the creation of the International Political Science Association in Paris, under the auspices of UNESCO, when eminent representatives of the four existing national associations (France, the United States, Canada, India) decided to become involved collegially in the development of political science.

Quincy Wright, Maurice Duverger, Jean Meynaud, François Goguel, Raymond Aron, André Siegfried, C. B. MacPherson, Adam Schaff, Denis Brogan, and Phedon Vegleris were among those promoters. No *politiste*, as we understand the term now, figured among these pioneers. They were jurists, philosophers, or graduates of classical studies, but they were all careful to give to the analysis of political power proper status according to reliable criteria. Some scholars, too, were capable of assimilating—as did Carl Friedrich, Stanislaw Ehrlich, or Karl Deutsch—the ancestors of political science (Solon, Plato, Aristotle, Saint Augustine, Machiavelli, Montesquieu, the Enlightenment philosophers, Aléxis de Tocqueville, and so on) and were capable at the same time of tackling with great perception the complexity of contemporary problems.

This generation produced thousands of books that cannot be ignored, developed instruction in a large number of universities and countries, educated thousands of *politistes* and political scientists, created hundreds of research institutes and journals. Undeniably, under its influence politics of parties, governmental decisions, power relationships among institutions, groups, and societies have become better clarified. Probably, the social order has benefited from it.

The Ways of Tradition

The political research of the 1950–1960 generation was concentrated in several domains, neglected by specialists in our time, but largely salvaged by the holders of political power, reminding, if necessary, those who might have forgotten that political science and practical politics cannot be separated.

This follows the great tradition of Montesquieu, whose most celebrated title—rarely given in full, *De L'Esprit des lois ou du Rapport que les lois doivent avoir avec la constitution de chaque gouvernement, les moeurs, le climat, la réligion, le commerce, etc.*—reveals the author's intention to analyze the political situation in its complex entirety. That is the tradition also, of the great ideological families that continue to dominate the world: Catholicism, Protestantism, liberalism, socialism, communism.

These traditional domains are the following:

The rational order and the spirit of justice. The concepts of order and justice stood as landmarks for more than two thousand years. These ideas favored the extensive liberation of men and the attenuation of their differences (free men vs. slaves, noblemen vs. serfs, natural equality, the rights of men and citizens, nonalienation, decolonization, racial integration, the new world economic order).

Many *politistes* took an interest in the works of those

who had long been considered philosophers, utopians, or doctrinarians, although they were very often the *politistes* of their time, men like Hugo Grotius, Jean Bodin, John Locke, Jean-Jacques Rousseau, Saint Simon, Proudhon, Karl Marx, or Lenin.

Since 1950 these themes have been taken up regularly in the world congresses and round-table discussions of the International Political Science Association. They constitute a means of privileged contact with colleagues from socialist countries of Marxist ideology, who need points of reference in order to prove the adequacy of their political regime according to the doctrine of scientific materialism.

National sovereignty and legitimacy. The great invention of the seventeenth century, developed by the Enlightenment and triumphant since the liberal bourgeois revolution, is the principle of national sovereignty. It has changed the entire world over the past century and a half, from the several states gathered in 1815 at the Congress of Vienna to the 149 member-states of the United Nations at present. The study of the upheavals that the concrete application of the principle of national sovereignty has engendered is a very fertile field in itself. The organization and functioning of political systems are deeply involved in it: parliamentary democracy, the presidential system, dictatorship of the proletariat, democratic centralism, or even the unitary state, federal state, and regional state.

Legitimacy is one of the most delicate questions, not for jurists but for *politistes*. It is the corollary of national sovereignty. What definition can be given to legitimacy, as much for a political system as for the political regime that governs it? By what means is legitimacy distinguished from nonlegitimacy? What values are attached to it?

For great contemporary works on the subject we are indebted to Carl J. Friedrich—one of the most prestigious political scientists—with titles such as *Man and His Government, Totalitarianism, Constitutional Government and Democracy,* and to Samuel Huntington's *Political Order in Changing Societies* and to Georges Burdeau with his *Traité de Science Politique.*

But Western *politistes* seem to be turning away from this serious theme, although the eleventh World Congress of the IPSA in Moscow in August 1979 returned to it under the cover of general themes like "peace and change in the world order" or "equilibrium of power and integration, as ways toward peace."

The Idea of power. The idea of power is not the exclusive property of political science. Economics takes a more particular interest in it even when it concerns political power. But it is undeniable that, since Machiavelli, this subject is one of the predilections of the political domain and is found inevitably in all works on political power.

Roberto Michels, Max Weber, Gaetano Mosca, Antonio Gramsci, for example, set forth very pertinent definitions of political power well before the development of political science—in the course of the study of political parties, the structure of societies, and the action of groups. Later authors took it up in a manner still unequaled. Bertrand de Jouvenel of the French school, Harold D. Lasswell, Charles Merriam, and Robert Dahl on the English-speaking side devoted their strengths and their talent to it.

"Political power," the equivalent of "power," should be understood both as the capacity of every political figure to act, whether or not he has the requisite authority, and as the expression of the invested authority. But the analysis of political power—as fundamental and interesting as it is—does not suffice to give a true image of political life. Power and political life do not function in a vacuum. The political environment contains institutions, decision mechanisms, power relationships, interests, and men.

Institutions and political mechanisms. This is the broad domain of political historians and constitutionalists such as Jean Dabin who defined political science as a science whose subject is the State and Marcel Prélot, for whom it was the science of power.

In this area, also, we find specialists of political ideas: in the beginning, historians, critical archivists like Jean Touchard or Jean-Jacques Chevallier concerned with doing historical criticism and comparative analysis; later, activists like Nicos Poulantzas appeared who were involved in political demonstration and in the logical explanation of an ineluctable evolution of political systems toward democratic socialism. Some students desire to know for the sake of intellectual satisfaction; some work with the conviction of arranging the elements of a science: political science. Others hold the political conviction of using acquired knowledge to institute another type of society.

But, basically, is there not a sort of mystification in seeming to contrast what should be considered science and what is held to be practice? Is it certain that broad analyses—those of American scholars for example—of liberal democracy are more scientific than those dedicated to scientific Marxism? Since 1953, several round-table discussions of the International Political Science Association have been devoted to this debate. They have had the essential merit of requiring East and West to confront each other by recourse to argument.

The Second-Generation Politistes

More and more numerous on the market, obliged to publish without respite in order to make a career in the profession, consulted as experts by decision makers, victims of their first success, *politistes* come to ask concrete questions about the reason for their discipline and about the place that they occupy in society.

This crisis-of-conscience phase began about 1960. Is political science useful? What can it offer that is concrete for the solution of the increasingly complex political, social, and economic problems in the world? First, a profound epistemological knowledge of the discipline and its objective was needed. This knowledge could have become possible only by means of a collection of monographs on all the accepted and imaginable subjects. Secondly, came the time of confrontation and the critical examination of an increasingly abundant documentation whose value lay in being translated into theoretical syntheses.

Political knowledge. Political knowledge was literary, philosophical, deliberate. Political science had little description or analysis. Any improvement of its standing required, then, an impressive effort at surveying the limits of the field that had been traced by the initiators of the evolution. Descriptions of political situations, of decision-making processes, of relationships among regimes and groups as well as case studies of political behavior and attitudes underwent what Bertrand de Jouvenel called "effervescence."

Each author, in the absence of rules and established, unquestioned norms, began by defining his own criteria to support his analysis. That done, he was constrained to make up his arsenal of information, references, quantifiable data, and facts capable of being linked in chains of causality. At the time, the most advanced were those who analyzed election results at the national level and, sometimes, at the regional and local levels.

Tables of results, maps of political representation, variation over time, voter shifts, analysis of the causes of failure and success, electoral behavior, were presented in a large number of works by a great many authors whose original model was the work of André Siegfried. *Politistes* like Maurice Duverger, Stein Rokkan, Avery Leiserson, and Erik Allardt distinguished themselves. Later, teams and research centers in each country specialized in electoral study to become—like the one at the University of Mannheim directed by Rudolph Wildenmann—large units of research and documentation, through the use of computers. The works of DeSmet, Evalenko, Fraeys of the *Université Libre de Bruxelles* and the documentation of CRISP are convincing examples that political science will be useful in electoral study as long as elections are one technique for choosing public officials.

Other domains attracted a great deal of attention and a certain amount of continuity as the following list indicates:

— *the study of local government* with specialists such as W. A. Robson, D. N. Chester, J. Djordjevic, G. Langrod, J. Wiatr
— *the study of political parties* with several authors such as J. K. Pollock, C. B. MacPherson, B. Akzin, A. Birch, H. Daalder, J. Blondel, K. von Beyme
— *the study of political attitudes* with, among others, Mattei Dogan, V. O. Key, Stephane Bernard, Austin Ranney, Warren Miller
— *the study of international relations* with Marcel Merle, Jacques Freymond, J. B. Duroselle, Max Beloff, M. Fainsod, Karl Deutsch, Stanley Hoffmann
— *the political study of economic development* with C. E. Lindblom, W. A. Robson, G. Heckscher
— *the study of interest groups* with J. Meynaud, H. W. Ehrmann, Daniel Bell, A. Ranney, David Truman, A. Leiserson
— *the study of polyethnic and multilingual societies* with J. Laponce, L. Dion, B. Akzin, K. D. McRae, A. Lijphart, A. Mazrui
— *the study of decentralization and public administration* with J. L. Quermonne, Bernard Gournay, G. Bergeron, S. Zawadski, S. V. Kogekar
— *the study of technocracy and bureaucracy* with Roger Grégoire, Georges Vedel, W. J. M. Mackenzie, M. Crozier
— *the study of political leadership* with J. Ziegler, R. Bhaskaran, R. Kothari, S. Verba, Mattei Dogan
— *the political study of elites, youth, women, religion* with René Rémond, Georges Lavau, Roy Macridis, Robert Lane, Suzanne Keller
— *the study of political finance* with A. Heidenheimer, R. S. Milne, J. Charlot

This sudden expansion led in its turn to the appearance of numerous journals (several hundred) and political collections in most publishing houses.

By force of circumstances, it provoked the creation in 1952 of the *International Bibliography of Political Science* whose first editor was Jean Meynaud.[6] Today, the *Bibliography* contains more than 100,000 references to books and journal articles in its index. In a parallel direction, the *International Political Science Abstracts* were created;⁷ their objective was to keep specialists informed quarterly of the content of recent works. This initiative came from the International Political Science Association, at the instigation of Jean Meynaud, H. R. G. Greaves, and Lannes Bruce Smith. Since 1961 the present director and editor, Serge Hurtig, has made it an excellent enterprise which can take pride in more than 35,000 abstracts.

Dictionaries and encyclopedias made their appearance to present again and again, in terms that excluded common language and by noncomparable examples, the usual meanings of the principal concepts of political science. Nevertheless, an effort toward common meanings was made under the auspices of COCTA by Giovanni Sartori and Fred Riggs.⁸ Progressively, the vocabulary became precise to the point of doing justice to Bertrand de Jouvenel for having insisted on this aspect of the discipline.

Whatever the reasons may be, political science is the only one to lack basic principles accepted by everyone. There are no basic concepts, simple enough to have only one meaning, having the same significance for everyone and capable of being handled with confidence by all; there are no simple relationships, accepted by everyone, to form the smallest elements of complex systems, and communally employed to construct models destined to simulate the complexity of real situations.⁹

This is the way *politistes* of the third generation, the present one, are oriented, somewhat in the manner of computers: vocabulary, universal elements, models, experimentation. We will return to this later.

Confrontation. The time of confrontation arrived. The discipline spread rapidly, like a drop of oil; first, in the industrialized countries of the West; then, toward the socialist countries of the East; finally, in chronological order, toward the developing countries in Asia, Africa, and Latin America. Not only did political science become entrenched by method and imitation. It also offered new subjects for study that induced specialists to travel abroad in ever larger numbers for the annual congresses of the American Political Science Association, for the triennial congresses of the International Political Science Association,¹⁰ and for numerous round-table discussions and seminars organized by the two large associations and by other national associations. Several hundred (between 1100 and 1200 since 1952) of these meetings have encouraged a vast movement of exchanges and cross-influences.

As John Trent said in chapter 2 above, noninstitutional contracts have played a large role: "The base of much contact between scholars can be traced to the international movement of individuals—through migration, foreign scholarships, guest professorships, internationally coordinated research projects, and editorial boards for publications."¹¹ This constant travel broke with the tradition of reflective study by the solitary man. What political science lost in intellectual depth by personal analysis, it regained by very commendable attempts at standardizing concepts, approaches, and research techniques stimulated by the confrontation.

The Third-Generation Politistes

Concepts and vocabularies, universal first principles and rational approaches, models and research techniques, experimentation, this defines the scope of the field of the third generation *politistes*.

The will to prove the scientific character of political science is firm. This is the great vogue of the behavioral approach, of functional analysis, of systematic analysis. This is the search for *a* political theory, for political models to assure political modernization (American modernization) of societies without shocks, by self-regulation; that once and for all will allow criteria to be set by virtue of which political decision makers will establish equilibrium between consensus and conflict. It is also the search for techniques of analysis: intensive and extensive, analogies and comparisons (comparative studies), intuitive and logical, qualitative and quantitative.

At one time, decision-making power was the theoretical concept toward which everything converged, and starting from which the political system organized itself. This generation was dominated by men who are now well known, such as David Apter, Gabriel Almond, Robert Dahl, David Easton, Giovanni Sartori, Samuel Finer, Georges Lavau.

But this search for the scientific characteristics of political science, with the use of models transposed from other scientific disciplines, will attract specialists formed in these other disciplines, such as social psychology, demography, anthropology, and sociology. Thus, political science has taken a polymorphic orientation, very heterogeneous, with the risk of wide dispersion.

Many scholars, conscious of the complexity of a larger and larger scientific field, wanted to put into the models a multitude of data and elements: culture, education, attitudes and behavior, orientations, choices, change, populations, electorates, groups, economic data, social indicators, and many other variables or factors. Socialization in the American sense, became the reference point par excellence.

In reality, they returned to the ancient and classical

double alternation of *determinacy and choice* on the one hand and *stability and change* on the other. Double alternation—or bipolar alternatives, according to the point of view—was complicated by the inference of ideologies and principally by the liberalism-Marxism controversy.

Political philosophers and *politistes* of liberal tradition, on one side of the Atlantic or on the other, could not refrain from including in their models the values of the society that they were analyzing. On the other hand, others belonging to the new Left as much in the United States as in Western Europe exercised their ingenuity to find a third means of political explanation, taking from liberalism and Marxism again what seemed to be suitable to the development of political societies. Scientific knowledge, as extended as it may be according to many, should allow better political theorizing.

In spite of the tendency, it is obvious that we cannot ignore works like those of Jurgen Habermas and of the Frankfort School, of Herbert Marcuse, Iring Fetscher, Milton Friedman, Gordon Tullock, for example. Research on peace, on the resolution of conflicts and on political and economic development on the world scale have found logical argumentation here, certainly subjective, but that inspires a goodly number of political decision makers. And by virtue of this, it is one of the elements which must be taken into account in studies on pluralism, polyarchy, bureaucracy, pressure groups. Strictly speaking, *"political purpose" inherent in the intellectual activity of the politiste is impregnated with this conditioning in ideological values*. Education, instruction, the diverse social and cultural milieus that form us lead us to value implicitly a certain ideal of life, thus producing the elements of political life that we approve.

Therefore, for several years there has been rapid progress in the theoretical formulation of scientific approaches and methods, but not necessarily as adapted to political analysis. The establishment of banks of political data (especially electoral) out of simulation exercises (which we support moreover) are worthy experiments, being uniquely destined to increase knowledge.

These approaches and methods, newly applied to political science, doubtless will not supply miraculous recipes for all those who must decide each day on the choice of policies to follow. However, they have the great merit of obliging *politistes* to organize their reflections according to a standardizable model and, consequently, of leading them to express themselves in a common language. Probabilist reasoning and the attempt to apply techniques that are as reliable as the waiting line theory, matrix analysis, stochastic processes, game theory, for example, open broad perspectives for political science.

The Future: Political Explanation or Political System?

No one can doubt the validity of very sophisticated works like those of Dennis Meadows,[12] Mihajlo Mesarovic, and Eduard Pestel.[13] They created a shock in the West as much as in the East, immediately producing two tendencies: limited growth and continuity in the work undertaken and an intuitive opposition to it, philosophical and political. But, as Karl Deutsch says in chapter one above: "Computers can assist thought but not replace it."[14]

For, in fact, everything depends on the level at which it occurs: in a rich and developed society or in a poor society that is perhaps condemned to underdevelopment; in a large entity or in a small group; in a political regime that favors the individual or in one that accords priority to the collectivity; in an authoritarian system or in a democratic system.

In effect, the Indian *politiste* may legitimately not conceive of political science as a system in the way an American colleague would. His political explanation necessarily will be that of his milieu as a function of his criteria and the immediate political options he faces. For his part, a head of state does not understand politics in the same way a local leader does. As for the rights of man, we know to what point they can evolve in time and space. And the democratic system, is it less or more effective than the authoritarian system? When will a computer be able to determine whether a system should be changed? What are the criteria for doing that?

Therefore, the great question for the future of political science is: is it a political explanation or a political system? One or the other or both?

The French and the Germans began more than ten years ago to ask the fundamental question that the title of a remarkable book of Alfred Grosser sums up with clarity: *Au nom de quoi? Fondements d'une morale politique*. Recently, American authors like Bruno Fritsch, Sheldon Wolin, and Anatol Rapoport have taken up that question. When one arrives at the last page in Alfred Grosser's book *L'explication politique,* the opening question has not been cleared up. What is political science? Where are the boundaries that necessity requires us to trace in relation to the other social sciences, if the response to the first question gives reliable criteria? That said, can it finally give the illusion of being a science as physicists understand that concept?

And we are convinced of having proved nothing, of having denounced nothing. The professionals of the discipline[15] cannot get excited about it because—in the effervescence of theories, models, comparative analyses, monographs and collections of data—they are looking for an object on which they still cannot agree. Until now, political men have not waited for recipes from political science to pursue their policies or implement political decision-making processes.

And the give-and-take that is so natural between empirical observations and conceptual elaboration is no longer a general practice. How many typologies are impressive theories whose harmony is undisturbed by any verifying reflection on reality! How many comparisons are built principally on a serene ignorance of comparative realities! As if one had the right to impose a schema on an entity inevitably impoverished by that imposition without being in a position to appreciate, even approximately, the extent of such an impoverishment! Comparison certainly improves understanding, but a minimum of previous knowledge is necessary to legitimate the comparison.[16]

Le Centre de Recherche et d'Information Socio-Politiques (CRISP) has laid out its route in the specific field of descriptive analysis of Belgian political life without attempting at any time to sketch its history, to undertake game theory. Its success and the audience acquired by means of the ordinary information that has flowed into permanent containers (Congo; financial groups; pressure groups; national, regional, and local institutions; electoral results) prove that a scientific discipline is forged slowly, not as a function of the fashions of the moment or of the original disciplines of those who do research, but by the accumulation of uncontested facts described in uniform language. Synthesis, in the form of theory or sets of hypotheses, will be achieved when the patiently assembled facts fit with the body of the methods of the social sciences.

What is true for CRISP is certainly true for every entity involved in political science. Twenty-five years of evolution have built up logistical bases in men and documentation. Even publishers' series take a futuristic orientation—*New Perspectives in Political Science* (Van Nostrand), *Foundations of Modern Political Science* (Prentice-Hall), *Key Concepts in Political Science* (Praeger) to cite only a few. Much remains to be demonstrated and proved.

Notes

1. "Sociology and political science" in "La science politique," *Revue de L'Enseignement supérieur*, Paris, S.E.V.P.E.N., no. 4 (1965), p. 59.
2. *Cahiers de la Fondation nationale des Sciences politiques*, no. 100 (Paris: A. Colin, 1959), p. 369.
3. See the critique, "Goals for Political Science: A Discussion," *American Political Science Review* 45, no. 4 (December 1951): 996-1024.
4. Jean Meynaud, *Introduction à la Science politique* (Paris: Colin, 1959), p. 345.

5. 12-16 September 1949, International Congress of Political Science; see A. Philippart, *Rapport de Synthèse sur les 20 ans de l'IPSA, 1949-69* (Brussels, 1969).
6. Established by the International Political Science Association with the collaboration of the Comité international pour la Documentation des sciences sociales (Paris: UNESCO), vol. 1, 1953; (additional works published in 1952 *et seq.*).
7. Volume 1 was published in 1951.
8. Conceptual and Terminological Analysis, an IPSA research committee.
9. In *De la politique pure* (Paris: Calmann-Levy, 1963), p. 11.
10. For example, the comparative table of world congresses of IPSA in the chapter by John E. Trent traces this quantitative evolution well (see p. 39 above).
11. See above, p. 41.
12. Dennis Meadows, *The Limits to Growth* (Washington, D.C.: Potomac Associates, 1972).
13. Mihajlo Mesarovic and Eduard Pestel, *Mankind at the Turning Point* (New York: E. P. Dutton, 1974).
14. See above, p. 17.
15. They now number in the thousands: about 16,000 professors, assistant professors, researchers, and members of large departments and institutions in the United States and about 4,000 for the 36 other member countries of IPSA.
16. *L'Explication politique* (Paris: Colin, 1972), pp. 137-38.

Bibliography

Alker, Hayward; Deutsch, Karl; and Stoetzel, Antoine. *Mathematical Approaches to politics*, vol. 8. Amsterdam and New York: Elsevier, 1973.

Almond, Gabriel, and Powell Jr., G. B. *Comparative Politics: A Developmental Approach: An Analytical Study*. Boston: Little Brown, 1966.

Apter, David. *The Politics of Modernization*. Chicago: University of Chicago Press, 1965.

Attali, Jacques. *Les modèles politique*. Paris: P.U.F., 1972.

Banks, Arthur, and Textor, Robert. *A Cross-Polity Survey*. Cambridge: M.I.T. Press, 1963.

Barents, Jan. *Political science in Western Europe: A Trend Report*. London: Stevens and Sons, 1961. (Proceedings of the IPSA Round Table of Opatija, 1959.)

Beloff, Max. *The Balance of Power*. London: G. Allen and Unwin, 1967.

Bergeron, Gérard. *Le fonctionnement de L'Etat*. 2d ed. Paris: A. Colin, 1965.

Bernard, Stéphane. *Les attitudes politiques en démocratie: Esquisse d'une typologie*. Bruxelles: Institut Sociologie U.L.B., 1968.

Birch, Anthony. *Representation*. New York: Praeger, 1971.

Boudon, Raymond, and Gremy, Jean-Paul. *Les mathématiques en sociologie*. Paris: P.U.F., 1971.

Bremer, Stuart. *Simulated Worlds: A Computer Model of Decision-Making*. Princeton: Princeton University Press, 1976.

Burdeau, Georges. *Traité de science politique*. 10 vols. Paris:

L.G.D.J., vols. I (1966), II (1967), III (1968), IV (1969), V (1970), VI (1971), VII (1972), VIII (1974), IX (1976), X (1977).
Charlesworth, James Clyde. *A Design for Political Science: Scope, Objectives and Methods.* Philadelphia: American Academy of Political and Social Science, 1966.
Coplin, William D. *Simulation in the Study of Politics.* 3d ed. Chicago: Markham Publ. Co., 1970.
Daalder, Hans. *Cabinet Reform in Britain 1914-1963.* Stanford: Stanford University Press, 1964.
Dahl, Robert. *Modern Political Analysis.* 2d ed. Englewood Cliffs, N.J.: Prentice-Hall, 1970.
———. *Who Governs? Democracy and Power in an American City.* New Haven: Yale University Press, 1961.
de Grazia, Alfred. *The Universal Reference System.* Political Science Series. Princeton: Princeton University Press, 1967.
de Jouvenel, Bertrand. *Du pouvoir: Histoire naturelle de sa croissance.* Paris: Hachette, 1972.
———. *The Pure Theory of Politics.* New Haven: Yale University Press, 1963.
Deutsch, Karl. *The Analysis of International Relations.* Englewood Cliffs, N.J.: Prentice-Hall, 1968.
———. *Nationalism and Social Communication: An Inquiry into the Foundations of Nationality.* 2d rev. ed. Cambridge, Mass.: M.I.T. Press, 1953.
———. Fritsch, Bruno; Jaguaribe, Helio; and Markovits, Andrei. *Problems of World Modeling: Political and Social Implications.* Cambridge, Mass.: Ballinger Publishing Co., 1977.
Dunner, Joseph. *Dictionary of Political Science.* New York: Philosophical Library, 1964.
Duverger, Maurice. *Méthodes de la science politique.* Paris: P.U.F., 1959.
Easton, David. *Analyse du système politique.* Paris: A. Colin, Collection Analyse Politique, 1974.
———. "The New Revolution in Political Science." *American Political Science Review* 63, no. 4 (December 1959): 1051-61.
Ehrmann, Henry W., ed., *Interest Groups on Four Continents.* Pittsburgh: University of Pittsburgh Press, 1960.
Elliott, Florence. *A Dictionary of Politics.* Harmondsworth: Penguin Books, 1969.
Ellul, Jacques, *L'illusion politique.* Paris: Robert Laffont, 1965.
Freund, Julien. *Qu'est-ce que la politique?* Paris: Le Seuil, 1965.
Friedrich, Carl J. *Constitutional Government and Democracy.* New York: Appleton-Century Crofts, 1950.
———. *Man and his Government: An Empirical Theory of Politics.* New York: McGraw-Hill, 1963.
———, and Brzezinski, Zbigniew. *Totalitarian, Dictatorship and Autocracy.* New York: Praeger, 1965.
Fritsch, Bruno. *Growth Limitation and Political Power.* Cambridge, Mass.: Ballinger Publishing Co., 1976.
Grosser, Alfred. *An nom de quoi? Fondements d'une morale politique.* Paris: Le Seuil, 1969.
———. *L'explication politique.* Paris: A. Colin, Cahiers no. 183 de la Fondation Nationale des Sciences Politiques, 1972.
Hoffmann, Stanley. *Contemporary Theory in International Relations.* Englewood Cliffs, N.J.: Prentice-Hall, 1960.
Huntington, Samuel. *Political Order in Changing Societies.* New Haven: Yale University Press, 1968.
International Bibliography of Political Science. Paris: C.I.D.S.S. and IPSA, UNESCO, annual volumes since 1953.
Lane, Robert. *Political life: Why People get Involved in Politics.* Glencoe, Ill.: Free Press of Glencoe, 1959.
Lapierre, J. W. *Essai sur le fondement du pouvoir politique.* Aix-en-Provence, Faculté des Lettres: Editiones Ophrys, 1968.
Laponce, Jean, and Smoker, Paul. *Experimentation and Simulation in Political Science,* vol. 8. Toronto: University of Toronto Press, 1972.
Lasswell, Harold D. *The Future of Political Science.* New York: Atherton Press, and London: Greenwood Press, 1963.
———. *A Pre-View of Policy Sciences.* New York: American Elsevier Publishing, 1971.
———, and Kaplan, Abraham. *Power and Society: A Framework for Political Enquiry.* London: Routledge and Kegan Paul, 1952.
Lavau, Georges. *Partis politiques et réalités sociales.* Paris: A. Colin, 1953.
Lindbolm, Charles E. *The Policy-Making Process,* vol. 6. Englewood Cliffs, N.J.: Prentice-Hall, 1968.
Lipset, Seymour Martin. *Politics and the social sciences.* New York: Oxford University Press, 1969,
———, and Rokkan, Stein. *Party Systems and Voter Alignments.* New York: The Free Press, 1967.
McCoy, C. A., and Wolfe, A. *Political Analysis: An Unorthodox Approach.* New York: Crowell, 1972.
Mackenzie, W. J. M. "The Political Science of Political Science." *Government and Opposition* 6 no. 3 (Summer 1971): 277-302.
MacPherson, C. B. "Report on Research in Political Science." *American Political Science Review* 68 (June 1954): 427-49.
MacRae, D. "Social Science and the Sources of Policy, 1951-1970." *P.S.* (APSA Newsletter) 3 (Summer 1970): 204-310.
Maddick, Henry. *Democracy, Decentralization and Development.* London: Asia Publishing House, 1963.
Malignon, Jean. *Dictionnaire de politique.* Paris: Cujas, 1967.
Marshall, T. H. "International Co-Operation in the Social Sciences." Reports and Papers in the Social Sciences, no. 21. UNESCO, 1964.
Merle, Marcel. *La vie internationale.* 3d ed. Paris: A. Colin, 1970.
Merriam, Charles. *Political power.* New York: Macmillan, 1964.
Merritt, Richard. *Systematic Approaches to Comparative Politics.* Chicago: Rand McNally, 1970.
Merritt, Richard, and Rokkan, Stein. *Comparing Nations: The Use of Quantitative Data in Cross-National Research,* vol. 15. New Haven: Yale University Press, 1966.

Meynaud, Jean. "International Co-Operation in the Field of the Social Sciences: A Tentative Balance-Sheet." Reports and Papers in the Social Sciences, no. 5/1956 et no. 13/1961, UNESCO.

———. *Introduction à la science politique*. Paris: A. Colin, Cahiers de la Fondation nationale des sciences politiques, no. 100, 1959.

———. *La science politique au XXéme siècle*. Lausanne: Université de Lausanne, Ecole des Sciences Sociales et Politiques, October 1955.

Morgenthau, Hans. *Politics Among Nations: The Struggle for Power and Peace*. 3d ed. New York: Knopf, 1961.

Parodi, Jean-Luc. *La politique*. Paris: Hachette, 1971.

Philippart, André. *Rapport de synthèse sur les 20 ans d'activités de l'AISP* (Synthesis Report on the IPSA 20 years Activities). Bruxelles: AISP, 1969.

Polec, X. *Dictionnaire de politique et d'économie*. Berlin: Waleter de Gruyter, 1967.

Poulantzas, Nicos. *L'Etat, le pouvoir, le socialisme*. Paris: P.U.F., 1978.

Powell, D. E., and Shoup, P. "The Emergence of Political Science in Communist Countries." *American Political Science Review* 64 no. 2 (January 1970): 572–88.

Merle, Marcel. *La vie internationale*. 3d ed. Paris: A. Colin, 1970.

Ranney, Austin. *Political Science and Public Policy*. Chicago: Markham, 1968.

Rapoport, Anatol. *Science and the Goals of Man: A Study in Semantic Orientation*. Westport, Conn.: Greenwood Press, 1971.

Rokkan, Stein. *Citizens, Elections and Parties: Approaches to the Comparative Study of the Process of Development*. New York: David McKay, 1970.

Schwartzenberg, Roger-Gérard. *Sociologie politique*. Paris: Domat-Montchrestien, 1971.

"La science politique." *Revue de l'Enseignement supérieur*, no. 4 (1965). Special issue on the discipline.

Sharkansky, Ira. *The Routines of Politics*. New York: Van Nostrand Reinhold, 1970.

Sills, David L., ed. *the International Encyclopedia of the Social Sciences*. New York: Macmillan and Free Press, 1968.

Somit, Albert, and Tanenhaus, Joseph. *The Development of American Political Science: From Burgess to Behavioralism*. Boston: Allyn and Bacon, 1967.

Sorkin, M., and Wolfe, A. "The Political Dimension in American Political Science." *Acta Politica* (Amsterdam) 5 no. 1 (October 1969): 43–61.

Steinbruner, John. *The Cybernetic Theory of Decision: New Dimensions of Political Analysis*, vol. 13. Princeton: Princeton University Press, 1974.

Verba, Sidney. *Small Groups and Political Behavior: A Study of Leadership*. Princeton: Princeton University Press, 1961.

von Beyme, Klaus. *German Political Studies, 1974*, vol. 8. London: Sage Publications, 1974.

Wolin, Sheldon. *Politics and Vision: Continuity and Innovation in Western Political Thought*. Boston: Little Brown, 1960.

Wynar, Lubomyr R. *Guide to Reference Materials in Political Science*. Rochester: N.Y. Libraries Unlimited Inc., 1968.

Young, Oran R. *Systems of Political Science*, vol. 13. Englewood Cliffs, N.J.: Prentice-Hall, 1968.

Developing Countries: Teaching Political Science*

RAUL BEJAR NAVARRO, FRANCISCO CASANOVA ALVAREZ, and LIAN KARP S.

Objectives for Study

Economic, social and political development is today the prime objective of the great majority of those countries, distinguished from the capitalistic countries (or the "First World") and the socialist countries with planned economies (the "Second World") by the generic term the "Third World."

It perhaps goes without saying that this term is analytically insufficient to bring into sharp focus the great differences among the societies it encompasses. These may be ranked on a scale which runs broadly from those which have not yet emerged from a tribal stage, to those which have already consolidated socioeconomic structures of the capitalist type. Such a classification contains so many variants that we may, with some justification, speak of "fourth," and even "fifth" worlds.

Be that as it may, and despite diversification, the concept of a Third World can be useful to identify two structural attributes which are common to all its members. These are backwardness and dependence as economic and social phenomena. These factors interact in what we may call an organic frame of underdevelopment, stagnation and misery.

Economic dependency, today, supplants the former colonial subjugation of the developing countries; the vestiges of the older political and social domination still persist in many. It is certainly in commerce, finance and technology that the brunt of economic dependency must be borne.

Within the existing structure of international commerce, factors such as low degrees of agricultural diversification, low levels of industrialization and hypertrophy of the tertiary sector, implacably condition dependency. Furthermore, inadequate technological development requires the import of technology to support the most advanced economic sector. Similarly, foreign capital is directed in an unbalanced manner toward sectors which are more highly developed and productive. As a result, the gap between the developed and non-developed sectors becomes wider and deeper, thus increasing the dependence of the entire economy. This distortion not only causes serious imbalances to impede progress in lagging sectors, or even broader regions of the economy, but also sets the stage for political and social tensions.

Another clear manifestation of dependency is the need to import current scientific paradigms from the industrialized countries. The development of an independent science is obstructed as much by incongruities between the stock of existing knowledge as by what successive scientific imports are applied to in countries with an extensive scientific infrastructure. It is reflected in all fields of science and technology but is logically greatest in those areas which depend most heavily on the rapid application of the latest information.

In the social sciences it may be shown, for example, that a great measure of research, teaching and professionalization is little more than a mirror image of processes which took place in the industrialized countries. This particular type of dependency is especially critical in fields like political science, where content is profoundly ideological.

Economic and social backwardness is, in part, also the sequence of dualistic (or pluralistic) structures. Not only is there a highly modernized sector which benefits from higher levels of development but, what is worse, internal structural mechanisms tend to magnify this difference rather than diminish it.

Such conditions have political repercussions which lead to instability and the spread of authoritarianism.

Moreover, the need to overcome economic stagnation

---

*Article from *International Social Science Journal*, Vol. 30, no. 1. © UNESCO 1978. Reproduced by permission of UNESCO.

and speed up the processes of development is greatest in countries where the population growth rate is high. Demographic explosions in developing countries lead, paradoxically, to the steady decrease of production capabilities in relation to the ever-increasing demands and needs of the population. Here again, lack of economic coordination and imbalance sow the seeds of rising demands that cannot be met, and bring a harvest of dissatisfaction, unrest, and still greater need which have repercussions throughout the political and social spheres, impeding their progress as well.

Internal development, conceived as a process of structural change rather than as the mere accumulation of goods and services, has at least three dimensions. In its economic aspects, the development of the backward countries requires a rapid and dynamic process of modernization. This, in turn, implies profound changes in the means and modes of production, in economic organization, in the framework of the use and accumulation of capital, in the mechanisms of marketing and distribution, and the development of a scientific and technological infrastructure. In addition, it is also necessary to break with dependency, both domestically and internationally, and to establish relationships of effective interaction on more egalitarian and equitable bases.

The requirements of social development derive not only from existing physical and material conditions of dependency and the hope for a better standard of living, but also from the fostering and inculcation of egalitarianism and the concepts of justice and social wealth which help to sustain and nourish all classes and strata of society. Regardless of the general level of development which may have been reached by a particular society, social development implies the reduction of disease, and the lengthening of life spans, as well as raising the standards of material and spiritual well-being. Implicit in such goals is the abandonment of traditional patterns of behavior, the adoption of modern technology, the improvement of channels for the distribution of social wealth, and in some relevant fashion, the establishment of new relationships which permit a more fruitful coexistence between the different classes of society. As in the case of economic development, it is necessary to break down the psychological and cultural barriers which prevent social change.

Political development, in turn, involves processes of institutional differentiation and specialization, and the participation of greater numbers of people in the political affairs of their community and nation. The redrawing of institutional lines of communication, the formation of alliances and agreements between and among social groups and sectors, the modernization of the administrative machinery of the State, communication between those who govern and those who are governed, promoting legitimacy and the credibility of government, and, above all, the overhauling of the global processes which affect the development of the Third World, are the principal matters involved.

It is obvious that the attainment of such goals requires efficient overall coordination and that it is the state which must assume responsibility for setting and reaching them. Only in this way is it possible to make the effort and to ensure continuity and internal sufficiency required by such endeavors. In this perspective it is clear that professional political scientists in developing countries must differ in fundamental objectives from their colleagues in the developed countries. For the former a capacity for honest and intelligent criticism, the ability to generate fresh options and new structures for social change, the updating of the administrative machinery of the state, a critical awareness of the problems of economic, social, and political marginality and dependence both domestic and international, and a clear social commitment, are the guidelines which must delineate intellectual effort. In addition, the political scientist in developing countries must be prepared to follow them in action.

The traditional theoretical framework of political science as generated in highly industrialized countries, focuses on the establishment of power, influence and authority as the characteristic processes of social control. On the other hand, the concept of order in developing countries tends to point up the potential political relevance inherent in nearly every aspect of daily life, even in those not directly related to government. In this sense, the content of a teaching program must include the political analysis of any social relationship where a difference of power and authority may exist.

In trying to assemble those elements that might better define the structural feature of developing countries it may be remarked that, given economic growth promoted mainly by private enterprise based on a government-created infrastructure, the state will try to frustrate attempts at change made by organized masses, by outlawing independent unions, using repressive measures and banning radical parties or groups.

Under this type of dependent political organization, operating in a sphere beyond formal regulation, the real practice of politics implies an explicitly coercive system which protects the basic social structure, its institutions and those symbolic values which support them by restraining individual behavior.

The emphasis placed on these practices is justified to the extent that political violence, as a form of governmental coercion, is used to maintain the status quo even though the capacity of a given political system may vary in its ability to react adequately to popular demands, by mobilizing and distributing resources, and strengthening or developing substructures such as political parties, lobbies and other pressure groups powerful enough to meet their demands. To some extent, this might convey the idea of the modernization of the political system in so far as it incorporates and integrates an effective bureaucracy. However, innovation requires sufficient flexibility to allow for possible changes; without such flexibility any alteration in the shareout of economic benefits creates a conflict which must be resolved by force.

Standard curricula dealing with political violence in all its manifestations are completely justified if it is not rejected a priori as irrational but is viewed as an ever-present force which performs a central role in the formation of the state, in the processes of industrialization, and may at a given moment open the way to change in a given social order.

Political science students should understand from the start that disorder, even violent disorder, may be interpreted as an early warning to those in power that a portion of society has adopted an attitude of rejection manifested by the existence of groups which have insufficient recourse to formal political processes.

It must be clearly understood that specific attitudes to the political process are conditioned by affiliation to particular socioeconomic groups; obviously the problems that afflict the politically weak often lie beyond the awareness of the politically powerful, both qualitatively and quantitatively. The authorities may simply ignore marginal groups, and generally maintain this attitude until problems are brought to their attention in a more or less dramatic fashion. The ground rules of politics in developing countries are products of a cultural context and a historical reality such that they allow only one team to win the game, since it so often happens that the players can write their own rules.

We may summarize our argument as follows.

Politics have since ancient times engaged human thought, yet efforts to treat the study of politics scientifically were started only in the second half of the nineteenth century; consequently, political science even in the universities of the most highly developed countries is still quite young. In underdeveloped regions, especially Latin America, the study of political science was first introduced into university curricula during the second half of the twentieth century, a relatively late start which explains its present lack of advancement.

Cultural dependency, one of the characteristics of underdeveloped societies, has biased the teaching of political science toward the focus, guidelines, concepts and values of highly developed countries, thus raising four basic problems in reaching a full understanding of the true nature of underdevelopment: (a) the adoption of universal theories which, because of their very nature, do not apply to specific and concrete situations, which require a different level of theoretical understanding; (b) the direct and mechanical "transplant" of theories to circumstances totally different from those which initially generated them; (c) the use of models and conceptual guidelines produced in developed countries provides at best an explanation of how things work in a world different from that in which they must be applied; (d) the use of theories and models of developed countries derived from typologies of their own systems and which constitute ideals of political formation rather than descriptions and explanations of the processes involved in their construction.

Third World countries must therefore produce general theories which can explain the realities of underdevelopment, its growth, direction and how it may be overcome. These theories would not necessarily conflict in any way with genuinely validated theory generated at a global level.

Theories to explain a particular reality are also required. It would seem imprudent to deny the value of certain models which, although they may fall short of explaining how things have come about, can tell us how they are at a given moment. The danger of importing theoretical models lies in the fact that, if the assumptions on which they are based are not made explicit, they favor purely mechanical imposition. These models can, of course, be useful if based on our knowledge of sociological factors, and we take into account the specific conditions which induced their creation and the underlying situation and values present at that moment.

As a result, political science faculties in Third World countries produced graduates who, lacking an adequate theoretical formation, can function only within the imperatives of a given ideology, which leads to behavioral dysfunction in the political environment and frustrates all attempts at change. For this reason, political science may appear to be an esoteric field unattractive and irrelevant to purposeful political change. The discipline must therefore earn its legitimacy by demonstrating its ability to generate valid theories and scientific bases for research.

The Search for Methodology

In overall terms, and aside from what could be considered adequate for a basic and general background, such as the philosophy and history of political theory and the feedback of other social sciences, the focus of a political scientist is directly concerned with the study of power phenomena from two methodological standpoints: the formation of power centers and their maintenance and extension. This means that the political scientist must be methodologically prepared to design systems of which the basic categories are: "How to organize power" and "How to extend and develop it" in contexts which, being defined by a power structure, possess, as a distinctive characteristic, a dynamism conditioned by interactions based on conflict situations.

"Power," "conflict," "organization," "development" and "systems," or "change," "disorganization," "domination," "stagnation," "public opinion" and so forth, are technical terms which constitute categories, concepts or notions to which the political scientist must address himself in order to substantiate philosophically, scientifically and ideologically, a specific theory and a congruent political praxis. Theory and praxis should form an inseparable unit dynamically adapted to the degree of social development of a given group or society whose political contradictions it seeks to resolve. These technical terms belong to the common interdisciplinary ground which extends beyond the disciplinary or even multidisciplinary spheres.

But since reality is different from what is established in educational and research centers, there is still a lack of theory, technique and paradigmatic form. Thus far, we can only point to assumptions, guidelines, or tentative criteria generated by an intellectual attitude or by the practices of individuals or groups working toward a given goal.

Consequently, the problem of assembling a pedagogic methodology for political science goes further and in some respects differs from that for the other social sciences, in which relatively acceptable solutions are to be found in conventional teaching methods. The search for an appropriate methodology should therefore begin with the logical approaches and techniques at present applied to the development of theories and praxis in ecology, organization and social planning, in other words, with the support of General Systems Theory, modal and time-dependent logic, operational research, especially the theory of decision-making, and informatics, as these are the fields in which concepts such as structure, control, dynamism, adaptation, forecasting, synergy, disorder and so forth, have been imbued with the greatest empirical precision and epistemological rigor. These terms provide a metalinguistic basis according to which categories, concepts and notions of political theory and praxis, such as those already mentioned, may be defined. Hence, if contemporary political science may be considered as interdisciplinary and even more, transdisciplinary, then its methodology must be oriented in this direction. In this case, only methods derived from the aforementioned fields will satisfy the minimum requirements for incorporation or consideration. This proposal is not new. We may cite works by Easton, Deutsch, Alker, Lange, Young, Dror, Lasswell, Helmer or Moisseev, where attempts along such lines have met with relative success.[1] Our purpose here is twofold: in the first place, to alert the scientific community, to the possibility, or even probability (if a paradigm of political science, whether completely formulated or fully generalized or not, may be said to exist) of an imminent scientific revolution (in the sense that T. S. Kuhn uses this term). Second, to confirm that at the moment political science, aside from its utopian (that is, Neo-Platonic) or pragmatic (that is, Neo-Machiavellian) guises, and in so far as it allows of binary treatments such as those applied in political historiography (Gramsci, Miliband), political sociology (Horowitz, Duverger), psychopolitics (Abkarian, Rapoport), political economy (Poulanzas, Zielinsky) and so forth, constitutes, in fact, a theory of social theories, that is, a body of knowledge of an interdisciplinary nature, and should therefore adopt a methodology of the same variety.

Up to this point, we have adopted an approach which tends to embody "convex" propositions, which should prove enlightening in the way conclusions may be drawn. But if we were now to suggest a dual approach, proposing a "concave" or synthetic form as well then, among other things, certain concepts and capacities required for the professionalization of the political scientist and practitioner must emerge. Some of these are:

The ability to design, set up, and operate power structures that generate social welfare according to predominant public interest.

Sufficient knowledge of social history to design, set up, and carry out politically viable solutions whose rationale concurs with the specific social restrictions of development.

Familiarity with the techniques which permit the prediction of future options, so as to be able to operate politically while confronting the processes of change (integrated or not) according to specific cost-benefit requirements within the limits of the possible and respecting the political and ecological boundaries.

Expertise in the formulation of tactics and strategies in the face of the conflicts inherent in social and economic stagnation, marginalization and dependency, as may be required by socialization, politicization, public opinion and participation, the capacity and flexibility to meet social, economic, cultural and other costs in society.

Experience and familiarity with the control problems of the society in which one lives, in order to apply administrative techniques, economic criteria and political potential on a nationwide basis without losing the necessary attention to detail, once a specific course of action has been chosen.

The ability to retrieve rapidly, from available institutional or contextual sources, information which allows the design and staging of scenarios in which processes of development may be simulated for the appropriate modernization of the political system.

Many other skills which are already well recognized, and therefore need not be mentioned here.

This approach requires that the political scientist have sufficient knowledge of the theory (as shown by his degree of awareness) and the praxis (as manifested by this active participation in, and effect on, reality) to master a methodology that includes: knowledge and ability to manipulate strategies involving the dynamics of change in relation to the political significance of hierarchically possible results, that is in relation to the power structures; to rely on and make use of talent, with both "hardware" and "software" attributes within the rational boundaries of the political system in which he acts. In other words, to discourse and to perform in a manner consistent with the social, political, psychosocial, economic, technological and military flexibility, required by the prevalent sets of interactions between political society and civil society, taken as a whole.

Although this second viewpoint is more enumerative and the first more enunciative, the conclusions, in so far as the methods and techniques to be embraced by political science plans and programs are concerned, are obviously similar, if not identical, in both instances.

Once it is accepted that political science is interdisciplinary, it is possible to determine the extent to which, by analysis or synthesis, the methodological content of curricula should cover matters derived from such areas as the theory of organization, theory of conflict, social ecology, etc., at present being worked out in an interdisciplinarian framework.

[Translated from Spanish]

Note

1. See, for instance: D. Easton, *The Political System* (New York: Alfred A. Knopf, 1967); O. Young, *Systems of Political Science* (Englewood Cliffs, N.J.: Prentice-Hall, 1968); K. W. Deutsch, *The Nerves of Government* (Glencoe, Ill.: Free Press, 1963); H. R. Alker, *Mathematics and Politics* (New York: Macmillan Co., 1965); H. Alker, K. Deutsch and A. Stoetzel, eds., *Mathematical Approaches to Politics* (Amsterdam, London, and New York: Elsevier Scientific Publishing Co., 1973); O. Lange, *Wstep do Cybernetyki Ekonomicznej* (Warsaw: Panstwowe Naukowe, 1965); Y. Dror, *Design for Policy Sciences* (New York: American Elsevier Publishing Co., 1971); H. D. Lasswell, *A Pre-View of Policy Sciences* (New York: American Elsevier Publishing Co., 1971); B. M. Gross, *The State of the Nation* (London: Social Science Paperbacks, 1966); O. Helmer, *Social Technology* (New York and London: Basic Books, 1966).

Bibliography*

Alker, H. R. *Mathematics and Politics*. New York: Macmillan Co., 1965.

───, Deutsch, K. W., and Stoetzel, A., eds. *Mathematical Approaches to Politics*. Amsterdam, London, and New York: Elsevier Scientific Publishing Co., 1973.

Deutsch, K. W. *The Nerves of Government*. Glencoe, Ill.: Free Press, 1963.

Dror, Y. *Design for Policy Sciences*. New York: American Elsevier Publishing Co., 1971.

Easton, D. *The Political System*. New York: Alfred A. Knopf, 1967.

Gross, B. M. *The State of the Nation*. London: Social Science Paperbacks, 1966.

Helmer, O. *Social Technology*. New York and London: Basic Books, 1966.

Lange, O. *Wstep do Cybernetyki Ekonomicznej*. Warsaw: Panstwowe Naukowe, 1965.

Lasswell, H. D. *A Pre-View of Policy Sciences*. New York: American Elsevier Publishing Co., 1971.

Young, O. *Systems of Political Science*. Englewood Cliffs, N.J.: Prentice-Hall, 1968.

AFRICA

Bogaert, J. *Human sciences in Black Africa, Bibliographic Guide (1945-1965)* (in French). Brussels: CEDES, 1966.

Bohnet, M. "Relations between Research Institutes and Governments in Developing Countries, with Particular Regard to Eastern Africa" (in German). *Internationales Afrika Forum* (Munich) (February 1971), pp. 121-26.

Ehrlich, C.; Engholm, G. F.; Goldthorpe, J. E.; and Powesland, P. G. "Social Studies at an African University College." *University Quarterly* (November 1955), pp. 56-63.

Gingyera-Pincycwa A. G. G., "The African political scientist and decision-making." *African Review* 5, no. 3 (1975), pp. 293-302.

Louw, Michael H. H. "Challenges for political science in South Africa." *Politikon* (June 1975), pp. 2-5.

Mazrui, A. A. "Political theory and national involvement in East Africa." *Cahiers d'Etudes Africaines* (The Hague-Paris) 9, no. 4 (1969), pp. 515-26.

Molnos, A. *Social Science Research in East Africa, 1954-1963, Kenya, Tanganyika, Uganda* (in German). Berlin and New York: Springer Verlag, 1965.

Mujaju, A. B. "Political science and political science research in Africa." *African Review* 4, no. 3 (1974), pp. 339-58.

ASIAN COUNTRIES

"Asian institutes of public administration." *Philippine Journal of Public Administration* (April 1958), pp. 108-47.

Wu Teh-Yao. "Teaching political science in Southeast Asia today." *Journal of Southeast Asian Studies* (March 1974), pp. 123-33.

*General bibliography on political science in developing countries was compiled by the editor.

CARIBBEAN REGION

Greene, J. E. "A review of political science research in the English-Speaking Caribbean: Toward a Methodology." *Social and Economic Studies* (Kingston) (March 1974), pp. 1-47.

Milacic, S., and Charbonneau, J.-P. *The Political Science of the Young Caribbean States* (in French). Cayenne: Centre universitaire Antilles-Guyanne, 1977.

CHILE

Donosa, L., and Zorbas, A. *The Present State of the Social Sciences in Chile* (in Spanish). Rio de Janeiro: Centro Latino Americano de Pesquisas en Ciencias Sociales, 1959.

Escobar Cerda, L. "The education of economics and administrative science in Chile" (in French). *Revue de la Société belge d'études et d'expansion* (Liège) (March/April 1959), pp. 201-7.

"Seven years of work by the Latin American Faculty of Social Science" (in Spanish). *Anales de la Facultad Latinoamericana de Ciencias sociales* (Santiago de Chile) (December/January 1964), pp. 203-8.

Wilhelmy von Wolff, M. *Current Trends in Political Theory* (in Spanish). Santiago: Editorial Juridica de Chile, 1969.

COLOMBIA

Arboleda, J. R. *The Social Sciences in Colombia* (in Spanish). Rio de Janeiro: Centro Latino Americano de Pesquisas en Ciencias Sociales, 1959.

Revesz, L. "Political science in Eastern Europe: discussion and initial steps." *Studies in Soviet Thought* (Freiburg) (September 1967), pp. 185-210.

Starosciak, J. "The development of administrative science in the socialist countries of Europe" (in French). *Revue administrative* (January/February 1966), pp. 67-71.

UNESCO. Social Science Clearing House. *The Social Science Activities of Some Eastern European Academies of Science.* Paris: UNESCO, 1964.

CONGO

Monnier, L. "Political Science Research in the Congo: Problems of Method and of Techniques" (in French). *Cahiers Économiques et Sociales* (Kinshasa) (September 1970), pp. 451-69.

———. "Problems of political science research in the Congo" (in French). *Informations Sciences Sociales* (August 1968), pp. 39-52.

Verhaegen, B., and Monnier, L. "Concrete problems and political science concepts in Africa, Applied to the Lower Congo" (in French). *Cahiers économiques et sociaux* (Leopoldville) (June 1963), pp. 79-91.

COSTA RICA

Campos Jimenez, C. M. *The Social Sciences in Costa Rica* (in Spanish). Rio de Janeiro: Centro Latino Americano de Pesquisas en Ciencias Sociales, 1959.

DEVELOPING COUNTRIES

Kriesberg, M. "Public Administration Teaching in Developing Countries: Objectives and Methods." *Revue Internationale des Sciences Administratives* 29, no. 3 (1963), pp. 247-51.

———. "Senior Civil Servants and the Teaching of Public Administration in Underdeveloped Countries." *Revue Internationale des Sciences Administratives* 23, no. 3 (1957), pp. 336-39.

"Social Sciences in the Third World" (in French). *Revue Internationale des Sciences Sociales* 21, no. 3 (1969), pp. 411-89.

EGYPT

Mustafa, A. A. al-R. *The Development of Political Science in Modern Egypt* (in Arabic). al-Qahirat, Mu'ahad al-Buhuth wal-dirasat al-'Arabiyat, Qism al-buhuth wal-dirasat altarihiyat wal-jughrafiyat, 1973.

ETHIOPIA

Clifford-Vaughan, F. "Public adminsitration education in Ethiopia" (in French). *Revue Internationale des Sciences Administratives* 29, no. 4 (1963), pp. 381-84.

LATIN AMERICAN COUNTRIES

Costa Pinto, L. A. "The Social Sciences in South America" (in Portuguese). *Educacao e ciencias socialis* (Rio de Janeiro) (August 1956), pp. 173-82.

Gillin, J. "The Situation of the Social Sciences in Six South American Countries" (in Spanish). *Ciencias sociales* (Washington) (February 1953), pp. 11-18.

Godoy, H. "Political Science and Latin American Development: A Comment on Prebisch's Report" (in Spanish). *Revista Latino-Americana de Ciencia Politica* (Santiago) (August 1970), pp. 352-58.

Grossman, J., comp. *Bibliography on Public Administration in Latin America.* Washington: Department of Cultural Affairs, Pan American Union, 1958.

Herring, P. "The social sciences in Latin America" (in Spanish). *Revista de Ciencias Sociales* (Puerto Rico) (December 1963), pp. 379-86.

Jordana de Pozas. "Administrative Sciences in Spanish- and Portuguese-Speaking Countries in 1954" (in French). *Revue Internationale des Sciences Administratives* 21, no. 3 (1955), pp. 532-45.

Kaplan, M. *Latin American Political Science at the Crossroads* (in Spanish). Santiago de Chile: Editorial Universitaria, 1970.

Moreno, F. J., and Rockefeller, R. C., eds. "Social research in Latin America." *American Behavioral Scientist* (September 1964), pp. 3-39.

Nun, J. "Notes on political science in Latin America" (in Portuguese). *Revista Brasileiro de Estudos Politicos* (Belo Horizonte) (July 1965), pp. 127-72.

Public Administration Clearing House. *Public Administration in Latin America: Opportunities for Progress through Technical Cooperation.* Washington: Pan-American Union, 1956.

Sanchez Sarto, M. "University teaching of the administrative sciences in Central America" (in Spanish). *Revista del ITAT* (Mexico City) (1960), pp. 113-23.

"Selected social sciences bibliography on the Central American countries" (in Spanish). *Ciencias politicas y sociales* (Mexico City) (April-September 1965), pp. 277-376.

Stavenhagen, R. "Problems of Social Science Documentation in Latin America." *America Latina* (January-March 1967), pp. 164-69.

Zimmerman, I. *A Guide to Current Latin American Periodicals: Humanities and Social Sciences*. Gainesville: Kallman, 1961.

LEBANON

Beckett, P., and Bent, F. "Letters from Beirut." *Public Administration Review* (Winter 1953), pp. 1-11.

MEXICO

Arnaíz, A. "Methodology and political science" (in Spanish). *Revista de la Facultad de Derecho de México* (April-June 1963), pp. 251-87.

Bejar Navarro, R. "The National School of Political Science and Social Sciences and the Mexican University Reform" (in Spanish). *Revista Mexicana de Ciencia Politica* (April-June 1968), pp. 173-90.

Bonfil Batalla, G., and Mendoza Navarro, R. "Social science periodicals: Mexico" (in French). *Revue internationle des sciences sociales* (Paris) (1967), pp. 244-56.

Carranca y Trujillo, R. "Safe steps by the National School of Political and Social Science" (in Spanish). *Ciencias Politicas y Sociales* (Mexico City) (July-September 1955), pp. 9-14.

Castano, L. *Themes of Mexican Political Sociology* (in Spanish), Mexico: Instituto de Investigaciones Sociales, Universidad Nacional Autonoma de Mexico, 1961.

"The teaching of international relations in the Political Science Faculty of Mexico: the 1976 Study Plan" (in Spanish). *Relaciones internacionales* (Mexico City) (January-March 1977), pp. 5-77.

"Functions and activities of the ENCEPS (National School of Political and Social Sciences, Mexico)" (in Spanish) (January-March 1969), pp. 119-99.

Gonzales Casanova, P. "The establishment of a development plan for social science" (in French). *Information sur les sciences sociales* (Paris) (February 1969), pp. 149-69.

Lopez Portillo, J. "The National Utility of Careers in Political Science" (in Spanish). *Ciencias Politicas y sociales* (Mexico City) (January-March 1957), pp. 77-102.

Mendietta y Nunez, L. "Origin, Organization, Goals, and Future of the National School of Political and Social Sciences" (in Spanish). *Ciencias Politicas y Sociales* (Mexico City) (July-September 1955), pp. 9-14.

Moedano, N. G. "The relation between folklore and political science, folkloric events and political events" (in Spanish). *Revista Mexicana de Sociologia* (May-August 1961), pp. 565-84.

Olguin, F. "Morphology of the National Institute of Political and Social Sciences" (in Spanish), *Ciencias Politicas y Sociales* (Mexico City) (January-March 1959), pp. 13-48.

Reyes Heroles, J. "Notes on the Significance of the Study of Political Science" (in Spanish). *Ciencias Politicas y Sociales* (Mexico City) (January-March 1957), pp. 103-17.

MIDDLE EASTERN COUNTRIES

International Committee for Social Sciences Documentation. *Retrospective Bibliography of Social Science Works Published in the Middle East: United Arab Republic, Iraq, Jordan, Lebanon, 1945-1955*. UNESCO, 1959.

Kwanry, H. A. "Ideas and Comments on the Teaching of Social Sciences in the Arab East" (in Arabic), *Al-Abhath* (March 1958), pp. 87-98.

PARAGUAY

"The Paraguayan School of Public Administration" (in Spanish). *Documentacion administracion* (Madrid) (August-September 1961), pp. 66-69.

THE PHILIPPINES

Abueva, J. V. "Some Notes on the Study of Public Administration and Politics in the Philippines." *Philippine Journal of Public Administration* (January 1957), pp. 5-11.

Lederle, J. W., and Heady, F. "Institute of Public Administration, University of the Philippines." *Public Administration Review* (Winter 1955), pp. 8-16.

SENEGAL

Thomas, L. V. "Social research in Senegal" (in French). *Information sur les Sciences Sociales* (June 1965), pp. 21-66.

Part II
POLITICAL SCIENCE IN INDIVIDUAL COUNTRIES

ARGENTINA

5

SEGUNDO V. LINARES QUINTANA AND ASSOCIATES*

Introduction: The State of Political Science in 1945

In the Republic of Argentina, as in most Latin American countries, the analysis of political institutions was carried out for a long time by the historical-juridical method, primarily by the study of constitutional texts. However, by 1945 Argentine scholars had accepted a new orientation of the political science discipline that followed a method that might be called in-depth analysis.

Whether this is a new political and constitutional science or a profound change within the old discipline, the clear and indubitable fact is that we are observing the restructuring and reorganization of political science, a discipline whose field is expanding at the present time to the point that the boundary that used to distinguish it from other similar sciences is blurred. This gives birth to many interdisciplinary areas.

For most Argentine political scientists, political science and constitutional law are integrated today into a single basic discipline—the sovereign science among sciences according to Aristotle. Its new and peculiar note is to emphasize Man, the great protagonist of the political scene, through whose virtues, passions, and defects the institutions live. A balanced and reasonable consideration of both the traditional approach and the new trends shows the way, correctly, to the reintegration of political and constitutional science with Man under the clear guidance of the Law. As Carl J. Friedrich says, "Political science without the Law is a mere ghost."[1]

The Evolution of Political Science Since 1945

THE INTELLECTUAL STRUCTURE OF THE DISCIPLINE

The process of structuring political science in Argentina, notwithstanding roots in its own politics, obviously has followed the generality and universality of every cultural science, as well as the social behavior of the world of politology (political science). Its present state allows us to delineate in synthetic form the scientific system that constitutes its essential structure in accordance with the dynamics of the political process to which it owes its existence.

In Argentina, as elsewhere, political science is a science of reality. Political science is the science of the political. Taken in its broadest sense, it is the science of political life, coinciding with public life (the *res publica*). This ontology of politics begins by assuming that political life *is* essential to human nature due to the fact that man is a political animal or a political being. The social human being is the determinant of political and public life.

What is the political environment that is determined? Every society is articulated for political action into a collective being, namely the people of the nation as an agent-subject of that community, acting through groups and political forces. On the other hand, that reality has an essence, an energy or potential that is its political power. This attribute of the political gives the science its center of attention.

---

*This paper was written under the direction of Dr. Segundo V. Linares Quintana, who wrote the Introduction: The State of Political Science in 1945, and Association Activities. The other contributors are: Héctor Rodolfo Orlandi: The Intellectual Structure of the Discipline; Mario Justo López: The Teaching of Political Science: Teaching in General; Alfredo N. Galletti: An Argentine Experience: The Specialized *Licenciatura* in Political Science; Juan R. Aguirre Lanari: Political Scientists in the World of Politics; and Germán J. Vidart Campos, The Present State and Future Perspectives of Political Science in Argentina. The translation from Spanish was done by Luis A. Oyarzun.

Placed in the pyramid of power, geometric and descriptive, that ascending energy of resistance—constitutive and electoral of the people—once it has reached the apex of the pyramid, finds itself in need of direction. It is met by the descending, subjective power of authority and obedience, that is to say, the government, which is ruled institutionally by a constitution. In our case this is the historic Constitution. As an initial premise, we say in the textbook, Political science: "Politics is a form of nationally based principles of behavior and of a basic knowledge of the people's power."

Since the political is the essence of politics, this form of human conduct and social behavior works in political life as an interactive process of the people's energy. This takes place in successive stages that, depending on their cultural beliefs and value systems, transcend the political struggle. By conquering or resisting power, or by exercising, transmitting, organizing, distributing, controlling, and participating in the use of political power—as immediate objectives—power and politics are conditioned and committed to leading objectives and ideological factors. The goal is to create a political order of coexistence and its dynamics and to establish a public political organization (a state, a government, a constitution). However, power for power's sake would lessen itself. Long-range political objectives would determine a conduct that would found, create, and guide—values, ends, goals—and would organize—by public order and the law—and integrate the community. These same objectives are found in scientific research and its methodological motivation. According to this second approach, political science is, in logical thinking, the science of politics.

Political science as the science of politics includes three general areas: (a) Politics as in applied (practical) science; (b) Political science as political theory; (c) Political philosophy, political history and political theory.

The vast area of political life that we have presented as a science appears from its very essence to be revealing truth. Thus, we include in political science epistemological knowledge and political philosophy—axiology, teleology—of the tradition inherited ever since the Aristotelian inception of the discipline. We understand it now as a modern, empirical science, as an organized and methodological body of knowledge that deals with the analysis, criticism, explanation and exegesis, verification, and transmission of political power and its phenomena. However, as a normative frame, the system implies a theory of order and as an empirical discipline, an interpretation of society. Thus, it answers the questions that come up in the political process: what is political life? and how does it work? Defined in qualitative terms, such a system rejects the order of stages in quantitative research and logically presupposes two crucial modern problems for the researcher or political scientist: (1) a relative unity of the object, and (2) a methodological procedure.

When political science is reduced to a mere science of power ("cratology"), in answer to the scientific question: "What is its object?" one synthetically alludes to political *power*. This leaves that theory and hypothesis infinitely open to the question: "What is the object like?" in relation to its extension and its intensity for any political phenomenon, because it definitely deals with processes, relations, acts, and decisions of power. Thus, is adopted an accurate criterion of unity and selective interest in reality that does not exclude but gives sense to all political interaction; to say nothing of the hypothesis of power in its broadest and most contemporary context, the political system. Most Argentinian political scientists have approached our science of power by starting with just such a permanent phenomenon of political life, although many-sided and polemical. Its essence, the potential energy of the people, makes possible, in its reciprocity, the relation of authority and obedience, extended to the specialized gamut of political problems.

Since Aristotle, the acknowledged father of political science in the traditional concept of knowledge, who considered it the supreme and sovereign science of Man, upon which all the other practical sciences are dependent in their actions, to Jean Bodin, who gracefully called it the princess among sciences on the boundary between private and public law, we come to the telesis of our José Manuel Estrada for whom all political science is contained in the idea of freedom. Following this is the reborn contemporary politology (political science), based on research and interdisciplinary techniques, leaving notoriously open the problem of mutual collaboration and necessary integration among the sciences, a process that is vitally operating in reality.

It is evident from the previous conceptual outline that political science, in its present state of development is not a science of nature, which is, nevertheless a determining factor in it; nor is it a science of ideal-mathematical objects that operate as models, but is a science of Man, a cultural and social science. On the one hand, are studies of human conduct or social behavior in the interaction of the political process of actions and decisions; on the other, is the science of the organizational structure, including its institutional-juridical form, and the revitalization of both of them in the dynamics of the political system with its demands, products, and influences. Therefore, the science of political reality is the science of a specific area of social life (the political one). This fact has acted as a catalyst forcing the politologist to request the collaboration of other social sciences rather than considering narrow concepts of inviolable autonomy.

Due to its own nature, political science assumes the role of an integrating science of all the cultural and social sciences, in order to produce a better knowledge—truth—and understanding—life—of that reality which is in the last instance one and the same. We include in this process of progressive integration, united by its commonality of object, power, affecting large areas of the political essence and existence. A few examples will suffice: ethics and political history, theory of the state and geopolitics, political and constitutional law, in the Aristotelian and classical doctrine, because in these disciplines the practitioners were practicing political science under another name. And to all this we add now contemporary sciences—the tripod of "conductism"—sociology, political psychology, and political anthropology; also economics and the science of public administration, demography and international affairs, not to mention the technological vehicle of cybernetics and mathematical statistics. The mutual aid and progressive integration are implicit in the use of plural political sciences, although in reality there is a single political science integrating, when fully developed, a restructured knowledge.

Our politologists have answered the imperative call of political science and of reality by structuring the system in certain ways. I will point up some of them as they are put into practice in our university research and teaching. First, there is political law whose content is political science. In its fundamental system, this includes a set of knowledge—theories—of society, politics, the state, law, government and the constitution, all seen from the point of view of politics, whose criterion of relative unity of the object, and the understanding of some concepts as antecedents of others, is determined by "the political," by political power, and by organizational phenomena conducive to public welfare. Such theories of power, organization, and objectives coordinate the system that we teach in our law schools and is integrated by (1) a theory of society; (2) a theory of the political act or of politics; (3) a theory of the state; (4) a theory of government or a constitutional theory, in the Spanish sense; (5) philosophy and world and Argentine political history.

Secondly, we consider *political and constitutional law*, a constitutional empirical science. It serves as the subtitle of the book *Constitutional Law and Political Institutions* by Dr. Segundo V. Linares Quintana, where we read "... instead of talking of a new political and constitutional science, in order to be more precise, we should speak of the new orientation that, at the present time, is predominant in the discipline... in fact, the limitations that once isolated political science, anthropology, sociology, psychology, economics, and other related sciences in watertight compartments are disappearing, and more and more political science and constitutional science are becoming one integrated discipline."[2]

In addition, following a similar scientific attitude with regard to the object and boundaries of political science, although without attempting to define it, a prototype list was put together by UNESCO in Paris in 1948, and circulated among us. Its open register of themes included: (1) political theory; (2) political institutions; (3) political parties, groups, and public opinion; (4) international affairs, divided into well-known subthemes. In integrating the political sciences it coincides, in substance, with the system of political law and with political and constitutional science. Since 1966, the University of Buenos Aires has had an in-depth course at the doctoral level on constitutional law and political science in the School of Law and Social Sciences. This course has been taught around different themes each year. Since 1970, it has been adopted with success for the plan of the specialized *licenciatura* in political science at the University of La Plata, founded and directed by Dr. Linares Quintana.

From the present state of knowledge world as well as Argentine politologists insist on the continuous task, as scientists and citizens, of vigorously structuring the discipline, always attentive to perceive the changes that are taking place in political life and that are constantly demanding a restructuring of the scientific system. In relation to that function, we leave in abeyance an implicit aspiration: the formulation of a genuine political method. That, due to its present impossibility, we must leave as an ideal mission for the future.

THE TEACHING OF POLITICAL SCIENCE:
TEACHING IN GENERAL

Thirty years ago, Professor Segundo V. Linares Quintana, in his report on "The Development of Political Science in Argentina" (published as part of the UNESCO volume entitled *La science politique contemporaine*), stated that José Manuel Estrada, who could be considered the founder of the discipline in this country, was the first Argentine to include this subject in his teaching of constitutional law, by adopting the political-historical method. In that report, its author reviewed the main scholars of these studies in this country and stressed the predominance of the constitutional-juridical approach being used.

Meanwhile, an important step in a new direction was taken on 11 October 1922 by the Executive Council of the Social Sciences and Law of the University of Buenos

Aires, by including in its curriculum of law studies a new subject entitled political law. In such a way the systematic study of the political reality was incorporated in the official program at the third level, with the double focus of general theory of the state and history of political ideas. The term "political law" was born in Spain in the days of its incipient constitutionalism, being, perhaps, a translation from the phrase *droit politique* used by Montesquieu and Rousseau. This subject had been added to the curriculum of the Spanish law school in the last decades of the nineteenth century. But outside the Spanish precedent, we have to consider in the creation of the new discipline the spirit of the times—the first postwar years—and the stimulus of foreign masters, such as Léon Duguit, Víctor Manuel Orlando Adolfo Posada, who through their masterly lectures delivered in the law school of the University of Buenos Aires, opened the new field.

Since then this subject has been incorporated in the curriculum of other national universities, in Córdoba, La Plata, del Litoral, and Tucumán. At present, the discipline exists in all of them under the same title. Also, it has been included in the curriculum of new national universities, as in the Social and Political Sciences and Law School of the Northeastern National University (Corrientes province); and in the following private schools: the Pontifical Catholic University of Argentina; the *Universidad del Salvador;* the Catholic University of La Plata; and in the University of Morón. On the other hand, in some law schools "political law" has given way to "political science and constitutional theory," as at the Catholic University of Santa Fé; or it is simply called "political science," as at the School of Juridical and Social Sciences at the *Universidad Nacional del Litoral* (Santa Fé).

Professor Linares Quintana introduced some thematic units of political science into his classes in constitutional law at the National University of Buenos Aires and of La Plata, years ago, and by so doing, renovated the traditional concepts of the discipline. In addition, the teaching of political science found its way outside law school curricula. There is a political science school at the national universities of Rosario, Cuyo (in the city of Mendoza), and a Department of Political Science at the National University of San Juan.

In every case, under one name or another, the new approaches of contemporary political science have been playing an expanding role in the context of the academic programs. The predominant influence has been that of American authors, or authors under American influence (Friedrich, Loewenstein, Brecht, Van Dyke, Lipset, Dahl, Easton, Almond, Deutsch, Sartori), and some French writers (de Jouvenel, Burdeau, Duverger, Aron, Prélot, Meynaud, Chevallier, Chapsal), and some Spanish writers (Sánchez Agesta, Xifra Heras, Verdú, Jiménez de Parga).

In spite of all kinds of obstacles, especially the lack of constitutional continuity and its serious repercussions in university life and scientific activities, Argentine political science professors have managed to accomplish their tasks at a very high level, keeping themselves up to date in order to give the best instruction to their students, to stimulate them to improve the theoretical approaches of the empirical investigation.

AN ARGENTINE EXPERIENCE: THE SPECIALIZED
LICENCIATURA IN POLITICAL SCIENCE

Different and also complex situations that we cannot analyze here have made it difficult to engage in scientific research about political science problems in Argentina. In order to study these problems, the selection of rigorous working methods requires a propitious climate that usually the Latin American reality does not offer very generously.

A science like ours—at the same time the oldest and the most modern, and in continuous transformation—whose limits still are not well delineated, demands not only complete dedication, but disinterested work in handling materials either elaborated or in raw form. This requires a rational intelligence and constant efforts, plus—in classical words—long study and a great love for the subject. Still, this alone is not enough. The scholar must, on the one hand, know the realities of the situation, and on the other, be able to generalize diversified knowledge (that comes criss-crossing from different disciplines), in order to achieve a synthesis and structures that have to be understood as the culmination of a process of interdisciplinary learning and background.

Some years ago, Dr. Segundo V. Linares Quintana set forth the general lines and the current status of political science in our country, in *Le développement de la science politique en Argentine,* a UNESCO publication of 1950. His work was based on different aspects, problems, and possibilities: historical developments, influences, theories, methods, perspectives, and so on. Precisely to this scholar belongs the merit of the original launching in our university circles of the valuable experience that we are recording here.

This contribution constitutes something like the founding chart of new projections for the study of political science in Argentina. Well known is the easy success of the so-called politologist—many of them of real merit indeed—who generally attempt to capture and interpret the changing concrete situations of political life, but often through circumstantial analysis that leads to predictions that are erroneous most of the time. The brilliance of articles addressed to large audiences through mass publication obscures sometimes—though not always—the serious and rigorous work carried out by scholars who achieve the rank of political scientists.

The experience mentioned above tended to form well-trained specialists. A specialized *licenciatura* for graduates in social sciences and law studies was the culmination of the tasks of the Institute of Political Science at the National University of La Plata between 1971 and 1973. In the first place, in order to carry out such a program, the institute had to obtain its own autonomy, although maintaining its interdisciplinary affinities with the Institutes of Public Law. Also, it intended to keep the juridical framework that would sustain the institutes, but allow the annexation of supporting political science disciplines that had been kept out until then.

The admission requirement was to be a lawyer or a graduate in law studies. In other words the *licenciatura* was reserved, with some exceptions, for law postgraduates, and its main character would be specialization. It gave a new dimension to what was understood as *licenciatura* in Argentina. It was not to begin studies leading to a doctorate, but to create and re-create subjects that were superficially treated in previous curricula, making the *licenciatura* a truly specialized degree, due to the fact that it required: (a) a previous university degree; and (b) the presentation and approval of a thesis, and besides, with some exceptions, those admitted to the program had broader knowledge. There was a qualitative selection, determined by the applicants themselves, without affecting the quantitative selection—in the good sense—based on an authentic, idealistic interest. (At the outset 120 students were accepted; most of them continued the studies, only a few dropped out.) From the start there was an awareness of a real need to fill a vacuum, a feeling of a certain weakness in our law curricula. As noted before, a good number of the graduate students were strong not only because of their degrees, but due to the knowledge and experience acquired in their professions and administrative positions, such as specialized ministry officers, administrators, bureaucrats, politicians, magistrates, career diplomats, members of the legislatures, and sociologists. There were a large number of doctors in juridical and social sciences, or in law and social sciences, but also there were a good number of university professors and secondary teachers. Those categories made up almost 40 percent of the student body, and if we add specialists on other related careers such as magistrates and legislators that percentage easily would reach sixty-five. Therefore only 25 percent had only a competency certificate (n some cases students could register without finishing their law or whatever other studies they were pursuing, but only on a probationary basis).

A "calling" for political science was a decisive factor in enrolling in these courses. Besides all the demands typical of any specialization, the system adopted had indisputable advantages: promotion based on conceptual evaluation rather than on a final testing of information, usually depending on themes chosen at random without any formative value. The lecture class was replaced by the seminar, with dialogue between students and teachers, leading many times to a continuation of the discussions beyond the required class time. Often at lunchtime, in nearby restaurants—in a more informal way—students and professors continued to treat their subject. The courses were intensive, covering two years, divided in four semesters, doubling, practically, the study time. Besides the required thesis, that must be defended in front of a tribunal formed by the professors of the course and chaired by the dean, the student had to write papers in the final period at the end of each quarter. The conceptual grading was based on the evaluation of the student's work during that period of time, the oral presentation of a freely chosen topic, after being questioned on general points or methodological problems, and also on how the student had worked out his paper and its bibliographical sources.

All this was complemented by the preparation of index cards, bibliographical guides, translation of texts unavailable in the market, and by gathering a specialized library. Also it was decided to create a political science publishing entity that would promote, among other things, the publication of a bulletin and of the best papers and theses.

The study plan followed the general outline and recommendations established in international projects, especially UNESCO, although leaving the teacher free to choose his themes and approaches, focusing preferably on national problems. Subjects were numbered correlatively from one to eight, under the general title of political science. The courses were outlined as follows: (1) political methodology; (2) political institutions; (3) contemporary political systems; (4) political forces; (5) Argentine political history; (6) Argentine political system; (7) political systems (another quarter); (8) foreign affairs and international politics. An effort was made to overcome the tradition of encyclopedic teaching by reaching to the great themes in a double approach: (a) by establishing adequate methodologies; (b) by clarifying the working methods through reading and discussions (for example, the Congress of the International Political

Science Association was the subject of an intensive mini-course). On the other hand, these subjects were approached by methods attuned to the inclusion of new problems and global studies—by using interdisciplinary correlation—although without ignoring specialized research.

In our judgment, our experience has been plentiful and generous in its results for the improvement of political science studies and for ample diffusion of their real and authentic content. A nucleus of specialists was formed and they have published important works and participated in different national and international environments. Groups of people who are interested in improving their political science knowledge have been tapped and they are anxious to renew their research.

Finally, we must credit the Political Science Association at the University of La Plata with the very auspicious idea of establishing the *licenciatura*.

Associational Activities

Associations. At most law and social sciences schools in Argentine universities there are specialized institutes of constitutional and political law, and some institutes of political sciences.

On 8 May 1957, the Argentine Political Science Association (affiliated with the International Political Science Association) was founded in the city of Buenos Aires with Dr. Segundo V. Linares Quintana as president. He still occupies that position. The association has held several scientific conferences in which the most important current themes of the discipline have been discussed, with the participation of distinguished foreign and national specialists.

Journals. The Argentine Political Science Association formerly published the *Revista Argentina de Ciencia Política,* under the direction of Dr. Segundo V. Linares Quintana. Publication ceased for financial reasons.

Special Publications. The Argentine Political Science Association has published several books, such as a Spanish translation of *Methods of Political Science* by Georges Burdeau, professor at the University of Paris; and *Political Forces and the Struggle for Power,* by the following foreign and national scholars: Pablo Lucas Verdú (Spain), César E. Romero (Argentina), Segundo V. Linares Quintana (Argentina), Germán J. Vidart Campos (Argentina), Themistocles Brandao Cavalcanti (Brazil), Carlos Sánchez Viamonte (Argentina), Jorge Xifra Heras (Spain), Alberto Ramón Real (Uruguay), Federico G. Gil (United States), Leopoldo Uprimny (Colombia), Jorge Aja Espil, Gregorio Badeni, Rodolfo Luis Ciri, Carlos Alberto Mayón, Zulema Escobar Bonoli, Edgardo R. Catterberg, Eusebio Angel Barriocanal, Luis R. M. Döllera Jofré (all of them from Argentina).

Political Scientists in the World of Politics

This theme implies a preliminary doubt. One should ask if correct scientific reasoning is helped by students of politics who act as militants in the political arena.

In this sense, we must remember Manuel García Pelayo, who reminds us of the plurality of formulation of the concept of a constitution and of juridical-political concepts in general, due to their polemical nature. Therefore "they find their *ratio* not in the desire for knowledge, but in the fitting instrument for the polemic with an adversary";[3] a political perspective that allows, however, a sometimes deeper perception of reality than is furnished by a neutral point of view.

Thus, it is possible to avoid the failure noted by Dr. Segundo V. Linares Quintana of

the political-social constitutions that astonished the world, at the end of World War I, by their originality and the theoretical perfection of their content, but did not fit the real world or the possibilities of those to be ruled by them. As Alcalá y Zamora indicated "it was the theorizing or professional constitutionalism developed by the two Germanic states, under the inspiration of men who were more cultured than wise, and more wise than prudent"; they forgot that, as Estrada had said, "political fantasies are sins that are purged not by the theoreticians, but by the people."[4]

Argentine political science has its deep roots in men with a general practical intuition and a doctrinal sediment. Cornelio Saavedra, president of the first Junta of Government (1810) noted an essential concept of constitutionalism: "There is no doubt that it is the people who confer the authority or power."[5]

Mariano Moreno in his passionate writings published to guide the new government of the country, develops concepts related to the doctrine that sought to reaffirm freedom in the face of the monarchic despotism they were challenging. It is particularly significant that in his article "On the Mission of the Congress" published by the *Gaceta,* Moreno proclaims the need of a firm constitution to guarantee the right of the people, and to reaffirm America's freedom and the state of law. In order to safeguard the latter he praises the separation-of-powers concept, lecturing on Rousseau and Montesquieu. Moreno, who wrote an introduction to a translation of the former's *The Social Contract,* talks about the social pact, sovereignty, general will, and even an eventual American federation, although he disagrees with Rousseau on religious matters.

The political doctrine of the first Junta of Government (May 1810) shows its initial experiences in the constitutional regulations of the first revolutionary decade, as well as in the draft constitutions of the 1813 Assembly and the abortive Constitutions of 1819 and 1826; it would find newer spokesmen and ideologists in the members of the 1837 generation who formed the Association of May: Esteban Echeverría, Juan Bautista Alberdi, Juan María Gutiérrez, Bartolomé Mitre, Domingo Faustino Sarmiento, Félix Frías, Vicente Fidel López, Tejedor Domínguez, Demetrio Peña, Marco Avellaneda, Quiroga Rosas, Benjamín Villafañe.

Esteban Echeverría, interpreting their common thought, wrote the *Socialist Dogma of the Association of May,* with a foreword, "Retrospective View of the Intellectual Movement in 'el Plata' since 1837," in which the author tries to determine the national essence by studying its history and its social elements. Therefore the use of the words "socialist dogma" is related to its social factors and has no relation to the usual political connotation. "May, Progress, Democracy": this is the formula of the 1837 generation. "These three pillars form the essence of our nationality," proclaims Echeverría, explaining the meaning of the dogma that expressed the ideology of May.

The 1837 generation, chastened by the tragic experience of the earlier internal dissensions, searches for the appropriate political formula for the country and studies its historical antecedents and its social configuration. Echeverría points out that "the starting point to define any political question must be our laws and existing statutes, our customs and our social situation.... Not to lose oneself in abstractions, not to lose sight of practical reality, to fix the eyes of the mind in the heart of hearts of our society."[6] These young men, many of whom took up arms to defend their political beliefs, were far from the theorizing constitutionalism mentioned above.

Juan Bautista Alberdi wrote the last of the symbolic words of the "dogma." He examines the unitary and federalist antecedents in our country as much in the colonial period as in the revolutionary period, postulating as a solution to the divisions, the political-social fusion of the antagonistic factions. As a consequence he conceived his political formula of a mixed government with a federal generic affiliation that does not ignore some unitary antecedents found in history and in the institutions. His famous *Fundamental Basis and Starting Points for the Political Organization of the Republic of Argentina,* explaining the ideas of his generation and inspiring the framers of the 1853 Constitution, rank him notably among the sharpest, most original, and transcendent Argentine political minds.

The influence exerted by Alberdi's book, as well as by the draft constitution that he sent to the Congress in 1853 at the suggestion of the deputy Juan María Gutiérrez, has been compared in impact to that of the *Federalist Papers* after the 1787 American Constitutional Convention. He emphasizes the enforcement of the natural rights of constitutionalism and the separation of powers. He proposes to open the sparsely populated Argentine territory to European immigration. To Govern Is to Populate was his slogan that inspired the philosophy of the constitution, under which the country had an astonishing development through a few decades of sustained progress.

Juan María Gutiérrez, another member of the 1837 generation, who formed a very close friendship with Echeverría and Alberdi, was the spokesman for the group in the Congressional Convention of 1853. Gutiérrez, as a militant politician, and as an intellectual of vast erudition, was faithful to his ideas when serving in several important public offices, among them the presidency of the National University of Buenos Aires. In 1868, during his term, the chair of Constitutional and Administrative Law was established.

Domingo Faustino Sarmiento was one of the most relevant and prolific writers and political militants of the period of our institutional organization. In his book *Facundo,* of polemic political inspiration, as has been pointed out by Linares Quintana, Sarmiento utilized a sociopolitical approach: "... his analysis pierced the most vivid, vibrating reality of Argentina, studying the defects and virtues of the rulers and relentlessly attacking their political vices and above all the *caudillismo*; and if he was unable to use the scientific means that de Tocqueville had at his disposal, he replaced them with his genius and direct observation resulting from his being many times protagonist in the political arena of the country."[7]

After the 1853 Constitution was approved, Sarmiento wrote his *Commentaries on the Constitution of the Argentine Federation.* In this publication he criticizes the Alberdi draft for its lack of originality and identifies it with the American Constitution, which brought him into another controversy. Alberdi stated that Sarmiento was wrong in interpreting the 1853 Constitution exclusively with North American criteria and ignoring the previous national antecedents. However, as Jorge A. Aja Espil says, neither Sarmiento's criticism nor Alberdi's defense is entirely justified. "As that publicist emphasizes, Sarmiento proposes to look at American jurisprudence and constitutional doctrine in order to safeguard the letter of the constitution. At the same time, Alberdi is pointing to 'the spirit of the national law' as the necessary guide for the correct interpretation of the Constitution."[8]

Sarmiento, who also wrote *Argiropolis* and many

other profound pages often polemical in character on constitutional matters, was above all an outstanding educator. Fraternal countries have proclaimed him "the teacher of America." Even after having occupied the most prominent public offices, including the presidency of this country, he prided himself on his career as an educator and identified himself on his visiting card, simply, as "school teacher."

Bartolomé Mitre was another prominent Argentine constitutionalist and politician who figured alongside the other eminent personalities already mentioned. Self-taught, as were the others, Mitre was a scientific military man, an eminent historian, a noted humanist. He also was by moral make-up and extended study, a man of the law; although he never wrote a systematic work, his juridical knowledge was vast and he participated eloquently in memorable legislative and constitutional debates.

It is impossible to capture in a few lines his political thought and the methods and approaches he used in his development.[9] Mitre was a forerunner of the modern integral approach, by using complex methodological tools to examine the history of the country, its sociological reality or by inspiring his countrymen with the highest values of natural law through a teleological approach in his lectures and his personal conduct.

During his political career Mitre shone as an orator in the debate on the San Nicolás de los Arroyos's agreement, and he personally wrote the report for ratification of the Convention of the state of Buenos Aires, that introduced important reforms in the Constitution of 1853. These reforms were used by the government of Buenos Aires, through the exertion of its original constitutional powers, to complete in 1860 the constitutional process, stressing the federal tone of the Constitution. Mitre was also one of the leading figures, among other illustrious participants, in the convention that reformed the Buenos Aires Constitution between 1870 and 1874. He also took part in the national convention for the reform of the Constitution in 1898, and was an outstanding member of the national legislature. Mitre's actions and thoughts as president of the republic, as a member of the opposition, as a party member, or as an influential journalist, show him as a learned practitioner of juridical science, and even though not possessing a university degree he justly and with great prestige occupied a place in the National Academy of Law.

Among other illustrious Argentine thinkers who participated in the national political life during the second half of the nineteenth century, we must mention José Manuel Estrada. Dr. Alberto G. Padilla says of Estrada: "Although second in the chronological order, he is the founder of the teaching of Constitutional law among us."[10]

Estrada was an eloquent orator. His class lectures, stenographically recorded, were published in 1877, as a text entitled *Course of Constitutional Law*. A revised edition appeared in 1927. His writings, including his famous speeches, were published in twelve volumes and entitled *Liberal Policies under Rosas's Tyranny*. He anticipated modern studies of Argentine political science by applying the historical-political method, which he endowed with admirable synthetical power in his conclusions. Estrada was a convinced and unselfish liberal Catholic, showing an uncompromising conduct when giving up his university chair in a memorable resignation.

The limitations of space do not allow us to mention a large number of other thinkers and professors who in the past century, as in the present one, also shared their political theorizing with active participation in Argentine public life. With this space restriction we avoid involuntary omissions that might occur in a more extensive listing.

The Present State and Future Prospects of Political Science in Argentina

The present and future of Argentine political science is focused on two fundamental themes.

In the first place, at the present time, we believe there is no consensus about what is understood as a political phenomenon. One part of the discipline equates politics with the state and considers politics as an activity related to the state. Another part of the discipline widens the field of politics and includes every phenomenon related to power—even if it is not state power—or to phenomena that influence the behavior of others. This expands the world of politics into regions beyond those reserved in the past to the state organization; this discrepancy, legitimate as it is, does not seem to be close to a solution in the near future. Political science will continue moving around partially different axes, according to the preference of the authors. Although we prefer the notion that politics encompasses only the phenomena that occur within the state or that are connected with it we nevertheless believe that the other doctrine will be more successful and that political science will go beyond the frame of state organization.

In the second place, there is also a lack of agreement between theories that argue whether political science is only descriptive, or if, besides being descriptive, it is also normative. One group of politologists conceives of political science as an empirical science, as a social science limited to an analysis of reality, abstaining from passing judgment or making critical evaluation. The neutrality implicit in this position leads to pure description, systematization and, perhaps, to a typology of political phenomena. On the other hand, without renouncing this first area of knowledge, another group adds evaluation. Not satisfied with the naked political fact, it aspires to know how politics should be as an ideal activity, it searches for the model, it tries to discover criteria of justice. Meanwhile, the first group relegates judgments of value to the content of political philosophy.

We must note that not all those who carry out purely empirical studies are following the first line of action. Some do not deny that it is legitimate within political science itself to evaluate the gathered data, but they abstain from doing it for the moment. In fact, only those who attempt to encompass the whole of the political world while leaving aside any judgment of values should be included with those who adhere to the empirical thesis of mere description.

We are convinced that, in the future, the second thesis will win. It would not be easy for the politologist to resist the innate tendency of the human mind to judge reality according to models seen as objectives and originating from a scale of values. Values are too much a part of human activity and cannot be ignored in the area of politics. It is not enough to study how values appear and how they are achieved in the political world. We must try to ascend to the level of seeking the ideal form of the value, in order to promote the image of the desirable regime that will incarnate that ideal value or set of values. Therefore we should not disregard this aspect of the political science content and, much less, deny to this study the same scientific quality of the empirical analysis of reality.

On the other hand, there are other artificial insertions in political science that are kept in university study programs, more for curricular reasons than out of scientific motivation. Two such elements are the history of ideas and political theory, and constitutional theory. It is common to find today both subjects formally included in the curricula of political science, perhaps with the idea of avoiding the proliferation of courses. We deem probable that in the future political theory and constitutional theory will become autonomous disciplines and in that way eliminate both subjects, which do not belong in the specific field of political science, this without denying the affinity and relation that they have with that area of studies.

Notes

1. Carl J. Friedrich, *Teoría y realidad de la organización constitucional democrática,* Spanish version by V. Herrero (Mexico City: Fondo de Cultura Económica, 1946), p. 556.
2. Segundo V. Linares Quintana, *Constitutional Law and Political Institutions,* vol. 1, p. 138.
3. Manuel García Pelayo, *Derecho constitucional comparado,* 1st ed. (Madrid, 1959), p. 29.
4. Segundo V. Linares Quintana, *Derecho constitucional e instituciones políticas,* 2d ed., vol. 1 (Buenos Aires, 1976), p. 467.
5. Bartolomé Mitre, *Historia de Belgrano y de la malependencia Argentina, Obras completas,* vol. 6 (Buenos Aires, 1940), p. 305.
6. Esteban Echeverría, *Ojeada retrospectiva sobre el movimiento intelectual en el Plata desde el año 37, Obras completas,* vol. 4 (Buenos Aires, 1873), p. 17.
7. Linares Quintana, *Derecho constitutional,* p. 212.
8. Jorge A. Aja Espil, *Lecciones de derecho constitucional* (Buenos Aires, 1971), p. 62.
9. Juan R. Aguirre Lanari, *Mitre, estampa moral de un político* (Buenos Aires: Imprenta del Congreso de la Nación, 1964); see also "Mitre y el derecho," lecture delivered at the Mitre Museum, on 25 June 1976.
10. Alberto G. Padilla, *Lecciones sobre la Constitución* (Buenos Aires, 1965), p. 101.

Bibliography

Dana Montaño, Salvador M. "Teoría General del Estado." Valencia, Venezuela: Universidad de Carabobo, 1963.
Fayt, Carlos S. "Derecho Político." Bs. As.: Abeledo-Perrot, 1962.
Legón, Faustino J. "Tratado de Derecho Político General." 2 vols. Bs. As.: Ediar, 1959.
Linares Quintana, Segundo V. "Derecho Constitucional e Instituciones Políticas: Teoría Empírica de las Instituciones Polícas." 2nd ed., 3 vols. Bs. As.: Editorial "Plus Ultra," 1976.
──────. "La Nueva Ciencia Política y Constitucional." Bs. As.: Academia Nacional de Derecho y Ciencias Sociales, 1969.
──────. "Tratado de la Ciencia del Derecho Constitucional." 2d ed. 5 vols. to date. Bs. As.: Editorial "Plus Ultra," 1977-1979.
Justo López, Mario. "Introducción a los Estudios Políticos: Teoría Política." 2 vols. Bs. As.: Editorial Kapelusz, 1969.
──────. "Manual de Derecho Político." Bs. As.: Editorial Kapelusz, 1973.
Natale, Alberto A. "Derecho Político." Bs. As.: Depalma, 1979.
Rodolfo Orlandi, Hector. "Ciencia Política: Teoría de la Política." Bs. As.: Editorial "Plus Ultra," 1975.
Sanchez Viamonte, Carlos. "Manual de Derecho Político." Bs. As.: Editorial Bibliográfica Argentina, 1959.
de Vedia y Mitre, Mariano. "Historia General de las Ideas Políticas." 13 vols. Bs. As.: Editorial Guillermo Kraft Ltda. (Vols. 11, 12, and 13 treat the history of Argentine political ideas.)
Vidart Campos, Germán J. "Derecho Político." Bs. As.: Aguilar, 1962.
See also, Pablo Lucas Verdu, Jorge Xifra Heras, Themistocles Brandao Cavalcanti, Federico G. Gil, Segundo V. Linares Quintana, Cesar E. Romero, Carlos Sanchez Viamonte, Jorge Aja Espil, Germán J. Vidart Campos and other authors under the direction of Segundo V. Linares Quintana, "Las Fuerzas Políticas y la Lucha por el Poder." Bs. As.: Editorial "Plus Ultra," 1974.

AUSTRALIA

6

COLIN TATZ and GRAEME STARR

In dealing with Australian political science since 1945 we are discussing almost its entire history. Very little happened before that year, or, in fact, for some years later. Nevertheless, the study of Australian politics and government does have some deep roots. Australia does not quite have its John W. Burgess or its Woodrow Wilson, but it does have counterparts in F. A. Bland and William Hearn. Bland, a distinguished academic and member of the Commonwealth Parliament, is often regarded as the father of Australian political science; Hearn (1826–1888) might best be regarded as its grandfather. Born in Ireland, Hearn was appointed Professor of History and Political Economy at the newly established University of Melbourne in 1854; late in his career he was elected to the Victorian colonial legislative council, of which he became unofficial leader after 1882.[1] His major study, *The Government of England: Its Structure and its Development,* was first published in 1867, the same year as Walter Bagehot's *The English Constitution* and Karl Marx's *Das Kapital.*

In spite of these promising origins, the growth of Australian political science was slow. As late as 1947, the journal of the Australian Institute of Political Science was still asking whether the "analysis, classification and the framing of hypotheses in the study of politics are sufficiently developed to admit it as one of the social sciences."[2] The question has still not been settled among students of politics. Debate continues over what to call the beast: Political Science, Politics, or Government. We do not agree on usage[3] but employ "political science" because it appears to conform more with international usage and the language of this volume.

The Growth of Academic Political Science

Politics and government were first taught in various courses in law, history, philosophy, economics and commerce departments, and in public administration tutorial programs offered early in the century by the University of Sydney. In 1918 a course entitled "Modern Political Institutions" (comprising studies in British political institutions and "international relations in law") was introduced in the bachelor of laws program at the University of Melbourne. It became available to bachelor of arts students in 1921, when a second course, "Modern Political Ideas," was also offered in law. The term "political science" was first used as the title of a course offered in 1919 as an appendage of a program in constitutional history under the responsibility of the professor of history and social science at the University of Queensland.[4] Courses in the broad area of politics were taught under the umbrella of commerce at the University of Tasmania from about 1920; the Department of History at the University of Western Australia began courses in political institutions in 1924.

Some notable developments in the 1930s began with the formation of the Australian Institute of Political Science in 1932. In 1934, Professor Garnet V. Portus was appointed as Professor of Political Science and History at the University of Adelaide. This department was concerned primarily with history and offered only one course in alternate years in political science. An interesting snippet of political science history occurred with Professor Portus's retirement. In 1951 G. W. K. Duncan was offered the Chair of History and Political Science. Earlier Sir Douglas Copland, an eminent economist, and Professor K. C. Wheare criticized this projected conjunction of the two disciplines. In 1953 the university's council "divided" the discipline: Professor Hugh Stretton became Professor of History and Duncan was offered the Chair of History and Political Science, with the prospect of becoming head of a new department called Politics. In January 1954 Sir Thomas Playford, the premier, objected to this title.[5] Politics, he said, was "the hurly-burly of the hustings" and he would prefer something like "political economy." In 1955 the council decided to make no nomenclature changes and the odd duality of Chairs in History and in History and Political Science remained until 1965—when a Politics Department was designated.

The most significant development was the establishment of a Department of Public Administration at the University of Sydney in 1935. It was fostered by New South Wales Premier Bertram Stevens, leader of the state's United Australian party (a forerunner of the present Liberal Party) government. Stevens, a former Treasury officer, had worked closely on problems of government and administration with F. A. Bland, the first professor in the new department. Bland—justly regarded as the father figure of Australian political science—had taught public administration in tutorial classes since 1914 and in the University of Sydney's Faculty of Economics since 1920. He served as a consultant to numerous government committees, public service boards, and ministries, and in 1929-1930 he was Visiting Professor of Government in New York. He retired from the Chair at Sydney in 1947 at the age of 65. He was elected to the House of Representatives as a Liberal party candidate in 1951, became chairman of the Public Accounts Committee in 1952, and served with distinction until 1961.[6] The scope in the Department of Public Administration was much wider than its name suggests and a broad range of courses in political institutions was offered.

The University of Melbourne, which created a subdepartment of political philosophy and modern political institutions in 1933 as a joint subsidiary of the departments of history and philosophy, gradually expanded its offerings in the discipline through the 1930s. In 1938 the university listed a School of History and Political Science, with courses in modern political institutions, international relations, constitutional and legal history, economic history, and political philosophy. A separate Department of Political Science was created in 1940 with William MacMahon-Ball as lecturer-in-charge. MacMahon-Ball—who had previously taught sociology, political philosophy, and political institutions—was appointed professor of political science in 1949 and occupied this position until 1968 when he was succeeded by Professor Alan F. Davies.

The discipline developed steadily but still slowly after World War II. In 1946 the University of Tasmania's History Department expanded the range of courses in politics; in 1956 a Department of Political Science was established under Professor W. A. Townsley, who served until 1975 when he was succeeded by Professor Harry Gelber. A similar expansion of courses at the University of Adelaide occurred with the appointment of Professor G. W. K. Duncan. At the University of Queensland, political science courses were the responsibility of the professor of history and social science until 1949. Then the department ceased to include economics and was renamed History and Political Science. Meanwhile, a further major development at the University of Sydney followed the retirement of Professor Bland, and the appointment of Professor P. H. Partridge to the Chair. The range of courses was widened, and the department was renamed Government and Public Administration—or, more commonly, simply Government. This name had some significance. The new department was not welcomed warmly at first; in fact, for some years the Faculty of Arts insisted that students obtain grounding in history and philosophy before proceedinig to "dubious" Government. The Philosophy Department at that time claimed some responsibility for teaching moral and political philosophy and objected to the new department using the terms "political science" or "political studies." Hence the name "Government and Public Administration," largely in deference to Australian Professor K. C. Wheare. His advice was sought commonly by Australian universities at that time: Wheare was then Gladstone Professor of Government and Public Administration at Oxford.

A further development, perhaps more significant in terms of subsequent research and graduate study, was under way in Canberra. Part-time classes in political science and public administration had been given by R. S. Parker at the Canberra University College, an affiliate of the University of Melbourne, as early as 1938. In 1944 and 1945, L. F. Crisp gave part-time courses to cadets of the Department of External Affairs (later Foreign Affairs). Crisp was appointed Professor of Political Science in 1949 and served there from 1950 to 1977 (including the period to 1970 as head of department). The name "Political Science" was chosen because of the link with the University of Melbourne. The Canberra University College ended its tie with Melbourne in 1960 when it became the School of General Studies, responsible for undergraduate teaching at the Australian National University. This university was established by the Australian Commonwealth Parliament in 1946 "to encourage and provide facilities for postgraduate research and study both generally and in relation to subjects of national importance to Australia." Postgraduate programs in the university's Institute of Advanced Studies were offered in the Research School of Social Sciences, where a Department of Political Science was created in 1951. This department functioned with one staff member (at reader level) for three years. The first Chair was established in 1956 for Professor Lester C. Webb, who was succeeded upon his death in 1962 by Professor Robert S. Parker. (The Australian National University still has two separate political science departments.)

This was the state of progress in Australian political science by the mid-1950s. Five of the nation's (then) seven universities had given "something approaching full recognition to the subject" and, as Professor R. N. Spann (successor to Professor Partridge at the University of Sydney) noted in 1955, the discipline had established its independence.[7] By that time a number of professional associations covering various fields in political science had been formed, and university teachers were beginning to give attention to the progress of the discipline. The crucial step in this direction was a Conference of University Teachers of Political Science, held at the Canberra University College on 28–30 August 1957, subsequently reported in the *Australian Journal of Politics and History* in August 1958. It provided the first opportunity for academic colleagues to meet to discuss teaching and research; it represented "a sort of stocktaking" of postwar work in the discipline and an opportunity to consider where it should be heading. Papers discussed were "Politics as a University Subject" by Professor P. H. Partridge, "Three and Four Year Courses in Political Science" by Professor L. F. Crisp, "The Teaching of Comparative Government" by H. A. Wolfsohn, "The Teaching of Public Administration" by Dr. B. B. Schaffer, and "The Study of International Relations" by Professor Gordon Greenwood. Professor Spann's report on the conference concluded with observations that portray the state of the discipline at the time:

the bent of the conference discussions confirms the view, as it has recently been expressed, that the average political scientist takes his stand somewhere between the historian's refusal to systematize and the sociological impulse to systematize too thinly. It is an uneasy stance, and one sometimes hard to defend. But it is where we are, and where many of our great predecessors were.

My final impression is summed up in Professor Partridge's contention that "political science must be problematic." He did not mean by this that it must necessarily deal with immediately and obviously burning issues; but that it is a dead thing unless it is to some point presented to us in the shape of problems to be solved, and problems in which we have a living interest. I wondered when I heard him say it, do we still carry about too much dead-weight? Do we often enough reflect on what interests us and concerns us in our own subject? Do we ask enough "what is living and what is dead" in political science?[8]

Subsequent developments were slow. The New South Wales University of Technology gave some courses in the 1950s and a School of Political Science was established in 1964 under the chairmanship of Professor Douglas McCallum when that institution became the University of New South Wales. A Department of Politics was established under Professor Rufus Davis with the commencement of Monash University, as the second university in Victoria, in 1962. In 1966 the University of Queensland established a separate Department of Government (Professor Colin A. Hughes), Western Australia a Department of Politics (Professor Gordon S. Reid), and the new Flinders University opened in South Australia with a discipline of Political Theory and Institutions (Professor David C. Corbett). In the following year, La Trobe University opened in Victoria with a Department of Politics under the chairmanship of Professor Hugo A. Wolfsohn. The University of New England, where a subdepartment of Public Administration had operated in the Faculty of Economics since 1961, established its Politics Department in 1971 with Colin M. Tatz as foundation professor. The most recent departments to be established were in 1972 at the Royal Military College in Canberra (Department of Government—Professor B. D. Beddie), and at Macquarie University in New South Wales where Politics has the status of a "discipline" under the chairmanship of Professor Don Aitkin in the School of History, Philosophy, and Politics. The universities of Newcastle and Wollongong (NSW), James Cook and Griffith (Queensland), Deakin (Victoria) and Murdoch (WA) do not have political science departments, though elements of the discipline are taught under other rubrics.

Throughout the 1960s and early 1970s, Australia also experienced the development of a number of undergraduate colleges of advanced education. In 1965 the national government decided to assist the states financially to create tertiary education institutions which were separate in function, but equal in status, to universities. Those consequently established—colleges of advanced education (CAEs)—have by "academic drift" become similar in role to universities and some have academic departments of considerable prestige. Many of these—notably Canberra College, Mitchell College in New South Wales, and a number of state colleges in Victoria—have given some emphasis to political science.[9]

Teaching Political Science

Political science in universities and colleges has developed from a few scattered courses and a handful of lecturers in the 1930s and a small number of incipient departments in the 1940s to a well-established discipline in most institutions today. The increase in the number of departments over the two decades since the mid-1950s is shown in table 6.1.

The number of political scientists—professional in the sense that they teach the subject—has naturally grown

Table 6.1 Political Science Departments in Universities and Colleges

STATE OR TERRITORY	1957	1977[1]	
	UNIVERSITIES[2] AND UNIVERSITY COLLEGES	UNIVERSITIES AND UNIVERSITY COLLEGES	COLLEGES OF ADVANCED EDUCATION[3]
Australian Capital Territory	Australian National University (ANU)	ANU	Canberra CAE
	Canberra University College	Royal Military College	
New South Wales	Sydney	Sydney	Taught in 11 colleges
		Macquarie	
		New England	
		New South Wales	
Victoria	Melbourne	La Trobe	Taught in 11 colleges
		Melbourne	
		Monash	
Queensland	Queensland	Queensland	Taught in 4 colleges
South Australia	Adelaide	Adelaide	Taught in 4 colleges
		Flinders	
Western Australia	. . .	Western Australia	Taught in 1 college
Tasmania	Tasmania	Tasmania	Taught in 1 college

SOURCE: G. Harman and R. Scott, *Teaching Politics in Colleges of Advanced Education*, APSA, 1975, pp. 46-55.

[1]This table does not include those universities that employ political scientists in more general social science departments.

[2]The list of universities in 1957 does not include the University of Western Australia and the NSW University of Technology, where some political science courses were taught.

[3]This information on colleges of advanced education is for 1975. Eight colleges had separate departments in 1975. There has been some growth in this area, notably in Victoria, where Politics is taught as a high school course.

accordingly. In 1958 it was possible to list all 44 academic political scientists on 1½ pages of a newsletter.[10] This list included a number of historians who also taught politics, and several part-time researchers. With these excluded or counted as fractions where appropriate, the number was about 39. By 1961 it had reached 61 and by 1977 it stood at 295 in the universities alone (see table 6.2). The largest department in 1957 was at Melbourne with 11½ members. By 1977, it had a 28 member teaching staff. Sydney had increased from 5 to 28, and the Australian National University from 5 to 44 political scientists in its various schools. Table 6.2 does not include political scientists teaching at CAEs where their numbers increased rapidly in the late 1960s and early 1970s. The full-time political science teaching staff in the colleges grew from 31 in 1970 to 49 in 1973 and 58 in 1974.[11]

The qualifications of academic staffs in the universities have also changed noticeably over the past two decades. In 1957, of the 27 full-time teachers at the rank of lecturer and above (tutors are normally part-time graduate students), only 9 had completed doctorates. In 1977 the figures were 208 at lecturer or above, of whom 118 had earned doctorates. The doctorate is now commonly considered an essential requirement for lecturing appointments (and there were 7 tutors with that qualification in 1978). The position is somewhat different at most of the CAEs.

In past years, many political scientists were recruited from outside the country and many Australians have felt a need to complete their academic training abroad. There is now a growing self-sufficiency in terms of the training of teachers of political science, although only 39.1 per-

Table 6.2 Political Scientists in University Political Science, Politics and Government Departments

RANK	1957	1977[a]
Professor	6½[b]	23
Associate Professor/Reader (+ Professorial Fellow)	1	22½
Senior Lecturer (+ Senior Fellow) (+ Senior Research Fellow)	10	77
Lecturer (+ Fellow + Research Fellow)	9½	86
Tutor	9	66½
Research Assistant	3	20
Total	39	295

SOURCES: The 1957 column is from L. F. Crisp, "Political Science in Australian Universities," *Vestes* 2 (June 1962): 26. The 1977 column is from a survey conducted by the authors.

[a]Note that the 1977 figures do not include political scientists at colleges of advanced education where a slightly different ranking system operates.

[b]The Queensland Chair was History/Political Science.

Table 6.3 Teachers of Political Science (Lecturers and Above): Sources of Qualification (in percentage)

COUNTRY	WHERE OBTAINED HIGHEST DEGREE %	WHERE OBTAINED PH.D. %
Australia	39.1	36.1
United Kingdom	34.3	27.8
United States	21.3	31.0
Other	5.1	5.3

SOURCE: Survey conducted by the authors.

cent of those at lecturer level or above now have their highest degrees from Australian universities (see table 6.3). A slightly lower proportion (36.1 percent) of those at these levels with completed doctorates received these qualifications in Australia. The other major source countries of political science qualifications are the United Kingdom and the United States. A point of interest is that of the 23 full professors of political science almost half came to Australia to pursue academic careers.

Student numbers provide the most dramatic indications of the post–World War II growth of the discipline. We have to estimate the number of undergraduates in 1945, but it is doubtful that there were more than about 400. Professor Spann noted in 1955 that there were about 800 in that year and the number had at least doubled in the postwar years.[12] By 1957 there were 1,276, of whom 128 were studying for honors degrees;[13] by 1961 this nearly doubled to 2,116, including 198 at honors level[14] (see table 6.4). In 1977–1978, 10,012 undergraduate students were in political science courses at the universities. Some 395 of these were studying for honors degrees, and a further 150 were preparing for honors with a further year of study beyond the pass degree. Up-to-date

Table 6.4 Students Enrolled in University Political Science Courses

LEVEL	1957	1961	1977/78
Undergraduate	1,276	2,116	10,012
Honors level	128	198	545[b]
M.A. (or M.Ec.) by thesis	11[a]	14	127
M.A. (or M.Ec.) by course work and thesis	—	—	106
Ph.D. by thesis	6[a]	9	108
Ph.D. by course work and thesis	—	—	1

SOURCES: *Australian Journal of Politics and History* 4 (1957): 91, for 1957; L. F. Crisp, "Political Science in the Australian Universities," *Vestes* (June 1962): 25–30, for 1961; survey conducted by the authors. Some universities provided numbers for 1977 and some for 1978.

[a]Crisp, *Political Science*, p. 25.

[b]Total of 545 honors students in 1977/78 includes 150 who were pursuing honors degrees as a further year of study beyond first degree.

figures for the colleges of advanced education are not available, but in 1973 5,415 students were taking some politics in CAE programs.[15]

Graduate studies have increased at a faster rate. Only 2 or 3 people pursued such studies in political science in the 1940s. In the period 1957–1961, 11 M.A. or M.Ec. (Master of Economics) degrees and 6 doctorates were awarded in the discipline, and in 1961 14 master's theses and 9 doctoral theses were in progress. By 1977–1978 233 students were enrolled for master's degrees and 108 for doctorates. Doctoral enrollments are heaviest among staff members who commonly have six or even eight years for completion on a part-time basis. Apart from the Institute of Advanced Studies at the National University, there are few full-time political science Ph.D. candidates. In the postgraduate field, several political science people are obtaining broader social science degrees: for example, the first 3 master of social science (interdisciplinary) graduates at New England completed their theses in political science.

Attention has been given from time to time to problems of teaching political science, most notably at the 1957 Australasian Political Studies (APSA) conference and at the 1973 APSA conference. Emphasis has been on questions of what should be taught and at what levels rather than on actual teaching methods. There has not been a great deal of innovation, and undergraduate courses at most universities follow a traditional pattern of two or three hours of lectures and one or two hours of tutorials per week, with term essays and tutorial papers required and a final examination. There have been some commendable attempts at developing case studies with some general utility,[16] and suggestions for more innovative approaches,[17] but these have not met with any great enthusiasm. Honors students normally attend additional seminars in their senior years and/or in an additional year beyond the pass program and usually present an honors thesis of 15,000 to 20,000 words. At these levels there has not been a significant emphasis on fieldwork or quantitative research methods except in some honors options. The trend in master's degree programs is to require some course work, but half the students currently enrolled are pursuing the degree by thesis alone (see table 6.4). Some consideration has been given to introducing course work into doctoral programs, but currently the Ph.D. is obtained by thesis alone (only one exception is noted in table 6.4). In contrast with the procedure in the United States, no courses are required beyond the M.A. and a graduate student does not normally have to satisfy any formal language or research-tool requirements. Australia still follows the so-called British tradition of an in-depth thesis for M.A. and Ph.D. requirements. In a discussion as to whether absence of Ph.D. courses could mean some level of "fraudulence" on the part of a lecturer-to-be, Professor Percy Partridge once said: "The best way to learn about any area of political science is to teach a course in it." Given the large number of staff with American higher degrees (see table 6.3), it is perhaps surprising that this British tradition persists so strongly.

A considerable diversity of courses is offered now, but a crudely typical four-year program can be described. This is based on our survey of universities and colleges, using the University of New England as a concrete base for the model. In almost every university, the first-year course consists of two semesters: more or less equal sections deal with an introduction to political ideas and an overview of Australian government and politics. Second-year courses tend to offer one-semester options in political theory, comparative politics (usually American, British, and European politics, and communist systems), international politics and political sociology. Some third-year programs include further courses in theory, behavior, and international politics, but the emphasis tends to be on public policy and administration, Asian politics, problems of political development, and advanced studies in Australian politics. Since the introduction of the semester system—which has replaced full-year courses in most universities during the past decade—there has been a trend among universities to make all courses above the first-year survey course available to both second- and third-year students, with no more depth or difficulty for the latter than for the former. Fourth-year and postgraduate courses tend to be more flexible and depend upon the interests of students and staff members. Only a few of the larger departments list courses as regularly available at the honors and master's levels. Student numbers at this level are still small enough to allow for tailor-made programs.

Some significant areas of relative inactivity are revealed by our survey. Law and legal studies receive very little emphasis beyond some elementary constitutional law in courses on federalism. Partly in consequence, where legal questions have become political issues (as they did in 1975 when a parliamentary crisis resulted in a governor-general dismissing a federal government thus leading to a general election) the tendency has been to look to lawyers rather than to political scientists for comment. While it is geopolitically sound that Australian students be taught the politics of South East Asia, Australia's Asian geographic location does not fully explain the dearth of interest in the continents of Africa and South America, or in the Middle East. Further, almost no attention has been given to race and ethnicity in Australia or to political anthropology. The latter is taught, not always well, in some anthropology departments. Very few courses are offered in general social issues or in specific policy areas, perhaps partly because there has not been a strong tradition of activism or commitment on social policies by Australian political scientists. With a few outstanding exceptions, moreover, the merging of professional and political activities has been marred by overcommitment and ideological luggage and has not contributed in any positive way to the development of the discipline. The general professional detachment of political scientists has resulted in their failure to make much worthwhile input into the resolution of many of the political and social problems of recent decades. Members of the discipline were not particularly visible during the antihanging, Vietnam, conscription, environmental, censorship, law reform, and constitutional crisis debates. Nor were they noticeably conservative. There is now a growing interest in policy studies, especially at the postgraduate level, and this may help overcome the limitations imposed by both commitment and detachment.

Political Science Associations

The discipline is served by two umbrella organizations: the Australian Institute of Political Science (AIPS), a broad-based organization interested in promoting a wide range of research in political, social, and economic areas, and the Australasian Political Studies Association (APSA), essentially a professional organization of academics. There are also several specialist-area associations—notably the Australian Regional Groups of the Royal Institute of Public Administration (RIPA) and the Australian Institute of International Affairs (AIAA). These are discussed in the chronology of their origins.

The AIPS was founded in 1932 to provide educational and research facilities for people interested in the study of Australian political, economic, and social problems. It prides itself on providing "a unique meeting point for many interests and viewpoints" and attempts to "contribute to the formation of forward-looking judgments on large political issues." The institute brings together academics, writers, members and officials from all political parties and groups, and politically interested lay people to participate in its seminars, forums, discussion groups, and other functions. Its main activities are an annual three-day summer school and a publications program. The summer schools have been organized since 1934, covering significant major issues each year. Recent schools have dealt with: Immigration and Growth (1971), Who Runs Australia? (1972), Foreign Policy (1973), Industrial Australia 1975-2000 (1974), Mass Media (1975), The Distribution of Wealth and Power (1976), and Rural Australia (1977). The proceedings of the schools are published in book form. The major AIPS publication is its journal the *Australian Quarterly.* It first appeared in 1929, to come under control of the institute some years later. It has since included articles by almost everyone of political or academic standing in Australia. It has wide circulation and a relatively short waiting period for publication—hence its popularity in the discipline.

The Australian regional groups of RIPA were organized as affiliates of the British RIPA, to advance the study of public administration and promote the exchange of information on the subject. RIPA provides a forum for academics and administrators in different organizations and different levels of government.[18] Seven regional groups (one in each state and one in the Australian Capital Territory) functioned more or less independently until 1958 when they began to cooperate in the organization of an annual conference. A steering committee set up to organize these conferences gradually acquired broader responsibilities: in 1975 it decided to establish a national council. In 1977 the council resolved to form an autonomous Australian institute which, as a result of a survey of its members, elected to retain the royal title. Through its national council, Australian RIPA is affiliated with the International Institute of Administrative Sciences and the Eastern Regional Organization for Public Administration (EROPA), which provides links with similar bodies throughout East Asia and the Pacific. Australian RIPA now has more than 3,500 members but no permanent staff. Each regional group determines its constitution, membership fees, and activities and these vary considerably across the country. In addition to organizing meetings, lectures, travel fellowships, and essay competitions, RIPA's main activities are its annual conferences (which are usually attended by about 300 delegates) and its publication program. The institute's quarterly *Australian Journal of Public Administration*—which was first edited by Professor F. A. Bland in 1937—now has more than 4,000 subscribers.

The Australian Institute of International Affairs was established in 1933 as an affiliate of the Royal Institute of International Affairs of Chatham House, London. It maintains close relations with similar bodies in Canada, New Zealand, India, Pakistan, and Nigeria. The AIIA is a federal body, with more than 2,000 members (including about 125 corporate members) in branches in the capital cities and a number of regional areas. The policy of the institute is determined by a Commonwealth council, which also appoints a director and elects a president and other officers annually. The governor-general of Australia is normally an office-bearer with the position of Visitor, and the institute's presidents have also been people of some distinction: the president elected in 1978, for example, was Sir Garfield Barwick, the Chief Justice of the High Court of Australia, and Sir Laurence McIntyre, a highly respected former diplomat, succeeded Professor T. B. Millar as director in 1976. The institute meets its purpose—which is "to stimulate interest in, and discussion and understanding of international affairs and foreign policy both among its members and the general public"—through its journal *Australian Outlook,* an extensive program of research and publication, annual conferences, and the sponsorship of regular public lectures. The annual Dyason lecturers have included such people as Bertrand Russell, Arnold Toynbee, William O. Douglas, Merle Fainsod, Gunnar Myrdal, and two notable South African spokeswomen, Margaret Ballinger and Helen Suzman. The Roy Milne Memorial Lecturers have included most Australian prime ministers, foreign ministers, and Federal Opposition leaders.

The youngest of the major organizations is APSA. Membership is open to teachers and researchers in political science and allied subjects in "Australia, New Zealand and overseas," and to others whose participation is held by the association's executive to be advantageous to political studies. APSA was formed in 1952 as an affiliate of the International Political Science Association. Its beginnings were unsteady. By 1955 it had held one or two business meetings at the periodical conferences of the Australian and New Zealand Association for the Advancement of Science (ANZAAS), but it was regarded at that time as stillborn because "no one has so far thought of anything useful for it to do."[19] But, soon after, the association established a permanent foothold. In 1956 it began publishing *APSA News,* a bulletin of short articles and notes of interest to teachers of politics. The *News* was replaced in 1966 by a more ambitious biannual journal, *Politics.* Under three editors (Professor Douglas McCallum, Professor Henry Mayer, and, currently, Dr. Dean Jaensch), *Politics* has become a very successful journal of articles and research notes by both new and established scholars. APSA publishes monographs of significant results of political research and a directory of political scientists in Australia. It also administers a Parliamentary Library Fellowship which annually enables a political scientist to take a one-year research post within the Commonwealth Parliament. The major activity of APSA is its regular conference. The first such meeting was the 1957 Canberra Conference of University Teachers of Political Science (discussed above) which was one of the most significant milestones in the development of the discipline. Subsequent conferences have been held annually in Canberra or the six state capitals. The first conference in a nonmetropolitan center was held at the University of New England at Armidale, New South Wales in 1977. That conference included 41 papers from Australian and overseas scholars (those from overseas included Brian Barry, Nathan Glazer, and J. Roland Pennock), and the 1978 conference at Adelaide, South Australia, included 53 papers. The Armidale and Adelaide conferences have produced a return to formal, tightly structured and tightly run forums for the discipline. The first (1957) conference was attended by 30 political scientists, while today the conferences normally attract about 200 people. APSA now has some 500 members, more than a quarter of whom are from outside Australia.

Research and Literature

In his 1950 summary of the condition of Australian political science for the UNESCO publication, *Contemporary Political Science,* Professor Geoffrey Sawer pointed out that it was a "time of remarkable opportunities for the students of Australia, since in almost every field of political investigation not merely the classic, but even the pioneer works still have to be written."[20] There were no comprehensive interpretive or even descriptive works on Australian government comparable with those on Britain and the United States—beyond a small book written by Sawer himself in 1948 as an elementary outline for first-year university students.[21] He attributed the "relatively backward conditions of academic research, writing and teaching dealing particularly with Australian government" partly to the fact that "Australian government, like its culture generally, has been derivative in character."[22] The Australian political system is, at least at its roots, a product of the marriage of the Westminster model of parliamentary government and the Philadelphia model of federalism. Such a conjunction inevitably produced peculiar offspring and it is surprising that it inspired so little research and so few publications by mid-century.

No great rush followed Sawer to fill this void. Professor R. N. Spann was able to point out five years later that political scientists were still slow to find methods of investigating Australia's peculiar practices, and they had to learn from overseas that even our political parties and pressure groups were worthy of academic study.[23] The first thorough treatment of the Australian party system was the American political scientist Louise Overacker's *The Australian Party System* (1952). Professor Overacker also produced one of the first comprehensive bibliographies on Australian politics—"Publications on Australia Useful to the Political Scientist: A Selective Survey" in *The American Political Science Review* in 1953[24]—in which she pointed out that there were many gaps to be filled before Australia could "find its Dicey, its Bagehot, its Jennings, its Bryce, and even its Brogan."[25] Overacker was followed a few years later by two other visitors, Josephine F. Milburn and Taylor Cole, who expanded on her listings in the areas of parties and groups with a further bibliographical article in the *American Political Science Review.*[26] These efforts inspired some activity and in 1958 the first major home-grown survey of the literature was produced by S. R. Davis and Colin Hughes as "The Literature of Australian Government and Politics" in the *Australian Journal of Politics and History.*[27] This really coincided with, and perhaps in part motivated, the beginnings of what one political scientist has recently referred to as "the explosion of knowledge, or at least of books and journals, that has occurred since the middle 1950s."[28] The conference, seminars, and other activities sponsored by the discipline's four key associations have provoked research, and their monographs and journals already mentioned, together with less exclusively political science journals (notably the *Australian Journal of Politics and History*), have provided the opportunities for publication. *Politics*—since its inception and especially under the influence of Professor Henry Mayer—has provided an invaluable service in recording the expanding bibliography of Australian politics. Indeed, Professor Mayer's other activities promoting research (and notably the publication in 1976 of the extremely useful *ARGAP—A Research Guide to Australian Politics and Cognate Subjects*)[29] have won him the unanimous appreciation of political researchers.

The recent expansion of the Australian political bibliography is also explained by the growing opportunities, encouragement, and facilities for research, especially with the development of the research schools at the Australian National University, and, of course, the sheer increase in the number of political scientists. The research departments at the Australian National University include a Political Science Department (which tends to emphasize Australian politics and Soviet and East European government), a History of Ideas Unit (which is primarily interested in the formation and history of concepts, systems of ideas or values, and ideologies in the period since the seventeenth century), and a Center for Foreign Politics (Western Europe)—all in the Research School of Social Science. A Department of International Relations (emphasizing international politics in the Asian-Pacific region) and a Strategic and Defense Studies Center are in the Research School of Pacific Studies. Other centers, notably the Center for Research on Federal Financial Relations, produce material of considerable value to political scientists. Including those at the research schools and centers, there are now at least 360 teachers of political science in the nation's universities and colleges. The research interests of these and nonacademic political scientists cover a wide area (see

Table 6.5 Professional Interests of Members of the Australasian Political Studies Association

SUBJECT	NO. OF ANSWERS	SUBJECT	NO. OF ANSWERS
Australian politics	111	Political opinion and communication	24
Comparative politics	88	Marxist theory	22
Public policy	68	Empirical theory	21
Third World; development; modernization	47	Methodology: epistemological and philosophical	18
Public administration	45	Methodology: other aspects	11
Normative theory; political philosophy	44	Political sociology	11
Political culture; ideologies; attitudes	43	Politics and psychology	9
International relations	37	New Zealand	3
Political change—violence, revolution, order, stability	29	Class analysis	2
		Urban studies	2

SOURCE: *APSA Directory of Political Scientists in Australasia – 1977/78*.
NOTE: Members of the Australasian Political Studies Association were asked to indicate their main three professional interests. Note that the survey included overseas as well as Australian members of APSA.

table 6.5), and most express a major professional interest in Australian politics. In the 1960s, Ph.D. scholars tended to look to pastures other than Australian for topics, resulting in a shortage of "Australianists" in the early 1970s. This pattern has begun to change.

The opportunities for research by academics are really quite good. Face-to-face teaching time for those above the rank of tutor in the universities rarely exceeds three to four hours per week (usually much more in the CAEs) and study-leave provisions have been very generous: academics at the rank of lecturer and above have traditionally enjoyed one-year's paid study-leave (with travel allowances) for every seven years of service. On the other hand, there has not been undue pressure on academics to publish (although this appears to be growing as the competition for university teaching positions increases). Further, the market for Australian publications is quite small: political scientists in Australia do not become wealthy on royalties.

In spite of the "explosion" since the 1950s, some observers of Australian political science have expressed surprise that more research has not been done. In 1973 British political scientist David Butler produced a book of essays on Australian government in which he drew attention to "the unworked lode."[30] Like Sawer more than twenty years earlier, Butler found Australian politics and government to be "extraordinarily little studied" and he made the point that "the great shortage of reflective analysis about the working of the Canberra system constitutes a reproach to the Australian political science community."[31] Indeed, Butler's observations had some validity. Many of the pioneering works had appeared since Sawer's 1950 report, but, still, very few books could be called classics on Australian politics. What is more, many areas were largely ignored by academic writers until discovered as fitting subjects for books by political journalists. This is especially so in such areas as political biography and election studies. Political science in Australia has virtually no tradition of fieldwork. Since the mid-1960s the federally funded Australian Research Grants Committee has provided money for Australian academics. As recently as 1977, the ARGC was urging political and other social scientists to apply for funds. It claimed few political scientists had sought funds since 1964 or funds of any magnitude. This may be due to the lack of "schools" of political science, or of departments as a whole engaging in expensive group projects. The number of joint research projects, even of jointly written articles, is remarkably few in Australian history and political science.

Australian political campaigns and election practices are peculiar and should have offered themselves as irresistible subjects for study. Until 1972, however, when journalists began to produce books in the American style of *The Making of the President,* there were few publications except for two or three relatively minor studies of by-elections or state elections[32] and some useful statistical material on electoral trends.[33] This situation has been remedied now and recent elections have produced some good analyses. Perhaps significantly, the best of these is a collection of essays, mainly by Australian writers, edited by Howard R. Penniman for the American Enterprise Institute for Public Policy Research.[34] The bibliography of Australian politics continues to be laced with names from overseas and many of their contributions have been in areas long neglected by local scholars.[35] This trend seems to be continuing. Australia in the 1970s won a place on the itineraries of many more visiting American, British, and Canadian political scientists, with the result that the nation's political system is being examined more closely than ever before. This has been very beneficial to the discipline in Australia. The turbulence of Australian politics in the 1970s—after more than twenty years of stable but relatively uninteresting government—inspired many more local scholars to look to the mine. The lode David Butler discovered in 1972 is no longer as unworked as when he surveyed it. Indeed, a useful bibliographical supplement in the May 1978 issue of the journal *Politics* provides 71 pages and some 500 listings and brief annotations of recent articles and other publications of relevance to political science in Australia.[36]

The Future

Can Australian political science sustain the expansion of the past two decades? There is considerable agreement that it cannot: that it has reached a plateau. Undergraduate student numbers are leveling off and in some areas of study they are declining quite markedly. Graduate student numbers are remaining stable or increasing slightly at a time when there are fewer and fewer prospects of new tertiary teaching positions. Tertiary education through 1986 is likely to be in a frozen but steady state. One result will be that university and college departments will be much more selective in their hiring policies. Perhaps the overall qualifications of their staffs will inevitably improve. But an unfortunate by-product of the moratorium on growth is that many staff members will be recruited for untenured, limited terms of three years. This produces both a morale and a disincentive problem. Lecturing positions will assuredly require doctorates. In many cases, the tutorship has lost its "apprenticeship" notion, as a training/research position leading to "higher things." It has become a competitively-fought-for, limited-tenure end in itself.

The discipline is becoming less incestuous as higher proportions of its graduates prepare for careers in the business and public service sectors. The "professionalization" of the federal and state public services has made them attractive to graduates generally. Political science has invariably been one of the "majors" sought in qualifications. The consequences of this trend are that some departments are now tilting the emphasis of their programs toward the more practical and vocational interests of their students.

There are other interesting indicators of the future. Some prospects are suggested by the growing interest in political studies at the secondary school level. Only the Victorian school system has courses in politics and government. In the other states it has been limited to at best a segment in broader social studies courses. Today, some experimental senior high school options are in political science in most states. If successful, they may be a source of both more and better-prepared tertiary students and of employment for political science graduates.

During the 1970s, governments, ministers, parliamentary committees, commissions, parties, individual politicians, and interest groups have tended to look to political science and the other social sciences for professional advisors and researchers. (Political scientists as such have not been sought out as think-tank advisors to premiers or ministers in the dramatic American sense of Kissingers or Brzezinskis.) As well as promoting research and publications of more general, rather than limited, academic interest, this trend also provides further avenues for employment for graduates as well as opportunities for teachers of political science to obtain valuable practical experience. Future demands for further career-oriented political science programs will probably be catered to by more university lecturers with practical as well as theoretical backgrounds. But there is still relatively little movement between elective politics and academic political science. Only three professional political scientists since Bland (A. J. Forbes and A. A. Staley who became Liberal party ministers, and Neal Blewett for the Labor party) have been elected to the Commonwealth Parliament, and there has been even less traffic in the other direction. It is hoped that the appointment of former Prime Minister E. G. Whitlam to a research position at the Australian National University could start a trend. There has been some movement in both directions between academia and the public service.

It is not easy to generalize about the present state of the discipline. Questions that confounded attempts to make such generalizations more than ten years ago are still as hard to answer.[37] There is no single outstanding institution, nor are there widely recognized prestige university departments. There are no definable "schools" of political science, renowned for any particular field of study or research approach. There is no identifiable "establishment"—or even agreement as to which local giants have made the greatest contributions to the world of political science. The discipline has few, if any, popularizers, except for a small number of newspaper columnists and feature writers. Significantly, the profession is still sufficiently small and homogeneous: it is free of divisions and competing "schools" and its conferences and conventions are friendly affairs. Australian political science certainly has some growing to do, but in the past two decades it has come of age.

Notes

1. See J. A. LaNauze, "Hearn and 'The Government of England'," *Public Administration* 30, no. 4 (December 1967): 303-10.

2. I. Milner, "The Field of Political Science," *Australian Quarterly* 19, no. 3 (September 1947): 57.

3. Tatz prefers "Politics" while Starr prefers "Political Science."

4. R. N. Spann, "Political Science in Australia," *Australian Journal of Politics and History* 1, no. 1 (November 1955): 88.

5. Ibid., p. 87.

6. For a summary of Professor Bland's career see "F. A. Bland: In Memoriam," *Public Administration* 26, no. 3 (September 1967): 283-86.

7. Spann, "Political Science," pp. 88-89.

8. R. N. Spann, "Political Studies: A Conference Report," *Australian Journal of Politics and History* 4, no. 1 (August 1958): 18.

9. G. Harman and R. Scott, eds., *Teaching Politics in Colleges of Advanced Education* (Canberra: Australasian Political Science Association, 1975).

10. "Staff List: Political Scientists at Australian Universities," *APSA News* 3, no. 3 (June 1958): 11-12.

11. Harman and Scott, *Teaching Politics*, p. 42.

12. Spann, "Political Science," p. 89.

13. *Australian Journal of Politics and History* 4, no. 1 (August 1958): 91.

14. L. F. Crisp, "Political Science in the Australian Universities," *Vestes* 5, no. 2 (June 1962): 28.

15. Harman and Scott, *Teaching Politics*, p. 41.

16. See C. A. Hughes, "Some Techniques of Teaching Politics and Political Research" (Paper presented at APSA Conference, Kensington NSW, August 1973).

17. See D. Stephens, "A Comment on Introductory Courses in Political Science," *Vestes* 18, no. 2 (1975): 118-22.

18. B. Moore, "Postcards from Abroad," *Australian Journal of Public Administration* 35, no. 3 (September 1976): 287.

19. Spann, "Political Science," p. 87.

20. G. Sawer, "Political Science in Australia," *Contemporary Political Science* (Paris: UNESCO, 1950), p. 323.

21. G. Sawer, *Australian Government Today* (Melbourne: Melbourne University Press, 1948).

22. Sawer, "Political Science," p. 323.

23. Spann, "Political Science," p. 86.

24. L. Overacker, "Publications in Australia Useful to the Political Scientist: A Selective Survey," *American Political Science Review* 47, no. 3 (September 1953): 844-57.

25. Ibid., p. 844.

26. J. F. Milburn and T. Cole, "Bibliographical Material on Political Parties and Pressure Groups in Australia, New Zealand and South Africa," *American Political Science Review* 51, no. 1 (March 1957): 199-219.

27. S. R. Davis and C. Hughes, "The Literature of Australian Government and Politics," *Australian Journal of Politics and History* 4, no. 1 (August 1958): 107-33.

28. D. Aitkin, "Trying to Keep the Right Hand Informed About the Left," *National Times,* 8 July 1978, p. 46.

29. H. Mayer et al., *ARGAP-A Research Guide to Australian Politics and Cognate Subjects* (Melbourne: Cheshire, 1976).

30. D. Butler, *The Canberra Model* (Melbourne: Cheshire, 1973).

31. Ibid., p. 3.

32. One notable exception is N. Blewett and D. Jaensch, *Playford to Dunstan* (Melbourne: Cheshire, 1971).

33. For some years the serious study of electoral statistics was left almost entirely to the efforts of Malcolm Mackerras of the Royal Military College.

34. H. R. Penniman, ed., *Australia at the Polls* (Washington, D.C.: American Enterprise Institute, 1977).

35. As examples, see the writings of Henry Albinski of Pennsylvania State University on the politics of foreign policy, David Butler of Oxford on elections, Louise Overacker on parties, and John R. Williams of West Virginia University on conservative parties.

36. H. Mayer, "Australiana—and Overseas," Supplement to *Politics* 13, no. 1 (May 1978).

37. J. McCallum, "Just Plain Boring or—?" *Quadrant* no. 35, 9, no. 3 (May-June 1965): 61-62.

Bibliography

Churchward, L. G. "Archival Memories." *Melbourne Journal of Politics* 4 (1971):69-72.

Crisp, L. F. "Political Science in Australian Universities." *Vestes* 5, no. 2 (June 1962).

———. "The Teaching of Political Sociology in Australia." In *The Teaching of Sociology in Australia and New Zealand,* edited by J. Zubrzycki, pp. 95-106. Melbourne: Cheshire, 1971.

Harman, G., and Scott, R., eds. *Teaching Politics in Colleges of Advanced Education.* Canberra: Australasian Political Studies Association, 1975.

Marshall, J., and Jaensch, D. *APSA Directory of Political Scientists in Australasia.* Australasian Political Studies Association, 1977-1978.

Mayer, H. "Australasian Political Science Association." *PS* (Spring 1972):195-96.

——— et al. *ARGAP: A Research Guide to Australian Politics and Cognate Subjects.* Melbourne: Cheshire, 1976.

Sawer, G. "Political Science in Australia." In *UNESCO, Contemporary Political Science: A Survey of Methods, Research and Teaching.* Paris, 1950.

Spann, R. N. "Political Science in Australia." *Australian Journal of Politics and History* 1, no. 1 (November 1955): 86-97.

——— et al. "The Australian Political Studies Conference, Canberra, August 1957." *Australian Journal of Politics and History* 4, no. 1 (August 1958).

7 AUSTRIA

PETER GERLICH, EMMERICH TALOS, and KARL UCAKAR

Introduction

Political science has been introduced into Austria only very recently, in spite of long traditions of legal and political studies and remarkable developments in earlier periods in the social sciences in general. The state of the discipline in Austria, therefore, remains still somewhat marginal. It is now established at the universities and partly even outside the universities, but continues to be confronted with many problems.

Most of these turn around the question of professionalization; first, the problem of professionalization on the university level: Political science is today practiced by representatives from various other fields with a great number of different theoretical approaches and research concerns. These drawbacks may, however, also be turned into an advantage and that is what the representatives of this young subject have been trying to do. One example has been the establishment of a rather active association. Another is the publication of a journal to maintain a level of discussion which may appear relatively intensive for such a small and recently established profession.

Professionalization, however, includes not only the institutionalization of organizations and their activities but also the conduct of university studies and curricula. Here one must note that Austrian university regulations are centralized, a matter of federal policy. The discussion of legal provisions for the introduction of courses of studies or the discussion on contents of laws, ordinances, and plans of studies is, therefore, not only of academic but also of political concern, and has not yet been completed.

Secondly, professionalization implies the problem of job realization for graduates. While the situation in the past has not been too bad, partly because of the very few graduates so far and partly because of the ability of those graduates to find jobs in other areas, great problems may arise in the future.

As can be understood easily the very recent introduction of the discipline has left a broad spectrum open to research, especially with regard to the Austrian political system. The whole broad range of open questions can be handled only partly by the limited research capacities of a small discipline. Nevertheless, Austrian political scientists have been trying to face up to this challenge and certainly will continue to do so.

The State of Political Science in 1945

The most remarkable fact about the development of political science in Austria as a discipline is that its establishment, compared with the United States or Western Germany, took place so very late, namely in the 1960s. For this reason, political science did not exist in 1945 as an institutionalized discipline within the social sciences even if questions belonging to political science according to today's understanding were traditionally treated in earlier periods under the title of political sciences (*Politische Wissenschaften*) or science of state (*Staatswissenschaft*).

Before 1945 political science questions were handled in close connection with problems of the legal sciences. J. Galtung has observed a correlation between socio-economic backwardness and a high proportion of lawyers among university graduates.[1] This hypothesis might be quite useful if one tries to explain the predominance of lawyers vis à vis social scientists in Austria. Up to roughly the middle of the nineteenth century, the political sciences played a role in the course of legal studies. They included problems of administrative science, of economics, and of fiscal science. What Blanke, Jürgens and Kastendieck have noted for the German Reich of the second half of the nineteenth century[2] applied similarly to the development in Austria. Political sciences were assigned the function of an appendix within the course of legal studies.[3] Even if theoreticians outside the universities and politicians, especially Austrian social democrats, noted at the turn of the century the importance of an independent political science,[4] further development of the field continued only in connection with or dependent on legal sciences: jurists decided what function political science should perform. An interesting illustration of this tendency is provided by the establishment of the course of study in state sciences at the Faculties of Law and State Science: In 1919, a course of study in state sciences was introduced. It did not, however, lead toward the possibility of entering the civil service. The course of study was shorter than that of legal studies which implied lower qualifications for its graduates.

A reform of this new course of studies took place only in the middle of the 1920s: the length of study was extended to eight semesters, but it still remained much less prestigious than the study of law, which continued to lead, as it does today, its graduates into all kinds of positions of public relevance within or outside the civil service.

During the First Republic (1918–1934) much scientific work was done outside the university which was of great relevance to political science (Renner, Bauer, Adler). The upswing of social research from the 1920s to the 1930s was connected with the names of Lazarsfeld, Zeisel, and Jahoda (*Österreichische Wirtschaftspsychologische Forschungsstelle*) but did not lead to immediate consequences for the institutional development of political science.

Austro-fascism from 1934 and Nazism after 1938 interrupted even these limited beginnings of social sciences in Austria. Many Austrian social scientists emigrated to the United States and, to some extent, influenced American political science (e.g., Lazarsfeld, Deutsch, Voegelin).

The Evolution of Political Science since 1945

The establishment of the Second Republic in 1945 did not mark a beginning for the introduction of political science. Here it is interesting to note the difference from the Federal Republic of Germany in which intense and finally successful efforts were undertaken to establish political science with special practical purposes. Among those were the attempt to overcome the past and to educate for democracy on all levels of the school system. Without initiatives coming from the outside, the resistance within the system of Austrian education, especially the universities but also the higher administration, could not be overcome, so that neither the establishment of political science as a university discipline nor the introduction of political education into the curricula of Austrian schools was possible.[5]

The question of establishing political science became a topic of discussion only in the 1960s. Why has political science as a scientific discipline finally been introduced into Austrian universities? In our opinion the following circumstances were of importance:

1. Initiatives from the outside: The activities of the OECD[6] did not remain without influence on scientific policy in Austria (a law for the promotion of research, 1967; a law introducing a course of social and economic studies).

2. Personal interests of scientists from different disciplines (legal science, philosophy, history, theology) who wanted to transcend the limits of their own fields.

3. A growing awareness of the possibilities or even necessity of practical uses of the social sciences. The feeling of a general crisis of society at the end of the 1960s played a certain role here. It led to a remarkable increase in social science involvement especially in the area of political planning in the Federal Republic of Germany. These aspects as well as the role that political science might play in the improvement of the legitimation of the political system exercised at least an anticipatory and latent influence in Austria.

4. The increased importance of social sciences vis à vis traditional scientific activity in comparison to the 1940s and 1950s, in consequence of which political science was introduced among the courses of study at the university level.

5. The promotion of political science as an independent social science discipline within the framework of the social democratic science policy which became relevant especially after the social democratic party took over the government in 1970.

What were the results of the developments of the 1960s?

1. The introduction of courses of studies on a legal basis.

2. The institutional and personal expansion of the discipline. In comparison to Western Germany, these developments have, however, been only marginal and the degree of professionalization of the discipline is still very low.

3. The beginning and continuation of political science research.

4. The problem of jobs for graduates. Generally it has to be pointed out that up to now there is no institutionalized access to job positions comparable with that of any other courses of study. Generally, one must add that the occupational options are very limited by the dominance of law graduates in the civil service and by the absence of access to the school system. Graduates so far have found jobs in

the following fields: research and teaching at the university (roughly 50 percent); service within the ministries, interest groups, and mass media; international organizations and institutions of adult education.[7] The present practice of development of necessarily individual strategies to find a job still constitutes quite a problem. With respect to the increasing figures of graduates the extension of possibilities to get jobs seems very necessary.

The establishment of political science in Austria did not come about without controversies. Certain political interests could not, however, nor could the predominance of law, prevent the establishment of political science teaching and research.[8]

THE INTELLECTUAL STRUCTURE OF THE DISCIPLINE

What we feel is the most remarkable aspect of the present situation has to be pointed out at the beginning: political science at present has still an integrative character in the sense that the problems treated could not be differentiated strictly from those of other disciplines. One could also say that political science has up to now by no means turned into a clearly differentiated social science discipline in this country. On the contrary, its structure reflects the special conditions of its establishment in the 1960s: the influence of different disciplines (law, history, etc.) has affected research structures and theoretical problems. This influence can be deduced from the fact that most of the political scientists presently active have come from other scientific disciplines.

Positions represented in teaching and research have been similarly affected. These positions extend from the traditional, normative, philosophical stance to the empirical, analytical, and critical theoretical standpoints. While the first position has, perhaps somewhat less than in the Federal Republic, moved into the background (together with the legal orientation), the two other positions appear more fashionable. As a recently published report has shown, the contents treated in political science in Austria have been to a large extent determined by the status of political science in the Federal Republic.[9] The reception of American political science characteristic of the Federal Republic during the 1960s has partly found its equivalent in the political science department of the Institute for Advanced Studies at Vienna, founded in 1962.[10]

THE TEACHING OF POLITICAL SCIENCE

Courses of studies, the academic curricula, are established by federal legislation in Austria. The first attempt to start a course of political science took place in 1965 at the University of Salzburg on the basis of the old Law Concerning the Study of Philosophy. In 1969 an Interfaculty Institute for Political Science was established there. Nevertheless, modern and satisfactory legal foundations for this course of study were missing. The introduction of political science as alternate subject in the Ordinance Concerning Diploma Examinations of Social and Economic Studies in 1966 was an important preparatory step in the direction of establishing such a foundation. The discussions that were carried on in the following years and which were concerned with the establishment of political science as an independent discipline were concluded successfully in 1971. The discipline of political science has now been included in the Federal Law Concerning the Courses of Studies in the Humanities and Sciences. Political science has thus been legally introduced as an independent course of study.[11]

In connection with this law, the establishment or the expansion of institutes of political science took place. In 1971 the Chair of the Philosophy of Politics and Criticism of Ideology at the University of Vienna was changed into the Institute for the Theory of Politics. Further, if limited, expansion of political science institutes took place in connection with the introduction of political science within the framework of the studies of social and economic sciences and in anticipation of tasks to be performed by institutes of political science in the reformed course of the study of law.

Institutes of political science were established at the Universities of Vienna (1974) and Innsbruck (1976). In spite of their traditional proximity to legal science, these new institutes considered themselves mainly oriented toward the social sciences, as can be seen from the fact that during the 1975 university reform when the old faculties of law were divided these two institutes were included in the new Faculties of Social and Economic Science.

The appendix of the 1971 federal law mentioned above includes a curriculum which the so-called ordinance of studies and the plans of studies at the different universities had to take into account. So far, an ordinance of studies has been issued by the Ministry of Science, but no plans of studies have been worked out on the university level. For this reason, the legal basis of the study is still the earlier Law Concerning the Study of Philosophy. Formally, the course of political science lasts for eight semesters. The precondition of graduation is the writing of a dissertation and the passing of strict examinations (*Rigorosen*) on the main and alternate fields as well as an additional examination on philosophy. There is no compulsory curriculum for the course of study. In practice, attendance at lectures, introductory seminars, and seminars is recommended. At present, political science can be studied at the universities of

Vienna and Salzburg. Aside from this, it is of a certain importance that political science can be studied as an alternate subject in the courses of study of the social and economic sciences. This includes the writing of master's theses and dissertations in the field of political science.

Within the framework of the Austrian universities, the following institutions of political science exist at present:[12]

NAME OF INSTITUTION	NUMBER OF SCIENTISTS	MAIN EMPHASIS OF RESEARCH
Institute of Political Science at the *Grund- und Integrativwissenschaftliche* Faculty at the University of Vienna	5	International politics, policies of integration, political conscience, political culture, political education, theory of the state, marginal groups, agrarian policy, science policy, security policy, conflict and peace research.
Institute of Political Science at the Faculty of Social and Economic Sciences at the University of Vienna	3	Legislative research, administrative research, social policy, welfare state planning, community history, development of electoral laws
Chair of Political Science at the *Geisteswissenschaftliche* Faculty at the University of Salzburg	4	Foreign policy, international policy, research on developing countries, interest group research, political education and socialization, electoral behavior
Chair of Political Science at the Faculty of Law at the University of Salzburg	4	Political theory, workers, movements, Austro-Marxism literature and practice
Institute for the Theory of Politics at the Faculty of Theology at the University of Salzburg[13]	3	History of political ideas, theory of science and knowledge, research methods, theories of revolution, political education, federalism
Institute for Political Science at the Social and Economic Science Faculty at the University of Innsbruck	3	Comparative politics, theories of democracy, the political system of Austria, theory of science, fascism, political culture

As an advanced institution of teaching and research outside the universities, the Institute for Advanced Studies and Scientific Research was established in Vienna in 1962. It has a Department of Political Science employing six scientific assistants. The main emphases of research are: administrative research, agrarian policy and international policy. The post-graduate course of study mentioned above which is carried on at this institute is primarily oriented toward research.

Concerning the further development of teaching one must mention the following legal regulations: on 15 June 1978 the Federal Ministry of Science issued an ordinance for the study of political science.[14] This ordinance is based on the curricula included in the 1971 federal law.[15] This federal law prescribes the following curriculum for the course of studies (i.e., subjects and examinations) leading toward a master's diploma.

First examination for the diploma:

1. Preliminary examinations in:
   a) Recent history
   b) Statistics for the social scientist
   c) According to the choice of the candidate, one of the following alternate fields:
      1. Introduction to the basic notions of economics and economic policy
      2. Introduction to the basic notions of the social sciences
      3. Introduction to social psychology
2. Fields of examination:
   a) Introduction to the history of political ideas and theories
   b) Basics of international politics
   c) Basics of law and the state as well as Austrian constitutional and administrative law
   d) Methods of empirical research

Second examination for the diploma:

1. Special precondition: knowledge of a living foreign language
2. Preliminary examination in recent Austrian constitutional and administrative history
3. Fields of examination:
   a) Political theory and history of ideas
   b) Comparative politics
   c) International politics and basics of international law
   d) Basics of the Austrian system of government and process of government

e) If political science has been chosen as the first course of studies, an alternate field, as for example:
   1. Constitution and government
   2. Philosophy of law and state
   3. Political economy
   4. Recent history
4. In addition, a diploma thesis must be presented

The course of studies laid down by the law and the ordinance now must be implemented by plans of studies at the different universities. The preparation of these plans is not yet finished. After their completion, the course of studies will be formally changed and conducted according to the new legal basis. The present study for a doctorate, old style, will then be replaced by the study for a diploma (roughly comparable to a master's degree) with the additional functional possibility of further study for a doctorate. At present it is difficult to judge whether the change in the course of studies will lead to an improvement in the job possibilities of political scientists.

As a further task for the political science teachers of the universities, their future participation in courses of studies in law has been included in the new Law Concerning the Course of Study of Law which was passed by parliament in 1978. Political science will have a function similar to that in the course of studies of social and economic sciences mentioned above. It will serve as an alternate additional subject and thus become a rather important part of the training of law students.

RESEARCH IN POLITICAL SCIENCE

Contributions. The results of research, which Austrian political science has produced so far, mirror the relatively brief history of this discipline in its modern sense. At the Institute of Political Science at the *Grund- und Integrätivwissenschäftliche* Faculty of the University of Vienna work has been done mainly in the field of international politics, especially politics of integration, as well as in the area of political education.[16] Research at the Institute of Political Science at the Faculty of Social and Economic Studies has been mainly in the fields of parliamentary research, social policy, and the political history of communities.[17] Contributions of the Chair of Political Science at the Faculty of Law at the University of Salzburg concern the area of the workers' movement and Austro-Marxism.[18] The main topic of research of the Chair of Political Science at the *Geisteswissenschäftliche* Faculty of the University of Salzburg is international relations, foreign policy, and neutrality policy.[19] In the areas of the history of political ideas and criticism of ideology, revolution research, and political education the research of the Institute for the Theory of Politics at the Theological Faculty of the University of Salzburg has led to concrete results.[20] The Institute of Political Science at the Social and Economic Sciences Faculty of the University of Innsbruck has, above all, done research concerning the theory of democracy.[21] The Institute of Advanced Studies in Vienna, which is, as has been mentioned, established outside the universities, has published research in the areas of socialization, administrative research, agrarian policy, and international politics.[22] At the University of Vienna, work has been done in the field of parliamentary studies.[23]

Methodology. During the first period of its establishment Austrian political science was, as regards methods, on the one hand very much influenced by American political science.[24] It was, therefore, oriented toward behaviorism and a rather unhistorical empiricism. On the other hand, traditional philosophical approaches did play a role.[25] Later on, a greater orientation toward the inclusion of the historical dimension of political and social developments was introduced.[26] Austrian political science is still very much influenced by the methodological concerns of systems theory, which had great influence in the beginning of the 1970s.[27]

ASSOCIATIONAL ACTIVITIES

Associations. Austrian political scientists founded a scientific association relatively late, namely in 1970, which corresponds to the belated development of the discipline. The "*Österreichische Gesellschaft für Politikwissenschaft*" (Austrian Political Science Association) includes among its statutory aims the promotion of political studies and research, the representation of the interests of Austrian political scientists, and the institutionalization of political science as an independent course of study at the Austrian universities.

The establishment of a course of study of political science on a legal basis, described above, was achieved at least partly as a result of the pressure group activities and especially expert opinions of the Political Science Association transmitted to parliament. Likewise, the association attempts to mediate in the present discussion on the concrete determination of the course of study for the diploma, since university teachers and students, who must agree on a plan of studies within this new system of the Austrian university government, hold very controversial points of view in this respect.

One of the most important tasks of the association is the promotion of communication among political scientists with respect to research and teaching. This aim is achieved by the publication of the *Österreichische Zeitschrift für Politikwissenschaft* (*Austrian Political Science Journal*) and by the organization of scientific congresses and the introduction of scientific work groups. Topics of the annual scientific congresses have so far been selected with the aim not to be limited to special interests but to make possible an integrative function by posing questions which are of more general interest. Such topics have included during recent years: "Equality in Austria"; "Thirty Years of the Second Republic"; "Political Education"; "The Fiscal Crisis of the State"; "Women in Society." The most important contributions to the congresses have been published in the *Austrian Journal of Political Science*.

The initiation of work groups for specific topics, which have a certain relevance in scientific and political discussion, for example "law and politics," "political education," and others, has likewise become an important activity of the association. The association annually elects a nine member board which conducts its affairs. It is elected by the general assembly of all members. In the composition of the board, the different scientific, regional, and political interests of the members have, as a rule, found representational expression.

Journals. A committee of editors has been asked by the Austrian Political Science Association to publish the "*Österreichische Zeitschrift für Politikwissenschaft*" (*Austrian Political Science Journal*).[28] Since 1972, this journal has been published quarterly by the Europa Verlag, Vienna. The task of this periodical, on the one hand, is to publish political science analyses which concern Austria and to present them in Austria itself to a broad reading public interested in the discipline. But, on the other hand, the content is by no means limited to regional topics. International and theoretical topics are included, also. Aside from political scientists, scientists of other related disciplines (economists, historians, lawyers, educators, sociologists) have published in the journal. Each quarterly journal is dedicated to a specific main topic.

Up to now the main themes have included: parliamentary affairs, political socialization, peace research, community politics and participation, international relations, bureaucracy, media and media policy, the welfare state, political economy, parties and democracy, administration and democracy, *Sozialpartnerschaft,* science and research policy, equality in Austria, thirty years of the Second Republic, law and politics, international politics, social and health policy, political education, methodological problems in the social sciences, minorities and nationality problems, the fiscal crisis of the state, communist parties in Western Europe, the debate on ideology within the parties, small states in the process of internationalization.

POLITICAL SCIENCE AND THE WORLD OF POLITICS

Politics and political institutions do, of course, influence the development of political science maybe especially so in Austria. The influence of politics and political interests can be concluded from different facts. For example, the establishment of a department of political science at the Institute for Advanced Studies, which was one of the initiatives leading to the establishment of the discipline, corresponded to the orientation of government circles toward the West, which had become dominant during the period of reconstruction after World War II. This intellectual predisposition did, of course, find its expression also within the social sciences.

The establishment of political science at the universities at the beginning of the 1970s has certainly been influenced by different factors: in neighboring countries, especially in the Federal Republic, political science was, at that time, developed much further than in Austria. To this it must be added that a social democratic government was formed in 1970.

Social democracy had long before advocated the expansion of modern social science, whatever was understood by this term. Certainly, those factors have played a role in the development of Austrian political science. They sometimes have been characterized as the "science of legitimation" or "science of crisis." However, one has to see that in Austria, unlike other countries, the immediate need for legitimation by a science of legitimation appears to be rather less urgent. Attention must be drawn to a system of rather stabilized mechanisms like the *Sozialpartnerschaft* or a politically highly integrated press which characterizes the Austrian political system.[29] However, certain political interests can be deduced from the selection of different main emphases of research: planning, parliamentary affairs, bureaucracy, welfare state, and political education among others.

From its very beginning the Austrian Political Science Association has put much emphasis on good relations with interested politicians, among other reasons to improve the position of the discipline vis à vis competing, well-established disciplines like the science of law or the philosophical analysis of science. In the course of these contacts it has with certain success always attempted to include on its board politicians who had a certain legitimacy because of their earlier studies and publications. On the other side, there are graduates of political science who are active in political affairs and hold functions in interest groups, parties, and public corporations.

Present State and Future Prospects of Political Science

After a development of roughly ten years of political science as an independent discipline some conclusions can be drawn about its present state. (1) The discipline is now established among the courses of study in the system of university education. (2) Political science has found its place within the framework of social science research even if many questions remain open. One of the problems of this very young discipline is the need to catch up with other, older disciplines. To this one must add the low degree of professionalization and institutionalization of political science (there are roughly only thirty political scientists which corresponds to probably 5 percent of the total political science personnel in the Federal Republic). These relatively few people are also responsible for the conduct of the courses of study. Since there are far too few university teachers, teaching takes up most of the time of the university personnel. In empirical as well as in theoretical research there are still many open questions in Austria. (3) The status of political science outside the universities has up to now been rather limited in its effects. Only a few political scientists have found positions in institutes of research outside the universities. Access to the administration and other occupational areas (media, adult education) is marginal, too. In other words: strategies for professionalization so far have not been too successful.

From the foregoing conclusions some aspects for future developments may be deduced. (1) Teaching at universities will undergo not inconsiderable changes after plans of study are finally passed. At present, it is difficult to judge what consequences these changes will bring in the level of education and the usability of the studies in job areas. (2) There will be, as until now, a broad field of areas of research which have to be covered by genuinely political science analyses. This concerns structure of the political system of Austria as well as international and theoretical questions. If the present state of professionalization is not changed the problems mentioned above will not be solved. Certain attempts toward an interdisciplinary research are not without interest and should be expanded in the future. (3) The next years will witness an increasing output of graduates. This will lead to an intensification of the job problem. The solution or nonsolution of this problem will certainly be of consequence for the further development of political science in Austria.[30]

Notes

1. J. Galtung, "Intellektuelle und Entwicklung," *Österreichische Zeitschrift für Politikwissenschaft* (hereafter cited as *ÖZP*) (1972/3): 75.
2. B. Blanke, U. Jürgens, and H. Kastendiek, *Kritik der Politikwissenschaft* (Frankfurt, New York, 1975), p. 38.
3. H. H. Fabris; G. Heinrich; H. Kramer; P. Kreisky; E. Schmidt, "Zum Politologenbedarf in Österreich," *ÖZP* (1973/4): 434.
4. N. Leser, *Zwischen Reformismus und Bolschewismus* (Vienna, Frankfurt, 1968), p. 80.
5. Fabris, "Zum Politologenbedorf," p. 437.
6. *OECD Research Report on Austria, Recommendations on Science Policy*, 1972.
7. Fabris, "Zum Politologenbedorf," p. 443.
8. Ibid., p. 441.
9. H. H. Fabris, "Abhängigkeiten der Kleinstaaten-Politologie," *ÖZP* 3 (1978): 370-75.
10. See, e.g., P. Gerlich and H. Kramer, *Abgeordnete in der Parteiendemokratie* (Vienna, 1969).
11. Compare B. Wicha, "Politikwissenschaft in Österreich," *ÖZP*, no. 1 (1972): 89-96.
12. According to responses to a survey by the Austrian Political Science Association, 1977, documented in: *ÖZP*, no. 4 (1976): 509-27.
13. The three Salzburg positions have been combined into an Institute of Political Science subordinate to the Academic Senate.
14. BGBl no. 259 / 15 June 1978.
15. BGBl no. 326 / 30 June 1971.
16. H. Schneider, *Politische Bildung in der Schule*, 2 vols. (Darmstadt, 1975); idem, *Die Leitbilder der Europapolitik* (Bonn, 1977); F. Windhager and H. Neisser, *Wie sicher ist Österreich?* (Vienna, 1978); C. Benard, "Realpolitikwissenschaft," *ÖZP*, no. 1 (1976).
17. P. Gerlich, *Parlamentarische Kontrolle im politischen System* (Vienna, 1973); idem, "Zur empirischen Machtforschung: Ansätz und Fragestellungen," *ÖZP*, no. 1 (1974); E. Talos, "Die Soziale Frage," *ÖZP*, no. 1 (1979); idem, "Zu den Anfängen der Sozial-politik," *ÖZP*, no. 2 (1976); K. Ucakar, "Die Entwicklung des Verbändewesens," in H. Fischer, ed., *Das politische System Österreichs*, 2d ed. (Vienna, 1977); idem and M. Welan, "Kommunale Selbstverwaltung und Konstitutioneller Rechtsstaat," in *Forschungen und Beiträge*, no. 1 (Vienna, 1978).
18. Leser, *Zwischen Reformismus;* idem, *Socialismus zwischen Relativismus und Dogmatismus* (Vienna, 1974); A. Pfabigan, "Die Rezeption der Marxschen Methode im Austro-Marxismus, *ÖZP*, no. 1 (1977); A. Pelinka, *Stand oder Klasse?* (Vienna, 1972).
19. K. Faupel, "Planung in der Außenpolitik—eine Inselwelt," *ÖZP*, no. 2 (1975).
20. F. Horner, *Die Sozialen Grundrechte* (Salzburg, 1974); H. Dachs, "Neuere Ansätze zur Revolutionsforschung," in *Zeitgeschichte*, no. 3 (1973-1974); idem, *Österreichs Geschichtswissenschaft und Anschlutz 1918-1930* (Salzburg, 1974).
21. See A. Pelinka, *Politik und moderne Demokratie* (Kronberg, 1976); idem, *Bürgerinitiativen—gefährlich oder notwendig?* (Freiburg, 1978).
22. Gerlich and Kramer, *Abgeordnete*; J. Krammer and G. Scheer, "Landwirtschaft und Kapitalismus in Österreich," *ÖZP*, no. 3 (1975); J. Krammer, "Österreich und die Dritte Welt," *ÖZP*, no. 3 (1978).
23. See H. Widder, *Organisationsprobleme im parlamentarischen Regierungssystem* (Salzburg, 1977).
24. See, e.g., Gerlich and Kramer, *Abgeordnete*, pp. 9-20.
25. Schneider, *ÖZP* (1975): 95.
26. Leser, *ÖZP*, no. 3 (1972): 89.
27. Gerlich, *ÖZP*, no. 1 (1972): 73.
28. The journal may be ordered from: Europa Verlag

Ges.m.b.H., Altmannsdorferstrasse 154-156, A-1232 Vienna, Austria.

29. See Fischer, ed., *Das politische System Österreichs,* 2d ed. (Vienna, 1977) for descriptions and analyses of the most important aspects of the Austrian political system.

30. In the fall of 1977 2,488 students (i.e., 15.1% of beginners in all courses of study) started a course of study of law, 2,352 (14.3%) chose the study of the social and economic sciences and 98 (0.6%) chose political science. These figures include beginners in all Austrian universities (P. Gerlich and H. Kramer, *Abgeordnete* (Vienna, 1978), p. 114).

Bibliography

Benard, C. "Realpolitikwissenschaft." *ÖZP,* no. 1 (1976).
Blanke, B.; Jürgens, U.; Kastendiek, H. *Kritik der Politikwissenschaft.* Frankfurt, New York, 1975.
Dachs, H. "Neuere Ansätze zur Revolutionsforschung." *Zeitgeschichte,* no. 3 (1973/1974).
⸺. *Österreichs Geschichtswissenschaft und Anschluß 1918-1930.* Salzburg, 1974.
Fabris, H. H. "Abhängigkeiten in der Kleinstaaten-Politologie." *ÖZP,* no. 3 (1978).
⸺; Heinrich, G.; Kramer, H.; Kreisky, P.; Schmidt, E. "Zum Politologenbedarf in Österreich." *ÖZP,* no. 4 (1973).
Faupel, K. "Planung in der Außenpolitik—eine Inselwelt." *ÖZP,* no. 2 (1975).
Fischer, H., ed. *Das politische System Österreichs.* 2d ed. Vienna, 1977.
Galtung, J. "Intellektuelle und Entwicklung." *ÖZP,* no. 3 (1972).
Gerlich, P. *Parlamentarische Kontrolle im politischen System.* Vienna, 1973.
⸺. "Zur Analyse des politischen Systems—Entwicklung eines Begriffsrahmens." *ÖZP,* no. 1 (1972).
⸺. "Zur empirischen Machtforschung: Ansätze und Fragestellungen." *ÖZP,* no. 1 (1974).
⸺, and Kramer, H. *Abgeordnete in der Parteiendemokratie.* Vienna, 1969.
Hochschulbericht 1978. Vienna, 1978.
Horner, F. *Die sozialen Grundrechte.* Salzburg, 1974.
Kramer, H. "Österreich und die Dritte Welt." *ÖZP,* no. 3 (1978).
Krammer, J., and Scheer, G. "Landwirtschaft und Kapitalismus in Österreich." *ÖZP,* no. 3 (1975).
Leser, N. "Politikwissenschaft zwischen Politik und Wissenschaft." *ÖZP,* no. 3 (1972).
⸺. *Sozialismus zwischen Relativismus und Dogmatismus.* Vienna, 1974.
⸺. *Zwischen Reformismus und Bolschewismus, Der Austro-Marxismus als Theorie und Praxis.* Vienna, Frankfurt, 1968.
OECD Research Report on Austria, Recommendations on Science Policy. 1972.
Österreichische Zeitschrift für Politikwissenschaft (Austrian Political Science Journal). Vienna: Europa-Verlag.
Pelinka, A. *Bürgerinitiativen—gefährlich oder notwendig?* Freiburg, 1978.
⸺. *Politik und moderne Demokratie.* Kronberg, 1976.
⸺. *Stand oder Klasse?* Vienna, 1972.
Pfabigan, A. "Die Rezeption der Marxschen Methode im Austro-Marxismus." *ÖZP,* no. 1 (1977).
Schneider, H. *Die Leitbilder der Europapolitik.* Bonn, 1977.
⸺. *Politische Bildung in der Schule.* 2 vols. Darmstadt, 1975.
Talos, E. "Die soziale Frage." *ÖZP,* no. 1 (1979).
⸺. "Zu den Anfängen der Sozialpolitik." *ÖZP,* no. 2 (1976).
Ucakar, K. "Die Entwicklung des Verbändewesens." In *Das politische System Österreichs,* edited by H. Fischer. 2d ed. Vienna, 1977.
⸺, and Welan, M. "Kommunale Selbstverwaltung und konstitutioneller Rechtsstaat." In *Forschungen und Beiträge zur Wiener Stadtgeschichte,* no. 1. Vienna, 1978.
Wicha, B. "Politikwissenschaft in Österreich." *ÖZP,* no. 1 (1972).
Widder, H. *Organisationsprobleme im parlamentarischen Regierungssystem.* Salzburg, 1977.
Windhager, F., and Neisser, H. *Wie sicher ist Österreich?* Vienna, 1978.

8

BELGIUM

ANDRÉ PHILIPPART*

Structure and Programs

Political science, what is it? Political scientists, what do they do?

Those are two questions often asked by politicians and Belgian universities.

Probably, a concise description of the state of political science in Belgium would show that Maurice Duverger is right.[1] Duverger believes that some research tends to create new forms of mystification. First, university mystification, because the status of political science is inferior to that of law, history, sociology, psychology, and economics. Second, methodological mystification, because research methods remain traditional, namely: reading, introspection, recollection; and when scientists resort to modern methods of analysis, it is by way of justification and alibis: content analyses, computations of correlation, factorial analyses, opinion surveys give a more scientific character to the work undertaken. And third, political mystification, because, in general, political scientists neglect the study of great political problems in order to perfect secondary and superficial analyses for fear of modifying the political structure. Those who do try for a global vision of problems fall back on the tradition of classical political science: political theory.

Should it be said, nevertheless, that, to return to the words of Maurice Duverger, "in a word, political science is generally taught in *Belgian* ["French" in the quotation] universities by amateurs rather than by professionals"? But the majority of great inventions that govern our technological society are the fruit of the work of amateurs.

What exactly is political science in Belgium?

THE UNIVERSITIES

The structure of political science has existed for more than half a century. The state universities of Gand and Liége were authorized by royal decree on 2 October 1893, to institute within the faculty of law, scientific degrees and diplomas for *candidat, licencié* and *docteur* of political science. At the Catholic University of Louvain and the Free University of Brussels schools of political and social science were created at the end of the last century. In the same period, the Free University of Brussels founded an Institute of Sociology which catalyzed research in the political sciences, essentially in the domains of political theory and elections. *L'Atlas des élections belges 1914–1954*[2] and *Les Elections belges— explication de la répartition géographique des suffrages*[3] constitute the best-known examples.

The schools of political and social science of the two free universities have been included for thirty years in ad hoc faculties autonomous at the level of authority but dependent, to a certain extent, for programs on the Faculties of Philosophy and Literature and of Law. At least, that was true at the beginning, until very clear tendencies toward scientific autonomy and specific instruction manifested themselves ten years ago. Thus, two institutes of political and social sciences existed until 1967 at the Catholic University of Louvain, at the bachelor's degree level (one for the French section, the other for the Flemish section) each institute being divided into a Department of Political Science and a Department of Social Sciences.

Since 1968 the French branch of this university has been organized in the manner of English-speaking universities, with a Department of Political Science further subdivided into groups: political science; international relations; public administration. The basic courses in the political area intended for bachelor's degree students in the political science group are: history of political science and social ideas; political science, first part; political instructions, second part; political life; contemporary policies; contemporary political thought; international re-

*The translation from French was made by Paula Lieberman and the editor.

lations theory; public administration theory; study in depth of political sciences; and comparative political systems.

Although this evolution toward an independent discipline appeared at the Catholic University of Louvain, that institution recently abandoned the departmental structure to return to a more classical faculty structure.

The evolution has been less sweeping at the Free University of Brussels. The remaining differences between it and Louvain, it is well to remember, arise from the complete freedom that the free universities have to elaborate their curricula as long as they respect the standards set for accreditation of university diplomas and scientific titles and for legal financing by the state.

The maturation of political science instruction at the Free University of Brussels seems to have been impeded by the preponderance given to the former School of Commerce when it merged in 1946 with the School of Political and Social Sciences (the merger is the basis for the creation of the Faculty of Social, Political and Economic Sciences, which acquired a unitary structure only in 1964).

The influence of the Institute of Sociology has been equally determinant. The essential subjects related to political science that are taught in it to future political scientists are: current problems of international politics; parliamentary history of Belgium; study in depth of questions of contemporary political history of Belgium; administrative law; general theory of the state; study in depth of questions of statutory law; parties, groups, and public opinion: first part; parties and groups, second part; the press and other mass media; study in depth of political science questions; origins and development of contemporary political doctrines and explanations of texts concerning them.

The study of political science is oriented differently at Brussels than at Louvain, in spite of a certain convergence at the end. At both places, the programs are designed in such a way that the holders of bachelor's degrees in political science can find work in public administration, the diplomatic corps, or even in private enterprises that have large administrative services. But the education given to *licenciés* at Brussels is more diverse than at Louvain where specialization appears more among the groups and in the subjects taught. In the area of research, political science seems to be favored less at Brussels than at Louvain, because it can scarcely develop at Brussels, except within the Institute of Sociology. However, this situation of relative dependence should not mystify us. The rise of political science depends finally, in Belgium as elsewhere, on people, on their quality and their will.

The predominance of sociologists at Brussels and jurists at Louvain is the result of the orientation formerly given to the schools; it is also the result of the difficulty of employing academic people who are only "political scientists." For this reason, the group of historical subjects (antiquity, Middle Ages, modern times, contemporary economic history of Belgium), sociology, political economics, social economics, administrative and public law still constitute the texture of political science studies.

The Catholic University of Louvain seems to have the most favored of all the political science units. Under the leadership of dynamic professors like W. Dewachter, H. Van Hassel and their colleagues, the department of political sciences of this university has developed intense research activity on Belgian political life, on the election results, on the formation of governments, on political elites, and so forth.

At the State University at Liège, political science remains dependent on the faculty of law; this is also the case at the State University at Gand. The law compels the state universities to integrate all new scientific disciplines into the five faculties of philosophy and literature, law, sciences, medicine, and applied sciences.

After studies in common with candidates in sociology and administration, the future political scientists are granted a degree in political science with the designation "Government" or "International Relations."[4] Specific courses, aside from contemporary history and the history of political doctrines, are: introduction to political science; parliamentary history of Belgium; diplomatic history; political geography; international organization; contemporary international relations; political science, and a group of juridical subjects, oriented especially to the European community.

It is undeniable that for fifteen years Belgian political scientists have had the opportunity to develop specific instruction in the university system. But it is also quite obvious that this instruction, in order to grow richer and to be enriching, should be centered on scientific research.

AUTONOMOUS CENTERS OF RESEARCH

Research in political science is done in part at the university and also, in large measure, in autonomous centers of research and documentation.

Centre de recherche et d'information sociopolitiques (CRISP). CRISP, although the most important research center, because of its method and objectives has remained on the fringe of the universities since its creation in 1958. However, CRISP, whether separate or not, will not be able to surpass the stage of information and documentation—which is essential for the growth of political science—if the universities do not consent to increased efforts and if the political sphere does not grant sufficient attention to the work of political science. Alas, it is a vicious circle.

Political science studies find an audience among Belgian politicians when they constitute for the latter, and when the latter are indeed willing to see in them, instruments capable of clarifying decision-making. These studies will become popular in academic circles as soon as academics become convinced that they can make themselves heard. At the moment, politicians ignore each other. No change seems to be taking shape, in spite of the audience and credibility of CRISP.

CRISP was founded by a team of men who wanted to study together the reality of the sociopolitical process in Belgium. In a society traditionally constructed on the system of *verzuiling* (segmented pluralism), this ambition implied direct access to diverse ideological and political families, as well as diverse linguistic communities. This necessity explains the concern of the founders to unite at the heart of CRISP personalities belonging to diverse tendencies, coming from the four universities and involved in complementary sectors by their research or their action.

Constituted as a cooperative society, financed—modestly, moreover—by the researchers themselves, CRISP at first applied itself to the morphology of groups: social, political, and economic, with particular attention to their methods of intervention and pressure on political decisions.

These studies appeared in a mimeographed *Courrier Hebdomadaire* (more than 800 in twenty years) furnished to fellow workers at cost and to subscribers at a price allowing for the expansion of the center's work. These weekly newsletters were complemented several years ago by the publication of syntheses—the *Dossiers pédagogiques*—intended to give a clear idea of the institutions, political system, and decision-making mechanism of Belgium.

CRISP published a basic work on financial groups: *Morphologie des groupes financiers* (second edition, January 1967) and since then has compiled a *Répertoire permanent* for following movements within groups, business agreements, mergers, and so on, and for delineating very exactly the Belgian domain of foreign industrial groups.

Later, CRISP organized a research team, combining theoreticians and activists, on the theme of "political decision-making in Belgium." A symposium with this title was published in Paris in the *Cahiers de la Fondation nationale des sciences politiques*, under the editorship of J. Meynaud, J. Ladriére, and F. Perin. The work includes a number of case studies (the school pact; the coal-mining crisis; the crisis over Belgian unity; the "single" law) but, especially, it presents an important synthesis on the foundations of Belgian political life.

Beyond the study of decisions and of collective actions, CRISP is especially attentive to the outcome of decisions, to the phenomenon of change in political life, and to the question of the threshold of politicization crossed by certain new problems in a developed society (technology; regional employment; water supplies; organization of health-care professions). Ideas about images and roles have attracted attention also and CRISP published an important work by F. Debuyst on *La fonction parlementaire en Belgique,* whose subtitle "Access mechanism and images," illuminates the contents.

CRISP formed a Congolese or Zairean section also which, since 1959, has studied Congolese ethnic-political groups, public figures, and the flow of events there. Each year, thanks to patient collection and very intense teamwork, it publishes a book of documents on Congolese politics, with special attention to their indigenous character. A special series, *Les Etudes du CRISP,* has published works on the secession of Kantanga (by J. Gerard-Libois) and the *muletiste* rebellion (by B. Verhaegen). In close cooperation with the *Institut national d'études politiques* (INEP) at Kinshasa, CRISP has copublished the journal *Etudes Congolaises* since 1961 and, in close liaison with the Congolese universities, it has taken the initiative in scientific publication on political or parapolitical themes. At the present time, collaboration is developing between it and the Congolese *Office national de la recherche et du développement.*

Most CRISP works are published anonymously. According to the directors of the center, that factor helps explain the success of the enterprise. The collection of documents and information, the research, and even the drafting assume a collective character which must appear rather confining to certain researchers or academics of individualist training. At CRISP, a human climate formed by reciprocal confidence, friendship, and a certain sense of humor seems to compensate for whatever may be harsh in the rule of collective work.

L'Institut belge de science politique. By statute, the *Institut belge de science politique* is the representative agent of Belgian political scientists. It was created in 1951 at the instigation of Professor Jean Meynaud, general secretary of the International Political Science Association, which was very young at the time. Canon Leclercq was its first president and M. P. Herremans its first general secretary.

Its founders considered it primarily a meeting place for men of different political and philosophical perspectives. They intended that it encourage free discussion of political ideas and problems with a view toward promoting political science studies.

Limited in its financial means, the *Institut* conserved its character of a learned society until 1964. It organized conferences and colloquiums which largely contributed to building its reputation. Some of its publications, moreover, are unchallenged works of political science which many political scientists have used; not theoretical studies, but rather presentations of certain concrete problems examined by specialists and by practitioners.[5]

Nevertheless, one of these works can be considered an important step in the evolution of political science in Belgium. The work of W. J. Ganshof van der Meersch, *Pouvoir de fait et règle de droit dans le fonctionnement des institutions politiques* has, in effect, *liberated* political science from excessive juridical formalism. The author called attention to the function of diverse groups in a constitutional regime undergoing transformation: political parties, professional organizations, trade-union organizations, and so forth.

This confrontation of ideas and opinions has undoubtedly enlarged the field of investigation. Since 1959 it has been continued in the journal *Res Publica* in which more than 400 studies have been published so far, especially on Belgian political questions: elections, political parties, government, Parliament, the linguistic question, and the equilibrium between the communities.

The program of the *Institut* is not, properly speaking, a program of pure research: but it is certainly fundamental and includes four broad orientations:

1. Research, inventory, and analysis of the archives of political parties, of politicians and of that which concerns them. From 1964 to 1967, forty-three microfilms were made, some of which contain information of great interest, especially concerning the finances of several large federations of the *Parti ouvrier* and *Parti socialiste belge*.

2. Regular publication since 1967 of an *Année politique* reporting decisions and consultations of the government, of parties, and of groups, studied at different levels and through the matters that dominated political activity. Above all, it is a question of an instrument for work, of a critical chronology of events, based as much as possible on authentic documents (reports, statements, interviews, proposals) and, failing that, on press analyses.

3. Continuing study of legislative elections, perpetuating thereby the analyses of 1958, 1961, and 1965, which carried forward those of CRISP.

4. Establishment of a "theoretical" library and a documentation service.

Since January 1979, the *Institut* has been divided into two autonomous institutes, according to the two dominant languages: the *Institut de science politique* (for the French language) and the *Vlaamse Politologisch Instituut* (for Flemish). This division indicates that political science is dependent on the dominant political movements, that it follows the trend of political power more than it influences it.

But, during the past twenty years in Belgium, political science should have had more working tools at its disposal: chronologies, specialized bibliographies, general bibliographies, political yearbooks, documents, weekly newsletters; collectively prepared for common ends.

Le Centre interuniversitaire de droit public. Since its creation in 1962, this center, under the authority of its founder and first president, Professor W. J. Ganshof van der Meersch, has published several works that concern political science, works that were conceived from a legal viewpoint, of course, but that cannot be ignored since they deal with political institutions. That is the case with the book by Jacques Velu, *La dissolution du Parlement*,[6] and the one by Herman De Croo and Philippe Seigneur, *Parlement et Gouvernement*,[7] and of Herman Van Impe, *Le role de la majorité parlementaire dans la vie politique belge*.[8] Works on federalism, on hearings and on regionalism can be added to this list.

Le Centre interuniversitaire d'histoire contemporaine. The interuniversity center has given great service to historians and also to political scientists. Because of space limitations the center's list of works cannot be enumerated.

Among the fifty-some publications that have appeared, the works most useful to political scientists are—by various authors: nine reports on the sources of contemporary Belgian history, 1957; by H. Haag: the personal archives of former Belgian ministers, 1963; by J. Dhondt and S. Vervaeck: bibliographic tools for the contemporary history of Belgium, 1960; by J. Willequet: documents useful for the history of the Belgian press, 1887–1914; by C. Levas: union of Catholics and liberals from 1838 to 1847, and a study of executive and legislative powers, 1960.

Interdisciplinary relations

Belgian political science is neither closed nor centralized and in truth there are almost no Belgian political scientists in the narrow sense of the term. There are historians, jurists, sociologists, economists, philosophers, and mathematicians. These specialists, by personal preference or as required by the reform of university instruction, became interested in political science and brought to it their experience and their methods.

Belgium is a pluralistic society, divided into several linguistic, political, philosophic, and religious groups at the heart of which instruction and *a fortiori* research are diversified according to men, circumstances, and structures. As a result, Belgian political science seems like a juxtaposition—indeed, like the superimposition of heterogeneous works that concern it in varying degrees. This abundance presents advantages and disadvantages.

Political science is neither a crossroads science nor a synthetic science and even less a residual science; it is a new science that in order to evolve needs permanent contact with the other scientific disciplines and, moreover, it is in their interest not to neglect it. On this point, Belgium is not in danger. On the contrary, its political and university structures make cooperative work necessary and require that political scientists have a varied education or a basic education in the traditional and legal subjects of university instruction.

At present, however, questions exist about whether the specific education of political scientists provides adequate access for careers, in the specialty itself. This situation keeps Belgian political science in a state of dependence relative to sociology, contemporary history, and constitutional law. Opinion and mass-media studies are dependent on sociologists (such as the competent and active team of Professor Thoveron that does systematic content analyses of the written, spoken, and filmed press during elections and INUSOP which conducts opinion surveys under the direction of Nicole Delruelle). The most important works on electoral sociology are the work of two commercial engineers and a geographer (Evalenko, Fraeys, and De Smet), who are occasional sociologists. It was as a political scientist that sociologist H. Janne posed the political problems that faced Belgium shortly after World War II in his *L'anti-Alcibiade ou la révolution des faits* of 1946.

Historians, whose courses remain dominant in political science studies, have tackled all the topics of interest: on electoral sociology there is R. Demoulin's *"Recherches de sociologie electorale en regime censitaire"* and on domestic politics J. Bariter's volume in the series *l'Histoire de Belgique*. On the Congolese question there are the numerous works of Professor J. Stengers. Parliament, institutions, and political life are dealt with in T. Luykx's *Politieke Geschiedenis van België*, and the structure of the Catholic party is the subject for the works of Aloïs Simon.

Jurists rank with historians as the most numerous authors of works close to political science. They teach constitutional law, administrative law, and, sometimes, the general theory of the state. In an annotated bibliography and, *a fortiori*, in an exhaustive bibliography of political science the following titles should be mentioned: the works already cited of W. J. Ganshof van der Meersch; A. Mast's *Overzicht van het belgisch grondwettelijk recht*; A. Molitor's *Les Sciences sociales dans l'Enseignement supérieur: Administration publique*; J. De Meyer's *Crisis der Europesche Staatsphilosophie* and *Elections dans les pays des communautés européennes et dans le Royaume-Uni*; Ch. Goossens's "Le bicaméralisme" in the *Revue internationale des Sciences administratives*; P. Wigny's "Les partis en droit public belge" in *Revue de Droit international et de Droit comparé* and his *Propos constitutionnels*; J. Dabin's *L'Etat ou la Politique, Essai de définition*; and H. Buch's *Les libertés individuelles dans la jurisprudence du Conseil d'Etat de Belgique*.

Other jurists who now specialize in social, economic, and fiscal law dealt with political science earlier in their careers—usually at the beginning (for example, L. E. Troclet who published in 1931, *Les Partis politiques en Belgique*). M. Grégoire, an ex-president of the *Institut belge de Science politique*—a lawyer at the Court of Appeals in Brussels—has written, in the past twenty years, some one hundred fundamental articles on Belgian political life. Political scientists frequently make allusion, in effect, to one or more of his articles when they examine aspects of Belgian political life (for example, V. Lorwin who wrote a chapter on Belgium in the book by R. Dahl, *Political Opposition in Western Democracies*. But with a few exceptions—such as J. Ladrière—Belgian psychologists, philosophers, and statisticians have little interest in political questions; social psychology, behavioral studies, political philosophy, and quantitative data are their domains.

Is political science in Belgium poorly served, then?

In fact, no, because for twenty years, in the university faculties, the *Institut belge de science politique* (IBSP), a young generation of political scientists with the help of "amateurs" has gained recognition, little by little.

The best representatives of this young generation have already received a broad education. However, they have adopted the habit of concentrating their studies on political science in terms of a concern for method and theory. Among others they include J. Buchmann who is greatly interested in methods of research and in European unification; F. Perin, an institutionalist; M. Boeynaems who is attentive to the functioning of ministerial cabinets; W. Dewachter whose field of activity is concentrated on the scientific analysis of elections; and F. Debuyst to whom parliamentary office represents a means of upward social mobility and remains one of the elements of political power.

A 500-page book would not suffice to represent the works on political science in Belgium.[9] Perhaps an inventory should be made some day in order to show the importance of the contribution of academics who were trained in the traditional disciplines.

Journals and Periodicals

Belgian political science has no difficulty in making itself known. Indeed, it enjoys a privileged position, for more than one hundred journals and periodicals are accessible. Among the most specific are *le Courrier Hebdomadaire* of CRISP and *Res Publica,* the quarterly journal of IBSP from 1959 to 1978 and of VPI since 1979. These two periodicals cover an important part of the documentation in political science. An informed specialist cannot neglect, however, *Les Annales de la Faculté de droit de l'Université de Liège; les Cahiers bruxellois, les Cahiers économiques de Bruxelles, Politica, Chronique de politique étrangère, La Revue générale belge, la Revue de l'Institut de sociologie de l'Université Libre de Bruxelles, la Revue Nouvelle, Rechtskundige Weekblad, Socialisme, Cepess, De Maand,* and *Socialistis che Standpunten.*

Trade unions, political parties and their study centers, industry, associations, cultural groups, communes, provincial economic councils publish intermittently, and at times with a wide circulation, journals and other information bulletins with basic articles and documentation useful in some ways to political science.

Given the philosophic and political viewpoints of most of these journals, all of them must be perused, because very often, yielding to conformist political habits, Belgian political scientists choose to publish their articles in journals whose ideological or religious point of view corresponds to their own. Also, this assumes a thorough knowledge of the political and philosophic "labels," the "coordinates" of each author.

Research and Work

The study of Belgian society absorbs a large part of the discipline's resources, either at the level of structures and institutions or on the more pragmatic plane of specific political questions.

Monographs proliferate on this subject; we shall say more: they endanger the spirit of synthesis. This is a rather striking tendency of political science in Belgium. Groups and men have become more specialized; and bridges must be built or monopolies will be established. At the present time, political theory is a rather neglected sector, except for the work carried out by S. Bernard in the domain of conflicts, consensus, and the typology of parties.

The study of political structures and institutions—in other words, the analysis of the political regime—is done in two categories. It is carried out by research organisms like the *Centre de droit public* that examines the topic from the institutional angle (such as the functioning of Parliament, the relationships between the powers, the constitutional control of powers) and by the *Centre de recherche et d'information sociopolitiques* which studies interest groups and political life.

For its part, the *Institut belge de science politique* has conducted research that is essentially documentary and is concerned with the archives of political parties, the preparation of a political yearbook, and the analysis of legislative elections.

A thorough study of political philosophy or the history of political ideas has been published in Ivo Rens's *L'introduction au socialisme rationnel de Colins.*[10] *L'Institut universitaire de sondage d'opinion publique* organizes and finances public opinion surveys of a sociopolitical nature. The two Catholic universities of Louvain have concentrated their efforts on European unification, aid to developing countries, the civil service, and electoral sociology.

The most numerous works are, nevertheless, produced by "independents" who have no other preoccupations and no other material means than to approach questions proper to Belgium; to the Congo (a former Belgian colony) and its accession to independence; to the language question and the problems of the ethnic communities (of which one of the most well-known specialists is M. P. Herremans); and to constitutional reform and the reform of public administration.

Conclusions

If we should issue a diagnosis of the state of political science in Belgium after more than twenty years of development, our disarray would be great and, depending on our mood, our opinion could be either most pessimistic or reassuringly optimistic.

Pessimistic, if based on the place that political science (in the broad sense) occupies in the faculties, and by the very limited financial resources that are invested in instruction and research.

Pessimistic, also, to the extent that the dispersion of work leads researchers to wonder about the interest and efficacy of political science. The amount of sponsored research reserved for the "political sciences" sector, which includes the administrative, commercial, diplomatic, economic, financial, political, and social sciences, is about 3 percent of the total amount for all the scientific disciplines.

And yet, Belgian political science in Belgium owes a lot to the imaginative effort bestowed on it by those who, numerous and passionate, dedicate their leisure to it and, sometimes, a part of their working time in the faculties, in the state administration, in public enterprises, in international institutions, and in parties and trade unions.

This situation of compulsory discretion attracts to political science dedicated persons for whom this science is second nature and who bring to it the richness of their experience and their knowledge.

Notes

1. Cf. his article "De la science politique considérée comme mystification," *Revue de l'Enseignement supérieur, la science politique*, no. 4 (1965): 13-22.
2. Roger DeSmet, René Evalenko, and William Fraeys, *Institut de sociologie Solvay*, 2 vols. (Brussels: Université Libre de Bruxelles, 1958).
3. Roger DeSmet and René Evalenko, *Institut de sociologie Solvay* (Brussels: Université Libre de Bruxelles, 1956).
4. This reform, adopted ten years ago, had an essential objective to adapt instruction to the new scientific requirements, taking into account the development of work undertaken in the administrative sciences on the one hand and the considerable progress of the international institutions and relations on the other hand. This reform should be favorable to political science in the long run.
5. *Aspects du regime parlementaire belge*. IBSP, 1st ser., no. 1, 1956; *Aspects de la société belge*, IBSP, 1st ser., no. 5, 1958; *Grands problèmes de la science politique contemporaine*, IBSP, 1st ser., no. 6, 1958; W. J. Ganshof van der Meersch, *Pouvoir de fait et règle de droit dans le fonctionnement des institutions politiques*, IBSP, 2d ser., no. 1, 1957; R. Urbain, *La Fonction et les services du Premier ministre en Belgique*, IBSP, 2d. ser., no. 2, 1958; F. Perin, *La démocratie enrayée, Essai sur le régime parlementaire belge de 1918 à 1958*, IBSP, n. s., no. 2, 1960.
6. (Brussels: Bruylant, 1966).
7. (Brussels: Bruylant, 1965).
8. (Brussels: Bruylant, 1966).
9. The *Institut belge de science politique* possesses a card index containing more than 6000 references to books and articles on political history, institutions, political parties, groups, elections, biographies and bibliographies, etc.
10. (Brussels: *Institut belge de science politique*, 1968).

Bibliography*

The periodicals in this list are standard media for articles and other materials of interest to political science.

(Les) Annales de la Faculté de droit de l'université de Liège.
Année politique (annual, since 1967).
(Les) Cahiers bruxellois.
(Les) Cahiers économiques de Bruxelles.
Cepess.
Chronique de politique étrangère.
Courier hebdomadaire (weekly mimeographed newsletter).
Dossiers pedagogiques (occasional papers).
(Les) Etudes du CRISP (monograph series).
Grands problèmes de la science politique contemporaine, IBSP, 1st series, no. 6, 1958.
De Maand.
De Meyer, J., *Crisis der Europesche Staatsphilosophie*, 1949.
Molitor, A., *Les Sciences sociales dans l'Enseignement: Administration publique*, 1958.
Politica.
Rechtskundige Weekblad.
Res publica (quarterly journal, since 1959).
(La) Revue de l'Institut de sociologie de l'université Libre de Bruxelles.
(La) Revue générale belge.
(La) Revue Nouvelle.
Socialisme.
Socialistesche Standpunten.

*Compiled by the editor.

BRAZIL

THEMÍSTOCLES BRANDÃO CAVALCANTI*

The development of teaching and research of political science in Brazil is rather recent. Only after the creation of graduate programs in 1965 was the first master's degree program in political science established by the Federal University of Minas Gerais. Only then did political science begin to be studied widely and independently through specific courses. Prior to the existence of master's degree programs, political science was included in undergraduate programs in schools of social sciences and in schools of juridical and social sciences. However, the *Foundation Escola de Sociologia e Política de São Paulo* (School of Sociology and Politics of São Paulo) had been offering graduate courses since 1941. Another relevant fact in the training of Brazilian political scientists has been taking place since the 1960s with the intensification of exchange programs with several European countries and with the USA. Since 1966 several institutions have sent specialized personnel abroad to work for Ph.D. degrees. Such programs have benefited the development of teaching and research in the field of political science.

Graduate programs in social and political sciences in Brazil "concern themselves with offering a Brazilian view of the social world, with locating specifically Brazilian social processes, and with preparing professionals in the fields of teaching and research who are sensitive to the problem of those values which give significance to the life of social and regional groups."[1] Such concerns can be identified in the graduate and undergraduate courses in political science which we shall list later.

Institutional Activities

A survey of several institutions was conducted for this study.[2] The survey was designed to identify the types of programs, undergraduate and graduate, that are being offered, participation in conferences, seminars, and round table discussions, national and international, the existence of journals for the dissemination of information relative to political science, and the use of any type of external funding to support teaching and research programs. The following list gives a general description of each institution:

Universidade Federal de Minas Gerais (Federal University of Minas Gerais). Its master's program began in 1976, and it has thesis projects and general research in the field of political science. The dissemination of information is done through the publication *Cadernos do Departamento de Ciência Política* (*Political Science Department Notes*). It participates in conferences and receives government funds.

Instituto Universitário de Pesquisas do Rio de Janeiro (IUPERJ) (University Institute of Research of Rio de Janeiro). It began its master's program in political science in 1969. It has thesis projects and general research. Its publication is *Revista Dados* (*Dados Review*). It participates in conferences and receives official funds.

Universidade Federal do Rio de Janeiro (Federal University of Rio de Janeiro). It has had an undergraduate program since 1939. Its publication is *Revista de Ciências Sociais* (*Social Science Review*). It has research, including thesis projects, in political science.

Pontifícia Universidade Católica de São Paulo (Pontifical Catholic University of São Paulo).** Its master's program began in 1973.

Universidade Estadual de Campinas (State University of Campinas). Its master's program began in 1974. It has research and thesis projects in political science. Its publication is *Revista do Instituto de Filosofia e Ciências Humanas* (*Review of the Institute of Philosophy and Human Science*).

---

*The author was assisted by Lídice Aparecida Pontes Maduro, researcher. The translation from Portuguese was made by Victor J. Rojas.
**The information on the master's program was obtained from CAPES (Coordenação do Aperfeiçoamento de Pessoal de nível Superior [Coordination for the Improvement of Higher Education Personnel].

Universidade de São Paulo (University of São Paulo). It has had a master's program since 1971 and a Ph.D. program since 1974. It does research, including thesis projects, in the field of political science. It receives official funds.

Universidade Federal do Rio Grande do Sul (Federal University of Rio Grande do Sul). Its master's program began in 1973. It has thesis projects and research. Its publication is *Revista do Instituto de Filosofia e Ciências Humanas* (*Review of Institute of Philosophy and Human Science*). It participates in conferences and receives official funds.

Universidade Católica do Rio de Janeiro (Catholic University of Rio de Janeiro). Its undergraduate courses began in 1957.

Universidade Federal Fluminense (Fluminense Federal University). Its undergraduate courses began in 1965. It has research and thesis projects, participates in conferences, and receives official funds.

Fundação Universidade de Brasília (University Foundation of Brazilia). Its master's program began in 1976. It participates in conferences. Its political science publication is entitled *Documentação e Atualidade Política* (*Documentation and Current Politics*). It has research and thesis projects.

Centro Brasileiro de Análise e Planejamento (CEBRAP) (Brazilian Center for Analysis and Planning). It has research and thesis projects. It participates in conferences, receives official funds, and publishes *Cadernos CEBRAP* (*CEBRAP Notes*), *Estudos CEBRAP* (*CEBRAP Studies*), and books.

Instituto de Direito Público e Ciência Política (INDIPO) (Institute of Public Law and Political Science). It offers graduate courses, has research, participates in conferences, and publishes *Revista de Ciencia Política* (*Political Science Review*).

According to the above information, Brazil has one doctoral program—at the University of São Paulo—and seven master's programs in political science—one in Rio de Janeiro (IUPERJ), one in Brazilia, three in São Paulo (UNICAMP, the University of São Paulo, and the Pontifical University of São Paulo), one in Rio Grande do Sul, and one in Minas Gerais. All the programs are carried out in institutions of higher learning in their respective states.

Regarding the two other institutions mentioned above, we have O Instituto De Direito Público e Ciência Política (INDIPO) (The Institute of Public Law and Political Science), of the Getúlio Vargas Foundation, whose objectives are to carry out studies and research in the field of public law and political science and to maintain scientific exchange with national and international institutions. Its activities include the organization of courses, lectures, and round-table discussions, as well as research and the publication of papers. Since 1960 INDIPO has offered a graduate program on methods and techniques for research in the social sciences which aims at training researchers in the field of the social and political sciences. The objective of the program is to give training in the preparation of research projects, including theoretical principles and systematization of all the phases of a given project. INDIPO also offers a program which deals with law and international politics, legislation, and foreign trade. Originated in 1973 at the graduate level, its objective is to offer scientific knowledge to people who are interested in international relations and foreign trade. In 1978 the program "Master's in International Economic Law" covered the following areas: juridical and political foundations of international economics; judicial systems of world economics; judicial systems of international trade.

Under INDIPO, there is also the *Centro de Pesquisa e Documentação de História Contemporanea do Brasil* (Center for Research and Documentation on Contemporary Brazilian History) which has been in operation since 1973. Its activities include five sections of research on contemporary Brazilian history, from the revolution in the 1930s to the current revolutionary movement. Those sections are:

Documentation. It deals with private archives of public figures and other personalities who worked in the political scene of the country.

Research. It develops projects relative to the post 1930s Brazilian model.

Oral history. It works with testimonies by politicians and public figures about events in Brazilian political life in the last fifty years.

The "Brasiliana" section (the section on collections of literary works on Brazil). It aims at the recovery of works devoted to the Brazilian intellectual production, edited between 1930 and 1945.

A dictionary of Brazilian historical biographies. It includes biographical information, by theme, on Brazilian political history from 1930 to the present.

Also INDIPO has a long tradition of research on elections, including several studies on election periods and, in general, on the legislatures.

The *Centro Brasileiro de Análise e Planejamento* (CEBRAP) (Center for Analysis and Planification) was founded in 1969 by a group of professors and researchers from the University of São Paulo. It is a nonprofit private organization devoted to study and research in the field of human sciences, specifically, to the study of Brazilian problems. CEBRAP does not offer a course of studies, but, in addition to research, gives assistance to businesses and government agencies. Its research includes: analysis of demographic problems; employment problems, urban problems of cultural assimilation and economic development; popular classes and urban social movements;

regional sociology; state, political parties, and electoral behavior.

In addition to the institutions mentioned above, we have the *Centro de Memória Social Brasileira* (Center for Brazilian Social Memoirs).[3] It was created by the *Conjunto Universitário Cândido Mendes* (Cândido Mendes University Group). It possesses information dating from 1930. In addition to archives on presidents of the republic, state ministers, governors, and politicians, it has documentation about recent history, as well as photograph archives. All documentation at the center is on microfilm.

Other sources of information are the data banks of the University Institute of Research of Rio de Janeiro and of the Federal University of Minas Gerais. The data bank of the University Institute of Research of Rio de Janeiro contains thirty-three survey studies and other data relative to ten Latin American countries.[4] Most of the data come from studies on Latin America done by North Americans. Five of those studies deal with Brazil. The Department of Political Science of the Federal University of Minas Gerais maintains a data bank for Brazilian states and municipalities.[5] The data cover individuals, municipalities, and states. The research deals mainly with Brazilian history from 1940 to 1969, but some data cover the period from 1872 to 1960. The work done here is also included in the data bank of the IUPERJ.

The Brazilian Association of Social Sciences[6] created a commission and a group for documentation in the social sciences. Their main objective is to prepare an information system on social research for teaching and documentation, which is available to people interested in the field of the social sciences. The system includes information on completed research, research in progress, thesis research in Brazil and in other countries, books, articles, and other recent publications. The information is published in the *Bibliografia Brasileira de Ciencias Sociais* (*Brazilian Bibliography on Social Sciences*) which is sponsored by the *Conselho Nacional de Ciência e Tecnologia* (National Council on Science and Technology) through the *Instituto Brasileiro de Bibliografia e Documentação* (Brazilian Institute on Bibliography and Documentation). This type of publication has been available since 1954. The latest volumes, 16 and 17, are dated 1972.

The Teaching of Political Science

Political science is part of the undergraduate curriculum in juridical programs in schools of philosophy and social sciences. The curriculum includes principles of political science, principles of Brazilian political organization, classical and contemporary concepts of political theory, as well as international politics. Master's and Ph.D. programs are much wider in scope. They include, in addition to practical courses on research methodology and statistics, theoretical subjects, studies on specific areas—through the general subject of development theory—and specific courses on the Brazilian reality.

Although some experts say that there are very few courses which deal with specifically Brazilian problems, we see that, according to Bolívar Lemounier, the master's programs at the IUPERJ and at the Catholic University of São Paulo, among others, have been doing more and more work relative to Brazil.[7] Their work includes courses, theses, research, and bibliography in the field of political science.

From the institutions which we researched, we obtained the following data regarding courses which are being offered in undergraduate and graduate programs in political science:

COURSES	UNDER-GRADUATE	MASTER'S
1. Introduction to Political Science	X	X
2. Political Science I, II	X	
3. Brazilian Political Organization I, II	X	
4. Comparative Political Structures	X	
5. Political Behavior	X	X
6. Political Theory I, II (Classical and Contemporary)	X	X
7. International Politics I, II	X	X
8. Political Sociology	X	X
9. Political Development	X	
10. Brazilian Political Thought I, II		X
11. Models of Political Analysis		X
12. History of Political Theories—Modern Age		X
13. Brazil: Political Institutions	X	X
14. Logic and Social Research	X	X
15. The Society in Rio Grande do Sul*		

*University of Rio Grande do Sul.

#	Course	Col A	Col B
16.	Political Development and Modernization		X
17.	Comparative Politics I, II		X
18.	State and Society in Brazil		X
19.	Political Participation and Behavior in Brazil		X
20.	Regional Political Studies		X
21.	International Relations		X
22.	Politics and Administration		X
23.	Planning, Approving, and Implementing Policies		X
24.	Policy Analysis	X	X
25.	Comparative Politics in Latin America	X	X
26.	Brazilian Political Theory	X	
27.	State and Political Organization	X	
28.	Political Parties in Brazil	X	
29.	Power and Development in Latin America	X	X
30.	Contemporary Political Theories	X	
31.	Brazilian Politics I, II, III, IV	X	X
32.	Brazilian History	X	X
33.	Political Analysis: Theory and Methods	X	X
34.	State and Development in Brazil I, II		X
35.	State Theory		X
36.	Political Ideologies in Brazil		X
37.	Political Party Theory		X
38.	Social Sciences	X	
39.	The Foreign Policies of the Great Powers		X
40.	Brazilian Foreign Policy		X
41.	Sociological Analysis of the State		X
42.	History of Political Thought		X
43.	Political Elites: The Actor and the System		X
44.	Social Theory and Political Order		X
45.	Topics in Sociology of Science and Scientific Politics		X
46.	Epistemology: Ideology and Political Action		X
47.	Cultural and Political Ideology		X
48.	Political Parties and Interest Groups		X
49.	Stratification and Social Mobility		X
50.	Theory of Organizations		X
51.	International Organizations		X
52.	Types of Modern States I, II, III		X
53.	Sociopolitical Participation in the Urban Context		X
54.	Hegemony Concepts in Political Theory		X
55.	Government Systems and Party Regimes		X
56.	Political Theory of Social Classes (Power Structures and Social Classes)		X
57.	Political Power and Social Classes		X
58.	Political and Social Problems in the Development of Latin America		X
59.	Methods of Analysis of Political Institutions (Analysis of Modern Institutions)		X
60.	Power and Politics in Black Africa		X
61.	The Cultural Context of Political Behavior		X
62.	Property and Power in Precapitalist Societies		X

COURSES	UNDER-GRADUATE	MASTER'S
63. Foundations of the Brazilian State (Theoretical Perspectives)		X
64. Sociological Theory		X
65. Statistics and Research Techniques		X
66. Studies on Brazilian Problems		X
67. Political Economics		X
68. Methodology I, II	X	X
69. Economic Theory		X
70. Latin-American Politics I, II		X
71. Legislatures: A Comparative Study		X
72. Integration and Dependence in Latin America		X
73. Introduction to International Relations		X
74. Formal Organizations		X
75. Policies and Urban Problems		X
76. Analysis of Public Policies in Brazil		X
77. Methodology of Historical Research		X
78. Brazilian Political History		X
79. Latin American History		X
80. Contemporary History		X
81. Brazilian Economic History		X
82. General Economic History		X
83. Classical Sociological Theory		X
84. Social Theory		X
85. Seminar: Thesis Orientation		X
86. Logic and Social Sciences		X
87. Social Change		X
88. Theory Formulation		X
89. Political and Social Structures in Brazil		X
90. Latin American Social Structures		X
91. Cause Analysis Strategy		X
92. Epistemological Roots of Some Classical Authors		X
93. Stratification and Occupational Structures in the City and State of Rio de Janeiro in the Second Half of the Nineteenth Century		X
94. Occupational Structures in Brazil		X
95. Evaluation of Policy Analysis		X
96. Urban Systems and Labor Market		X
97. Statistics I, II	X	X
98. Ideology and Politics		X
99. Urbanization and Cultural Assimilation		X
100. Racial Relations		X
101. Social Theory Applied to Brazilian Politics		X
102. Social Indicators of Development		X
103. Research Techniques I, II	X	X
104. Systematical Literature		X
105. Research Seminars		X
106. Society and Rural Cultures		X
107. Social Change Theory: Planning and Development		X
108. Comparative Analysis of Political Systems		X
109. Paradigms of Sociological Analysis		X
110. Latin-American Political Thought		X
111. Latin-American Political Systems		X

112.	Conflict Theory and International Asymmetry	X
113.	Classical Political Theory	X
114.	Epistemology: The Construction of an Object in Human Sciences	X
115.	The Organization of the State in Latin America	X
116.	Linguistic Analysis of the Political Speech	X
117.	The Transition from Colony to State in Brazil	X
118.	Politics and Development in Brazil	X
119.	Interdisciplinary Seminars	X
120.	State and Industrialization in Brazil	X
121.	The International System	X
122.	Property and Power in Precapitalist Societies	X
123.	Economic Politics	X
124.	Logic for Science	X
125.	Data Analysis	X
126.	Modern Political Theory	X
127.	Policy Analysis I (Decision Theory and Communication Theory)	X
128.	Policy Analysis II (Urban Politics)	X
129.	Brazilian Economics	X

Research in Political Science

Although research in political science at the universities can be characterized as incipient and sporadic, some topics attract special attention, especially among the institutions that we have studied. Some of the research can be considered traditional.[8] It deals with topics such as Brazilian political institutions, local power and patronage, political representation, electoral behavior, legislative behavior, public policies, social participation and political participation, union organization and political structure, comparative international politics, state and society, bureaucratization and political development. The information available verifies the fact that the aforementioned topics attract the attention of Brazilian scholars in political science. We were able to identify a total of 139 research projects (see the list below). The number of projects under each topic indicates the work done in recent years, but not the totality of the work done in the respective area. Some institutions mentioned the topics of interest but not the number of projects. From the data available, however, we can get a general view of the topics studied most commonly in recent times in Brazil. Many studies deal with the legislative branch of government, including the social composition of popular representation, the representatives' position regarding the functions of the legislature, as well as the lack of prestige in the position of legislators. Another source of interest is the organization of the State and the political parties. Special attention is given to political parties prior to the 1964 movement and to the perspectives for political liberalization and its influence on political representation.

Studies about regional problems are also frequent (9.35%). Most of the studies deal with the area in the south-central region. Almost no research has been done on the north-northeastern axis.

Studies dealing with the Brazilian social organization regarding socioeconomic determinants, formation of bureaucracies, employment modalities, and the relationships between the agrarian sector and other sectors, the position of private enterprise regarding the economic policies of the government, and national industry are among the many research projects which the following list attempts to classify:

RESEARCH TOPICS IN POLITICAL SCIENCE

1. Studies about the legislature: social composition, functions and position of the legislature in the contemporary world	28	(20.14%)
2. Organization of the state and political parties	17	(12.23%)
3. Regional political history—sociology of the regions	13	(9.35%)
4. Public policies	12	(8.63%)
5. The state and industrialization—private enterprise	11	(7.92%)
6. Brazilian political thought—study of ideology movements	10	(7.19%)

7. The teaching of the social and political sciences in Brazil and the participation of university students in the development of Brazil	7	(5.04%)
8. Brazilian social memoirs	7	(5.04%)
9. Latin-American integration: political and historical considerations regarding its basis, process, and meaning	6	(4.31%)
10. Elites and political institutions	6	(4.31%)
11. Demographic problems: analysis of population problems	5	(3.59%)
12. Class structures and urban social movements	5	(3.59%)
13. International politics	5	(3.59%)
14. The labor movement in Brazil	3	(2.15%)
15. Political participation of women in Brazil	3	(2.15%)
16. Armed forces and the state in Brazil, 1945–1969	1	(0.71%)
Total	139	(100%)

Theses in Political Science

The information regarding theses does not cover the entire period during which the master's and Ph.D. programs have been offered. Nevertheless, we were able to identify a total of 83 theses dealing with several topics in political science. Since it would be impossible to describe each thesis here in detail, we have grouped them by topic and have given the numerical distribution by topic. We can see that most of the studies (21.68%) deal with ideology and political movements, with special emphasis on nationalistic currents and on movements of party ideologies. The situation in metropolitan regions and the policies adopted by the responsible agencies also attract much interest for the preparation of theses. Some economic aspects related to political activities and to national development were the topic of analysis of 12.04% of the theses. Other theses deal with problems relative to the legislature, political parties, analysis of popular movements, political participation, and political behavior. The following list includes the main topics studied by graduate students working toward master's and Ph.D degrees in political science.

THESES IN THE FIELD OF POLITICAL SCIENCE

1. Ideology and political movements	18	(21.68%)
2. Public policies and conditions in metropolitan areas	11	(13.25%)
3. Economic development and power structures	10	(12.04%)
4. The legislative branch of government in Brazil	7	(8.43%)
5. Brazilian sociopolitical thought	7	(8.43%)
6. Political parties in Brazil	6	(7.23%)
7. Participation and political behavior	6	(7.23%)
8. Class structures and political power	5	(6.02%)
9. Local power and national development	3	(3.61%)
10. Participation of the military in politics	3	(3.61%)
11. International politics	3	(3.61%)
12. Studies about the popular political movement *populismo*	2	(2.41%)
13. Problems related to labor unions in Brazil	2	(2.41%)
Total	83	(100%)

Publications in the Field of Political Science

Publishing in political science is done mainly through journals that are affiliated with those institutions which offer master's programs and sponsor research. Those publications may be exclusively devoted to political science, or they may cover several social sciences. The earliest known publication is *Ciência Política* (*Political Science*), published by the *Instituto Nacional de Ciência Política do Rio de Janeiro* (National Institute of Political Science of Rio de Janeiro) from 1943 to 1945.

The *Revista de Ciência Política* (*Political Science Review*) of the *Instituto de Direito Público e Ciência Política* (INDIPO) (Institute of Public Law and Political Science) is a quarterly publication which since 1958 has been giving wide coverage to topics related to political science and public law. It publishes articles by national and foreign authors, as well as research findings and proceedings from round-table discussions sponsored by the institute. INDIPO has also been publishing a great deal of bibliographic information since 1951.

Revista Dados (*Data Review*) is a publication of the *Instituto Universitário de Pesquisas do Rio de Janeiro* (IUPERJ) (University Institute of Research of Rio de Janeiro), affiliated with the *Conjunto Universitário Cândido Mendes* (Cândido Mendes University Group). *Revista Dados* began publication in 1966. It publishes studies by professors and research from IUPERJ. It also publishes work in the social sciences, especially political science, by national and foreign authors. It is published three times a year.

Revista Brasileira de Estudos Políticos (*Brazilian Review of Political Studies*) was founded in 1956 by the

Universidade Federal de Minas Gerais (Federal University of Minas Gerais). Published once a year, it aims at stimulating research on public law and political science. In 1958 it began publishing research findings and monographs in a collection entitled *Estudos Sociais e Políticos* (*Social and Political Studies*) which so far includes 34 publications. The same university began publishing in 1974 *Cadernos do Departamento de Ciência Política* (*Department of Political Science Notes*) devoted exclusively to political topics.

Other important publications are the ones from the *Centro Brasileiro de Análise e Planejamento* (CEBRAP) (Brazilian Center for Analysis and Planning), which include three series:

Série Cadernos CEBRAP (*CEBRAP Notes*) with 28 issues published between 1971 and 1977.

Série Estudos CEBRAP (*CEBRAP Studies*) with 21 volumes published between 1971 and 1977.

Série Livros CEBRAP (*CEBRAP Books*) with 12 volumes published between 1971 and 1977.

In addition to those series, several professors and researchers from CEBRAP have published in specialized national and foreign journals, as well as in newspapers and in books from several publishers. All their publications deal with Brazilian problems in the general field of social sciences.

There are other university publications such as:

Revista do Instituto de Filosofia e Ciências Humanas (*Institute of Philosophy and Human Sciences Review*), published by the *Universidade Federal do Rio Grande do Sul* (Federal University of Rio Grande do Sul) once a year and covering social sciences.

Cadernos do Instituto de Filosofia e Ciências Humanas (*Institute of Philosophy and Human Sciences Notes*), published by the *Universidade de Campinas* (Campinas University). So far, two issues have been published under the responsibility of the Department of Political Science.

Revista do Instituto de Ciências Sociais (*Institute of Social Sciences Review*), published by the *Universidade Federal do Rio de Janeiro* (Federal University of Rio de Janeiro). First published in 1962 its publication was interrupted in 1967, but was resumed in August 1977. It is sponsored by professors from the Department of Social Sciences.

Documentação e Atualidade Política (*Documentation and Current Politics*), published by the University of Brazilia through its Department of Political Science. It was first published in 1976. It is a quarterly with the main objective of disseminating current and classical materials in political science and international relations. The review is published in conjunction with the Federal Senate.

Among the publications in political science that are not affiliated with universities or research centers are the following:

Ciência e Cultura (*Science and Culture*), published by the *Sociedade Brasileira para o Progresso da Ciência* (SBPC) (Brazilian Society for Progress in Science). It was first published in 1949. It covers all scientific topics, including studies and conference proceedings relative to the social sciences and political science.

Revista Política (*Political Review*) was first published in 1976. It is a publication of the political party *Alianca Renovadora Nacional* (ARENA) (Alliance for National Renovation). It is published through the *Fundação Milton Campos para Pesquisas e Estudos Políticos* (Milton Campos Foundation for Research and Political Studies) whose main purpose is the sponsorship of the ARENA political party. The magazine is devoted to the publication of studies in political science.

Participation in Conferences, Seminars, and Round-table Discussions

Generally speaking, the teaching and research personnel at the institutions which concern themselves with programs in political science demonstrate a great deal of interest in national and international conferences, seminars, and round-table discussions on their fields of studies. The institutions which we studied have been participating in the conferences of the International Political Science Association since 1952 and in other meetings since 1971. The following is a list of conferences, seminars, and round-table discussions, in Brazil and in other countries, in which Brazilian political scientists have participated:

In Brazil:

Brazilian Seminar on Population, São Leopoldo, Universidade do Rio dos Sinos (1973)

Conference of the Brazilian Society for Progress in Science, Recife (1974), Minas Gerais (1975), Brazilia (1976), São Paulo (1977)

Seminars entitled "Electoral Concentration and Dispersion in Minas Gerais," Minas Gerais (1975)

"The Minas Gerais Political Summit in the Old Republic," Belo Horizonte (M.G.) (1977)

Seminar on Legislature and Development—International Political Science Association—Rio de Janeiro (1974)

Seminar on "The Teaching of Political Science in Latin America," Belo Horizonte (1977)

"Points of View and Perspectives in the Institutionalization of Social Sciences Graduate Programs in Brazil," Rio de Janeiro (1974 and 1977)

Colloquium on the Training of Sociologists, Brazilia (1977)

International Seminar on Social Sciences and History, Campinas, São Paulo (1975)

Round Table on Political Science, Rio de Janeiro (1969)

Rio de Janeiro Meeting under the Auspices of the *Instituto Universitário de Pesquisas do Rio de Janeiro* (University Institute of Research of Rio de Janeiro) and the Club of Rome (1977)

Meeting of the Political Studies Group of the CLACSO, Rio de Janeiro (1971)

Franco-Brazilian Colloquium on International Politics, Rio de Janeiro (1971)

Seminar on Social Indicators of National Development in Latin America, Rio de Janeiro (1972)

International Seminar on Public Policies, Rio de Janeiro (1975)

Seminar on Elections and Institutional Order, Minas Gerais (1975)

In foreign countries:

Latin American Studies Association, Houston, Texas (1976 and 1977)

American Political Science Association, Washington, D.C. (1968 and 1969)

Southern Political Science Association, Gatlinburg (1968), Tenn. (1971), Atlanta (1976)

"The Scientific Study of International Relations, Present and Future," Mexico (1976)

Conferences of the Latin American Council on Social Sciences (CLACSO), Maracaibo and Quito (1974-1975)

International Conference on Sociology, Toronto (1974)

Latin American Conference on Sociology. San José, Costa Rica (1974)

Conference of the Canadian Association for Latin American Studies, Quito (1974)

Conference on the Crisis of Development, Italy (1974)

Seminar on New Ways for the Autonomous Development of the Third World, Greece (1975)

Participation in the Congresses of the International Political Science Association since 1952

Financial Support

The institutions which have graduate (master's and Ph.D.) and research programs in the field of political science in Brazil may receive financial support from national and foreign sources through scholarships for graduate students and through grants for researchers. Grants may be complete or partial. Among the main national funding agencies are the *Coordenação de Aperfeiçoamento do Pessoal de Nível Superior* (CAPES) (Coordination for the Improvement of Higher Education Personnel) and the *Conselho Nacional de Ciência e Tecnologia* (CNPq) (National Council on Science and Technology). Both organizations belong to the federal government. Such support is important in view of the fact that government policies tend to give funding preference to the exact sciences. CAPES has favored programs in the social sciences and CNPq, although it gives preference to technological fields, has given important support to the social sciences through research grants, making it possible to have a large number of social scientists doing field work.

Other organizations associated with public ministries also provide funding through a program of allocations for the preparation of theses for the master's and Ph.D. degrees, as well as for research. The *Instituto de Pesquisas Econômicas e Aplicadas* (IPEA) (Institute of Economic and Applied Research), an agency of the Ministry of Planification, and several agencies of the Ministry of Education and Culture and of the Ministry of the Interior are among the government agencies which contribute funds for the teaching and research of political science in Brazil.

Several international agencies are also a very important funding source. The most significant are the Ford Foundation and UNESCO which offer a large program of financial support for graduate studies and research in the field of political science. The following is a list of public and private Brazilian and international funding agencies:

National agencies:

Coordinação de Aperfeiçoamento de Pessoal de Nível Superior (CAPES) (Coordination for the Improvement of Higher Education Personnel)

Associação Brasileira de Ciência Política (ABCP) (Brazilian Political Science Association)

Banco Nacional de Habitação (BNH) (National Housing Bank)

Comissão de Estudo de Alternativa para o Desenvolvimento Brasileiro (CEADE) (Commission for the Study of Development Alternatives for Brazil)

Centro Brasileiro de Assistência Gerencial à Pequena e Média Empresa (CEBRAE) (Brazilian Center for Agency Assistance to Small and Middle-sized Businesses)

Conselho Nacional de Desenvolvimento Científico e Tecnológico (CNPq) (National Council for Scientific and Technological Development)

Financiadora de Estudos e Projetos (FINEP) (Financier of Studies and Projects)

Fundação Getúlio Vargas (FGV) (Getúlio Vargas Foundation)

Instituto Brasileiro de Desenvolvimento de Relações Inter-

nacionais (IBRI) (Brazilian Institute for the Development of International Relations)

Fundação Catarinense do Trabalho (FUCAT) (The Santa Catarina Labor Foundation)

Empresa Brasileira de Turismo (EMBRATUR) (Brazilian Travel Bureau)

Fundação de Amparo à Pesquisa (FAPESP) (Foundation for Assistance to Research)

PICD

Sociedade Brasileira de Instrução (SBI) (Brazilian Society of Instruction)

Departamento de Assuntos Universitários (DAU) (Department of University Affairs)

Programa de Estudos Conjuntos sobre Integração Econômica Latinoamericana (PECIEL) (Joint Program of Studies on Latin American Economic Integration)

Ministério do Interior (MINTER) (Ministry of the Interior)

Superintendência do Desenvolvimento do Nordeste (SUDENE) (Superintendence for the Development of the Northeast)

Conselho Federal de Cultura—Órgão do Ministério de Educação e Cultura) (MEC) (Federal Council on Culture—an Agency of the Ministry of Education and Culture)

International agencies:

Canadian International Development Agency (CIDA)

Centre d'Étude de Politique Étrangère (Center for the Study of Foreign Policy)

Consejo Latinoamericano de Ciencias Sociales (CLACSO) (Latin American Council on Social Sciences)

The Club of Rome

The Ford Foundation

The MISEREOR Foundation, Germany

The VENEVOLENTIA Foundation, Italy

Inter-American Development Bank

IDRC (Canada)

SAREC (Sweden)

NOVIPE (Holland)

International Political Science Association (IPSA)

The University of Michigan

UNESCO

International Social Science Council (ISSC)

Professional Associations

The Brazilian Political Science Association was founded by a group of professors and scholars in political science. Its president was Professor Themístocles Brandão Cavalcanti. It was installed on 23 September 1966. The ABCP is affiliated with the International Political Science Association.

Recently an interdisciplinary association was created at the graduate level. It is the *Associação Nacional de Programas de Pós-Graduação em Ciências Sociais* (National Association of Social Science Graduate Programs). Its main purposes are the protection of excellence in teaching and the integration of interdisciplinary activities, including graduate programs in political science, sociology, anthropology, and public administration, as well as in urban planning and social psychology.

From this study we can ascertain the present status of the teaching and research of political science in Brazil. Although we cannot classify it as excellent, we can be very optimistic about its development in view of the constant improvement of the teaching and research programs and in view of the increasing number of bibliographic materials about Brazilian topics.

Notes

1. *Catálogo de Cursos de Pós-Graduaçao—Coordenação do Aperfeiçoamento de Pessoal de Nível Superior* (CAPES). *Ministério de Educação e Cultura Catalog of Graduate Courses*—Coordination for the Improvement of Higher Education Personnel. Ministry of Education and Culture.

2. The research was conducted by sending a questionnaire to the universities and institutes which concern themselves with the teaching and research of political science in Brazil. Of the total questionnaires sent out 68% were answered. In addition to the questionnaires, we used data given by CAPES.

3. Neuma Aguiar. *Tendências atuais nas Ciências Sociais no Brasil* (*Current Tendencies in Social Sciences in Brazil*), mimeographed. Rio de Janeiro: IUPERJ, 1977.

4. Ibid.

5. Ibid.

6. Ibid.

7. Bolívar Lamounier, "O Ensino pós-graduado de Ciência Política no Brasil" ("Graduate Teaching of Political Science in Brazil"), *Revista Dados*, no. 14 (1977).

8. *Coordenação do Aperfeiçoamento de Pessoal de Nível Superior* (CAPES) (Coordination for the Improvement of Higher Education Personnel). *Ministério de Educação e Cultura* (Ministry of Education and Culture).

Bibliography

Cardoso, Fernando Henrique. *O modelo político brasileiro e outros ensaios*. São Paulo: Difel, 1972.

———. *Politica e desenvolvimento em sociedades dependentes*. Rio de Janeiro: Zahar, 1971.

Carvalho, Orlando de. *Ensaios de sociologia eleitoral*. Belo Horizonte: UFMG, 1962.

Cavalcanti, Themístocles, and Dubning, Reisky. *Comportamento eleitoral no Brasil*. Rio de Janeiro: FGV, 1964.

Faoro, Raymundo. *Os donos do Poder*. Porto Alegre: Globo, 1958.

Fernandes, Florestan. *A revolução burguesa no Brasil: ensaio de interpretação*. Rio de Janeiro: Zahar, 1974.

———. *Sociedade de Classes e Subdesenvolvimento*. Rio de Janeiro: Zahar, 1968.

Furtado, Celso. *Análise do modelo brasileiro*. Rio de Janeiro: Civilização Brasileira, 1972.

———.*A pré-revolução brasileira*. Rio de Janeiro: Fundo de Cultura, 1962.

Guerreiro, Ramos Alberto. *A crise do Poder no Brasil*. Rio de Janeiro: Zahar, 1961.

Ianni, Otávio. *Estado e capitalismo: estrutura social e industrialização no Brasil*. Rio de Janeiro: Civilização Brasileira, 1965.

———.*O colapso do populismo no Brasil*. Rio de Janeiro: Civilização Brasileira, 1968.

Jaguaribe, Hélio. *Brasil: crise e alternativas*. Rio de Janeiro: Zahar, 1974.

———.*Desenvolvimento econômico e desenvolvimento político*. Rio de Janeiro: Fundo de Cultura, 1962.

Lafer, Celso. *Brasil e Argentina no sistema das relações internacionais*. São Paulo: Duas cidades, 1973, 1956-1961, Ithaca: Cornell University Press, 1970.

———.*The Planning Process and the Political System in Brazil: A Study of Kubitschek's Plan*.

Lamounier, Bolívar. *Ideology and Authoritarian Regimes: Theoretical Perspectives and a Study of the Brazilian Case*. Los Angeles: University of California, 1974.

Leal, Victor Nunes. *Coronelismo, enxada e voto*. Rio de Janeiro: Forense, 1949.

Martins, Luciano. *Politique et développement économique structure de pouvoir et Système de décisions au Brésil*. Paris: Université de Paris, 1973.

Mendes de Almeida, Cândido. *Nacionalismo e desenvolvimento*. Rio de Janeiro: Instituto Brasileiro de Estudos Afro-Asiáticos, 1963.

Mercadante, Paulo. *A consciência conservadora no Brasil*. Rio de Janeiro: Saga, 1965.

Prado, Caio, Jr. *A revolução brasileira*. São Paulo: Brasiliense, 1966.

Soares, Glaucio Ary Dillon. *Sociedade e politica no Brasil*. São Paulo: Difel, 1974.

Sodré, Nelson Werneck. *História da burguesia brasileira*. Rio de Janeiro: Civilização Brasileira, 1964.

———.*História Militar do Brasil*. Rio de Janeiro: Civilização Brasileira, 1965.

Vianna, Francisco J. Oliveira. *Instituições políticas brasileiras*. Rio de Janeiro: José Olympio, 1951.

Weffort, Francisco Corrêa. *Populismo, marginalizacion y dependencia*. Costa Rica: EDUCA, 1973.

10

CANADA*

MICHAEL STEIN and JOHN E. TRENT

Introduction

This chapter is intended to sketch in a very tentative and abbreviated way some of the themes we are developing for a collective project on the development of political science in Canada.[1] These themes are naturally very broad in scope, sweeping in their assumptions, highly interpretative and impressionistic, and controversial.[2]

The focus of our concern is the more unique or distinctive characteristics and contributions of political science in Canada in comparison to what has developed in other Western countries. Paradoxically, despite the short history of the country, Canada has had a comparatively long political science tradition reaching back almost a century.[3] Similarly, although the population of the country is relatively small, numbering only about 23 million, Canada has the third largest political science community in the world after the United States and India, estimated at about 700 full-time university instructors. Despite its maturity and size, the discipline and profession of political science in Canada have tended to be downgraded or dismissed as largely derivative of that of other countries, particularly the United States, but also Britain and France. It is maintained that the paradigms, approaches, and tools of analysis used in the discipline have been imported, and that the problems selected for study are frequently those already initiated or being debated elsewhere; that the personnel teaching in the field are heavily foreign-born and foreign-trained, with little or no sensitivity to the history and nuances of the country; and that the quality of research and scholarship of Canadian political scientists in different subfields of the discipline is inferior to that of many other communities of comparable size and age.[4] It is also contended that the discipline and profession have had only a marginal impact on Canadian society itself, and in particular on its government and politics, and that their influence on the international political science community has been almost nil.

There is some truth in many of these allegations. However, it is our thesis that the denigration of Canadian political science, particularly by Canadians themselves, has been overstated and is largely unjustified. It is insensitive to the many unique characteristics of the discipline in Canada and the distinctive contributions made by our scholars in a variety of problem areas and subdisciplines. There is also an unawareness of the important influence which our political scientists and the discipline have had on the political process itself at critical junctures in our history. These oversights stem from a tendency to overemphasize what political science in Canada shares with other political science communities rather than what sets it apart. They stress the more spectacular global theoretical contributions to political science knowledge at the expense of the more incremental collective contributions to particular problem areas which are of an applied theoretical nature. There is also an exaggerated tendency to treat the discipline and profession in Canada as if it were a cultural monolith rather than composed of at least two separate though interrelated linguistic-cultural political science communities, English and French, and possibly other ideologically or regionally distinct subcommunities, each making its own unique contribution to political science knowledge. These oversights, in our view, stem largely from a proclivity in both the scholarly community in general and in the body of literature on the sociology of social science to neglect the important role which the indigenous (local) environment and culture tend to play in shaping the development, nature, and

---

*This chapter was presented as a paper at the 1979 IPSA Congress with the title "Distinctive Characteristics and Contributions of Political Science in Canada: The Influence of the Indigenous (Local) Environment and Culture on Disciplinary Development."

impact of a particular discipline and profession in a given society.

There are a number of important and distinct approaches to the study of the development of the social sciences, including: (1) the philosophy of science approach which emphasizes the logic of inquiry and the development of method in the social sciences (including Hempel, Nagel, Popper, Kuhn, Lakatos, Musgrave, Toulmin, and Brodbeck);[5] (2) the sociology of knowledge approach which examines the social origins of scientific ideas (for example, Marx and Mannheim)[6] and the importance of social organizations, educational institutions, and professional associations in the evolution of disciplines (including Merton, Shils, Ben David, and Eisenstadt);[7] (3) the history of social science approach which chronicles the changes in the content of the discipline in response to developments in professional organizations and in the international social science community (for example, Abrams, Clark, Oberschall, Schad, Furner).[8]

We believe that all of these approaches have considerable merit, but that none is sufficiently comprehensive to permit one to analyze a particular discipline's development within a broad, multidimensional framework.[9] In particular, with the partial exception of the third approach (empirical history of social science), there is a neglect in all of the preceding literature of the societal socioeconomic and cultural setting, both domestic and international, in which the discipline is spawned. We have, therefore, formulated a rough model which we feel can encompass the diversity and breadth of these larger environmental and cultural concerns.

Our model is an input-output framework of the "black box" variety familiar to students of David Easton[10] and of communications theory. The discipline and profession are placed within its domestic and international setting as shown in figure 10.1.

In this schema, which is intended to reflect broad trends over time, the focal point is the unique and innovative characteristics of the discipline in a particular society. They are portrayed as a product of the interplay of forces emanating from the society's internal socioeconomic and cultural environment and influences drawn from the external environment and filtered through the international social science community. Indigenous socioeconomic environmental and cultural influences include demographic and geopolitical conditions, historical crises, value conflicts, economic and social transformations such as those which occurred in the war years and during the depression. External influences mediated by the international social science environment include changes in paradigms, approaches and methods of inquiry, the identification and concentration on new problem areas, the establishment of institutional structures for the collection, storage and diffusion of international social science knowledge.

This model is intended to serve as a loose ordering device of the factors which in our view are most important in explaining the distinctive characteristics and innovative contributions of a discipline in a particular country. The local environment and culture are clearly primary in this respect. We will be attempting to apply this model in a global explanation of the development of political science in Canada in conjunction with several of our colleagues. We will be using it as a heuristic device to generate the following questions intended to guide both our own research and that of our collaborators in the various subdisciplines of political science in Canada: (1) What is the current state of political science in Canada? In other words, what are the major characteristics defin-

Figure 10.1 Input-Output Model of the Development of a Discipline in a Particular Society

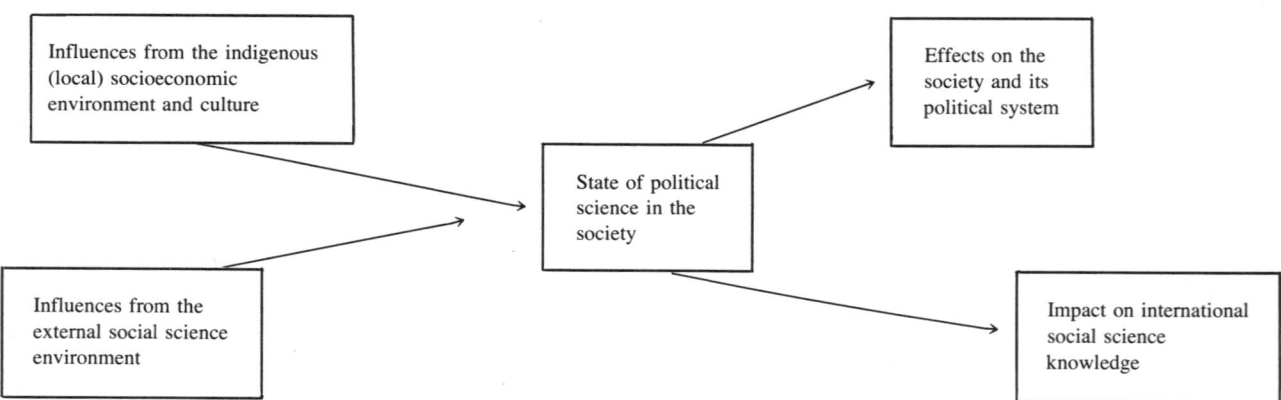

ing the discipline in Canada and distinguishing it from political science in other societies? (2) Why does political science in Canada have these characteristics? That is, what have been the major influences in the Canadian socioeconomic environment and culture which have shaped these distinctive characteristics, including Canada's population and demography, its geography, its cultural and linguistic makeup, its experiences of industrialization and urbanization, its historical crises. What have been the major influences from the international social science environment, particularly the United States and Western Europe? (3) What impact, if any, has political science in Canada had on Canadian society in general, and on Canadian politics in particular? Have the ideas of Canada's political scientists shaped the on-going political reality and influenced party debate and government policy-makers? Why or why not? Has Canada had any impact at all on the international social science community? Why or why not?[11]

The Current State of Political Science in Canada: Some Hypotheses

It is our thesis that the current state of political science in Canada may be roughly distinguished by the following characteristics: (1) it is eclectic in approach and tolerant of a variety of normative and ideological perspectives and disciplinary approaches; (2) it adopts a primarily synthetic, evolutionary, and cumulative rather than dialectical or discontinuous approach to knowledge; (3) it reflects greater innovativeness in case studies and theoretical applications than in pure theoretical contributions; (4) it fosters partial rather than holistic and sectoral rather than systemic studies.

A few examples should suffice to illustrate and provide some initial support for this description. First, with respect to its eclecticism and tolerance for different approaches, there are currently several quite different and rather antithetical schools of thought which have substantial followings within the discipline and the Canadian Political Science Association (CPSA)/Société canadienne de Science politique, including the behavioral school in Canadian and comparative politics, the neo-Marxist school in political economy, the public administration-public policy school. All of them are permitted and even encouraged to coexist in political science departments and curricula, in the executive committee and annual meeting of the Canadian Political Science Association, and in the mainstream journals and university presses.[12] Moreover, this pattern of eclecticism and tolerance for disciplinary diversity is not a recent development; there has always been a willingness in Canada to accept several schools of thought in political science simultaneously, including the formal-legal and political economy schools in the 1930s, and the institutional and behavioral schools in the 1950s and 1960s.[13] This pattern of tolerance and eclecticism in political science in Canada contrasts sharply with experiences in political science communities in some other Western countries, such as the United States, Britain, and France. In the United States, the tendency has been to embrace one school of thought at the expense of other, competing schools and to discourage fundamental differences of approach within departments and the American Political Science Association. Thus, the Marxist and neo-Marxist schools have generally met an unreceptive climate in the political science departments and associations of the United States, as did the behavioral school for a time before them. In Britain, behavioralism faced strong opposition for a long period, and still has no genuine legitimacy in the politics, philosophy, and economics departments of Oxford and Cambridge. The same is true for public administration and policy studies.[14] In France the deep cleavages between the Left and the Right have spilled over directly into the political and social science departments, which are delicately balanced between permanently warring or opposed pluralist and Marxist factions.

The second characteristic of a primarily synthetic, evolutionary, and cumulative approach to knowledge is closely related to the first. Since there is tolerance for diversity, there is likewise a willingness to incorporate the leading contributions of a number of these competing schools into the main body of disciplinary literature. Thus, political economy writings of disciples of Harold Innis such as Clark, Easterbrook, Watkins, and Levitt are read in Canada along with institutional writings such as Dawson, Ward, and Mallory, behavioral writings such as Meisel and Dion, and neo-Marxist literature such as Teeple, Naylor, Clement, and Panitch.[15] There are no sharp discontinuities in approach signifying changes in paradigms (although there are more and less popular approaches at different phases of the discipline's development). This pattern again appears to contrast with that of the United States, where sharp discontinuities do seem apparent, or some countries of Latin America, where there is virtually total adherence to one or another of the competing paradigms and total exclusion or ignorance of the contributions of rival schools.

The third characteristic of innovativeness in case studies and theoretical applications rather than pure theoretical contributions needs little elaboration. When one considers the important contributions to theories of comparative politics, international politics, political philosophy, and public administration and public policy, very few Canadian names come to mind. There is no

Canadian theoretical contribution equivalent to that of Dicey or Jennings in legal-institutional approaches to politics, to Lasswell, Merriam, Easton, Almond, or Deutsch in behavioral, systems, functionalist, and cybernetic studies, to Mosca or Pareto in elite approaches, to Morgenthau, Schelling, or Aron in balance of power or strategic theory in international relations, to Simon or Crozier in administrative theory, to Marcuse or Poulantzas in neo-Marxist thought. The leading Canadian contributions all appear to be theoretical applications such as Dawson and Mallory in legal-institutional studies, Porter and Clement in elite studies, Dion in group theory, Panitch in neo-Marxist political economy and neo-corporatism, and Simeon in federalism.[16] Several of the most acclaimed Canadian political science writings are also case studies: for example, Simeon's study of federal-provincial bargaining in the sphere of pensions, financial relations and constitutional revision; Meisel's exploration of electoral strategy and campaigning in the Canadian general election of 1957; Lemieux's analysis of the political subculture of the Isle D'Orleans of Quebec; Pinard's analysis of the rise of the Social Credit Party in Quebec in 1962; Mallory's study of the federal-provincial confrontation between the Alberta Social Credit and central government authorities; and Brecher's case studies of foreign policy decision-making in Israel.[17] The major exceptions to this pattern appear to be Macpherson's contributions to political theory (particularly his formulation of the concept of possessive individualism and his critique of liberal democratic theory) and Innis's contribution of "staple" theory in political economy and his concepts in communications theory.[18]

Fourthly, Canadian political studies tend to emphasize the part rather than the whole and the sector rather than the entire system to a greater extent than elsewhere (and allowing for a growing trend in this direction everywhere in the social sciences). Although there are some notable exceptions, few Canadian full-length books or articles attempt to encompass theoretically the entire political system, the complete formal machinery of government, the whole party system, the full history or life of a major political party, the global pressure-group system, the total elite structure, the entire federal system, or the whole Canadian foreign policy system.[19]

Of course, other characteristics could be included in this short list.[20] In addition, certain of these characteristics apply only to parts of the Canadian political science tradition. Thus the empirical and theoretical temper and the sectoral rather than systemic emphasis is more accurate in its description of political science in English Canada than in French Canada. Political science in French Canada has been much more given to constructing whole systems of thought and developing overall systemic approaches to such areas as groups, elites, the structure of government and administration, and the class structure in Canada.[21]

It is also worth relating these distinctive characteristics of political science in Canada to the more important contributions which Canadians have made to international political science as a whole. The qualities of eclecticism, tolerance, orientation to theoretical applications and case studies, and affinity for sectoral and partial studies may have enabled Canadians to blend a variety of approaches in a successful manner, thereby highlighting both the merits and shortcomings of different theoretical schools in political and other social sciences. They may have also enabled the discipline to develop a respectable inventory of partial or sectoral case studies upon which future theorists may build.

Explanations of the State of Political Science in Canada: Some Further Hypotheses

What accounts for the aforementioned distinctive characteristics of political science in Canada? If we refer to our heuristic model (figure 10.1), a number of factors come readily to mind. First, eclecticism in approaches is probably traceable to aspects of the Canadian environment and culture. Canada has a small population of 23 million spread out in a narrow rim north of the United States along a 4,000 kilometer continental expanse. It is loosely connected by the uneasy bonds of a common but conflictual history and political tradition, well-developed but sometimes chaotic transportation and communications links, nationally and regionally crosscutting but strong class divisions, and close but unequal regional economic ties and interests. The three most striking environmental and cultural traits of Canada are its harsh but rich climate and geography, its bilingual/bicultural and polyethnic makeup, and its close proximity to the much more powerful and culturally dynamic United States. This diverse, decentralized society of relatively autonomous regions and subcultures has managed to maintain its unity and political independence through a strong commitment to compromise, acceptance of difference and division, and the forging of a fragile, common identity composed of sometimes incompatible components. Some of these cultural characteristics have been carried over into the academic sphere, and have shaped the manner in which the members of the political science community, themselves a microcosm of the larger Canada, have related to each other. Tolerance for seemingly incompatible schools of thought, creating syntheses or at least striking compromises among philosophical or political antagonists, and constructing bridges across cultural chasms seem to characterize both the Canadian political and its academic experience.

Secondly, the synthetic and cumulative quality of disciplinary development in Canada can be particularly related to Canada's multifaceted intellectual and academic heritage. Canadian academic structures and content have always been a blend of indigenous factors and external influences, particularly from the United States, Britain, and France. The Canadian discipline and profession have never been entirely monopolized by one intellectual source. At various times in the past, largely British-inspired schools of constitutional law, economic history, and institutionalism have contended in Canada with American-inspired schools of political sociology and behavioral studies for dominance; French-inspired social Catholic and more recently neo-Marxist schools have likewise had a significant impact.[22] This resulted both from a general intellectual and cultural dependency on the important centers of Western learning and from the direct transmission of ideas by graduate students who had studied in these centers outside the country. The effect of this cross-fertilization has been a coexistence of what may be termed "mainline" and "marginal" schools within the Canadian discipline throughout its history.[23] In contrast to a Kuhnian conception,[24] Canadian political science has developed in an evolutionary rather than "revolutionary" manner, in much the same way as Canada's political history; it consists of the gradual absorption of ideas from abroad and their reworking to fit the peculiar conditions of the country. This pattern of absorption generally occurs without intense conflict among the rival groups for complete dominance, as has been the experience in political science in many other societies.

Thirdly, the tendency of political science in Canada to be innovative in case studies rather than in pure theoretical contributions may be linked to Canada's heavily derivative, dependent, and colonialist-tinged culture, which, however, gives expression to the more particularistic qualities of Canada within that external absorptive process. Until recently, Canadian culture has generally been regarded by its nationals as inferior to the "mother cultures" of the politically more powerful, historically rich, and populated countries of its origin (particularly Britain, France, and the United States). It is not surprising, therefore, that Canadian academics have often considered themselves to be primarily consumers rather than producers of academic ideas and importers of what is "best" in foreign scholarship. This kind of mentality has not tended to foster independent contributions or theoretical innovations. The potential for theoretical creativity has also been weakened by the proximity of larger and more dynamic centers such as the United States and Britain. The "brain drain" has robbed Canada of some of its more creative political and social scientists, including David Easton, Robert McKenzie, Anthony King, John Kenneth Galbraith, and Harry Johnson.[25]

Finally, the partial and sectoral approach to political science may reflect a general proclivity in Canada for managing narrow-gauge problems because of the intractability of so many large political questions in Canada.[26] It may also reflect the fragmented, regionalized, and segmented pattern of Canadian society and culture, and a distrust of holistic approaches which seem to attract scholars in the larger, "monocultural" countries such as the United States, Britain, and France. Global generalizations tend to be more open to questioning in societies that are defined as multicultural and regionally diverse.

One might be tempted to conclude from the foregoing that we are presenting a somewhat pessimistic and negative portrait of political science in Canada. Such is not our intention. As stated at the outset we generally view the current state of the discipline in Canada in a very positive light. The country and its culture have matured considerably in recent decades. Some speak of the current generation as the first to identify itself by Canadian criteria rather than by reference to the "imperial mother cultures." While it will still take several years for the recent, huge expansion of political scientists to be fully digested as mature, productive researchers, the publishing of important new studies is proceeding at present.

Even more important in our eyes, however, are what we consider to be the positive and potentially fruitful aspects of political science in Canada as described and explained in the four characteristics above. An eclectic tradition that is not afraid to seek what is best in other human societies and adapt it to its own use; a discipline that emphasizes tolerance and change through cumulative growth rather than conflict and stagnation; a political science that is skeptical enough of holistic theories to want to put them to the test in empirical cases surely has something to offer a world that is becoming increasingly interdependent and heterogeneous. Canada has required large doses of tolerance, understanding, and empathy even to exist. We may hypothesize that, in part, they have been provided in the political science textbooks, lectures, and policy advice which have been offered to the Canadian people.

These explanatory hypotheses are also somewhat speculative. There is a need to provide some empirical support for them by examining briefly the historical development of political science in Canada in two periods: (i) until 1945 and (ii) from 1945 to the present. In the course of doing so, we shall explore the following themes: the general state of the discipline in each period (bearing in mind our hypothesized four major characteristics); the intellectual structure of the discipline, including the general approaches and the areas or subfields developed in each period; some important contributions to research; the professional structures (such as departments, associations, journals) which were established; and the relationship between political science in Canada and the practice of politics.

The History and State of Political Science in Canada until 1945

The founding of political science in Canada is generally dated from the inauguration of the political economy department at the University of Toronto and the appointment of W. J. Ashley, a former Oxford don, to fill its full-time chair in 1888. In his inaugural address, entitled "What is Political Science?" Ashley defined the boundaries of the discipline in terms which are still applicable today: "It is systematic knowledge concerning the state of political society—concerning its constitution, its functions, the organs by which these functions are discharged, its relation to the individual and to other societies."[27] Ashley also argued presciently that political science should limit its field of inquiry to a narrower sphere than sociology and should include among its branches or allied concerns political economy, political philosophy, jurisprudence, municipal law, international law, and history. Its method of study should be largely historical and comparative.[28] He attempted to establish a curriculum in political science in Toronto along these lines.[29]

In the years which immediately followed, a number of other political science chairs and departments were established in the leading universities in English Canada.[30] There was even an attempt to establish a Canadian Political Science Association in 1913, composed of economists, lawyers and politicians as well as specialists in constitutional law and government;[31] however it had to be retarded until 1929, largely because of the intervention of World War I. At any rate, until the 1930s there were only a handful of political scientists holding full-time university positions, and most were trained primarily in law or economics. In the French Canadian universities, neo-Thomist social philosophy still held sway, and positivist social science was in general disrepute. There was not even a full-fledged social science department in Quebec until the mid-1930s, and political science was only initiated as part of a more general curriculum reform in this respect in 1938.[32]

The intellectual structure of the discipline at this early stage was shaped largely by two major influences: (1) the ideas generated in philosophy, law, and in social sciences such as sociology and economics in the nineteenth and early twentieth century, and (2) the ideas and institutional models emanating from the other political science communities in western Europe and the United States. The impact of the British universities was still preeminent, and therefore the major force on curriculum content was the British constitutional lawyers such as Maine and Dicey, and the British classical political economists such as Smith, Ricardo, and the Mills. However, the impact of the sociological positivists such as Comte, Spencer, and Durkheim was also felt to a degree as was that of the historical and dialectical (critical) school of Hegel and Marx. These influences entered Canada largely through the textbooks, journals, and graduate studies programs of the United States. Political science proper was comprised largely of the history of political theory, basic maxims or principles of politics culled from general introductory texts, constitutional histories or formal-legal writings by the most eminent jurists and constitutional law experts of the day.[33]

The community was still too small to make any large contribution to political or social science knowledge at this time. However, even at this early stage prior to the 1930s the political science and political economy writings of Stephen Leacock, Adam Shortt, O. D. Skelton, R. M. MacIver, and others were being widely read in Canada and elsewhere.[34]

The first flowering of the political science community in Canada occurred during the depression years of the 1930s. The original impetus for this development was the successful establishment of a Canadian Political Science Association in 1929, encompassing about thirty full-time political scientists, economists, sociologists, anthropologists, and constitutional lawyers.[35] It was followed quickly by the initiation of a regular quarterly journal, the *Canadian Journal of Economics and Political Science* (CJEPS), in 1935.[36]

The major force behind this maturation was the noted economic historian and communications theorist, Harold Adams Innis. Innis was responsible for pioneering what has come to be known as the political economy tradition in Canada, of which his own original work on "staple theory" stands as the most outstanding and durable contribution.[37] The ideas of Harold Innis extend beyond the economics of mere staple production, including that of fur, cod, wheat, and their effects on the economic, social, and political organization of the various regional communities of Canada. He also traced the linkages between primary production in the hinterland and the secondary and manufacturing processes of the larger industrial and commercial centers. Innis's insights stimulated a whole generation of economic historians, constitutional lawyers, political economists, political scientists, and sociologists to offer original interpretations of Canada, including Frank Underhill, F. R. Scott, Eugene Forsey, Hugh Aitken, W. T. Easterbrook, J. A. Corry, J. R. Mallory, C. B. Macpherson, and S. D. Clark.[38] These ideas, moreover, have found renewed receptivity among the contemporary generation of political economists and political scientists who have been instrumental in the revival of political economy in Canada. His later work on changing historical modes of communication, developed during the 1940s, likewise mobilized an incipient group of sociologists and communications theorists, such as Marshall McLuhan, although to a lesser extent.

But Innis's professional institutional contribution to the development of political science was equally impressive. Innis was a main force behind the formation of the association and journal, and was its first president. He actively encouraged theses, published bibliographies, and fostered research publications, often with the diligent assistance of his talented wife and collaborator, Mary Q. Innis. He was the chairman of the largest department of political economy in the country (at the University of Toronto) for many years and was embroiled in several of the leading early cases of academic freedom in the social sciences in Canada.[39]

The political economy school of the 1930s, although small, can be regarded as the mainstream Canadian political science school for the decade and perhaps also the most original and important contribution by Canada to the discipline as a whole. It was clearly a response to the perturbations of the depression. It encompassed virtually all of Canada's then-active political scientists, except for those who preferred to identify with R. McGregor Dawson's incipient institutional school.[40] The active debates of this community were recorded in the published proceedings of the annual meetings of the Canadian Political Science Association and in the pages of the *Canadian Journal of Economics and Political Science,* as well as in several leading books and edited collections of the period. Many of the discussions revolved around government policy and naturally spilled over into the political arena. Although Innis himself deliberately refrained from any direct political participation, several of his colleagues, including Frank Underhill, F. R. Scott, and Eugene Forsey, became involved actively in the organization of new political parties or movements such as the CCF (Cooperative Commonwealth Federation) and the labor movement. Others like Alexander Brady, J. A. Corry, R. A. McKay, and Henry Angus were drawn into the depression year deliberations over proposed revisions of the Canadian federal system and made substantial contributions to that great prewar document, the Rowell-Sirois Report on Dominion-Provincial Relations.[41] Still others abandoned their academic posts to accept Ottawa's call for expertise and assistance in government economic and industrial planning for World War II and postwar reconstruction.[42]

At the same time, French-Canadian universities were beginning to throw off their previous resistance to positivist social science. The battle against social catholicism and the neo-Thomist yoke had begun as early as the middle of the nineteenth century,[43] and had gained some impetus by the turn of the century within the confines of the Institut Canadien. Several noted lawyers and economists, notably Edouard Montpetit and Edras Minville, also raised their lonely voices in protest against this French-Canadian retardedness, during the early decades of the twentieth century.[44] But it was Père Georges-Henri Lévesque, a progressive cleric, who was the leading spirit behind the establishment of the first French-Canadian social science faculty, the Faculté des Sciences Sociales at Laval University in 1938. It quickly gained fame, and attracted to its courses some of the outstanding French-Canadian political figures of the postwar period, including Jean Marchard, Maurice Lamontagne, Claude Morin and even René Lévesque.[45] Its example was also emulated rapidly at the Université de Montréal, which created a similar faculty for evening students in 1942 and at several of the prominent *collèges classiques*. Although sociology preceded political science in its foundation and development in these institutions, firm groundwork had been laid for the postwar establishment in French Canada of separate political science departments, curricula, and the hiring of full-time specialists in the discipline.[46]

Even at this early stage, several of the distinctive characteristics of political science in Canada had already begun to manifest themselves. For example, despite the preeminence of the political economy school in the 1930s, and the sharp differences of ideological perspective which these ideas and the related depression conditions engendered, there was broad acceptance of diversity of opinion and ready tolerance of political radicalism within the Canadian political and social science community. Thus, at a time when socialism was challenging the major bastions of Canadian economic and political power for the first time, and facing strong resistance, outspoken advocates of socialism, of nationalization of industry and banking institutions, and harsh critics of the evils of the capitalist system were sheltered and given a platform within the universities, the professional associations, and the journals. Such leading academic radicals as Frank Underhill, F. R. Scott, and C. B. Macpherson were able to hold full-time university positions, or to organize and participate in radical political movements without seriously endangering their positions, or without fear of ostracism by their colleagues.[47] This trend was in sharp contrast with experience in other countries, such as the United States, where social scientists who challenged the system were sometimes treated harshly. (It also must be qualified to take account of the special conditions in French Canada, where opposition to left-wing radicalism of any color was strongly enforced by state and church authorities alike until well after World War II.)

Secondly, the synthetic, evolutionary, and cumulative approach to knowledge was preferred over a more dialectical view even at this stage. The proponents of the political economy approach did not set themselves in opposition to the constitutional-legal approach which preceded them, and they did not combat or discourage the efforts of R. MacGregor Dawson and others to develop a more institutional approach to the study of Canadian government during and immediately after World War II. Innis, and Adam Shortt before him,[48] devoted themselves to the careful accumulation of empirical data and case studies rather than to theoretical polemics, since they hoped to build an inventory of solid Canadian case materials from which scholars might draw in their future theoretical endeavors.

Thirdly, despite Innis's own impressive theoretical contributions, the main emphasis both in his scholarship and in that of his political economy and political science colleagues was on theoretical applications and case studies. Innis himself had set the pattern for this type of investigation in his graduate studies at the University of Chicago, where he reacted strongly against the large abstractions and theoretical models of his economics instructors and their mentors.[49] Innis believed in the inductive rather than deductive approach to knowledge, and he built his own ideas on a solid empirical foundation. "Staple theory," for example, was constructed out of rather dry and painstaking, detailed, case examinations of the fur trade in the Saint Lawrence valley, the cod fishing industry in the Maritimes, and the wheat farming and grain production of the Prairie provinces. A similar attitude was adopted by other early political economists.[50]

However, the tradition of partial and sectoral studies had not yet been initiated at this early stage. There were a few ambitious and not entirely successful attempts to synthesize knowledge about the totality of Canadian or Quebec society, economy, and government during this period.[51] There were also some forays by Canadian academics into the unchartered waters of public administration[52] and international relations studies.[53] Most scholarly efforts were confined, however, to examining in an integrated, interdisciplinary manner a particular Canadian policy question, a current problem of international diplomacy, or a case issue in public administration.[54]

The History and State of Political Science in Canada from 1945 to the Present

After World War II, Canada came increasingly under the economic control and cultural domination of its great southern neighbor, which had emerged as the leading world superpower. Not surprisingly, this influence extended to academic life, including political science. The indigenous tradition of the Canadian political economy gradually became submerged in the floodwaters of the American behavioral revolution and, for a time, lost all relevance for political scientists in Canada.

Before this occurred, however, political science was given an important additional injection by the proponents of the institutional school, led by that great pioneer in Canadian government studies, R. MacGregor Dawson. Dawson had begun teaching full-time at the University of Saskatchewan in the 1920s and later moved to the University of Toronto. Unlike Innis, however, he was trained as a constitutional lawyer and political scientist and in Britain rather than the United States. Dawson was disturbed by the lack of adequate information about the machinery of Canadian government, which he tried initially and unsuccessfully to overcome by distributing journalistic and government documentary materials in his classrooms.[55] He then turned to filling the gaps by his own research and writings.

This culminated in his ground-breaking textbook, *The Government of Canada,* first published in 1947 (and now in its fifth edition). He also wrote several other books and numerous articles on aspects of the federal legislature, executive, and public service in Canada, served on a royal commission investigating the need for administrative reform in Nova Scotia and fostered a number of different monographs by his former students on the structure of particular provincial governments.[56] The influence of Dawson and the institutional school parallelled earlier developments in other countries such as the United States and Britain, but it also gave to these concerns a decidedly Canadian coloration, by emphasizing the importance of delicately balancing the mechanisms of federalism with those of parliamentary government. Although a few observers considered this influence to have been diverting of more important political economy concerns,[57] most tend to regard the approach as complementary with earlier political economy and policy foci. This view is also prescient of current efforts to foster the coexistence of behavioral studies, policy analyses, and radical political economy approaches.

The number of academic political scientists in the postwar period remained at about the same level (about 30) until the late 1950s, and then began to rise steeply to meet the demands of rapidly increasing university enrollments[58] and intensifying interest in social sciences. Undergraduate political science students were encouraged to pursue graduate studies in the United States, Britain, and (later) France and to return to fill the growing number of available positions in political science in Canada. But the supply was still insufficient to meet the immediate needs of universities, so that many administrators and department heads turned to the United States and other countries to fill their complement of staff.

At the same time, the behavioral revolution in American political science was beginning to have a major impact on the state of political science in Canada. There had been direct influences from the writings of major American proponents of this approach, including Charles Merriam, Harold Lasswell, and Pendleton Herring in the pre-World War II period and David Easton, Gabriel Almond, Robert Dahl, and others in the immediate postwar period. There was also the indirect influence of American-trained political science graduates returning to teach in Canada, and the ever-burgeoning number of direct American recruits to Canadian universities.[59]

The behavioral school attempted to incorporate into the discipline of political science the findings of the emerging behavioral sciences in the United States and elsewhere, including sociology, anthropology, economics, systems theory, and cybernetics. It was, in the words of one of its major proponents, David Easton, both an intellectual tendency and a movement.[60] Its hope was to systematize in a scientific manner the body of available political knowledge by focusing on recurrent and observable political behavior patterns of individuals and groups of societies. In this way, it believed it would rid political science of the sterility of the constitutional-legal and institutional approaches, focus on the "guts" of politics, and through "scientific" approach and method, pave the way to a full maturation of the discipline.[61]

An important side effect of this movement was its stimulus of disciplinary and subdisciplinary specialization. Until the end of World War II, there were mostly combined departments in Canada of political science with economics, sociology, and anthropology. Subfields of comparative politics, international politics, and public administration were almost nonexistent in Canada: there were some courses offered in these specialties, but very few original contributions to research.[62] Since behavioralism had as its objective the systematizing of behavior patterns in all spheres of social life, it might have encouraged efforts at introducing new frameworks, approaches, models, or theories which could encompass social and political activities across disciplinary and institutional boundaries, national borders, and different levels of government. (That is, it might have produced interdisciplinary generalists capable of applying structural functionalism, systems, elite, group, culture, or game-theory approaches simultaneously to international, comparative, and Canadian fields and subfields).[63] Somewhat paradoxically, however, it had the opposite effect of multiplying the number of narrow specialists in each social science discipline. By the mid-1960s, political science had widely established itself as a separate university department and the major subdivisions within the political science discipline in Canada had begun to emerge, so that when the great expansion in university faculties and political science departments occurred in the late 1960s, hiring was conducted largely along these specialist disciplinary and subdisciplinary lines. It was not long before small but significant core groups of Canadian specialists in international politics, Western systems, communist systems, Third World studies, public administration and (later) public policy studies, provincial and municipal studies had emerged, established specialized panels at the annual meeting of the Canadian Political Science Association and begun to make their mark on the discipline. In a few cases, such as international politics, this even assumed a somewhat indigenous Canadian character,[64] although apart from the specifically Canadian subfields (such as public policy, provincial and municipal politics) this unfortunately has not been a general pattern.

Behavioralism had its most important impact in Canada on the development of studies of the Canadian political system. Following the pattern in the United States and elsewhere, it emerged in direct opposition to the legal-formal and institutional approaches which preceded it (political economy had already suffered a serious decline by the mid-1950s). Its attraction here, as elsewhere, lay in its promise to transform the study of Canadian politics into a genuine "science," with a body of well-defined and testable theoretical propositions. It also purported to take students of Canadian politics into important areas which had been neglected or disregarded by the legal-formal and institutional schools, including political parties, interest groups, political movements, elites, elections, and voting behavior. Finally, it actively promoted use of a wide variety of new quantitative techniques and empirical methods, including survey analysis and computer processing.

The beginning of behavioralism in Canadian political studies is generally dated from the publication of the first important voting-behavior study, that conducted by John Meisel into voter religious attitudes and behavior in Kingston in 1956.[65] It was followed almost immediately by a spate of similar voting studies, including Meisel's own book-length analysis of the Canadian general election of 1957.[66] Other leading figures promoting and contributing to the behavioral trend in Canadian political science were Jean Laponce, Fred Engelmann, Mildred Schwartz, Léon Dion, and Vincent Lémieux.[67] In addition to the attention given to elections and voting behavior in Canada, there was a rash of new studies in the 1960s and early 1970s on federal and provincial party organization, finance and behavior, interest groups, and elites.[68] Behavioralism has also influenced the way in which some of the more traditional Canadian political institutions have been reexamined or analyzed, including the federal system, the legislature, the public service, and the judicial system.[69]

The intellectual merits of the contributions made by behavioralists to Canadian political studies are generally recognized: they provided a strong empirical base for many of the later efforts at macro-hypothesizing and theorizing; they filled large voids in the available information about Canadian political institutions, particularly of the more informal variety; they corrected certain factual errors or misconceptions about our political processes attributable particularly to journalists and historians; and they encouraged much new theoretical discussion and interpretation of the pattern of Canadian politics. The shortcomings of the behavioral contributions have also been well documented: they encouraged attention to problems which were more susceptible to systematic inquiry or quantification than intrinsically interesting; they emphasized low-level empirical generalization at the expense of more controversial, abstract, and challenging hypothesizing and theorizing; they led political scientists into esoteric techniques of measurement and quantification which sometimes yielded little in the way of greater clarity or certainty about political life; they promoted intellectual laziness and dampened genuine creativity by encouraging validation or replication in Canada of hypotheses or theories generated elsewhere and having little or no relevance for the complex Canadian political reality; and they concealed in their assumptions important value biases which reinforced or encouraged a rather conservative, uncritical view of the Canadian system.

The influence of the behavioralists in Canada extended well beyond the intellectual content of political science curricula, the structure of political science departments, and the development of new research and publications. The leading promoters of this trend achieved preeminence within the profession itself by the late 1960s, and helped to engineer a formal split in 1968 from the economists in both the Canadian Political Science Association and its journal.[70] The first presidents and the secretary-treasurer of the newly created Canadian Political Science Association were all either sympathetic to or strong supporters of the behavioral approach, as were its initial joint French-English editors.[71] They stimulated rapid growth in the association's activities and annual budget, fostered an annual program which reflected the much greater subdisciplinary specialization and professional self-consciousness of Canadian political scientists, established the journal on a firm financial footing and ensured that its content reflected the new behavioral trends, and forged the first important links with the American and international political science communities.

The impact of political scientists in Canada on the world of politics and administration also increased considerably during this period, particularly at the federal level. Political scientists were called upon to act as consultants in such matters as constitutional reform, reorganization of the executive and higher public service, and federal-provincial relations. But the area of their greatest influence was undoubtedly that of French-English relations in Canada. The focal point for much of this activity was the Royal Commission on Bilingualism and Biculturalism, established by Prime Minister Pearson. The commission had as its research director and associate director two political scientists sympathetic to behavioral approaches and methods, Michael Oliver of McGill University and Léon Dion of Laval University, and it used David Easton as its major outside consultant; it also attracted a large number of both English and French-Canadian sociologists, historians, economists, and political scientists to its vast research team.[72] After almost four years of work, the commission finally produced a report of five volumes, published about ten research monographs, and released to scholars a large number of additional unpublished research studies it had commissioned. Its stimulus to other unassociated research studies and publications was also considerable. Most important of all, perhaps, it helped to create close ties between the two political science language communities of French and English Canada.

Although positivist social science was finally embraced in French Canada in the post–World War II period, political science tended to lag behind both economics and sociology in its development. The first full-time political scientist in French Canada was only hired in 1951, and the first permanent department was created in 1954, both at Laval University in Quebec.[73] Some impetus to the development of the discipline was also provided by the important contributions by political and social scientists to the Quebec counterpart of the Rowell-Sirois Commission, *La Commission royale d'enquête sur les problèmes constitutionnels* (Tremblay Commission) in 1954.[74] As the Quiet Revolution transformed the educational structure of Quebec, producing a large influx of new students, the numbers of political scientists in the francophone universities increased very rapidly. By the early 1970s, separate political science departments existed at all of the French-speaking universities in Quebec, at the bilingual University of Ottawa, and also at the newly created French-language universities in Sudbury, Ontario, and Moncton, New Brunswick. The old system of classical colleges had also been replaced by French-language CEGEPS, and these institutions had likewise established political science departments. The positions were filled by former undergraduates of the French-language universities who had pursued their graduate studies in the United States or in Europe (particularly France). These new recruits had been exposed to the behavioral approach, and they incorporated it into their analyses of the changing Quebec and French-Canadian political reality. There were important contributions made by francophones to voting behavior studies, to interest group theory and application, to elites, and to political parties and movements.[75] The *Canadian Journal of Political Science* had a regular French-language coeditor, and reserved about a third of its pages for French-language articles and reviews. Most important, a separate French-language political science association, the *Société canadienne de Science politique*, was established in 1964 to encompass the growing number of francophone political scientists who wished to have a supportive institution in order to function autonomously from the officially bilingual but actually English-dominated Canadian Political Science Association. The two associations cooperated in the work of the journal and a variety of other activities, thereby maintaining an uneasy coexistence through the turbulent period of French-English relations in the Canada of the 1970s. Several of the leading francophone political scientists also exercised considerable influence on the leading actors in the political process in Quebec and at the federal level, thereby helping to shape French Canada's strategy in its governmental and administrative dealings with its English-Canadian counterparts.[76]

In contrast to the United States and particularly Britain, the behavioral approach had not really faced strong opposition in Canada in its initial efforts to place its imprint firmly on the discipline. As a result, there never was a "behavioral revolution" in the sense in which this trend has been described in the United States.[77] Moreover, once implanted in Canada, behavioralism did not attempt to establish a monopoly position in political science or to impose its credo on the entire profession, as sometimes seemed to be the objective in its counterpart to the south. Almost from the beginning of its preeminence in Canada in the mid-1960s, behavioralism confronted criticism from a variety of different schools in both English and French Canada, including the so-called neoinstitutionalists, the public policy specialists, and the neo-Marxists and (later) radical political economists. The combined force of their attacks brought the brief reign of behavioralism to an abrupt end by the mid-1970s.

The neoinstitutionalists, as Donald Smiley has labeled them, included several members of the earlier school inspired and led by R. MacGregor Dawson in the 1940s and early 1950s, such as Norman Ward, Ted Hodgetts, Paul Fox, J. R. Mallory, W. F. Dawson, and, to a degree, Smiley himself. In their earlier writings, these individuals had kept closely to the nuts-and-bolts approach which Dawson had pioneered so effectively. Behavioralism had exposed some of the shortcomings of this approach; namely, that it failed to emphasize the important role that social and cultural forces have in shaping the institutions which comprise the basic machinery of government, and that it overemphasized the importance of the formal structures themselves and underemphasized the significance of individual actors, roles, and folkways which define the "real" political behavior behind these structures. The neoinstitutionalists absorbed these lessons and strove to modify and redefine their institutional concerns to include the aforementioned neglected factors. At the same time, they launched an effective counterattack against the behavioralists, whom they accused of overlooking the important constraints placed on individual and group actors by established structures, and the independent causal impact of formal institutions on political attitudes and behavior.[78]

The public policy specialists offered more of a revision than a critique of behavioralism. Among the most prominent spokesmen were Bruce Doern, Peter Aucoin, Vince Wilson, and Rick Van Loon. Following the lead of public policy and public administration analysts in the United States and abroad, and the call by David Easton for a postbehavioral revolution of relevance,[79] they pointed out that very little attention in the post–World War II period in Canada had been given to the policymaking structures, outputs and outcomes of the political process (or what Easton referred to as the black-box area of his well-known input-output model of the political system).[80] And yet, it is precisely this area which is of most crucial concern and interest to politicians and political observers. In aspiring to become "scientific," the behavioralists had tended to concentrate on the more tangential and less relevant data of politics.[81] There was a need to reorient the study of politics to policy and to apply the sophisticated analytical tools and methods of behavioralism to these central but neglected areas.

The neo-Marxists and (later) the radical political economists constituted a somewhat larger, more culturally diverse, and more strident group of critics than the other two. They included among their local elder mentors C. B. Macpherson and Stanley Ryerson,[82] and among their guiding spirits from outside Canada, C. Wright Mills, Gabriel Kolko, and Herbert Marcuse in the United States, Ralph Miliband and T. B. Bottomore in Britain and Nicos Poulantzas and Samir Amin in France.[83] In English Canada they were originally led in the late 1960s by a group of younger, mostly Toronto-based social and political scientists, including Ian Lumsden, Philip Resnick, Robert Laxer, Gary Teeple, Tom Naylor, and Leo Johnson. In French Canada they clustered around Jean-Marc Piotte, Gilles Bourque, and Nicole Laurin-Frenette. Their criticism of behavioralism centered on its neglect of the class dimension in politics and its conscious or unconscious identification with the status quo.[84] But they also rejected what they regarded as essentially alien liberal ideas imported from the United States and insufficiently attuned to the Canadian or Quebec social, economic, and cultural reality. Thus, neo-Marxism and neonationalism became closely intertwined, particularly in English Canada.

By the end of the 1960s, several political scientists of this school had become actively involved in the lively debate generated within the "Waffle" or left wing of the New Democratic Party concerning the evils of American economic and cultural imperialism. The academic component of this debate was led by two University of Toronto political economists, Mel Watkins and Abe Rotstein, and two Carleton University English professors, Robin Mathews and James Steele. They called for strong government measures to curb the extent of foreign and particularly American investment, ownership, and control of Canadian resource and manufacturing industries, restrictions on American content in the media and in academic curricula, and limitations on the hiring of Americans in Canadian universities. Their arguments were expanded on and empirically supported in a number of influential books on these topics, published primarily by political economists in the early 1970s, including Kari Levitt's *Silent Surrender,* Abe Rotstein's *Precarious Homestead,* Robert Laxer's *(Canada) Limited,* and Mathews and Steel's, *The Struggle for Canadian Universities.*[85] Watkins also had a direct impact on government foreign ownership policy and legislation by his research contribution to the *Report* of the Task Force on the Structure of Canadian Industry (or what became known as the Watkins Report) commissioned by the former finance minister, Left-Liberal and nationalist, Walter Gordon. This was followed by another report under the Consumer and Corporate Minister Herb Gray (the Gray Report) and finally by considerably diluted legislation establishing a Foreign Investment Review Agency (FIRA) in 1973.

The search for genuine, indigenous, Canadian, academic traditions to stem the tide of Americanization of our universities and the concern with American economic control led inevitably to a revival of the political economy tradition in the early 1970s. In English Canada, this first took the form of rediscovering the contributions of Harold Innis and of his most important followers among the political scientists, economists, sociologists, and historians.[86] But it soon led to efforts to push beyond those essentially non-Marxist frontiers, and to formulating a new, more radical approach to problems of advanced capitalism and the role of the state in the postwar Canadian and other Western economies. To some extent the stimulus was again external and there was heavy borrowing of concepts formulated by radical political economists and *dependencia* theorists from other countries such as Jurgen Habermas, James O'Connor, Stuart Holland, Ralph Miliband, Nicos Poulantzas, Louis Althusser, André Gunder Frank, Immanuel Wallerstein, Samir Amin, Perry Anderson, and others.[87] But there was also a genuine effort to foster studies and develop concepts more indigenous or applicable to Canada. A key promoter of this new intellectual trend is a Toronto-trained political economist, Daniel Drache, and its most notable adherents include political economists such as Mel Watkins and Tom Naylor, political scientists such as Leo Panitch, Philip Resnick, Garth Stevenson, and Larry Pratt, and sociologists such as Wallace Clement. A major vehicle for its promotion is the political economy section of the annual meeting of the Canadian Political Science Association, and the more recently established and related political economy network, a loosely linked grouping of local political economy specialists in the major academic centers across Canada. In French Canada, a smaller parallel *réseau* has been created which promises to offer stimulating new insights into the "statist" trends underlying the entire post-1960s *indépendentiste* phenomenon.

The intellectual fruits of this political economy revival have already begun to emerge in the form of lively papers and debates at the annual political science meetings, several contributions to published journals,[88] a collection of papers edited by Leo Panitch on *The Canadian State: Political Economy and Political Power* (1977),[89] and a published bibliography on Canadian political economy writings.[90] The interest in political economy has spread to other subdisciplines in Canada including comparative politics, international relations, and Canadian political thought; scholarly journals in two of these fields have been launched.[91] There has been a noticeable reactivation of interest in left-wing or socialist ideas among social science students in Canada, although not in left-wing political activity.⁹² At the same time there has been renewed interest in non-Marxist and liberal political economy ideas.

There are some signs that a similar trend is beginning to emerge elsewhere, particularly in Western Europe and in the Third World. However, in the United States, apart from a few isolated contributions in the comparative and international political science fields,⁹³ there does not appear to be a clear disciplinary movement in the political economy direction. Perhaps the increasing interaction among the different national political science communities will help stimulate a debate over the relative merits of this and other competing approaches, with corresponding benefits for the future of the discipline and profession as a whole. In particular, such a dialogue might lead to a more precise formulation of concepts in what is thus far a very rudimentary and shaky theoretical foundation underpinning the political economy approach.

Summary and Conclusion

It should be apparent from the preceding discussion that historical evidence both before and particularly since World War II tends to support the characterization of political science in Canada set out in the section on the current state of political science above. Even prior to World War II there were a number of competing but coexistent approaches, including the legal-formal and political economy schools.

After World War II, there was a rapid proliferation of ideas and schools of thought. Institutionalism, behavioralism, neoinstitutionalism, public policy, neo-Marxist, and radical political economy approaches followed one upon the other in rapid succession and were permitted to coexist without great debate or acrimony.⁹⁴ The intellectual contributions of these different approaches were regarded as complementary and cumulative: from the concentration of the legal-formal approach on the constitution to the political economy focus on the state and on policy concerns and the interdisciplinary nexus between the economic, social, and political; to the institutionalist emphasis on the nuts and bolts of government; to the behavioralists' concern for informal, mediating, political structures and social forces; to the neoinstitutionalist synthesis; to the policy analysts' desire to concentrate on the outputs and outcomes of government; to the neo-Marxist call for class-oriented, critical, and anti-status quo analyses; to the neopolitical economists' return to the interdisciplinary nexus between the economic and political and their search for indigenous concepts and tools of analysis.

Most of the contributions of these approaches were of an applied rather than basic theoretical nature; and yet they provided a series of fresh insights into the evolving and rapidly changing domestic social, economic, and political reality. Thus, Harold Innis's image of Canada as a staples producer in which metropolitan regions and hinterland areas existed in an unequal symbiotic relationship was particularly suitable to the chaotic conditions of the depression years; R. MacGregor Dawson's depiction of the machinery of parliamentary government and federalism in delicate balance fitted the more optimistic mood of the immediate post–World War II period; the behavioralist concept of Canada as a total sociopolitical system could readily encompass the fundamental societal changes then being implemented in Quebec; John Porter's elite analysis lay bare the nature of the unequal sociopolitical structure of English Canada in the 1960s and the unfulfilled aspirations of a society without genuinely equal social mobility; and Kari Levitt's view of Canada as a branch-plant economy captured the essence of an increasingly dependent, American-dominated country of the early 1970s. The partial and sectoral nature of most recent contributions may reflect the fragmented and unintegrated pattern of national politics emerging in recent years as much as the weaknesses in all the explanatory paradigms and the general rejection of any one predominant school in political science.

These characteristics distinguished political science in Canada from the pattern of the discipline and profession in other countries, but they have in no way derogated from the quality of the contribution which has been made by our colleagues. The historical evidence clearly contradicts the assertion that the discipline in Canada has been essentially derivative and that paradigms, approaches, and tools of analysis have generally been imported from outside the country. Except for the brief interlude in which behavioralism was dominant, indigenous or imported (and then substantially modified) approaches such as the political economy school, institutionalism, neoinstitutionalism, and neopolitical economy approaches have flowered throughout the almost 100 years of the discipline's existence in Canada. The political science personnel have not been overwhelmingly American-born or American-trained until recently, and this trend appears not about to be reversed. The quality of research is generally high and is certainly not inferior to that conducted elsewhere. The discipline has had more than a marginal impact on Canadian society and politics, as the contributions made to the Rowell-Sirois Commission, the Tremblay Commission, the Royal Commission on Bilingualism and Biculturalism and a host of other commissions, task forces, and agencies have illustrated. Finally, it is true that the influence of political science in Canada on international political science has been marginal at best, but this pattern may be changing under the impetus of the current neopolitical economy school. These generalizations are meant to apply to both English and French-speaking political scientists, although, as we have seen, in some periods the history of these two Canadian political science communities has diverged substantially, and this pattern may recur.

It will be necessary, of course, to explore these hypotheses further with reference to past, current, and future developments in Canada. More important, it will be useful to examine the ideal-typical characteristics of political science in Canada and their hypothesized explanation in comparative perspective, in order to highlight points of convergence and divergence with other countries. To what extent has the pattern of development in various countries been one of coexistence or conflict between the different approaches and schools of thought? How might one describe the pattern of evolution of the discipline: revolutionary or evolutionary? Has there been a cumulative or dialectical pattern of development? Are the contributions primarily to pure or applied theory? Are they holistic or sectoral? In this respect, the emphasis on the interaction of indigenous environmental and cultural factors and the political science discipline in each country should prove invaluable. Thus the discontinuous and paradigmatic pattern of development of American political science may be traceable to the revolutionary tradition in the American culture at large; the resistance of British political science to behavioralism may be related to the strong emphasis on embedded traditions and the deep-rooted conservatism of British society; and the uneasy balance between the two schools of liberal positivism and Marxism in political science in France may be traceable to the conflict between Left and Right over much of recent French history. We may, therefore, ask whether the political science of a country is basically consonant with or at cross-purposes with the culture and political systems of a society.

In short, the model developed to examine the evolution of political science in Canada, while admittedly very rudimentary, seems to have some heuristic value for the comparative sociology of political science in different societies.

Notes

1. Michael Stein, John Trent and André Donneur (eds.), *Aspects of Political Science in Canada: Fifty Years in the Development of a Discipline,* forthcoming.

2. One of our distinguished colleagues, Alan Cairns, writing on a similar topic several years ago, began his paper as follows: "The subject matter of this paper is not easy. There are gaps in our ignorance, but not many. In these circumstances the impressionistic overview which follows may be useful if its speculative basis is constantly kept in mind by the reader." (Alan C. Cairns, "National Influence on the Study of Politics," *Queen's Quarterly* 81, no. 3 (Autumn, 1974): p. 333). We have tried to diminish some of these "gaps in our ignorance" by conducting independent research and by mobilizing our colleagues to explore and gather information on their respective subdisciplines which can be used as a partial data base for our more global observations. Nevertheless, we readily acknowledge similar difficulties in our study and plead for similar indulgence and understanding from our readers.

3. The first full-time political scientist in Canada, W. J. Ashley, founded the University of Toronto's Department of Political Economy and launched the discipline in Canada in his inaugural lecture "What is Political Science?" See W. J. Ashley, "What is Political Science?" An Inaugural Lecture given in the Convocation Hall, University of Toronto, 9 November 1888 (Toronto: Rowsell & Hutchison, 1888). Ashley had previously been a fellow of Lincoln College, Oxford.

4. On these various points see James MacKinnon and David Brown, "Political Science in the Canadian University, 1969," in Robin Mathews and James Steele, eds., *The Struggle for Canadian Universities* (Toronto: New Press, 1969); Ellen and Neil Wood, "Canada and the American Science of Politics," in Ian Lumsden, ed., *Close the 49th Parallel: The Americanization of Canada* (Toronto: University of Toronto Press, 1970); Denis Smith, "What Are We Teaching: The Nationalization of Canadian Political Science," *Canadian Forum* 5 (June 1971): 4-5; Donald V. Smiley, "Must Canadian Political Science Be a Miniature Replica?" *Journal of Canadian Studies* 9, no. 1 (February 1974): 31-41; and Philip Goldman, "A Critique of the Dependency Model of Canadian Political Science," unpublished paper, CPSA, 1975. For a very different perspective, see Allan Kornberg and Alan Thorp, "The American Impact on Canadian Political Science and Sociology," in Richard Preston, ed., *The Influence of the United States on Canadian Development: Eleven Case Studies* (Durham: Duke University Press, 1972). The most balanced discussion of the issue appears in Alan C. Cairns, "Political Science in Canada and the Americanization Issue," *Canadian Journal of Political Science* (hereafter cited as *CJPS*) 8, no. 2 (June 1975): 191-234.

5. See Carl Hempel, *Aspects of Scientific Explanation* (New York: Free Press, 1965); Ernest Nagel, *The Structure of Science* (New York: Harcourt, Brace & World, 1961); Karl Popper, *The Logic of Scientific Discovery,* rev. ed. (New York: Harper & Row, 1965); Imre Lakatos and Alan Musgrave, eds., *Criticism and the Growth of Knowledge* (Cambridge: At the University Press, 1970); Stephen E. Toulmin, *Human Understanding* (Princeton: Princeton University Press, 1972), vol. 1; and May Brodbeck, ed., *Readings in the Philosophy of the Social Sciences* (London: Macmillan & Co., 1968).

6. See, for example, Karl Marx and Friedrich Engels, *The German Ideology,* ed. R. Pascal (New York: International Publishers Co., 1963), pp. 27-43; Karl Mannheim, *Ideology and*

Utopia, trans. Louis Wirth and Edward Shils (New York: Harvest Books, 1936), pp. 264-90.

7. For example, see Robert K. Merton, "Insiders and Outsiders: A Chapter in the Sociology of Knowledge," *American Journal of Sociology* (hereafter cited as *AJS*) 78, no. 1 (1972): 9-47; Robert K. Merton, "Social Conflict over Styles of Sociological Work," in J. Curtis and J. Petras, eds., *The Sociology of Knowledge: A Reader* (New York: Frederick A. Praeger, 1970); Edward Shils, "Tradition, Ecology and Institution in the History of Sociology," *Daedalus* 99, no. 4 (Fall 1970): 760-825; Edward Shils, "The Calling of Sociology," in T. Parsons, E. Shils, K. D. Naegele, and J. R. Pitts, eds., *Theories of Society* (New York: Free Press, 1961), 2: 1405-48; Joseph Ben-David, *The Scientist's Role in Society* (Englewood Cliffs, N.J.: Prentice-Hall, 1971); S. N. Eisenstadt, "The Sociological Tradition: Origins, Boundaries, Patterns of Innovation and Crises," in Joseph Ben-David and Terry N. Clark, eds., *Culture and Its Creators: Essays in Honor of Edward Shils* (Chicago: University of Chicago Press, 1977).

8. Philip Abrams, *The Origins of British Sociology: 1834-1914* (Chicago: University of Chicago Press, 1968); Terry N. Clark, *Prophets and Patrons* (Cambridge, Mass.: Harvard University Press, 1974); Anthony Oberschall, ed., *The Establishment of Empirical Sociology: Studies in Continuity, Discontinuity and Institutionalization* (New York: Harper & Row, 1972); Susanne P. Schad, *Empirical Social Research in Weimar Germany* (The Hague: Mouton, 1972); Mary O. Furner, *Advocacy and Objectivity, A Crisis in the Professionalization of American Social Science, 1865-1905* (Lexington, Ky.: University of Kentucky Press, 1975).

9. It will be impossible in the limited space available to review the relative merits and shortcomings of these approaches; however, it should be obvious that each provides only a partial view of the multifarious factors that shape disciplinary development.

10. See, for example, David Easton, *A Framework for Political Analysis* (Englewood Cliffs, N.J.: Prentice-Hall, 1965), p. 110.

11. Michael Stein and John Trent, "Aspects of Political Science in Canada: Fifty Years in the Development of a Discipline," Statement of Objectives, mimeographed, Toronto, 1977, 9 pp. These questions are all derived from figure 10.1.

12. Though particular journals and presses may give preference to some approaches over others; thus the *Canadian Journal of Political Science* is considered by some to favor behavioral writings.

13. For detailed evidence on this point see the two sections below on the history of Canada before and after 1945.

14. See F. F. Ridley, "Public Administration: Cause for Discontent," *Public Administration* (London) 50 (Spring 1972): 65-77, as cited in A. Paul Pross and V. Seymour Wilson, "Graduate Education in Canadian Public Administration: Institutionalizing Disciplinary Separatism," mimeographed, Ottawa, 1979, p. 6.

15. For example, see S. D. Clark, *The Developing Canadian Community*, 2d ed. (Toronto: University of Toronto Press, 1968); W. T. Easterbrook and M. H. Watkins, eds., *Approaches to Canadian Economic History* (Toronto: McClelland & Stewart, 1967); Kari Levitt, *Silent Surrender: The Multinational Corporation in Canada* (Toronto: Macmillan of Canada, 1970); R. MacGregor Dawson and Norman Ward, *The Government of Canada*, 5th ed. rev. (Toronto: University of Toronto Press, 1970); J. R. Mallory, *The Structure of Canadian Government*, 1st ed. (Toronto: Macmillan of Canada, 1971); John Meisel, *Working Papers on Canadian Politics*, 2d ed. (Montreal: McGill-Queen's University Press, 1974); Léon Dion, *Société et Politique: La Vie des Groupes* (Quebec: Les Presses de l'Université Laval, 1971), vols. 1, 2; Gary Teeple, ed., *Capitalism and the National Question in Canada* (Toronto: University of Toronto Press, 1972); R. T. Naylor, *The History of Canadian Business, 1867-1914* (Toronto: James Lorimer, 1975), vols. 1-2; Wallace Clement, *The Canadian Corporate Elite: An Analysis of Economic Power* (Toronto: McClelland & Stewart, 1975) and *Continental Corporate Power: Economic Elite Linkages between Canada and the United States* (Toronto: McClelland & Stewart, 1977); Leo Panitch, ed., *The Canadian State: Political Economy and Political Power* (Toronto: University of Toronto Press, 1977).

16. Dawson, *Government of Canada*; Mallory, *Canadian Government*; John Porter, *The Vertical Mosaic: An Analysis of Social Class and Power in Canada* (Toronto: University of Toronto Press, 1965); Clement, *Corporate Elite*; Panitch, *The Canadian State*; Dion, *Société et Politique* and "The Development of Corporatism in Liberal Democracies," *Comparative Political Studies* 10, no. 1 (April 1977): 61-90; Richard Simeon, *Federal-Provincial Diplomacy: The Making of Recent Policy in Canada* (Toronto: University of Toronto Press, 1972).

17. Simeon, *Federal-Provincial Diplomacy*; John Meisel, *The Canadian General Election of 1957* (Toronto: University of Toronto Press, 1962); Vincent Lemieux, *Parenté et politique: L'Organisation sociale dans l'Ile d'Orléans* (Quebec: Les Presses de L'Université Laval, 1971); Maurice Pinard, *The Rise of a Third Party: A Study in Crisis Politics* (Englewood Cliffs, N.J.: Prentice-Hall, 1971), and rev. ed. (Montreal: McGill-Queen's Press, 1975); J. R. Mallory, *Social Credit and the Federal Power* (Toronto: University of Toronto Press, 1976); Michael Brecher, *Decisions in Israel's Foreign Policy* (New Haven: Yale University Press, 1975).

18. See, for example, C. B. Macpherson, *The Political Theory of Possessive Individualism: Hobbes to Locke* (Oxford: Clarendon Press, 1962); idem, *The Real World of Democracy*, The Massey Lectures (Toronto: CBC Publications, 1965); idem, "Post-Liberal Democracy?" *CJPS* 30, no. 4 (November 1964): 485-98; idem, *Democratic Theory: Essays in Retrieval* (Oxford: Clarendon Press, 1973); Harold Adams Innis, *A History of the Canadian Pacific Railway* (London: P. S. King & Son, Toronto: McClelland & Stewart, 1923), esp. introduction and conclusion; idem, *The Fur Trade in Canada, An Introduction to Canadian Economic History*, rev. ed. (Toronto: University of Toronto Press, 1956), esp. conclusion; idem, *The Cod Fisheries: The History of an International Economy*, rev. ed. (Toronto: University of Toronto Press, 1954), esp. conclusion; idem, *Empire and Communications* (Oxford: Clarendon Press, 1950), esp. introduction, chaps. 3, 6.

19. Two major theoretical exceptions are: on the pressure

group system, Robert Presthus, *Elite Accommodation in Canadian Politics* (Toronto: Macmillan of Canada, 1973); on the elite structure, Porter, *Vertical Mosaic*. There are also some primarily descriptive texts or articles which are holistic in nature including: on the political system as a whole Dawson and Ward, *Government of Canada*, Mallory, *Canadian Government;* on the party system, Rick Van Loon and Michael Whittington, *The Canadian Political System: Environment, Structure and Process*, 2d ed. rev. (Scarborough: McGraw-Hill Ryerson, 1976); on the party system, F. C. Engelmann and M. A. Schwartz, *Canadian Political Parties: Origin, Character, Impact* (Scarborough: Prentice-Hall of Canada, 1975); on the formal machinery of government, Thomas A. Hockin, *Government in Canada* (Toronto: McGraw-Hill Ryerson, 1976); on the legislative system, Robert J. Jackson and Michael M. Atkinson, *The Canadian Legislative System* (Toronto: Macmillan of Canada, 1974); on the federal system, Donald V. Smiley, *Canada in Question: Federalism in the Seventies*, 2d ed. (Toronto: McGraw-Hill Ryerson, 1976).

20. For example, the discipline in Canada may exhibit simultaneously both great openness and deference to authority, and it may be more sympathetic to efforts at integrating political philosophy and empirical political studies than in other countries.

21. For example, Dion, *Société et Politique;* Gerard Bergeron, *Le Fonctionnement de l'Etat* (Quebec: Les Presses de l'Université Laval, 1965); Vincent Lemieux, "Pour une science politique des partis," *CJPS* 5, no. 4 (December 1972): 485-502; Gilles Bourque and Nicole Laurin-Frenette, "Classes sociales et ideologies nationales au Québec, 1760-1970," *Socialisme Québécois*, no. 20 (1970).

22. For a more detailed description of these external influences, see the two sections below on Canadian history before and after 1945.

23. For a definition of these concepts, see Irving Louis Horowitz, "Mainlines and Marginals: The Human Shape of Sociological Theory," in L. Gross, ed., *Sociological Theory: Inquiries and Paradigms* (New York: Harper & Row, 1963), pp. 328-83.

24. The Kuhnian conception of scientific development emphasizes the conflict between "normal" and "abnormal" or "revolutionary" science and the constant displacement of one paradigm by another. See Thomas S. Kuhn, *The Structure of Scientific Revolutions*, 2nd. ed. (Chicago: University of Chicago Press, 1970, esp. chaps. 1, 12. For a discussion of the application of Kuhnian ideas to the development of political science, see Sheldon Wolin, "Paradigms and Political Theories," in Preston King and B. C. Parekh, eds., *Politics and Experience, Essays Presented to Professor Michael Oakeshott on the Occasion of his Retirement* (Cambridge: At the University Press, 1968), pp. 125-57, and Jerome Stephens, "The Kuhnian Paradigm and Political Inquiry: An Appraisal," *American Journal of Political Science* (hereafter cited as *AJPS*) 17, no. 3 (August 1973): 467-88.

25. Easton, although Canadian-born and educated, has spent his entire career as a political scientist in the United States, although in recent years he has had a joint appointment at the University of Chicago and Queen's University in Kingston, Ontario. McKenzie and King have taught political science at the London School of Economics and University of Essex respectively, and Galbraith and Johnson (recently deceased) have taught economics at Harvard University and the University of Chicago respectively.

26. For example, the problem of constitutional revision, which has been on the political agenda in Canada since the country first sought dominion status in 1926.

27. Ashley, "What is Political Science?" p. 7.

28. Ibid., pp. 7 ff.

29. Ashley spent four years at the University of Toronto before joining the faculty of Harvard University. See Anne Ashley, *William James Ashley, A Life* (London: P. S. King & Son, 1932), p. 40.

30. They included Queen's University, whose department of Philosophy and Political Economy was developed after 1887 largely by Adam Shortt; McGill University, whose department of Political Science was headed by Stephen Leacock after 1901; and the University of Manitoba, which appointed A. B. Clark to its chair of political economy in 1909. See O. D. Skelton, "Fifty Years of Political and Economic Science in Canada," in *The Royal Society of Canada, Fifty Years Retrospect,* Anniversary Volume, 1882-1932 (n.p., n.d.), p. 87. The University of Montreal established a chair in political economy in its Faculty of Law in 1907. See Gustave Lanctot, "Rétrospective d'économie sociale au Canada français, 1882-1932," in the same volume, p. 51. The occupants of these chairs tended to emphasize the economics component of political economy, although some political philosophy, constitutional law, and principles of politics were also taught. See C. B. Macpherson, "On the Study of Politics in Canada," in H. A. Innis, ed., *Essays in Political Economy* (Toronto: University of Toronto Press, 1938), pp. 148-50.

31. Canadian Political Science Association, *Papers and Proceedings of the First Annual Meeting,* Ottawa, September 4-6, 1913 (Kingston, Ont.: Jackson Press, 1913), Introduction, Papers, and Discussions, Aims of the Political Science Association. The first president was Adam Shortt, formerly of Queen's University, then of the Civil Service Commission in Ottawa, James Mavor of the University of Toronto was the first vice-president, O. D. Skelton of Queen's University was secretary-treasurer, and the executive committee included such notables as Stephen Leacock of McGill and Edouard Montpetit of Université de Montréal, A. H. Lefroy, K.C., Toronto, Herbert B. Ames, M.P., Montreal, and President Walter C. Murray, LL.D., Saskatchewan. The opening address was delivered by Prime Minister Robert L. Borden.

32. See Maurice Tremblay and Albert Faucher, "L'Enseignement des Sciences Sociales au Canada de Langue Française," *Royal Commission Studies, A Selection of Essays Prepared for the Royal Commission on National Development in the Arts, Letters and Sciences, 1949-1951* (Ottawa: King's Printer, 1951), pp. 191-203. The first school of social sciences (Ecole des Sciences Sociales, Economiques et Politiques) was actually established at the Université de Montréal in 1920 under the direction of Edouard Montpetit, then a professor in the Law Faculty. However, this institution was not elevated to full university status, since its courses were evening courses and its

students did not require more than a twelfth grade (high school) diploma (p. 193). The School of Social Sciences, Economics and Politics of Laval was the first regular department having three years of full-time studies leading to a B.A., M.A., and eventually a doctoral degree, established under the direction of Père Georges-Henri Lévesque, O.P., in 1938. In 1943 it was transformed into a faculty (p. 197).

33. Macpherson, "Study of Politics," pp. 150 ff. The influence of Bryce, Lowell, Wilson and MacIver on a few courses in comparative government was also increasingly felt after 1920. See also, Annual Calendar of McGill College and University (Montreal: John Lowell & Sons, 1900-1930), McGill Archives, Montreal, Canada.

34. Macpherson, "Study of Politics," pp. 159-60; H. A. Innis, "Obituary: Stephen Butler Leacock (1869-1944)," CJEPS 10 (1944): 219; H. M. D. Clokie, "Canadian Contributions to Political Science," Culture, no. 3 (1942): 472. MacIver arrived in Canada from Oxford in 1915 and taught in Canada until 1927, when he left for Columbia University. He was chairman of the Department of Political Economy at Toronto from 1922 to 1927. His major contributions (written while he was in Canada) were: Community: A Sociological Study (London: Macmillan & Co., 1917, 1920) and The Modern State (London: Oxford University Press, 1926) reprinted five times until 1950.

35. See Canadian Political Science Association, Papers and Proceedings, vol. 2 (Ottawa, Ont., May 1930), Foreword, List of Officers, and Minutes; and the Canadian Political Science Association, List of Members, May 1935, July 1936. See also K. W. Taylor, "The Foundation of the Canadian Political Science Association," CJEPS 33, no. 4 (November 1967): 581-85.

36. See V. W. Bladen, "A Journal is Born: 1935," CJEPS 26, no. 1 (February 1960): 1-5. The journal was the successor of Contributions to Canadian Economics, established by Harold Innis in 1928 and published by the University of Toronto Press.

37. Innis's major contributions to "staple" theory, see note 18 above, were as follows: A History of the Canadian Pacific Railway (1923), The Fur Trade in Canada (1929), and The Cod Fisheries (1940). See also his Political Economy in the Modern State (Toronto: Ryerson Press, 1946), chap. 6. For an assessment of the contribution of staple theory to the Canadian political economy tradition, see Daniel Drache, "Rediscovering Canadian Political Economy," Journal of Canadian Studies 11, no. 3 (August 1976): 3-18, revised and reprinted in Wallace Clement and Daniel Drache, A Practical Guide to Canadian Political Economy (Toronto: James Lorimer & Co., 1978), esp. pp. 9-12. See also Mel Watkins, "The Staple Theory Revisited," unpublished paper, Canadian Political Science Association, May 1976.

38. See for example, Drache, "Rediscovering Canadian Political Economy," pp. 14-32.

39. Most notably, the effort to remove Frank Underhill from his history post at the University of Toronto. See Michael Horn, "The History of Academic Freedom: A Comment," CAUT Bulletin 24, no. 3 (December 1975): 14-15, and Douglas Francis, "The Threatened Dismissal of Frank H. Underhill from the University of Toronto, 1939-1941," CAUT Bulletin 24, no. 3 (December 1975): 16-21.

40. For an excellent description and critical discussion of this school and its adherents, see C. B. Macpherson, "The Social Sciences," in Julian Park, ed., The Culture of Contemporary Canada (Toronto: Ryerson Press, 1957), pp. 208-14.

41. Angus and McKay were regular commissioners, whereas Brady and Corry were commissioned to do special research studies.

42. For example, W. A. Mackintosh of the University of Toronto became acting deputy minister of finance, R. A. MacKay of Dalhousie University joined the Department of External Affairs. Their recruitment by Ottawa followed a time-honored pattern beginning with Adam Shortt in 1908 and including, among others, O. D. Skelton in 1925 and Clifford Clark in 1932.

43. See, for example, E. Parent, "Importance de l'Etude de l'Economie Politique" (Article lu devant l'Institut Canadien à Montréal), La Revue Canadienne 3, no. 86 (24 November 1846).

44. See Jean-Charles Falardeau, The Rise of the Social Sciences in French Canada (Quebec: Department of Cultural Affairs, 1967), chap. 1; Maurice Tremblay and Albert Faucher, "L'Enseignement des Sciences Sociales au Canada de Langue Française," in Royal Commission Studies, A Selection of Essays Prepared for the Royal Commission on National Development in the Arts, Letters and Sciences (Massey Commission), 1949-1951 (Ottawa: King's Printer, 1951), esp. pp. 191-93. The latter study labels the neo-Thomist school "L'école de la doctrine social chrétienne" and dates its impact particularly from the promulgation of the papal encyclical "Rerum Novarum" of Pope Leo XIII in 1891. The school, which was modelled on its Catholic counterpart in France, was firmly institutionalized in 1920 in the form of "Les Semaines Sociales du Canada" (pp. 191-92).

45. See Doris Lussier, "Le père Lévesque, lumière, force et ferment," Le Devoir (16 November 1978): 5.

46. Falardeau, Rise of Social Sciences, chap. 3. See also Jean-Charles Falardeau, "Social Sciences in French-speaking Quebec: Their Emergence and Evolution" (Paper delivered to the CPSA, Fredericton, New Brunswick, 1978), pp. 7 ff. The failure to establish separate departments or positions of political science at this stage had the unfortunate effect of retarding the growth of political science in French Canada even longer than the other social sciences.

47. One possible exception was Eugene Forsey, whose radical views and political activities may have generated official animosities which influenced his later decision to vacate his lectureship in political science at McGill University. Ironically, Underhill, Scott, and Forsey all adopted much more conservative ideological stances in their later years.

48. See Adam Shortt and Arthur G. Doughty, eds., Canada and Its Provinces (Toronto: Glasgow, Brook and Company, 1914-17), a 23-volume series on economic, social, and political problems published between 1914 and 1917. Among its principal contributors were such prominent early Canadian social scientists as O. D. Skelton, R. H. Coats, James Mavor, and A. B. Clark.

49. Robin Neill, *A New Theory of Value* (Toronto: University of Toronto Press, 1973), pp. 9 ff. Although influenced by Veblen and the Marxists, Innis did not adopt their ideological or theoretical perspectives.

50. Ibid., p. 39, n. 5. They included James Mavor, C. R. Fay, G. E. Jackson, and W. A. Mackintosh.

51. For example, in addition to the edited collection by Adam Shortt et al. cited n. 48 above, see Alexander Brady, *Canada* (Toronto: Macmillan of Canada, 1932); Edras Minville, ed., *Notre Milieu: Aperçu général sur la province de Québec* (Montreal: Editions Fides, 1942).

52. Most notably, the early public administration studies by R. MacGregor Dawson, *The Principle of Official Independence* (London: P. S. King, 1922) and *The Civil Service of Canada* (London: Oxford University Press, 1929).

53. For example, P. E. Corbett and H. A. Smith, *Canada and World Politics,* a study of the constitution and international relations of the British Empire (London: Faber & Gwyer, 1928) and J. T. P. Humphrey, *The Inter-American System: A Canadian View,* issued under the auspices of the Canadian Institute of International Affairs (Toronto: Macmillan Co., 1942), both essentially international law studies, and X. A. MacKay and E. B. Rogers, *Canada Looks Abroad* (London: Oxford University Press, 1938).

54. See, for example, Canadian Political Science Association, Annual Meeting, 1930-1934, *Papers and Proceedings* and *Canadian Journal of Economics and Political Science* (CJEPS) 1-11 (1935-1945).

55. An excellent example of these early efforts to provide this kind of information is Dawson, ed., *Constitutional Issues in Canada, 1900-1931* (London: Oxford University Press, 1933).

56. Dawson's books, in addition to *Constitutional Issues in Canada* (1933) (cited in note 55 above), included: *Official Independence* (1922), *The Development of Dominion Status, 1900-1936* (New York: Oxford University Press, 1937), *Government of Canada* (1947, 1st ed., revised by Dawson and Norman Ward in later editions), *Civil Service of Canada* (1929) (cited in note 52 above). His articles were published primarily in *Contributions to Canadian Economics* (prior to 1935) and in the *Canadian Journal of Economics and Political Science* (*CJEPS*) after 1935. He acted as a one-man commission in Nova Scotia investigating civil service reform. (See, Nova Scotia Royal Commission on Provincial Development and Rehabilitation, *Report on the Civil Service* (Halifax: King's Printer, 1944), as cited in A. Paul Pross and V. Seymour Wilson, "Graduate Education in Canadian Public Administration" cited above. Among the monographs on provincial governments which he fostered, all published by the University of Toronto Press, were: Frank MacKinnon, *The Government of Prince Edward Island* (1951), J. Murray Beck, *The Government of Nova Scotia* (1957), M. S. Donnelly, *The Government of Manitoba* (1963). See David E. Smith, "Provincial Government and Politics" (prepared for M. Stein, J. Trent and A. Donneur, eds., "*Aspects,*" p. 9). On Dawson's general influence, see J. H. Aitchison, ed., *The Political Process in Canada: Essays in Honour of R. MacGregor Dawson* (Toronto: University of Toronto Press, 1963), preface.

57. For example, see Macpherson, "Social Sciences," esp. pp. 210-11, and C. B. Macpherson, "After Strange Gods: Canadian Political Science 1973," in T. N. Guinsburg and G. L. Reuber, eds., *Perspectives on the Social Sciences* (Toronto: University of Toronto Press, 1974), esp. pp. 65-66.

58. C. B. Macpherson in "L'Enseignement de la Science Politique au Canada," *Revue Française de Science Politique* 4 (April-June 1954): 2 estimates the number of full-time university instructors of political science at 25 (p. 390). The number of academic political scientists had risen to 184 in 1965-1966 and to 517 in 1971. See R. R. March and R. J. Jackson, "Aspects of the State of Political Science in Canada," *Midwest Journal of Political Science* 11, no. 4 (November 1967): 435, and W. H. N. Hull, "The 1971 Survey of the Profession," *Canadian Journal of Political Science* (*CJPS*) 6, no. 1 (March 1973): 90.

59. See, for example, Cairns, "Americanization Issue," pp. 213 ff.

60. David Easton, *A Framework for Political Analysis* (Englewood Cliffs, N.J.: Prentice-Hall, 1965), p. 4. See also David Easton, "The Current Meaning of Behavioralism," in James C. Charlesworth, ed., *Contemporary Political Analysis* (New York: Free Press; London: Collier-Macmillan, 1967), pp. 13-16, and Robert A. Dahl, "The Behavioral Approach in Political Science: Epitaph for a Monument to a Successful Protest," *APSR* 55 (December 1961): 766. Easton uses the term "intellectual tendency," Dahl speaks of a "mood."

61. On the main tenets of behavioralism, see Albert Somit and Joseph Tanenhaus, *The Development of America Political Science: From Burgess to Behavioralism* (Boston: Allyn and Bacon, 1967), pp. 176-80. See also Easton, "Behavioralism," pp. 16-18.

62. See, for example, Macpherson, "Science Politique," pp. 394-95. Among the important pre- and immediate post-World War II contributions in these fields were: in comparative politics, Alexander Brady, *Democracy in the Dominions: A Comparative Study in Institutions* (Toronto: University of Toronto Press, 1947) (republished in later, revised editions in 1952 and 1958), and J. A. Corry, *Democratic Government and Politics* (Toronto: University of Toronto Press, 1946) (also revised in 1951 and later in collaboration with J. E. Hodgetts) in international politics, the three titles cited in note 53 above, and in public administration, the two books by MacGregor Dawson cited in note 52 above.

63. In fact, an emphasis on interdisciplinary studies was supposed to be a major tenet of behavioralists. On this point, see Somit and Tanenhaus, *American Political Science,* p. 179.

64. An important early force in this respect was the Canadian Institute of International Affairs, an organization encompassing academics specializing in international affairs, diplomats, and journalists. From its inception, it actively promoted studies in Canadian foreign policy and Canadian-American relations. Several of the early Canadian contributions to international relations were published under its auspices. See also Naomi Black, "Notes for a Future History: Canadian Contributions to the Study of International Relations" (prepared for M. Stein, J. Trent, and A. Donneur, eds., "*Aspects,*" esp. part 2).

65. John Meisel, "Religious Affiliation and Electoral Behavior: A Case Study," *CJEPS* 22 (1956): 481-95.

66. Meisel, *Election of 1957* (cited in n. 17 above). For a detailed list of these early voting studies, see Donald V. Smiley, "Contributions to Canadian Political Science Since the Second World War," *CJEPS*, 23, no. 4 (November 1967): 571-72.

67. Among their more notable intellectual contributions in this respect were: Jean Laponce, *People vs. Politics: A Study of Opinions, Attitudes and Perceptions in Vancouver-Burrard* (Toronto: University of Toronto Press, 1969); Fred Engelmann and Mildred Schwartz, *Political Parties and the Canadian Social Structure* (Scarborough: Prentice-Hall, 1967); Mildred Schwartz, *Public Opinion and Canadian Identity* (Berkeley: University of California Press, 1967); Dion, *Société et politique,* and *Le Bill 60 et la Société Québécoise* (Montreal: Hurtubise HMH, 1967), and numerous articles by Lemieux on electoral sociology in Quebec. Their influence over colleagues and students within their universities, the Canadian Political Science Association and the *Canadian Journal of Political Science* was even more important.

68. It would be impossible to cover such a large list in the limited space available here. For useful bibliographies on these topics, see Van Loon and Whittington, *Canadian Political System,* 2d ed. (Toronto: McGraw-Hill Ryerson, 1976), pp. 527-36, 538-41; Paul Fox, ed, *Politics: Canada* (Toronto: McGraw-Hill Ryerson, 1977), pp. 222-26, 275-85, 313-14, 350-54; and O. M. Kruhlak, Richard Schultz, and S. I. Pobihushchy, eds., *The Canadian Political Process,* rev. ed. (Toronto: Holt, Rinehart and Winston, 1973), pp. 517-23.

69. For example, see Allan Kornberg, *Canadian Legislative Behavior: A Study of the 25th Parliament* (New York: Holt, Rinehart and Winston, 1967), and S. R. Peck, "A Behavioral Approach to the Judicial Process: Scalogram Analysis," *Osgoode Hall Law Journal* 1 (April 1967).

70. The Canadian Political Science Association initially included political scientists, economists, sociologists, anthropologists under its umbrella. The sociologists and anthropologists withdrew from the association and established their own organization, the Canadian Association of Sociologists and Anthropologists (CASA) in the early 1960s. The political scientists and economists continued to operate autonomously within the same association and to publish a joint journal until 1968, when two separate associations, the Canadian Political Science Association and the Canadian Economics Association, were founded, and two journals, the *Canadian Journal of Political Science* (CJPS) and the *Canadian Journal of Economics* (CJE), were created.

71. The early presidents of the new association included Henry Mayo (1968-69), Donald Smiley (1969-70), Douglas Verney (1970-71), Gilles Lalande (1971-72), J. E. Hodgetts (1972-73), Jean Laponce (1973-74), John Meisel (1974-75), and Léon Dion (1975-76). The secretary-treasurer during those years was John Trent. The joint editors of the journal were initially Léon Dion and John Meisel (1968-71) and subsequently Vincent Lemieux and David Hoffman (1971-74).

72. On the contribution of political and social scientists to the Royal Commission on Bilingualism and Biculturalism since World War II, see also Smiley, "Contributions to Canadian Political Science," pp. 573-74.

73. See Falardeau, *Rise of the Social Sciences*, chap. 3. The first full-time political scientist was Léon Dion, who was retained by Père Lévesque in 1951.

74. On the contribution of (francophone) political and social scientists to the Tremblay Commission, see Jean-Charles Bonenfant, "Les Etudes Politiques," in Fernand Dumont and Yves Martin, eds., *Situation de la recherche sur le Canada français* (Quebec: Les Presses de L'Université Laval, 1962), pp. 76, 78, and François-Pierre Gingras, "L'essor des études politiques au Canada français," unpublished paper, *CPSA,* 1976, p. 10. The principal contributors (anonymously) to volume 2 on constitutional problems were Edras Minville and Père R. P. Arès on the state and on federalism. François-Albert Angers also wrote one of the annexes to the *Report* on *La centralisation et les relations fédérales-provinciales.* Bonenfant himself served as librarian and archivist. Minville and Angers were political economists, and Arès was (principally) a sociologist. The commission was largely manned by lawyers and businessmen, and unlike the Rowell-Sirois Commission and the B&B commission, the number of social science specialists was not large.

75. For a list of some of the more important French-language studies of this period (1960-76) see Gingras, "L'essor des études politiques," pp. 5 ff. On voting behavior studies, the numerous articles by Vincent Lemieux in *Recherches Sociographiques* and the *Canadian Journal of Political Science Revue Canadienne de Science politique* deserve special mention; on interest-group theory and application, the previously cited works by Léon Dion, *Société et Politique* and *Le Bill 60 et la Société Québécoise* are most noteworthy; on elites, see the articles in Richard Desrosiers, ed., *Le Personnel Politique Québécoise* (Montreal: Les Editions du Boreal Express, 1972) by Falardeau, Bonenfant, Boily, and Bourassai; on political parties and movements, see the articles by Lemieux, the collection edited by Réjean Pelletier on *Les Partis Politiques au Quebec* (Montreal: Hurtubise HMH, 1976), and Vera Murray, *Le Parti Québécois: de la fondation à la prise du pouvoir* (Montreal: Hurtubise HMH, 1976).

76. Most important in this respect were Léon Dion and Gérard Bergeron.

77. For example, by Easton and Dahl in "Behavioral Approach," p. 770. Dahl uses the term "revolt" rather than "revolution," but the implications are the same.

78. Smiley, "Miniature Replica?" p. 39.

79. See David Easton, "The New Revolution in Political Science," *ASPR* 63, no. 4 (December 1969): 1051-61. See also Theodore Lowi, *The End of Liberalism, Ideology, Policy and the Crisis of Public Authority* (New York: W. W. Norton & Co., 1969), esp. chap. 3, and Kenneth Dolbeare, "Public Policy Analysis and the Coming Struggle for the Soul of the Postbehavioral Revolution," in P. Green and S. Levinson, eds., *Power and Community: Dissenting Essays in Political Science* (New York: Random House, 1970), pp. 85-111.

80. For example, see David Falcone and Michael Whittington, "Output Change in Canada: A Preliminary Attempt to Open the 'Black Box'," unpublished paper, CPSA, 1972.

81. See, for example, Richard Simeon, "Studying Public Policy," *CJPS* 9, no. 4 (December 1976): 548.

82. Ryerson was the leading Marxist theoretician of the Communist party of Canada for many years. In recent years he has taught Canadian history at the Université de Québec à Montréal (UQAM). Among his writings, see *The Founding of Canada*, 2d ed. (Toronto: Progress Books, 1960, 1975) and *Unequal Union: Confederation and the Roots of Conflict in the Canadas, 1815-1873* (Toronto: Progress Books, 1968).

83. A somewhat different list is provided by Philip Resnick in "Towards a Class Analysis of Canada," unpublished paper, CPSA, 1972. He argues that "the works of contemporary Marxist and neo-Marxist writers, e.g., Baran and Sweezy's *Monopoly Capital*, Gunder Frank's *Development and Underdevelopment in Latin America*, Ralph Miliband's *The State in Capitalist Society*, André Gorz's *Strategy for Labour*, Sartre's *Search for a Method*, as well as the classics of revolutionary theory from Marx through Lenin, Luxemburg, Gramsci, Lukacs, Trotsky and Mao . . . provide valuable guidelines for a radical Canadian and Quebec social and political theory" (p. 3).

84. Ibid., pp. 1-2. See also pp. 4 ff.

85. Levitt, *Silent Surrender;* Abe Rotstein, *The Precarious Homestead: Essays on Economics, Technology and Nationalism* (Toronto: New Press, 1973), and *Getting it Back: A Program for Canadian Independence* (Toronto: Clarke Irwin, 1974); Robert Laxer, ed., *(Canada) Limited: The Political Economy of Dependency* (Toronto: McClelland & Stewart, 1973); Mathews and Steele, *Struggle;* Lumsden, *49th Parallel*.

86. See Resnick, "Class Analysis," pp. 9-15; Drache, "Rediscovering Canadian Political Economy."

87. See in particular the publications of Monthly Review Press, the *New Left Review, Socialist Register,* etc.

88. For example, Drache, "Rediscovering Canadian Political Economy," pp. 3-18, cited in note 37 above; Garth Stevenson, "Foreign Direct Investment and the Provinces: A Study of Elite Attitudes," *CJPS* 7, no. 4 (December 1974): 630-47; Wallace Clement, "The Changing Structure of the Canadian Economy," *Canadian Review of Sociology and Anthropology* (Special Summer Issue 1974): 3-27.

89. Panitch, *The Canadian State*. Among the better-known contributors to this important collection are: Reg Whitaker, Garth Stevenson, Henry Milner, Larry Pratt, Riane Mahon, Wallace Clement, and Dennis Olsen.

90. Clement and Drache, *A Practical Guide,* pp. 55-174.

91. They are: in comparative politics, *The Journal of Comparative Political Economy* (initiated in 1979) and in political theory, *The Canadian Journal of Political and Social Theory* (launched in 1977).

92. See John Meisel, "A Classic Dilemma," *Canadian Forum* (May 1979): 15-17.

93. See for example, Peter Katzenstein, ed., *Between Power and Plenty: Foreign Economic Policies of Advanced Industrial States,* special issue of *International Organization* 31, no. 4 (Autumn 1977); James R. Kurth, "The Political Consequences of the Product Cycle: Industrial History and Comparative Politics," *International Organization* 33, no. 1 (Winter 1979): 1-34; and for an excellent overall review of this literature, Peter Gourevitch, "The Second Image Reversed: The International Sources of Domestic Politics," *International Organization* 32, no. 4 (Autumn 1978): 881-911.

94. A somewhat similar perspective is adopted by Reginald Whitaker in his article, "Confused Alarms of Struggle and Flight: English-Canadian Political Science in the 1970s," *Canadian Historical Review* 60, no. 1 (March 1979): 1-18. However, he sees "the tendency today in political science faculties . . . of letting a thousand flowers bloom," and "the gains in tolerance and civility" arising therefrom as being largely a current rather than an historical phenomenon in the discipline (p. 9).

Bibliography

Bonenfant, Jean Charles. "Les Etudes Politiques." In *Situation de la recherche sur le Canada français,* edited by Fernand Dumont et Yves Martin. Quebec: Les Presses de l'Université Laval, 1962, pp. 75-82.

Bourinot, John George. "The Study of Political Science in Canadian Universities." *Proceedings and Transactions of the Royal Society of Canada for the Year 1889.* Vol. 7. Montreal, 1890.

Cairns, Alan C. "Alternative Styles in the Study of Canadian Politics." *Canadian Journal of Political Science* (hereafter cited as *CJPS*) 8, no. 1 (March 1974): 101-28 and comments by Ward, Mallory, Van Loon, and Whittington.

―――. "National Influences on the Study of Politics." *Queen's Quarterly* 81, no. 3 (Autumn 1974): 333-47.

―――. "Political Science in Canada and the Americanization Issue." *CJPS* 8, no. 2 (June 1975): 191-234.

Dawson, R. M. "Political Science Teaching in Canada" (a report to the Social Science Research Council, 1950). Reprinted in *Newsletter,* Canadian Political Science Association 2, no. 4 (March 1973).

Falardeau, Jean-Charles. *The Rise of the Social Sciences in French Canada.* Montreal, 1967, 67 pp. (*L'Essor des Sciences Sociales au Canada Français.* Quebec: Ministere des Affaires Culturelles, 1964).

Faucher, Albert. "La recherche des sciences sociales au Quebec: sa condition universitaire." In *The Social Sciences in Canada: Two Studies,* edited by Mabel F. Timlin and Albert Faucher. Ottawa, 1968.

Hodgetts, J. E. "Canadian Political Science: A Hybrid with a Future?" In *Scholarship in Canada, 1967: Achievement and Outlook,* edited by R. H. Hubbard. Toronto, 1968.

Hull, W. H. N. "The 1971 Survey of the Profession." *CJPS* 6, no. 1 (March 1973): 89-95.

Keirstead, B. S., and Watkins, F. M. "Political Science on Canada: Survey of Methods, Research and Teaching." Paris, 1950, pp. 171-77.

Kornberg, Allan, and Thorp, Alan. "The American Impact on Canadian Political Science and Sociology." In *The Influence of the United States on Canadian Development: Eleven Case Studies,* edited by Richard H. Preston. Durham: Duke University Press, 1972, pp. 55-98.

Lemieux, Vincent. "Les etudes avancées de Science politique dans les departments francophones" (Rapport commandité par la Commission Healy de concert avec la Société Canadienne de Science politique, Quebec) (February 1978).

Macpherson, C. B. "After Strange Gods: Canadian Political Science, 1973." In *Perspectives on Social Sciences in Canada,* edited by T. N. Guinsberg and G. C. Reuber. Toronto: University of Toronto Press, 1974.

―――. "On the Study of Politics in Canada." In *Essays in Political Economy,* edited by H. A. Innis. Toronto: University of Toronto Press, 1938, pp. 147-65.

March, R. R., and Jackson, R. J. "Aspects of the State of Political Science in Canada." *Midwest Journal of Political Science* 11, no. 4 (November 1967).

Skelton, O. D. "Fifty Years of Political and Economic Science in Canada." In *Fifty Years Retrospect* of the Royal Society of Canada, Anniversary Volume, 1882-1932. Ottawa: Royal Society of Canada, pp. 85-90.

Smiley, D. V. "Contributions to Canadian Political Science since the Second World War." *CJEPS* 33, no. 4 (November 1967).

Taylor, K. W. "The Foundation of the Canadian Political Science Association." *CJEPS* 33, no. 4 (November 1967): 581-85.

Wood, Ellen, and Wood, Neal. "Canada and the American Science of Politics." In *Close the 49th Parallel: The Americanization of Canada,* edited by Ian Lumsden. Toronto, 1970.

DENMARK

11

PETER NANNESTAD and ØYSTEIN GAASHOLT*

Introduction

The history of political science as an academic discipline *sui generis* in Denmark is rather short, both when measured by years and when compared to other countries with which Denmark shares important historical, cultural, and intellectual traits. Established as an independent study in 1958 at the University of Aarhus—at that time the younger and smaller of the existing Danish universities—Danish political science can look back at barely twenty years of existence.[1]

Not only did political science get off to a relatively late start in Denmark. Also, it had to start almost from scratch. An academic tradition from which the discipline could branch out in an evolutionary fashion simply did not exist. A deliberate creative effort was required.[2] Thus, political science is both a *young* and a *new* member of the Danish academic universe. This provides one important clue to the understanding of the state and shape of the discipline in Denmark as it appears to the observer today.

Another important clue to such an understanding is provided by the nature of the academic universe into which political science was introduced in 1958. One important feature of this universe is the tension—sometimes latent, sometimes manifest—which exists between influences from a Continental, especially German, tradition and from an Anglo-American tradition of thought, first and foremost in the humanities and the social sciences. At the most abstract level, this tension is expressed in rationalism versus empiricism, holistic theoretical systems versus partial theory, and a deductive versus inductive method. At the more concrete level, it is expressed in a "soft" approach to positive social science, leaning toward the humanities, versus a "hard" approach modeled after the natural sciences. We shall postulate that this tension is one of the main factors behind the conceptual and methodological diversification which—despite the limited size of its "scientific community"[3]—is a central characteristic of Danish political science, and that the tension between two traditions of thought also has enabled the discipline to keep away both from the Scylla of naive empiricism and the Charybdis of metaphysical speculation.[4]

The following overview will be divided into four parts, each covering an important aspect of political science as an organized academic activity. In the first part, an attempt will be made to draw up a rough map of the intellectual landscape of Danish political science and its main currents by describing some discernible lines of development. Against this background, an account will be given in parts two and three of the discipline's two central activities, teaching and research. In the final part, we shall examine briefly some aspects of the ever-changing relationship between Danish politics and Danish political science and the impact of this relationship on the development of the discipline.

The short time span of this overview of Danish political science implies that the wisdom of hindsight is not available to sift the materials and decide which contributions are profound and lasting in importance as opposed to surface squibbles or expressions of passing fads. The vagueness of the discipline's boundaries, which in Denmark by no means are congruent with institutional divisions and arrangements and which at the same time are impossible to draw according to content-based criteria, tends to reinforce these problems. It follows that the picture drawn in the following cannot claim to be purely

---

*Several of our colleagues have commented upon an earlier draft of this paper, written by the present senior author. Especially we would like to thank Ib Faurby, Martin O. Heisler, and Erik Rasmussen for their helpful remarks and criticisms.

descriptive—not to say objective—but also will and must reflect the authors' personal judgment.

The Intellectual Structure of the Discipline

In retrospect, we may speak of three main phases in the development of Danish political science, each of which has contributed to the theoretical currents discernible today. The first of these was the phase of identity formation. This phase was characterized by efforts to establish political science as an autonomous field of study, complete with its own conceptual tools and areas of knowledge—however embryonic. The second phase was the phase of consolidation: based on the foundations laid in the preceding phase, an expansion in research activities began to bridge the gaps in theoretical and empirical knowledge which had been so conspicuous in the infancy of the discipline. The last phase was a period of uproar, characterized by attempts to tear down some of the bridges which had been constructed and to erect others in their place.[5]

The main emphasis in this identification of phases in the development of Danish political science is on content rather than the chronology. From a purely chronological point of view, the phases overlap to a considerable degree. This is especially true of the two last phases, which almost coincide in time.

THE PHASE OF IDENTITY FORMATION

The task confronting the two scholars who were appointed in 1959 to the first chairs in political science was formidable: nothing less than to establish a brand new scientific subject without resort to any usable paradigm in the Danish academic universe, past or present. Both men were distinguished scholars. Neither was a political scientist: Poul Meyer had a background in law and was an expert in public administration, while Erik Rasmussen was an historian known for his work on, among other topics, Danish parliamentarism.

The first and overshadowing problem with which the "founding fathers" had to cope thus became the delimitation and identification of the proper scope of the new subject. Obviously, this involved the dual task of establishing a conceptual framework within which the relevant objects of the new study could be defined and connected theoretically, and formulating a method, in the broad sense of the term, based on an understanding of metatheoretical and philosophical foundations.

From the very beginning, there appears to have been remarkably little doubt that political science should not be allowed to degenerate into an appendix to history or into some kind of study of constitutional law, or into some kind of constitutional history, but should develop into a social science with its own identity, and, moreover, a social science rooted firmly in empirics as well as theory. This placed an additional constraint on the search for a suitable conceptual framework for the new subject: The merits of any such framework inevitably would have to be measured by its ability to encompass the realities of Danish political life.

It hardly is surprising that, under these circumstances, trends in American political science became highly influential. Perhaps the single most important sources of influence in the phase of identity formation in Danish political science were the methodological writings of Arnold Brecht[6] and the conceptual schemes presented by David Easton.[7] Within a very short time the main tenets of value relativism and intersubjective transmittable knowledge, and the notions of the authoritative allocation of values and of the political system, became firmly established as metascientific and conceptual conventions—not to say shibboleths—of the emerging Danish political science, receiving near-universal lip service. By the early 1960s, then, Danish political science had acquired at least the basic vocabulary of a discipline with an autonomous identity.

This quick and early adoption of the thoughts of Brecht and Easton as the cornerstone of the discipline raises two questions: What qualities in these thoughts made them attractive to the emerging discipline, and what were the consequences of their implantation into Danish political science? We shall not pretend to be able to answer these questions in full, but shall suggest some directions to go in seeking answers. With regard to the first question, it may be pointed out that the metascientific writings of Brecht did fit the prevailing philosophical mood and doctrines in Danish universities remarkably well. The dominating view of scientific method was British-American or neopositivist in orientation and had been for quite a while.[8] The influence from other continental schools of metascience, for instance hermeneutics, was much weaker in comparison. As far as the special attractiveness of Easton's writings was concerned, contemporary discussions indicate that it owed much to the definition of "politics."[9] This definition was the only one in rather widespread use which could be interpreted—at least until *Systems Analysis* appeared in 1965[10]—to imply a delimitation of politics from nonpolitics without reference to formal institutions of the state. Given the peculiarities of Danish political life, and especially the "corporatist" interplay of state institutions and interest organizations in the regulation of the labor market, any attempt to link the definition of politics to institutions of the state clearly must have appeared unrewarding in the Danish setting. By avoiding just this, the Eastonian definition seemingly was made to order.

The influence of the Eastonian framework appears less clear. But it may be pointed out that only a very limited part, if any, of the problems taken up and projects undertaken in Danish political research was derived directly from the Eastonian framework or linked to it in unequivocal ways. Moreover, the development of Danish political research, the problem areas taken up, and the priorities assigned to them, do not differ radically from the developments where Eastonian viewpoints did not find the same "official" adherence. This may in part be attributed to the generality, not to say vagueness, of the Eastonian framework. This vagueness was reinforced by a watering down of some key notions which accompanied the introduction of the framework to Danish political science. For one, the aspect-view often disappeared from sight, making the concept of the political system just a loose and convenient frame for the description and analysis of political institutions. Secondly, the system-persistence orientation which became especially visible in Easton's 1965 work normally was given only very limited attention. Thus, the Eastonian framework in the Danish setting was transformed into an unrestrictive umbrella under which scholars with widely different interests and viewpoints could pursue their research interests.

But if this view of the very limited *direct* influence of the Eastonian framework on Danish political research is tenable, it must, on the other hand, be admitted that the early adoption of the framework had a crucial *indirect* influence. By virtue of the very latitude of Easton's systems theory, it did not lead the emerging discipline into a cul-de-sac and did not preclude certain approaches and lines of inquiry. On the contrary, it opened wide possibilities for operating with various middle-range theories and viewpoints in most subareas of political research. This fact, taken together with the "psychological" shibboleth-role of the Eastonian framework in the phase of identity formation, may lead to the paradoxical conclusion that Easton's work had considerable influence on Danish political science, but negligible influence on Danish political research.

Lazarsfeld has pointed out that the task of "throwing bridges" implies that the main emphasis is placed on macrophenomena. This certainly holds true for Danish political science in the phase of identity formation. Phenomena at the aggregate level, such as parties[11] or the administration,[12] rather than the behavior of individuals, were made the main subjects of the first monographs produced by Danish political scientists.[13] Although, as we shall see, smaller units and lower levels of analysis by no means have been ignored, this emphasis on macrophenomena continues to represent an important trend within the discipline in Denmark.

THE PHASE OF CONSOLIDATION

The phase of consolidation, following the initial and tentative identity formation of the discipline, may be characterized by three main tendencies. First, the interest in discussing general theories, overarching theoretical frameworks, and metatheoretical issues in general, which had been so typical of the previous phase, clearly declined. The set of assumptions identified in the course of these earlier discussions now became more or less taken for granted, and the need to legitimize particular research problems and methods by the invocation of higher authorities such as Brecht and Easton was less and less urgent. Instead, middle-range theories were resorted to increasingly.

Secondly, this phase shows a growing interest in microphenomena and a turn away from the interest in political institutions per se. Stein Rokkan has noted that "the break-through toward a 'new science of politics' invariably occurred at the lowest level of the system, at the level of the 'unit citizen' defined in electoral law."[14] In accordance with that view, the shift in focus from institutions to individuals was set in motion by Danish electoral research.[15] As time went by, even subfields most often found resistant to the behavioral persuasion, as for instance the study of public administration[16] and foreign policy,[17] began reporting research on relevant aspects of individual behavior.

Finally, this phase is characterized by the increasing methodological and technical sophistication of the projects undertaken, bolstered by the easier access for scholars in the social sciences to computers and software,[18] and by the greater availability of government grants to finance large-scale and ambitious projects.[19]

In short, then, the phase of consolidation and beginning "gap-filling" in Danish political science was marked by a swing of the discipline as a whole[20] in a more wholeheartedly behavioral direction, as clearly witnessed by the bulk of projects and reports which originated in the late 1960s and early 1970s. Thus, a behavioral current emerged from this phase. Later developments within the discipline, most notably the Marxian challenge to the established political science, have by no means superseded this current,[21] although—as shall be seen—they have influenced it in several ways.

Much of the work within the behavioral current in Danish political science is, paradoxical as it may sound, at the same time both theoretical and atheoretical. It is theoretical in the sense that it relies on some fairly specific—albeit often implicit—theoretical foundation: A middle-range theory, model or framework, usually of American origin. This kind of relationship to theory has been referred to as "theory consuming,"[22] which is to say that the investigator draws on "established" theory for purposes of variable selection and explanation, as opposed to questioning and testing the theoretical notions with an eye to theory modification or theory building. This work is, therefore, atheoretical in the sense that it does not address itself to theoretical problems per se in efforts to change or construct theory. The Danish election studies mentioned above provide one example. These studies of the first national elections held in the 1970s were planned as nationwide sample surveys, including a three-wave panel.[23] The model which guided the planning and execution of the project clearly was borrowed from the Michigan SRC election studies, and their underlying social-psychological framework was thus imported to serve as the framework for Danish voting behavior research as well. The research group behind the Danish election studies gathered invaluable data, especially on the landslide election of 1973, and issued highly important reports.[24] Nowhere in these reports, however, do we find a discussion of the theoretical foundations upon which the work is based, not to say a discussion of the merits of the "Michigan model" vis-à-vis competing models of electoral behavior, such as rational-choice models.[25]

All in all, then, Danish political scientists whose works fall within the behavioral current have exhibited an astonishing degree of reluctance when it comes to theorizing, be it in proposing new conceptual models or in filling the gap between data and conclusions. Although we may be accused of betting after the race, we shall use an example from the research area of interest intermediation in the Danish political system as an illustration. Since World War I, the close interplay between interest organizations and institutions of the state in arriving at and executing political decisions in many fields has been a central feature of Danish politics. It is not an exaggeration to say that the growth in number of committees, steering boards, and so on—traditionally the vehicles for this kind of cooperation—has been explosive. This trend has been noticed and pointed to many times as an important empirical characteristic of the Danish political system. Nevertheless, and somewhat surprisingly, it took an article by Schmitter[26] to alert Danish political science to explore the possibilities contained in the notion of corporatism and the theoretical developments surrounding this notion.[27]

THE PHASE OF UPROAR

Like most other Western countries, starting in the late 1960s Denmark experienced a time of student unrest. Compared to what happened elsewhere, it was not particularly terrifying; one observer has, not unjustifiably, characterized it as decidedly a media event.[28]

The unrest constituted a two-pronged attack on the academic status quo. The main target was the power structure in the universities in which the incumbents of professorial chairs had the authority to make all important decisions, to the total exclusion of younger faculty members and students. Not surprisingly, therefore, the main carriers of the attack were the student organizations and a number of junior faculty members. One result was the University Act of 1970, which created an elaborate decision-making structure granting various degrees of influence to groups that had been virtually without formal power previously.[29]

The second target of the attack, especially in the humanities and the social sciences, was the curricula of the studies and thus—in a wider perspective—the direction taken by the disciplines. In political science, the attack was directed against what was somewhat vaguely called positivist tendencies. The themes were familiar: value relativism was denounced as a hollow and cowardly attitude, if not simply a cover for sheer conservatism, and most of the research conducted, especially in the behavioral current of the discipline, was castigated for its lack of relevance to the "real" social and political problems in the national and international settings. Again, this attack was borne mainly by the student organizations and some of the younger staff. In retrospect, then, the initial stages of the revolts in American and Danish political science look very much alike. The tenor of the criticism directed at "the establishment" was "radical" in the special American sense of this term. The authorities were Marcuse, Adorno, and Habermas rather than Marx, Lenin, and Mao and the demand was for a political science modelled after the continental tradition of thought or, at least, with more room for critical reflection. But quite soon, in the early 1970s, the course of developments in Denmark took a different direction. While it appears that in American political science much of the revolt was absorbed by "the establishment" of the discipline, in a process of conceptual and organizational integration,[30] marking the transition from behavioralism to postbehavioralism, the events in Denmark rapidly moved toward a polarization of the discipline. What had begun as a "radical" criticism of Danish political science became in the course of a few years firmly and explicitly Marxian, and the tenor of the debate followed suit. From being a criticism of weaknesses and aberrations in the "established" praxis of the discipline, it changed into a claim for the superiority of Marxism in understanding not only politics but society as a whole. Hence a Marxist current developed in Danish political science alongside the ruling behavioralist one. While the latter continued to dominate the faculty, or at least kept a balance of power in the institutes of the universities of Copenhagen, Aarhus, and Odense, the former quickly won the upper hand at the newly established university centers of Roskilde and Aalborg. Among the students, on the other hand, Marxism claimed the majority almost everywhere. Even in the predominantly non-Marxian institutes, consequently, Marxism became a force that had to be reckoned with. Obviously, the potential for conflict was great, perhaps not the least because the University Act provided ample opportunity for fighting power struggles under the guise of theoretical and methodological disagreements. While the lines of the most violent internal battles were typically drawn between faculty and students, it would be less than truthful to say that the opposing interests of Marxian and non-Marxian faculty members were always resolved in a cordial fashion and to the mutual satisfaction of both factions. In fact, one might be tempted to describe the situation as characterized by growing alienation and breakdown in communications: people learned to walk quietly in the halls and avoid confrontations.

One positive, substantive effect which the Marxian faction had on Danish political science as a whole during this period was a renewed interest in the role and functions of the state in modern society. While the series of political and economic crises facing the country after 1973 doubtless contributed to this interest, Marxian theory definitely deserves credit for its role in bringing political institutions back to the center of the stage in political science research.

The Marxian challenge is, however, by no means monolithic. Political scientists working within a Marxian framework usually profess their adherence to one of the three dominant schools of thought within Danish university Marxism: the capital-logical school, heavily dependent on German work; the structural school of Althusser and Balibar; and the Stamokap-school inspired by the ideological work of the official communist parties. Of these, the capital-logical school, by far the most abstract and antiempirical of the three, has been dominant until now.[31] But quite recently the capital-logical school appears to have lost ground in favor of the other two somewhat less doctrinaire schools of thought. Perhaps partly as a result of this development within the Marxian camp, Marxian and non-Marxian political scientists have slowly begun to emerge from the trenches and to enter into a constructive dialogue with one another. Still, Marxists tend to claim that the logical consistency and inclusive nature of their framework makes it superior, whereas non-Marxists, on the other hand, tend to point toward the deficiencies of Marxism with regard to empirical testability and methodological rigor. The fact is, of course, that each side stands to profit greatly by the insights offered by the other. As has often been noted, liberal social science in general, and behavioral political science in particular, frequently are guilty of fragmenting the object of study into manageable parts and isolating them from the context of culture and history.[32] The holistic nature of the Marxian approach doubtless provides a useful corrective to this tendency, calling attention to forces in human society which liberal social scientists have failed to take into consideration.[33] On the other hand, Marxian social scientists—at any rate those who orient their work toward the analysis of existing societies—stand to learn from the empirical method and more inductive mode of thought favored by non-Marxists. Indications are that Danish political science just now is entering into a period where such a mutual learning process is possible, and, indeed, has begun.

The Teaching of Political Science

Throughout most of its existence, the structure and content of the academic study of politics in Denmark has been changing continuously. The periods where curriculum-alterations have not been discussed, planned or implemented have been both short and infrequent. Many minor and major changes have been introduced to accommodate important conceptual developments which have taken place in the discipline. Other changes are due to pedagogical and didactical considerations. Still others have been introduced to adapt the study of political science to what was assessed to be demands from the prospective market for professional political scientists. And last but not least, a number of changes have been responses to student demands. As suggested above, the University Act of 1970 and its successors granted a great deal of influence to students, and consequently they have commanded considerable—in some instances even decisive—bargaining power in curriculum matters. Thus, the teaching of political science today represents the joint outcomes of both theoretical developments and intrauniversity and institute politics. This explains not only why curricula look as they do, but also why they may look somewhat different in different places.

Degrees in political science have been offered by the universities of Aarhus, Copenhagen, and Odense since 1958, 1965, and 1971, respectively.[34] Consequently, these three universities are the main centers for teaching political science in Denmark, although they are not the only ones. The university centers of Roskilde and Aalborg also offer courses in political science subjects. Due mostly to differences in the educational philosophy behind old and new universities, the degrees obtainable from the university centers of Roskilde and Aalborg are hardly comparable to the degrees offered by the old universities.

Political science students have a choice between two degrees, both of which are considered degrees in political science proper. They do, however, represent different emphases and somewhat different programs of study.

The oldest of the two is the degree of *Candidatus Scientiarum Politicarum* (*cand.scient.pol.*), established at the University of Aarhus in 1958, and still not obtainable from the other universities. Behind the establishment of this degree there appear to have been two decisive factors. First, in the previous decade, institutes of political science had been founded throughout Europe in keeping with the almost universal thrust toward the development of a science of politics after World War II—a thrust which also found expression in the founding of IPSA in 1949. Second, in Denmark there was a growing interest in establishing a new educational basis for recruitment to the civil service which traditionally had been totally dominated by professionals holding degrees in law and in economics.[35] A study which would combine relevant elements from the study of law and of economics with courses in political science subjects, including public administration and modern history, was envisaged.[36] It was hoped that such a study would produce professionals with profound insight into the composition and mechanics of modern government and politics, applicable to a variety of tasks in a variety of areas.

To some extent both of these considerations were mirrored in the new degree program. Like most Danish university studies, the study of politics consisted of two parts, a 2-year "undergraduate" part and a 3½-year "graduate" part, each made up of a series of compulsory courses and terminated by a series of oral and written examinations. The undergraduate part was composed of introductory political science, including sociology; economics (to the same extent as for students of economics); constitutional, administrative, and international law (to the same extent as for students of law); and statistical description of Danish society (to the same extent as for students of economics). Subjects in economics and law were taken together with students of economics and law. The "graduate" part was composed of courses on the constitution and political structure of Denmark and important foreign countries, including public administration; international politics and organizations; the history of political thought and of the principles of state; modern history; and elementary research methodology. Finally, as part of their study, students were required to submit a thesis of approximately 40,000 words on a topic within their chosen field of specialization.[37]

In 1965 still another degree program in political science was introduced at the universities of Aarhus and Copenhagen. This was the degree of *Candidatus Magisterii* (*cand.mag.*) with social science as the major subject in combination with a minor subject of the student's choice.

A primary consideration behind the establishment of this degree was the plan to reform the Danish high school (*gymnasium*), giving more room to social science subjects (*samfundsfag*) by adding a new track with an emphasis on the social sciences to the existing natural science and language tracks. The degree of *cand.mag.* with a major in social science was aimed primarily at preparing students for teaching social science within this new high school track.

The study for the degree of *cand.mag.* with a social science major was, consequently, envisioned as very broad. Economics, sociology, and political science were to contribute roughly equal shares. But due to the very outspoken reluctance, not to say opposition, which the new degree encountered from the more established social science disciplines, the responsibility of building up the program fell mainly into the hands of political scientists. The result was still another degree in political science. Initially, the structure and curriculum of the new program were alike at both universities, closely following the model provided by studies aiming at high school teaching careers in other fields. This model afforded a norm of four years of study for the major (*hovedfag*) and two years for the minor (*bifag*).[38] These structural features of the new program resulted in a political science degree which differed from the older one mainly in being more general in orientation while deemphasizing certain areas of study, in particular public administration and law.

After a series of changes and adjustments during the first years of both degree programs, a thorough revision of both programs was finally introduced in 1969. This reform was triggered by, among other things, a pending overload crisis due to the growing popularity of the studies of politics which expressed itself in growing enrollment numbers, while at the same time the institutes' teaching capacity remained severely limited mostly due to the short supply of qualified applicants for teaching and research positions in the institutes. Thus the accent of the reform on the structural side was on rationalization through coordination: large blocs of the two courses of study were made common for all students aiming at a degree in political science, regardless of kind.

The reform established an undergraduate curriculum common to both studies, consisting of compulsory courses in comparative politics; economics; statistics; sociology; and modern Danish history, terminated by a series of oral and written examinations. Furthermore, a sizable bloc of the graduate curriculum, courses in comparative politics and the history of political thought; international politics and organizations; selected issues in Danish politics; and research methodology, became shared by both degree programs. In addition to these common courses and the exams belonging to them, students aiming at the degree of *cand.scient.pol.* had to follow courses in constitutional, administrative, and international law—to the same extent as students of law—and public administration. They were also required to take a varying number of optional courses to provide an opportunity for specialization in accordance with individual wishes or career interests. Students aiming at the degree of *cand.mag.* with a social science major, on the other hand, were only required to take one additional course in sociology of law and to participate in an interdisciplinary social science seminar. The thesis requirement was upheld for both studies.

This structure continues to constitute the basic skeleton of the two programs in political science proper available to students in Denmark today, though lots of modifications have occurred since 1969. The central idea underlying this structure is to introduce the student to the basics of the discipline through compulsory undergraduate courses in order to provide a firm foundation for graduate level work involving great freedom of choice. Only in the university of Odense, where the degree program for the *cand.mag.* was introduced in 1971, is the structure somewhat different. There a large portion of the undergraduate curriculum is shared with students aiming at degrees in history and economics.

Through the first half of the 1970s, heated struggles were often fought between teachers and students, and within both groups as well, regarding course content. Quite naturally, given the history of the discipline, the conflict usually revolved around the problem of assigning a proper place to Marxism and Marxian theory in the curricula. The students generally demanded more (Marxian) theory, fewer empirical facts and methodology, and a greater emphasis on student projects. If a trend is to be pointed to in the development of the teaching of political science in Danish universities, it seems justifiable to contend that it has turned more theoretical, more pluralistic, more project-oriented, and more fragmented during the last decade.

Research in Political Science

Looking into the reviews and bibliographies in *Scandinavian Political Studies* and other relevant sources, almost no research was reported in 1960 and very little in 1966.[39] Since then, however, research activities have increased at an accelerating pace. Moreover, the size of projects undertaken has been growing, in part reflecting a trend away from individual scholarly work to collaborative efforts by political scientists from the same or from different institutes.

Several schemes could be used to classify the research areas which have commanded the greatest interest and produced the most noteworthy contributions. Excluding for the moment the important area of international politics, much of the research done can be organized easily into a set of categories essentially belonging to an Eastonian framework.[40]

This immediately brings out one important feature of Danish political science research. Most of the research done in the period under scrutiny here has been on topics related to input, conversion and feedback structures and processes at different levels of the polity. The allocation aspect, that is, the policy content of the output, has, however, been given very limited systematic attention. Many efforts have been made to elucidate *how* certain problems have been raised as "demands" and who did it, *how* the system of interest intermediation works, and *how* the final decision has been arrived at, whereas the question of *what* became the final content of the decision has largely been neglected. Most research has, furthermore, stopped short of examining the relationship between the political process and the policy outcomes.[41]

Still another general trait of Danish political science research deserves to be mentioned here. We are thinking of the conspicuous absence or near absence of a genuine comparative orientation in the bulk of the research which has been carried out. This is not to say, of course, that a comparative viewpoint has been totally lacking, or that international collaboration has not been taking place. With regard to the latter, the European Consortium for Political Research has played an important facilitating role. Nevertheless, as a whole, Danish political research has typically been rather ethnocentric in orientation. Given the central position of comparative politics in the teaching of political science in Danish universities and the close ties among the Nordic countries, this orientation seems hard to explain.

As mentioned above, the study of mass reactions and electoral behavior spearheaded the behavioral breakthrough in Danish political science, and constituted the first subfield within the discipline which was covered by comprehensive projects. The elections to the Folketing in the 1960s were made the object of ecological investigations which showed a clear relationship between ecological and political factors and demonstrated their considerable stability during that decade.[42] This project was followed by the nationwide sample-survey studies, conducted by a group of scholars from the universities of Copenhagen and Aarhus in connection with the national elections of 1971, 1973, 1975, and 1977. The surveys produced invaluable individual data for the analysis of the landslide elections of 1973, 1975, and 1977, which turned the established political landscape upside down. Although the possibilities of these data have by no means been exhausted, they have led to several reports issued by the research team[43] as well as by others.[44]

Another field which has been worked heavily by Danish political research is the study of parties, interest organizations, and popular movements and their interplay with formal institutions of the state, including the Folketing. The role played by particular organizations,[45] the interplay leading to certain decisions,[46] and the more general structural and process characteristics of the system of interest intermediation have been studied. Especially the final topic has drawn much attention lately. A multitude of approaches and models have been applied, including Downsian-inspired strategy models and the above-mentioned competing models for analyzing the relationship between interest organizations and institutions of the state, Erik Damgaard's "sector model,"[47] and the corporatism-model.[48]

Several aspects of the main output units of the polity, that is, the legislative and administrative systems, also have been made the objects of intensive studies.[49] The central work on the Danish Folketing in the 1970s is undoubtedly Erik Damgaard's study, based on the sector model alluded to above,[50] of the ways in which the parliament has adapted—or failed to adapt—to changes in the environment. Other aspects of the legislature covered by research are the recruitment of legislative elites[51] and the cleavage structures in the representation body.[52] The main and pioneering work in describing and analyzing the Danish administration as a whole has been done by Poul Meyer, utilizing several system theoretical frameworks.[53]

The study of international politics and international organizations constitutes another area in which a great deal of research has been carried out. Of all subdisciplines in Danish political science, this is undoubtedly the most diversified. The area has been dominated by studies of small state politics,[54] the politics of regional integration,[55] and last but not least international systems and subsystems,[56] including international organizations. Not surprisingly, Denmark's membership in the Common Market has increased the interest of Danish political scientists in these and related problems. Compared to, for example, Norwegian political science, peace research has played a rather insignificant role, although numerous studies of the politics of deterrence, defense, and disarmament have been done.

Political Science and the World of Politics

The relationships between political science and the world of politics constitute an intricate web of neutral influences. Clearly, political events may affect political science in many ways. Since the institutional framework as well as the supporting infrastructure of Danish political science are almost totally dependent on government money and government regulations, political events which directly or indirectly lead to changes in the priority assigned to the sector of education and research—or to changes in priorities within this sector—may affect the conditions of life for political science deeply. Political events may also change the focus of political research and have a profound effect on conceptual developments within the discipline. The events from the land-slide election of 1973 onward represent one particularly clear example of this spill-over from the world of politics into the world of political science. On the other hand, political science may influence the realm of politics either via theoretical insight and concrete research results made available to politicians and the public, or, indirectly, via political scientists pursuing political careers. Danish political science provides examples of all these kinds of interplay between political science and politics.

In the first place, the role of favorable political conjunctures in the establishment and rapid development of political science in Denmark should not be overlooked. Political science was established on the verge of a large expansion of the educational sector which, bolstered by an economic boom of previously unseen dimensions, was initiated in the early 1960s. The dominating viewpoint behind this expansion was expressed in what has been termed the social demand model. According to this view, all Danes should be given the opportunity to receive the education they want within the range of their personal abilities. Education, regardless of kind, was considered a valuable goal for the individual and for society as well.

Thus, political science rode high on the crest of the wave which swept an ever-increasing percentage of each youth cohort into the universities. At the same time, the growing public sector, and especially the growth of the central administration, created a seller's market for academic manpower, greatly facilitating placement of the first political science graduates in positions within the administration.

This situation came to a rather sudden end when, first, the political and, about six months later, the economic crisis struck Denmark in 1973-1974.[57] Like all other university activities, political science suffered budget cuts in the following years. Politicians concerned about the proper dimensions of the educational sector replaced the social demand model with a manpower demand model. Admission quotas, based on projections of the demand for graduates with different qualifications, were subsequently imposed. Rising unemployment numbers for graduates paved the way for this action. This led to a severe cut in the intake of students for the *cand.mag.* degree, while at the same time the employment situation for graduates in political science became increasingly difficult. In short, the series of crisis decisions after 1973 had a strong detrimental effect on the working conditions of political science in Denmark.

But the events of 1973-1974 also affected political research in Denmark in a substantive way. Although the understanding of the political landslide of 1973 was approached in different ways by different scholars, it did, as suggested above, stimulate renewed and widespread interest in political institutions and the interactions among them. The structural developments in interest intermediation and representation in particular were given high priority in Danish political research after 1973.[58]

The change which took place during this period in the attitudes of the public and politicians toward the educational sector, and especially toward research, may also be seen as a contributing force behind a growing interest in applied or at least applicable research. This is not to suggest that Danish political science had previously been totally confined to the ivory tower. One of the founding fathers, Poul Meyer, even made it a part of his definition of the task of political science to examine political decisions and processes to see whether they were "rational," and to let the politicians know if their decisions were not.[59] Both he and the other founding father, Erik Rasmussen, served periodically in advisory functions. Poul Meyer served as a member of several commissions and Erik Rasmussen on the Board of Overseers in the Danish Broadcasting System. Nevertheless, not until the mid-1970s did Danish political science begin to address itself to the solution of societal problems and political issues such as youth unemployment,[60] energy policies,[61] "economic democracy,"[62] and policies of regional development.[63] This beginning trend toward policy analysis may be seen, at least in part, as a response to the warnings sounded by many politicians, most notably the minister of education, Ritt Bjerregaard, to the effect that research now had to justify itself by being "useful" and "relevant."

The influence which Danish political science may have had on Danish politics is more difficult to assess. The area in which such an influence is most obvious is in terminology. Terms such as "the political system," "decision-making process," for instance, found their way quite quickly from the language of political science into the everyday vocabulary of Danish politicians. The concepts denoted by these terms have not always followed suit, however. Another link between political science and politics exists by virtue of those political scientists who made their way into the realm of political life. Again the founding fathers set the pace here: Both of them have been active in Danish politics.[64] Many of the students of political science, especially in the early years of the discipline, undoubtedly were motivated not solely by a scholarly interest in politics, but by a practical interest as well, and several of them pursued a political career successfully upon graduating. The national elections in the 1970s regularly returned a group of 4 to 6 political scientists to the parliament, and political scientists have been active in politics at other levels as well, ranging from the position of vice-secretary general of the UN[65] to positions within the Danish students' organization. To what degree they have been able to draw upon knowledge of political science may remain an open question.

Notes

1. Among the Nordic countries only Iceland can boast of a discipline of more recent vintage.

2. See Sven Henningsen and Erik Rasmussen, "Political Research in Scandinavia 1960-65: Denmark," *Scandinavian Political Studies* 1 (1966): 254-57 for an account of what did exist of a tradition of political research in Denmark prior to 1958.

3. This term is adopted from Thomas S. Kuhn, *The Structure of Scientific Revolutions* (Chicago, 1962).

4. This middle-of-the-road approach is clearly mirrored in the two volumes by Erik Rasmussen, *Komparativ Politik 1-2* (Copenhagen, 1968-69). Their mimeographed forerunners and later editions constituted the backbone of large parts of the study of political science during the 1960s and the first half of the 1970s, regardless of the place of study.

5. This distinction between "bridging the gaps" and "filling the gaps" strategies is adopted from P. F. Lazarsfeld, "Sociology," in *Main Trends of Research in the Social and Human Sciences* (Paris, 1960) vol. 1, *Social Sciences*, pp. 61-165.

6. Arnold Brecht, *Political Theory* (Princeton, 1959).

7. David Easton, *The Political System* (New York, 1953).

8. The main exponent of positivism in Danish philosophy at that time was undoubtedly Jørgen Jørgensen, who held the chair in philosophy at the University of Copenhagen from 1926 to 1964.

9. E.g., Poul Meyer, *Politisk videnskab* (Copenhagen, 1962), pp. 13-22.

10. David Easton, *A Systems Analysis of Political Life* (New

York, 1965). A certain disappointment with the view taken in this work, and especially with the restated definition of politics, is reflected in Erik Rasmussen, "Some Comments on the Concept of the Political System," *Scandinavian Political Studies* 5 (1970): 11-19. The essay shows how central this definition had been to the initial reception of the Eastonian framework.

11. Poul Meyer, *Political partier* (Copenhagen, 1965).

12. Poul Meyer, *Die Verwaltungsorganisation* (Göttingen, 1962).

13. In part, this must also be seen as a result of the need to produce a usable set of teaching materials.

14. Stein Rokkan, "Political Research in Scandinavia 1960-65: Norway," *Scandinavian Political Studies*, 1 (1966): 270.

15. The first study of individual behavior undertaken in Danish political science was Poul Meyer and Jens Jeppesen's study on nonvoting, *Sofavaelgerne. Valgdeltagelsen ved danske folketingsvalg* (Aarhus, 1964). The systematic study of electoral behavior, based on nationwide samples, started with the election of 1971.

16. E.g., Ole Nørgaard Madsen, Poul Meyer, Søren Winter, *Borger og komimune: Langå* (Aarhus, 1976).

17. Peter Hansen, Nikolaj Petersen, K. W. Redder, "Foreign Policy Attitudes of the Danish Population," Aarhus, 1969 (unpublished report).

18. This was an intended consequence of the establishment of regional computing centers at the universities of Aarhus, Odense, and Copenhagen in the early 1970s.

19. A short description of the development of what may be called the infrastructure of Danish political research is found in Peter Nannestad, "Political Science in Denmark: Trends of Research 1960-1975. Some Footnotes to a Bibliography," *Scandinavian Political Studies* 12 (1977): 85-104.

20. Of course, not all scholars active in Danish political science did follow this swing. Nevertheless, the quantitative and qualitative weight of those who did was sufficient to give this phase its characteristics.

21. A touch of this tension has been caught in a recent—unduly harsh—attack of one of the founding fathers of Danish political science, Poul Meyer, on the doctoral dissertation presented by Erik Damgaard (see note 27): Poul Meyer (without title) in *Politica* 9, nos. 3-4 (1978): 21-26. The apparent pragmatism of Danish social science, in casu sociology, has also been noted by Lazarsfeld, "Sociology." In Danish social science there exists a tradition—now represented particularly by the Socialforskningsinstitut (Institute of Social Research) in Copenhagen—of a "social problems approach" to knowledge about society. This tradition is followed by some of the work which would be relevant in this context.

22. Mogens N. Pedersen, "Om den rette brug af historiske materialer i statskundskaben: Nogle didaktiske overvejelser," *Festskrift til Erik Rasmussen* (Aarhus, 1977), pp. 235-72.

23. Since the Danish Folketing may be dissolved and an election called at almost any time, the timing of these surveys could not be foretold.

24. Ole Borre, Hans Jørgen Nielsen, Steen Sauerberg, Torben Worre, *Vaelgere i 70'erne* (Copenhagen, 1976).

25. Whereas the adoption of the Michigan model may have looked a rather uncontroversial choice in the late 1960s, the events in Danish politics in 1973 and later demonstrated how binding this decision could turn out to be. The landslide election of 1973 (and the following elections of 1975 and 1977) totally destroyed the traditional Danish party system, dating back to the 1920s, by doubling the number of parties in the Folketing (from 5 to 10), reducing drastically the strength of the old, established parties, and smashing time-honored party attachments. In this situation, the social-psychological framework dominating Danish electoral research inevitably led to a catastrophic view of the events—not unlike that adopted by most of the defeated politicians—and to a what-went-wrong approach to the understanding of the turmoil. Consequently, the search for explanatory factors has concentrated on irrational motives and drives in the voters.

26. P. C. Schmitter, "Still the Century of Corporatism?" in F. B. Pike and T. Strich, eds., *The New Corporatism* (London, 1974), pp. 85-131.

27. D. Dahlerup, C. Jarlov, L. Nørby Johansen, O. P. Kristensen, "Korporatisme-begrebet og studiet af samspillet mellem politiske institutioner," *Økonomi og Politik* 49 (1975): 317-44. A competing theoretical framework, owing far less than the corporatism model to foreign impulses and hence to a certain degree representing a counterexample, is developed in the doctoral dissertation by Erik Damgaard, *Folketinget under forandring* (Copenhagen, 1977).

28. Mogens N. Pedersen, "State and University in Denmark: From Co-existence to Collision Course," in Hans Daalder, ed., *Legislators and the University*, forthcoming.

29. A detailed account of the developments leading to this act as well as the institutional arrangements it created is found in Pedersen, "State and University."

30. See, e.g., Theodore J. Lowi, "The Politics of Higher Education: Political Science as a Case Study," in George J. Graham and George W. Carey, eds., *The Post-Behavioral Era: Perspectives on Political Science* (New York, 1972), and the second edition of David Easton, *The Political System* (New York, 1972), where the organizational and conceptual integration is described.

31. This is not considered the right place for a spelling out of the—sometimes quite subtle—theoretical differences in the viewpoints of these three schools.

32. E.g., Lazarsfeld, "Sociology."

33. Still "analysis of reality" (*realanalyse*) remains one of the tough problems of Marxist political science. If empirical material is used at all, it is often employed in a "case-consuming" fashion: data are used to illustrate a theory, the tenability of which is not questioned, rather than to test it. The distance between this practice and outright "data-filling" and manipulation is dangerously small.

34. The teaching for these degrees had been taken up in 1964, not awaiting the formal codification of the degrees.

35. Henningsen and Rasmussen, "Political Research," p. 255.

36. According to Poul Meyer, the reason for introducing public administration to the study of political science was that he had made this a condition for the acceptance of one of the two chairs in political science in 1959. See Poul Meyer, "For-

valtningslaere i Danmark 1958-1978," *Nordisk Administrativt Tidsskrift* (1978): 87. This is not confirmed by other sources.

37. Kgl. anordning af 1.8.1958. See also Poul Meyer, "Statskundskab ved Aarhus Universitet," *Nordisk Administrativt Tidsskrift* (1959): 233-38 (with summary in English).

38. The requirement of a minor subject was at least partially abolished in 1968, when the degree of *Candidatus Philosophiae* (*cand.phil.*) was introduced for students who wanted to graduate with a major subject only. It was, however, upheld for students aiming at the degree of *cand.mag.*

39. Henningsen and Rasmussen, "Political Research"; Stein Rokkan and Henry Valen, "Parties, Elections and Political Behavior in Northern Countries: A Review of Recent Research," in Otto Stammer, ed., *Politische Forschung* (Cologne, 1960), pp. 103-36; and Jan-Mogens Jansson, "Der Staatsapparat als Gegenstand der Politischen Wissenschaft in den Nordischen Ländern," in Stammer, *Politische Forschung*, pp. 137-51.

40. A helpful classification scheme, based on Eastonian categories, is found in Stein Rokkan, "Political Research in Scandinavia 1960-65: Norway," *Scandinavian Political Studies* 1 (1966): 275.

41. One particular example of the way in which the policy content of decisions is neglected in Danish political research may be taken from the study of public administration. Here, the problem of "rationality" and "efficiency" of decisions has traditionally been given high attention. Both rationality and efficiency have, however, been defined with reference to purely formal criteria, *i.e.*, criteria referring to the way in which decisions are made, instead of to their content. Thus, according to Poul Meyer, a decision is rational when it is based upon all relevant premises. See Poul Meyer, *Offentlig Forvaltning*, 2d ed. (Copenhagen, 1975), pp. 343-48.

42. Ole Borre and Jan Stehouwer, *Partistyrke og social struktur 1960* (Aarhus, 1968) and *Fire Folketingsvalg 1960-68* (Aarhus, 1970).

43. See note 24.

44. Ole Borre and Daniel Katz, "Party Identification and Its Motivational Base in a Multi-Party System," *Scandinavian Political Studies* 10 (1973): 69-112; Erik Damgaard and Jerrold G. Rusk, "Cleavage Structure and Representational Linkages: A Longitudinal Analysis of Danish Legislative Behaviour," in Ian Budge, Ivor Crewe, Dennis Farlie, eds., *Party Identification and Beyond* (New York, 1976), pp. 163-88; and Ole Borre and Jerrold G. Rusk, "The Changing Party Space in Danish Voter Perceptions," in Budge, Crewe, Farlie, *Party Identification*, pp. 137-62.

45. E.g., Jacob A. Buksti, *Et enigt landbrug? Konflikt og samarbejde mellem landbrugets organisationer* (Aarhus, 1974).

46. E.g., Henning Bregnsbo, *Kampen om skolelovene af 1958* (Odense, 1971).

47. Cf. note 27.

48. Cf. note 27.

49. Cf. Rokkan, "Political Research," p. 275.

50. Cf. note 27.

51. Mogens N. Pedersen, "Lawyers in Politics: The Danish Folketing and United States Legislatures," in Samuel C. Patterson, ed., *Comparative Legislative Behavior: Frontiers of Research* (New York, 1972), pp. 25-63; Mogens N. Pedersen, "Political Development and Elite Transformation in Denmark," *Sage Professional Papers 06-018* (Beverly Hills, 1976); and Kjell A. Eliassen and Mogens N. Pedersen, "Professionalization of Legislatures: Long-Term Change in Political Recruitment in Denmark and Norway," *Comparative Studies in Society and History* 20, no. 2 (1978): 286-318.

52. Damgaard and Rusk, "Cleavage Structure."

53. Meyer, *Offentlig Forvaltung*.

54. Ole Karup Pedersen, *Udenrigsminister P. Munch's opfattelse af Danmarks stilling i international politik* (Copenhagen, 1970); and Hans Branner, *Småstat mellem stormagter. Beslutningen om mineudlaegningen 1914* (Copenhagen, 1972).

55. Carsten Lehmann Sørensen, ed., *Politisk integrationsteori* (Aarhus, 1976).

56. Erling Bjøl, *Verdenshistorien efter 1945. vols. 1-3* (Copenhagen, 1972-1973). The main work on international organizations has been done by Peter Hansen, now vice-secretary general of the UN. See, e.g., Peter Hansen, *International Organization* (Copenhagen, 1975).

57. See above, note 25.

58. This development was actively encouraged by the Social Science Research Council, not the least through its grant policy.

59. Meyer, *Politisk videnskab*, pp. 9-12. As late as 1978 this view was reiterated by Meyer in *Politika* (1978): 21.

60. Carsten Jarlov and Lise Togeby, *Underbeskaeftigelse og underuddannelse: De 17- til 19-åriges arbejds- og uddannelsessituation i Århus kommune 1975* (Aarhus, 1977).

61. Jerome D. Davis and Bo Ander Svendsen, *Dansk naturgas—problemer og muligheder i 80' erne* (Aarhus, 1978).

62. Jacob A. Buksti, Ole P. Kristensen, Karen Siune, Palle Svenson, *ØD-undersøgelsen i Århus kommune* (Aarhus, 1978).

63. Peter Bogason, Leif Pedersen, Søren Villadsen, *Udvikling og Styring. Regionalpolitikkens muligheder i en udkantsregion* (Copenhagen, 1977).

64. Erik Rasmussen was chairman of the high school teachers' organization and had close personal ties to influential members of the radical-liberal party. Poul Meyer was active in the conservative youth organization prior to World War II and worked as a political columnist after the war.

65. See note 56.

Bibliography*

Anbro, Klaus, et al. *The Philosophy and History of the Social Sciences—Seen from the Angle of Critical Theory* (in Danish). Copenhagen: Akademisk forlag, 1972.

Bislev, Sven. "Political Science and Imperialism" (in Danish). *Politica* 4, nos. 1-2 (1971).

---

*Compiled by the editor.

Bjöl, Erling. "Research on Foreign Policy" (in Danish). *Fremtiden* 20, no. 3 (1965): 7-12.

Boolsen, Merete Watt, and Sørenson, Ole Aagaard. *Social Science Institutions and Publications in Denmark* (in Danish). Copenhagen, 1976.

Damgaard, Erik. "On a Definition of Politics and Its Consequences" (in Danish). *Politica* 3, no. 2 (1970): 23-29.

Danish Social Science Research Council, ed. *Aspects of the Organization of Social Science Research in Denmark.* Copenhagen, 1972.

Diderichsen, S. M., et al. *Research of Society: Research for Society?* (in Danish). Copenhagen: Reitzel, 1973.

Friis, Henning. "Collaboration among the Social Sciences" (in Danish). *Økonomi og Politik* 38, no. 3 (1964): 211-26.

Henningsen, Sven, and Rasmussen, Erik. "Political Research in Scandinavia 1960-65: Denmark." *Scandinavian Political Studies* (1966): 254-57.

Jansson, Jan-Mogens. "The State Apparatus as Object of Political Science in the Northern Countries" (in German). In *Politische Forschung*, edited by Otto Stammer. Cologne, 1960, pp. 137-51.

Lund, Niels. *Humanism, Ideological Criticism and Marxism in Scandinavian Social Science* (in Danish). Copenhagen: Studenterrådet ved Københavns Universitet, 1973.

Meyer, Poul. *Political Science* (in Danish). Copenhagen: Berlingske Forlag, 1962.

Munk, Knud Jorgen. "A Contribution to the Debate on the Methodological, Conceptual and Political Basis of the Social Sciences" (in Danish). *Politica* 4, no. 3 (1971): 35-53.

Nannestad, Peter. "Political Science in Denmark: Trends of Research 1960-1975: Some Footnotes to a Bibliography." *Scandinavian Political Studies* (1977): 85-104.

Pedersen, Mogens N. "On the Proper Use of Historical Materials in the Science of the State: Some Didactic Reflections" (in Danish). *Festskrift til Erik Rasmussen.* Aarhus, 1977.

———. "The Breakthrough of Behavioralism in Political Science. Some Footnotes Concerning Research Policy" (in Danish). *Politica* 5, no. 2 (1972): 13-33.

Pedersen, Ole Karup. "Conflict Research and the Political Sciences" (in Danish). *Økonomi og Politik* 40 (1960): 140-49.

Rasmussen, Erik. *Comparative Politics* (in Danish). 2 vols. Copenhagen, 1968-1969.

———. "Political Science and Society" (in Danish). *Statsvetenskapelig Tidsskrift*, no. 2 (1978): 93-98.

———. "Some Comments on the Concept of the Political System." *Scandinavian Political Studies* (1970): 11-19.

——— and Björklund, Stefan. "Values—Normativism in Social Science" (in Danish). *Statsvetenskapelig tidsskrift* 75, no. 1 (1972): 36-66 (two introductions and a debate).

Rokkan, Stein, and Valen, Henry. "Parties, Elections and Political Behavior in Northern Countries: A Review of Recent Research." In *Politische Forschung*, edited by Otto Stammer. Cologne, 1960, pp. 103-36.

Sørensen, Carsten Lehmann, ed. *Political Integration Theory* (in Danish). Aarhus, 1976.

Svensson, Palle. "On David Easton's General Theory." *Politica* 4, no. 5 (1971): 5-14.

Theory and Method in the Social Sciences (in Danish). Copenhagen: Planlaegningsrådet for de höiere uddannelser, 1972.

Note: Probably the most useful bibliographical keys to Danish political science are the bibliographies contained in *Scandinavian Political Studies*, vols. *1-11*, Oslo, 1966-1977 and the cumulative bibliography of main contributions in volume 12, Oslo, 1978. A special bibliography of titles in international politics and organizations by Nikolaj Petersen may be found in Niels Amstrup and Ib Faurby, eds., *Studier i dansk udenrigspolitik*, Aarhus, 1978.

12

FINLAND

ERIK ALLARDT

Intellectual Predecessors

The first two chairs in political science in Finnish universities were established shortly after World War I. Despite this comparatively late moment for the establishment of political science as an academic discipline, scientific analyses and discussions of matters related to the state and politics have, of course, a much longer history. During the nineteenth and early twentieth centuries at least four milieus or groups discussed problems which later became the object of academic political science. First, the German historical school of political economy under the leadership of Gustav Schmoller had a large following among Finnish historians and economists.[1] It represented a particular blend of social reform and conservative tendencies and focussed on such questions as national unity, the rise of the working class and socialism, the state and public policy. Second, academic sociology developed comparatively early in Finland under the inspiration of Edward Westermarck, who shared his time between the Finnish universities and London. Several of his pupils, such as Rafael Karsten, Gunnar Landtman, and Rudolf Holsti, wrote treatises about matters related to the development and rise of states and statehood from an evolutionary perspective.[2] Third, an important legal tradition, with considerable research activity in the fields of constitutional and public law, had developed shortly after the middle of the nineteenth century. Its rise was inspired partly by the fact that Finland from 1809 until its declaration of independence in December 1917 occupied a special position as a grand duchy within the Russian Empire, with the czar as the grand duke.[3] Fourth, since the early years of the twentieth century a socialist tradition developed in Finland. One leading Finnish socialist, Otto Wille Kuusinen, rose later to a high position as a theoretician within the Politburo of the Soviet Union.[4] The teachings and effects of these early socialist traditions in Finland, however, remained mainly outside the academic milieu and developments.

The State of Political Science after World War II

During the years immediately following World War II, there were four chairs in political science at Finnish universities and colleges: one each at the University of Helsinki, Åbo Academy, the Helsinki School of Social Sciences, which later became the University of Tampere, and the Swedish School of Economics. The name of the subject was translated from the German *Staatswissenschaft* or rather *Staatslehre* (in Finnish *valtio-oppi*, in Swedish *statslära*), and it kept this name despite the fact that political science (especially in the 1960s) was strongly oriented both toward behavioralism and American political science.

Still in the 1940s academic subjects in humanities and social science commonly had only one full-time teacher, the professor. In addition to the professor there were often some part-time lecturers (so-called docents), Ph.D.s with a small teaching burden, a small salary, other sources of income, and the potential to become a professor later. This was also the case in political science.

Despite the small number of full-time teachers in political science, there already was a great variety of intellectual orientations. The seeds of the behavioral revolution coming in the 1950s were there already. The professor of political science at the University of Helsinki, K. R. Brotherus, had been rector of the university and possessed a good position and reputation within the academic circles of the day. He represented, to a certain extent, the tradition of the German *Staatswissenschaft*, but in addition to the philosophy of the state and conceptual analysis he stressed strongly the importance of constitutional law and historical studies. However, two younger scholars, Yrjö Ruutu and Jussi Teljo, represented better the intellectual tendencies of the 1930s and the 1940s. Ruutu had in 1922 defended a doctoral dissertation about the nature of nationhood[5] and represented an organic conception of both the nation and the state. If

Ruutu represented tendencies typical of Continental Europe in the 1920s and 1930s, Teljo represented the empirical and behaviorally oriented political science of the future. Teljo (who in 1949 became professor at the University of Helsinki) had in the 1930s presented a doctoral dissertation directed against metaphysical conceptions of the state and introduced empirical studies of policy-making.[6] At the Swedish-speaking Åbo Academy in the city of Turku (which equals Åbo in Swedish) Sven Lindman had in the 1930s and 1940s conducted comprehensive studies of the actual functioning of parliamentarism and cabinet formation in Finland.[7] Lindman was closely related to the Uppsala School in Swedish political science with its focus on the modern history of decision-making and legislative state bodies.

Characteristic of the whole academic climate, not only in political science but in all the social sciences, during the years immediately following World War II was a strong belief in logical positivism and empirical social studies. It contributed later in the 1950s to an easy adoption of behavioralism with its emphasis on variables and quantitative techniques.

The Evolution of Political Science since 1945

THE INTELLECTUAL STRUCTURE
OF THE DISCIPLINE

From the early 1950s there has been a fairly rapid development and change in political science as an academic discipline. The crucial change in this period was the adoption of behavioralism and simultaneously a great increase in American influence upon curricula and research. It was, however, preceded by other developments in a similar direction and never became complete.

It is commonplace not only in Finland but also in many other countries to say that the period before World War II had been dominated by the German *Staatswissenschaft*. However, such a characterization should not be made without qualification since many different trends existed in the 1930s. The most important single work in the German tradition in the Finnish university environment was, no doubt, Georg Jellinek's *Allgemeine Staatslehre*. Jellinek was greatly concerned with the nature, necessity, and legitimization of the state; he was not opposed to historical studies of actual governmental praxis.[8] The founder of political science in Finland and the first professor of political science at the University of Helsinki, K. R. Brotherus, adhered quite closely to the doctrine of Jellinek. Brotherus defended the state against those who considered the state unnecessary or who took the side of society against the state, but he emphasized also historical, realistic studies of actual practices.[9] In this orientation Brotherus was influenced strongly by another international source, the book *Modern Democracies* by James Bryce.[10] This book, translated into Finnish in 1933, clearly influenced the style of teaching political science in the 1930s and 1940s, and favored descriptive comparisons of governmental and parliamentary practices in different, mainly Western, countries. Students who started their studies immediately after World War II at the University of Helsinki actually were confronted very little with the traditions from the German *Staatswissenschaft* but more with the style of Bryce's realistic political science. Among the more research-oriented students this style and manner was regarded often as irritatingly descriptive and theoretically unsatisfactory. It is also important to note that in 1950, shortly before behavioralism made its way into Finnish political science, Jan-Mogens Jansson (later a professor at the University of Helsinki), presented an important doctoral dissertation about Kelsen's theory of state which included a clear polemic against Jellinek's conceptions.[11] A kind of positivist political science was emphasized against older more "organic" and "normative" conceptions.

Behavioralism came into Finnish political science mainly during the second half of the 1950s. Clearly, it meant a new and engaging interest in the study of mass participation and the actual political behavior of political groups. Such empirical information came into great demand at a time when the apparatus of the political parties was growing.

The behavioralist revolution often has been described in terms of what tended to be de-emphasized during its heyday. It meant a decrease in the study of legal and constitutional foundations of the state and governmental bodies and a disappearance of theoretical and philosophical analyses of the nature of the state. In a certain sense, one can speak of a neglect of study of the institutional aspect.[12] The emphasis was on studying behavior, either of ordinary voters, or of political leaders such as parliamentarians or party activists, and the explanations were sought either in the social background of the actors or in sociopsychological processes. Studies mainly trying to assess the impact of formal political institutions were very few indeed. The most popular studies, or at least those carrying the greatest prestige, were voting studies. In retrospect it seems important to warn against exaggerated descriptions of this tendency. Also, those political scientists who carried out voting studies maintained an interest in the workings of political institutions. However, emphasis shifted from the study of formal state bodies and constitutional problems to the analysis of informal political institutions related to the party system.

During the 1950s and 1960s, political sociology was an important and at times the most visible part of the study of politics at Finnish universities. Also, it seems fair to say that political sociology (in contradistinction to behavioralism within political science proper) had a stronger and much more explicit relationship to social and political theory. Also, political sociologists were much more apt than behavioral political scientists to focus on major change in the society and to connect political change with societal master trends. Whereas a focus on the social and structural background of behavior in sociology meant a definite emphasis both on central sociological theory and on political problems, political scientists were both less inclined to relate their analyses to traditional social theory and more cautious in discussing controversial issues.

One should, however, avoid confusing a description of dominant tendencies such as the one presented above with a minute, total description of the field. All through the 1950s and 1960s the field of political science was broadening and new specialities were rising. Some very interesting studies on the foundations and prerequisites of democracy were published. The two most noteworthy dealt with the relationship between freedom and equality[13] and with the foundations of democracy in ancient Athens.[14] In 1960 an excellent and, in some respects, unique textbook on the Finnish political system was published by Jaakko Nousiainen (who later became professor of political science at the University of Turku).[15] This book is interesting because it reflects a tradition of a realistic, comprehensive description of political institutions which was kept alive all through the heyday of behavioralism. This tradition borrowed elements from the style of James Bryce; also, it adopted new elements. New international, fairly important sources of inspiration were the writings of Maurice Duverger, in particular his books on political parties and on political regimes of which the latter was translated into Finnish by Jussi Teljo in 1955.[16] However, during the decade from 1955 to 1965 it was mainly studies in the style of behavioralism of American political science that led to further discussions and scientific debates. Nevertheless, it cannot be overstressed that at the same time a tradition of realistic, systematic description of political institutions was kept alive and continued to be one of the very core elements of political science.

In any case, only toward the end of the 1960s were new developments with a stronger and independent interest in theory and theory formation observed among political scientists. Apparently, much behavioralism had come to stay, but new demands for theory and for considering the political context were beginning to be raised. The international student revolution of the second half of the 1960s and the new interest in Marxism appeared within Finnish political science also, but did not shake it, at least not in the same fashion as it affected the neighboring field of sociology. By 1978, no major scholarly book inspired mainly by Marxism had been published in academic Finnish political science. The new important theoretical attempts had their sources elsewhere than in Marxism. One important theoretical development was that inspired mainly by Karl Popper's new methodological orientation with its attack on raw empiricism and on the neglect of contextual, political variables.[17] Another was a new interest in policy analysis[18] which in Finland as elsewhere has been associated with a transition of emphasis from political sociology to political economy.[19] A third new development was an increased interest in systems analysis.[20] There was also a totally new interest in questioning the political science of the earlier decades combined with a new interest in a study of the history of the discipline.[21]

The increasing differentiation of political science did not mean new theoretical developments only. Also, new specialties and branches were institutionalized in the form of new, specialized academic jobs and research institutes. Among those, the specialties of public administration, international relations, and peace research probably were the three most important ones. The first two mentioned were institutionalized by especially created chairs and teaching jobs. The fields of both international relations on one hand, and conflict and peace research on the other were emphasized by the founding of governmental research institutes in the 1960s.

THE TEACHING OF POLITICAL SCIENCE

The period of the 1960s was in Finland (as in many other European countries) a decade of tremendous growth in higher education. New universities were founded, and the older, larger university departed clearly from the old rule to have only one or possibly two full professors in each academic subject. By the middle of the 1970s, political science departments with complete undergraduate and graduate programs existed at five universities, and there were associate professors in two other universities, one of them also offering an M.A. program in political science.[22] In 1976, the oldest and largest university, Helsinki, had a political science teaching staff of four full professors, two associate professors, one full-time lecturer, and seven full-time instructors.

Most universities have separate faculties of social sciences of which political science is a part. The social science faculties have tended to emphasize the common aspects of all social sciences, and, as a rule, the students graduating in political science have other social sciences as minors or auxiliary subjects. Political science has competed with economics in being the major subject chosen most often for the M.A. degree (the degree to which the undergraduate studies lead). Between 1946 and 1959, the University of Helsinki awarded 1,021 M.A. degrees in the social sciences. The major subject was political science for 29 percent of them, economics for 29 percent, sociology for 19 percent, social policy for 18 percent, political history for 2 percent, moral philosophy for 2 percent, and statistics for 1 percent. For the period 1960-1975 statistical data exist only on the number of master's theses accepted by the Faculty of Social Sciences. From 1960 to 1975 the Faculty of Social Sciences at Helsinki accepted 3,260 M.A. theses. Of those, 963 (30 percent) were in the field of political science. During the same period, the total number of accepted masters' theses in political science at all Finnish universities was 1,803 which means that the University of Helsinki represented slightly more than 50 percent of the output of political scientists in the country.[23]

Until the most recent years, classroom teaching at the social science faculties has focussed very much on the undergraduate studies. The main and completely decisive requirement for studies for the Ph.D. degree has been the Ph.D. thesis. This pattern is changing, although it has had a fairly rational explanation. Undergraduate teaching has emphasized many qualities of graduate work and reasearch requiring, for instance, a fairly comprehensive M.A. thesis. This pattern is due partly to the fact that Finnish students start their university studies at a fairly mature age, at 19 or 20, and that the studies for a M.A. in the social sciences and political science take about 6 years on the average. However, this average length is due partly to inefficiency in teaching and studying, and serious attempts are being made to shorten the studies both for the M.A. and the Ph.D. degrees. In any case, undergraduate teaching has contained many elements usually associated with Ph.D. programs.

The requirements for the Ph.D. thesis have been comparatively demanding, and the rule that Ph.D. theses have to be published as books remains in force. The theses are practically always based on research that has lasted several years. In 1961-65 a total of six Ph.D. theses in political science were accepted at Finnish universities, in 1966-70 eight and in 1971-75 eighteen.[24] Most Ph.D.s are clearly aiming at an academic career.

Only a small part of those completing M.A. degrees can be employed by the universities or in full-time research. Unfortunately, M.A.s with political science as a major subject cannot be separated from the other M.A.s in the social sciences. Generally, there has been a trend toward greater public employment of M.A.s from the social science faculties. This development has been furthered by new demands for work in the field of public planning. The older civil service jobs have been held mostly by lawyers who have been firmly rooted in the system and unwilling to make room for newcomers. According to a recent count of M.A.s in the social sciences who graduated from five universities in the academic years of 1971/72 and 1972/73, the state employed 28 percent, municipalities 22 percent, and joint organizations of local government 8 percent, whereas 25 percent were working in the private sector. In addition, the universities and the research councils employed 12 percent, and state-owned corporations 3 percent.[25]

MOST NOTEWORTHY DEVELOPMENTS IN RESEARCH

During the 30 years between 1945 and 1975, Finnish political science experienced both considerable proliferation of research activities and increased differentiation. New fields of specialization developed both substantially and methodologically. All the contributions cannot be described here, so references will be made to only the most noteworthy contributions in the most important fields of research. Therefore, the following account is limited mainly to developments in the field of voting studies as the most typical field of political science behavioralism, to political sociology, to the field of public policy, and to studies of international relations and peace research. In addition, some methodologically important new developments must be accounted for. During the last decade, they have been observable mainly in the study of public administration and in approaches to the study of the history of political science.

Despite the fact that voter surveys and studies of specific elections often are considered to be the most typical examples of behavioralism they have been neither common nor systematically conducted in Finland. The most notable exception is Pertti Pesonen's thorough analysis of the 1958 parliamentary elections.[26] The model for this study was clearly the large American voting surveys, in particular those conducted at the University of Michigan in Ann Arbor. Pesonen has also edited a large volume with papers about the elections in 1966, 1970, and 1972.[27] Actually, most of the larger Finnish voting studies have been ecological studies with the commune, the smallest administrative unit, as the main unit of observation and analysis. No doubt, this interest in ecological analysis was aroused by the abundance of ecological data. Some of the ecological studies were oriented more toward the presentation of data and techniques than toward the political content or the political implications of the findings. In particular, this is the case in Onni Rantala's depiction of the overall electoral geography of Finland, in which he presented data by regional units from all parliamentary elections, 1907-1958,[28] and in Risto

Sänkiaho's study of the results of the parliamentary elections, 1907–1962, in southern Finland.[29] The latter study focuses on the use of and analysis of the different solutions in factor analysis, whereas substantive information on actual politics is rather scarce. Both the political content and the information about the social background appear to be more abundant in some of the earliest ecological studies which were affected less by the political science trend of behavioralism and clearly influenced by research traditions other than the American voting studies. This is very true for Göran von Bonsdorff's comparative study from 1953 of liberal parties in the Nordic countries. It combines many different kinds of information, including electoral data, in a descriptive but systematic manner.[30] It is true also for Jaakko Nousiainen's doctoral dissertation of 1956 about communism in an eastern Finnish province.[31] His models for analysis are found mainly in the studies of Rudolf Heberle and in the French school of political geography founded by André Siegfried. Also Erik Allardt's predominantly ecological study from 1956 of political participation can be placed in this category. It was inspired by S. M. Lipset's early works but also has clear roots in the French electoral geography.[32]

However, during its period of dominance, the behavioralist approach exerted some kind of influence in almost all fields of political studies. In Olavi Borg's 1964 doctoral dissertation on the programs of the Finnish political parties, the method of analysis is cluster analysis and other correlational techniques while the aim is to specify ideological dimensions and to show what factors correlate with the dimensions.[33] Many studies of the Finnish Parliament were aimed at describing parliamentarian behavior in terms of social or psychological background factors without attempting to analyze thoroughly or to account for political processes. This was characteristic of a study of the social background of the members of the parliament,[34] of a study of the social roles of the members of the parliament,[35] and of some coalition theoretical studies of behavior in parliament.[36]

Political sociology has often been thought of as a twin to behavioral political science since they study the same kinds of topics and partly use the same kind of methods and variables. As already indicated, however, they have some obvious differences. The political sociologists, which actually meant sociologists studying politics, were more theoretically oriented than the behavioralists in political science. The sociologists were oriented toward the European founding fathers of macrosociology, such as Max Weber, Emile Durkheim, Vilfredo Pareto, and later also Karl Marx. Still, the socalled political sociologists, as a point of departure in their studies often used data about behavior. Also, they had strong ties to American social science as regards methods and approaches. The theoretical ties however, to the founding fathers of macrosociology were one of the factors contributing to the tendency among the political sociologists to attempt to tie political developments to societal master change. Data on political behavior were used to try to construct general theories about conflicts and solidarity,[37] or to build statistical models of societal master change.[38] The political sociologists by being more theoretical also tied their studies more closely to structural conflicts in the Finnish society than did the political scientists.[39] Among the political sociologists the explanations were sought in the social structure of the society, whereas very little attention indeed was paid to political institutions. The younger among the sociologists studying politics have indicated a special interest in the processes of nation-building and state-formation. In a country such as Finland, that formerly had been very rural, this implied a special emphasis on the social mobilization of the peasantry.[40]

The differences between the political sociologists and the behaviorally oriented political scientists tended to disappear or rather to become obsolete in the 1970s. Political scientists with a behavioralist stance tend to have stronger theoretical ambitions (as in a large-scale international comparison of the relationship between political processes and social patterns)[41] as well as greater daring to attack crucial problems (as in a very stimulating volume about the background of some populist movements in Finnish politics).[42]

Both political science behavioralists and political sociologists have emphasized the importance of cross-national comparative studies. Both groups had strong ties to the late Stein Rokkan, who played a great activating role in Finnish political studies. Finnish political scientists were coeditors with Rokkan[43] and authors of papers in books edited by him.[44]

As in the international social science community since the late 1960s, Finnish political science has had a new interest in public policy, in social indicators, and in social and public planning. In Finnish political science the most important example of this tendency was a large-scale study on democracy and equality in Finland, the so-called DETA project, led by Ilkka Heiskanen and Tuomo Martikainen. It published more than twenty special reports, the most important dealing with the nature and limitations of power within public administration, equalizing and unequalizing mechanisms in regional policies, the growth of the public sector, and the production of public goods in Finland.[45] Comprehensive studies of public policy were something new in the 1970s, and some very promising doctoral dissertations were presented. Probably, the two most noticeable studies dealt with the ability of public organizations (joint organizations of local government) to act as pressure groups,[46] and with the principles and practice of planning in local government.[47] Among the studies of public policy with implications for political science is a comparative study of the level of living and quality of life in the Scandinavian countries, Denmark, Finland, Norway, and Sweden.[48]

In a country with Finland's geographical location and history, studies in international relations naturally constitute an important part of the output in political science. The interest in this field was expressed, also, in the founding of two governmental research institutes, the Tampere Peace Research Institute, and the Foreign Policy Institute, in Helsinki.

International relations and peace research have certain differences as subfields of political science. In Finland, the latter tends to be more theoretical, whereas the former is descriptive, emphasizing realism as its foremost virtue. Of considerable theoretical interest is, for instance, *Militarization, Conflict Behavior, and Interaction,* a study by the director of the Tampere Peace Research Institute, Raimo Väyrynen.[49] Väyrynen, in his *Conflicts in Finnish-Soviet Relations* which analyzes three sensitive problem cases in the relations between Finland and the USSR,[50] formulates interesting theoretical propositions about sanctions generally used in the field of international relations. Actually, despite small resources, there is an abundance of interesting studies from the field of peace and conflict research. One very systematic study is a doctoral dissertation on variations in internal cohesion under different conditions of external pressures.[51]

In the field of international relations proper studies aiming to legitimize Finland's foreign policy have been increasing. At least, more studies are directly related to Finland's foreign political situation. Earlier, practically all works in the field of international relations focused on the world or on general theoretical problems. Among those, Risto Hyvärinen's doctoral dissertation about theoretical models for explaining international conflicts belongs to the latter category,[52] whereas Göran von Bonsdorff's many studies about the prerequisites for peace in the world are of the former category.[53] In both cases, it is a matter of taste whether they are considered parts of peace research or of the field of international relations. Also, in one doctoral dissertation of 1961 on Soviet attitudes toward nonmilitary regional cooperation,[54] and in another of 1971, based on content analysis of the foreign policy attitudes in the Finnish press,[55] no attempts are made to legitimize or particularly influence the interpretations of Finland's foreign policy in a specific direction. However, in some clearly academic studies from 1972,[56] 1973,[57] and 1975[58] the legitimizing tendencies are fairly obvious.

The last decade has seen an upsurge of theoretical, methodological studies either questioning former approaches or introducing new ones. The study of public administration in Finland has been influenced strongly by Ilkka Heiskanen's study on scientific strategies in administrative and organizational research.[59] It is directed against reductionist strategies because of their low informative value according to Karl Popper's terminology and favors contextual strategies. Theoretically related to the study of public administration are Hannu Nurmi's studies on rationality and public goods.[60] New in Finnish political science are some discussions of systems theory[61] and cybernetics.[62] Also, some interesting new attempts[63] study the relationship between political science and political ideas with the help of Feyerabend's anarchistic theory of knowledge[64] and John Galtung's ideas of a constructivist social science.[65]

ASSOCIATIONAL ACTIVITIES

The Finnish Political Science Association was founded in 1935. It is a scholarly organization whereas labor market problems as a rule are handled not by specific organizations of political scientists but by associations of all social science M.A.s or by general associations for people on the labor market with university degrees.

The most important tasks of the Finnish Political Science Association recently have been its publication program and its international contacts. It organizes meetings but they have declined in importance except perhaps for yearly two-day conferences with a great number of papers.

The Finnish Political Science Association became a member of the International Political Science Association (IPSA) in 1952. Also, it organized international seminars under the auspices of IPSA and other international organizations. The association has played an active part in inter-Scandinavian cooperation in the field. It took an active part in the establishment of the Scandinavian Political Studies yearbook in the mid-1960s and in the founding of the Nordic Political Science Association in the mid-1970s. The Finnish association has actively promoted the participation in both workshops and training seminars of the European Consortium for Political Research (ECPR) although the formal members of the organization are not the national associations but rather university departments.[66]

Membership figures have over the years remained fairly constant, around 320 to 360, but the nature of recruitment has changed. In the earlier years, the association had a membership composed mainly of politicians, high civil servants, and other groups with an interest in the rational discussion of politics. Some of them have remained members but, during the 1970s members were recruited more and more among academic teachers, researchers, Ph.D.s and graduate students. Thus, there has been a very clear trend toward professionalization.

The Finnish Political Science Association participated in the publication of *Scandinavian Political Studies* which was transformed from a yearbook into a quarterly journal in 1978. Domestically more important is the publishing of the quarterly journal *Politiikka* which contains articles in Finnish or Swedish with short English summaries. A book series mainly for the publication of doctoral dissertations in Finnish was started in cooperation with private publishers in 1958. A few publications of the association have been directed specifically at an international audience, such as *Democracy in Finland* (1960); *Finnish Foreign Policy* (1963); and *Essays on Finnish Foreign Policy* (1969).

POLITICAL SCIENCE AND THE WORLD OF POLITICS

The impact of political events on the development of political science in Finland is not easy to assess. The development of political science in a small country such as Finland naturally is affected strongly by the international scientific tendencies. Political events all over the world have similar effects. Nevertheless, there are clearly also some domestic impacts. Some specific impacts have been mentioned already. The rise of behavioralism and, especially, the interest in voting studies definitely had a relationship to the new demands for technical and instrumental knowledge by the expanding party bureaucracies. A virtual division of labor existed between behavioral political scientists and political sociologists. The political scientists focussed on detailed instrumental knowledge about factors influencing individual political behavior and the political sociologists undertook the task of social criticism to a much larger extent. Political sociology was clearly influenced by the basic cleavages and structural change in Finnish society. Also, the rise of studies in public policy had clearly some purely political undercurrents. Toward the end of the 1960s the bases of public policy and planning were clearly coming into the focus of political interest. Also, foreign policy studies have been influenced strongly by political events. All through the 1960s and 1970s, the Finnish government tried to increase its activity in the field of foreign policy, culminating in being host to the European Security Conference in 1975. This has meant a proliferation of reports and studies directly aiming at explaining Finland's foreign political situation.

The influence of political science on political events is even more difficult to measure. Political scientists like other social scientists have influenced greatly the language of public discussion during the decades after World War II. Also, many research findings and interpretations by political scientists have been used as political arguments. Still, it is very much an open question whether political scientists are influencing events or whether they are mainly legitimizing what has happened. The Finnish Political Science Association has not been used as a scholarly consultant to the government as apparently was the expectation when the association was founded.[67] In fact, there are no specific relations between the government and the discipline except that practically all Finnish universities are state owned and all of the Finnish Political Science Association's activities (including its publication program) are paid for entirely by the government. The association is, in some cases, asked to produce statements about committee reports or about appointments in the field of science policy, but so are a great number of similar associations.

Political scientists have been involved in practical politics. Several leaders and functionaries of the political parties have been trained in political science. Some professors in political science have participated in politics as chairmen of political parties or M.P.s. Over 10 percent of the members of the Finnish Parliament as well as several cabinet ministers during recent years have been university graduates with M.A.s in the social sciences. The implications should not be exaggerated. The majority of the Finnish M.P.s do not have university degrees.[68] However, the meaning of politics and participation in politics is not entirely clear. One recent interesting study about the position of the cabinet in Finnish politics has indicated that many forms of political decision-making have moved from the political institutions to the parties, to the interest organizations, and to governmental administrative bodies.[69] A large number of political and social scientists are employed in these bodies, and the influence of the discipline on decision-making might be greater than can be seen on the surface. However, the decision makers are rarely acting as political scientists as such but rather as holders of certain positions.

Notes

1. Fritz Ringer, *The Decline of the German Mandarins. The German Academic Community 1890-1933* (Cambridge, Mass.: Harvard University Press, 1969).

2. Rudolf Holsti, *The Relation of War to the Origin of State* (Helsinki, 1913); Gunnar Landtman, *The Origin of the Inequality of the Social Classes* (London: Kegan Paul, 1938); Rafael Karsten, *La Civilisation de l'Empire Inca: Un état totalitaire du passé* (Paris: Payot, 1952).

3. Yrjö Blomstedt, "A Historical Background of the Finnish Legal System," in J. Uotila, ed., *The Finnish Legal Sys-*

tem (Helsinki: Union of Finnish Lawyers Publishing Co., 1966).

4. O. W. Kuusinen, ed., *Marxismin-leninismin perusteet* (Moscow: Publisher of Literature in Foreign Languages, 1960).

5. Yrjö Ruutu (Ruuth), *Kansakunta, Poliittinen tutkimus* (Helsinki, 1922).

6. Jussi Teljo. *Valtio ja yhteiskunta Snellmanin valtiofilosofiassa* (Helsinki, 1934) and *Kansaneduskunta ja valtion tulo- ja menoarvio* (Jyväskylä, 1938).

7. Sven Lindman, *Statsrådet i Finland 1919-1934* (Uppsala; Skrifter utgivna av Statsvetenskapliga föreningen i Uppsala 4, 1935;) and *Studier över parlamentarismens tillämpning i Finland 1919-1926. Med särskild hänsyn till regeringsbillningens problem* (Åbo: Acta Academiae Aboensis, Humaniora 12, no. 1, 1937).

8. Georg Jellinek, *Allgemeine Staatslehre, Zweite durchgesehene und vermehrte Auflage* (Berlin: Verlag von O. Häring, 1905).

9. K. R. Brotherus, "Valtiotieteet," *Valtiotieteiden käsikirja 4,* (Helsinki: Tietosanakirjayhtiö, 1924).

10. James Bryce, *Modern Democracies,* 2 vols. (London: Macmillan & Co., 1923).

11. Jan-Mogens Jansson, *Hans Kelsens statsteori mot bakgrunden av hans rättsfilosofiska åskådning*, Commentationes Humanarum Litterarum, vol. 15, no. 5 (Helsingfors: Societas Scientiarum Fennica, 1950).

12. Erik Allardt, "Political Science and Sociology," *Scandinavian Political Studies*, vol. 4 (Oslo: Universitetsforlaget, 1969), pp. 11-21.

13. Jan-Magnus Jansson, *Frihet och jämlikhet: En studie över den politiska demokratin* (Helsingfors: Söderströms, 1952).

14. Tuttu Tarkiainen, *Die athenische Demokratie* (Zurich: Artemis Verlag, 1966).

15. Jaakko Nousiainen, *The Finnish Political System* (Cambridge, Mass.: Harvard University Press, 1971).

16. Maurice Duverger, *Les Partis Politiques* (Paris: Armand Colin, 1951). See also his *Les régimes politiques* (Paris, Presses Universitaires de France, 1948).

17. Ilkka Heiskanen, *Theoretical Approaches and Scientific Strategies in Administrative and Organizational Research: A Methodological Study*, Commentationes Humanarum Litterarum, vol. 39, no. 2 (Helsingfors, Helsinki: Societas Scientiarum Fennica, 1967).

18. Ilkka Heiskanen and Tuomo Martikainen, "On Comparative Policy Analysis: Methodological Problems, Theoretical Considerations and Empirical Applications," *Scandinavian Political Studies*, vol. 9 (Oslo: Universitetsforlaget, 1974).

19. See William C. Mitchell, "The Shape of Political Theory to Come: From Political Sociology to Political Economy," in S. M. Lipset, ed., *Politics and the Social Sciences* (New York: Oxford University Press, 1969).

20. Dag Anckar, *David Eastons politiska teori: En intern och extern modellkritik* (Åbo: Acta Academiae Aboensis, ser. A, vol. 50, no. 2, 1974). See also Ilmari Susiluoto, "Systeemiteoria politiikan tutkimuksessa: huomioita kotimaisesta keskustelusta" *Politiikka* 13 (1971): 230-42.

21. Erkki Berndtson, "Political Science in the Era of Post-Behavioralism. The Need for Self-Reflection," Scandinavian Political Studies, vol. 10 (Oslo: Universitetsforlaget, 1975). See also: Kari Palonen, *Politiikan tutkimuksen esteet ja mahdollisuudet valtio-opissa* (Helsinki: Institute of Political Science, University of Helsinki, Research Reports, ser. A, 1978).

22. Pertti Pesonen, "The Political Science Profession in Finland," Scandinavian Political Studies, vol. 12 (Oslo: Universitetsforlaget, 1978), pp. 29-33.

23. Pesonen, "Political Science Profession," pp. 33-36.

24. Dag Anckar, "Trends in Political Research: Finland" *Scandinavian Political Studies,* vol. 12 (Oslo: Universitetsforlaget, 1978), pp. 108-9.

25. Pesonen, "Political Science Profession," pp. 41-43.

26. Pertti Pesonen, *An Election in Finland: Party Activities and Voter Reactions* (New Haven, London: Yale University Press, 1968).

27. Pertti Pesonen, ed., *Protestivaalit, nuorisovaalit. Tutkielmia kansanedustajien vaaleista 1966, 1970 ja 1972* (Helsinki, Tampere: Ylioppilastuki, 1972).

28. Onni Rantala, *Suomen poliittiset alueet I. Poliittisten aatteiden levinneisyys 1907-1958*, 2d ed. rev. and enl. (Turku, 1970).

29. Risto Sänkiaho, *Puolueiden alueellinen kannatus Uudenmaan läänissä* (Helsinki, Helsingfors: Societas Scientiarum Fennica, 1973).

30. Göran von Bonsdorff, *Studier rörande den moderna liberalismen i de nordiska länderna* (Ekenäs: Skrifter utgivna av Fahlbeckska Stiftelsen, 1954).

31. Jaakko Nousiainen, *Kommunismi Kuopion läänissä* (Joensuu, 1956).

32. Erik Allardt, *Social struktur och politisk aktivitet* (Borgå: Söderströms, 1956).

33. Olavi Borg, *Suomen puolueet ja puolueohjelmat 1880-1964* (Helsinki: WSOY, 1965).

34. Martti Noponen, *Kansanedustajien sosiaalinen tausta Suomessa* (Helsinki: WSOY, 1964).

35. Matti Oksanen, *Kansanedustajan rooli* (Helsinki: Gaudeamus, 1972).

36. Pekka Nyholm, *Parliament, Government and Multi-Dimensional Party Relations*, Commentationes Scientiarum Socialium, vol. 2, (Helsinki, Helsingfors: Societas Scientiarum Fennica, 1972).

37. Erik Allardt, "Types of Protests and Alienation," in E. Allardt and S. Rokkan, eds., *Mass Politics, Studies in Political Sociology* (New York: Free Press, 1970), pp. 45-63.

38. Paavo Seppänen, "Dimensions and Phases of Change in Finnish Society," *International Journal of Politics* 4 (1974): 222-53.

39. Antti Eskola, "Perception of the Basic Cleavages of Finnish Society," *Journal of Peace Research* 7 (1970): 259-66. See also Erik Allardt, "Patterns of Class Conflict and Working Class Consciousness in Finnish Politics," in E. Allardt and Y. Littunen, eds., *Cleavages, Ideologies, and Party Systems* (Turku: Transactions of the Westermarck Society 10, 1964), pp. 97-131 and Elina Haavio-Mannila, "Sex Roles in Politics," Scandinavian Political Studies, vol. 5 (Oslo: Universitetsforlaget, 1970), pp. 209-40.

40. Risto Alapuro, "On the Political Mobilization of the Agrarian Population in Finland," *Scandinavian Political Studies*, vol. 11 (Oslo, Universitetsforlaget, 1976), pp. 51-76.

41. Tatu Vanhanen, *Political and Social Structures: Part I, American Countries 1880-1973* (Tampere: Institute of Political Science, University of Tampere, Research Reports, 1975).

42. Voitto Helander, ed., *Vennamolaisuus populistisena joukkoliikkenä* (Hämeenlinna: Karisto, 1971).

43. Erik Allardt and Stein Rokkan, eds., *Mass Politics: Studies in Political Sociology* (New York: Free Press, 1970).

44. E.g., Erik Allardt and Pertti Pesonen, "Cleavages in Finnish Politics," in S. M. Lipset and S. Rokkan, eds., *Party Systems and Voter Alignments: Cross-National Perspectives* (New York: Free Press, 1967), pp. 325-66.

45. E.g., Ilkka Heiskanen, *On Democracy, Equality, Efficiency and Justice as Criteria for Developing Local Government and Designing Linkages between the Central and Local Levels of Government* (Helsinki: Institute of Political Science, University of Hensinki, Research Reports, ser. C, deta 17, 1975). See also Tuomo Martikainen, *Julkisen sektorin kasvu Suomessa* (Helsinki: Institute of Political Science, University of Helsinki, Research Reports, ser. C, deta 13, 1975).

46. Voitto Helander *Julkisyhteisöt vaikuttajina* (Hämeenlinna: Karisto, 1971).

47. Krister Ståhlberg, *Teori och praxis i kommunal planering* (Åbo: meddelanden från Stiftelsens for Åbo Akademi forskningsinstitut, n.s. 4, 1975).

48. Erik Allardt and Hannu Uusitalo, "Dimensions of Welfare in a Comparative Study of the Scandinavian Societies," *Scandinavian Political Studies*, vol. 7 (Oslo: Universitetsforlaget, 1972), pp. 9-28.

49. Raimo Väyrynen, *Militarization, Conflict Behavior, and Interaction: Three Ways of Analyzing the Cold War* (Tampere: Tampere Peace Research Institute: Research Reports 3, 1973).

50. Raimo Väyrynen, *Conflicts in Finnish-Soviet Relations: Three Comparative Case Studies* (Tampere: Acta Universitatis Tamperensis, vol. 47, 1972).

51. Vilho Harle, *International Tension: An Application of Cohesion Theory and Event Analysis to East-West Relations during the Post-War Years* (Tampere: Institute of Political Science, University of Tampere, Research Reports 39, 1975).

52. Risto Hyvärinen, *Monistic and Pluralistic Interpretations in the Study of International Politics: A Methodological Examination*, Commentationes Humanarum Litterarum, vol. 24, no. 1 (Helsinki: Societas Scientiarum Fennica, 1958).

53. Göran von Bonsdorff, *Världpolitik i teknikens tidsålder* (Ekenäs, 1961). See also Göran von Bonsdorff, *Regionalismen i den internationella politiken* (Helsingfors: Söderström & Co., 1967).

54. Klaus Törnudd, *Soviet Attitudes towards Non-Military Regional Cooperation*, Commentationes Humanarum Litterarum, vol. 28 (Helsingfors: Societas Scientiarum Fennica, 1961).

55. Dag Anckar, *Partiopinioner och utrikespolitik* (Åbo: Acta Academiae Aboensis, ser. A, Humaniora 41, 1971).

56. Osmo Apunen, *Kansallinen realismi ja puolueettomuus Suomen ulkopoliittisina valintoina* (Tampere: Institute of Political Science, University of Tampere, Research Reports 28, 1972).

57. Harto Hakovirta, *Suomen läntinen integraatiopolitiikka ja puolueettomuuspyrkimykset 1947-1971*, (Tampere, Institute of Political Science, University of Tampere, Research Reports 30, 1973).

58. Harto Hakovirta and Raimo Väyrynen, eds., *Suomen ulkopolitiikka* (Jyväskyla: Gaudeamus, 1975).

59. Ilkka Heiskanen, *Theoretical Approaches and Scientific Strategies in Administrative and Organizational Research: A Methodological Study* 39, no. 2 (Helsingfors, Helsinki: Societas Scientiarum Fennica, 1967).

60. Hannu Nurmi, *Rationality and Public Goods: Essays in Analytic Political Theory*, Commentationes Scientiarum Socialium 9 (Helsinki, Helsingfors: Societas Scientiarum Fennica, 1977).

61. E.g., Dag Anckar, *Partisystem, withinputs och politiska resurser: några normativa iakttagelser kring partisystematiska demokratikonsekvenser i Finland* (Åbo: Meddelanden från Statsvetenskapliga fakulteten vid Åbo Akademi, se. B 43, 1975).

62. Ilmari Susiluoto, "Sosialismi ja systeemiajattelu," (with an English summary) *Politiikka* 20 (1978), pp. 3-20.

63. Kari Palonen, *Aatetutkimus aatekritiikkinä* (Helsinki: Gaudeamus, 1975).

64. Paul Feyerabend, *Against Method* (London: Humanities Press, 1975).

65. Johan Galtung, *Methodology and Ideology: Theory and Methods of Social Research*, vol. 1 (Copenhagen: Christian Ejlers, 1977).

66. Pesonen, "Political Science Profession," pp. 43-45.

67. Ibid., p. 44.

68. Ibid., p. 43.

69. Heiskanen, Ilkka, *Valtioneuvoston asema Suomen poliittisessa järjestelmässä* (Helsinki, *Valtioneuvoston Historia 1917-1966*, 3, 1975).

Bibliography

(In addition to the works appearing in the notes of this chapter)

Democracy in Finland, Studies in Politics and Government. Helsinki: Finnish Political Science Association, 1960.

Elovainie, Mauri K. and Huopaniemi, J. "Finland and the Study of International Relations 1960-64." *Cooperation and Conflict* 1, no. 27 (1965): 60-67.

——— and Lehtinen, R. *A Bibliography on International Relations Literature Published in Denmark, Finland, Norway, and Sweden 1945-60.* Stockholm: Utrikespolitiska institutet, 1972.

Heiskanen, Ilkka and Sinkkonen, Sirkka. *From Legalism to Information Technology and Politicization: The Development of Public Administration in Finland.* Institute of Political Science, University of Helsinki, Research Reports no. 31 (1974): 31.

Jansson, Jan-Magnus. "Der Staatsapparat als Gegenstand der politischen Wissenschaft der nordischen Ländern." In

Politische Forschung, edited by O. Stammer. (Cologne: Westdeutscher Verlag, 1960): 137-51.

Kastari, Paave. "The Historical Background of Finnish Constitutional Ideas." *Scandinavian Studies on Law* 7 (1963): 61-77.

Nousiainen, Jaakko. "Political Research in Scandinavia, 1960-65: Finland." *Scandinavian Political Studies* 1 (1966): 257-66.

Pesonen, Pertti. "Party Support in a Fragmented System." In *Electoral Behavior. A Comparative Handbook*, edited by Richard Rose (New York: Free Press, 1974): 271-314.

Uotila, Jaakko, ed. *The Finnish Legal System*. Helsinki: Union of Finnish Lawyers Publishing Co., 1966.

Uusitalo, Hannu. *Class Structure and Party Choice: A Scandinavian Comparison*. Research Group for Comparative Sociology, University of Helsinki, Research Reports, no. 10 (1975): 41.

13 FRANCE*

PIERRE FAVRE

Introduction

Perhaps much more so than for other countries the date 1945 is significant in the history of French national political science. Indeed, the period 1945-1950 may be considered that of the birth of French political science as an autonomous, scientific discipline. That political science became science so late in France may be surprising. As a matter of fact, this country has a very old tradition of reflection on politics (one thinks of Bodin, Montesquieu, Rousseau, Tocqueville). Since the nineteenth century, it has had a sociology which, with Durkheim and the Durkheimians, was elevated to the rank of the science of all social phenomena. Throughout the Third Republic, an intense politicization of society could have favored the appearance of a political science.

Yet nothing of the kind happened. For a number of reasons political science could not appear in France at the end of the nineteenth century. Sociology, born in the Faculty of Letters, too absorbed in its conquest of legitimacy through its combat with philosophy and the humanities, left political science to the jurists at the very time that the latter were bringing the science of the state back to the pure and simple study of juridical standards.[1] Of course, the famous Ecole libre des sciences politiques of rue Saint-Guillaume in Paris has been in existence since 1872, but its instruction, intended to prepare students for the important recruitment examinations for senior civil servants, is essentially economic, juridical, and historical.

As a result, during the first half of the twentieth century French political science existed only nominally. There was no scientific community of *politologues* representing itself as such, no scientific journals or centers of specialized research, and no textbooks. The few research workers were isolated. The breakthroughs of French political science before 1945 were the result only of individual efforts.

Therefore, this chapter will be centered on the history of a conquest carried out since 1945, a conquest of disciplinary autonomy and of "scientificity," even if at the outset—it will be established at the time of the examination of the present state of political science in France—the community of French political scientists, having become important, may appear to be profoundly divided and subject to the rivalry of sociologists who resent more and more the necessity of integrating political subject matter into their analyses.

An initial, quite central difficulty confronts those who wish to write the history of a discipline, whether the discipline appears to be formed or, as political science in France, is in the process of emerging. This difficulty results from the impossibility of really fixing the boundaries of a discipline, an impossibility which cannot be established here, but whose existence and the reasons for it are familiar to epistemologists. Therefore, should French political science, still in the process of formation, consist of all the works which by *institutional* origin were called political in nature (because they were, for example, written by a member of l'Association Française de Science Politique or by a professor at an Institut d'Etudes Politiques)? Or should it be limited to research having political phenomena as the subject (even though agreement does not exist—and, moreover, by nature, cannot exist—on the definition of the subject matter of political science)? In the following pages, a different route has been chosen, even though it allows numerous ambiguities to remain and—in the state of our research—is too intuitive. *Politologique* studies are identified as those which have been perceived socially as

---

*I wish to thank Professors Georges Lavau and Bernard Lacroix, who graciously agreed to read the first version of this chapter and whose critical remarks were very useful.

belonging to the domain of political science or those whose subject matter is usually termed political. In a word, this designation of the subject matter of political science is an empirical problem and not a theoretical question.[2]

The State of Political Science in 1945

Shortly after World War II, French political science began by taking possession of the areas of investigation which could be the most easily conceded to it, for it had explored them slightly already. In 1945 political science in France remained, therefore, as has often been written, the daughter of history and of law (also it is, in fact, the daughter of geography, since André Siegfried was a geographer). With rare exceptions, it had not yet put into practice new methods borrowed, for example, from psychometry or from the experimental sciences. It had, then, three preferred fields.

First, in France constitutional studies have always consisted of the comparative study and classification of political regimes and the functioning of political institutions, as well as the presentation of various political doctrines, projects for the reform of the state, and so forth. Such was the case, although unevenly, in the great Third Republic treatises on constitutional law of Joseph Barthélemy, Léon Duguit, A. Esmein, Maurice Hauriou, and Julien Laferrière, among others. This orientation was taken up again and even carried farther by the professors of civil law who succeeded the prewar generation. In 1943 Georges Burdeau published a study entitled *Le droit public et l'Etat* which became, in 1949, the first volume of his *Traité de science politique;* Georges Vedel and Maurice Duverger each published in 1948 a *Manuel de droit constitutionnel,* the second previously being entitled *Manuel de droit constitutionnel et de science politique*. The history of political ideas (a classical discipline, illustrated for example in 1932 by a book by A. Thibaudet, *Les idées polititques de la France*) and the history of political institutions became more and more the subject of studies and autonomous courses. Two books born of two schools of thought soon appeared, were used by generations of students, and put a mark on the discipline. They were the work of a professor of the Faculté de droit in Paris, Jean-Jacques Chevallier: *Les grandes oeuvres politiques de Machiavel à nos jours* (first edition 1949, second edition, 1976) and *Histoire des institutions et des régimes politiques de la France moderne* (the first edition, 1952, covers the period 1789-1945;[3] the second edition, 1972, is current through 1962).

As a second field of preference one could almost say that, in 1945 as throughout the century (and such a conception has not disappeared), contemporary political and social history belonged to the domain of the political sciences.[4] Often, this contemporary history was fragmented into national histories and enriched with social geography and economics (such as contemporary Germany, the United States, the British Empire). It was completed by contemporary diplomatic history. Some historical studies were more specialized, and inaugurated the French tradition of study of political parties: that was the case with André Siegfried's *Tableau des partis politiques en France* (1930) and François Goguel's classic, *La politique des partis sous la IIIe République* (1946).

The last area of preference for French political science in 1945 was much more specific and found its origins in the works of the French school of *geography* at the end of the nineteenth century. It was also the one which used the most rigorous analytical methods and was the closest to a scientific model: it concerned the study of elections. The situation was truly paradoxical: the masterwork in this domain appeared in 1913, the celebrated *Tableau politique de la France de l'Ouest sous la IIIe République* of André Siegfried. The very success of the work seemed to hinder the appearance of a true school of electoral sociology during the period between the two world wars, especially as André Siegfried himself did not publish the results of his next investigations (a course on southern France at the Collège de France). Therefore, not until shortly after World War II did the development of French electoral sociology take place: F. Goguel published electoral geography articles in the journal *Esprit* on each of the elections from 1945 to 1951; A. Siegfried in 1949 dedicated a work to *La géographie électorale de l'Ardèche sous la Troisième République,* and many of the first volumes of the collection of the "*Cahiers de la Fondation Nationale des Sciences Politiques*" were works of electoral sociology.[5]

The Evolution of Political Science since 1945

THE INTELLECTUAL STRUCTURE
OF THE DISCIPLINE

The trap of idealism (in the philosophical sense of the term) that the title of this paragraph harbors should be avoided. Everything, in fact, does not happen lightly at the intellectual level, as opposition between doctrines, between conceptions, and scientific methods. Knowledge of the structure (both intellectual and social) of a scientific discipline cannot really be acquired without the results of sociological works (of the type carried out by the sociology of science) taking this discipline as their object. Unfortunately, this is not the case for French political science and too many data are still lacking to present an explanatory picture. In fact, a discipline certainly is structured around problematical oppositions which can be indexed without too much difficulty, but this structure, though the most obvious, is not the only interesting one. The place of political science in the changing configuration of the diverse disciplines which share and dispute the field of the social sciences would have to be described. That description would include the variations during the last thirty years of the professional positions of political scientists (professors of law, nontenured teachers, researchers) and the evolutions of their strategy. Also, that would cover different stages of (1) the struggle for recognition of the scientific legitimacy of the study of politics and (2) the internal competition in the learned community for the monopoly of that legitimacy. Finally, that would include the different social determinants that may explain why specialized researchers in political science appeared so late. Thus, the extent to which the differences in social origin of political scientists conditions the intellectual structure of the discipline would have to be discussed. This agenda shows why its items can only be mentioned here. The research which would permit a response to these questions with regard to France has not been undertaken yet.[6]

THE TEACHING OF POLITICAL SCIENCE

The organization of the teaching of political science in France has been transformed considerably since 1945. Between 1945 and 1954, the situation was simple: only the Instituts d'Etudes Politiques (IEP)[7] issued diplomas mentioning political studies—diplomas obtained, in principle, after three years of attendance at school after the *baccalauréat*. Other institutions, principally the Facultés de Droit and the Facultés des Lettres, even if some of their instruction had a content close to that dispensed in the IEP, did not give diplomas in political science.

This situation should be clarified by three remarks. Enrollment in the IEP remains complementary. Students of the IEP almost always pursue simultaneously other, more traditional studies, such as a law degree or, less commonly, the degree in arts. Secondly, political science as taught in the IEP (and which is traditionally distinguished by the plural, *Sciences politiques,* covers an ill-defined domain, where general history, social geography, economics, law, the study of administrative institutions, the study of social questions, and international relations are side by side. Political science, in the narrow sense of the term, is rarely present there. Essentially, the IEP prepares students for the important administrative competitive examination and, especially, for the entrance examination for the prestigious Ecole Nationale d'Administration, created in 1945. Thirdly, the only instruction that challenges the monopoly of the IEP in the study of political science is that of the Facultés de Droit. Since the end of the nineteenth century, after a redistribution of disciplines the Facultés de Droit were obliged to teach political science, even though they gave it a very marginal place especially between the two world wars. The Facultés de Lettres do not in any manner award diplomas in political science and are totally absent from the process described (even if, here and there, in sociology, history, or philosophy some isolated instruction of political science exists).

Between 1954 and the intense movement for reforms that was born in the Facultés in the aftermath of the "events" of May 1968, political science became in the Facultés de Droit a recognized subject that accompanied legal studies systematically, although modestly. In this period, instruction and programs were set nationally. Therefore, all the Facultés de Droit in France devoted about 15 percent of their courses to topics related to political science. The list of these courses merits being reproduced: constitutional law and political institutions, methods of the social sciences, history of political ideas until 1800, history of political ideas since 1800, great contemporary political problems. Thus, the progress of political studies is obvious in the Facultés de Droit. In the same period, a third cycle of political science was instituted (a year of *Diplôme d'Etudes Supérieures* after the *Licence,* opening the possibility of writing a state thesis in political science) which allowed a true, although hurried, specialization in political science. Between 1954 and 1968 to 1970 a student who wanted to specialize in political science in France was compelled, practically speaking, to devote the major part of the time to strictly juridical studies, at least during the four years that followed the *baccalauréat*. To complete that education meant to pursue courses at other institutions: Instituts d'Etudes Politiques, departments of sociology of the Facultés de Lettres, seminars of the Ecole Pratique des Hautes Etudes, courses in history or philosophy somewhere else, and so on.[8]

Beginning in 1970, university regulation of political science improved considerably. The autonomy of the universities, written into the *Loi d'orientation* that was passed after May 1968, permitted them to multiply and diversify their courses in political science, indeed, to create specialized departments (such as the important Unité d'Enseignements et de Recherches de Science politique of the Université de Paris 1) or centers of specific research (Centre d'étude de la vie locale at Bordeaux, for example). The evolution seems to have been completed with the creation in 1978 of a *maîtrise* in political science, with a series of courses, including these required courses: analysis of political behavior, methods of political science and treatment of data, comparative institutions and political organizations, political philosophy and analysis of ideologies. A little earlier, a specialized competition destined to recruit professors of advanced study in political science had been created, thus accomplishing the separation of political science and law.

To conclude, one can thus enumerate the present stages of French instruction in political science (while neglecting some channels which are more particularized):

The *Licence* obtained, in principle, three years after the certificate of advanced study. Usually this degree remains unspecialized in political science (frequently the *Licence en Droit* or a diploma from an IEP)

The *maîtrise* specializing in political science, obtained in one year

The *Diplôme de IIIe cycle* in political science (in a Faculté de Droit or an IEP) obtained in one year, followed by a doctoral thesis of the *IIIe cycle* or of the state in political science, which requires from two (for a thesis of the *IIIe cycle*) to five years or more (for a state thesis) research.

Tenured teachers who have specialized in political science are recruited, either through a national competition (*l'Agrégation*) or, for the professors, through a two-step recruitment competition—University, Higher Council of the University Corps—for the *maîtres assistants*. In both cases, the state doctorate in political science and supplementary research works are required. Certain holders of the *doctorat ès Lettres*—obtained through considerable research often requiring more than ten years—are also professors of political science, as specialists in history, sociology, or the political life of a foreign country.

RESEARCH IN POLITICAL SCIENCE

The most noteworthy contributions. The state of political science in France in the years 1945 to 1950 has been described above. The present state of political science is described below. During the intermediate period (1950–1975) many contributions were made to political studies. Selecting those most worthy of attention is not an easy task. If, at different moments during those 25 years, and notably in 1950[9], 1960[10], 1965[11], and 1968-69[12], *politologues* of great renown had as their objective to take stock of the political science situation in France, the reader cannot simply be referred to their publications. How can a few lines present dozens of works and isolate theoretical currents? How can a single paragraph show relationships, point out doctrinal quarrels and institutional oppositions, and analyze the mutations of the communities of scholars? Therefore, of necessity, a listing will be made of the works cited most often. A catalog will be prepared of the recognized works by classifying them *according to the very criteria used most often during that period* when the unity of the discipline appeared relatively stronger than today.

The works of synthesis, with which it is customary to begin and which present systematically the subject matter and the methods and the results of political science frequently are born of university teaching. Certain ones, like the courses of Georges Vedel and Marcel Prélot, remain in mimeographed form. Others are presented in the form of textbooks, like those of Maurice Duverger (*Méthodes de la science politique,* first edition, 1954) and those of Madeleine Grawitz (*Méthodes des sciences sociales,* last edition, 1972) or a work like the *Introduction à la science politique* of Jean Meynaud (1959). One should set apart the monumental *Traité de science politique* of Georges Burdeau, in seven volumes that appeared from 1949 to 1957 (second edition, 9 volumes, 1966–1976), a systematic analysis of political regimes from a point of view which remains very juridical.

Political theory, whose subject remains controversial, is illustrated by the works of Bertrand de Jouvenel (*Du pouvoir,* 1947, *De la souveraineté,* 1955, *De la politique pure,* 1963) and, in a completely different direction, by those of Eric Weil (*Hegel et l'Etat,* 1950; *Philosophie politique,* 1956) and of Julien Freund (*L'essence du politique,* 1965). The articles of Raymond Aron subsequently collected in a volume under the title of *Etudes politiques* (1972) deserve mention here, also. The history of political ideas, whose specificity relative to political theory does not always appear clearly in this period, is the subject of many works, often in the tradition of Jean-Jacques Chevallier. Not everything can be cited, since the territory covered is immense. Its measure may be taken by referring to the important bibliographies in the two-volume textbook by Jean Touchard, Louis Bodin, Pierre Jeannin, Georges Lavau, and Jean Sirinelli, *Histoire des idées politiques* (first edition, 1959).

Political institutions are studied, sometimes from a broad comparative perspective, as in three works created in courses at the Sorbonne by Raymond Aron (*Dix-huit leçons sur la société industrielle,* 1962; *La lutte des classes,* 1964; *Démocratie et totalitarisme,* 1965), more often from the point of view of constitutional law as it pertains to political life, as in numerous textbooks (those for example of Maurice Duverger, André Hauriou, Marcel Prélot). Simultaneously, many works and articles describe the French political regime, whether in pedagogical syntheses (François Goguel and Alfred Grosser, *La politique en France*, fifth edition, 1975), or in more historical works (René Rémond, *La vie politique en France depuis 1789*, two published volumes, 1965, 1969, a third yet to appear; Jacques Chapsal and Alain Lancelot, *La vie politique en France depuis 1940*, fifth edition, 1979), or in doctoral theses on civil law (Pierre Avril, *Le régime politique de la Ve République*, second edition, 1967, Jean Gicquel, *Essai sur les pratique de la Ve République*, 1968), or in the chronicles of parliamentary life and law (Georges Berlia, Léo Hamon). At the same time, numerous foreign regimes are the subject of comprehensive studies, whether from a classical viewpoint dominated by constitutionalist preoccupations (as in the works of André and Suzanne Tunc, *Le système constitutionnel aux Etats Unis d'Amérique*, 2 volumes, 1954, or those of André Mathiot, *Le Régime politique britannique*, 1955, *La vie politique aux Etats-Unis et les tendances récentes*, 1956) or in a manner which couples contemporary history with political analysis (as in the studies of Alfred Grosser, *L'Allemagne de l'Occident, 1945-1952*, 1953, *La démocratie de Bonn, 1949-1957*, 1958, of François Fejto, *Histoire des démocraties populaires*, volume 1, 1952, volume 2, 1969).

The study of political parties has been dominated during the whole period by two authors, Maurice Duverger, on the one hand, with his masterwork *Les partis politiques*, 1951; Georges Lavau, on the other, with his 1953 book, a rejoinder to the preceding work, *Partis politiques et réalitiés sociales*, and especially by his articles ("*Partis et systèmes politiques: interactions et fonctions*," "*A la recherche d'un cadre théorique pour l'étude du Parti communiste français*"). The more classic works of Maurice Duverger have opened the way for a multitude of research articles, works, or theses (for example, those of Albert Mabileau, *Le Parti libéral dans le système constitutionnel britannique*, 1953, and of Jean-Louis Seurin, *La structure interne des partis politiques américains*, 1953). Of a different nature, certain books take the history of a partisan political tradition as their subject. Such is the celebrated study of René Rémond, *La droite en France de la première restauration à la Ve République*, third edition, 2 volumes, 1968). A little later, the study of pressure groups was added to that of parties (cf. the books of Jean Meynaud and that of Stanley Hoffmann et al. on *Le mouvement Poujade*, 1956). The many works that study electoral behavior cannot be listed here. The number of such specialists is large enough to permit the Fondation Nationale des Sciences Politiques (FNSP) to devote a volume (*Cahiers* of the FNSP) to each of the French national elections that took place between 1956 and 1967.

During this period, the specialists in social psychology have been working to lay the foundations for a political psychology: the best-known are Alfred Sauvy (*Le pouvoir et l'opinion, Essai de psychologie politique et sociale*, 1949, and *La nature sociale, introduction à la psychologie politique*, 1957) and Jean Stoetzel (*Les sondages d'opinion publique*, 1948, and *Psychologie sociale*, 1963).

The last sector where French research was abundant between 1950 and 1975 is that of international relations. Two principal currents existed during the time. One remained in the historical tradition, its most remarkable representatives being Pierre Renouvin and Jean-Baptiste Duroselle (see especially their *Introduction à l'histoire des relations internationales*, 1964). The other was more theoretical and originated in the fundamental work of Raymond Aron (*Paix et guerre entre les nations*, 1962). Among studies which focus on the role of geographic factors in international relations, one important work does not seem to have had the influence that one would expect: Jean Gottmann's *La politique des Etats et leur géographie* (1952).

To conclude this section, let us say again how misleading is a presentation which is made in several lines, and, therefore, omits some of the most eminent authors (not to mention that the choice of these authors is partly arbitrary and the omissions are numerous). To be sure, political science in France has progressed, thanks to the works of the most obvious masters of the discipline, but it has progressed just as much because during these years a true scientific community was formed, a community made up of more specialized researchers; of less productive or, rightly or wrongly, less well-known authors; of teachers absorbed in their pedagogic or administrative duties; of advanced students whose work gives rise to underground publications or unpublished monographs. A portrait of political science in France would show its true dimensions only if it included and put into perspective hundreds of books and articles whose accumulation has given life to the discipline. The bibliography cited previously, prepared in 1960 under the direction of Jean Meyriat, lists 603 works by 352 authors. Each of them played a part in making French political science a progressively more scientific discipline, recognized by universities. They all contributed to setting the direction it has taken.

Methodological Developments

The adjective "methodological" will be used here in its narrowest sense, meaning "techniques of the gathering and analysis of data." To treat the methods in political science in the broadest meaning (as in Durkheim's *Les règles de la méthode sociologique* or as in "the experimental method"), would have to take into account the progress in the very conception of the *politologique* position: development of the sociological method and the decline of juridical analysis, the appearance of a Marxist methodology, new space made for theorizing, reevaluation of the comparative method, or efforts at model-building.[13] In fact, the study of this progress is inseparable from the presentation of the present situation of French political science and from the sudden appearance in the discipline of schools which do not have the same methodological presuppositions. This progress, then, will be sketched in the last part of this chapter. The meaning having been so restricted, the methodological developments of French political science since 1945 appear tangible, especially in the techniques of observation and the analysis of data.

The development of techniques of observation and of gathering data has been considerable in the study of public opinion. Sample surveys have become systematic and the technique has been mastered. Unfortunately, and without exception, the data collected in this manner remain the property of those who direct the surveys and are not at the disposal of the entire scientific community. More recently utilized in political science but having acquired full citizenship already, is the technique of the nondirected interview which has shown itself to be rich. The progress of techniques to study opinion and social stereotypes has been paralleled in the development of greater systematization in exploiting existing data. Researchers analyze exhaustively yearbooks such as *Who's Who in France*, electoral lists, leaflets, and so forth. On the other hand, in spite of past examples, certain methods are still little practiced: for example, participant observation and ethnography.

Techniques for analysis of data should be improved especially in two directions (other techniques like cartography or graphic analysis not having made notable progress in political science). The first direction is the analysis of political discourse, which has taken in France the form of qualitative linguistic analysis of texts to bring to light and/or to make note of the effect on the discourse of the social conditions of its production.[14] The second direction is statistical analysis. Recent years have seen remarkable development in methods of automatic computation, notably multivariate analyses ("typological" analyses and factorial analyses principally), which has led in a roundabout way to the establishment of a bank of electoral data at the FNSP (unfortunately, the only such bank in France).

ASSOCIATIONAL ACTIVITIES

Associations

Only one national association exists in France, *l'Association Française de Science Politique* (AFSP), created in 1949 and administered by a council which has been presided over successively by André Siegfried, Jean-Jacques Chevallier, and François Goguel. The general-secretary of the AFSP is Jean-Luc Parodi, who succeeded Jean Charlot and Alain Lancelot. The association has about 600 members and organizes, usually in Paris at the FNSP, frequent study days, round tables, and discussion debates. Several specialized study groups have been created under its aegis: for instance, on French parliamentary studies, on the Socialist party, on the European Communist movement. In relation to the associational life in political science, France remains as centralized as in other domains. Thus, regional associations of political science do not exist, with the single exception of the Lorraine Political Science Group in Nancy (created in 1974). Late in 1981, the AFSP held its first full-fledged convention.

Journals

The only French journal devoted entirely to political science is the *Revue Française de Science Politique*, published under the sponsorship of the Association Française de Science Politique and presently edited by Georges Lavau.[15] Its content has evolved considerably since its creation in 1951. Until the late 1950s, the contributors were largely from the universities: professors of law, historians, philosophers. Then, the *Revue* became almost exclusively the organ of the research laboratories of the FNSP; the majority of the articles reported the results of factual work dealing with limited subjects. Recently the journal has been accepting articles which are much more diversified, emanating from researchers of varied backgrounds reflecting more faithfully the theoretical preoccupations that have appeared at the heart of the discipline.

Although the *Revue Française de Science Politique* is the only specialized journal in political science, it is not the only one that publishes political science articles. A considerable number of French journals of very varied nature are now publishing work that interests the discipline. These journals may be classified in four groups.

Sociology journals publish political sociology articles and less-specialized articles that include the political dimension. The principal representatives of this category are the *Revue Française de Sociologie; Actes de la Recherche en Sciences Sociales* (journal of the Centre de sociologie européenne directed by Pierre Bourdieu); *Cahiers Internationaux de Sociologie;* the *Archives Européennes de Sociologie,* and *Année sociologique*.

Journals on particular subjects include *Sondages*, published since 1938 by the Institut Français d'Opinion Publique; *Relations Internationales*, which remains primarily a historical journal; *Sociologie du Travail;* and the *Revue Française d'Administration Publique* which publishes articles about administrative science.

Less technical journals are directed more at a cultivated public than at the scientific community, which prefer studies on political life. These journals open their pages to political actors themselves and include *Pouvoirs* (subtitled "*Revue d'études constitutionnelles et politiques*," whose first number appeared in May 1977), *Project* (which, for example, publishes an analysis of the results by Alain Lancelot after each election), and *Revue Politique et Parlementaire*.

Finally, there are literary journals, that sometimes give an important place to articles of political theory or analysis because of the political and philosophical involvement of their staffs or their orientation toward the social sciences. They include *Esprit, Les Temps Modernes* (created by Jean-Paul Sartre), *Critique, Preuves*, and *Contrepoint*.

Special Publications

The oldest French collection of works of political science is the *Cahiers de la Fondation Nationale des Sciences Politiques*, whose first volume appeared in 1947 and which includes more than two hundred works. In the 1960s, the publications issued under the aegis of the FNSP became considerably diversified (collections of works and research, bibliographies, documentary indices, guides to research, atlas), to the point that in 1976 the Presses de la Fondation Nationale des Sciences Politiques were created, their activity being exactly comparable to that of the British and American university presses. These are the sole French publishers specializing in the political sciences (defined, it is true, very broadly). There is no equivalent to the collection of the *Cahiers* with any French publisher; the collection "SUP-Le politique" directed by G. Lavau at the Presses Universitaires de France ceased publication with its ninth work; the collection of paperbacks, *Politique*, of the *Editions du Seuil* (directed by J. Julliard) published many more books of political figures and essayists than scientific works; the collection *Sociologie politique*, also of the *Editions du Seuil*, is only on its fourth volume.[16] This is not to say that few books of political science are published in France; it is simply to state that studies of political science are published in a dispersed manner, and that it is necessary to look for them in the most diverse collections. Finally, many works remain unpublished, including reports of research conducted by contract between a team and an organ of public financing of research[17] and memoirs or theses written to obtain various university degrees.[18]

POLITICAL SCIENCE AND THE WORLD OF POLITICS

The impact of political events on political science. In choosing subjects to study, political science in France and perhaps in all Western democracies is heavily dependent on political events. Many researchers have as their principal objective to observe French political life at the very moment events occur (one of the principal centers of French research in political science is the well-named CEVIPOF[19] of the FNSP. As a result, there have been numerous works on elections (so frequent in France since 1958), on the Socialist party since its resurgence, on the construction of Europe, and so on. The trend is old; one can easily link the vogue of the theme of depoliticization with the end of the Fourth Republic and that of the personalization of power with the presidency of General de Gaulle, for two examples. Perhaps the majority of French political scientists are too absorbed in this, wishing at times to fight journalists on their own terrain[20] and for this reason they neglect research that is tied less to the present, especially those (in epistemology, political theory, or sociology) that could give a firmer base to empirical works.

Much more complex is the question of the influence of political events on the very conception of political science. Political events—and that is apparent especially for major events—are partly the product of social and cultural mutations, but they then crystallize these mutations by propagating, for example, new sensitivities. The most convincing example for France is that of the *événements*—a term that has become part of the language—of May–June 1968, which certainly seem to have introduced a new manner of conceiving politics, which has at least inspired a proliferation of works, often more militant than scientific, having politics as a subject. It remains true that the influence of political events in this domain is only secondary, and probably it modifies more the style of writing, the list of authors that it is good form to cite, the subjects of debates quickly becoming academic again, than the profound nature of the discipline.

Political scientists in politics. The status of the researcher or teacher in political science in France brings little material or symbolic satisfaction; the specialist is rarely known outside the circle of his peers; his books are easily rivaled by those of journalists or essayists; his income and his celebrity are not proportionate to those of the ruling class that he has constantly under surveillance. Obviously, this is not the place to discuss the historical and social reasons for this situation; what is important is to observe that, quite naturally, the *politologue* is going to look for the material and symbolic satisfaction that his discipline does not give him, in the very world that he studies, in the political world.

For certain among them, in truth very few, the conversion to politics is brought to fruition: the *politologue* has a true political career, he will be a minister (like Léo

Hamon or René Capitant), a deputy (like J. P. Cot), a senator (like Marcel Prélot) or indeed, a little more distant from the center of power, he will have a seat, like François Goguel, in the Constitutional Council, or even, but more rarely, he will serve on a ministerial staff. In reality, in the majority of cases, political involvement has been later than or parallel to the development of an academic career and is not really "reconversion." Success in politics in France scarcely seems to be the effect of a mastery of theoretical knowledge of politics.

Much more numerous are the *politologues* who content themselves with being in the background and are counselors, more electoral than political. During certain episodes in national political life, the influence of these counselors has not been negligible. Thus, during the attempt to shape a Socialist candidacy in a new style, in 1964 and 1965 for the first presidential election under universal suffrage (under the name of Gaston Defferre), the known experts and at times the inspirers, were G. Vedel, M. Duverger, and G. Lavau. Today, there are scarcely any specialists of electoral sociology who do not bring their knowledge to a party staff, for the Socialists as well as for the former majority.

Finally, some of them aspire to exercise a moral magistracy, to enlighten opinion or to counsel the prince by the public means of articles in the press; Raymond Aron, Maurice Duverger, and Alfred Grosser are the prototypes. The latter played this role even more in Germany, where he won the peace prize in 1975.

Only a rigorous investigation would make it possible to say whether the French *politologues* engage in political activity which becomes part of the hierarchy of political machinery at an upper level. The cultural influence on the dominant class is certainly important, to the extent that many political leaders are products of the Ecole Nationale d'Administration, (ENA) and that many students from the ENA attended Instituts d'Etudes Politiques. Yet, the instruction in the IEP is decided on in part by the same directing personnel, and the place for a critical political science or even for a technical political science is almost nonexistent there.

Relationships between the government and the discipline. Intellectuals in France have the reputation of being eternal opposers of power; at least they like to appear to be. As a result, political scientists, like philosophers and sociologists, are not the object of great solicitude from political leaders, even if the latter recognize their technical competence, principally in the electoral domain, and willingly call on them for consultation.

The result is that political science is a discipline poor in means, poor in the prestige of its research, poor in teachers and researchers, since it is a discipline whose practical utility and scientific legitimacy appear limited. The Instituts d'Etudes Politiques are the exception; their role in the formation of leaders allows them to have a privileged relationship to power. An indication of the reserve that political leaders feel toward political science can be found in the creation, in 1977, of an Institut des Sciences de l'Action (Institut Auguste Comte), conceived as a school for the development of decision makers of very high competence and experience, which did not attach itself to any institution of teaching or research in the social sciences and where the place made for political science was almost nonexistent.

The Present State of Political Science

Three traits appear to characterize the present situation of political science in France: (1) the subjects studied by political science remain few if one compares them with the list of what is usually included in the proper subject matter of this discipline; (2) French political science is divided into very individualized specialties which communicate little with each other; (3) political science in France has little scientific legitimacy to the extent that many works emanating from diverse sociological or historical schools deny it the capacity to deal with politics and propose other approaches to political subject matter.

Subjects studied by political science. It is probably vain to consider *in abstracto* the proper subject of a science; the distribution among the disciplines of the infinite number of subjects susceptible of scientific understanding constantly fluctuates in response to new principles of approach to these subjects (there is, for example, no permanently fixed subject for chemistry, biology, or geography). On the contrary, it is useful at a given moment to adjust the subjects concretely studied which are housed in a discipline. In order to confine itself to the number of specialized researchers and to the most numerous works, political science in France limits the main part of its research to several large subjects.

The first subject to which every French researcher ends up by devoting at least one project is electoral behavior. The heritage of André Siegfried is not lost. At the present time, the principal *politologues* who specialize in electoral behavior are Frédéric Bon, Jean Charlot, François Goguel, Jérôme Jaffré, Alain Lancelot, Guy Michelat, Jean-Luc Parodi, and Jean Ranger.

The study of elections, however, does not come quantitatively at the head of the list of favorite subjects of French political science. The most constantly studied domain is a vast block which is poorly delineated but which always situates itself in the shifting sands of traditional juridical studies of constitutional law and political institutions, and for which the content can at least be enumerated. Here one finds the second traditional subject for study: the examination of institutions, of the relationship among branches, the description of the mechanisms of governmental decision-making and of the mode of functioning of the *Assemblées*, more or less organized accounts of the unfolding of political life, and research on the institutional and political history. The researchers who devote themselves to this vast domain are too numerous to cite even those who are the most productive. On the other hand, it is necessary to give precise details about four specialties. First, contrary to what one would expect, this abundance of works on French institutions is not accompanied by reflection on the theory of democracy. For example, almost no works exist in France which study thoroughly—or even utilize—the concept of polyarchy with the exception of those of the sociologist François Bourricaud. Second, if the state and the balance of powers are the subject of many investigations, the study of the most coercive instruments of this state are strangely neglected by political scientists. Neither judicial power, nor the police, nor the army—with a few rare exceptions such as military studies which have had a very recent renaissance—are the subject of important works.[21] Third, on the contrary, among political forces, parties have been the subject of systematic research for a long time in France. After having been launched by the celebrated work of Maurice Duverger, in the sphere of theoretical analysis, they were reintroduced in 1971 with the publication of a little collection of texts chosen by Jean Charlot (specialist in the study of the Gaullist movement), *Les partis politiques* (Librairie A. Colin), which contributed much to introducing in France certain concepts of American political science. Fourth, the other political forces have had a mixed fate. Pressure groups, after the vogue of the 1960s, are scarcely studied any longer (except for peasant pressure groups); on the other hand, trade unions continue to arouse the interest of numerous researchers.

The third traditional subject of study is political thought or political philosophy (which is frequently studied under the guise of the history of political ideas) as well as political ideologies. The fourth subject is the political life of foreign countries, certain specific aspects within them, or certain types of political regimes. Among the current specialists, we should mention Alfred Grosser (Germany), Monica Charlot (Great Britain), Hélène Carrère d'Encausse (USSR), M. F. Toinet (United States), G. Hermet (authoritarian regimes), J. Leca (Maghreb), knowing full well that this list should contain dozens of other names in order to be complete. The final subject for political studies, international relations, is in the process of becoming accepted in France. Until recently, it belonged to the historical disciplines in the tradition of P. Renouvin and J. B. Duroselle. In addition to the numerous works dedicated to European integration, notably at the Centre d'Etudes des Relations Internationales (CERI) of the FNSP, the many articles by Pierre Hassner, the works of synthesis of Alfred Grosser, and the pedagogical works of Marcel Merle require notice.

Obviously, not all the research of French political science is concentrated in these five areas, but the several other domains of investigation are the subject of much less work, sometimes even carried out by a single team. Studies of political socialization (the works of Annick Percheron, of the FNSP) and studies on political communication and the mass media come to mind, as well as studies on local political life and on elites and political personnel (research has always existed in this area; several empirical investigations have already been done, the last one having been directed by Pierre Birnbaum). At last, in a final area, French research seems to be trying to make up for lost time; it is administrative science, an area where research is currently multiplying.[22]

On the other hand, four unknown regions appear in white on the map of French political science, four virgin regions where few explorers have yet ventured. (1) Epistemology, history, and sociology of political science, methodological investigation, theorizing[23], theoretical reflection on the treatment of data and the construction of models are still practiced only occasionally. (2) The study of public policy, administrative policy, social policy, the politics of education is still almost totally neglected. (3) Moreover, in France no works exist relative to political development, political mobilization, nor—what is at first glance more surprising—mass movements, civil strife, revolutions (if they are not in a strictly historical perspective). To use other terminology, French political science does not integrate the whole of social and political dynamics into its research. (4) Finally, research on political culture, collective representation, collective memory is also the exception, especially if the study of the results of opinion surveys as it is practiced in France, is excluded. If one looks more closely, these last two regions are not totally undeveloped, but, with rare exceptions (like the *Sociologie politique et religieuse de la Lorraine* by Serge Bonnet, 1972), it is necessary to turn to historians to find such studies. To give an example, French society of the Second or Third Republic has been the subject of more standard studies, with respect to social dynamics or collective protests, than France of the Fifth Republic.

The picture is mixed then. On a limited number of subjects, French political science has produced many, important studies; on other topics works exist, but in an exploratory phase; on still others—and not the least of them—the delay is considerable. French political science is clearly a science with a legacy; the broad orientations which were adopted in other times (resulting from a cyclical sharing of the social sciences among institutions of teaching and research at the end of the nineteenth century) are perpetuated for the most part. On some fronts breakthroughs have been made, but the complete restructuring of the discipline, to bring it up-to-date for the last quarter of the century, has not been accomplished.

Individual specialization. When one does not benefit from a broad historical perspective, the ruptures that mark the history of the sciences are difficult to perceive. However, it can be said with a minimum of risk, that French political science is (to adopt Kuhn's terminology) in a postparadigmatic phase; between 1950 and the middle of the 1960s, the scientific community was in agreement—if one looks at it from a distance—on the designation of subjects relevant to the discipline and on the different problems judged to be pertinent. In recent years, agreement has disappeared and the scientific field is divided into specialties (which are rarely "schools") which scarcely debate among themselves for they prefer to ignore each other. Five principal specialties can be enumerated, without denying that many French political scientists escape the ascendancy of one or the other and have individual orientations (such as the adherents of a *critical* political science in the wake of the Ecole de Frankfort[24]).

The first specialty is the one that will be called "the specialty of constitutionalist legal writers," whose most recent expression can be found in the journal *Pouvoirs* (see above) and which is the orientation of a great number of works.[25] By its methods (synthetic description of data that are immediately observable, married to juridical analysis), its subjects (study of political life and institutions), and the university status of its members, this specialty maintains the tradition of the Facultés de Droit in its approach to political phenomena.

The second specialty includes researchers who may be labeled "empiricists." Empiricism in political science, in its modern form, is often linked to the use of modes of mathematical treatment of data (factorial analysis, typological analysis); the data recorded on tape in many cases are electoral results, responses to opinion questionnaires, or else words from the statements of political men. The considerable development of works of this nature derives from the fact that they respond to an important social demand; the written or spoken news media in France make constant use of electoral predictions and simulations (without mentioning the forecasts made on the evenings of election days) as well as opinion surveys.

This social demand, at the same time that it multiplies research, imposes on it this particular form which allows its immediate exploitation for practical ends. Numerous researchers who devote themselves to recording "facts" may also be placed in the category of "empiricists." They collect facts by observation or gather them by analyses of the press; this recording then gives rise to a purely factual presentation. Many studies of French and foreign political life and of international relations are of this nature.[26]

The third specialty is Marxist; it finds its reference base in the works of the philosopher Louis Althusser, transposed to the domain of political institutions by an author of juridical training, Nicos Poulantzas. This specialty remains dominant, even if it is profoundly divided today, in the domain of community studies (those of Manuel Castells, of J. Lojkine) and in the domain of works on the state (Poulantzas, J. M. Vincent, research of the CERAT of Grenoble[27]).

The fourth specialty is searching among economic models for the principle of a renewal of the knowledge of politics. This specialty proposes bringing into play a veritable paradigm, "*interactionism*": collective action can be understood if one brings to light the mechanisms of the interaction of voluntary individual actions. The reference authors of this specialty are the neoclassical economists and the game theorists as well as Downs, Olson, and Hirschmann in the political domain. This specialty is in the process of consolidation; it holds conferences; it finds expression frequently in the journal *Contrepoint* or in *Analyses de la SEDEIS*. It has firm practical preoccupations: to ameliorate democratic institutions, to maintain pluralism in Western societies, to reflect on the values which allow basing the liberal system on theory.

The last specialty is that of the "sociologists" who aspire to establish explanatory propositions constructed according to methodological principles which have been common to the three founding fathers of sociology, Marx, Durkheim, Weber. These sociologists-political scientists follow the path of applied rationalism, that has been described by the epistemologist Gaston Bachelard, according to which facts must be explicated against the background of the common representations formed from practical experience and for it. Theoretical elaboration necessarily follows observation (or at least always gives it meaning), but should be validated by confrontation with the empirical data brought to light systematically. Adherents of this trend are J. P. Cot and J. P. Mounier who are authors of a textbook *Pour une sociologie politique* (Paris: Seuil, 1974), D. Gaxie and his *Le cens caché* (Paris: Seuil, 1978), B. Lacroix, who proposed a new reading of Durkheim, putting the political question at the center of the Durkheiman plan in *Durkheim et le politique* (Paris: Presses de la Fondation Nationale des Sciences Politiques, 1980).[28]

Obviously, this schema of five specialties is too analytical and many French political scientists are situated on the frontiers of two specialties or could even legitimately say that they belong to several or to none. It is equally clear that such a presentation would be complete only if one answered questions of the sort: What objective criteria can permit distinctions among different problems? What subjects are studied according to each of these approaches? According to what social logic do researchers divide themselves among these diverse specialties? What social group did they come from? What is their training? What institutions do they belong to? What are the social stakes of the theoretical battles existing at the heart of French political science? To what image of politics does each of the specialties lend credence? Such questions could be answered only if a sociology of French political science existed. As it does not, such a summary presentation of five specialties may be informative and instructive.[29]

The alleged lack of scientific legitimacy. French political scientists find their scientific serenity with difficulty, for they constantly encounter philosophers, sociologists, and historians who publicly announce their own claim to talk about politics and to talk about it with incomparably greater explanatory power. With exceptions—but some are illustrious[30]—philosophers, sociologists, and historians abandon the study of elections, of political institutions, and of the vicissitudes of political life to institutional political science; on the other hand, certain of them—and among the best known—demand the almost exclusive right to treat power and methods of domination legitimately.

It would be impossible, in the limited scope of this chapter, to present all those in the French intelligentsia who believe themselves to be competent to treat politics. It would be necessary to analyze works as different as those of numerous enlightened observers who paint a political and social picture of France (as Alain Peyrefitte in *Le mal français*) or those of the "new philosophers," whose political reflection has often been provoked by the reading of Solzhenitsyn, and who had their hour of glory in 1977 (André Gluksmann, *La cuisinière et le mangeur d'hommes; Essai sur l'Etat, le marxisme, les camps de concentration;* and *Les maitres penseurs;* B. H. Lévy, *La barbarie à visage humain*). To be consistent with the rules of scientific exposition, other works should be given a detailed presentation: those of the Marxist philosopher Louis Althusser whose new interpretation of Marx has had a considerable influence on contemporary French thought; those of philosophers who, like Cornélius Castoriadis or Claude Lefort, for twenty years have reflected on the Soviet bureaucracy, the movement of history, and the foundations of society; finally, those of psychoanalysts who, often nurtured on the teachings of Jacques Lacan, apply Freudian approaches, to power (see, for example, the books of Gilles Deleuze and Félix Guattari and of Pierre Legendre). The following discussion is limited to several authors, sociologists for the most part, about whom it can be said that they are all—in diverse forms—"leaders of schools," and who all include the analysis of politics in their investigations.[31]

For certain of them, this analysis leads moreover to a disintegration of politics: politics has exploded; the function of power is not found essentially in the relations of governor-governed, state-citizens, but is hidden in the multiple wheels of social organizations, whether they are directly repressive or are economic, cultural, educative, or domestic. The recent book by Michel Crozier (*L'acteur et le système* [Paris: Seuil, 1977], written in collaboration with E. Friedberg) can be read in this sense. Crozier starts from a definition of power as the process of exchange in an unequal situation; power is put into play in each negotiation where resources are involved which, in effect, are perpetually redistributed. In this approach the actors are considered as having the ability to conceive strategies, and this "liberty" makes the outcome of all competition unforeseeable. Power is no longer under state control (since no centralized system for guiding society can exist), but is multiplied at the heart of intermediate systems that the authors call "systems of concrete action" (for example, in regard to industrial organizations, a branch of an industrial group, and not a factory or a holding company). Nevertheless, the vision of M. Crozier is optimistic, for these systems are the center of regulatory phenomena which assure their survival in spite of the divergence of objectives of the actors. Therefore, the political scientist who follows M. Crozier should no longer dedicate his efforts to the study of what is the essence of politics (for example, the struggle for the monopoly of legitimate violence); he should study political decisions as the product of systems of action, as isolable and partial as the others.

At an opposing cardinal point of the intellectual field, a professor at the Collège de France, holder of the Chair of History of Systems of Thought, Michel Foucault, effects a comparable disintegration of politics; however, he is not close to Crozier either by his method, his structural history, his political involvement in the extraparliamentary groups of the Left, or his fundamentally pessimistic social conception. In his two works, *Surveiller et punir, naissance de la prison* and *La volonté de savoir* (Paris: Gallimard, 1975, 1976), Michel Foucault denies that power is concentrated in state machinery or that it is the property of a class. For him power is present in the whole social sphere; it goes across all institutions; it is at work in innumerable practices. In fact, power can only be comprehended by the examination of all the resources of the "technology of power" which is embodied as much in a school regulation, as in prison or hospital architecture, or as in the methods of apprenticeship in handling arms. What should be important to political science is to set itself up in the "microphysics of power," and to track down power in completely different places from those where one usually looks.

Far from wishing to disintegrate politics, the sociologist Alain Touraine places it at the center of his preoccupations. He attempts to construct a general sociological theory which permits an account of the relationship between society and politics beginning with an analysis of the social movement: *Production de la société* (Paris: Seuil, 1973); *La Voix et le Regard* (Paris: Seuil, 1978); *La prophétie anti-nucléaire* (Paris: Seuil, 1980). The social movement is the movement which animates all society because of the fact that it is divided into social classes. The ruling class and the dominated classes struggle for mastery of the means by which a society comes into being; these means are, for example, the representation, which exists in all collectivity, of the capacity that a society has to act on itself. In this context, Touraine centers his research on the study of particular social struggles (the student, antinuclear, and regionalist movements) where the actors of a new social movement appear to him to be operating. For Touraine, sociological knowledge is not separated from political action; the work of the sociologist should serve the development of social movements. The theoretical and practical ambition of A. Touraine has no equivalent in France in any contemporary work of political science; however, the sociological pertinence of his concepts remains to be demonstrated and his influence on present research in political science is weak. This is not the case with the following two sociologists.

The sociologist Raymond Boudon, known since his thesis devoted to *L'analyse mathématique des faits sociaux* (1967) and a study on *L'inégalité des chances* (1973) conducted in terms of analysis of systems, in his latest book, *Ordre social et effets pervers* (Paris: Presses Universitaires de France, 1977), seeks to furnish political sociology with new means for analyzing certain political facts. R. Boudon uses "methodological individualism" as his authority; sociological explanation may be discovered by taking the individual as a unit of analysis. The study of the modes of aggregation of individual actions allows it alone to explain social phenomena, on the condition that it is acknowledged that the result of the aggregation of individual actions is not simple (one thinks of the "Condorcet effect" and of its generalization by Arrow). R. Boudon becomes the theoretician of *perverse*, unwanted, and most often unfavorable effects, produced by the addition of unconcerted individual actions which have other goals. If R. Boudon still studies only a few examples which are directly political, his works provoke obvious developments in political sociology, since he gives a key to analysis for all situations where a logical structure unperceived by the social actors (as the celebrated structure put into play in the prisoners' dilemma) determines the outcome of interaction among the social actors.

Pierre Bourdieu, director of the Centre de sociologie européenne, professor at the Ecole pratique des hautes études (which became in 1975 Ecole des Hautes études en sciences sociales, Paris) devotes most of his present work to the study of the modes of symbolic domination and the social and cultural characteristics of the ruling and ruled classes. If he never deals with politics in the strict sense, he endeavors to institute a sociology which makes the traditional approach to political phenomena antiquated. Moreover, he does not refrain from harshly criticizing the dominating political science as he sees it being taught in the Instituts d'Etudes Politiques. He supports strict sociological determinism: the behavior of individuals is determined by their position in the social structure; the strategies that they believe that they choose freely result in fact from predispositions inculcated during the course of their socialization and which allow them practices suited only to what the objective future of their social class demands (the theory of *l'habitus*). The modes of domination by the ruling class may therefore be essentially modes of symbolic domination: by the school, by the culture, by holding the monopoly of the erudite language, by the power to impose the definitions of what will be legitimate practices. The principal writings by Bourdieu which challenge the political scientist will be found in two important works that the author has published recently: *La distinction* (Paris: Ed. de Minuit, 1979) and *Le sens pratique* (Paris: Ed. de Minuit, 1980).

French political science may appear today as confined to studies whose subject remains limited if they are compared to works of sociologists who insert politics in global theories of society. However, this relative inferiority is perhaps only temporary.

To be sure, it is impossible to foresee the evolution of French political science in the coming years; a political scientist knows better than anyone—and he understands it if he has read Popper—that one cannot be certain of the future. However, we will affirm our optimism (it is only a matter of personal sentiment, very subjective) as to what French political science will become; the analysis of politics should, in the space of a generation, become reunified and go through a new "paradigmatic" phase (always in the sense of Kuhn) during which a refined and reconsidered sociological method will give political scientists powerful intellectual means for comprehending politics. That will perhaps be a happy counterpart to the relative autarchy in which the discipline has lived up to now. The very weak penetration of foreign political science, especially British and American (which have no equal except for the very mediocre diffusion of French sociological and political works abroad) will have perhaps preserved an originality that will prove to be fruitful.

Notes

1. Cf. Duguit, who wrote in an article in the *Revue Internationale de l'Enseignement* in 1889 ("Le Droit Constitutionnel et la Sociologie"): "Political phenomena are those which are related to the origin and functioning of the State: they are essentially juridical phenomena; they are precisely the facts which form the domain of constitutional law, and this alleged political science is nothing other than constitutional law, that is, a branch of general science."

2. For a more extensive justification of this assertion, cf. my article, "La question de l'objet de la science politique à-t-elle un sens?," *Mélanges dédiés à Robert Pelloux* (Lyons: L'Hermès, 1980), pp. 123-42.

3. This history, published in 1952, leads the reader up to the contemporary situation of 1945. By comparison, the *Histoire constitutionnelle de la France* of Maurice Deslandres, whose three volumes were published between 1932 and 1937, remains "historical" because it ends in 1875.

4. The fact that "political science" is in the plural here relates in France to a specific conception within the discipline's field, cf. the section "The Teaching of Political Science," below.

5. In addition to Siegfried's book on the Ardèche, cf. the "Cahier" no. 1, *Etudes de sociologie électorale*, the "Cahier" no. 16, *L'influence des systèmes électoraux sur la vie politique* (under the direction of M. Duverger), the "Cahiers" 26 and 27, *Sociologie électorale, esquisse d'un bilan* by F. Goguel and G. Dupeux and *Géographie des élections françaises de 1870 à 1951* by F. Goguel. On the electoral sociology of this period, cf. the remarkable survey of the field by Georges Dupeux, "Le comportement electoral, revue des recherches significatives et bibliographie," *Current Sociology* 3, no. 4 (1954-55): 281-344.

6. The absence in France of a history and sociology of political science is an indication, among others, of the youth of the discipline; it has asserted itself too recently and has too many subjects to discover to take itself as a subject for scientific investigation.

7. The IEP in Paris was founded in 1945. It succeeded the celebrated Ecole libre des sciences politiques on rue Saint-Guillaume in Paris. Afterward, IEPs were established in Aix-en-Provence, Bordeaux, Grenoble, Lyons, Strasbourg, Toulouse.

8. Cf. a special issue of the *Revue de l'Enseignement Supérieur*, dedicated to "La science politique" (no. 4, October-November-December, 1965) and especially Georges Lavau's article, "La science politique et les cadres universitaires" (pp. 143-54).

9. Cf. the articles of R. Aron, Ch. Eisenmann, M. Duverger, F. Goguel, P. Renouvin, L. Kopelmanns in *La science politique contemporaine* (Paris: UNESCO, 1950), especially the article of R. Aron, "La science politique en France," and that of L. Kopelmanas, "L'enseignement et l'organisation de la recherche en matière de science politique en France."

10. See *La science politique en France*, annotated bibliography, under the direction of Jean Meyriat (Paris: Presses de la Fondation Nationale des Sciences Politiques, 1960), and Alfred Grosser, "La science politique en France," *Tendances*, no. 8 (1960). Cf. also the 1957 article by Roy C. Macridis and Bernard E. Brown, "The Study of Politics in France since the Liberation: A Critical Bibliography," *American Political Science Review* 51, no. 3 (September 1957): 811-26.

11. "La science politique," *Revue de l'Enseignement Supérieur*, 1965.

12. François Goguel, "Situation de la science politique en France," *Annuaire Suisse de Science Politique*, no. 8 (1968): 19-30, and Association Française de Science Politique, "L'état de la science politique en France" (mimeographed; debate introduced by Serge Hurtig), *Entretiens de samedi*, no. 10, (March 1969).

13. On the different types of models, cf. Raymond Boudon, "Modèles et méthodes mathématiques," in *Tendances principales de la Recherche dans les sciences sociales et humaines* (Paris, The Hague: Mouton/UNESCO, 1970), pp. 629-85. In political science the pioneer book has been that of Jacques Attali, *Analyse économique de la vie politique* (Paris: P.U.F., 1972), collection Systèmes-décisions, although the word "model" was understood in the narrow sense that it has in the expression "economic model."

14. For a survey of French work in the matter of analysis of political discourse, see the author's article "Analyse de contenu et analyse du discours, sur quelques critères distinctifs," in *Etudes offertes au Professeur E. de Lagrange*, (Paris: LGDJ, 1978), pp. 293-328. A journal devoted exclusively to research in political lexicography has been appearing since October 1980: *MOTS, Mots... Ordinateurs... Textes... Societes* (Fondation Nationale des Sciences Politiques).

15. In spite of its title, the *Revue du Droit public et de la Science Politique* opens its pages only occasionally to articles on political science. On the other hand, it grants a privileged place to constitutional law and to French and foreign parliamentary law.

16. We exclude collections of university textbooks from this enumeration; in France political science textbooks are frequently published in collections of juridical textbooks, since political science is taught principally in the Facultés de droit. Cf., for example, the works published in the collection *Thémis*

(directed by M. Duverger) at the Presses Universitaires de France; in the collection of the *Précis Dalloz* (Editions Dalloz); in that of the *Précis Domat* (Editions Montchrestien); and in the Collection *U* (*U* for Université) at Armand Colin.

17. CNRS (Centre National de la Recherche Scientifique); DGRST (Délégation Générale à la Recherche Scientifique et Technique) attached to the Secrétariat d'Etat à la Recherche; CORDES (Comité d'Organisation des Recherches Appliquées sur le Développement Economique et Social) attached to the Commissariat général du Plan.

18. The *Revue Française de Science Politique* has published since 1964, usually in its second issue each year, an "Etat des travaux inédits de science politique," of great utility but which is limited to mimeographed courses, memoirs, and theses to the exclusion of reports on research.

19. Centre d'Etude de la vie politique française.

20. Cf. the more and more frequent publication in *Le Monde* of articles in political sociology, emanating from political scientists, on the voters or the members of political parties, on candidates for election, on participants in political and trade union Congresses.

21. Without doubt, at the most elementary level, the reason is double: on the one hand, many French university students, ideologically on the Left, may remain too antiauthoritarian and antimilitary to accept devoting time to institutions that they do not like, or they may have a partisan involvement that leads them to write about repressive institutions in texts that are only militant. On the other hand, sociologists tend to emphasize the mechanisms of symbolic domination so much (see below) that they come to neglect the study of the repressive apparatus of the state.

22. Cf. the important treatise on *Science administrative,* by Jacques Chevallier and Danièle Loschak, 2 vols. (Paris: L.G.D.J., 1978). Political anthropology should be mentioned as having given rise to several remarkable publications (works of Georges Balandier, Pierre Clastres, Jean-William Lapierre), but in France it remains an institutionally independent discipline, much closer to sociology than to political science.

23. In regard to the term "theorizing," the reader is alerted to the fact that the theoretical representation which is talked about is used in the sense of sociology (the word "theory" refers here, in brief, to the system of propositions by which one tries to give an account of the subject studied as it is construed by the researcher). The expression "political theory" unfortunately remains very polysemous, since it is also used to name works on normative thought or works on political philosophy for example (the "political theory" of Plato or the "political theory" of Saint Thomas Aquinas). Moreover, as frequent as the study of political ideas of authors from the past is in France, works on political ethics are extremely rare; one can cite only a few works of J. Ellul and of A. Grosser.

24. Cf. the collection "Critique de la politique" (Payot, editor) directed by Miguel Abensour.

25. A characteristic example is given by a textbook of Dmitri-Georges Lavroff, professor at the Université de Bordeaux I, who, under the modern title of *Le système politique français* (Paris: Dalloz, 1975) offers a work which differs only slightly from classical treatises on "constitutional law and political institutions."

26. For a particular case, see the remarks by Jean Leca, "Crises et conflits au Proche-Orient," which was presented in an issue of the *Revue Française de Science Politique* (August 1974) devoted to "the October war and the new equilibrium in the Near East."

27. Centre d'Etude et de Recherche sur l'Administration Economique et l'Aménagement du Territoire.

28. Perhaps it is useful to note that the author of this chapter belongs to this specialty.

29. In a report presented in June 1980 to a colloquium of the French Political Science Association "Regards sur la science politique française," the author of this chapter proposed a different division into six problem areas ("La science politique française et ses problematiques," mimeographed). A revised version of this report was scheduled for publication in 1981 in a special number of *La Revue Française de Sociologie* devoted to political sociology.

30. Cf. the thesis for the *doctorat ès lettres* of Paul Bois, *Paysans de l'ouest: Des structures économiques et sociales aux options politiques depuis l'époque révolutionnaire dans la Sarthe* (Paris, The Hague: Mouton, 1960) which is a reevaluation of the works of André Siegfried on western France.

31. The December 1980 number of the *Revue française de Science Politique* was devoted to the presentation and discussion by different politologues (J. Leca, B. Jobert, F. Bon, Y. Schemeil, P. Favre) of the works of most of the sociologists cited in the following paragraphs. Cf., also in the *Revue française de Science Politique,* an article by M. and P. Favre on Michel Foucault in 1981.

Bibliography*

Aron, R. *Etudes politiques.* Paris: Gallimard, 1972.

―――. *Paix et guerre entre les nations.* Paris: Calmann-Levy, 1962.

Badie, B. and Birnbaum, P. *Sociologie de l'Etat.* Paris: Grasset, 1979.

Balandier, G. *Anthropologie politique.* Paris: PUF, 1969.

Bois, P. *Paysans de l'Ouest.* Paris: Mouton, 1960.

Burdeau, G. *Traité de science politique.* 3d ed. Paris: L.G.D.J., forthcoming.

Chapsal, J. and Lancelot, A. *La vie politique en France depuis 1940.* Paris: PUF, 1979.

Chevallier, J. J. *Les grandes oeuvres politiques de Machiavel à nos jours.* Paris: A. Colin, 1948.

―――and Loschak D. *Science administrative.* 2 vols. Paris: L.G.D.J., 1978.

Cot J. P. & Mounier, J. P. *Pour une sociologie politique.* 2 vols. Paris: Seuil, 1974.

Duverger, M., *Echec au roi.* Paris: A. Michel, 1978.

―――. *Les partis politiques.* 1st ed. Paris: A. Colin, 1951.

Goguel, Fr. *Chroniques électorales.* Paris: Presses de la FNSP, 1980.

*Compiled by the editor.

———— and Grosser, A. *La politique en France*. New ed. Paris: Colin, 1980.

Grosser, A. *Au nom de quoi? Fondements d'une morale politique*. Paris: Seuil, 1969.

Lancelot, A. *L'abstenstionnisme électoral en France*. Paris: Presses de la FNSP, 1968.

Michelat, G. and Simon, M. *Classe, religion et comportement politique*. Paris: Presses de la FNSP, 1977.

Poulantzas. N. *Pouvoir politique et classes sociales de l'Etat capitaliste*. Paris: Maspero, 1968.

Rémond, R. *La droite en France de la première restauration à la Ve République*. 3rd ed. Paris: Aubier, 1968.

Sfez, L. *Critique de la décision*. 2d ed. Paris: Presses de la FNSP, 1976.

FEDERAL REPUBLIC OF GERMANY

KLAUS VON BEYME

Introduction

Political science in West Germany was established relatively late, but the times are gone when a political scientist from Berkeley returning from West Germany in the mid-fifties could say: "There are fewer people teaching political science in all of Western Germany than in this department (Berkeley) alone."[1] Today in numbers of chairs West German political science has outnumbered all the other West European countries. This quantity abroad is occasionally also perceived in terms of qualitative representation, because of an ideological and theoretical fragmentation of the discipline which is greater than in the British and American countries. Measured by superficial, objective indicators of international participation in the congresses of the International Political Science Association (IPSA) West Germany is usually the fourth country in participation (after the U.S.A., Canada, and Britain) and ranks first among those countries whose language is not recognized as an official language of IPSA.

The State of Political Science in 1945

The new discipline had some roots in German intellectual history, though even the German Academy for Politics (Deutsche Hochschule für Politik) out of which emerged the largest political science department in Germany, the Otto Suhr-Institute in Berlin, was no equivalent to the Ecole des sciences politiques in Paris or to the London School of Economics and Political Science. Nevertheless the older German *Staatswissenschaften* had some impact on the founding fathers of American political science (Francis Lieber, J. W. Burgess, A. F. Bentley, and Charles Merriam).

A serious brain drain for German political science was caused by the Nazi period and the restrictions for the development of political science after the war. Eminent German-speaking scholars who had emigrated to the United States did not return, among them Hannah Arendt, Karl Deutsch, Lewis Edinger, Heinz Eulau, Gottfried Dietze, Arnold Heidenheimer, Carl J. Friedrich, Otto Kirchheimer, Henry Kissinger, Gerhard Loewenberg, Karl Loewenstein, Peter Merkl, Hans Morgenthau, Franz and Sigmund Neumann, Herbert Spiro, Leo Strauss, and others. Only a few returned, such as Arnold Bergstraesser, Ossip Flechtheim, Ernst Fraenkel, Carl J. Friedrich (part-time teaching in Heidelberg), Ferdinand A. Hermens, Fritz Morstein Marx, and Eric Voegelin.

Resistance to the new discipline among the established sciences was considerable. It arose among the conservatives because of their aversion to the "science of Reeducation" sponsored by the American occupation forces.[2] and among the other disciplines because of the suspicion that the science of politics "merely plucks the feathers from other disciplines and adorns itself with them."

Evolution of Political Science since 1945

THE INTELLECTUAL STRUCTURE OF THE DISCIPLINE

Until approximately 1965, the new discipline of political science experienced considerable qualitative difficulties. Methodological execution was predominantly provincial and antiquated. Almost no professional social scientists were available for chairs in political science. Lawyers, historians, philosophers, and journalists prevailed in the academic representation of the new discipline.

Theme selection of the growing discipline was narrowly restricted to domestic policy and theory usually was equated with the history of ideas. Professionalization increased with the creation of new teaching positions and with the development of a new generation trained in the social sciences. Compared to France and Britain the "Americanization" in approaches and methods was evident. However, due to the protest movement in the late

1960s, developments toward a narrow professionalization and the strengthening of behaviorist approaches were interrupted rather than facilitated.

RESEARCH IN POLITICAL SCIENCE

Methodological Developments

In the meantime, political science in Germany became well established and even abroad the growing methodological sophistication of empirical studies was recognized.[3] Political science was affected by the methodological debates in the neighboring disciplines which took place in the German tradition of the great debates, such as the debate on value judgments between Max Weber and the *Kathedersozialisten*. But political science was not leading in the new *Positivismus-Streit* between the followers of Popper in Germany and the neomarxist Frankfort school,[4] nor did it contribute anything like the debate between Habermas and Luhmann in sociology.[5] Political science in Germany—even more so than in the U.S.A.—remained dependent upon the concepts developed in sociology and in other social sciences. It did not soar to high levels of abstraction and its theory in Germany (apart from the normativists, the ontologists and the Straussians) was focused mainly upon reception. Narr, Naschold, and Senghaas, above all, can be credited with summarizing and propagating American theoretical approaches, in particular systems-theory. A new, more independent approach was developed in the theory of democracy, which attempted to link a systems-theory approach with the impetus of the leftist democratizing movement since the end of the 1960s.

German political science from the outset was highly fragmented in political outlook and metatheoretical views. Four main schools can be differentiated:

1. The normative-ontological school of Freiburg under Arnold Bergstraesser, which extended to Munich (H. Maier et al.) and which loosely amalgamated "single combatants" such as Eric Voegelin, Wilhelm Hennis, and Nikolaus Lobkowicz.

2. The early mainstream of political science was formed by traditional liberal institutionalists such as Theodor Eschenburg, Carl J. Friedrich, Ernst Fraenkel, Ferdinand A. Hermens, Eugen Kogon, or Dolf Sternberger, who hardly formed an integrated school with a common ideological background, but who had at least a minimal consensus about the normative implications of the discipline. Most of them were inspired by American political science.

3. Method-conscious behaviorists were concentrated in Cologne (König, Scheuch) and Mannheim (Wildenmann). To these could be added some of the younger scholars from the Institute of Political Science in Berlin directed by Otto Stammer. The work of Peter Christian Ludz on the German Democratic Republic became best-known abroad.

4. Marxist oriented political scientists were also single combatants such as Wolfgang Abendroth in Marburg, Ossip K. Flechtheim in Berlin or A. Gurland in Darmstadt. However, not these variants of non-Stalinist Marxism but rather the critical-dialectical school of Max Horkheimer, Theodor W. Adorno and Jürgen Habermas in Frankfurt, developed in philosophy and sociology and became the most influential new mainstream in the younger generation after the students' movement in the late 1960s.

Already before the war, Germans scholars tended to form schools and German social scientists have always tried to find a philosophical foundation for their work which might otherwise seem like isolated investigations and obscure methodologies. After a period of distrust in abstract philosophies as a consequence of the protest movement in the late 1960s, a new wave of abstract deductive theory influenced political science. The confrontation of the neo-Marxists and the established schools, which they lumped together under the rubric of "positivism"—if they did not prefer the notion "bourgeois science"—led to a rapprochement of the empiricists and the normative Straussians, at least in many questions of scientific recruitment of scholars and in educational and university policy matters.

A new wave of holistic theories spilled over into political science. On a highly abstract level, deductions of the actual political process from the "laws of the capital" became the fashion in a kind of typical German *Ableitungsliteratur,* which in its scholastic dimension was sometimes not understandable even to other Western neo-Marxists who had some impact on their respective countries, such as Poulantzas in France or Miliband in Britain. It was only after the conservative backlash in Germany, frequently labeled *Tendenzwende,* since 1972/73 that the more serious scholars among the *Staatsableiter* turned back to more empirical problems. A merger of approaches of neo-Marxist deductions and the policy sciences (Offe, Grauhan, Hirsch, Ronge) seems to be the trend of the late 1970s.

Most-Noteworthy Contributions

The most noteworthy contributions of German political science have changed over time. The liberals and the normatives—the two most important approaches in the 1950s—focused mainly on the institutions. Representation and parliamentary government were among the central topics, especially at Heidelberg (Sternberger school) or at Hamburg, where a group of younger scholars such as Steffani, Bermbach, Thaysen founded the first German periodical for "Parliamentary Affairs" (*Zeitschrift für Parlamentsfragen*). Opposition to the predominance of parliamentary studies came from the behavioral Cologne-Mannheim school, which focused on electoral behavior. But the schools of Sternberger and Hermens mostly agreed that the German proportional electoral law should be exchanged for the British system of a relative-majority electoral law.

On the other hand, a branch of the normative school combined with an institutional approach to advocate greater emphasis on government studies. W. Hennis polemicized against parliamentary studies, comparing politics to economics. He asserted that political scientists in Germany behaved like economists who try to substitute industrial economics and management studies for studies on participation and codetermination. A real breakthrough to modern governmental studies was achieved, not so much by old institutionalists, as by the younger generation of scholars who had adopted the insights of American policy science (such as F. W. Scharpf). Even the leftists started from the former preoccupation of postwar political science with parliamentarism. The neo-Marxist critique of the "bourgeois institutions" was opened under the catchword "debate on parliamentarism" (Agnoli, Euchner) and ended in rather unhistorical glorifications of the Soviet system (in its authentic form, not manipulated by the Leninists). Only later, did the neo-Marxists give up the institutional approach altogether and turn to abstract deductions of institutions and processes from the movements of capital. The school of Elmar Altvater in Berlin was the most successful in keeping a pure Marxist theory, aloof from the everyday quarrels of the Marxist sects and in developing considerable intellectual sophistication, though little political relevance.

Interest-group studies were a major innovation after the war, since the German tradition of a metaphysical elevation of the state as an actor above interests and groups, had led to a kind of "interest-group prudery," especially among the lawyers of the influential schools of Carl Schmitt, Ernst Forsthoff, and Werner Weber. Positivist evaluations of the activities of interest groups were attempted first in the institutes at Tübingen (Eschenburg) and Berlin (Stammer). The leftist wave in the early 1970s led to sharp criticism of the harmonious-equilibrium assumptions of older interest-group theories (Narr, Hirsch, Zeuner). The basic conflict between capital and workers was emphasized again and the study of trade unions and the labor movement turned toward conflict orientation. They became more and more isolated from the premises of interest-group research (especially in Marburg under Frank Deppe and others, and in Frankfurt under Brandt, E. Schmidt, and their collaborators). Moreover an enormous amount of scholarly and quasi-scholarly literature on working class conditions was coming out in the late 1960s.

Elite studies became popular at the end of the 1960s; they were based partly on social background-data (Zapf, P. C. Ludz, v. Beyme), partly on survey studies (Wildenmann, Kaltefleiter, Herzog). In the 1970s fewer elite studies were conducted than in the 1960s. One reason for this was again the impact of neo-Marxist thought, which was more interested in showing the restrictions of the "late capitalist system" (*Spätkapitalismus*) on the political actors than in tracing influences empirically between economic and political elites.

Recent recognition of the achievements of the policy sciences and neo-Marxist approaches have directed the interest of many German scholars to political output. Fields formerly ignored by the input-oriented political scientists have been taken into consideration, including social policy, economic policy, educational and research policies, and most recently under the impact of actual needs, labor market policies. This merger of approaches in political science and political economy developed a more economy-oriented approach in German political science. Until the 1960s, only a small minority of scholars centered in Berlin in the school of Gert v. Eynern tried to develop a kind of economic theory of politics under the heading of *Politische Wirtschaftslehre*.

Comparative politics was introduced by emigrés such as Fraenkel, Carl J. Friedrich, or Ferdinand A. Hermens. They had some followers in the second generation of political scientists in Germany (v. Beyme, Kaltefleiter, Nohlen, Nuscheler, Steffani and others), but area specialization was poorly developed. Almost no chair was specialized in one area. Even the specialist had to serve the "bread-and-butter students" with the basic all-round knowledge of a nonspecialization unheard of in the Western hemisphere. Only for East European studies did an interest sponsored by political institutions grow during the time of the cold war. But most of the East European study institutes (Berlin, Cologne, Munich) were dominated by lawyers and economists. Centers of GDR studies developed in Berlin and Erlangen. Area studies for the Third World were institutionalized for South Asia (Heidelberg), East Asia (Bochum, Berlin), Africa (Berlin), Near East (Hamburg), and Latin America (Freiburg, Hamburg, Bielefeld) but always with minor contributions from political science proper.

In the 1961 report of the German Research Association (Deutsche Forschungsgemeinschaft) for the first time three professorships of political science were claimed for every institute. The third was to be a specialist in international relations (Lepsius 1961). Only with the introduction of peace research institutes did specialized international relations develop. The most comprehensive and stimulating to date was established in the Hessian Foundation for Peace and Conflict Research at Frankfort. The interdisciplinary impulse (which mobilized not only social scientists in the narrow sense of the term but also theologians, pedagogues, psychologists, and historians) yielded to some extent to a professionalization of this new branch within the framework of political science. Although peace research was dominated initially by the critical approach of the Frankfort school, which utilized the results of aggression research by leftist-Freudians or Freudian-Marxists within the framework of political psychology (Senghaas), a bitter quarrel originated at the beginning of the 1970s in an effort to explain the character of peace research according to Marxist political and economic theories. The more traditional research on disarmament was in a defensive position (Czempiel, Forndran) for a while. Research interest was directed toward the internal aspects of the interconnections between armament and militarism (U. Albrecht, H. Haftendorn, F. Vilmar) or toward the external aspects of international class warfare, revolutionary movements, and the theory of imperialism (E. Krippendorff, D. Senghaas), the causes of wars (K. Gantzel, E. Weede), or international organization (V. Rittberger).

THE TEACHING OF POLITICAL SCIENCE

A striking difference from the American university system is that there is no developed graduate study system in Germany. Few special programs in German political science deserve the name "graduate studies." Normally, graduate studies take place in an archaic way of individual supervision of doctoral theses by university professors. This is done in a rather uninstitutionalized way by bilateral contacts and occasional meetings in special seminars with Ph.D. candidates.

Rarely we find a political science department in Germany. Only the institutes in Berlin and Munich are sufficiently large and differentiated to justify a department. Political science in German universities is included in different faculties, varying according to local traditions. Combinations with economics, other social sciences, or with a philosophy or history department are the most common arrangements.

Between 1960 and 1970, the number of chairs doubled. There were about 133 chairs of full professorships by 1976; if we include the equivalents in the pedagogical high schools and other academic institutions we get about twice as many posts at the top level. Including the equivalent of associate and assistant professors, the number of the teaching staff rises considerably. Between 1970 and 1975, 13 "red brick universities" were founded, most of which developed more teaching jobs in political science than the traditional universities had. As far as the contents of what is taught in political science is concerned, there are no reputational studies among scholars interviewed comparable to those of Somit and Tanenhaus in the United States. But if we take the courses offered in German universities as an indication of the shifting focus of reputation in the field, rather similar results could be found in West Germany: American surveys gave the highest prestige to comparative politics. Comparative politics ranks also highest among the subjects offered by political science institutes in Germany.

A striking difference from the U.S.A. is the higher prestige of political theory. In the 1950s it was predominantly disguised under the history of ideas; in the 1970s it was increasingly integrated into modern theory and methodology. The importance of comparative politics and modern political theory increased, the history of ideas has decreased. A slight increase is also to be found in international relations.

Theses figures indicate the average for West Germany. They hide two enormous regional differences: the differences in specialization of the staff in certain universities *and* the differences of the subjects taught for different curricula and degrees, varying with the regulations of the different *Länder* and their educational policies.

Few universities have enough chairs to offer a fairly balanced differentiation of the subjects. Still fewer uni-

Table 14.1 Subjects Taught in German Universities (in percentages)

SEMESTER	THEORY AND POLITICAL IDEAS	COMPARATIVE POLITICS	POLITICAL SOCIOLOGY/ECONOMICS	INTERNATIONAL RELATIONS
1950	18.2	32.9	28.0	20.7
1960	29.9	34.1	10.2	25.6
1970	18.7	50.5	11.5	19.1
1975	19.8	40.1	20.1	21.5

SOURCE: A. Mohr, "Anfänge zu einer Materialen Analyse" (Dissertation, Heidelberg, 1977), p. 90.

versities have a fair balance of metatheoretical positions and political views.[6] A line along the River Main approximately indicates the north-south division of the country. Some universities north of that line predominantly favor neo-Marxist views in political science (such as Frankfort, Marburg, Bremen, Oldenburg). The most notable exception to this rule is Cologne where conservative outlooks predominate. South of that line normative and positivist approaches usually are strong, the only exception being the recently founded University of Constance.

Most German students of political science until the middle of the 1970s aimed at the profession of a high school teacher in civics, which is the most striking difference from political science teaching in Western Europe and America. A very small percentage of those who got diplomas (which do not entitle them to enter school service) managed to go into public administration. Even after an enormous mobilization of social scientists in political careers, they are still discriminated against by recent federal and state civil service career regulations. Until the end of the boom, about a quarter of those who got a diploma or a doctorate was absorbed by university teaching jobs, a proportion that declined rapidly in the late 1970s.[7]

The future school teachers usually study political science in a combination with one or two other subjects of the former humanities faculties (most frequently philology and history), so that the degree of professionalization of teachers for civics education is comparatively low. Moreover, in some of the *Länder* the bulk of civics education in high school is still taught by teachers without any formal training in political science. Only in Baden-Württemberg do political science departments have a monopoly in the education of high school civics teachers. In some other *Länder* the share of political science is below 20 percent and the bulk is offered by economists and sociologists (Northrhine-Westphalia).

During the early 1970s, not only an improvement of the scholarly qualities of the subject was envisaged but especially a training of university students in didactic skills. This aim was realized only among teachers in the elementary schools, and failed largely among future teachers in high schools and in the universities.[8]

ASSOCIATIONAL ACTIVITIES

Associations. The German Political Science Association was founded in the late 1940s with the help of some emigrés working for the American occupation forces. It grew constantly and now includes about 800 members, most of whom are teachers at the university level. Associations for teachers of civics in high schools and bearers of a diploma of political science working in different professions exist apart from this merely science-oriented association.

Journals and Special Publications. The German Political Science Association since 1960 has run a periodical, the *Politische Vierteljahresschrift*. Its major competitor is the *Zeitschrift für Politik* with a half-century tradition. At present, it is a forum mostly for the more conservative and normative minded scholars in field. The critical school in the 1970s founded a periodical under the bewildering name *Leviathan* which quickly gathered the more leftist scholars and the equivalent of the "caucus group" in the United States. Within a few years, this periodical outsold the official periodical of the association. A minor periodical *Berliner Zeitschrift für Politologie* was transformed by the leftists into a periodical under the catchword *Sozialistische Politik*. Other leftist reviews like *Das Argument* or *Probleme des Klassenkampfes* are run only partly by political scientists. Since 1974 the German association publishes a yearbook *German Political Studies,* modeled on *Scandinavian Political Studies* with Sage (Beverley Hills, London).

Political Science and the World of Politics

THE IMPACT OF POLITICAL EVENTS ON POLITICAL SCIENCE

The most important event which has had an impact on political science was the conception of political science as a normative reeducation science, aiming at a contribution to transform West German intellectuals into good democratic citizens. Neo-Aristotelian approaches of the normative school and the liberal institutionalists were united under different flags for the same objective.

The second big impact on political science came as a consequence of the protest movement. A complete polarization took place in the social sciences, supported by increasing conflicts between the new government coalition (SPD-FDP) and the Christian Democratic opposition. The consequence was leftist orientation of many younger scholars in the field on the one hand, and a counterreaction of those who opposed the hegemonial claims of neo-Marxism on the other hand. Some organized in an association in defense of the freedom of science (*Bund Freiheit der Wissenschaft*), sometimes nicknamed as "professorial poujadism." The extreme horizontal mobility which characterized the German university system in the old days, particularly in political science, was cut down. Cooptation according to political views became frequent. In the time of backlash (*Tendenzwende*) the revolutionary search for immediate realization of principles in political practice affected some younger political scientists by the prime minister's decrees against the radicals and the so-called *Berufsverbot*. Even former liberals in the discipline began to overrate the subversive dangers of the leftist groups.[9] On the other hand, the neo-Marxists and a good part of the liberal press abroad overestimated the extent of the limitations on pluralism in West Germany. In proportion to the number of votes for the different communist parties, German political science has more Marxists employed in the universities than in the political science departments of most other West European countries. But the division of the country and the example of an authoritarian version of socialism on German soil, in the GDR, made the Marxist positions oriented toward the groups faithful to Moscow extremely weak—again in contrast to those countries in Europe where a Eurocommunist ideology developed in the dominant communist party.

POLITICAL SCIENTISTS IN POLITICS

The German tradition knows a sharp division between intellectuals and the state, atypical of most West European countries. Few of the grand old men in German political science were involved actively in politics, such as Carlo Schmid or Theodor Eschenburg. Only when the tendency toward a change in power affected political scientists in the late 1960s did a greater number of the younger specialists become active in politics. The sympathy of the majority belongs to the SPD, even after the *Tendenzwende*, which is a striking difference from the bulk of German university professors.

Active involvement in both political camps was frequent after 1969. Teachers of social sciences became most frequently ministers of education, if they managed to move into the political elite (von Friedeburg, SPD, in Hesse; von Oertzen, SPD, in Lower Saxony; Maier, CSU, in Bavaria; Vogel, CDU, in Rhineland-Palatinate; Glotz, SPD, in Berlin). Some politicians who graduated in political science became prime ministers in the *Länder* such as Kohl and Vogel (Rhineland-Palatinate), Schütz and Stobbe (Berlin).

The head of the Christian Democratic opposition, Helmut Kohl, took his Ph.D. in political science at Heidelberg. But still he prefers to be listed under the rubric *Staatswissenschaften* in the handbooks of parliament, which shows that political science still has a comparatively low reputation in the fields of politics.

On the whole, horizontal mobility between a political science career and the job of a professional politician decreased in the era of Schmidt's governments. The predominance of the lawyers in politics and public administration really was not affected by the temporary influx of social scientists.

RELATIONSHIPS BETWEEN GOVERNMENT AND THE DISCIPLINE

The relationships between government and the discipline of political science normally have been very weak. The development of the West German political system in the Adenauer era took place apart from the preoccupation of most political scientists. Major contributions in terms of advice given by scholars to governmental agencies and on mixed boards were made in the commissions for the reform of the electoral law (1955, 1968), which favored a relative majority system. But because of political obstacles the recommendations were not carried through. Another field of advice was planning and reform of the governmental system. Most specialists in domestic affairs have been consulted since 1968. Only minor reforms (introduction of parliamentary secretaries of state, reduction of the cabinet ministers) were carried through. In the most important commission on the constitutional reform which issued its report in 1976 only one political scientist was represented (Scharpf). The old predominance of constitutional law in all matters of major reform was still preserved. In the discussion of reorganization of the territory of the *Länder*, of fiscal reform, or the reform of the federalist system some political scientists played a certain role, but again they were a minority against lawyers and bureaucrats.

The situation of West Germany exposed to the frontier of the Communist sphere has led to all kinds of restrictions for Communists who want to enter the public service. Within the three parties of the Bundestag, it led to the development of a kind of anti-Marxist counterideology on the basis of a shallow understanding of Popper's critical rationalism. This took place, first in the FDP, then in the SPD and, later, even in the more modern wing of the CDU, opposed to the mere conservatism of the traditional Catholic ideology (Biedenkopf, Geissler, Kohl). Political scientists in this ideological movement of the "rent-a-Popper" type had some impact.[10] On the other hand some former university teachers of political science had some influence for a while within the left-wing of the SPD which—after the pragmatic Godesberg program—wanted to reopen the discussion in the debates on a long-term program (*Orientierungsrahmen* 1985) for leftist and neo-Marxist ideas (von Oertzen, Steffen).

The German research system so far knows very few institutes outside the universities concentrating on political analysis. The Max Planck Gesellschaft contains not a single social science institute. The work of the Max Planck Institute at Starnberg under von Weizsäcker and Habermas, attempted, at least to develop projects in sociology and political science under different labels. Some institutes run by the government for the advice of governmental agencies, such as the *Wissenschaft und*

Politik Foundation (Ebenhausen) or the Institute for Soviet Studies in Cologne, also employ political scientists. For the first time, political science got a chance to dominate most of the work in a recent foundation of the federal government, the Science Center in Berlin (*Wissenschaftszentrum*). Leading scholars in the field are among the directors of the different departments of the institute (Karl Deutsch, Frieder Naschold, Fritz Scharpf).

The Present State and Future Prospects of Political Science

At the time of reform, enthusiasm was accompanied by an increase in status and reputation of political science. In many universities, the number of political science students began to exceed the number of historians. After the restorative backlash, the boom in political science stopped. Younger scholars faced increasingly serious problems in finding jobs. The polarization of the discipline was weakening by the end of the 1970s. The danger that the German Political Science Association would split because of political and metatheoretical conflicts no longer exists. The time of abstract deductions in the name of systems-theory on the one hand or some kind of neo-Marxist "theory of the state," on the other hand, is gone. Again the efforts are united to develop empirical studies, predominantly in the field of policy sciences. But also on subjects which had been neglected altogether in the times of upheaval, such as parties and the representational system. In electoral studies the traditional adoption of approaches from the Nuffield school in Britain or the different achievements of American political science gave way to critical and creative development of concepts better adapted to European political science than those imported from the United States.[11] Polarization decreases, but pluralism is preserved to a greater extent than in most other West European countries. Therein, no doubt, lies the most fruitful potential of German political science.

Notes

1. P. H. Merkl, "Trends in German Political Science," *American Political Science Review* (1977): 1097.
2. C. Schrenk-Notzing, *Charakterwäsche* (Stuttgart: 1965), p. 148; H. J. Arndt, *Die Besiegten von 1945* (Berlin: Duncker & Humbolt, 1978).
3. D. P. Conradt, "The Development of Empirical Political Science Research in West Germany," *Comparative Political Studies* (October 1973).
4. T. Adorno et al., *Der Positivismusstreit in der deutschen Soziologie* (Neuwied: Luchterhand, 1969).
5. J. Habermas and N. Luhmann, *Theorie der Gesellschaft oder Sozialtechnologie?* (Frankfurt: Surhkamp, 1971).
6. Arndt, *Besiegten*.
7. D. Hartung et al., *Politologen im Beruf* (Stuttgart: Enke, 1970).
8. P. Ackerman, *Politiklehrer-Ausbildung* (Bonn: Bundeszentrale für politische Bildung, 1978), p. 44.
9. K. Sontheimer, *Das Elend unserer Intellektuellen: Linke Theorie in der Bundesrepublik Deutschland* (Hamburg: Hoffman & Campe, 1976), p. 154.
10. H. Spinner, *Popper und die Politik* (Berlin: Dietz, 1978), 1:39.
11. K. von Beyme, ed., *German Political Studies*, vol. 3 (Beverley Hills: Sage, 1978).

Selected Bibliography

Ackerman, P. *Politiklehrer-Ausbildung*. Bonn: Bundeszentrale für politische Bildung, 1978.
Adorno, Th. et al. *Der Positivismusstreit in der deutschen Soziologie*. Neuwied: Luchterhand, 1969.
Arndt, H. J. *Die Besiegten von 1945. Versuch einer Politologie für Deutsche samt Würdigung der Politischen Wissenschaft in der Bundesrepublik Deutschland*. Berlin: Duncker & Humbolt, 1978.
von Beyme, K. "Bibliographical Essay on the State of Research in Political Science in the Federal Republic of Germany." In *German Political Studies*, edited by K. von Beyme. Vol. 1, pp. 253-84. Beverley Hills: Sage Publications, 1974.
———. *Die politischen Theorien der Gegenwart*. 3d ed. Munich: Piper, 1976.
Blanke, B. et al. *Kritik der Politischen Wissenschaft*. Frankfurt: Campus, 1975.
Caciagli, M. "Il dibattito politologico nella repubblica federale tedesca." *Rivista italiana di Scienza politica* (1976): 561-87.
Conradt, D. P. "The Development of Empirical Political Science Research in West Germany." *Comparative Political Studies* (October 1973): 380-91.
Esser, J. *Einführung in die materialistische Staatsanalyse*. Frankfurt: Campus, 1975.
Grauhan, R. "Zur Ausbildungs—und Berufssituation von Politologen in der BRD." *Österreichische Zeitschrift für Politikwissenschaft* (1976): 425-36.
Habermas, J. and Luhmann, N. *Theorie der Gesellschaft oder Sozialtechnologie?* Frankfurt: Surhkamp, 1971.
Hartung, D. et al. *Politologen im Beruf*. Stuttgart: Enke, 1970.
Kastendiek, H. *Die Entwicklung der westdeutschen Politikwissenschaft*. Frankfurt: Campus, 1977.
Lehner, F. "Nostalgie einer Disziplin oder die Revolution, die nie stattgefunden hat." *PVS* (1974): 245-56.
Lepsius, M. R. *Denkschrift zur Lage der Soziologie und der Politischen Wissenschaft, im Auftrage der Deutschen Forschungsgemeinschaft*. Wiesbaden, 1961.
Maier, H. *Politische Wissenschaft in Deutschland. Aufsätze zur Lehrtradition und Bildungspraxis*. Munich: Piper, 1969.
Merkl, P. H. "Trends in German Political Science." *American Political Science Review* (1977): 1097-1108.

Mohr, A. "Anfänge zu einer materialen Analyse der westdeutschen Politikwissenschaft, dargestellt an den Determinanten der Institutionalisierung und der Lehre." Mag. Dissertation, Heidelberg, 1977.

Narr, W. D. "Entwicklung der Politologie—Entwicklung der Gesellschaft." *Kölner Zeitschrift für Soziologie und Sozialpsychologie* (1970): 98-120.

———— et al. *Theorie der Gesellschaft oder Sozialtechnologie: Neue Beiträge zur Habermas-Luhmann-Diskussion.* Frankfurt: Suhrkamp, 1974.

Naschold, F. *Politische Wissenschaft: Entstehung, Begründung und gesellschaftliche Einwirkung.* Freiburg: Albert, 1970.

Oberndörfer, D., ed. *Wissenschaftliche Politik.* Freiburg: Albert, 1962.

Pfotenhauer, D. "Conceptions of Political Science in Germany and the U.S. 1960-1969." *Journal of Politics* (1972): 555-601.

Sontheimer, K. *Das Elend unserer Intellektuellen: Linke Theorie in der Bundesrepublik Deutschland.* Hamburg: Hoffmann & Campe, 1976.

Spinner, H. *Popper und die Politik.* Vol. 1. Berlin: Dietz, 1978. Chapter 1.

Szlapczynski, J. *Nauka o polityce w RFN.* Warsaw: PWN, 1976.

GERMAN DEMOCRATIC REPUBLIC

15

KARL-HEINZ RÖDER and JÖRG FRANKE

Development and Tasks of the Political Sciences in the German Democratic Republic (GDR)

THE POLITICAL SUPERSTRUCTURE

The political sphere of social life is a central and complex object of research and teaching performed by the social sciences in the GDR. The political relations and activities are inseparably linked with the classes, the state, and the exertion of state power. The mutual relations of the classes and their interactions with the state power constitute the essence of the political relations. It is characteristic of politics that it serves the implementation of the fundamental class interests in all spheres of social life. Thus, the political activities of the classes, their parties, and other organizations comprise two fundamental directions within one process: (1) the formation of the political relations, and (2) the active influence on the other spheres of social life by means of political measures, most of all, state and legislative measures.

As a result of this complex set of relations social-scientific research into politics investigates three groups of interdependent connections: (1) the connections between the material (economic) relations and the political relations, (2) the essential connections within the political relations, and (3) the interrelations between politics and the other spheres of the superstructure. Political relations are a peculiar kind of relations between classes resulting from the economic relations that exist between them. They are ultimately economically determined and of necessity connected with the existence of political power. The special role and the specific function of the political relations are characterized by the fact that politics is the concrete expression of the economy. This means that the fundamental, that is, the economic, interests of the classes are immediately represented in their political actions. The political actions are of decisive significance for the implementation of these economic interests. The very fact that politics is a means for implementing the economic interests of classes leads to the conclusion that it is no passive result of the economic relations but, in turn, exerts an active influence on them, since the classes control the economic relations with political means in their own interests.

This reaction of politics to the economy under the conditions of the political power of the working class is expressed in the conscious implementation of the principle of the priority of the political approach for the solution of political problems. As the political relations are the immediate expression of the economic processes, they react more or less directly and more profoundly than other superstructure relations to changes of the economic basis. For this reason, a complex main research direction within the social sciences is to analyze and reveal how economic and social-class interests change to become political actions, organizations, and ideas. This requires the study of the emergence, formation, and development of the political organizations of society. At the same time, this involves analysis of the complicated, complex mediating process between the economy and politics and investigations into a variety of modifying factors, always taking into account the relative independence of the political relations of society.

Political relations exist as soon and as long as the state exists as the power organization of certain classes. The political relations, however, are not reduced to the actions of state power. They comprise the impact of the totality of class relations on the state power (home politics) and the relations among the states (foreign politics). From this it follows that the social sciences investigate the fundamental structure of the political relations in three directions: (1) the system of the practical political relations; (2) the political consciousness, which is the mental expression of the fundamental economic interests of the classes and at the same time reflects the practical political relations; (3) the system of the political organizations of society.

The changing character of the classes, their interests, and their position within the historical process and the type of state power will, in the course of the development of society, result in a change in the historically concrete character of the political relations. As a result of the socialist revolution, the political relations will acquire new content in the process of establishing a socialist society. Under socialism, the political relations maintain the essential characteristics on content and form which make them into a peculiar social phenomenon. The new qualitative stage of the political relations is reflected in three ways. First, the political relations between the working class and the class of cooperative farmers as well as with the other social strata become relations between allied classes with fundamental common interests. The alliance between the working class and the class of cooperative farmers is the political basis of socialist society. Second, the development of the creative and constructive character of politics assumes a decisive role. For the development of the political fight of the working class the relations between the class as a whole and its revolutionary party as its conscientious and organized vanguard has major significance. This relation will develop in the various stages of the fight for the extension of state power and its application as an instrument for building up socialism and communism. The constructive and creative character, however, also reflects itself, above all, in the development of the socialist state and its functions. And, third, in the socialist revolution, the long-lasting and complicated development process of the working masses to become the subject of politics and management of society begins. A characteristic phenomenon of developed socialism is the general social activity of the working people, who participate with high responsibility and competence in management and planning of social development. The main direction, along which the socialist state power develops, is the further development and perfection of socialist democracy.

The research activities of the social sciences in the GDR have always been directed toward the formation of the qualitatively higher level of political relations under socialism.[1] In this the dynamic process of revolution has significantly determined the tasks and research fields. Object, structure, theory, and methodology of the social sciences have both formed themselves and improved within this process of transforming the political relations.

Political Science Research in the German Democratic Republic

RESEARCH FIELDS AND THE RESULTS OF
RESEARCH IN THE LATE 1960S

1. Studies of the Marxist-Leninist theory of state and revolution; the leading role of the working class and its revolutionary party; society and state

2. Determination of the essence of fascism and the fascist state in Germany

3. Analyses of the Weimar Constitution of the Reich

4. Research into socialist constitutional theory on: the sovereignty of the people; alliance politics; socialist representation of the people and the overcoming of bourgeois divisions of power; the constitution, the law valid at present

5. Detailed analyses of the idea of power; of power and democracy

6. The type and forms of a state; the functions of a state

7. Creative initiative of the working people as a main characteristic of socialist democracy

8. The socialist state and the new laws underlying its development

9. Democracy and personality development

10. Socialist legal system

11. Theoretical basis of democratic centralism

RESEARCH FIELDS AND THE RESULTS OF
RESEARCH IN THE 1970S[2]

*Laws Inherent in the Developed Socialist Society
and the Gradual Transition to Communism*

1. Laws inherent in the further establishment of the developed socialist society and main questions of the gradual transition to building up communism (Institute for Social Sciences of the Central Committee of the Socialist Unity party [SED]; Academy of Sciences of the GDR)

2. Problems of materialist dialectics in the developed socialist society, particularly of the dialectics of productive forces and production relations; basis and superstructure; objective and subjective phenomena (Scientific Council for Marxist-Leninist Philosophy)

3. Fundamental problems of the political organization of socialism in the GDR and of scientific management and planning of socialist society. (Academy of Sciences of the GDR)

4. The sciences, scientific-technical revolution, and socialist society: research in which social and natural sciences cooperate (Academy of Sciences of the GDR)

*Laws Inherent in the Development
of the Socialist World System;
the Growing Cooperation of the Countries of
the Socialist State Community*

1. Fundamental problems of the formation and historical development of the socialist countries, particularly the USSR, as well as the socialist community of states; general laws and development stages inherent in the socialist world system (Council for the Science of History; Scientific Council for Research on Foreign Politics)

2. Main directions and prospects of the political, economic, ideological, and cultural development of peoples and states of the socialist community; socialist internationalism as a principle of the interstate relations of the socialist countries; the relation between national and international aspects in socialism; formation and development of socialist nations and their further approximation (Academy of Sciences of the GDR; Scientific Council for Research on Foreign Politics)

3. Fundamental theoretical problems of socialist economic integration; ways for further improvement of the planning of the integration processes, cooperation in the field of planning and the common planning activities of the Council for Mutual Economic Assistance (CMEA) member states; problems of structural development of the national economy and of specialization and cooperation in science, technology, production, and circulation; utilization of the money-commodity relations (Scientific Council for Problems of Socialist Economic Integration)

4. Problems of state management of the socialist economic integration and juridical regulations within CMEA (Council for Sciences of State and Law)

5. Problems arising in the development of the relations between socialist and nonsocialist countries (Scientific Council for Research on Foreign Politics)

Fundamental Problems of Economic Development in Establishing Socialism

1. Further improvement of the socialist production relations, development of socialist property and research on how the economic laws act under socialism (Scientific Council for the Political Economy of Socialism)

2. The dialectics of aims and means of socialist production, solution of the main task laid down by the 8th Congress of the Socialist Unity party (SED) as long-term orientation; the needs of the working people as the basis for planning (Scientific Council for the Political Economy of Socialism)

3. Laws inherent in the intensification of the national economic reproduction process in connection with rising labor productivity (Scientific Council for the Political Economy of Socialism)

4. Further elaboration of the scientific basis of socialist economic management and its application in practical economics; fundamental problems arising from the further improvement of management and planning of the reproduction process as well as from formation of economic and management organizations; development of the creative initiative of the working people (Scientific Council for Problems of Economic Management)

5. Problems of further improvement of national economic planning and scientific accounting (Scientific Council for Problems of Improvement of Planning and Scientific Accounting)

6. Fundamental problems of economy and labor organization; problems of further improvement of scientific labor organization, of distribution according to performance, utilization of the social labor capacity as well as the analysis and planning of labor productivity (Scientific Council for Problems of Economy and Labor Organization)

7. Problems of increasing the efficiency of socialist-integrated and other enterprises by intensifying the reproduction process (Scientific Council for Problems of Socialist Industrial Management)

8. Problems connected with the development of finances, money, and loans under socialism (Scientific Council for Problems of Improvement of Planning and Scientific Accounting)

Fundamental Problems Concerning the Development of Scientific-Technical Progress

1. Fundamental directions in the development of science and technology and criteria of the material-technical basis of the developed socialist society (Academy of Sciences of the GDR)

2. Main ways for accelerating scientific-technical progress as the essential basis for the establishment of the material-technical basis of socialism; interaction between scientific-technical progress and intensification of social production (Scientific Council for Economic Problems of Scientific-Technical Progress)

3. Main ways to the organic connection between science, technology, and production and the planned development of their interrelations; influence of scientific-technical progress on the development of national economic structure and efficiency (Scientific Council for Economic Problems of Scientific-Technical Progress)

4. Problems of improving management, planning, and economic stimulation of scientific-technical progress

5. Theoretical problems of organization and management of sciences; problems of implementation of the research results and of the efficiency of the scientific potential (Academy of Sciences of the GDR)

6. Influence of scientific-technical progress on the division and cooperation of labor and the formation of the content of labor; interrelations between scientific-technical progress and scientific labor organization; demands on training and further education of the working people (Scientific Council for Problems of Economy and Organization of Labor)

7. Problems concerning the history of sciences and their disciplines (Academy of Sciences of the GDR)

Further Growth of the Leading Role of the Working Class and Its Marxist-Leninist Party

1. Fundamental problems of the leading role of the working class and its Marxist-Leninist party; relations of party, class, masses in establishing the developed socialist society; problems of party structure and of internal party life

("Karl Marx" Party College at the Central Committee of SED)

2. Development of the working class, its character and its structure; development of the class of cooperative farmers in connection with the further development of the material-technical basis and socialist production relations in agriculture; social conditions and main directions of the approximation of the class of cooperative farmers, socialist intelligentsia, and other social strata toward the working class; problems of gradual overcoming the essential differences between mental and physical work, between urban and rural life (Institute for Social Sciences of SED; Scientific Council for Sociological Research)

3. Problems of development of mass initiative, innovation movement, socialist emulation, and collective work as an expression and requirement of the development of creative activities of the working class ("Fritz Heckert" Trade Union College)

Laws Underlying the Development of the Socialist State, Democracy and the Legal System in the Formation of the Developed Socialist Society in the GDR

1. Fundamental problems concerning the development of the socialist state, democracy, and law in the further establishment of the developed socialist society (Council for Research in the Sciences of State and Law)

2. Law and forms inherent in the development of socialist democracy as a result of the consolidation of working class power and the allied partners of the working class (Council for Research in the Sciences of State and Law)

3. Problems concerning the development of the socialist legal system, the increasing of the efficiency of socialist law, the consolidation and maintenance of socialist law (Council for Research in the Sciences of State and Law)

4. Problems concerning the improvement of efficiency and rationality of state management; factors and forms for the implementation of the growing economic role of the state; mass participation of the workers and application of modern methods in the course of preparation and implementation of decisions taken by the state (Council for Research in the Sciences of State and Law)

Fundamental Problems of Marxist-Leninist Ideology in the Establishment of the Developed Socialist Society and the Formation of Socialist Personalities

1. Fundamental theoretical and ideological problems of dialectical and historical materialism within the development of socialist society (Scientific Council for Marxist-Leninist Philosophy)

2. Elaboration of scientific foundations of communist personality education (Academy of Pedagogical Sciences of the GDR; Institute for Social Sciences of the Central Committee of SED; Institute for Higher Education)

3. On the development of Marxist-Leninist ethics and socialist morality; interrelations among material relations of socialism, socialist morality, and socialist personality development (Scientific Council for Marxist-Leninist Philosophy)

4. Dialectical and historical materialism as the ideological, cognitive, and methodological basis of social, natural, and technical sciences (Scientific Council for Marxist-Leninist Philosophy)

Fundamental Problems of Social Policy, the Socialist Way of Life and Demographic Development

1. Fundamental theoretical problems of social policy under socialism; influence of social policy on the development of class and population structure as well as the socialist way of life, particularly problems of meeting the demands of the working people, and of planning social processes; analysis of specific needs of families, working women, young people as well as elderly citizens (Scientific Council for Problems of Social Policy and Demography; Scientific Council for Sociological Research)

2. Problems of personality development in the process of work, of the intensification of socialist relations and mutual enrichment of social and personal life, further development of the socialist way of life (Institute for Social Sciences at the Central Committee of SED)

3. Laws and factors inherent in the demographic development in the process of establishing the developed socialist society in the GDR (Scientific Council for Problems of Social Policy and Demography)

Laws Underlying the Development of Socialist Culture, Particularly Problems of Education, Literature, and Art as Well as Language

1. Investigations into content and processes of education; development, planning, and forecasting of the integrated socialist educational system (Academy of Pedagogical Sciences of the GDR together with the Institute for Higher Education, the Central Institute for Vocational Training, and the Institute for Technical Schools)

2. Fundamental theoretical problems concerning the development of socialist culture; interrelations between work and culture under socialism (Scientific Council for Marxist-Leninist Cultural Sciences and Arts)

3. Fundamental theoretical problems of literature and art as well as problems concerning the interrelations of arts in the developed socialist society (Scientific Council for Marxist-Leninist Cultural Sciences and Arts)

4. Cultural heritage in a socialist society (Scientific Council for Marxist-Leninist Cultural Sciences and Arts)

5. Traditions and achievements of the multinational Soviet literature and the literature of the other member countries of the socialist community of states (Scientific Council for Marxist-Leninist Cultural Sciences and Arts)

6. Fundamental problems of Marxist-Leninist aesthetics (Scientific Council for Marxist-Leninist Cultural Sciences and Arts)
7. Language as a social phenomenon; laws inherent in structure, function, development, and social efficiency of language (Scientific Council for Linguistic Research)

Further Elaboration of a Marxist-Leninist Conception of History and the Utilization of the Progressive and Humanistic Heritage

1. Problems concerning the history of the revolutionary German working-class movement and the formation and development of its Marxist-Leninist party from its beginnings up to the present (Institute for Marxism-Leninism of SED)
2. Fundamental problems of the historical development of the German nation from its beginnings up to the development of the GDR as the result and the climax of the age-old struggle of the progressive forces of our people, particularly the working class under the leadership of its revolutionary party (Council for the Science of History)
3. Problems of the history of the GDR as a member of the socialist community of states, of its inner development and its foreign policy, particularly considering the development since the early 1960s (Council for the Science of History)
4. Problems of the historical development of the European nations; antifeudal peasants' movements, bourgeois and bourgeois-democratic revolutions and the impact of the Great Socialist October Revolution on the revolutionary movements in Europe (Council for the Science of History)
5. Theoretical and methodological problems of the historical science

Fundamental Problems Concerning the Present Development of the Revolutionary World Process

1. The growing influence of socialism in the international class fight; main directions and tendencies in the development of the international relation of forces; dialectics of the policy of peaceful coexistence and class fight; prospects for promoting the international process of detente, the fight for security and the development of international cooperation (Scientific Council for Research on Foreign politics; Scientific Council for International Workers' Movement)
2. Problems of the general crisis of capitalism in the presently increasing contradictions and instability of state monopoly capitalism (Scientific Council for Research on Imperialism)
3. Problems and prospects of economic and political integration in Western Europe (Scientific Council for Research on Imperialism)
4. Analysis of classes and strata (particularly of the working class) in the developed capitalist countries; problems of capitalist exploitation and anti-imperialist fight (Scientific Council for Research on Imperialism)
5. The crisis of the political system of imperialism; the present mechanism of political power in capitalist countries; analysis and critical assessment of the practical application of the imperialist state and legal system (Council for Research in the Sciences of State and Law)
6. Problems of the historical development of imperialism and opportunism in Germany and the Federal Republic of Germany as well as problems of recent history in selected main imperialist countries (Council for the Science of History)
7. Politics and ideology in present international social democracy (Institute for Social Sciences at the Central Committee of SED)
8. Investigations into the development of social forces and movements and into the policies of bourgeois and petty bourgeois parties in the Federal Republic of Germany (Institute for International Politics and Economics)
9. Problems concerning the history and present state of the national liberation movements and ways for promoting the unity of the anti-imperialist forces; development problems of nationally liberated countries (Scientific Council for Research on Foreign Politics)
10. Problems concerning the development of the international workers' movement in various countries; fundamental problems of strategy and tactics of the communist world movement (Scientific Council for International Workers' Movement)
11. Fundamental problems of the history of the international workers' movement, of the development of the relations among the fraternal parties of the socialist countries, particularly taking into account the role of the CPSU (Council for the Science of History)

Fundamental Problems of Marxist-Leninist Ideology in the Struggle between Socialism and Imperialism

1. Fundamental problems concerning Marx-Engels research and publication of their works as well as the fight against falsifications of Marx's and Engel's works; research on the sources, on the formation and development of Marxism-Leninism and its constituents (Scientific Council for Research on Marx and Engels)
2. Contributions to the further elaboration of strategy and tactics of the ideological struggle; analysis and critique of present anticommunism and its philosophical and political-ideological basis; critical assessment of the prevailing bourgeois, socioreformist, and revisionist theories, investigations into their function within the class struggle (Academy of Sciences of the GDR; Institute for International Politics and Economy)

3. Studies into the essence and social doctrine of Maoism; interpretation and critical assessment of the antisocial, anti-Soviet policies of the Maoist leadership in international affairs (Council for International Workers' Movement)
4. Critical assessment of anarchist, ultra-leftist, and Trotzkist theories and their impact on the workers' movement (Institute for Social Sciences of the Central Committee of SED; Institute for Marxism-Leninism of the Central Committee of SED)
5. Culture and art in the ideological class fight between socialism and imperialism (Scientific Council for Marxist-Leninist Culture and Art Sciences)
6. Critical assessment of the main directions of bourgeois historiography (Council for the Science of History)
7. Critical assessment of conceptual main lines of bourgeois educational policies and pedagogy (Academy of Pedagogical Sciences)

SCIENTIFIC COUNCILS IN THE GDR FOR RESEARCH WITHIN THE SOCIAL SCIENCES

SCIENTIFIC COUNCIL	SCIENTIFIC INSTITUTION
1. Scientific Council for Marxist-Leninist Philosophy	Institute for Social Sciences of the Central Committee of the SED
2. Scientific Council for Sociological Research	
3. Scientific Council for Marxist-Leninist Cultural Sciences and Art	
4. Scientific Council for International Workers' Movement	
5. Council for the Science of History	Institute for Marxism-Leninism of the Central Committee of the SED
6. Scientific Council for Research on Marx and Engels	
7. Scientific Council for Research in Economics, with oversight over:	Academy of Sciences of the GDR
Scientific Council for Political Economy of Socialism	Institute for Social Sciences at the Central Committee of the SED
Scientific Council for Problems of Economic Management	Central Institute for Socialist Management of the Economy of the Central Committee of the SED
Scientific Council for Problems of Socialist Economic Integration	
Scientific Council for Problems of Improving of Planning and Economic Accounting	Economic Research Institute of the State Planning Commission, Berlin
Scientific Council for Problems of Economy and Labor Organization	Central Research Institute for Labor at the State Secretariat for Labor and Wages, Dresden
Scientific Council for Problems of Socialist Industrial Management	"Carl Schorlemmer" Technical College, Leuna-Merseburg
Scientific Council for Social Policy and Demography	"Fritz Heckert" Trade Union College, Bernau
Scientific Council for Economic Problems of Scientific-Technical Progress	Research Unit at the Ministry for Science and Technology
8. Scientific Council for Linguistic Research	Academy of Sciences of the GDR
9. Scientific Advisory Committee, "Women in Socialist Society"	
10. Council for the Sciences of State and Law	Academy for the Sciences of State and Law of the GDR
11. Council for the Coordination of Pedagogical Research	Academy of Pedagogical Sciences of the GDR
12. Scientific Advisory Committee for Research on Youth Problems	Bureau for Youth Problems of the Council of Ministers of the GDR
13. Scientific Council for Research on Imperialism	Institute for International Politics and Economy
14. Scientific Council for Research in Foreign Politics	Institute for International Relations

Notes

1. Research complexes and main research directions are contained in the research program of Marxist-Leninist social sciences in the GDR, 1976–1980. Cf. *Einheit*, no. 9 (1975):1042–61.
2. Cf. *Einheit*, no. 2 (1975):153.

Bibliography

JOURNALS

Deutsche Außenpolitik.
Deutsche Zeitschrift für Philosophie.
Einheit. Zeitschrift für Theorie und Praxis des wissenschaftlichen Sozialismus.
IPW-Berichte. Zeitschrift des Instituts für Internationale Politik und Wirtschaft.
Staat und Recht.
Wirtschaftswissenschaft.

PERIODICALS

Abhandlungen der Akademie der Wissenschaften der DDR.
Aktuelle Beiträge der Staats- und Rechtswissenschaft.
Beiträge der Kritik der bürgerlichen Ideologie und des Revisionismus.
Internationale Reihe: Sozialismus—Erfahrungen, Probleme und Perspektiven.
IPW-Forschungshefte.
Jahrbuch der Internationalen Politik und Wirtschaft.
Reihe Grundfragen der Marxistisch-Leninistischen Philosophie.
Reihe Weltanschauung heute.
Reihe zur Kritik der bürgerlichen Ideologie.
Schriften der sozialistischen Wirtschaftsführung.
Schriftenreihe. Der Sozialistische Staat, Theorie—Leitung—Planung
Schriftenreihe ABC des Marxismus-Leninismus.
Schriftenreihe Blickpunkt Weltpolitik.
Schriftenreihe Recht in unserer Zeit.
Staats- und rechtstheoretische Studien.
Veröffentlichungen der Wissenschaftlichen Räte.

DICTIONARIES

Kleines politisches Wörterbuch. Berlin, 1978.
Kulturpolitisches Wörterbuch. Berlin, 1978.
Philosophisches Wörterbuch. 2 vols. Berlin, 1976.
Wörterbuch der Außenpolitik. Berlin, 1965.
Wörterbuch der Marxistisch-Leninistischen Soziologie. Berlin, 1977.
Wörterbuch der Ökonomie des Sozialismus. Berlin, 1973.
Wörterbuch der sozialistischen Jugendpolitik. Berlin, 1978.
Wörterbuch zum sozialistischen Staat. Berlin, 1974.

BOOKS 1976-1979 (SELECTED)

Adler, Frank and Jetzschmann, Horst. *Arbeiterklasse und Persönlichkeit im Sozialismus.* Berlin, 1977.
Die Arbeiterklasse der entwickelten sozialistischen Gesellschaft. Berlin, 1978.
Benjamin, Hilde. *Zur Geschichte der Rechtspflege in der DDR 1945 bis 1949.* Berlin, 1976.
Bürgerliche Staatsideologie. Berlin, 1979.
Dettenborn, Harry and Mollnau, Karl, A. *Rechtsbewußtsein und Rechtserziehung.* Berlin, 1976.
Dialektischer und historischer Materialismus, Lehrbuch. Berlin, 1976.
Doernberg, Stefan *et al. Außenpolitik der DDR. Drei Jahrzehnte sozialistische deutsche Friedenspolitik.* Berlin, 1979.
Die entwickelte sozialistische Gesellschaft. Wesen und Kriterien, Kritik revisionistischer Konzeptionen. Berlin, 1976.
Franke, Jörg. *Autonomie bürgerlicher Demokratielehren in den USA.* Berlin, 1978.
Friedländes, Paul and Liebscher, Gertrud. *Neokolonialismus in der Krise.* Berlin, 1978.
Friedliche Koexistenz in Europa. Entwicklungstendenzen der Auseinandersetzung zwischen Sozialismus und Imperialismus. Berlin, 1977.
Geschichte der SED—Abriß. Berlin, 1979.
Gottschling, Ernst. *Demokratie im Zerrspiegel.* Berlin, 1978.
Grahn, Werner and Wagner, Ingo. *Rechtliche und soziale Gleichheit im Klassenkampf.* Berlin, 1977.
Guliew, W. A.; Löwe, Bernd P.; Röder, K.-H. *Bürgerliches politisches System und Systemtheorie.* Widersprüche und Tendenzen, Berlin, 1978.
Hanke, Helmut and Rossow, Gerd. *Sozialistische Kulturrevolution.* Berlin, 1977.
Hartmann, Karl; Widerszpil, Stanislaw *et al. Arbeiterklasse und wissenschaftlich-technische Intelligenz in der entwickelten sozialistischen Gesellschaft.* Berlin, 1978.
Klein, Peter and Engelhardt, Klaus. *Weltproblem Abrüstung: Politische und ökonomische Probleme des Ringens um Rüstungsbegrenzung und Abrüstung.* Berlin, 1978.
Krüger, Joachim and Quilitzsch, Siegmar. *Zusammenarbeit und Annäherung in der sozialistischen Gemeinschaft.* Berlin, 1977.
Lieberam, Ekkehard. *Zur Krise der Regierbarkeit—ein neues Thema bürgerlicher Staatsideologie.* Berlin, 1977.
Marxistisch-Leninistische Staats und Rechtstheorie. Berlin, 1976.
Melzer, Helmut *et al. Arbeitskollektiv—Volksvertretung—Demokratie.* Berlin, 1976.
Mollnau, Karl A.; Schöneburg, Karl-Heinz; Weichelt, Wolfgang. *Macht und Recht—Einheit oder Gegensatz?* Berlin, 1976.
Reinhold, Otto. *Entwickelte sozialistische Gesellschaft und Arbeiterklasse.* Berlin, 1977.
Röder, Karl-Heinz. *Die Formel der "sozialen Demokratie," Staat und Demokratie in der Ideologie des Sozialreformismus.* Berlin, 1975.
―――― *et al. USA—Aufstieg und Verfall bürgerlicher Demokratie.* Berlin, 1976.
Sachse, Dieter *et al. Zur Agrar- und Bündnispolitik der SED bei der Gestaltung der entwickelten sozialistischen Gesellschaft.* Berlin, 1977.
Schmidt, Max. *Zu einigen aktuellen Fragen der Wirtschaftsbeziehungen zwischen sozialistischen Staaten und kapitalistischen Industrieländern.* Berlin, 1976.
Schneider, Wolfgang *et al. Die Arbeiterklasse und der Annäherungsprozeß der Klassen und Schichten.* Berlin, 1979.
Schöneburg, Karl-Heinz. *Revolutionärer Prozeß und Staatsentstehung.* Berlin, 1976.

Schüßler, Gerhard and Weichelt, Wolfgang. *Arbeiterklasse, Partei, Staatsmacht*. Berlin, 1976.

Schüßler, Gerhard et al. *Marxistisch-Leninistische Partei und sozialistischer Staat*. Berlin, 1978.

Schulze, Gerhard et al. *DDR—Gesellschaft, Staat, Bürger*. Berlin, 1978.

Söder, Günter. *Ökonomie—Politik—Wirtschaftspolitik*. Berlin, 1977.

Sorgenicht, Klaus. *Staat, Recht und Demokratie nach dem IX. Parteitag der SED*. Berlin, 1976.

Sozialismus und Demokratie. Die Demokratie in Theorie und Praxis der sozialistischen Länder. Berlin, 1977.

Sozialismus—Menschlichkeit, Freiheit und Demokratie. Berlin, 1977.

Sozialismus—Theorie und Praxis. Berlin, 1977.

Die sozialistische Gesellschaft, Wesen, Entwicklungen, Perspektiven. Berlin, 1977.

Staatsrecht der DDR, Lehrbuch. Berlin, 1978.

Vogt, Walter. *Integration—Politik und Ökonomie. Zu einigen politischen Aspekten der sozialistischen ökonomischen Integration*. Berlin, 1979.

Auf dem Wege der Wirtschaft des entwickelten Sozialismus. Berlin, 1978.

Weichelt, Wolfgang. *Der demokratische Inhalt der sozialistischen Staatsmacht*. Berlin, 1977.

Wissenschaftlicher Kommunismus, Lehrbuch. Berlin, 1977.

16

ICELAND*

ÓLAFUR RAGNAR GRIMSSON

Iceland is in that majority of nations where political science either does not exist or is entering the early stages of development, under the direction of only a few scholars in each country. Like political scientists in other such countries, Iceland's few scholars must cope with theoretical and analytical advances in a multitude of fields within the discipline, acquire a comprehensive knowledge of their own political system, teach and train students, and create from scratch a political science vocabulary in their native tongue. While providing an account of the development of Icelandic political science, this chapter will attempt, also, to present it as an example of the major problems involved in pioneering political science in countries where the discipline has no roots and, thus, must be transplanted from outside.

Political science came to Iceland as an academic discipline only about a decade ago. Following increasing demands in the late 1960s for new lines of study to be opened up at the University of Iceland—which for decades had consisted of traditional faculties of theology, law, medicine, languages, and Icelandic literature, together with minor studies in engineering and business administration—a Department of Social Science was established in the autumn of 1970, enabling Icelandic students to obtain a B.A. degree in political science and sociology. These disciplines were, however, without any roots in the Icelandic academic or social community; they did not even have acknowledged names in the Icelandic language. The preparations for the new department consisted of the issuance of the official decree and the appointment to teaching posts a fortnight before the department was opened of two Icelandic graduates who had just completed their studies in England and Sweden respectively; an American guest professor in sociology was hired during the first two terms; library facilities barely existed. The entrance of political science into Icelandic academia was thus more akin to the landing of the first astronauts on the moon than to the slow advance of the settlers through the Wild West—to use comparisons from the history of the New World.

Although in the decades following the Second World War a few Icelandic students had become acquainted with political science during their study of economics, history and other subjects in the Scandinavian countries, England, or the United States, a systematic analysis of the Icelandic political system was not instituted until Stein Rokkan and other directors of the Smaller European Democracies (SED) project decided in the mid-1960s to include Iceland, and employed the author of this chapter as a full-time researcher. The SED work inevitably consisted primarily of data gathering and preliminary analysis of the historical development of the Icelandic system since the middle of the nineteenth century. As no modern Icelandic history was available, the first research task was to establish what had actually taken place in the past one hundred years. Together with this author's doctoral thesis, "Political Power in Iceland Prior to the Period of Class Politics, 1845-1918," which grew out of the SED research, the material that was assembled under SED auspices, due largely to the encouragement of Rokkan and his fellow directors, was the foundation upon which the discipline primarily rested during its infancy in Icelandic academe. Thus, the SED project was the main source from which Icelandic political science advanced after the foundation of the Department of Social Science.

The following sections will provide a general account

---

*This chapter has been abridged and rearranged by the editor from ORG, "Pioneering Political Science: The Case of Iceland," *Scandinavian Political Studies* (1977):47-63, with the permission of the author.

of the development of the Department of Social Science at the University of Iceland during the first six years of its existence, with special emphasis on research in political science and related areas of sociology. As the former half of this period, 1970–1973, was characterized by the need to build up the teaching required for the B.A. degree, the research efforts have been almost exclusively restricted to the latter half, 1973–1976. In order to distinguish special aspects of the advancement of political science in Iceland the chapter is divided into the following sections: teaching; research; associational activities; future prospects. A list of publications and theses concerning Icelandic politics is provided at the conclusion of this chapter.

Teaching

The administrative organization and the need for integrated teaching led to extensive cooperation from the very beginning between the fields of political science and sociology within the Department of Social Science. This cooperation has furthered a joint analysis of political and social structures in Iceland and hindered the formation of administrative barriers that in some other places have prevented scholars basically interested in the same problems from approaching them together from the vantage points of distinct disciplines. So far as political science is concerned, the cooperative setup within the Department of Social Science has been particularly relevant in research on the social structure, especially class divisions and the urban-rural cleavage, and on the party-dominated mass media. Furthermore, it has been conducive toward providing the students with a wide-ranging background in social science and a broad analysis of Icelandic political and social development. Thus, the integration of teaching and research in political science and sociology has been a significant factor in establishing in Iceland during a relatively small number of years a body of social scientists who share each others' interests in a wide variety of areas.

The B.A. degree which the department awards is based on introductory courses in political science and comparative government, sociology, social anthropology, economics, psychology, statistics, methodology, social and political theory; furthermore, there are courses dealing with Icelandic political and social institutions and behavior patterns and their development from the early stages of modernization in the middle of the nineteenth century to the present. These subjects are all obligatory for every student. For those specializing in political science there are, in addition, courses in international relations, political sociology, and political philosophy as well as optional courses in mass media studies, the analysis of developing countries, philosophy, economics, and law. The degree is finally obtained by completing an extensive thesis (12,000–20,000 words) which generally requires independent research into Icelandic politics. The justification for the requirement concerning the size of the B.A. thesis, which admittedly exceeds that made in most places, is based on the need to employ the students' enterprise in the advancement of political science research in Iceland. The B.A. theses have thus contributed significantly to the data on Icelandic politics which have become available in the last few years. Although this practice has provided the students with valuable experience and enabled them to join the research undertaken in the department, it has, however, lengthened the normal time of study to four years.

When the Department of Social Science was established at the University of Iceland only two Icelandic teachers were appointed. In the following six years the number has increased to five. In political science, there are this author, professor, and Svanur Kristjánsson, lecturer; Thorbjörn Broddason is a lecturer in sociology, Haraldur Ólafsson is a lecturer in social anthropology; Thórólfur Thórlindsson was recently appointed guest lecturer in sociology. In addition, a professorship in sociology is vacant. During the last few years the teaching has been entirely in the hands of Icelandic staff members. Previously, the department employed on a temporary basis—for one or two terms—lecturers from Sweden, England, and the United States. With the present employment structure, the responsibility for teaching and research is now exclusively and permanently in the hands of Icelandic social scientists.

Although foreign teachers provided valuable international influence in the young department, their contribution to the advancement of social science in Iceland was fundamentally obstructed by the language barrier, which restricted their scope in the areas of both teaching and research; their inevitable unfamiliarity with Icelandic politics and history was furthermore a potential drawback to major analytical contributions. While it has been possible to teach individual courses in English, the creation of Icelandic concepts and the development of political science discourse in Icelandic have been essential prerequisites for the advancement of the discipline in the university and the community at large. The nature of the Icelandic language prevents the employment of the international social vocabulary, derived primarily from English. To this extent the establishment of these studies in Iceland is a much harder task than in most other countries where political science has been founded already. The translation of key concepts of the different social science disciplines has thus been a major occupation for the Icelandic staff members. Concept formation has to be a significant aspect of both teaching and research.

As the Icelandic language requires abstract concepts to indicate the concrete nature of phenomena, a characteristic which has probably been strengthened by the concreteness which farmers and fishermen in past centuries gave their discourse, it can be extremely difficult to translate the abstract notions which our colleagues in the more advanced places have so proudly created in abundance.

The following Icelandic terms will provide specific examples of what is involved in the obligation to provide translations of all relevant concepts in social science: political science—stjórnmálafraeði; elite—kjarni; pluralism—margraeði; ideology—hugmyndafraeði; socialization—félagsmótun; anomie—siðrof. All these terms are in international currency and used in a multitude of languages. In the Icelandic case, however, they have to be translated in a way which simultaneously fits the rules of the language and bears out the meaning of the concept. Such translations of hundreds of concepts are among the most important and the most unenviable tasks given to those responsible for introducing political science to a nation.

When the Department of Social Science was founded in 1970, it was given an administrative status outside the faculty structure of the university. In 1975 the department was amalgamated with three disciplines that had belonged to the Faculty of Arts: psychology, education science, and library science. This change became effective in the autumn of 1976, when the Faculty of Social Science was created. It is now the administrative residence of political science, sociology, and social anthropology, together with the other previously mentioned subjects. The new faculty has given social science a firmer basis within the University of Iceland and created more favorable administrative conditions for its advance.

Since the first three years of the department's existence were inevitably devoted to building up a succession of courses leading to the B.A. degree, not until 1973 had the necessary channels for graduation been fully established. By 1977 54 students had graduated from the department (three of whom graduated in 1972), 29 of those in political science and related areas of sociology, of whom 14 were in political science proper. As is brought out quite clearly in table 16.1 political science in Iceland follows the tradition of male dominance within the discipline. Whereas women constitute nearly half of all graduates from the department, they are less than a quarter of the political science graduates. While over a third of the male students choose politics as a field of specialization, the female students lean more toward studies of the family, education, and particular aspects of the social structure. Thus, the position of men and women in society at large is both reflected and maintained within the social sciences.

Table 16.1 Social Science Graduates from the University of Iceland: 1973–1976

SUBJECT MATTER	MEN		WOMEN		TOTAL	
All areas*	30	55%	24	45%	54	100%
Political science and related areas of sociology	18	62%	11	38%	29	100%
Political science	11	79%	3	21%	14	100%

*Sociology and political science as well as the subareas of social anthropology and criminology. Three of the students graduated in 1972.

To indicate the distribution of B.A. theses in the five specific research areas which are discussed in the following section on research, a classification of graduates (1973–1976), is provided; power structure 5, political parties 7, the *Althingi* (national assembly) 2, social structure 8, mass media 5. Though the *Althingi* has received a low proportion of B.A. theses, it should be noted that the research papers are primarily concentrated in that area. In addition, a few theses are yet to be completed.

Since social science did not grow out of traditional disciplines in Icelandic society and was, so to speak, transplanted from the outside, it was expected that graduates might find it difficult to obtain employment. Fortunately and somewhat surprisingly, however, this has not turned out to be the case. Graduates from the department are now posted within various institutions and agencies and already some seem to have established roots for the discipline within particular occupations. Some of the graduates in political science and the related areas of sociology are now employed in state institutions, either in administrative or research capacities, others work in the mass media, in interest organizations, or as teachers below the university level. One-third of the graduates have sought further education abroad.

Research

When the Department of Social Sciences, having established the teaching necessary for the B.A. degree, moved the emphasis in 1973 toward the advancement of research, it was decided to formulate a preliminary research policy for political science. Although the SED project and the author's thesis provided a certain basis from which it was possible to proceed, the key task would be to acquire a general perspective on all major aspects of the Icelandic system. The research policy was therefore constructed on the fundamental premise that a general mapping of all major system parts should be the primary endeavor. In such a way a sufficient overview could be established from which more detailed studies and intensive analytical and comparative efforts could be developed. It was estimated that it might take up to a decade for this preliminary task to be completed. Consequently by the early 1980s, the groundwork for a comprehensive and intensive analysis of Icelandic politics would have been laid.

On the basis of this policy the research program was divided into the following stages:

1. The power structure, a continuation of the research which preceded the establishment of the department
2. The party system, especially the emergence of the class parties and their development in recent decades
3. The legislative institutions with concentration on the *Althingi*
4. The coalition system, especially at the cabinet level
5. Interest organizations, their links to the parties and increasing involvement in the making of public policy
6. The civil service, the nineteenth-century colonial heritage and the major growth in the postwar period as far as institutional proliferation and ever-increasing professionalization are concerned
7. Election studies based on the analysis of historical data and on modern surveys
8. Local government, its organizational structure, links to national institutions, and recruitment functions.

In addition to these eight stages, the political science research program is supplemented by cooperation with the sociology branch of the department with respect to research in the following two areas: (a) the social structure, especially class and urban-rural cleavages; and (b) the mass media, especially its dominance by the parties. Thus, the entire research program consists of ten distinct stages.

The department has attempted to execute the research program by three separate yet interlocking means. The first involves independent research by staff members. The second is composed of the extensive B.A. theses which have been grouped together under teachers' supervision in order to form specific research efforts: some have dealt with the parties, others with aspects of the power structure or the *Althingi,* and so on. The third consists of cooperative research projects in which the students and staff members from different disciplines take part. The students have thus generally been highly involved in the advancement of Icelandic political and social research. The small size of the staff made this inevitable if reasonable progress were to be achieved in a relatively short time. The students' participation, even as early as in their second or third year of study, has proved to be very valuable—in some cases turning out excellent original work which has contributed some of the cornerstones of our present knowledge. The Icelandic experience thus seems to bear witness to the considerable research resources available in the student body, even at the undergraduate level. With systematic and patient direction, this resource can be employed to produce valuable material. Admittedly the students' contribution has been stronger with regard to empirical work and general data-gathering; it has inevitably lacked an analytical maturity. But in a virgin field the basic mapping is more essential for further progress than cosmological theorizing in the grand tradition.

So far, the realization of the previously described research program has been primarily restricted to stages 1 to 3, with some minor efforts concerning stages 4 and 5 and considerable emphasis on the two stages (a and b above) involving cooperation with the sociology branch of the department. In the next few years more efforts will be put into stages 4 and 5. Although stages 6 to 8 will have to wait until later in the 1980s for extensive treatment, some work has already been done on historical election analysis and local power structures. Thus, the ordering of the research tasks in the preliminary program has not been completely followed. It should, furthermore, be noted that in the immediate future particular emphasis will have to be put on publishing the research that has already been completed.

In order to provide a general but brief introduction to political science research at the University of Iceland, a summary follows of the main concerns in the chief research areas. The summary includes references to theses, publications and research papers that are listed at the end of the article. Interested scholars should thus be able to trace the works of particular relevance. However, as the research in all areas is still in progress, significant parts only exist in manuscript form or are still incomplete. The works referred to here therefore do not exhaust the available material. The account of the research has been divided into six components.

The Power Structure. Following the author's thesis on the Icelandic power structure from the emergence of modern politics in the early decades of the nineteenth century and through the period of independence politics, there has been considerable concentration in the department on extending this analysis to the more recent era of class politics. Among the specific exploratory emphases have been the interlocking of major institutions, the relationship between the political, economic, and cultural sectors as well as the institutional basis of the elite, its recruitment, social origins, and cohesiveness created by educational institutions and kinship ties. The research on the general character of the national power structure has been supplemented by individual case studies dealing with community power, such as Geirsson's 1976 study of the rule of socialist parties in an eastern town and Harðardóttir's 1975 examination of the respective influence of local councilors, building enterprises, and municipal bureaucrats in the planning of a major Reykjavík suburb. Among such case studies are Guðmundsson's 1976 preliminary investigation of the power exercised by different political and economic interests in the development of the University of Iceland and Vilhjálmsdóttir and Grímsson's 1975 analysis of women's leadership positions within the Icelandic political system; the latter study is part of a general report on the equality of men and women in Iceland which was prepared at the request of the Ministry of Social Affairs. Furthermore, a preliminary study was made by Valdimarsson of the role which different political institutions and other actors played in the formation of regional policy, contrasting the situation in the early 1950s with the present. This analysis was a contribution to a project which dealt with internal migration, with special emphasis on the Vestfirðir area.

Political Parties. The research in this area can be divided into two major components. The first consists of the analysis which Svanur Kristjánsson, lecturer, has conducted on the development of the Icelandic class parties in the interwar period, that is, from the emergence of class and ideological cleavages in the second and third decade of this century to the appearance of foreign policy, primarily the NATO/USA-base issue, as one of the fundamental factors in Icelandic politics. Kristjánsson's research deals with the complex interrelations between the parties and respective organizations of workers, farmers, employers, and cooperative societies, the parties' ideological characteristics, and the voting patterns of different occupational groups. Thus the research involves an attempt to deal in a systematic way with the period of class politics which succeeded the independence struggle. Kristjánsson's work provides a major cornerstone in the advancement of Icelandic political science. If it is linked to this author's thesis on nineteenth century and early twentieth century politics, one acquires a foundation for a comprehensive analysis of Icelandic politics from early modernization up to World War II.

The second component of the research on political parties consists of a number of B.A. theses that either analyze one of the major parties or deal with a fundamental issue in the development of the party structure. The merger of nationalism and laissez-faire ideology that characterized the origin of the Independence party is extensively treated by Guðmundsson in an analysis of its formation and how it became the largest party in the country. Einarsson's account of the Progressive party deals predominantly with its organizational structure, the links to the Cooperative Movement, and how it succeeded in establishing a strong urban following despite having been almost exclusively a rural party. The following significant aspects of the complex history of the Icelandic Left are treated in individual theses. Bjarnason describes the three major splits in the Social Democratic party that led to the formation of a successful Left challenger and the decline of the SDP electoral support from over 20 percent in the 1930s to below 10 percent in the 1970s. Thorkelsson examines the development in terms of organization and electoral strength from the Marxist-Leninist Communist party (CP) (1930-1938), through the United Socialist party (USP) (1938-1968) to the creation of the People's Alliance (PA) as a mass party which has achieved twice the size of the Social Democrats. The ideological development of these three successive parties is dealt with by Karlsson, who contrasts the CP, USP, and the PA in terms of Marxism, the class conflict, nationalism, democracy and parliamentarianism, the Icelandic cultural and historical heritage, the links to international communist and socialist movements, and the ownership of the means of production and general economic policy. The significance of foreign policy, especially the NATO/USA-base issue, as a fundamental cleavage in the postwar period is brought out in two theses. Ólafsson's deals with the development of party conflict in this issue area from Iceland's entry into NATO to the formation in 1956 of the first Left government that declared its intention to have the USA base removed. The second thesis, by Arnason, provides an analysis of the rise and fall of the National Preservation party (1953-1963) which campaigned almost exclusively on an antibase platform.

The Althingi. The research on legislative institutions and processes consists primarily of the following three focuses:

1. Interrelated minor research papers on the nature and characteristics of the party leadership in the *Althingi;* the issue specialization of different parliamentary parties and groups of M.P.s; the committee system; the relationship of M.P.s to their constituents; the nature and scope of party conflict in the *Althingi;* the increasing role of the government in legislative output; the growing influence of interest organizations and the civil service

2. An extensive survey based on interviews with M.P.s (1972-1973) focusing on their parliamentary work and

activities in other areas, thus bringing out their relationship with interest organizations and state bureaucracies, dealing also with the communication process within the *Althingi* and the flow of information to the M.P.s, and analyzing the characteristics of different parliamentary parties and leadership groups in terms of nationalism, localism, and party loyalties, with an attempt to show how the M.P.s view the Icelandic power structure

3. A few minor case studies of particular legislative processes, concentrating on how they reflect the power of respective actors both inside and outside the *Althingi*

Although a great deal of this research is piecemeal and still in progress, two theses, one by Ólafsson and one by Sigmundsdóttir, were completed in 1975 and a number of research papers are available. However, in the near future emphasis should be put on bringing the work in this area together in order to prepare the ground for publication of a comprehensive analysis of the *Althingi* and the forces at play in the legislative process.

The Social Structure. The rapid social change which has occurred in Iceland during the past 30 to 50 years and its effects on the political system make this research area a very significant and fruitful field for interdisciplinary studies. From the sociology side the chief contribution has come from lecturer Thorbjörn Broddason and his students. Broddason has also been the main director of the work on mass media which is described below. Among the primary concerns in this area have been the changes in population and occupational structure from the middle of the nineteenth century to the present and how the transformation of the stable rural society and the creation of modern urban Iceland have affected political and social institutions. At the present stage, the research efforts have led to individual research papers and theses dealing with particular topics, such as Héðinsson and Jóhannsson's on the social structure in a fishing town; Karlsson's on the reflection of social stratification in primary group relationships; the social origins of pupils in different educational institutions by Halldórsdóttir and Waage; and Ólafsson's study of how the recruitment of university students in the twentieth century reflects the changing social bases of this potential leadership group. Theses dealing with the characteristics of farmers by Thorgrimsdóttir, of tenants in the Reykjavík area by Sveinsson, of minority groups in Icelandic society by Jónsdóttir, and of the spread of literature among different occupational groups by Ólafsson also provide a wealth of interesting and useful material. Among other works in this field there is a brief analysis of the common notion of classlessness in Iceland by Broddason and Webb and a report on the quality of men and women in Iceland with respect to occupation, education, income, and leadership positions by Vilhjálmsdóttir and Grímsson. Following this report a more detailed study is being made of the social position of women in the Reykjavík area. The study will provide data on a number of relevant social and political behavior patterns of different occupational groups.

In addition to social stratification, which is the interlocking concern of the above mentioned research, the great migration from the rural parts of the country to the urban centers, especially Reykjavík, constitutes the other major focus of research in this area. Migration studies are an essential part of any analysis dealing with the formation of the fundamental urban-rural cleavage in modern Icelandic politics, which has made the center-periphery division a vital component of political development in Iceland. The primary research in this field consists of the Vestfirðir project which concentrates on migration from and within the Western Peninsula. The project involves data gathering on population changes in all the peninsula's communes (1850–1975), migration patterns in terms of family, age, sex, occupation, and other variables, the effects of economic and political changes, the role of governmental bodies—both national and local—as well as the administrative structure with regard to regional policy. Given the available manpower at the Department of Social Science, the assembled data will provide material for analysis for a number of years to come.

Mass Media. As all the major national and local papers during the last hundred years have been organs of political parties and the State Radio and Television has been dominated by party-appointed directors, the area of mass media research is highly central in the Icelandic case to the analytical interests of political science. Under Thorbjörn Broddason's supervision four theses have been written on the news selection processes in radio, television, and the press by Jónsdóttir, Pálsdóttir, Halldórsson, and Einarsdóttir and one by Jónsdóttir on the circulation of different party papers among various social classes in the Reykjavík area. In addition, this author has continued his work, begun as part of the SED project, on the history of the Icelandic press from the early period of independence politics to the present, with particular emphasis on the way in which the press has functioned as one of the main power bases of the party leadership. In 1973 a survey of radio and television listening and viewing patterns was carried out by Lárusson and the author.

Other Research Areas. In addition to the preceding five major research concerns, various other problems have been tackled in the department. So far as political science proper is concerned, the most significant are the author's work on cabinet coalitions in the postwar period and Guðmundsson's collection of local election data from the National Archives, covering the period from the commencement of local elections in the 1870s to the present. Such data have never before been available and in the future it will constitute highly fruitful material for the analysis of local power structures and their relationship to the national political system, of the emergence of class divisions and mobilization processes as well as changes in elite recruitment patterns. Apart from research on the social structure and mass media which has already been described, the concentration in the field of sociology has primarily been on the family and education. In addition, a small number of theses have been written in the fields of social anthropology and criminology, which have existed as subdisciplines within the department; however, a stronger emphasis on the former, under the direction of lecturer Haraldur Ólafsson, will undoubtedly achieve in the near future the same status within the new Faculty of Social Science as sociology and political science.

When the development of political science in Iceland reached the stage of publication, a series was started, called Islensk thjóðfélagsfraeði or Icelandic Social Science Publications (ISSP). Each volume will, in addition to the Icelandic main text, include an extensive summary and a key to all tables in English. Although three volumes have already been published, much greater emphasis must be placed on this activity in the future. Publication of existing research results will therefore constitute a major concern in the department during the next few years. The form of the ISSP series admittedly provides only a partial solution to the dilemma created by the two distinct audiences: the international body of scholars and the enlightened Icelandic public.

Associational Activities

Icelandic social scientists have established their own society and joined the two separate Nordic associations of political scientists and sociologists. The integrated nature of the Icelandic development and the comparatively small body of scholars have led to such twofold membership; however, a certain specialized division with respect to the two Nordic associations has already appeared within the Icelandic society of social scientists. Although size limitations and lack of financial resources will undoubtedly restrict the role of Icelandic scholars in the international community, it is clear that in addition to publication, professionalization and international integration will during the coming years mark the development of Icelandic political science. The results of greater amounts of research will indicate how far the discipline succeeds in establishing roots outside the university and to what an extent it will enjoy the support of a growing profession and a favorable network of national and international contacts.

Future Prospects

Although the development of political science in Iceland provides lessons drawn from only a single case, they indicate a general problem area that probably exists in many nations where the discipline has just been established. Similar problems will undoubtedly emerge if and when political science starts to be developed in those dozens of countries where it is not yet practised. The analytical strength of political science will depend increasingly on the ability to gain more extensive knowledge of the vast number of political systems that have emerged in recent decades. Scholars in the established Western powers within the discipline will for both internal and external reasons probably have growing difficulties in obtaining the necessary material on those countries and regions which are still almost or completely unresearched. Thus, the continuous extension of data available to political scientists will to an ever-growing degree most likely have to be the responsibility of the very small number of political scientists who work in the developing institutions within the discipline, and who face the same problems which have marked the Icelandic experience.

Bibliography

As the preceding account makes clear, the development of political science in Iceland has barely reached a stage characterized by continuous publications. The research at the Department of Social Science is still mainly available in the form of theses and research papers. Thus, it has been decided to list the publications, theses, and research papers in the previously discussed areas here. It is hoped that the following list will serve as a further indication of the research which has been conducted in the last few years. Access to the unpublished theses and research papers can be gained by contacting the department. Unfortunately, nearly all of them are at present only available in Icelandic.

Árnason, Ragnar. "Almenn athugun á tháttum löggjafarinnar og áhrifun emboettismanna á hana, einkum meœ tilliti til thingnefnda." [The Influence of civil servants on legislation, especially through Althingi committees]. Research Report, University of Iceland, 1972.

———. "Thjóðvarnarflokkur Islands." [The National Preservation Party]. Bachelor's thesis, University of Iceland, 1974.

Bjarnason, Dóra. "A Study of the Intergenerational Differences in the Perception of Stratification in Urban Iceland." Master's thesis, University of Keele, 1974.

Bjarnason, Guðmundur. "Fylgisthróun Althýðuflokksins 1916-1974." [Electoral strength of the SDP 1916-1974]. Bachelor's thesis, University of Iceland, 1975.

Broddason, Thorbjörn and Webb, Keith. "On the Myth of Social Equality in Iceland." *Acta Sociologica* (1975): 49-61.

Einarsdóttir, Hildur. "Kvennaárið 1975 i dagblöðum." [Women's year 1975 in the press]. Bachelor's thesis, University of Iceland, 1976.

Einarsson, Ingimar. "Framsóknarflokkurinn." [The Progressive Party]. Bachelor's thesis, University of Iceland, 1974.

Friðriksdóttir, Thórunn and Guðmundsdóttir, Esther. Samvinna thingmanna stjórnarflokkanna við thingmenn flokka stjórnarandstöðunnajr. [The Cooperation of government M.P.s with opposition M.P.s]. A research paper. University of Iceland, 1971.

Geirsson, Smári. Stjórnmaldaleg völd verkalýðsflokka i Neskaupstað i ljósi k jarnrœoiskenninga. [The Political power of working-class parties in Neskaupstað in the light of elite theories]. Bachelor's thesis, University of Iceland, 1976.

―――. "Political Power in Iceland Prior to The Period of Class Politics 1845-1918." Ph.D. dissertation, University of Manchester, 1970.

―――. "Iceland: Recent Althingi Elections." *Scandinavian Political Studies* 6 (1971): 195-200.

Grímsson, Ólafur Ragnar. "Iceland 1971: A Year of Political Change." *Scandinavian Political Studies* 8 (1973): 193-97.

―――. "Miostöð stjórnmalakerfisins." [The Center of the political system]. In *Reykjavik i 1100 ár* (1974): 226-54.

―――. "Utanrikshjónustan og útflutningsatvinnuvegirnir Skýrsla til utanrikisraoherra." [The Foreign service and the export industries]. Mimeographed. Report to the Foreign Minister, 1974.

―――. "The Icelandic Power Structure 1800-2000." *Scandinavian Political Studies* 11 (1976): 9-33.

―――. "Thróun islenskrar kjördœmaskipunar." [The Development of the Icelandic electoral system]. Mimeographed. Félagsvisindadeild, Háskóli Islands, no. 20 (1976).

―――. "The Icelandic Multilevel Coalition System." Mimeographed. Félagsvisindadeild, Háskóli Islands, 1976.

―――. and Lárusson, Erlendur. "Hlustendakönnun Rikisútvarpsins. Niourstödur og greinargerd." [Report on the state radio and TV listener's survey]. Mimeographed. Háskóli Islands, 1973.

Guðmundsson, Gestur. "Háskolar og aumagn." [Universities and capital]. Bachelor's thesis, University of Iceland, 1976.

Guðmundsson, Hallgrimur. "Stornmalatlokkar og aodragandinn ao myndun Sjálfstaeoisflokksins." [The Formation process of the IP]. Bachelor's thesis, University of Iceland, 1975.

―――. "Thróun hagsmunasamtaka." [The Development of interest organizations]. Research Paper, University of Iceland, 1972.

Halldórsdóttir, Helga and Waage, Kristin. "Uppruni nemenda." [The Origins of Students]. Bachelor's thesis, University of Iceland, 1975.

Halldórsson, Stefán A. "Heimsmynd fréttaskeytanna og islenskir hlioveroir." [The World view of news reports and Icelandic gatekeepers]. Bachelor's thesis, University of Iceland, 1975.

Harðardóttir, Steinunn. "Breioholt III. Skipulag og skipulagssjónarmio." [A Study of town planning: Breioholt III]. Bachelor's thesis, University of Iceland, 1975.

―――, Thorgrímsdóttir, Ragnheiður, and Karlsson, Örlygur. "Ferill rikisstjórnarfrumvarps." [The Legislative process of a government bill]. Research Report, University of Iceland, 1971.

Hédinsson, Elías and Jóhannsson, Ingi Valur. "Búseta og felagsleg lagskipting í Keflavik og Njarovik." [Settlement and social stratification in Keflavik and Njarovik]. Bachelor's thesis, University of Iceland, 1975.

Jónsdóttir, Sigríður. "Einstaklingar og hópar i minnihlutaáðstöðu." [Individuals and groups in minority positions]. Bachelor's thesis, University of Iceland, 1975.

Jónsdóttir, Sigurveig. "Fréttaval i rikisútvarpinu." [News selection in radio]. Bachelor's thesis, University of Iceland, 1974.

―――. "Fyrirspurnir á Althingi 1904-1972." [Parliamentary questions 1904-1972]. Research Paper, University of Iceland, 1972.

Jónsdóttir, Thorbjörg. "Könnun á útbreiðslu og notkun dagblaða i Reykjavik." [A Study of circulation and readership of Reykjavik dailies]. Bachelor's thesis, University of Iceland, 1973.

Karlsson, Örlygur. "Félagsleg mismunun og frumhópatengsl." [Social stratification and primary group relationship]. Bachelor's thesis, University of Iceland, 1976.

Karlsson, Stefán. "Hugmyndafraeði islenskra sósialista: Frá Kommúnistaflokki til Althýoubandalags." [The Ideology of Icelandic socialists: From the CP to the PA]. Bachelor's thesis, University of Iceland, 1974.

Kjartansson, Helgi Skúli. "Landbúnaðarmál á Althingi 1947-1962." [Agricultural issues in the Althingi 1947-1962]. Research Paper, University of Iceland, 1973.

Kristjánsson, Baldur. "Ráoahópar innan Althingis." [Althingi leadership groups]. Research Paper, University of Iceland, 1973.

―――, Bjarnason, Guðmundur, and Einarsson, Ingimar. "Ráðahópar innan Althingis." [Althingi Leadership Groups]. Research Paper, University of Iceland, 1971.

Kristjánsson, Svanur. "Íslensk verkalýoshreyfing 1920-1930." [Icelandic labor unions 1920-1930]. *Íslensk thjóð félagsfraeoi* 2; Félagsvisindadeild, Örn & Örlygur, 1976.

Mýrdal, Sigurjon. "Upphaf barnafraeoslumála á Althingi." [The Origin of children's education in the Althingi]. Research Report, University of Iceland, 1976.

Ólafsson, Hannes. "Íslenskir stúdentar." [Icelandic Students]. Bachelor's thesis, University of Iceland, 1975.

Ólafsson, Haukur. "Bandariskur her á Íslandi 1951–1956. Sjónarmio islensku stjórnmálaflokkanna." [The Policies of the Icelandic parties toward the USA base 1951–1956]. Bachelor's thesis, University of Iceland, 1975.

Ólafsson, Stefán P. "Íslenska stjórnkerfio i ljósi starfa thingmanna." [The Icelandic political system as reflected by M.P.s' activities]. Bachelor's thesis, University of Iceland, 1975.

―――. "Thingmenn og fjölmiolar." [The M.P.s and the mass media]. Research Report, University of Iceland, 1975.

Ólafsson, Thórir. "Bókmenntir og samfélag." [Literature and Society]. Bachelor's thesis, University of Iceland, 1975.

―――. "Fastanefndir Althingis." [The Althingi committees]. Research Report, University of Iceland, 1973.

Pálsdóttir, Katrín. "Fréttaval i islenska sjónvarpinu." [News selection in Icelandic TV]. Bachelor's thesis, University of Iceland, 1976.

Reynarsson, Bjarni. "Utanhéroðsthingmen 1931–1971." [Nonresidential M.P.s 1931–1971]. Research Paper, University of Iceland, 1971.

Sigmundsdóttir, Bergthóra. "Breytingar á thingniönnum við skilin." [The Change in Althingi membership when class politics replaced the independence struggle]. Research Paper, University of Iceland, 1972.

―――. "Kaupstaðaréttindi, ástoeour og ákvörounarferill." [Town rights: Causal and decision-making processes]. Bachelor's thesis, University of Iceland, 1975.

Sveinsson, Jón Rúnar. "Leigjendur i Reykjavik." [Tenants in Reykjavik]. Bachelor's thesis, University of Iceland, 1975.

Thorgrímsdóttir, Rangheiour. "Boendur." [Farmers]. Bachelor's thesis, University of Iceland, 1975.

Thorkelsson, Guðmundur Birkir. "Kommunistaflokkur Íslands. Sameiningarflokkur althýou-Sósialistaflokkurinn, Althýðubandulagið: Skipulags-og fylgisthróun 1930–1974." [The Organization and electoral strength of the CP, USP and PA 1930–1974]. Bachelor's thesis, University of Iceland, 1975.

Valdimarsson, Kristján. "Hagnýting kerfisgreiningar." [The Use of system analysis]. Bachelor's thesis, University of Iceland, 1976.

Vilhjálmsdóttir, Guorún Sigríður. "Innra skipulag og staoa nokkurra hagsmunasamtaka á Íslandi." [The Organizational structure of a few Icelandic interest organizations]. Research Paper, University of Iceland, 1972.

―――, and Grímsson, Ólafur Ragnar. "Jafnrétti kynjanna." [Equality of men and women in Iceland]. *Íslensk thjóðfélagsfraeði* 1; Námsbraut í thjóofélagsfraeðum, Örn & Örlygur, 1975.

17 INDIA*

IQBAL NARAIN and P. C. MATHUR

Introduction

Political science as a discipline of academic study and research is firmly established in India and, in the coming years, its intellectual output is likely to figure with increasing prominence on not only the university campuses, but also in a variety of public forums such as the press, parliamentary deliberations, and public administrators' confabulations. This befits the country's status as the world's most populous democracy, its rich heritage of political philosophy, and the seminal debates regarding political theory and practice which characterized its freedom struggle against British domination. India, with its unprecedented experiments with universal adult franchise and public ownership and control of remunerative and productive resources and its unparalleled diversity and variety of political institutions (including constitutionalism, federalism, judicial review, and decentralization of politico-administrative authority), and political processes (including associational activities, anomic violence, direct action, and moral protests) provides, in fact, a rich repository of political experience and a fertile laboratory for political analysis. It should, therefore, not be surprising if a large number of foreign scholars, belonging to a variety of social science disciplines, have focused their lifelong attention toward systematic elucidation of political values and political behavior in India. They have, thus, enriched not only our knowledge about Indian politics but also enlarged the territorial focus of the existing corpus of theories and conceptual frameworks in the discipline of political science as it had developed in the West and as it was transplanted into India under British auspices.

This chapter will present a synoptic overview of the state of the discipline of political science in India, highlighting the recent and emergent directions of change that have characterized the discipline during the last two decades or so. During its history of more than fifty years, political science in India has undergone a process of steady growth but in recent years the pace of change has quickened appreciably. This has posed, in turn, a variety of intellectual, methodological, and organizational challenges which will have to be tackled in the 1980s. We begin our analysis of the panorama of change by a brief overview of the characteristic features of political science as a university-based discipline in India. Thereafter, we identify the emergent trends in terms of syllabi input and research output. We conclude by a brief sketch of the handicaps and problem areas which will call for urgent action in the coming years. Partly on account of lack of detailed data and partly on account of our anxiety to make the chapter issue-oriented, we have refrained from giving itemized inventories either of study syllabi or of research trends but have concentrated on broad themes, highlighting the major contours of the discipline, which is firmly embedded in the intellectual ethos of the academic life in India.

An Overview of the Political Science Discipline

In its modern form as an academic discipline, political science was introduced in India sometime in the early 1920s as a subject for study in university teaching departments of history and law. Independent political science departments emerged rather slowly. For example, in 1938 only five universities had independent depart-

---

*This chapter was presented originally as a paper at the International Round Table on Non-Alignment and Special Meeting on Political Science in Developing Countries, organized by IPSA, the Indian Political Science Association, and the University of Calcutta, at the University of Calcutta, November 25-28, 1979. By permission of the authors.

ments of political science. The number increased to 15 by 1951, to 36 in 1967, and to 59 in 1971.* The dependent status of political science as a part, particularly, of history curricula during the first stages of growth influenced not only the status of the discipline but also the research foci and intellectual orientation of the earlier generation of political science scholars in India. Many of the scholars were trained in history departments and, thus, imbibed the conceptual frameworks and research methods flourishing in that discipline. More than half of the now existing independent political science departments are less than two decades old and have yet to establish their moorings in the changing academic world of India in which all disciplines in general and social science studies in particular are facing a variety of conceptual and methodological challenges.

UNIVERSITY LOCUS OF POLITICAL SCIENCE

A major institutional characteristic of political science, which stands out in sharp contrast to such social sciences as economics, management, sociology, and even public administration, is the fact that in the past it has been, essentially, a university-based discipline and even in the coming years it is likely to remain so, although a couple of nonteaching research centers and/or research institutes have already made their mark in the domain of political science in India. As noted above, political science studies in India began under the auspices of history departments and gradually became institutionalized as independent departments which became responsible for teaching as well as research. The Indian universities became repositories of several other intellectual disciplines at the same time as political science studies began under their auspices. However, in regard to many of these disciplines, one finds today that a host of organizations have sprung up outside the university framework which not only supplement the work done by their university counterparts but also provide a challenge to them in terms of professional competence, faculty recruitment, and research output. The case of economics comes readily to one's mind in this context as one notes that the bulk of research studies in the discipline are being undertaken in governmental or nongovernmental research centers and institutes, with university faculties having to compete with these organizations (not all of them are nonteaching but almost none undertakes undergraduate teaching) for material, financial, and personnel resources. The university-based political science scholars certainly do not face a competitive challenge of this order from the handful of the research centers and institutes, most of which started to function during the 1950s and early 1960s. Most of these centers and institutes are, moreover, characterized by a specialized orientation and have been chartered to study only selected segments of the vast domain covered by the university departments of political science. The Indian Institute of Public Administration, New Delhi (established in 1955), has for example concentrated only on the administrative dimension of political science, while the Indian School of International Studies, New Delhi (now merged with the Jawaharlal Nehru University) has dealt mainly with international relations aspects. The Center for the Study of Developing Societies, Delhi (established in 1963) was, no doubt, conceived on a broader canvas but it has also remained practically confined to studies relating to government and politics in India which is only a fragment of the totality of political science studies in the Indian universities. Taking into account only the territorial specificities of India, there is no well-organized research center to study the various aspects of modern Indian political tradition and reality. Similarly, apart from the handful of recently started area studies centers, there is no organization for undertaking studies in the field of comparative politics (with special reference to developing countries) which occupy a very important niche in the political science curriculum in India. Such examples can be multiplied.

STEADY GROWTH IN STUDENT ENROLLMENT

Another striking feature of political science studies in India is the spectacular popularity of these courses, not only at the undergraduate and postgraduate teaching centers, but also in terms of enrollment in correspondence courses which have become a part of the university system only in the 1970s and which have great potential. The continuous steady growth in student enrollment in political science courses all over India has, no doubt, its positive aspects. However, the academic bonuses on this account are partly offset by the inertia and confusion engendered by the proliferation of undergraduate students located in small towns and even big villages who have no access to any library which is well-stocked with testbooks, let alone standard journals. The teachers in these institutions find it difficult, if not impossible, to keep themselves abreast of the latest advancements in political science studies. Rapid multiplication of such colleges, some of which undertake postgraduate teaching also, poses a formidable challenge to advanced scholars in political science, who have to keep in view constantly the built-in limitations of teaching and research in such

---

*By 1980 the number had reached 76.—ED.

underequipped institutions which in some cases tend to dominate the decision-making forums in the universities on account of their voting strength. The growing number of undergraduate (and to some extent correspondence course) students tends to set a limit to introduction of innovations such as revision and upgrading of academic syllabi in the domain of political science and makes a large proportion of the political science faculty in India prone to view their role primarily as transmitters of political science knowledge (if not just information) rather than producers of original ideas and insights. The University Grants Commission (UGC) has, to be sure, already taken note of the problem and has launched a variety of programs to offset the handicaps. However, it is too early to assess the impact of faculty improvement programs. Till a large number of political science scholars arrive at routine competence even the more advanced teachers and researchers cannot make a significant dent in situations of institutional inertia.

THE DICHOTOMY OF RESEARCH AND TEACHING

Partly as a corollary of the ever-growing student enrollment, a balanced partnership between research and teaching could not develop even in university departments, let alone postgraduate and undergraduate colleges. Worse still, the two regard each other as dichotomous. We are thus far from a situation in which the latest research feeds into and enriches teaching and in which research stereotypes are given an intellectual jolt in the classroom. The poverty of political science in India can in part be traced to the fact that the world of research and the world of teaching have, by and large, been kept apart from each other. This is what perhaps also explains the paradox of outdated textbooks coexisting with the most up-to-date research in substantive and methodological terms.

SENSITIVITY TOWARD PARADIGM-CONFLICTS

In spite of this, a major intellectual characteristic of political science in India is the emergence of sensitivity toward problems of paradigm-conflict and paradigm-choice that is to be found among the ranks of political science scholars to a degree unparalled among other social science scholars in India. While all the intellectual disciplines in India are subject to the *problematique* of making a choice between liberal and Marxist assumptions and approaches toward research and teaching, the academic tensions on account of the adherents of each of these paradigms, challenging each other's basic concepts, approaches, and research methods have surfaced more sharply in the domain of political science in India as compared to other disciplines, where the scholars have not engaged in such sharp polemical exchanges as political science scholars have done. For example, the ideological cleavage between liberalism and Marxism would raise its head virtually at all gatherings of political science scholars in India on the issue of functionalism or structural-functional analyses. Taking into account the fact that each of these contending paradigms is unmistakably identified with a superpower, it is difficult to foresee the final outcome of the debate about the ideological parameters of political science. We can only hope that the present trend of peaceful coexistence, if not convergence of these conceptual frameworks, will continue in the years to come and the emergent generations of political science scholars will not wait for a final settlement on this score before launching upon their own studies. In fact, what is distressing at times is the fact that the polemics both among the traditionalists and the behavioralists on the one hand and the liberals and the Marxists on the other become the be-all and end-all of the efforts of political scientists in India.

CHANGE WITH CONTINUITY

Finally, we would like to emphasize that, despite its institutional inertia and ideological cleavages, political science in India has been undergoing a series of changes, especially after the 1950s. Syllabi are being modernized at all levels; growing theoretical orientation is being imparted both to study and research; scholars are devoting themselves to new themes and adopting a whole range of new research technologies and their intellectual outputs are gaining greater circulation both internationally and inside the country through such media as journals, conferences and symposia. At the August 1979 World Conference of the International Political Science Association as many as 39 political scientists went to Moscow from India and 9 of them served as panel chairmen. Winds of change are certainly flowing through the corridors of political science departments and research centers in the country. Although some of us would like the pace to be accelerated still more, we have to keep in mind the fact that political science, globally speaking, is a discipline of great antiquity where the element of change has to coexist with a great deal of substantive continuity.

Political science being predominantly a university based discipline in India, its teaching dimension is naturally much more prominent, although in recent years its research profile has also come into its own. Political science teachers are now undertaking a greater variety of research activities as compared to their predecessors in the earlier phases of institutionalization of the discipline as a medium of teaching undergraduate and postgraduate students. The political science syllabi in India remained static for several decades with political science teachers going through the same syllabi year after year. More recently, however, there is an emerging trend toward dynamic interaction between teaching and research. Political science teachers are thus beginning not merely to utilize the newly available research to chisel new courses of study but also are undertaking a variety of research projects to develop new components of political science syllabi.

Emerging Trends in the Content of Syllabi

INTERDISCIPLINARY IMPULSION OF SYLLABI REFORM

Animated debates about changes in undergraduate as well as postgraduate syllabi have, in fact, become a noticeable feature of the political science faculty in India with many departments periodically overhauling their courses of study which had remained virtually static for over three to four decades. The most dramatic change in this regard has occurred in relation to courses devoted to the history of political thought (HPT) which actually amounted earlier to a chronological description of Western political thought during its ancient and medieval phases. Today courses encapsulating the latest theoretical and methodological advances in the domain of political science have been introduced under the rubric of modern political theory (MPT). While the HPT courses not only commanded great prestige, they virtually placed a premium on inculcation of a historical descriptive approach which focused mainly on legal-formal entities, underplaying the teacher's research function because India-based political science scholars, in any case, had very few opportunities to embark upon firsthand research into the tangled web of Western political thought with its 2,000 years of history of intellectual refinement. The MPT courses, although they have already aroused impassioned polemics about their class bias and ideological undertones, would place a premium on methodological innovations and empirical research and exhort the political science scholars to give up their traditional conceptual frameworks in favor of new models and methods of theory building which are not merely empirical but are also governed by the possibility of an intersubjective consensus so that different scholars can arrive at their own conclusions after conducting their own investigations. In a sense, these MPT courses do not contain anything new and represent merely a compendium of theories, concepts, and methods adopted from a number of other disciplines but the introduction of such courses in the domain of political science has already created wide ranging stirrings. These have made political scientists not merely more research conscious but have also impelled them to acquire a great deal of familiarity with other disciplines from which the substance of the MPT courses is drawn. While in the past political science has been heavily irrigated by thought streams originating in disciplines like philosophy, law, and history (and Indian HPT teachers rightly emphasized the amount of time and energy required to understand and transmit the resultant "mix"), no political science teacher in India today can afford to be out of touch with the latest advances in disciplines like sociology, social anthropology, economics, management, and public administration.

INCLUSION OF COURSES ON GOVERNMENT AND POLITICS

Another emergent zone of change in the political science syllabi relates to introduction of courses on government and politics of India. Historically speaking, the pedigree of these courses can be traced to courses on British constitutional history which were an integral part of political science syllabi from the earliest days but which, with the passage of time, yielded place to courses devoted to Indian constitutional history. The change involved a shift in the territorial referent only with the conceptual approach and research methods undergoing hardly any change. The courses on government and politics in India (GPI) still bear, of course, the genetic imprint of the circumstances in which they developed, but they certainly require the concerned teachers to imbibe and communicate much more than a formal, legal analysis of governmental institutions. The emphasis in such courses is being gradually shifted to the study of political behavior, political processes, and political culture. In fact, even undergraduate students in several departments have begun to become familiar with the empirical realities of Indian politics rather than just memorizing details about the status, powers, and functions of various constitutional functionaries. At another level, an attempt is clearly visible all over India to bring about a greater degree of integration between courses devoted to various facets of Indian government, with courses focussed on different aspects of Indian political thought. As a result of the labors of a number of pioneering scholars, courses relating to modern Indian political thought (MIPT) had begun to take shape even before 1947 and many universities have duly incorporated them into their political science syllabi. Even after sustained labors of scores of dedicated scholars, these courses seem to remain underintegrated with the rest of political science syllabi. Logically speaking, MIPT courses should provide sustenance to the students' efforts to understand the structure and process of Indian politics. The task of enriching them with MIPT courses, though undertaken at several political science departments, still remains to be done. In the years to come one may expect the scope of this intellectual integration to be widened to ancient Indian political thought (AIPT) also so that political science students can form a coherent portrait of government and politics in India in terms of the continuities and changes in Indian political tradition. If this change is to be brought about, the orientation of AIPT to individual thinking will have to yield place to concept-based study.

COMPARATIVE POLITICS

A reorientation comparable to that which GPI courses are undergoing but, on a much broader level, is affecting the traditional courses on comparative constitutions which are well on the way to being brought in line with the courses on comparative politics which most political science departments have adopted all over the world. Courses focussed on the constitutions of the UK, USA, USSR, France, and Switzerland have been a staple item of political science syllabi ever since the discipline took roots in India. These courses have undergone a good measure of substantive and methodological changes in recent years, becoming, in the process, much more theory-oriented with their comparative framework being constantly enlarged to include noninstitutional political phenomena as well. In fact, the range of comparison has been further widened to include non-Western political systems, especially political systems of Afro-Asian countries whose political experience is much more relevant for India than those of developed industrial societies of the West. The courses on comparative constitutions had, in fact, become over the years, very highly routinized at the teaching level and political science scholars in India would hardly entertain any thought of undertaking field research on their own in this subfield. However, since the mid-1960s the teaching materials as well as research methods in this area have undergone a veritable revolution with political science scholars in India matching the strides taken by their Western counterparts. The research output of the International School of International Studies and the establishment of several area studies centers (with regard to which the pioneering initiative came from the political science department of the University of Rajasthan in the form of establishment of the South Asia Studies Center in 1964) have made it possible to introduce full-fledged courses on government and politics of such regions as South Asia, West Asia, East Africa, and South East Asia in the political science syllabi, which have thus been enriched by the enlargement of their territorial coverage and comparability.

INTERNATIONAL POLITICS AND
PUBLIC ADMINISTRATION

It is also noteworthy that various departments of political science in the country are no longer content with the mere teaching of the history of international relations; they have switched over to the teaching of international politics. More importantly, theoretical orientation in the teaching of this subfield is on the increase. Meanwhile the debate about this subfield becoming an independent discipline continues, as is the case of public administration also. The syllabi of public administration have, by and large, remained confined to traditional grooves, in spite of the fact that there is a lot of scope to develop problem- and policy-oriented study and research in the subfield.

COURSES IN RESEARCH METHODOLOGY

The foregoing changes in the substantive focus of political science syllabi have produced an inevitable compulsion to introduce courses relating to research methodology which would enable political science students to launch empirical research on their own. Such courses on research methodology have been included in the syllabi of disciplines like economics and sociology for a long time, but they represent a major innovation in the domain of political science, taxing to the utmost not only the intellectual resources of the students but also of even the well-established departments which find it difficult to recruit teachers to handle these courses from a political science perspective. In spite of these obvious difficulties, several political science departments have gone ahead and introduced courses relating to research methods under the generic name and style of "Political Analysis and Research Methods." This in the years to come, should result in the emergence of a new breed of political science scholars who are well versed in the methods and techniques of data collection and data analysis. This may also result in a greater influx of students to political science departments as courses in research methodology would enable graduates to claim a larger share of jobs in the expanding research market on account of their familiarity with such investigatory tools as survey research and content analysis.

Emerging Trends in Research

The foregoing survey of the dominant and emergent themes in the political science syllabi primarily focusses on the teaching dimension of political science. However, the most notable characteristic of political science in India has been that, although political science teachers have been making regular research contributions, the field of research in the discipline has been dominated by non-Indian scholars drawn from a variety of intellectual backgrounds and academic disciplines; even full-time political science researchers with no or little teaching responsibilities have, with a few distinguished exceptions, been content to labor in the shadow of these intellectual giants who have virtually brought into being a new discipline of political science. At any rate, the contributions made by non-Indian and/or nonpolitical scientists have resulted in the inculcation of a new orientation toward almost all substantive as well as methodological aspects of political science as it flourished till the mid-1950s in India. The issues of nationality and disciplinary orientation are not, normally speaking, relevant in the case of intellectual discourses, but the pattern of development of political science in recent years in the context of India makes one conscious of these factors. In a short period of less than two decades the two-thousand-year-old discipline of political science has undergone a series of remarkable reorientations most of which have been initiated by scholars belonging to other disciplines (the range of other disciplines including not only other social sciences but even life sciences and physical sciences) with the result that in order to function as a good political scientist today one has to become a multidisciplinary or transdisciplinary scholar familiar with a growing range of theories, models, and research methods and techniques, some of which are not part of political science syllabi even in many developed countries.

The interfusion of political science with other disciplines has acquired an additional transdisciplinary dimension in the case of India on account of the fact that Indian politics has attracted a large number of foreign scholars belonging to diverse academic backgrounds who have popularized a corresponding variety of conceptual categories and research methods for political analysis. Political science scholars in India can ill afford to ignore these conceptual frameworks and methodological innovations, not only because they focus on Indian political realities but also because many of them illuminate a greater range of political behavior in India than do the existing approaches and techniques already encapsulated in the political science syllabi. The GPI courses (including courses on modern Indian political thought, public administration in India and state politics in India) have, thus, to be revised at short intervals in order to keep up with the veritable flood of first-rate empirical studies which are also embellished with seminal conceptual frameworks. What is true of GPI courses is also true, in varying degrees, of other segments and subfields of political science; the upshot being that a great deal of transdisciplinary orientation has become a sine qua non for political science scholars in India. This is especially so if one wants to keep abreast of and contribute one's own bit to the growing literature on the analysis of Indian politics.

Sociologists and social anthropologists have, for example, conducted a large number of research studies into various nooks and corners of India's political structure and political culture, using (and inventing) a battery of concepts, models, and research techniques which have withstood the test of replication, not only inside but outside India (most notably in South Asia). Many of these analytical tools and techniques were indeed developed as part of a broad theoretical scheme and the concerned scholars have had to modify them after testing them in the Indian soil. Given such an intellectual pedigree, political science scholars attempting to research into Indian political realities simply cannot afford to ignore the conceptual and empirical vocabularies developed by sociologists and social anthropologists engaged in analyzing the same phenomena but from different disciplinary perspectives. Yet the very effort to acquire a multidisciplinary orientation cuts into the time available for political science scholars to develop their own disciplinary perspective and insights, besides placing them at a relative disadvantage in the overall competition for research funds and other resources. Thus far political science scholars (teachers as well as researchers) have been happy to imbibe the research output of scholars belonging both in substantive and methodological terms to other disciplines. But, over the coming decades, the political scientists would also like to contribute their bit to the interdisciplinary pool, shifting themselves from an exclusively receiving end to a giving end and, ultimately, to a mutually rewarding and academically reinforcing relationship of give-and-take. That is at once a challenge and promise for political scientists in India.

Limitations of Traditional Research Techniques

The current fecundity of nonpolitical science theoretical constructs and methodological techniques in political science research is all the more pregnant with beneficial as well as baneful consequences in view of the historical concentration of Indian political science scholars (most of them being or becoming university and college teachers) in studies pertaining to constitutional and institutional aspects of government and politics in India. It would have been, realistically speaking, well nigh impossible for India-based Indian political scientists to undertake firsthand research enquiries either in the history of Western political thought or even in the field of comparative constitutions. It is, therefore, not surprising that most political science research up to the 1940s was confined to a field in which data were readily available in India itself. Moreover, the fact that the discipline of political science had its organizational roots in history departments had equipped political science scholars with research techniques and tools which were highly appropriate for research into such historical topics as constitutional development in India. Consequently, a large majority of the first-generation political science scholars in the country addressed themselves to research studies in this field, relying upon archival and library sources for their data. The trend has persisted even today with a number of doctoral theses being regularly produced on themes in the field of constitutional development, using historians' research techniques. The focus of legal-formal studies of government institutions and constitutional developments was, however, enlarged as early as the 1930s to include studies on the nature and methods of the freedom struggle launched by a variety of Indian political activists. Very soon, another dimension was added to political science studies in India by a band of political science scholars who began systematic explorations into the political thought of these political activists themselves. With the attainment of independence and enactment of the Constitution of India in 1950 the attention of political science scholars was drawn toward the new legal-formal structures and institutions and a large proportion of doctoral theses in the domain of political science are still devoted to such themes, using analytical techniques borrowed from the disciplines of law and history rather than the more sophisticated research methods which are common to various social sciences.

During the late 1950s and early 1960s, the research scenario in the context of political science in India underwent a great change as theories and techniques from other social science disciplines like sociology, social anthropology, and even economics began to shake the political scientists from their traditional moorings in constitutional history, institutional comparisons, and legal-formal descriptions. The 1960s thus turned out to be a period of great excitement and ferment as political scientists were exposed to positivistic research methods and many of them enthusiastically launched empirical research with the aid of the technology that goes with these methods. However, as noted earlier, also, even as the first crop of research work in such subfields as voting behavior, *panchayati rai,* and state politics was being harvested, the conceptual premises of the research technology came under severe attack creating doubts and dampening the enthusiasm of the younger scholars for empirical research. The ensuing liberal-Marxist confrontation further dried up the research enthusiasm of political scientists for project-research inasmuch as project fundings were more or less tied up with the issue of choice of research methods. Most funding agencies relied upon the canons and criteria of positivistic research methodology for judging the eligibility of research proposals for financial support. But the hesitant political scientists missed the opportunity partly as they did not want to be caught in the web of controversy and partly because they were ill-equipped in analytical political theory and methods and techniques of political research.

The research dimension of political science in India continues, therefore, to be dominated by the traditional techniques of historical-institutional-legal-formal analyses. The result was that very few out of the large number of political scientists in India could make a mark on the international research scene. Even taking a national perspective, one can hardly be satisfied with the quality of research output that we have been able to maintain during the past three decades or so. While researchers have paid no attention to analyses of Western political thought or Western political systems, even the studies of Indian political thought or Indian political systems have not yet reached the level of sophistication that one would look for in a discipline as rich in theory as political science. At another level, our empirical probes into the working of non-Western political systems have just begun to take shape, while our research initiatives in the subfield of public administration have remained confined to India with an overemphasis on local government and development administration and a sustained neglect of economic policy and public enterprise management. On account of India's role in its development, nonalignment has been a favorite topic of research but sophisticated analyses of India's foreign policy in the context of the international political system are yet to be made.

The fact that most political science researchers in India have concentrated on Indian themes is natural and quite welcome. Most of these research efforts have, however, been molded in the historical-institutional-legal-formal approach and outstanding empirical research studies have emanated from only a few political science departments. In contrast to the rather meager research output of Indian political scientists, the foreign, mainly Western, scholars have published scores of outstanding empirical research studies focussed on government and politics in India including its international relations and public administration dimensions. Even in regard to modern Indian political thought and the Indian National Movement the most outstanding contributions have come from British, Australian, and U.S. scholars. Soviet scholars have also produced some studies which provide stimulating insights. With the exception of a handful of scholars, even this subfield is characterized by the dominance of non-Indian scholars, most of whom do not belong to the discipline of political science in a strict sense of the term. This underlines, once again, the need for developing an interdisciplinary orientation among political science researchers in India even for the study of various facets of MIPT. Empirical research and familiarity with methods and techniques of scientific enquiry (including historical method and logical reasoning) would thus seem to be a sine qua non for political science teachers and researchers even in relation to subfields where the object of study is values and thought systems. The sooner the gaps in this respect are bridged, the better would be the research prospects in the domain of political science in India.

Current Handicaps and Problem Areas

Political science as an academic discipline is thus well established in India even though, for the time being, its teaching dimension is much more developed than its research output. This is a long-term generalization which offers an overview of developments during the last fifty years of the flourishing existence of the discipline in India. We would, nevertheless, like to emphasize that this long-term trend is certainly being modified by the emergence of an accent on research in the last twenty years or so. To some extent Indian political scientists are already coming forward in larger numbers to undertake empirical analyses of various dimensions of government and politics in India. The more important of these somewhat new themes are studies of election politics and voting behavior, legislative and rural elite, political culture and political socialization, judicial behavior, political economy, and so on. The research enthusiasm is, however, being somewhat dampened on account of several factors, the most prominent of which is the relative unfamiliarity of political scientists with the methods and techniques of research which scholars belonging to other social sciences have successfully employed. The handicap imposed upon the political scientists by the traditional syllabi which made no provision for training in research methodology is, of course, being partially offset by recent inclusion of courses on research methods and political analyses. As part of immediate and short-term efforts to offset the handicap, both the ICSSR and UGC had launched a series of local, regional and all-India training courses in research methodology. Since the mid-1970s, however, they have been assigned a lower priority. The result is that only a tiny fraction of the vast political science faculty in Indian universities and colleges has been covered by such courses and, every year, hundreds of new teachers are being recruited who should be exposed to the training courses if we expect them to match the sophisticated research output which is being regularly produced by scholars belonging to other social science disciplines.

THE SWITCHOVER TO REGIONAL LANGUAGES

The 1950s and 1960s (precisely the era during which political science was undergoing reorientation in India) saw the emergence of popular sentiment in favor of a switchover to regional languages as the medium of instruction at all levels, including undergraduate and postgraduate studies. Before the emergence of political demands to this effect, higher education (including research) was almost entirely conducted in the English language with all scholars keeping in touch with each other through the medium of books and journals in that language. The formation of "linguistic states" in 1956 and the break-up of the two states which defied the formula of one-language-one-state, namely Bombay and Punjab in 1960 and 1966, respectively unleashed powerful political movements advocating total abandonment of English as a medium for teaching. Even the most advanced students in most Indian universities have already begun the process of changeover from English to regional languages, although many scholars genuinely feel that adequate teaching aids and teaching materials do not exist in most of these regional languages, let alone the question of systematic scientific research being carried out through the medium of these languages. The advocates of the changeover have, however, tended, by and large, to brush aside these misgivings and the switchover has already been made in the case of undergraduate teaching all over India. Most university postgraduate teaching departments have also made considerable progress in this direction. Thus, within the next few years, Indian universities will be producing students and recruiting teachers with nil or negligible familiarity with the vast amount of literature available in the English language which has been the *lingua franca* of the academic community in India for a long time. All social sciences in general and political science in particular are, thus, bound to be profoundly affected by the linguistic switchover. Unless appropriate steps are taken, the abruptness of the changeover will impose an additional handicap on the teaching and research in the domain of these disciplines whose growth is even today sustained mainly on the basis of output in the English-speaking world. Although non-English-speaking countries like France, Netherlands, Germany, USSR, and Japan are also making significant research contributions, their output reaches the social sciences scholars in India mainly through the medium of the English language.

In the absence of detailed information about the extent and consequences of the switchover to regional languages in different parts of India, we are not in a position to offer reliable all-India generalizations in this regard. However, with reference to the discipline of political science in the states which have switched to Hindi as the medium of university and college teaching, it has been observed that students and teachers there are facing a severe crisis of the dearth of literature (textbooks, journals) and other academic requisites such as good quality translations of the great classics and other basic texts). The state of helplessness is being recklessly exploited by underqualified writers who are amassing sizeable personal fortunes by putting out low-quality "notes" and "how-to-pass books" which present badly distorted materials, solely from the point of view of enabling the Hindi-medium students to cram in enough "points" to secure "pass" marks in the university examinations. The need of the hour is, therefore, for political science scholars to turn their attention toward the large gaps in the literature available in the various regional languages so that the switchover from English to regional languages does not result in academic discontinuity in the form of a steep fall in the academic standards attainable by the future generations of India to whom English and other non-Indian languages would be accessible only indirectly.

TRANSLATION ROLE OF POLITICAL SCIENCE TEACHERS

The linguistic switchover in terms of teaching is likely to have more profound and far-reaching consequences in the case of political science than other academic disciplines. This is so because political science in India is practically confined to university and college campuses and there are not many centers and/or institutions conducting advanced research only, that may be relatively immune to the public pressures for a changeover to regional languages for conducting their academic work. Moreover, the experiences of various government-sponsored translation schemes has not been very satisfactory, at least in the domain of political science. The only viable method to ensure a steady flow of original and translated literature in political science would, then, seem to lie in the political science teachers themselves coming forward in larger numbers to perform the urgent task of producing good quality, teaching materials. In this connection, the initiative taken by the political science department of the University of Rajasthan to combine the teaching and translation functions in the same person by creating full-time posts of lecturer-cum-translators seems to offer positive possibilities.

NEED FOR INFRASTRUCTURAL DEVELOPMENT

The discipline of political science has been sustained, over the years, in India by steady increases in student enrollment but, in the coming years, it would be necessary to pay greater attention to the development of its infrastructure. This could take the form of the creation of viable regional and local associations of political science teachers and researchers; publication of standard journals in various regional languages; and creation of institutional facilities for conducting periodic refresher and research methodology courses according to a plan which may aim to cover at least one teacher in each political science department in all the universities of the country. Present-day *ad hocism* in running research methodology courses is not helpful. While some progress has been registered in all these directions in the past, political science as a discipline still remains underinstitutionalized, especially if one were to compare it with other social sciences like economics, management, sociology, and even public administration which has emerged on the Indian academic scene only during the past three decades or so. A comparative scrutiny of the research grants made available by the UGC and ICSSR over the past ten to fifteen years would immediately reveal the poor allocation of their funds and other facilities to the political science scholars, most of whom are still ploughing their lonely furrows in undergraduate and postgraduate lecture rooms, while their colleagues in other social sciences are handling at first-hand research projects, taking advantage of their greater familiarity with sophisticated research methodologies and the relative abundance of professional amenities like standard journals and periodical conferences. Professional teachers of political science banded together, no doubt, under the forum of the Indian Political Science Association in the late 1930s but the subsequent career of this body has been rather checkered and, barring some efforts made in recent years, the organization has certainly failed to provide the type of academic leadership which its counterparts in other disciplines in India, not to mention the Western ones, have been able to provide. With the national association trying to take off academically, it is no surprise to discover that political scientists in India have hardly made any efforts to organize local and regional associations where they could meet frequently and discuss their common problems in an atmosphere of greater interpersonal familiarity. On the positive side, it certainly augurs well for the discipline that the attention of political scientists in India has been drawn toward both these professional handicaps and that efforts are already on the way not only to upgrade the all-India association academically but also to link it up with well-organized state level associations. In that lies, at least partly, the future of political science in India.

Bibliography*

Adams, J. W. L. "Henley and Hyderabad." *Indian Journal of Public Administration* 4, no. 1 (January–March 1958): 66–78.

Appadorai, A. "Role of the Teacher of Political Science."

---

*Compiled by the editor.

Indian Journal of Political Science 32, no. 1 (January–March 1971): 1–13.

———. "Teaching and Research in International Relations." *Indian Journal of Politics* 5, no. 1 (January–June 1971): 19–36.

———. "University Teaching in International Relations in India." *India Quarterly* 10, no. 1 (January–March 1954): 52–71.

Asirvathan, E. "Study of Political Science in India." *Indian Journal of Political Science* 16, no. 1 (January–March 1955): 1–22.

Bains, J. S. "State of Political Science in India." *Indian Journal of Political Science* 32, no. 2 (October–December 1971): 393–444.

Batria, P. *Studies in Political Science*. Agra: Lohamandi, 1956.

Bhambrhi, C. P. "Political Science in India: Academic Colonialism and Lessons for the Third World." *Economic and Political Weekly* (Bombay) 10, no. 18 (3 May 1975): 731–35.

———. "Teaching of Political Science in Indian Universities: Some Observations." *Political Science Review* 9, nos. 3–4 (July–December 1970): 337–46.

Bhaskaran, R. "Political Science Sub Specie Aeternitatis." *Indian Yearbook of International Affairs* 1, no. 52 (1952): 172–78.

Bhatt, V. R. "A Plea and a Scheme for an Integrated Study of Social Aim and the Law." *Journal of Karnatak University* 2, no. 2 (June 1958): 37–44.

Bradley, P. "Potentials for Public Administration Research in India." *Indian Journal of Public Administration* 5, no. 2 (April–June 1959): 163–73.

Chacko, C. J. "The Teaching of Political Science in India." *Education Quarterly* (New Delhi) 5, no. 19 (September 1953): 155–61.

Chakravarti, R. "Is There a Science of Politics?" *Calcutta Review* 146, no. 1 (January 1958): 11–28.

———. "New Aspects of Political Science." *Calcutta Review* 145, no. 1 (October 1957): 79–88.

"The Constitution of the Indian Political Science Association." *Indian Journal of Political Science* 14, no. 1 (January–March 1953): 79–85.

Damle, Y. B. "Social Science Periodicals: India" (in French) *Revue internationale des sciences sociales* 19, no. 2 (1967): 214–26.

Dexter, L. A. "Politicians, Science and Scientists." *Indian Sociological Bulletin* 1, no. 3 (April 1964): 18–21.

Farrer, D. G. "The Political Scientist as a Technological Ombudsman: A Sorcerer's Apprentice?" *Political Scientist* 11, no. 2 (January–June, 1975): 1–12.

Hajjar, Sami G. "The professional literature of Indian Political Science: A Comparative Study" *Political Science* 1 (January 1977): 67–85.

Halappa, S. S. "The Study of Public Administration in India." *Indian Journal of Political Science* 16, no. 2 (April–June 1955): 158–64.

Juergensmeyer, M. "Teaching Political Theory in India." *Indian Journal of Political Science* 32, no. 4 (October–December 1971): 445–54.

Kogekar, S. V. "Inquiry into the Teaching of Political Science." *Indian Journal of Political Science* 14, no. 1 (January–March 1953): 50–55.

——— and Appadorai, A. *Political Science in India*. Delhi: Premier Publishing Co., 1953.

Majunedar, B. "Presidential Address" (Current Trends in Indian Political Science). *Indian Journal of Political Science* 13, no. 1 (January–March 1952): 19–34.

Mukerji, K. P. "Nature, Scope and Methods of Political Science." *Indian Journal of Political Science* 15, no. 4 (October–December 1954): 273–82.

Panikkar, K. M. "Inaugural Address to Political Science Conference at Hyderabad, 27.12.51" (Current Trends in Indian Political Science). *Indian Journal of Political Science* 36, no. 3 (July–September 1975): 207–23.

Proceedings of the annual meeting of the Indian PSA. Indian Journal of Political Science 14, no. 1 (January–March 1953): 66–72.

Proceedings of the 15th Annual Conference, Aligarh. Indian Journal of Political Science 14, no. 1 (January–March 1953): 55–65.

Rai, H. "Political Theory: New Viewpoint in Meaning and Method." *Indian Journal of Political Science* 30, no. 4 (October–December 1969): 350–61. (Indian political science at the threshold of a methodological orientation.)

Sharma, S. K., ed. *Political Science in Independent India* 2 vols. Chandigarh: Goodwin Publishers, 1976. (Presidential addresses delivered to the Indian Political Science Association.)

Srivastava, G. P. "The Empirical and Anti-Intellectual Approach to Political Science." *Indian Journal of Political Science* 15, no. 4 (October–December 1954): 305–12.

———. "Towards Integrated Approach in Social Sciences." *Journal of Social Sciences* (Agra) 1, no. 1 (January 1958): 9–20.

"Study of Political Science and International Relations in India." *Indian Yearbook of International Affairs* 1 (1952): 238–45.

Thakirrdas, F. "The Expanding Frontier of Political Science." *Indian Journal of Political Science* 34, no. 4 (October–December 1973): 397–428.

Tyagi, A. R. "Systems Approach to Political Science." *Indian Journal of Political Science* 7, no. 2 (July–September 1973): 177–85.

UNESCO, *The Teaching of the Social Sciences in India*. Paris, 1956.

Varma, S. P. "A Plea of Critical Political Science." *Political Science Review* 14, nos. 3–4 (July–December 1975): 1–16.

Venkatarangaiya, M. "The State of Political Science in India." *Indian Journal of Political Science* 36, no. 3 (July–September 1975): 207–23.

Appendix*

UNIVERSITIES

The following is a list of universities in India where political science as a separate discipline and other social sciences are taught, both at M.A. and B.A. levels and doctoral research is conducted:

1. Agra University, Agra
2. Aligarh Muslim University, Aligarh
3. Allahabad University, Allahabad
4. Andhra University, Waltair
5. Annamalai University, Annamalainagar
6. Awadhesh Pratap Singh University, Rewa
7. Banaras Hindu University, Varanasi
8. Bangalore University, Bangalore
9. (Maharaja Savaji Rao) University of Baroda, Baroda
10. Berhampur University, Berhampur
11. Bhagalpur University, Bhagalpur
12. Bhopal University, Bhopal
13. University of Bihar, Bihar
14. Bombay University, Bombay
15. University of Burdwan, Burdwan
16. University of Calcutta, Calcutta
17. University of Calicut, Calicut
18. University of Cochin, Hill Palace
19. University of Delhi, Delhi
20. Dibrugarh University, Dibrugarh
21. Garhwal University, Srinagar
22. Gauhati University, Gauhati
23. Gorakhpur University, Gorakhpur
24. Gujrat University, Ahmedabad
25. Gujrat Vidyapith, Gujrat
26. GuruNanak Dev University, Amritsar
27. Himachal Pradesh University, Simla
28. University of Hyderabad, Hyderabad
29. University of Indore, Indore
30. Jabalpur University, Jabalpur
31. Jadavpur University, Calcutta
32. Jamia Millia Islamia, New Delhi
33. University of Jammu, Jammu Tawi
34. Jawaharlal Nehru University, New Delhi
35. Jiwaji University, Gwalior
36. University of Jodhpur, Jodhpur
37. Kalyani University, Kalyani
38. Kanpur University, Kanpur
39. Karnatak University, Karnatak
40. University of Kashmir, Srinagar
41. University of Kerala, Trvandrum
42. Kumaun University, Nainital
43. Kurukshetra University, Kurukshetra
44. Lalit Narayan Mithila University, Darbhanga
45. University of Lucknow, Lucknow
46. University of Madras Chepauk, Madras
47. Kamaraj Madurai University, Madurai
48. Magadh University, Bodh Gaya
49. Marathwada University, Aurangabad
50. Meerut University, Meerut
51. Mysore University, Mysore
52. Nagpur University, Nagpur
53. University of North Bengal, Darjeeling
54. North Eastern Hill University, Shillong
55. Osmania University, Hyderabad
56. Patna University, Patna
57. Poona University, Pune
58. Punjab University, Chandigarh
59. Punjabi University, Patiala
60. Rabindra Bharati University, Calcutta
61. Rabisankar University, Raipur
62. Rajasthan University, Jaipur
63. Ranchi University, Ranchi
64. Rohilkhand University, Barelly
65. Sambalpur University, Sambalpur
66. Sardar Patel University, Kaira
67. University of Saugar, Saugar
68. Saurasthra University, Rajkot
69. Shivaji University, Kolhapur
70. South Gujrat University, Surat

*The three lists in this appendix are adapted from a paper by Nirmal Bose, "Political Science in India: A Search for an Identity," presented by him to the International Round Table on Non-Alignment and Special Meeting on Political Science in Developing Countries at the University of Calcutta, November 25-28, 1979.

71. Sreemati Nathi-Bai Damodar Thackersey Women's University, Bombay
72. Sri Venkateswara University, Tirupati
73. University of Udaipur, Pratapnagar
74. Utkal University, Bhubaneswar
75. Vikram University, Ujjain
76. Visva Bharati, Birbhum

RESEARCH INSTITUTES AND ASSOCIATIONS

A. N. Sinha Institute of Social Studies, Patna
Academy of Political and Social Studies, Pune
Ahmedabad Management Association, Ahmedabad
All-India Institute of Local Self-Government, Bombay
All-India Management Association, New Delhi
All-Indian Panchyat Parishad, New Delhi
Association of Universities, New Delhi
Association of Voluntary Agencies for Rural Development, New Delhi
Bangalore Management Association, Bangalore
Behavioral Sciences Center, New Delhi
Bihar Council of Public and International Affairs, Patna
Bombay Management Association, Bombay
Calcutta Management Association, Calcutta
Center for Development Studies, Trivandrum
Center for Policy Research, New Delhi
Center for Studies in Peace and Non-Violence, Tirupati
Center for the Study of Developing Societies, New Delhi
Center for Urban Studies, New Delhi
Center of Applied Politics, New Delhi
Center of Social Studies, Surat
Council for Political Studies, Calcutta
Council for Social Development, New Delhi
Council of Social and Cultural Research, Ranchi
Delhi Management Association, New Delhi
Forum of Free Enterprise, Bombay
Gandhi Peace Foundation, New Delhi
Gandhian Institute of Studies, Varanasi
Gokhale Institute of Public Affairs, Bangalore
HCM State Institute of Public Administration, Jaipur
Harold Laski Institute of Political Science, Ahmedabad
Indian Academy of Social Science, New Delhi
Indian Council for Africa, New Delhi
Indian Council of Historical Research, New Delhi
Indian Council of Peace Research, New Delhi
Indian Council of Social Science Research, New Delhi
Indian Institute of Asian Studies, Bombay
Indian Institute of Management, Ahmedabad
Indian Institute of Mass Communication, New Delhi
Indian Institute of Public Administration, New Delhi
Indian Institute of Public Opinion Private, New Delhi
Indian Management Association, Indore
Indian Political Science Association, Madras
Indian Public Administration Association, New Delhi
Indian School of Political Economy, Pune
Indian Society for International Law, New Delhi
Indian Society of Criminology, Madras
Institute for Techno-Economic Studies, Madras
Institute of Asian Studies, Hyderabad
Institute of Behavioral Science, Bihar
Institute of Constitutional and Parliamentary Studies, New Delhi
Institute of Defense Studies and Analyses, New Delhi
Institute of Management Studies, Bombay
Institute of Public Administration, Lucknow
Institute of Social Studies, Calcutta
Jayaprakash Narayan Institute of Political Philosophy, Madras
Kasturba Institute of Rural Studies, Patna
Kerala Academy of Politics, Trivandrum
Kerala Institute of Marxist Studies, Trivandrum
Kumarappa Institute of Gram Swaraj, Jaipur
Lal Bahadur Shastri National Academy of Administration, Dt. Dehra Dun
Madras Institute of Development Studies, Madras
National Institute of Community Development, Hyderabad
National Institute of Rural Development, Hyderabad
North East India Council for Social Science Research, Meghalay
Press and Public Relations Association, Fire Brigade
Professor Periaswamy-Thayammal Institute for Research and Advanced Study in Social Science, Madras
Rajasthan Institute of Social Science Research, Jaipur
Shivalik Center in Behavioral Science and Education, Saharanpur
State Institute of Community Development and Panchayati Raj, Hyderabad
Subhas School of Social and Political Studies, Calcutta
Tata Institute of Social Science, Bombay
Tribal Research Bureau, Bhubaneswar
University Grants Commission, New Delhi
Vidya Bhawan Rural Institute, Udaipur
Xavier Institute of Social Services, Ranchi

JOURNALS

Journals in political science, international relations, and public administration in India (the list is not exhaustive)
Administrative Change, Janata Colony, Jaipur (biannual)
Agra University Journal of Research, Agra University, Agra (quarterly)
Calcutta Review, University of Calcutta, Calcutta
Civic Affairs, Kanpur (monthly)
Contemporary, New Delhi (monthly)
Economic and Political Weekly, Sameeksha Trust Publication, Bombay
Gandhian Perspectives, Institute of Gandhian Studies, Varanasi (biannual)
Indian Journal of Behavioral Science, Institute of Behavioral Science, Magadh University, Arrah (biannual)
Indian Journal of Political Science, Indian Political Science Association, Panjab University, Chandigarh (quarterly)
Indian Journal of Politics, Department of Political Science, Aligarh Muslim University, Aligarh (quarterly)

Indian Journal of Political Studies, Department of Political Science, University of Jodhpur, Jodhpur (biannual)

Indian Journal of Public Administration, Indian Institute of Public Administration, New Delhi (quarterly)

Indian Political Science Review, Department of Political Science, University of Delhi, Delhi (biannual)

India Quarterly, Indian Council of World Affairs, New Delhi (quarterly)

International Studies, Jawaharlal Nehru University, New Delhi (quarterly)

Journal of Constitutional and Parliamentary Studies, Institute of Constitutional and Parliamentary Studies, New Delhi (quarterly)

Journal of Government and Political Studies, Punjabi University, Patiala (biannual)

Journal of Karnataka University Social Science, Department of Political Science, Karnataka University, Dharwar

Journal of the Local Self-Government Institute, All-India Institute of Local Self-Government, Bombay (quarterly)

Journal of North-East India Council for Social Science Research, Shilling (half-yearly)

Journal of Parliamentary Information, Lok Sabha Secretariat, New Delhi (quarterly)

Journal of Political Science, Postgraduate Department of Political Science, DAV College, Jullender (biannual)

Journal of Social Research, Council of Social and Cultural Research, Bihar, and Department of Anthropology, Ranchi

Journal of State Politics and Administration, Department of Political Science, Sambalpur University, Sambalpur (biannual)

Law Quarterly, Journal of the Indian Law Institute, New Delhi

Lok Prashashan (in Hindi), Madhya Pradesh Hindi Granth Academy, Bhopal (quarterly)

Loktantra Sameeksha (in Hindi), Institute of Constitutional and Parliamentary Studies, New Delhi

Marxist Review, Calcutta (monthly)

Nagarlok (Urban Affairs) (in Hindi), Indian Institute of Public Administration, New Delhi (quarterly)

Modern Review, Calcutta (quarterly)

Peninsular Review of Politics, Department of Political Science, Madurai Kamaraj University, Madurai (quarterly)

Political Change, Department of Political Science, Institute of Correspondence Studies, University of Rajasthan, Jaipur (biannual)

Political Science Review, Department of Political Science, University of Rajasthan, Jaipur (quarterly)

Political Science Today, Nehru Memorial Postgraduate College, Mansa (biannual)

Political Scientist, Department of Political Science, University of Ranchi, Ranchi (biannual)

Radical Humanist, New Delhi (monthly)

Rajya Shastra Samiksha (in Hindi), Department of Political Science, University of Rajasthan, Jaipur (biannual)

Rashtra (in Bengali), Calcutta (quarterly)

Review of Politics, Department of Political Science, Magadh University, Center Cegrah (biannual)

Review of Public and International Affairs, Bihar Council of Public and International Affairs, Patna (biannual)

Review of Public and International Affairs, Patna (biannual)

Social Defense, Department of Social Welfare, New Delhi (quarterly)

Social Science Research Journal, Panjab University, Chandigarh (three issues a year)

Social Scientist, Indian School of Social Sciences, Trivandrum (monthly)

Socialist Perspective, Council of Political Studies, Calcutta (quarterly)

South Asia Studies, University of Rajasthan, Jaipur (biannual)

Teaching Politics, Department of Political Science, University of Delhi (quarterly)

18

JAPAN*

TAKASHI INOGUCHI

Introduction

This chapter attempts to achieve the following two goals. First, it will describe how political science in Japan has evolved for the last thirty-five years since 1945 and delineate its major features in terms of: (a) the intellectual structure of the discipline; (b) its infrastructure for teaching; (c) major research fields and methods; (d) its associational activities; and (e) the relationships between political scientists and the world of politics. Second, it will point out some directions in which political science in Japan is likely to evolve from now on. The discussion will involve both shifting weights of various fields of study and some institutional reforms necessary to invigorate its contribution to the world intellectual community.

The State of Political Science in 1945

In 1946, Maruyama Masao, one of the then emerging leading political scientists in Japan, noted in an essay entitled "Political Science as Science": "Political Science in Japan has no tradition worth reviving. All is up to its future development."[1] Dissatisfied with the past legacies of political science in Japan, he finds the major cause in the political structure of modern Japan since 1868. (Political science was first taught in 1877.) He argues that whether political science can develop, as in the U.S. and the U.K., depends largely on the existence of civil freedom whereby one can study the world of politics with independence and openness. Without significant interaction between political science and the world of politics in terms of conceptual development and practical contributions, political science could not possibly grow. Before World War II, European intellectual achievements were introduced and interpreted sometimes even without having much relevance to the world of politics in Japan. The distance between political science and the world of politics was immense.

Although what Maruyama asserted in 1946 holds basically true, close examination of prewar publications reveals that conditions for the postwar development of Japanese political science had been prepared before 1945. Arduous absorption of Western intellectual achievements enabled students of politics to start vigorously to develop Japanese political science after 1945. Not only Marxist methodology but also positivist methodology like Max Weber's and other intellectual traditions especially of the 1920s had been so familiar to Japanese students of politics in 1945 that it was very easy to learn and utilize social science concepts and methods now coming from the U.S. while strengthening the indigenous development of political science in Japan.[2]

The Evolution of Political Science since 1945

Thus it is not surprising that the Japanese Political Science Association (JPSA) was established as early as 1948. If we restrict ourselves to those teaching in univer-

---

*An earlier version of this chapter was commented upon by Joji Watanuki (Sophia University) and Yoshinobu Yamomoto (Saitama University). Masato Ninomiya (the University of Tokyo) and Masahiko Noro (the Japan Foundation) helped me to locate some materials. I wish to acknowledge gratefully their constructive criticisms and valuable help. The chapter was written basically in Geneva 1977–1978 when I had a grant from the Japan Foundation, to which I am grateful. A minor revision was made subsequently. Of course, the responsibility for the views expressed is solely my own. (Note on Japanese names: in the text of this chapter, a family name comes first and a given name comes afterward, following the Japanese custom.)

sities, there are about 600 political scientists in Japan. (Comparable figures in other fields of study are as follows: economics, about 4,000; commerce and business administration, about 1,500; law, about 2,000; history, about 2,000; sociology, about 1,300.)[3] However, if we include those who specialize in political history and philosophy and area specialists as well as political science graduate students and other nonuniversity-affiliated political scientists, the number becomes easily more than 2,000. In 1979, the JPSA had about 1,000 members and the Japanese Association of International Relations (JAIR) about 1,000, with about 200 persons belonging to both. The rate of expansion is steady but somewhat slow, due in part to the fragmented institutional setting which political scientists have to face in universities and the very limited number of university posts available to aspiring students of politics. There is no single political science department in Japan. However, Japanese political science has been making notable advances for the last thirty-odd years. Its activities have been expanding and its perspectives have been broadened, especially for the last fifteen years.

THE INTELLECTUAL STRUCTURE
OF THE DISCIPLINE

One of the most important features of the discipline is that it is like a "consociational democracy" in the sense that some of the important historical, institutional, and sociological divisions are kept largely intact within the still small Japanese political science community. Interaction between scholars of different specializations or different persuasions is not difficult, but not frequent and intense enough for cross-fertilization. Not only cleavages like traditionalists versus behavioralists and Marxists versus non-Marxists but also all sorts of differences in interest and background help retain this fragmentation under the facade of a grand coalition, all despite some recently strong forces that encourage more interaction.

Thus it is not easy to depict some major strands in the intellectual structure of the discipline without slighting some currents possibly as important as the following three which we believe are likely to be most salient in shaping Japanese political science for the next quarter century as they have been for the past quarter century. The first is the continuing emphasis on political philosophy and political history—the more traditional subjects in political science. Many political scientists specializing in political theory deal with classical political theory. The second strand is the growing—and healthy and natural—tendency to specialize in Japanese politics. More students of politics are specializing and publishing in this field, especially during the last fifteen years. The third is an increasing emphasis on international relations as Japanese overseas activities—largely economic—have expanded during the last twenty years.

First, the continuing emphasis on philosophy has to do in part with the prewar tendency of introducing and interpreting Western intellectual achievements. The writings of classical political philosophers like Aristotle, Machiavelli, Locke, Rousseau, Hobbes, and Marx are one of the favorite fields of study for many aspiring students of politics. So are the studies of Japanese philosophers and thinkers, due in no small part to Maruyama's influential works on Japanese intellectual history. In addition to those political scientists specializing in political philosophy, many students of philosophy have graduated from departments of not only Western but also Chinese and Sanscrit philosophy.

The emphasis on political history is also due in part to the chair system still retained in some universities. Many students of political history specialize in European political history rather than that of other countries, although those specializing in Japanese political history are largest in number. The emphasis on history also represents the tendency to deal with the world of politics in fairly concrete and descriptive terms rather than abstract and analytical terms in many studies of politics. In this sense, too, traditionalists are very strong in Japanese political science. Formal political theories like that of party competition, for instance, have not yet found a receptive audience in Japanese political science, although many political science concepts and methods have been introduced from the U.S. since 1945. In addition to those political scientists who work on history, a far larger number of historians graduated from history departments, probably ten times as many.

Second, the increasingly strong interest in Japanese politics is a natural phenomenon. Although the need to analyze elections scientifically was preached by Japanese social scientists as early as the 1920s, it came to be practiced only after 1945.[4] Until about 1960 Japanese politics as a subject of study did not particularly outnumber other subjects in terms of the publication of academic works by political scientists. There are three major reasons for that: (a) the prewar legacy of introducing and interpreting Western intellectual achievements continued. Western classical philosophy and European diplomatic and political history carried an unmatched weight before 1945. Then came the tide of introducing and interpreting American political science. Many Japanese political scientists were busy learning from it—and still are. However, for the last fifteen years, many of the concepts and methods of American origin have come to be adapted and used effectively in the study of Japanese politics; (b) sociologists, psychologists, and statisticians have been equally active in working on political attitudes and behavior. In the early postwar years they went ahead of political scientists, using survey research and other behavioral methods. Only in the last twenty years have political scientists come to match them. There have also been many studies jointly undertaken by political and nonpolitical scientists in this field of study; (c) Japanese political scientists have become more self-confident at studying Japanese politics on its own terms. Although the concepts and methods employed are often of American origin, some indigenous concepts and methods have also been born, such as a fairly sophisticated predictive model of electoral outcomes tailored to the Japanese electoral system of nontransferable votes and multimember constituencies and an ecological analysis of the voter-candidate relationship which has tended to be spatially concentrated and fixed.

Third, interest in international relations has grown during the last twenty years. This is evident from the number of members of the two political science associations. The JAIR though established only in 1956 has now come to match the JPSA in membership. Several major subgroups exist within those specializing in international relations: (a) those who specialize in Japan's foreign relations, whether historical or contemporary, comprise the majority; (b) a large number specialize in the politics of other, mostly non-Western, countries and regions; (c) traditional diplomatic historians work on largely European and American diplomatic history; (d) a sizable number are more behaviorally oriented scholars; (e) a fairly large number of specialists are doing strategic studies; (f) another fairly large number are pursuing peace/conflict studies; (g) more recently, those who work on the international political economy have been increasing, especially in the younger generation.

If we look at the intellectual structure of the discipline in terms of the general outlook of political scientists, the following three features, which apply to Japanese social science in general, must be noted.[5]

First, Japanese political scientists are still parochial in the sense that they do not pay much attention to how their works are related to works on the world's frontiers of knowledge and how they could contribute to the world intellectual community. They tend to pay almost exclusive attention to the Japanese audience, whether highly specialized or more general. This is due in part to the use of the Japanese language which few people outside Japan can read. It is also due in part to the fact that Japanese political scientists have a huge domestic market for their writings, which are thus often tailored to the preference of the general audience, most importantly white-collar employees, businessmen, and bureaucrats as well as students. More recently, however, parochialism has been slowly eroding due to the growing size of the Japanese political science community which increases internal interactions; and because of the growing exposure to and participation in international academic activities.

Second, there is a fairly large gap between empiricists and theorists. Empiricists tend to devote their energy to detailed description whereas theorists tend to play with concepts without much reference to substance. This phenomenon is universal: however, it may be more pronounced in Japan. More recently, however, the interactions between them have been noticeable for the reasons stated above as well as for the slowly changing graduate training which puts greater emphasis on acquiring more comprehensive knowledge and skill than before.

Third, there is also a fairly pronounced tendency among political scientists to be largely indifferent to how their works might contribute to policy formation. On the one hand, many political scientists work on subjects which have little to do with currently disputed issues of social and political importance; rather they tend to be very academic. On the other hand, a sizable number of political scientists are often occupied with selling policy advice to politicians, bureaucrats, businessmen, labor union leaders, and/or a general audience without providing a solid academic basis. This feature has been changing recently due to the increasing awareness of the need for political scientists to contribute actively to the democratic process of shaping policies and influencing policy outcomes on the basis of academic research.

THE TEACHING OF POLITICAL SCIENCE

Undergraduate Level. The teaching of political science has been somewhat hampered by the intellectual divisions which are the partial consequence of the institutional structure of the universities. Indicative of difficulties in teaching political science is the absence of departments of political science. About 50 percent of political science professors belong to departments of law which accommodated political science or its predecessor, *Staatslehre,* in the preceding century. About 20 percent of them belong to departments of international relations or of foreign languages and studies. Most are international relations or area specialists. The remaining 30 percent belong to other university units like departments of general education, of social sciences, of politics and economics, institutes of social sciences, of oriental culture, or of policy science.

There are basically three types of political science curricula. One is the most traditional curriculum centered around political theory and philosophy, political and diplomatic history (mainly Japanese, European, Chinese, and American), public administration and international relations. This curriculum is often tailored to the need of those who take higher civil service or bar exams in which a small number of political science subjects are included, along with the more dominant law and economics subjects. The second type is more oriented toward international relations, consisting of international relations, international law, international economics, political and diplomatic history (which covers more non-Western countries and regions) and foreign language(s) (normally English, but another area-language in case of area specialists). This curriculum was born after 1945, partially influenced by the academic development in the U.S. A third type is emerging in a few places, which has the policy-oriented curriculum using general systems-theory concepts and techno-economic methods. Though its impact on Japanese political science is yet to be seen, it will certainly become a new way of organizing political science curricula, encompassing social and engineering sciences.

Undergraduate teaching of political science consists generally of lectures and seminars. Professors give lectures to a huge number of students, 100 to 300 on the average, and a written final exam (once a year) is the normal, often sole, requirement for credit. Seminars are smaller in size, ranging from 5 to 30 students. An oral presentation and a seminar paper on subjects of the students' choice within the confines of the seminar's focus are normal requirements for credit.

Graduate Level. The graduate curriculum normally runs parallel to the three types of the undergraduate curriculum. However, graduate teaching is normally smaller than undergraduate teaching in time and budget. Institutionally and financially, graduate teaching has not been given greater attention than undergraduate teaching. This small size has until recently been well suited to a system of producing future scholars for a very small political science job market. This has been especially so when a professor finds the successor to his chair within his own department. However, the system has manifested many deficiencies and reform plans have been proposed and discussed for the last ten years. There are two fundamental weaknesses in graduate teaching. First, the graduate training of political science has been impaired more seriously by the lack of political science departments. Since undergraduate education in political science is generally thought to be an appendage to the teaching of other practical matters such as law, economics, and language expertise, its lack is partially justifiable. However,

graduate education is another matter. Since graduate education runs parallel to undergraduate education, the teaching of political science at the graduate level is also divided, even within the same university. Thus, despite the presence of a sizable number of political science professors in the same university, resources have not been utilized adequately in graduate teaching. Rather, some gradual changes within each unit—especially in peripheral units—have been taking place without formal change in the facade of the institutional divisions. They include emphasis on behavioral training, emphasis on international relations and developing countries, and creation of policy science courses. Whether these changes can bring about fundamental transformation is yet to be seen.

Secondly, graduate education is often not a major concern for many professors of political science. Institutionally and financially, graduate teaching is treated as an appendage to undergraduate teaching. To some extent, the strange combination of laissez-faire on the part of professors and self-reliance on the part of students has existed. Normally, course requirements have been minimal (a seminar paper and an oral presentation once or twice a year) and many graduate students have tended to develop their academic interest and specialization early—and stick with them. This has tended to exacerbate the already serious fragmentation of the discipline and the weakness in communication and cross-fertilization between the subdisciplines. More recently, however, professors have come to devote more time and energy to graduate teaching as the somewhat medieval character of graduate teaching has shown more deficiencies than merits. More interaction has come to take place at various levels: between professors and students; crosscutting through various subdisciplines within political science, and crosscutting between various universities. Especially, the political science associations that have been intensifying their activities and the increasing project-oriented research practice which needs better communication and cooperation have come to play an important role in encouraging more interaction which is, in turn, likely to bring about favorable consequences to the intellectual structure of Japanese political science.

RESEARCH IN POLITICAL SCIENCE

Most Noteworthy Contributions

There is an impressive number of publications in Japan, despite the institutional weaknesses mentioned. It is estimated that "over a thousand genuine academic social science books are published annually in Japan, each selling, on the average, several thousand copies."[6] If we confine ourselves to academic political science books, the best guess one can come up with is that something like 100 to 200 books are published each year. It is, thus, not an easy task to select a certain number of books in political science as the most noteworthy contributions. There must be some cirteria for selection. The major criteria we adopt in this attempt are international competitiveness and contribution. In other words, we ask the following question: In what fields of study can Japanese political scientists compete most effectively with scholars on the academic frontiers of the world and thus make significant and original contributions to the world intellectual community? Thus our selection is certainly biased. One can notice that works on Japanese domestic politics and foreign relations as well as on Japanese and Chinese political and diplomatic history are well represented in the list below. This is largely because in these fields of study Japanese political scientists have been able to make important contributions to the world intellectual community both in quality and quantity. Thus it should not be taken that there are no other important contributions in other fields of study like European diplomatic history, political philosophy, comparative politics, and public administration.

For the sake of convenience, I use the following five fields of study: (a) political theory and political philosophy; (b) political attitude and behavior; (c) political institutions and processes; (d) political and diplomatic history; (e) international relations and comparative politics. I list an English version when there are both Japanese and English versions (asterisked) even if the contents are somewhat different. When there is only an English version, it has double asterisks. Space being limited, I omit the romanized original Japanese-language titles entirely.

Political theory and political philosophy. In this field, contributions to Japanese intellectual history are most important. Outstanding among them is Maruyama Masao. It should be mentioned that there is an important contribution to mathematical social theory in the Arrow tradition by Murakami Yasusuke.

Aruga Hiroshi, *The Reformation and German Political Thought*, 1966.
Fujita Shozo, *The Dominant Principle of the Emperor State*, 1966.
Fukuda Kanichi, *Modern Political Thought: Its Foundations*, 1970.
———, ed., *Western Europe and Japan in Political Thought*, 2 vols., 1961.
Hiromatsu Wataru, *The Origin of Marxism*, 1969.
Ishida Takeshi, *Law and Politics in Modern Japanese Intellectual History*, 1976.
Kamishima Jiro, *The Intellectual Structure of Modern Japan*, 1961.
Katsuta Yoshitaro, *A History of Modern Russian Political Thought*, 1961.
Kyogoku Junichi, *Modern Democracy and Political Science*, 1969.
Maruyama Masao, *Studies in the Intellectual History of Tokugawa Japan*, 1952 (1977)*.
———, *Thought and Behavior in Modern Japanese Politics*, 1956–57 (1963)*.
Matsumoto Sannosuke, *A Study of the Political Thought of "Kokugaku"*, 1957.
Murakami Yasusuke, *Logic and Social Choice*, 1968.**
Nambara Shigeru, *The State and Religion*, 1942.
Oka Yoshisato, *Politics*, 1971.
Onogawa Hidemi, *A Study of Late Ch'ing Political Thought*, 1969.
Royama Masamichi, *The Development of Modern Political Science in Japan*, 1949.
Sasaki Takeshi, *Machiavelli's Political Thought*, 1970.
———, *Sovereignty, Opposition Rights, Tolerance*, 1973.

Political attitude and behavior. Works on Japanese political attitude and behavior are predominant. It is important to note that many such works have been done not only by political scientists (e.g., Kyogoku and Miyake) but also by sociologists (e.g., Watanuki and Matsubara), psychologists (e.g., Ikeuchi and Tanaka), and statisticians (e.g., Hayashi and Nisihira).

Akuto Hiroshi, *American Political Culture*, 1980.
Ikeuchi Hajime, ed., *A Study of Civic Culture*, 1974.
Institute of Statistics and Mathematics, ed., *Japanese National Character*, 3 vols., 1959, 1971, and 1975.
Ishida Takeshi, *Japanese Society*, 1971.*
Ishikawa Akihiro, *Social Change and Workers' Consciousness*, 1975.
Jiji Tsushinsha, ed., *Postwar Japanese Parties and Cabinets*, 1981.
JPSA, ed., *The Formation and Structure of Political Attitudes in Contemporary Japan*, 1971.
Kohei Shinsaku, *Political Consciousness at a Time of Transition*, 1980.
Kyogoku Junichi, *An Analysis of Political Consciousness*, 1966.
Matsubara Haruo, *The Attitudes of Japanese Youth*, 1974.
Miyake Ichiro et al., *A Study of Voting Behavior at Different Levels*, 1967.
Nagai Yonosuke, *A Study of Political Consciousness*, 1971.
Nakamura Kikuo, ed., *Contemporary Japan's Political Culture*, 1975.
NHK Public Opinion Research Institute, ed., *Japanese Consciousness*, 2 vols., 1975 and 1980.
Ogawa Koichi et al., *Progressive Voters in Big Cities*, 1975.
Tanaka Yasumasa, *The Science of Communication*, 1969.
The "Study-of-the-Japanese" Group, ed., *Party Support by Groups*, 1975.

Political institutions and processes. Works on Japanese political institutions and processes are predominant. Here again not only political scientists (e.g., Masumi and Muramatsu) but also sociologists (e.g., Watanuki) and statisticians (e.g., Nisihira) have made important contributions to this field.

Contemporary Urban Policy, 12 vols., 1972-1973.
Fujiwara Hirotatsu, *Japanese Political Consciousness*, 1958.
Ide Yoshinori, *The Politics of Local Self-Government*, 1972.
Iizuka Yoshiaki et al., *Tides toward Coalition Politics*, 1979.
Institute of Social Science, University of Tokyo, ed., *Post-War Reforms*, 8 vols., 1974-1975.
Ishida Takeshi, *Organizations and Symbols in Contemporary Politics*, 1978.
JPSA, ed., *Parties and Bureaucracy in Contemporary Japan Since 1955*, 1968.
_____, *Pressure Groups in Japan*, 1960.
Kataoka Hiromitsu, *Administrative State*, 1976.
Masumi Junnosuke, *The Political System of Contemporary Japan*, 1969.
_____ and R. A. Scalapino, *Parties and Politics in Japan*, 1961.*
Matsushita Keiichi, *Political Configurations in Contemporary Japan*, 1962.
Miyake Ichiro and Muramatsu Michio, eds., *Dynamics of City Politics in Kyoto*, 1981.
Miyazato Seigen, *U.S. Rule of Okinawa*, 1966.
Murakami Yasusuke et al., *'Ie' Society as a Civilization*, 1979.
Muramatsu Michio, *Postwar Japanese Bureaucracy*, 1981.
Nisihira Sigeki, *Cross-national Comparisons of Elections*, 1969.
_____, *Japanese Elections*, 1972.
Oka Yoshitake, ed., *The Political Processes of Contemporary Japan*, 1958.
Otake Hideo, *Political Power and Economic Power in Contemporary Japan*, 1979.
Public Administration, 5 vols., 1976.
Sakagami Nobuo, *Japanese Electoral Institutions*, 1977.
Soma Masao, ed., *National Elections and Party Politics, 1945-1976*, 1977.
Takabatake Michitoshi, *Parties and Elections in Contemporary Japan*, 1980.
Takane Masaaki, *Japanese Political Elites*, 1976.
Taniuchi Akira et al., eds., *Modern Public Administration and Bureaucracy*, 2 vols., 1974.
Tomita Nobuo, *Perspectives on Parliamentary Politics*, 1978.
Tsuji Kiyoaki, *Studies in Japanese Bureaucracy*, 1952.
Watanuki Joji, *Politics in Postwar Japanese Society*, 1978.*
_____, S. P. Huntington and M. Crozier, *The Crisis of Democracy*, 1975.*

Political and diplomatic history. Works on Japanese and Chinese political and diplomatic history are predominant. More than 60 percent of the works listed below belong to this category. At the same time, there are some important contributions made to the fields of political and diplomatic history of Southeast Asia, North America, and Western and Eastern Europe.

Bamba Nobuya, *Japanese Diplomacy in a Dilemma: New Light on Japan's China Policy, 1924-1929*, 1972.*
Banno Junji, *The Establishment of the Meiji Constitutional System*, 1972.
Banno Masataka, *China and the West, 1958-1961: The Origins of the Tsungli Yamen*, 1964.**
_____, *Studies in Modern Chinese Diplomatic History*, 1970.
Eguchi Bokuro, ed., *Studies on the Russian Revolution*, 1968.
Eto Shinkichi, *Studies in Modern Chinese Political History*, 1969.
_____, *Studies in the Political History of East Asia*, 1969.
Hosoya Chihiro, *A History of the Siberian Intervention*, 1955.
_____ et al., eds., *A History of Japanese-American Relations*, 3 vols., 1970.
_____ and Saito Makoto, eds., *The Washington Treaty and Japan-US Relations*, 1978.
Inoguchi Takashi, *The Comparative Study of Diplomatic Style: China, Britain, Japan*, 1978.
Inoki Masamichi, *A Biography of Yoshida Shigeru*, 2 vols., 1978-79.
Ito Takashi, *A Study of the Early Showa Political History*, 1970.
JAIR, ed., Issues devoted to *Japanese Diplomatic History*, 21 vols., 1956-.
_____, *The Road to the Pacific War*, 8 vols., 1962-63.
Kim Yongjak, *A Study of Nationalism in the Late Yi Korea*, 1975.
Kosaka Masataka, *The Rise and Fall of Classical Diplomacy*, 1978.
Masumi Junnosuke, *Studies in the History of Japanese Political Parties*, 5 vols., 1965-1979.
Mitani Taichiro, *The Establishment of Japanese Party Politics*, 1968.
_____. *On Taisho Democracy*, 1974.
Miwa Kimitada, *Matsuoka Yosuke*, 1970.
Miyake Masaki, *A Study of the Japanese-German-Italian Triple Alliance*, 1975.
Momose Hiroshi, *A Study of Soviet-Finnish Relations*, 1970.
Nagazumi Akira, *The Dawn of Indonesian Nationalism: The Early Years of the Budi Utomo, 1908-1918*, 1972.*
Nakamura Takafusa, ed., *Japanese Economy and Politics During the Occupation*, 1979.
Ng Chiautong, *A Study of the Republic of Formosa 1895*, 1970.
Ogata Sadako, *Defiance in Manchuria*, 1964.*
Saito Makoto, ed., *Domestic Politics and Foreign Policy of Contemporary America*, 1961.
Saito Takashi, *International Politics during the Inter-war Period*, 1978.
_____, *Studies in the Pre-World War II History*, 1965.
Sato Seizaburo and Roger Dingman, eds., *Modern Japan's Attitude Toward the Rest of the World*, 1974.
Seki Hiroharu, *The Establishment of the Modern East Asian International Environment*, 1966.
Shindo Eiichi, *Woodrow Wilson and the International Order*, 1974.
Shinohara Hajime and Mitani Taichiro, eds., *Political Leadership in Modern Japan*, 1965.

——— and Yokoyama Shin, eds., *Political Leadership in Modern States*, 1964.
Takagi Yatsuka, ed., *Studies in Japanese-American Relations*, 2 vols., 1970.
Taniuchi Akira, *The Establishment of the Stalinist Political System*, 1970.
———, *Reflections on Socialism*, 1978.
Tominaga Yukio, *A Historical Analysis of German-Soviet Relations, 1917-1925*, 1979.
Yamada Tatsuo, *A Study of the Kuomintang Left*, 1980.
Yano Toru, *A Political History of Contemporary Thailand and Burma*, 1968.
Yokoyama Shin, *Studies in Modern French Diplomatic History*, 1964.

International relations and comparative politics. Works on Japan's external relations are predominant although Japanese political science as a whole has come to acquire a more global outlook for the last fifteen years than before in terms of area specialization as well as in terms of conceptualization. It is also worth noting that an increasingly large number of behaviorally oriented works have been done in this field.

Banno Masataka, *An Analysis of Modern Diplomacy*, 1971.
——— and Eto Shinkichi, eds., *East Asian International Politics*, 1968.
Hayashi Kentaro et al., eds., *Japan's International Environment*, 10 vols., 1978-1979.
Hosoya Chihiro and Watanuki Joji, eds., *Foreign Policy Decision-Making System: A Japanese-American Comparison*, 1977.
Inoguchi Takashi, *The Quantitative Analysis of International Relations, Peking, Pyongyang, Moscow, 1961-1966*, 1970.
———, *International Political Economy*, 1982.
Irie Keishiro and Ando Masashi, eds., *The International Relations of Contemporary China*, 1975.
Ishii Yoneo, *Thailand: A Rice-Growing Society*, 1979.*
JPSA, ed., *The Political Processes of International Detente*, 1970.
Kamiya Fuji, *Perspectives on Contemporary International Politics*, 1966.
Kamo Takehiko and Yamamoto Yoshinobu, eds., *International Politics of Interdependence*, 1979.
Kataoka Tetsuya, *Resistance and Revolution in China*, 1974.**
Kawai Hidekazu, *Party and Class: The Volte-Face of Contemporary British Politics*, 1978.
Kawata Tadashi, *Imperialism and Power Politics*, 1964.
Maeda Hisashi, *A History of Disarmament Negotiations*, 1968.
Mushakoji Kinhide, *Behavioral Science and International Politics*, 1972.
——— and M. A. Kaplan eds., *Japan, America and the Future World Order*, 1976.**
Nagai Yonosuke and Iriye Akira, eds., *The Origins of the Cold War in Asia*, 1977.**
Nakajima Mineo, *Contemporary China: Its Politics and Ideology*, 1966.
Nishihara Masashi, *The Japanese and Sukarno's Indonesia*, 1975.**
Nishimura Fumio and Nakazawa Seiichiro, eds., *Contemporary Soviet Politics and Diplomacy*, 1978.
Okabe Tatsumi, *The Foreign Policy of Contemporary China*, 1971.
———, *The People's Republic of China's Policy Toward Japan*, 1976.
Sakamoto Yoshikazu, *International Politics in the Nuclear Age*, 1967.
Seki Hiroharu, *Foundations of International Systems Theory*, 1971.
Shiratori Rei, *Political Development*, 1968.
Tokuda Noriyuki, *The Political Dynamics of Maoism*, 1977.
Watanabe Akio, *The Okinawa Problem*, 1970.*
Yamamoto Mitsuru, *Japan's Economic Diplomacy*, 1973.
Yano Toru, *A History of Japan's Southern Expansion*, 1975.

Methodological Developments

There are a number of "schools," each of which clusters around a particular, influential professor. For instance, Japanese intellectual history has been enormously influenced by the example set by Maruyama. In schools not only methods but also style of writing, subjects dealt with, and conclusions arrived at tend to reflect the minds and habits of the founding fathers of the schools. However, with the exception of the Maruyama school, which has a most distinctive method and style, we separate methods from schools, and we do not deal with the latter.

The more traditional methodology. There have been serious efforts in Japanese political science to understand and grasp the essence of Japanese logic unique or peculiar to Japanese culture. Noteworthy among them are, first, that dealing with Japanese intellectual history. With sharp insights into the logic of Japanese thinkers and philosophers, Maruyama has constructed a paradigm of Japanese intellectual history. He has developed a methodological tradition by which key intellectual elements are abstracted in such a way that the social-political structure and its endogenous momentum for self-transformation are revealed. Matsumoto Sannosuke, Ishida Takeshi, Fujita Shozo and others have done works using the same method.

A second area of study has considered Japanese political culture. A small number of political scientists have developed indigenous political theories by which the Japanese political system is presumably better understood than by those imported from the U.S. or Europe. Kyogoku Junichi, Oka Yoshisato, and Kamishima Jiro have developed frameworks more sensitive to prominent cultural aspects which are important in understanding

Japanese politics. More influenced by the American concept of political culture, Ishida Takeshi and Uchiyama Hideo have made a methodological contribution in this field.

A third methodological group has concerned itself with the logic of inquiry. There coexist strongly antithetic traditions of inquiry: Marxist versus non-Marxist, critical versus empirical, structuralist versus behavioralist. The debates between the adversaries are generally not those of confrontation but of peaceful coexistence based on territorial separation, adopting some things from each other. Thinkers on the logic of inquiry like Habermas have not appeared in Japanese social science. It must be noted, however, that students of Marx and Marxism have done highly sophisticated, if close to Talmudic, philological and historical works on Marx. Also Maeda Yasuhiro's recent works on dialectics are worth mentioning. In addition to these political scientists working on the logic of inquiry, there are a large number of Marxist scholars in history, economics, and sociology, a sizable number of critical thinkers in philosophy and sociology, and a few structuralists in anthropology.

The more scientific methodology. The more scientifically oriented methodological developments may be classified in five groups. First, survey research which has been increasingly used as a vehicle to analyze political attitude and behavior. Major opinion polls have been conducted by leading newspapers (such as *Asahi* and *Mainichi*), the NHK (the Japan Broadcasting Association), the Institute of Statistics and Mathematics, the Clean Election League, and the Prime Minister's Office. In this field of study, statisticians, sociologists, and psychologists have been equally active and productive. However, there is not yet a survey research center or a university-based computer center which is "friendly" to social scientists in terms of services. Hayashi Chikio and his associates have published books and articles on such broad topics as electoral behavior and national character. Hayashi Chikio, Kyogoku Junichi, Takabatake Michitoshi among others have constructed mathematical predictive models of electoral outcomes on the basis of opinion and social cues of individuals, a model which is tailored to the nontransferable vote, multimember constituency electoral system. These models have been utilized with some success for predictive purposes every time general elections have been held since the mid-1960s. Ikeuchi Hajime and his associates have done a study of civic culture as part of Sidney Verba's project. Miyake Ichiro and his associates have done a study in the Michigan tradition on different voting patterns according to national, prefectural, and district levels. Watanuki Joji and his associates have been working with American and British colleagues on a very large-scale, cross-national comparative study of electoral behavior. Tanaka Yasumasa has done a study in the Illinois tradition on the cross-cultural psycholinguistic analysis of Japanese political attitudes toward nuclear weapons. There are also those, including Soma Masao, Shiratori Rei, and Miyakawa Takayoshi, who have been working energetically on Japanese electoral politics for quite a long period. Akuto Hiroshi has argued recently on the basis of the Study-of-the-Japanese survey that, when there are no clear-cut class cleavages, as in contemporary Japan, life-style plays a most important role in distinguishing party support and other political attitudes, having replaced such variables as income, occupation, sex, education, and subjective class consciousness. Besides electoral behavior surveys, Ori Kan has done a study of political institutionalization at grass-roots level and Okamura Tadao has done a political socialization study in the Chicago tradition.

A second development, content analysis, has been fairly frequently used by psychologists and sociologists like Ikeuchi Hajime and Tsujimura Akira for the analysis of newspapers. Then a small number of political scientists began analyzing the content of official newspapers. Eto Shinkichi and Okabe Tatsumi have done an interesting study on China's policy toward Japan, based on the *People's Daily*. Inoguchi Takashi has done a quantitative study of triangular relations among China, North Korea, and the Soviet Union, on the basis of a friendship-hostility index constructed by use of content analysis and multidimensional scaling. Along the same line, he has been working on the dynamics of realignment among Vietnam, China, and the Soviet Union from 1964 to 1980. Mushakoji Kinhide and Watanabe Akio have independently done studies on Japanese political leaders' cognitive maps. Usui Hisakazu has done a content analysis of the style of persuasion of Japanese political leaders. Ikeuchi Hajime and his associates have done a content analysis study on the Japanese-American relationship, skillfully constructing a conflict-cooperation scale on the basis of Japanese newspapers. On domestic politics, Inoguchi Takashi has done a study on election pledges of Japanese political parties, using the common categories for content analysis, with mainly European colleagues. Though computer linguistics and artificial intelligence techniques have been making rapid progress within and outside Japan, Japanese political scientists have not yet stored them as one of their methodological armors.

Not many studies use experimentation, a third methodology, in Japanese political science. Some major exceptions are the following: Seki Hiroharu has done a simulation study of the international system in the Northwestern University tradition, with some notable revisions including the trade sector in the model. Mushakoji Kinhide has done an interesting gaming study with three options (accommodation, boycott, and confrontation) in the context of Japanese-American negotiations, using Japanese and American students. Umemoto Takao and his associates have constructed a computer-simulation model of the Prisoner's dilemma.

There are few students in the scientific-methodological field of aggregate data analysis. Kyogoku Junichi has done a study of large-scale world trends (ca. 1960) by using principal component analysis in the early Yale tradition. Kyogoku, Takabatake Michitoshi, and Ogata Norio have done a study of the support base (or *jiban*) of candidates who normally develop a patron-client relationship in some spatially concentrated areas. Takabatake has also developed a quadratic programming analysis for electoral analysis. Inoguchi Kuniko has constructed econometric models of dependency, using nineteen Latin American data. More recently, Inoguchi Takashi has been working on the relationship between the economy and the polity, focusing on the mass public's government support and the government's macroeconomic policy-making. Uno Kimio has been working on the impact of environment destruction on the patterns of party support at the prefectoral level. More sociologically oriented are studies on voting behavior by Watanuki Joji, on social mobility by Yasuda Saburo and Tominaga Kenichi and his associates, and on elites by Aso Makoto, Mannari Hiroshi, and Takane Masaaki.

The fifth methodological group concerns itself with mathematical models. Formal models of negotiations and communication have been constructed by Kinhide Mushakoji, using among others the switching theory in electrical engineering. Yamamoto Yoshinobu has constructed probabilistic models of war expansion. Yamamoto and Tani Akira have constructed a computer simulation model of a foreign policy maker's cognitive map, with respect to the Japanese-Chinese peace and friendship treaty of August 1978. Inoguchi Takashi and Miyatake Nobuharu have constructed two models of the Soviet-Japanese salmon catch negotiations of 1957–1977. One of them is a structural equations model on the basis of the concept of quasi budgeting. The other uses the state space model derived from modern control theory. Both models are very successful in explaining as well as predicting negotiation outcomes. Onishi Akira has done a simulation study of anti-Japanese sentiments in Southeast Asia. Inoguchi Kuniko has modeled the five major response patterns of forty non-oil-exporting Third World countries to the oil crisis of 1973-1976, using regression equations. On the domestic scene, Inoguchi Takashi has built a general model of elections to explain and predict electoral outcomes by party with four basic political and economic variables. Yakushiji Taizo has examined effects of government intervention on the development of the Japanese automobile industry, using the Kalman filter. Noguchi Yukio and his associates have done an interesting study of Japanese budgeting. Sakakibara Eisuke and his associates have constructed models of the politico-economic dynamics of the treasury's road construction investment policy. Although world modeling studies associated with the Club of Rome and the LINK projects have been done in Japan, no Japanese political scientist has been actively involved in either of them.

ASSOCIATIONAL ACTIVITIES

Associations. There are three major associations in political science and a number of others loosely related to political science. The oldest one is the Japanese Political Science Association (JPSA), founded in 1948. The other two are the Japan Association of International Relations (JAIR), dating from 1956 and the Japan Association of Public Administration (JAPA) of 1950. In terms of associational activities, the JAIR is the most active of the three, publishing its journal three times a year and sponsoring workshops and conferences, occasionally with the International Studies Association of the U.S. and the British Association of International Studies.

There are a number of other related associations. They include: the Japan Association of International Law (1897) with a large number of political and diplomatic historians in its membership; the Association of Asian Political and Economic Studies (1948); the Japan Association of Southeast Asian Studies (1966); the Japan Peace Studies Association (1973); the Japanese Sociological Association (1923); and the Japanese Association of Theoretical Economics (1934).

Journals. The JAIR publishes *International Relations* (three times a year); the JPSA *The Annals of Political Science;* the JAPA *The Annals of Public Administration;* the JAIL *The Journal of International Law and Diplomacy* (quarterly); the AAPES *Asian Studies* (quarterly); the JASEAR *Southeast Asian Research* (annually); the JPESA *Peace Studies* (annually); the JSA *Sociological Review* (quarterly); and the JEA *Quarterly Review of Theoretical Economic Studies.* Besides these, there are a number of other journals. They include: *International Affairs* (monthly), *Japanese Annals of International Affairs* (in English), and *Communism and International Politics* (quarterly), all edited by the Japan Institute of International Affairs; *Asian Economies* (quarterly) and *The Developing Economies* (quarterly in English) both from the Institute of Developing Economies, *Southeast Asian Studies* (quarterly in English and in Japanese) edited by the Center for Southeast Asian Studies, Kyoto University; *Afro-Asian Linguistic-Cultural Research* (annually in English and in Japanese) edited by the Institute of Afro-Asian Linguistic-Cultural Research, Tokyo University of Foreign Studies; *Peace Research in Japan* (annually in English) edited by the Japan Peace Research Group; *The Japan Interpreter* (quarterly in English) edited at the Center for Japanese Social and Political Studies; and *The Japan Echo* (quarterly in English) edited at the Japan Echo. Furthermore, there are a large number of university or departmental bulletins. The importance of these bulletins reflects the lack of nationally based major journals which adopt the anonymous referee system of accepting/rejecting publication. Instead, the publication practice of somewhat medieval character still dominates the Japanese political science community. Perhaps more than 95 percent of political science journal articles are published outside the three national political science journals, mostly in university or departmental bulletins or less importantly in more journalistically oriented general magazines.

Special publications. There are special publications by the JPSA and the JAIR. The JPSA published *Publications on Political Science in Japan* annually in English from 1965 to 1975. It was terminated in 1976. The JAIR has published its quarterly newsletter since 1977.

POLITICAL SCIENCE AND THE WORLD OF POLITICS

The Impact of Political Configurations on Political Science

Political configurations—rather than political events—in which Japanese political scientists have found themselves have had a deep impact on political science in Japan. There are two basic political facts: since 1955 the Liberal Democratic party (LDP) has been in power without interruption and since 1945 Japan has not been involved in any military conflicts with foreign countries. These two basic political facts have inevitably influenced the minds of many political scientists and thus their products. For one example, the very personalistic politics within LDP and some other parties has sometimes made it cumbersome (and dull) for many political scientists, who are influenced by the armchair tradition, to break into the world of politics for systematic empirical analysis. Journalists and nonuniversity affiliated researchers write about it more often. In addition, the monopoly of power by the LDP and the inability of opposition parties to throw the LDP out of power have made somewhat unattractive the rational theory of party competition in which party positions are assumed to change flexibly according to voters' preference distribution although the recent fluidity of the political situation has created a situation in which the theory attracts some political scientists' attention. Also, social cleavages in Japan, which are less clear-cut than in many West European and North American countries, have hindered the development of the social-group theory of electoral behavior. Its explanatory power tends to be small. The Japanese electoral system of nontransferable votes and multimember constituencies complicates the situation because in that electoral system local situations and electoral tactics matter very much. More positively, the element of the fairly stable patron-client relationship has prompted Kyogoku and his associates to invent an operationally defined concept of electoral support base.

Another example of the effect of the basic political facts on political science is that the weak class cleavages, further muted by the high economic growth of the 1960s and early 1970s, have led Watanuki to coin the notion "cultural politics" as the best framework for understanding Japanese politics, and Akuto to argue that life-style is an unusual but most important determinant of party support. Turning to the foreign side, the inability of oppositions to share or take power has bred the tendency to ideologize the party's foreign policy positions more than necessary on both sides of government and opposition. The inability and lack of need to take a hardheaded look at foreign policy options on the part of the opposition and the inability and unwillingness to explain its positions cogently and patiently on the part of the government have brought about a situation in which many of Japan's foreign policy debates were often made in a somewhat superfluous manner short of the standard of academic discourse. The recent increase in the number of international relations specialists equipped with solid empirical-analytical methodology is expected to be accompanied by a change in this respect. Finally, the comfortable "umbrella" that was extended to Japan by the U.S. for many years and the consequent passivity of Japan's foreign policy during the third quarter of this century tended to make the Japanese perspectives less than commensurate with Japanese external economic relations in terms of width and depth. Thus the number of serious scholars specializing in a specific area or country or subject and being able to offer, when needed, a cogent analysis of the issue concerned was somewhat limited. This tendency has been rapidly changing, especially since the early 1970s, when some basic assumptions of Japan's foreign policy since 1945 were partially shaken.

Thus, both in Japanese domestic politics and foreign relations, the impact of the given political configurations on political science has been great.

Political Scientists in Politics

The notion of social science as the opposition science had some notable influences in Japan. Social scientists, especially political scientists, tended to stay aloof from the government. This tendency has been changing, starting in economics—a more "advanced" and somewhat more technical discipline—and then slowly permeating into political science. A sizable number of political scientists are involved in the government-sponsored deliberation councils or those close to the government on such subjects as industrial structure, urban problems, external economic policy, electoral laws, the constitution, and foreign policy. However, unlike the U.S. where political appointments are made, career bureaucrats in Japan play a far more important role in decision-making and the role of these councils is very limited. A far smaller number of political scientists and economists play the role of informal advisors to the prime minister and other influential politicians and are not thought to be as powerful as, say, some of their American counterparts like Kissinger. Also a number of political scientists are involved in politics, occasionally advising leaders of various sectors to adopt a particular set of policies formulated by their like-minded private groups. In a few cases, social scientists, most of whom are economists, win elections (more local than national) and become professional politicians. More at the grass-roots levels, a sizable number of political scientists play active roles for such causes as community services, neighborhood facilities, and property rights as well as for antiwar and human rights. However, when political scientists have something to say in public about the currently debated issues, they generally write not in academic journals but in the more mass-oriented newspapers and weekly or monthly magazines and in a way that is different from the basic academic style and standard of discourse.

Relationships between the Government and the Discipline

Relationships between the government and the discipline have been weak. The government hardly thinks that political science can be of use whereas the discipline as a whole never pretends to be practical—nor does it wish to be. There is no fundamental reform plan either in the Ministry of Education or in universities in this respect. Yet recently discernible on the part of the Ministry of Education is the tendency to emphasize, and invest in, new departments and research centers in international studies and policy science. Whether this tendency will develop in a way to trigger a series of drastic changes in the relationships between the government and the discipline is not clear, but it does not seem very likely that the relationships will change very much in the near future when we take into account the formidable institutional rigidity of Japanese universities.

The Present State and the Future Prospects of Political Science

Political science in Japan is largely confined to the Japanese academic community. It has made more contributions to international scholarship in terms of providing rich and detailed description and analysis than in theoretical and methodological innovations. The fields of study which are likely to develop further in the near future include: Japanese politics, East Asian studies and Southeast Asian studies, international relations, and quantitative political analysis.

Japanese Politics. Japanese political scientists have produced an impressive number of largely descriptive studies providing rich data which are utilized and "processed" for further analysis by political scientists at home and abroad. More recently, processed products—rather than raw materials—have been produced by Japanese political scientists, especially in electoral behavior and mathematical political analysis. Also, more studies using comparative theoretical perspectives and advanced methodological armories have been done.

East Asian and Southeast Asian Studies. Japanese scholarship in East Asian studies has been notable, producing impressive works on the basis of primary materials. Especially in modern Japanese and Chinese political and diplomatic history, Japanese scholars have made important contributions to the international academic community, helped in part by the fact that many non-Japanese specialists on Japan and China can read Japanese-language works. More recently, Japanese scholarship in Southeast Asian studies has been progressing rapidly in making international contributions. While retaining a good tradition of solid empirical description and analysis, it is expected to make further theoretical and methodological contributions.

International Relations. Although many works in international relations have been oriented primarily for domestic consumption until recently, gradual changes are taking place. A few students have done some important work with originality and with a regard for the evidence, especially in Japan's foreign relations and international relations in that part of the world. With increasingly broadened perspectives and with the innate sensitivity to complexity, it is expected that Japanese political science will contribute more to international scholarship in this field of study.

Quantitative Political Analysis. Japanese political scientists have made some important contributions to quantitative political analysis and will increase their contributions in the near future. Despite the overall conservatism in terms of restructuring Japanese political science on the part of a large number of Japanese political scientists, a sizable number of social scientists including statisticians, economists, and political scientists are keen to develop and use mathematical methods in political analysis. Given the relative ease of communication among academic disciplines and across national boundaries due to the use of the universal language, this field of study has been making rapid progress in Japanese political science.

In order for political science in Japan to make important contributions to the world community more actively than before, a number of weaknesses mentioned above have to be overcome. In addition, some necessary reforms may be fruitful if attempted with commitment.

Institutionally, departments of political science must be independent of other departments, most importantly of the department of law, to which most political scientists have been an appendage for a century. Without independent undergraduate and graduate curricula in political science, the discipline cannot expect to do very much especially in view of the growing need to cope with increasingly complex problems at home and abroad. More specifically, the still prevalent form of graduate training in political science (the early and narrow specialization without adequate systematic training) must be changed and restructured so that a systematic exposure to more comprehensive subject matter and a familiarity with more than one intellectual tradition can be achieved. In a radical restructuring of graduate training both in conceptual and institutional terms, Japanese political science can hope to become more fully integrated in, and actively lead with others, the mainstream of the world intellectual life. More immediately, it may be useful to do two things: create more opportunities for some excellent works by Japanese scholars to be made available in English translation to the world community; and expose more aspiring Japanese students of politics to the frontiers of the world academic community. Vigorous efforts have been made for the last twenty years in realizing both of these goals under the auspices of various foundations like the Japan Foundation, academic associations, and other organizations like the International House of Japan and the Japan Center for International Exchange. Their outcome is yet to be seen.

To conclude, despite all the weaknesses described above, Japanese political science has a lot of potential to contribute more actively to the world academic community in the common pursuit of universal truths and practical solutions, helped by its solid empiricist tradition and increasingly broad perspectives.

Notes

1. Maruyama Masao, "Kagaku toshiteno seijigaku," in *Gendai seiji no shiso to kodo,* rev. ed. (Tokyo: Miraisha, 1964), pp. 341-59.
2. Royama Masamichi, *Nihon niokeru kindai seijigaku no hattatsu* (Tokyo: Jitsugyonihonsha, 1949); Watanuki Joji, personal communication, 1978.
3. Mombusho gakujutsu kokusai kyoku, *Kenkyusha kenkyukadai soran: Jimmon Shakai kagaku hen*, vol. 2 (Tokyo: Nihon gakujutsu shinkokai, 1979).
4. Watanuki Joji, personal communication, 1978.
5. Watanuki Joji (1976) "Japan," in *Social Sciences in Asia 2* (Paris: UNESCO, 1976).
6. Ibid., p. 40.

Bibliography

There are a number of bibliographies of works on political science. The following are especially useful. For English-speaking readers the last mentioned work is most convenient. The JPSA's annual publication, *Annals of Political Science,* has had a section on political science works published in the preceding year since 1953. The JPSA published *Publications on Political Science in Japan* annually in English from 1965 to 1975. The JAIR published in 1979 a massive bibliographical work reviewing major works in international relations and area studies in Japan since 1945, entitled *The Study of International Relations in Japan*. The Japan Foundation publishes biannually a bibliographical work on Japanese studies in English. The chapter on political science was written by Sato Seizaburo and Omori Wataru in 1974, 1976, 1978, 1982; "Political Science," in *An Introductory Bibliography for Japanese Studies*, pt. 1 of vols. 1, 2, and 3. Also, see pp. 211-13 of this essay.

19 KOREA

KE SOO KIM

Introduction

Even though a conscientious attempt will be made to follow the "model outline for national and regional chapters," suggested by the editor, it would be difficult to survey the history of political science in Korea without considering the particular circumstances surrounding the birth and development of the discipline in Korea. Not until 1945, when the country was freed from Japanese colonial rule, did the concern for the study and teaching of modern political science emerge in Korea, and in August 1946 the first political science department was founded in the country. Ever since the birth of the discipline in 1946, political science as well as the political scientists in Korea have been affected sensitively by the sociopolitical changes in the larger society and, consequently, it is necessary to indicate the nature of such changes whenever pertinent in order to establish an overview of the history of political science in Korea.

For the sake of convenience, the history of political science in Korea can be divided into three distinct periods: from 1945 to 1953, from 1954 to 1961, and from 1962 to the present. The periodic division is not without arbitrariness, but there are discernible changes in the major trends and concerns of the Korean political science in each of the periods. The three periods in the history of the Korean political science correspond also to the major political changes in Korea. It is undeniable that the political changes exerted certain, if not decisive, influences on the path of development of the discipline in Korea. This is not to say, however, that the three periods in the history of the Korean political science are by any means disjunctive: the contention is only that there are discernibly different tendencies in each of the periods, and that there are noticeable shifts of emphasis and concern in the study of politics from one period to another.

The State of Political Science in 1945: The Embryonic Period

The birth of the discipline in Korea dates back to 1945. For some 70 years—from 1876 to 1945—the study of politics in Korea had been in an embryonic stage, or perhaps dormant. Two historical considerations help explain the unusually lengthy embryonic stage which Korean political science had undergone.[1] One is the overwhelmingly powerful influence of Confucianism in all aspects of the lives of the Korean people for an extended period of time. As the official ideology of the Yi dynasty (1392-1910), Confucianism reigned supreme in all aspects of the lives of the Koreans, including academic activities. The enlightened elites in the Yi dynasty, the Confucian scholars, were the very pillars of the traditional society, and it was extremely difficult, if not impossible to expect from them any political thinking or activity that even slightly transgressed the reigning Confucian *Weltanschauung*. Even when the Yi dynasty was forced by external pressures to "open" itself to Japan and the world beyond in 1876, thereby exposing the traditional society to foreign influences from Western civilization, most of the enlightened elites in the society, rather than taking a receptive posture, clung to the old *Weltanschauung* and failed in constructively reconciling the old with the new, the indigenous with the foreign.[2] One result of this was the delayed "birth" of modern political science in Korea.

Another historical consideration which helps explain the lengthy dormant period for the study of politics in Korea is the Japanese colonial rule from 1910 to 1945. Under the Japanese, all kinds of political activity and thinking on the part of the Koreans were severely repressed as part of the colonial policy. During the 1910-1945 period, therefore, Japanese colonial domination over Korea played a decisive role in forcing Korean political science to remain dormant. It must be noted, however, that there were a few isolated attempts at writing Korean history—especially political history and diplomatic history—from a consciously nationalist standpoint.[3] Also, various Western political ideologies found their way to the Korean intellectuals, especially after the conclusion of World War I. Liberal ideology in the form of the Wilsonian doctrine of self-determination and the socialist ideology from the newly established Soviet Russia were outstanding examples. These ideologies tended to encourage nationalist aspirations and sentiments among Korean intellectuals.[4]

Finally, in this period a privileged few had the opportunity to receive higher education in the arts and sciences, mostly in colleges and universities in Japan. Through some of these people the German *Staatswissenschaft* was introduced to Korea. The "study of the state" was an imported field of study in Japan and was reimported from Japan to Korea. Though imported in an indirect way, the *Staatswissenschaft* had considerable influence among some Korean intellectuals. Yet, an indigenous development of modern political science did not materialize in Korea. Thus, internal and external factors and reasons—Confucianisim and the Japanese colonial domination—played major roles in keeping Korean political science in a lengthy dormant state.

The First Period (1945–1953): The Germinating Period

The period 1945–1953, which may be said to constitute the germinating period for Korean political science, was a time in which many radical changes occurred in Korean society. The liberation from Japanese domination in 1945 was followed immediately by intense ideological conflicts between Right and Left. In the midst of that sociopolitical turmoil, two separate governments were established in south and north Korea in 1948, each claiming its own legitimacy. Only two years later the Korean war broke out, as the North Korean communists launched a surprise attack against the South in June 1950. Not until 1953 could the South Korean government, which had been forced to move its headquarters to Pusan, return to Seoul. The major trends and tendencies in political science can be characterized by several considerations.

First, the intellectual leaders in political science were in large measure the products of Japanese higher education.[5] Since Japanese political science had considered the study of politics only a marginal part of the study of the state and jurisprudence, the tendency toward legalistic and traditional approaches in political science was reflected rather faithfully in the academic activities of the forerunners of Korean political science in this period. As American political science in its early stage was influenced heavily by German scholarship, so was Korean political science heavily influenced by Japanese approaches to the study of politics. In particular, specialists in public law—constitutional law, administrative law, and international law—played a major role in the teaching of political science. Historians—especially experts in political history and diplomatic history—contributed their share to the development of Korean political science. This was the time when public law specialists and historians, rather than political scientists proper, assumed intellectual leadership in the discipline, and heavy influences of Japanese political science were manifest in the political science curricula in the colleges and universities.[6]

A second consideration is the effect of Japanese colonial rule. Korea had only a few professional schools and only one university, with Japanese faculty occupying most of the teaching positions. It was a part of Japanese colonial policy in Korea to suppress higher education among the Koreans. With the liberation of the country, the Japanese faculty departed from Korea, along with all other Japanese who had been in Korea, and the institutions of higher education in Korea now had to be filled and led by all-Korean faculties. At the same time, a number of private colleges and universities were founded following the liberation of the country. Seoul National University was established in August 1946, in accordance with the National University Plan issued by the U.S. Military Government as part of the higher education policy in the new nation. A Department of Political Science was established in the School of Arts and Sciences of Seoul National University in August 1946. The same year, the Bosung Professional School and Yonsei Professional School were upgraded to become the Korean University and Yonsei University, respectively, and the newly established universities added two more departments of political science. Proliferation of political science departments also extended to women's colleges and universities, as the Ewha Women's College and the Sukmyong Woman's College added two more departments of political science in 1950 and 1952.

Major difficulties which the Korean political science faced included the lack of a sufficient number of qualified political scientists for teaching and research, the problem of formulating political science curricula in the face of the obviously inadequate teaching facilities, and the problem of securing bibliographic materials for teaching and research.[7] In many political science departments, consequently, the academic backgrounds and orientations of the faculty were the decisive factors in determining the real content of the curricula. Courses in public law, economics, and history tended to predominate. Among political science courses proper, emphasis was usually placed on political thought and political philosophy. For instance, courses in "the theories of sovereignty" and "the theories of the state" constituted core areas of study in the discipline. Historical approaches to political institutions and political ideology were also part of the trends in this period. Graduate courses in political science did exist in some universities but, due to the shortage of qualified teachers, the graduate schools in this period remained in large measure rather nominal.[8]

A third factor in this period was that Korean political science found it extremely difficult to remain entirely unaffected by the intense ideological conflicts that plagued the entire society. All the major issues—unification, the nature of the government to be established, and so on—inevitably entailed intense ideological conflict among various political inclinations ranging from the extreme right to the radical left. Korean political scientists in this period were, in fact, very much involved in the pros and cons of the various ideologies, and much of their work in this period was of the kind that explicated and propagated the various political isms.[9] During the period 1948 to 1953, however, the general ideological consensus among Korean political scientists gradually emerged, and was inclined toward liberal democracy. Of course, the Korean War only worsened the conditions for a healthy development of political science in Korea. Under the extremely adverse circumstances, each political scientist had to do his best in teaching and research.

Fourthly, toward the end of 1953, some twenty leading political scientists had a meeting at the provisional campus of Seoul National University (SNU) in Pusan, and resolved to establish a scholarly association for Korean political scientists. The Korean Political Science Association (KPSA) was thus founded in October 1953.[10] The association remained in name only for the next three years, without producing any visible academic activities or works. Even so, the KPSA did perform at least a symbolic function, proclaiming to the outside world that the Korean political scientists were now united in an independent academic discipline. Furthermore, it cannot be denied that the association did in a small way provide a channel for the exchange of ideas and academic cooperation among Korean political scientists.

A fifth consideration is the participation of the UN Forces in the Korean war which had an unanticipated consequence of awakening interest in international politics among Korean political scientists.[11] But there were not yet any regular courses in international politics offered in political science departments, and not until the late 1950s did Korean political scientists begin to engage in serious research in international relations.

The Second Period (1954–1961): The Period of Initial Growth

As the armistice agreement was concluded in 1953, the Korean government returned to Seoul from its provisional location in Pusan of the previous three years. With the suspension of hostilities, everything seemed to be returning to normalcy. Political instability, however, was on the increase, due to mounting distrust of people toward the Syngman Rhee regime and rampant corruption in the party in power. The overthrow of the Syngman Rhee regime by the students in April 1960 gave birth to the Second Republic in Korea, but a military coup d'état a year later brought that regime to an early end. For Korean political science, however, the 1954–1961 period was one of rapid initial growth and development.

This period marked a considerable growth in the number of political scientists and teachers in the political science departments. A considerable number of people who had had their undergraduate training in the Japanese universities received graduate degrees from the various Korean universities in the years 1949 and 1950. And in the years 1953 to 1956 the Korean universities began to produce a number of graduate-degree holders whose educational backgrounds were purely Korean. These people gradually came to occupy the teaching positions in the various political science departments, with the consequence that the average age of political science teachers in Korea became quite young.[12] Yet, the general academic trends dominant in the previous period tended to continue through the late 1950s.

Along with the increase in the number of political scientists, there was also an increase in the number of fields of study within the discipline. New fields of study were added to the old ones. In particular, the fields of international organization and international politics witnessed remarkably rapid growth and expansion. New courses in comparative government and politics were also initiated. Perhaps the most remarkable development was the introduction of the field of public administration. Instrumental to the introduction of public administration were the scholarly exchange programs which had been established between SNU and the University of Minnesota during the years 1957–1958. As an immediate outcome of those programs, a graduate school of public administration was founded in SNU in 1959. The Graduate School of Public Administration played a significant role in enhancing the quality of graduate studies in general, and in introducing empirically oriented approaches to the study of politics in Korea. In the same period, a number of original works and translations of foreign works were published in the fields of political parties, parliamentary institutions, and political processes.[13] In teaching political science, the emphasis still centered on undergraduate training. The graduate schools were still weak and few in number, but the number of graduate enrollments grew steadily, especially after 1957.

This period also witnessed a rapid increase in the volume of publications. Original works and translations of foreign books, articles, and essays were published in the various fields of the discipline. Some 305 books—original works and translations—were published during the years 1945–1955. Of the 305 some 52 percent were published in 1954–1955, compared with 28 percent in 1953.[14] After 1955 the rate of growth in the volume of publication did not slow down, due mainly to the fact that almost every university and college decided to publish its own journal in the social sciences.[15] At the same time, quite a few popular monthly magazines continued to carry articles and essays written by political scientists, which were read widely by college students and intellectuals in general.[16]

In terms of methodologies and approaches, the traditional orientations still predominated in this period as before. But in the books published—especially those that dealt with introductory materials—there was a noticeable concern with the definitions, scope, and methodology of political science. This contrasted with the tendencies of earlier years when political ideologies were the main concern of political scientists. A conscious concern for a systematic, scientific political science was emerging slowly in this period. Among the widely read foreign books were those by Harold J. Laski, Charles E. Merriam, and Robert M. MacIver.[17] Laski's works in particular were widely read and taught. All of these undoubtedly contributed to laying the foundations for the development of modern political science in Korea. Toward the end of this period, American behavioral political science was introduced in Korean political science. At the first annual meeting of the Korean Political Science Association, in December 1958, a report was made on American behavioralism by a person who had participated in the APSA's annual meeting that year.[18] In 1959 the first issue of the official journal of the KPSA, *Political Science,* was published, and it carried an article entitled, "The Role of Behavioralism." Also, around this time Harold D. Lasswell's works were being translated and introduced.

The Korean Association of International Relations (KAIR) and the Korean Association of Public Administration (KAPA) were both founded in 1956. There were no significant academic activities in the two associations until 1963. The membership of these three associations—KPSA, KAIR, and KAPA—was in large measure overlapping.

Until 1960, when the Syngman Rhee regime was overthrown by the students' uprising, the political scientists' posture toward the government was one of detached criticism. Numerous essays and articles were written by political scientists explicating the basic principles of liberal democracy. The government and the party in power, however, did not launch any significant attempt to restrict and regulate academic freedom on the university campuses in the country.

The Third Period (1962 to the present): The Period of Rapid Growth

The period of military rule that followed the 16 May military revolution that had brought the Second Republic to an end came to an end itself when power was turned over to a civilian government and the Third Republic was established. These events, plus the proclamation of the Yushin Reforms on 17 October 1973, form the backdrop for the developments in Korean political science during this period. Searching efforts to bring about the full maturation of the field is the hallmark of Korean political science over the last decade and a half. In this respect, the field is only a reflection of the momentous social, economic, political, and cultural changes that have been occurring throughout these years. On the other hand, there has been a great deal of ferment within the field itself, since the fruits of political science research in the West, particularly in the U.S., have been introduced into Korea at an accelerating pace. On the whole, this has led to epochal achievements during these years that go far beyond anything previously seen in Korean political science and which have contributed significantly to the maturation of the field. It may be argued on the basis of this development that the field has been transformed abruptly both in qualitative and quantitative terms.[19]

For one thing, the number of political scientists has increased greatly. There were 165 persons teaching either political science or public administration in 1965 but there were substantially more than twice this number of political scientists in 1974. Some 386 names appeared on the Korean Political Science Association membership roster published in the latter year and some 320 of them held teaching positions in colleges or universities.[20] This figure alone reflects an almost twofold increase over 1965. Of course, an important factor in this growth was the expansion and increase in the number of departments of public administration. In fact, it is rare these days to find a college without a department of public administration although not a few lack a political science department.

The number of members of the association holding the Ph.D. has also been on the increase. There was scarcely more than a handful of such persons in 1965, but 170 members had this qualification ten years later. Thus, in 1975, 45 percent of the entire membership of the Korean Political Science Association held the Ph.D. Breaking this down by sources: 101 had been awarded by Korean universities; 50 by U.S. universities; 8 by West German and Austrian universities; 3 by Japanese universities; and one each by British and French universities. In other words some 27 percent of the association membership in 1975 held the Ph.D. from a Korean university and thirteen percent from a U.S. university.[21] However, the number of holders of the Ph.D. from a Korean university increased suddenly in 1974, the final deadline set for the screening of dissertations for doctoral degrees awarded under the old system.

The relative order of the subfields of Korean political science in 1965 by percentage of specialists was as follows: international politics: 18 percent; public administration: 17 percent; political theory: 15 percent; political processes: 15 percent; comparative politics: 12 percent; political history: 9 percent; Korean politics: 7 percent; and public law: 7 percent.[22] In 1974 the ranking of public administration and political theory was reversed, as was that of political processes and comparative politics. Hence, despite the increase in the number of political scientists, the constellation of interests remained much the same. Of special interest is the fact that the subfield of Korean politics remained at the bottom of the list. Moreover, the number of political scientists claiming this specialty decreased from eleven to eight over this decade.[23] This lack of enthusiasm for the study of Korean politics stands in sharp contrast with the situation in the U.S. where the majority of political scientists devote themselves to the study of American political processes. One can only suppose that there are many factors which obstruct the expression of a normal level of interest in domestic politics on the part of Korean political scientists.

Another change has been in the curricula of political science departments which have gradually grown in scope and diversity. In the same way, research activities have become broader, both in terms of the topics pursued and the geographical localities encompassed. Furthermore, as the interest in political processes rather than simply in institutions and structures has increased, political scientists have begun lecturing on topics such as public policy decision-making, public opinion, propaganda, political psychology, and political sociology. This marks a major change from the days when lectures on political parties and parliamentarianism were predominant. Interest in methodology and area studies has been on the upswing also. This is reflected in the growing number of departments which have courses on topics such as the methodologies of political science, systematic political science, political science theory, the political theory of developing countries, and the political characteristics of the major regions of the world. Area studies typically cover Asia, the Middle East, Latin America, and Africa as well as communist-bloc nations including Communist China and the Soviet Union. In fact, courses have mushroomed to the point that serious difficulties have begun to arise in the drawing up of curricula. There is a growing feeling that some consolidations must take place, perhaps in the format of a model curriculum.

College education has become popular and widespread over the last decade or so. Graduate programs in diplomacy and political science as well as public administration have been created. As a result master's theses in political science and public administration have appeared in great numbers in recent years and Ph.D. dissertations under the new system began appearing around 1971. The critical assesment of the content and effectiveness of graduate education has thus become an issue within the field.

The increased concern with methodology has led to a heightened awareness of the demands of empiricism and more empirical research has been done. As the traditional approaches were being replaced gradually by the new empirical approaches, the works and textbooks by Lasswell, Easton, Deutsch, and Eulau, among others came to occupy a central place, replacing those by Laski, MacIver, and Merriam. With the introduction of American behavioral political science, the behaviorally oriented political scientists in Korea gained considerable prestige in the discipline.[24] The introduction of American behavioral political science had many significant impacts on Korean political science in arousing general interest in the "scientific" study of politics, as well as in broadening the scope of inquiry for political scientists. However, behavioral political science was not received without certain resistance among some political scientists in Korea. Such resistance was, in the main, emotional rather than logical in nature.

Political scientists have become more and more specialized. The field and even the subfields have been divided into as many specialized areas as would seem possible and yet this trend appears likely to continue. In addition to this kind of expansion the present decade has also seen an increased interest in problem-oriented research focused on issues such as modernization, national security, the reunification of Korea, and the North-South gap. Finally, interest in international politics, comparative politics, and specialized area studies has grown apace.

Also, concern with Western democracy has declined considerably, and increasing interest was now centered on nationalism in general and nationalism in the developing countries in particular. This tendency was particularly manifest toward the end of this period.

Korean political science was still very dependent upon American political science in many respects.[25] However, the issue of the "Koreanization" of the discipline has also arisen.[26] It has provided a stimulus for research in Korean political history, government, and politics. At the same time, the Koreanization attempt has had a significant impact on the study of political theory, public administration, and international politics. Nevertheless, Koreanization still remains an aspiration rather than a reality.

Political scientists have frequently been the recipients of research grants awarded by the Songgok Foundation and the Ministry of Education. These funds have been a major contributing factor in the growth of research activities, especially field surveys. More recently, grants have been awarded also to political scientists by the Vocational Training Assistance Foundation and the Samsong Cultural Foundation, but in these cases the number of recipients has been extremely limited and the funds have not been of much assistance in meeting the costs of field surveys. Actually, the Ministry of Education's grants are about the same as those awarded by private foundations in terms of amounts and grant periods. The major contribution they make is, therefore, more a reflection of their considerably greater availability to political scientists all over the country. These funds have been made available since the late 1960s. In addition to supporting and stimulating individual research, the ministry has promoted the establishment of political science research institutes at most universities; without regard to whether the circumstances in a particular instance warranted such a move, one might add. In the same way the Korean Unification Center has provided funds to many academic institutions to enable them to establish research institutes devoted to studying the problems of national security and national reunification.

Since the last half of the 1960s, the Korean Political Science Association has been rather active in academic activities. Ever since 1966, an annual seminar on a given theme has been a regular practice and, in addition, four to five monthly seminars per year have been regularly held since 1968. The *Korean Political Science Review* (*KPSR*), which had been only intermittently published (volume 1 in 1959, volume 2 in 1967, volume 3 in 1969, volume 4 in 1970), has become a regular publication since 1970. The official journals of the Korean Association of International Relations and the Korean Association of Public Administration have been published regularly since their inception in 1963 and 1967, respectively. (See Appendix, Table 19.1.) Due to the increase in membership of the KPSA, the association organized local chapters in the 1970s. Local chapters in Pusan, Taegu, and Kwangju were organized in 1970, 1971, and 1974, respectively. The KPSA was now a national organization.

Interest in international scholarly exchanges has increased appreciably within the Korean Political Science Association. As a result, the association became a member of the International Political Science Association (IPSA) in September 1967 and delegates were sent to the Eighth Congress of IPSA held in Munich, that year. Delegates were sent again in 1973 and 1976 to the meetings in Montreal and London.

Another noteworthy occasion along these lines was the First Joint Conference of the Korean Political Science Association and the Association of Korean Political Scientists in North America held in Seoul, June 9-12, 1975. The Second Joint Conference was held in 1977 in Seoul, and subsequent meetings were planned for every two years.

Finally, the association has also sponsored a considerable number of valuable publications. Apart from the *Journal,* its first efforts along these lines were two titles brought out in 1965; one of these was a book entitled *Modern Political Science* and the other a collection of monographs in English entitled *Readings in Political Science.* Then, in 1971, a compilation of papers by twenty-six Korean political scientists was published by the association under the title *The Theory of Democracy.* A major project in which nearly every political scientist in Korea had a part was the *Dictionary of Political Science* which was completed between 1973 and the end of 1975. Meanwhile, in 1974, an update of the collection of monographs in English was brought out under the new title of *Readings in Contemporary Political Science.* This and the original of some ten years earlier contributed toward the diffusion of the work of contemporary American political scientists in Korea. In addition to these publication activities, the association has also formed a committee to deal with the curricular problems mentioned earlier. The curricula currently in use in colleges and universities across the country have been collected, analyzed, and evaluated with the idea of drawing up a model curriculum.

Another noteworthy trend in this period was that a few political scientists made an exit from the academy to occupy high positions in the government and seats in the National Congress. A number of practising political scientists continued to maintain close contacts with the party in power in advisory capacities. Several political scientists were appointed to seats in the National Congress (a new system under the Yushin Reform since 1973), and a handful of political scientists were appointed to positions in the Blue House (special assistants, counsellors to the president, and so on). In other words, there was a noticeable tendency among some political scientists to show an active interest in practical politics and administration.[27]

However, since the Emergency Measures proclaimed under the Yushin system—which drastically limit freedom of expression—political scientists have been practically prohibited from any criticism of the government and its policies. As a consequence, studies on national security, national unification, communist countries, and so forth, have tended to attract much interest by political scientists.

The Present State and the Future Prospects

Although political science in Korea is only thirty years old, the rate of growth and development of the discipline has been rather remarkable. Statistics show that from 1945–1972 the total number of copies of books and articles which dealt with political issues in general was 150,837.[28] It is not a small figure, considering the overall size of the country. Perhaps the rapid sociopolitical changes which the Korean society has undergone in the past thirty years is a factor that is related to the rapid growth and expansion of the discipline. For good or evil, political scientists in Korea have had ample political experience, and the abundance of such political experience is perhaps reflected in the rate of growth of the discipline.

However, only after the latter part of the 1960s did Korean political science begin to develop substantially in terms of quantity and quality. Contributing to this development was the heavy impact of American behavioral political science. Unfortunately, however, in the process of incorporating American behavioral political science, there was a tendency for empirical research in Korea to be isolated from the democratic ideals, or political philosophy, which was the foundation of empiricism in America. As a consequence, it has been difficult for Korean political scientists to arrive at a consensus on the ultimate goal of the discipline. Ever since the 1960s, various and often dissonant ideals, concepts, and approaches have coexisted in the discipline, and there is no sign of amelioration in this regard. Current circumstances surrounding Korean political science, it seems, tend only to aggravate the situation. Perhaps, Korean political science needs more time to arrive at a general and desirable consensus on the ultimate goal of the discipline in Korea.

Notes

1. Wha Ryong Kim, *Chongchi-hak* [Political science] in *Hanguk Hyundae-sa Daekae* [Modern history of Korean culture] (Seoul: Institute of National Cultural Research, Korea University, 1976), 2:242.

2. Ibid., pp. 243–48.

3. Ibid., p. 249.

4. Ibid., p. 251.

5. Ke Soo Kim, *Hanguk Ui Hakbo–Chongchi-hak* [History of Korean scholars—political science], Seoul Daehan-Ilbo, 13–27 January 1972.

6. Ibid.

7. Ibid.

8. Ke Soo Kim, *Hanguk Chongchi-hak—Hyonwhang kwa Kyonghyang* [Korean political science—status and trends] (Seoul: Ilchokak, 1969) pp. 20–23.

9. Daehan Minguk Kuhae Doso-Kwan [National Assembly Library of ROK], *Chongchi-Haengchong-Bopriul Ronmoon Chong Mokrok, 1945–1972* [An index of Korean periodicals on politics, administration and law, 1945-1972] (Seoul: National Assembly Library of ROK, 1973).

10. Choong Souk Suh, "8.15 iwho ui Hanguk Chongchi Hak-kae" [Korean political science since 15 August 1945], *Hanguk Chongchi Hakhae-Bo, Changkan-Ho* [Korean political science review] 1 (Seoul: Ilchokak, 1959) 186.

11. Kim, [History of Korean scholars].

12. Kim, [Korean political science], pp. 20–23.

13. Daehan Minguk Kukhae Doso-Kwan [*Index*], pp. 1–538.

14. Ke Soo Kim, "History of Korean political science, 1945-1955" in *Haksool-chi* (Seoul: Kunkuk University, 1970), 11: 170–173.

15. Daehan Minguk Kukhae Doso-Kwan [*Index*], pp. 781–855.

16. *Sassangkae, Chayou-Saekae, Sacho, Hanguk Pyongron*, and *Saekae* were the most popular monthly magazines.

17. Kim, [Korean political science] pp. 67–75.

18. Hanguk Chongchi Hak-hae [KPSA], *Hanguk Chongchi Hakhae-Bo* [KPSR] (Seoul: Ilchokak, 1959), 1.

19. Daehan Minguk Kukhae Doso-Kwan [*Index*], pp. 1–538.

20. Ke Soo Kim, "Hanguk Chongchi-hak ui Hyonwhang kwa Moonjae-choom" [The status and problems of KPS], *Report of the First Joint Conference of the Korean Political Science Association and the Association of Korean Political Scientists in North America* (Korean edition) (Seoul: KPSA, 1975), p. 52.

21. Ibid., pp. 52–53.

22. Kim, [Korean political science], pp. 98–99.

23. Ke Soo Kim, "The Study of Political Science," in Korean National Commission for UNESCO, ed. *The Study of Social Science in Korea* (Seoul: Bom-moon-sa, 1977), p. 15.

24. Kim, [Korean political science], pp. 51–61.

25. Ibid., pp. 62-75. Byong-Man, Ahn, "The Impact of American Political Science on Korean Political Science," *Korean American Studies Review* 9 (1976) 43-44.

26. Kim, "Study of Political Science," pp. 14-15; [The status and problems of KPS], p. 54. Ahn, "Impact of American Political Science," pp. 45-46.

27. Kim, "Study of Political Science," p. 14; [The status and problems of KPS], pp. 53-54; [History of Korean scholars].

28. Daehan Minguk, Kukhae Doso-Kwan [*Index*], pp. 1-538; Kim, "Study of Political Science," pp. 17-19.

Bibliography

Ahn, Byong Man. "The Impact of American Political Science on Korean Political Science." *Korean American Studies Review*, American Studies Association of Korea 9 (1976).

Daehan Minguk Kukhae Doso-Kwan [National Assembly Library of the Republic of Korea]. *Chongchi-Haengchong-Bopriul Ronmoon Chong Mokrok, 1945-1972* [An index of Korean periodicals on politics, administration and law, 1945-1972], Seoul: National Assembly Library of Republic of Korea, 1973.

Kim, Ke Soo. "Hanguk ui Chongchi-hak yeongku" [The study of political science in Korea]. In *Hanguk Sahae Kwahak Yeongku* [The study of social science in Korea] edited by the Korean National Commission for UNESCO. Seoul: Bom-moon-sa, 1977.

———. "Hanguk Chongchi-hak ui Hyonwhang kwa Moonjae-choom" [The status and problems of Korean political science]. *The Korean Editing report of the First Joint Conference of the Korean Political Science Association and the Association of Korean Political Scientists in North America*. Seoul: Korean Political Science Association, 1975.

———. *Hanguk Chongchi-hak—Hyonwhang kwa Kyonghyang* [Korean political science—status and trends]. Seoul: Ilchokak, 1969.

Kim, Wha Ryong. "Chongchi-hak" [Political Science]. In *Hanguk Hyundac-sa Daekae* [Modern history of Korean culture]. Vol. 2. Seoul: Institute of National Cultural Research, Korea University, 1976.

Appendix

DEPARTMENTS AND PERSONNEL

According to available statistics, Korea has 50 departments including the departments of Public Administration and a total of about 8,000 students since 1965. Since then, there has been little change.

MEMBERSHIP OF KOREAN POLITICAL SCIENCE ASSOCIATION (KPSA)

Year	1965	1970	1975
Number	165	262	385

ADDRESSES OF MAJOR POLITICAL SCIENCE ASSOCIATIONS

Korean Political Science Association (KPSA)
Rm. 203 Namdo Bldg.
119, Suhsomun-dong, Choong-ku, Seoul, Korea

Korean Association of International Relations (KAIR)
Rm. 1006 Daiwu Center Bldg.
286, Yang-dong, Choong-ku, Seoul, Korea

Korean Association of Public Administration (KAPA)
Same as KPSA

Table 19.1 Korean Journals

NAME	SIZE OF CIRCULATION (BOOKS)	EDITOR	ADDRESS	FREQUENCY (FOR 1 YEAR)
KPSR[1]	1,000	Director of the editorial committee	KPSA office	1
KIRR[2]	1,000	Director of the editorial committee	KAIR office	1
KPAR[3]	1,000	Director of the editorial committee	KPSA office	1

[1]KPSR—Korean Political Science Review
[2]KIRR—Korean International Relations Review
[3]KPAR—Korean Public Administration Review

THE NETHERLANDS

ANDRIES HOOGERWERF

The Early History

In the beginning the earth of political science in the Netherlands was without form and void. Just as in the period before World War II, there was in 1945 not one professorate, not one student, not one department, not one periodical in political science in the Netherlands. Even the name "political science" and its Dutch equivalent *politicologie* were unknown in this country.

However, there were politics. There were also people who studied political phenomena in a scientific way. They were mainly lawyers and historians, and to a lesser degree economists, philosophers, and sociologists.[1] As early as the seventeenth century there were, at various Dutch universities, chairs for politics, sometimes called *politica* and *retorica*. In the nineteenth century and the first half of the twentieth century political phenomena were studied within the framework of disciplines such as public philosophy, constitutional law, and history. Thus, names of several prepolitical scientists can be mentioned: Hugo Grotius in the seventeenth century, J. de Bosch Kemper, J. R. Thorbecke and A. Kuyper in the nineteenth century; and among others, W. A. Bonger and R. Kranenburg in the twentieth century. They studied, also in a more empirical way, political phenomena and, in doing so, used the scientific knowledge and insights from other countries.

We shall not go further into the early history of Dutch political science, since it was discussed in detail in *Contemporary Political Science* (Paris, 1950).

Development since 1948

The birth of political science as an independent science in the Netherlands dates from 1948. In that year, the first Dutch professor of political science was appointed. His name was J. Barents.[2] He took the chair in the newly established Department of Political and Social Sciences at the University of Amsterdam. At the Catholic University of Nijmegen, L. G. A. Schlichting became, in 1950, professor of Survey of National and International Trends and Tendencies, later changed to Political Science, Journalism and Mass Communication. The (Protestant) Free University in Amsterdam followed, in 1953, with the appointment of J. J. de Jong. Later, came appointments of full and associate professors of political science or one of its subfields at the University of Leyden (1963), the University of Groningen (1971), Erasmus University in Rotterdam (1973), the University of Utrecht (1973), the Interfaculty Delft en Rotterdam (1974) and Twente University of Technology (1975), whereas the Catholic School for Economics in Tilburg appointed a lecturer (associate professor) of sociology of state and public administration. At the present time almost all Dutch universities have one or more chairs of political science or of its subfields. The first three professors were originally lawyers. About half of the present full and associate professors of political science studied initially in a different field than political science, usually sociology or law.

Full-fledged departments of political science have existed at the University of Amsterdam since 1948, at the Free University in Amsterdam since 1955, at the Catholic University of Nijmegen since 1969 and at Erasmus University in Rotterdam since 1978. In addition to these, the University of Leyden has had a political science program for graduate students since 1969. Twente University of Technology has had, since 1976, a department of public administration, where political science is one of the four key subjects.

---

*The author thanks Liz Kerver-Garnett for her translation and the Dutch professors and lecturers in political science for their comments on a draft of this chapter.

Since 1967 the field of political science has been regulated by the Academic Statute. Its contents are very brief. The political science department falls under the School of Social Sciences. The candidate's (B.A.) examination in political science includes political science as a major, methods and techniques of social research, and three fields, chosen by the school from sociology, cultural anthropology, sociology of non-Western civilizations, psychology, history, economics, or any other field. The M.A. examination, leading to the Dutch *doctorandus* degree, which is not the same as the doctor's degree, includes a major in political science and two minors.[3]

In 1969, through a change in the Academic Statute, three legal political specializations were set up in the law department, namely international relations, public administration, and political science. After the candidate's (B.A.) examination in law, the students can take an M.A. examination in one of these specializations. The M.A. examination in the political science specialization includes political science, international relations, Dutch and comparative constitutional law, and two other fields at the option of the student.[4]

The number of students with political science majors grew gradually. On the first of September 1978 the number at the University of Amsterdam was 924, at the Free University in Amsterdam 338, at the Catholic University in Nijmegen 328, at the State University in Leyden 88, and at Erasmus University Rotterdam 87, a total of 1,765.

For a long time, the number of graduates remained low, since there were only two full political science departments (at the two universities in Amsterdam). Moreover, especially at the University of Amsterdam, the study took very long in the beginning and the number of dropouts was high. Officially the study program took five years, but studying eight to nine years was not exceptional.

The number of graduates in political science per year increased as follows:[5]

April	1967	126
May	1969	166
January 1	1972	321
October 1	1973	458
September 1	1978	904

As of 1 September 1978, the number of graduates (in terms of having passed the M.A. examinations) of the various political sciences departments were:

University of Amsterdam	541
Catholic University of Nijmegen	78
Free University in Amsterdam	219
State University in Leyden	66
Total	904

Since 1948, the number of completed Ph.D. dissertations in political science at Dutch universities is as follows:

University of Amsterdam	21
Catholic University in Nijmegen	5
Free University in Amsterdam	12
University of Leyden	8
Erasmus University Rotterdam	2
Total	48

The growth of political science in the Netherlands can also be seen in the growth of the Dutch Political Science Association, founded in 1950. Another indication of the development of Dutch political science is the establishment of journals in the field of political science and related areas. Since 1965, *Acta Politica, Journal of Political Science,* has been published quarterly. Other relevant Dutch magazines are *Beleid en Maatschappij* (Policy and Society) published since 1973, *Beleidsanalyse* (Policy Analysis) since 1946, *Civis Mundi* (the earlier *Oost-West*) since 1961, *International Spectator* since 1946, *Openbare Uitgaven* (Public Expenditures) since 1965 and *Transactie* (Transaction: Journal of Peace Research) since 1972.

Research and Publications

Because of the small number of political scientists in the Netherlands, the amount of political science research and the number of political science publications remained very small for a long time after 1945. In total, about two hundred political science books and a few hundred political science articles in periodicals have now been published by Dutch political scientists in the Netherlands.

Using these publications, we shall try to give a short survey of research and publications. A condensed trend report, such as this, has, of course, its drastic limitations. We shall concentrate here on books. In this respect the survey strives for completeness. Articles will be named only occasionally.

The summary will attempt to keep as much as possible to political science, that is to say, to publications by persons who teach and/or have studied political science.[6] In a number of cases, however, to give insight into the process of development of political science as an independent science, a few publications from others than political scientists will be mentioned.

Primarily, the widely known division of political science into subfields is used as a guide to this puzzle. In this summary the following subfields will be treated: general introduction to political science; research methods and techniques; the Dutch political system (including studies on electoral behavior, political parties, parliament, interest groups, and provincial and local politics), comparative politics, international relations, the study of political theories, public administration, and policy studies.

THE OBJECT OF RESEARCH: GENERAL
INTRODUCTION TO POLITICAL SCIENCE

There has been till now pretty much a general agreement among Dutch political scientists on the limits and division of the concrete field of research in political science. Through the years, the division given in *Contemporary Political Science* in 1950 has often been cited with agreement, namely (here summarized): (1) political theory; (2) political institutions; (3) parties, groups, and public opinion; (4) international relations.[7]

The opinions of political scientists in the Netherlands differ however on a more abstract definition of the object of political science, that is, on a scientific definition of politics. We shall now give a survey of them, using mainly the general introductions to political science that have been published in the Netherlands so far.

Barents published an exploration of the field in 1948. He defined political science as the science that studies the life of the state. As important branches, he mentioned the history of theories of the state, and the state in practice as well as its history.[8] In 1961 Barents published his *Political Science in Western Europe: A Trend Report*, that is mainly a literature review.[9]

In 1958 de Jong issued a syllabus in which the political process is seen as the central object of political science. In a lengthy definition, building on Easton among others, the political process is described as: "the total of behaviors and interactions between persons and groups in the tension field between the authority of the state and the people... in so far as these behaviors and these interactions [can] result in actions by this state authority, which intend to bring about general [re-]allocations of immaterial values, that are justice oriented and can be maintained by a strong arm."[10]

Also in 1958, a reader appeared under the editorship of van der Land that not only contains a summary of the history of political theories but also an analysis of the democratic process, a description of the political systems of sixteen countries and an exposition of international relations.[11] It did not give a characteristic definition of politics.

In 1963 Daudt endorsed in an address Easton's definition of the object of political science as "the authoritative allocation of values for a society." In more concrete terms he described this object as: (1) the political theories and intellectual currents that try to set norms for the usage of power in states and (2) the institutions that in fact exercise the power according to one or another norm system.[12]

In 1968 Valkenburgh came with an introduction to political science that actually is a theoretical exposition of problems related to political power. According to the author, politics deals in the first place with the struggle for power and in the second place with the goal that is strived for with the acquired power, namely molding society.[13]

In 1972, Hoogerwerf's condensed and introductory survey of political science appeared. It concentrates on the different theoretical approaches in terms of (respectively) the state, the political system, policy, power allocation, conflict, and change. Politics is defined as public policy as well as its formation and its effects.[14]

In 1973, Kuypers published a book on basic concepts of politics. He sees a political process as a process of policy formation, policy execution, and the acquisition of power in an organized or nonorganized political system. Central, for him, is policy, which he defines as the combination of, first, the goals chosen by one or more actors, for himself or for a group; second, the chosen ways and means; and, third, the chosen points of time.[15]

In 1973, Tudyka wrote a booklet on *Kritische Politikwissenschaft* (critical political science) in which he says: "The basic paradigm in a critical political analysis forms the relationship between classes, their conflicts."[16]

In 1976 under the editorship of van Schendelen a book appeared on the basic themes of political science, in which eleven Dutch colleagues give a review of theory formation and empirical research. The political system, political influence, decision-making, allocation, integration, and conflict, are among the themes.[17]

Concluding, we can say that Dutch political scientists, from the beginning, agreed, in general, on the concrete objects of political science, but, differed just as much in their opinions on the definition of politics in more abstract terms. A few terms that appear in many of the definitions are: the state, allocation, power, policy, conflict, and related concepts. These terms can be viewed also as indications of different theoretical approaches in political science.

EMPIRICAL-THEORETICAL APPROACHES

Publications that are written totally on a theoretical level are rare in Dutch political science. Dutch political scientists seem to tend more toward empirical research in combination with theory formation rather than toward pure theory formation. The themes of the few theoretical studies can be described as the state, power, conflict, integration, policy, distribution system, and (in-)stability.

State theory has a central place in Barents's approach (1948), in that of some professors of public law, such as Donner and Couwenberg, and also in a number of publications from a Marxist point of view.[18]

The earlier mentioned introduction by Valkenburgh (1968) is about political power.[19] In regard to conflict,

Valkenburgh gave in 1969 a game-theoretical approach including a conflict model for computer simulation.[20] De Vree's Ph.D. dissertation (1972) is entitled *Political Integration: The Formation of Theory and its Problems*. This book is not only about integration but also about more general problems around theory formation.[21]

The introduction by Kuypers (1973) deals, above all, with policy. This attempts to reason consequently from a goals-means scheme.[22] Van den Doel (1975) does something similar but in a different way in his book on democracy and welfare theory. He tries to integrate a number of economic principles, especially of the "new political economy," with those of political science and of public administration.[23] In 't Veld's dissertation (1975) on majority system and welfare theory is also in this area of the new political economy.[24] While the three authors just mentioned analyze to an important degree in terms of rationality, van Gunsteren published in 1976 a critique on the "rational central-rule approach in public affairs" in a theoretical study on planning.[25] Rosenthal, van Schendelen, and Scholten follow the same course in this matter in their 1977 book on public administration.[26] In a book on public policy edited by Hoogerwerf policy is defined differently from Rosenthal et al., in terms of goals and means, but the book leaves room for different views on policy.[27]

The problem of distribution, also from a theoretical perspective, is central in a book by van den Doel and others, about equality and inequality in the Netherlands (1975).[28]

The dissertation of Noordzij (1977) deals with system and policy.[29] The concept of the political system and especially the definition given by Easton was already used on a large scale for a long time by Dutch political scientists.[30]

Rosenthal's dissertation (1978) is on *Political Order: Rewards, Punishments and Political Stability*.[31] So far, not one special book of a theoretical nature has been written in Dutch political science on political change, development, and revolution, although these subjects have received some attention.[32]

To the theory-oriented publications can also be added the already mentioned introductions by Hoogerwerf (1972) and van Schendelen et al. (1976). Both pay attention to most of the theoretical approaches in the terms of this section.

RESEARCH METHODS AND TECHNIQUES

The choice of research methods and techniques shows a relationship to the geographical orientation in political science. The rise and development of political science in the Netherlands is, above all, influenced by political science in the United States. Literature in English, especially from the United States, is used a lot in teaching and research. French and German political science, viewed in the Netherlands as being more traditional and less behavioral, have been less influential in the Netherlands. Since the end of the 1960s though, interest in German literature has been growing in the Netherlands, especially among Marxist political scientists.

The traditional, historical-legal-philosophical approach, that was the usual one in prepolitical science publications on political phenomena, still has its followers, of course. Especially in the beginning of Dutch political science, at the end of the 1940s and in the beginning of the 1950s, the traditional approach stimulated among others, the so-called institutional approach. Besides this, there was also a more quantitative and behavioral approach, starting in the 1950s. This approach shows a lot of resemblance to that in other social sciences, especially sociology and psychology. Since the 1960s it has dominated Dutch political science, but the traditional approach is still very much alive.

The behavioral revolution of the 1950s and 1960s and the postbehavioral revolution of the 1960s and 1970s in American political science, have not passed the Netherlands unnoticed. However, both revolutions took a moderate course in the Netherlands and did not lead to major conflicts.

Even though the first Dutch professors of political science—Barents, de Jong, and Schlichting—were all originally legal scholars, they did not shy away from conducting an electoral study in 1954 that, in its theoretical basis and methodological-technical details, was strongly influenced by American behavioralists of that day.[33] If the intentions and assumptions of the behavioralists can be summarized in the way Easton[34] did (1962)—with key words such as verification, techniques, quantification, and pure science—then it can be said that a large number of Dutch political scientists were and are behavioralists. But the more traditional, mostly historical-legal-philosophical, methods have also stayed current and accepted in Dutch political science.

The later postbehavioral revolution, of which a few key words such as engagement, relevance and action can be pointed out (Easton, 1970)[35] had and still has influence on Dutch political science, almost as unmistakably as the behavioral revolution. Though it is certainly not to be said that all Dutch political scientists have accepted this creed of political relevance to the same extent and to the last letter, it seems to be clear that many political scientists are concerned, more than before, about the political relevance of their research. Many still do research according to behavioral methods and techniques, but more than before keep an eye on the public interest and hold a critical view regarding the existing society and the existing political system.[36]

Handbooks on research methods and techniques have

not yet been written by Dutch political scientists. They are generally furnished by American colleagues and by Dutch sociologists. Of course, studies by Dutch political scientists on certain methodological-technical subjects have appeared. Illustrative are the dissertations of Mokken (1970) entitled *A Theory and Procedure of Scale Analysis with Applications in Political Research*[37] and of Stokman (1977) on *Roll Calls and Sponsorship: A Methodological Analysis of Third World Group Formation in the United Nations*.[38]

THE DUTCH POLITICAL SYSTEM

The Dutch political system was first analyzed from a political science point of view by de Jong (1951) in his dissertation on political organization in western Europe since 1800. His approach was mainly institutional-legal, but was pioneering through his analysis of, for example, the relationship between party organization and the party group in parliament.[39] This also applies to his publication on the political structure in the Netherlands since 1945.[40]

In 1965 the lawyer Couwenberg edited a reader on *Problems of Democracy*. In several articles the shortcomings of the Dutch political system are described from a democratic point of view.[41]

For a great deal of time since 1945, the Dutch political system has apparently shown to an important extent the same characteristics as in the prewar period. Changes did occur, however, mainly since the second half of the 1960s. Among others, the laborious course of cabinet formation and interim cabinet crises led to a widespread feeling that something was wrong with the Dutch political system. Political dissatisfaction and polarization increased, together with a striving for less fragmentation and further democratization. Dutch political science reflected and analyzed the contrast between the periods. Illustrative of this is that Daalder in 1964 gave his address on leadership and passivity in Dutch politics and in 1974 spoke about politicians and politicization in the Netherlands.[42]

In 1967 Kuypers came out with a book in which he called the Dutch political system sick. He described the nature of the sickness as a failing political game. The core of the sickness lay, in his opinion, in the way in which cabinets are formed and influenced in the Netherlands.[43]

Lijphart published in 1968 his study on *The Politics of Accommodation: Pluralism and Democracy in the Netherlands*. The paradox that he pointed out was that the Netherlands, despite deep religious and ideological cleavages, still had a stable political democracy and an effective government. The picture that Lijphart presented was essentially that of the period from World War II until 1965. The book was written in 1966. In the second edition of his book, Lijphart also tried to explain the changes in Dutch politics since 1967, using an amended theory of pluralism.[44]

Building on Lijphart and others, van den Berg and Molleman published a book in 1974 on what they called the crisis in Dutch politics. According to them this crisis concerns the legitimacy of the political system. The reasons they try to find are, on the one hand, a drifting away from fragmentation and confessionalization, and on the other hand a striving for democratization and an aversion against an all-regulating government.[45]

In a 1975 book on democracy in the Netherlands, van Putten sees the problems mainly in the unequal distribution of political power. He expects improvement through, among others things, a further democratization in the form of a functional parliamentary decentralization, through which the voter gets a say in every important field of public policy.[46]

Theoretically, these diagnoses and remedies regarding the Dutch political system may be divided into approaches in terms of power and authority (especially Daalder, van den Berg/Molleman, and van Putten), integration and conflict (especially Kuypers and Lijphart) and distribution (especially van den Berg/Molleman and van Putten). Remarkably, one has hardly or not at all looked for an explanation of the crisis in public policy itself. Van den Berg and Molleman do mention the dislike for the all-regulating government. But the enormous growth of public policy and the possible ineffectiveness of much of this has received little attention.

In addition to these publications on the Dutch political system as a whole there are a number of publications on specific elements of this system, namely: citizens, political parties, the parliament, and interest groups.

Electoral Behavior, Political Opinions and Political Participation

The collaboration in research between Dutch political scientists from different universities has concentrated on electoral research for a long time. This research started in 1956 with a local electoral panel survey in *Nieuwer Amstel*.[47] Also in 1956 the first report appeared on the behavior and opinions of Dutch voters, based on a nationwide survey. The research—at the time really modern—was set up on behalf of a national advisory committee on the electoral system and on legal regulations for political parties.[48] One of the members of the committee was de Jong, a political scientist.

In the same year de Jong published a book that was based largely on a comparison of electoral and opinion data from a large number of countries.[49] The Dutch interest in electoral research was apparent also in Daudt's dissertation (1961) on floating voters and the floating vote: a critical analysis of American and English election studies.[50]

The political scientists from the Free University conducted a nationwide survey among voters in 1967.[51] In 1971, 1972, and 1977 there were again nationwide voting studies, but now under the leadership of a team of political scientists from all relevant Dutch universities. The day-to-day coordination was in the hands of researchers from the University of Amsterdam in 1971, from Nijmegen in 1972, and from Leyden and Tilburg in 1977. Each of those electoral studies was subsidized by the Dutch organization for the advancement of pure science.[52]

What is called electoral research here is in fact much more. The situation is more like this: data are collected on the occasion of the Second Chamber elections about a large number of important variables in relation to opinions, behavior, and positions of the Dutch electorate. The questionnaires are formulated so that the collected data, as far as possible, are comparable over the years and with other countries.

Each of the nationwide electoral studies resulted within a few months, sometimes even within a few weeks after election day, in a first publication, in which a number of important survey results were published.[53] Various topics were discussed such as the relationship between party choice and age, income, and religion and changes that occurred in those relationships, the correlation of various political opinions with party choice and different forms of political participation. After the first publications, the electoral studies led to a large number of other publications in professional periodicals but also as reports and dissertations. These publications concentrate on political participation, political opinions, and voting behavior. Examples are the report of Irwin and Molleman (1972) on *Political Participation in the Netherlands*,[54] the dissertation of van der Maesen (1974) on participation and democracy[55] and a report by Daemen (1978) on political culture in the Netherlands.[56] Besides the voting studies, there is a dissertation of Jacqueline Schokking (1958), an early Dutch study in the area of political participation, on women in Dutch politics.[57] A Dutch dissertation on political opinions is the one by the social psychologist Middendorp, entitled *Progressivism and Conservatism: The Fundamental Dimensions of Ideological Controversy and Their Relationship to Social Class*.[58]

Political Parties

As to political parties, Dutch political science has mainly studied their history, their institutional structure, and their programs.[59]

Initially, the history of political parties was studied by historians and lawyers.[60] Often the description was integrated with reflections on a (considered) desirable development. An example is the book by Couwenberg (1960) on the Dutch party system and the future[61] and that by Verkade on *Democratic Parties in the Low Countries and Germany*.[62]

Van der Land, a political scientist, published in 1962 a dissertation on the foundation of the Pacifist Socialist party.[63] In 1973 a study and documentation center for Dutch political parties was set up in Groningen, with support from the Dutch organization for the advancement of pure science. In this setting, Lipschits (1977) published an introduction to the history of the Dutch political parties[64] and a study on the Protestant-Christian current up to 1940.[65]

Besides the (parliamentary) history of the political parties, their institutional structure, as seen through their statutes, has also been studied in a systematic-comparative way by, among others, de Jong (1951)[66] and Lipschits (1965/66).[67] A systematic-comparative analysis of party programs is attempted by de Bruyn (1971),[68] among others. Waltmans wrote on Dutch political parties and national thought in 1962.[69]

As we have seen in the preceding section, the opinions, behavior, and social positions of voters were the object of research repeatedly. Something similar also applies to the members of parliament as we shall see in the next section. The opinions and behavior of those who are active in the party organization, however, have so far hardly been studied in the Netherlands. This is even more remarkable, when one realizes that a start in this direction was made by prepolitical scientists like Bonger (1934) and Kranenburg (1956).[70]

Parliament

In the Netherlands, the study of parliamentary history is predominantly practiced by historians and lawyers. The research on the history of governmental institutions in a broader sense has, among other works, resulted in a dissertation of Cramer (1958) on parliament and press in relation to the government[71] and a study by the jurist Duynstee on cabinet formation.[72]

So far political scientists have been busy mainly with the opinions and behavior of members of parliament, insofar as these can be learned by means of a questionnaire among members of parliament. Daalder (1975) edited a reader on parliament and political decision-making in the Netherlands.[73] Van Schendelen (1975) wrote his dissertation on parliamentary information, decision-making, and representation.[74] Besides this, he has published, together with Rosenthal and Scholten, various smaller studies on parliamentary opinion and behavior.[75] Thomassen (1976) published a dissertation in which the distance between voters and representatives was studied empirically, based on a comparison of data from surveys among voters as well as among members of parliament.[76] Kooiman (1976) came out with a book of a more general nature, based on questionnaires among members of the Second Chamber in 1968 and in 1972.[77] Various more formal institutional studies on the Dutch parliament have appeared both from political science and from the legal side.[78]

Politically Active Interest Groups

In 1959 a predominantly theoretical publication appeared, to which also political scientists contributed, on the influence of organized groups in social and political life.[79] Two years later the New Zealander Robinson received his Ph.D. from the Free University in Amsterdam with a dissertation on *Dutch Organized Agriculture in International Politics*.[80] The European Institute at the University of Amsterdam published a report on pressure groups in the European Economic Community in 1965.[81] After that the focus of research on pressure groups shifted somewhat to the influence and effectiveness of groups. In 1971 two reports appeared in which the central question was the degree to which an action group reaches its goals.[82]

In 1973 the sociologist Braam completed a dissertation on the influence of business on government, in which he measured this influence in an original way.[83] Two years later a book by the political scientists Mokken and Stokman et al. (1975) appeared, in which they attempted to measure the economic and political power of enterprises, based on an original use of the position method.[84] Braam started from the perception of problems and attempts at influence of companies and tried then to determine to what extent the enterprises achieved their goals in the sphere of government. Mokken et al. took as a starting point the position of business directors and managers and determined to what extent accumulation of positions occurred to certain people and thereby also to certain companies. The old methodological discussion between the decision approach and the position approach in the measurement of power and influence was stimulated anew through these publications.[85]

The research on political parties, parliament, and interest groups can, at least partially, be characterized as research on certain aspects of political elites. Besides this, there is more elite research in the Netherlands. Thus, there is among others, a study done by Kooiman and others on the relationship between political leaders and top civil servants.[86]

Provincial and Local Politics

Dutch political scientists have done practically no research on the politics of the eleven provinces so far.[87] However, on the occasion of the elections of the Provincial Estates, questionnaires were given to voters within the framework of political representation research.[88]

More research has been done regarding local politics. In the first place, the distance between citizens and city governments was measured in one town by means of oral questionnaires among citizens, municipal council members, and civil servants.[89] In Leyden, a study was set up on the political relationships in municipalities. Data were gathered from three sources: an oral survey in 1971 and 1972 of a sample of the population and of the mayors, two aldermen, and two councillors in each of 79 Dutch cities; statistical material from all Dutch municipalities (census data since 1880 and the political color of councilors and aldermen in 1962, 1966, and 1970); and data on all mayors on January 1 of the years 1930, 1950, and 1970.

Part of the material has been published in two reports. A book by Morlan (1974), an American political scientist, deals with the opinions of citizens and members of the city government in 79 municipalities, among other things, on the mayor, the composition of the committee of mayor and alderman, and the relationship between voters and representatives.[90] A report by Daalder and others (1974) contains data on city council elections in 1970 in all (then) 872 Dutch municipalities, among other things, distributed by degree of urbanization.[91] The data include the participating parties, the voter turnout, the political color of the municipal councils and of the aldermen, and a short historical survey of the political balances of the city council elections since 1931. Dittrich wrote a dissertation on relations among parties in Dutch municipalities.[92]

Comparative research on local public policy, attempting to explain characteristics of the local community, has been started recently by political scientists in the Department of Public Administration in Enschede. This is done partially with financial support from the Ministry of Interior.

COMPARATIVE POLITICAL SCIENCE

A predecessor of students of comparative political science in the Netherlands was the constitutional law scholar Kranenburg, with his books on general public law and on comparative constitutional law, in which political phenomena received much attention also.[93] A beginning to comparative political science was given by de Jong in 1951 with his dissertation on political organization in Western Europe after 1800.[94] Here, according to the institutional country-by-country approach, changes in the political systems of Great Britain, France, Belgium, and the Netherlands since 1800 were dealt with. The author discussed among other things, suffrage, politically active interest groups, political parties, the parliament, the cabinet, and the position of the head of state, all in relation to each other. In his following book (1956) de Jong compared electoral and public opinion data from various European countries.[95]

In 1960 Daalder's dissertation on organization and reorganization of the British cabinet since 1914 appeared.[96] In the 1960s the study of comparative political science in the Netherlands was limited mainly to articles by Daalder and Lijphart.[97] Lijphart's typology of democratic political systems also had a lot of influence internationally. Starting from two criteria, namely the homogeneity or the fragmentation of the political culture on one hand and cooperative or competitive styles of political elites on the other, he arrived at a fourfold division of cartel, pacification, centripetal, and centrifugal democracies.[98] In 1977 Lijphart built his earlier studies on "consociational democracy" into an international comparative book on *Democracy in Plural Societies: A Comparative Exploration*.[99] It can be noted that the well-known Dutch fragmentation delivered an important Dutch contribution to comparative political science. Somewhat along the same line is the dissertation of de Swaan on *Coalition Theories and Cabinet Formation* (1973). As is well stated in the subtitle, this is "a study of formal theories of coalition formation applied to nine European parliaments after 1918."[100] The unique way in which a relationship between formal theories and empirical research is laid is especially interesting.

Comparative in nature and focusing on public policy, are the dissertations of Aquina (1974) on science policy in the Netherlands, the Federal Republic of Germany, and Great Britain, and of Slomp (1977) on agricultural policy in the Soviet Union and in China at the time of collectivization in each country.[102]

Research on Eastern Europe is, in the Netherlands, mainly done by Slavists and historians, and very little by political scientists. Besides the dissertation just mentioned, Kuypers's dissertation (1954) must be named in this connection. Kuypers, originally a lawyer, and later professor of political science, wrote this study on the Russian problem in the Soviet idea of the state.[103] In 1978 Jurrjens published a dissertation entitled *The Free Flow: People, Ideas and Information in Soviet Ideology and Politics*.[104]

Aspects of the problem of development are illustrated in the dissertations of van Niekerk (1972) on populism and political development in Latin American[105] and of Hoetjes (1977) on corruption in the public life in developing countries.[106]

INTERNATIONAL RELATIONS

Since the Dutch scholar Hugo Grotius wrote his *De jure belli ac pacis* in 1625, the study of international relations has been closely connected to the study of international public law and of political history. The first postwar professors of international relations were originally lawyers, like Tammes and van der Molen, or historians, like Vlekke. Lawyers and historians supported the Dutch Association for International Affairs and the periodical *International Spectator*, as well as *Oost-West* (East-West), later changed to *Civis Mundi*.

An authority in the field of international public law, Verzijl, published a book on the United Nations[107] in 1945. Tammes followed with a book on international organizations in 1951.[108] In both cases, the legal aspects were central. The approach of Vlekke was mainly historical. This is shown clearly in his 1948 book on the relationship between the United States and Western Europe and in his 1953 study on the bipolarization between Washington and Moscow.[109] Also within the framework of a historical approach the foreign policy of the Netherlands was studied. Well-known examples are the two-volume work of Smit on the history of Dutch foreign policy[110] and a study of van Campen, entitled *The Quest for Security: Some Aspects of Netherlands Foreign Policy 1945–1950*.[111]

Surveys of the study of international relations and of the authors' own views are given in orations by Vlekke (1956) on the study of international statecraft,[112] by Baehr (1966 and 1970) on education and research in international relations and the study of foreign policy,[113] by Lijphart (1969) on paradigms in international relations,[114] and by Tudyka (1972) on changes in the interests regarding the study of international relations.[115] Besides these, there are more detailed publications by Boasson (1963)[116] and Tudyka (1971)[117] then still working in Germany.

Also, some studies by political scientists with a historical approach deal with somewhat more limited subjects. Examples are the studies by Biegel (1954) on the Arab League,[118] by Sandberg (1959) on Germany as an object and subject in international politics,[119] by Lipschits (1962) on French politics from 1939–1941 in the Levant,[120] and by van Staden on NATO.[121]

A more behavioral approach can be found in a number of other publications. The Dutch political scientist Baehr received his Ph.D. from Georgetown University in Washington, D.C., in 1964 with a dissertation, partially based on roll call analysis, on *Dilemmas in United States Foreign Policy in the United Nations with Regard to Problems of National Self-Determination*.[122] In the same year, Valkenburgh, a sociologist and later professor of political science, received his Ph.D. with a dissertation on people in the cold war, in which survey data, besides other materials, were used.[123] In 1966 Lijphart, then still working in the United States, published his book on the

Dutch policy toward western New Guinea, entitled *The Trauma of Decolonization*.[124]

The Dutchman Letterie defended in 1971 a dissertation on individual competitive behavior as a function of attitudes, perceptions and pay-off conditions in an experiment with triads of subjects.[125]

In the same year, Lipschits published a more general book on simulations in international politics.[126] Later Baehr made a survey of the United Nations.[127] In 1977 appeared Stokman's dissertation on roll calls and sponsorship: a methodological analysis of Third World group formations in the United Nations.[128] A report on the Dutch foreign policy elite was also written by Baehr and others.[129]

The problems of European integration have received a lot of attention within the framework of the study of international relations. A series of publications on the organization and the policy of the European Community came from the John F. Kennedy Institute in Tilburg, under the leadership of the jurist Alting von Geusau.[130] De Vree received his Ph.D. in 1972 with a study about theory formation on political integration.[131]

A second focus of attention is the problem of peace and war. Röling, a lawyer, became initiator and leader of peace research in the Netherlands and of the Peace Research Institute in Groningen. From his hand appeared, among others, books on war and peace (1963) and on peace research.[132] The Study Center for Peace Research in Nijmegen produced a number of publications.[133]

A third subject, that has received attention in the last few years, is the role of multinational corporations and of trade unions in international politics.[134]

POLITICAL THEORY

Political science publications in the field of the history of political ideas are comparatively scarce in the Netherlands. For a long time Dutch students of political science had to get their knowledge of political theories from Plato to the present day to an important extent from foreign handbooks by Sabine, Theimer, Touchard, and others. Moreover, a Dutch translation of fragments of works of political thinkers from Plato to Roosevelt proved of good use for teaching.[135] Besides these, a reader edited by van der Land gave, among other things, a brief survey of the history of political theories.[136] In 1971, Vloemans, a philosopher, published a history of social and political philosophy.[137] Lastly, there appeared in 1977 an extensive book by Van Gunsteren and Lock, in which classical political theories, mainly since Machiavelli, are dealt with.[138]

However, these were preceded by publications of more limited scope. In 1946, a book by J. Suys on political principles appeared, regarding the problems of world government.[139] In 1952 Barents published a short introduction to the thinking of Machiavelli[140] and in 1958 a study entitled "Democracy: An Unagonized Reappraisal."[141] In 1964, Hoogerwerf's dissertation on Protestantism and progressiveness appeared, which analyzed opinions of Dutch Protestants on change and equality. It was based on written material from the beginning of the nineteenth century on one hand, and on a mass survey on the other.[142] Stassen received his Ph.D. in 1969 with a dissertation on the idea of democracy.[143] In the same year appeared a book by Lipschits on the Left and Right in politics.[144] In 1971 Sizoo came out with a dissertation on the political thinking of the Right.[145] Various studies from others than political scientists on political ideas have been published also.[146]

PUBLIC ADMINISTRATION

The position of public administration is seen in different ways in the Netherlands: as an independent science, as a subfield of political science, and as the whole of the sciences that together study public administration. In this section, as in the other sections, we shall limit ourselves as much as possible to political science publications on public administration. In so far as necessary for a coherent picture, nonpolitical science publications will be mentioned, too. In 1942 G. A. van Poelje, a lawyer, published the first general introduction to public administration.[147] It was strongly institutional and legal in nature. Brasz et al. followed in 1962 with an introduction to public administration.[148] Besides institutional elements, it contained more behavioral aspects. Its setup was multidisciplinary (sociological-legal-economic). The ecological approach in public administration stands central in this book. Hence, the political, legal, economic, sociocultural and other environments of public administration are treated amply. In connection with a study tour to the United States, Brasz published in 1964 a little book on the American study of public administration.[149]

In 1977, Rosenthal, van Schendelen, and Scholten, all political scientists, came out with an introduction to the study of public administration for which they also made use of other sciences. The three main subjects in this introduction are organization, policy, and political environment.[150]

Until now, Dutch public administration specialists have mainly been busy with research on the organization of public administration, but gradually they are paying more attention to the political environment and the decision-making process.

Aspects of the organization of public administration are, among others, described in the dissertations of the sociologist van Braam (1957) on civil servants and bureaucracy in the Netherlands,[151] of Brasz (1960) on municipal governments as an element of the Dutch system of social control,[152] of Leemans (1967) on the unity of government in large cities,[153] and of van Ruller (1972) on the problem of agglomerations[154]. Besides these, there can be mentioned, among other things, the research done by Kottman and others on coordination among departments.[155]

The political environment, and especially the relationship between government and citizens, was the central theme in a project of the Free University in Amsterdam. The collaboration between public administration specialists and social psychologists in this project led in 1974 to the publication of four books: Filet, on participation of citizens in public administration; Huismans and Siegerist, on what Dutch citizens think of the government; de Jong, on the organization and procedures of a couple of administrative organizations; and Smit, on the contacts between administrative organizations and individual citizens.[156] In connection with this, Faber's dissertation (1974) on mayors and democracy can be mentioned also.[157] Breunese (1976) made public administration research itself the object of study.[158] Studies on decision-making will be dealt with in the next sections.

POLICY STUDIES

Decision-making, besides organization, has been one of the central research objects in public administration for a long time. This can be seen in Dutch introductions to public administration and also in the dissertations of Scholten (1968) on the Socio-Economic Council and ministerial responsibility,[159] of Kooiman (1971) on governmental decision-making in San Francisco[160] of Klinkers on openness in government,[161] and of the sociologist Menting on the decision-making process at the top level of the post office.[162]

More frequently, especially since the last decade, and partially in connection with decision-making, the contents and effects of policy and the policy process have been studied systematically. This can be seen in the establishment of new periodicals. Since 1965 in the field of public finance the journal *Openbare Uitgaven* (Public Expenditures) has appeared. The committee for the development of policy analysis, set up by the Secretary of Finance, has published since 1972 *Beleidsanalyse* (Policy Analysis). Since 1972, the periodical *Beleid en Maatschappij* (Policy and Society) has appeared. Especially in this last journal, political scientists, besides economists, lawyers, and sociologists, take an active part.

In Dutch political science, interest in the study of public policy was present from the beginning. The policy concept takes a central place in Kuypers's description of the research object of political science. Moreover, in political science theory formation and research, he tries to think systematically in terms of means and goals (the so-called final approach). This appears not only in the terminology that he uses, among others, in his book on basic political concepts (1973), but also in the setup of the nationwide election study in 1967, which was partially led by him.[163]

The study of public policy also stands central in two books published by Hoogerwerf and others in 1972 and in 1978.[164] To a lesser degree this applies also to a book by van den Doel et al. on equality and inequality in the Netherlands.[165] In the introduction to the study of public administration by Rosenthal et al. (1977) policy and planning together form one of the three main parts.[166] Important aspects of public policy are also treated in the dissertations of Aquina (1974) on science policy in four countries;[167] of Snellen (1975) on approaches to strategy formulation;[168] of van Gunsteren (1976) on planning;[169] and of Ringeling on policy liberty of civil servants.[170] Systematic comparative research on municipal public policy has just been started by Dutch political scientists, although as early as 1956 an interesting dissertation on the structure of municipal expenditures was published by someone other than a political scientist.[171]

Political Science and Politics

THE INFLUENCE OF POLITICAL EVENTS
ON POLITICAL SCIENCE

World War II was a catalyst for establishing political science in the Netherlands. Other important factors, that had been operating already, were the growing volume of public policy and the increasing need of insight into possibilities to influence public policy. Barents refers to this, when he comments in his 1948 booklet, that political science can show the different possibilities regarding goals, ways, and means of the state on the one hand, and on the other, show which conditions must be met if there is to be a political democracy.[172]

People in political and administrative circles, at least at the Ministry of Education and Sciences, considered it important to establish political science departments. This is shown, among other things, by the support of the ministry in starting political science departments, regulating them in the Academic Statute of 1967, and establishing chairs of political science and its subfields. All Dutch universities, including the private ones, need the cooperation of the ministry for creating chairs. To appoint full and associate professors this cooperation is also necessary for state universities but not for private institutions. Initially, the University of Amsterdam needed also the agreement of the city council to appoint full and associate professors.

In 1947 political problems arose around the first appointments in the department of political and social sciences at the University of Amsterdam. Three nominations, presented by the city council of Amsterdam (Dr. J. Suys for political science, Dr. S. Kleerekoper for economics, and Dr. J. Presser for history) were refused by the secretary of education on formal grounds (a single nomination). It was generally assumed that the secretary of education, Dr. J. Gielen (Catholic People party) feared a leftist trend at the department of political and social sciences. When the matter came up a second time in the city council, the majority voted against Dr. Suys and in favor of Dr. J. Barents. In the end Barents was appointed, as well as the initially refused candidates for economics and history.[173]

In 1969 and thereafter, serious conflicts developed in the political science department at the University of Amsterdam and later also at other universities, especially at the Catholic University in Nijmegen. A number of professors and staff members were opposed by activist students and staff members, mostly of a Marxist persuasion. The activists demanded far-reaching influence—farther than the University Administration Reform Act of 1970 allows—for students on the contents of the curriculum, on procuring and prescribing literature, on appointing the members of the scientific staff, and on other decisions regarding teaching and research. Moreover, they demanded that their own political ideals be totally served by teaching and research. In connection with this, they primarily used political criteria for appointing staff, for procuring and prescribing literature, and for other decisions regarding teaching and research. A number of professors turned against these tendencies, since they saw this as an infringement on the scientific character and quality of teaching and research. This resulted in demonstrations, occupations of buildings, lecture strikes, appeals, court cases, long-lasting legal skirmishes, lots of headlines in the newspapers. On the outside, things seem to have slowly returned to normal, but tensions and conflicts still exist at various political science departments in the Netherlands. The unmistakable effect of the conflicts is that much valuable time for teaching and research has been lost. Since 1969 occupational mobility among Dutch professors of political science is according to Dutch standards extraordinarily high. Moreover, the reputation of political science seems to have been damaged by all the publicity on tensions and conflicts, which is felt in the labor market, too. Various publications discuss fully the course of the conflicts and their backgrounds.[174]

POLITICAL SCIENTISTS IN POLITICS

Through the years, as far as is known, about one-third to two-thirds of the Dutch political science graduates have been working in politics. More than once, political science professors have sat on committees to advise the government. Several Dutch political scientists have been members of the cabinet or of parliament. In this respect, one can even talk about the overrepresentation of political scientists—at least compared with the number of political scientists—among university graduates.[175]

From table 20.1 it can be seen that political science graduates are mainly employed in three areas: the machinery of government, various other politically active groups, and education. Initially, about one-third of the graduates went into each of these three fields. Slowly it seems, proportionally fewer political scientists than before work for the government and more for other politically active groups. Within the category of education, university education is losing ground to secondary education.

The fact that political scientists are spreading more evenly over the various branches than before, can on the one hand be interpreted as positive. It can mean that certain jobs, such as in secondary education and in politically active groups, are more open to political scientists than before. However, more negative interpretations are possible, too. For example: the professional identity may have become less clear. Government and university education have comparatively less professional attraction for political scientists than before. The growth of staffs in university education is stagnating, even when there is an increase in the number of students. Probably, partially due to the conflicts between Marxists and others in political science, the government is less willing than before to appoint political scientists.

The manifest demand for political scientists is still very limited in the Dutch labor market. An analysis of personnel want ads for governmental and private organizations (except for trade and industry) for graduate level and comparable functions in the first half year of 1977 revealed that only 1 percent of the 1,095 cases asked for a political scientist and also 1 percent asked for a public administration graduate. For economics, this was 23 percent and for law 31 percent. Opposite this, the latent demand for political scientists and public administration graduates can be called large, if one assumes that political scientists and public administration graduates are qualified for policy functions. Fully half of the examined advertisements referred directly or indirectly to a policy functionary and, especially, policy preparation was mentioned.[176] The job for the future shall be to turn the latent into a more manifest demand for political scientists and public administration graduates.

DUTCH GOVERNMENT AND POLITICAL SCIENCE

There is practically no interference from the Dutch government with the content of political science teaching.

Table 20.1 Positions Held by Dutch Political Science Graduates

NATURE OF POSITION	1967	1969	1972	1973
Education:				
University education	23.0	27.1	26.2	17.4
Secondary education	4.3	1.2	3.8	14.7
Subtotal:	27.3	28.3	30.0	32.1
Government:				
National government	19.0	17.5	17.2	10.9
City, province, corporate bodies, etc.	7.1	7.8	7.8	9.8
International and supranational organizations	4.8	5.3	4.0	1.1
Subtotal:	30.9	30.6	29.0	21.8
Politically Active Groups:				
Trade and commerce	11.1	13.3	9.9	7.7
Press, radio and TV	6.3	3.6	3.4	4.3
Nonuniversity research institutes	4.0	3.0	2.5	3.3
Employers organizations and trade unions	2.4	2.4	0.9	1.1
Research bureaus of political parties	2.4	1.8	1.2	—
Social work	1.6	1.2	1.2	1.1
Member, Second Chamber	—	1.2	0.6	—
Private institutions, societies, foundations, etc.	—	—	5.0	14.1
Subtotal:	27.8	26.5	25.7	31.8
Other:				
(without vocation, housewife, military, service, died, postgraduate studies, unknown)	14.0	14.7	15.3	14.3
Total in percent	100%	100%	100%	100%
Total number	126	166	321	458*

SOURCES: *Acta Politica* 2, no. 3 (1966/67): 245; ibid. 4, no. 4 (July 1969): 484; ibid. 7, no. 3 (July 1972): 364; ibid. 10, no. 1 (January 1975): 59.

*Sample N = 132.

The regulations in the Academic Statute, regarding political science departments, say nothing on the content of political science, as has been pointed out already. Indirectly though, the government does influence political science through not approving the creation of chairs, through the size of the university budget, through subsidies and contracts for research, and through not appointing political scientists to the civil service.

All Dutch universities, including private ones such as the Free University in Amsterdam and the Catholic University in Nijmegen, are funded 100 percent by the state. However, this generosity has its limits. The last few years, the government tried to halt the rising university expenditures. According to regulations and also in practice, moreover, the staff-student ratio in the social sciences, including political science, is considerably lower than in the natural, medical, and technical sciences.

Political science research in the Netherlands is financed almost totally through the government. This happens, in the first place, in the form of financing the personnel and material costs of the political science departments through the university budgets. Secondly, another flow of money comes through research contracts. The volume of this source, though, is very limited since governmental agencies contract for political scientists only occasionally. For public administration specialists, this situation is somewhat more favorable. Thirdly, the government also gives subsidies for political science research. This occurs through the Dutch organization for the advancement of pure research (ZWO). Without the support of this organization, a number of important political science research projects could not have been undertaken. The volume of this support however, leaves much to be desired. Of the total support given by ZWO in the years 1971-1975, never more than 5.7 percent has gone to all of the social sciences (law, economics, sociology, psychology, political science, history, and others). About three-fourths went to the natural sciences, of which astronomy alone received each year more than all of the social sciences together.[177] Until now, Dutch political science has always received less, and mostly much less, than 1 million florins in subsidies annually. Political scientists have tried to increase this amount by, among other things, stimulating the quality and quantity of subsidy requests via the *Nederlandse Stichting voor Politicologisch Onderzoek* (Dutch Foundation for Political Science Research), established in 1975. This private foundation has set out to promote political science research in the Netherlands. In early 1979 the name was changed to the Dutch Foundation for Research in Politics and Public Administration (*Nederlandse Stichting voor Wetenschappelijk onderzoek inzake politiek en openbaar bestuur*).

Balance and Perspectives

During the thirty years in which political science in the Netherlands has existed as an independent branch of science, there has been unmistakably major advancement in knowledge and insight. Concept and theory formation on political phenomena have advanced. Methods and techniques to study political phenomena are known and used according to present-day standards of the social sciences. In all subfields of political science, important studies have been undertaken. The scientific knowledge of the Dutch political system, of political behavior, and of voter opinions, political parties, interest groups, parliament, and civil servants, that was almost nonexistent in 1945, has grown considerably since then. The international literature, mainly in English, has been made accessible for the Netherlands. The number of Dutch political science books, nil in 1948, has grown in the last thirty years to about 200 and the number of political science articles in periodicals to several hundred. The personnel potential of Dutch political science has increased from almost nothing in 1945 to about 25 full and associate professors and several scores of staff members, spread over 9 universities. The number of graduates increased to about 900 and the number of political science students to about 1,800.

Still, there is much to be desired. Seen from a political science point of view, the political map of the Netherlands is still a white area with only a few dashes. Political science knowledge is fragmented. There is more analysis than synthesis. A policy is lacking for stimulating accumulative work through trend reports, review articles, surveys, coherent research programs, division of tasks, and research coordination among the various universities. Not only as a result of a shortage of manpower and of synthesis-directed activity, but also as a result of a shortage of scientific knowledge, there is still not one political science book that gives a good, up-to-date survey of the Dutch political system and its parts. There are no separate books that, based on empirical research, give a current survey of Dutch political culture, electoral behavior, political parties, interest groups, parliament, governmental bureaucracy, cabinet formation, Dutch public policy, political division of power, municipal and provincial political systems, local and provincial public policy, the role of the Netherlands in international politics, and the changes that have come in all of this—to mention a few subjects that are each worth several books. Important and large areas of research (such as the contents, preparation, determination, execution, and effects of public policy) lie practically untouched from a political science point of view.

Financial support by the government for teaching and research in political science is much too limited, compared to the natural sciences. Moreover, the government rarely asks for a political scientist in its job openings. The idea that one can deal with political phenomena with only intuitive reasoning and not with empirical scientific knowledge is still spread widely in the Netherlands, including governmental circles.

If Dutch political science wants to take the place that is due to it in the interest of science and of Dutch society, it must demonstrate, more than now, that it deserves this. Not only should more financial and personal resources be made available to teaching and research, but also the circle of political scientists should make higher demands on them. Political science efforts should, more than so far, be directed to teaching and research and less to administrative tasks and conflicts among themselves. With combined efforts Dutch political scientists should strive to extend the financial possibilities for teaching and research and publications, and to improve the position of political scientists in the labor market. The road to further development and recognition of Dutch political science seems to be difficult, but, seeing what has been accomplished during the last thirty years, it is not impossible.

Notes

1. J. V. Rijpperda Wierdsma and G. A. Hintzen, "Political Science in the Netherlands," in *Contemporary Political Science: A Survey of Methods, Research and Teaching* (Paris: UNESCO, 1950), pp. 280-93.

2. The first teacher of political science was J. Suys. See his *De rechten van de mens* (Amsterdam, 1977) and *Politiek en vrede* (Arnhem, 1955).

3. Article 110 and 111 of the Academic Statute.

4. Article 22 quinquies and article 22 sexies of the Academic Statute.

5. Data from *Acta Politica* (July 1969): 484; (July 1972): 364; (January 1975): 59. For 1978, information from the administrations of the universities. I thank them for procuring these and other relevant data.

6. This survey builds upon, among others, J. Barents, *Political Science in Holland* (Paper delivered at the seventh round table of the International Political Science Association, 1959);

bibliographies in *Acta Politica;* publications mentioned in this chapter with their bibliographies.

7. See, e.g., J. J. de Jong, *Wetenschap en politiek* (Utrecht, 1953), p. 11 and H. Daudt, *Enige recente ontwikkelingen in de wetenschap der politiek* (Leiden, 1963), pp. 6, 26.

8. J. Barents, *De wetenschap der politiek: Een terreinverkenning* (The Hague, 1953), pp. 25, 26.

9. J. Barents, *Political Science in Western Europe: A Trend Report* (London, 1961).

10. J. J. de Jong, *Politicologie: Een syllabus en studiewijzer* (Amsterdam, 1958), pp. 10, 11.

11. L. van der Land, ed., *Repertorium van de sociale wetenschappen, deel I, Politiek* (Amsterdam, Brussels, 1958). Cf. J. Niezing, *Inleiding tot de politieke sociologie* (Assen, 1966) and *Massamedia en politiek: Vierentwintig essays ter nagedachtenis aan prof. mr. L.G.A. Schlichting* (Utrecht, 1968).

12. Daudt, *Enige recente ontwikkelingen,* pp. 6, 16.

13. P. Valkenburgh, *Inleiding tot de politicologie: Problemen van maatschappij en macht* (Amsterdam, 1968), p. 5.

14. A. Hoogerwerf, *Politicologie: Begrippen en problemen* (Alphen aan den Rijn, 1972), p. 37; idem, *Politiek in beweging: Een bundel politicologische schetsen* (Alphen aan den Rijn, 1971); idem, ed., *Verkenningen in de politiek*, vols. 1, 2 (Alphen and den Rijn, 1976).

15. G. Kuypers, *Grondbegrippen van politiek* (Utrecht, Antwerp, 1973), pp. 18, 19.

16. Kurt P. Tudyka, *Kritische politikwissenschaft* (Stuttgart, 1973), pp. 23, 39.

17. M. P. C. M. van Schendelen, ed., *Kernthema's van de politicologie* (Meppel, Amsterdam, 1976).

18. J. Barents, *De taak der politieke wetenschap: verruiming van inzicht* (The Hague, 1948); C. W. van der Pot, *Handboek van het Nederlandse Staatsrecht*, ed. A. M. Donner, (Zwolle, 1977); S. W. Couwenberg, *De omstreden staat: Ontwikkeling en problematiek van de staatstheorie in de twintigste eeuw* (Alphen aan den Rijn, 1974); R. J. B. Bergamin et al., *De cultuurstaat* (Deventer, 1976); S. Stuurman, *De theorie van de staat en het ontstaan van de EEG* (Amsterdam, 1975); idem, *Kapitalisme en burgerlijke staat: Een inleiding in de Marxistische politieke theorie* (Amsterdam, 1978).

19. Valkenburgh, *Inleiding tot de politicologie.*

20. P. Valkenburgh, *Anatomie van het conflict: Een modeltheoretische benadering* (Alphen aan den Rijn, 1969); see also R. Kroes, *Conflict en radicalisme* (Meppel, 1971); cf. Tudyka, *Kritische,* 1973.

21. J. K. de Vree, *Political Integration: The Formation of Theory and its Problems* (The Hague, 1972); idem, *Het stervensuur van Leviathan?* (Alphen aan den Rijn, 1974).

22. Kuypers, *Grondbegrippen.*

23. J. van den Doel, *Demokratie en welvaartstheorie: Een inleiding in nieuwe politieke economie* (Alphen aan den Rijn, 1975-1978).

24. R. J. in't Veld, *Meerderheidsstelsel en welvaartstheorie* (Leiden, 1975).

25. Herman R. van Gunsteren, *The Quest for Control: A Critique of the Rational-Central-Rule Approach in Public Affairs* (London, 1976).

26. U. Rosenthal, M. P. C. M. van Schendelen, and G. H. Scholten, *Openbaar bestuur: Organisatie, beleid en politieke omgeving* (Alphen aan den Rijn, 1977).

27. A. Hoogerwerf, ed., *Overheidsbeleid* (Alphen aan den Rijn, 1978).

28. J. van den Doel and A. Hoogerwerf, eds., *Gelijkheid en ongelijkheid in Nederland: Analyse en beleid* (Alphen aan den Rijn, 1975).

29. G. P. Noordzij, *Systeem en beleid* (Meppel, Amsterdam, 1977).

30. J. A. J. de Vries, *Belastingheffing in beweging: Een onderzoek van de resistentie en stabiliteit van het belastingpolitieke systeem in het bijzonder tegen de achtergrond van de Europese integratie* (1968).

31. U. Rosenthal, *Political Order: Rewards, Punishments and Political Stability* (Alphen aan den Rijn, 1978).

32. A. Hoogerwerf, *Verandering van politieke stelsels* (Alphen aan den Rijn, 1969).

33. *Kiezer en verkiezing: Verslag van een onderzoek met betrekking tot de verkiezing van 1956 in Nieuwer-Amstel voor de Tweede Kamer der Staten-Generaal* (Amsterdam, 1963).

34. David Easton, "Introduction: The Current Meaning of Behavioralism in Political Science," in James C. Charlesworth, ed., *The Limits of Behavioralism in Political Science* (Philadelphia, 1962), pp. 7, 8.

35. David Easton, "The New Revolution in Political Science," *Acta Politica* 5, no. 2 (January 1970) : 208-21.

36. Daudt, *Enige recente ontwikkeingen,* pp. 6, 7, 24, 25; idem, "Politicologie en politieke praktijk," in van Schendelen, *Kernthema's,* pp. 262-94.

37. R. J. Mokken, *A Theory and Procedure of Scale Analysis with Applications in Political Research* (Den Haag, 1970).

38. F. N. Stokman, *Roll Calls and Sponsorship: A Methodological Analysis of Third World Group Formation in the United Nations* (Leiden, 1977).

39. J. J. de Jong, *Politieke organisatie in West-Europa na 1800* (The Hague, 1951).

40. J. J. de Jong, "Politieke structuur sinds de bevrijding," in *Oosthoek's Encyclopedie* (Utrecht, 1955), 16:402-29.

41. S. W. Couwenberg, ed., *Problemen der democratie,* vol. 1 (Den Haag, 1965) and vol. 2 (Den Haag, 1967). See also H. A. Brasz, H. Daudt et al., *Democratic anno 1967: Werking en feilen van een systeem* (Meppel, 1967).

42. H. Daalder, *Leiding en lijdelijkheid in de Nederlandse Politiek* (Assen, 1964), idem, "Politici en politisering in Nederland," in H. Daalder, ed., *Polistisering en lijdelijkheid in de Nederlandse politiek* (Assen, 1974).

43. G. Kuypers, *Het politieke spel in Nederland: Diagnoses, remedies en een suggestie* (Meppel, 1967), pp. 38.

44. Arend Lijphart, *The Politics of Accommodation: Pluralism and Democracy in the Netherlands* (Berkeley, 1968 and 1975).

45. J. Th. J. van den Berg and H. A. A. Molleman, *Crisis in de Nederlandse politiek* (Alphen aan den Rijn, 1974), pp. 61, 62.

46. J. van Putten, *Demokratie in Nederland* (Utrecht, Antwerpen, 1975); idem, *Ontevredenheid over politiek* (Meppel, 1971).

47. *Kiezer en verkiezing.*

48. *De Nederlandse kiezer: Een onderzoek naar zijn gedragingen en opvattingen* (The Hague, 1956).
49. J. J. de Jong, *Overheid en onderdaan* (Wageningen, 1956).
50. H. Daudt, *Floating Voters and the Floating Vote: A Critical Analysis of American and English Election Studies* (Leiden, 1961).
51. *De Nederlandse kiezer in 1967* (Amsterdam, 1967); *Kiezen in 1967: Eindverslag van het nationaal kiezersonderzoek 1967* (Amsterdam, 1977).
52. *De Nederlandse kiezer '71* (Meppel, 1971); *De Nederlandse kiezer '72* (Alphen aan den Rijn, 1973); *De Nederlandse kiezer '73* (Alphen aan den Rijn, 1973); *De Nederlandse kiezer '77* (Voorschoten, 1977); *The Dutch Voter 1972-1973*, vols. 1 and 2 (Nijmegen, 1974); C. J. Wiebrens, G. A. Irwin, and J. Verhoef, *Vragen en vraagstellingen van de nationale kiezersonderzoekingen: Een evaluatie* (Leiden, 1976).
53. See note 52.
54. G. A. Irwin and H. A. A. Molleman, *Political Participation in the Netherlands* (Leiden, 1972); F. J. Heunks, *Aliënatie en stemgedrag* (Tilburg, 1973).
55. C. E. van der Maesen, *Participatie en democratie* (Amsterdam, 1974).
56. H. H. F. M. Daemen, *Burgerzin en politiek systeem* (Enschede, 1978).
57. J. C. Schokking, *De vrouw in de nederlandse politiek: Een inleidend onderzoek* (Assen, 1958); see also L. J. Gubbels, *Veranderingen in politieke betrokkenheid bij gehuwde vrouwen: Een exploratieve studie* (Nijmegen, 1977); idem, *Vrouwen en politiek: Een literatuurstudie* (Nijmegen, 1978).
58. C. P. Middendorp, *Progressiveness and Conservatism: The Fundamental Dimensions of Ideological Controversy and Their Relationship to Social Class* (The Hague, 1978).
59. A. E. Bronner and R. de Hoog, *Politieke voorkeur: Oordelen en beslissen* (Amsterdam, 1978); J. J. van Cuilenburg, *Lezer, krant en politiek* (Amsterdam, 1977); G. W. Noomen, *Beweren en motiveren* (Amsterdam, 1977).
60. I. Lipschits, "Geschiedschrijving over de Nederlandse politieke partijen: Reactie en aanvulling," in *Bijdragen en medelingen betreffende de geschiedenis der Nederlanden* (1976), 1, 3:455-88.
61. S. W. Couwenberg, *Het nederlandse Partijstelsel in toekomst perspectief* (Den Haag, 1960).
62. W. Verkade, *Democratic Parties in the Low Countries and Germany* (Leiden, 1965).
63. L. van der Land, *Het ontstaan van de Pacifistisch Socialistische Partij* (Amsterdam, 1962).
64. I. Lipschits, *Politieke stromingen in Nederland: Inleiding tot de geschiedenis van de Nederlandse politieke partijen* (Deventer, 1977).
65. I. Lipschits, *De protestants-christelijke stroming tot 1940* (Deventer, 1977); see also J. van Putten, *Vrijheid en welzijn, Over socialisme en de toekomst van onze samenleving* (Deventer, 1977); Bertus Boivin, Herman Hazelhoff, Bert Middel, and Bob Molenaar, *Opkomst, ontwikkeling en betekenis van Nieuw Links* (Deventer, 1978); J. Th. M. Bank, *Opkomst en ondergang van de Nederlandse volksbeweging* (Deventer, 1978).

66. de Jong, 1951, *Politieke organisatie;* H. Daalder, "Parties and Politics in the Netherlands," *Political Studies* 3 (1955): 1-16.
67. I. Lipschits, "Partijbestuur en fractie," *Acta Politica* 1, nos. 1-4 (1965/1966) :154-71; see also F. A. Hoogendijk, *Partijpropaganda in Nederland* (Amsterdam, Brussels 1971).
68. L. P. J. de Bruyn, *Partijkiezen: Systematischvergelijkende analyse van de partijprograms voor de Tweede Kamerverkiezingen 1971* (Alphen aan den Rijn, 1971).
69. H. J. G. Waltmans, *De Nederlandse politieke partijen en de nationale gedachte* (Sittard, 1962).
70. W. A. Bonger, *Problemen der demokratie: Een sociologische en psychologische studie* (Batavia: Groningen, 1934); R. Kranenburg, *Politieke organisatie en groepspsychologie* (Haarlem, 1956).
71. N. Cramer, *Parlement en pers in verhouding tot de overheid* (Leiden, 1958).
72. F. J. F. M. Duynstee, *De kabinetsformaties 1946-1965* (Deventer, 1966).
73. H. Daalder, ed., *Parlement en politieke besluitvorming in Nederland* (Alphen aan den Rijn, 1975); see also idem and S. Hubée-Boonzaaijer, "Sociale herkomst en politieke recrutering van Nederlandse Kamerleden in 1968," *Acta Politica* 5, no. 3 (April 1970) :292-333 and 5, no. 4 (July 1970 : 371-416; idem, *Kamers en Kamerleden* (Leiden, 1971); idem and Jerold G. Rusk, "Perceptions of Party in the Dutch Parliament," in Samuel Patterson and John C. Wahlke, eds., *Comparative Legislative Behavior; Frontier of Research* (New York, 1972), pp. 143-98; J. P. van der Geer and H. de Man, *Analysis of Responses to Issue Statements by Members of the Dutch Parliament 1972* (Leiden 1974); idem and J. P. van de Geer, "Partij-afstanden in de Tweede Kamer der Staten-Generaal," *Acta Politica* 12, no. 3 (July 1977) :289-345.
74. M. P. C. M. van Schendelen, *Parlementaire informatie, besluitvorming en vertegenwoordiging* (Rotterdam, 1975).
75. U. Rosenthal, M. P. C. M. van Schendelen and G. H. Scholten, *Ministers, Ambtenaren en Parlementariërs in Nederland* (Groningen, 1975); H. T. J. F. van Maarseveen and M. P. C. M. van Schendelen, *Proces van wetgeving: Een onderzoek naar de snelheid van wetgeving in Nederland, (1961-1970)* (Groningen, 1976); M. P. C. M. van Schendelen, *Terugtred van de wetgever* (Groningen, 1976).
76. J. J. A. Thomassen, *Kiezers en gekozenen in een representatieve demokratie* (Alphen aan den Rijn, 1976).
77. J. Kooiman, *Over de Kamer gesproken* (The Hague, 1976).
78. E. van Raalte, *Het Nederlandse parlement* (The Hague, 1974); cf. de Jong, *Politieke organisatie;* A. Vondeling, *Tweede Kamer: lam of leeuw?; Synopsis* (Leeuwarden, 1976).
79. J. J. de Jong et al., *Pressiegroepen* (Utrecht, 1959); J. Barents, ed., *Pers, propaganda en openbare mening* (Leiden, 1956).
80. A. D. Robinson, *Dutch Organized Agriculture in International Politics, 1945-1960* (The Hague, 1961).
81. *Pressiegroepen in de E. E. G.* (Deventer, 1965).
82. *Aktie en doeltreffendheid* (Nijmegen, 1971); W. Kok, C. Meyer, and G. van Ruiten, *Protest tegen Progil: Een on-*

derzoek naar de achtergronden en uitwerkingen van een protest (Groningen, 1971).

83. G. P. A. Braam, *Invloed van bedrijven op de overheid: Een empirische studie over de verdeling van maatschappelijke invloed* (Meppel, 1973). G. P. A. Braam et al., *Collectieve acties* (Meppel, 1976).

84. H. M. Helmers, R. J. Mokken, R. C. Plijter, and F. N. Stokman, *Graven naar macht: Op zoek naar de kern van de Nederlandse economie* (Amsterdam, 1975).

85. A. J. A. Felling, *Lokale macht en netwerken: Een methodologische terreinverkenning* (Alphen aan den Rijn, Brussels, 1974); idem, *Sociaal-netwerkanalyse* (Alphen aan den Rijn, Brussels, 1974); *Acta Politica* 8, no. 2 (April 1973).

86. S. J. Eldersveld, S. Hubée-Boonzaaijer, and J. Kooiman, "Het politieke process in de ogen van hoge ambtenaren en politici: Een eerste verkenning," in *Politisering van het openbaar bestuur* (Den Haag, 1974); *Elite en buitenlandse politiek in Nederland* (The Hague, 1978); D. Th. Kuiper, *De voormannen: Een sociaalwetenschappelijke studie over ideologie, konflikt en kerngroepvorming binnen de gereformeerde wereld in Nederland 1820-1930* (Meppel, 1972).

87. H. A. Brasz, *Toezicht op gemeentebesturen* (Alphen aan den Rijn, 1964).

88. Heunks, *Aliënatie;* and Thomassen, *Kiezers*.

89. *Burgers kijken naar hun gemeente* (Nijmegen, 1971).

90. R. L. Morlan, *Gemeentepolitiek in debat: Opvattingen van bestuurders en bevolking* (Alphen aan den Rijn, 1974).

91. H. Daalder, K. L. L. M. Dittrich, R. P. van den Helm and J. Verhoef, *Gemeentepolitiek in kaart gebracht* (Leiden, 1974).

92. K. L. L. M. Dittrich, *Partij-politieke verhoudingen in Nederlandse gemeenten: Een analyse van de gemeenteraadsverkiezingen 1962-1974* (Leiden, 1978).

93. R. Kranenburg, *Algemene Staatsleer* (Haarlem, 1955); idem, *Inleiding in de vergelijkende staatsrechtswetenschap* (Haarlem, 1955).

94. de Jong, *Politieke organisatie*.

95. J. J. de Jong, *Overheid en onderdaan* (Wageningen, 1956).

96. H. Daalder, *Organisatie en reorganisatie van de Britse regering 1914-1958* (Assen, 1960); idem, *Cabinet Reform in Britain, 1914-1963* (Stanford 1963 and Oxford 1964).

97. H. Daalder, "Parties, Elites, and Political Developments in Eastern Europe," in Joseph La Palombara and Myron Weiner, eds., *Political Parties and Political Development* (Princeton, 1966), pp. 43-77; idem, "On Building Consociational Nations: The Cases of the Netherlands and Switzerland," in S. N. Eisenstadt and Stein Rokkan, eds., *Building States and Nations* (Beverley Hills, 1973), 2: 14-31; Arend Lijphart, ed., *Politics in Europe: Comparisons and Interpretations* (Englewood Cliffs, N.J., 1969).

98. A. Lijphart, "Kentering in de Nederlandse politiek," *Acta Politica* 4, no. 3 (April 1969) : 231-47.

99. A. Lijphart, *Democracy in Plural Societies: A Comparative Exploration* (New Haven, 1977).

100. A. de Swaan, *Coalition Theories and Cabinet Formation: A Study of Formal Theories of Coalition Formation Applied to Nine European Parliaments after 1918* (Amsterdam, 1973).

101. H. J. Aquina, *Beleidswetenschap en wetenschapsbeleid: De ontwikkeling en de optimaliteit van het wetenschapsbeleid in Nederland, vergeleken met die in de Bondsrepubliek Duitsland en Groot-Brittanië* (Nijmegen, 1974); idem and A. Hoogerwerf, *Wetenschapsbeleid in opbouw* (Alphen aan den Rijn, 1971).

102. J. F. W. Slomp, *Het landbouwbeleid in de Sowjet-Unie en de volksrepubliek China ten tijde van de collectivisatie in beide landen* (Nijmegen, 1977).

103. G. Kuypers, *De Russische problematiek in het Sowjet-staatsbeeld* (Wageningen, 1954); M. J. Broekmeyer, *De arbeidersraad in Zuidslavië 1950-1966: Een hoofdstuk uit de bevrijding van de arbeid* (Meppel, 1968) and *Oost-Europastudies in Nederland: Inventarisatie en evaluatie, Rapport van de koördinatiecommissie Oost-Europa* (Amsterdam, 1974).

104. Rudolf Th. Jurrjens, *The Free Flow: People, Ideas and Information in Soviet Ideology and Politics* (Uithoorn, 1978).

105. A. E. van Niekerk, *Populisme en politieke ontwikkeling in Latijns Amerika* (Rotterdam, 1972); idem, *Populism and Political Development in Latin America* (Rotterdam, 1974).

106. B. J. S. Hoetjes, *Corruptie in het openbare leven van ontwikkelingslanden* (Leiden, 1977); A. Hoogerwerf, *Verandering van politieke stelsels* (Alphen aan den Rijn, 1969); Gerrit Huizer, *Peasant Rebellion in Latin America* (Harmondsworth, Middlesex, 1973); P. C. Verton, *Politieke dynamiek en dekolonisatie: De Nederlandse Antillen tussen autonomie en onafhankelijkheid* (Alphen aan den Rijn, 1977); W. F. Wertheim, *De Lange mars der emancipatie: Herziene druk van Evolutie en revolutie* (Amsterdam 1977).

107. J. H. W. Verzijl, *De nieuwe bond der Verenigde Naties* (Amsterdam, 1945).

108. A. J. P. Tammes, *Hoofdstukken van internationale organisatie* (The Hague, 1951).

109. B. H. M. Vlekke, *Amerika en wij* (Roermond, 1948); idem, *Tweespalt der wereldrijken; De tegenstelling tussen Oost en West in wezen en wording* (Haarlem, 1953).

110. C. Smit, *De buitenlandse politiek van Nederland*, 2 vols. (The Hague, 1946).

111. S. I. P. van Campen, *The Quest for Secruity: Some Aspects of Netherlands Foreign Policy 1945-1950* (The Hague, 1958); idem, *The Imperator: Consequences of Frustrated Expansion* (The Hague, 1978).

112. B. H. M. Vlekke, *Over de Studie der Internationale Staatkunde* (The Hague, 1956).

113. P. R. Baehr, *Onderwijs en onderzoek in de internationale betrekkingen* (Meppel, 1966); idem, *De studie van de buitenlandse politiek: Toegang tot de internationale betrekkingen* (Meppel, 1970).

114. A. Lijphart, *Paradigmata in de leer der internationale betrekkingen* (Amsterdam, 1969).

115. Kurt P. Tudyka, *Wandel des Erkenntnisinteresses an internationalen Beziehungen* (Nijmegen, 1972).

116. C. Boasson, *Approaches to the Study of International Relations* (Assen, 1963).

117. Kurt P. Tudyka, *Internationale Beziehungen: Eine Einführung* (Stuttgart, 1971).

118. L. C. Biegel, *De Arabische Liga: Een belangrijke phase in de strijd om de politieke eenheid in de Arabische wereld* (Amsterdam, 1954).

119. H. W. Sandberg, *Duitsland, 1945-1955, object en subject van internationale politiek* (Amsterdam, 1959); L. E. L. Sluimers, *De Brits-Russische entente van 31 augustus 1907 gezien als verwezenlijking van Bismarcks "cauchemar des coalitions"* (Amsterdam, 1957).

120. I. Lipschits, *La politique de la France à Levant 1939-1941* (Amsterdam, 1962).

121. A. van Staden, *Een trouwe bondgenoot, Nederland en het Antlantische Bondgenootschap (1960-1971)* (Baarn, 1974).

122. P. R. Baehr, *Dilemmas in United States Foreign Policy in the United Nations with Regard to Problems of National Self-Determination* (Washington, D.C., 1964).

123. P. Valkenburgh, *Mensen in de koude oorlog: Sociologische bijdrage tot de kennis van internationaal politieke conflictsituaties* (Meppel, 1964); idem, *Viergesprek over oorlog en vrede* (Arnhem, 1968).

124. Arend Lijphart, *The Trauma of Decolonization: The Dutch and West New Guinea* (New Haven, 1966).

125. J. W. Letterie, *Individual Competitive Behavior as a Function of Attitudes, Perceptions and Pay-off Conditions in an Experiment with Triads of Subjects* (University of North Carolina, microfilm).

126. I. Lipschits, *Simulaties in de internationale politiek* (Deventer, 1971).

127. P. R. Baehr, *De Verenigde Naties: Ideaal en werkelijkheid* (Utrecht, Antwerp, 1976).

128. F. N. Stokman, *Roll Calls and Sponsorship: A Methodological Analysis of Third World Group Formation in the United Nations* (Leiden, 1977).

129. P. R. Baehr et al., *Elite en buitenlandse politiek in Nederland* (The Hague, 1978).

130. F. A. M. Alting von Geusau, *European Organizations and Foreign Relations of States: A Comparative Analysis of Decision-Making* (Leiden, 1962); idem, *Beyond the European Community* (Leiden, 1969); idem, *European Perspectives on World Order* (Leiden, 1975).

131. de Vree, *Political Integration;* Kees van der Pijl, *Een Amerikaans plan voor Europa: Achtergronden van het ontstaan van de EEG* (Amsterdam, 1978); K. P. Tudyka, *Marktplatz Europa: Zur politischen Oekonomie der Europäischen Gemeinschaft* (Cologne; 1975).

132. B. V. A. Röling, *Over oorlog en vrede*, 1968; idem, *Polemologie: Inleiding tot de wetenschap van oorlog en vrede,* 3e druk, 1973, idem, *Volkenrecht en vrede* (Deventer, 1973); Fenna van den Burg et al., *Vrede en oorlog: Opstellen voor prof.mr. B. V. A. Röling* (Amsterdam 1977); Robert J. Akkerman, Peter J. van Krieken, and Charles O. Pannenborg, eds., *Declarations on Principles: A Quest for Universal Peace* (Leiden, 1977).

133. Graham Lock, *"Stalinism" as a Deviation from Class Struggle* (Nijmegen, 1976); W. K. Polder, *Internationalisering van de Koncernfinanciering* (Nijmegen, 1978); J. Roebroek, *Krisis en inflatie* (Nijmegen, 1978).

134. Tudyka, *Internationale;* idem, *Wandel;* idem, *Gesellschaftliche Interessen and auswärtige Beziehungen* (Nijmegen, 1978); idem et al., *Macht ohne Grenzen und grenzenlose Ohnmacht* (Frankfurt, 1978); S. Stuurman, *De theorie van de staat en het ontstaan van de E.E.G.* (Amsterdam, 1975).

135. M. Bodlaender, ed., *Politeia: Groote mannen over staat en maatschappij* (Amsterdam, Brussels, 1950), vol. 1, *Van Plato tot Kant*, vol. 2, *Van Napoleon tot Roosevelt*.

136. L. van der Land, ed., *Repertorium van de sociale wetenschappen* (Amsterdam, Brussels, 1958), vol. 1, Politiek.

137. A. Vloemans, *Politeia: Geschiedenis van de sociaal-politieke filosofie* (Den Haag, 1971).

138. Herman van Gunsteren and Grahame Lock, *Politieke theorieën* (Alphen aan den Rijn, 1977).

139. J. Suys, *De nieuwe politiek: Over politieke beginselen in dezen tijd* (Amsterdam, 1946).

140. J. Barents, *Inleiding tot het denken van Machiavelli* (Assen, 1952).

141. J. Barents, *Democracy: An Unagonized Reappraisal* (Den Haag, 1958); idem, *H. P. G. Quack: Zijn leven en werk* (Assen, 1959).

142. A. Hoogerwerf, *Protestantisme en progressiviteit; Een politicologisch onderzoek naar opvattingen van Nederlandse protestanten over verandering en gelijkheid* (Meppel, 1964).

143. J. L. Stassen, *Over democratie* (Rotterdam, 1971).

144. I. Lipschits, *Links en rechts in de politiek* (Meppel, 1969).

145. J. Sizoo, *Inzake rechts, Verkenning van een politieke gedachtenwereld* (Meppel, 1971); R. A. Roe, *Links en rechts in empirisch perspectief* (Amsterdam, 1975); J. van Putten, *Vrijheid en welzijn: Over socialisme en de toekomst van onze samenleving* (Deventer, 1977).

146. W. Banning, *Hedendaagse sociale bewegingen* (Arnhem, 1967); S. W. Couwenberg, *Modern socialisme: Achtergrond, ontwikkeling, perspectief* (Alphen and den Rijn, 1972); P. Kroes, *New Left—Nieuw Links—New Left* (Alphen aan den Rijn, 1975); Arthur Lehning, ed., *Michael Bakunin: Selected Writings* (New York, 1974); H. de Vos, *Geschiedenis van het socialisme in Nederland in het kader van zijn tijd*, 2 vols. (Baarn, 1976).

147. G. A. van Poelje, *Algemene inleiding tot de bestuurskunde* (Alphen aan den Rijn, 1942).

148. H. A. Brasz; A. Kleijn; J. in 't Veld; D. A. P. W. van der Ende, *Inleiding tot de bestuurswetenschap* (The Hague, 1975).

149. H. A. Brasz, *De studie van het openbaar bestuur* (Alphen aan den Rijn, 1964).

150. U. Rosenthal, M. P. C. M. van Schendelen, and G. H. Scholten, *Openbaar bestuur: organisatie, beleid en politieke omgeving* (Alphen aan den Rijn, 1977).

151. A. van Braam, *Ambtenaren en bureaucratie in Nederland* (Zeist, 1957).

152. H. A. Brasz, *Veranderingen in het Nederlandse communalisme: De gemeentebesturen als element in het stelsel van sociale beheersing* (Arnhem, 1960); idem, *Toezicht op*

gemeentebesturen, (Alphen aan den Rijn, 1964); idem, *De bestuurlijke organisatie van de Hoeksche Waard* (Amsterdam, 1968).

153. A. F. Leemans, *De eenheid in het bestuur van de grote stad* (The Hague, 1967); idem, *Changing Patterns of Local Government* (Den Haag, 1970).

154. H. van Ruller, *Agglomeratieproblematiek in Nederland* (Alphen aan den Rijn, 1972).

155. R. H. P. W. Kottman, *Coördinatie bij de centrale overheid* (Amsterdam, 1976); idem, *Succes- en faalfactoren bij commissies* (Amsterdam, 1978). Cf. *Onderzoek naar de bestuurlijke organisatie,* no. 1, Literatuur-rapport, Instituut voor Bestuurswetenschappen (Rijswijk, 1972) no. 2, Eindrapport (The Hague, 1975); *Bestuursorganisatie bij de kabinetsformatie 1971,* Rapport van de commissie interdepartementale taakverdeling en coördinatie (The Hague, 1971).

156. B. C. Filet, *Kortsluiting met de bureaucratie: Over participatiemogelijkheden van burgers bij het openbaar bestuur* (Alphen aan den Rijn, 1974); S. E. Huismans and E. Siegerist, *Burger en overheid: Een analyse van wat de Nederlandse burger vindt van de overheid* (Alphen aan den Rijn, 1974); L. de Jong, *Bestuur en publiek: Verslag en interpretatie van een onderzoek naar de organisatie en werkwijze van enkele lokale bestuursdiensten* (Alphen aan den Rijn, 1974); O. Smit, *Participatie in bestuurlijke besluitvorming: Verslag van een onderzoek naar het contact tussen bestuursorganisaties en individuele burgers* (Alphen aan den Rijn, 1974).

157. S. Faber, *Burgemeester en democratie* (Alphen aan den Rijn, 1974).

158. J. N. Breunese, *Bestuurskundig onderzoek* (Driebergen, 1976).

159. G. H. Scholten, *De Sociaal-economische raad en de ministeriële verantwoordelijkheid* (Meppel, 1968); idem, *Politiek en bestuur* (Alphen aan den Rijn, 1972).

160. J. Kooiman, *Besturen is beslissen: Besluitvorming bij de overheid in San Francisco* (Meppel, 1971).

161. L. E. M. Klinkers, *Openbaarheid van bestuur* (Den Haag, 1974).

162. C. L. Menting, ... *hij is in vergadering: Een sociaal-psychologische veldverkenning naar beslissingsprocessen in de top van een grote organisatie* (Deventer, 1976).

163. G. Kuypers, *Grondbegrippen van politiek* (Utrecht, Antwerpen, 1973); *De Nederlandse kiezer in 1967* (Amsterdam, 1967); *Kiezen in 1967: Eindverslag van het nationaal kiezersonderzoek 1967* (Amsterdam, 1977).

164. A. Hoogerwerf, ed., *Beleid belicht; Sociaalwetenschappelijke beleids-analyse, deel 1 en 2* (Alphen aan den Rijn, 1972; idem, ed., *Overheidsbeleid* (Alphen aan den Rijn, 1978).

165. J. van den Doel and A. Hoogerwerf, eds., *Gelijkheid en ongelijkheid in Nederland; Analyse en beleid* (Alphen aan den Rijn, 1975).

166. Rosenthal, van Schendelen, and Scholten, *Openbaar bestuur.* See also U. Rosenthal and G. H. Scholten, *Crisis en continuiteit: Economische zaken, de oliecrisis en andere turbulenties* (Alphen aan den Rijn, 1977).

167. Aquina, *Beleidswetenschap;* idem and A. Hoogerwerf, *Wetenschapsbeleid in opbouw: Een terreinverkenning* (Alphen aan den Rijn, 1971).

168. I. Th. Snellen, *Benaderingen in strategieformulering; Een bijdrage tot de beleidswetenschappen* (Alphen aan den Rijn, 1975); P. J. A. Idenburg, *Politieke strategie en tactiek* (Amsterdam, 1977), Joost Smiers, *Cultuur in Nederland 1945-1955; Meningen en beleid* (Nijmegen, 1977).

169. van Gunsteren, *Quest for Control.*

170. A. B. Ringeling, *Beleidsvrijheid van ambtenaren: Het spijtoptantenprobleem als illustratie van de activiteiten van ambtenaren bij de uitvoering van beleid* (Alphen aan den Rijn, 1978).

171. C. van den Berg, *De structuur van de gemeentelijke uitgaven* (Leiden, 1956). See also J. D. Hilferink, *Gemeentelijke investeringsbeslissingen* (Den Haag, 1974).

172. Barents, *De taak,* pp. 42, 43.

173. P. R. Baehr and G. H. Scholten, "Conflicten over de politicologie aan de Universiteit van Amsterdam: Een verzameling documenten," *Acta Politica* 8, no. 4 (October 1973): 370.

174. *Acta Politica* 8, no. 3 (October 1973); H. Daalder, "The Dutch Universities between the New Democracy and the New Management," *Minerva* 12 (2 April 1974): 221-57; Henry L. Mason, "Reflections on the Politicized University: 2. Triparity and Tripolarity in the Netherlands," *AAUP Bulletin* 60, no. 4 (December 1974) : 383-400, also published in *Wetenschap en Democratie* 3 (March 1975) : 209-30; Arend Lijphart, "Dutch Universities in the Seventies," *Newsletter* (International Council on the Future of the University) 4, no. 1 (November 1977) : 1-7; *Wetenschap en Democratie* 1 (September 1974) : 6-14; ibid. 4 (June 1975) : 255-70; ibid. 2, no. 1 (September 1975) : 46-50; ibid. 2, no. 4 (June 1976) : 271-74. For a Marxist view see Miklos Racz, *Universiteit en klassenstrijd* (Amsterdam, 1972).

175. G. van Benthem, van den Bergh, et al., Intellectuelen tussen macht en wetenschap (Amsterdam, 1973); Philip C. Bom, *Academocracy: American Scholarship and Statesmanship in the Sixties* (Amsterdam, 1976); A. Hoogerwerf, "Macht en onmacht van sociologen en politicologen," *Beleid en maatschappij* 1, no. 3 (March 1974) : 86-94; *Politicoloog, Beroepenmonografieën,* Directoraat-generaal voor de arbeidsvoorziening (The Hague, 1974).

176. Unpublished manuscript, Vakgroep Politicologie Onderafdeling der Bestuurskunde, THT, Enschede.

177. Nederlandse organisatie voor zuiver-wetenschappelijk onderzoek, *Jaarboek 1976* (The Hague, 1977), p. 42.

Selected Bibliography

BOOKS

Baehr, P. R. *Onderwijs en onderzoek in de internationale betrekkingen.* Meppel, 1966.

―――― and Scholten, G. H. "Conflicten over de politicologie aan de Universiteit van Amsterdam," *Acta Politica* 8, no. 41 (October 1973) : 370-516.

Barents, J. *Political Science in Western Europe: A Trend Report.* London, 1961.

Daalder, H. *Politisering en lijdelijkheid in de Nederlandse politiek.* Assen, 1974.

Daudt, H. *Enige recente ontwikkelingen in de wetenschap der politiek.* Leiden, 1963.

van Gusteren, Herman and Lock, Grahame. *Politieke theorieën.* Alphen aan den Rijn, 1977.

Hoogerwerf, A. *Politicologie: Begrippen en problemen.* Alphen aan den Rijn, 1972.

———. ed., *Overheidsbeleid.* Alphen aan den Rijn, 1978.

Kuypers, G. *Grondbegrippen van politiek.* Utrecht/Antwerp, 1973.

Lijphart, Arend. *The Politics of Accommodation: Pluralism and Democracy in the Netherlands.* Berkeley, 1968 and 1975.

Rijpperda Wierdsma, J. V. and Hintzen, G. A. "Political Science in the Netherlands." In *Contemporary Political Science: A Survey of Methods, Research, and Teaching.* Paris, 1950.

Rosenthal, U., van Schendelen, M. P. C. M., and Scholten, G. H., *Openbaar bestuur: organisatie, beleid en politieke omgeving.* Alphen aan den Rijn, 1977.

Valkenburgh, P. *Inleiding tot de politicologie: Problemen van maatschappij en macht.* Amsterdam, 1968.

van Schendelen, M. P. C. M., ed. *Kernthema's van de politicologie.* Meppel/Amsterdam, 1976.

Stuurman, S. *Kapitalisme en burgerlijke staat: Een inleiding in de marxistische politieke theorie.* Amsterdam, 1978.

JOURNALS

Acta Politica (Journal for Political Science)
Beleid en Maatschappij (Policy and Society)
Bestuurswetenschappen (Administrative Sciences)
Internationale Spectator (International Spectator)
Transactie (Journal for Peace Research)

21 NEW ZEALAND

RAY GOLDSTEIN and JOHN HALLIGAN

Introduction

New Zealand is an island nation, geographically isolated and small in area and population. These and other factors limit the scope for development of political science as a discipline. The country supports six universities—a relatively large number for its three million people—and five of them teach political science.

Political institutions and university traditions are English and Scottish in origin and New Zealand political science has retained an affinity with those countries. Nevertheless, frequent visits by and appointments of scholars from the United States (and, to a more limited extent, other countries as well) have contributed to the diversification of the field of study. Developments in American political science, while influential, have mingled with the stronger British tradition to produce the present mixed character of the discipline. Political science is also affected by factors internal to New Zealand, such as its intimate society, fairly homogeneous population, and the discipline's initially close links to the teaching of history.

For more than half its existence, political science in New Zealand was confined practically to one institution. A multiuniversity discipline has emerged only in the past twenty years. Its uneven evolution can be seen by examining the sequence of major events during this period. The first chair was established in 1938, the second chair twenty-five years later. A journal devoted to political science began to be published in 1948, but a professional association was not formed until 1974.

A decade of accelerated growth began in the 1960s. Departments more than doubled in size and course options multiplied. This eventually affected the discipline through a substantial increase in postgraduate research and greater communication and collaboration between members of different departments. This paper is the first to attempt an overview of these developments.

The State of Political Science in 1945

The end of World War II has often been described as a point when New Zealand assumed full nationhood. The modern two-party system was well established even if its incubation had occurred largely during the crises of depression and war. In 1940 the centenary of New Zealand (dating from her establishment as a crown colony of Great Britain in the nineteenth century) provided a fillip to national consciousness. Among the publications commissioned to celebrate this event was the first book that resembled in form a systematic study of politics as we know it today.[1] But in 1945 political science still did not exist as a discipline within the four largely autonomous colleges that comprised the University of New Zealand. The university's calendar included prescriptions for two courses in political science and single courses were offered for many years in at least two of the constituent colleges, but they were not taught by qualified political scientists.

Degrees had been awarded in political science as early as 1883, but not by departments of political science. Courses in political economy and political philosophy were offered first at Otago University College in 1871 and toward the end of the century at Christchurch and Auckland University Colleges, but under the auspices of other disciplines. This situation continued until the 1920s. James Hight became professor of history and political science at Canterbury University College in 1920, although the position was usually referred to as history "with" or "including" political science. A course entitled either history of political philosophy or political science was available at Auckland University College from about 1923 but was taught initially by professors of constitutional law and philosophy and later by members of the philosophy department. A diploma in public administration was also offered at Auckland in the 1930s, but derived mainly from the needs of local body officials and was a college rather than a departmental course.

It had been recognized as early as 1886 (by the then prime minister, Sir Robert Stout) that Wellington, as the seat of parliament, should have provision for the teaching of political science in its university college. Fifty years elapsed before action was taken to realize his vision. It eventually occurred in response to requests from the newly formed Institute of Public Administration for a course suitable for public servants. Recognition of the need to develop the relationship between the university and the public service led to the funding of the first specialist department in the discipline's history at the Victoria University College of Wellington. But the department's orientation was to reflect its origins, and to take the form of subjects encompassed by the term "public administration" and in particular its diploma program in public administration.

Prior to the appointment of a director, a strong case was made for expanding the role of the new department from that of educating public servants to the equally important function of educating the public.[2] These views may well have been influential because politics was taught in the department from the beginning and the first director took up his appointment in 1939 with the title of professor of political science. The first professional political scientist in New Zealand, Leslie Lipson, was an imaginative choice for an incipient discipline. As a graduate of Oxford and the University of Chicago, his training benefited from their different traditions. This was reflected in his research which combined analytical and historical approaches and encompassed political science and public administration.[3]

Courses had been in operation for a short period before being suspended until 1946 because of the war. During this period appointees to positions in the department had public administration backgrounds, particularly because the practice rapidly developed of recruiting talented public servants who had completed the postgraduate diploma of public administration. By the time of Lipson's departure for the United States in 1946, political science was established, but only at one institution in New Zealand, and no traditions or body of research existed.

The Evolution of Political Science since 1945

THE INTELLECTUAL STRUCTURE OF THE DISCIPLINE

Prior to the middle of the twentieth century the study of New Zealand politics was undertaken largely by travelers from overseas, or by historians who wrote from the point of view of their discipline. Both have remained as important sources of studies—overseas academics continue to make important contributions and history has been the progenitor of some political science departments and an important influence on many political scientists.

In the postwar years Victoria University College was the focus of developments in the discipline. Additions to the department's staff were increasingly political scientists, and eventually its title became the School of Political Science and Public Administration. An enterprising Political Science Society first produced the *Journal of Political Science* in 1948 and later the school assumed responsibility for its publication. As the only university with a department specializing in political science until the early 1960s (and because of its location in the capital city) it attracted overseas scholars. Little research emanated from elsewhere until political historians began to extend their interests to contemporary politics, and more than twenty years passed following Lipson's appointment before political science departments were established in the other universities.

The development of the discipline outside Wellington followed the dissolution of the University of New Zealand and reflected increased interest in the social sciences. A position in political science had been created in 1948 within the history department at Otago University, but the recruitment of additional staff with political science training did not occur until the early 1960s. Separate political science departments were eventually created at Canterbury in 1963, Auckland in 1964, and Otago in 1967.

These nascent departments received the imprint of the traditional affiliation of political science with history (and to a lesser extent with philosophy). The initial staff consisted mainly of members of the existing history departments. Two foundation chairs were filled by the appointment of members of the history departments of the same university (one of whom was also a specialist in political philosophy and the history of ideas). The third foundation chair was filled by an American political philosopher. The newest university, Waikato, opened in 1966 with courses in politics offered within the school of social sciences. The initial appointee became the first professor there in 1970.

At one stage it was thought that departmental traditions might emerge based on existing specialties, namely, political philosophy at Canterbury University, institutions and pressure groups at Victoria University, and parties and elections at Auckland University.[4] Because of growth and diversification these characterizations no longer apply to Auckland and Wellington. Political philosophy is now relatively more prominent at Otago while Canterbury is more concerned with empirical studies. Otherwise, it is difficult to discern any deliberate pattern of specialization.

THE TEACHING OF POLITICAL SCIENCE

Despite the relatively small number of departments teaching political science (or politics or political studies as it is termed by some departments), it is not easy to summarize the teaching programs. This is because a wide variety of courses are offered (many of which are unique to one university) and their development, in some cases, has been disjointed and discontinuous. However, some generalizations can be made regarding factors which have affected teaching programs. Following their initial establishment, growth in all departments but Victoria occurred in several stages: first, undergraduate courses were extended to all levels; second, course options were increased; and third, masters degree courses were introduced. Subsequent to these phases all departments experienced staff turnover and alteration of their teaching programs. The final stage was the acceptance of Ph.D. candidates by departments which occurred increasingly in the 1970s.

In 1979 the 5 political science departments had a total of 47 tenured teaching staff (Waikato 6, Otago 6, Canterbury 9, Auckland 10, Victoria 16, conducting approximately 106 undergraduate and 62 postgraduate courses. Bachelors, masters, and doctors degrees in political science are awarded by each of these universities, and advanced degrees in the cognate fields of public administration and international politics can be gained at Victoria University of Wellington. Several specialized degree programs exist (including a diploma in local government and administration at Auckland and a masters in public policy at Victoria). Courses of a political nature are also taught in the history department at Massey University (Palmerston North) and in the social studies departments of some of the 8 teachers colleges (most notably at Auckland and Christchurch), but these are not included in this discussion.

Notwithstanding its long history the School of Political Science and Public Administration at Victoria University of Wellington grew slowly following its prewar establishment until the general expansion of universities in the 1960s. From the beginning the school had offered a diploma course in public administration and as early as 1950 a full program of undergraduate and graduate courses. A Chair in Public Administration was created in 1966. At present the school is administered by an elected chairman, currently the first woman professor of political science in New Zealand. The teaching program consists of 2 first-year, 12 second-year, 22 third-year courses, and 23 courses for the one year honors degree programs in either political science, public administration, or international politics. In addition, the school contributes courses to the diploma in social work, the master of recreational administration, and to the faculty program for the master of public policy degree (the successor to the diploma in public administration), the only one of its kind in New Zealand. As the largest department, the school offers the widest range of courses in the country and has led the way in the fields of public administration, South Pacific, Asian, and international politics. Its proximity to the central institutions of government is reflected in many of the course offerings.

The Department of Political Science at the University of Canterbury (Christchurch) had, within two years of its establishment in 1963, developed a range of undergraduate and postgraduate courses. An initial emphasis on political philosophy has shifted under its second professor (and chairman) to empirical studies. The teaching program consists of a first-year introductory course, 5 second-year options, 6 third-year courses, and 12 postgraduate courses. The M.A. Honors program requires a combination of course work and a thesis; it is the only one in New Zealand to include a mandatory research-methods course and a statistics requirement. In addition, the department contributes courses to a faculty liberal arts program and has been associated with the university's journalism department. Its teaching program recently has been innovative in the areas of political sociology and political psychology.

The Department of Political Studies at the University of Auckland grew out of the History Department to become the second largest in New Zealand. Its location in the biggest metropolitan area has influenced both research and teaching. Several courses were pioneered there, including those on Maori and other minority groups, psephology, comparative urban politics, fascism and right-wing totalitarianism, and Australian politics. A more recent development has been its diploma course in local government administration, which remains unique in New Zealand. At present, the department is administered by its first professor, and the teaching program consists of 3 first-year, 7 second-year, 8 third-year, and 11 postgraduate courses. The M.A. and Honors program requires coursework or a combination of courses and a thesis. The department also teaches 5 undergraduate courses in the university's Asian politics program.

The Political Studies Department at the University of Otago (Dunedin) took over an existing program of undergraduate instruction from the History and Political Science Department and developed a range of courses at all levels. Presently there are 2 first-year, 6 second-year, 6 third-year and 10 fourth-year courses. Under the department's first professor, who presently administers the department, there has been an attempt to develop sequences in political philosophy, New Zealand politics, and international relations. Despite the department's small size, diverse course offerings exist including American, Commonwealth, and New Zealand politics, international relations, modern Chinese politics, politics of totalitarian states, selected political thinkers and problems of political philosophy, Marxism, Latin-American, Middle Eastern, and Eastern European politics and comparative government.

Since 1966 politics has been taught at Waikato University within the schools of Social Sciences and Humanities. This small and most recent politics faculty offers a teaching program consisting of 2 first-year, 7 second-year, and 10 third-year courses, as well as additional selected topics for the honors and masters programs. Three mainstreams are taught: comparative government, political sociology, and political theory. Despite the limitations imposed by staff size, a surprising range of courses exists, especially at more advanced levels (including international relations, public administration, public opinion, political sociology, politics of change, and politics of the Middle East and of the Asia/Pacific regions). Noteworthy is the inclusion of subjects on the fascist state, and normative questions related to dependent economies (including Latin America).

In summary, the five universities offer a fairly comprehensive range of courses among them. The first-year introductory courses at two institutions include comparisons of the political structure of two states (U.S.A. and USSR at Auckland; New Zealand and Japan at Canterbury), while the others emphasize political philosophy and New Zealand politics. The second-year offerings are more diffuse, but tend to include options on political philosophy (all five), politics in New Zealand, international relations, and comparative politics as well as particular area studies. Two have a scope and methods course, while Victoria runs several basic public administration courses. At the third-year level all offer courses on international relations, most on political philosophy, and the majority on research methods, while two have courses on political sociology, comparative politics, public administration, and public opinion. In addition, most teach more specific country-oriented courses.[5]

The range of postgraduate courses tends to reflect the research interests of the teaching staff. All departments presently teach courses on political theory and area studies (in particular, Asian states) while four do so on political sociology, international relations, and comparative politics. Other specialized courses are held at all universities, but the greatest number are at Victoria, which offers three separate postgraduate-degree programs in political science, public administration, and international politics.

Occasionally some rationalization of the teaching programs is suggested, but so far the specialization that does exist is influenced by local conditions and the orientations of departmental chairmen rather than by conscious collaboration. Auckland, located in the largest metropolitan area, has relatively more concern with problems of urban and minority group politics, while Victoria tends to center on administrative problems of central government and foreign affairs. During times of national economic growth rationalization of course structures is not encouraged, but if New Zealand continues in a state of restricted growth the pressures for coordinated specialization, particularly at the postgraduate level, may increase.

RESEARCH IN POLITICAL SCIENCE

The lack of agreement upon frameworks or classification schemes in the discipline is particularly relevant in New Zealand where some of the highly specialized areas of political science are not represented. Traditional areas such as public administration, international politics, political philosophy, and comparative government have firm roots. The term political sociology has attracted a measure of support as a focus for organizing research, as have for example, public policy and Marxist political economy. Otherwise it is more appropriate to write of tendencies (rather than traditions or schools) that have changed with the local growth of the discipline. In the first half of the postwar period research was more historical, descriptive, and institutional. With the expansion of the profession there has been greater diversity in conceptual, methodological, and theoretical interests.

Owing to editorial limitations on space and references this review of noteworthy contributions is restricted to book-length works on New Zealand politics. To assess them, conventional categories have been adopted where substantial studies exist and merit consideration. To do otherwise is to record the omissions rather than the accomplishments, and for that reason methodological developments are not given separate treatment. A number of important books in other fields, in particular political philosophy and contemporary area studies, are neglected, including several outstanding works by New Zealand political scientists.[6]

As mentioned above, the prehistory of the study of politics in New Zealand is based on the observations of visitors from Western Europe and resident historians. New Zealand's experiments in democracy and social legislation of the late nineteenth and early twentieth century attracted eminent scholars such as André Siegfried and Lord Bryce. Otherwise, historians, some with a constitutional or economic orientation, were the main academic observers of New Zealand politics until the 1950s.

Following the introduction of political science as an autonomous university discipline, two books on New Zealand politics appeared. The first, a government publication by a journalist surveyed the main institutions of government and included the first analysis of the backgrounds of members of parliament and cabinet ministers.[7] In 1948, a substantial study of New Zealand government and politics, Lipson's *Politics of Equality,* was published by the University of Chicago Press. His method was to combine history with a contemporary analysis of the main aspects of the political system, including public administration.

The precedent set by Lipson was not followed by other studies of similar scope and depth. Almost fifteen years elapsed before another book was published on any aspect of New Zealand politics. The most singular lack in the short history of New Zealand political science has been a general text published in the postwar years corresponding either to L. F. Crisp's *Parliamentary Government of the Commonwealth of Australia* or to R. MacGregor Dawson's *The Government of Canada,* that has with successive editions been updated and is still in use today.

A paucity of secondary works on New Zealand politics has, until recently, impeded the writing of a successor to Lipson. In fact, no political science book on New Zealand has achieved a revised or second edition. Because of the small number of studies, research in a particular area is often significant by virtue of its very existence. It will stand without competitors until eventually it becomes outdated but not necessarily superseded.

The constitutional approach to New Zealand government was particularly influential in the 1950s but was related to the operation of the political system. Thus Scott's book, *The New Zealand Constitution,* combined an analysis of laws and practices.[8] The indefinite quality of a mainly unwritten constitution and its conventions and arguments for alternatives to certain aspects of the framework have encouraged intermittent debate. Issues such as a written constitution, a bill of rights, a second chamber, and the term of parliament have been considered by political scientists.[9] A current need is for research on issues that have emerged (or reemerged) during the 1970s, such as government action in breach of constitutional conventions.[10]

It is ironic that the House of Representatives (the existing lower house) has not been as well researched as bicameralism and the defunct upper house, the Legislative Council. The failure and abolition of the latter body in 1950 has received extensive treatment in Jackson's historical outline and analysis.[11] An examination of the role of the back-bench MP in the 1950s in relation to parliament as well as to the party and constituents[12] extended knowledge beyond groundwork laid in the 1940s.

Otherwise the legislature in New Zealand has been even more neglected by political scientists than elsewhere. An exception is Austin Mitchell's work which views parliament within the structure and processes of party government and draws particular attention to the importance of the party caucus within the parliamentary system.[13] The first book devoted to parliament for more than thirty years was recently published but was confined mainly to aspects of parliamentary reform.[14]

Political parties have held a central interest for political scientists. An apparently rigid two-party system, highly disciplined members of parliament, and the role of the caucus ensured the importance of parties in the political system, especially in the immediate postwar years. The formal descriptions of party organization and activities of the 1950s were incorporated into an important work by Milne that has remained the single comprehensive study.[15] The foci of research have been on the two major political parties; the more successful in gaining and retaining office, the National party, has been studied less than the Labour party. Recent research on the subject is contained in Levine's work.[16]

The triennial general elections in New Zealand have attracted more academic attention than any other subject. Initial commentaries on selected aspects of the event were superseded by the introduction of electoral surveys in 1957. There followed a succession of studies based on surveys of the 1960, 1963, and 1966 elections and the introduction of an ecological approach to electoral statistics. The most important of these was the collaborative publication on the 1960 election.[17]

The Nuffield studies of British elections have been more influential as models than American research such as that of the Survey Research Center at the University of Michigan. Similarities between the electoral contexts of Britain and New Zealand (plus the training of the authors concerned) fostered research which replicated British studies, including the significance of the "cube law," and more recently the utility of the concept of "swing."[18] Other studies have examined the relationship between class and voting, uniformity in electoral opinion between elections, and the floating voter.

Despite the "investment" in electoral research in New Zealand the return in terms of substantial published results has not been high. Mitchell observed in 1969 that because mistakes were repeated in successive voting surveys as a result of a lack of communication among departments, "this has precluded any concerted, coordinated inquiry into the New Zealand voter."[19] Other surveys have been conducted since (and the data from prior surveys reworked) but our knowledge of electoral behavior has not been advanced substantially. Only the 1960 and 1978[20] elections have received extensive analysis and no national electoral surveys have been undertaken by political scientists. A number of questions, such as political change in the electorate, require immediate attention. The impression remains that electoral studies are marking time; the promise of research undertaken has yet to be realized.

Interest in public opinion and attitude research is growing in New Zealand although this has not resulted in much sustained research. Systematic information about public opinion has been collected by private survey research organizations but only since 1968. No single university-based survey research center exists, although a proposal for one at Victoria University was under discussion from 1964 until 1978. A modified multiuniversity scheme was proposed at the 1977 conference of political science departments but no progress on it has been made. Recent publications include a selective outline of public opinion taken at the time of the 1975 election.[21]

A firm tradition of public administration was established by the first department of political science and by Lipson's study of 1948, but the number of academic positions in this subject has always been small and publications have tended to be addressed to the practitioners rather than to an academic audience. The New Zealand Institute of Public Administration has sponsored a journal that contains many useful examinations of aspects of public administration, and has published a series of publications entitled "Studies in Public Administration" based on its conferences. The latter have focused on such topics as welfare, local government, bureaucracy, and decentralization. The unevenness in quality of the institute's publications detract only partially from the contributions they have made to the understanding of the machinery of government.

The only general study of government administration was written by a highly rated administrator, who had participated also in the teaching program at Victoria University.[22] The work of Betts and Brookes remains the only case study of a city council, but the characteristics of the local government system have now been given a comprehensive treatment (Bush, 1980).[23] It is more difficult to appraise the contributions of political scientists to the reports of government enquiries such as the Royal Commission on the State Services in 1962. Two important departures from the conventional approaches have been written by American political scientists. A study of various dimensions of the work of executive-level administrators (Smith, 1974) introduced survey research methods to public administration.[24] A major recent publication investigates the transference to New Zealand of the office of ombudsman and its institutionalization in the political system.[25]

The dominant mode of analysis of New Zealand's foreign policy and involvement in international relations has been historical and has emphasized the country's isolation and colonial origins—in short, its dependence on Britain.[26] The first book on New Zealand's foreign policy by a political scientist was written by an American.[27] He challenged local interpretations by asserting that only the threat of external aggression caused the revision of New Zealand's policy of depending on Great Britain for its security. Although this analysis was later updated by others to include the greatly expanded relationship with the United States, only one general book by a political scientist in New Zealand has since been published, Richard Kennaway's *New Zealand Foreign Policy 1951-1971*.[28] Kennaway's analysis closely resembles that of a diplomatic historian or correspondent: it is topical, chronological, and largely nontheoretical (for example, a question not raised is whether process makes a difference for policy outcome).

A few other extensive studies concentrate on aspects such as Australian-New Zealand relations, the ANZUS alliance, external aid policy, or public opinion on foreign affairs. More limited research takes the form of numerous articles, conference papers, and postgraduate theses. The New Zealand Institute on International Affairs provides a useful outlet for nongovernmental analysis in the form of occasional books, pamphlets, collections of conference and seminar papers, and (since 1976) its own magazine. A similar, but more limited, service is provided by the annual foreign policy school held by the extension department of the University of Otago. Anthologies on politics in New Zealand contain little or no material on foreign policy or international relations.

Government publications on foreign affairs still provide the basic source of information for most assessments. The Ministry of Foreign Affairs publishes a quarterly official journal and has also issued in 1972 a collection of official documents for the period 1943-1957.[29] The historical publications section of the Department of Internal Affairs has produced several volumes on specific topics like New Zealand's relations with the United States and Japan prior to, including, and immediately following World War II.

Political science research on international relations and foreign policy remains limited, nonsystematized, nonquantitative, and largely noncumulative. Huge gaps exist in almost all areas, even within the still dominant focus on security studies, and the definitive analysis of foreign policy-making in New Zealand has yet to be written.[30]

Other dimensions of the political system have been partially researched. Political culture, the subject of impressionistic commentaries by visitors since the nineteenth century, has since received exploratory treatment based on systematic empirical research. Policymaking remains a familiar but largely unresearched process (although the performance of the third Labour government in some policy areas has been surveyed).[31] An initial approach has been made to the study of interest groups based on case studies.[32] The lack of a substantial study of the political role of the Maori and other Polynesian citizens may be accounted for by their relative political inactivity and the former's separate representation in parliament. Political change is one other topic in need of serious research although a general introduction is available.[33]

Austin Mitchell once criticized the tendency "to lag behind developments overseas and to reflect them mainly by imitation, applying the techniques to New Zealand but not developing them. There are implications also for political science today in the strictures of two sociologists who have concluded that political sociologists in New Zealand (and Australia)

have remained content with "intuitive" statements within the context of comparative studies with a strong historical and institutional bias. The few empirical studies that provide factual evidence are descriptive only, and do not concern themselves with the theoretical implications of their findings. The research is mostly conventional, and merely replicates studies conducted in Britain and the United States.[35]

A more pressing need is for research on the major aspects of the political system that is up-to-date and pertinent to contemporary problems of New Zealand society. Institutions such as cabinet, parliament, and the public service, and processes such as policy-making are sorely in need of systematic and continuing study.

Notice has been given of the maturation of the discipline by the broader range of publications now available on New Zealand politics.[36] The immediate future should produce a respectable range of significant studies if current research ambitions are fulfilled. The harbingers include the publication in 1979 of two introductory books on the political system.[37]

ASSOCIATIONAL ACTIVITIES

Associations. New Zealand political scientists have belonged to the Australasian Political Science Association (APSA) and continue to contribute to its conferences and journal, *Politics*. However, with the growth of the discipline it was felt that a local professional association was needed.[38]

The New Zealand Political Studies Association was formed in September 1974 at an interdepartmental political science conference held at Canterbury University, Christchurch. This meeting appointed interim officers and agreed that the association should produce a periodical newsletter and hold regular conferences, and the first issue of the association's *Newsletter* appeared in the summer of 1975. Subsequently, the constitution was approved and officers elected, including an editor of publications and local area coordinators in the university cities of New Zealand, two overseas coordinators in Australia, and one coordinator for teachers colleges.

Membership grew to approximately 300 in 1978, but currently it is around 150. Three successful conferences have been held (Wellington, May 1976, Auckland, August 1977, and Christchurch, May 1980), a membership directory published,[39] and a political economy section approved.

The association is funded solely by membership fees from individuals and a few institutions (mainly universities and libraries). This places serious constraints on its further development. To overcome some of these problems, informal arrangements have been made: one university department (currently Canterbury University) hosts the national office and provides free or subsidized secretarial and related services; some conferences are timed and located so as to coincide with the triennial interdepartmental meetings funded by the Vice-Chancellors' Committee; and the Newsletter, *POLS*, is printed at reduced cost by the host university's printing department. If the association is to develop into a soundly based organization it will have to consider other means of raising revenue and providing services on a more formal basis.

In addition to the above-mentioned activities, the association's constitution commits it to pursue inter alia the following objectives: sponsorship of public lectures, summer schools, and study groups; assistance to publications dealing with social or political questions; development of a political and social internship program; facilitation of faculty exchanges; development of a research institute for the study of political, economic, and social questions of interest to New Zealand; and cooperation and affiliation with other associations or societies having similar objectives.[40] These special activities either remain in the conception stage or are barely into infancy.

Journals and Special Publications. Perhaps the most important attempt to expand the association's activities is in the area of publications. At present, the only professional journal in the field published in New Zealand is *Political Science*. Since 1951 this scholarly publication has been produced in the School of Political Science and Public Administration at Victoria University of Wellington. Two issues appear per year and current priorities in order of preference are: politics in New Zealand, Australia, and the South Pacific, and Asia and the Pacific; but articles on other subjects are also published. The editorial advisory board consists of the heads or chairpersons of all five departments of political science in New Zealand universities. The New Zealand Political Studies Association has expressed interest in developing a closer relationship with the journal (possibly having it become the association's official journal), but to date this has not eventuated. A special publication series for the association has also been suggested and preliminary arrangements made to develop this, but at present commercial publishers provide the main outlet for lengthier works.

Other specialized journals and publications exist as well. The New Zealand Institute of Public Administration sponsored the twice-yearly *New Zealand Journal of Public Administration* from 1937 until 1978 when it was replaced by a more popularly styled and more frequently produced magazine called the *Public Sector*. The institute also regularly publishes monographs which usually are expanded versions of papers from its annual conferences. The New Zealand Institute of International Affairs publishes both books and pamphlets, and since 1976, an official journal, the bimonthly *New Zealand International Review*. *Local Authority Administration* is edited by a member of the Department of Political Studies at the University of Auckland. Occasionally, articles of interest to political scientists appear in local professional journals of other disciplines and in the journals published by student political studies societies such as *Politik* (later *Political Studies Monthly*) at Auckland and *Historical and Political Studies* at Otago. The life span of the latter publications is typically short, the quality rather uneven, and the circulation limited.

POLITICAL SCIENCE AND THE WORLD OF POLITICS

The Impact of Political Events on Political Science. The influence of political events on the discipline can be discerned from research on political science. The triennial elections for parliament in New Zealand have received the most constant attention by political scientists. Since the 1957 elections there has been increasing interest in case studies of particular electorates and of the general results. Discrete events are another source of studies. The election of a Labour government in 1972 and the promise of significant changes in New Zealand society encouraged research on the performance of the party in office. Another inducement has been legislation of an innovative nature or with far-reaching consequences. A good example is the Local Government Act of 1974 which if implemented would effect the greatest constitutional change in New Zealand since 1876. Trends in politics that appear significant for the political system are a third source of research. Recent examples include a decline in the institution of parliament, the growth of executive power, and the loss of confidence by the public in the institutions of government.

Political Scientists in Politics. Political scientists have not been prominent in the membership of political institutions; none have been elected to parliament but several have become members of councils of local authorities. It is more common for them to be involved in party organizations, although they usually have given their time to the Labour party rather than the National party, or have acted as unofficial advisors to these parties. Members of the profession frequently have been political commentators on radio and television, and this has occasionally resulted in criticism from party politicians at the highest level.

Relationships between Government and the Discipline. The relationship between the discipline and government takes many forms. Political scientists have been appointed to royal commissions and boards of inquiry or to the commissions of statutory bodies. Submissions to parliamentary select committees have regularly been made on bills that propose important changes in areas such as electoral reform, the parliamentary term, the reintroduction of a second chamber, a written constitution, and a bill of rights. Members of the profession also have been involved with the various royal commissions on parliamentary allowances and conditions and recently on such civil liberties subjects as public access to government information.

This relationship also has been fostered by numerous graduates in political science and public administration who are employed in the government service or in ancillary occupations (or who occasionally have entered public life). Courses such as the now defunct diploma of public administration and the current masters of public policy degree at Victoria University ensure that these contacts are maintained at a more advanced level. In addition, the links between the discipline and practitioners have been encouraged through the institutes of international affairs and public administration, organizations in which political scientists have held executive positions. A less visible link results from frequent lectures given by faculty to various government departments' training courses and to government-sponsored conferences.

The Present State and Future Prospects of Political Science

The discipline has entered a new phase of its development, the consequences of which are important yet difficult to discern. Owing largely to New Zealand's economic situation university departments that were previously preoccupied with expanding teaching programs and then with consolidation now face the possibility of retrenchments in staff positions. This may induce a reassessment of teaching programs, particularly at advanced levels, and lead to a better balance between the diverse range of courses available in each department and the overall requirements of the discipline.

The effects of economic restraints on research, however, are likely to be more negative than positive. Research funds for political scientists have always been limited (indeed research into social sciences generally in New Zealand has been poorly funded); and thus projects requiring expensive funding are even less likely to receive support. This could effectively preclude, for example, development of a national survey research facility or participation in international schemes for computer data analysis. Departments and individual scholars may find it even more difficult to acquire the services of research assistants, and the professional association will be hard pressed to expand its research activities as originally envisaged. Depending on the form which these restraints take, basic source materials could become less readily available, and international professional contacts (already tenuous) reduced.

As there are many areas of politics in New Zealand requiring substantial study, this prospect is serious indeed. Many fine scholarly works are written in New Zealand, but they have been less forthcoming on New Zealand. The question remains how the latter can be furthered in both quantity and quality. One hopeful sign is the manifest concern of departments to increase their offerings in the area of New Zealand politics, and to employ a growing number of New Zealanders with overseas education and experience (although women and Maoris, in particular, remain grossly underrepresented, for a variety of reasons).

In the face of a partial reemergence of the original factors that hindered the development of political science in New Zealand, a challenge is clearly presented. At the very least it should stimulate a period of serious self-examination, perhaps leading to the creation of new means of furthering excellence in both teaching and research.

Notes

1. L. Webb, *Government in New Zealand* (Wellington: Department of Internal Affairs, 1940).

2. J. C. Beaglehole, *A School of Political Studies* (Wellington: New Zealand Council for Educational Research, 1938).

3. L. Lipson, *The Politics of Equality* (Chicago: University of Chicago Press, 1948).

4. A. V. Mitchell, *People and Politics in New Zealand* (Christchurch: Whitcomb & Tombs, 1969), p. 7.

5. A useful listing of most political science courses taught in New Zealand universities in 1980 is contained in *POLS* 5 no. 2 (December 1980).

6. Much good research remains unpublished, usually as masters and doctoral theses. This material is not always accessible and therefore has been omitted. Information about political research in New Zealand is contained in *Political Science* 26, no. 1 (July 1974): 82–85 and in the *Newsletter* of the New Zealand Political Studies Association (currently titled *POLS*).

7. L. Webb, *Government in New Zealand* (Wellington: Department of Internal Affairs, 1940).

8. K. J. Scott, *The New Zealand Constitution* (London: Oxford University Press, 1962).

9. See, e.g., L. Cleveland and A. D. Robinson, eds., *Readings in New Zealand Government* (Wellington: Reed, 1972).

10. A relevant new work by a specialist in constitutional law is G. W. R. Palmer's *Unbridled Power: An Interpretation of New Zealand's Constitution and Government* (Wellington: Oxford University Press, 1979).

11. W. K. Jackson, *The New Zealand Legislative Council* (Dunedin: University of Otago Press, 1972).

12. R. N. Kelson, *The Private Member of Parliament and the Formation of Public Policy* (Toronto: University of Toronto Press, 1964).

13. Mitchell, *People and Politics*.

14. J. Marshall, ed., *The Reform of Parliament* (Wellington: New Zealand Institute of Public Administration, 1978).

15. R. S. Milne, *Political Parties in New Zealand* (London: Oxford University Press, 1966).

16. S. Levine, *Politics in New Zealand* (Sydney: George Allen and Unwin, 1978).

17. R. M. Chapman, W. K. Jackson, and A. V. Mitchell, *New Zealand Politics in Action* (London: Oxford University Press, 1962).

18. See, e.g., A. McRobie and N. S. Roberts, *Election '78: The 1977 Election Redistribution and the 1978 General Election in New Zealand* (Dunedin: John McIndoe, 1978).

19. Mitchell, *People and Politics*, p. 7.

20. H. Penniman, ed., *New Zealand at the Polls: The General Election of 1978* (Washington, D.C.: American Enterprise Institute for Public Policy Research, 1979).

21. S. Levine and A. Robinson, *The New Zealand Voter* (Wellington: Price Milburn, 1976).

22. R. J. Polaschek, *Government Administration in New Zealand* (Wellington: New Zealand Institute of Public Administration, 1958).

23. T. M. Betts, *Betts on Wellington: A City and Its Politics*, ed. R. H. Brookes (Wellington: Reed, 1970).

24. T. B. Smith, *The New Zealand Bureaucrat* (Wellington: Cheshire, 1974).

25. L. B. Hill, *The Model Ombudsman* (Princeton: Princeton University Press, 1976).

26. A prominent work by an historian is F. L. W. Wood's *New Zealand in the World* (Wellington: Department of Internal

Affairs, 1940). While emphasizing these and other traditional explanatory factors, Wood argues that the tendency to follow Great Britain did not preclude New Zealand from, on occasion, pursuing her own foreign policy. See also his later book, *Political and External Affairs* (Wellington: Department of Internal Affairs, 1958).

27. B. K. Gordon, *New Zealand Becomes a Pacific Power* (Chicago: University of Chicago Press, 1960).

28. R. Kennaway, *New Zealand Foreign Policy 1951–1971* (Wellington: Hicks Smith & Sons, 1972).

29. New Zealand Ministry of Foreign Affairs, *New Zealand Foreign Policy: Statements and Documents, 1943–1957* (Wellington: Government Printer, 1972).

30. An example of current efforts to fill these gaps is the collection in J. Henderson, W. K. Jackson, and R. Kennaway, eds., *Beyond New Zealand: The Foreign Policy of a Small State* (Auckland: Methuen, 1980).

31. R. Goldstein and R. Alley, *Labour in Power* (Wellington: Price Milburn, 1975).

32. L. Cleveland, *The Anatomy of Influence* (Wellington: Hicks Smith & Sons, 1972).

33. W. K. Jackson, *New Zealand: Politics of Change* (Wellington: Reed, 1973).

34. Mitchell, *People and Politics,* p. 8.

35. C. V. Baldcock and J. Lally, *Sociology in Australia and New Zealand: Theory and Methods* (Westport, Conn.: Greenwood Press, 1974).

36. See especially Levine, *Politics in New Zealand.*

37. L. Cleveland, *The Politics of Utopia: New Zealand and Its Government* (Wellington: Methuen, 1979) and S. Levine, *The New Zealand Political System* (Sydney: George Allen and Unwin, 1979).

38. Political scientists frequently participate in other professional conferences, including those on Asian studies, history, and sociology.

39. *Newsletter* 1, no. 3 (Spring 1975) and up-dated in *POLS* 6, 1 (1980).

40. In 1980, the New Zealand Political Studies Association became an associate member of the International Political Science Association.

Selected Bibliography

Betts, G. M. *Betts on Wellington: A City and Its Politics.* Edited by R. H. Brookes. Wellington: Reed, 1970.

Chapman, R. M.; Jackson, W. K.; and Mitchell, A. V. *New Zealand Politics in Action: The 1960 General Election.* London: Oxford University Press, 1962.

Cleveland, L. *The Anatomy of Influence: Pressure Groups and Politics in New Zealand.* Wellington: Hicks Smith & Sons, 1972.

Cleveland, L. *The Politics of Utopia: New Zealand and Its Government.* Wellington: Methuen, 1979.

Cleveland, L. and Robinson, A. D., eds. *Readings in New Zealand Government.* Wellington: Reed, 1972.

Goldstein, R. and Alley, R., eds. *Labour in Power: Promise and Performance.* Wellington: Price Milburn, 1975.

Gordon, B. K. *New Zealand Becomes a Pacific Power.* Chicago: University of Chicago Press, 1960.

Henderson, J.; Jackson, W. K.; and Kennaway, R., eds. *New Zealand Foreign Policy: A Reader.* Wellington: Methuen, 1979.

Hill, L. B. *The Model Ombudsman: Institutionalizing New Zealand's Democratic Experiment.* Princeton: Princeton University Press, 1976.

Jackson, W. K. *The New Zealand Legislative Council: A Study of the Establishment, Failure and Abolition of the Upper House.* Dunedin: University of Otago Press, 1972.

———. *New Zealand: Politics of Change.* Wellington: Reed, 1973.

Kelson, R. N. *The Private Member of Parliament and the Formation of Public Policy: A New Zealand Case Study.* Toronto: University of Toronto Press, 1964.

Kennaway, R. *New Zealand Foreign Policy 1951–1971.* Wellington: Hicks Smith & Sons, 1972.

Levine, S. *The New Zealand Political System.* Sydney: George Allen and Unwin, 1979.

———, ed. *Politics in New Zealand.* Sydney: George Allen and Unwin, 1978.

Levine, S. and Robinson, A. *The New Zealand Voter: A Survey of Public Opinion and Electoral Behaviour.* Wellington: Price Milburn, 1976.

Lipson, L. *The Politics of Equality.* Chicago: University of Chicago Press, 1948.

McRobie, A. and Roberts, N. S. *Election '78: The 1977 Election Redistribution and the 1978 General Election in New Zealand.* Dunedin: John McIndoe, 1978.

Marshall, J., ed. *The Reform of Parliament: Papers Presented in Memory of Dr. Alan Robinson.* Wellington: New Zealand Institute of Public Administration, 1978.

Milne, R. S. *Political Parties in New Zealand.* London: Oxford University Press, 1966.

Mitchell, A. V. *Government by Party: Parliament and Politics in New Zealand.* Christchurch: Whitcombe & Tombs, 1966.

———. *People and Politics in New Zealand.* Christchurch: Whitcombe & Tombs, 1969.

Penniman, H., ed. *New Zealand at the Polls: The General Election of 1978.* Washington, D.C.: American Enterprise Institute for Public Policy Research, 1979.

Polaschek, R. J. *Government Administration in New Zealand.* Wellington: New Zealand Institute of Public Administration, 1958.

Scott, K. J. *The New Zealand Constitution.* London: Oxford University Press, 1962.

Smith, T. B. *The New Zealand Bureaucrat.* Wellington: Cheshire, 1974.

NORWAY*

STEIN KUHNLE

Introduction

Norway cannot boast a long tradition of disciplined scholarship and teaching in the field of politics. Political science (*statsvitenskap*) did not exist as a subject before World War II, but was introduced at the University of Oslo—Norway's only university at the time—in 1947: the decisive initiative was taken by the great teacher of constitutional law, Professor Frede Castberg. The initial courses were taught by scholars trained in law and in history. It took some time before it was possible to establish a distinctive teaching position for the new subject; the first docent, Thomas Wyller, was appointed in 1957. The first regular chair was not established until the summer of 1965, and was held for a few years by Knut Dahl Jacobsen before he moved on to take the Chair of Public Administration at the University of Bergen.

The decisive thrust toward the development of a systematic discipline of politics had not come from the university, however. The bulk of the Norwegian work on politics had been done in independent academic research institutions without explicit teaching functions. Four of these still play a significant role in Norwegian political science:

— the Christian Michelsen Institute in Bergen, established in 1929, active in political research since 1938.
— the Institute for Social Research in Oslo, established in 1950, active in political research practically from the start and operating a distinct Division of Political Studies since 1955.
— the Norwegian Institute of Foreign Affairs, established in 1960, mainly active as a documentation and information center, but also engaged in long-term research in the field of international relations.
— the International Peace Research Institute, established in 1959 as a division within the Institute for Social Research but given independent status from January 1, 1966; active in a wide range of fields within the sociology of economic, cultural, ethnic, and national conflicts and responsible for a number of empirical studies of immediate interest to students of politics.

A fifth research institute, the *Polhøgda Foundation*, also established during the 1950s became an important center for research on the politics of the Arctic and the ocean by the late sixties.

The Evolution of Political Science since 1945

THE INTELLECTUAL STRUCTURE
OF THE DISCIPLINE

Until 1967, only one political science department existed: in Oslo. An Institute of Sociology was established at the University of Bergen in 1967. Stein Rokkan transferred some of his activities from the Michelsen Institute to the university and was appointed professor of sociology with special responsibility for a new subject, comparative politics.

The 1960s represented on the whole a decade of extraordinary academic expansion in Norway. By 1960 the institute in Oslo could boast only two regular teaching positions and three recruitment posts. Ten years later, the respective figures were fifteen and three. The institute in Bergen rapidly developed into a genuinely multisubject

---

*This contribution is essentially a revised and shortened version of two articles Stein Rokkan and the author wrote for *Scandinavian Political Studies* "Political Research in Norway 1960–1975: An Overview" 12 (1977):127–56 and "The Growth of the Profession: Norway" 12 (1977):65–73. *SPS* is published jointly by Universitetsforlaget, Oslo, and Sage Publications, Beverly Hills, London.

social science department; by 1976 it had appointed three full professors in public administration and organization theory, two in sociology, one in economics, and one in social administration and social policy. The economics division split off and formed an independent institute in 1977. While the institute in Oslo teaches political science as an integrated discipline, the Bergen institute has divided it into two separate subjects: comparative politics and public administration and organization theory. The number of permanent positions in the two subjects had risen to fifteen by 1975. Since 1972 expansion in terms of new positions has stagnated in both Oslo and Bergen due to a ministry resolution that the two largest universities had reached a ceiling, and allocations for further positions were stopped almost completely.

Further developments have since taken place at the Universities of Trondheim and Tromsø, both established in 1968. These institutions both offer teaching in social science subjects: political science has not been set up as a separate, independent discipline, but integrated into a broader range of social sciences.

A number of regional colleges were established in 1969 and 1970. By 1975 four of these offered education in political science, under the name public administration or social politics: Agder Distriktshøgskole, Kristiansand; Rogaland Distriktshøgskole, Stavanger; Hedmark/Oppland Distriktshøgskole, Lillehammer, and Nordland Distriktshøgskole, Bodø.

THE TEACHING OF POLITICAL SCIENCE

During the early years political science could only be studied for a graduate degree called *Magister Artium* which required some 6 to 7 years of concentrated study after university entrance. The University of Bergen introduced a multidiscipline social science degree called the *Cand. Polit.* in 1966. The undergraduate part of this degree called for a combination of three different subjects over 4 to 5 years, and the graduate degree required a further 3 to 4 semesters of concentrated work in one of the subjects. Graduate degrees of this new type were offered in comparative politics from 1967 and in public administration from 1969 onwards. The *Cand. Polit.* degree was subsequently introduced in Oslo as well, and represented from 1969 onward an alternative to the *Mag.Art,* but with a much stronger concentration on political science subjects than was the case in Bergen.

With the multilevel *Cand.Polit.* scheme students are offered opportunities to take one-year courses (*grunnfag*), three-semester courses (*mellomfag*), and full three-year study schedules (*hovedfag*). A number of students take the shorter courses in political science and combine these with other social science subjects or with history. The total student load, particularly at the lower levels, increased rapidly during the 1960s. The steep growth at the University of Oslo came to an end in 1969, with the level stabilizing over the last few years. The number of students grew rapidly in Bergen through 1975, but recently signs of a levelling off have been observed.

The yearly production of upper-level graduates (*Mag. Art.* or *Cand.Polit.*) is still small in proportion to the total student load. Table 22.1 gives a picture of the trend: the slow growth until about 1965, the acceleration after the introduction of the *Cand.Polit.* degree. Very few Norwegian students have gone abroad to study political science. According to information kept by the Norwegian Political Science Association *five* Norwegians have acquired either an M.A. or a Ph.D. in political science in the United States and only *one* Norwegian has graduated in Sweden!

Instead of scanning the organization and the contents of the various curricula in the political science subjects for the undergraduate and graduate levels and changes over time, let us in an indirect way give an idea of topics emphasized in teaching by indicating some trends in the fields of concentration in graduate theses. By far the greatest number of theses has been produced on political institutions of various kinds: government, parliament, legislation, administrative decision-making. Within this broad category data reveal a trend toward greater emphasis on local decision-making studies. In the early 1960s there was a heavy concentration on studies of parties and organizations. This is still an important field of specialization, and the trend has been to focus more and more on organizations and their relationship with government. Over the last few years we have seen a growing interest in the political systems of foreign countries. Interest in pure theory and in the history of political ideas has never been widespread in Norway and has even declined further lately. In a classification of all 256 theses produced between 1960 and 1975 we found that only seven were written on political ideas. Table 22.2 gives a crude idea of fields of concentration in graduate theses produced during the sixteen-year period.

Table 22.1 Number of Graduates in Political Science 1950–1975, by Sex

TIME PERIOD	MEN	WOMEN
1950–59	58	4
1960–64	22	0
1965–69	54	3
1970–75	168	9
Total	302	16

Table 22.2 Magazine Articles and Candidates' Political Theses by Field 1960–1975

THESIS TOPICS	NO.	%
Theory, political ideas	7	2.7
Mass media, public opinion, political socialization	14	5.5
Electoral research: surveys and ecological analysis	10	3.9
Parties, organizations	55	21.5
Elites: recruitments, behavior	16	6.2
Political institutions: government, parliament, legislation, administrative decision-making, local dec.-mak. studies	101	39.5
Political systems of foreign nations, developmental research, developing countries	11	4.3
International politics, foreign politics of nations (incl. Norway)	42	16.4
Total	256	100.0

RESEARCH IN POLITICAL SCIENCE

Introduction

Political research has been a growth industry in Norway since the late 1950s. The expansion on the research front paralleled the expansion of teaching staffs and the increase in student loads. The overall expansion—evidenced for example by data on research projects and research grants—was accompanied by an increasing diversification of efforts, geographically no less than thematically. The establishment of a strong research milieu in Bergen during the second half of the 1960s produced a climate of healthy competition which made for higher standards. And recently, we have seen a rapid expansion of research facilities and research activities in Trondheim and Tromsø and at the district colleges. This extraordinary expansion of research activities has of necessity produced a great increase in the rate of publication. I cannot possibly go into details of all projects or all publications: no attempt will be made to cover all fields in equal depth. The main emphasis will be on the development of a tradition of empirical and analytical research and on the few extant examples of systematic conceptualization and model-building. Focus shall be almost exclusively on studies of conditions, structures and processes within national territorial communities.[1] This overview is essentially an update of earlier accounts published in *Scandinavian Political Studies*.[2]

The Institutional Infrastructure

The bulk of the research activities covered in this report took place within seven institutes: the university departments in Oslo and in Bergen, the five independent research centers.

The extraordinary increase in student loads during the 1960s made it difficult to build up adequate research facilities within the university departments. In Oslo a considerable proportion of the research work initiated by staff members in the university department was in practice carried out in the independent research institutions. The Institute for Social Research remained the headquarters of the program of electoral research, the Institute for Peace Research played a similar role in studies of the international system, and the Norwegian Institute of Foreign Affairs organized a number of projects in such fields as European cooperation, the Middle East conflict and Atlantic military strategy. It proved easier to build up research facilities within the broader department established in Bergen in 1967, but even there some of the research work continued to be carried out within other institutional frameworks. The Michelsen Institute continued its program in comparative politics and served as the headquarters of a Europe-wide facility, the Data Information Service set up by the European Consortium for Political Research. Further infrastructure developments took place at the periphery of the university. Two large-scale research projects, the Conditions of Living Survey and the Study of the Distribution of Power, had to establish their own temporary headquarters outside the university framework. Another major institution, the Norwegian Social Science Data Services,[3] was housed by the university but was formally a federal organization under the research council.

Models and Conceptual Frameworks

The technology of the data revolution produced a dramatic break with the earlier traditions of single-scholar documentary research; the "new science of politics" set itself off from history and constitutional jurisprudence through its concentration on the developing methods of sampling, standardized data gathering and automated mass analysis. But this emphasis on technological innovation did not in itself guarantee the development of a systematic discipline of political analysis. The mushrooming organizations of pollsters and social surveyors and the increasingly powerful generations of computers opened up extraordinary possibilities for research but also increased enormously the intellectual responsibilities of the analysts. It became easier to assemble data and easier to manipulate them, but it also became easier to produce statistical nonsense and to get lost in sheer numerology. Happily, the revolution in the technology of research was paralleled by a vigorous, if not always concerted, revival of interest in theory construction, in the formulation of models, and in the systematization of frameworks for the design of research and the strategy of analysis. Since the early 1950s this "data-theory" dialectic had conditioned the development of all the social science disciplines and had found particularly clear-cut expression in the field of political analysis.

The data-theory gap became a concern of political analysts in most countries in the West throughout the 1960s. It was perhaps less discussed in the circles where the study of politics remained a branch of traditional history, but it became an increasingly important issue among all students concerned with developing a truly comparative and cross-national discipline of political analysis.

In Scandinavia a number of attempts were made during the 1960s to take up the challenge of this gap between theory and data in the study of politics. Most of these theoretical formulations reflected developments in *sociology*. In fact, there was a marked tendency toward a merger of research traditions at the borderline between sociology and empirical and statistical politics. Developments were much slower on the other frontiers of interdisciplinary exchange. There were scattered explorations of the possibilities of systematic application of formal models of decision-making. In 1965 the anthropologist Fredrik Barth made imaginative use of paradigms from the theory of games and the political scientist Knut Midgaard tried to systematize the implications of these paradigms for the study of negotiations. Elements of the March-Simon-type models of organizational decision-making gained ground during the 1960s; the pioneers in this tradition were Knut Dahl Jacobsen and Johan P. Olsen.[4] The decisive thrust toward an economization of political analysis came in the 1970s, however; Gudmund Hernes made innovative use of Coleman's exchange models, not only in concrete analyses in 1974 of transactions within Parliament but with even greater impact in his 1975 analyses of concepts of power and powerlessness.

But the bulk of the efforts at theorizing remained heavily sociological in style and in orientation. Explicitly sociological frameworks for political analysis were developed by Erik Allardt in Finland, Ulf Himmelstrand in Sweden, Vilhelm Aubert, Johan Galtung, Stein Rokkan, Ulf Torgersen, Francesco Kjellberg, and Øyvind Østerud in Norway.

A trend toward a concentration on developmental and ecological dimensions of the national polity can be seen in the work of a number of Norwegian social scientists. Vilhelm Aubert broadened his 1960 study of the origins and functions of lawyers in Norwegian society into an overall inquiry in 1962 into the growth and interlinkages of the professional elites and suggested ways of using such data in an approach to the sociology of nation-building and national integration. This work was carried one step further by Ulf Torgersen in his 1972 analyses of the development of a variety of elite groups in Norway and in his sketch of a general sociology of the professions. Interestingly, this interest in the growth of core elites of nation builders was coupled with an intensified concern with developments at the *peripheries* of the nation, particularly in the economically and culturally backward communities of the north, the last area to enter into the national system of communication and exchange. Francesco Kjellberg's 1975 work on *Political Institutionalization* has contributed important insights into the interlinkages between local social structure and governmental organizations. His analyses are based on field work experiences in northern Norway as well as in a rural community in Sardinia.

This work parallels other endeavors on the border between sociology and politics. Johan Galtung has tried to make operational a general "center-periphery" dimension and to formulate hypotheses about the consequences of differences in positions on such a scale. In later papers the elements of this dimension—geographical, economic, social, cultural, and political—have been analysed in further detail and a model has been suggested for the generation of hypotheses about the consequences of movements toward disequilibria in rankings on each of the elementary attributes. This style of model-building draws its strength from the important Yule-Lazarsfeld tradition of attribute combinatorics and has very direct applications in survey research and in aggregate comparisons of the type pioneered by Karl Deutsch and his colleagues at Yale. In a series of articles in the *Journal of Peace Research* and other international media Galtung has demonstrated great versatility in the development of multilevel models of interaction within the word community. His work in 1973 on the cosmologies of different civilizations goes still further in theoretical generality, but has not yet reached the stage of synthesis.

Parallel theoretical developments have taken place within the long-term program of electoral research carried forward since 1956 at the Institute for Social Research in Oslo and the Michelsen Institute in Bergen. Valen and Katz's studies were from the outset focused on the political effects of the historical processes of change in Norwegian society: the continuing spread of urban settlement, the exodus from the primary economy, the increase in the size and complexity of work organizations, and the consequent changes in occupational structure. The basic design of the studies was formulated in a two-dimensional location chart for variables by Rokkan in 1962. One dimension was structural: from attributes of the total nation through a series of subsystem attributes to attributes of the member-citizens. The other dimension was historical and developmental: the variables were time-specified at each level of the national polity, from the total state of the system in its geopolitical environment to the behavior of the constituent organizations, collective units, and individual actors.

The early studies focused on the latest phases of change in Norwegian society: the years since World War II. But the program was gradually broadened to try to piece together a complete "statistical history of Norwegian politics" by Rokkan in 1966. The theories of social, cultural, and political mobilization formulated by Karl Deutsch and Daniel Lerner and brought into a developmental model by Gabriel Almond, Lucian Pye and their associates proved an important stimulus for the Norwegian program.

What was new in the Norwegian effort was the attempt to pin down a number of threshold points of local development through the accumulation of time series data for all distinguishable communities within the nation. This effort generated an interest on the part of Rokkan and Valen in 1964 in the identification of the crucial dimensions of the emerging Norwegian party system. A first, still incomplete, formulation of a basic model for comparisons of stages in the development of party systems was published in 1967 by Lipset and Rokkan and was spelled out in greater detail in a volume published in 1970 by Stein Rokkan. The model represents a first step in the operationalization of the politically central dimensions of Talcott Parsons's A-G-I-L paradigm. It first suggests ways of locating the historically given party oppositions (whether local or nationwide) in a two-dimensional diagram and then proceeds to specify conditions for the development of particular types of alignments within the framework of this classification.

The early work on the genealogy of party systems quickly led to analyses in greater historical depth. Stein Rokkan became increasingly interested in the development of a general model of the interaction of geopolitics and geoeconomics in the structuring of the territorial systems of Western Europe. The first attempts in this direction were published by Rokkan in 1971 and offered arguments for the construction of a conceptual map of Europe.

Several younger scholars have taken up the challenge of macrohistorical comparisons but have found it advisable to stick to the most-similar systems approach: they have concentrated their efforts on the Nordic countries.

Of these analyses the richest in theoretical implications is probably the one by Øyvind Østerud: this focuses on the early agrarian structures in Denmark, Norway, and Sweden and seeks to explain differences in the style and content of peasant politics against the background of information on land tenure systems, levels of commercialization, and links to the urban economies.[5] Østerud's work is of particular interest because of its emphasis on the inherited structures, the contrasts in historical legacies before the decisive waves of democratization and mobilization at the end of the nineteenth century. William Lafferty and Stein Kuhnle have concentrated on the first waves of political change from the 1880s onward. Lafferty's 1971 book on *Economic Development and the Response of Labour in Scandinavia* subjected the well-known Bull-Galenson theories to a critical test by bringing together a variety of data and analyses in an effort to explain the differences between Denmark, Norway, and Sweden in their rhythms of industrialization and in the character of the consequent mobilization of urban and rural workers. In two follow-up volumes he tried in 1972 and 1974 to analyze the data for Norway within a broader framework of ecological theory. Stein Kuhnle's work parallels Lafferty's but covers a longer span of time. His initial analyses in 1975 covered the interaction between sociocultural modernization (economic development, urbanization, schooling) and political mobilization across four Nordic countries, and his 1978 work compares rhythms of welfare legislation over a period of more than one hundred years.

These various efforts at macrohistorical analysis have obviously been influenced to some extent by the revival of Marxist theorizing in academic circles since the mid-1960s. The true believers have on the whole had only minimal impact on theory development but the repeated clashes between humanistic vs. scientistic interpretations of the Marxian oeuvre have stimulated fresh attempts at general reformulations of the implicit models of historical dynamics. The leading Norwegian Marxologist Jon Elster[6] has exerted considerable influence on political sociologists in Norway and has helped them refine their analyses of processes of change. Gudmund Hernes has combined elements from Marxist historical materialism, modern development economics as well as systems theory in an effort to formulate a general model of structural change.[7] This formalization of notions of dialectic feedback holds great promise but clearly calls for further specification and testing in concrete analyses of processes of sociopolitical change.

Mass Reactions and Electoral Behavior

Systematically designed surveys of political opinions, attitudes, and behaviors have been organized since 1957 under a joint program of electoral research at the Institute for Social Research and the Michelsen Institute.

The first reports on the surveys carried out at the time of the 1957 election were published in 1959 but it took several years before the general results of the analysis work could be presented to the public. A major event in the history of the program was the publication in 1964 of the principal report on the local surveys conducted in the southwest of Norway. Henry Valen's book with Daniel Katz in 1964 was the first broad presentation of facts and findings from a pioneering study of party activities and voter reactions in Norway. The parallel analyses of the nationwide data collected in 1957 have not been presented in any single report, but have found their way into a variety of technical reports and interpretive statements of Rokkan from 1963 to 1970 and by Rokkan and Valen in 1964. The pressure of other work did not make it possible to organize a further nationwide survey at the election of 1961, but some secondary analysis was subsequently carried out on the basis of Gallup data for the dramatic period of mobilization against entry into the Common Market from 1961 to 1962 by Rokkan and Valen and by Rokkan and Høyer.

By the time of the next national election, however, there was so much interest in public circles in this type of research that grants were made to the program both from the government and the Research Council. A nationwide panel survey was carried out before and after the election of 12–13 September 1965. The focus was again on the political effects of the processes of change in Norwegian society and on this occasion there were for the first time since the war really significant movements in the dependent variables: a marked increase in turnout and a sizeable reduction in the strength of the governing party. To explore the effects of one major change in the technology of electioneering a study of differences between communes with and without television coverage was built into the design: this necessitated a separate interview operation in districts of the north not having TV. The nationwide sample interviewed in 1965 was interviewed again at the equally dramatic election of 1969.

These panel data offered extraordinary opportunities for analysis and a number of important reports were published in the early 1970s: we cite the detailed analysis of the dimensionalities of electoral choice undertaken by Henry Valen in cooperation with Phil Converse of the Ann Arbor team in 1971 and Valen and Martinussen in 1972; the innovative work on political resources and modes of participation carried out by Willy Martinussen from 1968 to 1973 as well as interesting contributions by Ragnar Waldahl in 1974 to the study of face-to-face communication about political issues.

The extraordinary mobilization of support across party lines for and against entry into the European Community offered a fresh challenge to the Norwegian team of electoral analysts. The panel interviewed in 1965 and 1969 was interviewed again in 1973 and was even sent a mail questionnaire at the time of the local and provincial elections of 1975. A few reports have already been produced by Valen and Rokkan on the basis of this unique set of panel data. Based on other collections of opinion data, and ecological data, researchers at the Institute for Peace Research have analyzed variations in attitudes to membership in the European Community.[8]

The joint program went far beyond the organization of sample surveys, however. A central element in the program was the development of a time series archive of coded information on the political, economic, social, and cultural structure of each commune in Norway. This archive has involved a great deal of work and is still in full development: it was transferred to the Norwegian Social Sciences Data Services in 1971 and incorporates more than 15,000 variables covering a period of close to 140 years—from the 1840s to 1976. The early analyses of this material simply helped to check the reliability of the data collected by the survey method. The first publications of Rokkan and Valen in 1964 and of Rokkan in 1966 reviewed evidence of the patterns of regional variations in the strength of the parties and in the level of participation; the later ones focused on variations in the local conditions of political mobilization and made use of extensive information on the activities of different parties at the level of the commune. One of the first reports brought in an important developmental variable: the politicization of local elections through the breakdown of the traditional territorial oppositions and the entry of nationally organized parties. This work was subsequently followed up in a 1967 historical study by Hjellum of rates of politicization.

In recent years, the group organized by Stein Rokkan in Bergen has pushed these analyses of historical trends at the local-regional level several steps further. Stein Kuhnle has studied in 1972 and 1975 processes of suffrage extension and political mobilization since 1814 and Frank Aarebrot has tried out a series of regression models in a study of the decisive waves of increases in registration and turnout from 1876 to 1897.[9] Lars Svåsand has focused attention on the spread of popular movements and party organizations in the 1970s and 1980s and also published in 1973 a statistical analysis of the first two-party contest in Norwegian history, the election of 1882. The period from 1900 to 1936 has also been extensively studied on the basis of information now in the NSD archives of commune data. Gabriel Øidne has reviewed in some detail the fate of the *Venstre*, the dominant party of opposition to the central urban establishment in the important election of 1903. Sten Sparre Nilson has looked at the variations in the Republican votes at the referendum held in 1905 and correlated them with the votes in the two consultations on prohibition organized in 1919 and 1926.[10] William Lafferty carried out in 1974 detailed ecological analyses of commune data on the speed of industrialization and the radicalization of the labor movement from 1910 to 1924. And Terje Sande has opened up a new field of research on developments at the local level by analyzing in some detail data on the impact of electoral realignments on increases in communal budgets, tax rates, and indebtedness from 1910 to 1924, a period of accelerated expansion of infrastructure equipment and social services.[11] The joint program of electoral research was broadened during the 1960s to cover the mass media. A number of important contributions to the study of the impact of changes in the technologies and the economics of the mass media on political alignments in Norway has been undertaken in Oslo and Bergen.

Among the many inquiries organized in this field four groups are of particular importance:

— the detailed historical-statistical studies of the political economy of the press undertaken by Svennik Høyer in 1961, 1973, 1975

— the analyses of survey evidence of the importance of newspaper reading for active vs. passive voters in different local settings, originally presented in an article by Stein Rokkan and Per Torsvik, later developed in further depth by Torsvik

— the content analyses of party campaign materials, newspaper articles, and stories in weekly magazines carried out by Svennik Høyer in 1963, 1975; Sigmund Grønmo in 1975; Per Arnt Pettersen in 1975; and Per Torsvik in 1973

— the studies of the impact of television during the 1960s and 1970s carried out by Per Torsvik in 1967; Henry Valen in 1967; and Helge Østbye in 1972

The Norwegian program of electoral research has been carried forward in close cooperation with social scientists in other countries. Special mention should be made of Stein Rokkan, who wrote several programmatic statements on the potentialities of comparative electoral research and took the lead in organizing an *International Guide to Electoral Statistics*. The first volume, covering fifteen countries of Western Europe, was published in 1969.

Parties, Interest Groups and Popular Movements

In recent years there has been a marked tendency to devote greater resources to the study of variables at higher levels of the system: to treat such variables as dependent and worthy of explanatory efforts in their own right rather than as independent and intervening variables in the study of the mass electorate. Early examples are represented by Henry Valen who established an archive of data about candidates at the *Storting* elections of 1957 and 1961 and also collected information about party organizations and party membership in each commune.

The first analysis to be published on this basis by Rokkan and Valen in 1964 focused on the relationship between local politicization and candidate recruitment. Much more detailed analyses of candidate characteristics were published in 1966 by Valen. Following up this work at a different level of the system, Torstein Hjellum in 1967 analyzed the composition of the lists of candidates presented at local elections in the west of Norway and tried to pinpoint the effects of the emergence of partisan conflicts on the recruitment of leaders from different social strata. This paralleled Francesco Kjellberg's study in 1965 of the professionalization of local politics in an isolated community in the north. These early studies were followed up in the second half of the 1960s within a broader program of research on local politics at the University of Oslo. Francesco Kjellberg and Audun Offerdal organized several studies from 1967 to 1974 of the personnel of city councils and also encouraged a set of initial inquiries into local budgetary processes.

But much still remains to be done on the history of Norwegian party developments. Academic historians have recently begun to take a serious interest in the emergence and early structuring of the parties.[12] Among political scientists, Ulf Torgersen carried out in 1961–1962 a series of painstaking analyses of the growth of the urban parties in the 1880s and 1890s and has looked into principles and procedures of member recruitment. This set of studies was later followed up in 1966 through an analysis of changes in the systems of representation on the national party conventions from the early period of indirect elections through the brief period of run-off majority elections to the period of PR contests after 1920. Torgersen's historical studies of party structure go further in sociological depth than any others thus far carried out and constitute important elements in a broad program of studies of changes in the recruitment and functions of Norwegian elite groups in the decades before and after the extension of the suffrage.

The period of run-off majority elections from 1906 through 1918 has been opened up for detailed research by Tertit Aasland. Her study of 1965 of the party labels of the candidates and the second-round coalitions in the five elections held in this period is of great interest and points to a number of challenging tasks of statistical analysis as well as raising important questions about variations in party strategy under the impact of changes in the rules of the electoral game. She has also conducted a thorough study of the developments which led up to the organization of a nationwide Agrarian party during World War I.[13]

The further developments from World War I to the entry of the Labor party into the national establishment have given rise to a great deal of excited speculation and controversy but have not as yet been subjected to systematic scrutiny. Torgersen and Lafferty have studied in great detail the struggle between the different factions of the Labor party during the crucial years after the Russian Revolution. Knut Heidar has established an archive of biographical information on the elites of the Labor party and has analyzed in some detail the relationships between trends in recruitment and changes in ideology.

The crisis years of the 1930s have been attracting increasing attention both among historians and political scientists. Nils Ørvik's history of the conflicts over foreign policy gives fascinating details about the tense years from 1928 to 1933: the trend toward a polarization of the political forces, the traces of *Verfemung* and militarization. But solid monographs on this phase of near-disintegration are still missing. The early work of Sten Sparre Nilson on the background of the Quislingites has been followed up by Rolf Danielsen, Stein Ugelvik Larsen, and Jan-Petter Myklebust. They have built up an important file of biographical information on all members of the *NS*, the Norwegian National Socialist party, and Larsen and Danielson have carried out some initial analyses of this material. Jan-Petter Myklebust has aggregated the membership figures by commune and tried to analyze the fit between membership development and voting strength.

The history of the Labor party after its accession to power has so far mainly been described in official accounts. The only academic studies of internal developments in the party organization are by Fredrik Hoffman of the short-lived split in the party ranks over the atomic rearmament of Germany and by Knut Heidar on recruitment and deradicalization.

The détente among the parties during the period from 1945 to 1961 has been the subject of a great deal of discussion by H. F. Dahl. Ulf Torgersen has recently gone into this process in some detail and has tried to throw light on dilemmas of party strategy in the phase of de-ideologization.[14]

All students of political parties have in one way or another had to face up to the existence of the parallel network of interest organizations and popular movements. At the level of unit statistics the linkages between the two channels of influence can be studied through the collation of information about joint positions and memberships. Henry Valen looked into these linkages in his studies of party personnel and Ottar Hellevik and Gudmund Hernes have explored the configurations of organizational commitments in great detail in their work on the members of the *Storting*. Parallel studies by Olsen, Egeberg, and Sætren, of the organizational links of functionaries within the central administrative organs are underway within the "Power" program.

Stein Rokkan in 1963 and 1966 called attention to the challenging tasks of research inherent in the two-tier system of public decision-making.[15] A number of inquiries has focused on the relationships between the "numerical-electoral" and the "organizational-functional" channels of influence on central decision makers.[16] Jorolv Moren reviewed trends toward an institutionalization of functional representation across Western Europe and worked extensively with the American scholar Kvavik in a broader study of interest organizations in Norwegian politics. Moren also edited with Hallenstvedt and others a useful collection of analyses of the "votes count, resources decide" thesis.[17]

This theme has become central in the current program of research on Power in Norwegian society. Gudmund Hernes and Johan P. Olsen are developing new approaches to the conceptualization of the multiplicity of channels of influence in the modern industrial state and have gathered a vast amount of fresh data for the testing of alternative models. Johan P. Olsen and his associates within this large-scale program are applying elements of organization theory in an effort to explain variations in the degree of interpenetration between governmental agencies and organized social interests: which are the principal factors making for higher or lower likelihood of such interpenetration and what are the strategies open to interest organizations in their interaction with public power structures?[18] Gudmund Hernes and his associates are conducting detailed inquiries into the linkages between business corporations, branch organizations, and governmental agencies and have sketched the contours of a theory of sources of change in mixed "market-command" economies.[19]

Institutions of Government and Processes of Policy Production

Most of the efforts within the empirical-statistical school of politics have focused on the feedback units of the political system: citizens as subjects of government; citizens as claimants; as voters; or citizens as subjects without citizen rights. Attention has been devoted to their economic, social, and cultural situation, their opinions and attitudes, their alternatives of action, and their actual decisions. A few studies have cut across several levels of the polity but have then restricted themselves to one single analytical task, say, the recruitment of incumbents to higher-level roles, or the interlinkages among units and across levels through crosscutting careers and through role cumulations.

The extensive studies by Aubert and Torgersen of the recruitment of elite personnel in Norway exemplify possible approaches to such a mixed strategy. They have both accumulated large masses of unit statistics but their essential concern has been to fit their numerical findings into broader theoretical interpretations of the characteristic trends of development in Norway.

Another outstanding example of cross-level analysis is Knut Dahl Jacobsen's meticulous case study in 1964 of the conflict between administration and Parliament over the organization of services for agriculture from 1874 to 1899. The theme of the study is a standard subject of administrative history, the development of a distinct unit of the national bureaucracy, yet the unit is not studied in isolation but in the wider context of overall changes in the balance of political forces and in cultural modes of interaction. The study is of great potential value in the planning of comparative research on the functions of bureaucracies and representative organs in the process of nation-building and points to crucial issues in the study of the emerging nation-states in the developing areas of the world.

Jacobsen's study suggests a cyclical movement of expansion, contraction, and "de-traction" in the growth of bureaucracies under the pressure of new demands from lower levels in the system: once new channels of influence and action have been institutionalized the leeway for administrative discretion increases and the chances for new disturbances decrease. Interestingly, this line of cyclical interpretation has recently also gained ground among professional historians.[20] Ulf Torgersen has on several occasions pointed to the great flexibility of the Norwegian administrative elite, its capacity for survival. This is clearly a theme of great importance in the analysis of breaks in recruitment traditions: at which points in time were the sons of the "official" families most likely to opt out of the normal careers and what were the typical alternatives? This is a central question in the study of the fate of the radical groups of the 1920s and the "domestication" of the Labor party.

However far social scientists plan to go in the production of time series analyses, our knowledge and understanding of the processes of national development will essentially reflect the work of professional historians. This is not the place for a detailed review of historical research on facets of nation-building in Norway, but students of politics might want references to a few outstanding examples of analyses and interpretations: such as Kaartvedt's and Dahl's.[21] Among political scientists, or political sociologists, mention must be made of Ottar Hellevik's volume on the *Storting* as an elite body and of Gudmund Hernes's thesis which represents a distinctive innovation in the study of legislative bargaining behavior.[22] Hernes demonstrates the great potentialities of Coleman-type procedures in the analysis of resource aggregations and coalition strategies. The M.P.s interviewed in 1966 have just been approached for a second round within the framework of the "Power" study: this should create an ever richer data base for the analysis of conflicts and coalitions at the legislative level.

A history of the central administration is nearing completion. Jacobsen has analyzed the crucial changes under the impact of democratization in the second half of the nineteenth century, while Johan P. Olsen has organized a series of studies of the central apparatus of the state within the "Power" program.[23] Olsen has been a pioneer in the use of the tools of organization theory in the study of administrative decision-making and implementation. He studied local budget-making in 1972 and the structuring of universities in 1971 and 1972 and he is currently engaged in a series of investigations of the linkages among the administrative apparatus, the network of interest organizations, and the various agencies of the electoral-legislative channel.

The Ministry of Foreign Affairs and the diplomatic service have been subjected to detailed research at the Oslo Institute for Peace Research by Galtung, Ruge, and Hveem. A variety of studies of influences on foreign policy have been undertaken within the peace research group as well as within the Norwegian Institute of Foreign Affairs and the Polhøgda Foundation. Kjell Skjelsbæk has followed up ideas originally formulated by Johan Galtung in a series of studies of voluntary organizations at the international level; parallel studies have been pursued at the Nordic level by Abraham Hallenstvedt and Aira Kalela, Jaakko Kalela, and Raimo Lintonen in Finland. Within the "Power" program a series of studies of policy response to the multinational corporations have been carried out by Helga Hernes in 1973 and Harald Knudsen in 1974. Olav Knudsen made a major contribution to the study of the role of the shipping interests in Norwegian foreign policy in 1972 and Finn Sollie and his associates at the Polhøgda Foundation opened up in 1974 a field of very immediate concern in the current geopolitical situation: the study of the politics of the ocean and the seabed. The Norwegian Institute for Foreign Affairs has throughout the period been dominant in the fields of strategic analysis as noted by Holst in 1967 and in European studies, examined by Saeter in 1971.

In the study of domestic politics we can also register a marked increase over the years 1965–75 in the number of systematic studies of policy processes and policy outputs. Such inquiries have been pursued at all levels; local, provincial, national.

An early study in the style of the American analyses of sources of variation in state budgets was Eldrid Nordbø's research on local service offerings in the social sector.[24] Francesco Kjellberg, Karl-Erik Brofoss, and Tore Hansen have done pioneering work on municipal budgets[25] and the Norwegian Social Science Data Service has built up a large file of information, commune by commune, on rates of taxation and types of expenditure. Harold Baldersheim has been heavily engaged in research on the relationship between central and local authorities in 1972 and 1977. A first historical study of changes in policy outputs at the local level was recently completed by Terje Sande: this focuses on a period of explosive growth in communal activity, the period from 1913 to 1923. Sande has cooperated with the American scholar Richard Hofferbert on a cross-national study of time-series data for local- and provincial-level expenditures and has tried to develop a set of models for the explanation of changes in the steps of incrementation in the allocation process.[26]

Ulf Torgersen has pioneered another type of policy study within specific urban settings. He and his collaborator Lars Gulbrandsen have been engaged for some time in a study of policies of public housing and their consequences for the behavior of different categories of clients.

Parallel studies of decision-making at the intermediate level of territorial organization, the *fylke,* have been undertaken by Per Stava in 1973 and Torodd Strand in 1975. This is a field of great importance. The decision to introduce direct elections to the *fylkesting* and to build up stronger administrative units at this level is bound to add to the strains between center and periphery in the Norwegian system and will also have consequences for the recruitment and the careers of party activists.

Another set of agencies likely to be the targets of thorough inquiries in the future are those of the Social Security Administration. Else Øyen carried out a pioneering study of the implementation of welfare measures in 1974 and Jon Eivind Kolberg in 1974 reviewed data in the NSD archive on variations in social security payments across regions and types of communes.[27]

Only a handful of attempts have thus far been made to subject policy-making processes at the national level to systematic scrutiny. Alf-Inge Jansen has carried out an initial study of steps in the formulation of science policies, mainly within the research councils. Per Arnt Pettersen has written a thesis on factors affecting decisions on labor market policy[28] and Odd Handegaard has been looking into the complex processes of bargaining characterizing policy-making in the fishery sector of the economy.[29]

Aubert's pioneering studies in the sociology of law have stimulated a great deal of interest in the role of the judiciary in Norwegian politics. Aubert has shown how content analyses of court decisions can contribute to our understanding of the politics of the courts. Torgersen in 1963 concentrated on the politics of recruitment and has given us an illuminating comparison of the supreme courts in Norway and the U.S.

There is still no adequate academic presentation of the essentials of Norwegian political institutions. The American political scientist Storing prepared a handy little textbook in the early 1960s but this is very traditional in its approach and will have to be rewritten in the light of the detailed research under way. Leiv Mjeldheim's textbook of 1969 is much better and ought to be translated. Ulf Torgersen published in 1964 the first version of what promises to become a useful compendium for students.

Comparative Cross-National Research

All political research proceeds by comparisons: comparisons over time, comparisons of the characteristics and behavior of actors and collectivities, comparisons of localities, comparisons of total political systems. Whatever the method, any systematic treatment of politics must resort to comparative analysis. The expanding comparative politics movement has brought into analytical focus a broader range of units than was usual in earlier treatments. Traditional political analysis tended to stick to the one nation or to the one cultural area: the cross-system comparisons rarely went beyond simple juxtapositions. The comparative politics movement of the 1950s was vastly more ambitious: its professed aim was systematic analysis across all extant units of territorial government. During the late 1960s and early 1970s there was a movement back toward more region-specific comparisons: comparisons within culturally distinctive areas of the world. The movement should promote detailed, contextually grounded comparisons region by region before proceeding to develop paradigms for global analysis. In fact, the 1970s was to see a distinctive upsurge of Europe-centered comparative research, in some cases covering all of Europe, in others Western Europe only or even smaller areas such as the Nordic countries. The European Consortium for Political Research contributed decisively to this upsurge, encouraging more and more younger scholars to become interested in comparing findings across neighboring countries and to reflect on possible models for the explanation of similarities or contrasts.

Norwegian political sociologists and political scientists took an active part both in the early and in the later phases of this movement. Johan Galtung and his colleagues at the Institute of Peace Research were enthusiastic "globalizers" and brought together information on the entire range of territories across the world. Nils-Petter Gleditsch in fact produced in 1970 a Norwegian equivalent of the *World Handbook*. The group was heavily involved in comparative survey research and took a lead in the organization of a cooperative project across Eastern and Western Europe under the auspices of the ISSC Center in Vienna.[30]

The group of election analysts in Oslo and Bergen also did their best to advance comparative analysis, not only at the concrete level of survey findings (Campbell and Valen in 1961; Rokkan and Campbell in 1960) but also at the level of model development and theory construction (Lipset and Rokkan in 1967; Rokkan, Verba, Viet, and Almasy in 1969; Rokkan in 1970). The Michelsen Institute played an important role in this movement, and also served as the secretariat of the International Committee on Political Sociology, as Allardt and Rokkan indicated in 1970 and in 1971 became the headquarters of one of the agencies of the European Consortium for Political Research: the Data Information Service. This service has not only served as a clearinghouse for information about research activities in the different countries of Western Europe but has also taken direct steps toward organizing data files for comparative analysis. The service has been particularly active in the promotion of teaching packages for training in cross-national analysis. One of the current projects calls for the production of a workbook and a corresponding data set for "comparative analyses of center-periphery structures" in Europe. The Bergen group has also been active in developing a facility for computer cartography of regional variations within Europe and hopes to build up, on this basis, a network of contributors to a joint data bank for studies of center-periphery contrasts in Europe.[31]

Comparative research at the Nordic level has been heavily influenced by the model proposed by Erik Allardt in 1975 in launching his four-country survey of dimensions of welfare. Norwegian political scientists have been less active at this level of synchronic analysis but have concentrated on diachronic inquiries, on the macrosociology of developments over longer spans of time. In this field a number of significant contributions have been made over the last fifteen years. Stein Rokkan developed in 1971, 1973, and 1975 a series of models for the explanation of historical contrasts in the structuring of political systems in Western Europe. Derek Urwin[32] and Øyvind Østerud[33] have done extensive work on agrarian structures and their consequences for political developments, whereas William Lafferty has carried out corresponding research on comparative industrial developments. Stein Kuhnle has collaborated with Peter Flora and his group on the comparative analysis of conditions making for early or late adoption of different types of welfare legislation.[34] Kjell Eliassen and Lars Svåsand were actively engaged in 1975 in comparative research on the formation of different types of popular movements and political parties in Western Europe. Torodd Strand

compared in 1976 regional policy outputs in Norway vs. Sweden and the entire Bergen group is currently about to throw itself into yet another cross-national venture: a study of territorial tensions and ethnic contrasts within the nation-states of Western Europe. Whatever the quality of these multifarious ventures, there can be little doubt about the vitality of the comparative politics movement in Norway. There is no turning back to a strictly national political science. The discipline can no longer be kept within the bounds of the one nation-state.

ASSOCIATIONAL ACTIVITIES

Associations. The Norwegian Political Science Association (*Norsk Statsvitenskapelig Forening*) was founded in the early 1950s. The association is a member of the International Political Science Association and has always had one representative on its council. In 1975 the association joined with the national associations of the other Nordic countries to form the Nordic Political Science Association.

The main activity of the Norwegian association has concentrated on the annual conferences. The number of participants at these conferences—which take place every fall—has varied between 30 and 40, but over the last few years participation has increased to between 60 and 80. These figures can hardly be evaluated without taking into consideration the small community of political scientists in Norway. Over the past few years, the association has had about 100 to 120 dues-paying individual members.

The themes of the annual conferences are decided upon by the board each year. Themes have been chosen on the unwritten principle that priority should be given to subjects likely to interest all political scientists whatever their current occupational position, and thus the conferences are not organized in order to attract primarily the academic community. The conferences of recent years have discussed the following themes:

1973: Multi-national corporations

1974: The education of political scientists and the needs of Norwegian society

1975: Access to information from governmental bodies and private business and policy research: public planning of social science research

1976: The study of power: the Norwegian project on the study of the distribution of power in Norway.

In 1977 and 1978 the association moved toward a workshop model. In 1977 the conference was divided into three groups: (a) political science as a tool for the analysis of the relationship between government and organizations; (b) political science as a tool for the study of the relationship between government and business; (c) political science as a tool in the work on local government reforms. In 1978 the conference was divided into four workshops: (a) local planning; (b) women and work; (c) problems of bureaucracy; (d) Norway and the international economy. The activity of the organization has been gradually escalated in recent years, partly as a reflection of a widened representation on the board, which until 1974 was composed entirely of political scientists in Oslo. From 1974 the board has included at least one representative from Bergen, and from 1975 on, one representative from the districts. It should be noted that 65 percent of all candidates in political science live and work in Oslo, 11-12 percent live and work in Bergen, while the rest work in other cities, a few even outside cities. Close to 4 percent work in other countries as members of the Norwegian diplomatic corps.

Journals. The Norwegian Political Science Association publishes no journal of its own, but cooperates in the joint Nordic venture: *Scandinavian Political Studies* which until 1978 was an annual publication (12 volumes produced since 1966) but which was made a quarterly journal from January 1978. So far the association has found the Norwegian market too small for a separate Norwegian journal. Many political scientists also regularly contribute to the *Tidsskrift for samfunnsforskning*, which is a general social science journal in Norwegian.

Since 1974 a newsletter (*Statsviteren*—"the political scientist") has been published quarterly and distributed to political science candidates as well as to institutions, organizations, and the media.

Special Publications and Other Activity. Since all of the association's activities are voluntarily based, very little has been written in the name of the association. But over the last few years, political scientists have demonstrated an increasing interest in using the organization more actively for common purposes. For example: First, the board of the organization has established several subgroups to deal with subjects of special interest to political scientists: one on the future organization of research in Norway; one on access to information from public organs or governmental administrative bodies; and one on local policy research. This last group, with Francesco Kjellberg as chairman, has published a report on ongoing projects in local government and policy research. The report gives information about the title of the project, the analytic focus, available publications, and the date of the expected end of project. Secondly, the organization evaluates public initiatives affecting political scientists *qua* political scientists and makes comments or statements on these. And finally, the organization has started to keep better track of the employment which political scientists have been able to find, and has made efforts to assemble more systematic statistics on the "when, where, what, and how" of Norwegian political scientists.

POLITICAL SCIENCE AND THE WORLD OF POLITICS

The Impact of Political Events on Political Science

It is quite obvious that a number of research topics have been raised as a consequence of political events. One of the most conspicuous examples from Norway is the effect of the referendum on Norwegian membership in the European Common Market.[35] Another example, and maybe much more important for the development of political science in Norway, is the comprehensive study of the distribution of power in Norway: this is the single most resource-demanding social science research project ever to have been undertaken in Norway. The Power group has taken up for detailed scrutiny a great number of contemporary political questions and problems: in what way are organizations and business firms integrated with governmental bodies; to what extent are governmental decisions influenced by various organizations and groups; how are economic resources distributed and what are the effects of actual distributions; why has there been an increase in ad hoc organizations—and who makes the best of this novel channel of influence? These are just a few examples, but they all demonstrate that political problems of the day influence political research.[36] Likewise, one could argue that the contemporary financial problems of local governments have given impetus to local government research and relationships between different levels of political authority.

International political events all the time influence research profiles of our specialists in the field of international relations. The most recent example is a study by Hveem in 1977 about the impact of the New Economic World Order on Norway. Generally it is fair to say that a great deal of research is inspired by political events of various types, or simply by observed present-day problems. But this does not imply that all active research is steered in this way.

Political Scientists in Politics

Of all political scientists graduated in Norway since 1950, only two have become representatives in the Norwegian parliament, the *Storting*. Thus, few political scientists have gone into party politics at the national level. Information on representational activity at lower levels is lacking.

On the other hand, political science has clearly established itself as a distinctive academic discipline and has begun to produce a phalanx of younger experts for the various agencies of the public sector. But the discipline has still far to go toward recognition as a full-fledged profession on the level of law or economics in the Norwegian central administration. Political scientists are sometimes, but not as frequently as might be expected "objectively," consulted by governmental commissions to give expert advice and are sometimes also invited to be full participants of such commissions. As the number of political science graduates in governmental agencies increases, and as the increasing amount of research on a widening range of topics becomes more visible, we may expect an increase in the use of political science expertise in governmental commissions.

It should also be mentioned that some political scientists have been—or still are—politically appointed secretaries of cabinet ministers, where they have played important roles as carriers of political science knowledge.

Relationships between the Government and the Discipline

Political scientists have gradually become more visible in governmental circles. This has partly had the effect that political scientists once in a while, and recently more often, are sought for advice. But it has also had the effect that government departments offer more and more resources for social science and political science research. The most outstanding example is the study of the distribution of power which has been financed directly by the prime minister's office and which has offered a variety of opportunities for fresh data-gathering and innovative conceptualizations. A substantial share of the funds allocated to political research is now channeled through government departments. A number of research projects have been launched on the basis of cooperation between government agencies and academic researchers: by cooperation I mean that government officials do not necessarily define research "needs" unilaterally.

The Present State and Future Prospects of Political Science

Political science is a young discipline in Norway, but it has established a firm footing in the academic and political milieux quickly. The overview of research trends has given some quick information on the areas of political research in which Norwegian political scientists are engaged as well as some indication of future directions of research activities.

The large-scale government-sponsored power study has laid the basis for a number of follow-up analyses. Quite rare data bases have been built up: nationwide survey data on organizational and political participation of citizens; interviews with officers of nationwide organizations; interviews with civil servants, members of Parliament, and other elite groups; structural data on business firms and branches; historical data on lawmaking. The project will provide researchers and students with materials of crucial importance for our understanding of the channeling of pressures on decision makers and decision implementers in the Norwegian polity. The Norwegian Social Science Data Service will play an important role in future research activities. The service has established huge archives of various sorts of data: mass opinion data; ecological data on the levels of the municipality and the province; Parliamentary roll-call data; biographical data on M.P.s and cabinet ministers; local government budget data; electoral data for all levels. The different kinds of data cover long time spans: for example, data on all municipalities since 1837 or on all M.P.s since 1814. The consolidation of this service has meant a tremendous increase in the opportunities for political research and in the opportunities for the combination of different types of data.

Rich opportunities now exist for testing hypotheses about longitudinal trends of national development, as for example relationships between different levels of political authority, center-periphery; economic modernization, mass political mobilization, and elite transformation. Even studies of changes in mass opinion and attitudes are now possible on a time-series basis.

On the other hand, there is also reason to believe that a lot of the research to be done in the immediate future will center around the contemporary problematics of democracy, bureaucracy, and the welfare state. The acceleration of social security budgets in recent years clearly argues for a greater concentration of research efforts in this field. And the rapid increase in public budgets and in the relative size of the public sector calls for analyses of the interlinkages between democratic and bureaucratic structures. The uncovering of great inequalities in the distribution of political and economic resources among citizens, organizations, firms, and territorial units has created a solid basis for further inquiries into the current controversies over the alleged failures and the dilemmas of the democratic welfare state. Both the government, the public, and the political science community take a great interest in these issues.

Notes

1. Readers interested in Norwegian literature on international relations should consult the following references: (a) accounts of Nordic research on international relations have regularly been given in the biennial journal *Cooperation and Con-*

flict. An early review of Norwegian studies was given by Nils Ørvik in vol. 1, no. 1, pp. 79-84. This was later expanded into a book-length bibliography of the literature on foreign policy from 1905 to 1965 (Ørvik, 1968), (b) the activities of the Nordic institutions active in international relations through 1965 were described by two official committees: Nordisk Udvalg vedr. forskning af international politik. Forskning af international politik. Stockholm, April 1965, 99 pp. (Nordisk udredningsserie 1965:4); Fredsforskningsutredningen. Internationellt fredsforskningsinstitut i Sverige, Stockholm, Norstedt och Söner, 1966, 61 pp. (Statens off. utredningar, 1966:5), (c) the Nordic Cooperation Committee on International Politics, a body set up by the Nordic Council to promote cooperation in the fields of international relations and peace research, issues a quarterly *Newsletter* which provides details of a variety of research projects in the five countries. The activities of the Oslo Institute for Peace Research are reflected in its quarterly, *Journal of Peace Research*.

2. Stein Rokkan, "Political Research in Scandinavia 1960-1965: Norway," *Scandinavian Political Studies* 1 (1966): 268-80; Stein Kuhnle and Stein Rokkan, "Political Research in Norway 1960-1975: An Overview," *Scandinavian Political Studies* 12 (1977): 127-56.

3. For details on this organization see S. Rokkan and B. Henrichsen, "Building Infrastructures for Social Science Research," *Research in Norway* (1976) : 11-15.

4. For further developments, see the recent volume by James March and Johan P. Olsen, *Ambiguity and Choice in Organizations* (Bergen, Oslo: Universitetsforlaget, 1976).

5. Öyvind Österud, "Agrarian Structure and Peasant Politics in Scandinavia" (Ph.D. diss. LSE, London: 1974); cf. also idem, "The Class Quality of the Peasantry," *Scandinavian Political Studies* 11 (1976): 35-50.

6. See especially *Nytt syn på ökonomisk historie* (Oslo, Pax, 1971).

7. G. Hernes, "The Logic of Functional Analysis," Mimeographed (Bergen, Institute of Sociology, 1971); 'Structural Change in Social Processes,' *American Journal of Sociology* 82, no. 3 (November 1976): 513-47.

8. N. P. Gleditsch, Tord Höivik, and Ottar Hellevik, "Noen enkle modeeler for valg of folkeavstemninger," *Tidsskrift for samfunnsforskning* 15, no. 3 (1974): 233-68; Ottar Hellevik, *Gallup demokratiet* (Oslo: Det Norske Samlaget, 1972); N.P. Gleditsch and Ottar Hellevik, *Kampen om EF* (Oslo: Pax, 1977).

9. Frank H. Aarebrot, *Political Mobilization in Norway 1876-1897* (Bergen: Institute of Sociology, 1976).

10. Sten Sparre Nilson, *Politisk avstand ved folkeavstemninger* (Oslo: Gyldendal, 1972).

11. Terje Sande, *A Decade of Local Government Boom: Norway 1913-1923* (Bergen: Institute of Sociology, 1976).

12. See, e.g. Rolf Danielsen and Alf Kaartvedt in Kaartvedt (1964, Vol. II), and Leiv Mjeldheim (1973).

13. Tertit Aasland, *Fra Landmannsorganisasjon til Bondeparti* (Oslo: Universitetsforlaget, 1974).

14. Ulf Torgvisen, "The Trend Toward Political Consensus," in E. Allardt and S. Rokkan, eds., *Mass Politics* (New York: Free Press, 1970).

15. Rokkan's model of the two tiers has provided the basis for an interesting critique of his scheme for the explanation of variations in the structure of party systems: Robert R. Alford and Roger Friedland, "Nations, Parties and Participation: A Critique of Political Sociology," *Theory and Society* 1 (Fall 1975): 307-28; cf. Robert R. Alford, "Paradigms of Relations Between State and Society," in Leon Lindberg et al., eds., *Stress and Contradiction in Modern Capitalism* (Lexington, Mass.: D.C. Heath & Co., 1975), pp. 145-60.

16. See Rokkan, "Votes Count, Resources Decide" (1975).

17. J. Moren, ed., *Den kollegiale forvaltning* (Oslo: Universitetsforlaget, 1974).

18. See Johan P. Olsen, ed., *Politisk organisering* (Oslo: Universitetsforlaget, 1978).

19. See Gudmund Hernes, ed., *Forhandlingsökonomi og blandingsadministrasjon* (Oslo: Universitetsforlaget, 1978).

20. See especially, Jens Arup Seip, *Fra embedsmannsstat til ettpartistat* (Oslo: Universitetsforlaget, 1963), and idem, *Utsikt over Norges historie* (Oslo: Gyldendal, 1974).

21. Alf Kaartvedt et al., Det Norske Storting gjennom 150 år, 4 vols. (Oslo: Glydendal, 1964); Ottar Dahl, "Grupperinger i Stortinget 1892-1897, belyst ved voteringsdata," *Historisk Tidsskrift* 50, no. 3 (1971): 215-84.

22. Ottar Hellevik, *Stortinget—en sosial elite?* (Oslo: Pax, 1969); Gudmund Hernes, "Interest, Influence and Cooperation: A Study of the Norwegian Parliament (Ph.D. diss., Johns Hopkins University, 1971).

23. Morten Egeberg, Johan P. Olsen, and Harald Saetren, "Organisasjonssamfunnet og den segmenterte stat," *Kirke og Kultur* 1, no. 5 (1975): 257-72; 2, no. 6 (1975): 368-78.

24. Eldrid Nordbø, *Kommunenes ytelser i sosialsektoren*, mimeographed (Oslo: Institute of Political Science, 1967).

25. See Andrew Cowart, Tore Hansen, and Karl-Erik Brofoss "Budgetary Strategies and Success at Multiple Decision Levels in the Norwegian Urban Setting," *American Political Science Review* 69, no. 2 (June 1975): 543-58; Francesco Kjellberg and Tore Hansen, "Municipal Expenditures in Norway: Autonomy and Constraints in Local Government Activity," *Policy and Politics* 4 (1976): 25-50.

26. See the reference in note 11 above. See also Richard Hofferbert et al., "Financing Education in Federal Systems," mimeographed (Binghamton, N.Y.: Project Papers, Center for Social Analysis, State University of New York at Binghamton, 1977).

27. Cf. Kolberg's contribution to the series of reports on the "Conditions of Living" survey: J. E. Kolberg, N. Kildal, and A. Viken, *Uförepensjon og samfunnsstruktur* (NOU 1977 vol. 2) (Oslo: Universitetsforlaget, 1977).

28. P. A. Pettersen, *Naeringer, arbeidsmarked og sysselsettingspolitikk: sosial og geografisk omfordeling av arbeidskraft* (Oslo: Institute for Social Research, 1975).

29. Odd Handegaard, "Administrasjon og kilienter" (Master's thesis, University of Oslo, 1967).

30. H. Ornauer, H. Wiberg, A. Sicinski, and Johan Galtung, eds., *Images of the World in the Year 2000* (The Hague: Mouton, 1976); cf. also the contributons to A. Scalai, R. Petrella, S. Rokkan, and E. K. Scheuch, eds., *Cross-National Comparative Survey Research* (London: Pergamon, 1977).

31. See the report by Jens Lorentzen and Stein Rokkan in European Political Data Newsletter 19 (1976).

32. Derek W. Urwin, *From Ploughshare to Ballot Box: The Politics of Agrarian Defence in Europe* (Bergen: Institute of Sociology, 1973).

33. See note 5 above. Note also his comprehensive new book on developmental theories and historical change, Öyvind Österud, *Utviklingsteori og historisk endring* (Oslo: Gyldendal, 1978).

34. Stein Kuhnle, "The Beginnings of the Nordic Welfare States: Similarities and Differences," *Acta Sociologica* 21 (1978), supplements.

35. Henry Valen, "Norway: 'No to EEC'," *Scandinavian Political Studies* 8 (1972):214-26.

36. See notes 18 and 19.

Selected Bibliography

Aarebrot, Frank H. "Political Mobilization in Norway 1876-1897. Bergen: Institute of Sociology, 1976. (*Cand. Polit.* Thesis).

Aasland, Tertit *Fra Landmannsorganisasjon til Bondeparti.* Oslo: Universitetsforlaget, 1974.

———. "Valgordningen 1906-1918," *Historisk Tidsskrift* 44, no. 4 (1965): 267-97.

Allardt, Erik. *Att ha, att älska, att vara: Om välfärd i Norden.* Lund: Argos, 1975.

——— and Rokkan, Stein, ed. *Mass Politics: Studies in Political Sociology.* New York: Free Press, 1970.

Aubert, Vilhelm. *Norske jurister fra 1814 til den annen verdenskrig.* Oslo: Institute for Social Research, 1960.

Aubert, Vilhelm, et al. *The Professions in Norwegian Social Structure 1720-1955: Tables 1-2.* Oslo: Institute of Social Research, 1962.

Baldersheim, Harald, "Kommunane som klienter i regionalplanlegginga." *Plan og Arbeid* 2 (1972).

———. *Patterns of Central Control over Local Service Provision in Norway.* Ph.D. dissertation, LSE, London, 1977.

Barth, Fredrik. *Political Leadership Among Swat Pathans.* 2nd ed. London: Athlone Press, 1965.

Campbell, A. and Valen, Henry. "Party Identification in Norway and the United States." *Public Opinion Quarterly* 25, no. 4 (1961): 505-25.

Converse, Philip and Valen, Henry. "Dimensions of Cleavage and Perceived Party Distances in Norwegian Voting." *Scandinavian Political Studies* 6 (1971): 107-52.

Cowart, Andrew, Hansen, Tore, and Brofoss, Karl-Erik. "Budgetary Strategies and Success at Multiple Decision Levels in the Norwegian Urban Setting." *American Political Science Review* 69, no. 2 (June 1975): 543-58.

Dahl, Hans Fredrik. *Fra klassekamp til nasjonal samling.* Oslo: Pax, 1969.

Dahl, Ottar. "Grupperinger i Stortinget 1892-1897, belyst ved voteringsdata." *Historisk Tidsskrift* 50, no. 3 (1971): 215-84.

Egeberg, Morten, Olsen, Johan P., and Saetren, Harald. "Organisasjonssamfunnet og den segmenterte stat." *Kirke og Kultur* 5 and 6 (1975): 257-72; 368-78.

Eisenstadt, S. N. and Rokkan, Stein. *Building States and Nations.* Vols. 1 and 2. Beverly Hills: Sage Publications, 1973.

Elster, Jon, *Nytt syn på ökonomisk historie.* Oslo: Pax, 1971.

Galtung, Johan. "Balance of Power and the Problem of Perception." *Inquiry* no. 3 (1964): 277-94.

———. "Foreign Policy Opinion as a Function of Social Position." *Journal of Peace Research* 1, nos. 3-4 (1964): 206-31.

———. "A Structural Theory of Imperialism." *Journal of Peace Research* 8, no. 2 (1971): 81-118.

———. "A Structural Theory of Integration." *Journal of Peace Research* 5, no. 4 (1968): 375-95.

———. *Verdiorientering og sosial posisjon: en forelöpig analyse av et gallup-utvalg.* Oslo: Institute for Social Research, 1961.

——— and Ruge, Mari Holmboe. "The Structure of Foreign News: Presentation of the Congo, Cuba and Cyprus Crises in Four Norwegian Newspapers." *Journal of Peace Research* 2, no. 1 (1964).

Gleditsch, Nils P. *Norge i verdenssamfunnet. En statistisk årbok.* Oslo: Pax, 1970.

——— and Hellevik, Ottar. *Kampen om EF.* Oslo: Pax, 1977.

———, Höivik Tord, and Hellevik, Ottar. "Noen enkle modeller for valg of folkeavstemninger." *Tidsskrift for samfunnsforskning* 15, no. 3 (1974): 233-68.

Grönmo, Sigmund. "Skillelinjer i partipolitikken 1969-1973. Noen virkninger av EF-striden." *Tidsskrift for samfunnsforskning* 16, no. 2 (1975): 119-53.

Gulbrandsen, Lars and Torgersen, Ulf. "Market Interests and Moral Indignation: The Political Psychology of Housing Price Regulations in Post-War Oslo." *Scandinavian Political Studies* 9 (1974): 75-101.

Hallenstvedt, Abraham, et al. *The Nordic Transnational Association Network: Structure and Correlates.* Mimeographed. Helsinki: University of Helsinki, Institute of Political Science, Research Report C:3, 1975.

Handegaard, Odd. "Administrasjon og klienter." Master's thesis, Oslo, 1967.

Heidar, Knut. "Partielite og politikk. Arbeiderpartiets organisasjonselite som bakgrunn for etterkrigstidas fortsatte avradikalisering." *Tidsskrift for samfunnsforskning* 15, no. 4 (1974): 314-41.

———. *Stortinget—en sosial elite?* Oslo: Pax, 1969.

Hellevik, Ottar. *Gallupdemokratiet: Bruk og misbruk av menings-målinger.* Oslo: Det Norske Samlaget, 1972.

Hernes, Gudmund. "Interest, Influence and Cooperation: A Study of the Norwegian Parliament." Ph.D. dissertation, Johns Hopkins University, 1971.

———. "The Logic of Functional Analysis." Mimeographed. Bergen: Institute of Sociology, 1971.

———. *Makt og avmakt.* Oslo: Universitetsforlaget, 1975.

———. "Political Resource Transformation." *Scandinavian Political Studies* 9 (1974): 147-70.

———. "Stortingets komitesystem og maktfordelingen i partigruppene." *Tidsskrift for samfunnsforskning* 4, no. 1 (1973): 1-29.

———. "Structural Change in Social Processes." *American Journal of Sociology* 82, no. 3 (November 1976): 513-47.

——— ed. *Forhandlingsökonomi og blandingsadministrasjon*. Oslo: Universitetsforlaget, 1978.

Hernes, Helga. "The Visible Hand of the Multinational Corporation: A Review." *European Journal of Political Research* 1, no. 3 (1973): 265-92.

Hjellum, Torstein. *Partiene i lokalpolitikken*. Oslo: Gyldendal, 1967.

Hoffman, Fredrik. "Da apparatet var på ferie—Påskeoppröret 1958." In *Påskeoppröret 1958*. Oslo: Pax, 1966.

Holst, Johan Jörgen. *Norsk sikkerhetspolitikk i strategisk perspektiv*. Vols. 1 and 2. Norsk Utenrikspolitisk Institutt, 1967.

Höyer, Svennik "Avisen og dens lesere." Speech delivered at the Nordic Meeting for Journalistic Research, University of Århus, June 1963.

———. "Political Commitment and Audience Coverage: An Analysis of Norwegian Newspapers." Paper read at the UNESCO Seminar, Bergen, 1961.

———. "Temporal Patterns and Political Factors in the Diffusion of Newspaper Publishing: The Case of Norway." *Scandinavian Political Studies* 10 (1975): 157-70.

———. "En transaskjonsmodell for studiet av pressen." *Tidsskrift for samfunnsforskning* 14, no. 2 (1973): 81-105.

Hveem, Helge. *En ny ökonomisk verdensorden og Norge*. Oslo: Universitetsforlaget, 1977.

———. *International Relations and World Images: A Study of Norwegian Foreign Policy Elites*. Oslo: Universitetsforlaget, 1972.

Jacobsen, Knut Dahl. "Informasjonstilgang og likebehandling i den offentlige virksomhet." *Tidsskrift for samfunnsforskning* 6, no. 2 (1965): 147-60.

———. "Public Administration under Pressure: The Role of the Expert in the Modernization of Traditional Agriculture. *Scandinavian Political Studies* 1 (1966): 69-93.

———. *Teknisk hjelp og politisk struktur*. Oslo: Universitetsforlaget, 1964.

Judge, Anthony and Skjelsbaek, Kjell. "Transnational Associations and their Functions." In *Functionalism: Theory and Practise*, edited by A. J. R. Groom and Paul Taylor. London: University of London Press, 1973.

Kaartvedt, Alf, et al. *Det Norske Storting gjennom 150 år*. 4 vols. Oslo: Gyldendal, 1964.

Kjellberg, Francesco. "Kommunalforskning—perspektiv og muligheter." *Tidsskrift for samfunnsforskning* 8, nos. 2-3 (1967): 219-31.

———. *Political Institutionalization*. London, New York: John Wiley & Sons, 1975.

———. "Politiske konsekvenser av standardisering av offentlige ydelser." *Tidsskrift for samfunnsforskning* 15, no. 2 (1974): 138-53.

———. "Politisk lederskap i en utkantkommune." *Tidsskrift for samfunnsforskning* 6, no. 1 (1965): 74-90.

———, ed. *Kommunalpolitikk*. Oslo: Universitetsforlaget, 1971.

——— and Hansen, Tore. "Municipal Expenditures in Norway: Autonomy and Constraints in Local Government Activity." *Policy and Politics* 4 (1976): 25-50.

——— and Offerdal, Audun. "Politisk rekruttering. Nominasjoner ved kommunevalg." *Tidsskrift for samfunnsforskning* 12, no. 4 (1971): 299-323.

——— and Olsen, Johan P. "Det kommunale selvstyre." *Tidsskrift for samfunnsforskning* 9 no. 1 (1968): 1-18.

Knudsen, Harald. *Kontroll med internasjonale konsern*, Arbeidsnotat 24, Maktutredningen. Bergen, 1974.

Knudsen, Olav. "Skipsfart og internasjonal politikk: Et teoretisk perspektiv." *Internasjonal Politikk* 2 (1972): 175-201.

Kolberg, Jon Eivind. *Trygde-Norge*. Oslo: Gyldendal, 1974.

——— et al. *Uförepensjon og samfunnsstruktur*, NOU 1977 Vol. 2. Oslo: Universitetsforlaget, 1977.

Kvavik, Robert. *Interest Groups in Norwegian Politics*. Oslo: Universitetsforlaget, 1975.

Kuhnle, Stein. "The Beginnings of the Nordic Welfare States: Similarities and Differences." *Acta Sociologica* 21 (1978) supplements, pp. 9-36.

———. *Patterns of Social and Political Mobilization: A Historical Analysis of the Nordic Countries*. London, Beverly Hills: Sage Publications, 1975.

———. "Stemmeretten i 1814." *Historisk Tidsskrift* 51, no. 4 (1972): 373-90.

Lafferty, William M. *Economic Development and the Response of Labor in Scandinavia*. Oslo: Universitetsforlaget, 1971.

———. "Industrialism and Labor Radicalism in Norway: An Ecological Analysis." *Scandinavian Political Studies* 7 (1972): 157-76.

———. *Industrialization, Community Structure and Socialism: An Ecological Analysis of Norway 1875-1924*. Oslo: Universitetsforlaget, 1974.

———. "Radikaliseringen av det norske arbeiderparti." *Tidsskrift for samfunnsforskning* 10, no. 2 (1969): 192-214.

Larsen, Stein Ugelvik and Danielsen, Rolf, eds. *Fra Ide til Dom*. Oslo: Universitetsforlaget, 1975.

Lipset, Seymour M. and Rokkan, Stein, eds. *Party Systems and Voter Alignments*. Glencoe: Free Press, 1967.

Lorentzen, Jens and Rokkan, Stein. Report in *European Political Data Newsletter* 19 (1976).

March, James, and Olsen, Johan P. eds. *Ambiguity and Choice in Organizations*. Bergen, Oslo: Universitetsforlaget, 1976.

Martinussen, Willy. "The Development of Civic Competence: Socialization or Task Generalization." *Acta Sociologica* 15, no. 3 (1972): 213-27.

———. *Fjerndemokratiet*. Oslo: Gyldendal, 1973. (also published in English, 1977[?]).

———. "Political Awareness and Other Social Resources." *Scandinavian Political Studies* 6 (1971): 153-70.

———. "Politisk oppmerksomhet og politisk bakgrunn."

Tidsskrift for samfunnsforskning 9, no. 4 (1968): 253-74.

Midgaard, Knut. *Strategisk tenkning*. Oslo: Norsk Utenrikspolitisk Institutt, 1965.

———. "Strategy and Ethics in International Politics." *Cooperation and Conflict* 5, no. 4 (1970): 224-40.

Mjeldheim, Leiv. *Organisasjon, nominasjon og interesseaggregering: Ein studie av Venstre i landskrinsane 1906-1918*. Mimeographed. Bergen: Institute of History, 1973.

———. *Politiske prosessar og institusjonar*. Oslo: Universitetsforlaget, 1969.

Moren, Jorolv. *Staten og naeringslivet*. Bergen, Chr. Michelsen Institute, 1962.

———. ed. *Den Kollegiale Forvaltning*. Oslo: Universitetsforlaget, 1974.

Myklebust, Jan Petter. *Hvem var de norske nazistene? Sammenheng mellom sosial, ökonomisk og politisk bakgrunn og medlemsskap i Nasjonal Samling*. Bergen: Institute of Sociology, 1974. (*Cand. Polit.* thesis).

Nilson, Sten Sparre. *Politisk avstand ved folkeavstemninger*. Oslo: Gyldendal, 1972.

Nordbö, Eldrid. *Kommunenes ytelser i sosialsektoren*. Oslo: Institute of Political Science, 1967. (*Mag. Art.* thesis).

Offerdal, Audun. "Kumulering, ressursar og representasjon." *Tidsskrift for samfunnsforskning* 15, no. 1 (1974): 29-59.

Öidne, Gabriel. "Venstres valgnederlag i 1903. Politiske strömninger ved århundreskiftet i Norge." *Historisk Tidsskrift* 51, no. 1 (1972): 37-69.

Olsen, Johan P. "Alternative beslutnigsprosedyrer i organisasjoner." *Tidsskrift for samfunnsforskning* 13, no. 1 (1972): 25-50.

———. "Kreativitet og organisasjon." *Tidsskrift for samfunnsforskning* 11, no. 3 (1970): 228-38.

———. "On the Theory of Organizational Choice." Ph.D. dissertation, University of Bergen, 1971.

———. " 'Organization', 'Government,' and the Study of Universities." *Administrative Science Quarterly* 16, no. 1 (1971).

———. "Public Policy-Making and Theories of Organizational Choice." *Scandinavian Political Studies* 7 (1972): 45-62.

———. "Voting, 'Sounding Out,' and the Governance of Modern Organizations." *Acta Sociologica* 16, no. 3 (1972): 267-83.

———, ed. *Politisk organisering*. Oslo: Universitetsforlaget, 1978.

Örvik, Nils. *Sikkerhetspolitikken 1920-39*. Vols. 1-2. Oslo: Tanum, 1961.

Östbye, Helge. *Om innföring av fjernsyn i Norge*. Bergen: Institute of Sociology, 1972. (*Cand. Polit.* thesis).

Österud, Öyvind. "Agrarian Structure and Peasant Politics in Scandinavia." Ph.D. dissertation, LSE, London, 1974.

———. "The Class Quality of the Peasantry: A Conceptual Exploration." *Scandinavian Political Studies* 11 (1976): 35-50.

———. *Utviklingsteori og historisk endring*. Oslo: Gyldendal, 1978.

Öyen, Else. *Sosialomsorgen og dens forvaltere*. Oslo: Universitetsforlaget, 1974.

Pettersen, Per Arnt. "Elite Perceptions of Welfare Equality: Frame of Reference for an Analysis of Storting Representatives' Positions on Welfare Problems in Norway Since 1900." *Scandinavian Political Studies* 11 (1976): 77-91.

Rokkan, Stein. "Cities, States and Nations: A Dimensional Model for the Study of Contrasts in Development." In *Building States and Nations*, edited by S. N. Eisenstadt and Stein Rokkan. Vol. 1. Beverly Hills: Sage Publications 1973.

———. "Dimensions of State Formation and Nation-Building." In *The Formation of Nation States in Western Europe*, edited by Ch. Tilly. Princeton: Princeton University Press, 1975.

———. "Electoral Mobilization, Party Competition and National Integration." In *Political Parties and Political Development*, edited by Lapalombara and Weiner. Princeton: Princeton University Press, 1966.

———. "Entries, Voices, Exits: Towards a Political Generalization of the Hirschman Model." *Social Science Information* 13, no. 1 (1974): 39-53.

———. "Nation-Building and the Structuring of Mass Politics." In *Political Sociology: A Reader*, edited by S. N. Eisenstadt. New York, London: Basic Books, 1971.

———. *The Nationwide Election Survey 1957: Basic Tables*. Bergen: Chr.Michelsens Institute, 1960.

———. "Norway: Numerical Democracy and Corporate Pluralism." In *Political Oppositions in Western Democracies*, edited by R. A. Dahl. New Haven: Yale University Press, 1966.

———. "Political Research in Scandinavia 1906-1965: Norway." *Scandinavian Political Studies* 1 (1966): 268-80.

———. "Valgsamfunnet og organisasjonssamfunnet." In *Ökonomi og Politikk*. Bergen: Chr.Michelsens Institute, 1963, pp. 21-30.

———. "Votes Count, Resources Decide." In *Makt og Motiv, Et festskrift til Jens Arup Seip*. Oslo, Universitetsforlaget: 1975.

———, ed. *Approaches to the Study of Political Participation*. Bergen: Chr.Michelsens Institute, 1962.

———, and Campbell, A. "Norway and the United States of America." *International Social Science Journal* 12, no. 1 (1960): 69-99.

——— and Henrichsen, Björn. "Building Infrastructures for Social Science Research." *Research in Norway* (1976): 11-15.

——— and Höyer, Svennik. *Samfunnsvitenskapelige undersökelser omkring den dommende folkeavstemning om Norges inntreden i EEC: en redegjorelse og et forslag*. Bergen: Chr.Michelsens Institute, 1962.

——— and Valen, Henry. "Regional Contrasts in Norwegian Politics. In *Cleavages, Ideologies and Party Systems*, edited by E. Allardt and Y. Littunen. Helsinki: Westermarck Society, 1964.

——— and Meyriat, Jean, eds. *International Guide to Electoral Statistics, Vol. 1: National Elections in Western Europe*. Paris: Mouton, 1969.

——— et al. *Citizens, Elections, Parties*. New York: David McKay, 1970.

——— et al. *Comparative Survey Analysis*. Paris: Mouton, 1969.

Ruge, Mari Holmboe. "Norske utenrikstjenestemenn 1905–1965. En analyse av rekruttering og sosial bakgrunn." *Tidsskrift for samfunnsforskning* 6, no. 3 (1965): 213–34.

Saeter, Martin. *Det politiske Europa: Europeisk integrasjon: Teori—Ide—Praksis*. Oslo: Universitetsforlaget, 1971.

Sande, Terje. *A Decade of Local Government Boom: Norway 1913–1923*. Bergen: Institute of Sociology, 1976. (Cand. Polit. thesis).

Seip, Jens Arup. *Fra embedsmannsstat til ettpartistat*. Oslo: Universitetsforlaget, 1963.

———. *Utsikt over Norges historie*. Oslo: Gyldendal, 1974.

Skjelsbaek, Kjell. "Transnasjonale organisasjoner. Vekst og virksomhet." *Internasjonal Politikk*, no. 1 (1973): 89–105.

Sollie, Finn et al. *The Challenge of New Territories*, Stockholm: Scandinavian University Books, 1974.

Stava, Per. "Theories of Public Policy Making and the Location of Norwegian District Colleges and Universities." *European Journal of Political Research* 1, no. 3 (1973): 249–64.

Strand, Torodd. "Administrative betingelser for regional planlegging. Erkjennelse av et problem." *NordReFo* 3 (1975).

———. *Geographic Policies: A Comparative Study of Norway and Sweden*. Ph.D. dissertation, Institute of Sociology, Bergen, 1976.

Svåsand, L. "The Development of Party Fronts: Cleavage Lines in Norway in the General Election of 1882." *International Journal of Politics* 4, nos. 1–2 (1974): 141–60.

———. "Stortingsvalget 1882: geografiske og ökonomiske variasjoner i oppslutningen om Höyre og Venstre." *Historisk Tidsskrift* 4 (1973): 314–28.

——— and Eliassen, Kjell A. "The Formation of Mass Political Organizations: An Analytical Framework." *Scandinavian Political Studies* 10 (1975): 95–121.

Torgersen, Ulf. *Landsmøtet I norsk partistruktur*. Mimeographed. Oslo: Institute for Social Research, 1966.

———. *Norske politiske institusjoner*. Oslo: Universitetsforlaget, 1964. (Later published in *Det Norske Samfunn*, edited by N. Ramsöy. Oslo: Gyldendal, 1968.

———. *Profesjonssosiologi*. Oslo: Universitetsforlaget, 1972.

———. "The Role of the Supreme Court in the Norwegian Political System." In *Judicial Decision-Making*, edited by G. Schubert. New York: Free Press, 1963.

———. "Sosiale klasser, politiske partier og politisk representasjon i norske bysamfunn, 1. 1885–87, 2. 1900 og 1903." *Tidsskrift for samgunnsforskning* 2, no. 3 (1961): 162–81.

———. "The Trend Toward Political Consensus: The Case of Norway." In *Mass Politics*, edited by E. Allardt and S. Rokkan. New York: Free Press, 1970.

———. "Universitetet og politikken." *Tidsskrift for samfunnsforskning* 2, no. 1 (1961): 17–36.

Torsvik, Per. *Ukepressen—en innholdsanalyse*. Bergen, 1973.

———. *Valgkampen i fjernsyn og radio*. Oslo: Universitetsforlaget, 1967.

Urwin, Derek. *From Ploughshare to Ballot Box: The Politics of Agrarian Defence in Europe*. Bergen: Institute of Sociology, 1973.

Valen, Henry. "Norway: 'No to EEC'." *Scandinavian Political Studies* 8 (1972): 214–26.

———. "The Recruitment of Parliamentary Nominees in Norway." *Scandinavian Political Studies* 1 (1966): 121–66.

——— and Katz, Daniel. *Political Parties in Norway: A Community Study*. Oslo: Universitetsforlaget, 1964.

——— and Martinussen, W. *Velgere og politiske frontlinjer*. Oslo: Gyldendal, 1972.

——— and Rokkan, S. "The Norwegian Program of Electoral Research." *Scandinavian Political Studies* 2 (1967): 294–305.

——— and Rokkan, S. "Regional Contrasts in Norwegian Politics." In *Cleavages, Ideologies and Party Systems*, edited by E. Allardt and Y. Littunen. Helsinki: Westermarck Society, 1964.

——— and Torsvik, P. "Ökningen i valgdeltakelsen ved kommunevalget i 1963 og Stortingsvalget i 1967." *Tidsskrift for samfunnsforskning* 8, nos. 2–3 (1967): 187–218.

Waldahl, Ragnar. "Politisk engasjement og velgerstabilitet." *Tidsskrift for samfunnsforskning* 15, no. 2 (1974): 117–37.

Appendix

MEMBERSHIP OF THE NORWEGIAN POLITICAL SCIENCE ASSOCIATION SINCE 1945:

(a) *Norsk Statsvitenskapelig Forening* was established in the early 1950s.

(b) Membership below 50 up until 1973.

(c) During the last 5-year period the membership has averaged c.100.

ADDRESS OF THE NORWEGIAN POLITICAL SCIENCE ASSOCIATION:

Norsk Statsvitenskapelig Forening
Institute of Political Science
P.O.Box 1097
Blindern, Oslo 3
Norway

President 1978–1979:
Bernt Krohn Solvang
Institute of Political Science
University of Oslo
P.O.Box 1097
Blindern, Oslo 3
Norway

PUBLICATIONS:

The Norwegian Political Science Association publishes the quarterly journal *Scandinavian Political Studies* jointly with the political science associations of Denmark, Finland, Iceland, and Sweden.
Circulation: c.1500

Editors 1978–1980: Harald Sætren, Tor Saglie, and Morten Egeberg.
All three at
The Institute of Sociology and Political
Studies/University of Bergen,
Christiesgt 15–19,
5014 Bergen-Univ, Norway

Editorial policy:
Scandinavian Political Studies is open to all Nordic scholars active in political research as well as to scholars from other countries contributing to records on the five countries. To ensure the highest possible quality, no article will be accepted until it has been judged by at least one referee from another country. We shall continue to distinguish between research articles and surveys of current events. We hope to be able to bring regular surveys of recent elections and other recent developments in each country, not necessarily in each issue, but at least twice a year. We shall not bring ordinary book reviews but will from time to time commission review articles covering larger bodies of recent literature. We shall no longer publish yearly bibliographies as in the earlier series: instead we have decided to issue a selective bibliography every third year.

As a quarterly, The Nordic Political Science Association hopes to make *Scandinavian Political Studies* an effective organ for the exchange of information about research, about findings, about methods, and about efforts of theory construction, not only across the five Nordic countries, but among all scholars interested in the advancement of the discipline.

The Norwegian Political Science Association publishes in addition a newsletter, *Statsviteren,* which is issued quarterly with a circulation of about 350.

STATISTICAL INFORMATION ON POLITICAL
SCIENCE DEPARTMENTS, STUDENTS, AND
GRADUATES.

(a) Number of permanent teaching positions in political science subjects in 1978:
—at the Institute of Political Science, Oslo: 18
—at the Institute of Sociology and Political Studies, Bergen: 15

In addition, there are political scientists in tenured teaching positions at a number of district colleges, altogether between 15 and 20.

A few political scientists hold tenured positions at the universities of Trondheim and Tromsø where political science is integrated into a broader social science subject.

(b) Total number of students in political science in 1975:
in Oslo: c.360
in Bergen: c.300

(c) Total number of graduates during the period 1950–1975: 302
About 20–25 students have graduated each year since 1975.

23 PAKISTAN

A. SALEEM KHAN

Politics is the royal and political art assigned the task of directing man to happiness by having a philosopher-king as ruler.
           Abu Nasr al-Farabi, 870-950 A.D.

Politics is the first of the three practical sciences aiming at Man's welfare in this world and bliss in the next, attainable only if government is rooted in the legal and completed by the political sciences (*ulum-i-Shariya, ulum-i-Siyasia*).
           Abu Hamid al-Ghazzali, 1058-1111 A.D.

The prayer of every Muslim and Pakistani is: "O Lord, Increase my knowledge." Islamic injunctions order every Muslim man and woman to seek knowledge, even if it means going to a distant land like China. In order to know his Creator, a Muslim must know himself first. Such convictions of the Muslim people particularly in an Islamic republic like Pakistan orient them toward enormous love for *ILM*, that is, knowledge. The sciences of politics, government, and public administration have been viewed by Muslim scholars in medieval as well as modern times as extremely necessary for building a happy religious and social order. Islam does not believe in the separation of church and state. There is no demarcation such as "Render unto Caesar the things that are Caesar's, and unto God the things that are God's." Muslim political theorists, whether the Falasifa or the writers on *Adab* (Mirrors for Princes)[1] abstained from the advocacy of the theory of two swords. The science of politics, theoretical and applied, is placed by them in the category of religious and moral sciences (*ulum i Diniya wa Akhlaqiya*). Al Ghazzali in his book *The Munqidh* places politics in the line of sciences connected with ethics and religion, unlike logic, mathematics, astronomy.[2] The great galaxy of medieval Muslim political theorists, whether al Ghazzali, al Mawardi (974-1058 A.D.), Nizam ul Mulk Tusi (1017-1091 A.D.), Zia ud din Barani of the Indo-Pakistani subcontinent (1283-1358 A.D.), or several others unanimously declared that religion and politics were twins. The web of a twin-brother relationship between Shis and Kaimurs, the former symbolizing patriarchy in *din* (religion) and the latter in government is established by them. As such, the study of politics, government, and administration constituted special academic syllabi in the medieval Muslim *madrasas* at Baghdad, Cairo, and the metropolitan town, Delhi, under the Delhi sultans (1206-1526 A.D.). The royal princes and the offspring of the aristocracy destined to be future administrators (*qazis, wazirs, muqtis*) were coached thoroughly in this discipline under expert *ulema* and literati of repute. The immense popularity of the discipline is obviously noticeable from the overwhelming compilation of political treatises of the genre of philosophical works of Ibn i Abir Rabi of the ninth century A.D., Farabi and many others and the *adab* literature produced by al-Ghazzali, Barani, and their group, in order to train properly the future sultans, *wazirs* and the bureaucracy in the idiom of good government. They have constantly admonished the ideal Muslim sultans and their ruling junta to administer the affairs of God's creation judiciously and responsibly so that even "an old woman does not retire to bed hungry." A slight default in discharging their obligation would make them liable to condemnation in the innermost pit of hell.[3]

Following the failure of the War of Independence of 1857, total political control over the subcontinent was acquired by the British rulers to the detriment of Muslim rule and cultural ascendancy. The university education existing in Pakistan by and large till a few years ago really was started by the British with the prime aim of producing clerks on cheaper wages for the white bureaucrats. Lord Macaulay's wisdom dominated the educational syllabi and instruction in the Anglo-vernacular institutions with English as the medium of instruction and examination. According to the authors of the *University Year Book of Pakistan*, 1976, university education as it is understood in this part of the world actually began with the establishment of the University of Punjab, Lahore, in 1882. The University of Dacca in former East Pakistan enjoyed the same parental position in respect to the other universities of Pakistan, which were created after obtaining independence on 14 August 1947.[4] The undivided Indo-Pakistani subcontinent witnessed the establishment of universities on the model of London University much earlier (1857), when the Anglo-vernacular universities of Calcutta, Bombay, and Madras were set up in the regions now constituting the Republic of Bharat.[5]

Historically speaking, Pakistan has had a checkered career in terms of prominence of arts and letters flourishing in ancient and medieval periods. The fine archaelogical remains of Mohan-Jo-Daro and Taxila indicate the existence of advanced institutions of higher learning. In fact, fourth-century-B.C. Taxila had the honor of instruction by an erudite scholar who was particularly, a political philosopher, Kautilya, the celebrated author of *Arthasastra*, a monumental work on statecraft, government, and administration. Following the Muslim conquest of Sind in the eighth century A.D., Multan had the reputation of being a magnificent seat of learning and Lahore soon followed suit. The Muslim sultans of Indo-Pakistan were great patrons of learning and scholarship and Muslim scholars from various nooks and corners of the world, finding life uneasy because of the Mongol menace, selected Delhi and other cities of the land as suitable abodes. Brilliant works on Muslim political ethics, government, and administration were compiled by Fakhr-i-Muddabir, Zia ud-din Barani, Ali Shihab Hamadani, among others.[6] A thriving Muslim educational system suiting the requirements of the times prevailed, but the Sikh domination of Punjab and NWFP brought about a marked decline. The British administered a further setback by replacing the Persian language with English. Thus an oriental mode of learning gave way to an English-medium educational system with a considerable bias in favor of Western art, science, and literature to the neglect of the native ethics and tradition. Government jobs under the British were open only to those who were coached in the English medium. Sir Syed Ahmed Khan, looking to the tide of the times, set up a Mohammadan college at Aligarh in 1877 to cater to this need. A happy blending of Muslim, oriental, and Western learning formed the syllabi of this *madrassa*. Here the Muslim youth was inspired to equip itself with the necessary contemporary knowledge and skill along with grooming in Muslim nationalism, ultimately resulting in the establishment of the Islamic Republic of Pakistan in 1947.

University Education in Pakistan

The universities of the Punjab and Dacca were the only two institutions of higher learning and research in those parts, which from 1947 constituted the Dominion of Pakistan. Whereas Dacca now belongs to the Republic of Bangladesh since 16 December 1971, the University of Punjab alone can be styled as the mother of all universities in present-day Pakistan. Not only in the diverse fields of trade, commerce, industry, technical development, and administration did Pakistan start from scratch, but in the field of educational development similar bottlenecks were also encountered. Soon after independence, the University of Sind at Jamshoro, Sind, saw the light of day. At present there are twelve universities in Pakistan and, with the exception of the universities of Agriculture at Faisalbad (Lyallpur) and of Engineerig and Technology at Lahore, the following ten provide advanced studies in science and liberal arts:

University of Punjab, Lahore, 1882
University of Sind, Hyderabad, 1947
University of Peshawar, 1950
University of Karachi, Karachi, 1951
Quaide-Azam University, Islamabad, 1965
University of Baluchistan, Quetta, 1970
Allama Iqbal University, Islamabad, 1974
University of Gomal, Dera Ismail Khan, 1974
University of Multan, Multan, 1975
Islamia University of Bhawalpur, Bhawalpur, 1975[7]

The Structure of education. In view of the fact that a preponderant number of our young students and scholars seek higher education in the universities of the United States, an awareness regarding the various levels of our educational system must be imparted. Our educational system as given to us by the British since the nineteenth century, and with some rudimentary changes after independence, follows basically two streams. The first includes primary education for students from the age of five to six years through the first few years of middle school. Secondary school education for the next two years entitles the pupil to a secondary school certificate. Higher secondary or intermediate education in science, arts, and commerce consists of another two-years duration in higher secondary colleges.[7] The second is the degree course, resulting in the award of a B.A., a B.Sc., or a B. Com. Such degrees consist of another two years' study and are offered in degree colleges. A large number of these institutions are government-run. The education reforms of 1969-1970 introduced B.A. and B.Sc. Honors courses comprising a three years' course in the major and minor subjects in the various universities of Pakistan. The academic results were very productive, but due to political troubles this scheme in general fizzled out within a couple of years. M.A. M.Sc. studies are offered in general in the various universities of Pakistan, comprising a two years' course. In some disciplines, some colleges run by the government as well as private bodies have been permitted to offer M.A. M.Sc. courses. After a B.A. Honors degree a candidate is permitted to obtain M.A. M.Sc. in one year. Universities in Pakistan are now offering M. Phil. and Ph.D. programs in disciplines where facilities for research guidance are available. The M. Phil. program is of two years' and Ph.D. is of three years' duration after and M.A. M.Sc. in the major subject.[8]

From December 1971, following the induction into office of a civilian people's government, a new education policy (1972-1980) was devised and enforced, making a greater commitment to the promotion of higher learning, education, and research. As indicated earlier, several new universities, centers of advanced studies, regional area study centers, institutes of Pakistan studies, and a University Grants Commission have been established. In addition to the regional institutes of Pakistan studies, a national institute of Pakistan studies has been set up at the University of Quaid-e-Azam, Islamabad. Special mention of these institutes is viewed as necessary, because they offer educational facilities at higher postgraduate levels in areas drawing upon political science, such as culture, history, sociology, government, and administration of the regions concerned.[9]

The Semester System. The British system of education has undergone profound changes in our universities. The traditional system of examination of a purely external and annual nature is being replaced by the semester system of evaluation and examination grading. The *Reports of Study Groups on University Teachers, Students and Problems* issued in the mid-1970s hit hard at the declining standards of education in the country. For remedying the situation, the introduction of the semester system involving the teacher and the pupil more closely in the educational exercise has been suggested.[10]

The State of Political Science in 1947

In prepartition Indo-Pakistan, political science as an independent subject in general existed only at the undergraduate level, that is, up to a B.A. or lower. Very few universities had assigned it an independent place. The Muslim University Aligarh, the torchbearer and the beacon light in terms of Indo-Muslim educational tradition and national aspirations separated the departments of history and political science only in August 1948. Hitherto, some courses or papers in political science were included in history courses and an M.A. degree was awarded at the end of two years through purely external examinations in the discipline of history. The approach to the study of political science was purely normative. For history M.A. degrees, three political science courses out of eight were compulsory; Political Thought from Plato to the Present Day; Comparative Government including India plus U.K., U.S.A., USSR, and Switzerland; and the Constitutional Development of India from 1857 till 1947. In 1948 when the M.A. in political science at Aligarh was introduced, an overwhelming number of students, compared with history students, sought admission, testifying to the enormous popularity of the discipline from the start. The chairman of the department was an Oxford-trained scholar with matchless academic accomplishment, the late Professor Mohammad Habib.

In Pakistan, on the western side, the University of Punjab alone functioned as a university. It had several good postgraduate colleges offering political science at the M.A. level. The political science faculty in independent Pakistan was largely India-trained and Punjab-trained. The demand for political science forged ahead and, as the new universities came into being, departments of political science were created also. As a whole, among the social sciences, the subject of political science both at the undergraduate as well as the postgraduate level has proven to be more inviting than history. Sometimes in some universities the discipline of economics shows slightly more enrollments.[11]

Out of the ten universities in present Pakistan providing education at the higher, postgraduate level in the various disciplines of social sciences, seven have full-fledged departments of political science. The Quaid-e-Azam University at Islamabad has not yet opened a separate department of Political Science but in the department of History, Pakistan studies, international relations, and public administration courses dealing with it are being offered.

Like the above-mentioned university, the University of Gomal at D.I. Khan has refrained from opening a Department of Political Science on the plea that a full-fledged Department of Political Science at the University of Peshawar is already offering postgraduate studies in this discipline. The Allama Iqbal University at Islamabad is in a class by itself. Its former name "People's Open University" is self-explanatory, for it offers a different kind of program, emphasizing adult literacy in the general scheme of studies. However, in the Department of Social Sciences great weight is given to areas of study drawing upon political science.

University Postgraduate Studies

At present, the following universities are offering postgraduate studies in the major discipline of political science, including subdivisions like international relations and public administration.

UNIVERSITY OF PUNJAB, LAHORE, 1882

This university has various postgraduate departments, three constituent colleges and 106 affiliated colleges with almost all offering civics at the intermediate and political science at the B.A. level. Some of its colleges offer M.A. studies in political science with the government college for boys being high in calibre and having rich traditions. The number of students reported is 5,040. The Department of Political Science of the university is located on the new campus and has in the M.A. final third semester 32 students and in the fourth semester 31 students appeared for their examination. M. Phil. has 3 students and the Ph.D. program has 4 scholars on the rolls. B.A. Honors does not function at present.

The faculty consists of about ten members with Professor M. U. Chughtai, D. Phil Cantab, U.K., as full Professor of Political Science. The chairmanship of the department under the rotation principle introduced in the universities among the first three senior faculty members since 1974 is currently held for two years by Sajjad Naseer, M.A. ABD, University of Massachusetts, Amherst, U.S.A. It does not publish any journal but the seminar library is well-stocked.[12]

UNIVERSITY OF SIND, JAMSHORO, 1947

This university has the singular honor of being the first university created in Pakistan to illuminate the large tract of land constituting the province of Sind. Apart from a wide variety of different postgraduate departments including the Department of Political Science it has 78 affiliated colleges. In some of these colleges, postgraduate studies are being provided in Political Science as an M.A. discipline. The university and the colleges have 13,330 students and 1,347 members in the teaching faculty. In the university alone there are 2,785 students and the faculty strength is reported as 386.

The Department of Political Science offers M.A., B.A. Hons., M.Phil. and Ph.D. programs. It has a faculty of 15 with Nazeer Ahmed Moghul as full professor and Zahida Ashraf, assistant professor, as chairman.[13]

UNIVERSITY OF PESHAWAR, 1950

When Quaid-e-Azam Mohammad Ali Jinnah, father of the nation, visited the historic Islamia college, Peshawar, the miniature Aligarh Muslim University, in April 1948, he promised the young students the bounty of a seat of knowledge from which the rays of learning will spread all over Central Asia.[14] In fulfillment of the promise of the founding father, Liaquat Ali Khan, the first prime minister of Pakistan, laid the foundation stone of the University of Peshawar with the insignia May the Lord Increase My Knowledge. Occupying a thriving campus in the vicinity of the scenic beauty of the Khyber hills only thirty-five miles from the Pakistan-Afghanistan border at Torkham, the university is unique in that it provides comprehensive education from nursery school to the high doctoral level, in various faculties such as humanities, physical sciences, law, engineering, medicine, agriculture, home economics, and commerce. Its academic and administrative jurisdiction extends over the colleges in the settled as well as remote tribal areas excluding Bannu, D. I. Khan, and Waziristan. The colleges in picturesque Dir, Swat, Chitral, and Parachinar are all affiliated with it. In all, it has 2 constituent and 28 affiliated colleges. The student enrollment in the university is 4,109, while in the affiliated colleges it numbers 11,323. The faculty strength in the former is 462 and in the latter 658. The discipline of political science is taught in about 23 colleges at the undergraduate level. Originally the Department of Political Science was combined with the Department of History. Because of the pressurizing demand of the young the department in August 1962 saw the light of day as an independent postgraduate unit of study and research in the discipline of political science with a heavy bias toward international relations and public administration. The author of this chapter who had been associate professor in the combined Department of History and Political Science was transferred to become chairman. The enrollment has been very heavy since its inception. Based on the availability of resources and activities the normal admissions are: 45–50 (with a previous M.A.); 40–44 (with a M.A. Final after dropouts). Diploma classes in international relations and public administration of one academic year duration have 35–45 students in each class.

Arrangements for the Ph.D. and M.Phil. exist in the department. At present two scholars are working for their Ph.D. and five for their M.Phil. One scholar, Nazir Kakakhel, Lecturer in Political Science, Government College for Boys, Nowshera, has already obtained the degree of Ph.D. as an internal candidate with a dissertation on the "Emergence of the State in Early Islam

(622–644.A.D.)." Since the University of Peshawar does not provide M.A. studies in the fields of international relations and public administration the Department of Political Science leans heavily on them in its course content. The teaching faculty is comprised of six full-time members, three having Ph.D. degrees from the U.K. and the U.S.A. and three having double M.A. and law degrees from home universities. The semester system of teaching like the Universities of Punjab and Sind has been in operation for the last three years and is showing very productive results, to the satisfaction of both the faculty and the student body. The department is the largest social science unit in terms of student enrollment. A large number of students seek admission in order to perform favorably in the Central Superior Service examinations held by the Federal Public Service Commission and in reality the course content as well as academic guidance provided in the department have given them a safe entry into these coveted posts. Every year an average of eight alumni succeed in this as well as the public services examinations of the Provincial Public Service Commission, Peshawar.[15] Departments of international relations and public administration are expected to come into existence shortly, since the community demand is reaching a very high pitch. The department publishes an annual journal entitled *Leader* with six issues having been printed so far. The contributors are the faculty and the student body of the department. The journal covers both academic and topics of general interest in the English language. It is quite interesting, that while the various universities teaching political science have permitted the teaching and the answering of examination papers in the Urdu language, the Peshawar university at the B.A., M.A., and research levels has the English language as the required medium. The consensus of academicians and university administrators runs to the effect, that until sufficient reliable material is available in the Urdu language, academic standards should not be allowed to deteriorate by permitting Urdu as the medium of teaching and examination. The seminar library has about five thousand books and journals.

UNIVERSITY OF KARACHI, 1951

The third university established in West Pakistan after independence, the University of Karachi, was intended to serve the huge commercial city of Karachi which has the largest population, now amounting to about four million. The university's jurisdiction extends to the Karachi division only. It has various departments and 44 affiliated colleges. Student enrollment in the university is 7,986 and in the colleges is 62,300. The university faculty consists of 430 members and the colleges have 1,658 members. The Department of Political Science was established in 1953 under the chairmanship of a fine scholar, the late Ilyas Ahmed, author of several works. It has a faculty of 13 with Dr. Manzoor-ud-din Ahmed, Ph.D. Columbia, as full professor. At present he is attached to the South Asian-Pakistan Study Program, Columbia University. The breakdown of students in the department is as follows: 93 (with a previous M.A. of whom 27 are male); 138 (with a final M.A. of whom 73 are female); B.A. Honors: 49 (first year), 83 (second year); 48 (third year). Some scholars are working for their Ph.D. and M. Phil. The seminar library has about 5,000 books and a journal was published until three years ago entitled *The Journal of Political Science*.[16]

UNIVERSITY OF BALUCHISTAN, QUETTA, 1970

Although territorially Baluchistan is the largest of the four provinces of Pakistan, it is the smallest in number of inhabitants with a total population of about 2.6 million. The university exercises jurisdiction over the 16 affiliated colleges, one constituent college, and some postgraduate departments, with a student strength of 1,231 students in the affiliated colleges and 826 students in the university. Similarly, the faculty strength in the former is 256 and in the latter 74.[17] The Department of Political Science was opened in 1972 and is engaged in building up. It has about fifteen students in the M.A. previous and final classes with no honors program. However, students are encouraged to offer a thesis in lieu of M.A. papers. The faculty consists of seven full-time and part-time members with Salah ud-din working for his Ph.D. at Columbia University, New York. At present, the chairmanship of the department is held by Mahmud Ali Shah, M.A., LL.B., Karachi. The seminar library is not well-stocked and no journal is being printed.

ISLAMIA UNIVERSITY, BHAWALPUR, 1975

This university aims primarily at the integration of Islamic values with modern thought. Its territorial jurisdiction covers the whole of Bhawalpur division. It is both a teaching and an affiliating institution. It has five affiliated colleges with 2,500 students and a faculty of 379. The university teachers number 21 and its political science department which opened in early 1976, is headed by Abdul Hamid Khan, M.A., Karachi. It has a very small number of students and follows the conventional system of examinations and courses of the Punjab University. No journal or publications stand to its credit so far. Political science at the undergraduate level is being taught in the five colleges from which part-time teachers in the department of political science are obtained. Being a new department it will take some time to grow.[18]

UNIVERSITY OF MULTAN, 1975

Under the new education policy with a view to meeting the increasing demand in the southern regions of the province of Punjab for ameliorating the condition of the common man this institution was created. Its territorial jurisdiction extends over the whole of the Multan division. It is both a teaching and an affiliating university with some postgraduate departments including the Political Science Department and 24 affiliated colleges. The number of students is 400 in the university and 7,528 in the colleges. The teaching faculty in the university is 24 and in the affiliated colleges 969. In the Political Science Department, the M.A. classes have a very limited number of students with four faculty members. No B.A. Honors or M.Phil. and Ph.D. programs have been started so far. It is in the process of development. Political science is a very popular subject at the undergraduate level in the affiliated colleges.[19]

Structure of the Discipline of Political Science

The intellectual structure of the discipline of political science has assumed new dimensions during the past five to ten years. Before 1947 and until the 1950s, the discipline was viewed as a normative science and heavy emphasis was laid upon its philosophical, legal, and institutional aspects. In general, at the B.A. level two papers were required in the subject of political science with the first paper devoted to the principles of political science and the second to comparative government, (called "modern constitutions," that is, of the U.K., U.S.A., USSR, and India or Pakistan). The recommended sources of study were *Political Science and Government* by W. Garner, *Political Science* by Raymond Gettel, *Political Theory* by Asirvatham, *Principles of Political Science* by Mazhar ul-Haq. Similarly, for the second paper books like *Governments of Europe* by W. B. Munro, *Government of United States of America* by W. B. Munro, *Theory and Practice of Modern Government* by H. Finer, *Comparative Constitutions* by K. K. Aziz, were recommended.

At the postgraduate level of study, also, the courses were imbued with the spirit of the old tradition, placing their main emphasis upon philosophical, legal, and institutional aspects. However, far-reaching changes have been incorporated in political science since the 1960s. By now, our departments have been able to obtain the services of a sizable number of faculty members trained in the modern methodology and behavioral complexion of the discipline from various American and European universities. So, accordingly, the courses of studies in the subject have been revised and an interdisciplinary approach, practical relevance to domestic socioeconomic requirements, and the absorption of home cultural values have been accommodated. Now the departments of political science in the older universities, that is, Karachi, Sind, Punjab, and Peshawar, are teaching compulsory or required courses in the basic areas of political philosophy with a heavy course content in Muslim political philosophy and comparative political systems, including some Asian and African countries; the genesis of Pakistan, public administration; and international relations with emphasis upon Third World countries. Optional courses are being given in local government, international law, international organization, specialized courses in foreign policies, political philosophy, and comparative politics. All courses, whether required or optional, draw heavily upon the ideology, culture, and Pakistani situation, as well as the general Muslim and Afro-Asian situation. Education, including university education in Pakistan, is treated as a vital humanizing, socializing, and skill-giving force. The general consensus in the country is: "Pakistan has been established in the name of Islam. It would not only remain a citadel of Islam but would become a model for other Muslim states in the world."[20] A comprehensive educational policy is also under preparation, and it seeks to harmonize the two branches of knowledge, secular and religious, so that the younger generation is able to develop the qualities of mind and heart advocated by the founding fathers of the country.

A major breakthrough in the uniform designing of courses for all the departments of political science in the various universities of Pakistan occurred with the publication of the *Draft Proposals on Curriculum For B.A. and M.A. in Political and International Relations*, which was prepared by the Curriculum Revision Committee comprised of eminent political scientists of the country, and was set up by the University Grants Commission in July 1976.[21] These recommendations have since been enforced in Pakistan while allowing some flexibility to different universities considering their regional requirements and aspirations. The exercise of revising the curriculum was undertaken with the following objectives in mind:

1. A minimal level of standards should be attained throughout the country.
2. The scheme of courses should be revised to incorporate, so far as possible, the latest developments in the field.
3. The study and training in the two disciplines should be brought in line with and be made useful to national requirements.
4. The proposed scheme of courses should be prepared,

keeping in view the human and material resources available in the country.

5. The scheme should serve as a guideline and should have sufficient flexibility to accommodate individual teacher's expertise and the autonomy of the relevant bodies of the universities.[22]

RECOMMENDATIONS FOR THE B.A.
IN POLITICAL SCIENCE

1. The duration of the course shall be two academic years or four semesters with at least four hours teaching in a week.
2. To provide reading material on the lines of the proposed scheme of courses it will be necessary for textbooks to be written. The committee recommends appointment by the University Grants Commission of four editorial bodies, each assigned the task of writing a textbook.
3. Orientation of teachers through seminars, refresher courses and summer programs is an essential precondition for the introduction of the new scheme. Appropriate steps should, therefore, be taken by the University Grants Commission in this direction.

B.A. Political Science (Pass)

Semester 1
PSC.301   Political Theory
          Paper A.

Political Science: nature and scope; subdivisions, namely, public administration, international relations, comparative politics, local govt; methods of study; approaches such as disciplinary, interdisciplinary and behavioral

Concept of State: traditional, modern, and Islamic concepts
organization of the modern state and its forms: unitary, federal, parliamentary, presidential, democratic, totalitarian, autocratic; structure of govt: legislative, executive, and judicial; political processes: electorate, political parties, interest and pressure groups, public opinion; individual and the state: law, rights, and liberty

Semester 2
PSC.302   *Political Theory:* contemporary ideologies: Marxism, communism, socialism, individualism, fascism, authoritarianism; United Nations: main organs and their working; political systems: definition, components, functions, and types; system analysis with particular reference to Gabriel Almond and David Easton; political development and concepts of development and change

Books Recommended

Rodee Anderson, Clymer et al.,   *Introduction to Political Science* (New York, 1967)

Pennock & Pennock,   *Introduction to Political Science*

Semester 3
PSC.401   Political Systems of China, U.K., and U.S.A.

Books Recommended

Ivor Jennings,   *Cabinet Government* (Cambridge University Press), latest ed.

Samuel Finer,   *Comparative Government,* latest edition, 1974

George Kahin,   *Major Governments of Asia* (Lahore: National Book Foundation), latest ed.

Roy Macridis and Robert Ward,   *Modern Political Systems of Europe,* vol. 1 (Englewood Cliffs, N.J.: Prentice-Hall), latest ed.

Semester 4
PSC.402   *Government and Politics of Pakistan*
   i. Bases of Muslim nationalism in South Asia
   ii. Contribution of Sir Syed Ahmad Khan, Dr. Mohd Iqbal and Quaid-e-Azam Mohammad Ali Jinnah in the making of Pakistan
   iii. Constitutional development since 1947
   iv. Constitution of 1973
   v. Political process with special reference to the functioning of the parliamentary system, federalism, and political parties
   vi. Pakistan in world affairs

Books Recommended

I. H. Qureshi,   *Struggle for Pakistan*

Khalid bin Syed,   *Political System of Pakistan*

S. M. Ikram,   *Modern Muslim India and Birth of Pakistan*

Syed Hassan Riaz,   (Book in Urdu)

Safdar Mahmood,   (Book in Urdu)

Ministry of Law, Govt of Pakistan,   *Constitution of the Islamic Republic of Pakistan, 1973*[23]

RECOMMENDATIONS FOR THE M.A.
IN POLITICAL SCIENCE

For an effective implementation of the proposed scheme of courses, the committee makes the following recommendations:

1. To acquaint the teachers with the latest developments in the field of study, seminars, refresher courses, and short-term training abroad should be provided.
2. To improve the qualifications of the teachers, M.A. Phil. and Ph.D. programs in the subject must be introduced.

Scholarships for higher studies abroad must be established also.

3. Promotion of interdepartmental teaching and research in political science, public administration, international relations and area studies to maximize the utilization of the available trained personnel.

4. The number of teachers should be increased considerably.

5. Since the reading material suggested for the various courses is not available easily in the country, it is recommended that export committees be appointed to select books and articles for printing by the concerned agencies in the country.

6. Steps may be taken to improve library facilities.

7. To provide incentive for study and research a professional journal of international standing should be published.

SCHEMES OF COURSES FOR THE M.A. IN
POLITICAL SCIENCE IN ALL UNIVERSITIES

The scheme is framed on the basis of the following considerations:

1. The minimum credit hours requirement for the master's degree program will be 60.

2. There will be 9 required courses in each discipline. Each required course will be for 4 credit hours.

3. Each student will be required to specialize in one of the proposed fields. For this purpose be will have to take at least 4 courses from the selected field of specialization.

4. A student may be allowed to write a dissertation on an approved subject in lieu of two elective courses (i.e. 8 credit hours).[24]

Draft Proposals for the Syllabus of M.A. Political Science

Minimum credit hours requirement: 60
Required Courses:
  i) Political Theory (Western)
  ii) Political Theory (Muslim)
  iii) Political Systems (Developed)
  iv) Political Systems (Developing)
  v) Pakistan Movement
  vi) Goverment and Politics of Pakistan
  vii) Public Administration
  viii) Basic Factors in International Relations
  ix) Methodology/Political Sociology/Political Modernization and Development

  Each of the above noted courses will be for 4 credit hours.

The following are the four fields of specialization. A student will be required to take at least four courses in the field in which he is specializing:

  i) Political Theory
  ii) Comparative Politics
  iii) International Relations
  iv) Development Administration and Local Government

Field 1 *Political Theory*
  i) Plato and Aristotle
  ii) Marx, Lenin, and Mao
  iii) Contemporary Political Thought
  iv) Ghazzali and Ibn-i-Khaldun
  v) Shah Wali Ullah and Iqbal
  vi) Contemporary Muslim Political Thought
  vii) Hobbes, Locke, and Rousseau

Field 2 *Comparative Politics*
  i) Theories of Comparative Politics
  ii) Studies in Political Systems
  iii) Theories of Modernization and Development
  iv) Political Systems of Iran, Turkey, Pakistan
  v) Indian Politics
  vi) Study in African State Systems
  vii) Political Systems of Selected Latin-American States
  viii) Political Systems of Selected States of the Middle East
  ix) Political Systems of Selected Western European States

Field 3 *International Relations*
  i) International Relations since 1945
  ii) International Organization
  iii) International Law
  iv) Foreign Policy Analysis
  v) Politics of International Economic Relations
  vi) Foreign Policy of Pakistan
  vii) Foreign Policy of Major Powers
  viii) Foreign Policy of India
  ix) Foreign Policy of Iran, Turkey, and Afghanistan
  x) Politics of the Middle East

Field 4 *Developmental Administration and Local Government*
  i) Developmental Administration
  ii) Comparative Public Administration
  iii) Personnel Administration
  iv) Organizational Theory and Behavior
  v) Administrative Management
  vi) Public Administration in Pakistan
  vii) Local Government Administration
  viii) Comparative Local Government
  ix) Financial Administration
  x) Administrative Law
  xi) Planning and Development

Some guidelines for the required courses together with suggested readings have been given in this respect. As regards optional courses, it was thought expedient to leave it up to the relevant bodies of the universities to frame details according to their requirements and the availability of qualified teachers and sufficient reading material.

Political Philosophy (Western). The courses may be designed to provide grounding in the evolution of Western political thought from Plato to Laski, with a focus on the political thought of most representative thinkers of major political movements. This study should be made relevant to the requirements of modern times.

Books Recommended

George H. Sabine,	*History of Political Theory*
William Ebenstein,	*Modern Political Thought: The Great Issues*
Judd Herman,	*Political Thought from Plato to the Present*
Chester Maxey,	*Political Philosophies*

Political Theory (Muslim). The course may be designed to investigate the origin, development, and application of major political concepts of Islam in the light of Holy Quran, Sunnah, and the writings of Muslim jurists, philosophers, and other scholars: for example, Mawardi, Ibn-i-Khaldun, Farabi, Ghazzali, Tusi, Shah Wali Ullah, Afghani, Abduh, and Iqbal. This course is to include a section relating to the application of Islamic political concepts to modern conditions.

Books Recommended

M. M. Sharif,	*A History of Muslim Philosophy,* vols. 1 and 2 (relevant portions)
E. I. J. Rosenthal,	*Political Thoughts in Medieval Islam*
Manzoor ud din Ahmed,	*Muslim Political Theory in the Modern Age*
Mohammad Iqbal,	*Reconstruction of Religious Thought in Islam*

Some books in Urdu.

Political Systems (Developed). This course is designed to acquaint the students with the political systems of three developed countries from among the Federal Republic of Germany, France, U.K., U.S.A. and USSR. These systems are studied to gain a good understanding of the history, social structure, economy, ideology, formal and informal political institutions, and the process of political development.

As an introduction to this course, the students may be initiated into recent methods of comparative politics with particular reference to the structural, functional, and systematic models of Gabriel Almond and David Easton.

Books Recommended

Almond and Powell,	*Comparative Politics: A Developmental Approach*
David Easton,	*A Frame-Work of Political Analysis*
Wiseman,	*The Political System–Some Sociological Approaches*
Almond and Verba,	*Civic Culture*
Macridis and Ward,	*Modern Political Systems of Europe,* vol. 1
Robert Dahl,	*Pluralist Democracy in the United States*

Political Systems (Developing). The course is designed to focus on political processes of at least three countries from among the following: People's Republic of China, Egypt, India, Malaysia, Nigeria, and Turkey. These systems should be studied so as to develop a clear understanding of their history, social structure, economy, ideology, formal and informal political institutions, and the processes of change and political development.

The study should proceed on the lines of functional, structural, and systemic models of comparative politics with particular reference to current writings on modernization and development.

Books Recommended

Gabriel A. Almond and J. S. Coleman,	*The Politics of the Developing Areas*
Almond and Powell,	*Comparative Politics: A Developmental Approach*
Macridis and Ward,	*Modern Political Systems of Asia*
G. Kahin,	*Major Governments of Asia*
W. H. Morris-Jones,	*Government and Politics of India*
N. D. Palmer,	*The Indian Political System*
D. J. Waller,	*Government and Politics of Communist China*
Edward Shils,	*Political Development in the New States*
Burch and Cole,	*Asian Political Systems*
H. B. Sharabi,	*Government and Politics of the Middle East in the Twentieth Century*

The teachers are advised to prepare a reading list containing up-to-date material relating to the political systems to be studied. Students should be asked to consult material from reputable journals in this field.

Pakistan Movement. This course will examine in depth major political, constitutional, social, cultural, and economic forces leading to the establishment of Pakistan. The course is to focus particularly on the major landmarks in the history of the Muslim political movement such as the Aligarh movement, Muslim response to

Hindu religio-political and cultural movements; the Muslim stand vis-à-vis constitutional reforms from 1892 to 1935. Establishment of the all-India Muslim League; Khilafat Movement; Fourteen Points of Jinnah; the Lahore Resolution; the Cripps Proposals; the Cabinet Mission Plan; and the Indian Independence Act of 1947.

The roles of Sir Syed Ahmad Khan, Mohsin-ul-Mulik, Viqar-ul-Mulk, Maulana Mohammad Ali, Dr. Mohammad Iqbal and Quaid-e-Azam Mohammad Ali Jinnah are to be studied in fairly good detail.

Books Recommended

S. M. Ikram,	*Modern Muslim India and the Birth of Pakistan*
I. H. Qureshi,	*Struggle for Pakistan*
Chaudhury Mohammad Ali,	*The Emergence of Pakistan*
M. A. H. Ispahani,	*Factors Leading to the Partition of India*
Abdul Hamid,	*Muslim Separatism in India*
S. S. Pirzada,	*Foundations of Pakistan*
S. S. Pirzada,	*Evolution of Pakistan*
G. Allana,	*Quaid-e-Azam Jinnah*
Saleem Qureshi,	*Jinnah and the Making of a Nation*

Some Books in Urdu

Government and Politics in Pakistan. The course is designed to deal with the ideology of Pakistan and its significance in the political and constitutional development; political and constitutional development since 1947, impact of bureaucracy, military, pressure groups (*Ulemas,* students, trade unions) on the political processes, role of political parties, the press, etc. The course should also discuss economic growth and social change and the problems of national integration. The 1973 constitution and its working should be studied in detail with a focus on the problems of federalism.

Books Recommended

Khalid Bin Syeed,	*Political System of Pakistan*
Manzoor-ud-din Ahmed,	*Pakistan—The Emerging Islamic State*
Howard Wriggins,	*Pakistan in Transition*
G. W. Chowdhury,	*Constitutional Development in Pakistan*
G. W. Chowdhury,	*Democracy in Pakistan*
Wayne Wilcox,	*Pakistan—Consolidation of a Nation*
Ralph Braibanti,	*Bureaucracy in Pakistan*
Henry F. Goodnow,	*Civil Service in Pakistan*
Hasan Askari Riazvi,	*Military and Politics in Pakistan*

Public Administration. The course is designed to acquaint students with the basic concepts of public administration. The course may include topics like approaches and methods of study of public administration, planning, organization (formal and informal), decision-making, bureaucracy, administrative behavior and responsibility, authority, leadership, human relations, personnel management, and developmental administration.

Books Recommended

J. M. Pfiffner and Presthus,	*Public Administration*
Harold Koontz and Cyril O'Donnell,	*Principles of Management*
Pfiffner and Sherwood,	*Administrative Organization*
L. D. White,	*Introduction to the Study of Public Administration*
Herbert A. Simon,	*Administrative Behavior*
March and Simon,	*Organization*
Gerald D. Bell,	*Organization and Human Behavior*
Sidney, Mailick, and Vanress,	*Administrative Behavior*

Basic Factors in International Relations. This course is designed to give a proper understanding of the basic factors and operational principles of international relations with a view to acquainting the student with a rational, analytical, and systematic grasp of the stresses and strains of the contemporary international system.

Books Recommended

K. J. Holsti,	*International Politics*
Hans J. Morgenthau,	*Politics Among Nations*
Joseph Frankel,	*International Politics: Conflict and Harmony*
Vernon Van Dyke,	*International Politics*
Palmer and Perkins,	*International Relations*

Study of Research Methodology. This course will cover recent developments in the field of methodology and comparative politics.

Books Recommended

H. V. Wiseman,	*The Political System—Some Sociological Approaches*
William J. Goode and Paul K. Hatt,	*Methods in Social Research*

Vernon Van Dyke,	*Political Science: A Philosophical Analysis*
Abraham Kaplan,	*The Conduct of Inquiry*
Leon Festinger and Daniel Katz,	*Research Methods in Behavioral Sciences*
Charlesworth,	*Contemporary Political Analysis*

Political Sociology. The course is designed to study the various strands of social and political behavior constituting political sociology. An attempt will also be made to emphasize the importance of sociology in the study of political processes.

Books Recommended

Michael Rush and Philip Althoff,	*An Introduction to Political Sociology*
W. G. Runciman,	*Social Science and Political Theory*
Oran R. Young,	*System of Political Science*
Karl W. Deutsch,	*The Nerves of Government: Models of Political Communication and Control*
Lucian W. Pye, ed.	*Communication and Political Development*

Theories of Change—Political Modernization and Development. This course will evaluate the theories and comparison of major patterns of political modernization, values, and ideology in relation to institutional change, national identity, social communication, and the process of nation-building; the role of social groups in the political processes, the problems of local government; resources and urbanization; charismatic leadership, and mass movement.

Books Recommended

Finkle and Gables Welch, C. E., Huntington	*Political Modernization*
Edward Shils,	*Political Development in New States*
David Apter,	*Politics of Modernization*

Interest in Political Science

As pointed out earlier, the discipline of political science has become increasingly popular as an elective and as a major subject at the postgraduate and undergraduate levels on account of the personal interest of the young people and also because of the returns it offers in terms of lucrative future careers. Among the social science subjects in the Northwest Frontier Province, it is the most popular subject. A brief statistical record of admissions during a recent session will indicate how the enrollment is flooding undergraduate classes despite the efforts of the respective admission committees.

Islamia College, Peshawar, Admissions, 1976-77

	1st yr	2d yr
Civics	102	119
Economics	70	92
History	83	90

Jinnah College for Women, Peshawar, Admissions, 1977-78

	1st yr	2d yr
Civics	39	65
Economics	35	35
History	25	25
	3d yr	4th yr
Political Science	20	15
Economics	10	...
History	3	...

Frontier College for Women, Peshawar, Admissions, 1976-77

	3d yr	4th yr
Political Science	64	50

Edwards College for Boys, Peshawar, Admissions, 1976-77

	4th yr	2d yr
Political Science	52	...
Civics	...	62
Economics	42	49
History	38	72

Other social science disciplines attract much smaller numbers of students and the same interest is reflected by the students at the postgraduate level. In other provinces, the disciplines of civics and political science are very popular but some competition comes from psychology in the cases of women and economics in the case of men. If the colleges and the postgraduate departments in political science were to increase facilities and exercise no bar upon admissions, the turnover would be much higher. Each year the University of Peshawar produces about 100 M.A.'s in political science and about 300 B.A.'s with political science as an elective subject.[25]

In Pakistan, a large number of private candidates in service and otherwise are allowed to take the B.A. and M.A. examinations in nonscientific disciplines and a second annual examination called the Supplementary is also permitted. So, the production of M.A. candidates in political science in the country is about seven hundred. The tendency of the best degree holders is to appear for the Central and Provincial Public Service Commission examinations in order to join the elite civil services. The reports of these commissions have indicated that political science graduates have been faring above average. The Department of Political Science, University of Peshawar, has earned greater distinction by giving to these services the best male brains of the province to serve the needs of the teeming millions in the nation who are awaiting fulfillment of their rising expectations. While teaching the discipline, the efforts of the faculty are directed toward the creation of social and political awareness among the young graduates to serve the cause of the Pakistani masses and humanity in general as the special appeal and commitment of their subject. Among the male graduates after the first choice of civil services the second preference is toward joining the teaching profession at the college and university levels. Within the last fifteen years or so, an explosion has taken place in terms of the provision of inland-trained lecturers by the political science departments in the universities of Punjab, Karachi, Sind, and Peshawar. The department at Peshawar has performed a valuable service by providing every college in the province, even in distant Miranshah or Chitral, with lecturers in the disciplines of civics and political science. This, indeed, is the most positive contribution in producing ideology-oriented and production-centered teachers to train the youth for future responsibilities.

METHODOLOGICAL DEVELOPMENTS:

Enormous interest is being shown in the methodological study of political science. Research methods in social sciences, use of questionnaires, interview techniques, and behavioral techniques are not only taught comprehensively at the M.A. level, but they are also employed while writing assignments, dissertations, and Ph.D. theses. However, a major bottleneck of resources and equipment is preventing greater speed. At the B.A. level on an all-Pakistan basis, various faculty members have been selected to write textbooks in the discipline.[26] It is sincerely hoped that these books will bear the imprint of modern approaches, techniques, and methodology in general. The students are encouraged to express their recommendations and appreciation of the themes and course contents more profusely than before. The discipline is leaning more heavily toward anthropology, social psychology and economics. The teachers concerned before introducing, for example, the subjects of comparative politics, public administration and international relations place sufficient emphasis upon the modern approaches and relevant models of Almond and Coleman, David Easton, Kaplan, Lasswell, and Elton Mayo. As such, the discipline is receiving a new orientation in the classrooms and in research but it will take some time for Pakistani teachers to produce more books containing new methodological developments. The very fact that a consensus on this issue exists and a pioneer effort has been made guarantees a hopeful future.

ASSOCIATIONAL ACTIVITIES

The all-Pakistan Political Science Association was founded in 1950 under the presidency of the late Maulvi Tamiz ud-din from East Pakistan who was a distinguished ex-speaker of the National Assembly of Pakistan, the federal legislature under the 1962 Constitution of Pakistan. The association has a written constitution and is registered with UNESCO. The second president was Ishtiaq Hussain Qureshi, a scholar of eminent distinction in the history and politics of the subcontinent. In December 1972, the author of this chapter was elected president. The present secretary of the association is Professor Muneer ud din Chughtai, Professor of Political Science, University of Punjab, Lahore. Professor Aziz Ahmed served as an elected secretary from the early 1960s till November 1971, and the association owes profound gratitude to his leadership in organizing its activities. He retired from service as Professor and Chairman, Department of Political Science, University of Karachi, some years ago, and is available for detailed information about the association at Karachi. General conferences were held at Lahore 1951, Peshawar 1957, Karachi 1964, and at Karachi again in 1968.

The association has to its credit four printed proceedings containing the papers read at these conferences and copies can be obtained from the former secretary. Its membership is open to all teachers and degree holders in the discipline of political science. It is handicapped by financial impediments because member subscriptions cost the nominal sum of Rs 12 (U.S. $1.20) and there is only a very meager grant from the Federal Ministry of Education. It really needs the active interest and support of political scientists, at home and abroad, of the government, and of sister professional associations. The cost of holding general conferences has risen tremendously and the universities' hospitality has been almost impossible to get during the past few years. Some older associations in other social sciences and physical sciences have been receiving preferential hospitality by the universities in the country. Now, with the coming into existence of the departments of political science at the Universities of Baluchistan, Multan, and Bhawalpur, the prospects that the association will gain fresh vigor have brightened. It is worth mentioning, that a Pakistan-wide seminar of representative teachers from the various departments of political science and the colleges from the four provinces was held at Baragali, NWFP, in July 1972. The author, a member of the home university of

Peshawar, was selected as the convenor/leader, with Professor M. U. Chughtai, Punjab University, and Asrar Hussain of the home university as other leaders. The participants were the teachers of the discipline and numbered about two dozen. The major areas touched were the role of ideology in the constitution-making process in Pakistan, foreign policy of Pakistan, the secession of East Pakistan, the causes, factors, and the recognition of Bangladesh by Pakistan, the need for new research methodology in political science, and the interdisciplinary approach.[27]

Journals. So far there is no independent journal of political science in the country. The scholars and patrons of the discipline, however, are publishing research papers in the journals of the various universities and research organizations. Some of the most notable are the *Journal of the University of Peshawar, Journal of the Academy for Rural Development, Peshawar,* and the *Journal of the Pakistan Administrative Staff College.* The faculty of the discipline of political science has been producing publications, some of which are cited below:

G. W. Chowdhry, formerly of the University of Dacca, East Pakistan:
Constitutional Development In Pakistan, London, 1969.
Democracy In Pakistan, Dacca, 1963
Pakistan's Relations with India, London, 1968
Last Days of United Pakistan, London, 1974

Manzoor ud-din Ahmed, University of Karachi, Pakistan:
The Emerging Islamic State, Karachi, 1966

Afsar Saleem Khan, University of Peshawar:
Political Theory of Delhi Sultanate, Delhi, 1961
The Fatawa-i-Jahandari of Zia ud-din Barani, Lahore, 1972

Hasan Askari Rizvi, University of Punjab, Lahore:
Military and Politics in Pakistan, Lahore

M. A. Chowdhri, Department of Political Science, University of Dacca, East Pakistan:
The Civil Service of Pakistan. Dacca, 1963.

Dr. Waheed us-zaman, Dean, Faculty of Social Sciences, Quaid-e-Azam, Islamabad:
Quaid-e-Azam Mohammad Ali Jinnah: Myth and Reality, Islamabad, 1977

Qureshi Ishtiaq, H., formerly president of all-Pakistan Political Science Association;
Struggle for Pakistan, Karachi, 1965
The Muslim Community of the Indo-Pakistan Sub-Continent, The Hague, 1962
Pakistan, An Islamic Democracy, Karachi
Ulema In Politics, Karachi, 1974

Masood Ahmed Khan:
Comparative Politics, Lahore, 1977

Political Science and the World of Politics

THE IMPACT OF POLITICAL EVENTS ON POLITICAL SCIENCE

The impact upon political science of local, domestic, and international political events is tremendous. The politics of underdevelopment; the pressing need for developmental state activity; challenges of hunger, disease, ignorance, international multipower politics, Great-Power rivalry; and, above all, a general yearning for overall security are some of the vital issues flooding the reflections of the students and the faculty of this discipline. How may the house be set in order, and how may these baffling problems be tackled by the full use of the instructions of patriotism, national identity, selfless effort, and inclinations of world citizenship? The discipline is required to play its full role in answering these questions. Representative groups of students and teachers were interviewed in this connection and their views are recorded briefly.

According to the Peshawar group:[28]

"Political science means a program for the aggregation and channelization of men's interests and needs in their private as well as publicly organized life."

"The problems and issues that this subject deals with are virtually as infinite and complex as the varied wishes of the individual and his collectivities. The subject could thrive only if it effectively incorporates within its scope this sense of realization."

"In Pakistan the subject has a fertile and novel area for research. The political behavior of the Pakistani electorate could be successfully investigated and its weakness and trends fruitfully analyzed. Institutional stability and the lack of it could also be effectively probed by political scientists and, thus, with the help of this subject the politics of all such developing areas may be cleaned and developed. It could be shown how politics might be made less vulnerable to friction, violence, factionalism, and abuse. In short, political science has to face a great humanitarian challenge in areas like Pakistan and other developing countries, where a healthy consensus is weak enough to get overshadowed by self- and power-seeking individuals and groups."

"On the global level it would be vain to emphasize the precarious situation of humanity split up among numerous sovereign states, vying with one another, jockeying for advantage and benefit in a world of dwindling resources. With a nuclear incubus hanging upon their subconscious, the political leaders and citizens alike are undergoing the torture of an uncertain tomorrow. In this highly somber and volatile international milieu, the value of political science, aiming at its basics of coordination and accommodation, suggests itself inevitably. George Bernard Shaw could never be more correct than to say—it is a science which alone can save mankind from destruction."

A group of political science teachers and postgraduate students from the Department of Political Science, University of Baluchistan visiting the University of Peshawar was interviewed by the author in early 1978. It stated:

> "Our discipline offers an appeal of a happy and a prosperous tomorrow. It identifies individual good with social advantage. Questions of what is mine and what is thine are very satisfactorily answered by it. The society and the government are means to an end and not ends in themselves. They demand legitimacy and obedience for what they offer by way of security and happiness to the community."
>
> "In Pakistan and other developing countries the science of politics bears special relevance. Its emphasis upon modernization and development along with ideological values holds the key to a better tomorrow. Gone are the days when Machiavellis, Hitlers, and Mussolinis inspired us. Times have approached when political philosophers like Dr. Mohammad Iqbal, Jamal ud-din Afghani, Shah Wali Ullah, and Bertrand Russell set the right path before us. In the words of the national poet Iqbal:
>
> God Almighty has created man for the service of others,
> Otherwise for His Own Worship the animals were quite enough.

The impact of contemporary political events upon the course content of political science is also no less deep. The courses have been modernized and made very up-to-date as the Scheme of Courses prepared by the Committee on Political Science under the auspices of the Pakistan University Grants Commission, cited earlier, very clearly indicates. Methodological developments, Third World political systems, their foreign policies, bipolar and multipolar world politics, political sociology, and political development with special reference to Pakistan have been accommodated.[29]

POLITICAL SCIENTISTS IN POLITICS

Young graduates of political science have shown more interest in terms of careers in the civil service, teaching positions, banks, industry, and private business than participation in practical politics.[30] A large number of political scientists are selected for the foreign service of Pakistan. They have become career diplomats and comprise a large proportion in the civil administration as policy makers and practical administrators. Very few have joined political parties, contested in national and provincial elections or have become ministers. In Pakistan mature persons from the aristocratic, *ulema,* and legal profession have been entering practical politics, the assemblies, and the ministries. Excepting the Department of Political Science of the University of Punjab, the departments have come into existence only during the last few years. It is premature to expect their alumni to enter practical politics, for professional service careers guaranteeing a secure livelihood are more inviting than participation in practical politics. However, the Department of Political Science of the University of Peshawar had Waheed Akhtar from Campbellpur on its rolls in the early 1960s. With a masters degree in political science, he entered politics as a member of the People's party. He was first elected a federal senator under the 1973 Constitution and in the elections of March 1977 he was elected a member of the Federal National Assembly. The Department of Political Science, University of Punjab, also reports its ex-student, Asad Masud as an MNA (member of the Federal National Assembly). In the next few years as political stability returns to Pakistan, it is expected that more political scientists will enter practical politics.

RELATIONSHIPS BETWEEN THE GOVERNMENT AND THE DISCIPLINE

Several political scientists are serving in the government as bureaucratic officials and diplomatic agents. They are selected from the universities by the government to work on syllabus committees, national commissions, and as organizers of government-sponsored seminars and symposia. Students from the departments of political science have been selected to represent their country in delegations to the People's Republic of China and to Japan. From the Peshawar department two female postgraduate students, Zahida Niazi and Riffat Sardar, went to the People's Republic of China and Japan in 1976 in student delegations. An increasing awareness is dawning that the government must extend participation to political scientists at the student and teacher level in nation-building activities. The teachers particularly expect to serve as government advisors in the fields of external foreign policy formulation as well as internal public policy drafting.

The Present State and Future Prospects of Political Science in Pakistan

Since the tide of rising expectations is in full swing, the departments of political science in the universities and in the degree colleges fully deserve expansion in terms of physical facilities. In view of the enormous student interest in seeking admissions to this discipline, expansion of the faculty, seminar libraries, physical accommodations, and research equipment must be arranged for. It is not because of a lack of awareness regarding the utility and useful role of the subject, that this expansion has been handicapped. It is the bottleneck of available resources that prevents better organization, including expansion, rather than an inadequacy in realizing the usefulness of the discipline. Pakistan ideology, movement, political system, public administration, foreign relations, and local government constitute the basic areas of study in this discipline and their thorough understanding will provide fundamental tools for creating greater integration, cohesion, adaptation, penetration, and identification in the minds of the young graduates, who are destined to be the leaders and the citizenry in Pakistan tomorrow.[31]

Notes

1. See E. I. Rosenthal, *Political Thought in Medieval Islam* (Cambridge: At the University Press, 1968), p. 23.
2. See H. K. Sherwani, *Muslim Political Thought and Administration* (Lahore, 1963), p. 145.
3. A. Saleem Khan, *The Fatawa-i-Jahandari of Zia ud-din Barani*, (Lahore, 1972), pp. 122-23.
4. Islamabad: University Grants Commission, 1977, p. 1.
5. Ibid.
6. Khan, *Fatawa-i-Jahandari*, pp. 54-55.
7. *Universities Year Book*, p. 3.
8. Ibid.
9. Ibid., p. 14.
10. See the three reports published by the University Grants Commission, Islamabad, especially the *Report on Student Problems*, p. 77. It is worth mentioning here that with a population of about 70 million in Pakistan 2% of the relevant age group are enrolled in the institutions of higher learning, as against 50% in the U.S., or 175 out of 10,000 in Pakistan, 3,700 in the U.S., and 217 in India. Similarly, the GNP spent on research and development in Pakistan is 0.3%, in the U.S. 3.40%, and in India 0.45%. See *Varsities*, May-June 1977, p. 38.
11. *Universities Year Book*, p. 25.
12. Ibid., pp. 16, 36, 54. Some data come from questionnaires sent by the author to the departments.
13. Ibid., pp. 55-78.
14. The father of the nation, who died in September 1948, had a special love for this college. He donated much of his personal fortune to three institutions: Islamia College, Sind, Peshawar; Madrasa; and Muslim University, Aligarh.
15. *Universities Year Book*, pp. 121-23. The department has produced roughly 600 young M.A.'s, mostly engaged in jobs throughout Pakistan, and has had an alumni association since 1972.
16. Ibid., pp. 144-45.
17. Ibid., pp. 213.
18. Ibid., pp. 237, 243.
19. Ibid.
20. From the address of the Central Education Advisor, delivered 2 March 1978.
21. Islamabad: University Grants Commission, 1976, pp. 1-5.
22. Ibid., p. 5.
23. Ibid., pp. 5-7.
24. The Department of Political Science, University of Peshawar, has introduced these courses for the B.A. and M.A. levels, effective from the academic session of 1978. Departments in other universities are taking suitable steps to implement the proposals. This report of the committee is very illuminating with regard to the structure of the discipline, mode of teaching, library facilities, and the need for a professional journal. See note 21, pp. 3-4.
25. See the university results in March and April 1978.
26. Masoor Ahmed of the Department of Political Science, Punjab University, produced his first work in Urdu, "Comparative Politics," Lahore, 1977.
27. For a record of the proceedings, contact Dr. Kazmi, in charge of the seminar, Department of Physical Chemistry, University of Peshawar.
28. Interview conducted by the author in November 1977.
29. See note 21.
30. The results of the FPSC, Pakistan, March 1978, showed that eight of nine former students of the Department of Political Science, University of Peshawar, passed the written examination.
31. The existing pay structure for university and college faculty, after considerable liberalization since May 1977 is:
1. Lecturer—Rs. 900-50-1150/60-1750 per month
2. Asst. prof—Rs. 1350-75-1650/100-2150 per month
3. Assoc. prof.—Rs. 2250-100-2750 per month
4. Professor—Rs. 2600-125-3225 per month

This salary, in addition, carries a 30 percent housing allowance, a conveyance/car allowance, and some other allowances along with free medical aid. For promotion, teaching experience and research contributions are the required criteria.

Selected Bibliography

Admission records of selected colleges in Peshawar, 1976-77, 1977-78.
Anderson, Rodee, Carlton Clymer, et al., *Introduction to Political Science*. New York: McGraw Hill, 1976.
Daily Pakistan Times, Rawalpindi edition.
ud-din Hasan, Syed Ahmed. "Political Science Departments in the Universities of Pakistan." (Article in Urdu). *Daily Mashriq*, 25 August, 1977.
Interviews by the author with selected faculty and student representatives of the Departments of Political Science, December-February, 1977-78.
Irish, Marian D. *Political Science, Advance of the Discipline*, 1968.
Khan, Afsar Saleem. *The Fatawa-i-Jahandari of Zia ud-din Barani*. Lahore, 1972.
Replies to questionnaires issued to various Departments of Political Science, Universities of Pakistan, March-April 1978.
Report of Study Groups on Student Problems in Universities. Islamabad: University Grants Commission, 1975.

Report of Study Groups on University Teachers' Problems. Islamabad: University Grants Commission, 1974.

Rosenthal, E. I. *Political Thought in Medieval Islam.* Cambridge: At the University Press, 1968.

Sherwani, Haroon Khan. *Muslim Political Thought and Administration.* Lahore, 1963.

Universities of Pakistan Year Book. Islamabad: University Grants Commission, 1976.

University Calendars of Sind, Karachi, Punjab, and Peshawar, published by these universities annually.

Varsities. Islamabad: Journal of University Grants Commission, May–June, 1977.

24 POLAND
KAZIMIERZ OPAŁEK

Introduction

The development of political thought in Poland corresponds in substance to more generally observable patterns. Political science in the contemporary sense began to take shape in recent times—since the turn of the century—and its rise as a distinct discipline occurred in the period after World War II. The study of politics, however, has a long tradition in Poland, with two branches that must be mentioned. The first is political philosophy, having its outstanding representatives in the Middle Ages (Stanisław of Skarbimierz and Paweł Włodkowić), in the period of the Renaissance (Jan Ostróg and Andrzej Frycz Modrzewski), and in that of the Enlightenment (Hugo Kołłątaj and Stanisław Staszic).[1] The second is the literature pertaining to current political problems. In political philosophy, axiological considerations have prevailed, while in the writings on current questions practical proposals of concrete solutions have done so. However, many times both types were interconnected and mingled with considerations on ethical, legal, and economic topics in a way typical of periods in which the social disciplines were not yet separated.[2]

In times when Poland was deprived of national independence (1795–1918), the development of academic political thought was visibly restrained. "Unofficial" political thought, however, derived new incentives from unceasing strivings for independence together with arising social problems and spread—both in the country and in exile—beyond the sphere of legality of the states occupying Polish territories.

The decline of the maximalist philosophy and the influence of positivist conceptions of science became pronounced in Poland at the end of the last century, contributing to the shaping up of the program of "political sciences" (in the plural as disciplines dealing separately with different facts or aspects of politics). This program determined for a long time the research practice, consisting of the dispersion of scholarly activities, carried on as a rule within other, already separate, social disciplines such as history, the study of law, political economy, and sociology—quite frequently rather on their periphery only. It determined also the educational activities, which consisted of creating (even before independence was regained, in parts of the country where the political regime was more liberal) "schools of political sciences," that aimed at supplementary education or persons studying other social sciences.[3] These traits were also characteristic of the interwar period (1918–1939), in which the influence of the French conception of *sciences politiques* was visible.[4] In the domain in question, as in the whole scientific life of the country, the period of the Nazi occupation (1939–1944) was marked by severe personal, institutional, and material losses. Scientific work was carried on in hiding and isolation, education in secret universities.

The State of Political Science, 1945–1949

After World War II, research and education were quickly restored, while the plural conception of "political sciences" still prevailed. Two factors were decisive. First, the tradition of investigating different aspects of politics within such disciplines as the theory of the state, constitutional and international law, political economy, modern history, and political sociology. Second, the existence of specialized studies in particular fields of politics (foreign, social, economic, cultural policies, etc.). In effect, research and education in sciences commonly called "political" were performed by scholars of different specializations, favoring various theoretical conceptions, using various methods and research techniques, and differing in their conceptual apparatus. Also it was manifest in the activities of scientific associations and institutes, undertaking research on different problems of politics within other, programmatically cultivated social sciences,[5] as well as in education in the schools of political sciences founded at the universities of Warsaw, Cracow, Łódź, and Poznań. These schools were similar in character and aims to those of the preceding period.

One factor producing a certain spontaneous integration of political science during this period was the existence of two main orientations in scope and methods: the *juristic* one, concentrating on the problems of the state and of legal regulation in the field of politics, and the *sociological* one, drawing attention to the wide range of formal and informal manifestations of political life, studied from the point of view of facts and not their legal regulation.[6]

These orientations led later to alternative proposals of integrating political sciences on the base either of the juristic theory of the state or of political sociology.

The Evolution of Political Science since 1949

THE INTELLECTUAL STRUCTURE OF THE DISCIPLINE

In spite of the shortcomings mentioned above, the attainments of political science in Poland increased and became visible. Consequently, among scholars interested in problems of politics and establishing mutual contact in schools of political sciences, grew a consciousness of affinity and a need to tighten their bonds in scientific research. This tendency was intensified by programs of integration, spreading to the social sciences in mid-century. In Poland, as in other countries, steps were taken toward unification in research, consisting of creating theories of interdisciplinary range, of introducing common methods and research techniques, and of bringing closer the conceptual apparatus of various social sciences. Also attempts were made at coordinating research efforts on related topics and at interdisciplinary cooperation in research. For the stabilized social sciences, it amounted to the enrichment and modernization of the tools of research and a widening of the scope of problems beyond the traditional limits. For political science, integration was something more, leading up to the creation of an autonomous discipline, in place of political sciences forming parts of history, sociology, the study of law, and political economy.[7]

At the same time, the narrow empiricism and "hyperfactualism" were criticized. The role of theories—of both general and middle-range—in the social sciences was appreciated anew, while demands for scientific accuracy in these theories increased, in comparison with the earlier, "humanistic" stage of the social sciences when theorems were based on data of undetermined representativeness and influenced by the scholar's intuition and his own uncontrolled experience.[8] In political science in Poland this tendency was of particular importance, as it was conducive to the unification and separation of the discipline and opposed to the collecting of crude data in various unrelated domains.

Most important, however, for the intellectual structure of the discipline, was its basis after mid-century on the theory and methodology of historical materialism which, as a general theory of society and its evolution, made it possible to organize the vast amount of factual data from the field of politics, and provide tools for their explanation and interpretation as manifestations of general patterns in social life. Historical materialism contains also theses pertaining specifically to politics and giving inspiration to scientific reflection on the political phenomena of our time. Namely, the founders of Marxism, on the bases of concrete analyses of political life—of the state, political parties, diplomacy, wars, and so on—formulated general theses on the mechanisms of politics, on their dependence upon economics and relations of social classes, on the ancillary role of the state in relation to the economic basis, on revolutionary changes of the social-political structure, on the dictatorship of the proletariat and its state—to mention only the fundamental theses. The influence of historical materialism and the successive deepening of its application contributed to the unification of political science, and was decisive in the specific intellectual traits of this discipline in Poland.

This evolution in political science found its expression in vivid theoretical-methodological discussions. In the first phase—in the 1950s and 1960s—they pertained mostly to the general meta-scientific problems of the theory of political science and methods of the latter. The Polish tradition of political sciences in the plural was commonly attacked, but the views and postulates as to the character, structure, scope, and relation to other social sciences differed widely. Cautious postulates of the gradual integration of political sciences met with proposals for a "strong" integration, having its base in the theory of the state or political sociology; and with radical views on the principal separateness of political science as a branch of social science. The application of Marxist methodology was also commonly accepted but the views differed—in accordance with the standpoints already mentioned—whether in political science the Marxist methods concretized in the domains of history, sociology, the study of law, and political economy ought to be adopted, or whether specific concretization of Marxist methodology ought to be elaborated in political science.[9]

In the second phase of discussions—in the 1970s—detailed theoretical and methodological conceptions were worked out concerning various aspects of politics and particular methods and research techniques. These contributions, however, constitute a separate topic dealt with below under "Research in Political Science." In shaping up the intellectual structure of political science some organizational measures played an important role also. These are described below under "Associational Activities."

THE TEACHING OF POLITICAL SCIENCE

Parallel to these changes in political science, the problem of new forms of education was entered upon. The schools of political sciences gradually died out. Teaching based on the new principles started from the introduction in 1964 of the course of lectures entitled "Foundations of Political Science" as an obligatory subject in some faculties and specializations of the academic schools. In 1968, this subject became obligatory for all faculties and specializations. The course lasts alternatively one to two semesters, depending on the type of studies, and ends with an examination. The program of this course, after several changes, is composed of the following parts: (1) fundamental problems of Marxist political theory, (2) the political system and its functioning, (3) contemporary political movements and doctrines, (4) socioeconomic politics of Poland, (5) foreign policies of Poland and contemporary international relations, and (6) political consciousness.[10] Since 1964, a number of textbooks for this subject have appeared, some of them specially adapted to the main types of studies. We have now a basic textbook, collectively prepared.[11] Special units, called studies of political science, were created in all academic schools for organizing the teaching of the subject.

The introduction of this course was accompanied by the organizing of different forms of education for the junior scientific staff. The main forms since 1967 are postgraduate (doctorate) studies in political science. They are situated in the most important scientific centers of the country, in which institutes of political science were created (in the universities of Warsaw, Cracow, Poznań, Wrocław, Katowice and Gdańsk). The institute in Warsaw was afterward (1976) transformed into a faculty. Until 1977 the institutes educated 239 doctors of political science and 22 assistant professors, including 8 doctors in 1971, 18 doctors in 1972, 28 doctors and 2 assistant professors in 1973, 43 doctors and 3 assistant professors in 1974, 53 doctors and 5 assistant professors in 1975, 39 doctors and 4 assistant professors in 1976, and 50 doctors and 8 assistant professors in 1977. In 1978, 111 persons attended postgraduate studies (Warsaw 46, Katowice 27, Cracow 20, Wrocław 13, Poznań 5). At present there is a growing number of persons working on theses qualifying for assistant professorships. All institutes, however, also employ scholars who are qualified in other branches of social science.

Institutes of political science are the main organizers of research. This research is conducted also by institutes of social-political sciences, created in the main academic technical schools. These institutes, however, are not authorized to confer scientific degrees. Also, we have in Poland some academic schools in which teaching and research in political science has an important place (Military Political Academy, Academy of Social Sciences in Warsaw).

Since 1970 graduate studies in political science have been organized in the institutes of political science. Until 1977, the masters degree was obtained by 486 persons. In 1978 we had 1,774 students (Warsaw 525, Katowice 554, Poznań 297, Wrocław 245, Cracow 153).

All these activities are supported by an institution that reports to the Ministry of Science, the Academic Education and Technology-Methodological Center of Education in Political Science in Warsaw. In the beginning, its tasks were limited to methods of teaching and preparing didactic materials. In recent years, the center started its own research work.

RESEARCH IN POLITICAL SCIENCE

Most Noteworthy Contributions

Special attention must be paid to two great research projects of an interdisciplinary character and executed jointly by all academic centers of the country.[12] The first of them deals with problems of local power in Poland (the functioning of the national councils, in the first place). The research started fifteen years ago. It is directed by the Institute of State and Law of the Polish Academy of Sciences, headed by S. Zawadzki. The results are published in a special journal *Problemy Rad Narodowych* [Problems of national councils] and in separate publications. This research gave rise to comparative research on local power on an international scale, undertaken on Polish initiative since 1970 under the direction of J. Wiatr. The second project, on "The model of political culture in Socialist Society," was initiated in 1976. It is directed by the Faculty of Social Sciences of the Silesian University in Katowice. After the first stage of preliminary theoretical-methodological studies, empirical research is now being conducted. The starting point for this project was the session of the Polish Political Science Association (Poznań 1975). Afterward, a round-table conference of IPSA on political culture was organized (Cracow 1977).

Noteworthy contributions are those in the field of Marxist political theory. The work of a special research team of the Methodological Center of Education in Political Science under the direction of A. Bodnar must be mentioned. These works aim at elaborating a theory of politics as an empirical theory corresponding to the postulates of the contemporary methodology of social sciences. Their attention is focused on the problem of explanation in political science. The ideological function of this branch of science is also much debated. Here belong also studies of A. Bodnar on the relation of politics to economics, those of J. Wiatr on the relation of politics and ideology, and of K. Opałek on law and politics and on the role of various other social norms and values in politics.

Research on the political system is undertaken mainly in Warsaw and Poznań. The works in Warsaw (Institute of Basic Problems of Marxism-Leninism and Academy of Social Sciences) concentrate on the role of the Marxist-Leninist party in the socialist political system while those in Poznań are concerned with other organizations that form parts of this system (National Unity Front, United Peasants' Party, Democratic Party, trade unions, students associations, etc.). The recent history of the workers movement in Poland is being investigated by the Wrocław center (M. Orzechowski, B. Pasierb).

The Gdańsk center under direction of K. Podoski specializes in problems of public policy. Some attainments of the scholars of Warsaw (A. Rajkiewicz and his disciples) must be mentioned here also.

Research in contemporary international relations is concentrated in the Polish Institute of International Affairs in Warsaw (R. Bierzanek, J. Symonides and others). The main topics are international organization, relations among socialist countries, the European system of security and disarmament, and Polish-German relations.

The Cracow center specializes in contemporary political doctrines. The most important works are those by M. Sobolewski and M. Waldenberg on socialist political thought and on neoliberal and conservative doctrines.

Methodological Developments

After the phase of preliminary discussions in the 1960s more detailed investigations into methodological problems were developed. One of the recent interesting attempts in the general methodology of political science is based on the attainments of the Poznań school of social sciences methodology, laying stress on the adaptational dependence of social phenomena, discovered by historical materialism, and formulating postulates of "humanistic interpretation" together with the assumption of the rationality of social actions, political among them.[13] It is an original conception in Marxist methodology, very much debated and having adherents but also opponents.

Particular methods and research techniques are being developed also. There is a marked tendency to build them consistently into the general methodology of historical materialism. Present methodological orientations and attainments illustrate the collective work *Methodo-*

logical and theoretical problems of political science (1975), dealing with such topics as the methodological status of Marxist political science, quantitative methods and research techniques, behavioral methods, comparative research, institutional-juristic methods, systems analysis, and conceptual-terminological analysis. Still more and more influential are the methods and techniques of empirical social sciences, mostly of sociology, and systems analysis. The applications of theories of behavior, of decisions, and of the general theory of action in the version of praxeology, elaborated by the Polish philosopher, T. Kotarbiński, must be noted also.[14]

One can still speak about a methodological pluralism, due partly to the many-sidedness of the subject matter of political science and partly to the fact that the process of integration of political science is far from being finished.

ASSOCIATIONAL ACTIVITIES

Associations. Poland joined the IPSA in 1950 as the seventh national member and the first one from a socialist country. Simultaneously, the process of the formation of the Polish Political Science Association (PPSA) was started. The first stage of this process was finished in 1955. PPSA was built, then, as a federation of scientific associations in which problems of political science were undertaken. Later (1959) PPSA was reorganized according to the model of other scientific associations, and from this time on it has been based on the principle of individual membership. The main organs of the association are: a general assembly of delegates (convening in the normal course every three years); an executive, revisory commission; and a court of arbitration. There are four special sections of the executive: of research on political relations in the national economy; on local power; on international relations; and on the theory and methodology of political science. The presidents of PPSA have been: M. Lachs, 1959-1962; S. Ehrlich, 1962-1964; J. Wiatr, 1964-1967; K. Grzybowski, 1967-1970; Z. Rybicki, 1970-1972; K. Opałek, 1972-1976; and J. Wiatr, 1976-1979. PPSA has now 575 members—scholars and distinguished politicians—organized in 12 territorial branches (Warsaw 174, Cracow 56, Poznań 56, Wrocław 46, Lublin 26, Toruń 31, Katowice 24, Gdańsk 49, Zielona Góra 13, Szczecin 23, Bydgoszcz 27, Łódź 50).[15]

The activities of PPSA consist of stimulating the development and popularization of political science and of integrating disciplines interested in research on political phenomena. These purposes serve: scientific meetings of territorial branches with lectures given by members or invited guests, from Poland and abroad; public lectures in different social circles; national and international scientific conferences. Until now PPSA has organized 7 (statutory) conventions, 9 scientific sessions, 1 symposium, and 5 international conferences, including 2 IPSA round tables in connection with meetings of the executive committee (Jabłonna 1966, Kraków 1977).

PPSA since joining IPSA has participated actively in all World Congresses and in the majority of special round-table conferences. Representatives of Poland have been elected systematically to the executive committee of IPSA (S. Ehrlich, 1958-1967; J. Wiatr 1967-1973; K. Opałek 1973-1979). Polish political scientists have been among paper givers at the congresses (7 at the 1976 congress in Edinburgh) as well as among convenors and chairmen of the sections. Also they have been organizers of groups of specialists. Since 1970, J. Wiatr has been the chairman of the Committee of Comparative Research on Local Power of IPSA.

The section on Research on Political Relations in the National Economy of the PPSA is affiliated, as a national committee, to the Association Internationale des Relations Professionelles. The chairman of this section, Z. Rybicki, has been a member of the executive committee of this organization since 1973.

The institution supervising and subsidizing PPSA is the Polish Academy of Sciences. In 1972 the Committee of Political Science of this academy was created. It is, like other committees of the Polish Academy of Sciences, a representative of the discipline, coordinating and partly organizing research; there is close cooperation between this committee and the PPSA.[16]

Journals. The main journals are *Studia Nauk Politycznych* (*Studies in Political Science*) edited in Warsaw since 1967 by the Methodological Center of Education in Political Science. It was a quarterly till 1977, and is now a bimonthly. The circulation amounts to 1,700 copies. Editor in chief is now A. Bodnar (previously K. Opałek).

The PPSA publishes in English a yearbook, *Polish Round Table*. In 1967-1976 6 volumes appeared, including 3 double ones. The circulation amounts to 700 copies. The editor in chief is now L. Pastusiak (previously S. Ehrlich and J. Wiatr). At present, an edition of this yearbook in Russian is being prepared.

There are also some specialized journals, such as *Problems of National Councils*, already mentioned, and *Sprawy Międzynarodowe* [Foreign affairs], published by the Polish Institute of International Affairs. Besides, the Institutes of Political Science in the main scientific centers publish a series of *Political Science Reviews*.

Special publications. The materials of all conventions, sessions, symposia, and international conferences of PPSA appear in mimeographed editions, some of them also in book form. Thirty mimeographed papers, presenting attainments of political science in Poland, were distributed at the 1976 IPSA Congress in Edinburgh. A similar publication, but in book form, was distributed at the next 1979 congress in Moscow. In cooperation with the Belgian Political Science Association one issue of the quarterly *Res Publica* (no. 1, 1973) was fully designed for publishing contributions of Polish political scientists, and in the following year a special number of Polish *Studies in Political Science* (no. 3, 1974) appeared, containing papers of Belgian authors. A similar cooperation took place with the Finnish association: there was an issue of the journal, *Politiikka* (no. 1, 1977) with Polish contributions and an analogous number of *Studies in Political Science* is now being prepared.

Political Science and the World of Politics

THE IMPACT OF POLITICAL EVENTS ON POLITICAL SCIENCE

Political science in Poland is Marxist and Socialist not only in the sense of being based on the theory and methodology of historical materialism, but also in laying stress on political phenomena and processes specific to the Socialist countries, Poland in particular, and on problems of international relations from the point of view of the role played by the Socialist community and Poland as a member of it. Poland's becoming a Socialist country and successive phases of the evolution of its political system have markedly influenced the choice of problems subjected to investigation. The same can be said about events in international politics, considered from the Polish perspective.

Consequently, in research on the political system special attention has been paid to specific traits and evolution of the Socialist state and party systems. Attention is focused on the characteristics and functions of the Marxist-Leninist party, the Polish United Workers party in particular. An important place in research is occupied by the public policies of the socialist state in their development, again with emphasis on the events in the Polish People's Republic. The same applies to the recent research on socialist political culture.

Within the range of international relations problems visibly influenced by current political events are investigations on the coexistence of states with different social-political systems, on the Socialist community and its role in the present world, on the foreign policy of Poland with stress on its crucial points of reference in the sphere of global political processes, of those in the Socialist community, as well as in the sphere of bilateral relations (e.g., Poland-Germany). In research on contemporary political movements and doctrines, special attention is paid to the Communist movement and various kinds of Socialist doctrines.

At the same time, problems of internal and international politics of countries with differing political systems are by no means overlooked. The essential trait of research is aimed at discovering correlations and interactions of political forces of the present world and changes and various phases of these relations since World War II.

POLITICAL SCIENTISTS IN POLITICS

The role of the political scientist was earlier more visible in foreign than in domestic politics. Almost from the rise of the Polish People's Republic, they acted in foreign politics as advisors, experts, sometimes even combining scholarly work with functions in practical politics. This remains the case today. In this domain, also, the first scientific institutions were created with the main task of preparing analyses of and reports on problems of international politics for the government. The most important of them is the Polish Institute of International Affairs, connected with the Ministry of Foreign Affairs.

In the last two decades, the postulate of basing political decisions on scientific data has been advanced more and more firmly and to some extent achieved. This is indubitably connected with progress in research as well as in quantity and quality of the staff of political and other social scientists. The number of scholars playing roles of experts in the sphere of internal politics is growing also, and still more frequent are cases of their entering the field of practical politics.

Characteristic of the present situation is the appointment of permanent and ad hoc mixed commissions of politicians and experts for preparing political decisions on the party level, on that of the government, and on that of ministries. The function of permanent political advisors in particular domains and problems was created. Important tasks in preparing political expertise and analyses is now fulfilled by the Institute of Basic Problems of Marxism-Leninism, founded in 1974.

RELATIONSHIPS BETWEEN THE GOVERNMENT
AND THE DISCIPLINE

Taking into account that the initial state of political sciences lacked the status of a distinct discipline, the organizational and administrative measures supporting the initiatives of the scholars themselves, which became pronounced in the 1950s, were of considerable importance, especially at the beginning of the process of consolidating the discipline. This support started with the resolution of the XIII Plenary Assembly of the Central Committee of the party on the educational tasks of political science in academic schools (1963), and found expression in further resolutions. It was followed by measures taken by the Ministry of Science, Academic Education, and Technology, which has created the system of teaching political science, and contributed to the organization of research in this discipline. The latter task is now fulfilled mainly by the body of political scientists, representing the discipline in the Polish Academy of Sciences—Committee of Political Science.

One must mention further the organizational and financial support of the government for national and international activities of that committee and the PPSA, and frequent contacts of the politicians with political scientists, especially in the PPSA, consisting in giving and attending lectures and discussing political problems.

The Present State and Future Prospects of Political Science

As characteristic traits of the development of political science in Poland one must underline, on the one hand, the long-standing traditions of investigations and teaching in this domain, while on the other hand one must be aware of the short period—of about twenty years—of planned, organized efforts both in research work and in academic teaching. The integration of political science is advanced, but not wholly accomplished. A considerable part of the staff of the discipline consists still of the scholars whose scientific background is the study of law, history, sociology, and the political economy, and who have fully or partly moved over to political science. Alongside them is a still growing number of young scholars who specialized in political science in the course of undergraduate and postgraduate studies, supplemented many times by studies abroad. In a short time certainly quite a lot was done through international cooperation in research, in the education of the young scientific staff, and in academic teaching. The state of political science of Poland is fairly well advanced when compared with the situation in other countries.

The prospects for the future are propitious. There are promising attainments, and justifiable expectations of further progress because of the following favorable circumstances: First, the advantages of employing the theory and methodology of historical materialism, the heuristic value of which has been tested successfully in many fields; second, the Polish traditions of political philosophy and theory; third, the widely recognized achievements of Polish philosophy, logic, and the methodology of science, constituting an important aid in investigations in political science; fourth, the ample opportunities for exchange of opinions and of cooperation at the international level, especially within the activities of IPSA; fifth, the still increasing number of well-trained scholars; and sixth, the introducing of various forms of teamwork that unite scholars with different specializations and provide forums for wide discussions in the scientific meetings and conferences organized by the Committee of Political Science of the Polish Academy of Sciences and by the PPSA.

Notes

1. K. Grzybowski, comp., *Historia Doktryn Politycznych i Prawnych* [History of political and legal doctrines] (Warsaw, 1967) and monographic studies: L. Ehrlich, *Pawel Włodkowic i Stanislaw ze Skarbimierza* (Warsaw, 1954); W. Voisé, "Doktryna politycznoprawna Jana Ostroroga" [The political-legal doctrine of John Ostroróg], *Państwo i Prawo* 6 (1954); idem, *Andrzeja Frycza Modrzewskiego nauka o państwie i prawie* [Theory of State and law of Andrew Frycz Modrzewski] (Warsaw, 1956); K. Opalek, *Hugona Kołłątaja poglądy na państwo i prawo* [Hugo Kołłątaj's conceptions of State and law] (Warsaw, 1952); B. Szacka, *Teoria i utopia Stanisława Staszica* [Theory and utopia of Stanislas Staszic] Warsaw, 1965).

2. K. Opalek, "Problem integracji w naukach politycznych" [Problem of the integration of the political sciences], *Nowe Drogi* 1 (1973): 88.

3. M. Zychowski, "Nauki polityczne w świecie współczesnym" [Political science in the contemporary world], *Studia Nauk Politycznych* 1 (1968): 183.

4. S. Ehrlich, "Die politischen Wissenschaften in Polen," *Schweizerisches Jahrbuch für politische Wissenschaft*, 1968, p. 59.

5. W. Rolbiecki, comp., *Towarzystwa naukowe w Polsce* [Scientific associations in Poland] (Warsaw, 1972), ch. 5.

6. K. Opalek, "Charakterystyka nauk politycznych: Stan i perspektywy ich rozwoju w Polsce" [Characteristics of political science: State and perspectives of its development in Poland], *Studia Nauk Politycznych* 2 (1972): 13.

7. J. Wiatr, "Nauki polityczne: charakter i perspektywy" [Political science: its character and perspectives], *Kultura i Społeczeństwo* 4 (1963): 3-10; K. Opalek, "Prospects of Integration and development of Political Science in Poland," *Res Publica* 15, no. 1 (1973): 22.

8. S. Ossowski, *O osobliwościach nauk społecznych* [On the peculiarities of social sciences] (Warsaw, 1962), p. 205.

9. The more important studies of this period are the following: A. Schaff and S. Ehrlich, "La conception du matérialisme en science politique," in *La science politique contemporaine*, (Paris, 1950); J. Hochfeld, "Marksizm a socjologia stosunków politycznych" [Marxism and sociology of political relations], *Studia Socjologiczno-Polityczne* 1 (1958); M. Zychowski, "Nauki polityczne" [Political science], *Nowe Drogi* 12 (1966); J. Ładosz, "Polityka a walka klas: uwagi o znaczeniu terminu polityka" [Politics and class struggle: remarks on the meaning of the term 'politics'], *Studia Nauk Politycznych* 1 (1968); J. Banaszkiewicz, "Marksistowska socjologia polityczna. Tendencje i perspektywy" [Marxist political sociology. Tendencies and perspectives], *Studia Nauk Politycznych* 3 (1969); A. Lopatka, "Polityka i politologia" [Politics and politology], *Życie Szkoły Wyższej* 12 (1970); J. Steperski, "Niektóre problemy rozwoju nauk politycznych w Polsce Ludowej" [Some problems of development of political science in Poland], *Studia Nauk Politycznych* 5 (1970); S. Widerszpil, "Przedmiot marksistowskiej socjologii życia politycznego. Socjologia a nauki polityczne" [The subject of the Marxist sociology of political life. Sociology and political science], in *Problemy struktury i aktywności społecznej* [Problems of social structure and activity] (Warsaw, 1970); W. Zakrzewski, "Z problematyki nauk politycznych" [Some problems of political science], *Krakowskie Studia Prawnicze* 3 (1970). Cf. Ehrlich, "Politischen"; Opalek, "Problem integraji"; and Wiatr, "Nauki polityczne."

10. According to the program introduced by the Ministry of Science, Academic Education and Technology on 20 Sept., 1977.

11. *Podstawy nauk politycznych* [Foundation of political science], 1st ed. (Warsaw, 1975) 2d ed. (Warsaw, 1977).

12. For references, see the selected bibliography at the end of the chapter.

13. P. Buczkowski and L. Nowak, comps., "Kilka uwag o przedmiocie nauk politycznych" [Some remarks on the subject of political science], *Studia Nauk Politycznych* 4 (1977).

14. See esp. T. Kotarbiński's, *Traktat o dobrej robocie* [Treatise on good work], (Łódź, 1955).

15. This order is chronological.

16. Data contained in this section are based mainly on the *Bulletin* of the PPSA, no. 1 (Warsaw, 1977).

Selected Bibliography to Chapter 24

Bierzanek, R. *Współczesne stosunki międzynarodowe* [Contemporary international relations]. Warsaw, 1972.

Biskupski, K. *Problemy ustrojoznawstwa* [Problems of political structure]. Toruń, 1968.

Bodnar, A. *Ekonomika i polityka: Podstawowe zależności* [Economics and politics: Basic interdependences]. Warsaw, 1978.

———. *Problemy polityki gospodarczej P.R.L. w 25-leciu* [Problems of the economic policies of the Polish People's Republic 1944-1968]. Warsaw, 1972.

Bodnar, Artur, and Best, Paul, "Political Science in Poland." *Political Science* (Spring 1976): 218.—ED.

Cetwiński, O. *Zagadnienie wyjaśniania i uzasadniania w nauce o polityce* [Problems of explanation and inference in political science]. Warsaw, 1979.

Ehrlich, S. *Grupy nacisku w strukturze politycznej kapitalizmu* [Pressure groups in the capitalist political structure]. Warsaw, 1962.

———. *Władza i interesy* [Power and interests]. Warsaw, 1967. *Funkcje państwa socjalistycznego* [Functions of the Socialist State]. Warsaw, 1977.

Gebethner, S. *Ustrój polityczny P.R.L.* [The political system of the Polish People's Republic]. Warsaw, 1976.

Gołębiowski, J. *Ideologia i polityka współczesnej socjaldemokracji* [Ideology and politics of the contemporary social democratic movement]. Warsaw, 1974.

Groszyk, H. *Francuska konĉepcja nauki politycznej* [The French conception of political science]. Warsaw, 1968.

Grzybowski, K. *Ojczyzna—naród—państwo* [Homeland—nation—state]. Warsaw, 1970.

Langer, T. *Amerykańska wersja analizy systemowej w nauce o państwie* [The American version of systems analysis in the science of government]. Warsaw, 1977.

———. *Typ i forma państwa socjalistycznego* [Type and form of the Socialist State]. Poznań, 1977.

Łopatka, A. *Kierownicza rola partii komunistycznej w stosunku do państwa socjalistycznego* [The controlling role of the communist party in relation to the socialist state]. Poznań, 1963.

———, ed. *Marxizm-Leninizm i polityka* [Marxism-Leninism and politics]. Warsaw, 1979.

Michalska, A. *Podstawowe prawa człowieka w prawie wewnętrznym a pakty praw człowieka* [Fundamental human rights in the internal law, and pacts of human rights]. Warsaw, 1976.

Opałek, K., ed. *Metodologiczne i teoretyczne problemy nauk politycznych* [Methodological and theoretical problems of political science]. Warsaw, 1975.

———. *Z. zagadnień teorii polityki: System polityczny; Interesy, wartości, normy polityczne. Decyzje polityczne* [Problems of political theory: Political system; political interests, values, and norms; Political decisions]. Warsaw, 1978.

Orezechowski, M., ed. *Polska, naród, państwo: Z badań nad myślą polityczną P.P.R. 1942-1948* [Poland, nation, state: Studies in the political thought of the Polish Workers' Party, 1942-1948]. Wrocław, 1972.

Ostrowski, K. *Rola związków zawodowych w polskim systemie politycznym* [The role of trade unions in the Polish political system]. Wrocław, 1970.

Pastusiak, L. *Komputery a polityka* [Computers and politics]. Warsaw, 1976.

Rajkiewicz, A., ed. *Polityka społeczna* [Public policy]. Warsaw, 1976.

Redelbach, A. *Front Jedności Narodu: Model i funkcjonowanie frontu narodowego w P.R.L.* [National Unity Front: Model and functioning of the national front in Polish People's Republic]. Warsaw, 1978.

Rybicki, Z. *System rad narodowych w P.R.L.* [The system of National Councils in the Polish People's Republic]. Warsaw, 1971.

Ryszka, F. *Wstęp do nauki o polityce* [Introduction to political science]. Warsaw, 1976.

Sobolewska, B. and Sobolewski, M. *Myśl polityczna 19 i 20 w. Liberalizm* [Political thought of the 19th and 20th century Liberalism]. Warsaw, 1978.

Sobolewski, M. *Partie i systemy partyjne świata kapitalistycznego* [Parties and party systems of the capitalist world]. Warsaw, 1974.

Sufin, Z. *Planowanie przyszłości˙społeczeństwa* [Planning of the future of the society]. Warsaw, 1975.

Waldenberg, M. *Wzlot i upadek Karola Kautsky ego: Studium z historii myśli społecznej i politycznej* [Rise and fall of Karl Kautsky: A study in history of social and political thought]. 2 vols. Cracow, 1972.

Wesołowski, W. *Klasy, warstwy i władza* [Classes, strata, and power]. Warsaw, 1974.

Wiatr, J. *Czy zmierzch ery ideologii? Problemy polityki i ideologii w świecie współczesnym* [Decline of the epoch of ideology? Problems of politics and ideology in the contemporary world]. Warsaw, 1968.

———. *Społeczeństwo, polityka, nauka* [Society, politics, science]. Warsaw, 1973.

Widerszpil, S., ed. *Problemy struktury i aktywności społecznej* [Problems of social structure and activity]. Warsaw, 1970.

Wojtasik, L. *Psychologia propagandy politycznej* [The Psychology of political propaganda]. Warsaw, 1975.

Wołczew, W. *Podstawowe zagadnienia marksistowskiej teorii polityki: Polityczna problematyka materializmu historycznego* [Basic problems of the Marxist political theory: Political problems in historical materialism]. Warsaw, 1978.

Zamkowski, W. *Dyktatura, suwerenność, demokracja* [Dictatorship, sovereignty, and democracy]. Wrocław, 1974.

Zawadzki, S. *Państwo dobrobytu; Doktryna i praktyka* [The Welfare State: Doctrine and practice]. Warsaw, 1970.

———. ed. *Spor o istotę państwa* [Contention on the notion of the State]. Warsaw, 1961.

Z badań nad kulturą polityczną [Studies on political culture]. Warsaw, 1977.

SWEDEN

25 RESEARCH*

OLOF RUIN

Swedish research on politics during recent decades has not been confined to the departments of political science in Sweden. Research of this kind has also occurred in other university departments as well as outside the universities. The major portion of the country's political research however has taken place within the framework of political science.

The Background

The content and focus of an academic discipline is determined by a series of different background factors. In a discussion of the background of Swedish political science it is appropriate to examine five such factors: (a) the intellectual tradition within the discipline, (b) international contacts and influences, (c) the domestic network of contacts, (d) funding, and (e) the relations between society and political science research.

The Intellectual Tradition. Swedish political science research, is based on quite a long tradition in comparison with the other Nordic countries. A chair, the Johan Skytte professor of discourse and politics, was established as early as 1622 at the University of Uppsala. The scholars holding this chair did not however concentrate on the study of politics until the 1840s. During the first half of the twentieth century a similar study of politics was introduced at the Universities of Lund, Gothenburg, and Stockholm. These pedigrees in themselves may seem modest. Slightly more than one hundred years, however, is not an insignificant period of time in a rapidly developing scientific discipline characterized by swift changes in focus and methods.

The content of Swedish political science research before 1945 was dominated by three main currents. Each of these currents was oriented toward another academic discipline.

One current was related to constitutional law. Many political scientists devoted their attention to the study of written law: its background, substance and application. The focal point of this interest was the 1809 Instrument of Government, the second oldest written national constitution in the world. Special attention was given to the question of the origin and influences shaping this constitutional document. One school of thought stressed the influence of foreign doctrines, another school emphasized the importance of the national tradition.

A second line of analysis in political science was influenced by the discipline of history. Political events of various kinds in a fairly recent past were analyzed. Particular interest was devoted to the study of the development of different political institutions and processes. An analysis restricted to written law was viewed as not providing an adequate picture of the functioning of different institutions and procedures. Much attention centered on the evolution of parliamentarism, primarily in Sweden but also in a number of other countries. Numerous studies, based on vast source material, dealt with the formation, dissolution, and inner working procedures of governments. The expressed purpose of these studies was to elucidate the successive shifts in power in the relationships between the head of state, parliament, and the government.

A third current in political science finally gravitated toward philosophy and the history of ideas. Classical political thought as well as modern ideologies were regarded as a major line of inquiry in political science. Works were published on various bodies of ideas, their

---

*This chapter is reprinted from *Scandinavian Political Studies*, vol. 12, with the permission of the author.

background, historical development, the correctness of their appraisals of reality.

At the end of the Second World War, each of these lines of inquiry in Swedish political science was dominated by an outstanding figure: Fredrik Lagerroth, Axel Brusewitz, and Herbert Tingsten. Fredrik Lagerroth, who was at the University of Lund, mainly concentrated on a study of written laws and their origin; he passed away in 1974. Axel Brusewitz was at the University of Uppsala. Among his accomplishments was an inspiring leadership of the extensive research on the evolution of parliamentarism. Brusewitz died in 1950, shortly after he had retired. Lastly, at the University of Stockholm there was Herbert Tingsten, the most dynamic of the three. His major area of research was the analysis of ideas. Herbert Tingsten left political science in 1946 when he was appointed editor in chief of *Dagen Nyheter,* the largest morning newspaper in the Nordic countries. New editions of his writings in political science were published during the subsequent decades; for example, his major work on the historical development of the political thought of the Swedish Social Democrats was published in English as *The Swedish Social Democrats* as recently as 1973.[1]

Although Swedish political science in the period before 1945 was characterized by three main currents, each dominated by one man, it would be too much to say that the discipline was divided into three independent parts. On the contrary, these three currents were intimately interconnected with each other; Lagerroth, Brusewitz, and Tingsten were at home in all of them at the same time as they symbolized one. A noticeable feature of Swedish political science during this period was indeed the ability of political scientists to fuse perspectives and ways of thinking found in law, history, and philosophy into a single study of the institutions and processes of central importance in political systems.

International contacts. The contacts of Swedish political scientists with political science in other countries can take many different forms: research on political conditions in other countries, teaching at foreign universities, participation in international arrangements of various kinds, reading of literature, and acting as host to foreign researchers visiting Sweden. Instances of all of these forms can be found in recent decades.

The rhythm and substance of these contacts varied in earlier periods. Before the Second World War there was not very much political science to keep in touch with. Sweden was one of the few countries where political science existed at all as an independent and well-established discipline at the universities. On the other hand, it was not so uncommon that Swedish political scientists themselves lived abroad and conducted research on political conditions in other countries. A series of studies was also published on political institutions and practices in other countries besides Sweden alone. But since many of these studies were written in Swedish they have unfortunately remained almost unknown outside the Nordic countries.

During the years immediately following the Second World War political science became established in several other countries, amongst them Denmark and Norway. At times during these years the contacts between Swedish political science and that in countries outside Scandinavia could have seemed to be less intensive than the contacts of, for example, the expanding young discipline in Norway. Contacts between American and Norwegian research in political science thus appeared to be somewhat closer than those between American and Swedish research. Young Swedish political scientists had a strong tradition of their own for support and therefore did not feel as great a need to travel abroad to receive their education. Furthermore, Swedish social scientists did not have the same opportunities to receive scholarships for studies abroad as did, for example, their Norwegian colleagues.

Nevertheless, as was mentioned above, by the 1960s and 1970s Swedish political science had become well integrated into the international network of contacts within the discipline.

One exceedingly important area of contacts for Sweden is American political science. Now it is almost a general rule that young Swedish political scientists study for a period at a university in the U.S. Many have participated in the courses arranged by the Institute of Social Research (ISR) in Ann Arbor; the department in Gothenburg is a member of the ISR. Projects, consisting of both American and Swedish political scientists and based on American and Swedish data, have been started. American political scientists pop up very often in the academic environment in Sweden. Sweden, it seems, has come to be regarded as an example of a small, and consequently easily surveyed, postindustrial society which is valuable to include in comparative research. So far Sweden has tended both to encounter and to attempt to solve at an early point in time the problems which appear to be common to postindustrial societies.

Another important area of contacts now is European political science. Contacts with the rest of Europe have mainly developed during the 1970s. At the beginning of the decade the European Consortium for Political Research (ECPR) was formed. Sweden, like the other Nordic countries, has been very active in this organization. Every year, for example, roughly twenty Swedish scholars participate in the annual Joint Sessions of Workshops; every year young Swedish political scientists also participate in the courses organized by the ECPR. A sense of community within European political science is gradually beginning to develop.

Domestic Network of Contacts. The pattern of contacts within Swedish political science, as well as between disciplines, has of course also been of significance for the development of political science research.

The pattern of internal contacts *within* each of the five departments of political science has naturally varied; a fifth department was established at Umeå in the early 1960s. Certain common conditions have however had an impact on intradepartmental contacts. The explosion in enrollment during the 1960s was dramatic at some departments of political science. The small number of professors, who were supposed to fulfill a large portion of their duties in the form of research, became largely occupied with administrative tasks. University lecturers, an expanding category of university teachers, were almost entirely occupied with teaching undergraduate courses. The substantial amount of research, which was conducted during these years in spite of everything, was mainly done by younger researchers and doctoral candidates.

Contacts among the five departments of political science have been frequent and beneficial. Regular consultations have taken place. There have been several research projects consisting of personnel from two or more departments. Since the beginning of the 1970s the graduate studies programs have been revised and now a similar program exists at all five departments. Some instruction has even been provided on a joint basis; graduate students from the five departments convene during a shorter period for intensive instruction. One reason for this organized cooperation has been quite simply the realization that individually the five departments of political science are relatively small with limited resources, but together they constitute a not insignificant research unit. Parallels have been drawn at times with American conditions. The size and the capacity of the five Swedish departments, viewed as one unit, correspond to a department at one of the large U.S. universities with a vital research program. Staff mobility among the Swedish departments has however not been achieved; persons who receive their doctoral degree at one department seldom move to another department.

The organized cooperation existing among the country's five departments of political science has been facilitated by a fairly good intellectual climate. Naturally there have been intellectual disputes between individual political scientists. To be sure, there has periodically also been a rather intense and bitter debate within the discipline. But a more permanent division of the discipline into various groupings with divergent approaches, hostile to one another, has not occurred. It is perhaps characteristic that two of the "new" currents in political science during the postwar period—the behaviorist movement and the Marxist influences during the late 1960s and the 1970s—have not generated the intense dissensions which have characterized political science in a number of other countries. Comparatively widespread agreement prevailed, when behaviorism was eventually introduced at all departments, that the new approach was important and essential. Those who may have felt sceptical were fairly silent. There also prevailed a rather large indifference to the Marxist influences. Of course some individuals were firmly committed for or against. A majority remained fairly uninvolved, however.

Contacts *between* political science and other disciplines have been rather infrequent in Sweden. Here, as in other countries, various circles have advocated more cooperation and an exchange of ideas among traditional academic subjects. There has been much talk of multidisciplinary and problem-oriented research. Although these demands were frequently expressed, fairly few research institutes in Sweden concentrated on a single problem area and consisted of researchers trained in different traditional disciplines. However, several plans for establishing such research institutes were being discussed, and by 1977 some of these plans had come a long way toward implementation.

Funding. In Sweden the resources for political science research, and social science research in general, are simultaneously both remarkably limited and rather sizable.

The scarcity of resources pertains to permanent research positions. It is often acknowledged and criticized that the number of professorships in political science is remarkably small. At present, there are only nine professors of political science in Sweden. In terms of population, Sweden is larger than its three neighboring countries. But Denmark, Finland, and Norway each have a larger number of professorships than Sweden.

Funds for short-term research projects in Sweden are more readily available; however, there are three major sources of funding for such projects: the Swedish Council of Social Science Research, the Bank of Sweden Tercentenary Fund, and various bodies involved in sectoral planning. Council research grants have increased even after taking inflation into account. The Tercentenary Fund was established in connection with the 300th anniversary of the Bank of Sweden. The amount of money allocated annually must be regarded as considerable for Nordic conditions. During the first ten years of the fund's existence, Swedish political science had received a total of 20 million crowns from the fund. The funding of social science research by bodies involved in sectoral planning has primarily occurred during the 1970s. This form of funding has expanded rapidly. There has been a steady increase in appropriations to various authorities for research and development. A large portion of these funds has been used to commission research concerning various social problems.

In a study on Swedish social science research, commissioned by the Office of the Chancellor of the Swedish Universities, Dick Ramström, a business economist at the University of Uppsala, has attempted to make a rough estimate of the total amount of funds available to social science research in Sweden during one year, 1973-74. The amount was estimated to be approximately 77 million crowns. A little over half of the amount was in the form of revenues received by the universities within the framework of the regular government budget. Roughly 17 million was obtained in the form of grants from various funds, primarily from the Swedish Council of Social Science Research and the Tercentenary Fund. Roughly the same amount—approximately 16 million—came from bodies involved in sectoral planning. The bulk of this research is financed by funds administered by central and regional public bodies. The ability of different social science disciplines to attract money from funds and sectoral bodies varies. Political science is not among the least successful. The most successful disciplines in this respect are psychology and education.[2]

The Relations between Society and Political Science. Swedish society naturally influences the content and focus of the nation's political science research in various ways. This influence can vary both in degree and directness.

One influence, even if weak and indirect, consists in the mere fact that the political scientist in selecting research tasks is influenced by problems which happen to be of current interest to the society he or she is living in. In addition there is a growing tendency on the part of political scientists, as well as other social scientists, to stress explicitly the social relevance of the research they wish to undertake. The emphasis on one's research as being of significance for society is partially a response to a traditional criticism which has been levelled at the universities for being isolated from society. This sort of emphasis, however, appears especially urgent if external funding is desired by a project and if this funding is based, in part, on judgments concerning the project's relevance for society. For example, the Tercentenary Fund applies such criteria of relevance in giving priority to project applications.

A sectoral funding of research naturally enough leads to both a strong and direct influence on the content of a research program. The research which is carried out must be of direct value to politicians, administrators, and planners in their area of activity. In the case of political science, this type of research has been initiated by both the authorities funding the projects and university researchers who have inquired if there was an interest in an analysis of certain specific questions. Many examples of this sort of practical research can be mentioned: inquiry commissions concerning constitutional reforms have given research tasks to the departments of political science; the Swedish Broadcasting Corporation has turned to political scientists to analyse certain aspects of the content of radio programs; local government bodies have sponsored research dealing with planning; the central administrative agency for higher education has financed various projects concerning university administration; immigration authorities have commissioned research concerning the political socialization of immigrants in Sweden.

Another form of direct societal influence on the choice and orientation of research tasks in political science is quite simply the practical experience of the political scientist in politics and administration. Movement back and forth between a university position and employment outside the universities is not common in Sweden. The system of appointing university positions militates against this sort of shuttle traffic. Rather often, however, university-employed political scientists are utilized as experts for limited periods in the administration. Furthermore many political scientists are politically active; in the elections in September 1976 for example, three university teachers of political science were elected to parliament. Some of the university-employed political scientists who have served as experts or held political office have eventually left the universities for good; others have returned however and contributed their practical experiences and observations to the departments' political research.

General Features

The general lines of development followed by contemporary political science research in Sweden resemble for the most part trends that can be discerned in the discipline in the Western world. This resemblance can in itself be viewed as an indication that international influences have played an especially important role among all the different factors determining the development of the discipline. Swedish political scientists have largely worked within the same frames of reference as political scientists in other countries; they have tended to be influenced by and refer to the same theoretical works.

During the first part of the 1960s what is usually called the behavioristic wave in political science had swept through the departments at all universities. The group that was mainly responsible for introducing this movement to Sweden was that comprised of Jörgen Westerståhl and his associates, especially Bo Särlvik. Westerståhl had been appointed professor at the University of Gothenburg in 1951. The department of political science there was the first in Sweden to offer thorough training in quantitative techniques; it was also the first to carry out large-scale projects concerning political behavior of the masses. Studies of both voters and the mass media had been begun in the 1950s. This behavioristic wave was of course largely influenced by the American example. The fact that it did not sweep through the whole of Sweden until fairly late can be taken as an indication of the fact that during the 1950s relatively few Swedish researchers had studied at American universities where sociological perspectives and quantitative methods stood at the forefront. At the same time it should be pointed out however that Sweden had something of a tradition of its own in this field. As early as 1937 Herbert Tingsten had published *Political Behavior*, a pioneering work on the study of mass behavior.

During the 1960s the general mood in Swedish political science, as in political science in many other countries, was characterized by optimism. Many political scientists entertained fairly high hopes concerning the possibilities of evolving a general theory of politics and political behavior based on empirical findings. These hopes stemmed from a fairly strong belief in the methodological and technical innovations which at this time were being incorporated into Swedish political science. Considerable energy was expended in specifying aims and formulating clear definitions of concepts. There was a wave of enthusiasm for attempts to measure various phenomena by using quantitative methods.

During the 1970s a certain reaction occurred in Swedish political science, as in other countries. The optimism concerning the possibility to generalize on the basis of common theoretical assumptions and vast amounts of data has diminished. The multiplicity of theoretical perspectives has persisted; the difficulties in comparing data from different political systems still exist. Criticism has also been levelled at an alleged preoccupation with aspects lending themselves to operationalization and measurement. This emphasis has been felt to lead to a neglect of certain areas of research. A naive attitude is also considered to have been displayed at times toward the role of values in the research process.

This new climate, which naturally is observable in varying degrees in most of the social sciences, has not however meant that Swedish political science has discarded the concern for methodology and techniques, which emerged during the 1960s. On the contrary, this persistent concern is among other things illustrated by the fact that obligatory instruction in methods and techniques has expanded at all the departments of political science. Now however, the complexity of the research process is stressed more than during the previous decade. An interest in analyzing the discipline's intellectual structure has also manifested itself in political science: how problems are formulated, how operationalizations are conducted, how conclusions are drawn, and so on. Young scholars representing this new form of awareness in Swedish political science are, for example, Jan Erik Lane in Umeå, Evert Vedung in Uppsala and Björn Wittrock in Stockholm.

During the 1970s in Swedish political science there have occurred certain shifts in the selection of research subjects, which correspond to a well-known international trend; naturally there are areas which have continued to be perennial objects of research and concern.

One shift of this kind is the current focus on policy studies. To be sure, research centering on specific policy areas was conducted prior to the 1970s. In the 1960s a number of such studies were published, such as Bo Jonsson on the policy toward the Swedish ore fields around the turn of the century,[3] Sven-Ola Lindeberg on Swedish unemployment policy during the 1920s,[4] and Hans Wieslander on Swedish defense policy in the 1920s.[5] A new feature in the 1970s was an analysis of contemporary policy in various areas. Lennart J. Lundquist began to publish books and articles dealing with environmental policy.[6] In the middle of the decade a very large policy-oriented project, known as the Politics as Rational Action Project, was started at the University of Uppsala. In principle, it was to comprise all the active researchers at the department, and its objective was to elucidate and explain, on the basis of a rational theory, a series of different policy decisions in Sweden. At about the same time a number of political scientists at the University of Stockholm embarked on a study of the education and research policy of a number of countries. In Gothenburg, finally, a project was launched on nuclear power and energy policies in Sweden.

An additional shift in the selection of research subjects is a revived interest in the major institutions and procedures of the political process. Of course this interest also existed to some degree during the 1960s, but the input side of politics was strongly accentuated during the decade: electoral behavior, the formation of opinion, parties and organizations. Now in the mid-1970s, Bo Bjurulf at the University of Lund is in charge of a study of the Swedish remiss procedure of consultation; at the University of Gothenburg a study of the Swedish system of inquiry commissions is in progress; at the University of Stockholm studies concerning the working procedures of the government and parliament have been started.

In subsequent parts of this essay a more detailed account of the subjects researched in contemporary Swedish political science will be given. To do so it is of course necessary that the material be organized in some suitable way. Unfortunately, no one principle of classification is completely adequate while any combination of principles is difficult to apply consistently because of overlapping. In an essay on the development of Swedish political science in the postwar period in *Scandinavian Political Studies* vol. IV, Olof Ruin divided his subject according to five different dimensions: nature, level, region (i.e., area), point of time, and sector.

Of these five dimensions, one—level—seems to be especially suitable to a more detailed presentation of recent research in Swedish political science. The largest research project undertaken by Swedish political scientists during this period took the dimension of level as one of its points of departure: the project involved a study of local government in Sweden from a number of different perspectives. Interest in international politics, which had earlier been documented in Swedish political science, was intensified, as witnessed by a series of new studies. To these two levels can of course be added a continued—and still dominant—interest in politics at the "national" level, particularly Swedish politics, but to some extent also non-Swedish. This primary stress on level does not mean however that such dimensions as area, time, and sector have been totally ignored.

The fact that a great deal of Swedish work in political science can be arranged according to level reveals one of the weaknesses of this scientific effort, for there is not very much written on the interaction between levels or on such processes as steering and decentralization.[7] One scholar who has been active in this field however, is Lennart Lundquist, originally associated with the University of Lund but now professor at the University of Copenhagen. His most important work is *Means and Goals of Political Decentralization*. It is often quoted, even outside of Sweden; the model of decentralization developed in this study has aroused a remarkable amount of attention.

Political Theory

The field of political theory encompasses a broad sphere. Principles of classification and distinctions in it often vary. One distinction has been upheld with remarkable tenacity in Swedish political science: the distinction between normative and empirical theories. Normative theories refer to theories concerning what the nature of politics ought to be, whereas empirical theories refer to theories constructed for application in empirically oriented research. The desire to maintain this sharp distinction is related to a tradition which has been very strong in Swedish intellectual life. It has been repeatedly emphasized, although less during the 1970s than in previous decades, that a distinction must be maintained between propositions containing an evaluation and propositions containing a statement about reality. The truth of the latter can be verified but not that of the former.

Normative Theory. Few Swedish political scientists have themselves produced theories on what the nature of politics ought to be. On the other hand, there are many Swedish political scientists who have devoted themselves to the study of normative theories formulated by others. The analysis of political thought and ideologies, as already emphasized, has a fairly long tradition in Swedish political science. The emphases in this type of analysis have varied. Among others, Leif Lewin and Evert Vedung have sought to systematize various conceivable approaches to the analysis of political ideas and ideologies.[8]

One branch of the analysis of political thought and ideologies is historically oriented. The development of ideas and ideologies has been studied. Recent examples of works of this kind are Nils Elvander's study on Swedish conservative thought 1865-1922,[9] Reidar Larsson's examination of theories of revolution in Russia,[10] and Daniel Tarschys's analysis of the concept of the state in both classical and Soviet Marxism.[11] Two scholars who have manifested a continuous interest in this type of the analysis of political thought are Elias Berg at the University of Stockholm and Stefan Björklund at the University of Uppsala.[12]

An analysis of ideas and ideologies can also have many other focal points. In addition to the delineation of the historical development of ideas, the degree of truth in appraisals of reality can be verified and the logic of arguments can be tested. Herbert Tingsten, as mentioned, is the outstanding figure in Swedish political science representing this broad analysis of political thought and ideologies. He did not write any new works in this area during the 1960s but he did eagerly interject his views into the contemporary debate on the role of ideologies in politics. With great persistence he argued the thesis of the end of ideologies.[13] This occurred before the radicalism of the 1960s had gained momentum and Marxism had experienced a renaissance. Moreover, this thesis had been formulated by Tingsten long before Daniel Bell published his famous book, *The End of Ideology*. Tingsten's thesis was challenged in Sweden by other political scientists. One of them was Leif Lewin who published a study of the debate on a planned economy which had been carried on during four decades.[14]

As a rule, ideological writings with their built-in values and descriptions of reality have not been utilized in the construction of empirically oriented theories in Swedish political science. This is largely a consequence of the sharp distinction maintained in political theory between normative thought on what the nature of politics ought to be and the construction of instruments for the analysis of reality. In at least one area however the gap between normative and empirical theories has been bridged. This concerns the study of the problems of democracy: ideological writings on democracy have been analyzed at the same time as models for empirically oriented research on democracy have been constructed.

In Swedish political science there is a tradition of analyzing the problems of democracy. Again Herbert Tingsten is a forerunner in this area. In 1946 he wrote a book entitled *The Problem of Democracy,* which appeared in English translation in 1965.[15] Elias Berg published a work entitled *Democracy and the Majority Principle.*[16] The problematic dimension of democracy, which has received particular attention during the late 1960s and early 1970s, was the implications of democracy in the sense of congruence between the will of the majority and the policies of the government vis-à-vis democracy in the sense of citizen participation in political decisions. Within the framework of the earlier mentioned research project on local government, which will be presented in more detail below, a model emphasizing the first aspect was constructed.[17] Another model was presented by Leif Lewin in a book that contained a systematic survey of American academic literature during the postwar period relating to the problems of democracy.[18] These diverse American writings were classified into two groups: the functionalists and the normativists. The latter group included those writers who considered democracy to be implemented to the same extent that the people participate in the political decision-making process. In an article in *Scandinavian Political Studies,* vol. 9, Olof Ruin stressed that the demands for participation by individuals in the decision-making processes in various spheres of society easily pave the way for more corporativism, that is, for an intensified incorporation of interest organizations into the machinery of government.[19] The interest in the participation dimension of democratic theory during the late 1960s and the early 1970s was a natural reflection of political conditions in Swedish society; more than before, people voiced demands to participate in decisions which directly affected them.

Empirical Theory. The interest in the second dimension of political theory—the construction of theoretical tools for use in empirically oriented research—increased greatly during the 1960s. One of the leading Swedish political scientists with this type of theoretical orientation was Gunnar Sjöblom; he is now professor at the University of Copenhagen. This orientation was clearly a result of the general interest in methodology and orientation was clearly a result of the general interest in methodology and techniques which now began to assume prominence. Consequently, Swedish political scientists, like political scientists in many other countries, were strongly influenced by a number of American theorists. Most of these theorists were subsequently cited in Swedish works. There were, however, two theorists whose ideas were particularly influential in Swedish political science. Moreover these two theorists appear to some degree as opposite poles: David Easton emphasizing a systems perspective and Anthony Downs emphasizing actors who behave rationally.

The influences of David Easton's ideas arrived first. His book, from 1953, *The Political System* was read quite early, among others by a group of young scholars at the University of Lund. Most members of this group, in a way uncommon for Swedish political science, subsequently moved to different universities around the country. Easton's first book served as a general plea for greater systematization, categorization, and classification of political data than had been common in the highly descriptive Swedish political science during the early postwar period. It was Easton's books from the 1960s, however, which were most frequently cited. Many Swedish works presented the major features of his system in considerable detail. In contrast it was less usual to allow his framework of analysis to permeate entirely a study or to attempt to refine various features of Easton's theory.[20] Easton's role in Swedish political science, although large, was chiefly restricted to providing a common framework of reference for many scholars.

Anthony Downs with his book, *An Economic Theory of Democracy,* to a greater extent than Easton has directly shaped research in Swedish political science. His theory of parties as a team of individuals desiring to gain political office through maximizing votes was developed in various directions. The goals assumed to explain the behavior of parties were differentiated in a variety of ways; several secondary goals were included; the conceptual apparatus was refined. It is correct to say that utilization of rational models in explaining political behavior has formed a special school in Swedish political science.

The pioneer in Swedish political science of this actor-oriented research is Björn Molin. In 1965 he published a study of the political conflict in Sweden during the late 1950s over supplementary pensions.[21] The book constituted both an independent elaboration of Downs's reasoning and an application of a scheme of analysis, formulated by Molin, to this important issue in Swedish politics. Additional empirical studies in Sweden applying a goals-means approach have been mainly conducted in the area of party research. The major Swedish theoretical work of this genre is Gunnar Sjöblom's book from 1968, *Party Strategies in a Multiparty System:* the book is often quoted in Nordic political science literature but is surprisingly little utilized outside the Nordic countries.[22] The book builds upon both the approaches of Downs and Easton. It can be viewed as an attempt to bridge the gap between actor-oriented and systems-oriented theories.[23]

A Marxist-inspired critique of the main currents in Swedish political science has been rather limited within the discipline. It is characteristic that two of the existing criticisms are levelled at the systems-oriented theory and the actor-oriented theory respectively. In 1971 Maj Palmberg, who is a member of a research group at the University of Uppsala on problems of the developing countries, published an article containing a critical discussion of the kind which is now fairly common, challenging Easton's theory and especially the theories of Almond, Apter, and Pye.[24] Lennart Berntsson criticized Downs and the Swedish elaborations of his theory.[25] Both Palmberg and Berntsson were critical of these American political scientists and their followers in Sweden for having neglected the significance of actual economic structures and consequently, according to Palmberg and Berntsson, also condemned themselves to conducting research of a superficial nature.[26]

It should be finally noted that the growing interest among Swedish political scientists during the 1960s in constructing theoretical tools for empirical analysis has primarily focussed on the formulation of schemes of analysis and definitions of concepts. The construction of formal models has been comparatively rare. Two examples of the construction of such models however are Bo Bjurulf's model for studying legislative voting behavior[27] and Leif Lewin's model for aggregate analysis presented in the book, *The Swedish Electorate 1887-1968.*[28] Two useful textbooks, written by Ingemar Lindblad and Björn Söderfelt respectively, for teaching methodology and research techniques in political science have been published during these years.[29]

Analysis of Arguments. One contemporary line of inquiry in Swedish political science—simultaneously related to both the traditional interest in the analysis of ideas and ideology and to the growing interest of the 1960s in the construction of tools to be used in empirically oriented research—is the analysis of arguments. There are a remarkable number of studies of political debates and the arguments presented in these debates.

These analyses of arguments have had a variety of purposes and varying focal points; at times several purposes have been combined in one study. Three different purposes however stand out as central. One aim had been simply to interpret and present the nuances in the content of a debate; the subject matter of the debate is thus regarded as of essential importance. A second aim has been to attempt to dissect the logical structure of a debate and examine the interrelationships between arguments; here the manner of conducting a debate on a political problem appears as crucial. A third aim finally has been, through an analysis of arguments, to attempt to explain other facets of the actors' behavior; in this case the actors in the debate are of prime interest, not the content or the structure of the debate. This third type of analysis of arguments is directly related to the interest in actor-oriented theories which has characterized Swedish political science.

Arguments can be analyzed with the use of quantitative techniques. To date, this type of analysis of arguments has been mainly conducted at the departments at Gothenburg, Lund, and Stockholm; the technique developed at the University of Stockholm was presented in *Scandinavian Political Studies,* vol. 7, written by Magnus Isberg, Anders Wettergren, and Björn Wittrock.[30] The major purpose of the research conducted at the University of Gothenburg has been to analyze the attributes and content of large amounts of text in quantitative terms; a good presentation of the technique used is given by Jörgen Westerståhl in a book on objectivity in news reporting.[31] At Lund and Stockholm there has also been a concern with using quantitative content analysis to attempt to comment on the behavior of the "debaters."

Many analyses of arguments which are not based on quantitative methods can also be mentioned: the debate on religious instruction in Swedish schools by Karl-Göran Algotsson,[32] the Swedish debate on the EEC by Mats Bergquist,[33] the international debate on research and society by Sverker Gustavsson,[34] the Swedish debate on the state church by Carl Arvid Hessler,[35] the Swedish foreign policy debate in connection with the Korean war by Barry Holmström,[36] the Swedish debate concerning the formation of governments by Olof Ruin,[37] and the debate on the Norwegian-Swedish union at the turn of the century by Evert Vedung.[38]

The large interest of Swedish political science in the analysis of arguments is unusual. International forerunners or parallels are few; an often quoted American work however is R. A. Levine's *The Arms Debate.* In fact, this focus on the analysis of arguments can be designated as a distinctive Swedish tradition.

Local and Regional Politics

Politics at the local level was the most neglected level of politics in Swedish political science for a long time. Accordingly, at the beginning of the 1960s there was hardly any research dealing with local government politics in Sweden or in other countries. Most of the Swedish studies that did exist were influenced by administrative law. The situation was radically changed when a large project on local government politics was started in 1965.

The decision to select local government politics as the object of a huge research endeavor is indicative of the trends of the 1960s. Swedish local government politics was in the midst of a tremendous transition. As a result of a steady migration, three-fourths of the population were already living in built-up areas; parallel with this, local government services had rapidly expanded and had become more diversified; local government units had successively been merged into larger units. In the early 1950s the number of local government units (the communes) was reduced from 2,500 to 1,000, and during the 1960s the number was expected to decline to less than 300. The future form of government at the local level was a topic of public discussion. Within the discipline, research on local politics also appeared tempting. The field was totally unresearched. Furthermore, comparisons aiming at generalizations would be easy to do. There were a large number of units to analyze; they had a similar organization and similar functions.

The organization and funding of the local government research project is also illustrative of the spirit of expansion during the 1960s. The project included all five departments of political science and was led by a board of directors consisting of one person from each department. The chairman of the board was Jörgen Westerståhl. The project was financed by the newly established Tercentenary Fund. The grants from the fund eventually came to a total of approximately 5 million crowns. The major portion of these grants was paid out in the form of salaries for younger researchers. The actual research was largely done in the form of dissertations. Nearly forty dissertations have been published within the framework of the project.

The major topic of inquiry of the local government project may be formulated as a study of the relationship between different types of communes and two sets of values: democratic values and efficiency values. By democratic values was meant values related to local government activities viewed as popular government; efficiency values referred to conditions relating to local governments as producers of public services. The data which were the foundation for the various studies of the project were chiefly collected from a sample of thirty-six communes. The communes were selected according to criteria of size and density of population. The project was divided into a number of subprojects. The subprojects dealt not only with the communes at the local level. Significant attention was also devoted to the activities of county councils (*landsting*). Each subproject, based on joint data, consisted in general of researchers from more than one department.

The results of the local government project, as mentioned, are presented in a large number of dissertations. It is not possible to list them all and their authors. In addition, a series of five volumes has been published. The series contains a presentation of the research program,[39] the forms of citizen information,[40] the nominating process of the parties,[41] parties and organizations at the local level,[42] and the activities of the county councils.[43] A final presentation summarizing all the results is still not complete. It is evident already, however, that activities vary with the size of the commune: this is true of the frequency of political discussion, the number of elected officials and full-time employees, the voters' opportunities to meet politicians, the nature and intensity of election campaigns, participation in the nominating process, membership in parties and organizations, the degree of agreement between voters and elected officials. One circumstance has been emphasized rather strongly. At the same time as the large cities have the best provision of services, they also contain the largest proportion of persons dissatisfied with services. On the other hand, in the small rural communes where the standard of service is lowest, fairly widespread satisfaction with services prevails. This paradoxical condition has been labelled by the local government research project the "service paradox."

The local government research project has entirely dominated Swedish research dealing with politics at the local level. It must be noted however that research on local politics has occurred on a limited scale in addition to the project. Two examples are: Bengt Owe Birgersson, Sören Häggroth, and Gunnar Wallin at the University of Stockholm who have analyzed the extent of political and social activities in a newly built suburb of Stockholm,[44] and Gunnel Gustafsson and Harry Forsell at the University of Umeå who have studied the relationship between political decision-making and structural change in communes which are expanding or are depressed.[45]

The strong concentration on research dealing with local politics which characterized Swedish political science for several years is now past. Few scholars are currently active in this area. Most of the doctoral candidates who did their research within the framework of the local government project have left the universities; persons remaining have changed their focus of interest. This de-emphasis is per se illustrative of Swedish research policy. For periods of a few years it is often possible to obtain quite substantial resources for research in a specific area but it is difficult to secure more permanent resources which would make possible a continuous concentration in a specific area.

An interest in research concerning conditions at the next level above the local level—the regional level—has arisen in recent years. No extensive studies in this area have been presented. This interest is centered at the departments at Lund and Umeå. At Lund the emphasis is on an analysis of the Swedish counties (*län*), their decision-making structures, planning activities, and relations with local government units; earlier many researchers at Lund had been involved in studying the county councils within the framework of the local government research project.[46] At Umeå prime weight has been attached to a study of the organization of regional planning and the relation of the region to the national political system. Inasmuch as Umeå is located in Norrland, which geographically is the largest region of Sweden, it is natural that the department should adopt an interest in regional problems in a comparative perspective. Contacts have been developed with other university disciplines focusing on regional questions, government agencies responsible for regional policy, and, finally, with regional research conducted in other countries.

National Politics

In terms of volume, there is still a predominance of research dealing with political conditions at an intermediate level: the "national" level. Above all, this research has focused on Sweden. To some extent, other political systems have also attracted attention.

The research on non-Swedish conditions with one exception has been of a disparate nature. A series of contributions to this research can be enumerated: Göran Lindahl has written about Uruguay,[47] Olle Nyman about West German federalism,[48] Thomas Hart about China,[49] Tom Bryder about industrial relations in Great Britain,[50] Harald Hamrin about the Italian Communist Party.[51] During this period a number of scholars, independent of one another, have also exhibited an interest in the Soviet Union: Jurij Borys,[52] Åke Dellenbrant,[53] Reidar Larsson and Daniel Tarschys. The only regional area outside Sweden which has been the focal point of political science research that is not of a more sporadic nature is Africa.

The interest of Swedish political science in Africa commenced when Gören Hydén presented a study of the dominant party in Tanzania[54] and Lars Rudebeck wrote a work on the dominant party in Tunisia.[55] Hydén and Rudebeck have been involved in a general discussion of different approaches to the study of politics in the developing countries.[56] Göran Hydén later received a position in Africa; he has additionally published a number of works on African politics.[57] Lars Rudebeck remained in Sweden. He has written articles concerning theories of development.[58] Around him have gathered several doctoral students all of whom are working in the area of African politics. Dissertations have been published or are forthcoming concerning conditions in Ethiopia, Ghana, Lesoto, and Nigeria.[59] This interest of Swedish political science in Africa and not equally in conditions in Asia or Latin America is not exactly easy to explain.[60] Accidental circumstances have contributed to this development. It must be underscored, however, that Swedish public opinion has long been committed to the black liberation struggle in Africa, that Africa is a major recipient of Swedish development aid, and that the Scandinavian Institute of African Studies is located in Uppsala.

The bulk of the literature written in Swedish political science about politics at a national level, as noted, deals with Sweden. Earlier this chapter mentioned some examples of debates conducted at a national level or concerning national policies. Other works can be grouped in terms of a number of phases into which political decision-making processes can be divided: voters, mass media, interest organizations, parties, parliament and the cabinet and their internal bodies, and, finally, the government administration.

There is a disinclination to center attention on dimensions of a political process other than these "phases." Few studies employ theoretically based concepts as a point of departure. Studies which in a single sweep cover this entire process are also rare. In general, Swedish political scientists have not produced any studies which attempt to analyze and describe the Swedish political system in toto. There is an unwillingness in Swedish political science to adopt broad perspectives. The discipline is still more microoriented than macrooriented. Some British and American political scientists, in contrast, have written books that adopt a macroperspective: Joseph Board, Donald Hancock, and Dankwart Rustow.[61] Furthermore, a few Swedish works elucidate the decision-making process at the national level in terms of a single concrete issue. Terry Carlbom has analyzed the processes preceding the decision in parliament to establish a number of new institutions of higher learning,[62] Olof Ruin the process leading to a new system of financing university studies, and Lars F. Tobisson the evolution of the decision to grant public employees the right to collective bargaining.[63] This type of analysis of decision-making processes can be expected to increase as a result of the growing interest during the 1970s in policies: the origin of a policy is one dimension of policy analysis.[64]

Voters. The emergence of an interest amongst Swedish political scientists in political behavior and the use of quantitative techniques was intimately related to the starting of research on voters and electoral behavior. This research has been led by Bo Särlvik at the University of Gothenburg. A long series of general elections has been examined: all regular parliamentary elections starting with the 1956 election until the present. This is a fairly unique series. Several different aspects of electoral behavior and the party system in Sweden have been analyzed on the basis of data from these elections: the significance of socioeconomic status and origin, the saliency of the Left-Right continuum, the degree of stability and change in voting behavior. The results of these studies have been published in a series of articles; several have appeared in *Scandinavian Political Studies*.[65] Since Bo Särlvik has taken a position as professor at the University of Essex, the leadership of electoral research in Sweden has been assumed by one of his colleagues, Olof Petersson at the University of Uppsala.[66] Lars Ricknell at Umeå has attempted to analyze voting behavior in a number of constituencies in northern Sweden employing partially new techniques.[67]

The electoral studies at the Gothenburg department, in turn, have generated a series of additional projects. One of these is the project on representative democracy. For one of the studies within this project, a set of data on voters has been compared with a set of similar data on members of parliament. The results have been published in the book, *Riksdagen representerar svenska folket* ("The Riksdag represents the Swedish people") by Sören Holmberg.[68] One of the most surprising results of Holmberg's study was a tendency, if a Left-Right scale was applied, among the members of parliament to be farther to the Left on various issues than their voters.

It should be added that during the 1970s there has been a growing interest in research on political socialization by Swedish political scientists. This interest is concentrated in Stockholm and Umeå. At the Stockholm department there is a project examining the political socialization of immigrants in Swedish society; immigrants recently received the right to vote in local and regional elections. The project is led by Thomas Hammar and Ko-Chih Tung;[69] Hammar in the 1960s published a study of Swedish immigration policy.[70] Gunnel Gustafsson at the University of Umeå has written works in this area.[71]

Mass Media. Mass media research of significant proportions has occurred in Swedish political science. Most of this research, but not all of it, has been done at the Gothenburg department under the direction of Jörgen Westerståhl. It is not surprising that one and the same department has concentrated on both electoral research and mass media research. Various dimensions can be applied to mass media research. Three frequently mentioned dimensions of this kind are: content, use, and structure. All three of these dimensions are represented in the media research at Gothenburg. One example of research focusing on content is the earlier mentioned studies commissioned by the Swedish Broadcasting Corporation. The purpose was, with the use of quantitative content analysis, to attempt to ascertain the objectivity in news reporting in certain instances;[72] the criteria used to determine objectivity have been criticized, resulting in a lively discussion on methods in this area.[73] One example of research concerned with the effects of using mass media is a project started during the 1950s on the political significance of the press; this research has led to other projects with a similar focus. Presently a project on the functions of the press in society is under way under the leadership of Lennart Weibull. Finally one example of a study more oriented toward analyzing the structure of media is a work by Stig Hadenius, Jan-Olof Sveveborg and Lennart Weibull on the growth of the Social Democratic press.[74] Stig Hadenius has additionally published several studies, among others, one dealing with the major news agency in Sweden.[75] Structure-oriented studies on mass media have also been published by scholars at other departments. Ingemar Lindblad at the University of Stockholm has written a work on the Swedish Broadcasting Corporation,[76] and Torbjörn Vallinder at Lund has examined the daily press and politics in Sweden.[77]

Interest Organizations. It is repeatedly emphasized, not least by foreign observers, that organizations are very strong in Sweden. Most conceivable interests are organized; the rate of organization among potential members is very high; interest organizations play an exceedingly important role in the political system. Against this background it is not surprising that the interest in the study of these organizations has been sizable in Swedish political science. This interest began during the 1940s with books by Jörgen Westerståhl and Gunnar Heckscher and has been sustained through the subsequent decades. During the 1960s many monographs on national interest organizations and affiliate associations were published: on the Metal Workers' Union and the Agricultural Workers' Union by Pär-Erik Back,[78] the Municipal Workers' Union by Ingemar Lindblad,[79] the Typographers' Union by Bertil Björklund,[80] the farmers' organizations by Gunnar Hellström,[81] the consumer cooperative movement of Olof Ruin,[82] on the Association of Swedish County Councils by Rolf Ejvegård,[83] the Swedish Employers' Confederation by Lennart Lohse,[84] automobile associations by Olle Söderberg,[85] the "peoples high-school" teacher association by Bengt Bogård.[86] During the same decade two books dealing with Swedish organizations in a total perspective were published. One by Pär-Erik Back considered the role of interest organizations in politics in 1870–1910; his thesis was that this role was already significant then.[87] The other one by Nils Elvander covered the situation today.[88]

During the first half of the 1970s somewhat fewer studies in this area of research were published than previously. Simultaneously, however, the public debate on interest organizations became more intense. The discussion concerned democracy inside the organizations and the growing tendency to incorporate interest organizations into the public administration. The first aspect is dealt with in a research project on democracy in trade unions, which was started at the University of Uppsala under the direction of Leif Lewin.[89] The second aspect has been commented on by political scientists in the public debate but has not yet been a subject of serious research. It is common amongst political scientists, perhaps under the influence of Gabriel Almond's ideas about the functions of articulation and aggregation, to express themselves in normative terms concerning a division of roles in a political system between interest groups and political parties. Nils Elvander has taken up and elucidated this general problem in connection with a study of a central area of policy: Swedish tax policy during the postwar period.[90] He concluded that the differences in "style of articulation" both amongst the parties themselves and amongst different types of interest organization are so great that it is not at all possible to speak of any general differences between parties and organization in this respect.

Political Parties. The interest in the study of political parties does not have quite as strong a tradition in Swedish political science as the study of interest organizations. A marked increase in this interest has occurred recently, however. For example, there has been a research project concerning the structure and functioning of the political parties; similar to the local government research project, this was a joint project involving the five departments. Several different dimensions of the activities of the political parties have been examined within the framework of the project as well as outside it.

One dimension of the party research has concerned the internal organization and activities of the parties. Sten Berglund has published a theoretically oriented work on the interaction between members and leaders within a party.[91] He is now directing a project on support and discontent in political parties. Agne Gustafsson has dealt in an article with the party congresses[92] institutions which have successively increased in importance. Carl Gunnar Peterson has written a book on the youth organization of the Social Democratic party.[93] A second dimension involves the activities of the parties in the electoral arena. Much light has been shed on this dimension. Magnus Isberg, Anders Wettergren, Jan Wibble, and Björn Wittrock have analyzed party behavior in the electoral arena on the basis of interviews with party politicians and the earlier mentioned quantitative analysis of election propaganda from the 1960, 1962, 1964, and 1966 elections.[94] Several researchers such as Paula Uddman and Jan Åse Wickleus have concentrated on the parties' behavior during a single election campaign, the 1968 election to the lower chamber of the bicameral Riksdag, which still existed then, Kai Kronvall, with a somewhat different focus, has analyzed the parties during the 1970 election—the first election to the unicameral Riksdag.[95] Dan Brandström has examined the nomination process in the parties for this election.[96] A third dimension of party research, finally, concerns party activities in the parliamentary arena. Bo Bjurulf, by himself[97] and together with Nils Stjernquist,[98] has analyzed the voting behavior of the parties. Hans G. Andersson has written a book dealing with the activities of the parties in the Riksdag.[99] Lastly an overall description of the Swedish party system is provided in a book by Pär-Erik Back.[100]

The feature of the contemporary Swedish party system which has attracted most attention internationally was the stability in the distribution of party strength and thus the roles of the parties. To be sure, the electoral support of the parties has varied; even pronounced shifts have occurred in some elections. But, until 1976, the three non-Socialist parties remained in opposition and the Social Democratic party remained in government as the party had done since the autumn of 1932 with the exception of one hundred days in 1936. In an often quoted article in the book, *Political Oppositions in Western Democracies,* Nils Stjernquist has analyzed the dilemma of the non-Socialist parties as opposition parties, on the one hand, and as participants in a political system where compromises are common, on the other hand.[101]

Parliament and Government. A new constitution came into force in Sweden on 1 January 1975; a major overhaul of the former constitution however had already been undertaken a few years earlier. This entailed a unicameral parliament, changes in the period of office, and a new electoral system. The constitutional changes were preceded by a lengthy period of investigation and inquiry. Two political scientists—Nils Stjernquist and Jörgen Westerståhl—have been especially active participants in this work; other political scientists have been active in the public debate concerning these issues. No extensive research concerning these major institutions of government and their internal bodies had been conducted on a parallel basis with the work of the inquiry commissions. Attention, as emphasized and exemplified earlier, was centered primarily on the input side of politics.

In connection with the one-hundredth jubilee of the bicameral Riksdag, however, several analyses concerning parliament were published by political scientists. These works dealt with: the evolution of the bicameral system by Olle Nyman, the social composition of parliament by Lars Sköld and Arne Halvarson, the work and the procedures of the Riksdag by Nils Stjernquist, the control function of a parliamentary committee on the constitution and simple questions by Nils Andrén, and finally the popular referenda by Gunnar Wallin.[102] No studies on the working procedures of the cabinet, on the other hand, were published. Hans Meijer, who had earlier published a work on the system of inquiry commissions, presented in an article in *Scandinavian Political Studies*, vol. 4, a follow-up analysis of certain aspects of this important instrument for preparing legislation at the disposal of a government;[103] in the same volume Lars Foyer offered a survey of social science research presented in the reports of the inquiry commissions.[104] The problem of the formation of governments—a classical subject in Swedish political science—however also now attracted a certain amount of interest. In a book Olof Ruin discussed the party negotiations concerning the formation of governments in Sweden during the postwar period;[105] Henrik Hermerén published a more general work on the formation of governments in multiparty systems.[106]

Administration. The final stage in a roughly sketched decision-making process, that is, the administration, at last during the years 1960-1975 began to receive somewhat greater attention. This occurred against the background of the rapidly expanding importance of the administration in the political system in Sweden as elsewhere. In 1950 Gunnar Heckscher in an article in *Statsvetenskaplig Tidskrift* (the journal of political science) had urged political scientists to undertake research concerning the structure and functioning of public administration in Sweden; shortly later he published a study on Swedish administration at work, which remained the major publication in this area for many years.[107] A very useful description of the contemporary organization of Swedish government administration, authored by Björn Molin, Lennart Månsson, and Lars Strömberg, was published in 1969.[108] A more theoretical analysis of the role of the administration in the political system was made in a book by Lennart Lundquist.[109] Two large-scale interview studies of bureaucrats in the ministries and central administrative agencies were done independently of each other at the departments at Gothenburg and Stockholm. Results from the study done at Gothenburg have been presented in a book by Ulf Christoffersson, Björn Molin, Lennart Månsson, and Lars Strömberg;[110] so far only the preliminary results of the second study have been published in an article in *Canadian Public Administration* written by Tom Anton, Claes Linde, and Anders Mellbourn.[111]

Another area of adminstrative research is the study of public enterprises. This part of governmental activity increased in importance in the late 1960s. In 1974 Roger Henning published a book dealing with the attitudes of the political parties toward state enterprise but primarily focusing on the organization of the largest state concern, AB Statsföretag.[112]

After this phase-by-phase survey of published research concerning politics at a national level, it remains to make two reflections.

The first reflection pertains to the dimension of time. Most of the research presented here deals with contemporary phenomena or those of the immediate past. Now a certain distance in time to the subject of one's research is no longer maintained, as was still the rule a couple of decades ago; the reason for this distance was mainly a desire to obtain some perspective. But of course, parallel with this emphasis on contemporary phenomena politics, occasional works focusing on periods in the comparatively remote past have also continued to be published. Works having a common feature of concentrating on some period of the nineteenth century can be enumerated. Elmer Nyman has written a book about the power to confiscate printed matter and freedom of the press in the late eighteenth century and the early nineteenth century,[113] Bo Westerhult about the evolution of the offices of bailiwick officials during the 1800s and early 1900s,[114] Stefan Björklund about the opposition at the 1823 Riksdag,[115] Gunnar Wallin about election campaigns and their outcomes during the period 1860-1884,[116] Per Sundberg about ministerial crises during the 1880s and 1890s,[117] Torbjörn Vallinder about the suffrage movement in Sweden at the end of the nineteenth century,[118] and Olof Wennås about aspects of Swedish elementary education policy during the 1800s.[119] A study dealing with the first decade of this century is Yngve Myrman's analysis of the power struggle in industrial relations during 1905-1907.[120] Some of these works can be classified as constitutional history but others cannot. The field of constitutional history, which once dominated Swedish political science, was not, however, especially prominent during the period 1960-1975. But the outstanding Swedish scholar in this field during this century, Fredrik Lagerroth, continued to publish works in this area up until his death in 1974. In a book published in 1970 he compared the work to revise the constitution and the resulting reforms during the postwar period with the 1809 Instrument of Government.[121] Studies employing a long-term historical perspective seem to have become fairly common once again in political science in many countries. There is a renewed concern to analyze long-term trends in various areas at the same time as advances in computer techniques facilitate studies of this kind. So far there are not many studies of this kind in Swedish political science. In 1972 however, Leif Lewin published a work on trends in Swedish electorate during the period 1887–1968;[122] he was able to utilize both data on changes in the occupational structure of the electorate and election statistics. Daniel Tarschys has in his research also displayed a proclivity to adopt a long-term perspective. This is evidenced firstly by an analysis of the budgetary argumentation of central administration agencies, which he and Maud Eduards have done,[123] and secondly by an initial presentation of his ongoing research on the expansion of the public sector.[124]

The second reflection, which there is reason to make, is that a lack of comparisons continues to characterize Swedish research on politics at a national level. The bulk of the published research is centered on Sweden, a modest portion deals with other countries. Comparisons of similar phenomena in several different countries, in contrast, are quite rare. The comparative studies which do exist deal chiefly with the Scandinavian countries. Ingemar Glans has published a study on the left-wing socialist parties in Denmark and Norway;[125] Claes Olof Olsson and Lennart Weibull have compared the selection of foreign news by news agencies in the Nordic countries;[126] Nils Elvander has analyzed the role of the state in the settlement of labor disputes in those countries.[127] A textbook comparing various dimensions of politics in the Nordic countries has been written by Ingemar Lindblad, Claes Wiklund, and Krister Wahlbäck.[128] Nevertheless it is surprising that there are not more comparisons of various aspects of the political systems of the Scandinavian countries. This deficiency is often noted and regretted. The similar social, economic, and political structure of the Nordic countries ought to have stimulated comparative research long ago. A reversal seems to be in progress now—viewed from a Swedish vantage point. A theoretical interest in the problems of comparison, irrespective of the countries involved, is reflected in a research project being carried out by Sverker Gustavsson and Evert Vedung in Uppsala. Furthermore, several concrete comparative research projects focusing on the Nordic countries are in progress. This greater desire to compare phenomena in the Nordic countries is also manifested in the formation of research groups within the framework of the recently founded Nordic Political Science Association; these research groups comprise representatives from all the Nordic countries.

International Politics

Debates concerning the academic discipline to which the study of international politics properly belongs are not uncommon. Such discussions have also occurred in Sweden, even if they have not generated much heat. There have been two main lines of argument. According to the first, international politics is not essentially different from politics in general. By and large the same theoretical traditions have made their mark on both the study of international politics and the study of politics at other, lower levels of analysis. The foreign policy decision-making processes of the various states—processes of primary importance for politics at the international level—are also closely connected to other decision-making processes at the national level. One consequence of this view of the closeness between the study of politics at different levels has been to maintain that international politics constitutes an obvious part of political science. The second line of argument is just the opposite of the first. It maintains that international politics is essentially different from other forms of politics. The international system lacks political agents of the type that regulate the activities of national political systems. The study of international politics lies moreover in greater proximity to general conflict theory. International politics should therefore not be regarded as a subdiscipline of political science. It would be more natural to create instead a separate academic subject, which could comprise not only the study of international politics but also a general study of international problems and patterns of behavior.

The study of international politics constitutes at present an integral part of political science in Sweden. At the same time institutes for peace and conflict research, independent of the political science departments, have been established at the Universities of Gothenburg, Lund, and Uppsala. At the political science departments, international politics has been incorporated into all levels of instruction; several positions in political science are held by persons who have done their research largely or entirely in the area of international politics; many doctoral candidates have chosen to specialize in international politics; through the years *Statsvetenskaplig Tidskrift*, the journal of the profession, has contained a sizable number of articles on international politics.

At the same time as international politics appears as a crucial and self-evident part of political science in Sweden, there are variations as in other fields of political science in the amount of research at the departments. At the departments of Umeå and Uppsala the research in this area has been sporadic. The largest amount of research activity has developed at the departments at Lund and Stockholm. At the University of Lund one of the two professors at the department, Hans F. Petersson, has specialized exclusively in international politics. At the University of Stockholm intimate contacts exist between the department and the Swedish Institute of International Affairs, which has a research section; several teachers and researchers at the department of political science thus are simultaneously employed at this institute.

Research on international politics, strictly speaking, can boast of a fairly long tradition in Swedish political science. It is sufficient to recall the internationally well-known writings of Rudolf Kjellén on geopolitics during the first decades of this century. At the same time it is correct to say that the contributions to research on international politics had been rather meager before 1960. In fact, it is not until the period 1960-1975 that activity in this area came into full swing. As is common practice concerning research on international politics, the Swedish research published during these years can be divided into studies employing a systems-oriented approach and an actor-oriented approach. These two approaches have been employed in roughly equal proportions.

Among the systems-oriented studies, three works form a separate group on the basis of their common interest in analyzing global patterns related to war and peace. The first of these works is Hans F. Petersson's study, *Power and International Order*.[129] His study analyzes a dimension of politics which has generally been given much attention in Swedish political science: normative statements. The "debate" which is analyzed was an international discussion of power, peace, and international order at the end of the First World War. The second work is Kjell Goldmann's *International Norms and War between States*.[130] This work also reflects an interest in the analysis of arguments. He analyzes the official justification by governments for going to war; what are the causes and effects of these justifications, what conventions and norms are referred to in these justifications, what are the differences in the choice of justifications by various types of states? A concern with the problem of war finally also prevades in Peter Wallensteen's study, *Structure and War: On International Relations 1920-1968*.[131] The origins of international conflicts and war are examined during a fifty-year period with reference to different patterns of relations between states.

A separate systems-oriented project has been carried out at the Institute for International Affairs under the leadership of the institute's research director, Kjell Goldmann; Goldmann has simultaneously held a position at the department of political science. The main aim of the project has been to study and measure fluctuations between tension and détente in European politics during the postwar period.[132] Roger Wall has analyzed bipolarization as a general phenomenon in the international system.[133]

During the entire postwar period in Sweden there has been a marked interest in organized international cooperation. Initially this interest was especially associated with the United Nations. In Swedish political science however no major work on the world organization has been produced; some articles—published and unpublished—have however been written about various aspects of the UN's activities. A similar interest, which so far has not resulted in any important works in political science, has been exhibited toward regional organizations like the European Community and the Nordic Council.[134] Research projects on various dimensions of integration in these regions however have been started; a study on European integration is being written by Gunnar Sjöstedt. Finally there are works published on specialized international organizations. Torsten Landelius has written a work on the ILO,[135] Gunnar Sjöstedt a study of OECD.[136]

The actor-oriented research in international politics has had nation-states as its focal point during the period 1960-1975; research now in progress however includes other actors on the international scene, such as multinational corporations.[137] Gunnar E. Jervas has in a book on the processes of international conflict presented a general model for the study of the development of conflicts between states with reference to motives and alternative courses of action of the major actors in these conflicts.[138] The actor-oriented research can be divided into three groups: (a) patterns of behavior, (b) doctrines and (c) policy formation.

One type of behavior is negotiating. Lars-G. Stenelo has written a work entitled *Mediation in International Negotiations*.[139] This kind of study is unusual in Swedish political science. It is concerned with a problem which is important not only at an international level but also at other levels, and it also focuses attention on two key political mechanisms in a decision process—negotiations and mediation—and not, as often is the case, on a "phase" of a decision process. A colleague of Stenelo at Lund, Christer Jönsson, has written a case study on the negotiating behavior of one state, the Soviet Union.[140] The conclusions in this book are based on both an analysis of the literature and the concrete negotiations which led to the nuclear test ban treaty. The actual policy area of international politics dealt with in Jönsson's book, security and armaments policy, has of course also received attention in Swedish research. Two scholars who are active in this area are Ingemar Dörfer[141] and Gunnar E. Jervas.[142]

Criticism as a means of conducting foreign policy is the theme of a new research project that has been begun in Lund under Lars-S. Stenelo. The main focus is on Sweden and the criticism the Swedish government has levelled at the U.S.A. and the USSR with regard to both the dominant influence of these countries within world politics in general and the substance of their actual policies. The principal thrust of the project is to ascertain and appraise the effects of this criticism.

Doctrines are an aspect of foreign policy. In official statements a country formulates the goals and means for its foreign policy conduct.[143] Krister Wahlbäck is working on a comparative study of neutrality doctrines in Europe; it is only natural for a Swedish political scientist in this case to pay special attention to Swedish neutrality policy. Wahlbäck's study is also concerned with Finland. A work which deals entirely with Finland's foreign policy doctrine has been written by Katarina Bodin.[144] Another country with a special position between the blocs is Yugoslavia. Lars Nord has published a work entitled *Nonalignment and Socialism,* dealing with Yugoslav foreign policy in theory and practice.[145] Even this study is an analysis of a doctrine—the doctrine of nonalignment—and its application in a series of conflicts affecting Yugoslavia. Naturally several books on foreign policy with a broader focus than merely doctrines have also been published. Nils Andrén, for example, has written a survey of Swedish foreign policy since 1945.[146]

An interest in studying foreign policy decisions also exists in Swedish political science. This interest however has not been large, just as it so far has not been large regarding the origin of other types of policy decisions. Krister Wahlbäck has published a work on Swedish foreign policy vis-à-vis Finland during 1935–1940, including the formation of this policy;[147] he has also studied the Scandinavian defense negotiations preceding the adoption of foreign policy positions by Denmark, Norway, and Sweden in 1949.[148] Thomas Hart has been engaged in research concerning the foreign policy perceptions of elites.[149] Ingemar Dörfer, in his book *System 37 Viggen, Arms, Technology and the Domestication of Glory,*[150] has analyzed the process leading to the decision to build the Viggen. Naturally it can be discussed whether an analysis of a defense policy decision, which this was, should be mentioned at all in a survey of research on international politics. A reference to this very point in this chapter can be viewed as a practical illustration of the fact that it often is difficult and unproductive to draw clear lines between research on international politics and research concerning other aspects of politics.

Effects on Society

In the introduction it was emphasized that Swedish society naturally influences the content and focus of the country's political science research in various ways. To some extent the reverse is also true.

It is not easy to determine the degree of influence which the results of political science research have had on the workings of society. Seldom have these results made the major headlines; nor is there one single work in political science, published during the period 1960–1975, which has profoundly changed opinion makers' and decision makers' views of society. The effects of political science research have been of a more specific nature.

The local government research project, for example, provides an excellent illustration of the possibilities open to political science research to influence a process of reform within a limited sector. During the past ten years, the national government has been relatively concerned with various aspects of local democracy. In 1969 there was a decision on public subsidies for local party organizations; a system of substitute representatives in local government councils was introduced the same year; in 1970 an inquiry commission on local democracy was appointed; five years later the commission published a report on local government organization and information. These various measures were accompanied by frequent references to the results published by the local government research project.

The propensity of opinion makers and decision makers to heed and utilize the results of a discipline's research is naturally dependent upon the reputation which the particular discipline's research and its scholars may happen to have in a society. Judgments concerning political science research and political scientists vary, of course. There are many groups outside the universities which generally feel that studies oriented toward political science are uninteresting; problems which are perceived as urgent are not included in the area of political science research. There may be other groups which are not necessarily negative toward political science research in general, but they find Swedish political science research uninteresting due to its cautious approach and lack of broader perspectives. Negative attitudes of this kind surely exist. Nevertheless, Swedish political science has a good reputation in society. The honesty and reliability of the discipline create respect.

There is a paradoxical aspect of the relations between

political science research and society. On the one hand, the very subject matter of political science research is potentially of an antiestablishment nature: the study of relationships of power in society. Persons holding positions of power have reason to feel skeptical and uneasy in relation to researchers whose field of inquiry involves an analysis of these positions. On the other hand, political scientists have revealed a tendency to merge with the establishment or at least to maintain close contacts of a friendly nature with individuals in positions of power. Many persons who have received a doctor's degree in political science have been absorbed into the public administration and the interest organizations; many scholars who remain at the universities, as mentioned earlier, are utilized as experts in various connections. Swedish political science simultaneously contains a potential for criticism of society and is well-integrated in society. This delicate balance constitutes both a dilemma and an asset.

Notes

1. *The Swedish Social Democrats* (Bedminster, Totowa, N.J., 1973).
2. Dick Ramström, *Social Science Research in Sweden Today and Tomorrow* (Uppsala: Department of Business Administration, University of Uppsala). The study was commissioned by the Office of the Chancellor of Swedish Universities.
3. *Staten och malmfälten: En studie i svensk malmifältspolitik kring sekelskiftet* (Stockholm: Almgvist & Wiksell, 1969) (with English summary).
4. *Nodhjalp och samhällsneutralitet: Svensk arbetsloshetspolitik 1920-1923* (Lund: Uniskol, 1968).
5. *I nedrusthingens tecken: Intressen och aktiviteter kring försvarsfrägen 1918-1925* (Lund, 1966).
6. *Miljovårdsförvaltning och politisk struktur* (Stockholm: Prisma & Verdandi, 1971) (with English summary); "Environmental Duality and Politics: Some Notes on Political Development in 'Developed' Countries," *Social Science Information* 12, no. 2 (1973): 43-65; "The Comparative Study of Environmental Policy," *Policy Studies Journal* 1, no. 3 (1973): 138-43.
7. A recent work with such a steering perspective is Benny Hjern, *Statsbidrag som styrmetod* (Göteborg: Studies in Politics) (1976).
8. Lewin, "Om studiet av de politiska ideologiernas innehåll och funktion," *Statsvetenskaplig Tidskrift* 75, no. 4, (1972): 437-438; Vedung, "Innehållslig och funktionell idéanalys," ibid. 77, no. 1 (1974): 1-20, and "The Study of Contents and Functions of Political Ideas," *Scandinavian Political Studies* 10 (1975): 185-208.
9. *Harald Hjärne och Konservatismen: Konservativ idédebatt i Sverige 1865-1922* (Stockholm: Almqvist & Wiksell, 1961).
10. *Theories of Revolution: From Marx to the First Russian Revolution* (Stockholm: Almqvist & Wiksell, 1970).
11. *Beyond the State: The Future Polity in Classical and Soviet Marxism* (Stockholm: Läromedelsförlagen, 1972).
12. Bjorkland, *Politisk teori* rev. ed. (Stockholm: Aldus/Bonnier, 1970).
13. *Från idéer till idyll: Den lyckliga demokratien* (Stockholm: Norstedt, 1966).
14. *Planhushällnings-debatten* (Stockholm: Almqvist & Wiksell, 1967) (with an English summary).
15. *Demokratíns problem*, 4th ed. (Stockholm: Aldus/Bonnier, 1961); *The Problem of Democracy* (Totowa, N.J.: Bedminster Press, 1965).
16. (Gothenburg: Akademiförlaget, 1965).
17. Jörgen Westerståhl, *Den kommunala självstyrelsen I: Ett forskningsprogram* (Stockholm: Almqvist & Wiksell, 1970; and "Demokratidebatt," *Statsvetenskaplig Tidskrift* 74, no. 4 (1971): 371-76.
18. *Folket och eliterna* (Stockholm: Almqvist & Wiksell, 1970).
19. "Participatory Democracy and Corporativism: The Case of Sweden," *Scandinavian Political Studies* 9 (1974): 171-82.
20. An attempt at such refinement is made in Harry Forsell, *Struktur-omvandling och kommunala seslut*, mimeographed (Umeå, 1972) (with an English summary).
21. *Tjänstepensionsfrågan: En studie i svensk partipolitik*. (Gothenburg: Akademiförlaget/Gumpert, 1965) (with an English summary).
22. Lund: Studentlitteratur, see also Sjöblom, "Partimodeller och beslutsanalys," *Statsvetenskaplig Tidskrift* 70, no. 4 (1967): 293-317.
23. A rather intensive debate on the theoretical problems of the analysis of party behavior was pursued in *Statsvetenskaplig Tidskrift*: Stig Hadenius, "Partiers beslutprocess och tjänstepensions-fragan," 68, no. 4 (1965): 343-64; Sjöblom, "Analys av partiers beteende. Diskussion om ett avsnitt i Björn Molins doktorsavhandling," 68, no. 4 (1965): 365-88; Erik Moberg, "Partimodeller och beslutsanalys—en replik" 71, no. 3 (1968): 220-37, and "Modeller för politiska partiers handlande," 69, nos. 2-3 (1966): 127-37; Sjöblom, "Replik på Mobergs replik," 71, no. 3 (1968): 238-48.
24. "Den funktionalistiska utvecklingsteorin," *Häften för kritiska studier* 4, nos. 1/2 (1971): 31-66.
25. *Politiska partier och sociala klasser*. (En analys av partiteorin i den moderna statskunskapen och marxismen) (Staffanstorp: Cavefors, 1974).
26. A lively discussion of Berntsson's critique was published in *Statsvetenskaplig Tidskrift* in 1976 and 1977; see notes by Sjöblom, Göran Hermeren, and Berntsson.
27. "Från minoritetsparlamentarism till majoritetskoalition. En studie av riksdagens rösträdningar 1925-38," *Statsvetenskaplig Tidskrift* 75, no. 2 (1972): 125-88; "A Probalistic Analysis of Voting Blocs and the Occurrence of the Paradox of Voting," in R. G. Niemi and H. F. Weissberg, eds., *Probability Models of Collective Decision-Making* (Columbus: Merrill, 1972), pp. 232-51.

28. Lewin, Bo Jansson, and Dag Sörbom (Stockholm: Almqvist & Wiksell, 1972).

29. Lindblad, *Om den politiska vetenskapens grundar*, (Stockholm: Almqvist & Wiksell, 1972); Söderfelt *Statsvetenskapsliga metoder* (Stockholm: Almqvist & Wiksell, 1972).

30. Magnus Isberg, Anders Wettergren, and Björn Wittrock, "A Technique for Structural Content Analysis of Party Propaganda," *Scandinavian Political Studies* 7 (1972): 83-105.

31. *Objektiv nyhetsförmedling* (Gothenburg: Akademiförlaget, 1972).

32. *Från katekestvang till religionsfrihet: Debatten om religionsundervisningen i skolan under 1900-talet* (Stockholm: Rabén & Sjögren, 1975).

33. *Sverige och EEC*, (Stockholm: Norstedt, 1970) (with an English summary).

34. *Debatten om forskningen och samhället: En studie i några teoretiska inlägg*, (Stockholm: Almqvist & Wiksell, 1971), (with an English summary).

35. *Statskyrkodebatten* (Uppsala: Almqvist & Wiksell, 1964) (with an English summary).

36. *Koreakriget i svensk debatt* (Stockholm: Rabén & Sjögren, 1972).

37. *Mellan samlingsregering och tvaparti-system: Den svenska regeringsfrågen 1945-1960* (Stockholm: Bonnier, 1968).

38. *Unionsdebatten 1905: En jämförelse mellan argumentationen i Sverige och Norge* (Stockholm: Almqvist & Wiksell, 1971).

39. Westerståhl, *Den kommunala självstyrelsen I: Ett Forskningsprogram* (Stockholm: Almqvist & Wiksell, 1970).

40. Bengt-Owe Birgersson, Harry Forsell, Torsten Odmark, and Lars Strömberg, *Den Kommunala självstyrelsen 2: Medborgarna informeras* (Stockholm: Almqvist & Wiksell, 1971).

41. Bengt Barkfeldt, Dan Brändström, Uno Simm, and Lars Zanderin, *Den Kommunala självstyrelsen 3: Partierna nominerar* (Stockholm: Almqvist & Wiksell, 1971).

42. Sven-Rune Bergqvist, Alf Gunnmo, Lars-Erik Klason, *Den kommunala självstryelsen 4: Partier och organisationner. Aktivitet och verksamhetsformer under senarer delen av 1960-talet*, (Stockholm: Almqvist & Wiksell, 1975).

43. Leif Johansson, Lars-G. Nilsson, and Harry Peterson, *Den kommunala självstyrelsen 5: Landstingskommunerna. En studie av politik och förvaltning på regional nivå* (Stockholm: Awe Geber, 1975).

44. *Att leva i Salemstaden: Politisk aktivitet, servicebehov och trivsel i en ny Stockholmsförort* (Stockholm: Statens institut för byggnadsforskning, 1973).

45. *Strukturomsvandling och politisk socialisation* (Umeå, 1972); *Strukturomvandling och kommunala beslut*, mimeographed (Umeå, 1972) (with English summary).

46. Their first major project was published in 1977: Björn Beckman, *Regional förvaltning och regional planering: En undersökning av planeringsprocess, planinnehåll och planeffekter i länsprogram 70* (Lund: University of Lund, 1977).

47. *Uruguay's New Path, A Study in Politics During the First Colegiado, 1919-1933* (Stockholm: Library and Institute of Ibero-American Studies, 1962).

48. *Der Westdeutsch Föderalismus: Studien zum Bonner Grundgesetz* (Stockholm: Almqvist & Wiksell, 1960).

49. *The Dynamics of Revolution: A Cybernetic Theory of Modern Social Revolution with a Study of Ideological Change and Organizational Dynamics in the Chinese Revolution* (Stockholm, 1972).

50. *Power and Responsibility: Contending Approaches to Industrial Relations and Decision-Making in Britain 1963-1971* (Lund: Gleerup/Liber Läromedel, 1975).

51. *Between Bolshevism and Revisionism: The Italian Communist Party 1944-47* (Stockholm: Scandinavian University Books, 1975).

52. *The Russian Communist Party and the Sovietization of the Ukraine* (Stockholm: Norstedt, 1960).

53. *Reformists and Traditionalists: A Study of Soviet Discussions About Economic Reform 1960-1965* (Uppsala: Statsvetenskapliga föreningen, 1972).

54. *TANU, yajenga nchi. Political Development in Rural Tanzania* (Uniskol: Scandinavian University Books, 1968).

55. *People and People: A Study of Political Change in Tunisia* (Stockholm: Almqvist & Wiksell, 1967).

56. Rudebeck, "Politik och samhällsutveckling. Synpunkter i anslutning till Göran Hydéns avhandling," *Statsvetenskaplig Tidskrift* 72, no. 2 (1969): 163-83; "Utvecklingsbegreppet i modern statskunskap," *Statsvetenskaplig Tidskrift* 74, no. 1 (1971): 1-18.

57. *Stat och förvaltning i Afrika* (Stockholm: Almqvist & Wiksell, 1973).

58. "Developmental Pressure and Political Limits: A Tunisian Example," *Journal of Modern African Studies* 8, no. 2, (1970): 173-98; "Political Development: Towards a Coherent and Relevant Theoretical Formulation of the Concept," *Scandinavian Political Studies* 73, no. 5 (1970): 21-63; *Utveckling och politik* (Stockholm: Wahlstrom & Widstrand, 1970).

59. For example, Michael Ståhl, *Ethiopia: Political Contradictions in Agricultural Development* (Stockholm: Rabén & Sjögren, 1974); Björn Beckman, *Organizing the Farmers: Cocoa Politics and National Development in Ghana* (Uppsala, 1976); Onesimo Silveira, *Africa South of the Sahara: Party Systems and Ideologies of Socialism* (Uppsala, 1976).

60. However, in 1976, was published James Walch, *Faction and Front: Party Systems in South India, New Delhi* (Stockholm).

61. Board, *The Government and Politics of Sweden* (Boston, Houghton Mifflin, 1970); Hancock, *Sweden: The Politics of Postindustrial Change* (Hinsdale, 1972); Rustow, *The Politics of Compromise: A Study of Parties and Cabinet Government in Sweden*, (Princeton: Princeton University Press, 1955).

62. *Hogskolelokaliseringen i Sverige 1950-1965* (Stockholm: Almqvist & Wiksell, 1970).

63. *Framväxten av statstjänstemännens förhandlingsrätt: En studie av en beslutprocess* (Stockholm: Jurist och samhällsvetarförbundets, 1973).

64. Among the remarkably few biographies of Swedish politicians are Ivar Anderson, *Otto Järte* (Stockholm: Bonnier, 1965); Knut Petersson, *En bondedemokrat: Alfred Petersson i Påboda* (Stockholm: Norstedt, 1965); Leif Kihlberg, *Karl Staaf* (Stockholm: Bonniers, 1962), vol. 1, 1860-1905, (Stock-

holm: Bonnier, 1963) vol. 2, 1905-1915, pp. 476. Also, Clarence Nilsson has written a book on the role of Liberal Sam Stadener in shaping church policy, *Sam Stadener som kyrkopolitiker*, (Uppsala: Almqvist & Wiksell, 1964).

65. "Politisk rörlighet och stabilitet i valmankåren," *Statsvetenskaplig Tidskrift* 67, no. 4 (1964): 185-219; "Skiljelinjer i valmanskåren," *Statsvetenskaplig Tidskrift* 68, nos. 2-3 (1965): 141-83; "Party Politics and Electoral Opinion Formation: A Study of Issues in Swedish Politics 1956-1960," *Scandinavian Political Studies* 2 (1967): 167-202; "Partibyten som mått på avstånd och dimensioner i partisystemet," *Sociologisk forskning* 5, no. 1 (1968): 35-82; "Socioeconomic Determinants of Voting Behavior in the Swedish Electorate," *Comparative Political Studies* 2, no. 1 (1969): 99-135; *Electoral Behavior in the Swedish Multi-Party System* Ph.D. diss., University of Gothenburg, 1970). "Socioeconomic Position, Religious Behavior and Voting in the Swedish Electorate," *Quality and Quantity* 4, no. 1 (1970): 95-116; "Voting Behaviour in Shifting 'Election Winds': An Overview of the Swedish Elections 1964-1968," *Scandinavian Political Studies* 5 (1970): 214-83; "Stabila väljare och partibytare," *Statsvetenskaplig Tidskrift* 78, no. 3 (1975).

66. "The 1973 General Election in Sweden," *Scandinavian Political Studies* 9 (1974): 219-27; *Change in Swedish Political Behaviour* (Lund: Liber Läromedel/Gleerup, 1975).

67. *Politiska Regioner: Studier i regionindelningsproblematik* (Umeå: University of Umeå, 1976).

68. *Riksdagen representarer svenska folket, Empiriska studier i representativ democrati* (Lund: Studentlitteratur, 1974) (with English summary).

69. Hammar and Tung, "Political Science Perspective on Migration Studies," *Migration Research in Scandinavia* (Helsinki: Ministry of Labor, 1974): 91-116; *Invandrare och politik: En intervjuundersökning våren 1973 om samhållsinformation, myndigheter och politik* (Södertalje: Kommuns informationskontoret, 1975).

70. *Sverige åt svenskarna: Invandringspolitik, utlänningskontrou och asylrätt 1900-1932* (Stockholm, 1964).

71. *Strukturomvandling och politisk socialisation* (Umeå, 1972) (with English summary); "Political Socialization of Swedish Children," in R. Niemi, ed., *The Politics of Future Citizens: New Dimensions of Socialization* (San Francisco: Jossey-Bass, 1974).

72. Jörgen Westerståhl, *LKAB-konflikten i Radio och dagspress* (Gothenburg: Statsventenskapliga institutionen, 1971) *Objectiv nyhetsförmedling* (Gothenburg: Akademiförlaget, 1972).

73. Gunnar Andrén, Lars Ericsson, O. Ohlson, and Torbjörn Tännsjö, "Från objekivitet till ökad genomsnittlighet," in *Häften förkritiskastudier* 5, no. 6 (1972): 6-30.

74. "The Social Democratic Press and Newspaper Policy in Sweden," *Scandinavian Political Studies* 3 (1968): 49-69; *Partipress: Socialdemokratisk press och presspolitik 1910-1920*, (Stockholm: Rabén + Sjögren, 1970).

75. *Nyheter från TT. Studier i 50 års nyhetsförmedling,* (Stockholm: Bonniers, 1971); (with Lennart Weibull) *Press, radio, tv. En bok om massmedia*, 2d rev. ed. (Stockholm: Aldus/Bonnier, 1973).

76. *Etermediernas värld* (Stockholm: Bonnier, 1970).

77. *Gleerup* (Lund, 1968).

78. Pär-Erik Back, *En klass i uppbrott: Den fackliga lantarbetarrörelsen uppkomst och utveckling* (Malmö: Framtiden, 1961) and *Svenska metallindustriarbetarförbundets historia* (Stockholm: Förbundets Förlag, 1963).

79. Ingemar Lindbland, *Svenska kommunalarbetarförbundet 1910-1960* (Stockholm: Tiden, 1960) (with English summary).

80. Bertil Björklund, *Svenska typografförbundet: Studier rörande Sveriges äldsta fackförbund* (Stockholm: Tiden, 1965) (with English summary).

81. Gunnar Hellström, *Föreningsdemokrati och förtroendemannakår inomjordbrukets föreningsrörelse i början av 1950-talet* (Halmstad: LTs Förlag, 1964) and *Jordbrukspolitik i industri samhället med tyngpunkt på 1920—och 30—talen* (Stockholm, 1976).

82. Olof Ruin, *Kooperative Förbundet 1899-1929* (Lund: Gleerup, 1960) (with English summary).

83. Rolf Ejvegård, *Landstingsförbundet: Organisation, beslutsfattande, förhållande till staten* (Stockholm: Landsstingsförbundet, 1973).

84. Lennart Lohse, *Arbetsgivarnas inställning till föreningsrätt arbetarskydd och arbetstid i statsvetenskaplig belysning* (Stockholm: Svenska-Arbetsgivareforeningen, 1963).

85. Olle Söderberg, *Motororganisatione i Sverige: Bakgrund, grupperingar, aktivitetar* (Stockholm: Rabén & Sjögren, 1966).

86. Bengt Bogärd, *Svenska folkhögskolans lärareförening och staten 1902-1970: En studier i organisationsflytande* (Stockholm: Rabén & Sjögren, 1974).

87. *Sammanslutningarnas roll i politikken 1870-1910* (Lund: Studentlitteratur, 1967) (with an English summary).

88. *Interesseorganisationerna i dagens Sverige* (Lund: Gleerup, 1969).

89. Axel Hadenius, *Facklig organisationsutveckling. En studie av Landsorganisationen i Sverige* (Uppsala, 1976); Leif Lewin, *Hur styrs facket? Om demokratin inom fackföreningsrörelsen* (Uppsala, 1977).

90. "The Politics of Taxation in Sweden 1945-1970: A Study of the Functions of Parties and Organizations," *Scandinavian Political Studies* 7 (1972): 63-82; *Svensk skattepolitik 1945-1970: En studie i partiers och organisationers funktioner* (Stockholm: Rabén + Sjögren, 1972).

91. *Masspartiet som kommunikationssystem*, Mimeographed (Umeå, 1972) (with an English summary).

92. In Pär-Erik Back, ed., *Modern Demokrati*, 4th rev. ed. (Lund: Gleerup, 1970).

93. *Ungdom och politikk: En studie av Sveriges socialdemokratiska undgomsförbund* (Stockholm: Frihet, 1975).

94. *Partierna inför väljarna: Svensk valpropaganda 1960-1966*, (Stockholm: Statsvetenskapliga Institutionen/ Allmänna förlaget, 1974).

95. *Politisk massakommunikation i ett flerpartisystem, Sverige—en fallstudie* (Lund: Studentlitteratur, 1975).

96. *Nommeringsförandet vid riksdagsval. En studie av partiernas kandidatnomineringar inför 1970 års riksdagsval* (Stockholm: Allmänna Förlaget, 1972).

97. "Från minoritetsparlamentarism till majoritetskoalition: En studie av riksdagen rösträkningar 1925-1938," *Statsvetenskaplig Tidskrift* 75, no. 2 (1972): 125-88; "A Simulation Analysis of Selected Voting Procedures," *Scandinavian Political Studies* 8 (1973): 37-68.

98. "Party Cohesion and Party Cooperation in the Swedish Parliament in 1964 and 1966," *Scandinavian Political Studies* 5 (1970): 129-64; "Partisammanhållning och partisamarbete," *Statsvetenskaplig Tidskrift* 71 no. 4 (1968): 35-405.

99. *Vad gör partierna i riksdagen? Mål, taktik och arbetsformer* (Stockholm: Studentförbundet Naringsliv och samhälle and Forum, 1969).

100. *Det svenska partiväsendet* (Stockholm: Almqvist & Wiksell, 1967).

101. "Sweden: Stability or Deadlock?" in Robert Dahl, ed., *Political Oppositions in Western Democracies* (New Haven: Yale University Press 1968).

102. Arthur Thompson, ed., *Samhälle och Riksdag* (Stockholm: Almqvist & Wiksell, 1966), pts. 1-5.

103. *Från uppslag till betänkande: Studie i kommittépolitik och kommittéarbete* (Lund: Gleerup, 1965). "Bureaucracy and Policy Formulation in Sweden," *Scandinavian Political Studies* 4 (1969): 103-16.

104. "The Social Sciences in Royal Commission Studies in Sweden," ibid. 4 (1969): 182-203.

105. *Mellan samlingsregering och tva partisystem: Den svenska regeringsfragen 1945-1960* (Stockholm: Bonnier, 1968); "Patterns of Government Composition in Multi-Party Systems: The Case of Sweden," *Scandinavian Political Studies* 4 (1969): 71-87.

106. *Regeringsbildninger i flerpartisystem* (Lund: Studentlitteratur, 1975).

107. See *Statsventenskaplig Tidskrift* 1950:1, pp. 42-52, and Gunnar Heckscher, *Svensk Statsförvaltning i arbete* (Stockholm, 1952).

108. *Offentlig förvaltning, Stats- ochs kommunalförvaltningens struktur och funktioner*, 4th rev, ed. (Stockholm: Bonnier, 1976).

109. *Miljövårdsförvaltning och politisk struktur* (Uppsala: Prisma, Stockholm: Verdandi 1971) (with English summary).

110. *Byråkrati och politik* (Stockholm: Bonnier, 1972).

111. *Canadian Public Administration* 16, no. 4 (1973): 627-51.

112. *Staten som förtag. En studie av Statsföretag AB:s mål, organisation och effektiviteten* (Stockholm: Rabén & Sjögren, 1974).

113. *Indragningsmakt och tryckfrihet 1785-1810* (Ph.D. dissertation, Stockholm, 1963) (with English summary).

114. *Kronofogde, häradsskrivare, länsman: Den svenska fögderiförvaltiningen 1810-1917* (Lund: Gleerup, 1965) (with English summary).

115. *Oppositionen vid 1823 ärs Riksdag: Jordbrukskris och borgerlig liberalism* (Uppsala, Almqvist & Wiksell, 1964) (with English summary).

116. *Valröelser och valresultat, Andrakammarvalen i Sverige 1866-1884* (Stockholm: Ronzo, 1961) (with English summary).

117. *Ministarerna Dildt och Åkerhielm: En studie i den svenska parlemtarismens förgårdar* (Stockholm: Ronzo, 1961) (with English summary).

118. *I kamp för demokratin, Rösträttsrörelsen i Sverige 1886-1900* (Stockholm: Natur & Kultur, 1962) (with English summary).

119. *Striden om latinväldet: Idéer och intressen i svensk skolpolitik under 1800-talet* (Stockholm: Almqvist & Wiksell, 1966).

120. *Maktkampen på arbetsmarknaden 1905-1907: En studie av de icke-socialistika arbetarna som faktor i arbetsgivarpolitiken* (Stockholm: Statsvetenskaplig Institutionen, 1973).

121. *Två svensk regeringsformer* (Lund: Gleerup, 1970); *Den svenska monarkin inför rätta: En författningshistorisk exposé* (Stockholm: Rabén & Sjögren, 1972).

122. Lewin, Bo Jansson, and Dag Sörbom, *The Swedish Electorate 1887-1968* (Stockholm: Almqvist & Wiksell, 1972).

123. (With Maud Eduards) *Hur de svenska myndigheterna argumenterar för högre anslag* (Stockholm: Liber Förlag, 1975).

124. For instance, "The Growth of Public Expenditure: Nine Modes of Explanation," *Scandinavian Political Studies* 10 (1975): 9-31.

125. *De socialistiska folkpartierna i Danmark och Norge: En komparativ organisasjonsstudie* (Lund: Institute of Political Science, 1965).

126. "The Reporting of News in Scandinavian Countries," *Scandinavian Political Studies* 8 (1973): 141-67.

127. "The Role of the State in the Settlement of Labor Disputes in the Nordic Countries: A Comparative Analysis," *European Journal of Political Research* 3 (1974): 363-83.

128. *Politik i Norden: En jämförande oversikt* (Stockholm: Aldus/Bonnier, 1972) (with the cooperation of Carl-Einar Stålvant).

129. (Lund: Gleerup, 1964).

130. (Stockholm: Läromedelförlagen, 1971).

131. (Stockholm: Rabén & Sjögren, 1973).

132. Goldmann, "East-West Tension in Europe, 1946-1970: A Conceptual Analysis and Description," *World Politics* 26, no. 1 (1973): 106-25; *Tension and Détente in Bipolar Europe* (Stockholm: Esselte Studium, 1974).

133. *The Dynamics of Polarisation: An Inquiry into the Process of Bipolarisation in the International System and Its Regions 1946-1970* (Stockholm: Institute of Political Science, 1975).

134. Carl-Einar Stålvant, "Sweden: The Negotiations with the EEC," *Scandinavian Political Studies* 8 (1974): 236-45; Claes Wiklund, "The Zig-Zag Course of the Nordek Negotiations," *Scandinavian Political Studies* 5 (1970): 307-36.

135. *Workers, Employers, and Government: A Comparative Study of Delegations and Groups at the International Labor Conference, 1919-1964* (Stockholm: Norstedt, 1965).

136. *OECD-samarbetet: funktioner och effekter* (Stockholm: Statsvetenskapliga, 1973).

137. Lars Thunell, *Political Risk and International Business: A Study of Multinational Corporations Investment Behavior* (Stockholm: University of Stockholm, 1977).

138. *Internatiella konfliktprocesser: En generell modell för studiet av mellanstatliga konfliktförlopp* (Stockholm: Wahlström & Widstrand, 1973).

139. (Lund: Studentlitteratur, 1972).

140. *The Soviet Union and the Test Ban: A Study in Soviet Negotiating Behaviour* (Lund: Studentlitteratur, 1975).

141. *Strategiska doktriner i Väst* (Stockholm: Rabén and Sjögren, 1974); *Kärnvapendoktriner i Väst*, Mimeographed (Stockholm: Ministry of Defense, 1974).

142. *Från Kärnvapen till gerilla: Om modern strategi*, (Stockholm: Almqvist & Wiksell, 1972); *Från hotbild i öst och väst till svensk försvarsplanering* (Stockholm: Liber Förlag/Allmänna-flaget, 1975).

143. Katarma Brodin, *Studiet an utrikespolitiska doktriner: Teori och tva empiriska tillampningar* (Stockholm, 1977).

144. "Finlands aktiva neutralitetspolitik," *Världspolitikens dagsfrågor* 11 (1975).

145. *Nonalignment and Socialism: Yugoslav Foreign Policy in Theory and Practice* (Stockholm: Rabén and Sjögren, 1974).

146. (With Åke Landqvist) *Svensk utrikespolitik efter 1945* (Stockholm: Almqvist & Wiksell, 1965); translated as *Power Balance and Non-Alignment: A Perspective on Swedish Foreign Policy* (Stockholm: Almqvist & Wiksell, 1967).

147. *Finlands frågor i svensk politik 1937–1940* (Stockholm: Norstedt, 1964).

148. *Norden och blockuppdelningen 1948–49* (Stockholm: Rabén and Sjögren, 1974).

149. *The Cognitive World of Swedish Security Elites*, 1976.

150. (Oslo: Universitetsförlaget, 1973).

SWEDEN
TEACHING AND ASSOCIATIONAL ACTIVITIES*

NILS ELVANDER

Academic teaching in political science has a relatively long history in Sweden compared with the other Nordic countries. "Statskunskap," as it is called in Swedish, emerged as an independent discipline in Uppsala in the middle of the nineteenth century and around the turn of the century at the universities in Lund and Gothenburg and in 1935 in Stockholm. New chairs in political science were founded at the new universities in Umeå and Linköping in 1965 and 1975 respectively.[1]

Until the 1950s political science was a minor academic subject at all levels of examination. There were no departments in the modern sense; the whole staff usually consisted of one full professor and one docent (assistant professor). At the end of the 1940s, the first elements of a department organization were introduced: a few administrative assistants and teaching positions (without tenure) for the undergraduate level. But still the professor alone was responsible for all graduate education. Needless to say, the output of candidates for the two highest degrees, *Licentiat* and *Doktor* (roughly comparable to the American Ph.D. and the old German doctor's degree) was very small. Between 1901 and 1950, only 47 persons graduated with the *Licentiat* degree in political science in the whole country, and the figure for the doctor's degree was 58.[2] The situation in other academic disciplines was similar to this pattern.

The low productivity of graduate education was not the only problem. There were also serious economic and social problems for the graduate students. Scholarships and state subsidies covering printing costs for dissertations were introduced as late as the end of the 1940s. The average age of the doctors was nearly forty years. The typical Swedish dissertation was a thick and solid volume which had the character of one man's life achievement. Widespread criticism against this old-fashioned system led to a reform of graduate education and the doctor's degree. Inspired by the American Ph.D. system, the reform was passed by the Riksdag in 1969 and had been carried through successively in the beginning of the 1970s. The two old degrees were abolished and a new degree, called *Doktorsexamen* (Ph.D.), was improved, and the size of the dissertation was cut down with the help of such measures as the rules for publishing subsidies.

The effects of the reform have not been systematically evaluated; however, we can already see some positive results in political science. The output of dissertations has increased considerably, partly as a result of the reform; this aspect will be discussed later. The new doctors are about ten years younger and the dissertations are much shorter than before the reform. Qualitative standards have been maintained at an acceptable level, partly through the new system of methodological courses and intensified research guidance. New categories of teachers have been engaged in instruction and guidance work; the single professor is no longer solely responsible for all graduate education. By and large, the reform of 1969 has created some positive conditions for the future development of political science research in Sweden, although much remains to be done—particularly concerning the construction of positions in the academic career after the Ph.D.

The 1960s was the decade of grand reforms at all levels of education in Sweden. The undergraduate level at the universities was affected in many ways; these reforms have important indirect consequences for graduate education, and therefore something must be said about them. In order to meet the increase in the number of

---

*This study appeared in *Scandinavian Political Studies*, vol. 12, and is reprinted by permission of the author.

students in the "open" faculties (natural science, humanities, and social science) with sufficient teaching resources, an administrative system of "automatic" allocation of positions in correspondence to the influx of students was created around 1960. At the same time, a new category of teachers, the university lecturer, was introduced. New branches outside the old universities and a whole new university (the fifth, in Umeå) were founded in the middle of the 1960s. In 1969, a reform of the curriculum system was decided, according to which undergraduate studies at the open faculties should be better planned and better adapted to the needs of the labor market than the old system of "free" studies.

The curriculum reform weakened the position of political science in relation to other social science subjects. This effect was partly due to the fact that a new, cross-disciplinary social science subject was created for the education of school teachers, whereas political science had dominated in the traditional education of teachers in the social sciences. Together with a general decline in the number of students at the beginning of the 1970s, the reform of 1969 led to a drastic reduction of the student population and a slight reduction of the teaching staff in political science. The fluctuations in student numbers are illustrated in table 25.1.

The table shows that student numbers peaked in 1967, when the total figure was more than ten times higher than in 1975. The same drastic decrease took place at the level of second-term studies, where student registrations dropped from a total of 1,037 in 1969 to 162 in 1975. Through this development the recruitment base of graduate studies was eroded, which can also be demonstrated by registration figures (usually the highest undergraduate level): a decline from a total of 254 in 1969 to 65 in 1975.[3]

During the period of rapid expansion of the student population a great number of teaching positions were established, thanks to the system of automatic allocation of teaching resources. Many of these positions were lectureships with tenure, but the bulk of the teaching load was carried by nontenured junior teachers. It should be mentioned here that a Swedish university lecturer has a full-time teaching position; no research work is required from him. In the last few years, however, lecturers have been given some opportunity to take part in graduate education, mostly in the form of research guidance work. Of course some lecturers are doing research work of their own, but on the whole the category cannot be regarded as belonging to the research staff. This is something specific to Sweden; the system has no correspondence in the other Nordic countries—nor in any other modern countries for that matter.

The expansion of the teaching staff for undergraduate education was not accompanied by a corresponding increase in research positions, also typical of Swedish university policy. A few so-called associate professorships in political science were established in the middle of the 1960s, but still the number of chairs is much lower than in Denmark and Norway.[4] The number of docent positions—a nontenured position with appointment for only 6-9 years, although with possibilities for extension—has also been kept down. On the other hand a new category of so-called research associates (*forskarassistent*) was introduced in the beginning of the 1960s and was expanded a little as a consequence of the reform of the doctor's degree.[5] The typical research career after the Ph.D. is now the following: research associate, docent, professor. The development of the research staff in political science is demonstrated by table 25.2.

The gloomy picture of scarce resources becomes a little brighter, however, if we add to the ordinary staff two types of nontenured positions. There is one category of research positions—mostly research associates—which has been created and financed by special research

Table 25.1 Undergraduate Students at Swedish Universities and Branches 1963–1975: First-Time Registrations for First-Term Studies in Political Science

TERM		UPPSALA	LUND	GÖTEBORG	STOCKHOLM	UMEÅ	BRANCHES	TOTAL
Autumn	1963	358	298	118	397	—	—	1,171
"	1965	421	317	223	721	124	—	1,806
"	1967	421	290	412	806	207	465	2,601
"	1968	319	240	312	729	215	319	2,134
"	1969	367	302	287	597	122	191	1,866
"	1970	319	193	306	380	94	160	1,452
"	1971	181	158	146	211	62	125	883
"	1973	73	158	52	177	31	70	561
Spring	1974	59	78	46	130	31	60	404
"	1975	34	25	25	90	19	47	240

SOURCE: Stig Brewitz, "Vad gör statsvetaren? En kartläggning av bakgrund, yrkesverksamhet och karriärvägar för personer med högre akademisk examen i statskunskap," Uppsala universitet, Enheten för pedagogiskt utvecklingsarbete, mimeo, 1975.

Table 25.2 Department Staffs in Political Science at Swedish Universities 1960–1975 (Autumn Term)

UNIVERSITY	FULL PROFESSORS	ASSOCIATE PROFESSORS	DOCENTS	RESEARCH ASSOCIATE	LECTURERS (TENURED)[5]
Uppsala					1
1960	1		1		4
1967	1	1	1	1	2
1975	1	1	2	3	
Lund					1
1960	1		1		3
1967	1	1	3	1	3
1975	1	1	1	2	
Göteborg					
1960	1		1	1	1
1967	1		1	1	3
1975	1		1	1	
Stockholm					2
1960	1	⅓	1		5
1967	1	1⅓	2		6
1975	1	1⅓	2	2	
Umeå					1
1967	1				
1975	1		1	1	2

SOURCE: Brewitz, "Väd gör statsvetaren?"

projects with external funding from the Research Council, or the Bank of Sweden Tercentenary Fund. In this way many doctoral students and young doctors have been salaried during their full-time research work. As an example it ought to be mentioned that the large Local Government Project employed about 15 research associates at all universities during the most intensive period of project work at the end of the 1960s. The other type is the part-time teaching position, such as "extra" lecturer, assistant, amanuensis which gives their holders some time for research work. This category of positions is very important as a complementary source of research funding in addition to scholarships and full-time research positions. As an illustration the following figures from the Department of Political Science in Uppsala can be given: in 1960 there were 7 positions of this kind, in 1967 the number was also 7, and in 1975 it was 8. In 1974 about 20 persons in the whole country with licentiate or doctor's degrees or the new Ph.D. occupied such positions.

Let us now turn to the results of graduate education in political science. We shall begin with the development of student numbers, which is illustrated in table 25.3. The table demonstrates that student numbers have increased

Table 25.3 Graduate Students at Swedish Universities 1963–1975: Registrations for Licentiatexamen, Doktorsgrad and Doktorsexamen in Political Science (Non-Active Students Excluded)

TERM		UPPSALA	LUND	GÖTEBORG	STOCKHOLM	UMEÅ	TOTAL
Autumn	1963	28	21	12	55	—	116
"	1964	27	22	11	55	—	115
"	1965	29	31	16	60	3	139
"	1967	38	29	29	47	11	154
"	1969	54	40	35	55	23	207
"	1970	45	45	33	51	21	195
"	1971	39	48	47	53	21	208
"	1972	59	58	40	51	17	225
"	1973	56	48	49	50	15	218
"	1974	57	49	47	58	15	226
"	1975	54	33	36	59	17	199

SOURCE: Brewitz, "Väd gör statsvetaren?"

Table 25.4 Graduate Examination in Political Science 1960–1975

TIME PERIOD	LICENTIATEXAMEN	DOKTORSGRAD	DOKTORSEXAMEN	TOTAL
1960–64	22	9	—	31
1965–69	42	12	—	54
1970–74	40	14	29	83
1975	—	1	10	11

Source: Brewitz, "Väd gör statsvetaren?" p. 70.

in a rather modest way. The enormous expansion of the undergraduate level in the middle of the 1960s was never followed by a corresponding increase at the graduate level. This is partly due to the fact that the recruitment base at the higher undergraduate levels was drastically reduced in the beginning of the 1970s, as was demonstrated above. However, the modest increase in the number of graduate students which is still going on would have been impossible without the great undergraduate expansion. Many students who started political science studies at the end of the 1960s are now working with their doctoral dissertations. This time lag probably explains more of the relatively high number of students at the graduate level today than the stimulating effects of the Ph.D. reform in 1969.

As regards examinations, the Ph.D. reform probably stimulated output in two ways. Those who had studied for the old degrees had to finish their dissertation work at the beginning of the 1970s before the expiration of the old system. The new Ph.D. was off to a flying start with a high number of examinations in the period 1970–75, as is demonstrated by table 25.4.[6]

In order to give a picture of the areas of interest in dissertation work we shall now present a tentative classification of topics of dissertations. The table is based on a survey of all political scientists who graduated between 1950 and 1973. The figures should be taken with reservation because distinctions between the headings are often hard to draw. It should also be pointed out that only 81.4 percent of the population responded, which may partly explain that, for instance, election research has such a low figure. However, table 25.5 gives some indications of main trends of research in dissertation work, particularly when the old degrees are compared with the new Ph.D.

The table indicates a shift of emphasis away from political theory and history of political ideas, and from constitutional history and public law in the dissertations of the old type, towards an increasing interest in public administration and political institutions in the new Ph.D. dissertations. The same trend can be observed if the material is divided into time periods according to the time of examination: public administration, for instance, is advancing at the expense of political theory and constitutional history. International politics and international organizations did not attract much interest before 1965, but the area has been steadily advancing since then. Finally, it should be pointed out that the vanishing interest in political parties and interest organizations in the Ph.D. dissertations before 1974 is a causal phenomenon; in

Table 25.5 Topics of Dissertations in Political Science 1950–1973. Divided into Examination Categories

RESEARCH AREA	LICENTIAT-EXAMEN		DOKTORS-GRAD		DOKTORS-EXAMEN		TOTAL	
	N	%	N	%	N	%	N	%
Political theory and history of political ideas	18	15	8	19	—	—	26	15
Mass media, political opinion, and political socialization	36	30	14	34	5	36	55	31
Election research	1	1	—	—	—	—	1	1
Political parties and interest organizations	10	8	7	17	—	—	17	10
Public administration and political institutions	34	28	4	10	6	43	44	25
Political systems for foreign countries	7	6	1	3	1	7	9	5
International politics and international organizations	8	7	5	12	2	14	15	9
Constitutional history and public law	6	5	2	5	—	—	8	4
	120	100	41	100	14	100	175	100

Source: Brewitz, "Väd gör statsvetaren?" p. 7. The classification has been changed somewhat.

1974-75 several dissertations were presented within this field.

An important aspect of the results of graduate education in political science is the occupational career of the graduated political scientist. In what fields of the labor market did they find jobs? The aforementioned survey gives some basic information: 82 percent of those who answered in 1974 were employed in the public sector and only 14 percent in the private sector. The dominant fields of occupation are university teaching (34%), school teaching (14%) and public administration (33%).[7] These are the traditional fields for political scientists: the average percentages for comparable sectors of the labor market in the period 1890-1970 are 26, 31, and 27 respectively. Since 1960, however, the university career has expanded considerably, whereas school teaching has decreased.[8]

This tendency is also illustrated in table 25.6, particularly as regards the period 1970-73. The figures reflect the great expansion of graduate examinations after 1960, and particularly after 1965. No less than 73 percent of those who have university employment have graduated in the period 1965-73; for school teaching and public administration the corresponding figures are 67 and 61 respectively. This means that most of the many new positions which were created during a period of rapid growth of the public sector are occupied by young people. There will be very few openings in the traditional fields of employment for political scientists who are graduating in the future, so they will have to look for other occupations, such as private industry jobs.

In table 25.7 we find the total survey population divided among various types of occupations and examinations. The table shows that only a few persons were occupied in fields other than teaching and public administration. In the latter field the distribution among the three types of examination is similar to the distribution in the total population. The doctor's degree is overrepresented in university teaching, and the licentiate degree is totally dominant in school teaching. A great majority of the doctors (both types) are occupied at universities or in public administration, whereas the licentiate category is more evenly divided among the three main fields. Some of the political scientists with licentiate degrees have reached high positions in public administration and interest organizations. According to the survey, 44 percent of all graduated political scientists working in the administrative sector have leading functions. This is good evidence of the usefulness of graduate studies in political science. It should be mentioned here that about 60 percent of those who have administrative occupations have conducted dissertation research within the fields of mass media, political opinion, public administration, and so on, and that about half the people who have studied one of these fields have such occupations. On the other hand, research in political theory and history of ideas is more frequent among political scientists who have university positions.[9]

Finally, something should be said about the professional organization of graduated political scientists in Sweden. Such an organization was formed in 1970 as a sort of national union of the old local university clubs. The name is *Statsvetenskapliga Förbundet*, and the aims are the following: to represent the interests of the political science discipline vis-à-vis the state; produce external information about research and other activities (this is mainly done through the journal *Politologen*); promote cooperation between the departments of political science, particularly concerning graduate teaching; and represent Swedish political science in contacts with IPSA and other international organizations, particularly in the Nordic area.[10] Most of these aims have been successfully

Table 25.6 Main Occupations of Graduated Political Scientists Divided into Time Periods of Examination 1950-1973

TIME PERIOD	UNIVERSITY TEACHING		SCHOOL TEACHING		PUBLIC ADMINISTRATION		TOTAL	
	N	%	N	%	N	%	N	%
1950-54	1	2	5	19	5	9	11	8
1955-59	1	2	1	3	5	9	7	5
1960-64	14	23	3	11	12	21	29	20
1965-69	17	28	10	37	18	31	45	31
1970-73	27	45	8	30	17	30	52	36
Total	60	100	27	100	57	100	144	100

SOURCE: Brewitz, "Väd gör statsvetaren?" p. 11.

Table 25.7 Occupations of Graduated Political Scientists Divided into Types of Examination

EXAMI-NATION	UNIVERSITY TEACHING		SCHOOL TEACHING		PUBLIC ADMINISTRATION		BUSINESS ADMINISTRATION		LIBRARIES		JOURNALISM		RESEARCH OUTSIDE UNIVERSITY		TOTAL	
	N	%	N	%	N	%	N	%	N	%	N	%	N	%	N	%
Licentiatexamen	30	50	26	96	42	74	3	100	3	60	7	88	9	60	120	69
Doktorsgrad	22	37	1	4	11	19	—	—	2	40	1	12	4	27	41	23
Doktorsexamen	8	13	—	—	4	7	—	—	—	—	—	—	2	13	14	8
Total	60	100	27	100	57	100	3	100	5	100	8	100	15	100	175	100

SOURCE, Brewitz, "Väd gör statsvetaren?" p. 11.

fulfilled. It should be pointed out that the *Statsvetenskapliga Förbundet* has nothing to do with the economic interests of the members; those interests are usually taken care of by professional unions, such as the University Teachers Union and other unions within the national top organization SACO.

Membership in the *Statsvetenskapliga Förbundet* is open to all graduated political scientists and for graduate students as well. The number of members has increased from 11 in 1971 to 162 in 1975. About 50 percent of the graduated members have occupations outside university departments. Such "external" members are regarded as an important resource; they are represented on the governing board, and some of them take an active part in connection with the annual meetings.

Notes

1. Uppsala has the oldest chair (in 'Latin Eloquence and Political Science') in the world, founded in 1622. The chair in Linköping is a personal professorship for the university president, Hans Meijer.
2. Conny Blom and Birgitta Pikwer, "Vem blev forskare och vad blev forskaren." Delrapport I inom UKÄ-projektet *Forskarutbildningens resultat 1890-1970*, mimeographed, 1976, p. 21.
3. Brewitz, "*Vad gör statsvetaren?*" (see source, table 25.1).
4. The term associate professor is somewhat misleading. Although the Swedish title is *biträdande professor* and the salary range is lower than for full professors, the position has almost the same functions as full professor and is tenured.
5. One of the three research associates in Uppsala belongs to the Department of Peace Research, but the holder of this position is docent in political science, and part of his teaching is carried out at the Department of Political Science.
6. Brewitz's figures for the years 1960-1973 are based on a survey of all graduated political scientists in 1974. The survey was answered by 81.4%, which means that the figures are too low. According to Blom and Pikwer, "*Vem blev forskare,*" p. 21, the total number of examinations in 1961-1970 was 94 for the licentiate degree and 30 for the doctor's degree. The figures for 1974 and 1975 are based on reports from the political science departments in *Politologen,* official publication of the Political Science Association.
7. Brewitz, "*Vad gör statsvetaren?,*" p. 9. The category public administration includes a few leading positions in interest organizations.
8. Revised versions of appendix table 2 in Blom and Pikwer, "*Vem blev forskare,*" p. 88. The share of the university career increased from 17% in 1951-60 to 36% in 1961-70; the corresponding figures for the school sector are 44% and 17%.
9. Brewitz, "*Vad gör statsvetaren?,*" pp. 12, 13, 16.
10. *Politologen,* no. 1, 1971.

Bibliography

Berntsson, Lennart. *Politiska partier och sociala klasser.* Staffanstorp: Cavefors, 1974.

Berwitz, Stig. "Vad gör statsvertaren? En kartlaggning av bakgrund, yrkesverksamhet och karriarvagar för personer med hogre akademisk examen i statskunskap." Uppsala: Enheten for pedagogiskt utvecklingsarbete, mimeo, 1975.

Blom, Conny, and Birgitta Pikwer. "Vem blev forskare och blev forskaren." Delrapport I inom UKA-projektet *Forskarubildingens resultat 1890-1970,* mimeo, 1976.

Eliassen, Kjell. "The Founding of the Nordic Political Science Association." *Scandinavian Political Studies* 11 (1976):167.

Foyer, Lars. "The Social Sciences in Royal Commission Studies in Sweden." *Scandinavian Political Studies* 4 (1969): 71-87.

Gustavson, Sverker. *Debatten om forskningen och samhallet: En Studie i nagra teoretiska inlagg.* Stockholm: Almqvist & Wiksell, 1971, with English summary.

Hadenius, Stig. "Partiers beslutsprocess och tjanstpensionsfragan." *Statsvetenskaplig Tidskrift* 69, no. 4 (1965): 343-64.

Hammar, Thomas, and Ko-Chih Tung. "Political Science Perspective on Migration Studies." In *Migration Research in Scandinavia*. Helsinki: Ministry of Labor, 1974, pp. 91-116.

Isberg, Magnus, Anders Wettergren, Björn Wittrock. "A Technique for Structural Content Analysis of Party Propaganda." *Scandinavian Political Studies* 7 (1972): 83-105.

Jervas, Gunnar E. *Internatiella konfliktprocesser: En generell modell for studiet av mallanstatliga konfliktforlopp*. Stockholm: Wahlstrom & Widstrand, 1973.

Lewin, Leif. *Folket och eliterna*. Stockholm: Almqvist & Wiksell, 1970.

———. "Om studiet av de politiska ideologiernas innehall och funktion." *Statsvetenskaplig Tidskrift* 75, no. 4 (1972): 437-38.

Lindblad, Ingemar. *Om der politiska vetenskapens grundar*. Stockholm: Almqvist & Wiksell, 1972.

Moberg, Erik. "Modeller for Politiska partiers handlande. "*Statsvetenskaplig Tidskrift* 69, nos. 2-3 (1966): 238-48.

———. "Partimodeller och beslutsanalys—en replik." *Statsvetenskaplig Tidskrift* 71, no. 3 (1968): 220-37.

Ramström, Dick. *Social Science Research in Sweden Today and Tomorrow*. Uppsala: Department of Business Administration, n.d.

Rudebeck, Lars. "Political Development : Towards a Coherent and Relevant Theoretical Formulation of the Concept." *Scandinavian Political Studies* 73, no. 5 (1970): 21-63.

Ruin, Olof, "Political Science in Sweden in the Postwar Period." *Scandinavian Political Studies* 4 (1969): 171-82.

Sjöblom, Gunnar. "Analys av partiers beteende. Diskussion om ett avsnitt i Bjorn M Molins doktorsavhandling." *Statsvetenskaplig Tidskrift* 68, no. 3 (1965): 365-88.

———. "Replik på Mobergs replik." *Statsvetenskaplig Tidskrift* 71, no. 3 (1968): 238-48.

Vedung, Evert. "Innehallslig och funktionell idéanalys." *Statsvetenskaplig Tidskrift* 77, no. 1 (1974): 1-20.

———."The Study of Contents and Functions of Political Ideas." *Scandinavian Political Studies* 10 (1975): 185-208.

Westerståhl, Jörgen. *Den kommunala sjalvstyrelsen I : Ett forskningsprogram*. Stockholm: Almqvist & Wiksell, 1970.

———. "Swedish Local Government Research." *Scandinavian Political Studies* 2 (1967): 276-80.

SWITZERLAND*

MONICA WEMEGAH WITH THE COLLABORATION OF DANIEL FREI

The Birth of Political Science in Switzerland

POLITICAL SCIENCE : A SUPERFLUOUS SCIENCE

Although political science began developing in the United States at the beginning of the twentieth century and in Europe after the Second World War, Switzerland has avoided this evolution. How can this lack of interest be explained in a country where it is well known that politics is everybody's affair? Should not political science interest a people whose democratic traditions enable each citizen to learn about public life and thus about political affairs?

It is, however, precisely because of their great experience in communal and public affairs that the Swiss have long deemed superfluous a science that would teach them the way their state was functioning. To their eyes, practical experience made scientific analysis quite useless. Many saw in political science a passing fashion from abroad and held it in suspicion. There was a fear that the study of politics would lead to a politicization of science or to the "scientification" of politics. It was considered unacceptable that politics, which was everybody's affair, would become that of a few specialists, even if they were political scientists.

The stability of the Swiss political system is another factor which accounts for the reticence of the Swiss toward political science. Unlike other Western countries, Switzerland was preserved from this century's great wars and upheavals, consequently it has not experienced the governmental and constitutional crises which have racked belligerent countries. The Swiss have not felt in the same way the need to study possible weaknesses in the mechanisms of public life, since political reality has not seemed to differ from what the founders of Switzerland had written in the 1848 constitution.

State problems were thus approached for a long time from the exclusive angle of public law and institutions. Until very recently, law was considered a discipline both necessary and sufficient for a good understanding of Swiss politics. Since, however, it fails to take into account the observations of political science, the purely legal analysis inevitably neglected several important facets of the political system and resulted in a somewhat one-sided knowledge of the Swiss state. Thus, the public law approach precluded a comprehensive study of democracy, federalism, or the Swiss administration. Similarly, many single aspects of the state, such as the formation and functioning of interest groups or political parties, were of essentially no interest to social scientists. In fact, foreign scholars were the first to draw attention to the peculiarities of the Swiss political system. Marcel Bridel wrote in 1951: "There are no works by Swiss professors which are specifically concerned with political science. Only foreigners have produced such works."[1]

POLITICAL SCIENCE OR POLITICAL SCIENCES

In light of the preceding discussion, it is hardly surprising that political science has remained for so long in a state of underdevelopment that can only be corrected over a period of many years. It would, however, be wrong to think that in the absence of political science in Swiss academic publications and even more particularly in universities, the study of public life was neglected

---

*This chapter has emerged from the work of a committee set up by the Swiss Political Science Association to examine the state of the discipline in Switzerland. Monica Wemegah drafted this shortened version and Daniel Frei completed it on a number of points. Roy Preiswerk, former president of the association, initiated the research.

completely. Although political science was practically unknown until the 1960s, most of its subject matter was contained in the traditional social sciences, such as history, law, philosophy, or economics, which have always been of great importance in Switzerland.

All of these fields deal with the problems of the state and power in their different aspects although their main object is not necessarily to analyze public life. Thus, history may be one of the most fruitful ways of learning about political societies. The entire field of public law also supplies indispensable knowledge about the institutional framework in which political behavior is situated. Similarly, economics touches on problems of the state in so far as the state plays an increasingly important, even essential role in the administration of scarce resources. Other fields which are important links to the study of politics are psychology, geography, and in particular sociology. They provide political science with indispensable information on such things as the make-up of society, public opinion, and group dynamics.

One of the obstacles in the way of introducing political science in Swiss universities lay precisely in the excellence of some traditional disciplines. The development of what is commonly known as the political sciences seemed to render useless, or little wished for, the expansion of an autonomous political science. Thus, in the few university centers which taught politics during the first half of this century (the School of Social and Political Sciences in Lausanne and the Graduate Institute of International Studies in Geneva), one did not meet political science students, properly speaking, since they remained indebted—to a great extent—to their education in the field of the traditional disciplines. They were students of the political sciences, not of political science as a complete and specialized study.

THE PIONEERS OF AN AUTONOMOUS
POLITICAL SCIENCE

The fact that political science managed to take root in Switzerland all the same is a result of the double influence of political science from abroad and the growing number of Swiss scholars, in particular professors of public law and history, who were interested in the workings of Swiss political life. We can identify several generations of political scholars who left their mark on the development of political science since 1945. Even before this date, there were historians, philosophers, and jurists involved with the problems of states and governments. Many of them were members of the New Swiss Society, which has been a source of much thought in the study of politics ever since its creation in 1914. Political thought was also encouraged in 1939 when the Foundation Pro Helvetia was set up for the purpose of maintaining and developing the Swiss spiritual heritage.

The real pioneers of political science, however, appear in the 1940s. It was then that historians such as Jean-Rodolphe de Salis or Hans Nabolz, economists like Emil Küng and especially jurists like Max Imboden of Basle, Hans Huber of Berne, Werner Kägi of Zurich, Marcel Bridel of Lausanne, and Maurice Battelli of Geneva—to mention only a few—started studying the problems of federalism, democracy, or economics in a perspective that went beyond the rigid framework of their own respective disciplines. Without minimizing the role of history, economics, or philosophy professors, however, the Swiss jurists were the first political scientists in the true sense of the word. In the French-speaking part of Switzerland, Marcel Bridel was the first to approach with greater freedom problems which public law shares with political science. It is therefore not a coincidence that Bridel was elected vice-president of the International Political Science Association (IPSA), which was founded in 1949 upon a UNESCO initiative. UNESCO also called upon the jurists Marcel Bridel and Hans Huber when it launched, in 1948, an international survey on the position of political science in the world. Thanks to his participation in the first IPSA conferences which were held in Zurich (1950), the Hague (1952), and Stockholm (1955), Bridel was able to establish invaluable contacts with many political scientists, Jean Meynaud in particular. The latter was to play, as secretary-general of the IPSA, an important role in the propagation of political science in Europe and Switzerland. At the second IPSA meeting, Switzerland was already able to submit an important contribution on the subject "Direct Democracy in the Swiss communes." Encouraged by this success and greatly influenced by the personality of Jean Meynaud, Bridel became convinced of the necessity to create a Swiss political science association. However, when he called for a meeting in Lausanne to this end, his efforts met with failure. "My colleagues' thoughts were not yet ripe. In their opinion, political science should be left to the foreigners with serious political and economic crises in their countries. What purpose could political science serve in a model state like Switzerland, the best of all possible worlds?"[2]

Fortunately, Bridel's initiative was taken over a few years later by Jacques Freymond, the director of Geneva's Graduate Institute of International Studies at that time. Freymond was also influenced by foreign thought in political science, particularly American, and had more luck than his predecessor. When he relaunched the idea of a Swiss political science association in 1959, attitudes were open to it this time.

The Development of Political Science

THE CREATION OF THE SWISS POLITICAL
SCIENCE ASSOCIATION

Aims. The Swiss Political Science Association (SPSA) held its constitutive assembly on 18 April 1959 at the Graduate Institute for International Studies. Many important Swiss officials and members of the academic world attended the meeting. The aim of the SPSA was to promote the development of political science in Switzerland. To this end, it considered pursuing the following activities:

- To encourage and develop the teaching and study of political science in Switzerland

- To facilitate the propagation of information on important progress in the field of political science

- To organize conferences, debates and meetings in order to favor personal contacts among political science specialists both in Switzerland and abroad

- To ensure Swiss representation in international political science meetings

- To establish contact with competent international associations[3]

Members. This vast program paved the way for a radically new approach to political science in Switzerland. Its development was entrusted to the Association Committee presided over by Jacques Freymond. It consisted of six members, mostly jurists. This was just one of many peculiarities which distinguished this committee. Another lies in the important role played by French-speaking circles. Out of its forty-two founding members, only five came from the Swiss-German part of the country. It is also relevant to mention that Geneva was the place of its creation and that the two first volumes of the SPSA bore exclusively French titles.

Another main trait of the SPSA was, and still is, its open attitude toward nonacademic circles. While remaining strictly scientific, the SPSA was anxious to lay a bridge between academic, governmental, and economic circles interested in Swiss political life. Thus, it has never been an exclusive club reserved for specialists such as jurists, historians, sociologists, and political scientists. It has been open from the outset to politicians, governmental officials, economists, and journalists. Thanks to this policy of openness, the membership of the SPSA has increased regularly to the respectable number of 470 members in 1978 (26 of whom are collective members). The committee has expanded similarly from 6 members in 1959 to 17 members in 1978. It is true that the committee opened more slowly to the nonacademic world. Five of the six original committee members were academics, although, as we have seen, none of them was a political scientist in the true sense of the term. For years, the committee was almost exclusively composed of academics and particularly of representatives of universities wishing to introduce political science courses. Gradually, however, the committee opened up to the private sector and public administration, and counts journalists and civil servants from both the federal and cantonal governments among its members today.

Activities. Annual meetings are an important means of action for the SPSA. These meetings provide valuable opportunities for contact between scholars of different linguistic and academic backgrounds on the one hand, and between "analysts" and "practitioners" of Swiss political life on the other hand. In the attempt to clear up a misconception about the role of the political scientist in Swiss society, the SPSA organizes periodic meetings where politicians and political scientists engage in public debate. The 1973 congress, for example, was entirely devoted to the subject "Politics and Political Science." Many other meetings were called to emphasize the specificity of political science in relation to similar fields. The roles of the Federal Council, political parties, Parliament, and professional associations were among the subjects discussed at numerous congresses of the association. A few years ago, however, the format of the congress was changed. The congresses are now held every second year, and instead of being devoted to only one subject, a large number of subjects is discussed in work groups which meet several times in the months preceding the congress. This new format helps to dismantle the intellectual and institutional barriers which plague our decentralized university system. It also promotes the participation of the association membership, since it makes possible increased contributions, suggestions, and criticism.

In accordance with its objectives, the association also encourages contact with other scientific organizations. On the international level, the SPSA was granted collective membership in the International Political Science Association (IPSA), thereby entitling it to represent Switzerland in this international body. Jacques Freymond, the first president of the SPSA, was immediately elected to the Executive Committee of the IPSA and, in 1964, became president of the association for a three-year term. Since 1977, Switzerland has been represented on the Executive Committee of the IPSA by Daniel Frei, the current president of the Swiss Political Science Association. The SPSA also maintains close ties with the European Consortium for Political Research (ECPR), whose main objective is to provide a solid basis and the necessary material conditions for bringing European political science professors and researchers together. Furthermore, many members of the SPSA regularly attend common workshops organized each year by the ECPR and providing Swiss political scientists with the opportunity to present the results of their research and to compare them with studies done by political scientists from abroad.

On the Swiss level, the SPSA became a member of the Swiss Society for Human Sciences (SSHS) in 1961 and has been receiving regular subsidies from that society since 1974 to organize its congress and publish its Swiss *Political Science Year Book*. New prospects for the development of the field appeared with the creation of the Social Sciences Section of the SSHS in January 1976. This section, which groups the SPSA, the Swiss Society of Sociology, the Swiss Society of Psychology, and the Swiss Society of Statistics and Economics, could become an additional means for promoting political science in Switzerland, since the branches which make up the section are relatively undeveloped. The SPSA also seeks contact with numerous other bodies with similar preoccupations, such as the Foundation for Confederal Collaboration in Solothurn or the Institute for Local, Regional, and National Planning of the Federal Polytechnical University in Zurich.

Publications. The SPSA created several publications "to facilitate the propagation of information on important progress made by political science in Switzerland."[4] Most such scientific information appears in the *Political Science Year Book* which has been published yearly since 1961. It provides an accurate picture of the main trends in Swiss political science research. The editorial committee, replaced in 1969 by a single editor, has chosen to alternate its publications by devoting them sometimes to a variety of subjects and sometimes to a specific topic such as the problem of federalism (1964), Swiss foreign policy (1966), the Federal Council (1967), public administration (1977), and political systems of the cantons (1978). Whereas the volumes mentioned contain studies focusing on a general subject chosen in the field of political science research, many other volumes (1968, 1970, and 1975) deal with the discipline of political science itself in order to draw attention to its different concepts, approaches, and methods. Such clarification is necessary because political science is still young in Switzerland and remains in search of its identity and place in Swiss society. "Political scientists," remarks Roy Preiswerk, "cannot claim a long secular tradition such as their colleagues in law, history, and economy. This may be the reason why they periodically feel the need to review what they have undertaken, list the work in progress, and reevaluate work completed."[5]

During the first six years of its existence, the year book propagated not only scientific, but also political information. Thus, part of the year book was regularly devoted to current Swiss politics. It is only in 1967 that *The Swiss Political Year* became a separate publication under the patronage of the association. On the other hand, the year book has always included an annual bibliography of Swiss political science publications, which provides the scholars and members of the association with basic reference material and an indispensable research tool. The first bulletin published by the SPSA in collaboration with the Swiss Society for Sociology appeared in October 1972. The *Bulletin* is published four times a year and is intended to increase the amount of information available to the members of the SPSA and particularly to universities where political science is involved in the long and difficult process of institutionalization.

THE INSTITUTIONALIZATION OF
POLITICAL SCIENCE

The Situation in 1959. One of the main objectives of the SPSA is to establish political science firmly at the university level. At the moment of its creation in 1959, political science occupied a vast range of positions all the way from total absence in the curriculum to recognition as one of the essential branches of the social sciences. Particularly in the German-speaking part of Switzerland, political science confronted resistance and even hostility from universities for a long time. In comparison with the universities of the French-speaking region, these universities are still behind today and are catching up only slowly. This situation is the result of a converging of regional differences in history, politics, and culture, which can be mentioned only briefly here.

Thus, Swiss-German reticence toward political science can be mainly accounted for by the fact that it is the traditional center of political and economic power of the confederation. As such, it has therefore a tendency to favor a strictly juridical analysis of the state, by emphasizing the conditions that must be fulfilled in order for the state to function according to the rules of the constitution. This approach, remarks Erich Gruner, makes it possible for the Swiss Germans to avoid thinking about the problems of political power and thus avoid any feelings of "remorse" with respect to the other linguistic regions.[6] The French-speaking part of Switzerland expresses great interest in all questions dealing with power and the formation of opinions precisely because of its minority position. Furthermore, this part of the country was influenced heavily by the early development of political science in France, and it is more open to new developments in general, as seen in the presence of the many international organizations on its soil. In addition, French-speaking universities are ahead of the German-speaking ones by the fact that they have been teaching "political sciences" since the beginning of the century. Lausanne created a School of Political and Social Sciences in 1902, and Geneva followed suit in 1915 with its Faculty of Economic and Social Sciences, to which the Graduate Institute of International Studies (GIIS) was added twelve years later. This institute is the only postgraduate institute in Switzerland today which is engaged in both teaching and research in the political sciences. As we have seen earlier, however, these do not represent a homogeneous science but group the various sciences that deal with the state in one form or another.

Yet this familiarity with the concept of political sciences made it much easier to introduce political science in French-speaking universities. Thus, it is not surprising that the first political science professorships were created in 1959 in the cities of Lausanne and Geneva. It is not surprising either that during the first six years these professorships were held by foreign professors[7] until Swiss political scientists could be trained to take over.

The Evolution in the 1960s. For the rest of Switzerland, the situation did not evolve in the 1960s, although it still remained more favorable in the French-speaking part of the country than in the German-speaking. Thus, at the University of Neuchâtel, political science was attached to the Institute of Sociology and Political Science and no professorship was created. At Fribourg, the Faculty of Law, Economics, and Social Sciences went on conferring political science degrees made up of various faculty teachings. In Basle and Zurich, where there was neither a political science department nor an institute, political science problems were studied in the framework of public law. At the Saint-Gall Graduate School of Economics and Social Sciences, political questions were approached from the angle of economics, a fact which can be explained from the very nature of the school. The University of Bern deserves a special place for having created in 1960 an *ad personam* professorship in the sociology of Swiss politics for Erich Gruner. He was awarded this professorship on the basis of his eminent work in social history, and he is the only Swiss political scientist who holds a research professorship with the National Fund.

The Present Situation. In terms of the number of professorships, the French-speaking part of Switzerland still leads the country by the same amount as it did in the 1960s. Thus, the University of Lausanne now has two-and-a-half political science professorships, and the Political Science Department of the University of Geneva is in the process of creating a third one. Elsewhere, the progress of political science in academic structures goes on at a slower pace. Thus, during the 1970s, the universities of Neuchâtel, Zurich, and Saint-Gall were each endowed with a single political science professorship, whereas in Fribourg, a permanent course is devoted to political science within the Faculty of Law, Economics, and Social Sciences. To this day, the University of Basle still does not have a professorship, or courses which could be considered political science in the strict sense of the term. It is only thanks to the interest of professors in related fields that political science is not entirely ignored.

Therefore, even if the academic situation of political science has greatly improved during this decade, it is still not entirely satisfactory. In fact, as long as political science does not manage to get solidly rooted in all Swiss university structures, it will find itself deprived, both materially and intellectually, of the necessary means for its unrestricted development in teaching as well as research.

THE EVOLUTION OF POLITICAL SCIENCE RESEARCH

Research Orientation. Political science research in Switzerland is strongly influenced by Swiss political pragmatism on the one hand, and foreign political science, mainly American, on the other hand. These two factors account - to a great extent - for the atrophy of political science research in some fields as shown in the accompanying chart.

One has to admit however that this chart does not cover all forms of political science research in Switzerland. It has been elaborated according to the studies published in the year book bibliography and is therefore not necessarily complete. However, we can deduct from it general tendencies in Swiss research during the past twenty years. There are two striking elements. In the first place, it is surprising to discover how much Swiss political science, under direct American influence, has become involved in empirical research. Thus, the lack of political theory, which was already noticeable during the 1959-1966 period, grew worse in the 1967-1977 period. Topics in political science and political thought did not add up to more than 15 percent of all research undertaken during the last ten years. Furthermore, if one examines the empirical orientation of research, it appears that political science conducts its research more and more from an institutional point of view. Political and administrative institutions are in fact, the only fields of academic inves-

26.1 Political Science Research in Switzerland

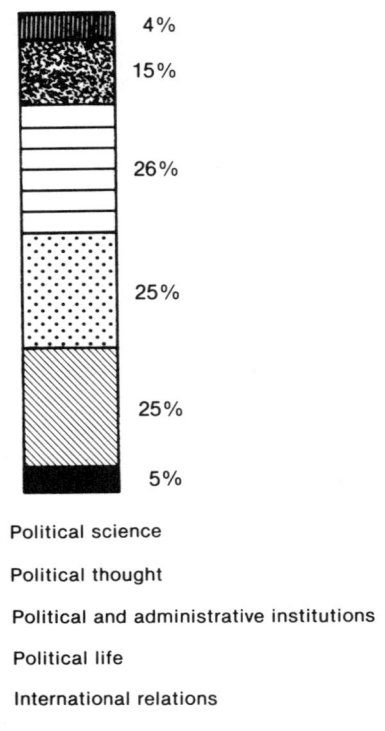
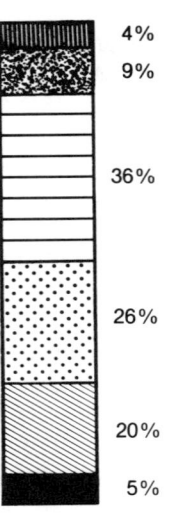

According to Roland Ruffieux
1959-66

According to Monica Wemegah
1967-77

- Political science
- Political thought
- Political and administrative institutions
- Political life
- International relations
- National and regional studies

tigation which have gained importance during the last decade. They presently cover about one-third of all political science research.

It is true that the orientation of political science research in a given country is determined equally by the political temperament of its inhabitants. Thus, one may suppose that a similar investigation on the position of research in Italy would have revealed a preponderant interest in theoretical and political studies. Such an orientation could be accounted for by the ideological struggles and class conflicts that prevail in the Italian peninsula. One should not forget either that research is often a matter of persons. In the German-speaking part of Switzerland, for example, where law faculties are very strong and conservative, faculty members still prefer to train new jurists rather than political scientists. From the standpoint of all possible investigation, however, political science represents a field of research, much of which has lain fallow and needs to be developed immediately.

Amplitude of Research. The amount of research undertaken in Switzerland appears rather modest compared to other countries such as Belgium, France, and the Federal Republic of Germany, not to mention the United States. This situation can be accounted for by several institutional, political as well as financial factors. Thus, unlike France, for instance, where the creation of a National Political Science Fund favors financial state intervention in the field of teaching, research, and publications, there is no such support for political science in Switzerland. Until the end of the 1960s, political science was sporadically subsidized by the Pro-Helvetia Foundation, the Swiss Society of the Humanities, or the National Scientific Research Fund, but such subsidies were small and never continuous.

It should be mentioned that until 1968, political science was an unknown field for the national fund and could not be found on the list of the twenty areas subsidized by the fund. Such subsidies as existed for political science could be found under "sociology and professional orientation" or "political economy and business." Political science was first mentioned as a distinct branch in the national fund's 1968 annual report, although it is listed together with sociology. Adding to this the fact, which appears insignificant on first sight, that political science is still today expressed in the plural (the rubric reads "sociology and political sciences"), we can understand the road left to be travelled by political science before it will be recognized as a complete and specialized field.

What are the subsidy policies of the National Scientific Research Fund with regard to our field? Is Swiss political science the poor cousin of the social sciences in the way that American political science is? In order to answer this question, we have compared subsidies granted to some of the main traditional disciplines of the humanities. Thus, during the 1968-1971 period subsidies evolved favorably, though modestly, passing from 5 to 10 percent of total social science subsidies. So, political science improved its position during this period with respect to economics and law which were then less subsidized. During the 1971-1974 period, however, political science subsidies did not stop dropping in relative as well as in absolute terms. Despite a slight improvement starting in 1975, political science has since remained the least favored field and thus does indeed appear to be the poor cousin of the social sciences in Switzerland.

Political Science and the World of Politics

To say something about the relationship between political science and the Swiss world of politics is quite a difficult task. For reasons mentioned above, political science, for a long time, was not accepted by those who made decisions on behalf of the universities. The reluctance to accept the rationale of political science still prevails to some extent among the Swiss political elite. Apart from the long-standing feeling that, in a semidirect democracy like Switzerland, everybody is too much an expert in politics to need any scholarly advice, and the general preference for a legalist type of analysis, there are important additional motives which support this reluctance.

The first is that many politicians seem to be frightened by the very questions social scientists ask. This has to be seen against the background of the Swiss political system, which is run by an all-party coalition and has aptly been described as a "consociational" democracy or "government by cartel," working primarily by smooth and discrete bargaining among interest groups. It goes without saying that, in such a system, the analytical zeal exhibited by political scientists to shed light on decision-making processes and on the relative impact of interest groups may be perceived not only as an unsuitable element, but as a kind of threat to the confidential political intimacy of those concerned. However, in Switzerland all social scientists are facing this problem.

Another reason can be seen in the general tendency to be observed among Swiss political decision makers and bureaucrats to identify social sciences with leftist tendencies. Switzerland never had a proletariat offering a base for a radical-socialist mass movement, and the country's basic structure remains traditional and conservative, the small townships surrounded by rural areas still constituting the main feature of the Swiss population infrastructure. Thus, there is a strong trend toward the support of middle-class values and political moderation. Hence a general distrust against anything or anybody seeming—correctly or not—to represent ideas opposed to the status quo. Unfortunately and due to some regrettable misunderstandings, political science is largely considered to constitute such a suspect "revolutionary" force.

Yet, this rather gloomy picture would not be complete without taking into account an aspect pointing in the opposite direction: the smallness of the country and thus the necessity to make the best use of the scarce resources available. Since Switzerland as a sovereign nation wants to perform all functions belonging to a modern state, the political system finds it hard to forego the help of qualified advisers. In Switzerland, a great many tasks which, in large states, are considered to be the genuine domain of professional staff are performed on a part-time basis or by voluntary work. This system to overcome structural scarcity is called the "militia system"; its most salient application is the Swiss army which, apart from a small instruction staff corps, has no full-time staff let alone permanent staff and operates completely on a spare-time basis. However, the militia system is constantly and increasingly being applied to other fields too. For the Swiss political scientist, this led to gradual involvment in the decision-making process, usually by means of joining one of the many expert committees, advisory groups, and so forth, set up by the government. Thus, despite the general reluctance on the part of the political elite toward political *science*, political *scientists* are fairly well integrated into the world of politics. To put it briefly: although political science is distrusted, political scientists are generally quite welcome. At least, one can say that political scientists in Switzerland do not risk becoming isolated in a kind of academic ivory tower—on the contrary, some political scientists even feel quite sad sometimes about their often too heavy investment of time and effort required by participating in consulting work of various kinds.

In the past few years, this close interaction network between political scientists and the decision-making process led to a new form of cooperation. Several political and societal problems were raised by the growth of a postindustrial society becoming increasingly unmanageable by traditional methods, and the government decided to call on the universities for a more systematic and more scientific analysis of the sociopolitical system. They set up a series of so-called national research programs attempting to focus the research potential available on the most burning problems the Swiss political, social, and economic system is faced with. At least three of these programs have an immediate bearing upon the field of political science: the programs regarding the analysis (and improvement) of political decision-making processes, regional politics, and social integration. The programs are endowed with considerable funds to be administered during a period of five years by the National Scientific Research Fund and they can be expected to tie up a large part of the political science research infrastructure available in Switzerland. They also offer a new challenge and a chance of being heard by those whom the political scientists desire to reach. Therefore, maybe the place of political science in the Swiss world of politics will be quite different—and hopefully better—within the coming years.

A Note on the Teaching of Political Science in Switzerland

The current teaching of political science in Switzerland very much reflects the various concepts of the discipline. Whereas in Geneva and in Zurich modern curricula have been established which lead to a systematic, empirically oriented social science training, political science as taught at other places is—to a lesser or greater degree—integrated into a more general framework of humanities or public law or public administration. As an illustration, the following are samples of titles of courses currently being taught at Swiss universities:

Basle:
Socio-Political Utopias and Counter-Utopias
The Positions of the Trade Unions in Switzerland
Ideology and Critique of Ideology

Berne:
Press and Information in Eastern Europe
Local and Regional Planning
Marxism and Eurocommunism
The Rise and Decline of Collective Security
Violence and Politics

Geneva:
Introduction to Political Science
Political Science Methods
Conflict and Cooperation in Regional Integration
The Use of Computers in the Social Sciences
Comparative Politics
Political Behavior
Public Administration
Political Sociology of the Arab World
The Practice of Technical Cooperation
The Revision of International Development Strategies
Introductory Quantitative Methods
International Relations Theory

Lausanne:
Political Participation in Switzerland
Political Institutions
Language and Politics
History of Political Ideas
The Middle East Conflict

Saint Gallen:
Eurocommunism
Guerilla Warfare and Nuclear War

Zurich:
International Organizations
Political Science Methods
The Causes of War
The Executive Power
Local Politics: Introduction
Security Policy of Switzerland
Chinese Foreign Policy
Theories of Justice
Regional Economic Policy

As to the pedagogical methods used, no generalization seems to be possible. It can be said that practically all methods are being used, from the classical-type lecture in the big lecture theater to the face-to-face tutorial. Increasingly, emphasis is being laid on small-group teaching and project-oriented "learning by doing," especially at those universities which prefer empirical approaches.

Notes

1. Marcel Bridel, "Etat et méthodes de la science politique suisse," in *La science politique contemporaine, Contribution á la recherche, la méthode et l'enseignement* (Paris: UNESCO, 1951), pp. 68–78.
2. Interview with Marcel Bridel by the author.
3. Article 4 of the *Statuts de la SPSA*.
4. Ibid.
5. Preface to *Annuaire suisse de science politique* (Bern: Paul Haupt Verlag, 1975).
6. Erich Gruner and Roland Ruffieux, "Politische Wissenschaft in der Schweiz," *Politische Vierteljahrsschrift* 3 (1966): 483–93.
7. Jean Meynaud and John Goormaghtigh.

Bibliography

The Swiss Political Science Association publishes an annual comprehensive *Political Science Bibliography* listing all books and articles written by Swiss political scientists as well as publications about Switzerland authored by foreign colleagues. This bibliography is part of the *Annuaire Suisse de Science Politique*. The main periodical publication is the Political Science Annual (*Annuaire Suisse de Science Politique*), published in German and in French since 1961 by Paul Haupt Publishers, Berne. It offers a representative view on current Swiss activities in the field of political science. The Swiss Political Science Association also issues a quarterly newsletter, called *Bulletin*, distributed to all of its members.

Annuaire suisse de science politique. Volume 1, 1961.

Bridel, Marcel. *Précis de droit constitutionnel et public suisse*. 1959.

Chenaux-Repond, Dieter. "Politische Wissenschaft als Universitätstudium." *Neue Zürcher Zeitung*, 16 June 1961.

———. "Standart, Aufgaben und Problem der Politischen Wissenschaft in der Schweiz." *Neue Zürcher Zeitung*, 17 April 1960.

Fondation De Pro Helvetia. *Pro Helvetia 1939-1964*. Zurich: Orell Füssli Verlag, 1964.

F. R. "Stand der politologischen Forschung in der Schweiz—Notizen zum Kongress der Schweizerischen Vereinigung für politische Wissenschaft." *Neue Zürcher Zeitung*, 3 December 1975.

Fueter, Edouard. "Die Wissenschaft von der Politik." *Revue universitaire suisse*, no. 2 (1951).

Gautier, Léopold. "Les débuts de la Nouvelle Société helvétique." In *La Suisse—Annuaire national*. Nouvelle Société Helvétique, 1954.

Giig, Peter, and Gruner, Erich. "Die schweizerisch Politik als Forschungsgegenstand." *Wirtschaftspolitische Mitteilungen*, January 1968.

Gruner, Erich, and Ruffieux, Roland. "Politische Wissenschaft in der Schweiz." *Politische Vierteljahresschrift* 3 (1966).

Institut Universitaire de Hautes Etudes Internationales. *Hei 50, 1927, 1977*. Geneva, 1977.

Junker, Beat; Gilg, Peter; Reich, Richard. *Geschichte und Politische Wissenschaft*. Bern: Francke Verlag, 1975.

Meynaud, Jean. *La science politique au XXème siècle*. Paris: Imprimeries R. Faulon, 1955.

———. "Sciences politiques et science politique." Paper read at the Fondation de l'Association suisse de science politique, 18 April 1959, Geneva.

Reich, Richard. "Politische Wissenschaft in der Schweiz." *Neue Zürcher Zeitung*, 30 March 1963.

Ruffieux, Roland. "Die schweizerische Vereinigung für politische Wissenschaft und die Pflege der Politischen Wissenschaft in der Schweiz." *Politischen Vierteljahresschrift*, March 1966.

———. "La science politique en Suisse durant l'année 1966." *Annuaire suisse de science politique*, 1967.

———. "La Science politique en Suisse: situation et perspective." *Annuaire suisse de science politique*, 1968.

———. "La Suisse contemporaine—Etat des travaux." *Revue française de science politique*, 1960.

de Salis Jean-R. *Réflexions sur l'étude de la science politique*. Lausanne: Imprimérie des Arts et Métiers, S. A., 1966.

Schindler, Dietrich. "Die politische Wissenschaft und ihre Pflege in der Schweiz." *Neue Zürcher Zeitung*, 13 and 14 January 1961.

———. "Die Staatslehre in der Schweiz." *Jahrbuch des öffentlichen Rechts der Gegenwart* 25 (1976): 255-79.

———. "Zur Lage der Staatslehre und der politischen Wissenschaft in der Schweiz." *der Staat*, 1964.

Stauffer, Pierre André. "La politologie cherche sa place sociale." *La Suisse*, 24, 25 and 26 December 1975.

UNESCO. *La science politique contemporaine, contribution à la recherche, la méthode et l'enseignement*. Paris, 1951.

WRD. "Aspekte politologischer Forschung in der Schweiz." *Neue Zürcher Zeitung*, 14 August 1975.

UNION OF SOVIET SOCIALIST REPUBLICS

SOCIALIST POLITICAL SCIENCE*

V. E. CHIRKIN

Along with further differentiation, use of mathematical-logical methods, and extensive application of the systems approach to the study of phenomena and things, one of the leading trends in science in the second half of this century is the process of integration. This applies fully to the social sciences as well, including those that are directly associated with various aspects of social administration.

This tendency has also clearly appeared in the disciplines concerned with the political organization of society, government, and law. Since the beginning of the 1960s the opinion has become increasingly widespread that it is necessary to establish a special branch of knowledge to study interdisciplinary problems of social management and even the organizational establishment of a special course of study in those higher educational institutions whose graduates enter the field of social administration (law schools, institutes of the national economy, etc.).

This viewpoint is being implemented in some socialist countries, albeit in differing forms. Some higher educational institutions have introduced courses in political science, organization science, and so forth; chairs of political sciences have been established, and sometimes departments of political science and law.

The differing views on the matter of integration of the "political sciences"[1] can be explained, on the one hand, by epistemological factors and, on the other, by needs of a practical character.

The epistemological causes are associated chiefly with the extensive employment of the systems approach in science. Data accumulated in study of the "elementary components" have shown that none of the institutions of the political organization and political system of society function in isolation. Changes in the character of the functioning of one of them cause changes in others, a process which has emerged quite clearly, for example, in studying the role of the public in the functioning of the organs of government.

Discussion of the problem under examination has also been prompted by practical needs of personnel training. The professionalization of the personnel of the government apparatus and voluntary organizations, combined with interdisciplinary training of professionals, is presently acquiring special significance. But it is no secret that the graduates of some higher educational institutions devoted to the humanities are not trained precisely in the general-political interpretation of questions and in selection of optimal forms of social administration under changing conditions.

Proposals to improve the system of political sciences[2] can be divided into four principal groups. They are: (1) expansion of the bounds of theory of government and law or public law by partially changing their purview, introducing additional "politological" topics but retaining the previous name of each discipline; (2) organization of a special branch of knowledge—the theory of direction of society, the science of management of social processes, the science of governmental administration, a science of the state; (3) singling out a "political sci-

---

*This article was published originally as "On the Question of Socialist Political Science", *Soviet Law and Government*, vol. 13, pp. 32-46, © 1974 by M. E. Sharpe, Inc. Reprinted by permission of M. E. Sharpe, Inc. Translation from *Pravovedenie*, 1973, no. 4.

ence," "science of politics," having the purpose of teaching not only the political structures of society (including capitalist) but even foreign and domestic policy as it changes; and (4) establishing special courses in the theory of the political organization of society, the political system, and the science of government administration in those higher educational institutions whose graduates work to a greater or lesser degree in the field of managing the development of society.

The first group of proposals is advanced exclusively by specialists in the theory of state and law, governmentalists, including, as a rule, faculties of colleges of law.... They have been presented in works by the Soviet scholars N. P. Farberov, P. E. Nedbailo, A. P. Kositsyn, G. S. Ostroumov.... In their presentations at an international symposium of specialists in the theory of state and law, Kositsyn and Ostroumov observed that "the Marxist-Leninist theory of state and law must be regarded as both a political and a legal descipline." At the same time, these scholars, plus Farberov and Nedbailo, regard as essential "a certain degree of reform" in the teaching of the course in the theory of state and law by incorporation of the topics "The State and Political Parties," "The State, Law, and the Individual," and so forth. In their opinion, "It is possible and necessary to speak of political science as a combination of disciplines including the general theory of state and law, as well as other legal disciplines, the theory of scientific communism, the theory of sociopolitical organizations (for example, organization of the party, organization of the soviets), sociology, and other disciplines that now study or in the future will study political problems."[3] Kositsyn and Ostroumov object to the establishment of a separate political science but recognize that "the segregation of political science as a special set of scholarly disciplines might attract closer attention on the part of the scholarly community to problems associated with political theory and practice and to the political struggle presently in progress between socialism and capitalism."[4]

Essentially similar positions are adopted by D. A. Kerimov and G. B. Gal'perin, who describe the theory of state and law as the "universal political-legal discipline."[5]

This approach is also expressed in the three volumes that have appeared of the four-volume textbook *Marxist-Leninist Theory of State and Law* [Marksistsko-leninskaia teoriia gosuderstva i prava] (Moscow, 1970–1972). This textbook includes chapters showing that its politological aspect has undergone development....

The other three groups of scholars rely principally on the notion that the new branch of knowledge has in fact already come into being and that discussion now should be essentially only about giving it organizational recognition. At the same time, unlike the proponents of maintaining the existing system of disciplines, whose disagreements are in any case not fundamental, the views of these scholars are marked by a variety of emphases.

The second group offers the most radical proposals: to separate the discipline of social management and to establish as a scholarly category "system of the administration of society"[6], a discipline on the organs and norms for managing society.

A. E. Mushkin believes that "the science of the organs and norms of administration of society" has been called upon to become an independent branch of the society (along with history, ethics, political economy, and others), and some disciplines (those of jurisprudence, for example) should be regarded merely as parts of the first-named field. The discipline of the agencies and norms of administration of society should include: disciplines pertaining to the organs and norms of control of primitive society, class society, and communist society.[7] The literature has commented that this concept looks at things in an entirely new way. However, Mushkin's proposal to "deprive" the discipline of state and law of independent standing by converting it into a branch of the discipline of organs and norms of management of society, and the latter into a branch of the science of management in general, has generally been received critically.[8]

Finally, a similar proposal, albeit on a narrower plane, was introduced by V. A. Perttsik. He thinks that a special course, "Fundamentals of the Organization of Communist Self-Administration" should be introduced as soon as possible in some higher educational institutions.[9]

Like the writers in the first group, the proponents of the viewpoint just discussed have attempted to implement their ideas, specifically by establishing special courses in colleges of law and publication of learned works, teaching aids, and the like. The largest work of this kind was the book by V. S. Osnovin devoted to social administration of society, published in Voronezh in 1971 as a text for students taking a special course on the subject.

The broad approach to treating the theory of the administration of society as a separate entity provoked objections on the part of some teachers of the course in the principles of political science (Poland) and of legal disciplines. Thus the Polish scholar E. Wiatr spoke in no uncertain terms against courses in political science and the sociology of politics similar to those disciplines in the capitalist countries.[10] V. G. Afanas'ev offers a cautious reply on this subject. While recognizing the need to treat general problems of administration of economic, social, and intellectual processes in society, he also feels that "it is hardly worth arguing at the present moment whether the general theory of administration of society is a science unto itself distinct from the other social sciences."[11]

M. I. Piskotin spoke out directly against recognizing such a science. He writes that "the science of administration of the development of socialist society," or "a science of management of social processes," can have no area of its own to investigate qualitatively separate from the subject of existing social sciences. Such a science would lump the problems of these disciplines together in a purely mechanical way, with no internal unity. "The result," writes Piskotin, "is a sort of limitless science of sciences" that "does not provide any deeper knowledge of the life of society and can only lead to loss of the specialization of scholarly research that has now come into being."[12]

The third group of scholars is represented by advocates of what is termed socialist political science. They speak in favor of founding a discipline having that name and subject. Proponents of this standpoint also reveal various nuances. Thus B. A. Shabad speaks only of the need for an interdisciplinary theoretical study of the corresponding problems, without deciding in advance whether a special branch of knowledge should be established in the organizational sense. Changes in Soviet society, he writes, quite forcefully advance the problem of positive treatment of fundamental theoretical problems of policy and government, including the laws of development of the political realm of society.[13] Shabad looks at the question as it applies to Soviet society. F. M. Burlatskii pictures this branch of knowledge much more broadly. In his opinion, the theory of politics or science of politics should concern itself with the study of government, parties, other associations, the forms of participation of citizens in political life, public opinion, management of sociopolitical processes, international relations, international organizations and institutions, and political ideology....[14]

There are some writers who flatly oppose the setting up of a distinct political science. Their views are put forth in *The Marxist-Leninist General Theory of State and Law. Basic Institutions and Concepts* [Marksistsko-leninskaia obshchaia teoriia gosudarstva i prava. Osnovnye instituty i poniatiia] (Moscow, "Iuridicheskaia literatura" Publishing House, 1970), which states on page 19 that "objections to the creation of a new, independent political science are justified."...

Finally, a special position is held by members of a fourth group of scholars. They emphasize not an autonomous political science but a course in this subject that might vary in content and name. A majority of them feel that its area is study of the political organization of society in its structural and functional aspects, and study of the political system of socialism.

However, when it comes to more exact definition of the area to be studied by this field, serious disagreements arise among the proponents of this viewpoint. Some of them think that the basis of the course is study of power, while others propose to build it on the basis of the institutions of constitutional law studied in the sociological aspect, with inclusion of a number of supplemental topics. "The science of constitutional law," writes P. Peska, "must not confine itself to simple description of sociopolitical institutions." It is called upon primarily to analyze the carrying out of the provisions of constitutions, which "closely approximates the range of problems called socialist political science."...[15]

Other writers express themselves even more cautiously. Thus W. Wewerka writes that introduction of a course in political science (even when the subject is understood as above) requires prior solution of many questions pertaining to the relationship between that discipline and the theory of state and law, history, the economic disciplines, and some other branches of knowledge.[16]

Soviet writers (particularly S. S. Alekseev) understand this field to be the theory of the political organization and political system of socialist society, which might be taught in a number of higher educational institutions as a special methodological course.[17] E. V. Lisnevskii... is close to this viewpoint.[18] Nedbailo, without challenging the validity of singling out the theory of the political organization of society as an independent discipline, observes, however, that on the general level it falls into the system of sciences comprising scientific communism.[19]

In the writings of some Soviet scholars one finds discussion not of setting up a special discipline (a question that is not settled by administrative measures, for it is essential that the very categories of the new discipline attain maturity) but of the pragmatic purposes of introducing in some higher educational institutions, initially as an experiment, a special course in the theory of the political organization of society—political system—which is essential for the training of competent personnel in the field of government administration and for work in social organizations. They feel that such a course should serve as the basis for the future creation of a special science (say, the theory of the political system of socialist society), if the practical need for it is demonstrated in the course of teaching. It is not always obligatory that a science become a course of study. The opposite process is also possible, in which case the introduction of a special course may serve as catalyst for the birth of a new science, for its organizational "budding."... The Soviet philosopher V. V. Nikolaev proposes that the general theory of the state and the theory of the socialist state should be separate disciplines, and he offers a definition of the subject of the latter.[20]

A number of Soviet... writers have favored establishing a whole list of management disciplines for various areas. Thus the economist A. Birman calls for the development in the USSR "of a special science on the organization of management of the economy."[21] A large group of lawyers, historians, and economists, the authors of *Scientific Foundations of State Administration in the USSR* [Nauchnye osnovy gosudarstvennogo upravleniia v SSSR] (Moscow, 1968), regard it as necessary to establish a special field—the science of state administration. Other proposals have also been advanced.

This survey... (although we have been unable to offer detailed characterizations...) convinces us that interest in the range of problems comprising political science has increased considerably in the past decade.

Notes

1. A number of articles published in journals of philosophy and law have been devoted to this problem. See also A. E. Mushkin, *Gosudarstvo i pravo—istoricheskie raznovidnosti organov i norm upravleniia obshcestvom* (Leningrad: Leningrad University Press, 1969); F. M. Burlatskii, *Lenin, gosudarstvo, politika* (Moscow; "Nauka" Publishing House, 1970).

2. The term "political sciences" is here employed in the narrow sense. It refers to the sciences studying the political organization of society or its major components.

3. See *Sovetskoe gosudarstvo i pravo*, no. 7 (1968): 22; *Pravovedenie*, no. 3, (1968): 151.

4. See *Sovetskoe gosudarstvo i pravo*, no. 7 (1968): 22.

5. See *Akual'nye voprosy sovetskogo gosudarstva i prava v period stroitel'stva kommunizma* (Leningrad: Leningrad University Press, 1967) p. 8.

6. See Iu. E. Volkov, *Sistema upraveleniia obshchestvom i ee razvitie v protsesse formirovaniia kommunisticheskikh obshchestvennykh otnoshenii* (author's abstract of doctoral dissertation, Sverdlovsk, 1955), p. 1.

7. See *Vestnik LGU*, issue 1, (1968): 111; A. E. Mushkin, *Gosudarstvo i pravo—istoricheskie raznovidnosti organov i norm upravleniia obshcestvom* (LGU, 1969).

8. See *Sovetskoe gosudarstvo i pravo*, no. 12 (1970): 140.

9. See *Kratkie soobshcheniia i doklady o nauchno-issledovatel skoi rabote* (Irkutsk, 1965).

10. See E. Wiatr, "Nauki polityczne: charakter i perspektywy," *Kultura i spoteczénstwo*, no. 4 (1963).

11. V. G. Afanas'ev, *Nauchnoe upravlenie obshchestvom* (Moscow: Nauka Publishing House, 1968), p. 380.

12. *Nauchnye osnovy gosudarstvennogo upravleniia v SSSR* (Moscow, Nauka Publishing House, 1968), p. 40.

13. See *Sovetskoe gosudarstvo i pravo*, no. 8 (1968): 89.

14. See F. M. Burlatskii, *Lenin, gosudarstvo politika* (Moscow, Nauka Publishing House, 1970) pp. 150-51.

15. *Acta Juridica*, vol. 7, fasc. 3-4, 1965: 300.

16. See *Právnik*, no. 9 (1966): 833.

17. See *Sovetskoe gosudarstvo i pravo*, no. 5 (1965).

18. See E. V. Lisnevskii, *K voprosu o predmete i zadachakh politicheskoi nauki: Tezisy itogovoi nauchnoi konferentsii iuridicheskogo fakul'teta za 1966 god* (Rostov-on-Don, 1967).

19. See P. E. Nedbailo, "Marksistsko-leninskaia filosofiia i iuridicheskaia nauka," *Kommunist Ukrainy*, no. 6 (1967): 88; idem, *Vvedenie v obshchuiu teoriiu gosudarstva i prava* (Kiev, 1971), p. 54.

20. See V. V. Nikolaev, *Sovetskoe sotsialisticheskoe gosudarstvo* (Moscow, 1968), p. 8.

21. See *Sovetskoe gosudarstvo i pravo*, no. 1 (1965): 58.

UNION OF SOVIET SOCIALIST REPUBLICS
TASKS OF SOCIAL SCIENCE DEPARTMENTS*

V. ELIUTIN

The Twenty-fourth Congress of the CPSU has defined the principal directions of the further movement of our society toward communism and has armed the party and people with a scientifically based socioeconomic program that corresponds to the new potentials and requirements of developed socialist society.

This program ascribes a major role to education as a powerful factor in social and scientific-technological progress. The congress set as an important task the further improvement of the entire system of education on the basis of the achievements of modern science.

In carrying out the decisions of the Twenty-fourth Congress of the CPSU in the field of higher education, we are fully aware of the enormous responsibility we bear to the party, the people, and the country, for the role of higher education in scientific and technological progress is exceptionally large. The development of science and the introduction of its achievements into production depend to a great degree on the personnel and education of the professionals trained by the higher educational system.

Today we have moved to the culminating state of the introduction of universal secondary education. The higher educational institutions bear part of the responsibility for successful attainment of that goal. They train the teachers and help to develop the curricula and textbooks for the secondary schools, thereby exercising a significant influence on the level of its work.

In order to solve successfully the tasks of the building of communism, the personnel graduated from the higher educational institutions must completely master modern methods of management, possess a feeling for the new, envisage prospects of development, find the most effective paths for solution of problems that arise, and utilize the knowledge and experience of others. Toward this end, one must study constantly, assimilating the very latest achievements of science and practical experience, and raise one's level of theoretical ideas.

The Soviet higher school is today an enormous and important sphere of state activity. It consists of 811 higher educational institutions, including 52 universities, and it trains people for all branches, for all the most important directions of development in science and technology, and for all areas of the economy and culture.

The higher educational institutions employ 348,900 research and teaching workers, including 11,600 with the doctorate and 111,100 with the candidate's degree. Our teachers, raised by the Communist party, are performing as a sacred duty the behest of the great Lenin to give to the people—the workers and peasants—the entire resources of knowledge accumulated by humanity, instill in tomorrow's professionals the lofty humanist qualities of serving the people, and train them as patriots and internationalists and active fighters for the triumph of the ideas of scientific communism. In the last five-year plan, the higher schools carried out important work in raising the quality of instruction and communist upbringing of the students. In that period, over 7 million professionals

---

*This article was published originally as "Tasks of the Social Science Departments of Higher Educational Institutions at the Present Stage," *Soviet Law and Government*, vol. 12, pp. 25-50, © 1973 by M. E. Sharpe, Inc. Reprinted by permission of M. E. Sharpe, Inc. Translation from *Kommunist*, 1972, no. 1.

and semiprofessionals (*spetsialisty*) with higher and secondary education were trained.

The Twenty-fourth Congress of the CPSU has presented us new and more complex tasks. During the Ninth Five-Year Plan, we are to train approximately 9 million professionals and semiprofessionals, to extend training of personnel in new and promising spheres of science and technology, and to equip youth better with modern knowledge, skills in organizational and sociopolitical work, and the ability to apply scientific knowledge in practice.

At the All-Union Rally of Students, Comrade L. I. Brezhnev spoke clearly about the traits of the contemporary Soviet professional: a person who has mastered well the fundamentals of Marxist-Leninist theory, who sees clearly the political goals of the party and country, who has broad scientific and practical training and a thorough knowledge of his own specialty. The Soviet professional today is an able organizer, capable of applying the principles of scientific organization of labor in practice. He is able to work with people, values collective experience, listens to the opinions of his comrades, and critically evaluates what has been achieved. And, of course, the professional of today is a person of high culture and broad erudition; all in all, a genuine intellectual of the new, socialist society.

This is why it is so important that future professionals deeply master fundamental scientific and technical knowledge.

Highly significant is the development of creative capacities in students and of their skills in information search, the ability to find their way independently in the most recent literature in the field. All this demands systematic perfection of the content and methods of teaching and broad introduction of modern technical means of instruction into the learning process.

In training professionals it is necessary to consider not only the present state of a given science, branch of the economy, and production technology but also their prospects for development. For the student entering college today will be advancing the economy and culture at the end of our century and the beginning of the twenty-first century. In this connection it is very important to determine the optimal content of education in each specialty, to develop, as it is now the custom to say, a "model" of the professional of the years 1980–2000, and to use it as a guide in improving the educational process.

Under contemporary conditions, economic education of personnel is acquiring ever-increasing importance. One of the most important tasks of the higher and the specialized secondary schools is further improvement of the economic training of the graduates entering the economy and active participation by the faculty in implementing the decree of the CPSU Central Committee "On Improving the Economic Education of Working People." The Ministry of Higher and Secondary Specialized Education of the USSR is developing a set of measures to improve instruction in political economy and revise curricula and syllabi in economics and engineering economics, providing for deeper study of economic theory, production economics, providing for deeper study of economic theory, production economics, the scientific organization of work and management, as well as computer technology and its use in economic calculations. The task is being posed of developing an organic interconnection between the teaching of the specialized disciplines and the economic disciplines. Only if matters are thus organized will it be possible to create in each institute an atmosphere of special attention to economic knowledge and to attain a situation in which future professionals always approach the solution of technical problems of any kind in terms of concrete economic analysis.

Teaching of the Social Sciences Must Rise to the Level of the New Tasks

The Communist party ascribes particular significance to Marxist-Leninist education of personnel. Thorough and creative study of the heroic history of the CPSU, of philosophy, political economy, and scientific communism, plays a decisive role in developing the students' communist world view, a high level of party loyalty and ideological conviction, and is an essential part of their general scientific training.

In his speech at the All-Union Rally of Students, Comrade Brezhnev emphasized that "it is possible to assimilate critically a specialty, to become an active participant in our building of communism and a carrier of party policy to the masses only if one has mastered Marxist-Leninist theory. The teachings of Marxism-Leninism are the foundation and an inseparable component of the knowledge of a professional in any field."

And in this regard the departments of social sciences (*kafedry obshchestvennykh nauk*) of the higher educational institutions play the leading role. They are supposed to help students master the dialectical materialist method of acquiring knowledge and of transforming reality, as well as the laws of social development.

Recently, the departments of socioeconomic disciplines have considerably raised the ideological-theoretical and methodological level of teaching Marxist-Leninist theory. The past five-year plan saw completion of the transition to a new, logically consistent system of teaching the social sciences in the higher educational institutions. Today each student has the chance to master an integrated and structured system of philosophical, economic, and sociopolitical views and to study thoroughly the history of the CPSU. Introduction of the course in scientific communism in all the country's higher educational institutions was exceptionally important. It facilitated in many ways improvement in the communist upbringing of the student youth.

The USSR Ministry of Higher and Secondary Specialized Education and the USSR Academy of Sciences have taken steps to prepare and publish textbooks in the social disciplines for higher educational institutions. Textbooks of Marxist-Leninist philosophy and scientific communism have already been issued to them. Work on the political economy textbook is nearing completion. The last five years have seen the publication of a large volume of instructional and methods literature in the social sciences that will aid students and teachers.

Making wide use of party documents, the achievements of science, and the experience of society, instructors have begun to present Marxist-Leninist theory more deeply and with more support, to tie it more closely to present-day life, and to demonstrate the leading role of the Communist party in the building of socialism and communism.

The teaching of social sciences in the higher educational institutions is proceeding under the banner of deeper study of the great theoretical heritage of Lenin. Lenin's role in the creative development of Marxist theory, the international essence of Leninism, the significance to world history of Lenin's activity in the revolutionary transformation of society have come to be presented more fully and comprehensively.

The rise in the level of teaching of the social sciences facilitated the organization of special courses on current problems in the social sciences and on methodological problems of the disciplines central to each. Special courses of this kind have been introduced in Moscow, Leningrad, Kiev, the Urals, and Tomsk universities, and in the following institutes in Moscow: National Economy, Mining, Economic Statistics, and a number of others.

Class sessions combining coverage of the questions in the syllabus with discussion of student papers and reports and with the organization of discussions on the most important problems of the course have become widespread.

In recent years, social science departments have done major work in improving teaching and have achieved successes in organizing the learning process at a high scientific level. I have in mind primarily the social sciences departments of Moscow, Leningrad, and Kiev universities, the Bauman Higher School of Technology in Moscow, the Moscow Institute of Steel and Alloys, the Leningrad Shipbuilding Institute, and other higher educational institutions.

We know that a high level of class sessions means not only that they are significant in terms of scholarly subject matter but also that they influence students and produce a need for deep and systematic study of Marxist-Leninist theory. Each teacher has to strive toward the goal that his words will teach the student to penetrate into the essence of that theory, think creatively, correctly analyze sociopolitical events and social phenomena, and provide an accurate evaluation of them.

Successful work to shape a Marxist-Leninist world view in the student youth largely depends on the influence of social science departments, on the departments of general science and specialized subjects, and on the establishment, to use Lenin's words, of an intimate union of materialist philosophers with natural scientists. The higher educational institutions face a major task—strengthening the ideological, methodological, and atheist content of the teaching of mathematics, physics, chemistry, biology, and the other natural and specialized disciplines. Here there is a need for the constant assistance of the departments of social sciences. They bear responsibility for the ideological and political direction of the entire learning process and of all the work to train professionals in the higher educational institutions.

While recording positive achievements in teaching the social sciences, we must at the same time direct attention to significant shortcomings in this work.

We still have departments of social sciences that do not pay the necessary attention to improving the quality of lectures and seminar sessions, do not organize systematic discussion of the texts of lectures, mutual visits at class sessions, and exchanges of experiences among instructors. There are cases in which instructors do not prepare properly for classes, conduct them at low levels of theory and methods, do not make use of the achievements of contemporary scholarship, and do a weak job of connecting the questions under discussion with the practice of building communism. Serious attention is not always paid to critiques of current bourgeois and revisionist doctrines.

The inadequate level of instruction in the social sciences naturally has a negative effect on shaping a Marxist-Leninist world view in future professionals, reduces their interest in studying social sciences, and thus harms the cause of communist education of the student youth.

Demands for improved training in Marxism-Leninism and for improved communist training of future professionals, put forth by the Twenty-fourth Congress, dictate the need to improve the teaching of the social disciplines in higher educational institutions, to perfect the scholarly content of courses in the history of the CPSU, philosophy, political economy, and scientific communism, and to intensify the connection of Marxist-Leninist theory with life and with the practice of the building of communism.

It is the most important duty of teachers in the social disciplines to reveal to the consciousness of each student the grandeur of the tasks posed and being resolved by the party in the new five-year plan. Particular attention has to be directed to a thorough explanation of the political and economic conclusions in the documents of the Twenty-fourth Congress of the CPSU. Study of the congress documents will facilitate mastery of a Marxist-Leninist understanding of the fundamental questions of domestic and foreign policy of our party and of the Soviet state.

It is a task of prime importance for the social sciences departments to promote systematic study by students of the works of Marx, Engels, and Lenin, in intimate connection with the current problems of our day. Teachers have the function of instructing students to master Marxist-Leninist theory independently, to work on primary sources, to discover the laboratory of scientific thinking, and to demonstrate the permanent significance of the theoretical heritage of Marx, Engels, and Lenin. However, there are still social science teachers who present Marxist-Leninist teachings in isolation from the previous development of social thought, who present it as a collection of absolute truths that one can only memorize.

We know how Lenin warned against taking this path in the study of Marxist theory and the shaping of a communist world view. "You would be making a tremendous mistake," he said, addressing Komsomol members at the Third All-Russian Congress of the Russian Communist League of Youth, "if you tried to draw the conclusions that one can become a communist without assimilating what has been accumulated by human knowledge. It would be erroneous to think that it is enough to master communist slogans and the conclusions of communist science without assimilating the sum of knowledge of which communism is itself a consequence. Marxism is an example of how communism appeared out of the sum of human knowledge." (*Poln. sobr. soch.*, vol. 41, p. 303.)

It is necessary to fix and develop further the valuable experience of study and propaganda of Leninism accumulated in higher education institutions during the period of preparation for and celebration of the centennial of Lenin's birth.

Today a militant, scientifically argued, and purposeful criticism of modern bourgeois ideology and of "Left" and Right revisionism—those reactionary theories that seek most actively to influence the youth by propagandizing a false revolutionism, pessimism, and debauchery in private life—is more pertinent than ever. It will facilitate the shaping of professionals in the spirit of irreconcilability to any manifestations of bourgeois ideology, profound belief in the greatness of the ideas of communism, and devotion to the theory of Marxism-Leninism.

Improved teaching of the social sciences under present conditions also requires solution of a number of major problems of scientific method and education. Improving the teaching skills of all instructors also is largely dependent on this.

As we know, in our country teaching of the science of Marxism in the higher schools was introduced in the earliest years of Soviet power. Since that time, vast and valuable experience in the teaching of Marxist-Leninist theory in the higher educational institutions has been accumulated. Recently, the ministry has taken steps to improve the techniques of teaching the social science disciplines. The All-Union Conference on Scholarly Methods, devoted to generalization of experience in teaching the history of the CPSU, philosophy, political economy, and scientific communism, was of undoubted value in this regard. The conference analyzed the achievements of the departments in instructing and training students, defined tasks, and developed concrete recommendations in this field.

In accordance with the recommendations of the conference, questions are being studied of teaching economic disciplines in the institutes to improve the qualifications of social sciences teachers who are attached to Moscow, Kiev, and Leningrad universities, the Moscow institutes of aviation and finance, and a number of higher educational institutions. It is necessary to create an atmosphere more favorable to work in the sphere of methods and to regard it as one of the most important branches of scientific research.

Introduction of modern technological developments in the instruction process is very important. Serious work to manufacture visual aids, tapes, and other technical aids is under way at the Urals Polytechnical Institute, Nikolaevsk Shipbuilding Institute, and the Kiev institutes for civil engineering and civil aviation engineers. This experience should be disseminated.

Television and film courses in philosophy, political economy, and scientific communism can play a major role in teaching the social sciences, as can utilization of popular science films. In this regard, much has been done in the Institute for Improvement of Qualifications at

Leningrad University, which has prepared catalogues of movie films and slides for the teaching process. The ministry has decided to publish and distribute these aids to the higher educational institutions.

Following the experience of Voronezh University and the Novosibirsk Institute of Electrical Engineering, which have prepared instructional segments from the film *Chronicle of a Half Century*, the Vuzfilm Studio has undertaken to make prints of these excerpts for higher educational institutions. Not long ago a commission from the ministry accepted an instructional film made by the studio for the course in Marxist-Leninist philosophy. It was titled *Consciousness, Its Origin and Essence*. A number of instructional films are being prepared in political economy and scientific communism.

The professionals trained by Soviet institutes and universities will meet the high standards set for them by the party and the people at the present stage in the building of communism if a consistent, scientific, integrated communist world view is shaped in them, if knowledge of Marxist-Leninist theory becomes a matter of deep personal conviction, and if feelings of high civic responsibility and responsibility to party and people for the affairs and life of society are cultivated. The instructional staff plays an enormous role in this process.

The social sciences departments must achieve an organic interconnection, continuity, and logical structure in teaching the history of the party, Marxist-Leninist philosophy, political economy, and scientific communism. This means that each teacher must have a good knowledge not only of his own subject but of all the component parts of Marxism-Leninism.

In this connection it should be observed that improvement in the level of teaching of the history of the CPSU depends to a significant degree on how deep the knowledge of instructors themselves is in the sphere of Marxist-Leninist philosophy, political economy, and scientific communism, and whether they have a thorough mastery of the dialectical materialist method of cognition and revolutionary transformation of reality and of the laws of social development.

Teachers of party history must more closely associate the treatment of each question in the course with the present day, with current tasks in the building of communism, and with the international revolutionary movement. Special attention must be given to comprehensively laying bare the scientific character of the policy of our party, to the growth of its leading role in the building of communism, to the objective treatment of the history of development of the Soviet state, and to the truthful presentation of the historical path traversed by the Soviet people. Illumination of the extremely rich experience of the CPSU in the building of socialism and communism, and its significance for the international communist movement, should occupy an important place in teaching the course in CPSU history.

Teachers of Marxist-Leninist philosophy are called upon to demonstrate the interconnection and mutual determination of dialectical and historical materialism as a single philosophical discipline and its significance for developing the strategy and tactics of the communist and workers' parties. Thorough explanation of dialectics as the method of cognition and transformation of reality is a task of first importance. Lenin repeatedly emphasized that, lacking a mastery of the materialist dialectic, it is impossible to assimilate Marxism and its creative and revolutionary character.

Serious attention must be given to shedding light on fundamental questions in historical materialism—the methodological foundation of all social sciences. Teachers must equip students with a knowledge of the general laws of social development and the distinctive ways in which they function under the conditions of the building of socialism and communism, must comprehensively disclose the content of the fundamental works of the classical figures of Marxism-Leninism, and must make wide use in the teaching process of the achievements of modern science and practical experience.

In the sphere of the teaching of political economy, analysis of the objective laws of economic development, the specific features of their manifestations under the conditions of a developed socialist society, and the mechanism of their utilization in the practice of the building of communism must be advanced to the foreground. The importance of this task increases further in connection with the resolution recently adopted by the party central committee on improving the economic education of working people.

It is the duty of teachers of political economy to teach the professionals of tomorrow to employ in practice the Leninist principles of management of social production. It is necessary to demonstrate more vividly in the instructional and educational process how our people are solving the historical task of broadly joining the revolution in science and technology with the advantages of the socialist economic system.

It is important to make clear the policy of the CPSU in realizing the Combined Program of Further Deepening and Improving Collaboration and Development of Socialist Economic Integration of the COMECON countries. It is necessary in lectures and at seminars to make a deeper analysis of the features distinguishing economic relationships in advanced socialist society, the system of laws and categories and the mechanism of their operation under socialism, and the means to improve Leninist principles and methods of management.

Students' work on Marxist-Leninist theory culminates with the course in scientific communism. It arms them with knowledge of the laws, paths, and forms of class struggle of the proletariat, of socialist revolution, the sociopolitical laws of modern social development, and the emergence and functioning of the communist social order. Teachers of this discipline, basing themselves on the knowledge obtained by students with regard to the history of the CPSU, Marxist-Leninist philosophy, and political economy, are to go deeply into the theory and practice of the building of communism, the laws of development of the world system of socialism, problems of the international workers and national liberation movement, as well as the struggle of the CPSU and other Marxist-Leninist parties for unity of the socialist countries and of the international communist movement. In the teaching of scientific communism an important place must be occupied by questions of management of sociopolitical processes and communist education of the working people.

A most important task is that of strengthening the struggle against the ideology of anticommunism in its present form and against reformist and revisionist conceptions, the exposure of falsifiers of Marxist-Leninist theory, of CPSU history and Soviet society, and of the communist and workers' movements, to which special attention was directed by the Twenty-fourth Party Congress and the November (1971) Plenum of the CPSU Central Committee.

The teaching process is the central link in the entire system of communist upbringing of future professionals. It provides an organic supplement to the diverse and many-faceted ideological-education work in extracurricular time-work which embraces the entire sociopolitical life of a higher educational institution.

As the experience accumulated in recent years demonstrates, plans of ideological-education work drawn up for the entire period of a student's stay in the institute or university are of great importance in solving the problem of communist training. These plans define the role and place of each subdivision of a higher educational institution in the political training of the youth, the forms and methods for influencing the student, with proper consideration for his individual characteristics, his life experience, and the demands made by society on the future professional. The implementation of such plans promotes intimate contacts among teachers of social, natural, and specialized sciences and the more effective solution of the entire set of problems of shaping a communist world view in student youth.

One of the most important tasks of higher education posed by the Twenty-fourth Congress of the CPSU is arming young professionals with the skills of organizational and sociopolitical work and with the ability to apply in practice the knowledge they have acquired. This task derives directly from the Marxist-Leninist principle of unity of theory and practice, the process of instruction and ideological education. It is associated with the demands being made at the present stage of development of socialist society on persons with higher education.

Every higher educational institution offers extensive opportunities for acquiring the needed skills in work with the masses by active participation in a variety of public activities. However, these opportunities are not by any means being used to the full. Many of our young professional people, upon graduating from an institute, still prove to be unprepared to organize the socialization of a work force and to resolve problems of sociopolitical life. It is therefore necessary that the higher educational institutions, the social sciences departments, and other departments persistently seek effective paths and forms for solution of this problem and reach each student with ideological-education work.

In this connection, I would like to cite the interesting experience in socialization work at the Moscow Institute of Engineering Physics. Here all instructors in the natural sciences, scientific, specialized, and socioeconomic departments annually gather at a conference that has already become a tradition, to discuss questions associated with forms and methods of work with students, and to exchange experience in the socialization of future professionals in the course of the educational process. They work out recommendations for all departments.

Recent years have seen the birth of all-union competitions for student works on problems of the social sciences, a practice that stimulates a creative attitude on the part of students to a study of Marxist-Leninist theory. Hundreds of such works have been awarded certificates and prizes as the result of the last three such competitions. The Fourth USSR Competition of Student Works, devoted to the Twenty-fourth Congress of the CPSU and the fiftieth anniversary of the USSR, is now in progress. Hundreds of thousands of students have already decided to write papers on problems of the heritage of Lenin, on the materials of the Twenty-fourth Congress, and on questions of the practical implementation of the planned program of sociopolitical and economic development of our country. The first student conferences on theory have taken place.

Schools for the young lecturer, people's "universities," and "academic departments" of volunteer occupations have proved to be interesting means of actively involving students in the process of ideological education. These forms of educating the youth as communists have attained broad popularity in our institutes and universities. They facilitate a deepening and reinforcement of the acquired knowledge of social and other sciences, enlarge students' theoretical horizons, instill in them habits of ideological work and skill in lecturing, and facilitate the development of creative capacities. In many higher educational institutions, students' work as lecturers has been raised to the level of a volunteer civic profession.

In the past two years, yet another new form of involving students in the work of agitation and propaganda has developed in the higher educational institutions—agitation tours. Today preparatory work is under way for the Second All-Union Agitation Tour, to be devoted to propagandizing the decisions of the Twenty-fourth Congress of the CPSU.

The All-Union Leninist Inspection (*zachet*) is a form of sociopolitical training of youth that has firmly entered into, and justified itself in, the arsenal of means and forms of work of ideological socialization. In the course of the inspection, demands have increased on Komsomol members, their grades, voluntary activity, and participation in the research and work done by the higher educational institution. Its significance is that it provides a sociopolitical evaluation of every Komsomol student and makes it possible to determine the degree to which knowledge of Marxist-Leninist theory has become his personal ideological conviction.

Student construction brigades have been a good school for socialization of youth in labor and political ideology. Here, socially useful labor—organized on the principles of voluntary participation, self-management, and a high level of responsibility of each for the common cause—is combined with extensive sociopolitical and cultural mass work among the people on collective and state farms and in the work forces of construction projects. Student construction brigades testify to a rise in civic maturity and activity on the part of Soviet youth.

An important consequence of all the work of higher educational institutions, social organizations, and social sciences departments has been a close rallying of the Soviet student body around the Communist party and its Leninist central committee. The All-Union Rally of Students vividly demonstrated the high level of political consciousness of our youth and its boundless devotion to the ideals of communism.

The Soviet student body is playing a constantly increasing role in the country's sociopolitical and cultural life. Its best representatives have been elected to the Supreme Soviets of the union and autonomous republics and to local soviets of working people's deputies.

For the successes achieved in study and civic activity, a large group of students has been decorated with orders and medals of the Soviet Union. Lenin Jubilee Medals were awarded to all participants in the rally. This is evidence of our party's high evaluation of students' work in mastering scientific knowledge.

The decisions of the Twenty-fourth congress of the CPSU have produced a new upsurge of sociopolitical activity and labor enthusiasm on the part of Soviet students. Close contacts with industrial enterprises are being established by higher educational institutions. Contracts are being signed regarding collaboration with collectives of workers, and unified plans of socialization and cultural mass work are being drafted. The new tasks in the realm of socialization of the student youth have posed the question of introducing periods of social and political practice for them at institutions of higher education.

The system of such periods of practical work presumes the involvement of all students in active sociopolitical activity and the development in them of habits of mass work on immediate issues and on political and organizational work. This will facilitate further improvement of the scientific system of communist socialization of the youth and will tie all its forms together, giving them deeper content.

However, serious shortcomings also exist in the ideological activity of the higher educational institutions. It is no secret that not all our students acquire deep knowledge at an institute or university in the area of Marxist-Leninist theory or the required ideological and political tempering. Many of them receive unsatisfactory and mediocre grades in examinations on the social sciences, and some commit immoral acts and disturb public order.

Further improvement in the work of communist socialization of the students must be based on scientific synthesis of accumulated experience and profound study of current problems in the communist socialization of future professionals. The role of departments of social sciences is great in this regard.

Soviet scholars and teachers have done a good deal in the sphere of scientific treatment of theoretical and practical questions in the communist socialization of the youth. Specifically, a number of studies of the theoretical heritage of Marx, Engels, and Lenin on these matters have been carried out. The Ministry of Higher and Secondary Specialized Education of the USSR is coordinating the efforts of scholars at higher educational institutions who are interested in problems of communist socialization and is organizing interdisciplinary studies in this field. One of the first steps in this direction was the creation, in association with the ministry, of a learned council for coordination of research into problems of communist socialization of student youth. The council is unifying the work of many staffs at higher educational institutions, of prominent social scientists and teachers, and of representatives of a number of republic ministries of higher and secondary specialized education. The plan of scientific research for 1971-1975 has already been adopted. Represented in this plan are various schools of thought in the treatment of this problem; the most important topics, leading organizations, and most important researches are stipulated.

Training and Upgrading of Teachers of Social Sciences in Higher Education

The Communist party ascribes major significance to training and upgrading instructors in the social sciences. The level of teaching of Marxist-Leninist theory and the degree to which it is assimilated by students depends in the final analysis on instructional staffs. An uninterrupted improvement in the qualitative composition of social scientists and improvement of their qualifications are conditions for the further improvement of the teaching process, development of research work in the higher educational institutions, and the successful solution of problems of communist socialization of the student youth.

In carrying out the resolution of the Central Committee of the CPSU "On Measures for Further Development of the Social Sciences and Elevation of Their Role in the Building of Communism" and the joint decree of the CPSU Central Committee and the USSR Council of Ministers "On Improving the Training of Research and Research-Teaching Personnel," the higher educational institutions carried out considerable work in improving the qualitative makeup of instructors in social science departments.

At present there are about 27,000 teachers of social sciences employed in the country's higher educational institutions, including 719 holding the doctorate (*doktora*) (or 2.6 percent) and 12,447 holding the candidate's degree (*kandidaty*) (or 46 percent). Consequently, nearly half the teachers of party history, philosophy, political economy, and scientific communism have the candidate's or doctor's degree. In the past five years, the total number of teachers in departments of social sciences increased by 8,000, or 43 percent.

In accordance with the decree of the CPSU central committee on the social sciences, as well as the recommendation of the conference of heads of departments of socioeconomic disciplines and teachers in higher educational institutions, there has been an improvement in the work of certification and recertification of teachers and in filling department staffs through competitions. In certifying instructors, the departments and learned councils have begun to analyze in more detail the teachers' scholarly and teaching activity and their work in the communist education of students. The delivery of lectures at a high ideological-political and technical level and the conducting of regular work in research methods and in socialization are absolute conditions for admission to the posts of heads of departments, professors, and lecturers (*dotsenty*).

At the same time, we cannot be satisfied with the results achieved. The rising standards for training future professionals and for their education in Marxism-Leninism makes necessary further improvement in the entire system of training and improvement of teachers' qualifications. Moreover, highly qualified personnel presently available are by no means evenly distributed.

In a number of higher educational institutions, the direction of departments of social sciences has been assigned to persons who do not have degrees or ranks. Although in recent years many instructors in social sciences departments have defended doctoral dissertations, the demand for persons holding the doctorate is still high. This testifies to the fact that more attention must be given to questions of training and improving the qualifications of instructors, their assignment and proper utilization.

Graduates of these departments and divisions of universities provide good recruits to the ranks of instructors and graduate students. A number of universities have organized the training of specialists in scientific communism and CPSU history. This will certainly have a favorable influence on the quality of training of researchers and teachers in higher educational institutions in these disciplines.

As we know, graduate students are the principal source of instructional personnel in the social disciplines. Measures to enlarge and improve the work of graduate students have recently been taken. A supplemental examination in the history of the discipline in which they will work has been introduced for graduate students in the social sciences who lack specialized education when they submit the minimal requirements for application for the candidate's degree. Seminars in theory are organized for them in their departments, at which current problems in Marxist-Leninist theory are discussed. Graduate students have begun to prepare better for work as teachers, to study educational methods in higher education and teaching techniques. However, the work of graduate students needs further improvement. During the past five years, 4,563 persons have been accepted into full-time graduate work in CPSU history, political economy, philosophy, and scientific communism. Of these, 994 defended dissertations within the proper time period, and 1,235 presented dissertations to be defended. These indices cannot be regarded as satisfactory.

It is necessary to improve significantly the selection of

young professionals capable of scholarly work for admission to graduate study. The training of graduate students must be concentrated in departments that have persons who hold the rank of professor, persons who hold the doctor's degree, and highly qualified lecturers (*dotsenty*).

As we know, higher educational institutions have been granted permission to relieve from teaching duties persons who hold the candidate's degree who have achieved serious results in research into particular problems and to transfer them to the status of research associate (*nauchnyi sotrudnik*) for up to two years to enable them to complete their doctoral dissertations. From 1962 to 1970, 742 persons in the social sciences departments of the country's higher educational institutions were transferred to the status of research associate, of whom 219 (or 30 percent) defended doctoral dissertations on time, and 160 (or 24 percent) presented them for defense. This is undoubtedly a solid addition to the professorial and instructional staffs of the departments of social disciplines. We should make wider use of this form of training highly qualified personnel. At the same time, it is necessary to concern ourselves with using them more effectively. The agencies for administering higher education, the rectors and social sciences departments of higher educational institutions have to improve their selection of teachers for the posts of senior research associates.

Under today's conditions, systematic improvement of the qualifications of instructional staffs is of the very greatest importance. During the past five years, a network of institutes for raising the qualifications of social science teachers has been established, and it has been fruitful. However, the existing potentials of the institutes cannot assure improvement of the qualifications of all teachers. In order to keep up with current necessities and meet the high demands he faces as an educator of future professionals, an instructor must take a refresher course not less often than once in five years. However, our institutes are able to provide such retraining only once in ten to twelve years. Urgent measures must be taken to change the existing situation.

An increase in recruitment to institutes for refresher training will naturally improve the situation somewhat, but it will not solve the problem in its entirety. Therefore, it is proposed to open departments of refresher training in the immediate future in major centers of science, which will enroll primarily instructors who work in the higher educational institutions of that city. An important form of improving instructors' qualifications is the internship (*stazhirovka*), but it is rarely used.

At the same time, it must not be forgotten that internships and institutes and departments for refresher training cannot guarantee a constant rise in the skill of instructors, deepening of the scholarly content of their lessons, or the conduct of the latter on a high level of ideology and theory. A teacher must not only follow the development of science and technology day by day but must systematically engage in research, improve his ability as teacher, lecturer, and orator, must present an example to his students in his attitude toward work, his passion and involvement, his conduct, his moral and external image. In other words, the Soviet instructor must be a real political preceptor to whom student youth will always be attracted. And toward that end he must do a great deal indeed to improve himself. Without this, it will be impossible to assure a high level of instruction, to establish a creative atmosphere in the department and the educational institution.

Today it has become obligatory in higher educational institutions for instructors to engage not only in teaching but research. By providing a direct connection between the teaching process and the development of science, scientific research constantly enriches teachers with new knowledge, and this in turn facilitates training of highly qualified professionals.

Let us briefly consider certain questions associated with research by faculty members of higher educational institutions.

In the research of departments of CPSU history, much attention is being paid to identifying the leading role of the party in preparing and carrying out the Great October Socialist Revolution and in the building of socialism and communism in our country. Major research in party history, which describes the multifaceted activity of Lenin and the Communist party, has been published. Questions reflecting the activity of the CPSU in leading the heroic struggle of the Soviet people during World War II have also had comprehensive treatment.

Some progress has been made in working out a number of problems of philosophy. Problems of Lenin's advancement of Marxist philosophy and his theoretical heritage have been central to the attention of philosophers in higher educational institutions in recent years. Research has also been conducted in such important directions as problems of materialist dialectics, epistemology and logic, philosophical questions of natural science, and others. Increased attention began to be given to study of the dialectics of social development, methodological questions in the social sciences, problems of humanism, the structure of the social mind, and problems of culture.

Scholars in higher educational institutions are engaged in working out current theoretical problems of developed socialist society, the creation of the basis of communism in material goods and technology, and the improvement of relationships of production.

In speaking of scientific research in economic theory, it is necessary to take note of such special features as deepened treatment of Lenin's theoretical heritage on questions of the political economy of socialism, the increasing ties of theoretical research with the practice of building communism (in which connection the qualitative features and advantages of developed socialist society are taken into account), more fundamental treatment of the scientific bases of the course in the political economy of socialism, and improvement of its structure.

A great deal has been accomplished in developing research in the field of scientific communism. In works prepared by professors and instructional staffs of higher educational institutions, the experience of the world revolutionary movement and practice in the building of socialism and communism are being generalized; rich factual material is being analyzed; more attention is being given to the special features of the current stage of the world revolutionary process, the properties of construction of socialism and communism, and problems of scientific management of socialist society.

While pointing to the large contribution departments of social sciences have made to the treatment of current problems of Marxist-Leninist theory, it is necessary at the same time to emphasize that the potentials of scholars in higher educational institutions are by no means being used to the full. As already noted, some 27,000 instructors in the social sciences are at work in the higher educational system. And if the work of this army of scholars was rationally organized, if their efforts were channeled into solving the most pressing theoretical problems in the science of Marxism-Leninism, if a clear-cut coordination of the higher educational institutions with the institutes of academies of science were established, we would achieve more substantial successes in the development of the social sciences. The present procedure for research work in the higher educational institutions cannot yet satisfy us. The choice of topics for investigation is often random. There are cases in which the authors pose problems that are clearly invented, not associated with practical goals, and of no scientific value. In some scholarly works and texts we find incorrect formulations and judgments that distort Marxist-Leninist theory.... Primitive presentations of the most important problems in the theory of Marxism-Leninism can be found.

Concrete social research is important in gaining knowledge of processes in the life of society. Recently they have become a widespread phenomenon in higher educational institutions. Concrete social researches have been the basis for publication of a number of monographs and dissertations for the doctor's and candidate's degrees. However, it is still too early to speak of major successes in this regard. This is to be explained to a certain degree by the fact that concrete social research in higher educational institutions is often pursued by persons who lack the required methodological training or experience in sociopolitical, scholarly, and teaching activity. In the literature that draws conclusions from the results of such studies, an empirical, superficial description of factual material and of phenomena in the life of society is often looked at objectivistically, detached from class and party positions.

At present, a certain contradiction can be seen between the scale of the research conducted in the social sciences field and the organizational forms of guidance to and coordination of research work. The absence of clear-cut and real coordination in the organization of research in the social sciences field has a particularly negative effect on the preparation of candidate and doctoral dissertations. This unavoidably leads to duplication, pettiness of theme, and the fact that a number of problems escape the attention of the scholarly community....

Very few dissertations are written on major, key theoretical problems of a methodological character. Problems in the criticism of the principal kinds of anticommunism today and the major concepts of bourgeois revisionism and reformism are being poorly treated. There are very few dissertations on these questions....

Many shortcomings also exist in the activities of the learned councils. The required atmosphere of high standards and adherence to scientific principle in the discussion of dissertations has not yet been established. Defense of dissertations often occurs without thorough and comprehensive discussion. All this testifies to the need to improve the standards that must be met by levels of dissertations and heightened responsibility on the part of learned councils.

Proceeding from the decisions of the Twenty-fourth Party Congress, the ministry proposes to develop in the immediate future a long-range plan of scholarly research in the socioeconomic sciences field over the next ten to fifteen years. In this connection, a long-range plan for all-union and interinstitutional learned conferences and symposia will be drawn up.

It remains to expand voluntary forms of organization and coordination of scholarly work and involvement of academic associations and learned councils on interdisciplinary problems, and to activate the work of the social sciences sections of the ministry's council on science and technology.

In devoting greater attention to development of scientific research in the higher educational institutions, the ministry believes that it must, above all, be associated with the solution of the principal task facing the institutes and universities—training of highly qualified professionals. Research must exercise a direct influence on the teaching process and raise its level.

Thus, higher education faces the task of furthering, by every measure and means, the training of professionals who will meet the demands of the present stage in the movement of our society toward communism and the developing revolution in science and technology.

THE SOVIET POLITICAL SCIENCE ASSOCIATION*

WILLIAM SMIRNOV

The Soviet Political Science Association (SPSA) was established in 1960. Its activities are a reflection of the development of the political sciences in the Soviet Union and of the growing need for greater cooperation between specialists in different spheres of knowledge investigating political problems. The SPSA is "a voluntary scientific association of people who engage in studies in the political sciences, established in accordance with Article 51 of the Constitution of the USSR" (Article 1 of the Charter adopted on 11 May 1978). The association is affiliated with the USSR Academy of Sciences and functions under the auspices of the Social Sciences Section of the Academy's Presidium.

The association's supreme body is its All-Union Conference, which convenes at least once a year. The conference sets the guidelines for the association, discusses research papers and reports on topical problems in the political sciences, elects the president, vice-president and general secretary, the executive committee and auditing commissioner.

There are territorial sections of the association in six cities, and it also has sections on various spheres of science and groups on fundamental problems.

The association's basic tasks are defined as: the promotion of creative work in the political sciences—their development in a spirit of democracy, humanism, and social progress; the participation in measures to enhance the political standards of the people and popularization and dissemination of political knowledge; criticism of unscientific theories and views in the political domain; the strengthening of understanding and international cooperation between political scholars.

Lately Soviet scholars have been working on a wide range of problems in the political sciences. The effectiveness of that work depends in many respects on the coordination of various researches in this field. The SPSA has an important part to play in coordinating these researches.

One of the latest undertakings in this sphere was a symposium "Political Relations: Planning and Forecasting," sponsored jointly by the SPSA, the Soviet Sociological Association, the USSR Philosophic Society, and the Soviet International Law Association. The All-Union SPSA Conference in May 1978 discussed "The New Constitution of the USSR and the Tasks in Political Studies."

Since 1975, the association has been putting out a yearbook. Each edition is devoted to a certain theme. The 1975 yearbook (Moscow, Nauka Publishing House, 1976) was devoted to the topic, "International Relations, Politics and Personality"; the 1976 yearbook was on "Peaceful Coexistence and Social and Political Development"; the 1977 yearbook was on "Political Relations: Planning and Forecasting."

The articles and reviews cover topical issues extensively debated by Soviet and foreign researchers.

The yearbook extensively reports achievements of the political sciences in the socialist countries. The said issues carried reviews of papers by scientists from the GDR, Hungary, Poland, and Rumania at the Tenth Congress of the International Political Science Association and articles by authors from Bulgaria and Cuba on questions of peaceful coexistence.

The yearbook also carries information and reference material on the activities of the SPSA and bibliographical reviews of Soviet political literature.

The association has been actively promoting international contacts in recent years. It is a member of the In-

---

*Reprinted from *Social Sciences: USSR Academy of Sciences* 10, no. 3 (1979): 203–5. By permission of the editorial board.

ternational Political Science Association (IPSA) and takes an active part in the functioning of its bodies (notably, SPSA President G. Shakhnazarov is a vice-president of IPSA), as well as in international political science congresses, conferences, meetings, and symposia and also in sessions of national political science associations.

In September 1977, SPSA representatives for the first time attended a congress in Rabat, Morocco, of the African Association of Political Science, formed in 1974 by the national associations of a number of African countries. In August–September 1977 SPSA members attended a round-table conference on "Political Culture" sponsored by IPSA in Cracow. In April 1978, representatives of the Soviet and Finnish national political science associations met for the first time in Helsinki, where they exchanged information on political research in both countries. They also signed a cooperation protocol between the two associations.

In August 1978 an SPSA delegation took part in a round-table discussion on "Technocracy and Its Control with Special Reference to the Developing Countries," sponsored by IPSA in Rio de Janeiro. Representatives of the Soviet and Brazilian associations exchanged information on the functioning of their organizations and the development of the political sciences in their countries.

SPSA cooperation with the political science associations of the socialist countries is steadily expanding. In April 1977 a conference of representatives of these associations and an international symposium on "Current Problems of the Development of the Political Sciences and a Critical Analysis of the Present State of Bourgeois Politology" was held at Lidice, Czechoslovakia.

The Eleventh World IPSA Congress was held in the summer of 1979 in Moscow. The preparations for the congress occupied a key place in the work of the SPSA in 1978–1979. A national organizational committee of thirty-seven members has been set up. It has held a number of national scientific conferences on the topics of the congress. Collections of papers submitted by the Soviet delegation have been published in Russian, English, and French. The committee has in many ways promoted the expansion of business contacts with national political science associations in other countries.

At a meeting with members of the IPSA Program Committee, in March 1978 in Moscow, Vice-President of the USSR Academy of Sciences P. Fedoseyev stressed that politologists had a special responsibility for molding constructive political consciousness in their countries. On behalf of Soviet scientists, he expressed the conviction that the Moscow IPSA congress would be a forum for the scientific discussion of outstanding problems of mankind in the name of humanism and social progress.

Bibliography*

Akademija Nauk SSSR. *Construction of Communism and the Social Sciences. Materials of the Session of the General Assembly, 19–20 October 1962* (in Russian). Moscow: Izdatel'stvo Akademii Nauk SSSR, 1962. (Research program in the USSR.)

Alekseev, S. S., and Chirkin, V. E. "On the System of Sciences Which Study the Problems of the Political Organization of Society, the State and the Law" (in Russian). *Sovetskoe Gosudarstvo i Pravo* 35, no. 5 (May 1965): 45–52.

Bibič, A. "Political Science in the USSR, Czechoslovakia and Poland" (in Serbo-Croatian). *Politička Misao* (Belgrade) 2, no. 3 (September–December 1965): 87–98.

Bociurkiw, B. R. "The Post-Stalin 'Thaw' and Soviet Political Science." *Canadian Journal of Economics and Political Science* 30, no. 1 (February 1964): 22–48.

Brodersen, A. "Soviet Social Science and Our Own." *Social Research* 24, no. 3 (August 1957): 254–86.

Brunner, Georg. *Political Sociology in the USSR* (in German). Wiesbaden: Akademische Verlagsgesellschaft, 1977.

Capecchi, V., and Munari, F. "Dogmatism and Empirical Research in the Social Sciences in the USSR" (in Italian). *Mulino* (Bologna) 13, no. 3 (March 1964): 350–59.

Černacklj, V. N. "Politics as a Sociological Category" (in Russian). In *Filosofija, ėkonomika, sovremennost*. Leningrad, 1978, pp. 76–94.

Česnokov, K. I. "The Correlation between the Social Sciences and the Place of Scientific Communism among Them" (in Russian). *Voprosy Filosofii* (Moscow) 19, no. 3 (1965): 20–31.

———, ed., *Methodological Questions in the Social Sciences* (in Russian). Moscow: Moscow State University, 1966.

Chapkarine, A. V., et al. "Social Science Education in the Institutions of Higher Education of the USSR" (in French). *Revue internationale des sciences sociales* 11, no. 2 (1959): 163–224.

Churchward, L. G. "Towards a Soviet Political Science," *Australian Journal of Political History* 12, no. 1 (April 1966): 66–75.

Čikvadze, V. M., and Zivs, S. L. "New Trends in Legal Sovietology and Our Tasks" (in Russian). *Sovetskoe Gosudarstvo i Pravo* 40, no. 3 (March 1967): 54–64.

Denisov, A. I., and Lejst, O. E., eds. *History of Political Teachings* (in Russian). Moscow: Juridiceskaja Literatura, 1978.

Dmitriev, A. V., and Ketzerov, N. M. "The Object of Bourgeois Political Sociology" (in Russian). *Učenye Zapiski* (Leningrad gosudarstvennyj Universitet naučnoissledovatel'skij Institut kompleksnyh sociologičeskih Issledovanij) 5 (1969): 15–24.

*Compiled by the editor.

Eliutin, V. "Improving the Quality of the Teaching of Social Sciences in Institutions of Higher Education" (in Russian). *Kommunist* 13 (September 1955): 28-38.

Fedoseyev, P. "The 24th USSR Party Congress and Principal Research Orientations in the Social Sciences Field" (in Russian). *Kommunist* (Moscow) 49, no. 1 (January 1972): 56-77.

Goormaghtigh, J. "International Relations as a Field of Study in the Soviet Union." *Yearbook of World Affairs* 28 (1974): 250-61.

Gorbunov, I. S. "On the Interdependence of Economics and Politics" (in Russian). *Učenye Zapiski* (Komi gosudarstvennij pedagogičeskij institut) (Syktyvkar) 6 (1958): 129-51.

"The Human Sciences in Research in the Soviet Union" (in French). *Annuaire de l'URSS* (Strasburg) (1966): 535-94.

"Human Sciences Research in the Soviet Union" (in French). *Annuaire de l'URSS* (Strasburg) (1968): 779-849.

Il'jašenko, K. "Some Results and Further Tasks of the Social Science Professorships of the Universities of the Republic (Moldavia)" (in Moldavian). *Kommunist Moldavii* (Kišinev) 3, no. 5 (May 1958): 15-21.

"The Imposing Program of Construction of Communist Society and Tasks of the Soviet Legal Sciences" (in Russian). *Sovetskoe Gosudarstvo i Pravo* 1 (January 1959): 3-13.

Inago, T. "The Development of Political Science in the USSR" (in Japanese). *Hôsei Ronshû* (Nagoya) 35 (March 1966): 1-46.

Ivanov, S. S., and Rahmaninova, E. A. "Concerning Elaboration of the Course 'History of the Soviet State and Law'" (in Russian). *Sovetskoe Gosudarstvo i Pravo* 3, no. 8 (August 1961): 134-38.

Jampol'skaya, C. A. "A Methodology of the Science of Administration" (in Russian). *Sovetskoe Gosudarstvo i Pravo* 35, no. 8 (August 1965): 12-21.

Javič, L. S. "On the Problem of the Methodology of Legal Science" (in Russian). *Sovetskoe Gosudarstvo i Pravo* 33, no. 5 (May 1963): 71-79.

Keček'jan, S. G., and Fed'kin, G. I. *The History of the Political Studies* (in Russian). Moscow: Gos. izd-vo jurid. lit-ry, 1955.

Klováč, J., and Tlustý, V. "Remarks on the Relation between Political Science and Sociology of Politics" (in Czech). *Sociologicky Časopis* (Prague) 3, no. 3 (1967): 245-56.

Konstantinov, F. "Political Theories and Political Practice: On the Results of the Fourth Congress of IPSA" (in Russian). *Kommunist* 35, no. 16 (1958): 86-102.

Konstantinov, F. V. *Marxism-Leninism in Higher Education* (in Russian). Moscow: Gosudarstvennoe Izdatel'stvo političeskoj literatury, 1957.

———. "Sociology and Politics" (in Russian). *Voprosy Filosofii* (Moscow) 16, no. 11 (1962): 3-18.

Kuhlberg, S. "Political Science in the Soviet Union" (in Swedish). *Politiikka* (Helsinki) 7, no. 3 (1965): 81-86.

Kurin, D., and Morov, N. "University Social Science Teaching" (in Russian). *Kommunist* 35, no. 17 (December 1958): 60-63.

Kuznecova, S. I., ed. *A Scientific Bibliography from the Fundamental Library of Social Sciences of the USSR Academy of Sciences* (in Russian). Moscow: Nauka Publishing House, 1967.

Langrod, G. "The Revival of Administrative Science in the USSR and in the People's Democracies" (in French). *Revue internationale des sciences administratives* 29, no. 1 (1963): 22-29.

Lasina, M. V. "Some Methodological Questions of Research on the Sociopolitical Sphere of Social Life" (in Russian). *Učenye Zapiski* (Moscow Pedagogical Institute) 387 (1970): 291-315.

Lavigne, P. "The New Methodological Trends of Soviet Juridical Science" (in French). *Annuaire de l'URSS* (Strasburg), 1965, pp. 123-43.

Léon, V. "The Social Sciences in Eastern Europe" (in French). *Revue de l'Est* 2, no. 3 (July 1971): 155-71.

Lorincz, L. "The Development and Place of Soviet Administrative Science" (in Russian). *Allam-és Jogtudomány* (Budapest) 12, no. 2 (1974): 201-29.

Lucas Verdu, P. "Structural Conditioning and Cultural Levels and Styles of Political Science" (in Spanish). *Revista internacional de Sociología* (Madrid) 23, nos. 91-92 (July-December 1965): 341-64.

Lunev, A. E. "The Soviet Science of Administrative Law after 60 Years" (in Russian). *Sovetskoe Gosudarstvo i Pravo* 11 (November 1977): 60-66.

Materials of the All-Union Conference of Heads of Departments of Social Sciences (in Russian). Moscow: Gospolitizdat, 1958.

Mills, R. M. "On Theory in Search of Reality: The Development of United States Studies in the Soviet Union." *Political Science Quarterly* 87, no. 1 (March 1972): 63-79.

Mohov, N., and Lutčenko, A. "Problems in Teaching the Social Sciences in the Higher Educational Establishments" (in Russian). *Kommunist* 13 (September 1955): 28-38.

"The Most Important Achievements in the Field of Natural and Social Sciences" (in Russian). *Vestnik Akademii Nauk SSSR* 35, no. 3 (March 1965): 11-94.

Nahlik, S. E. "International Organizations as Subjects in the Light of Soviet Science" (in Polish). *Pańi i Prawo* 31, no. 10 (October 1976): 52-66.

Ojanen, Juhani. "About Political Science Research in the USSR" (in Finnish). *Politiikka* 20, no. 1 (1978): 45-53.

Nordenstam, G. "Destalinization in Soviet Political Science." *Acta sociologica* 7, no. 3 (1963): 131-50.

Pfaff, D. *Development of Soviet Legal Science* (in German). Cologne: Verlag Wissenschaft und Politik, 1968.

"Political Studies: History and the Present" (in Russian). *Sovestskoe Gosudarstvo i Pravo* 45, no. 1 (January 1972): 62-72.

Powell, David E., and Shoup, Paul. "The Emergence of Political Science in Communist Countries." *American Political Science Review* (June 1970): 572-88.

Robinson, T. W. "Game Theory and Politics: Recent Soviet Views." *Studies in Soviet Thought* (December 1970): 291-315.

Rogger, H. "Politics, Ideology, and History in the USSR: The Search for Coexistence." *Soviet Studies* 16, no. 3 (January 1965): 253-75.

Romaskin, P. S. "On the Tasks of the Institute of State and Law during the Present Period" (in Russian). *Sovetskoe Gosudarstvo i Pravo* 31, no. 1 (January 1961): 13-23.

Rozin, V. P., ed. *Methodological Questions of the Social Sciences*. Leningrad: Izdatel'stvo leningradskogo universiteta, 1968.

Sisakjan, N. M. "Essential Results in the Fields of Natural and Social Sciences in 1965" (in Russian). *Vestnik Akademii Nauk SSSR* 36, no. 3 (March 1966): 14-135.

Sivak, A. F. "Some Methodological Problems of Political Science Research" (in Russian). *Učen. Zap. Kaf. obšč. Nauk Vuzov Leningr.* 9 (1977): 153-58.

Skilling, G. "In Search of Political Science in the Soviet Union" (in Portuguese). *Revista brasileira de Estudos politicos* 19 (July 1965): 173-91.

Slavin, V. "The First Annual Meeting of the Soviet Political Science Association" (in Russian). *Sovetskoe Gosudarstvo i Pravo* 31, no. 7 (July 1961): 131-35.

"The Soviet Political Sciences." *Politiikka* 1 (1978): 1-82.

Stefanov, N. K. *Theory and Methods in the Social Sciences* (in Russian). Moscow: Progress, 1967.

Susiluoto, I. *About the Development of Political Science in the Soviet Union: An Historical and Sociological Interpretation of the Science* (in Finnish). Mimeographed. Helsinki: University of Helsinki, Institute of Political Science, 1973.

———. "History and Political Sciences in the Soviet Union" (in Finnish). *Politiikka* 15, no. 1 (1973): 35-42.

———. "On Soviet and Western Political Science" (in Finnish). *Politiikka* 12, no. 1 (1970): 71-82.

Theen, R. H. W. "Political Science in the Soviet Union." *Problems of Communism* (May-June 1972): 64-70.

———. "Political Science in the Soviet Union." *World Politics* (July 1971): 684-703.

Time, Space and Politics: Soviet Studies in the Political Sciences. Moscow: Social Sciences Today Editorial Board, USSR Academy of Sciences; New York: Four Continents Book Corp., 1977.

Topornin, B. "Social Sciences in the USSR" (in French). *Information Social Science* 3, no. 4 (December 1964): 106-22.

USSR Upravlenie usebnyh zavedenij. *Bibliography of Social and Political Literature* (in Russian). Moscow: Gos. izd-vo kul'turno'prosvetitel'noj lit'ry, 1955.

Vyshinsky, A. Ja. "A Few Problems in the Field of Soviet Legal Science" (in Russian). *Sovetskoe Gosudarstvo i Pravo* 4 (1953): 10-26.

White, R. K. "Social Science Research in the Soviet Bloc." *Public Opinion Quarterly* 28, no. 1 (September 1964): 20-26.

Wilder, E. "Social Research in Soviet Bloc Countries." *American Behavioral Scientist* 6, no. 5 (January 1963): 3-4.

Woronitzin, S., ed. *Bibliography on Social Research in the Soviet Union 1960-1970* (in German). Munich: Verlag Dokumentation, 1973.

Zor'kin, V. D. "Critic of the Positivist Conception of the Political and Juridical Science Ideologization" (in Russian). *Gosudarstvo, pravo, demokratija* (Moscow) (1978): 184-98.

Zvorikine, A. "The Social Sciences in the USSR: Situation and Trends" (in French). *Revue internationale des sciences sociales* 16, no. 4 (1964): 634-52.

Zvorykin, A. A. "A Structural Analysis of Publications in the Field of Social Studies in the Soviet Union, 1960-1965." *Social Research* 33, no. 4 (Winter 1966): 552-61.

28 UNITED KINGDOM
JACK HAYWARD

Introduction

At the outset one is faced with the problem of how to describe those people engaged in the teaching and research of politics in Britain, given the widespread reluctance to accept the denomination "political scientist," yet it is difficult to find an acceptable alternative that is both less pretentious and not so modest or clumsy as to be unduly diffident. Partly because the status of the study of politics as one of the social sciences is relatively new and because many of its senior practitioners were frequently trained within the humanities or law, there has been a reluctance to segregate the subject from others. Furthermore, there has been a particularly British self-consciousness about engaging introspectively in a systematic examination of the rationale of one's practical activities. Except when under pressure to do so by the requirement to deliver an inaugural lecture, professors of politics in Britain seldom concern themselves with the identity and boundaries of their discipline in the way that sister disciplines like sociology are prone to indulge with an obsessive intensity, perhaps because in their case the indigenous tradition has been more easily penetrated by foreign ideas. Even on the formal occasions when they may feel called upon to express their views on the nature of politics as an academic discipline, there has been an increasing tendency in recent years for inaugural lecturers to eschew the general survey in favor of the examination of a specific problem,[1] which allows them to avoid the embarrassment of questioning their fundamental assumptions. Like Dickens we prefer to let sleeping dogs lie.

However, there remains the practical problem of finding a substitute for the term "political scientist" which probably remains a misleading self-description in the British context. I shall adopt the locution "politist" because it conveys (to me at least) the increasing aspiration to become a social scientist, particularly among the younger members of the profession, without laying claim to having as yet fully attained it. Ironically, in the light of its parents, the Webbs, the London School of Economics and Political Science Department of Government—in conjunction with the other great pillar of British political studies, Oxford—has been a stronghold of the hostility to "political science" in Britain since Michael Oakeshott's succession to Harold Laski in mid-century. In place of the reforming spirit which saw the study of politics as intended to contribute to the alleviation of human misery and oppression, there came a supercilious skepticism about the capacity of Reason to improve Man's lot. Although some British politists play an active part in politics, Laski's kind of involvement has also been frowned upon by those who have advocated a political science devoted to a value-free accumulation of knowledge of the real political world rather than one nourishing an ambitious concern to ameliorate it. This self-imposed modesty has both reflected and perhaps contributed to the view of Britain's political elite that the academic study of politics has little to offer them. By one of those ironies of history, the inaugural meeting of the Political Studies Association (PSA) of the United Kingdom on 23–24 March 1950 coincided with the death of Harold Laski, who had been scheduled to deliver the keynote address. With Laski departed much of the 1940s' reforming zeal and the new PSA, whose creation was prompted by external forces, watched over rather than led the subsequent developments in the academic study of politics. For to lead would have implied some sense of direction and those who guided the destinies of the PSA could not discern clearly "where the study of politics was going, if it was going anywhere at all," as the first editor of the association's journal *Political Studies* frankly put it a quarter of a century later.[2]

The Emergence of an Organized Profession

Prior to World War II, the discipline of politics led a hole-and-corner existence in British universities, its few practitioners usually tucked away inside departments of economics, history, or law or as isolated fellows in Oxford and Cambridge colleges. Three chairs had been established, first the Gladstone Chair in Oxford (1912), then London (1914), and finally Cambridge (1928) but there were few supporting teachers of politics, the Oxford colleges relying primarily upon their philosophy and history fellows to undertake such tuition. Public administration teachers already had an organization—the Public Administration Committee of the Joint University Council of Social Studies—thanks to the National Association of Local Government Officers' concern to promote the training of local officials. A number of journals were in existence—*International Affairs* (from 1922), *Public Administration* (from 1923), *Political Quarterly* (from 1930), and *Politica* (from 1934)—the first three continuing to flourish, while *Politica,* suspended during World War II, was not revived subsequently. But despite the publication of some important books by the distinguished pioneers who paved the way for the postwar cohort, this period corresponds to the prehistory of the discipline in Britain. In this sphere, though less so than in so many others, World War II helped to reduce the inertial pressures of past practice and prejudice. It enriched the capacity of a small generation of politists, thanks to their direct inside experience of the working of British government, which proved alas to be a purely temporary breakdown in the compartmentalization of British public life. William Robson (who as the link with IPSA played a key part in the creation of the PSA) recalls: "In 1946-7 I started a course at L.S.E. on the Central Government and the Civil Service. Its only novelties were the inclusion of such topics as the internal organization of departments, the intelligence, information and public relations functions, and the role of the Cabinet Secretariat, all of which were the result of my wartime experience in the Civil Service."[3] There was also greater official support for politics teaching and research through the University Grants Committee in the 1947 to 1952 quinquennium, following the recommendations of the Clapham Committee on the Provision of Social and Economic Research (note the absence of any mention of politics) which reported in 1946. A modest expansion in academic posts resulted. During the decolonization process that was such a feature of the late 1940s and 1950s, a number of politists and constitutional lawyers, most notably Sir Ivor Jennings, were called upon to advise both the British and the newly independent governments about the political and administrative arrangements necessitated by the breakup of the British Empire. Yet, none of these developments would have, of themselves, prompted the creation of a professional association of politists, had the initiative not come—characteristically—from outside Britain, a country more inclined to respond to an external challenge than to seize the initiative itself.

As a result of the UNESCO initiative, leading to the creation of IPSA, William Robson of the LSE explored the possibility of creating a national association in Britain, working initially with the warden of Nuffield College, Oxford, Norman Chester, and Denis Brogan at Cambridge. What to call the new association was an immediate issue and despite Robson's preference for IPSA's term "political science," the opposition of Oxford led to the choice of "political studies." As Sir Norman Chester recalled, "There was a feeling that 'studies' was a wider umbrella than 'science,' a particularly important consideration when so much of the writing was political history."[4] Even this term proved too restrictive for Cambridge and at Brogan's insistence it was widened to include allied subjects. Thus, in the recruiting circular sent out in November 1949, it was stated that "The precise scope of the Association would require full consideration. At the moment it is suggested that membership should be open to all University teachers in Political Theory and Institutions, Government and Public Administration, Constitutional and Administrative Law, International Relations, International Law and similar subjects."[5] This typically eclectic compromise persisted. Despite the promise to give full consideration to the association's scope, it never really received this searching inquiry and the latitudinarian approach to political studies helped the new association to recruit a hundred members. Apart from holding an annual conference, usually in London or Oxford, the PSA's chief aim was to establish a journal, which it was able to launch in 1953 thanks to the agreement of the Oxford University Press, secured by the PSA's first chairman, Norman Chester.

Defining the Subject One Is to Teach

One must start from the fact that there is no agreement among British politists and (fortunately) no authority to impose a common pattern about what constitutes their subject matter and their methodology. Concluding his recollections of the evolution of British political studies in a pessimistic key, Sir Norman Chester noted

the failure of any central core of accepted learning or theory to emerge. When there were only a few books this lack was concealed by the fact that all established teachers had read the same books. This was why it was comparatively easy for, say, a modern historian to become a well-accepted teacher of politics quite quickly. All that was needed, in addition to the knowledge of British, American, and French history they possessed, was the reading of a dozen or so standard works and an interest in contemporary affairs. Moreover, the fact that, with a few exceptions, those teaching politics had been undergraduates at Oxford, the London School of Economics, or Cambridge, in that order of numbers, added to the cohesion. The sheer weight of new publications and of new undergraduate courses has killed that cohesion.[6]

When one adds to this the increasing number of universities engaged in undergraduate and postgraduate teaching and research, as well as the growth of new courses in polytechnics, the scope for diversity and dissent is enormous. One may make the best of a bad job and with Bernard Crick argue that "Since we are not a discipline but a problem-area parasitic upon other disciplines, mainly History and Philosophy, we might as well try to act like a parasite rather than an elephant; give up the claim to an exclusive domain, our own palace graveyard, but buzz and sting promiscuously everywhere, searching out the political implications of (and within) so many other subjects and proselytise in the immense field of political education in the schools."[7]

However, when one looks closely at what is actually taught to students of politics in Britain, the chaos is more apparent than real. Part of the credit for the degree of consensus that exists is to be attributed to the fact that a few big graduate schools still dominate the training of future politics teachers. Furthermore, despite the autonomy of each university (but not the polytechnics) in devising its own courses and teaching methods, comparability is secured by the institution of the external examiner, whereby the standards and practices of each university's teaching is subject to annual scrutiny by a senior member of the teaching staff of another university. This informally achieves a measure of cohesion in practice that one would not be entitled to expect from the freedom of the members of each institution to indulge their own imagination in the matter of undergraduate and postgraduate course design and teaching.

When one compares the content of what is taught to British undergraduates in the late 1970s with what was offered in the late 1940s, one is struck by the virtual elimination of such subjects as British Constitutional History. To some extent this reflects a threefold decline in the importance attached to each of the constituent elements of that subject. While the historical element has receded in importance, what has survived is an emphasis upon contemporary history, without delving into the medieval origins of Parliament. Furthermore, courses are less parochial in their focus, making up in space for what is lost in the dimension of time. For although international relations has sometimes been developed as a separate discipline, it generally remains part of the course in politics and is increasingly recognized as an indispensable part of such a course. Lastly, the study of the formal constitution has declined almost to the vanishing point as more fashionable concerns, first with political parties, then pressure groups, political socialization, political communication, and public policy, were added to the curriculum. Just as the influence of political sociology transformed the study of political institutions, so administrative theory has enlivened the study of public administration.

The emergence of politics as a discipline in its own right meant that it ceased to be taught merely as an adjunct of other subjects or even as a joint subject with one or two other social science or arts subjects. Special honors degrees emerged, which meant that even those traditional courses that had been given pride of place because of the close links of the embryonic study of politics with them, now had to compete with new specialisms. Thus, political philosophy (whose importance derived in part from the fact that philosophy, like history and law, had been one of the disciplines from which politics became differentiated) has tended to receive relatively less emphasis. For example, whereas it was earlier taken for granted that the history of political thought should be a compulsory component of any course in politics, it has had increasingly to fight to maintain this position, both against nonphilosophical courses and from newer courses in empirical or normative political theory.

Another change of emphasis that can be detected is the shift from the undergraduate study of a few First World countries—notably the U.S.A., France, and the USSR—to an interest in comparative politics, to the study of Third World countries, and to political development. Furthermore, there has been a relative decline in the study of countries that have had historic links with Britain, notably through the colonial empire, whether they be pre–World War II white Commonwealth or newer black Commonwealth countries. Area studies have become more popular than studies with an exclusive focus on a particular country, allowing comparisons to be facilitated among states that share certain cultural characteristics.

Literacy rather than numeral facility still has pride of place, with few politics departments offering courses on statistical and survey techniques, combined with opportunities to apply them in undergraduate dissertations. This has an effect upon the kind of research undertaken at the postgraduate level, although there are opportunities to develop these skills at those postgraduate schools which have embraced the behavioral persuasion most completely, notably Essex in England and Strathclyde in Scotland. While the development of a variety of one-year postgraduate courses, helped in some cases with funding from the Politics Committee of the Social Science Research Council, has made for a more diversified training than the purely research thesis, the "apprenticeship" mode has held its own as the most esteemed form of postgraduate qualification in the recruitment to academic positions. While the doctorate has not yet become the sine qua non of appointment to politics posts in Britain, it has become increasingly common.

Unlike some other countries, the growth in numbers and the increased professional importance attached to published research has not dwarfed the traditional emphasis upon the small group-teaching of undergraduates. Despite the substantial increase in student numbers and the constraint exercised by the public sources of funding that have resulted in a deterioration in the ratio of students to academic staff, stress is laid upon personal supervision of students, not merely at the postgraduate but at the undergraduate level. While Britain has avoided the worst extremes of the publish-or-perish mentality, nevertheless politists are aware that promotion depends in no small measure upon scholarly publications. Gone are the days when, as W. J. M. Mackenzie has recalled, he was able in the 1930s to switch from teaching classics to politics, learning "political science while I taught it" and in 1948 to secure appointment to a Chair of Government in Manchester when he "had really published nothing"; a time, furthermore, when "'Research' was scarcely yet a concept; the thing was not to 'do research' but to 'write a book.'"[8] These comments naturally lead us to a consideration of the published work of the postwar decades.

The British Research Response to the Behavioral Challenge

Compared with the vast output produced by American political scientists, the British contribution—like that of the politists of almost any other country—is bound to appear puny. One would be happier if one could argue that what is absent in quantity is made up in quality but despite the necessarily subjective nature of such a judgment, I find it hard to dissent from Sir Norman Chester's stern assessment: "A good part of the articles and books published in the last 15-20 years fall below the high standards expected of an academic profession."[9]

The initial British response to the behavioral revelation that appeared to be gripping American political science in the late 1950s was either lukewarm—in the case of David Butler's *The Study of Political Behaviour* (1958)[10]—or trenchantly critical—Bernard Crick's *The American Science of Politics* (1959)—and though this approach acquired able advocates in Britain, they were often politists from America like Richard Rose or a Frenchman, Jean Blondel, who had enthusiastically embraced the American challenge. Perhaps the best indicator of the characteristic British politists' response to behavioralism is to be found in W. J. M. Mackenzie's writings, notably his book on *Politics and Social Science* which represented a rare attempt to come to grips with the new, nontraditional ways of engaging in political study as a social science.

Mackenzie, who built up in the 1950s and early 1960s probably the best department of politics in Britain in terms of its scholarly publications, typically affirms: "I see 'the discipline' as a group of people rather than as a set of principles, as a continuing debate rather than as an enquiry in the style of natural science...."[11] Although, more than most of his fellow British politists, Mackenzie has taken the trouble to familiarize himself with not only the behavioral approach but many other alternative methodological approaches, he was representative of his inductivist colleagues in asserting that "methodology comes after practice, not before it" or again that "on the whole, it seems better to let questions of methodology arise incidentally out of questions of substance...."[12] While prepared to concede that an American behavioral political scientist was trained to organize his material in a more disciplined way, interdisciplinary cross-fertilization was to be achieved less by expensively funded teamwork than by individual scholars eclectically disregarding the traditional frontiers between disciplines.

> In describing and explaining politics we carry a bag of different intellectual tools, using each tool for its own job and not worrying too much about a general theory of tools.... The craftsmanship... was an individual skill, not different in character from scholarship in other humanities and not dependent on formal teaching of technical procedures. Each book stood alone, and each author had his own standards of arrangement and evidence, so that there was no cumulative advance in knowledge, no pretense at science.[13]

However, the new wave of social science professionalism was not entirely to be denied. Just as in the U.S.A., where the foundations funding research gave a fillip to behavioral research, the establishment of the Social Science Research Council in 1965, coinciding as it did with a substantial increase in the numbers of politists appointed to university posts and in the numbers of graduate students, promoted a more systematic and less idiosyncratic approach to research. While it would be wrong to exaggerate the practical extent of the change, the intent may be gleaned from the following checklist sent to those who were selected by the SSRC Politics Committee to vet research grant applications:

Contribution

Is the proposed research likely to make a new/significant contribution to theory, method, or factual information?

Is it likely to have any practical application?

Would there be any partial benefit, even if the full objectives were not attained?

General

Does the application as a whole reflect knowledge, planning and capability in the application?

Is research on this topic worth supporting?

Aims and Methods

Are the aims of the research sufficiently clear?

Will the proposed methods and techniques enable the objectives to be attained?

Context

Is there similar/related work (past or current) not mentioned in this proposal of which the applicant should be aware?

Is the proposed research merely replicating work which has been carried out elsewhere?

Planning

Are the qualifications and experience of the research staff suitable for the project?

Is the size of the research staff appropriate for the research?

Are the time-scale and scheduling of the work appropriate and realistic to the aims of the research?

Is the equipment appropriate?

Are the suggested costs realistic?

While most research grant applications remained in the tradition of the artisan managing on a shoestring budget and not contemplating employing a research assistant, it was now possible to conceive more ambitious, collective projects that had hitherto been usually ruled out. Collaborative research became fashionable, with conferences arranged to secure a problematic meeting of minds. However, as the sources of finance have diminished, artisan techniques have retrieved some of their attractions.

While it is a necessarily selective and somewhat arbitrary exercise to pick out the most noteworthy contributions by British politists since 1945, one may make a start by saying that the loss of interest by American scholars in the traditional areas like the history of political thought and political theory has meant that British contributions have had the field more to themselves. The names of Isaiah Berlin, Michael Oakeshott, John Plamenatz, and Brian Barry particularly come to mind as individuals who have had the most impact in those fields where personal inspiration rather than teamwork holds its own. Naturally enough, the concern with British politics and administration has been a major research preoccupation. The most continuous postwar tradition has been the Nuffield election studies which have made psephology one of the rare subjects in which quantification has had a field day. British and American collaboration in the shape of *Political Change in Britain* by David Butler and Donald Stokes has provided the most searching examination of British voting behavior, although in the 1970s the work of Ian Budge, Ivor Crewe, and their associates at the University of Essex has taken up the subject and extended it in new directions. Robert McKenzie's *British Political Parties* was a pathbreaking book in 1955 and Richard Rose's *The Problem of Party Government* in 1974 was a thoroughly and authoritatively researched study. The Study of Parliament Group, in which Bernard Crick long played an active role, represented a rare attempt to build a bridge between official insiders and academic outsiders. Crick's *The Reform of Parliament* (1964) reflected the reformist, Laskian urge to improve our institutions which Richard Crossman, ex-politist turned politician, sought to give effect as Leader of the House of Commons in 1966-1968. Another innovative venture was the establishment in 1963 of the Institute of Local Government Studies (Inlogov) not only to provide management training for British local officials but to advance the study of public administration, from which a stream of interesting publications has come.[14]

Others have been less exclusively concerned with Britain, such as Samuel Finer in *The Man on Horseback* and Philip Williams in his superb study of the French Fourth Republic, *Crisis and Compromise* (1964) that exemplifies a strong British interest in French politics which has remained active throughout the postwar period. The study of interest groups and public policy has been a flourishing field in Britain, ranging from Finer's *Anonymous Empire* in 1958 to one of the most impressive case studies, that of Wyn Grant and David Marsh, *The Confederation of British Industry* (1977). A notable problem for those seeking to do research on British politics has been official secrecy. As Hugh Heclo and Aaron Wildavsky (two transatlantic scholars who were able successfully to brave Treasury imperviousness) have put it: "The executive fortress is proclaimed sacrosanct. Those inside who do not wish to be seen make common cause with those outside who could try to see but do not. The Constitution is their common pretense."[15] We shall return to this problem in discussing the relationship between politists and the real political world.

The Political Studies Association of the UK

We dwelt at some length, earlier in this chapter, on the origins of the PSA because the highly circumspect way in which it was launched conveyed in the most eloquent fashion the degree of self-doubt and caution that were the hallmarks of many of Britain's postwar politists. Rather like people who emerge from a dark tunnel into brilliant sunlight, there was a tendency to blink with bewildered myopia and to venture forward only in a tentative fashion. Nevertheless, one would be churlish not to recognize the real achievements of the founding fathers or to ignore the genuine difficulties confronting them. As we saw, the new association, as well as playing a full and active part in the work of its parent organization, IPSA, rapidly instituted an annual conference and established a journal that until 1969 published only three issues annually, after which *Political Studies* appeared quarterly. What is perhaps more surprising is that professional energies were almost exhausted by the initial effort and thereafter its activities went little if at all beyond these vital preliminary steps. The PSA settled down to an intimate and cozy if episodic life, in which conviviality and the exchange of gossip helped to impart a sense of cohesion. As Ivor Crewe wrote in 1975, at a time when a determined attempt was made to shake up this state of affairs, "I enjoyed the old PSA meetings. But academic conferences reflect the discipline's self-image. The customary thinness of numbers and activities, the pervading atmosphere of gentle muddle, the cultivated casualness of approach all reflected an underlying lack of confidence in political science as an academic subject."[16]

The PSA's Executive Committee had, perhaps inadvertently, become a self-recruiting and self-perpetuating oligarchy that seldom had to face a contested election. So, it came as something of a shock when, at the Twenty-Fifth Anniversary Oxford conference in 1975, almost a full slate of candidates (Brian Barry dropping out on accepting a post abroad) presented themselves for election against the outgoing executive committee and secretary. As one of those who made what he thought was a gesture in support of the need for change—*vingt-cinq ans, c'est assez*—without believing that it would produce more than a token response, I must confess that we had underestimated the extent to which disquiet at the immobilism of the PSA was common among the membership. The eight candidates advocating a more assertive PSA were all elected and it may be of some interest to quote from the unprecedented fly sheet manifesto circulated. It will be clear that to regard the items in this program as radical would be a reflection on the preceding inertia rather than a testimony to the revolutionary propensities of the challengers.

The elections for the PSA executive committee are being contested by a group of people who have not stood before but offer themselves this year in the belief that the PSA needs a change of management. While they span a wide range of fields and methodological outlooks, they are united by a desire to make the PSA a more effective body, better adapted to meeting the needs of a large and scattered membership. Among the ideas so far suggested by people in this group are:

(i) The committee should take a more active role in planning the annual conference . . . should actually exert itself to think of subjects for the conference.

(ii) The journal should be used to carry association news and provide a forum for the discussion of matters of professional and disciplinary concern, as well as a place for publishing learned articles.
(iii) The committee should take the lead in setting up a variety of meetings at which faculty and graduate students with common research interests can get together, either on a regional or on a national basis.
(iv) On the basis of offering a real service to members (including a lively and interesting journal) it should be possible to mount a campaign to bring in the many university and polytechnic teachers who have not in the past joined the PSA. This would strengthen the resource base of the association and enable it to do a better job.

Above all, the members of the group pledge themselves to bring more imagination and energy to the conduct of the association's affairs and on that basis ask for your vote.

It would probably be both tedious and tendentious to expatiate about the extent to which this program has been attained. Suffice to say that the annual conference has become a much more elaborate affair, with far more papers being discussed by more participants. The establishment of a newsletter has provided the channel for information but—through no fault of its energetic editor, Jeffrey Stanyer—not a forum for discussion. The number of research activities sponsored by the PSA has grown substantially, with specialist groups proliferating. Polytechnic and women members of the PSA have played a much more prominent role than in the past, notably on the executive committee. Despite successive increases in the membership fee to meet, inter alia, the cost of expanding activities, the number of members was quickly increased from under six hundred to over seven hundred: approximately three-quarters of the potential membership. (This does not include the new categories of graduate member and corporate member, the latter being instituted in 1977 to help fund curriculum and graduate training activities, as well as to finance a biennial heads of department conference.) A major recent PSA activity was to act as host to the Tenth IPSA Congress in Edinburgh in 1976, which proved a great success, without ruining the PSA as it threatened to do at one stage.

The PSA's journal *Political Studies* has a far wider circulation than the membership of the association and has often published contributions from foreign politists, particularly from the U.S.A., Canada, and Australia. We saw earlier that in 1945 there were only three politics journals in existence. Thereafter *Parliamentary Affairs* (1947) preceded the establishment of *Political Studies* in 1953, which in turn was followed by *Government and Opposition* (1966), the *British Journal of Political Science* (1971), *Teaching Politics,* and *Policy and Politics* (1972). In addition to these journals with a general coverage (although they tend to have a British emphasis) are an increasing number of more specialized journals such as the *British Journal of International Studies* (1975), some relating to a particular area, like *Soviet Studies,* the *Journal of Common Market Studies,* and most recently *West European Politics* (1978). Other specialist outlets for research by politists include the British Political Sociology Yearbook, which first appeared in 1974. All this amounts to a formidable quantity of published work with which to keep up.

The Politist and the World of Politics

We have already seen that during the Second World War and in its decolonization aftermath a select few were either temporarily absorbed into government work, which they were able to observe as participants, or were called upon to give advice that was frequently acted upon. Thereafter, the barrier between the politists and the world of politics was reestablished. Jim Sharpe has perceptively discussed the experience of British academics by comparison with their American colleagues, who live in a society more receptive to the influence of social scientists upon the policy-making process.

Such an exalted place for social science has no parallel in the British political tradition. On the contrary, it is profoundly suspicious of the university world altogether and social science in particular.... The epitome of the government's response to a policy problem in the United States is to select the professor with the highest reputation in the field, give him a generous research budget and put him on a contract. The epitome in Britain is to set up a committee of inquiry made up largely of distinguished practitioners in the chosen policy field with a token academic who may or may not be invited by his colleagues to organize research.[17]

Although some 1960s Royal Commissions (Donovan on trade unions and employers' associations, Redcliffe-Maud on local government) did appoint a social scientist research director, in other cases (Fulton on the civil service and Kilbrandon on the constitution) a politist and member of the commission unofficially assumed the role of research director. There is not much evidence that the research actually influenced the reports' recommendations. Politists were encouraged by the "what's wrong with Britain" reformism of the 1960s to address themselves to these and other problems. The 1970s have contributed the governability of Britain, the rise of nationalism within the United Kingdom (leading to a new interest in devolution), and British membership of the EEC, all of which brought constitutional matters, for decades dismissed as of negligible significance, back to the forefront of concern.[18]

The involvement of politists in politics has taken various forms. The most obvious is election to local councils or to the House of Commons, much more rarely elevation to the House of Lords as a life peer. A rare example of a British politist who had a distinguished political career since 1945 was Richard Crossman. After serving on Oxford City Council while he was a don, he spent nearly twenty years as a back-bencher prior to his six years as a cabinet minister. His diaries, only published after an important legal skirmish, are a mine of information and views about the working of the political and administrative executive, deliberately intended to provide a conducted tour behind the normally impenetrable veils of official secrecy.[19] Interestingly, Crossman, having written an extensive introduction to Walter Bagehot's classic *The English Constitution,* was taken with the idea of "prime ministerial government," suggested by another Labour politist, John Mackintosh, whose untimely death in 1978 (at a time when he was most unusually combining a professorship in Politics with being an M.P.) prevented him from following up his fine book on *The British Cabinet* with a study of Parliament that would have been illuminated by his years as an M.P. Much more common, partly because it can be combined with one's job as an academic, is service on a local council, often involving the chairmanship of important council committees. At a rough estimate, about 15 per cent of politists, at some stage of their career, will have stood for election to a local council and probably about 10 per cent would have been elected. Conscious of the rather tenuous ties between politists and the political world, the PSA has encouraged civil servants and M.P.s to become members and has established a research assistant scheme for M.P.s, recruited from among graduate students working on some aspect of British government, as ways of strengthening the link.

Earlier mention of the Fulton Report on the civil service, in which an Oxford politist, Norman Hunt (later Lord Crowther-Hunt, who served as a junior minister in the Labour government under Harold Wilson), played an influential part, reminds us of one of its consequences—the creation of a Civil Service College in 1968. This has afforded modest scope for an academic input into the short in-service training courses that have provided the staple fare of the college. Thus most of the younger senior officials will have acquired a nodding acquaintance with the politist's mode of thinking about public administration but because of the very limited time devoted to such instruction, its significance can easily be exaggerated. An imaginative attempt to build a bridge between the academics interested in policy studies and the public decision makers in the shape of a "British Brookings" misfired in 1978, owing to the jealousies of some of the existing policy studies institutes and the fact that official support came characteristically too little and too late. A by-product of this failure to imitate an American model, which further confirms the contrasting top-level political cultures in the two countries, has been the amalgamation of the Centre for Studies in Social Policy and of Political and Economic Planning into the Policy Studies Institute. The Royal Institute of Public Administration attempts to provide a meeting ground for academics and senior civil servants, its director-general being formerly a politit, member of the Central Policy Review Staff, and senior official at the Department of Industry. The Institute of Strategic Studies provides a close link between politicians and senior officials concerned with defense policy and the academic specialists, while the Royal Institute of International Affairs continues to maintain its close links with the Foreign Office, with civil servants sitting on advisory groups monitoring research projects.

Intermediate between the civil service and the politician proper has emerged the small group of special advisers to ministers—usually one or two per minister—who perform in an embryonic way a few of the functions of the much more developed *cabinet ministériel* system in France. Some of these advisers are politists by training, notably the head of the Prime Minister's Policy Unit, Dr. Bernard Donoughue, who has served both Sir Harold Wilson and James Callaghan. It should be made clear, however, that the politists who are appointed to such positions are indebted more to factors other than their academic expertise for their preferment. The involvement of politists in political activity tends to be markedly more evident in the case of the Labour party than in the Conservative party, which doubtless reflects the tendency of politists in general to be disproportionately left-wing in their political loyalties. There are practical problems involved in British politists becoming full-time politicians because universities are reluctant to give academics more than a limited period of unpaid leave of absence, after which they are expected to choose between one career or the other. This has not proved an insuperable problem in other countries.

Conclusion

At a time when some of the leading proponents of a behavioral science of politics have sounded the retreat and begun to rehabilitate institutional and evaluative studies, the more complacent among British politists may feel reassured that far from being the rearguard they are once again part of the main body. Nevertheless, there is a great deal of disquiet among politists about their standing among their academic colleagues and in relation to the wider society. Sir Norman Chester's frank view is that "Within the world of scholarship I doubt whether we rank very high," while "Our professional services are not greatly in demand except in new countries and by the mass media and generally speaking are not recognized as giving us claims to speak with special authority on the subjects we teach."[20] By contrast with some other countries, in Britain

> Politics departments produce neither politicians nor public officials—nor, indeed, anything else recognizable. Of all the social sciences, in fact, Politics seems the most resolutely to cultivate a humanities outlook, offering knowledge about modern society, it is true, but largely for its intrinsic interest rather than for any use value. The minority of students who enroll believing in their youthfully unsophisticated way that the purpose of understanding the world is to change it are soon disabused, as much by the attitude of their teachers as by the realities of life.... Politics departments respond to, and in turn reinforce, the British cult of the amateur.[21]

This cult has been less fashionable since the 1960s but the attempt to develop a more professional attitude to the subject of politics involves an uphill struggle in Britain. Because the proliferation of departments of politics has spread scarce talent thinly, decimating such centers of excellence as there were in the 1960s, an increased responsibility has fallen upon the professional association to attempt to bring together those capable of innovating in particular fields as well as to impart a general impetus. The decreasingly insular character of "political studies" in Britain, thanks in part to organizations like the European Consortium for Political Research (in which Politics Departments from the UK are particularly well represented) or IPSA itself, will help to provide an impetus for change from without to assist the ferments of change within.

Notes

1. Preston King, ed., *The Study of Politics: A Collection of Inaugural Lectures* (London: Frank Cass, 1977).
2. Wilfrid Harrison, "The Early Years of *Political Studies*," *Political Studies* 23 (June–September 1975): 184. The early chapters of this twenty-fifth anniversary issue in honor of the PSA are an indispensable source of information about the postwar development of politics as an academic discipline in Britain, particularly the chapter by Sir Norman Chester.
3. W. A. Robson, "The Study of Public Administration Then and Now," *Political Studies* 23 (June–September 1975): 195.
4. Norman Chester, "Political Studies in Britain: Recollections and Comments," *Political Studies* 23 (June–September 1975): 153.

5. Ibid., p. 152; cf. 153-54.
6. Ibid., p. 163.
7. Bernard Crick, "Chalk-dust, Punch-card and the Polity," *Political Studies* 23 (June-September 1975): 180. See also Bernard Crick and Alex Porter, eds., *Political Education and Political Literacy* (London: Longman, 1978).
8. W. J. M. Mackenzie, *Explorations in Government* (London: Macmillan & Co., 1975), pp. xxi, xxvi-xxvii.
9. Chester, "Political Studies," p. 162.
10. See the interesting review of David Butler's book by Andrew Hacker, "Political Behaviour and Political Behavior," *Political Studies* 7 (February 1959): 32-40.
11. Mackenzie, *Explorations*, p. ix.
12. Ibid., p. xxxii, and W. J. M. Mackenzie, *Politics and Social Science* (Harmondsworth: Penguin Books, 1967), p. 43.
13. Mackenzie, *Politics and Social Science*, pp. 64-65; cf. 68-69.
14. R. A. W. Rhodes, "The State of Public Administration: An Evaluation and a Response," *Public Administration Review* (June 1974): 27.
15. *The Private Government of Public Money* (London: Macmillan & Co., 1974), p. 341.
16. "Britain's Most Backward Social Science," *Times Higher Educational Supplement*, 11 April 1975, p. 5. For a sympathetic portrait of the way the PSA had worked, see the contribution by the then secretary to the twenty-fifth anniversary issue: Peter Woodward, "The P.S.A. Today," pp. 202-7.
17. L. J. Sharpe, "The Social Scientist and Policy-making: Some Cautionary Thoughts and Transatlantic Reflections," *Policy and Politics* 4, no. 2 (December 1975): 11-12.
18. See Richard Rose, "The Constitution: Are We Studying Devolution or Break-up" in Dennis Kavanagh and Richard Rose, eds., *New Trends in British Politics: Issues for Research* (London: Sage, 1977), chap. 2. See also the editors' introduction and Nevil Johnson, *In Search of the Constitution* (Oxford: Pergamon Press, 1977), especially chapters 3 and 7.
19. Richard Crossman, *The Diaries of a Cabinet Minister*, ed. Janet Morgan. 3 vols. (London: Hamish Hamilton and Jonathan Cape, 1975, 1976, and 1977).
20. Chester, "Political Studies," p. 161.
21. F. F. Ridley, *The Study of Government: Political Science and Public Administration* (London: G. Allen & Unwin, 1975), p. 210.

Select Bibliography

"A Generation of Political Thought," *Government and Opposition* 15, nos. 3-4 (1980).

Dennis Kavanagh and Richard Rose, eds. *New Trends in British Politics: Issues for Research*. London: Sage, 1977.

Preston King, ed. *The Study of Politics: A Collection of Inaugural Lectures*. London: Frank Cass, 1977.

J. Lovenduski. *The Political Science Profession in the United Kingdom*. Centre for the Study of Public Policy, University of Strathclyde (March 1981).

W. J. M. Mackenzie. *Politics and Social Science*. Harmondsworth: Penguin Books, 1967.

Political Studies 23 (June-September 1975). PSA anniversary issue, also published as F. F. Ridley, ed. *Studies in Politics*. Oxford: Oxford University Press, 1975.

F. F. Ridley. *The Study of Government: Political Science and Administration*. London: G. Allen & Unwin, 1975.

UNITED STATES OF AMERICA

29

EVRON M. KIRKPATRICK and WILLIAM G. ANDREWS

Introduction

Politics have been studied throughout recorded history, but political science as an organized, learned discipline has very recent origins. Political science was studied and taught in the United States before 1900. However, not until well into the twentieth century did it come of age, either in the more important aspects of method and substance or in the quantity of data produced, amount of substantive knowledge, and number of professional scholars.[1] Perhaps 15,000 trained political scientists are living in the United States today. This is substantially more than had lived in the entire history of civilization until some recent year—say, 1930. By no definition had there been as many as 1,000 political scientists by the time the American Political Science Association was formed in 1903. If political science is defined by the significant known writing, the number was more likely less than 500. More political scientists receive Ph.D. degrees in one year now than all those who existed in 1900, perhaps even as recently as 1930. By recent count, 118 American universities offer Ph.D. degrees in political science now, compared to no more than half-a-dozen in 1900.

The explosive increase in the literature of political science is especially clear. In 1900, perhaps as late as 1930, a political science student could have read all the literature in the discipline while undergoing undergraduate and graduate education. Now, such a student hardly can read all the literature in one or two specialized fields. Few new books were advertised or even reviewed or listed in the early issues of the *American Political Science Review,* which began publication in 1906. Today, they number more than a thousand in each annual volume. In 1900, even in 1930, all the books and articles on Congress, state legislatures, even legislatures in general could have been listed on a few pages. Today, such a list requires a large volume. Moreover, political scientists in the United States produce 95 percent of all literature in the discipline, even though significant increases are taking place elsewhere in the world.

Data are being accumulated at an increasingly rapid rate. The Inter-University Consortium for Political and Social Research, the Survey Research Center, the Roper Center at Williams College, the Yale Data Center, and other archives across the country are collecting, processing, and developing storage and retrieval systems that provide easy access to important data that could not even have been collected in 1900, let alone stored in any quickly retrievable fashion. The development of the science of statistics, the computer, the sample survey, content analysis, easy and rapid travel and communication are all elements in the complete transformation of the study of politics in twentieth-century America. They help to account both for the great increase in the volume of data, research, and important publications and for the revolution in the character and quality of the work done.

However, quantity is not the most interesting and certainly not the most important aspect of the recent development of American political science. Beyond numbers lies the substantive growth that has been produced by a greater consciousness of being political scientists and concern about what that means; greater methodological awareness; greater commitment to science *qua* science; and greater recognition of the need to distinguish problems of value (normative theory) from problems of description (empirical theory). Perhaps the most important substantive growth was generated by methodological awareness and methodological scruples.

Those developments, in turn, were largely responses to the impact of the natural sciences upon political science and the other sciences of mankind. Those forces stimulated in American political scientists a desire to make their work more scientific and launched an era of methodological preoccupation. Especially since 1945, American political scientists have devoted much energy to examining the subject matter and goals appropriate to a science of politics and to the position of political science in a general social science. During that period, many of them have, with much anxiety, turned to the analysis of their own work and that of their colleagues in an effort to identify and examine the assumptions, procedures, modes of explication and description, and the nature of the findings that characterize the body of scholarship known as political science; many have become methodologists. Perhaps this can be summarized by saying that American political science has arrived finally at being a science.

American Political Science Since 1945

INTELLECTUAL STRUCTURE

The questions asked and the answers sought by contemporary American political science fall into two quite different categories that delineate the intellectual structure of the discipline at its most basic level. One set of questions calls for answers that may be described as empirical theory; the other set calls for answers that may be described as normative theory. The distinctions between them furnish a basis for examining the intellectual structure of contemporary American political science. A less abstract aspect of the discipline's intellectual structure concerns its component subfields, a topic that lends itself better to statistical treatment.

Empirical Theory

In political science, empirical theory is concerned with the behavior of individuals as they participate in political processes and institutions. It seeks to understand and explain political behavior, political processes, political institutions, and their interaction. Empirical theory not only collects facts; it interprets, explains, predicts. Theory is not anecdote or gossip. Anecdote, gossip, fact, case history, biography all provide experience vicariously for those who do not or cannot get it firsthand. However, they are only part of empirical theory and empirical science.

Science involves theory as well as facts. The empirical sciences are systems of theories. They guide the collection of data, the gathering of facts, the classification of facts, the ordering of phenomena, and the testing of hypotheses.

Empirical scientists hold that knowledge is not to be had merely by coming face to face with raw data or naked facts. Empirical theory continually anticipates what it finds, it seeks always to clothe the unknown with some attributes of the known. It interprets facts.

The business of empirical scientists is to invent theories so as to understand, to bring order out of confusion, to explain, to predict. Then, they must test those theories continuously, trying to prove them false. The tools, techniques, and methods for testing will depend on the nature of the subject. The more those theories withstand the tests, the more they supply the capacity to control the political environment.

However, empirical theory does not provide ends or goals or wisdom. It supplies only information. It may give data that can change the environment. The wise use of that information can create a humane and just social and political order. However, empirical theory can never answer questions about the ends and goals of political life. Normative theory is required for that.

Normative Theory

Normative theory is oriented to the inner world of human beings, to their hopes, aspirations, dreams, values. Unlike empirical theory, it seeks to provide the moral imperatives, or at least the moral understanding, to permit the existence of a decent, humane, civilized community. Unlike empirical science, normative theory does not study the *actual* hopes, aspirations, and values. Normative theory does not describe but examines what ought to be; it is concerned not with what people value but what they should value; it does not explain existing political systems, but illuminates the characteristics they should have. Its subject matter encompasses the ends government and politics should serve, the obligations of citizens, the vision they should have of themselves and their interrelationships.

Normative questions are vitally important; answers to them affect everyone's lives. Yet, some political scientists deny that normative theory can be related to politics. They claim that "ought" and "ought not" are meaningless terms or that any meanings assigned to them are arbitrary; that words of obligation merely state preferences; or that people cannot act differently than they do; or that "ought not" acts can never be identified with certainty. The acceptance of such claims would eliminate normative political theory as a subject for rational examination.

Another argument holds that normative questions are not a proper concern of political science because they are not subject to analysis by the methods—hypothesis, deduction, observation, experiment, corroboration—appropriate to the empirical world. The difficulty lies in the difference between description and prescription. The methods of dealing with the latter differ greatly from those for the former.

Other political scientists assert that the most important questions about political life are normative and to exclude them would condemn the discipline to triviality. They and their critics have argued the matter for decades, with no end in sight. In any case, many American political scientists always have been concerned with normative questions. Normative inquiry continues to rank with empirical inquiry as an important and legitimate mode of study of political life.

Subfields

Another consideration in delineating the intellectual structure of political science is the distribution of attention among subfields. No standard and generally followed identification of subfields has ever emerged in American political science. However, the most frequently used breakdown includes American government and politics, comparative government and politics, international or world affairs, political theory, research methods, and public administration. Some indication of the relative interest in the various subfields is given by the distribution of articles published in the *American Political Science Review* for 1978–1979: American politics, 36.1 percent; comparative and international politics, 20.8 percent; political theory and theorists, 29.2 percent; and research methods, 13.9 percent.[2] A more direct and substantial indicator is the fields of interest listed by APSA members in the 1973 association directory. The approximate numbers are given below:

Foreign and Cross-National Political Institutions and Behavior

Analysis of particular systems or subsystems	1393
Decision-making processes	742
Elites and their opposition	559
Mass participation and communications	338
Parties, mass movements, secondary associations	773
Political development and modernization	1301
Politics of planning	169
Values, ideologies, belief systems, political culture	1069
Aggregate total	6344

International Law, Organization, and Behavior

International law	400
International organization and administration	668
International politics	1587
Aggregate total	2655

Methodology

Computer techniques	222
Content analysis	91
Epistemology and philosophy of science	323
Experimental design	78
Field data collection	112
Measurement and index construction	120
Model building	211
Statistical analysis	384
Survey design and analysis	351
Aggregate total	1892

Political Stability, Instability, and Change

Cultural modification and diffusion	164
Personality and motivation	138
Political leadership and recruitment	290
Political socialization	502
Revolution and violence	566
Schools and political education	142
Social and economic stratification	127
Aggregate total	1929

Political Theory

Systems of political ideas in history	554
Ideological systems	484
Political philosophy (general)	927
Methodological and analytical systems	368
Aggregate total	2333

Public Policy: Formulation and Content

Policy theory	354
Policy measurement	196
Economic policy and regulation	204
Science and technology	192
Natural resources and environment	214
Education	261
Poverty and welfare	245
Foreign and military policy	887
Aggregate total	2553

Public Administration

Bureaucracy	482
Comparative administration	283
Organization and management analysis	250
Organization theory and behavior	485
Personnel administration	234
Planning, programming, budgeting	272
Politics and administration	765
Systems analysis	113
Aggregate total	2884

U.S. Political Institutions, Processes, and Behavior

Courts and judicial behavior	645
Elections and voting behavior	987
Ethnic politics	268
Executives	515
Interest groups	421
Intergovernmental relations	372
Legislatures	911
Political and constitutional history	499
Political parties	932
Public law	609
Public opinion	491
State, local, and metropolitan government	1027
Urban politics	738
Aggregate total	8415

AGGREGATE GRAND TOTAL 29,005

Those figures reflect, of course, the interests of persons who belonged to the APSA at the time the *Directory* was compiled (1972). Therefore, they should show full spectra of age and career of the members. Another perspective on subfield distribution may be obtained from the lists of doctoral dissertations completed in recent years. Those data should give some indication of the interests of those political scientists, mainly younger ones, who will be determining the intellectual structure of the discipline in future decades. The lists for the five most recent years available include the following number of dissertations for the various subfields:[3]

Doctoral Dissertations in Preparation and Completed, 1978–79

	'75	'76	'77	'78	'79	Total
Foreign and cross-national political institutions and behavior	255	214	203	189	140	1001
International law, organization, and politics	106	78	78	70	60	392
Methodology	8	12	5	4	5	34
Political stability, instability, and change	17	27	36	25	28	133
Political theory	91	105	77	72	70	415
Public policy: formulation and content	65	54	63	83	61	326
Public administration	52	58	70	37	81	298
U.S. political institutions, processes, and behavior	185	156	144	152	143	780
Subtotals	779	704	676	632	588	3379

Translated into percentages for comparative purposes, the two sets of figures look like this:

	Directory	Dissertations All	Dissertations U.S. Only
Foreign and cross-national	21.9	29.6	19.7
International affairs	9.2	11.6	10.4
Methodology	6.5	1.0	40.8
Political stability, etc.	6.7	3.9	4.1
Political theory	8.0	12.3	13.1
Public policy	8.8	9.6	11.2
Public administration	9.9	8.8	13.5
United States	29.0	23.1	27.3
	100.0	99.9	100.1

The second column of figures in the list above exaggerates the differences between the *Directory* list and the dissertation list because it includes foreign political scientists who will, in all likelihood, return to their homelands after completing their doctoral work and, therefore, will not become part of American political science.

They tend to work more heavily in comparative government and international affairs than do their American colleagues. When the second-column figures are adjusted to take this into account, the differences from the *Directory* are not so pronounced, as column 3 indicates. The *Directory* and dissertation figures differ, also, in that the *Directory* permitted the members to list several fields of interest, whereas the dissertation writers appear in only one field. The effects of those differences on the subfield structure is not known. The difference is greatest in political theory, a 5.1 percentage point gap. Yet, the number of dissertations in that field has declined over the past five years. Public administration and public policy showed signs of more moderate growth. The losses were spread more evenly. Political stability, etc., seems to be hit the hardest. Perhaps the safest conclusion is that the subfield structure in American political science is sufficiently mature and that the base is so substantial that dramatic shifts are not likely to occur. Probably, American government will continue to attract the greatest share of interest, with comparative government a fairly close second, and international affairs, political theory, public policy, and public administration grouped closely, each drawing about half as much attention as the two leaders.

TEACHING

American political science is overwhelmingly a college and university teaching discipline. About 12,000 (77.4 percent) of an estimated 15,500 political scientists in the United States are employed in academic jobs, 9,000 as full-time faculty members, 2,000 as part-time faculty members, and 1,000 in research, administration, and so forth. About 85 percent of the full-time and 65 percent of the part-time faculty members hold Ph.D. degrees.

Most political science teachers are members of political science departments. In 1978–1979, 796 such departments employed 7,000 political scientists full-time and 1,075 part-time. The 118 such departments with Ph.D. programs housed 2,700 full-time and 275 part-time political science faculty members. The 165 departments with M.A. programs had 1,800 full-time and 400 part-time political science faculty members. The remaining political science teachers were employed in undergraduate combined departments and in two-year colleges. Each type housed about 1,000 full-timers, while the former had 425 and the latter 500 part-timers.[4]

One measure of the result of their labors is their degree production. From 1973 through 1978, they awarded between 850 and 900 Ph.D. degrees in political science, public administration, and international relations annually with total graduate enrollments in Ph.D. programs ranging between 5,500 and 6,500. The number of M.A. degrees awarded in the same fields hovered around 3,000 annually during that period and the number of undergraduate degrees was 30,000 to 33,000 per year.[5]

While separate departments of political science did not develop in the U.S. until the late nineteenth and early twentieth centuries, the study of politics in the United States extends back to the beginnings of our colleges and universities. At that time, it was incorporated mainly into courses in "ethics," and instruction tended to be didactic. Unhappily, the study of politics was "conducive to neither productive scholarship nor inspired instruction."[6]

The late nineteenth and early twentieth centuries brought significant changes. In almost all areas of teaching and research, the German university became the model. The traditional fields were broken down into special fields. Social science became history, politics, economics, sociology. Within a short time new departments were established and new professional associations formed. The American Academy of Political and Social Science was created in 1889 and the American Political Science Association in 1903. These changes were accompanied by new specialized publications like the *Political Science Quarterly* (1886) and the *American Political Science Review* (1906).

By the turn of the century, teachers were supplementing the classics (Plato, Aristotle, Hobbes, Locke, Rousseau, Bentham, Mill, the Federalist Papers) with Tocqueville, Bryce, Wilson, Burgess, Dunning, Goodnow, the Willoughbys, Ford, Bagehot, Dicey, Wallas, and Lowell.

The changes taking place brought an emphasis on creative and productive scholarship. The intensity and vigor of scholarship in the European universities was reproduced in America. As Somit and Tanenhaus make clear, this gave rise to significant problems that were important at the turn of the century and continue to be important. One of the most significant was the production of scholars with little knowledge about or interest in teaching. Although teaching was their primary responsibility, they "often lacked the most rudimentary conception of how to transmit their knowledge to others."[7] By 1979 the situation had not changed much. Everett Carll Ladd reports that a clear majority of the faculty has never published anything—book or article—and yet the profession has a norm or model that emphasizes research.[8] Ladd points out that "A model is ascendant in academe, positing what faculty *should be doing*, that is seriously out of touch with what they *actually want to do*. The model is as well profoundly at odds with the primary goal of promoting the best possible teaching—that is, the best educational experience—in the nation's colleges and universities."[9]

Scholarly competence and academic achievement were, and are, defined in terms of publication. "All but the most obtuse graduate students quickly realized that books and articles, rather than scintillating lectures, paved the road to advancement... promotions and raises had a closer relationship to the length of one's bibliography than to the quality of one's pedagogy."[10] Nonetheless, most academics do not think of themselves as "scholars" or "scientists" but as teachers and, while a great volume of printed work is produced, nearly three-fifths of all persons employed full time as university or college teachers have never published any book, written or edited by themselves or in collaboration with others.[11]

Thus, the problem of teaching—of good teaching—has been with us since the beginning. The problem has been exacerbated by increasing specialization in courses and research, by the publication pressures that have increased as the expansion of higher education has ended, by the production of more Ph.D.s than there are teaching positions, by the greatly increased number of students who are not adequately prepared for college work. These factors are forcing more attention to teaching, curriculum, and the structuring of programs. The graduate curriculum is being revised to train political scientists for jobs outside academia, in government or industry. This has led to a renewed interest in and emphasis on policy studies and to the development of useful skills in mathematics, statistics, computer programming, languages, and the like.

At the undergraduate level, it has led to a reevaluation of requirements and insistence upon broader and more structured undergraduate programs. Many colleges and universities have been going through such evaluations and the Harvard University study and report have stimulated others.

From its very inception, the American Political Science Association has been interested in improving teaching at all levels—precollegiate as well as collegiate.[12]

The first annual meeting of the association in 1904 had a section on "Instruction in Political Science" under the chairmanship of W. A. Schaper, University of Minnesota. Schaper reported at the second annual meeting in 1905 in a memorandum entitled "What Do Students Know About Government Before Taking College Courses in Political Science?"[13]

This interest has continued in committees, subcommittees, and task forces. Annual meetings have featured discussions about teaching; seminars and conferences have been held; scores of papers have been written. Foundation grants have made books and articles possible; at one time, a weekly educational radio program was sponsored. Most recent activities have been publication by APSA of the *NEWS* (formerly *DEA NEWS*), a quarterly newspaper for teachers, *SETUPS* (Supplementary

Empirical Teaching Units in Political Science); workshops on topics such as data analysis, personalized system of instruction, simulations, learning theories and strategies, case method, teaching constitutional law, judicial process, and constitutional methods. Instructional research monographs have been published, including *A Guide to Library Resources in Political Science, Simple Simulations, Using Computers,* and *U.S. Census Data for Political and Social Research.*

The association also has conducted for teachers a series of Seminars on Ethical Issues in Political Science. The seminars aimed at illustrating ways of dealing with ethical problems in the more descriptive and theoretical courses. A new series of seminars was offered in 1980. A full report on the educational programs in recent years can be found in the executive director's annual report in *PS.*[14]

The success of these activities provides ample evidence of genuine concern in the discipline for improving teaching at all levels. Committees representing various segments of the discipline have developed the programs and have served in advisory roles. An overall Committee on Educational Programs and Policy reviews the programs and reports to the APSA Council. The endorsement of these programs by the association members and officers has contributed to widespread interest in improving teaching.

All this should lead to more forthright recognition of teaching as a primary responsibility of the college teacher. Certainly, it has done so in a number of institutions; and more attention is being paid to teaching as one of the important criteria for pay increases and promotions.

RESEARCH

The Behavioral Revolution

By 1945, research by American political scientists had accomplished much. Their scholarship had generated more knowledge about the institutions and processes of government in their country and, to a lesser extent, in other parts of the world, than had ever been known before. This included the loci of power in society and the operations of that power in and on government; the organization of government; the cultural and psychological determinants of political behavior; electoral and legislative processes; decision-making; the character and types of political leadership; the variant relations of ideology to leadership; and so forth. They had learned more than would have been thought possible when the American Political Science Association was organized in 1903.

The increase in published works and in educational and professional activity was striking. Between the first publication of the *American Political Science Review* in 1906 and 1910, it contained only 14 advertisements for books (2.8 per year) and between 1911 and 1920 only 25 (2.5 per year). By the period 1941 through 1950, the number had grown to 230 (23.0 per year), by 1961 through 1970 to 1,456 (145.6) and by 1971 through 1979 to 2,016 (224). This very rough measure of the quantity of new work that publishers believe will interest political scientists indicates the great expansion within the profession.[15] With this expansion came a new self-consciousness by political scientists about their corporate identity, purposes, and organization. Out of the new self-consciousness and self-scrutiny grew what has been called the behavioral revolution.

Influenced by developments in the natural sciences, in mathematics and statistics, in the other social sciences, and perhaps even more by such students of science and the scientific method as Morris R. Cohen, more and more political scientists expressed dissatisfaction with the research work done in political science and with the results it produced. They criticized the formalism, the aridity, the legalism of much political science. They protested the lack of recognition by political scientists of the research of other disciplines, particularly psychology, sociology, anthropology, and psychiatry. They were unhappy about the bulging inventory of facts with no relation to theory, the extent that untenable assumptions and premises influenced and distorted findings, the failure to make better use of new developments in statistics, the amount of so-called political science that served no function but to bolster the value premises of the author, the lack of comparative data and of comparability of data collected. In brief, they accused the profession of dignifying sloppy, impressionistic, crudely empirical, and prejudiced research with the name of science.[16]

Dissatisfaction and criticism produced ferment that produced change. The change was based on the criticisms and on the call for new units of analysis, new methods, new techniques, and the development of systematic theory. A good example of this criticism in the early postwar period is *The Political System* by David Easton.[17] Easton's appeal for the development of theory is an effective restatement for political science of the plea for theory rather than crude empiricism by Cohen.[18] Easton's volume is a most effective criticism of the state of the discipline at that time. Easton, his fellow critics, and those whose work grew out of that criticism were labeled "behavioralists" and their approach was designated "political behavior."

The word "behavioral" describes a wide variety of people, propensities, and activities. A number of different, sometimes contradictory, sets of assumptions, methods, techniques, and data are identified with the political behavior movement. It includes political scientists with a special interest in or enthusiasm for psychology, cultural anthropology, sociology, structural functionalism, systems analysis, developing areas, comparative politics, voting behavior, survey research, epistemology, and the scientific method. Initially, the only definite requirement was desire for a change in how political science was conceived and practiced, a change in the direction of attempting to be more systematic and scientific.

Despite the variety of interests and talents among the carriers of the behavioral revolution, its salient characteristics can be identified: (1) at least initially, it rejected institutions as the basic units of analysis and sought to put in their place the behavior of individuals in political situations; (2) it emphasized the unity of the social sciences and used the name "behavioral sciences" to describe that unity; (3) it advocated much more precision, especially for observing, classifying, and measuring data; (4) it urged strongly the use of quantitative formulations wherever possible, specifically far greater use of the modern science of statistics; (5) it insisted on the separation of empirical from normative statements and, in many cases, left the impression or, in fewer cases, asserted that normative propositions have no place in political science; (6) in the early stages, at least, it tended to deprecate most past work, including the classics; (7) it defined the construction of systematic, empirical theory as the goal of political science; (8) it involved a high sense of professionalism based on the conviction, shared, to be sure, by many traditional scholars, that political science would and should be a scholarly enterprise characterized by skills, commitments, and findings that would distinguish it from the speculations and writings about politics by nonpolitical scientists, from gossip, from plain reporting.

Of course, not all the characteristics attributed to the political behavior movement were found in any one individual. The term "political behavior" was a sort of umbrella, capacious enough to shelter a heterogeneous group united by their dissatisfaction with various aspects of the discipline.

Although the political behavior movement reached full flower after 1945, it had a long history before then. Almost all of the behavioral criticisms made after 1946 had been voiced long before. Almost all types of work advocated by behavioralists had been done by some political scientists decades earlier, except work dependent on new techniques or new machines. Both proponents and critics of the behavioral tendency exaggerated the extent to which it broke with the past.

Among pioneer political scientists, Woodrow Wilson and James Bryce displayed protobehavioral tendencies by urging their colleagues to get out of the library and into the field.[19] J. W. Burgess[20] and A. Lawrence Lowell[21] asked for and produced better comparative literature. In 1908 Graham Wallas[22] complained of the misuse of psychology by political scientists and Arthur Bentley[23] urged students of politics to concentrate on the study of human behavior and on functional relations and group processes. However, the most influential behavioralist before 1945 was Charles Merriam, brilliant developer of the political science department at the University of Chicago. He argued that political science was paying inadequate attention to scientific work in social psychology, biology, sociology, ethnology, and statistics.[24] Merriam's most distinguished student, Harold Lasswell, was a leader among those who carried the behavioral torch into the period after 1945. Other leading political scientists in the postwar period who had been trained or influenced by Merriam were Leonard White, Quincy Wright, Harold Gosnell, Roscoe Martin, V. O. Key, Gabriel Almond, Avery Leiserson, Herman Pritchett, Robert Dahl, Herbert Simon, David Truman, David Easton, Ithiel de Sola Pool, and Alfred and Sebastian de Grazia. Besides Merriam himself, two members of the department he headed (Wright and White) and five of his students (Almond, Key, Lasswell, Pritchett, Truman) became presidents of the APSA.

During the time that most of those scholars were making their marks in the political science world, an enormous growth in college enrollments was beginning; political science departments expanded; an ever-increasing number of Ph.D. degrees were awarded; research money became more plentiful; the Social Science Research Council—founded by Merriam and directed by E. Pendleton Herring—brought funds and leadership. The resulting progress of the behavioral emphasis especially after 1945 was greater than anyone might have expected in the 1930s.

Behavioralism Regnant

Between 1945 and the mid-1950s, the term "political behavior" or "behavioralism" represented both an approach and a challenge, an orientation and a reform movement, a type of research and a rallying cry, "hurrah"-terms and "boo"-terms. Often, debate about behavioral techniques and methods was accompanied by vituperation; discussions aimed at vanquishing adversaries more often than clarifying issues. Advocates of the behavioral approach provided more promise than performance.

Nevertheless, behavioralism became the dominant, though certainly not the exclusive, orientation of political scientists very quickly after World War II. An institutional reflection of the speed with which the behavioral approach was assimilated into all major fields of the discipline is found in the programs of the annual meetings of the American Political Science Association. In 1956 the association recognized formally the interest of a substantial number of its members in behavioral studies by including in that program a series of panel discussions devoted to political behavior. By 1959, however, studies utilizing the behavioral approach had begun to appear in most traditional fields of research in politics and special panels on that subject were abandoned. The results of behavioral studies were reported and discussed in regular panels on political parties, legislation, international relations, public administration, and so on.

As it became absorbed into the mainstream of American political science, behavioralism exercised a determinative influence on the focus of the discipline. It had a large impact on the vocabulary of political science, the criteria of relevance, the canons of evidence, the training of graduate students, the character of work produced, and the standards of excellence in the discipline. The movement and its products came to enjoy a great deal of success during the postwar period. It generated excitement and respect for its accomplishments; its members have held a large number of offices in the American Political Science Association; scholarly journals have been filled with articles produced by those associated with it.

The behavioral movement gained control of the "commanding heights" of the American political science profession during those years, especially the leading offices of the American Political Science Association and its *Review*. However, it seems unlikely that its ranks ever have included a majority of American political scientists or even produced the bulk of the discipline's literature, if all appropriate professional media are taken into account. In any event, no definition of the movement exists that would permit such a determination to be made.

Many factors account for the rapid spread of the behavioral orientation in addition to its contributions of knowledge in the discipline. Among the most important are: (1) its deep roots in political science, dating at least to the turn of the century and involving some of the most distinguished scholars in the profession; (2) its tendency to move political science in the same direction as the other social sciences; (3) its identification with new tools such as survey research, computer analysis, and mathematical applications that have undoubted importance for any discipline involved in the study of mass aggregates; (4) its ability to generate funds and organizational support when they were needed most; (5) its association with many political scientists of high ability and productivity; (6) the receptivity of many distinguished traditional scholars to the new ideas and their willingness to give them an opportunity to develop; (7) the excitement generated among colleagues and graduate students by early behavioral studies; (8) the central relevance of behavioral concepts, methods, tools, goals, and results to the tasks of political science as perceived by a great majority of the profession.

Because the behavioralist broom swept so broadly and generally through American political science after 1945, specification of its impact is difficult and dangerous. Nevertheless, some areas of special importance deserve separate mention. Perhaps the most significant were those that applied advanced concepts and techniques from psychology, statistics, and mathematics.

Starting from the conviction that the individual in political situations is the proper focus of the discipline, many behavioral political scientists in the United States undertook research on politically relevant beliefs, values, and personality structures. They brought to an age-old interest in those matters the application of recently developed concepts, methods, and techniques. For instance, Freud's discovery of the method of free association and his development and refinement of in-depth interviewing had put new tools at the disposal of political scientists interested in politically relevant patterns of cognition and valuation.[25] The development of a modern science of statistics and its application to the problem of sampling large populations made possible the collection of accurate information about the attitudes of masses by investigating the subjectivities of a limited number through sample surveys. Emphasis on the subjective aspects of political life stimulated interest in questionnaire development, sampling techniques, scale construction, attitude measurement, tests of validity and reliability, and a host of other problems. The substantive consequences of this emphasis were an increased interest in the relations of politics to personality, in voting behavior, in political culture, and in political socialization.[26]

Behavioralists also harnessed psychology and statistics for use in electoral research. Especially after 1955, they churned out studies of the social, psychological, and institutional determinants and consequences of voting behavior. They did studies on the influence—if any—of such social factors as religion, age, economic class, family, race, ethnic background, and occupation on voting behavior.[27] They did motivational studies which attempted to analyze the psychological determinants of the influence of social factors on voting behavior by focusing attention on voter perceptions rather than on objective social affiliations. The behavioral approach also stimulated increased work on other types of election studies, including analyses of the causes and consequences of straight and split-ticket voting, interparty competition, party cohesiveness, and the development of election typologies.

The obvious value of mathematics and statistics in the study of such areas as political personality and electoral behavior led a number of American political scientists of behavioral persuasion to develop or acquire skills with those tools. A knowledge of statistics came to be regarded increasingly as a necessary, rather than only a desirable, asset for political scientists. Examinations in statistics took place alongside language examinations as requirements for a Ph.D. degree. About the same time, the modern computer appeared in the discipline. Political scientists learned computer programming and other skills to enable them to use such machines and methods. All this stimulated interest in and concern for a more adequate collection of quantifiable data. New data archives were established. The use of that equipment and data was extended to undergraduate teaching with the development of appropriate handbooks and manuals.

Behavioralists contributed importantly to the development of the area of comparative politics in the postwar period. Their interest flowed largely from their commitment to empirical theory and the corollary conviction that an empirical theory of politics must take into account the full range of varieties of political experience. The result was a veritable explosion of new literature in the comparative field that tended to emphasize the newer areas of investigation such as political socialization, political culture, leadership, and political development. Also, many scholars developed a new consciousness about the comparability of data. A vast literature of books, monographs, and articles has been produced, multiplying by many times the substantive knowledge of the varieties of politics.[28]

Political scientists in the behavioral movement, believing in the unity of the social sciences, borrowed concepts, approaches, techniques, and vocabulary from other social sciences. Not all these borrowings supported, or were even consistent with, other premises of the behavioral orientation, but in their enthusiasm for interdisciplinary collaboration, some did not seem to notice. Through such borrowing, structural-functionalism and general-systems theory entered the discipline. So did such concepts as modal personality, national culture, ideal types, cognitive dissonance, and others too numerous to mention. The borrowed concepts are still being sorted out; it is too early to say which are most useful to the study of politics.

Studies in all fields of political science showed the impact of the behavioral movement. The fields were as diverse as international politics, comparative government, the judicial process, public administration, the study of legislatures and legislation, and local government. A few examples are: the work of Herman Pritchett, Glendon Schubert, Alan Westin, and Jack Peltason on the courts and the judicial process; the massive generation of data and effective analysis of voting behavior at the Survey Research Center; the work on administrative behavior by Herbert Simon, James March, and Fred Riggs; the study of community power structure by Edward Banfield, Robert Dahl, and by Robert Agger and his coworkers; the work on comparative political cultures by Sidney Verba, Gabriel Almond, and Lucian Pye; the studies on developing nations by James Payne, Robert Ward, James S. Coleman, and Samuel Huntington; the effective research on political socialization and the psychological dimensions of political behavior; the publications in the field of parties, elections, and voting behavior by Samuel Eldersveld, Leon Epstein, Allen Sindler, Duane Lockard, Dwaine Marvick, Donald Stokes, Philip Converse, Warren Miller, and Austin Ranney; the work in international politics by Vernon Van Dyke, Ernest Haas, James Robinson, James Rosenau, Morton Kaplan, David Singer, Richard Snyder, and Karl Deutsch. To name a few is unfair, of course, to those who are omitted and to a great many who have made important contributions to more than one field.

Of course the development of American political science since 1945, led in large part by scholars of the behavioral persuasion, cannot be examined only in isolation. The problems, preoccupations, and technological and social developments of the society in which it exists have influenced it in crucial ways. As always, the impact of the environment was reflected in the political scholarship of the period. Certainly, the enormous expansion in the study of comparative politics was partly a consequence of increased ease and speed of transportation and communication, of the availability of Fulbright grants and foundation funds that, in turn, reflected the increased interest of the United States in other parts of the world. No doubt, the cold war stimulated the great expansion of the body of literature on the Soviet Union and communism. Finally, a much larger government provided greatly increased research funds (to produce knowledge to help it solve pressing problems of American society) to support work that could not have been done otherwise.[29]

Challenges to Behavioralism

In 1967 a leader of the movement declared that "behaviorism" had become "the new orthodoxy" of political science, "at least until some new generation of rebels comes along."[30] Two years later, another of its leaders announced in his presidential address to the American Political Science Association that the "developing behavioral orthodoxy" was being challenged already by "the post-behavioral revolution."[31] Of course, behavioralism had been criticized throughout its history, but by 1969 the critics had become more vigorous, better organized, and more vituperative. Also, some of them expressed new anti-intellectual attacks, radically different from those of the earlier periods.

The newer criticisms fall into three main classes: (1) criticism from within the movement, directed at alleged shortcomings in applying the scientific method; (2) intellectual criticism from outside, directed at both methodological and substantive matters; (3) activist criticism from outside, directed at its alleged conservative bias. All three of these categories deserve at least brief examination, as that will help to clarify the present intellectual status of the discipline.

Self-criticism. This category has two principal purposes, the first prompted by the scientific attitude that all scholarly work should be subjected to criticism. Scientific work must be reported and challenged for proof of reliability and validity. Only rigorous, critical testing and checking by the investigators themselves and their critics can ensure scientific impartiality and objectivity. This criticism rests on Karl Popper's proposition that scientific objectivity is "the product of the social or public character of the scientific method," not of the scientist's own impartiality.[32]

The second purpose of self-criticism serves the need for scientific communication among scholars in a field of study. Scientists must speak to one another continuously and in the same language, one determined by their scientific experience of public observations, experiments, and theories. To be public, replicable, and testable, work must be published and understandable in detail by colleagues, though not necessarily by the lay reader. Any consequent replication and testing, as reported in later communications, advances the field further in its continuous pursuit of knowledge and understanding.

As a result of that commitment to science, the best behavioralists are self-critical, criticize their colleagues' work freely, and accept criticism from others freely. However, they assume shared goals and approaches and agreement on the proper purposes and central focus of political science. Therefore, they deal mainly with questions of insufficient evidence, unwarranted generalization, improper use of statistics or mathematics, sloppy sampling techniques, unreliability, inadequate validation of scales and measurement instruments, and related matters. As with all other sciences and learned disciplines, such criticism serves as the basis for continuing revision, refinement, and progress.

Outside intellectual criticism. At every stage in the development of the behavioral movement it has met criticism from outside its ranks. Some has been moderate, some severe; some justified, some not. Among the most vigorous and persistent critics have been such scholars of established reputation as Leo Strauss, David Butler, Herbert Storing, Hans Morgenthau, Christian Bay, Sheldon Wolin, Bernard Crick, Henry Kariel, Robert Horowitz, and Walter Berns.[33]

The criticism has been wide-ranging and vigorous. Generally, the critics have focused on the following: that the behavioral approach has produced political science that is *parochial* because it ignores history, *shallow* because it rejects the classics, *imitative* because it follows slavishly often-mistaken notions of the work of other disciplines, *pretentious* because it uses unfamiliar polysyllabic words, *deceptive* because its precision is often spurious, *sterile* because it deals only with easily answered, trivial questions, *dull* because of its studied neutrality, *immoral* because it turns aside from normative questions, and *unreadable* because its statistics and mathematics require knowledge not possessed by most political scientists. Perhaps most telling is the accusation that the behavioral approach has not kept its promises, that it has not constructed an empirical political science or an empirical theory of political behavior, despite the expenditure of an incalculable amount of time, money, and energy.

Also, this category of critic attacks the assumption that the scientific study of politics is desirable, spells out limitations on the use of quantitative techniques and methods, deplores studies of voting behavior that ignore politics, asserts that behavioral political "science" is designed to manipulate and control people. They insist that the behavioralists transmute time- and space-bound findings into universal principles of politics and thereby enshrine the status quo in a permanent place in the political science heavens. They argue that behavioralist pluralism stands in the way of dealing with our pressing problems. They insist that democratic theory needs restructuring badly and that behavioral research pays little attention to the substantive goals that were so important to some of its early proponents and that are equally important today.

Finally, in spite of its substantive contributions, the behavioral approach has been accused, too often, of emphasizing method to the exclusion of all else. The behavioral approach is associated with many technical innovations, including survey methods, test instruments, statistical analysis, content analysis, small-group experiments, scaling techniques, mathematical models, and game theory. However, to equate them with the political behavior movement is to equate ends with means. The technical innovations followed new conceptions of political process and political system. They are tools, necessary for generating data and analyzing aspects of public authority and public life that had not been susceptible previously to systematic investigation.

Furthermore, the behavioral attention to technique has had salutary side effects. It has made many more political scientists conscious of their goals, procedures, and findings. Its interdisciplinary focus has awakened many political scientists to the existence of alternative approaches, orientations, goals, and methods open to those who study human affairs. It has stimulated wide dissemination of knowledge from other disciplines. Furthermore, the theoretical emphasis has led to a more concerted effort to discover uniformities and regularities. It may even have aided in reviving interest in the political classics.[34] All this has improved substantive studies of political life and public authority.

These intellectual critics of behavioralism do not represent any one political or philosophical viewpoint. Some are conservatives, some liberals, some radicals. Almost without exception, they have presented their criticism in reasoned arguments, participating in a rational dialogue, and they have had impact.

Outside activist criticism. In the 1960s and 1970s, a comprehensive new attack was launched against the entire political science profession in the United States and its basic norms, although the behavioral movement was its principal target. The attack coincided with the assault on many institutions of American society by tactics of direct action. A heterogeneous group, mostly associated with the radical politics of the so-called New Left carried it out. Some of the charges repeated those of the outside intellectual critics, though in a new key. No summary can do justice to the criticism, but the following essential accusations may provide a sense of the positions advanced:

1. Virtually all American political science has a conservative bias that grows out of accepting rather than combatting the corrupt, materialist, imperialist, racist, repressive, unjust American society. Because American political science aims at understanding, not changing, society and proceeds by description and analysis, not action, it has accepted a conservative ideology.
2. The norms and organization of the political science profession (and of other learned disciplines) impose the conservative bias through its definitions of excellence, standards of evidence, and system of rewards.
3. The behavioral persuasion is *especially* reprehensible because (a) it fosters undue concern for method and precision as compared to substance; (b) it advocates constructing a *science* of politics and maintaining a research posture of detachment; (c) its language and research procedures result in work that is abstracted from desperate human needs.
4. Political scientists have been inadequately concerned about the normative aspects of their work. They have ignored the pressing problems of the day and have been corrupted by relations with government and foundations.
5. Political scientists have accepted false gods of reason, objectivity, and freedom when (a) a rational response to misery is inhuman; (b) objectivity is neither possible nor desirable; (c) freedom for noxious ideas should not be permitted.

Several noteworthy aspects of this indictment distinguish it from earlier disagreements and debates in political science. The new criticisms are basically political, rather than turning on questions of intellectual assumptions, methods of inquiry, and the status of findings. Also, the older controversies assumed a shared purpose of studying politics with a view to increasing the understanding of political life. The new critics condemn political science for precisely that purpose—for making understanding rather than action the goal. They attack political scientists' political commitments and actions, rather than dealing with questions of scholarly inquiry. Finally, and most important, they are more radical because the reason, objectivity, and freedom they attack as false gods are the very foundation of the scholarly ethic. Since at least the eighteenth century, these values have been central in all learned disciplines. They have been accepted as essential to scholarship, science, and the pursuit of truth. Of course, they have been attacked before in our time. Nazis, Fascists, Communists, and assorted other tyrants have denounced reason as enfeebling, objectivity as a sham, and defined truth to serve their purposes of the moment. Various versions of revolutionary truth have been propounded, including Aryan truth, proletarian truth, and Fascist truth. However, those assaults originated outside the profession. The activist critique is the first political attack on the learned discipline to originate among its own members. That makes its threat to the very processes of national debate especially serious.

Fortunately, so far at least, the activists have attracted little support in the profession. Few political scientists agree that their colleagues are indifferent to human suffering or that passionate concern, unguided by reason, is a sure and exclusive route to human progress. The commitment by most American political scientists to rational inquiry resting on intellectual freedom and a large measure of objectivity remains unshaken. The replacement of reason by force as a basis for the discipline has not found broad acceptance in the profession and seems unlikely to do so.

American political science has changed greatly in its relatively short life as an academic discipline. It has come to accommodate a wide variety of approaches, methods, and orientations. It thrives on debate and controversy. It seems well aware that it could not survive the loss of reason, objectivity, and freedom.

Political Science and the Political World

There is the statesmanship of thought and there is the statesmanship of action . . . the man who has the time, the discrimination, and the sagacity to collect and comprehend the principal facts and the man who must act upon them must draw near to one another and feel that they are engaged in a common enterprise.

Woodrow Wilson—political scientist, college teacher, college president, president of the American Political Science Association, governor of New Jersey, president of the United States—spoke these words in his presidential address to the association in 1910, two years before he was elected president of the United States.

Throughout the existence of political science as an organized discipline, most political scientists have shared this view. In the history of the association, important persons from public life have played a significant part in its activities. Lord Bryce, as well as Wilson, was president of the association; so was Simeon Baldwin. President Harry Truman was a life member of the association and spoke more than once at a plenary session. Hubert Humphrey—college teacher, mayor of Minneapolis, United States senator, vice-president, and Democratic presidential candidate—was a lifelong member, frequent participant, and vice-president of the association.

Many political scientists have been active participants in politics, including running for public office. During 1978-1979, the national office of APSA did a survey of political scientists who have been elected to public office: a total of 97.[35] The list includes one president of the United States (Wilson); one vice-president (Humphrey); six United States senators (Harris, Humphrey, Thomas, Hatfield, Moynihan, and Tower); nine present and six former members of the House of Representatives; four governors, and many state legislators, city council members, and mayors.

In addition, many political scientists have been active in political campaigns, worked in the offices of senators and representatives, served in appointive positions in the national and state governments. Some notable examples include Henry Kissinger (secretary of state), Robert Wood (secretary of Housing and Urban Development), Daniel Patrick Moynihan (United Nations ambassador), John A. Perkins (undersecretary of Health, Education and Welfare), Harold Chase (deputy assistant secretary of Defense), Matthew Holden, Jr. (commissioner of the Federal Energy Regulatory Commission), Mark A. Siegel (White House—special assistant for public policy), Richard Cheney (chief of staff in President Ford's White House), David Adamy (director of finance—Wisconsin), Arthur Naftalin (director of administration—Minnesota), Zbigniew Brzezinski (White House—special assistant for national security), Jeane Kirkpatrick (United Nations ambassador).

Today, with more Ph.D.s being produced than there are college and university teaching positions, many political scientists, political science departments, and university administrators are concerned with modifying both undergraduate and graduate programs to train students more effectively for jobs in government, political parties, legislative bodies, city halls. In addition—apart from the lack of jobs—many colleges and universities have a genuine desire to develop programs that will meet public needs more adequately.

This desire is long standing. In 1940, at the APSA Annual Meeting in Chicago, Joseph P. Harris submitted a report of the Committee on Relations with Public Officials. The report contained nine recommendations, including that "political science departments should follow a deliberate policy of rendering public service to governments within their areas and conducting research studies of significant local governmental problems" and "that political science departments should seek in various ways to establish effective and cooperative relations with public officials."[36]

Political scientists and the association have followed those and other recommendations of the committee in the years since. Recent programs of the American Political Science Association have included, for example, the Congressional Fellowship Program (since 1953), which brings young political scientists to spend a year working for members of Congress—half the year for a senator or Senate committee, half the year for a member of the House of Representatives or a House committee; fellowships for young political scientists to work for a year with the Republican and Democratic national committees; and the State Legislative Service program that enabled young political scientists to work with state legislatures.

Also, the association has been called on by presidents of the United States to assist in special projects. President Truman, for example, asked the association to study soldier voting and make recommendations. The association did so and President Truman sent the report to the Congress asking for and getting passage of the legislation recommended.[37] President Kennedy asked the association to review the situation again in 1961 and, on the recommendation of Vice-President Humphrey, President Johnson asked for another review in 1966.

In the early 1940s, the association established a committee on Congress. After four years of study, the committee presented a comprehensive report in 1945. In part as a result of the work of the committee, Congress established a Joint Committee on the Organization of Congress. The chairman of the APSA committee, George B. Galloway, became staff director of the joint committee and all but one of the recommendations of the APSA committee were included in the joint committee report.[38] More recently, with a grant from the Carnegie Corporation, the APSA sponsored a "Study of Congress" that resulted in the financial support of research on Congress by individual scholars, the publication of a number of books and articles growing out of the research, and testimony by scholars before congressional committees on problems of congressional organization. The Carnegie-financed "Study of Congress" was directed by Ralph Huitt, University of Wisconsin, and Robert Peabody, Johns Hopkins University, and books produced by the project were published in a series by Little, Brown and Company.

In 1963 the association took the initiative to set up a commission to "review past experience, consider the implications of future radio and television debates between presidential candidates, and make recommendations regarding format and procedures for such debates if they are held." A report was issued in 1964.[39]

In 1946 the American Political Science Association created a Committee on Political Parties at its annual meeting in Cleveland. The committee centered its attention on the condition and improvement of *national* party organization. The committee issued a report in 1950 entitled "Toward a More Responsible Two Party System."[40] The report elicited much discussion in the public forum as well as in the profession.

Also, a great many political scientists go into university administration which takes them some distance into the political world. The national office of APSA did a survey of political scientists who have been or are college or university presidents or chancellors.[41] At least 70 political scientists have been in the past and another 61 are so at present. The list includes a number of distinguished political scientists; Woodrow Wilson and A. Lawrence Lowell are perhaps the best known.

Associational Activities

The American Political Science Association, founded in 1903, had a slow but steady growth from then until World War II. In the postwar period, the association participated in the phenomenal expansion that characterized the whole of higher education. The number of colleges and universities grew rapidly, enrollments skyrocketed, faculties expanded, the number of independent departments of political science tripled, membership in the APSA pushed upward rapidly. In 1950 there were 1,859 colleges and universities; in 1977, 3,130. In 1950 enrollments were 2,296,592; in 1982, 12,300,000. As late as 1960, there were only 466 political science departments; in 1979 there were 1,350. APSA membership was 5,126 in 1950, approximately 13,000 in 1979.[42]

The association is the major professional organization in the United States for those (both in the U.S. and in other countries) engaged in study, teaching, and research on politics and for persons engaged or interested in public affairs.[43] In addition, there are eight regional associations: Southern, Pacific Northwest, Midwest, Western, National Capitol Area, New England, Northeastern, Southwestern; and thirty state political science associations. Six regional associations publish journals and hold annual meetings; the state associations hold annual meetings and engage in some other activities, but most do not publish journals.[44]

The American association seeks to provide services to its members, including facilitation of research, teaching, and professional development. Association membership is composed primarily of political scientists doing research and teaching in colleges and universities, although a fourth of its members are employed elsewhere: government, journalism, business. As employment opportunities in higher education become more limited (as they have been the last few years and as they will continue to be through most of the 1980s), more political scientists will pursue careers outside academia, in government, research and consulting firms, and private business and industry. Association programs and publications have been modified gradually in anticipation of this development.[45]

For convenience, the association activities may be thought of in three main categories: publications, advancing the profession, and programs and services.

Publications. All members receive three periodical publications, the *American Political Science Review*, a scholarly quarterly containing research reports and book reviews; *PS*, a quarterly journal that contains articles on the profession and reports on association official activities: minutes of meetings, reports of the executive director, treasurer and association committees; *NEWS, for Teachers of Political Science*, a quarterly newspaper on teaching and learning materials.

The *Review* is the oldest, most substantial, and important of the periodicals. Also, it ranks far-and-away as the most prestigious journal in the discipline.[46] From its initial volume in 1906 until 1949, it had only three editors. W. W. Willoughby served until 1917, John H. Fairlie until 1925, and Frederic A. Ogg until 1949. Terms tended to be shorter thereafter. Ogg's successor, Taylor Cole, served four years and was followed by Hugh Elsbree for two and Harvey Mansfield for ten. Austin Ranney was editor from 1965 through 1970, Nelson Polsby from 1971 through 1977, Charles Jones from 1977 through 1981, and Dina A. Zinnes since then.[47]

In addition to these periodical publications, the association has published a number of monographs. These include: *Research Support for Political Scientists: A Guide to Sources of Funds for Research Fellowships, Grants and Contracts; Guide to Graduate Studies in Political Science; Careers and the Study of Political Science: A Guide for Undergraduates; Career Alternatives for Political Scientists: A Guide for Faculty and Graduate Students; A Directory of Black Americans in Political Science;* a series of instructional resource monographs and two series of supplementary empirical teaching units in political science.[48]

Advancing the profession. The association has a number of programs for professional development, protection of professional rights, representing professional interests, and collecting data and providing information to the profession. These include such programs as workshops and publications on career alternatives; the Congressional Fellowship Program—an internship program for academics, journalists, and federal officials; the Black Fellowship Program to support graduate education for blacks; a Committee on Professional Ethics and Academic Freedom to handle cases arising from college or university decisions on tenure and employment; representing the interests of political scientists with Congress, federal and state governments, and other scholarly organizations; collecting and publishing data and information on staffing, salaries, enrollments, and resources through an annual survey of departments; maintaining a roster of women, blacks, and Chicanos in political science.[49]

Programs and services to members. The association conducts an annual meeting for exchange of scholarly and professional information; an employment service, including a retired professors registry, a credential referral service, a personnel service—with a monthly newsletter listing positions available to political scientists, and an annual meeting placement service.

The annual meeting of the APSA is the principal regular political science conference in the United States. It has been held every year since 1903 and attracts an average of about 2,500 registrants, about one-third to one-half of whom participate on the official program of scholarly panels and round tables.[50] The papers presented on the program are published as the *Proceedings of the Annual Meetings* by Xerox University Microfilms. Also, some 100 book publishers and related firms exhibit their products at the meetings.

In the field of education, which has been a concern of the association throughout its history, the association has a range of publications, conferences, workshops, and seminars to assist college and high school faculties in course preparation and curriculum planning.

The association also undertakes special projects, usually with grant support, to create more resources for political science research. Currently, in cooperation with the American Historical Association, the APSA has developed *Project 87: An Interdisciplinary Study of the Constitution*. The project provides research fellowships and grants for studies of the Constitution.

For a complete review of APSA activities, including financial reports, see *PS*, summer and fall issues.

Structure. As the association grew in membership over the decades, its administrative structure changed correspondingly. The original 214 individual and institutional members of 1903 had little need for anything more than a president (elected annually), an executive council, a secretary-treasurer, and (after 1906) a managing editor for its *Review*. An assistant secretary-treasurer was added before World War II, but otherwise the structure remained the same until 1949. All of the offices were, of course, part-time responsibilities.

The structure was overhauled completely in 1949. The executive council was replaced by a six-member council (president, president-elect, executive director, chairman of the program committee, and two persons appointed by the president) and a sixteen-member executive committee. A permanent secretariat was established in Washington with a small staff headed by an executive director. The first two directors, Edward Litchfield (1950-1953) and John Gauge (1953-1954), served part-time. Evron M. Kirkpatrick (1954-1981) served full-time, as does Thomas E. Mann (1981-).[51]

Notes

1. Much of the material in the introduction to this chapter and in the sections on Intellectual Structure and Research was revised, adapted, and augmented by the editor from Evron M. Kirkpatrick, "The Impact of the Behavioral Approach on Traditional Political Science," in Austin Ranney, ed., *Essays on the Behavioral Study of Politics* (Urbana: University of Illinois Press, 1962), pp. 1-29 and "From Past to Present," in Donald M. Freeman, ed., *Foundation of Political Science: Research, Methods, and Scope* (New York: Free Press, 1977), pp. 3-41. The other sections were written for this volume, mainly by Kirkpatrick.

2. *PS* (American Political Science Association newsletter) (Fall 1979): 461.

3. These lists are published in the fall number of *PS* each year.

4. These data are drawn from "Political Science Faculty and Student Data," *PS* (Summer 1979): 334-36. Similar reports are published annually in *PS*. See them for more specific and detailed statistics.

5. Ibid.

6. For an account of what was being taught and where, see Anna Haddow, *Political Science in American Colleges and Universities 1636-1900* (New York: Appleton-Century, 1939);

the early period is covered in parts 1 and 2. Also, see the excellent study by Albert Somit and Joseph Tanenhaus, *The Development of American Political Science* (Boston: Allyn and Bacon, 1967); the above quotation is from pp. 10-11. Somit and Tanenhaus provide the best available account of the development of political science in America. Chapter 2, "Pre-History and Origins," has a brief section on American higher education before 1800.

7. Somit and Tanenhaus, *Development*, p. 39.

8. "The Work Experience of American College Professors: Some Data and an Argument" (Paper delivered at the Annual Conference of the American Association for Higher Education, Washington, D.C., April 16-19, 1979), p. 11.

9. Ibid., pp. 13-14.

10. Somit and Tanenhaus, *Development*, p. 39.

11. Ladd, "Work Experience," p. 2.

12. See the mimeographed study done by Cora Prifold, "A History of the American Political Science Association's Activities in the Field of Secondary Education in Government, 1904-1962" (Washington, D.C.: American Political Science Association, 1962).

13. Ibid.; see also *Proceedings of the American Political Science Association* 1 (1904): 31; 2 (1905): 207-8; 3 (1906): 28.

14. See the summer issues of *PS*. The most recent report is in *PS* 14, no. 3 (Summer 1981). See also the APSA brochure "Programs and Services for Members of the American Political Science Association."

15. Beginning with 1968, advertisements for books in *PS*, the association newsletter, are included. They number about one-seventh of the total for the relevant years.

16. See Kirkpatrick in Ranney, *Essays*, for a more extensive citation of relevant literature.

17. (New York: Alfred A. Knopf, 1953).

18. Morris R. Cohen, *Reason and Nature: An Essay on the Meaning of the Scientific Method* (New York: Harcourt, Brace & Co., 1931).

19. Woodrow Wilson, *An Old Master and Other Political Essays* (New York: Charles Scribner's Sons, 1893); James Bryce, *The American Commonwealth*, 2 vols. (New York: Macmillan Co., 1888).

20. *Political Science and Comparative Constitutional Law*, 2 vols. (Boston: Ginn and Co., 1891).

21. *Government and Parties in Continental Europe*, 2 vols. (Boston: Houghton Mifflin, 1896); *The Government of England*, 2 vols. (New York: Macmillan Co., 1908).

22. *Human Nature in Politics*, 2d ed. (London: Constable; Boston: Houghton Mifflin, 1915).

23. *The Process of Government* (reprint ed., Bloomington: Principia, 1949).

24. "The Present State of the Study of Politics," *American Political Science Review* (May 1921): 173-85; *New Aspects of Politics* (Chicago: University of Chicago Press, 1925).

25. See Robert E. Lane, *Political Ideology: Why the American Common Man Believes What He Does* (New York: Free Press, 1962); *Political Thinking and Political Consciousness: The Private Life of the Political Mind* (Chicago: Markham, 1969); Lucian Pye, *Politics, Personality, and Nation Building* (New Haven: Yale University Press, 1962); Harold D. Lasswell, *Psychopathology and Politics* (Chicago: University of Chicago Press, 1930); *Power and Personality* (New York: Norton, 1948); and Robert Rubenstein, *The Shaping and Sharing of Power in a Psychiatric Hospital* (New Haven: Yale University Press, 1966); *A Preview of Policy Sciences* (New York: American Elsevier, 1971).

26. See, for examples, Fred I. Greenstein, *Personality and Politics* (Chicago: Markham, 1969); Lasswell, *Power and Personality;* James C. Davies, *Human Nature in Politics: The Dynamics of Political Behavior* (New York: John Wiley & Sons, 1963).

27. See S. M. Lipset, "Political Sociology: 1945-1955," in W. Zetterbery, ed., *Sociology in the United States of America* (Paris: UNESCO, 1956); P. H. Rossi, "Four Landmarks in Voting Research," in E. Burdick and A. J. Brodbeck, eds., *American Voting Behavior* (Glencoe: Free Press, 1949); Heinz Eulau, *Recent Developments in the Behavioral Study of Politics* (Stanford: Stanford University, 1961).

28. See the bibliography in Carl J. Friedrich, *Man and His Government: An Empirical Theory of Politics* (New York: McGraw-Hill, 1963), and articles dealing with comparative politics in David L. Sills, ed., *International Encyclopedia of the Social Sciences*, 17 vols. (New York: Macmillan Co., 1968).

29. See Saad Z. Nagi and Ronald G. Corwin, eds., *The Social Contexts of Research* (New York: Wiley-Interscience, 1972).

30. Ithiel de Sola Pool, ed., *Contemporary Political Science: Toward Empirical Theory* (New York: McGraw-Hill, 1967), pp. vii-viii.

31. David Easton, "The New Revolution in Political Science," *American Political Science Review* (December 1969): 1051.

32. *Logic of Scientific Discovery* (London: Hutchinson, 1959); *The Poverty of Historicism* (New York: Harper & Row, 1964); *The Open Society and Its Enemies* (New York: Harper & Row, 1963); *Conjectures and Refutations: The Growth of Scientific Knowledge* (London: Routledge and Kegan Paul, 1962), esp. chaps. 16-20.

33. Hans J. Morgenthau, *Scientific Man vs. Power Politics* (Chicago: University of Chicago Press, 1946), and "Power as a Political Concept," in Roland Young, ed., *Approaches to the Study of Politics* (Evanston: Northwestern University Press, 1958), pp. 66-77; Bernard Crick, *The American Science of Politics* (Berkeley and Los Angeles: University of California Press, 1959); D. E. Butler, *The Study of Political Behaviour* (London: Hutchinson, 1959); Henry S. Kariel, *The Decline of American Pluralism* (Stanford: Stanford University Press, 1961); Herbert J. Storing, ed., *Essays on the Scientific Study of Man* (New York: Holt, 1962), esp. essays by Leo Strauss, Irving L. Horowitz, and Walter Berns; Christian Bay, "Politics and Pseudopolitics: A Critical Evaluation of Some Behavioral Literature," *American Political Science Review* (March 1965): 39-51 and "Behavioral Research and the Theory of Democracy," in Henry S. Kariel, ed., *Frontiers of Democratic Theory* (New York: Random House, 1970), pp. 327-51; Sheldon Wolin, "Political Theory as a Vocation," *American Polit-

ical Science Review (December 1969): 1062-82; Charles A. McCoy and John Playford, eds., *Apolitical Politics: A Critique of Behavioralism* (New York: Thomas Y. Crowell, 1958).

34. Pool, *Contemporary Political Science*.

35. For the list and pictures of some, see *PS* 12, no. 2 (Spring 1979): 217-23.

36. Joseph P. Harris et al., "The Relations of Political Scientists with Public Officials," *American Political Science Review* 35, no. 2 (April 1941): 339.

37. See *Voting in the Armed Forces*, Message from the President of the United States Transmitting the Report of the Special Committee on Service Voting, American Political Science Association, with Recommendations for the Enactment of Appropriate Legislation. House Document no. 407, 82d Cong., 2d sess., 29 March 1952 (Washington, D.C.: Government Printing Office, 1952).

38. See the *American Political Science Review* 40, no. 2 (April 1946): 340.

39. See *Report of the Commission on Presidential Campaign Debates of the American Political Science Association* (Washington, D.C.: American Political Science Association, 1964).

40. *American Political Science Review* 44, no. 3, pt. 2 (September 1950).

41. For details and pictures, see *PS* 11, no. 4 (Fall 1978) and 12, no. 1 (Winter 1979): 30.

42. For an estimate of the number and characteristics of political science faculty and students, see *PS* 12, no. 3 (Summer 1979): 334-36. For a study of the characteristics of political science departments, see *1978-1979 Survey of Departments* (Washington, D.C.: American Political Science Association, 1979).

43. Membership in the American Political Science Association is open to persons all over the world and, in fact, APSA has a large number of members in other countries. Lord Bryce not only was a member but was president of APSA. At the present time, Anthony King, University of Essex, is a member of the APSA council and administrative committee.

44. A list of the regional and state associations is in *PS* 12, no. 1 (Winter 1979): 31-35.

45. See Jack L. Walker's "Challenges for Professional Development for Political Science in the Next Decade and Beyond," *PS* 11, no. 4 (Fall 1978): 484-90; James P. McGregor, "Government Job Hunting in Washington," *PS* 11, no. 4 (Fall 1978): 492-98; William J. Siffin, "Portents and Prospects: Graduate Study and the Profession," *PS* 10, no. 1 (Winter 1977): 10-11; Robert S. Friedman, "Non-Academic Careers for Political Scientists," *PS* 10, no. 1 (Winter 1977): 14-15.

46. Albert Somit and Joseph Tanenhaus, *American Political Science* (New York: Atherton, 1964), pp. 89-98.

47. Somit and Tanenhaus, *Development*, pp. 94-97, 155-57, and recent *APSR* issues.

48. A complete list of publications is printed in *PS*. See *PS* 12, no. 1 (Winter 1979): 48-49 and 12, no. 3 (Summer 1979): 381-83.

49. For fuller description of these programs, see the Report of the Executive Director in *PS* each year, for instance, *PS* 12, no. 3 (Summer 1979): 340-69. The report includes information on the annual meeting, publications and information exchange, research and publication awards, political science education, professional equality, professional rights, governing the association, departmental services, professional placement, scholarly cooperation and liaison, governmental liaison, international political science, special projects, and membership services.

50. For detailed, specific statistics, see the annual meeting reports in *PS*. The annual meeting in 1979 had 185 scheduled events including APSA official committee meetings and functions and unaffiliated group activities. On the program were 127 official APSA panels and 1,350 individual participants. Annual meeting attendance was approximately 3,500.

51. Somit and Tanenhaus, *Development*, pp. 93, 150-52.

Bibliography*

In addition to the listings below, a number of publications of the American Political Science Association present information on the development of political science in the United States. They are advertised in the *American Political Science Review*.

Almond, Gabriel A., and Coleman, James S., eds. *The Politics of Developing Areas*. Princeton: Princeton University Press, 1960.

Bailey, Stephen K., and associates. *Research Frontiers in Politics and Government*. Washington: Brookings Institution, 1955.

Bay, Christian. "Politics and Pseudopolitics: A Critical Evaluation of Some Behavioral Literature." *American Political Science Review* (March 1965): 39-51.

Beard, Charles A. *An Economic Interpretation of the Constitution of the United States*. New York: Macmillan Co., 1913.

Beardsley, P. L. "Political Science: The Case of the Missing Paradigm." *Political Theory* 2, no. 1 (February 1974): 46-61.

Bentley, Arthur F. *The Process of Government*. 1949. Reprint. Bloomington: Principia, 1980.

Brams, Steven J. *Game Theory and Politics*. New York: Free Press, 1975.

Buchanan, William. *Understanding Political Variables*. 2d ed. New York: Charles Scribner's Sons, 1974.

Buehrig, Edward H., ed. *Essays in Political Science*. Bloomington: Indiana University Press, 1966.

Burgess, J. W. *Political Science and Comparative Constitutional Law*. 2 vols. Boston: Ginn and Co., 1891.

Butler, D. E. *The Study of Political Behaviour*. London: Hutchinson, 1959.

Charlesworth, James C., ed. *Contemporary Political Analysis*. New York: Free Press, 1967.

———. *A Design for Political Science: Scope, Objectives,*

---

*Compiled by the editor.

and Methods. Philadelphia: American Academy of Political and Social Science, 1966.

———. *The Limits of Behavioralism in Political Science*. Philadelphia: American Academy of Political and Social Science, 1967.

Clinton, R. L., ed. *Population and Politics: New Directions in Political Science Research*. Lexington, Mass.: Lexington Books, 1973.

Cochran, C. E. "Political Science and 'the Public Interest'." *Journal of Politics* 36, no. 2 (May 1974): 327-55.

Cohen, Morris R. *A Preface to Logic*. New York: Holt, 1944.

———. *Reason and Nature: An Essay on the Meaning of the Scientific Method*. New York: Harcourt, Brace & Co., 1931.

Crick, Bernard. *The American Science of Politics*. Berkeley and Los Angeles: University of California Press, 1959.

Dahl, Robert A. "The Behavioral Approach in Political Science: Epitaph for a Monument to a Successful Protest." *American Political Science Review* (December 1961): 763-72.

———. *Modern Political Analysis*. Englewood Cliffs, N.J.: Prentice-Hall, 1963.

———. *A Preface to Democratic Theory*. Chicago: University of Chicago Press, 1956.

Davies, James C. *Human Nature in Politics: The Dynamics of Political Behavior*. New York: John Wiley & Sons, 1963.

Deutsch, Karl W. *Nationalism and Social Communication*. Cambridge and New York: MIT Press and John Wiley & Sons, 1953.

Downs, Anthony. *An Economic Theory of Democracy*. New York: Harper & Row, 1957.

Easton, David. *A Framework for Political Analysis*. Englewood Cliffs, N.J.: Prentice-Hall, 1965.

———. "The New Revolution in Political Science." *American Political Science Review* (December 1969): 1051-61.

———. *The Political System*. 2d ed. New York: Alfred A. Knopf, 1971.

Eckstein, Harry, and Gurr, Ted Robert. *Patterns of Authority: A Structural Basis for Political Inquiry*. New York: John Wiley & Sons, 1975.

Edelman, Murray. *The Symbolic Uses of Politics*. Urbana: University of Illinois Press, 1964.

Elken, S. L. "Political Science and the Analysis of Public Policy." *Public Policy* 22, no. 3 (1974): 399-422.

Eulau, Heinz. *The Behavioral Persuasion in Politics*. New York: Random House, 1963.

———, and March, James G., eds. *Political Science*. Englewood Cliffs, N.J.: Prentice-Hall, 1969 (prepared for the Behavioral and Social Science Survey Committee of the National Academy of Sciences and the Social Science Research Council).

Freeman, Donald M., ed. *Foundation of Political Science: Research, Methods, and Scope*. New York: Free Press, 1977.

Friedman, Robert S. "Nonacademic Careers for Political Scientists." *PS* (Winter 1977): 14-15.

Friedrich, Carl Joachim. *Constitutional Government and Politics*. New York: Harper & Brothers, 1937.

———. *Man and His Government: An Empirical Theory of Politics*. New York: McGraw-Hill, 1963.

Fries, S. D. "*Staatstheorie* and the New American Science of Politics." *Journal of the History of Ideas* 34, no. 3 (July-September 1973): 391-404.

Gaus, John M.; White, Leonard D.; and Dimock, Marshall E. *Frontiers of Public Administration*. Chicago: University of Chicago Press, 1936.

Goals for Political Science. New York: Sloane, 1951.

Goodnow, Frank J. *Politics and Administration*. New York: Macmillan Co., 1900.

Greenstein, Fred I., and Lerner, Michael, eds. *A Source Book for the Study of Personality and Politics*. Chicago: Markham, 1971.

———, and Polsby, Nelson W., eds. *Handbook of Political Science*. 8 vols. Reading: Addison-Wesley, 1975.

Gunnell, John. "Social Science and Political Reality: The Problem of Explanation." *Social Research* (Spring 1968): 159-201.

Haas, Michael, and Kariel, Henry S., eds. *Approaches to the Study of Political Science*. Scranton, Pa.: Chandler, 1970.

Haddow, Anna. *Political Science in American Colleges and Universities, 1636-1900*. New York: Appleton-Century, 1939.

Harmon, Robert B. *Political Science: A Bibliographical Guide to the Literature*. New York: Scarecrow Press, 1965; supplement, 1968; supplement 2, 1972.

Holler, Frederick L. *The Information Sources of Political Science*. 5 vols. Santa Barbara: ABC-Clio, 1975.

Holt, Robert, and Turner, John E., eds. *The Methodology of Comparative Research*. New York: Free Press, 1970.

Horowitz, Irving Louis. *Foundations of Political Sociology*. New York: Harper & Row, 1972.

Howard, D. "A Politics in Search of the Political." *Theory and Society* (Amsterdam) 1, no. 3 (1974): 271-306.

Huntington, Samuel P. *Political Order in Changing Societies*. New Haven: Yale University Press, 1968.

Hyneman, Charles S. *The Study of Politics: The Present State of American Political Science*. Urbana: University of Illinois Press, 1959.

Irish, Marian D., ed. *Political Science: Advance of the Discipline*. Englewood Cliffs, N.J.: Prentice-Hall, 1968.

Jaros, Dean, and Grant, Lawrence V. *Political Behavior: Choices and Perspectives*. New York: St. Martin's Press, 1974.

Kariel, Henry S. "Disarming Political Science." *Polity* 5, no. 1 (1972): 3-18.

———. *Saving Appearances: The Reestablishment of Political Science*. North Scituate: Duxbury, 1972.

———, ed. *Frontiers of Democratic Theory*. New York: Random House, 1970.

Kenski, H. C., and Kenski, M. C. "Teaching Political Development at American Universities: A Survey." *Western Political Quarterly* 28, no. 3 (September 1975): 567-78.

Key, V. O. *Politics, Parties and Pressure Groups*. 5th ed. New York: Crowell, 1964.

Kirkpatrick, Samuel A. *Quantitative Analysis of Political Data*. Columbus: Merrill, 1974.

Kort, F. "The Multiple Dilemma of Political Science." *Modern Age* 16, no. 1 (1972): 15-24.

Landau, Martin. *Political Science and Political Theory*. New York: Macmillan Co., 1972.

Lane, Robert E. *Political Thinking and Political Consciousness: The Private Life of the Political Mind*. Chicago: Markham, 1969.

Lasswell, Harold D. *The Future of Political Science*. Chicago: Atherton, 1963.

―――. *Politics: Who Gets What, When, How*. New York: McGraw-Hill, 1936.

―――. *Power and Personality*. New York: W. W. Norton, 1948.

―――. *Psychopathology and Politics*. Chicago: University of Chicago Press, 1930.

―――. and Kaplan, Abraham. *Power and Society*. New Haven: Yale University Press, 1950.

Latham, Earl. "The Group Basis of Politics: Notes for a Theory." *American Political Science Review* (June 1952): 376-97.

Lazarsfeld, Paul F.; Berelson, Bernard; and Gaudet, Hazel. *The People's Choice: How the Voter Makes Up His Mind in a Presidential Campaign*. 3d ed. New York: Columbia University Press, 1968.

Lerner, Daniel, and Lasswell, Harold D., eds. *The Policy Sciences: Recent Developments in Scope and Methods*. Stanford: Stanford University Press, 1951.

Lipset, Seymour Martin. *Political Man: The Social Bases of Politics*. Garden City: Doubleday, 1960.

―――, ed. *Politics and the Social Sciences*. New York: Oxford University Press, 1969.

McCoy, Charles A., and Playford, John, eds. *Apolitical Politics: A Critique of Behavioralism*. New York: Thomas Y. Crowell, 1967.

McGregor, James P. "Government Job Hunting in Washington." *PS* (Fall 1978): 492-98.

Macridis, Roy C. *The Study of Comparative Government*. Garden City: Doubleday, 1955.

Melanson, Phillip H. *Political Science and Political Knowledge*. Washington, D.C.: Public Affairs, 1975.

Merkl, Peter H. "Where Is American Political Science Going?" (in German). *Zeitschrift zur Politik* 24, no. 2 (June 1977): 163-94.

Merriam, Charles E. *New Aspects of Politics*. Chicago: University of Chicago Press, 1925.

―――. "The Present State of the Study of Politics." *American Political Science Review* (May 1921): 173-85.

Mills, Walter Thomas. *The Science of Politics*. New York: Funk & Wagnalls, 1887.

Mitchell, William C. *Sociological Analysis and Politics*. Englewood Cliffs, N.J.: Prentice-Hall, 1967.

Morgenthau, Hans J. *Politics among Nations*. 4th ed. New York: Alfred A. Knopf, 1967.

Murphy, Robert E. *The Style and Study of Political Science*. Glenview: Scott, Foresman, 1970.

Newman, A. S.; Baer, M. A.; and Patterson, J. W. "Political Scientists: What Do They Know about Politics?" *American Political Quarterly* 3, no. 2 (April 1975): 189-200.

O'Brien, D. C. "Modernization, Order, and the Erosion of a Democratic Ideal: American Political Science 1960-1970." *Journal of Developmental Studies* 8, no. 4 (July 1972): 351-78.

Pennock, J. Roland. "Political Science and Political Philosophy." *American Political Science Review* (December 1951): 1081-85.

Pool, Ithiel de Sola, ed. *Contemporary Political Science: Toward Empirical Theory*. New York: McGraw-Hill, 1967.

Popper, Karl. *The Logic of Scientific Discovery*. New York: John Wiley & Sons, 1961.

―――. *The Open Society and Its Enemies*. New York: Harper & Row, 1963.

―――. *The Poverty of Historicism*. New York: Harper & Row, 1969.

Prifold, Cora E. "A History of the American Political Science Association's Activities in the Field of Secondary Education in Government, 1904-1962." Mimeographed. Washington, D.C.: American Political Science Association, 1962.

Pye, Lucian W., and Verba, Sidney, eds. *Political Culture and Political Development*. Princeton: Princeton University Press, 1965.

Ranney, Austin, ed. *Essays on the Behavioral Study of Politics*. Urbana: University of Illinois Press, 1962.

Reid, H. "Contemporary American Political Science in the Crisis of Industrial Society." *Midwest Journal of Political Science* 16, no. 3 (August 1972): 339-66.

Reid, H. G., and Yanarella, E. J. "Political Science and the Post-Modern Critique of Scientism and Domination." *Review of Politics* 37, no. 3 (July 1975): 286-316.

Rice, Stuart A. *Quantitative Methods in Politics*. New York: Alfred A. Knopf, 1928.

Riker, William H. *The Theory of Political Coalitions*. New Haven: Yale University Press, 1962.

Rogow, Arnold A. *Politics, Personality and Twentieth-Century Political Science*. Chicago: University of Chicago Press, 1969.

Rosen, Paul L. "Science, Power, and the Degradation of American Political Science." *Polity* 9, no. 4 (1977): 463-80.

Schwartz, D. C. "Toward a More Relevant and Rigorous Political Science." *Journal of Politics* 36, no. 1 (February 1974): 103-37.

Siffin, William J. "Portents and Prospects: Graduate Study and the Profession." *PS* (Winter 1977): 10-11.

Sills, David L., ed. *International Encyclopedia of the Social Sciences*. 17 vols. New York: Macmillan Co. and Free Press, 1968.

Simon, Herbert A. *Administrative Behavior*. New York: Macmillan Co., 1947.

Smith, Barbara Leigh; Johnson, Karl F.; Paulsen, David Warren; and Shocket, Frances. *Political Research: Methods, Foundations, and Techniques.* Boston: Houghton Mifflin, 1976.

Smith, David G. "Political Science and Political Theory." *American Political Science Review* (September 1957): 734-46.

Smith, Edward Munroe. "The Domain of Political Science." *Political Science Quarterly* 1, no. 1 (1886): 1-8.

Somit, Albert. *Political Science and the Study of the Future.* Hinsdale: Dryden, 1974.

———, and Tanenhaus, Joseph. *American Political Science: A Profile of a Discipline.* New York: Atherton, 1964.

———, and Tanenhaus, Joseph. *The Development of American Political Science: From Burgess to Behavioralism.* Boston: Allyn & Bacon, 1967.

Sorauf, Frank J. *Perspectives on Political Science.* Columbus: Merrill, 1966.

Spragens, T. A., Jr. *The Dilemma of Contemporary Political Theory; Toward a Postbehavioral Science of Politics.* New York: Dunellen, 1973.

Storing, Herbert J., ed. *Essays on the Scientific Study of Politics.* New York: Holt, Rinehart & Winston, 1962.

Stretton, Hugh. *The Political Sciences: General Principles of Selection in Social Science and History.* New York: Basic Books, 1969.

Tinker, I. "Non-academic Professional Political Scientists." *American Behavioral Scientist* 15, no. 2 (November-December 1971): 206-12.

Truman, David B. "Disillusion and Regeneration: The Question for a Discipline." *American Political Science Review* (December 1965): 865-73.

———. *The Governmental Process.* New York: Alfred A. Knopf, 1951.

Tufte, Edward R. *Data Analysis for Politics and Policy.* Englewood Cliffs, N.J.: Prentice-Hall, 1974.

Tullock, Gordon. *Toward a Mathematics of Politics.* Ann Arbor: University of Michigan Press, 1967.

Van Dyke, Vernon. *Political Science: A Philosophical Analysis.* Stanford: Stanford University Press, 1960.

———. *Teaching Political Science: The Professor and the Polity.* Atlantic Highlands: Humanities Press, 1977.

Voegelin, Eric. *The New Science of Politics.* Chicago: University of Chicago Press, 1952.

Waldo, Dwight. *The Administrative State.* New York: Ronald, 1948.

Walker, Jack L. "Challenges for Professional Development for Political Science in the Next Decade and Beyond." *PS* (Fall 1978): 484-90.

Walter, Oliver, ed. *Political Scientists at Work.* Belmont: Duxbury, 1971.

Wasby, Stephen L. *Political Science: The Discipline and Its Dimensions.* New York: Charles Scribner's Sons, 1970.

Wilson, Woodrow. *Congressional Government: A Study in American Politics.* Boston: Houghton Mifflin, 1885.

———. "The Study of Administration." *Political Science Quarterly* (June 1887): 197-222.

Wolfe, Alan, and Surkin, Marvin, eds. *An End to Political Science: The Caucus Papers.* New York: Basic Books, 1970.

Wright, Quincy. *The Study of International Relations.* New York: Appleton-Century-Crofts, 1955.

Young, Oran. *Systems of Political Science.* Englewood Cliffs, N.J.: Prentice-Hall, 1968.

Young, Roland, ed. *Approaches to the Study of Politics.* Evanston: Northwestern University Press, 1958.

30

YUGOSLAVIA

ADOLF BIBIČ

Introduction

If political science is to be taken as a special branch of social science studied at the university level and at that level systematically investigating political phenomena, then it has to be admitted that political science in Yugoslavia has no long tradition. Only after World War II were courses in political science offered at our universities.

In itself, this does not mean that in this country there had not previously been contributions to political thought and political science. Progressive movements, the principal factor of growing national and social consciousness and emancipation, led to original political analyses. Among the precursors of contemporary political science were primarily the exponents of socialist thought, which, since the second half of the nineteenth century, had been more and more active in the social and political life of nations and nationalities which, in 1918, were united by the course of history in one common state.

In old Yugoslavia (1918–1941), however, political science did not become established as a discipline of higher learning. Academic pursuits, in particular in the sphere of social sciences, were all rather traditionally oriented. Political knowledge was conveyed, as a rule, by generally normatively oriented sciences of state and public law; this was, it may be added, a characteristic of most of the countries in the more highly developed part of Europe, to which the Yugoslav state was very strongly subordinated, not only economically but also intellectually. The more progressive impulses, which in the 1930s started to penetrate our universities, as well as the first elements of the sociological views of political development, were not capable of changing this basic picture at that time.[1]

The national liberation war against Fascism (1941–1945), which at the same time meant a socialist revolution, was creating conditions for an indigenous development of social science disciplines and, thus, of political science.

However, political science was acquiring more realistic chances to establish itself as an academic discipline only on the basis of the social and political transformation taking place in the new socialist society. The decisive factor in this direction was—after the conflict with Stalin—the clear-cut determination of all the leading socialist forces (1950) for the concept of self-management, which, during the subsequent thirty years, exercised a decisive influence on the democratization of social and political life and created for the social sciences an ever bigger field for free development and an active role in the society. The position of social sciences was decisively influenced also by the role performed by Yugoslavia in international relations, by its independent way expressed both in the nonalignment movement and in the solidarity with progressive movements all over the world.

Such a development of domestic policy and such an international role of Yugoslavia were, among other factors, related to the need that political relations both at home and elsewhere in the world be systematically and continuously studied and that the insights about the nature, forms, and role of politics be presented in an organized manner at the academic level.

The idea that political science should be constituted as an integral part of scientific pursuits in our country was affirmed in the Program of the League of Communists of Yugoslavia (1958) where the need for the development of political sciences is explicitly urged.[2] In the same year the Institute of Social Sciences was founded in Belgrade; the institute had a special section for legal and political science. With organized postgraduate courses in political science and with the beginning of empirical research on political relations, it gave—in addition to some other initiatives at some law schools—the first pioneering impulse to the development of political science in Yugoslavia.[3] In the beginning of the 1960s this impulse was followed by a definitive institutionalization of political science at the university level: in the years 1960–1961 there were founded the Higher Schools of Political Sciences in Belgrade, Ljubljana, and Sarajevo, and the Faculty of Political Sciences in Zagreb (1962). At these schools, which, in due course, were transformed into faculties within the university (this being the status of Zagreb Faculty of Political Science from the beginning), political science, more or less closely bound up with other social science disciplines, became the object of a self-contained study, and inquiry into political relations a systematic and continuous task.

Political science, institutionalized in this way, not infrequently significantly enriched by the political-theoretical thought of social practice, has during the last two decades attempted to give a more precise outline of the nature of the discipline, and to delineate its basic articulation. On the basis of insights gained in this way, interacting with world political science, it started to develop the profile of politological study and research.

The Concept of Politics and of Political Science

WHAT IS POLITICS?

Witnessing throughout the world lively discussions about politics as the subject of political science, we should not be surprised that for more than two decades highly intensive discussions about this topic have been going on in Yugoslavia. From the very start, the initiatives for establishing the new discipline had to cope with at least two obstacles. First, with reference to the established academic disciplines, especially in the sphere of law, it was necessary to make explicit what constitutes the specific subject of this new aspirant to academic status. Second, it was imperative to provide an answer to the question of what constitutes the need for political science in a society which proclaims that the state "is withering away" and which relates socialism with self-management.

The line of demarcation as regards the established legal disciplines (and this line was from the very beginning advocated by those in favor of political science) was not hard to mark. On the one hand, even inside the legal disciplines themselves some keen supporters of the emerging discipline were appearing.[4] They were weakening the traditional normativism in jurisprudence and advocating the need for political science—arguing chiefly that modern, empirical research methods should be introduced into the study of political institutions. On the other hand, it was becoming increasingly obvious that the legal sciences, focusing on the state and the public law, may deal in part with political problems but do not treat them exhaustively.

With a few exceptions outside the discussions about the subject of the new discipline, the discussions about the essence of politics have produced an almost unanimous opinion that politics cannot be identified with the state or political science with the theory of the state.[5] Politics is, it was argued, in some respects, narrower than the state, while, on the other hand, it is a concept broader than the state.

In spite of its critical attitude toward identifying politics with the state, political science in Yugoslavia has never denied, and also today does not deny, that the study of the state constitutes one of the most important elements of political science. Gradually, but not without critical remarks,[6] there emerged in Yugoslav political science a view of politics which stresses the difference between politics in the narrower and politics in the broader sense of the term.[7] By politics in the narrower sense, allowing for some oversimplification, we generally refer to that social activity which comprises the activity carried on by the state,[8] the influence exercised by social factors on the state and the influence exercised by the state in guiding society. On the other hand, politics in the broader sense of the term, allowing for certain nuances, is understood to comprise in addition to the activity carried on by the state and the dialectic between the state and the society (hence, in addition to politics in the narrower sense) also any management of the society or of its parts and the adjusting of parts with the society as a whole.[9]

With such an articulation of politics as the subject of political science there emerged a roughly formulated answer to the second question, specifically: does not the orientation toward socialist self-management and in this sense also toward the withering away of the state mean that the specific subject of political science, politics itself, is withering away?

In discussions about the essence of politics and about the subject of political science views also arose claiming that since politics is an expression of the class society it represents in socialist society but a residue of the past and is withering away or rather should wither away just like the other categories of the class society. Politics as social reality and as a term was claimed to become, in due course, completely replaced by the socialist self-management.[10] Such a narrowing down of politics, however, is not a typical answer to be found in contemporary Yugoslav politology. Most of the authors discussing this problem believe—while making a distinction between politics in the narrower and in the broader sense—that self-management and politics are not mutually exclusive.[11] Some take an extreme point of view, claiming that all self-management relations are political relations.[12] Others attempt to distinguish between those self-management relations which can be qualified as political and those which do not have a political character.[13] Understandably, this has its consequences for the conception of the scope and content of the subject of political science.

Although discussions about politics and about the subject of political science cannot be regarded as completed, it should be pointed out that the result obtained in the discussions held so far is clear: in contemporary Yugoslavia, political science has not only established for itself the right to existence but is also—in the opinion of Jovan Djordjević, one of its outstanding protagonists—in a sense becoming the central social science.[14]

POLITICAL SCIENCE, POLITICAL PHILOSOPHY, POLITICAL SOCIOLOGY

A definition of the subject of political science cannot bypass the question of what is the relation between political science and political sociology and the relation between political science and political philosophy. Even if these questions have not been the objects of broader discussions in Yugoslavia, they have nevertheless been, in various periods, actively present in defining the status of political science.

Political Science and Political Philosophy. In discussions about the essence of politics and of political science the philosophical problems of political science have been treated from various angles. Here it may be suitable to mention discussions about the problem of evaluation in political science,[15] or discussions about the relation between philosophy and politics[16] or between ethics and politics.[17] Our interest, however, centers on viewpoints concerning the question of the existence and the nature of political philosophy. Although there are not many authors who have explicitly formulated views on this question, there are also in our country a few writers strongly in favor of political philosophy as a separate discipline or at least strongly emphasizing the philosophical aspects of political activities and of political science.[18] Even if these views are at times divergent, they share the common characteristic in that they see in political philosophy (in contradistinction to political science) a normative value theory or at least they emphasize strongly the teleological elements. In particular some writers, with reference to the European movement for the renewal of political philosophy, attempt to give a detailed definition of the subject, state the tasks of this practical philosophical discipline,[19] and demarcate it from modern political science. Following Aristotle's conception of politics and thus defining politics as "rational action in the community"[20] they take a sharply defined stand against the modern conception of politics as technique, as the struggle for power. In terms of their vision of the world as an "association of self-managing communities"[21] they plead for a renewal of the philosophy of politics which would put into the foreground purposeful political action in the service of higher ethical goals: freedom, happiness, human dignity. It is almost unnecessary to stress that such a view of the tasks of political philosophy is rather critical of the prevailing empirical-descriptive political science, even if it does not negate its results.[22] Other writers, on the other hand, put more emphasis on the relation between political philosophy and political science, claiming even that "the science of politics in a broader sense includes also political philosophy."[23]

Political Science and Political Sociology. The sociological view of politics is essential in establishing modern political science. But does such a view render the establishing of a separate discipline—political sociology—impossible? In case of a positive answer there comes the question of the nature of such a discipline and of its demarcation as regards political science. Discussions about the subject of political sociology appeared almost simultaneously with the first major discussions about the subject of political science,[24] while new attempts to clear this question were made in some more recent works dealing with politico-sociological problems or bearing such titles as "Political Sociology."[25] One of the most recent sources says: "The subject of political sociology should be the study of interaction between social and political problems. Basically, these are: the conditions and causes in which arise and operate political phenomena; social functions of the dominant political relations—are they in the service of the reproduction of the existing social relations or are they constructing new ones on the ruins of the old ones; the social perspectives of politics—the withering away and the socializing of its functions."[26] When another writer in his most recent book finds that "in our opinion political sociology deals with the complex analysis of the interactions between various social subjects and the apparatus of public government"[27] and emphasizes that, especially in Marxian politology, there can be no sharp distinction between political sociology and political science, he defines the difference between the two as follows: "In a slightly simplified sense, the difference lies in that political sociology takes its start from society and its structure and studies the influence that society exercises on the development and results of the political process, whereas political science takes its start from the political sphere and studies its internal dynamics and its influences on society."[28]

DIFFERENTIATION AND INTEGRATION OF POLITICAL SCIENCE

Statements such as those quoted in the preceding paragraphs about the demarcation between political science and political philosophy and political sociology, respectively, are evidence that the field of politology is becoming increasingly differentiated in Yugoslavia. For, just as from one particular angle, political philosophy and political sociology may be regarded as subjects belonging to another social discipline, so from another angle—as it has been argued—they are in fact part of the broader complex of political science. In this way, the internal articulation of political science becomes enriched with related disciplines. This poses the question of the relation of political science to related branches of inquiry, and at the same time brings forward the question of integration within political science itself.

It is evident that a conception of political science that would be founded merely on special disciplines, even if these would occasionally deal with some global aspects of politics, would find itself in an impasse of one-sided reductionism, unless it had an adequate complement in political science as a general, integral, politological discipline. In recent years, a number of Yugoslav politologists have been pointing out the need to establish a discipline which would comprise sociological, sociological-philosophical, and historical-dynamic approaches.[29] Such an integral, synthesizing science of politics studying political forms, political activities, and opening new possibilities for direct management of society creates, in social and political affairs—in conjunction with the existing special politological disciplines—a crystalizing nucleus around which it will only be possible for political science to become "definitively" established as an independent discipline of modern social sciences.

POLITICAL SCIENCE AND MARXISM

The fact that in past decades Yugoslav political science has constantly concerned itself, among other things, with discussions about Marxism in relation to political science is not surprising when one takes into account that the great majority of the Yugoslav politologists, in establishing the grounds for political science, use Marxism as their cardinal point of reference and when one understands how these issues were treated in the past and in part continue to be treated at present in the worldwide politological arena.[30] The founding fathers of Yugoslav political science had to examine critically both the thesis which purely and simply reduces Marxism to an ideology and the thesis which regards Marxism as economic determinism. In both cases, in fact, political science would be deprived of its legitimate raison d'être: in the first case because both Marxism and political science are reduced to a pragmatic-instrumental level, and, in the second, because one-track, rigid economic determinism subordinates politics completely to the laws of a different sphere, specifically the economic. In the critical examination of the dogmatism and pragmatism of socialist practice and in the critical examination of the positivistic conception of the relation between ideology and science in Yugoslav political science, views have been formed about the relation between Marxism and political science, chiefly from the aspect of basic contributions of Marx and later Marxists to the scientific understanding and changing of politics. From the opinions propounded, and they do differ on individual points,[31] it might be appropriate to mention a few issues that have essentially influenced or continue to influence the very conception of political science in Yugoslavia.

First, in the criticism of tendencies which have attempted or continue to attempt to isolate Marxism as a cultural-historical phenomenon and as theory, Yugoslav political science has made a fairly intensive study of the historical sources of Marxism and, by extension, of political science founded on Marxism. A number of studies have been carried out and published subsequently, studies dealing with the problems of the relation between Hegel's philosophy and Marx's political theory.[32] These studies have disclosed how deeply Marx's and Marxian thought is conditioned by the European philosophical tradition as well as what is its critical relation to that tradition. This fact is particularly obvious in Marx's distinction between (civil) society and the (political) state as well as in his unveiling of the dialectical connections between the two. For the establishing and purposeful guiding of political science this has provided a significant insight: specifically, that between the social forces of the society (classes, etc.) and the state, or rather the political system, there does not exist a relation of identity only but also of differences—and this was in view of some traditional one-sided identification, extremely stimulating for establishing and developing political science.

Second, an "archeological excavation" of the classic Marxian thesis about the withering away of the state has occurred. On this point, Yugoslav political science and political thought dissociated themselves from the *étatist* interpretation of politics and state. The rehabilitation of the theory of the withering away of the state was pivotal for the fundamental orientation not only of political practice but also of political science in our country. This has entailed a number of consequences for the conception of the fundamental categories of political science, the political system, and especially of the political system of socialism.

Third, such a distinction between the state and society, as well as the thesis about the withering away of the state, have brought into focus the problems of distinguishing between socialization and nationalization, between socially owned and state-owned property; also, they have revived and sharpened the contradictions between Man and citizen in contemporary politics, including politics in postrevolution societies.

Fourth, related to this was the emergence of bureaucratism and the subsequent criticism of bureaucratism as well as the problem of political alienation in general and of political alienation in socialism in particular.

Fifth, parallel to the criticism of the "political state" and political alienation, stimulated through the need for further development of socialism, emphasis was focused on that central constituent element of Marxism which Marx and after him many other Marxists called a free association of producers. This idea was the central stimulation for advancing self-management as a law underlying society in the transitional period, and all this has served to revitalize the socialism-democracy issue.

Sixth, such a conception of the Marxian contribution helped Yugoslav political science to discover in Marxism great significance not only for new social content but also for new political forms of socialism. This in turn was highly stimulating for the development of political science entitled not just to provide convincing arguments for current policy but also to help to develop elements of politics and the political system which would ensure a maximum of interrelation between personal initiative and common interest.

Such a conception of the relation between Marxism, politics, and the state was, we believe, highly favorable for establishing and developing political science in Yugoslavia. In the process of becoming established, political science was from such points of departure in a better position to dissociate itself from the absolutist principles of the traditional theory of the state. As regards the one-sided economistic reductions, the emerging political science was becoming more sensitive to the increasingly complex dialectic of relations between political and social life; in the focus of its attention the contradictions of interests started to enter, as they did also in the political system of the transitional period. In such an orientation political science was developing—as can be understood readily—not only on the basis of a specific understanding of the relation between Marxism and politics but also through searching for a way of developing a specific political system of socialist self-management in our country and through forming a vision of the new needs for a gradual democratization of contemporary international relations. At the same time, the development of political science in our country was influenced significantly by contemporary world politology, to which political science in Yugoslavia has been from the very beginning (critically) open.

Major Foci of Attention

Although Yugoslav political science is articulated in fields which are becoming increasingly numerous it is possible to identify several central common accents in them.

Here four of such major foci of attention are briefly outlined: (1) interests and politics, (2) class dimension and the national dimension of politics, (3) monism and pluralism, and (4) socialism, self-management, democracy. These aspects are closely interrelated and they will be dealt with separately here only for analytical purposes.

INTERESTS AND POLITICS

In their theoretical discussions of politics, political science, and the political system, Yugoslav politologists have been paying and continue to pay particularly great attention to the relation between interests and politics.[33] If there is one constant tendency in political science in our country, it is the increasingly explicit recognition of the significance of interests in both political theory and political practice. The most significant contribution to this was undoubtedly made by the self-management orientation, which is based on the assumption that the political system of socialism should allow as much space as possible to *direct* articulation and aggregation of interests; this specific orientation of interests, it should be added, has also been influenced and continues to be influenced by the general standpoints of political science in Yugoslavia, discussed earlier. Particularly the insight that political reality, including the politics of the socialist community, contains essential contradictions necessarily focused the attention of social thought and also of young politology on the problems of contradictions arising in socialism. The recognition of contradictions is thus the first stage in recognizing the problems of varying interests as far as the political science of a socialist country is concerned.[34] The point at issue is not simply that the contradictions between the elements of the past and the elements of socialism in a society of a transitional period were given emphasis; Yugoslav politology and social thought have been paying increasing attention to the contradictions *inside* the socialist society itself. In this sense, analyses have been made of, for example, the contradictions stemming from social property,[35] the contradictions due to different kinds and different character of work, the contradictions entailed by the application of the rule of remuneration according to the work performed, the contradictions between the state and self-management, between the working class and other working people and their official representatives, "their own bureaucracy."

The gradual discovery of contradictions in political life, and especially in the society of a transitional period, sooner or later had to lead to an affirmation of the problems related to the pursuit of interests in our political science. To substantiate and illustrate this statement, several typical opinions of Yugoslav authors concerning the relation between politics and interests can be quoted. To mention one or two: "The interest is the determining category in politics.... Politics is usually regarded as the sphere in which conflicting interests between individuals and social groups are to be solved."[36] "Whatever has been said so far justifies us in concluding that the category of interest, or rather the category of class interest, not only clearly belongs to the categorical apparatus of Marx's theory but represents one of the fundamental concepts of Marxian politics and social theory."[37] Still more clearly is the significance of the problems of interest for politics and for political science emphasized by Najdan Pašić:

> At the basis of the political organization of society lies the conflict of interests.... To speak of politics thus means to speak of interests, i.e., of the way in which in the sphere of conducting the general affairs of the society various interests of social groups are interrelated, mutually opposed as well as adjusted in a global social community. The history of the social sciences, and especially of the science studying politics as special field of social life, provides a sufficient basis for the conclusion that the category of interest represents a fundamental concept and instrument of political analysis. Likewise, the category of interest occupies a central place in the development of the materialistic view of politics and of the laws underlying political life.[38]

As it has been developed during the last three decades in Yugoslav politology, the approach to politics from the viewpoint of interest shows (allowing for some simplification) in particular the following characteristics. At its most general, theoretical level, politics is defined in terms of interests. The interests are not to be taken in economic reductionist terms. Emphasis is laid on economic interests as well as on moral, cultural, scientific, and other interests and on their significance for political life. Although the category of *class* interests performs the central role, the problems of interests are not reduced to undifferentiated class interest or to more class interests but relate also to the interests of other strata and groups, and also to the interests pursued by the individual as worker and citizen. Great emphasis is laid on the specific way of articulating, aggregating, and integrating interests in the political system of self-management as it is being developed in Yugoslavia. The problems of the "common interest" also appear in a new light. The common interest is pursued not merely by the state but also by all the subjective forces of the society, to which, in addition to the sociopolitical organizations and some other forms of associations also belong culture and science. Along with theoretical works dealing with the problems of interests there are becoming increasingly important empirical studies of how interests are articulated and aggregated through the delegate system in the political system of Yugoslavia.[39] In the treatment of the problems of interests, Yugoslav political science pays particular attention also to the question of national interests and to the relation in which national interests stand to other, specifically class, interests.

CLASS DIMENSION AND NATIONAL DIMENSION OF POLITICS

The relation between the class dimension and the national dimension of politics has topical significance for Yugoslav political thought and political science not simply because of the multinational structure of contemporary Yugoslav society or because of the role which the national question occupied in the recent history of Yugoslav nations and nationalities. These were beyond doubt the two factors stimulating the thought to seek answers for coping with the national question. It was, however, a characteristic of Yugoslav political thought (and continues to be a characteristic of contemporary political science in Yugoslavia) that the national question was not viewed as a partial problem but understood (and continues to be understood) as an epoch-marking question intimately related to the political emancipation and the social transformation of the contemporary world. The national question is not only the dominant question of the nineteenth century but also one of the main questions of the twentieth century. All the big upheavals of the twentieth century—world wars, anticolonial revolutions, socialist revolutions—have also brought into focus the national question.[40] The national question is related not just to the fate of national minorities and small nations in the present-day world. This question occasionally refers even to the existence of individual nations, it refers to relations among nations inside individual multinational political systems, as well as to the relations among nations on the world scale. The national question not only is a topical issue in "classical" countries, which are known to have this problem, but comes up also in places where it was believed to have been definitively solved. It is present in capitalist countries, in developing countries, and in socialist countries. In a sense we might even speak of a genuine renaissance of the national question.[41]

Therefore it is not accidental that Yugoslav political thought and political science have been, particularly since the mid-thirties, paying extraordinary attention to the question of the nation[42] and that the discussions about the national phenomenon have expanded greatly, particularly in recent years. Although the direct impulses for the treatment of the national question often came from a need to cope with our concrete problems and also (in the recent period) from coping with the reemergence of certain nationalistic phenomena,[43] Yugoslav political thought and political science have dealt with this question not simply in political-pragmatic terms but in the context of broader discussions of the essence of the nation, its definition, its place in contemporary social development, its relation to the problem of socialism; they have dealt with it in a critical confrontation with the spiritualistic and other idealistic theories of the nation as well as with certain views advocated by some Marxist authors.[44]

One of the essential aspects of the treatment of the national phenomenon in our political science is represented precisely by the relation between class interests and national interests. This question was articulated in crystal-clear form during the National Liberation War, whose principal specific characteristic was the interrelatedness of national and social liberation.[45] While the revolution has solved the national question in its global political sense, it could not, as elsewhere, bring a solution to all aspects of the national question. The residues of the old nationalistic mentality, the inherited inequality in the development of the individual nations and nationalities, resistance against the pressures of unitaristic-centralistic tendencies[46]—all this has given rise to certain national hard feelings and conflicts. Yugoslav political practice responded to these phenomena by endeavoring to provide for increasing independence of individual nations and nationalities and to effect a suitable transformation of federalism. The fundamental principle in this was the requirement that the national interest must not be reduced to the merely specific linguistic or to some broader cultural-autonomous interest. Even the political interest of the nation, to be expressed in its statehood, cannot in itself be sufficient. The basic foundation for national freedom is economic sovereignty, that is, the right of the nation to dispose of the surplus product that it has created.

This is the point where the problems of national interest actually meet with the problems of the working class and of all the working strata of the society. Yugoslav political thought and political science here stress emphatically that as long as the working class is not in command over the means, conditions, and results of its labor, that as long as somebody else—private owners, alienated centers of economic power, or the state monopoly—disposes of the results of his work, so long one cannot speak of an accomplished social emancipation.[47]

In view of the fact that the emancipation of the working class can proceed only if it is accompanied by a harmonious relation between the class interest and the national interest it is understandable why a nation can be fully free not simply when it is culturally and politically but also when it is economically emancipated. A free disposal of the results of its labor is both the framework and the condition of pursuing its interest in the cultural and political spheres. Therefore, the problem of self-management, which openly and radically poses the question of class interest, refers not only to democracy in the working organization or in the school but also to the position and role of the nation—which necessarily has an influence on the specific form of federalism and the political system of a multinational socialist society in general.

This is the stand on which Yugoslav political thought and political science have also formed and continue to form their view of the relation between national and international interests.[48] Just as they resisted any a priori hierarchical setting up of the relation between the class interest and the national interest, so they opposed both abstract internationalism and narrow-minded nationalism. Such a view of the relation between the national and the international has had significant consequences for the understanding of the international solidarity and of the relations between the individual sections of the contemporary socialist movement, and of the relations between socialist, developed, and developing countries. The struggle for a new international economic order, seriously supported by Yugoslav political thought and science,[49] is founded on the understanding that national freedom is real only when based on a sovereign disposal of the national wealth and when economic relations with other nations are based on terms of equality. Such a conception of the relation between the national and the international has also been and continues to be the source for the orientation for the nonalignment policy, understood by Yugoslav political thought and science also as a factor of social progress. The dialectic of class interests and national interests is hence one of the central issues of contemporary Yugoslav political science, both in its views of international relations and in its understanding of the articulation and integration of interests in the political system of self-management. The point we are here concerned with—and this point is emphasized also in Yugoslav political science—is not merely the increasing freedom and independence of nations but also an increasingly close cooperation in cultural, political, and economic fields.

MONISM AND PLURALISM

The third important focus in Yugoslav political science, indicating a permanent tendency in its development, is the increasingly clear orientation for a specific pluralism in political theory and practice, particularly in the theory and practice of the political system of socialist self-management. Pluralism was already characteristic of the structure of the socialist revolution in Yugoslavia, which in addition to national liberation features had distinctive social features through the participation of all the important strata of workers. The multinational structure of our society, remarkably well affirmed during the revolution and during the last three decades playing a decisive role in forming political thought and political science as well as in the practical work of structuring the political system, was opposed to a one-sided, unitaristic reductionism. From the very beginning self-management as a term covering the strategic orientation of socialism in Yugoslavia actively opposed any kind of a mechanistic-centralistic monism and paved the way for a plurality of initiatives from individuals and social groups in our society. The polydimensional conception of the contradictions and interests which was, as already mentioned, gaining momentum in practical politics and political thought, denied the real and potential recurrence of centralist monism in social thought and in political life itself. In the current big debate concerning the relation of monism and pluralism[50] Yugoslav political science has not been confronted with a dilemma imposed on it from outside; rather, it was faced with a question that has been under its scrutiny in one form or another for several decades. A result of such a critical examination was at both the theoretical and political level a clear decision for a specific form of pluralism, which has meant and means also a fairly specific conception of unity (''monism'') for socialist society.

Thus, it would be wrong to assume that the explicit determination for a specific pluralism (that is, for the ''pluralism of self-management interests,'' or rather for ''self-management pluralism''), adopted in the second half of the 1970s in the political thought and political science of Yugoslavia, came up as a sudden, complete novelty. The idea of a specific form of pluralism in Yugoslav political thought and political science has been *implicit* ever since the beginning of the idea of self-management and, as such, is related to all those sources which refer to the self-management orientation of Yugoslav socialism. In its confrontation with the practice of one-dimensional monism, Yugoslav political thought and science have emphasized the significance of basic initiative in socialism.

But, also, the *explicit* orientation for a specific form of pluralism did not emerge all of a sudden but went through several stages of development. We might say that the explicit orientation for pluralism emerged concretely in the second half of the 1960s when the implicitly pluralistic content of self-management started to acquire a sporadic, pluralistic label. This tendency—sometimes troubled by inappropriate uses of the term—subsequently found recognition also in some official documents, notably in the document ''The Socialist Alliance of the Working People Today,'' passed in 1970 at the republican conference of the Socialist Alliance of the Working People of Slovenia.[51] This document explicitly aimed at ''ensuring through the methods of work and through the various institutions of self-management a steady growth of the pluralism of authentic interests in our society.''[52] The idea of a specific pluralism in Yugoslav society was emerging in politological discussions and investigations in the following years in a smaller extent (and again not without contradictions caused by some controversial uses of this term),[53] but in its totality it could establish itself only when, in the new Constitution (1974) and in the legislation stemming from it (in particular the Associated Labor Act) it gained new support for the development of self-management. The principal contribution toward elaborating and affirming this idea was given in 1977 by Edvard Kardelj in his work ''Directions in the Development of the Political System of Socialist Self-Management.''[54] This work has given a new impetus to the development of a specific pluralism in both Yugoslav political thought and political science in relation to the political system of Yugoslavia and to the theoretical aspects of the problem in question. In terms of the ''pluralism of self-management interests'' or ''self-management pluralism'' the idea of pluralism had been accepted as a designation of the political system of socialist self-management. In this way there was, on the one hand, theoretically affirmed and clearly formulated the long-range tendency in the development of the Yugoslav political system, whereas on the other hand this brought along a more open area for the interests growing from the framework of the self-management socialist orientation.

In very recent years we have been witnessing the emergence of a considerable output dealing with the problem of interests and in particular with the theoretical and empirical content of the specific pluralism of self-management interests,[55] while at the same time there have occurred attempts at a clear demarcation of this kind of pluralism with regard to various other conceptions of pluralism in contemporary political science. The results achieved so far in the still on-going investigations and discussions might be summarized briefly under the following points:

1. Yugoslav political practice and political science have rejected the idea according to which pluralism is incompatible with Marxism.

2. In its structure of interests, a socialist society is also pluralistic—the political system of the socialist society must recognize this fact and ensure that all *legitimate* interests become institutionally operative in the political system.

3. The pluralism that is suited for a political system of socialist self-management is essentially different from the political pluralism of the classical multiparty system, and it differs also from the pluralism that is being shaped in

some other socialist conceptions; "the pluralism of self-management interests" is both in its class foundation and in its aim essentially different also from classical "analytical pluralism."[56]

4. "The pluralism of self-management interests" is, therefore, no pluralism of *arbitrary* empirical interests; rarther, it is a conception based on a multitude of interests in which the interests of the working class in association with the interests of all the working people have a dominant role in the society. Hence, the apparent paradox that Yugoslav political thought related the self-management pluralism with acceptance of the dictatorship of the proletariat.

"The pluralism of self-management interests" has a wide sphere in which to affirm itself: from self-management in the material production and in the field of labor in general, in the local community and in the commune, in the self-managing community of interests, via the regulating of relations between the nations and nationalities in the republic, the province, and the federation, to the role of sociopolitical and social organizations and to the entire operation of the delegate system inside associated labor and at the level of global sociopolitical communities.

When the more recent Yugoslav analyses seek to find out why the implementation of this self-management pluralism does not in every respect meet present expectations, they are at the same time pointing out that self-management pluralism can be developed and deepened only if in the self-management system itself a broad recognition is given to all the subjective forces, in which the strategic role is and must be played (within the setting of the organized socialist consciousness) by the League of Communists.

The conception of self-management pluralism is, accordingly, a class conception involving also the question of the integration of the self-management interests. Therefore, this conception necessarily includes also the monistic aspect of the political system—not in its classical form but transformed or rather in the transformation on the basis of self-management principles pursuing the possibility for the widest possible direct articulation of the various interests of the working (and otherwise articulated) socialist social basis and superstructure.

SOCIALISM, SELF-MANAGEMENT, DEMOCRACY

The meeting point which integrates all the endeavors of the politologists in Yugoslavia—as will be understood readily from what was said above—is socialism based on self-management.[57] Without assuming that the empirical forms developed by socialist practice in Yugoslavia should be taken as a general "model" to be followed by others, political science in Yugoslavia pursues the view that self-management in one form or another represents one of the fundamental laws underlying the transitional period. Following Marx's (and Engels') thesis about the self-emancipation of the proletariat, his theory about the withering away of the state, his conception of social emancipation, his analysis of revolutionary experiences, in particular of the Paris Commune, Lenin's conception of the Soviets as well as other revolutionary experiences, including—last, but not least—the experience gained in our own revolution, Yugoslav socialist thought and political science have in the development of our specific way of socialism been shaping a concept of socialism which had a highly critical attitude toward the then-prevailing views. In this concept of socialism the category of *social* ownership is of key importance for the negation of any monopolistic ownership; this category contains as its immanent element the self-management of the workers and on this basis—along with the overcoming of the class nature of society and the elimination of exploitation, along with the expansion of self-management over the entire society and with the withering away of the state—a gradual elimination of the dualism between those who rule and those who are ruled.[58]

Yugoslav politologists and social scientists see in self-management the central point from which to shape a political system in Yugoslavia and a perspective within which in specific forms its development and socialism as a world process are being determined. Self-management expands the horizons of socialism and for socialism, and thus also of political science, for it brings forth new views and new solutions as regards the relation between politics and economics, between classes, social strata, and the political system, between society and political power. Self-management transforms the relations between micropolitics and macropolitics, and broadens the sphere of the political to the state-level sphere. Self-management is based on the sphere of work (associated labor) and from here it expands over all other spheres of social life. At the same time, self-management represents a new way of establishing relations between the various spheres of social life, between material production and public services in particular. Self-management also transforms the traditional sphere of political power, not merely by reaffirming the problem of the control of power but also by demanding the socialization of power. Self-management is also a powerful criticism of the unlimited power of the state apparatus, of bureaucratism and of other centers of alienated power based on technocracy or some other form of elitism. Likewise, as we have seen, self-management enters into the solving of the national question, into the structure and conception of federalism. The effects and the forms of self-management exert an influence also on such classical fields of state policy as foreign policy, national defense, and social self-protection. And also social planning acquires new dimensions and a new content in socialism on the self-management basis.

Yugoslav political scientists in general realize that self-management conceived in this way is only starting on its way in Yugoslav society and that there is thus still a considerable discrepancy between the norm and the real.[59] Self-management is no static model; rather, it is a process not free from standstills, aberrations, and even retrogressions. It contains a number of specific contradictions due to the still disproportionate difference between the norm and the factual distribution of power,[60] to the persisting contradiction between social ownership and the remnants of the ownership monopolies, to the contradiction between the production for needs and that for the market. Significant in this respect is the fact that Yugoslav political thought and political science are becoming increasingly aware of these contradictions and are trying to find ways to resolve them—but not in the form of monopolizing power or ownership but rather through "opening" the sociopolitical system for new suggestions and incentives.

Parallel with the development of its own specific concept of socialism and self-management, Yugoslav social thought and political science have formed their own view of democracy, especially of democracy in socialism. This concerns, at bottom, only different aspects of one and the same problem.[61] Socialism, based on the self-management perspective, necessarily had to and has to bring into focus also the problem of democracy in socialism and by doing this to stimulate political science to adapt its stands to such concepts of democracy as could be advanced as an alternative to *self-management democracy*.[62]

The concept of democracy as it has been developing in recent decades in Yugoslav social thought and political science could be (allowing for some schematic simplification necessitated by the shortage of space) summed up in the following characteristics. Socialism is, by definition, a democratic society which must ensure more room for personal and common initiative than is available in any class society. Democracy is not merely a concept limiting itself to the particular procedure for selecting the rulers from the political groups competing for power.[63] At the same time, given the necessary formal procedural assumptions, democracy has to be explicitly goal-oriented and defined as to its content. Therefore, socialist self-management democracy is not just a political concept; democracy is a concept integrated in its tendency and intention; democracy does not denote merely democratic provenance and democratic control of the state apparatus but it extends over all the spheres of social life, from economic relations via public services to representative organs of the state, which are gradually losing their character of power. Self-management democracy by its nature involves the masses and by its essential tendency represents direct democracy.[64] As an explicitly class-oriented conception of democracy it aims at the same time to overcome the class nature of society and politics and along with this to explicate and affirm the authentic pluralistic nature of socialist society and politics ("the pluralism of self-management interest").[65]

What has been said of self-management applies also to self-management democracy. Although extremely rich in its potential for future development, it is by virtue of its realization so far only in the beginning stage of a historical process within which it can realize all its dimensions to the fullest extent. It is not only the relatively modest material possibilities which preclude a fuller realization of self-management democracy; there is also the particular degree of people's consciousness, the psychology of everyday life fraught with traditional ideas of ownership and power which impede the full realization of direct self-management democracy. But in spite of the discrepancy between the vision and the reality, as found by Yugoslav political science to exist in Yugoslav political reality, the responsibility of self-management democracy is thus not diminished but rather increased—the responsibility to seek in opposition to oligarchic subordination and elitistic skepticism for new ways and possibilities for ever greater freedom for Man.

Fields of Political Science

POLITICAL THEORY

A cursory inspection of the world and of our own literature will readily reveal that political theory is that discipline (or field) of political science which is most difficult to define.[66] Political theory is here understood as that discipline and field of political science which describes political phenomena, shapes the fundamental politological categories, reveals the relations between political and other social phenomena, elucidates political relations and processes, and seeks to identify the tendencies and regularities in political life. In this sense political theory is the introductory, basic, and general discipline of the science of politics or at least it contains introductory, basic, and general observations and findings as regards a given field of politics and political science.

If such a working conception of political theory is accepted, there can be no doubt that at this point we must take into account also some of the aspects mentioned earlier: the problems of the essence and scope of politics; the relation between what is class-determined and the national, between interests and politics; the problems of democracy, socialism, and self-management are also problems and concepts of political theory. Likewise, it should not be overlooked that the fields of political science to be discussed later have significant theoretical components to a lesser or greater degree (this is in particular true of the history of political thought, of the theory of the state, of international relations). Bearing all this in mind we should point out that there are in political science in Yugoslavia actually more theoretical constituent elements than one might assume merely on the basis of the titles of works: the works published in fact only seldom contain in their titles the expression "political theory"[67] and only by way of exception concern themselves with the definition of the concept itself. To what has been outlined so far we should add that Yugoslav authors often speak about political theory without using that name. Here we are referring to those cases in which authors do not by political science or by the science of politics understand merely a sum total of the individual disciplines but use "political science" or a similar term (foundations of political science, general political science, general politology) to denote what is otherwise commonly called political theory.

Therefore, contributions to political theory are to be found also in works dealing with general problems of politics and of the political system, or in works giving general or introductory outlines of politology, or dealing with problems relevant to all the disciplines of political science.[68]

A comprehensive evaluation of these contributions would require a more detailed analysis of these works, and this would clearly go beyond the scope of the present chapter. But in order to gain some additional insight into some of the political-theoretical dimensions of political science, we shall seek to elucidate some categories and problems, which have been either in connection with the already mentioned ones or in relation to them particularly brought into focus by Yugoslav political science during recent decades. Here we are referring specifically to the problems of the political system (sociopolitical system), of political representation, of political development, and to the relation between what is factual and what is value-oriented (and related to the relation between political science and political ideology).

In the first place it should be underlined that the development of political science in Yugoslavia was truly significantly influenced by the introduction and specific treatment of new terms which make it possible to deal with political institutions, political relations, and political processes as a complex whole, taking into account both the internal contradictions in the political sphere itself as well as the dialectical relations between politics and the socioeconomic and other environment. I am here in particular referring to the term *political system* (sociopolitical system), which has as one of the fundamental and most general categories of politics and political science during the last two decades completely superseded some of the previous terms (e.g., the state, the state system), which took to the phenomenon of politics a much more institutional and partial approach. The political system (sociopolitical system) is being defined by the Yugoslav politologists[69] in such a way that the use of this term involves a dynamic conception of the relation between the political power and the social structure and of the relations between the classes and the forms of the political system; at the same time they seek to define the general indicators needed for identifying the degree of independence of the political system and to reveal the typical and specific tendencies in the development of contemporary political systems as well as to reveal the significance of the structural changes within them. In this way the category of the "political system," used by some authors also to denote a special discipline of the political science, is to be clearly demarcated from some of the narrower concepts, particularly the state, and from some broader terms, in particular the political structure and the political process.

The second aspect of political-theoretical discussions which has been receiving increasing attention from Yugoslav political science during the last three decades is the problem of (political) representation. Yugoslav authors[70] have been discussing not merely the historical evolution of the principle of political representation but also the characteristics of some of the more recent theories of representation. They have reconstructed the critique of political representation in the classical and in the more recent Marxian (Marx, Engels, Lenin, Gramsci) literature and have analyzed the conceptions of representation as originating from the practice of the development of postrevolutionary socialist society. The results of these critical examinations focus attention on the limits of political representation as the fundamental principle for the constituting of parliament, or corresponding bodies of state power; but at the same time they argue that in the political system of a society in its transitional period political representation should be transformed in such a sense that representation would increasingly integrate the sphere of labor and the sphere of politics.

The third sphere of the political-theoretical character to be emphasized here relates to the problems of political development. If one were to view these problems simply in terms of how often the term *political development* has been used, one could without hesitation find that political science in Yugoslavia has not been paying any particular attention to this question. But this could mean not that the problems of political development have not been studied but that they have been treated with little attention. These problems appear both in the works devoted to the treatment of political systems in developing countries[71] and in works dealing with the development of the political system of socialism, in particular with the political system of socialist self-management.[72] But the problems are coped with, of course, also in works concerned with the general problems of the political system, politics, and social development.[73] Without quoting particular works we shall take the liberty to sum up some basic stands related to that complex of problems which are designated in world literature as "political development":

1. Political development should not be viewed as an isolated category. Political development occurs in the context of economic development and in the context of social development in general.

2. Political development has to be viewed in relation to the development of socioeconomic relations. Political development is not a mechanical consequence of economic development but is a result of intricate interactions between economic development, changes in class and social structure, people's consciousness, etc.

3. Political emancipation is an important aspect and criterion of political development. But, without economic emancipation, the results of political emancipation remain necessarily limited and imperiled.

4. There exists no universal "model" by which a political system should follow its course of development. In political development there is always the dialectical interplay of the universal and the particular, which does not admit of static and epigonic patterns of development but in each stage calls for a new creative initiative and new forms.

5. The essential criterion of political development is Man's ability, in cooperation with other people, to overcome the social and political alienations (monopolies), gradually to overcome the division between those exercising power and those subject to it, and to create such conditions in which the actual development of the creative initiatives and abilities of everybody is accompanied by a real possibility to meet Man's authentic needs and interests.

Such constituent elements of "political development," finally, lead us to the issue of what is the relation between values and facts in political science. Even if this question has not been solved by unanimous agreement,[74] it must be emphasized that most Yugoslav politologists favor the view that facts and values cannot in political science become mechanically separated and abstractly opposed to each other.[75] Political science cannot be "value-free" but is always, in overt or covert form, a science actively committed to the object of its inquiry. If such a stand is not immune from big dangers (the problem of distinguishing between what is value-oriented and what is factual is necessarily related to the problem of the relation between the political approach and the scientific one), then it is not hard to understand the complexity of the relation between political science and political ideology. Among Yugoslav politologists the opinion prevails that political science and political ideology are neither identical or a priori antagonistic. Neither of them can readily dispose of sociopolitical practice and both can either mutually support or hinder each other. The contradiction between political science and political ideology will last as long as there are essential contradictions of interests in society.

HISTORY OF POLITICAL THEORIES AND
CONTEMPORARY POLITICAL IDEAS

In the Yugoslav conception of the development of political science, the history of political ideas has a recognized status for the very reason that most authors emphasize that this history contains a significant source for the history of political science.[76] Besides, it should not be overlooked that the high degree of (positive) socialist ideological commitment calls for special attention to be paid to the history of Marxism and of socialist ideas in general, to the sources which have been instrumental in forming socialist political ideas, and also to those trends of thought which socialist thought—and particularly socialist thought in Yugoslavia—has been or continues to be confronted with. Our openness to the outer world has in a sense directed Yugoslav political science to concern itself, among other things, also with the ideas of the Third World, and especially with some aspects of these political ideas. Therefore, taken as a whole, the history of political ideas occupies in Yugoslavia a place much more prominent than that indicated merely by its presence in academic courses offered at the faculties of political science and at some other faculties in our country.

Among the systematic investigations in this field, mention should first be made of *Istorija političkih i pravnih teorija* [History of political and legal theories] by Radomir Lukić,[77] one of the rare authors seeking to give a possibly detailed definition of the scope and nature of this discipline. *Oris zgodovine političkih teorij* [An outline of the history of political theories] by Jože Goričar[78] extends in part to that period where the more recent and modern political thought is followed up by Juraj Kolaković.[79] Within this group, one must mention also some anthologies of the history of political thought, provided by their editors with more or less extensive accompanying studies.[80] The next biggest, one might say, set of issues from this field is the history of socialist ideas which is also given great emphasis in some of the books mentioned. Several works have been devoted to analyzing the important representatives of Utopian socialism,[81] history of Marxism,[82] individual representatives and schools of Marxism,[83] and to other representatives of socialist thought.[84]

If such attention has been paid to the history of the political socialist (political) thought this does not imply that during the same period Yugoslav political science was not, to a greater or lesser extent, dealing also with other significant representatives and trends of political ideas. In the last three decades there have appeared—in addition to translations of some of the most important classical works from the history of political thought—numerous works (sometimes as introductory studies, some as monographs) dedicated to the political thought of Greek philosophers and to some of the most important representatives of modern political thought. In recent years works have been published dealing with fascism and neofascism,[85] Catholicism,[86] elitism,[87] political theory of instrumentalism.[88] Of great significance for our political science, which unfortunately has not yet managed to produce a survey of the development of the political ideas of Yugoslav nations and nationalities, are also the studies dealing with the great individual representatives of the political thought in our country.[89]

Anybody wishing to study the history of the socialist revolution and the development of the socialist (self-management) idea in Yugoslavia and of its contemporary results will of course need to take into full account the works of Josip Broz Tito[90] and Edvard Kardelj, both recently deceased.[91] A useful contribution toward understanding the genesis and development of the idea of self-management, which plays such an important part in recent Yugoslav history and an increasingly significant part in the world, is represented also by sizeable anthologies published in recent decades and dedicated to self-management and the workers' movement[92] and to self-management and Marxism.[93]

As already mentioned, Yugoslav politologists have also shown an active interest in the political thought of the developing countries, as in the problems of socialism and developing countries,[94] Arab socialism,[95] socialism in Africa,[96] Left-oriented ideas of Latin America,[97] and the development of the nonalignment doctrine in individual developing countries.[98]

This brief survey of some of the principal topics in the history of political thought—to be taken as an indication of some of the principal trends and as illustration, which is applicable also to other points in the present chapter—demonstrates that in recent decades Yugoslav political science has become enriched by numerous works signifying an expansion of both the themes and the area of its field. Even if some areas of this discipline remain inadequately covered, the horizons have been expanded and deepened.

THE THEORY AND PROBLEMS OF THE STATE

Less than thirty years ago in Yugoslavia the theory of the state was that central discipline which was understood as political theory *tout court*. Such a position of the theory of the state was in accordance with the Central European tradition, strengthened by the increased role of the new Yugoslav state ("revolutionary étatism") and under considerable influence of the then-current Soviet theory of the state. The subsequent position of the theory of the state in Yugoslavia is characterized by its relativization: instead of remaining in the role of *the* discipline absorbing all the fundamental insights of political theory, the theory of the state or rather the science of the state has increasingly become just one of the disciplines studying one of the extremely significant (and from some angles the most significant) political institutions of society. Such a shift in the conception of the state and of the theory of the state was substantially due to the classical Marxian conception of the state and was supported by the experiences (negative as well as positive) of socialist practice and by the results of contemporary political science.

Although it would not be possible to claim that political science in Yugoslavia has studied the role of the contemporary state to an adequate degree, it can be said, on the other hand, that it has remained free from making the mistake which some other politologists make when ignoring the state as a problem of political science. Yugoslav political thought and political science reject an absolutization of the state as well as a utopian underestimation of the state.[99] The awareness of the ever-growing role of the state in the modern world, irrespective of differences in the sociopolitical system, is just as present in political science in this country as is the awareness that the social effects of the growing power of the state need to be assessed in each case with special reference to the concrete circumstances.[100]

At the outset we should mention that during the recent three decades there have appeared in Yugoslavia a greater number of works which deal with the fundamental and theoretical problems of the state.[101] They vary in content, but taken in cross section, they deal particularly with the question of the definition of the state, with various theories of the state, the origin of the state, the development and changes of the state, the activity and function of the state, state organization, form and type of states. The problem of sovereignty is also a regular feature in the systematic treatment of the state as well as the subject of some monographs.[102] Also well worth mentioning is the attempt to establish a special "political theory of the state"[103] whose task it would be "to find out how the state makes particular political decisions and which factors determine a state policy made up of a series of such decisions as well as how these decisions are carried into effect and how such a policy operates, i.e. does it pursue its aims successfully or not."[104] Such tasks, it would appear, are successfully tackled from some aspects, for example, by works in which Yugoslav authors discuss the role of the contemporary state, the phenomenon of étatism, parliamentarism, bureaucracy, the role of the state in developing countries,[105] or in which they analyze the relations between the state and the religion,[106] the historical development of the intervention of the state in the economy,[107] or the economic role of the state in some areas of the developing countries.[108]

During the last three decades, Yugoslav political thought and political science have paid special attention to the theme of the state and socialism. Our own development of the socialist revolution made it necessary immediately after World War II to strengthen the apparatus of the new state power, but also practical examples from socialist practice of that time pointed in the same direction. But the needs of the development of socialism in Yugoslavia soon came into antagonism with such a strengthening of the state, while the exterior and interior circumstances in the late 1940s and the early 1950s stimulated careful critical thought about real and possible deformations of socialist development, later branded as "personality cult." All this caused Yugoslav political thought and political science to be concerned rather critically with the thesis that the class struggle becomes sharper and sharper in socialism and that therefore the role of the state must be strengthened, including its repressive apparatus.[109] Opposing this thesis with reference to the thought of K. Marx, F. Engels, and V. I. Lenin,[110] Yugoslav authors have, as it has been mentioned, been reaffirming the problem of the withering away of the state in socialism. Therefore it stands to reason that systematic works about the state today also contain a chapter dealing with the withering away of the state.

In this context, it should be pointed out that the thesis about the withering away of the state does not mean to Yugoslav authors an anarchistic negation of the state, hence also not a weakening of that role of the state which is still indispensable and will remain indispensable for a long time to come. Likewise, this thesis does not exclude the possibility that the state, particularly in some spheres, may for a period become stronger: such a strengthening might in given circumstances (e.g., after a socialist revolution, after an anticolonial revolution) represent an indispensable means for the initial socialist transformation of society or for the consolidation of national freedom and independence. But, sooner or later, in the development of the state in a transitional period there arises a need to set up relations which would mean "a withering away of the state." In Yugoslav theory and practice the "withering away of the state" is related to the self-management project; and the relation between self-management and the state has also been one of the themes discussed in political thought and political science in Yugoslavia.[111]

It follows from what has been said that the placement of the state in political thought and political science in Yugoslavia has been relativized, although it continues to receive considerable attention. Some concrete studies point to a direction in which, we believe, political science as regards the state should profitably become more firmly oriented: to a historical and contemporary study of the role of the state, of the influence of class and other social factors upon the state and to the relation between the contemporary state and social development.

POLITICAL PARTIES AND SOCIOPOLITICAL ORGANIZATIONS

One positive outcome of the dialectical conception of the relations between the state and society in Yugoslav political thought and political science is represented by the ever-growing interest in the problems of the political parties (and sociopolitical organizations). The overcoming of abstract globalism and legalistic institutionalism has been related to the increasingly clearer understanding that is necessary in order to study the dynamic forces of the political system, including political parties. A result proceeding from this understanding was a relatively comprehensive, if unevenly distributed, output of works which from various points of view speak about political parties. Several works have been published which deal with political parties in a systematic way.[112] Also, general works on political science as a rule contain a chapter on political parties.[113] A significant contribution toward the understanding of contemporary political parties has been made by texts discussing the concept of the revolutionary avant-garde as expounded by significant Marxian thinkers[114] or analyzing the role and program of parties in contemporary socialist movements,[115] and in individual political systems of other countries.[116] The party phenomenon has been elucidated also in some historical analyses of the development of political parties in the history of the individual Yugoslav nations.[117]

The theory of political parties in Yugoslavia has been concerned also with some fundamental questions discussed in world political literature; additionally, Yugoslav authors have introduced into the general treatment of political parties some specific topics or have offered specific answers to some questions. Thus, like most other authors, they could not avoid the problem of the origin and development of political parties, the defining of political parties, the organization of political parties, the relations inside political parties (democracy, autocracy), party systems, functions of political parties.

In contradistinction to some classical texts about political parties (like the well-known book of Duverger), which in their treatment of the contemporary phenomenon of political parties lay the principal stress on the question of organization, Yugoslav politologists—while paying full attention to the question of organization and, we may add, to the ideology of political parties—focus attention also on the problem of class and social structure of political parties.[118] In doing this, they are trying to work out the criteria by which empirical analysis should elucidate the complex relationship between political parties and basic groups, notably classes, in contemporary political systems. As far as the internal structure of political parties is concerned, individual authors deal, in particular, with the factors of bureaucratization and oligarchization of political parties as well as with the factors of their internal democratization.[119] Considerable attention has been paid to the relation between the party system and the question of democracy or autocracy in a political system. Critics have questioned the views that provide only abstract answers to this all-important issue and do not take into account concrete historical analysis. Just as a multiparty system in given circumstances has meant and still can mean a significant advance in the democratization of a given political system, so also a one-party system, even if not free from specific dangers, can in a different kind of circumstance represent a progressive step in the democratization of society. From the arguments advanced by Yugoslav authors it follows generally that, in fact, the future of democracy does not lie in a party system, which would invariably mean a monopolization of the political initiative, but rather in a nonparty, direct democracy.[120] In their general analysis of the causes and functions of political parties as an expression of a specific degree in the development of class structure, Yugoslav authors are thus taking up "futurological" ideas about political parties: in the same sense as they speak about the "withering away" of the state they pose also the question of the "withering away" of political parties when circumstances no longer justify them.[121]

Such a general context might make it easier to understand why Yugoslav political and politological terminology—when referring to the political system of Yugoslavia—does not speak of the "political party" but rather of sociopolitical organizations.[122] Without entering here into a discussion of the role of these organizations we might mention that these "delicate topics" are becoming increasingly the subject of systematic treatment and of empirical studies. Great attention is paid by political thought and political science above all to the League of Communists of Yugoslavia (LCY) as the leading ideological and political force of Yugoslav society. Several rather more general works have come out which discuss the role of the League of Communists in the political system of socialist self-management.[123] In recent years there have appeared in periodicals and in book form more and more works analyzing the role of other sociopolitical organizations: the Socialist Alliance of the Working People,[124] the Federation of Trade Unions,[125] the Union of Socialist Youth.[126] Although these analyses of sociopolitical organizations may not yet all be wholly free from normativism, this field is also increasingly becoming a subject of empirical investigation. Thus, there have been discussions about the social structure of the League of Communists, about its basic organization, the ideological views of its members, about the role of the League of Communists in big cities and in "big systems."[127] Empirical analyses have been made and continue to be made of certain aspects of the activity pursued by other sociopolitical organizations. It can be said that in spite of the delicate nature of this kind of theme—which is the case not only in Yugoslav society—this highly significant aspect of the political system of contemporary society is also becoming increasingly accessible to scientific investigation.

INTEREST GROUPS, SOCIAL ORGANIZATIONS, ASSOCIATIONS

Considering the emphasis currently given in political science in Yugoslavia to the relation between interests and politics it is not at all surprising that political science continues to pay great attention to the problems of interest groups, social organizations, and associations. Yugoslav politologists have been considering these questions from both the viewpoint of the fundamental concepts and political theory and from the standpoint of the nature and function of the interest groups in the political system of Yugoslavia as well as from some other points of view. The basic point of departure was the view that there is no contemporary society and no contemporary political system—no matter how they might differ in their class-social structure or the degree of democracy—in which exists a perfect homogeneity of interests. This is true of both the Western democracies and the socialist countries as well as the developing countries.[128]

In discussing the general, conceptual problems of

interest groups, Yugoslav politologists have pointed out the difference between and at the same time the complementary nature of the concept of interest groups and the concept of social class.[129] By laying emphasis on various points they have attempted to define the content of "interest group" and the relation in which this concept stands to related terms, in particular to "pressure groups."[130] Depending on the fundamental conception of the interest group, various authors suggest different classifications of interest groups: some include under this category a very wide spectrum of groups, including even the army and "groups occupying a key position within the political system,"[131] while others define the category in somewhat narrower terms.[132] Other authors, again, underline the significance of informal interest groups.[133] In our survey we have also come across investigations of interest groups in individual foreign countries[134] and attempts at a conceptualization of interest groups in the study of international relations.[135]

Special attention (though not sufficient) has been paid by Yugoslav politologists to the problems of interest groups in Yugoslavia.[136] Here our politology proceeds from the fundamental assumption that the problems of interest groups are a topical concern also in societies of the transitional period. This is true in particular of the political system of socialist self-management as it is being formed in Yugoslavia. In large-scale transformations triggered by the socialist revolution our politologists have been discovering the causes for the essential restructuring of interests and interest groups, while in the self-management orientation they identified that factor which has given to the structure and role of interest group a special significance.[137] The category of interest groups is here taken often in very broad terms; it includes also all the units of associated work[138] and the linkage between the self-management base and the global political system.[139] Even when focusing on the field of the association of citizens and working people, covered by the terms "social organizations" and "associations," researchers find that not only is the number of such organizations growing constantly but also that the interests voiced through such organizations are becoming increasingly varied.[140] This kind of organization, in which they see not only general functions but also instruments of control, the adjusting and even the withering away of political power,[141] are becoming an increasingly important constituent part of the sociopolitical system itself. This has been recognized also in the new constitution of the S.F.R.Y., which gives to the field of the association of interests still greater formal emphasis, whereas the sociopolitical organizations, in particular the Socialist Alliance of the Working People, pursue this intention of the constitution in practice. In view of all this, it is understandable that in recent years the social organizations and associations have become the object of politological research—as regards the political and legal foundations, the classification criteria, the aims and motives of associations, membership, internal organization and as regards the position of these organizations within the global sociopolitical system.

Within the framework of the problems of interest groups, Yugoslav politologists, like their professional colleagues in other countries, have also encountered the question of the general evaluation of the so-called group approach to politics or of analytic pluralism.[142] The overall balance shows in addition to certain negative items also positive ones. The group approach to politics—such would be a rough summary concerning the implications of this question—has made a significant contribution to political science because it reached beyond the individualistic explanation of politics, because it unveiled the idealistic mystifications of the "general interest," and because it demanded and stimulated the empirical analysis of politics as a political *process*. While on the one hand this approach has in opposition to the legalistic institutionalism and sociologistic globalism pushed into the foreground the dynamic aspects of politics, it has, on the other hand, by ignoring or negating the class concept, failed to elucidate the long-range, particularly revolutionary aspects of the transformation of society and politics.

INTERNATIONAL RELATIONS

The discipline studying international relations is one of the youngest but nevertheless well-established disciplines in Yugoslav political science. The constitution and subsequent development of this discipline was doubtlessly influenced decisively by the active, nonaligned foreign policy of Yugoslavia, by the significance of international relations for contemporary social development in general as well as by the needs of the pedagogical practice itself. Since this is a very young discipline we should not be surprised that the first phase of its development was characterized by discussions above all about methodological questions, about the scope of its subject and the like.[143] These efforts in due course produced the first results—results to be seen in a number of systematic outlines of the science of international relations.[144] It might be claimed safely that—despite some open questions—this discipline has thus marked out the boundaries of its subject, that it has determined its fundamental structure and thus defined the long-range perspective of its development. Likewise, the first works appeared in which a condensed survey of the theories of international relations in the contemporary world are outlined.[145]

In their definition of the subject to be studied under the heading of International Relations, Yugoslav authors, as a rule, reject the conception according to which international relations as a discipline should mean only a sum of the disciplines studying the individual aspects of international relations.[146] Likewise, they reject an equation of international relations with interstate relations. The critical attitude toward equating international relations with the relations among the states entails, above all, consequences for the number of the exponents or subjects of international politics. Although some authors speak of international relations as relations "among political-territorial complete societies—which are today states"[147] there is none who regards the state as the only subject of international relations. R. Vukadinović thus cites the following among the subjects of international relations: (1) the state, (2) international organizations, (3) international economic organizations, (4) various movements, (5) the church, (6) nations, (7) groups of people inside individual states, (8) man as an individual subject of international relations.[148] V. Benko ranks among the subjects of international relations the following: (1) states, (2) international governmental organizations, (3) international nongovernmental organizations, (4) social classes, (5) intellectual and cultural groups, (6) religious groups of supranational character, (7) international pressure groups, and (8) multinational companies.[149] V. Dimitrijević classifies the international subjects into the following groups: (1) national subjects of international relations, (2) international subjects of international relations, (3) supranational subjects of international relations.[150] Insisting on the requirement that international relations not be equated with interstate relations, thus, does not mean that the Yugoslav science of international relations negates the significance of the state as a subject of international relations.[151]

The expansion of subjects studied under the heading of international relations from the state to other exponents of international politics—while taking into account the real role of the state—signifies in our circumstances a considerable shift forward in political science. A positive shift, we believe, is to be seen, also, in the attempt to define the various factors affecting international relations in concrete terms as much as possible. The Yugoslav science of international relations recognizes the specific role of individual factors but at the same time—in opposition to monocausal explications—brings forth a greater number of factors to be considered in analyzing international relations, such as geographic, demographic, economic, legal, psychological, scientific-technological, military, national, and ideological.[152] As a rule the authors stress the importance of economic factors as primarily essential for the understanding of international relations, but at the same time reject the monistic absolutization of this factor, which leads into economism.[153] In contradistinction to some other schools, Yugoslav authors seek the laws underlying international relations.[154]

The central or at least one of the most important categories of the science of international relations is considered by Yugoslav specialists to be found in the international community.[155] While rejecting the nihilistic or legal-institutionalist views of the international community,[156] they seek to identify those social and political forces which integrate the international community into a real whole. In doing this, they point out, for example, that in the international community we are concerned with "a historically defined form of a social organization pursuing the relation among state-organized and other social communities, which is at bottom conditioned by the achieved degree of material and social development in domestic frameworks and by the general tendencies of historical developments in worldwide dimensions."[157] Considering the role performed in the past and today by the world market in the setup of the international community, some authors (emphasizing the need to take a sociological view of the international community) point out that the study of the international community is broader in its scope than that of international political relations.[158] Others, again, seek the constituting basis for an international community in the common interests of the integral parts of the community or in the common goals of the community.[159] However, the nuances in defining the international community are all based on recognizing the importance of the mutual economic ties and the resulting interconnections. The international community is becoming a real community through the increasing circulation of ideas and people. The world taken as a whole has common interests because there exists the possibility of self-destruction through the development of nuclear arms.[160]

But our literature does not point out merely the forces integrating contemporary mankind into an international community (to be seen also in the emergence of contemporary international organizations) but also it recognizes the factors still dividing the international community. A consequence of the existing world market as created by capitalism is not only the increasing mutual dependence in economic terms but also a growing inequality between the technologically advanced and the developing countries. The question of how to resolve this contradiction of the contemporary world—along with the contradiction of the forces of domination and those of emancipation—is a fundamental problem encountered and coped with in the international community and accordingly one of the basic problems of the contemporary science of international relations.[161] The struggle for a new international economic order[162] is in this context becoming one of the most important pursuits in the science of international relations.

In what has been said above, we have touched the subject which fundamentally underlies politics as pursued by socialist Yugoslavia and at the same time represents one of the basic issues in the political science of Yugoslavia: the question of nonalignment. Nonalignment as policy, as a political doctrine, and as a movement is the subject of numerous studies and monographs[163] and is at the same time a prominent, integral part of international relations as a special discipline. All the more significant, outlines of international relations discuss the nonalignment issues.[164] Although the authors of books on international relations discuss the question of nonalignment in different chapters and under different titles,[165] they reject the one-sided explanations of nonalignment, which take the nonalignment policy to be a short-range phenomenon, related only to the confrontation between the blocs and the cold war and which should thus lose its raison d'être in the new circumstances of détente and direct negotiations between the superpowers. Relating the nonalignment policy to the anti-imperialist revolution of nations, they search for the deeper roots of nonalignment in the effects of the anticolonial revolution, in the resistance against the division of the world into blocs, in the tendency to reject the policy of force and domination, in the tendency for democratic and equal rights in international political and economic relations, in the need to secure world peace, and in the need for a more rapid economic and social development of technologically underdeveloped countries.

The nonalignment policy, it is stressed by many Yugoslav authors, is at the same time a manifestation of the struggle for national *emancipation* of peoples and of their striving for increasing cooperation and *integration*. In his well-known study, *Historical Roots of Non-Alignment*, Edvard Kardelj, who has given to this idea special emphasis, expressed, we might say, the general position of Yugoslav political thought and political science in saying, "The nonalignment movement is not a subjectivist construct or an ephemeral phenomenon at a given moment in the international situation but a long-range sociohistorical factor of historical necessity."[166] Owing to such importance of nonalignment for the contemporary world another Yugoslav author has drawn a logical conclusion in writing that "the elaboration of theoretical questions of the nonalignment movement is of fundamental significance for further development of the science of international relations."[167]

OTHER FIELDS OF POLITICAL SCIENCE

Understandably, the fields of political science briefly outlined above cannot exhaust all the subjects discussed and studied by Yugoslav writers in the postwar period and in particular during the last two decades. Here we would like to mention a few fields which in the future will require at least as much attention as has been paid to the disciplines discussed above. First, we are referring to public administration, which has in our country some significant representatives who treat it as part of political science.[168] Also, we should not bypass the problems of political culture closely associated with the problems of political ideology and public opinion,[169] which also have a fine future in our political science. A detailed study should be made of the problems of contemporary socialism: Yugoslav authors deal with them in several important works.[170] Nor should we overlook comparative political systems, a field of great significance for political science and political practice. Within this framework a detailed analysis would elucidate the contributions made by Yugoslav political scientists to the study of the political systems of the developing countries.[171]

Institutionalization of Political Science

INSTITUTIONALIZATION OF THE STUDY OF POLITICAL SCIENCE

The basic institutions in which political sciences are studied at the academic level in Yugoslavia are the faculties of political sciences: Faculty of Political Sciences in Belgrade, Faculty of Sociology, Political Sciences, and Journalism in Ljubljana, Faculty of Political Sciences in Sarajevo, and Faculty of Political Sciences in Zagreb. The founding of faculties of political sciences in Yugoslavia resulted from the awareness that the social development must be based on increasing conscious guidance, which, however, must proceed from a richly articulated, direct initiative of the society and must become integrated into a full-scale concept, including the decisive role of the subjective factor. The faculties of political sciences as an integral part of the subjective forces of society should form a profile of professional workers who with their analytical capability, based on a deeper understanding of social and political phenomena, would be able to unveil the anatomy of social relations and contradictions and who would with their knowledge and orientation based on socialist self-management contribute their share toward a national and democratic resolution of these contradictions.

Since no comparative studies are available it is rather difficult to outline the development and current pedagogical functions of the faculties of political science in Yugoslavia.[172] The first thing to be stated is that the faculties have, since they were founded, been undergoing considerable transformation as regards the syllabuses, the internal articulation of professional profiles which they form, the functions which they perform, and the mechanisms by means of which they are related to the broader society. It is, however, possible to say that the development of these faculties (to some extent the faculty in Zagreb is an exception here) has one characteristic in common: they have been developing from a fairly general and unified syllabus, on the basis of which a fairly general profile of the politologist was formed, to a considerably differentiated syllabus, through which, on the one hand, the profile of the politologists has become rather more concrete and, on the other, the faculties also started to train, in more or less close connection with the politological profile, profiles of experts in other social sciences. Thus the Faculty of Political Sciences in Belgrade offers academic courses in politological studies in the sociopolitical line and in the international line; closely related to politology are courses in journalism and courses for prospective teachers of Marxism and self-management. On the other hand, courses in social security work and social security policy have become, it might be said, fairly independent of the basic study of political science. As regards the syllabus, study at the Faculty of Sociology, Political Sciences, and Journalism in Ljubljana is even more specialized with a broad interdisciplinary basis. The faculty has five lines of studies, which are based to a considerable extent on interdisciplinary courses in the first two years but later on are subdivided into ten more specialized lines: the study of political sciences with a sociopolitical and with an international orientation; the study of sociology with an orientation for analytic research, for personnel and organization work, and for social security work; the study of journalism with a sociopolitical and with an informative-organizational orientation; the study of self-management including the foundations of Marxism; and the study of total national defense with a pedagogical and a military-administrative orientation. At the faculty in Sarajevo the studies are pursued along the following distinct lines: the study of political sciences, the study of sociology, the study of journalism, and the study of the total national defense.

In its external organization the study at the Sarajevo faculty closely resembles the organization of studies in Ljubljana; however, it differs in two respects: on the one hand, the profiles of studies are much more separated and, therefore, the number of courses attended by all students is much smaller, and, on the other, these profiles are not internally as articulated as those coming from the corresponding faculty in Ljubljana. Clearly specific is the structure of the syllabus at the Faculty of Political Sciences in Zagreb. Here a broad, theoretical, and unified politological study (including the study of Marxist theory and of self-management) has been preserved. The study of journalism, introduced in recent years also at this faculty, is only a specialist course complementing the study of politology or the study in some other faculty; the study of the total national defense has, as in other faculties, a specific character.

From what has been said above and from surveying the syllabuses of the individual faculties of political sciences it is now possible to draw some tentative conclusions about the study of political science in Yugoslavia. The study is based on the nucleus of the politological disciplines consisting, roughly speaking, of political theory, history of political theories, the political system and the political institutions of contemporary Yugoslav society, comparative political systems, international relations, and numerous other disciplines or fields. This basic fund of politological disciplines is then combined with other disciplines of social sciences, differently in different faculties, but in all of them, including, for example, political economy, the economic system of Yugoslavia, history of Marxism and the topical problems of Marxism, certain philosophical disciplines, methodology. While there is a considerable number of basic politological and other disciplines included in the syllabuses to be followed by all students in all the Yugoslav faculties, there are also considerable differences as regards the number and kinds of fields, their allocation in various years of study, the relation between theoretical and practical knowledge, the relation between politological and nonpolitological disciplines, the amount of purely technical and methodological subjects in the syllabus. On the whole it might be said, allowing for some simplification, that there emerge three basic tendencies as they appear in the profile of studies. (1) The syllabus and thus also the profile of the politologist is expressly theoretically-philosophically accentuated—leading to a fairly comprehensive profile of the prospective politologist (Faculty of Political Sciences in Zagreb). (2) The syllabus is solidly theoretically based but oriented toward a rather more articulated profile of politologists (the faculties of political science in Belgrade and in Ljubljana, with the remark that the profile of the politologist in Ljubljana is conceived on a more interdisciplinary level and does not have the same articulation as that in Belgrade). (3) The profile of the politologist is fairly differentiated from other profiles and correspondingly to a lesser extent based on interdisciplinary studies (Faculty of Political Sciences in Sarajevo).

The differentiation of social needs has additionally required that the faculties, as already said, gradually introduce other profiles. This has affected and will continue to have an influence on the scope of politological studies and on the profile of the politologist. Without any great risk, it can be predicted that the syllabuses at the faculties of political sciences, which in recent years have been influenced more and more by the requirements of the direct users of the services, will continue to change, even if the fundamental outlines of the profile of the politologists are established.

Speaking of the study of political sciences, we must not forget that in Yugoslavia this study is pursued in various forms and at various levels. With regard to whether the students pursuing academic courses are at the same time employed or devote all of their time to the study and are thus present every day in the process of studying, we distinguish between what we call literally full-time study and study combined with work. The developmental trend goes in the latter direction. In addition to graduate studies, Yugoslav faculties offer postgraduate courses also. Postgraduate courses are attended by a considerable number of students; at the faculties of political sciences in Belgrade and Zagreb they are articulated internally. At the faculty of political science in Ljubljana they are more interdisciplinary while in Sarajevo they are held at the university level. Postgraduate studies in political science are organized also by other institutions, thus for instance by some research institutes (Institute of Sociological and Political-Legal Research in Skopje), by Marxist centers, but always in close cooperation with the faculties of political and related social sciences.

Graduates from the faculties of political sciences—and here we are referring primarily to politologists—subsequently work in various fields of social and political life.[173] A number of them teach the relevant subjects in secondary schools, a great many are employed in working organizations (organizations of associated labor), organs of sociopolitical communities (such as the commune, socialist republics, socialist autonomous provinces, federation), further in sociopolitical organizations, in mass media agencies, in agencies for international relations, in research organizations, and at universities.

INSTITUTIONALIZATION OF RESEARCH WORK

To write a more detailed account of the research carried on by political science in Yugoslavia it would be necessary beforehand to prepare a study of the organizational and professional potentialities as well as of results in the research field. Since such a study does not exist, we have, unfortunately, in our presentation of the activity in question limited ourselves to the general institutional framework and the tendencies underlying it. It has also to be taken into account that the present outline of political science in Yugoslavia covers research work at least partly.

The faculties of political sciences are not merely pedagogical institutions but also research institutions for the field of political and related sciences (to the extent that they are pursued). Their research activity has gradually managed to obtain its own relatively independent base in research centers and institutes. Thus the Faculty of Political Science in Belgrade has the Institute of Political Studies and the Center of International Studies; the Faculty of Sociology, Political Sciences, and Journalism in Ljubljana recently founded a research institute, bringing together several previously established centers, among them the Center for Politological Research. A corresponding research institute is organized at the Faculty of Political Sciences in Sarajevo, while the Faculty of Political Sciences in Zagreb has its Institute of Political Sciences. Within the framework of research organized in these units more or less systematic and continued research work in the field of political and related sciences is going on, a result of which are numerous reports and books, published either by the faculties or in cooperation with publishing houses that are increasingly interested in the politological output.[174]

Organized research work in the field of political studies is carried on not only in the faculties of political sciences and in their research units but also in research organizations of other faculties as well as outside the university. In this connection it is necessary to mention, for instance, the Belgrade Institute of Social Sciences, the Institute of the International Politics and Economy (including the former Institute of the International Workers' Movement), also in Belgrade. Other institutions include the Institute of Sociological and Political-Legal Research in Skopje, the Institute of Socioeconomic Research in Titograd, the Law Faculties, the Institute of Sociology in Ljubljana, Marxist Centers, and Academies of Arts and Sciences.

Although research activity in the field of political science, to the results of which the political and social thought of socialist practice has made no small contribution, has been carried on in Yugoslavia mostly in specialized research institutions, it should be emphasized that numerous important politological works represent the result of individual research efforts. This is in part bound up with the traditional manner of research, while to some extent this has been influenced by the need to establish political science and the individual politological disciplines. The developmental trend, however, is oriented toward bigger research projects, as for example instanced by the projects "The Implementation of the Delegate System," "European Security and Cooperation," "Sociopolitical Organizations."[175]

Special attention is paid by Yugoslav research workers to the developing countries. Thus, there exist some specialized agencies working on the problems in these countries. We might single out the already mentioned Institute of International Politics and Economy in Belgrade, which in the past contributed a significant share to the study of these countries and which continues with its work, the Institute for Developing Countries in Zagreb, and the Center for the Cooperation of Yugoslavia with Developing Countries in Ljubljana.[176]

Particular mention should be made of the research program carried on in the International Center for Public Enterprises in Developing Countries in Ljubljana. Its work is centered around the research projects: Workers' Self-management and Participation in Decision-Making as a Factor of Social Change and Economic Progress in Developing Countries; The Role of the Public Sector in Developing Countries; Planning in Public Enterprises in Developing Countries; Education and Training of Personnel in Public Enterprises in Developing Countries; Management of Transfer and Development of Technology in the Public Sector in Developing Countries.[177]

PROFESSIONAL ASSOCIATIONS OF POLITICAL SCIENTISTS

Yugoslav political scientists are organized in associations for political sciences in socialist republics and provinces. These associations are freely associated in the Union of Political Science Associations of Yugoslavia, which has its center in Belgrade. The individual associations each have their own statute which specifies the tasks as well as sources needed for organizational and professional activities. It may be said that the associations are based on identical or at least similar assumptions in all the republics and provinces and that they pursue the same tasks, though with varying degrees of activity. These associations are professional organizations of political scientists but anyone else who makes a contribution to the development of political thought is eligible for membership. The tasks of the associations are above all to foster and popularize the development of political science, to unite and affirm the work of political scientists, to monitor and stimulate instruction in political sciences at schools, to cooperate in the programming and publishing of politological literature, to foster cooperation with related societies in Yugoslavia and abroad, and in an organized way to cooperate—following the delegate principle—in the sociopolitical system.

As a rule, these associations are organized in regional sections for the reason that such an organization permits a higher degree of influence exerted by the members on the activity of an association. It is not easy to assess the actual degree of activity of the associations because detailed information about this is not available. Still, on the basis of empirical observation and some reports[178] it can be stated that in recent years the republican and provincial associations have been organized more strictly, that they have sought to increase the number of their members, and that they are developing their activity not only at the level of executive organs but also in the base, in individual sections. Likewise there is growing cooperation between the associations throughout Yugoslavia, as well as on a bilateral basis. Also, the interest in international cooperation has become stronger. Their role is becoming more pronounced also in sociopolitical organizations and in the political system in general, in accordance with the increased emphasis given by the Constitution to the role of associations in general.

At the same time, it is possible to say that in recent years the Union of the Political Science Associations of Yugoslavia has speeded up its activity. Founded in 1954, the union is increasingly effective in connecting Yugoslav political scientists and their professional associations, in affirming political sciences, and in international cooperation. According to its statute, adopted at the Third Congress of Yugoslav politologists (January 1978), the highest forum of the union is its assembly, consisting of ten delegates from each of the republican or provincial associations, while its work is directed by the presidency, consisting of the chairman, three vice-chairmen, chairmen of the republican and provincial associations, of one delegate from each of the republican or provincial associations, and the secretary-general of the union. In addition to the day-to-day adjusting and fostering of the activities of the individual associations the union is especially active in organizing scientific meetings. Thus it has, in cooperation with IPSA, organized two round tables: (1) "The Relations between Civil and Military Powers in the Modern State"; (2) "Political Science in Europe" (Opatija, 1959); and (1) "Participation and Self-Management as a Factor of the Transformation of Contemporary Political Systems"; (2) "Class Interest and National Interest in Multi-National Communities" (Dubrovnik, 1975). Professional circles followed with special attention such meetings as "Federalism and the National Question" (Novi Sad, 1971), "Interests: Theoretical Conception, Articulation, and the Struggle of Interests in Our Society" (Ljubljana, 1973), the Third Congress of the Politologists of Yugoslavia (Belgrade, January 1978), at which the following topics were discussed: (1) "The Current Situation in Political Sciences in Yugoslavia," (2) "Theory and Topical Issues of the Political System of Self-Management," divided into contributions under the headings: Principles of Responsibility, specifically in the delegate system; Position and Role of the Commune in the Political System of Socialist Self-Management.

The union publishes its own publications (such as materials presented at its scientific meetings), stimulates—in cooperation with republican and provincial associations—publishing activity in the field of political sciences, in which respect the direct initiative of its members is decisive. In the periodical literature in which appear politological texts or political texts with theoretical relevance we should mention in particular: *Arhiv za pravne i društvene nauke, Socijalizam, Marksistička misao* and *Gledišta* (Belgrade); *Naše teme, Politička misao, Kulturni radnik* (Zagreb), *Teorija in praksa* (Ljubljana), *Pregled* and *Opredeljenja* (Sarajevo), *Pogledi* (Skopje), *Praksa* (Titograd), and *Savremenot* (Novi Sad). In Yugoslavia a few reviews are published in foreign languages, relevant for an understanding of Yugoslav political thought and science, thus: *Socialist Thought and Practice* (published in Belgrade in English, Russian, German, Italian, Spanish, French, and Arabic), *Socialism in the World* (published in Belgrade in English), and *Survey* (published in English in Sarajevo). The Union of Political Sciences Associations of Yugoslavia has also given the initiative for the study of the profile of the political scientist. A specialized meeting devoted to this study was held in 1979. It should also be pointed out that from its very beginning the union has been an active supporter of international cooperation in the field of political sciences. As a member of IPSA, the union has participated in organizing the activity of this international organization, it has stimulated and continues to stimulate bilateral international cooperation among politologists and their associations, and it has supported and continues to support active participation of Yugoslav politologists at IPSA congresses. It is to be expected that the activity of the Union of Political Science Associations of Yugoslavia will continue to grow and will become more articulated, corresponding to the activity in its basic units in republics and provinces.

Political science associations—both as the union and in individual republics and provinces—are thus becoming a significant factor in the development and advancement of political science, a factor of professional consciousness increasingly integrating itself in the broader values of socialist self-management and of the contemporary world, a factor integrating politological endeavors both inside Yugoslavia and in establishing communications between Yugoslav political science and political science in the broader world. That there exist a great many possibilities in this field which our associations have not as yet followed up or have only just realized is clearly beyond doubt. This is in no small degree due both to the open nature of the Yugoslav society and to the dynamics in political science in Yugoslavia and in the contemporary world in general.

Results, Problems, Perspectives

What are the results, the problems, and the perspectives of political science in Yugoslavia?

On various occasions, particularly in the recent period, Yugoslav political scientists have tried to answer these questions. It is now in order for us, at the end of our outline of the scope and institutional development of political science in Yugoslavia, to attempt to provide an answer.

It is no exaggeration to state that political science in Yugoslavia has achieved results from several aspects in the last two decades. Among them, we shall single out those which we find particularly significant.

Political science has defined and elucidated the essence of politics in the political system of socialist self-management and at the same time firmly established the new discipline—politology—as one of the central disciplines of modern social sciences in our country.

Political science has contributed—using methods of modern empirical research—to the insights in the functioning of the political system of socialist self-management and also to the transformation of this system. Also, it has elaborated a methodological-theoretical framework for comparative research on contemporary political systems, especially of the political systems of developing countries and has begun research work on this basis.

It could be added that a mood, rooted in the conception of a dialectical relationship of theory and practice, against a "value-free" political science has been accompanied by a deeper methodological consciousness to increase the cognitive role of political science. But this does not mean that the contribution of our political science to the normative aspects of political culture of Yugoslav society could be underestimated and in the coming years diminished.

In interaction with the political thought of social practice, which has, in many respects, contributed essentially to the development of political science, political science in Yugoslavia has been, to a greater or lesser extent, exposing and also investigating problems which, with their implications, may be interesting also for political science outside Yugoslavia. Among these problems the following deserve, in our opinion, to be mentioned especially: the extension of the scope of politics from the problems of the state and power to the field of the management of society and its parts (socialist self-management); the clarification of the dialectic between socioeconomic relations and the political system, especially the political system of socialist self-management; the actualization and concretization of the national phenomenon in political processes of contemporary societies; the establishing of dialectical interrelations between class interests and national interests and the shaping of the influence exercised by the national structure of society on the formation of the specific federalism of a multinational society; the revealing of the contradictions existing in a society of a transitional period; the exposition of the problems of articulation and integration of interests in the political system of socialist self-management and in the society of the transitional period in general; the critique of the principle of political representation; a critical examination of the relation between the rulers and the ruled (problems of bureaucratism, technocratism, and other forms of elitist alienation) in the political system of socialism and in the political system of socialist self-management; new foci of attention in the conception of socialism, particularly as related to the free association of producers, that is, to self-management, and to the reevaluation of the concepts of democracy as well as to the shaping of a concept of self-management democracy based on the pluralism of self-management interests; the problems of the role played by the "subjective factor" in the socialist self-management society; and the shaping of principles, goals, and means of the nonalignment policy. Irrespective of how some of the problems dealt with were present (or were emerging) in the work of contemporary political thought and political science throughout the world, an impartial assessment could not deny that political science in Yugoslavia inasmuch as it brought them into sharp focus—even if the posed questions could be answered in different ways—has enriched the content and expanded the horizons of contemporary political science.

In view of all this, however, it should not be overlooked that the development of political science in Yugoslavia has weaknesses on its record. In particular we have to accept the criticism that political science has not as yet wholly overcome normativism. Also, it needs to be mentioned that the research of political phenomena as regards the sociopolitical system of Yugoslavia and the contemporary world still remains too much fragmented. Also, there are aspects of politics which politological research has hardly touched so far.[179]

In spite of these and some other weak points there are no reasons whatsoever for a pessimistic view as regards the further development of political science in Yugoslavia. First, it should be stated that Yugoslav political scientists have realized clearly which are the weaknesses among them; this was apparent at the Third Congress of Yugoslav political scientists, held in the beginning of 1978. Next we must say that political science in Yugoslavia is developing in a social climate favoring a growing role and practical relevance of social sciences in general and of political science in particular. This is manifesting itself also in the principle that social and political scientists shall, via appropriate mechanisms, participate directly in the elaboration of decisions. And a deep need is felt that the role of (political) science as regards social planning and development of the Yugoslav society should be growing in the future. In spite of this, however, the contradictions between science and politics, to a greater or lesser extent present everywhere in the world, are not and cannot be overcome once and for all. But the fundamental political orientation of society and the institutional integration of (political) science into the developmental processes of society promise to political science—which has already so far enjoyed wide social support—increased possibilities for further development. That this development will be dependent to a considerable degree upon the interactions between our political science and political science in the contemporary world is, on the basis of experiences gained so far and of permissible predictions, beyond any doubt.

Notes

1. On the development of political science in Yugoslavia, see, e.g., Jovan Djordjević, "Osnovna pitanja političkih nauka" [Fundamental questions of political science] in J. Djordjević, ed., *Socijalizam i demokratija* (Belgrade: Savremena administracija, 1962). See also *Political Science in Yugoslavia* (Belgrade: Union of Political Science Associations of Yugoslavia, 1979).

2. *The Program of the League of Yugoslav Communists* (LCY) (Belgrade: Jugoslavija, 1958), p. 234: "Socialist society devotes special attention to the progress of social and political sciences. Advanced social and political sciences, which reveal and determine the laws of the development of modern society and of its consciousness, are a powerful factor in progressive social development and the development of Man's social being."

3. This institute has given impulse also to research in other fields, e.g., sociology.

4. See Radomir D. Lukić, Gorazd Kušej, Jože Goričar and others.

5. Cf. Jovan Djordjević, *Politički sistem* [The political system] (Belgrade: Savremena administracija, 1977), p. 50; Adolf Bibič, *Kaj je politična znanost?* [What is political science?] (Ljubljana: Komunist, 1969), p. 18.

6. This position was criticized, e.g., by Branko Caratan. See Branko Caratan, *Socijalizam i politika* [Socialism and politics] (Zagreb: Centar za aktualni politički studij, 1972), p. 34.

7. Such position is defended, e.g., by Radomir Lukić, *Istorija političkih i pravnih teorija* [History of political and legal theories] (Belgrade: Naučna knjiga, 1956), pp. 20-23; Radomir Ratković, "O predmetu i mestu političkih nauka" [On the subject and placement of political science] in *Ogledi o problemima savremenog društva* (Belgrade: Kultura, 1961), p. 130.

8. For the definitions of politics in a narrower sense, see, e.g., Radomir Lukić, *History*, p. 23.

9. Typical definitions of politics in the broader sense (along with differentiating it from politics in the narrower sense) are to

be found in: Najdan Pašić, *Klase i politika* [Classes and politics] (Belgrade: Rad, 1974), p. 40; Bibič, *What Is Political Science?* p. 24; Radomir Lukić, *Politička teorija države* [Political theory of the state] (Belgrade: Savez udruženja pravnika Jugoslavije, 1962), p. 15; Stevo Gaber, *Politikata i političkata nauka* [Politics and political science] (Skopje: Naša knjiga, 1975). On the subject of political science see also Radoslav Ratković, *Osnovi nauke o politici* [Foundations of political science] (Belgrade: Institut za političke studije FPN, 1977); Stojan Tomić, *Politički profesionalizam* [Professionalism in politics] (Belgrade: Radnička štampa, 1975).

10. See Caratan, *Socialism*, p. 34.

11. Gaber, *Politics*, p. 44; Bibič, *What Is Political Science?* p. 56.

12. Leo Geršković, "Political System of Yugoslavia as a Teaching Subject" (Paper delivered at the Symposium of the Yugoslav Political Science Association, Zagreb, March 30-31, 1965).

13. Pašić, *Classes*, pp. 38-39.

14. In *Political Science in Yugoslavia*.

15. For examples, see *Marks i savremenost* [Marx and contemporary epoch] (Belgrade: Institut za izučavanje radničkog pokreta—Institut društvenih nauka, 1964), esp. pp. 174-84.

16. Arif Tanović, "Filozofija, politologija i politika" [Philosophy, politology and politics], *Dijalog*, no. 3, 1977, pp. 21-31.

17. Vojan Rus, "Politika i moral u socijalizmu" [Politics and morality in socialism] in Adolf Bibič and Pavle Novosel, *Politička znanost—Predmet i suština* [Political science—subject and substance] (Zagreb: Naprijed, 1971), pp. 323-33.

18. See, e.g., Andrija Krešić, "Politika i ljudska zajednica" [Politics and human community], Introduction to *Država i politika* [The state and politics], by Andrija Krešić and Radoslav Vujičić (Belgrade: Sedma Sila, 1960); Vanja Sutlić, *Bit i suvremenost* [Being and contemporaneity] (Sarajevo: Veselin Masleša, 1967), pp. 385-405. This aspect has been especially underlined by Ante Pažanin, *Filozofija i politika* [Philosophy and politics] (Zagreb: FPN, 1973).

19. Pažanin, *Philosophy and Politics*.

20. Ibid., p. 65.

21. Ibid. p. 72.

22. Ibid. pp. 50, 74, n. 118.

23. This is the position of V. Stanovčić in his contribution on political philosophy in *Politička enciklopedija* [Political encyclopedia] (Belgrade: Savremena administracija, 1975), p. 747.

24. See, e.g., Adolf Bibič, "Sociologija političkog život a" [Sociology of political life], *Naše teme*, no. 5, 1962, pp. 682-92.

25. Miroslav Pečujlić, *Horizonti revolucije:Studije iz političke sociologije* [Horizons of revolution: studies in political sociology] (Belgrade: Institut za političke studije FPN, 1970); Radoš Smiljković and Miroslav Pečujlić, eds., *Politička sociologija* [Political sociology] (Belgrade: Radnička štampa, 1978); Vladimir Goati, *Politička sociologija* [Political sociology] (Belgrade: Mladost, n.d.).

26. Radoš Smiljković, "Politička sociologija" ["Political Sociology"], in Smiljković and Pečujlić, *Political Sociology*, p. 14.

27. Goati, *Political Sociology*, p. 18.

28. Ibid. p. 23.

29. Such a general political science has been defended by R. Lukić, Branko Caratan, S. Sokol, and by others.

30. As to the different treatment of the relation between political science and Marxism in world political science we can quote the extremely negative positions of Dante Germino, *Beyond Ideology* (New York: Harper and Row, 1967); the more balanced stand of Maurice Duverger, *Méthodes de la science politiques* (Paris: FUF, 1959), and Arnold Brecht, *Political Theory* (Princeton: Princeton University Press, 1959); the critical and at the same time favorable position of Umberto Cerroni, *Crisi ideale e transizione al socialismo* [The ideological crisis and transition to socialism] (Rome: Editori Riuniti, 1977), pp. 89ff. ("Esiste una scienza politica marxista?"); and the affirmative position of Julian Hochfeld, "Marksizm a socjologia stosunków politycznych" [Marxism and sociology of political relations], *Studia Socjologiczno-polityczne*, no. 1, 1958. For a position on this question by a Soviet author see, e.g., F. M. Burlackij, *Lenin: Gosudarstvo: Politika* [Lenin: The state: Politics] (Moscow: Nauka, 1970).

31. The relation between Marxism and political science is treated by all the authors who have written in Yugoslavia on general problems of political science. For examples see Caratan, *Socialism*, p. 11; Djordjević, "Fundamental Questions," p. 514; Gaber, *Politics*, p. 10; Jovan Mirić, *Rad i politika* [Labor and politics] (Zagreb: Centar za kulturnu djelatnost SSO Zagreb, 1978), p. 13; Najdan Pašić, *Classes*, chap. 2; Obrad Pejanović, *Marks i politika* [Marx and politics] (Belgrade: "Export-Press," 1969); Davor Rodin, *Marxova misao zajednice* [Marx's conception of the community] (Belgrade: Velika edicija "Ideja," 1974).

32. See Adolf Bibič, *Zasebištvo in skupnost: "Civilna družba" in država pri Heglu in Marxu* [Particularism and community: "Civil society" and state in Hegel and Marx] (Ljubljana: Mladinska knjiga, 1972).

33. On the relation of interests and politics see, e.g., Adolf Bibič, "Prispevek k teoriji interesov" [A contribution to the theory of interests], *Teorija in praksa* 9, nos. 11-12 (1972): 1620-35, 10 nos. 1-2 (1973): 95-100; Albin Igličar, *Pravni sistem in družbeni interesi* [Legal system and social interests] (Ljubljana: Partizanska knjiga, 1978); Jovan Mirić, *Interesne grupe i politička moć* [Interest groups and political power] (Zagreb: Centar za aktuelni politički studij, 1973); Najdan Pašić, *Interesi, institucije, ideologije* [Interests, institutions, ideologies] (Belgrade: Institut za politički studij FPN, 1977); Žarko Puhovski, *Interesi i zajednica* [Interests and community] (Zagreb: Liber, 1975).

34. Rade Aleksič, *Dijalektika socijalizma: Prilog marksističkoj teoriji o društvenim suprotnostima* [Dialectics of socialism: a contribution to the Marxist theory of social contradictions] (Belgrade: Vuk Karadižić, 1975). The problem of contradiction is treated in many works of Edvard Kardelj. See especially Edvard Kardelj, "Protislovja pri graditvi socializma" [Contradictions in socialist construction] in *Problemi naše socialistične graditve* (Ljubljana: DZS, 1963); Mito-Hadži Vasilev, *Protislovja v socializmu* (Ljubljana: CZ, 1958).

35. Among many works see Edvard Kardelj, *Protislovja*

družbene last-nine v sodobni socialistični praksi [Contradictions of social ownership in contemporary socialist practice] (Ljubljana: DZS, 1976).

36. Mirić, *Interest Groups*, pp. 35, 46.

37. Vukašin Pavlović, "Upotreba kategorije interesa u marksističkoj društvenoj teoriji i društvenoj nauci: Teorijskometodološke kontraverze" [The use of categories of interests in Marxist social theory and social science: Theoretical-methodological controversies] in Gjoko Tozi and Kiro Zrmanovski, eds., *Demokratskiot pluralizam na samoupravuvanje* [Democratic pluralism of self-management interests in the political system of socialist self-management] (Skopje: Republički centar za ideološko-političko obrazovanje i studii, 1978). On interests, see also, inter alia, the contributions of Petre Georgievski, Milan Matić, Denko Malevski, Mijat Damjanović in the same publication.

38. Pašić, *Interests*, p. 5.

39. See note 57 below.

40. Cf. Najdan Pašić, *Nacionalno pitanje u savremenoj epohi* [National question in the contemporary epoch] (Belgrade: Radnička štampa, 1973), chap. 1.

41. Ibid.

42. On the national question, see, e.g., Josip Broz Tito, *Nacionalno vprašanje in revolucija* [National question and revolution] (Ljubljana: DZS, 1978); Edvard Kardelj, *Razvoj slovenskega narodega vprašanja* [The development of the Slovene national question] (Ljubljana: DZS, 1957, the first edition in 1939 was under the pseudonym Sperans); Vladimir Bakarić, *Društvene klase, nacija i socijalizam* [Social classes, nation and socialism] (Zagreb: Skolska knjiga, 1976); Todo Kurtović, *Komunisti i nacionalne slobode* [The communists and national liberties] (Sarajevo: Oslobodjenje, 1975); Pašić, *Classes;* Ernest Petrič, *Mednarodnopravno varstvo narodnih manjšin* [The protection of national minorities in international law] (Maribor: Obzorja, 1977); Rudi Rizman, *Marksizem in vprašanje naroda* [Marxism and the question of nation] (Ph.D. diss., Ljubljana, 1978); Stipe Šuvar, *Nacionalno i nacionalističko* [National and nationalistic] (Split: Marksistički centar, 1974); Dragan Taškovski, *Resnica o makedonskem narodu* [The truth about the Macedonian nation] (Ljubljana: DZS, 1976).

43. On sources and forms of nationalism see, e.g., Živko Sučurlija, *Društvena anatomija nacionalizma* [Social anatomy of nationalism] (Belgrade: NIP "Mladost," s.s.).

44. See the works of Edvard Kardelj; Zvonko Lerotić, *Nacija: Teorijska istraživanja društvenog temelja i izgradnje nacija* [Nation: theoretical investigations of social basis and building of nations] (Zagreb: Kulturni radnik, 1977); Šuvar, *National and Nationalistic*.

45. Cf. Josip Broz Tito: "V čem je specifičnost osvobodilne borbe in revolucionarne preobrazbe nove Jugoslavije" [What are the specific characteristics of liberation war and revolutionary transformation of the new Yugoslavia?] in Tito, *National Question*, pp. 88-97.

46. Kardelj, *Development*, p. 48.

47. Edvard Kardelj, *Problemi naše socialistične graditve*, ix, [Problems of our socialist construction] (Ljubljana: DZS, 1974), p. 232.

48. On internationalism see *Proleterski internacionalizam u teoriji i praksi* [Proletarian internationalism in theory and practice] (Sarajevo: Marksistički studijski centar SKBiH "Veljko Vlahvic," 1978). See also Aleksandar Grličkov, *Evropa u očima komunista* [Europe in the eyes of Communists] (Zagreb: Informator, 1977), p. 110ff.

49. Anton Vratuša, *Profiles of Nonalignment* (Georgetown: Ministry of Foreign Affairs, Guyana, 1978).

50. Examples of this debate are: William E. Connolly, *The Bias of Pluralism* (New York: Atherton Press, 1969); Rainer Eisfeld, *Pluralismus zwischen Liberalismus und Sozialismus* (Stuttgart: Kohlhammer, 1972). For approaches to this question in some socialist countries see, e.g., the works of Asen Kožarov, *Monizm i pljuralizm v ideologii i politike* [Monism and pluralism in ideology and politics] (Moscow: Izdat, "Progress," 1976); Stanislaw Ehrlich, "Rzecz o pluralizmie," *Kultura i spoleczenstwo* 21, no. 4 (1977): 61-81. The revival of the discussion of pluralism is connected also with the appearance of Eurocommunism, which has caused, as in Italy, sharp debates on this question.

51. *Socialistična zveza delovnega ljudstva danes* [The socialist alliance of working people today] (Ljubljana: Zal. republiške konference SZDL Slovenije, 1970).

52. Ibid., p. 94.

53. As in Mirić, *Interest Groups*.

54. Edvard Kardelj, *Smeri razvoja političnega sistema socialističnega samoupravljanja* [Directions in the development of the political system of socialist self-management], 2d ed. rev. (Ljubljana: Komunist, 1977; 1978). Available also in translation: Edvard Kardelj, *Democracy and Socialism* (London: Summerfield Press, 1978).

55. An illustrative collection could be found in *Demokratskiot pluralizam na samoupravnite interesi vo političkiot sistem na socialističkoto samoupravuvanje*. See also: Najdan Pašić, *Pluralizam interesa i politički sistem* [Pluralism of interests and political system] (Belgrade: Delta Press, 1978).

56. Mahmut Bakhali, *Interesne grupe i marksistička teorija politike* [Interest groups and Marxist theory of politics] (Belgrade: FPN, 1970); Mirić, *Interest Groups*.

57. It is clear that the political and scientific literature on self-management in Yugoslavia is so numerous that only a small sample can be quoted here. See, e.g., J. B. Tito, *Self-management*. Great theoretical and political contributions to this field were given by the late Edvard Kardelj in several of his works, particularly those collected in: *Problemi naše socialistične graditve* [Problems of our socialist construction] (Ljubljana: Državna založba Slovenije, 1954-1974), vols. 1-9; Vladimir Bakarić, *Socijalistički samoupravni sistem i društvena reprodukcija* [Socialist self-management system and social reproduction] (Zagreb: Informator, 1974); Dušan Bilandzić. *Društveni razvoj socijalističke Jugoslavije* [Social development of socialist Yugoslavia], 5th ed. (Zagreb: Centar društvene djelatnosti SSOH, 1978); Aleksandar Hristov: *Samoupravnata kontrola i samoupravnata odgovornost* [Self-management control and self-management responsibility] (Skopje: Naša kniga, 1973); Ljubomir Jakimovski, *Socijalističkoto samoupravuvanje* [Socialist self-management] (Skopje: Komunist, 1977); Neca Jovanov, "Aspekti teoriske koncepcije samoupravljanja u Jugoslaviji" [Aspects of theoretical conception of self-management], *Kulturni radnik* 32, no. 4 (1979):

3–50; Bogdan Kavčič, *Sodobni sociološki problemi samoupravljanja v podjetjih* [Contemporary sociological problems of self-management in enterprises] (Ljubljana: Delavska enotnost, 1972); Boris Kidrič, *Zbrano delo* [Collected works], vol. 4 (Ljubljana: Cankarjeva založba, 1976); Ivan Kristan, *Samoupravljanje* [Self-management] (Ljubljana: Cankarjeva založba, 1975); Stipe Šuvar, *Samoupravljanje i alternative* [Self-management and alternatives], 3d ed. (Zagreb: Centar za kulturno djelatnost SSO, 1978); Jovan Djordjević and Najdan Pašić, eds., *Teorija i praksa samoupravljanja u Jugoslaviji* [Theory and practice of self-management in Yugoslavia] (Belgrade: Radnička štampa, 1972); Zoran Vidaković, *Korak nazad, dva koraka napred* [A step backwards, two steps forwards] (Belgrade: Komunist, 1971). Jovan Djordjević, Najdan Pašić, Balša Špadijer, eds., *Društvanopolitički sistem SFRJ* [Sociopolitical system of Yugoslavia] (Belgrade: Radnička štampa, 1976); Milojko Drulović, *L'autogestion a l'epreuve* (Paris: Fayard, 1978); Djordjević, *Political System;* Dušan Bilandžić, *Historija Socijalističke federativne republike Jugoslavije* [History of the socialist federative republic of Yugoslavia] (Zagreb: Školska knjiga, 1976); Edvard Kardelj, *Socialism and democracy;* Boštjan Markič, *Izbori i kadrovska politika* [Elections and politics of personnel recruitment] (Belgrade: Delta Press, 1978); Vladimir Mitkov, *Samoupravuvanjeto osnova na opštestveno-politički ot sistem na SFRJ* [Self-management basis of sociopolitical system of SFRJ] (Skopje: Komunist, 1976); J. B. Tito, *Self-management:* Drago Božič-Savin Jogan, *Samoupravljanje v komuni* [Self-management in the Commune] (Zagreb: Globus, 1974); Majda Strobl, Ivan Kristan, Ciril Ribičič, *Ustavno pravo Jugoslavije* [The constitutional law of Yugoslavia] (Ljubljana: PF-DDU Univerzum, 1978).

58. For definitions of socialism, see Jovan Djordjević, *Socijalizam i demokratija* [Socialism and democracy] (Belgrade: Savremena administracija, 1962), pp. 26–41. See also Branko Pribičević, *Socijalizam—svetski proces* [Socialism as a world process] (Belgrade: Partizanska knjiga—OOUR "Monos," 1979), p. 24.

59. See the discussion in the journal *Gledišta* 18, no. 6 (1977).

60. Cf. Bogdan Kavčič and Vojko Antončič, *Samoupravna urejenost in gospodarska uspešnost delovnih organizacij* [Self-management and economic efficiency of working organizations] (Ljubljana: DE, 1978); Josip Županov, *Samoupravljanje i društvena moć* [Self-management and social power] (Zagreb: Naše teme, 1969).

61. On socialism and democracy, see, e.g., Djordjević, *Political System*, p. 199; Kardelj, *Democracy and Socialism;* Ćazim Sadiković and E. Kardelj, "Socialistična demokracija v jugoslovanski praksi" [Socialist democracy in Yugoslav practice] in *Problemi naše socialistične graditve,* 4; Dmitar Mirčev, *Participacija, samoupravljanje, demokratija* [Participation, self-management, democracy] (Ph.D. diss., Ljubljana: FSPN, 1977); Ćazim Sadiković, *Kriteriji demokratije* [Criteria of democracy]; Vučina Vasović, *Demokratija i politika* [Democracy and politics] (Belgrade: Radnička štampa, 1973).

62. Among several works which could be quoted, one can mention Stipe Šuvar, *Samoupravljanje i alternative* [Self-management and alternatives] (Zagreb: Centar za kulturnu djelatnost SSOH, 1978).

63. This is the approach of Joseph Schumpeter and his contemporary followers of "democratic elitism." See J. Schumpeter, *Capitalism, Socialism and Democracy*, 3d ed. (New York: Harper & Brothers, 1950).

64. Bora Jevtić, *Neposredna demokratija: Politički interesi samoupravnog društva* [Direct democracy: political interests of self-management society] (Belgrade: Institut za pol. studije FPN, 1974).

65. Harold Laski predicted that a genuine pluralism would be possible only in a society without class domination. See H. Laski, *A Grammar of Politics* (London: George Allen and Unwin, 1967), p. 13.

66. As to the different uses of the term one has only to compare the positions as expressed by, e.g., Klaus von Beyme, *Die politischen Theorien der Gegenwort Eine Einführung* (Munich: Piper and Co., 1972), p. 16; Ralph C. Chandler, "Political Theory as History, Philosophy, and Science," in Donald M. Freeman, ed., *Foundations of Political Science Research, Methods, and Scope* (New York: Free Press, 1977), p. 123; Wolf-Dieter Narr, *Theorie-begriffe und Systemtheorie* (Stuttgart: Kohlhammer, 1971).

67. An example is: Jovan Djordjević, *Elementi političke teorije i društvenopolitički sistem samoupravnog socijalizma* [Elements of political theory and sociopolitical system of self-management socialism] (Belgrade: ICS, 1975).

68. For example, Caratan, *Socialism;* Gaber, *Politics;* Kardelj, *Democracy and Socialism;* Mirić, *Labor and Politics;* Pašić, *Classes;* Ratković, *Foundations.*

69. See the works of Djordjević, Pašić, Ratković cited in notes 67 and 68.

70. Milan Matić, *Političko predstavljanje: Razmatranje u oblasti političke teorije* [Political representation] (Belgrade: Radnička štampa, 1974).

71. *Politički sistemi i pokreti u nerazvijenim zemljama* [Political systems and movements in underdeveloped countries] (Belgrade: IIRP, 1964); Stane Južnič, *Kolonializem in dekolonizacija* [Colonialism and decolonization] (Maribor: Obzorja, 1980).

72. Kardelj, *Democracy and Socialism.*

73. Djordjević, *Political System.*

74. See, e.g., the debate in *Marx and Contemporary Epoch* 2, pp. 176–77.

75. Mirić, *Labor and Politics*, p. 47; Adolf Bibić, *Politična znanost. Ideologija. Politika* [Political Science, ideology, politics] (Ljubljana: Komunist, 1978); Ante Marušić, *Sociologija znanja i marksizam* [Sociology of knowledge and marxism] (Zagreb: Skolska knjiga, 1977).

76. Djordjević, "Fundamental Questions," p. 501.

77. Lukić, *History.*

78. Jože Goričar, *Oris zgodovine političnih teorij* [An outline of the history of political theories], *Od antike do industrijske revolucije* (Ljubljana: Cankarjeva založba, 1959).

79. Juraj Kolaković, *Historija novovjekovnih političkih teorija* [History of modern political theories] (Cakovec: Zrinski, 1976).

80. Andrija Krešić and Radoslav Vujičić, *Država i politika*

[State and politics], 2 vols. (Belgrade: Sedma sila, 1968); Nerkez Smailagić, *Historija političkih doktrina* [History of political doctrines], 2 vols. (Zagreb: Naprijed, 1971).

81. Mile Joka, ed., and Introduction to *Preteće naučnog socijalizma* [Forerunners of scientific socialism] (Zagreb:, Školska knjiga, 1978).

82. Predrag Vranicki, *Historija marksizma* [History of Marxism], Drugo preradjeno i prošireno izdanje, 2 vols. (Zagreb: Naprijed, 1971 and other editions).

83. Radoslav Ratković, *Politička teorija austromarksizma* [Political theory of Austro-Marxism] (Belgrade: Institut za izučavanje MRP, 1965).

84. Halim Mulaibrahimović, *Marksizam i anarhizam* [Marxism and anarchism] (Sarajevo: Marksistički studijski centar, 1978).

85. *Fašizam i neofašizam* [Fascism and neofascism] (Zagreb: FPN—Centar društvenih djelatnosti SSOH, 1976); Branko Pribičević et al., *Fašizam i neofašizam* (Belgrade: Savremena administracija, 1977).

86. Zdenko Roter, *Cerkev in sodobni svet: Razvoj katoliškega nauka o socializmu, komunizmu, marksizmu in ateizmu* [The church and contemporary world...] (Ljubljana: Cankarjeva založba, 1973).

87. Dušan Žubrinić, *Marksizam i teorija elita* [Marxism and theory of elites] (Zagreb: Skolska knjiga, 1975).

88. Ivan Babić, *Politička teorija instrumentalizma* [Political theory of instrumentalism] (Zagreb: FPN-Liber, 1971).

89. E.g., Desanka Savičević, *Društvena i politička teorija i kritika u radovima Dimitrija Tucovića* [Social and political theory and criticism in the works of Dimitrij Tucović] (Belgrade: Rad, 1972); Jovan Djordjević, *Svetozar Marković i savremenost* [Svetozar Marković and contemporaneity] (Belgrade: Ideje, 1978).

90. Josip Broz Tito, *Zbrana dela* [Collected works] (Ljubljana: Komunist in Borec, 1978–). A recent edition of Tito's selected works in five volumes is now available, under the titles: vol. 1, *Referati s kongresov KPJ (ZKJ)* [Reports at the congresses of CPY (LCY)]; vol. 2, *Delavski razred in Zveza komunistov Jugoslavije* [The working class and the league of communists of Yugoslavia]; vol. 3, *Nacionalno vprašanje in revolucija* [National question and revolution]; vol. 4, *Samoupravljanje* [Self-management]; vol. 5, *Jugoslavija v boju za neodvisnost in neuvrščenost* [Yugoslavia in the fight for independence and nonalignment]. All these volumes were published in Ljubljana: DZS, 1977–1978.

91. Kardelj, *Problems* and other works.

92. Nikolić Miloš (and Štambuk, Vladimir, Vol. III) ed. *Samoupravljanje i radnički pokret* [Self-management and workers' movement] 3 vols. (Belgrade: IC Komunist, 1973).

93. Predrag Radenović and Živko Surčulja, *Marksizam i samoupravljanje* [Marxism and self-management] (Belgrade: Službeni list SFRJ, 1974).

94. Stane Južnič, *Socializem in dežele v razvoju* [Socialism and developing countries] (Ljubljana: Komunist, 1969).

95. Stojan Gligorić, *Arapski svet i socijalizam* [Arab world and socialism] (Belgrade: IMRP, 1973).

96. Ivan Iveković, *Afrika i socijalizam* [Africa and socialism] (Belgrade: Komunist, 1976); Jokica Hadži-Vasileva, *Socijalistička opredeljenja u tropskoj Africi* [Socialist orientations in tropical Africa] (Belgrade: IMRP, 1973).

97. Ljubomir Paligorić, *Političke doktrine levice u Latinskoj Americi* [Political doctrines of the Latin American Left] (Belgrade: IMRP, 1972).

98. Bojana Tadić, *Nesvrstanost u teoriji i praksi medjunarodnih odnosa* [Nonalignment in theory and practice of international relations] (Belgrade: IMRP, 1976).

99. This position can be found in any serious treatment of the state in our country.

100. So it is generally estimated that the role of the state immediately after the anticolonial revolution can be used and in fact is used as an important force of social transformation.

101. Radomir Lukić, *Teorija države i prava* [Theory of state and law] (Belgrade: Naučna knjiga, 1953), vol. 1, *Teorija države* [Theory of state]; Oleg Mandić-Smiljko Sokol, *Država* [The state] (Zagreb: Informator, 1977); Najdan Pašić, *Savremena država* [The contemporary state] (Belgrade: BIGZ, 1976).

102. Svetoslav Radovanović, *O suverenitetu države u savremenim uslovima...* [On the sovereignty of the state in contemporary conditions...] (Ph.D. diss., Novi Sad, 1977).

103. Lukić, *Political Theory*.

104. Ibid., p. 29.

105. Cf. Pašić.

106. Zdenko Roter, *Katoliška cerkev in država v Jugoslaviji 1945–1973* [Catholic church and the state in Yugoslavia 1945–1973] (Ljubljana: CZ, 1976).

107. Nikola Vućo, *Državna intervencija u privredi, Istoriski razvoj* [The state intervention in economics, historical development] (Belgrade: Savremena administracija, 1975).

108. Novica Blagojević, *Ekonomska uloga države u nerazvijenim afričkim zemljama* [The economic role of the state in the underdeveloped African states] (Belgrade: Institut za izučavanje medjunarodnog radničkog pokreta, 1975).

109. E.g., Edvard Kardelj, *Problemi naše socialistične graditve* [Problems of our socialist construction] (Ljubljana: DZS, 1964), 6: 57.

110. K. Marx, *Critique of Hegel's "Philosophy of the Right" and other works;* F. Engels, *Anti-Dühring*; V. I. Lenin, *State and Revolution*. This idea is also contained in Gramsci's works.

111. Blažo M. Petrović, *Država i samoupravljanje* [The state and self-management] (Belgrade: ZAK, 1976).

112. Radomir Lukić, *Političke stranke* [Political parties] (Belgrade: Naučna knjiga, 1966); Stjepan Pulišelić, *Političke stranke kao faktor suvremenog političkog sistema* [Political parties as a factor of contemporary political system] (Zagreb: Naprijed, 1971); Radoš Smiljkovič, *Sociologija političkih stranaka* [Sociology of political parties] (Belgrade: ICS, 1976).

113. Djordjević, *Political System;* Pašić, *Classes*.

114. Radoš Smiljković, *Lenjinova koncepcija partije* [Lenin's conception of party] (Belgrade: FPN, 1966); Ivo Petrinović, *Partija radničke klase u koncepciji Antonija Gramscija* [Gramsci's conception of the party of the working class] (Split: Matica Hrvatska, 1967).

115. E.g., Branko Pribičević, *Socijalizam—svetski proces*

[Socialism as a world process] (Belgrade: Partizanska knjiga—"Monos," 1979).

116. Dan Gjanković, "Političke partije u SAD" [Political parties in USA], *Politička misao* 1, no. 3 (1964): 11-67.

117. Dragoslav Janković, *O političkim stankama u Srbiji XIX veka* [On political parties in Serbia in the nineteenth century] (Belgrade: Prosveta, 1951); Vaso Bogdanov, *Historija političkih stranaka u Hrvatskoj* [History of political parties in Croatia] (Zagreb: NIP, 1958).

118. See, e.g., the quoted works of R. Lukić and R. Smiljković.

119. R. Lukić, "O suzbijanju birokratizacije i tehnokratizacije političkih stranaka" [On fighting the bureaucratization and technocratization of political parties] in *Komunisti i samoupravljanje* (Zagreb: FPN, 1967); Stjepan Pulišelić, "Političke stranke kao faktor suvremenog političkog sistema" [Political parties as a factor of contemporary political system] in S. Pulišelić, ed., *Političke stranke kao faktor* (Zagreb: Naprijed, 1971).

120. See *Program of the LCY*, p. 244; Lukić, *Political Parties*.

121. Lukić, *Political Parties*, speaks of "social conditions of withering away of political parties," of "the process of withering away of political parties" and of the "political life without political parties."

122. This term is used to characterize the changes in the role of political organization in a political system of socialist self-management.

123. See, e.g., Živko Marković, *Samoupravljanje i avantgarda* [Self-management and vanguard] (Belgrade: Radnička štampa, 1976); Gojko Stanič, *Družbena slojevitost ZK Slovenije* [Social stratification of the league of communists of Slovenia] (Ljubljana: FSPN, 1975).

124. E.g., Ilija Vuković, *The Socialist Alliance of the Working People of Yugoslavia in Political System of SFRY* (Belgrade: Savremena administracija, 1975).

125. Vukašin Pavlović, *Sindikat i politički sistem* [Trade unions and the political system] (Belgrade: Radnička štampa, 1974).

126. Lolić Marko, *Mladost revolucije: SKOJ—Savez socijalističke omladine Jugoslavije* [The youth of revolution: FCYY—Federation of Socialist Youth of Yugoslavia] (Zagreb: Centar za kulturnu djelatnost SSO Zagreba, 1979); Divna Mirkoć-Lebl, *Omladinska organizacija kao faktor formiranja društvenog profila mladih* [Youth organization as a factor of building of social profile of the young generation] (Belgrade: IDN, 1972).

127. There were some scientific and political conferences on these topics.

128. Jovan Djordjević, "Interest Groups in Yugoslavia," in H. W. Ehrmann, ed., *Interest Groups on Four Continents* (Pittsburgh: University of Pittsburgh Press, 1960).

129. Cf. Pašić, *Classes*, p. 220; Mirič, *Interest Groups*, p. 14.

130. There are some nuances in defining these terms in our politological literature.

131. Djordjević, *Political System*, pp. 785-86.

132. E.g., Adolf Bibič, "Interesne skupine kot predmet politične znanosti" [Interest groups as a subject of political science], *Aṅthropos*, nos. 3-4, 1970.

133. Djordjević, *Political System*, p. 786.

134. Gavro Altman, *Političko grupisanje u SAD* [Political grouping in USA] (Zagreb: Naprijed, 1964).

135. Vlado Benko. "Mednarodne skupine pritiska" [International pressure groups], *Aṅthropos*, nos. 3-4, 1970, pp. 33-43.

136. In addition to the cited works of J. Djordjević, Najdan Pašić, Jovan Mirić, are the examples of Miodrag Zecević, *Društvene organizacije i udruženja* [Social organizations and associations] (Belgrade: Institut za politicke studije FPN, 1976); Stane Kranjc, *Interesna združenja občanov v SRS* [Interest groups of citizens in SR Slovenia] (Ljubljana: FSPN, 1971).

137. Pašić, *Classes*, p. 222, and others.

138. As Mirić, *Interest Groups*, p. 140, includes in the "institutional interest groups" also the "working organization as an interest group."

139. Djordjević, *Political System*, p. 787, includes in the interest groups also the "chamber of the associated labor" as a part of the assembly system. See also Mirić, *Interest Groups*.

140. Kranjc, *Interest Groups*; Začević, *Social Organizations*.

141. Djordjević, *Political Systems*, p. 790; Zečević, *Social Organizations*, p. 10.

142. Mahmut Bakhali, *Interesne grupe i marksistička teorija politike* [Interest groups and Marxist theory of politics] (Belgrade: FPN, 1970).

143. Dj. Ninčić, "Metodologija proučavanja medjunarodnih odnosa" [Methodology of the study of international relations], *Arhiv za pravne i društvene nauke*, nos. 3-4, 1960.

144. Among general works on international relations can be quoted: Vlado Benko, *Mednarodni odnosi* [International relations] (Maribor: Obzorja, 1977); Vojin Dimitrijević and Radoslav Stojanović, *Osnovi teorije medjunarodnih odnosa* [The foundations of theory of international relations] (Belgrade: Službeni list, 1977); Velibor Gavranov and Momir Stojković, *Medjunarodni odnosi i spoljna politika Jugoslavije* [International relations and foreign policy of Yugoslavia] (Belgrade: Savremena administracija, 1972); Vladimir Ibler, ed., and Introduction to *Medjunarodni odnosi* [International relations] (Zagreb: Naprijed, 1971); Branimir M. Janković, *Teorija i stvarnost u nauci o medjunarodnim odnosima* [Theory and reality in the science of international relations] (Belgrade: Savremena administracija, 1977); Milan Šahović, *Medjunarodni odnosi i društveni napredak* [International relations and social progress] (Belgrade: Radnička štampa, 1977); Radovan Vukadinović, *Medjunarodni politički odnosi* [International political relations] (Zagreb: Centar za aktualni politički studij, 1974).

145. Radovan Vukadinović, *Teorije o medjunarodnim odnosima* [Theories of international relations] (Zagreb: Centar društvenih djelatnosti Saveza OH, 1978).

146. Benko, *International Relations*, pp. 181-82; Ibler, *International Relations*, p. 15.

147. See Dimitrijević and Stojanović, *Foundations of Theory*, p. 13.
148. Vukadinović, *International Political Relations*, pp. 116-37.
149. Benko. *International Relations*, pp. 247-94.
150. In Dimitrijević and Stojanović, *Foundations of Theory*, pp. 141-96.
151. Ibler, *International Relations*, p. 16; Vukadinović, *International Political Relations*, p. 19.
152. See the cited works of Benko, Dimitrijević, Stojanović, Janković.
153. See Vukadinović, *International Political Relations*, pp. 81-82.
154. E.g., Benko, *International Relations*, p. 233.
155. Leo Mates, "Neki problemi nauke o medjunarodnim odnosima" [Some problems of the science of international relations], *Medjunarodni problemi*, no. 1, 1963.
156. Gavranov and Stojković, *International Relations*, p. 25.
157. Ibid.
158. Benko, *International Relations*, p. 230.
159. Ibler, *International Relations*, p. 42.
160. Vukadinović, *International Political Relations*.
161. Problems of inequality as an international problem are treated by all important authors on international relations in our country.
162. *Novi medjunarodni ekonomski poredak* [The new international economic order] (Belgrade: IMPP, 1977).
163. Bora Jevtić, *Medjunarodna uloga nesvrstanosti* [International role of nonalignment] (Belgrade: Rad, 1976); Edvard Kardelj, *Zgodovinske korenine neuvrščenosti* [Historical roots of nonalignment] (Ljubljana: Komunist, 1978); Leo Mates, *Nesvrstanost: Teorija i savremena praksa* [Nonalignment: theory and contemporary practice] (Belgrade: Institut za medjunarodnu politiku i privredu, 1970); Ranko Petković, *Teorijski pojmovi nesvrstanosti* [Theoretical conceptions of nonalignment] (Belgrade: Rad, 1974); Tadić, *Nonalignment*; Anton Vratuša, *Profiles of Nonalignment* (Georgetown: Ministry of Foreign Affairs, Guyana, 1978).
164. Benko, *International Relations*, pp. 130, 329; Vukadinović, *International Political Relations*, p. 283.
165. See Dimitrijević and Stojković, *Foundations of Theory*, for a discussion of the form of relations in international communities, complementary to the collective security; see also Vukadinović, *International Political Relations*, on types of international relations.
166. Kardelj, *Historical Roots*, p. 15.
167. Janković, *Theory and Reality*, p. 15.
168. Eugen Pusić, *Problemi upravljanja* [Problems of administration] (Zagreb: Naprijed, 1971).
169. Stane Južnič, *Politična kultura* [Political culture] (Maribor: Obzorja, 1973); Radoslav Ratković, *Ideologija i politika* [Ideology and politics], 3d ed. (Belgrade: Institut za političke studije FPN, 1976); Ivan Šiber, *Socijalna struktura i politički stavovi* [Social structure and political attitudes] (Zagreb: Centar za aktuelni politički studij, 1974).
170. See, e.g., Branko Pribičević, *Socijalizam svetski proces* [Socialism as a world process]; Branko Caratan, *Tradicije oktobra i suvremenost* [Traditions of October Revolution and our time] (Zagreb: Globus, 1977); Zorica Priklmajer-Tomanović, *Socijalizam i demokratija u koncepcijama zapadnoevropskih komunističkih partija* [Socialism and democracy in the conceptions of West-European Communist parties] (Belgrade: Institut za MRP, 1973).
171. Najdan Pašić, *Uporedni politički sistemi* [Comparative political systems] (Belgrade: Institut za političke studije FPN, 1962); Aleksander Fira, *Prilog proučavanju političkih sistema buržoaske demokratije* [Contribution to the research of political systems of bourgeois democracy] (Belgrade: VŠPN, 1964); Vučina Vasović, *Savremeni politički sistemi* [Contemporary political systems] (Belgrade: Savremena administracija, 1976); Jovan Djordjević, *Politički sistem—Politički sistemi i pokreti u nerazvijenim zemljama* [Political systems and movements in underdeveloped countries] (Belgrade: IIRP, 1964); Stane Južnič, *Latinska Amerika: Društvena struktura i politički sistemi* [Latin America: social structure and political systems] (Belgrade: IMPP, 1968); Anton Belber, *Vojaška vladavina v Afriki* [Military rule in Africa] (Ljubljana: Partizanska knjiga, 1974); Janko Rupnik, *Ustavnost, demokracija in politični sistem* (Maribor: Obzorja, 1975).
172. This section is based on the status of the faculties, on the curricula, and in particular on a meeting of Yugoslav faculties of political science, held 12-13 April 1979 at the Faculty of Sociology, Political Science, and Journalism in Ljubljana. The materials of the Third Congress of political scientists of Yugoslavia (January 1978) are also taken into account.
173. These fields are, e.g., education, research, sociopolitical organizations, local communities, organizations of associated labor, sociopolitical communities, journalism, public administration.
174. Many important books on political science have been published by the Institute of Political Studies at the Faculty of Political Science in Belgrade; the Zagreb Faculty has published its books in a special *Politička misao* (political thought) series; the Faculty in Ljubljana has been publishing in cooperation with *Obzorja*, Maribor, a special series under the title *Sociological and Political Science Library*. Some faculties have been publishing special journals.
175. For detailed information on research work in political science, consult the research institutions and the self-management communities of interest, responsible for the research.
176. The center concentrates its work on economic aspects of the cooperation.
177. For further information on the work of this center, see the *Bulletin* of the International Center for Public Enterprises in Developing Countries.
178. For further information on this topic see *Political Science in Yugoslavia* (note 1 above) and *Arhiv za pravne i društvene nauke* 61, no. 3 (July-September 1978).
179. Among recent discussions to be mentioned are contributions published in journals: *Gledišta* 18, no. 6 (1977); *Dijalog*, no. 3, 1977; *Teorija in praksa* 15, nos. 1-2 (1978); *Naše teme* 23, no. 4 (1979).

Bibliography

Aktualni problemi politične znanosti [Topical problems of political science] (Ljubljana: VŠPV, 1966).

Benko, Vlado. *Mednarodni odnosi* [International relations] (Maribor: Obzorja, 1975).

Bibič, Adolf. *Kaj je politična znanosti'* [What is political science?] (Ljubljana: Komunist, 1969).

_____. *Politična Znanosti', Ideolog'a, Politika* [Political science, ideology, politics] (Ljubljana: Komunist, 1978).

_____, and Pavle, Novosel. *Politička Znanost—Predmet i suština* [Political science—subject and substance] (Zagreb: Naprijed, 1971).

Caratan, Branko. *Socijalizam i politika* [Socialism and politics] (Zagreb: Center za aktualni politički studij, 1972).

Čemerlić, Hamdija. "Razvoj političkih nauka u Bosni i Hercegovini" [Development of political science in Bosnia and Herzegovina], *Arhiv za pravne i društvene nauke*, no. 3, 1978.

Dimitrijević, Vojin, and Stojanović, Radoslav. *Osnovi teorije medjuna-rodnih odnosa* [The foundations of theory of international relations] (Belgrade: Službeni list, 1977).

Dimitrov, Evgeni. "Stanje i problemi političkih nauka u SR Makedoniji" [Position and problems of political sciences in SR of Macedonia], *Arhiv za pravne i drustvene nauke*, no. 3, 1978.

Djordjević, Jovan. "Osnovna pitanja političkih nauka" [Fundamental questions of political science] in J. Djordjević, *Socializam i demokratija* (Belgrade: Savremena administracija, 1962).

_____. *Politički sistem* [Political System] (Belgrade: Savremena administracija, 1977).

_____. "Stanje i problemi političkih nauka" [Position and problems of political science] *Gledišta*, no. 6, 1977.

Gaber, Steva. *Politikata i političkata nauka* [Politics and political science] (Skopje: Nasa Knjiga, 1975).

Gerskovic, Leo. "Political System of Yugoslavia as a Teaching Subject." Paper delivered at the Symposium of the Yugoslav Political Science Association, Zagreb, March 30-31, 1965.

Gjanković, Dan. "Politička nauka-danas" [Political science today], *Zbornik Pravnog fakulteta u Zagrebu*, no. XII, 1962.

Goati, Vladimir. *Politička Sociologija* (Belgrade: Mladost, n.d.).

Kardelj, Edvard. *Democracy and Socialism* (London: The Summerfield Press, 1978).

Lukić, Radomir. *Istorija političkih i pravnih teorija* [History of political and legal theories] (Belgrade: Naucna knjiga, 1956).

Mates, Leo. "Neki problemi nauke o medjunarodnim odnosima" [Some problems of the science of international relations], *Medjunarodni problemi*, no. 1, 1963.

Mirić, Jovan. *Rad i politika* [Labour and politics] (Zagreb: Izd. Centra za društvenu djelatnost SSO, 1978).

Ninčić, Dj. "Metodologija proucavan ja medjunarodnih odnos" [Methodology of the study of international relations], *Arhiv za pravne i društvene nauke*, nos. 3-4, 1960.

Pašić, Najdan. *Klase i politika* [Classes and politics] (Belgrade: Rad, 1978 ed.).

_____. "Politička nauka u samoupravnom društvu" [Political science in self-management society], in *Fakultet političkih nauka, 1968-1980/Visoka škola političkih nauka 1960-1968* (Belgrade: FPN, 1980).

_____. "Društveni uslovi razvitka marksističke političke nauke" [Social conditions of the development of marxist political science], *Socijalizam*, no. 3, 1964.

Pažanin, Ante. *Filozofija i politika* [Philosophy and politics] (Zagreb: FPN, 1973).

Pecujlic, Miroslav. *Horizonti revolucije: Studije iz političke sociologije* [Horizons of revolution: studies in political sociology] (Belgrade: Institut za političke studije FPN, 1979).

Podunavac, Milan. "O mogućnosti zasnivanja metateorije marksističke politikologije" [On the possibility of a metatheory of marxist politology], *Naše teme*, no. 4, 1979.

Political Science in Yugoslavia (Belgrade: Union of Political Science Associations of Yugoslavia, 1979).

Ratković, Radomir. "O predmetu i mestu političkih nauka" [On the subject and placement of political science], *Ogledi o problemima savremenog društva* (Belgrade: Kultura, 1961).

_____. *Osnovi nauke o politici* [Foundations of political science] (Belgrade: Institut za političke studije FPN, 1977).

Smiljkovic, Rados, and Pecujlic, Miroslav, eds. *Politička Sociologija* (Belgrade: Radnička Stampa, 1978).

Tanović, Arif. "Filozofija, politologija i politika" [Philosophy, politology and politics], *Dijalog*, no. 3, 1977, pp. 21-31.

Tomic, Stojan. *Politički professionalizam* [Professionalism in politics] (Belgrade: Radnička stampa, 1975).

Vasović, Vučina. *Demokratija i politika* [Democracy and politics] (Belgrade: Radnička stampa, 1973).

Vukadinović, Radovan. *Teorije o medjunarodnim odnosima* [Theories of international relations] (Zagreb: Centar za društvenu djelatnost SOH, 1978).

APPENDIX 1

POLITICAL SCIENCE IN SELECTED COUNTRIES

COUNTRY	FIRST TAUGHT	ASSOCIATION FOUNDED	NUMBER OF POLITICAL SCIENTISTS	DOMINANT APPROACH
Argentina	1922[1]	1957	not available	Traditional
Australia	1919	1952	375	None
Austria	1965	1970	30	Behavioral
Belgium	1893	1951	not available	None
Brazil	1939[2]	1966	not available	Traditional
Canada	1888	1929	about 700	None
Denmark	1958	after 1958	not available	Behavioral and Marxist
Finland	1922	1935	320–360	Behavioral/Traditional
France	1945	1949	600	Traditional
Germany, East	n.a.	1974	150	Marxist
Germany, West	1945	late 1940s	800	Behavioral
Iceland	1970	early 1970s	5	Behavioral
India	before 1938	before 1944	76 departments	Traditional
Japan	1877/1945	1948	600[6]	Traditional
Korea	1946	1953[3]	385	Traditional
Netherlands	1948	1950	1,000	Behavioral
New Zealand	1938[4]	1974	144[7]	Traditional
Norway	1947	early 1950s	100–120	Behavioral
Pakistan	1947	1950	300	Traditional
Poland	1964	1950–1955	575	Marxist
Sweden	1622/1840s	1970	162	None
Switzerland	1902	1959	470	Traditional
USSR	1967	1960	360	Marxist
United Kingdom	1912[4]	1950	900–1,000[5]	Traditional
United States	1876	1903	15,000	Behavioral
Yugoslavia	1958	1954	not available	Marxist

Most of the above data were drawn from the foregoing chapters of this volume. 1. Political law. 2. Graduate courses. 3. Inactive until 1956. 4. First chair. 5. Over 700 in British Political Studies Assn. 6. University and college faculty. The associations have 2,000 members. 7. Members of the association in 1981.

APPENDIX 2

INTERNATIONAL POLITICAL SCIENCE ASSOCIATION CONGRESSES

YEAR	LOCATION	PARTICIPANTS	COUNTRIES	PRESIDENT	PAPERS
1950	Zurich	80	23	Quincy Wright (USA)	9
1952	The Hague	220	31	Quincy Wright (USA)	57
1955	Stockholm	275	36	William A. Robson (UK)	25
1958	Rome	320	31	James K. Pollock (USA)	77
1961	Paris	425	46	Jacques Chapsal (France)	59
1964	Geneva	494	43	Sir Norman Chester (UK)	94
1967	Brussels	754	56	Jacques Freymond (Switz.)	146
1970	Munich	894	46	Carl J. Friedrich (USA)	259
1973	Montreal	1,144	56	Jean Laponce (Canada)	327
1979	Moscow	1,466	53	Karl Deutsch (USA)	
1982	Rio de Janeiro			Candido Mendes (Brazil)	

NUMBER OF MEMBERS AND ROUND TABLES

	MEMBERS			ROUND TABLES		
YEAR	COLLECTIVE	ASSOCIATE	INDIVIDUAL	NO.	PARTICIPANTS	COUNTRIES
1949	4	—	—	—	—	—
1950	8	—	—	—	—	—
1951	12	—	—	—	—	—
1952	18	8	52	—	—	—
1953	18	8		2	58	16
1954	20	8		1	46	13
1955	23	20	232	—	—	—
1956	25	26		1	33	14
1957	23	6		1	38	14
1958	25	26	425	—	—	—
1959	24	27		1	41	13
1960	25			1	41	15
1961	26	58	442	—	—	—
1962	26			1		
1963	26			1		
1964	29	68	420	2	59	17
1965	29	85		1	36	17
1966	29			2	91	19
1967	30	194	520	1	24	13
1968	33			1	40	17

(*continued*)

NUMBER OF MEMBERS AND ROUND TABLES

	MEMBERS			ROUND TABLES		
YEAR	COLLECTIVE	ASSOCIATE	INDIVIDUAL	NO.	PARTICIPANTS	COUNTRIES
1969	33	207	510	3	128	32
1970	33	198		—	—	—
1971	33	175		1	64	22
1972	33	169		1	53	19
1973	34	167	450	1	17	8
1974	36	162		3	50+	18+
1975	36	155		8	155	27
1976	37	152	532	NA	NA	NA
1977	36	91	690	NA	NA	NA
1978	36	97	847	5	80	19
1979	36	114	980	3	68	12
1980	36	130	871	4	72	16
1981	NA	NA	NA	4	64	21

Source: IPSA Secretariat.

APPENDIX 3

INTERNATIONAL POLITICAL SCIENCE
ASSOCIATION FINANCIAL REPORTS,
1955–1980

			RECEIPTS			EXPENDITURES		
YEAR	MEMBERSHIPS	UNESCO SUBSIDY	GRANTS	CONGRESSES	OTHER	CONGRESSES	OTHER	BALANCE
1955+	2,417	7,658	4,000	—	9,198	9,044	13,893	390
1956	2,964	7,540	6,000	—	3,201	—	13,732	5,973
1957	3,330	7,518	23,500	—	4,087	—	38,717	−282
1958	4,082	7,500	7,680	15,500	4,220	23,703	16,870	−1,601
1959	4,300	7,540	19,747	—	5,922	—	38,572	−1,063
1960	4,713	7,540	17,567	—	377	—	22,247	7,950
1961	4,770	9,000	13,400	2,650	9,247	20,339	17,391	1,336
1962	5,020	9,000	—	—	589	—	17,730	−1,121
1963	4,599	9,000	—	—	2,069	—	17,650	991
1964	5,990	9,000	9,219	30,876	6,049	37,220	29,000	−5,086
1965	8,955	9,000	5,666	—	3,722	—	28,450	−1,016
1966	9,094	9,000	7,731	—	3,796	—	31,677	−2,046
1967	11,743	10,000	27,109	32,268	4,550	45,622	29,576	10,472
1968	13,084	10,000	8,041	—	3,927	—	31,495	3,557
1969	12,831	11,249	45,067	—	3,962	—	63,183	9,926
1970	14,401	11,000	15,500	62,539	5,625	67,013	38,851	3,201
1971	16,396	11,443	6,540	—	5,941	—	41,251	−931
1972	17,457	11,508	7,150	—	3,063	—	49,937	−6,759
1973	19,453	12,750	—	100,350	13,286	103,163	47,111	3,201
1974	14,953	12,734	—	—	16,344	—	43,485	−5,036
1975	16,405	13,421	—	—	88,503	—	40,266	−1,409
1976	NA	NA	NA	—	NA	—	NA	NA
1977	23,265	14,748	10,450	—	20,680	—	73,711	4,568
1978	27,091	25,200	18,500	—	21,087	—	91,144	734
1979	30,662	12,632	20,318	74,201	20,175	70,777	77,568	9,643
1980	37,686	18,346	19,348	—	53,570	—	139,227	10,277

SOURCE: IPSA Secretariat.

APPENDIX 4

GENERAL SECRETARIES OF THE INTERNATIONAL POLITICAL SCIENCE ASSOCIATION

François Goguel (France) 1949–1950
Jean Meynaud (France) 1950–1955
John Goormaghtigh (Belgium) 1955–1961

Serge Hurtig (France) 1961–1967
André Philippart (Belgium) 1967–1976
John E. Trent (Canada) 1976–

Source: IPSA Secretariat

APPENDIX 5

INFORMATION ON INTERNATIONAL POLITICAL SCIENCE ASSOCIATIONS

ASSOCIATIONS	PERSONNEL	PUBLICATIONS	MEETINGS/REUNIONS
AFRICA Département de science politique, Université de Tanzanie, B.P. 35036 Dar Es Salaam, Tanzania	*President:* Dr. Mohamed Bouzidi, Faculté de Droit, 24, rue Oum Errabia, Rabat (Agdal) Morocco *Secretary General:* Dr. S. S. Mushi	*A.A.P.S. Bulletin*. Editor: Dr. S. S. Mushi, Département de science politique, Université de Tanzania, B.P. 35036, Dar-Es-Salam, Tanzania	Conférence bi-annuelle
ARGENTINA Solis 443, 2°p., Dto, "C" Buenos Aires (1078), Republica Argentina	*President:* Professor Segundo V. Linares Quintana, Facultad de Derecho, Universidad de Buenos Aires, Republica Argentina	*Método de la Ciencia Política* (version espanola). Editor: Georges Burdeau *La Ciencia Política y la Lucha por el Poder.* Varios autores	
AUSTRALASIA Department of Political Science, Research School of Social Science, Australian National University Canberra A.C.T. 2600	*President:* Peter Loveday *Executive Officer:* Margrit Sedlacek	*Politics.* Editor: Dr. Dean Jaensch, Flinders University, Discipline of Politics, Bedford Park, South Australia 5042 *APSA Monographs.* Editor: Dr. Dean Jaensch, Flinders University	August-September, various locations (Monash University, 1981)
AUSTRIA A-1060 Vienna Stumpergasse 56	*President:* Raoul F. Kneucker, Fonds zür Förderung der Wissenschaftlichen Forschung *Secretary:* Werner Pleschberger	*Österreichische Zeitschrift für Politikwissenschaft.* Editors: Ernest Kouba, Emmerich Talos, Karl Ucakar	
BELGIUM (Walloon) Avenue Louise 339-341, rte 23 B-1050 Brussels	*President:* Professor Charles Goosens, Université de Liège *Director:* André Philippart, 43, rue des Champs-Elysées, 1050 Brussels	*Res Publica.* Editor: Wilfried Dewachter	
BELGIUM (Flemish) E. Van Evenstraat 2B B-3000, Louven	*President:* Hugo Van Hassel, Katholieke Universiteit Leuven *Secretary:* Maurice Boeynaems		
BRAZIL Sociedade Brasileira de Instruçao Praca XV de Novembro 101 Rio de Janeiro, Brazil 21-231-2946	*Administrator:* Martha Pimenta De Moraes	*Revista de Ciência Política.* Editor: Armando de Oliveira Marinho	

(continued)

ASSOCIATIONS	PERSONNEL	PUBLICATIONS	MEETINGS/REUNIONS
BULGARIA 1040 Sofia, Sofia University "Kliment Ochridsky" Boulevard Rousky 15	*President:* Professor Dimitar Dimitrov, Higher School of Economics "Karl Marx" *Secretary:* Ivan Nedev		Sofia University— December
CANADA Carleton University Room 1403, Arts Tower Ottawa, Ontario K1S 5B6 613-231-7160	Canadian Political Science Association *President:* Walter D. Young, University of Victoria, Victoria, B.C. V8W 2Y2 *Secretary-Treasurer:* V. Seymour Wilson	*Canadian Journal of Political Science/La revue canadienne de science politique*. Editors: John Courtney, University of Saskatchewan, and Jean Crete, Laval University	Annual, late spring location varies
Département de science politique, Université du Québec à Montréal CP 8888, Montréal, P.Q. H3C 3P8	Société québécoise de science politique *President:* Paul Painchaud *Secretary-Treasurer:* Jacques Bourgault	*Bulletin* (jointly with la Société québécoise de science politique). Editors: V. Seymour Wilson and Michel De la Durantaye	
CHINA 7th Fl., 100 Hengyang Rd. Taipei, Taiwan	*President:* Lien Chan, National Taiwan University *General Secretary:* John C. Kuan, National Chengchi University	*Occasional Papers.* Editor: Tsai Chang-wen, National Taiwan University	December—Taipei
CZECHOSLOVAKIA Narodni 18, 116 91 Praha 1 Czechoslovakia 20 38 38, 20 38 66	*President:* Milan Matous, Institut of Marxism- *Secretary:* Bela Malikova	*Bulletin of Czechoslovak Association of Political Science*. Editor: Dr. Josef Blahoz	
DENMARK Institute of Political Science Aarhus University Universitetsparken DK-8000, Aarhus C. 06/13011	*President:* Erik Damgaard, Aarhus *Treasurer:* Steffan Zetterholm	*Newsletter*.	
FINLAND Department of Political Science University of Helsinki Aleksanterinkatu 7, 6 krs. 00100 Helsinki 10 191 2662	*President:* Dr. Ilkka Heiskanen *Secretary:* Kirsti Aaltonen	*Politiikka (Quarterly).* Editor: Harto Hakovirta *Politiikka & yhteiskunta.* Editor: Kirsti Aaltonen *Politiikan tutkimuksia.* Editor: Ilkka Heiskanen	January—varies April—Helsinki

FRANCE

27, rue Saint-Guillaume
75341 Paris Cedex 07
260.39.60 Postes 752,778 et 669

President: François Goguel
Secretary-General: Jean-Luc Parodi
Assistant: Guillaume Parmentier

Revue française de science politique.
Director: Georges Lavau

Bulletin de L'A.F.S.P.
Editor: Jean Luc Parodi

GERMANY

Von-Melle-Park 15
D-2000 Hamburg 13
040/4123-2425

President: Manfred Hattich, Tutzing

Politische Vierteljahresschrift.
Editor: Prof. Dr. Ulrich v. Alemann, Westdeutscher Verlag, Faulbrunnenstr. 13, D-6200 Wiesbaden

Academy of Sciences of the GDR
Institute of Theory of State and Law
108 Berlin, Otto-Nuschke-Strasse 10/11

President and Secretary-General: Dr. Karl Heinz Roder

Staat und Rechts.
Editor: Akademie fur Staat-und Rechtswissenschaft der DDR, 1502 Postdam/Babelsberg, August-Bebel-Strabe 89

GREECE

7, rue Tassopoulou
Aghia Pazaskevie,
Athens

President: Phedon Vegleris, Athens University
Secretary-General: George Cortogiogis

Les forces sociales et politiques en Grèce
Editor: "Exantas," 4, rue Delphoz, Athens (t.t. 144)

HUNGARY

Tarsadalomtudomanyi Intézet
1068 Budapest Benczur 33
Hungary

President: Lakos Sandor

Tarsadalomtudomanyi Kozlemények.
Editor: Halay Tibor

Allam es Jogtudomany.
Editor: Szabo Imre, Budapest 1, Orszaghaz 30

Politikai Foiskola Kozlemenyei.
Editor: Tomori Lajos, Budapest XIV, Ajtosi Durer 19

INDIA

Department of Political Science
University of Jodhpur, New Campus
Jodhpur (Rajasthan) 342001

President: J. Ramachandran, Director of College Education, Government of Tamilnadu, Madras
Secretary-General and Treasurer: Dr. L. S. Rathore, Jodhpur

News Bulletin (quarterly).
Editor: L. S. Rathore

Annual Conferences

Indian Journal of Political Science.
Editor: B.A.V. Sharma, Hyderabad

(continued)

ASSOCIATIONS	PERSONNEL	PUBLICATIONS	MEETINGS/REUNIONS
ISRAEL			
Department of Political Studies Bar-Ilan University Ramat-Gan	*President*: Daniel J. Elazar, Bar-Ilan University *Secretary-General*: Giora Goldberg		
ITALY			
Via dei Colli Farnesia, 202 00100 Roma	*President*: Professor Franco Valsecchi *Secretary*: Mario d'Addio, Instituto Studi Storico Politici, Universita di Roma, Roma		
JAPAN			
Faculty of Law, Rikkyo University 3-34-1 Nishi Ikebukuro, Toshima-ku, Tokyo	*President*: Prof. Jiro Kamishima *Secretary-General*: Prof. Michitoshi Takabatake	*Annals Newsletter*.	Annual Conferences
KOREA			
Room 203, Namdo Building, 119 Suh So Mum-Dong, Chong-ku, Seoul 23-9887	*President*: Bae-Ho Han, Korea University *Secretary-Treasurer*: Sang-Il Han, Kukmin University	*Korean Political Science Review*. Editor: Sang-Woo Rhee, Segang University	
LEBANON			
P.O. Box 3865, Beirut	*President*: Bechir Aridi		
MEXICO			
Av. Anillo Periférico Oriente No. 2500 Col. Rinconada Coapa, Mexico D.F. 5 94 38 34	*President*: Lic. Enrique Gonzalez Pedrero, Edif. A-11 cubiculo No. 111 ENEP-ACATLAN, Av. Alcanfores y San Juan Totoltepec, San Mateo, Naucalpan, Edo. de México *Secretary-General*: Lic. Roberto Salcedo Aquino		Annual Meetings
MOROCCO			
Faculté de droit, B.P. 721 Rabat	*President*: Mohamed Bouzidi, 24 rue Oum Errabia, Rabat (Agdal)		

NETHERLANDS
P.O. Box 19770
1000 GT, Amsterdam, Holland
020-5252951

President: J. K. De Vree, Europa Instituut University of Amsterdam
Secretary-Treasurer: Dr. Max Jansen

Acta Politica.
Editor: Dr. K. Koch
Business correspondence: Boom Publishing Cy., P.O. Box 58, Meppel
Editorial correspondence: Faculteit der Sociale Welenschappen, Erasmus University, P.O. Box 1738, 3000 D. R. Rotterdam

Annual Conferences—May

NEW ZEALAND
Department of Political Studies,
University of Otago,
P.O. Box 56,
Dunedin

President: G. A. Wood, University of Otago
Executive Secretary: M. H. Gold, University of Otago

Pols.
Editor: S. W. Greif, University of Otago

NORWAY
Agder Regional College
P.O. Box 607, N-4601
Kristiansand S
042-27040

President: Bernt Krohn Solvang
Secretary: Finn Holmer Hoven

Statsviteren.
Editor: Paul G. Roness

September—Annual Meetings

PAKISTAN
214 E.I. Line, Karachi

President: A. Saleem Khan

PHILIPPINES
Department of Political Science
University of the Philippines
Diliman, Quezon City 3004

President: Loretta Makasiar Sciat, University of the Philippines
Secretary: Shirley C. Advincula, Ateneo University

Philippine Political Science Journal.
Editor: Loretta Makasiar Sciat

POLAND
00-330 Warszawa, Palac Staszica
ul. Nowy Swiat 72
26 77 70

President: Artur Bodnar, Centralny Osrodek Metodyczny Studiow Nauk Politycznych, 00-046 Warszawa, Nowy Swiat 69
Secretary-General: Dr. Pawel Gieorgica

Studia Nauk Politycznych.
Editor: COM SNP, Committee of Political Sciences of Polish Academy of Sciences, 00-046 Warszawa, Nowy Swiat 69, Poland

April—Warsaw

Polish Round Table.
Editor: Polish Association of Political Sciences, Research Institute on Contemporary Capitalism, 125/127 Jerozolimskie Ave., 02-017 Warsaw, Poland

(*continued*)

ASSOCIATIONS	PERSONNEL	PUBLICATIONS	MEETINGS/REUNIONS
RUMANIA			
Soseana Kiseleff, No. 49 Bucarest 1, cod. 7000	*Président*: George Macovescu, Université de Bucarest, Bucarest 1, cod. 7000	*Vittorul Social.* Association romaine des sciences politiques et Académie des sciences sociales et politiques, 11 rue Onesti, Bucarest 1, cod. 7000	September
SOUTH AFRICA			
P.O. Box 486 Pretoria 0001	*President*: G. C. Olivier *Secretary-Treasurer*: A. du Plessis	*Politikon.* Editor: Michael Sinclair	
SPAIN			
Plaza de la Marina Espanola 9 Madrid 13. c/o Centro de Estudios Constitucionales 2415000	*President*: Manuel Ramirez Jimenez, Universidad de Zaragoza, Facultad de Derecho, Zaragoza, Spain *Secretary-General*: Julian Santamaria Ossorio, Universidad Complutense, Madrid *Executive-Secretary*: Dora Schilling		
SWEDEN			
Department of Political Science University of Gothenburg S-41124 Gothenburg	*President*: Jorgen Westerstahl *Secretary-General*: Rutger Lindahl	*Politologen.* Editor: Cecilia Runnstron, Dept. of Political Science, FACK, University of Stockholm, S-10691 Stockholm *Statsvetenskaplig Tidskrift.* Editor: Torbjørn Valinder, Dept. of Political Science, University of Lund, FACK, S-22005, Lund	
SWITZERLAND			
Université de Neuchâtel, Institut de sociologie et de science politique, Pierre-à-Mazel 7, 2000 Neuchâtel (038) 25 72 05	*Président*: Ernest Weibel *Secretary-General*: Philippe Oertlé	*Annuaire Suisse de Science Politique.* Correspondance à caractère scientifique: Dr. Gerhard Schmid, Steinengraben 79, 4051 Basel *Année Politique Suisse.* Correspondance à caractère scientifique: Dr. Peter Gilg, Forschungszentrum fur Schweizerische Politik, Neubruckstrasse 10 3000 Berne	

TURKEY

Siyasal Bilgiler Fakultesi
Cebeci-Ankara

President: Bahri Savci
Vice-President: Nermin Abadan-Unat
Secretary-General: Ersin Onulduran, Faculty of Political Science, University of Ankara, Cebeci-Ankara

Turk Parlamentoculugunun: Demokrasiyi Kurami, trns.

Demokrasiyi denetim Mekanizmalari Uluslarasi Uluslarasi politika.
For all publications please contact the President

January of each year

USSR

Institute of State and Law,
USSR Academy of Sciences,
ul. Frunze 10, Moscow, USSR 2911709

President: Georgii Shakhnazarov
Secretary-General: William Smirnov

Annual
Editor: D. A. Kerimov

UNITED KINGDOM

Department of Government
University of Manchester
Manchester 13 9PL
061 273 7121 Ext 5657

Chairman: Geraint Parry
Secretary: Ms. V. Randall, School of Social Sciences, Polytechnic of Central London, 32-38 Wells St., London W1P 3EG
Executive Secretary: Lynn Dignan

Political Studies.
Editor: L. J. Sharpe, Nuffield College, Oxford

Newsletter.
Editor: Joni Lovenduski, Dept. of European Studies, University of Loughborough, Loughborough, Leicester

Politics
Editor: Jean Woodall

April—location varies

USA

1527 New Hampshire Ave. N.W.
Washington, D.C. 20036
202-483-2512

President: Seymour Martin Lipset, Dept. of Political Science, Stanford University, Stanford, California 94305
Executive Director: Thomas Mann

American Political Science Review.
Editor: Dina A. Zinnes, 50 C. Lincoln Hall, University of Illinois, 702 So. Wright St., Urbana, Illinois 61801

PS.
Editor: Catherine E. Rudder

September—location varies

VENEZUELA

Av. 8 No. 81-11
Apartado (P.O. Box 361) Maracaibo
(061) 84810

President: Hermann Petzold-Pernia, Instituto de Filosofia del Derecho, Universidad del Zulia, Apartado 526, Maracaibo

Actividades Politologicas.
Editor: Associacion Venezolana de Ciencia Politica, Apartado (P.O. Box) 361, Maracaibo

Annual Meetings—Maracaibo

YUGOSLAVIA

11000 Belgrad
Proleterskih brigada 74

President: Jovan Djordjević
Secretary-General: Stojan Tomić
Executive-Secretary: Danka Firaunović

Archive for Juridical and Social Science.
Editor: Federation of Jurists Associations of Yugoslavia

twice a year

SOURCE: IPSA Secretariat.

BIBLIOGRAPHY OF WORKS ON POLITICAL SCIENCE IN COUNTRIES NOT INCLUDED IN THIS VOLUME*

Bulgaria

Savova, E. "Social science institutes of the Bulgarian Academy of Sciences" (in French). *Informations sur les Sciences Sociales* (June 1968): 221-27.

U.S. Bureau of the Census. *Bibliography of social science periodicals and monograph series: Bulgaria, 1944-1961*. Washington: NSF, 1961.

Communist Countries

"The development of legal science in socialist countries" (in Russian). *Sovetskoe Gosardustvo Pravo* (September 1969): 13-32 (Hungary, Poland, USSR).

Powell, D. E., and Shoup, P. "The emergence of political science in communist countries." *American Political Science Review* (June 1970): 572-88.

Czechoslovakia

Association internationale de science politique. *Czechoslovakian Political Science at the IPSA Congress in Brussels* (in French). (Prague: Svoboda, 1968).

Heretik, S. "Marxism and the problem of the integration of social sciences" (in Slovakian). *Ekonomický Časopis* (Bratislava) (May/June 1963): 223-36.

Knapp, V. "On the principal trends of development of legal science in Czechoslovakia" (in Russian). *Sovetskoe Gosardustvo Pravo* (June 1963): 104-11.

Kolaja, J. "Czechoslovak sociology: A history of the interaction between science and politics" (in Spanish). *Revista Mexicana de Sociologica* (September/December 1963): 1095-1125.

Starnovsky, B. "The organization of research in the human sciences in the Socialist Republic of Czechoslovakia" (in French). *Informations sur les Sciences Sociales* (March 1964): 40-53.

Hungary

Berenyi, S. "On the position and tasks of legal and administrative sciences" (in Hungarian). *Allam es Igazgatas* (September 1964): 817-24.

Brunner, G. *New development trends in Hungarian political science* (in German). Cologne and Ehrenfeld: Bundesinstitut für Ostwissenschaftliche und Internationale Studie, 1967.

Kulesar, K. "Hungaro-Soviet colloquium on the use of sociological methods in legal science" (in Hungarian). *Jogtudomanyi Közlony* (Budapest) (October/November 1967): 619-23.

———. "The legal and political sciences and social practice in Hungary" (in Hungarian). *Allam es Jogtudomany* (Budapest) (January/March 1964): 3-58.

Louniev, A. J. "Problems of the concrete utilization of sociological research methods in the legal sciences field" (in Hungarian). *Jogtudomanyi Közlony* (Budapest) (April 1966): 173-77.

Markoja, I. "The state of legal and political sciences and their tasks" (in Hungarian). *Jogtudomanyi Közlony* (Budapest) (April 1964): 202-14.

Martonyi, J. *Administrative sciences in Hungary since 1945* (in French). Szeged: Hungaria nyomda, 1961.

Nagy, L. *Bibliography of legal and political sciences, 1962-1963* (in Hungarian). Budapest: Kozgazdasagi es Jogi Kiado, 1965.

———. *Hungarian Legal Bibliography, 1958-1959* and *1960-1961* (in Hungarian). Budapest: Kozgazdasagi es Jogi Kiado, 1961, 1962.

*Compiled by the editor.

———; Veredy, K.; Nagy, I. "Hungarian bibliography of legal and political sciences, 1962-1963." *Acta juridica* (July-December 1963): 445-62, (January-June 1964): 201-20.

Peteri, Z. "Bourgeois political science and the Marxist-Leninist theory of State" (in Hungarian). *Allam es Jogtudomany* (Budapest) (January-March 1964): 59-87.

Rozsa, G. *Social science research and orientation problems of scientific organization* (in Hungarian). Budapest: Akademiai Kiado, 1965.

"Some general characteristics of the development of the social sciences" (in Hungarian). *Magyar Tudomanyos Akademia tarsadalmi-torteneti Osztalyanak Kozlemenyei* (Budapest) (July-December 1965): 293-314.

Szamel, L. *The Hungarian science of public administration* (in Hungarian). Budapest: Kozigazdasagi es Jogi Kiado, 1977.

Szigeti, J. "The role of the social sciences development in the socialist conscience" (in Hungarian). *Magyar Tudomanyos Akademia tarsadalni-torteneti Osztalyanak Kozlemenyei* (Budapest) (July-December 1965): 333-47.

Tibor, Polgar, ed. *The position of the Marxist political science in the social science system and its impact on the practice of socialist construction* (in Hungarian). Budapest: Tudomanyos Ismerettejeszto Tarsulat, 1977. Mimeographed.

U.S. Bureau of the Census. *Bibliography of Social Science Periodicals and Monograph Series: Hungary, 1947-1962*. Washington: GPO, 1964.

Vas-Zoltan, P. "Basic formation of political science" (in Hungarian). *Magyar Tudomany* (September 1967): 587-601.

———. "An independent political science or complex sociological research?" (in Hungarian). *Magyar Tudomany* (November 1966): 679-86.

Veszi, Beda, "Actuality of political science and duties of the construction of socialism" (in Hungarian). *Kulpolitika* 1 (1977): 55-62.

Israel

Cohen, L. "International Relations at Hebrew University." In R. Bachi, ed. *Scripta Hiersolymitana*. Jerusalem: Hebrew University, 1956, pp. 281-91.

Dror, Y. "The teaching of public administration in Israel." *Philippine Journal of Public Administration* (January 1960): 61-72.

Italy

"The administrative sciences in Italy" (in French). *Revue internationale des sciences administratives* 37, nos. 1-2 (1971).

"Associazione Italiana di Scienze Politiche e Sociali." *PS* (Washington) (Spring 1972): 196.

Battaglia, F. "The university and political science" (in Italian). *Sociologia* (Rome) (May 1968): 141-78.

Benedetti, F. "Difficulties and prospects of a center of political studies in Italy" (in Italian). *Spettatore internazionale* (Rome) (May-June 1969): 305-16.

Benevenuti, F. "The science of public administration as a system" (in Italian). *Revista internazionale di scienze sociali* (July-August 1957): 314-27.

Bobbio, N. "Essays on political science in Italy" (in Italian). *Storia e Politica* (October-December 1968): 544-70.

———. "Political science in Italy; teaching and disciplinary autonomy" (in Italian). *Tempi Moderni* (April-June 1963): 45-53.

———. "Social and political studies in the Italian university today" (in Italian). *Politico* (Pavia) (June 1973): 316-27.

Brunello, B. *Problems of Politics as a Science* (in Italian). Bologna: Patron, 1961.

Bruni Roccia, G. *The Foundation of Political Science* (in Italian). Milan: Guiffre, 1965.

Duclos, P. "New methods and techniques in political science" (in Italian). *Revista internazionale di scienze sociali* (January-February 1957): 11-24.

Firpo, L. "The Faculty of Political Science" (in Italian). *Politico* (Pavia) (December 1967): 667-85.

Fisichella, D. *Themes and Methods in Political Science* (in Italian). Florence: Sansoni, 1971.

Fotia, M. "Political science in Italy" (in Italian). *Storia e Politica* (October-December 1968): 544-70.

Gangemi, L. "Sociology and politics: bibliographic notes" (in Italian). *Studi economici* (Naples) (May-August 1963): 200-20.

Italian Bibliography of the Social Sciences 1961 (in Italian). Milan: Vita e Pensiero, 1962 (political science is pp. 99-124.

Italian Bibliography of the Social Sciences: Economics, Political Science (in Italian). Milan: Vita e pensiero, 1960.

"Italian bibliography of the social sciences" (in Italian). *Rivista internazionale di scienze sociali* (Milan) (November-December 1958): 533-69.

Leonardi, F. "Educational reform and political science in parliament" (in Italian). *Sociologia* (Rome) (January 1968): 7-40.

Leoni, B. "A lamentable balance sheet: The under-development of political science in Italy" (in Italian). *Politico* (March 1960): 31-41.

———. "Professor Leoni's talks on the faculties of political science" (in Italian), *Politico* (Pavia) (September 1956): 422-29.

———. "Value judgments and political science" (in Italian). *Politico* (Pavia) (May 1957): 86-94.

Lombardi, F. "The 'moral and social sciences' and our times" (in Italian). *Problemi Umani* (Rome) (October 1956): 19-56.

Marongiu, A. "The value of the history of political institutions" (in Italian). In *Scritti di Sociologia e Politica in Onore di Luigi Sturzo,* vol. 2. Bologna: Nicola

Zanichelli, 1953, pp. 437-62; and *Politico* (Pavia) (December 1953): 305-28.

Marradi, A. "The reform of the political science faculty" (in Italian). *Mulino* (Bologna) (February 1965): 144-53.

Medici, G. "The science of administration in its aspect and scope" (in Italian). *Produttivita* (June 1957): 517-20.

Musio, G. "Politics, culture, and methodology" (in Italian). *Belfagor* (Florence) (July 31, 1956): 447-53.

Napoleoni, C. "Political science and economics" (in Italian). *Futuribili* (January 1969): 27-37.

Pasquino, G. "Recent research trends in political science" (in Italian). *Mulino* (Bologna) (January-February 1970): 150-62.

Passigli, S. "The Italian conception of political science" (in German. *Politische Vierteljahresschrift* (July 1971): 162-200.

———. "Political science" (in Italian). *Rassegna italiana di Sociologia* (April-June 1966): 287-318.

Pellizzi, C. "The human sciences in Italian universities" (in Italian). *Rassegna italiana di Sociologia* (April-June 1960): 3-13.

Pototschnig, M., and Vito, F. "Political studies in Italy" (in French). Communication to the seventh Round Table of IPSA, September 1959.

———. "Political studies in Italy" (in Portuguese). *Revista de Direito público e Ciência política* (May-August 1962): 39-69.

"Research policy in the social sciences" (in Italian). *Scienze sociali* (Bologna) (April 1972): 3-131.

Sani, G. "Is a new political sociology really necessary?" (in Italian). *Rassegna italiana di Sociologia* (Florence) (January-March 1969): 108-22.

Sartori, G. "The field of political science in Italy today" (in Italian). *Mulino* (March-April 1970): 205-22.

———. "In search of political sociology" (in Italian). *Rassegna italiani di Sociologia* (October-December 1968): 597-639.

———. "Philosophy of politics and empirical science of politics" (in Italian). *Studi politici* (Florence) (September 1953-February 1954): 348-77.

———. "Political science" (in Italian). *Politico* (Pavia) (December 1967): 688-701.

———. "Political science and retrospective knowledge" (in Italian). *Studi politici* (Florence) (June-August 1952): 52-74.

———. "When will there be a faculty of political and social sciences?" (in Italian). *Rassegna italiani di Sociologia* (October-December 1965): 503-14.

Scaramozzino, P. "The development of political science faculties in Italy" (in Italian). *Politico* (Pavia) (December 1963): 920-31.

Spreafico, A. "Political studies in Italy" (in Italian). *Tempi moderni* (Rome) (January-June 1964): 31-41.

Stoppino, M. "Some observations on political science and democracy" (in Italian). *Federalista* (Milan) (December 1961): 261-66.

"A timely initiative in the field of public administrative study" (in Italian). *Studi economici* (January-April 1961): 186-87.

Valles, A. de. "The theoretical and didactic problem of the administrative sciences" (in Italian). *Rivista trimestrale di diritto publico* (Milan) (October-December 1957): 771-83.

Vidal, E. "Considerations on the problem of the relations between politics, morals, law, and economics" (in Italian), pp. 527-68. In *Scritti di Sociologia e Politica in Onore di Luigi Sturzo*. Vol. 2. Bologna: Nicola Zanichelli, 1953.

Vito, F. "Current trends of political studies" (in Italian). *Rivista internazionale di Scienze sociali* (Milan) (July-August 1956): 287-95.

———. "Political and social studies in the impending university reform" (in Italian). *Studi di Sociologia* (Milan) (April-June 1964): 178-82.

———. *Political Studies in Italy* (in Italian). Milan: Vita e pensiero, 1964.

———. "The reform of schools of economics, commerce, and political science" (in Italian). *Rivista internazionale di scienze sociali* (March-April 1957): 97-114.

Watson, J. R., and Negri, G. *Teaching and Research in the Field of Public Administration* (in Italian). Bologna: N. Zanichelli, 1960.

Weber, M. *The Method of the Historico-Social Sciences* (in Italian). Bologna: N. Zanichelli, 1958.

Portugal

Magalhaes Godinho, V. "On interdisciplinary investigation in the human sciences" (in Portuguese). *Revista de Economia* (Lisbon) (September-December 1964): 141-53.

Münke, S. "The autonomy of political science" (in French). *Estudos politicos e sociais* (Lisbon) 2, no. 2 (1964): 437-64.

Rumania

Moldovan, D. R. "The contents of research in the domain of social and political sciences." *Revue roumaine des sciences sociales. Serie Sociologie* (Bucharest). 1971, pp. 13-17.

"The political sciences in the Socialist Republic of Rumania" (in French). *Res publica* (Brussels) 13, no. 5 (1971): 697-782.

Stoicoiu, V. *Legal Sources and Bibliography of Rumania*. New York: Praeger, 1964.

Trasnea, O. *Political Science: An Historico-Epistemological Study* (in Rumanian). Bucharest: Editura politica, 1970.

———. "Political science and relations with boundary disciplines" (in Rumanian). *Revista de Filozofie* (Bucharest) 14, no. 11 (1967): 1225-36.

———. "Reflections on the current state of political theory" (in Rumanian). *Revista de Filosofie* (Bucharest) 18, no. 1 (1971): 17-26.

U.S. Bureau of the Census. *Bibliography of Social Science Periodicals and Monograph Series: Rumania, 1947–1961.* Washington: NSF, 1961.

Spain

"Activity of the Institute of Political Studies" (in Spanish). *Impuestos de la hacienda publica* (Madrid) (October 1961): 625–27.

Bernard, S. "The relation of theory and practice in political science" (in Spanish). *Revista de estudios politicos* (Madrid) (September–October 1960): 119–40.

Dana Montano, S. "The object, purpose, and methods of political science" (in Spanish). *Revista de estudios politicos* (Madrid) (September–October 1968): 175–210.

———. "Observations on the study program of the School of Political Science of the National Coastal University" (in Spanish). *Revista de estudios politicos* (Madrid) (November–December 1969): 209–64.

Djordjevich, J. "The relation of theory and practice in political science" (in Spanish). *Revista de estudios politicos* (Madrid) (May–June 1959): 207–30.

Fraga Iribarne, A. "Note on the principal national systems in contemporary political science" (in Spanish). *Informacion juridica* (Madrid) (March–April 1955): 201–20.

Fueyo, J. "About current political knowledge" (in Spanish). *Revista de estudios politicos* (September–October 1967): 5–27.

Ganon, I. "Political science as an autonomous science and as sociology" (in Spanish). *Revista de estudios politicos* (May–August 1963): 35–73.

Garcia Arias, L. "Definition and general bibliography of the science of international relations" (in Spanish). *Revista de estudios politicos* (May–June 1957): 247–75.

Garrido Falla, F. "Current trends in the training of higher civil servants" (in Spanish). *Revista de administracion publica* (Madrid) (May–August 1956): 47–68.

———. "Public administration as a subject-matter of legal and non-legal sciences" (in Spanish). *Revista de administracion publica* (May–August 1957): 9–63.

Gonzalez Pedrero, E. "On the methodology of political science" (in Spanish). *Ciencias politicas y sociales* (July–September 1960): 413–27.

Hernandez-Rubio, J. M. "New directions and possible themes of current political science" (in Spanish). *Boletin informativo de Ciencia politica* (Madrid) (June 1970): 5–23.

Jordana de Pozas, L. "Organization and administrative sciences in Spain" (in Spanish). *Revue internationale des sciences administratives* (Brussels) 23, no. 1 (1957): 1–16.

Kaplan, M. "New directions and possible themes of current political science" (in Spanish). *Aportes* (April 1970): 125–66.

Langrod, G. "The new school of administration in Spain" (in French). *Revue administrative* (Paris) (May–June 1961): 302–8.

Maravall, J. A. "The history of political thought, political science, and history" (in Spanish). *Revista de estudios politicos* (Madrid) (November–December 1955): 25–65.

Murillo Ferrol, F. "The crisis of the problem 'theory and practice' in political science" (in Spanish). *Anuario de filosofia del derecho* (Madrid). 1954, pp. 101–33.

Ollero, C. "Political science and sociology" (in Spanish). *Revista de estudios politicos* (Madrid) (September–October 1954): 39–57.

———. "The present evolution of political science" (in Spanish). *Cuadernos hispano-americanos* (Madrid) (October 1954): 3–15.

———. "The theory of the State and constitutional law in the system of political law as political science" (in Spanish). *Informacion juridica* (Madrid) (October 1954): 819–32.

Perales, L. "The present organization of the study of law and political economy in Spain" (in French). *Cahiers de l'Association nationale des Docteurs en droit* (Paris) (October–December 1962): 91–95.

Ramirez, M. "Face and form of political sociology" (in Spanish). *Revista de estudios sociales* (Madrid) (January–April 1971): 211–17.

Sanchez Agesta, L. "Crisis of politics as a moral science" (in Spanish). *Revista de estudios politicos* (Madrid) (September–October 1956): 3–17.

Uribe Villegas, O. "Thoughts on the specific subject-matter of political science" (in Spanish). *Ciencias politicas y sociales* (July–September 1960): 453–68.

Xifra Heras, J. "About political science" (in Spanish). *Revista del Instituto de Ciencias sociales* (Barcelona). 1964, pp. 11–54.

Ycaza Tigerino, J. "Notes for a study on political systems" (in Spanish). *Revista de estudios politicos* (Madrid) (January–February 1954): 175–85.

Thailand

Raksasataya, A. "The study of political science in Thailand." *Ratthasart Nites* (November 1965–January 1966): 30–46.

Turkey

Abadan, Y. "The importance of law and the political sciences in the universities" (in Turkish). *Ankara Universitesi siyasa Bilgiler Fakultesi Dergisi* (December 1959): 50–57.

———. "Philosophy of law and sociology in Turkey" (in German. *Archiv für Rechtsund Sozialphilosophie* 43, no. 4 (1957): 519–30.

Ataov, T. "The teaching of international relations" (in Turkish). *Ankara Universitesi siyasa Bilgiler Fakultesi Dergisi* (June 1960): 181–202.

Bilge, A. S. "The teaching of international politics" (in Turkish). *Ankara Universitesi siyasa Bilgiler Fakultesi Dergisi* (March 1961): 102–17.

Meray, S. L. "Symposium on the teaching and study of international law" (in Turkish). *Ankara Universitesi siyasa Bilgiler Fakultesi Dergisi* (March 1960): 215-31.

"Political science in Turkey. A report by the Turkish Political Science Association" (in French). *Information sur les sciences sociales* (Paris) (March 1964): 68-73.

U.S. Bureau of the Census. *Bibliography of Social Science Periodicals and Monograph Series: Turkey, 1950-1962*. Washington: NSF, 1964.

Uruguay

Solari, A. E. *The Social Sciences in Uruguay* (in Spanish). Rio de Janeiro: Centro latino americano de pesquisas en ciencias sociales, 1959.

Venezuela

Silva Michelena, J. A. *The Present State of the Social Sciences in Venezuela* (in Spanish). Rio de Janeiro: Centro latino americano de pesquisas en ciencias sociales, 1960.

INDEX

Aalborg, University of, 136–37
Aaltonen, Kirsti, 420
Aarebrot, Frank H., 261, 269–70
Aarhus, University of, 132, 136–37, 139, 141, 430
AAPES *Asian Studies,* 215
Abadan, Y., 429
Abadan-Unat, Nermin, 425
Abd el Malek, Anouar, 16, 23, 25
Abelson, Robert, 12, 17, 20, 25, 198
Abendroth, Wolfgang, 170
Abensour, Miguel, 167
Abir, Rabi, Ibn i, 275
Abkarian, 59
Åbo Academy, 144–45
Abrams, Philip, 112, 125
Abueva, J. V., 62
Abu Nasr al-Farabi, 5, 275
Academic Education and Technology-Methodical Center of Education in Political Science (Poland), 293, 295
Academic Statute (Netherlands), 228, 236, 238–39
Academies of Arts and Sciences (Yugoslavia), 402
Academy for Rural Development, Journal of the, 287
Academy of Pedagogical Sciences of the GDR, 180, 182
Academy of Political and Social Studies (India), 205
Academy of Sciences (GDR), 178–79, 181–82
Academy of Sciences (USSR), 342, 351
Academy of Social Sciences (Poland), 293
Ackerman, P., 175
Acta Politica (Netherlands), 228, 238

Actes de la Recherche en Sciences Sociales, 159
Activists, 2, 49
Adamany, D. W., 24–25
Adams, J. W. L., 202
Adamson, Walter L., 25
Adamy, David, 375
Advincula, Shirley C., 423
Adelaide, University of, 74–75, 77
Adler, Alfred, 12, 86
Adler, Frank, 183
Adorno, Theodor W., 12, 20, 25, 28, 135, 170, 175, 182
Advanced Studies, Institute for (Austria), 90
Afanas'ev, V. G., 337, 339
Afghani, Jamal ud-din, 288
African Political Science Association, 5, 37, 41, 352
Afro-Asian Linguistic-Cultural Research, Institute of, 216
Agder Distriktshøgskole (Norway), 257
Agger, Robert, 372
Aggregate data analysis, 13, 215
Agnoli, 171
Agra University (India), 204
Agrégation,l (French certification), 157
Aguiar, Neuma, 109
Aguirre Lanari, Juan R., 73
Ahmed, Aziz, 286
Ahmed, Bashiruddin, 22
Ahmed, Ilyas, 279
Ahmed, Manzoor-ud-din, 279, 284, 287, 289–90
Ahmedabad Management Association (India), 205
Ahn, Byong-Man, 226

Aitchison, J. H., 128
Aitkin, Don, 76, 84
Aja Espil, Jorge A., 70–71, 73
Akhtar, Waheed, 288
Akkerman, Robert J., 243
Akuto Hiroshi, 211, 214, 216
Akzin, B., 50
Alapuro, Risto, 152
Alberdi, Juan Bautista, 71
Albinski, Henry, 84
Albrecht, U., 172
Alcalá y Zamora, 70
Alekseev, S. S., 338, 352
Aleksič, Rade, 406
Alexander, Herbert, 24–25
Alford, Robert R., 269
Algotsson, Göran, 306
Ali, Chaudhury Mohammad, 284
Ali, Maulana Mohammad, 284
Aligarh movement (Pakistan), 283
Aligarh Muslim University, 204, 277–78, 289
Alker, Hayward R., Jr., 13, 21–26, 53, 59–60
Allahabad University (India), 204
Allama Iqbal University (Pakistan), 276–77
Allana, G., 284
Allardt, Erik, 13, 21, 25, 44, 50, 148, 151–52, 259, 266, 269–70, 273
Alley, R., 255
Alliance for National Renovation party (Brazil), 107
All-India Management Association, 205
All-India Muslim League, 284
All-Indian Panchyat Parishad, 205

I am greatly indebted to Mr. Norman Plyter, director of Brockport's Academic Computing Center for much technical assistance in preparing this index.

All-Pakistan Political Science Association, 286
All-Union Agitation Tour (USSR), 346
All-Union Conference on Scholarly Methods (USSR), 343
All-Union Leninist Inspection (USSR), 346
All-Union Rally of Students (USSR), 341, 346
Almasy, 266
Almond, Gabriel, 15–16, 23, 25, 44, 51, 53, 68, 114, 119, 260, 270, 275, 281, 286, 306, 310, 370, 372, 379
Althingi (Iceland), 187, 189–90
Althoff, Philip, 285
Althuser, Louis, 122, 136, 164
Alting von Geusau, F. A. M., 235, 243
Altman, Gavro, 410
Altvater, Elmar, 171
American Academy of Political and Social Science, 368
American Historical Association, 377
American Political Science Association, 1–2, 51, 108, 113, 364, 366, 369–71, 375–77, 379
American Political Science Association *Directory*, 366–67
American Political Science Review, 81, 364, 366, 368–69, 371, 376–77, 379
American Sociological Association, 2
Ames, Herbert, B., 126
Amin, Samir, 16, 23, 25, 122
Amsterdam, Free University of (Protestant), 227, 233, 236, 238
Amsterdam, University of, 227–28, 232–33, 236–37
Amstrup, Niels, 143
Analyses de la SEDEIS, 163
Analysis, techniques of, 51
Anarchism, 11
Anbro, Klaus, 142
Anckar, Dag, 151–52
Anderson, Ivar, 316
Anderson, Perry, 122
Anderson, Rodee, 281, 289
Andersson, Hans G., 310
Andhra University (India), 204
Ando, Masashi, 213
Andrén, Gunnar, 317
Andrén, Nils, 311, 314
Angers, François-Albert, 129
Angus, Henry, 117, 127
Annales de la Faculté de droit de l'Université de Liège, Les, 98–99

Annals of Political Science, The (Japan), 215, 218
Annals of Public Administration, The (Japan), 215
Annamalai University (India), 204
Année politique, 96, 99
Année sociologique, 159
Anthropology, 12
Anthropos, 42
Anton, Tom, 311
Antončič, Vojko, 408
ANZUS alliance, 251
Appadorai, A., 44, 202
Approaches, logical, 12
APSA News, 80
Apter, David, 51, 53, 285, 306
Apunen, Osmo, 152
Aquina, H. J., 234, 236, 242, 244
Aquinas, Saint Thomas, 167
Aquino, Roberto Salcedo, 422
Arab League, 234
Arboleda, J. R., 61
Archives Européennes de Sociologie, 159
Ardrey, Robert, 10, 19, 25
Area studies, 249
Arendt, Hannah, 169
Arès, Père R. P., 129
Argentine political science: associational activities, 69; evolution since 1945, 65; general areas, 65; as integrating science, 67; intellectual structure, 65; in 1945, 65; present state and future prospects, 72–73; the specialized *licenciatura*, 68–69; its teaching in general, 67–68; in the world of politics, 69, 71–72
Argument, Das (German journal), 173
Arhiv za pravne i društvene nauke (Yugoslavia), 404
Aristotle, 5, 9, 65–67, 173, 208, 282, 368, 385
Arnaíz, A., 62
Arnason, Ragner, 189, 191
Arndt, H. J., 175
Aron, Raymond, 44, 47–48, 68, 114, 157–58, 161, 166–67
Aronson, E., 20
Arrow, Kenneth, 211
Arton, Raymond, 44
Aruga, Hiroshi, 211
Ary Dillon Soares, Glaucio, 24
Asahi (Japanese newspaper), 214
Ashby, W. Ross, 22, 25
Ashford, Douglas E., 25
Ashley, Anne, 126
Ashley, W. J., 1, 116, 124, 126
Ashraf, Zahida, 278

Asian Economics, 215
Asian Studies (Japan), 215
Asian Studies, Institute of (India), 205
Asirvatham, E., 44, 203, 280
Aso, Makoto, 215
Associated Labor Act (Yugoslavia), 390
Association Française de Science Politique, 154, 159, 166
Association Internationale des Relations Professionnelles, 295
Ataov, T., 429
Atkinson, Michael M., 126
Attali, Jacques, 53, 166
Aubert, Vilhelm, 259, 263, 265, 270
Auckland University College (NZ), 246–48, 253, 349
Aucoin, Peter, 121
Australasian Political Science Association, 78–82, 252
Australian and New Zealand Association for the Advancement of Science, 80
Australian Institute of International Affairs, 79–80
Australian Institute of Political Science, 74, 79–80
Australian Journal of Politics and History, 76, 81
Australian Journal of Public Administration, 80
Australian National University, 75, 77–78, 81, 83
Australian Outlook, 80
Australian political science, 74; associations, 79–81; future, 83; growth, 74–76; origins, 74; research and literature, 81–83; teachings, 76–79
Australian Quarterly, 80
Australian Research Grants Committee, 82
Austrian political science: associational activities, 89–90; evolution since 1945, 86–87; intellectual structure, 87; introduction, 85; journals, 90; in 1945, 87–88; present state and future prospects, 90–91; research, 89; its teaching, 87–88; and the world of politics, 90
Austrian Political Science Association, 89–91
Austrian Political Science Journal, 89–90
Austro-Marxism, 89
Autarchy, national, 15
Avellaneda, Marco, 71
Avril, Pierre, 158

Awadhesh Pratap Singh University (India), 204
Axelrod, Robert, 20, 25
Azia, K. K., 280

Babić, Ivan, 409
Baccalauréat (French degree), 156
Bachelard, Gaston, 163
Bachelor of Arts degree: in Iceland, 185–89; in Netherlands, 228; in New Zealand, 248; in Pakistan, 276, 278–81, 285–86, 289
Bachelor of Commerce degree, in Pakistan, 276
Bachelor of Science degree, in Pakistan, 276–77, 280
Back, Pär-Erik, 309–10, 317
Badeni, Gregorio, 70
Badie, B., 167
Baehr, P. R., 234–35, 242–44
Baer, M. A., 381
Bagehot, Walter, 74, 81, 361, 368
Bailey, Stephen, K., 379
Bains, J. S., 44, 203
Bakarić, Vladimir, 407
Bakhali, Mahmut, 407, 410
Balandier, Georges, 16, 23, 25, 167
Baldcock, C. V., 255
Baldersheim, Harold, 265, 270
Baldwin, Simeon, 375
Balibar, 136
Ballinger, Margaret, 80
Baluchistan, University of (Pakistan), 276, 279: 286, 288
Bamba, Nobuya, 212
Banaras Hindu University (India), 204
Banaszkiewicz, J., 297
Banfield, Edward, 372
Bangalore Management Association (India), 205
Bangalore University (India), 204
Bank, J. Th. M., 241
Bank of Sweden Tercentenary Fund, 301–2, 322
Banks, Arthur S., 13, 21, 25
Banning, W., 243
Banno, Junji, 212
Banno, Masataka, 212, 213
Barani, Zia ud din, 275–76
Barber, James D., 13, 21, 25
Barents, J., 45, 53, 227, 229–30, 235–37, 239–44
Bariter, J., 97
Barkfeldt, Bengt, 316
Barnes, Samuel H., 25
Baroda, University of (India), 204
Barriocanal, Eusebio Angel, 70
Barry, Brian, 81, 260, 359

Barth, Fredrik, 259
Barthélemy, Joseph, 155
Barwick, Sir Garfield, 80
Basic Problems of Marxism-Leninism (Poland), 294, 296
Basle, University of (Switzerland), 331, 334
Batelli, Maurice, 328
Bator, Francis, 22, 25, 343
Batria, P., 203
Battaglia, F., 427
Bauer, 86
Bauman Higher School of Technology (USSR), 342
Baxter, Sandra, 25
Bay, Christian, 17, 25, 373, 378–79
Beaglehole, J. C., 254
Beard, Charles A., 11, 20, 379
Beardsley, P. L., 379
Beck, J. Murray, 128
Beckett, P., 62
Beckman, Björn, 316
Beddie, B. D., 76
Beer, Samuel H., 23, 25
Behavioralism, 13–14, 42–43, 113, 118–24, 128, 145–46, 148, 208, 222–23, 230, 234, 302–3, 358, 368
Behavioral Sciences Center (India), 205
Behavioral Studies, Institute of (India), 205
Bejar Navarro, R., 62
Belber, Anton, 411
Beleid en Maatschappij (Netherlands), 228, 236
Beleidsanalyse (Netherlands), 228, 236
Belgian political science: autonomous centers of research, 94–96; conclusions, 98–99; interdisciplinary relations, 96–98; journals and periodicals, 98; research and work, 98; structure and programs, 93–96; in the universities, 93–94
Belgian Political Science Association, 295
Belgrade Faculty of Political Sciences (Yugoslavia), 384, 400–402, 407
Belgrade International Politics and Economy Institute, 402
Bell, Daniel, 50, 304
Bell, Gerald D., 284
Beloff, Max, 50, 53
Benard, C., 91–92
Ben-David, Joseph, 36, 45, 112, 125
Benedetti, F., 427
Benedict, Ruth, 20, 25

Benevenuti, F., 427
Benjamin, Hilde, 183
Benko, Vlado, 399, 410–411, 412
Bent, F., 62
Bentham, Jeremy, 368
Benthem, G. van, 244
Bentley, Arthur F., 169, 370, 379
Berelson, Bernard R., 13, 21, 25, 29
Berenyi, S., 426
Berg, C. van, 244
Berg, Elias, 304–5
Berg, J. Th. J. van den, 231, 240
Bergamin, R. J. B., 240
Bergen, University of (Norway), 256–58, 274
Bergeron, Gérard, 50, 53, 129
Bergh, van der, 244
Berglund, Sten, 310
Bergquist, Mats, 306
Bergqvist, Sven-Rune, 316
Bergstraesser, Arnold, 169–70
Berhampur University (India), 204
Berlia, Georges, 158
Berlin, Isaiah, 359
Berliner Zeitschrift für Politologie, 173
Bermbach, 171
Bernard, Stéphane, 50, 53, 98, 429
Berndtson, Erkki, 151
Berne, University of (Switzerland), 334
Berns, Walter, 373, 378
Berntsson, Lennart, 306, 315, 325
Bertalanffy, Ludwig von, 22
Berufsverbot (German decree), 174
Best, Paul, 297
Betts, T. M., 251, 254–55
Beyme, Klaus von, 5, 44, 46, 50, 55, 171, 175, 408
Bhaglapur University (India), 204
Bhambrhi, C. P., 203
Bharat, Republic of, 276
Bhaskaran, R., 50, 203
Bhatt, Anil, 22
Bhatt, V. R., 203
Bhawalpur, Islamia University of (Pakistan), 276, 279, 286
Bhopal University (India), 204
Bialer, Seweryn, 25
Bibič, Adolf, 352, 405–6, 410
Biedenkopf, 174
Biegel, L. C., 234, 243
Bierzanek, R., 294, 297
Bihar, University of (India), 204
Bihar Council of Public and International Affairs (India), 205
Bilandžić, Dušan, 408
Bilge, A. S., 429

Birch, Anthony, 44, 50, 53
Birgersson, Bengt Owe, 307, 316
Birman, A., 339
Birnbaum, Pierre, 162, 167
Bisco, Ralph, 21
Biskupski, K., 297
Bislev, Sven, 142
Bjarnason, Dóra, 192
Bjarnason, Guðmundur, 189, 192
Bjerregaard, Ritt, 140
Bjøl, Erling, 142–43
Björklund, Bertil, 309, 317
Björklund, Stefan, 143, 304, 311
Bjurulf, Bo, 303, 306, 310
Black, Naomi, 128
Black Fellowship Program (US), 377
Bladen, V. W., 127
Blagojević, Novica, 409
Blahoz, Josef, 420
Bland, F. A., 74, 80, 83–84
Blanke, B., 85, 91–92, 175
Blewett, Neal, 83–84, 97
Blom, Conny, 325
Blomstedt, Yrjö, 150
Blondel, Jean, 5, 50, 358
Blücher, Viggo Count, 13
Board, Joseph, 308, 316
Boasson, C., 234, 242
Bobbio, N., 427
Bociurkiw, B. R., 45, 352
Bodin, Jean, 5, 10, 49, 66, 154
Bodin, Katarina, 314
Bodin, Louis, 157
Bodlaender, M., 243
Bodnar, Artur, 293–95, 297, 423
Boeynaems, M., 97, 419
Bogaert, J., 60
Bogärd, Bengst, 310, 317
Bogason, Peter, 142
Bogdanov, Vaso, 410
Bohnet, M., 60
Boily, 129
Bois, Paul, 167
Boivin, Bertus, 241
Bom, Philip C., 244
Bombay Management Association, 205
Bombay University, 204
Bon, Frederic, 161, 167
Bone, Hugh A., 25
Bonenfant, Jean-Charles, 45, 129, 230
Bonfil Batalla, G., 62
Bonger, W. A., 227, 232, 241
Bonnet, Serge, 162
Bonsdorff, Göran von, 148–49, 151–52
Boolsen, Merete Watt, 143

Borden, Robert L., 126
Borg, Olavi, 148, 151
Borre, Ole, 141–42
Borys, Jurij, 308
Bose, Nirual, 204
Bosung Professional School, 220
Bottomore, T. B., 122
Boudon, Raymond, 14, 22, 26, 53, 164
Boulding, Kenneth E., 12, 20, 26
Bourassai, 129
Bourdieu, Pierre, 159, 164
Bourgault, Jacques, 420
Bourguiba, Habib, 16
Bourque, Gilles, 122, 126
Bourricaud, François, 47, 162
Boutmy, Emile, 47
Bouzidi, Mohamed, 419, 423
Bowie, Robert R., 22, 26
Bozeman, Adda B., 10, 19, 26
Braam, G. P. A. van, 233, 235, 242–43
Bradley, P., 203
Brady, Alexander, 117, 127–28
Braibanti, Ralph, 284
Brams, Steven J., 379
Brandström, Dan, 310, 316
Brandt, Willy, 171
Branner, Hans, 142
Brasz, H. A., 235–36, 240, 242–43
Brazilia, University of, 107
Brazilian Association of Social Sciences, 102
Brazilian Bibliography on Social Sciences, 102
Brazilian Center for Analysis and Planning, 101, 107
Brazilian Center for Agency Assistance to Small and Middle-sized Businesses, 108
Brazilian Institute for the Development of International Relations, 108–9
Brazilian Institute on Bibliography and Documentation, 102
Brazilian National Council on Science and Technology, 102
Brazilian political science: courses of study, 102–5; financial support, 108–9; institutional activities, 100–102; overview, 100; participation in conferences, 107–8; professional associations, 109; publications, 106–7; research, 105; research topics, 105–6; its teachings, 102–5; theses, 106
Brazilian Political Science Association, 108–9

Brazilian Review of Political Studies, 106
Brazilian Society for Progress in Science, 107
Brazilian Society of Instruction, 109
Brazilian Travel Bureau, 109
Brecher, Michael, 23, 26, 114, 125
Brecht, Arnold, 10, 19, 26, 68, 133–34, 140, 406
Bregnsbo, Henning, 142
Bremen, University of (FRG), 173
Bremer, Stuart, 17, 24, 26, 53, 69
Breunese, J. N., 236, 244
Brewitz, Stig, 321–25
Bridel, Marcel, 44, 327–28, 334–35
Bridgman, Percy W., 12, 20, 26
Brinton, Crane, 24, 26
British Association of International Studies, 215
British Journal of International Studies, 361
British Journal of Political Science, 360
British political science: associational activities, 359–61; conclusion, 362; definition, 356–58; emergence, 355–56; introduction, 355; journals, 360–61; most noteworthy research contributions, 358–59; research, 358–59; and the world of politics, 361–62
British Political Sociology Yearbook, 361
Broadhead, R. S., 45
Brodbeck, A. J., 378
Brodbeck, May, 112, 124
Broddason, Thorbjörn, 186, 190, 192
Brodersen, A., 352
Broekmeyer, M. J., 242
Brofoss, Karl-Erik, 264, 269–70
Brogan, Denis W., 6, 48, 81, 356
Bronner, A. E., 241
Brookes, R. H., 251, 254
Brotherus, K. R., 144–45, 151
Brown, Bernard E., 166
Brown, David, 124, 131
Brunello, B., 427
Bruni Roccia, G., 427
Brunner, Georg, 352, 426
Brunswick, E. Frankel, 20
Brusewitz, Axel, 300
Brussels, Free University of, 50, 94
Bruyn, L. P. J. de, 232, 241
Bryce, James, 81, 127, 145–46, 151, 249, 368, 370, 375, 378–79
Bryder, Tom, 308
Brzezinski, Zbigniew, 10, 19, 26, 83, 375

Buch, H., 97
Buchanan, James M., 20, 26
Buchanan, William, 379
Buchmann, J., 97
Buczkowski, P., 297
Budge, Ian, 142, 169, 359
Buehrig, Edward H., 379
Buenos Aires, National University of, 71
Buenos Aires, University of, 67–68
Buksti, Jacob A., 142
Bull, 260
Bulletin (of Swiss Political Science Association), 330, 335
Bund Freiheit der Wissenschaft, 173
Burch, Betty B., 275
Burdeau, Georges, 47, 49, 53, 68, 70, 154, 157, 167, 419
Burdick, Eugene, 378
Burdwan, University of (India), 204
Bureaucracy, study of, 50, 52, 386, 396
Bureau for Youth Problems of the Council of Ministers (GDR), 182
Burlackij, F. M., 406
Burg, Fenna van den, 243
Burger, Edward J., Jr., 26
Burgess, John W., 74, 169, 368, 370, 379
Burke, Edmund, 3, 10–11
Burlatskii, F. M., 338–39
Burns, Sir Alan, 23, 26
Burrell, Sidney A., 22, 26
Bush, 251
Butler, David, 13, 21, 26, 82–84, 358–59, 363, 373, 378–79

Cabinet Secretariat (UK), 356, 359
Cabinet Mission Plan (Pakistan), 284
Caciagli, M., 175
CAE (College of Advanced Education) (Australia), 76–77, 82
Cahiers Internationaux de Sociologie, 159
Cahiers bruxellois, 98–99
Cahiers de la Fondation Nationale des Sciences Politiques, 95, 160
Cairns, Alan C., 45, 85, 124, 128–29
Calcutta, University of, 194, 204
Calcutta Management Association, 205
Calicut, University of (India), 204
California, University of (Berkeley), 41
Callaghan, James, 362
Cambridge University, 113, 278, 356
Campbell, Angus, 13, 266, 270, 272
Campbell, Donald T., 26

Campen, S. I. P. van, 234, 242
Campinas, State University of (Brazil), 100, 107
Campos Jimenez, C. M., 61
Canadian Association for Latin American Studies, 108
Canadian Association of Sociologists and Anthropologists, 129
Canadian Economics Association, 129
Canadian Institute of International Affairs, 128
Canadian International Development Agency, 109
Canadian Journal of Economics, 129
Canadian Journal of Economics and Political Science, 35, 116–17, 120–21
Canadian Journal of Political Science, 121, 124, 129
Canadian political science: current state, 113; in French Canada, 114, 120–22; introduction, 112–13, 124; before 1945, 116–18; since 1945, 118–23; schema, 112–13; some hypotheses, 113; summary and conclusion, 123–24; and the world of politics and administration, 120
Canadian Political Science Association, 35, 41, 113, 116–17, 119–22, 124, 129
Canadian Public Administration, 311
Canberra University College, 75–77
Cand. Polit. degree, in Norway, 257–58
Candidat degree, 93; in Belgium, 93
Candidatus Magisterii degree, in Denmark, 137–38, 140
Candidatus Philosophiae degree, in Denmark, 142
Candidatus Scientiarum Politicarum degree, in Denmark, 137–38
Cândido Mendes University Group, 102, 106
Canterbury University College (NZ), 246–48, 252, 349
Capacity, 14
Capecchi, V., 352
Capitant, René, 161
Caratan, Branko, 405–6, 408, 411
Cardoso, Fernando Henrique, 109
Carey, George W., 141
Carlbom, Terry, 308
Carleton University (Canada), 122
"Carl Schorlemmer" Technical College (GDR), 182
Carranca y Trujillo, R., 62
Carrère d'Encausse, Hélène, 162
Carvalho, Orlando de, 109

Castano, L., 62
Castberg, Frede, 256
Castelbajac, Ph. de, 22, 30
Castells, Manuel, 163
Castoriadia, Cornelius, 164
Catholicism, 48
Catholic School for Economics (Netherlands), 227, 232, 235
Catholic University of La Plata (Argentina), 68
Catholic University of Santa Fé (Argentina), 68
Catterberg, Edgardo R., 70
Cavalcanti, Themistocles Brandão, 70, 73, 109
CEBRAP Books (Brazilian series), 107
CEBRAP Notes (Brazil), 101, 107
CEBRAP Studies (Brazil), 101, 107
CEGEPS (French-Canadian colleges), 121
Čemerlić, Hamdija, 412
Center for Applied Politics (India), 205
Center for Brazilian Social Memoirs, 101–2
Center for Development Studies (India), 205
Center for Japanese Social and Political Studies, 216
Center for Policy Research (India), 205
Center for Research and Documentation on Contemporary Brazilian History, 101
Center for Social Studies (India), 205
Center for Studies in Peace and Non-Violence (India), 205
Center for the Cooperation of Yugoslavia with Developing Countries, 403
Center for the Study of Developing Societies (India), 195, 205
Center for Urban Studies (India), 205
Central Committee of the CPSU, 341, 344–47
Central Institute for Socialist Management of the Economy (GDR), 182
Central Institute for Vocational Training (GDR), 180
Central Policy Review Staff (UK), 362
Central Research Institute for Labor at the State Secretariat (GDR), 182
Centre de sociologie européene (France), 159
Centre d'étude de la vie locale (France), 156

Centre d'Etude de la vie politique française, 160, 167
Centre d'Etude . . . sur l'Administration . . . du Territoire (France), 163, 167
Centre d'Etudes des Relations Internationales (France), 162
Centre for Studies in Social Policy and . . . Economic Planning (UK), 362
Centre international de coordination des recherches sur l'autogestion, 42
Centre interuniversitaire de droit public, 96, 98
Centre interuniversitaire d'histoire contemporaine, 96
Cepess, 98–99
Černacklj, V. N., 352
Cerroni, Umberto, 406
Česnokov, K. I., 352
Cetwiński, O., 297
Chacko, C. J., 203
Chakravarti, R., 203
Chan, Lien, 420
Chandler, Ralph C., 408
Chang-wen, Tsai, 420
Chapkarine, A. V., 352
Chapman, R. M., 254–55
Chapsal, Jacques, 68, 158, 167, 414
Character, national, 12
Charbonneau, J.-P., 61
Charlesworth, James C., 6, 45, 54, 128, 285, 379
Charlot, Jean, 50, 159, 161–62
Charlot, Monica, 162, 167
Chase, Harold, 375
Chenaux-Repond, Dieter, 335
Cheney, Richard, 375
Cherry, Colin, 22, 26
Chester, Sir Norman, 5, 44–45, 50, 356, 358, 362–63, 414
Chevallier, Jacques, 167
Chevallier, Jean-Jacques, 47, 49, 68, 157, 159, 167
Chicago, University of, 118, 126, 247, 370
Chirkin, V. E., 352
Chowdhri, M. A., 287
Chowdhry, G. W., 284, 287
Christchurch University College (NZ), 246, 248
Christian Democratic Union (Germany), 173–74
Christian Michelsen Institute (Norway), 256–60
Christian Social Union (Germany), 173–74
Christie, Richard, 20, 26

Christoffersson, Ulf, 311
Chronique de politique étrangère, 98–99
Chughtai, Muneer Ud Din, 278, 286–87
Churchward, L. G., 84, 352
Churdrisard, L. G., 45
Ciencia Política (Argentina), 70
Čikvadze, V. M., 352
Ciri, Rodolfo Luis, 70
Civil Service College (UK), 361
Civis Mundi (Netherlands), 228, 234
CLACSO (Latin American Council on Social Sciences), 41, 108–9
Clapham Committee on the Provision of Social and Economic Research (UK), 356
Clark, A. B., 126–27
Clark, Clifford, 127
Clark, S. D., 113, 117, 125
Clark, Terry N., 112, 125
Clastres, Pierre, 167
Clean Election League, 214
Clement, Wallace, 113–14, 122, 125, 127, 129
Cleveland, L., 254–55
Clifford-Vaughn, F., 61
Clinton, R. L., 380
Clokie, H. M. D., 127
Club of Rome, 17, 108–9, 215
Clymer, Carlton, 281, 289
Coalition theory, 17
Coats, R. H., 127
Cochin, University of, 204
Cochran, Charles E., 380
COCTA, 51
Cognition, 10–11
Cognitive dissonance, 12
Cohen, L., 427
Cohen, Morris, 369, 378, 380
Coherence, 14
Cole, Allen B., 275
Cole, H. S. D., 24, 26
Cole, Taylor, 81, 84, 376
Coleman, James S., 23, 25, 259, 264, 275, 286, 372, 379
Collection U (French book series), 167
Colliard, C. A., 47
Cologne, University of (FRG), 173
Columbia University (US), 1–2, 127, 279
COMECON, 344
Comité d'Organisation des Recherches Appliquées . . . (France), 167
Comité international pour la documentation des sciences sociales (France), 53

Common Market Studies, Journal of (UK), 361
Communication, theory of, 14
Communism, 42, 48, 374
Communism and International Politics, 215
Communist party (Iceland), 189
Communist party of the Soviet Union (CPSU), 340–48
Comparative government, study of, 43, 221, 233–34, 249, 256–57, 366, 372
Comparative Research on Local Power, Committee of (IPSA), 295
Comparative survey studies, 15
Competition of Student Works (USSR), 345
Computers, 17, 52
Comte, Auguste, 116
Conditions of Living Survey (Norway), 258
Condorcet, Jean, 10, 19, 26, 164
Conductism, 67
Conflict theory, 17
Confucianism, 219–20
Congo, study of, 53
Congressional Convention (Argentina), 71
Congressional Fellowship Program (US), 375, 377
Congress of Vienna, 49
Connolly, William E., 407
Conradt, David P., 175
Conservative party (UK), 362
Constance, University of (FRG), 173
Constitution: of Argentina, 71–72; of United States, 71
Constitutional and Parliamentary Studies, Institute of (India), 205
Constitutional Convention (United States), 71
Constitutional Council (France), 161
Constitutionalists, 49
Constitutional law, 2, 299
Constitutional-legal approach, 118–19
Content analysis, 13, 17, 214
Contrepoint (France), 160, 163
Contributions to Canadian Economics, 127
Converse, Philip, 13, 261, 270, 372
Cook, James, 76, 84
Cooperation and Conflict (Norway), 268–69
Cooperative Commonwealth Federation (Canada), 117
Cooperative Movement (Iceland), 189

Coordination for the Improvement of Higher Education Personnel (Brazil), 108–9
Coordination of Pedagogical Research, Council for (GDR), 182
Copenhagen, University of, 136–37, 139, 141, 304–5
Copland, Sir Douglas, 74
Coplin, William D., 54
Corbett, David C., 76, 128
Córdoba, University of (Argentina), 68
Cornell University (US), 1
Corry, J. A., 117, 128
Cortogiogis, George, 421
Corwin, Ronald G., 378
Costa Pinto, L. A., 61
Cot, Jean-Pierre, 161, 163, 167
Cotler, Julio, 16, 24, 26, 118
Courrier Hebdomadaire (Belgium), 95, 98–99
Courtney, John, 420
Couwenberg, S. W., 229, 231–32, 240–41, 243
Cowart, Andrew, 269–70
Cox, Richard H., 11, 20, 26
Cracow, University of (Poland), 292–94
Cramer, N., 232, 241
Cratology (science of power), 66
Crete, Jean, 420
Crewe, Ivor, 142, 260, 359
Crick, Bernard, 357–59, 363, 373, 378, 380
Cripps Proposals, 284
Crisp, L. F., 75–78, 84, 250
CRISP (Center of Research and Sociopolitical Information (Belgium), 53, 94–95, 98
Critical archivists, 49
Critical epistemology, 11
Critique (France), 160
"Critique de la politique" (French book series), 166
Cromwell, Oliver, 16
Crossman, Richard, 3, 359, 361, 363
Crowther-Hunt, Lord, 361
Crozier, Michel, 23, 26, 50, 114, 164
Cuilenberg, J. J. van, 241
Curtis, J., 125
Cuyo, National University of, 68
Cybernetics, 14
Czempiel, 172

Daalder, Hans, 5, 50, 54, 141, 231–34, 240–42, 244–45
Dabin, Jean, 49, 97
Dacca, University of (Pakistan), 276
Dachs, H., 91–92
Dados Review (Brazil), 24, 100
Daemen, H. H. F. M., 232, 241
Dahl, Hans Fredrik, 263, 270
Dahl, Ottar, 264, 269–70
Dahl, Robert A., 12, 15, 18, 21–22, 26, 49, 51, 54, 68, 97, 114, 119, 128–29, 275, 318, 370, 372, 380
Dahlerup, D., 141
Dahlstrom, E., 45
Dalhousie University (Canada), 127
Damgaard, Erik, 139, 141, 143, 420
Damjanović, Mijat, 407
Damle, Y. B., 203
Dana Montaño. Salvador M., 73, 429
Danish Broadcasting System, 140
Danish political science: intellectual structure, 133–36; introduction, 132–33; phase of consolidation, 134–35; phase of identity formation, 133–34; phase of uproar, 135–36; research, 138–39; its teaching, 133–34; and the world of politics, 139–40
Darwin, Charles, 10
Data banks, 52
Data Information Service (ECPR), 258, 266
Data Review (Brazil), 106
Daudt, H., 229, 231, 240–41, 245
Davidson, Philip, 24, 26
Davies, Alan F., 75
Davies, James C., 378, 380
Davis, Jerome D., 142
Davis, Rufus, 76
Davis, S. R., 81, 84
Dawson, R. MacGregor, 113–14, 117–18, 121, 123, 125–26, 128–29, 250
Dawson, W. F., 121
Deakin, University of (Australia), 76
Debuyst, F., 95, 97
Decision making, political, 51–52
De Croo, Herman, 96
Defense Studies and Analyses, Institute of (India), 205
Defferre, Gaston, 161
de Gaulle, Charles, 160
De Imaz, Jose L., 16, 24, 26
De Jong, J. J., 227, 229–34, 240–42, 244
De la Durantaye, Michel, 420
Délégation Générale à la Recherche Scientifique et Technique (France), 166
Deleuze, Gilles, 164
Delhi, University of, 204
Delhi Management Association, 205

Dellenbrant, Åke, 308
Delruelle, Nicole, 97
De Maand, 98–99
De Meyer, J., 97, 99
Democracy, 392–93, 397, 405
Democracy, theory of, 15
Democratic centralism, 49
Democratic party (Poland), 294
Democratic party (US), 375
Demoulin, R., 97
Denisov, A. I., 352
Department of Political Science Notes (Brazil), 107
Department of University Affairs (Brazil), 109
Derathé, Robert, 11, 20, 26
Deslandres, Maurice, 166
Desrosiers, Richard, 129
De Smet, Roger, 50, 97, 99
DETA (Finnish research project), 148
Dettenborn, Harry, 183
Deutsch, Karl W., 13, 21–24, 26, 32, 34, 44, 48, 50, 52, 54, 59–60, 68, 114, 169, 175, 223, 259–60, 285, 372, 380, 414
Development Alternatives for Brazil, Commission for the Study of, 108
De Vree, J. K., 230, 235, 240, 243, 423
De Vries, J. A. J., 10, 240
Dewachter, W., 94, 97, 419
Dexter, L. A., 203
Dhondt, J., 96
Dibrugarh University (India), 204
Dicey, A. V., 81, 114, 116, 368
Dickens, Charles, 355
Diderichsen, S. M., 143
Dietz, Gottfried, 169
Dignan, Lynn, 425
Dilthey, Wilhelm, 11, 19, 27
Dimitrijević, Vojin, 399, 410–12
Dimitrov, Dimitar, 420
Dimitrov, Evgeni, 412
Dingman, Roger, 212
Dion, Léon, 45, 50, 113–14, 120, 125–26, 129
Diplôme d'Etudes Supérieures degree, in France, 156–57
Dittrich, K. L. L. M., 233, 242
Djordjević, Jovan, 50, 385, 405–6, 408–9, 411–12, 425, 429
Dmitriev, A. V., 352
Docteur degree, in Belgium, 93
Doctorandus degree in the Netherlands, 228
Doctorat ès Lettres, in France, 157
Doctor of Philosophy degree: in Australia, 78; in Brazil, 101–2, 106,

Doctor of Philosophy degree (*cont.*) 108; in Finland, 147; in Korea, 223; in the Netherlands, 228; in New Zealand, 248; in Pakistan, 278–81, 286; in Sweden, 320, 323, 325; in the United States, 367–68, 370, 372, 375
Documentation and Current Politics, 101
Doern, Bruce, 121
Doernberg, Stefan, 183
Dogan, Mattei, 21, 44, 50
Doktor degree, in Sweden, 320, 323, 325
Doktora degree, in USSR, 347–48
Dolbeare, Kenneth, 129
Dollard, John, 12
Dollera Joffre, Luis R. M., 70
Dominguez, Jorge I., 26–27
Dominguez, Tejedor, 71
Donnelly, M. S., 128
Donner, A. M., 229, 240, 243
Donneur, André, 124–25, 128
Donosa, L., 61
Donoughue, Bernard, 362
Dörfer, Ingemar, 314
Dossiers pédagogiques (Belgium), 95, 99
Doughty, Arthur G., 127
Douglas, William O., 80
Downs, Anthony, 12–13, 20, 27, 139, 163, 305–6, 380
Drache, Daniel, 122, 127, 129
Dror, Y., 59–60, 427
Drulović, Milojko, 408
Dubning, Reisky, 109
Duclos, P., 427
Duguit, Léon, 67–68, 154, 166
Duke University, 41
Dumont, Fernand, 129
Duncan, G. W. K., 74–75
Dunn, Delmer, 24, 27, 146
Dunner, Joseph, 54
Dunning, 368
Dupeux, Georges, 166
Durkheim, Emile, 116, 148, 154, 158, 163–64
Duroselle, Jean-Baptiste, 50, 158, 162
Dutch Association for International Affairs, 234
Dutch Foundation for Political Science Research, 239
Dutch Foundation for Research in Politics and Public Administration, 239
Dutch political science: balance and perspective, 239; development since 1948, 227–28; early history, 227; empirical-theoretical research approaches, 229–36; financing, 238–39; full-fledged departments, 227; and the government, 237–39; influence of political events on, 236–37; object of research, 229; political scientists in politics, 237; and politics, 236–37; positions held by graduates, 238; research and publications, 228–36; research methods and techniques, 230
Dutch Political Science Association, 228
Dutch political system: electoral behavior, 231–32; interest groups, 233; parliament, 232–33; political parties, 232; provincial and local politics, 233; study of 231–33
Duverger, Maurice, 48, 50, 54, 59, 68, 93, 146, 151, 154, 157–58, 161–62, 166, 307, 406
Duynstee, F. J. F. M., 232, 241
Dye, Thomas R., 22, 27

Easterbrook, W. T., 113, 117, 125
Eastern Regional Organization for Public Administration (Australia), 80
Easton, David, 5–6, 22–23, 27, 45, 51, 54, 59–60, 68, 112, 114–15, 119, 125–26, 128–29, 133–34, 140–42, 151, 223, 229–31, 240, 275, 281, 286, 305–6, 369–70, 378, 380
Ebenhausen, 175
Ebenstein, William, 283
Echeverría, Esteban, 71, 73
Eckstein, Harry, 380
Ecole des Hautes études en sciences sociales (France), 165
Ecole libre des sciences politiques (France), 154, 166, 169
Ecole Nationale d'Administration (France), 156, 161
Ecole Pratique des Hautes Etudes (France), 156
Economic and Applied Research, Institute of (Brazil), 108
Economic development, study of, 50, 52
Economic Management, Scientific Council for, Problems of (GDR), 179, 182
Economic Problems of Scientific-Technical Progress, Scientific Council for (GDR), 179, 182
Economic Research Institute of the State Planning Commission (GDR), 182
Economic Statistics Institute (USSR), 342
Economics, Scientific Council for Research in (GDR), 182
Edelman, Murray, 380
Edinger, Lewis J., 22, 26, 169
Eduards, Maud, 312, 318
Egeberg, Morten, 263, 269–70, 274
Eguchi, Bokuro, 212
Ehrlich, G., 60
Ehrlich, L., 297
Ehrlich, Stanisław, 48, 294–95, 297, 407
Ehrmann, Henry W., 50, 54, 410
Eiconics, 12
Einarsdóttir, Hildur, 190, 192
Einarsson, Ingimar, 189, 192
Eisenmann, Charles, 166
Eisenstadt, Schmuel N., 10, 19, 21, 27, 44, 112, 125, 242, 270
Eisfeld, Rainer, 407
Ejvegård, Rolf, 309, 317
Elazar, Daniel, 422
Eldersveld, S. J., 242, 372
Electoral research, 53, 250, 259–62, 266, 303, 309, 371–72
Eliassen, Kjell A., 142, 266, 325
Elite recruitment, 17
Elites, study of, 50–51
Elitism, 395, 407
Eliutin, V., 353
Elken, S. L., 380
Ellul, Jacques, 54, 167
Elovainie, Mauri K., 152
Elsbree, Hugh, 376
Elster, Jon, 260, 270
Elvander, Nils, 304, 310, 312
Empire building, 15
Empiricism, 12–13, 209, 247–48, 263, 292, 303–5, 383–84, 397
Ende, A. P. W. van der, 243
Engelhardt, Klaus, 183
Engelmann, Fred, 120, 126, 129
Engels, Friedrich, 11, 124, 181, 343, 346, 391, 393, 396, 409
Engholm, G. F., 60
Enlightenment, 48–49
Epstein, Leon, 372
Erasmus University (Netherlands), 227–28
Ericsson, Lars, 317
Erikson, Erik H., 12, 20, 27
Eschenburg, Theodor, 170–71, 174
Escobar Bonoli, Zulema, 70
Escobar Cerda, L., 61
Eskola, Antti, 151
Esmein, A., 154
Esprit (France), 160

Esser, J., 175
Essex, University of (UK), 126, 309, 357, 359, 379
Estrada, José Manuel, 66–67, 70–72
Eto, Shinkichi, 212, 214
Etudes Congolaises (Belgium), 95
Etudes du CRISP, Les (Belgium), 95, 99
Etzioni, Amitai, 20, 27
Euchner, 171
Eulau, Heinz, 6, 169, 223, 378, 380
Eurocommunism, 407
Europe, Western, 52
European Consortium for Political Research, 5–6, 41, 138, 258, 265–66, 300, 329–30, 362
European Economic Community (EEC), 41, 139, 233, 235, 261, 267, 306, 313, 361
European Journal of Political Research, 5
European Security Conference, 150
Evalenko, René, 50, 97, 99
Ewha Women's College, 220
Experimentation, 13, 214–15
Explication des textes, 11
Eynern, Gert von, 171

Faber, S., 236, 244
Fabris, H. H., 91–92
Faculté de droit (Paris), 155
Faculté des Lettres, 156
Facultés de Droit, 156
Faculty of Sociology, Political Sciences, and Journalism, Ljubljana (Yugoslavia), 384, 400–402, 407, 411
Fagen, Richard, 24, 26
Fainsod, Merle, 50, 80
Fairlie, John, 376
Faisalbad, University of Agriculture at (Pakistan), 276
Fakhr-i-Muddabir, 276
Falardeau, Jean-Charles, 127, 129
Falcone, David, 129
Falk, Richard A., 17, 25, 27
Fanon, Frantz, 16, 23, 27
Faoro, Raymundo, 110
Farabi, 275, 283
Farberov, N. P., 337
Farlie, Dennis, 142
Farrer, D. G., 203
Fascism, 374, 395
Faucher, Albert, 126–27, 129
Faupel, K., 91–92
Faurby, Ib, 132, 143
Favre, M., 167
Favre, Pierre, 167

Fay, C. R., 128
Fayt, Carlos S., 73
Federal Council (Switzerland), 329
Federal Council on Culture (Brazil), 109
Federalist Papers, 71
Federal Law Concerning the Courses of Studies . . . (Austria), 87
Federal Polytechnical University (Switzerland), 330
Federal Senate (Brazil), 107
Federal state, 49
Federation of Trade Unions (Yugoslavia), 397
Federations, 15
Fed'kin, G. I., 353
Fedoseyev, P., 353
Fejtö, François, 158
Felling, A. J. A., 242
Fenno, Richard F., 22, 27
Fernandes, Florestan, 110
Festinger, Leon, 12, 20, 27, 285
Fetscher, Iring, 11, 20, 27, 52
Feyerabend, Paul, 149, 152
Filet, B. C., 236
Financial groups, study of, 53
Financier of Studies and Projects (Brazil), 108
Finer, Herman, 280
Finer, Samuel, 44, 51, 281, 359
Finkle, 285
Finnish political science: associational activities, 149; evolution since 1945, 145–46; intellectual predecessors, 144; intellectual structure, 145; research, 147–49; its teachings, 146–47; and the world of politics, 150; after World War II, 144–45
Finnish Political Science Association, 149–50, 352
Fira, Aleksandar, 411
Firaunović, Danka, 425
Firpo, L., 427
Fischer, H., 91–92
Fisichella, D., 427
Five-percent barrier, 16
FLACSO, 41
Flechtheim, Ossip, 169–70
Flinders University (Australia), 76–77
Flora, Peter, 13, 21, 27, 266
Fluminense Federal University (Brazil), 101
Foltz, William J., 22, 26
Fondation Nationale des Sciences Politiques, 158–60, 162
Forbes, A. J., 83
Ford, 368, 370

Ford Foundation, 5, 108–9
Foreign Investment Review Agency (Canada), 122
Foreign Policy, Center for the Study of (France), 109
Foreign Politics, Scientific Council for Research on (GDR), 178–79, 181–82
Formanek, Miloslav, 420
Forndran, 172
Forsell, Harry, 307, 315–16
Forsey, Eugene, 117, 127
Forsthoff, Ernst, 171
Forum of Free Enterprise (India), 205
Fotia, M., 427
Foucault, Michel, 12, 20, 27, 164, 342
Foundation for Assistance to Research (Brazil), 109
Foundation for Confederal Collaboration (Swiss), 330
Foundation Pro-Helvetia (Switzerland), 328, 332
Foundations of Modern Political Science (book series), 53
Fourteen Points of Jinnah, 284
Fox, Paul, 121
Fox, Robin, 19, 32
Foyer, Lars, 311, 325
Fraenkel, Ernst, 169–71
Fraeys, William, 50
Francis, Douglas, 127
Frank, André Gunder, 122, 130
Frank, Philipp, 12, 21, 27
Franke, Jörg, 183
Frankel, Joseph, 284
Frankfort, University of, 173
Frankfort School, 52, 163, 170, 172
Frederickson, George M., 27
Free Democratic party (Germany), 173–74
Freeman, Donald M., 377, 380, 408
Frei, Daniel, 327, 329
French political science: alleged lack of scientific legitimacy, 164–66; associational activities, 159; associations, 159; evolution since 1945, 155–61; impact of political events on, 160; individual specialization, 163–64; intellectual structure, 155–56; introduction, 154–55; journals, 159–60; methodological developments, 159; in 1945, 155; political scientists in politics, 160–61; present state, 161–66; relations with government, 161; research, 157–58; special publications, 160; subjects studied,

French political science (*cont.*)
161, 163; its teaching, 156–57; and world of politics, 160
Freud, Sigmund, 12, 164, 172, 212
Freund, Julien, 54, 157
Freymond, Jacques, 50, 328–29, 414
Frías, Félix, 71
Fribourg, University of (Switzerland), 331
Friðriksdóttir, Thorunn, 192
Friedberg, E., 164
Friedeburg, 174
Friedland, Roger, 269
Friedlandes, Paul, 183
Friedman, Milton, 12, 20, 27, 52
Friedman, Robert S., 379–80
Friedrich, Carl J., 10, 16–17, 19, 22, 24, 27, 44, 48–49, 54, 65, 68, 73, 169–71, 378, 380, 414
Fries, S. D., 380
Friis, Henning, 143
Fritsch, Bruno, 24, 26, 27, 52, 54
Fritz Heckert Trade Union College (GDR), 180, 182
Fueter, Edouard, 335
Fueyo, J., 429
Fujita, Shozo, 211
Fujiwara, Hirotatsu, 212
Fukuda, Kanichi, 211
Furner, Mary O., 112, 125
Furtado, Celso, 110

Gaber, Steva, 406, 412
Gables, 285
Gaige, John, 377
Galbraith, John Kenneth, 115, 126
Gal'perin, G. B., 337, 339
Galtung, Johan, 85, 91–92, 149, 152, 259, 264–65, 269–70
Game theory, 12, 17, 52
Gand, State University of (Belgium), 93–94
Gandhian Institute of Studies, 205
Gandhi Peace Foundation, 205
Gangemi, L., 427
Ganon, I., 429
Ganshof van der Meersch, W. J., 96–97, 99
Gantzel, K., 172
Gapotchka, Marlen, 6, 45, 256
Garcia Arias, L., 429
Garcia Pelayo, Manuel, 70, 73
Garhwal University (India), 204
Garner, W., 280
Garrido Falla, F., 429
Gaudet, Hazel, 13, 21, 29
Gauhati University (India), 204
Gaus, John M., 380

Gautier, Léopold, 335
Gavranov, Velibor, 410
Gaxie, D., 163
Gdańsk, University of (Poland), 293–94
Gebethner, S., 297
Geer, J. P. van der, 241
Geirsson, Smári, 189, 192
Geissler, 174
Gelber, Harry, 75
General Systems Theory, 59
Geneva, University of, 331, 334
George, Alexander, 13
Georgievski, Petre, 407
Gérard-Libois, J., 95
Gerlich, Peter, 91–92
German Academy for Politics, 169
German political science (Democratic Republic): councils for social sciences research, 182; development and tasks, 177–78; fields and results in late 1960s, 178; fields and results in 1970s, 178–82; journals and periodicals, 183; political superstructure, 177–78; research, 178–82
German political science (Federal Republic): associational activities, 173; associations, 173; evolution since 1945, 169–75; impact of political events on, 173–74; intellectual structure, 169–70; introduction, 169; journals and special publications, 173; methodological developments, 170; most noteworthy research contributions, 170–72; in 1945, 169; political scientists in politics, 174–75; present state and future prospects, 175; relations with government, 174; research, 170–72; its teaching, 172–73; and world of politics, 173
German Political Science Association, 173
German Political Studies, 173
German Research Association (FRG), 171
Germino, Dante, 406
Gersković, Leo, 406, 412
Gerth, Hans, 19
Gettel, Raymond, 280
Getúlio Vargas Foundation (Brazil), 101, 108
Ghazzali, Abu Hamid al-, 275, 282–83
Gibbs, Willard, 14
Gicquel, Jean, 158
Gielen, J., 237

Gieorgica, Pawel, 423
Gil, Federico G., 70, 73
Gilden, Hilail, 20
Gilg, Peter, 335, 424
Gillin, J., 61
Gingras, François-Pierre, 129
Gingyera-Pincycwa, A. G. G., 60
Gjanković, Dan, 410, 412
Glans, Ingemar, 312
Glazer, Nathan, 81
Gledišts (Yugoslavia), 404
Gleditsch, Nils-Petter, 265, 269–70
Gligorić, Stojan, 409
Glotz, 174
Gluksmann, André, 164
Goati, Vladimir, 406, 412
Godoy, H., 61
Goguel, François, 45, 47–48, 154, 157, 159, 161, 166–67, 417, 421
Gokhale Institute of Public Affairs (India), 205
Gold, M. H., 423
Goldberg, Giora, 422
Goldman, Philip, 124
Goldmann, Kjell, 313, 318
Goldstein, Ray, 255
Goldthorpe, J. E., 60
Gołębiowski, J., 297
Gomal, University of (Pakistan), 276–77
Gonzales Casanova, P., 62
Gonzalez Pedrero, E., 429
Goode, William J., 284
Goodnow, Frank J., 380
Goodnow, Henry F., 284, 368
Goormaghtigh, John, 44, 334, 353, 417
Goosens, Charles, 97, 419
Gorakhpur University (India), 204
Gorbunov, I. S., 353
Gordon, B. J., 255
Gordon, Walter, 122
Gorer, Geoffrey, 12, 20
Goričar, Jože, 394, 405, 408
Gorz, André, 129
Gosnell, Harold, 370
Gothenburg, University of (Sweden), 299–300, 306, 309, 311–12, 320
Gottmann, Jean, 158
Gottschling, Ernst, 183
Gourevitch, Peter Alexis, 27, 129
Gournay, Bernard, 50
Gover, Geoffrey, 27
Governability, 14
Governing, 14
Governing capabilities, 15
Governing capacity, 14
Government, 2

Governmental performance, 15
Government and Opposition (UK), 360
Government College for Boys, Nowshera (Pakistan), 278
Graham, George J., 141
Grahn, Werner, 183
Gramsci, Antonio, 49, 59, 129, 393, 409
Grands problèmes de science politique contemporaine (Belgium), 99
Grant, Lawrence V., 380
Grant, Wyn, 359
Grauhan, R., 170, 175
Grawitz, Madeleine, 157
Gray, Herbert, 122
Gray Report (Canada), 122
Grazia, Alfred de, 54, 166, 370
Grazia, Sebastian de, 370
Greaves, H. R. G., 51
Green, P., 129
Green, Reginald, 24, 28
Greene, J. E., 61
Greenstein, Fred, 12, 20, 378, 380
Greenwood, Gordon, 76
Grégoire, M., 97
Grégoire, Roger, 50
Grémy, Jean-Paul, 53
Grief, S. W., 423
Griffith, University of (Australia), 76
Grímsson, Ólafur Ragnar, 189–90, 192–93
Grličkov, Aleksandar, 407
Groningen, University of (Netherlands), 227
Grønmo, Sigmund, 262, 270
Gross, Bertram M., 60
Gross, L., 126
Grosser, Alfred, 5, 23, 27, 52, 54, 127, 157–58, 161–62, 168
Grossman, J., 61
Groszyk, H., 297
Grotius, Hugo, 49, 227, 234
Gruner, Erich, 330–31, 334–35
Grzybowski, K., 294, 297–98
Guattari, Felix, 164
Gubbels, L. J., 241
Gúðmundsdóttir, Esther, 192
Gúðmundsson, Gestur, 189, 192
Gúðmundsson, Hallgrimur, 191–92
Guerreiro, Ramos Alberto, 110
Guinsburg, T. N., 128
Gujrat University (India), 204
Gujrat Vidyapith University (India), 204
Gulbrandsen, Lars, 265, 270
Guliew, W. A., 183
Gumplowicz, Ludwig, 19, 27

Gunnell, John, 380
Gunnmo, Alf, 316
Gunsteren, Herman R. van, 230, 235–36, 240, 243–45
Gurr, Ted Robert, 380
GuruNanak Dev University (India), 204
Gustafsson, Agne, 310
Gustafsson, Gunnel, 307, 309, 316
Gustavsson, Sverker, 306, 312, 325
Gutierrez, Juan Maria, 71
Gwan, Sung-Kyun, 422

Haag, H., 96
Haas, Ernst, B., 15, 22–23, 27, 372
Haas, Michael, 380
Haavio-Mannila, Elina, 151
Habermas, Jürgen, 11, 20, 27, 52, 122, 135, 170, 174–75, 214
Habib, Mohammad, 277, 432
Hacker, Andrew, 363
Haddow, Anna, 377, 380
Hadenius, Stig, 309, 315, 317, 325
Hadži-Vasileva, Jokica, 409
Haftendorn, H., 172
Haggroth, Sören, 307
Hajjar, Sami G., 45, 203
Hakovirta, Harto, 152, 420
Halappa, S. S., 203
Haldane, J. B. S., 10, 19, 27
Halldórsdóttir, Helga, 190, 192
Halldórsson, Stefán A., 190, 192
Hallenstvedt, Abraham, 263, 270
Halvarson, Arne, 311
Hamadani, Ali Shihab, 276
Hamid, Abdul, 284
Hamilton, Alexander, 9
Hammar, Thomas, 309, 317, 325–26
Hamon, Léo, 158, 160–61
Hamrin, Harald, 308
Han, Bae-Ho, 422
Han, Sang-Il, 422
Hancock, Donald, 308, 316
Handegaard, Odd, 265, 269–70
Hanke, Helmut, 183
Hansen, Peter, 141–42
Hansen, Tore, 217, 264, 269–70
Haq, Mazhar ul-, 280
Harðardóttir, Steinunn, 189, 192
Harle, Vilho, 152
Harman, G., 77, 84
Harmon, Robert, B., 380
Harold Laski Institute of Public Administration (India), 205
Harris, Joseph P., 375, 379
Harris, Oren, 375
Harrison, Wilfrid, 45, 362
Hart, Thomas, 308, 314

Hartmann, Karl, 183
Hartung, D., 175
Harvard University, 1, 41, 126, 368
Hasan, Syed Ahmed ud-din, 289
Hassner, Pierre, 162
Hatfield, Mark, 375
Hatt, Paul K., 284
Hattich, Manfred, 421
Hauriou, Maurice, 154, 157
Hayashi, Chikiu, 214
Hayashi, Kentaro, 211, 213–14
Hayek, Friedrich von, 12, 20, 28
Hazelhoff, Herman, 241
HCM State Institute of Public Administration, 205
Heady, Ferrel, 62
Health plans, national, 16
Hearn, William, 74–75
Heberle, Rudolf, 148
Heckscher, Gunnar, 50, 309, 311, 318
Heclo, Hugh, 23, 26, 28, 359
Héðinsson, Elias, 190, 192
Hedmark/Oppland Distriktshøgskole (Norway), 257
Hegel, Georg, 10, 19, 116, 386
Heidar, Knut, 263, 270
Heidelberg, University of, 174
Heidenheimer, Arnold, 50, 169
Heinrich, G., 91
Heiskanen, Ilkka, 148–49, 152, 420
Heisler, Martin O., 132
Helander, Voitto, 152
Hellevik, Ottar, 263–64, 269–70
Hellstrøm, Gunnar, 317
Helm, R. P. van der, 242
Helmer, O., 59–60
Helmers, H. M., 242
Helsinki, University of, 144–45, 147
Helsinki School of Social Sciences, 144
Hempel, Carl, 112, 124
Henderson, J., 255
Henning, Roger, 311
Henningsen, Sven, 140–43
Hennis, Wilhelm, 170–71, 175
Henrichsen, B., 269, 272
Heretik, S., 426
Herman, Judd, 283
Hermeneutics, 11
Hermens, Ferdinand, 169–71
Hermeren, Göran, 315
Hermerén, Henrik, 311
Hermet, G., 162
Hernandez-Rubio, J. M., 429
Hernes, Gudmund, 259–60, 263–64, 269–70
Hernes, Helga, 217, 264

Herremans, M. P., 95, 98
Herring, E. Pendleton, 61, 119, 370
Herzog, 171
Hessian Foundation for Peace and Conflict Research (FRG), 172
Hessler, Carl Arvid, 306
Heunks, 242
Hibbs, Douglas A., Jr., 21, 28
Higher Education, Institute for (GDR), 180
Higher education, Soviet, 340–41
Higher Schools of Political Science (Yugoslavia), 383–84
Hight, James, 246
Hilferink, J. D., 244
Hill, L. B., 254–55
Himachal Pradesh University (India), 204
Himmelstrand, Ulf, 259
Hinckley, Barbara, 28
Hintzen, G. A., 239, 245
Hiromatsu, Wataru, 211
Hirsch, 170
Hirsch, Fred, 24, 28
Hirsch, Paul, 28
Hirschmann, 163
Historical and Political Studies (NZ), 253
Historical materialism, 292
Hitler, Adolf, 10, 19, 28, 288
Hjellum, Torstein, 217, 261–62
Hjern, Benny, 315
Hobbes, Thomas, 9, 208, 282, 368
Hochfeld, Julian, 297, 406
Hockin, Thomas A., 126
Hodges, Herbert, 19, 28
Hodgetts, J. E., 121, 128–29
Hoetjes, B. J. S., 234, 242
Hofferbert, Richard, 265, 269
Hoffman, David, 129
Hoffman, Fredrik, 217, 263
Hoffmann, Stanley, 50, 54, 158
Hofstadter, Richard, 19, 28
Höivik, Tord, 269
Holden, Matthew, Jr., 375
Holland, Stuart, 122
Holler, Frederick L., 380
Holmberg, Sören, 309
Holmström, Barry, 306
Holst, Johan Jörgen, 217, 264
Holsti, K. J., 284
Holsti, Ole R., 13, 21, 28
Holsti, Rudolf, 144, 150
Holt, Robert T., 380
Hoog, R. de, 241
Hoogemdijk, F. A., 241
Hoogerwerf, Andries, 229–30, 235–36, 240, 242–45

Horkheimer, Max, 11, 20, 28, 170
Horn, Michael, 127
Horner, F., 91–92
Horowitz, Irving, 59, 126, 378, 380
Horowitz, Robert, 373
Hosoya, Chihiro, 212–13
Hoven, Finn Holmer, 423
Howard, D., 380
Höyer, Svennik, 217, 261–62, 272
Hristov, Aleksandar, 407
Hubbée-Boonzaaijer, S., 241–42
Huber, Hans, 328
Hudson, Michael C., 13, 21–22, 28, 32
Hughes, Colin A., 76, 81, 84
Huismans, S. E., 236, 244
Huitt, Ralph, 376
Huizer, Gerrit, 242
Hull, W. H. N., 45, 128–29
Hume, David, 11
Humphrey, Hubert, 375
Humphrey, J. T. P., 128
Hunt, Norman, 361
Huntington, Samuel P., 10, 15, 19, 26, 28, 49, 54, 285, 372, 380
Huopaniemi, J., 152
Huq, Mazhar ul-, 280
Hurtig, Serge, 5, 51, 166, 417
Huxley, Julian S., 10, 19, 28, 234
Hveem, Helge, 217, 264, 267
Hydéns, Göran, 308, 316
Hyderabad, University of (India), 204
Hyneman, Charles S., 380
Hyvarinen, Risto, 149, 152

Ianni, Otavio, 110
Ibler, Vladimir, 411
Iceland, University of, 185–89
Icelandic political science: associational activities, 191; future prospects, 191; minor research areas, 190–91; origins, 185–86; research, 187–89; research on mass media, 190; research on parliament, 189–90; research on political parties, 189; research on power structure, 188–89; research on social structure, 190; its teaching, 186–87
Icelandic Social Science Publications, 191
ICPSR consortium, 5
Ide, Yoshinori, 212
Idenburg, P. J. A., 244
IDRC (Canada), 109
Igličar, Albin, 406
Iizuka, Yoshiaki, 212
Ike, Nobutaka, 23, 28
Ikeuchi, Hajime, 211, 214

Ikram, S. M., 281, 284
Il'jašenko, K., 353
Imboden, Max, 328
Imperialism, Scientific Council for Research on (GDR), 181–82
Improvement of Qualifications, Institute for (USSR), 343
Imre, Szabo, 421
India, 52
Indian Academy of Social Science, 205
Indian Council for Africa, 205
Indian Council of Historical Research, 205
Indian Council of Peace Research, 205
Indian Council of Social Science Research, 202, 205
Indian Independence Act, 284
Indian Institute of Management, 205
Indian Institute of Mass Communication, 205
Indian Institute of Public Administration, 195, 205
Indian Institute of Public Opinion, 205
Indian Management Association, 205
Indian National Movement, 200
Indian political science: change and continuity, 196–97; comparative politics, 198; courses in research methodology, 198; current handicaps and problem areas, 201; dichotomy of research and teaching, 196; emerging trends in research, 198–99; emerging trends in syllabi content, 197; inclusion of courses on government and politics, 197; interdisciplinary impulsion of, 197; international politics and public administration, 198; introduction, 194; journals, 205–6; limitation of traditional research techniques, 199–201; need for infrastructural development, 201–2; overview, 194–95; research institutes and associations, 205; sensitivity toward paradigm-conflicts, 196; steady growth of enrollment, 195–96; switchover to regional languages, 201; translation role of political science teachers, 201–2; universities where taught, 204; university locus of, 195
Indian Political Science Association, 194, 196, 202, 205
Indian Public Administration Association, 205

Indian School of International Relations, 195
Indian School of Public Economy, 205
Indian Society for International Law, 205
Indian Society of Criminology, 205
Indore, University of, 204
Inglehart, Ronald F., 25, 28
Inkeles, Alex, 13, 16, 20–21, 23, 28
Innis, Harold, 113–14, 116–18, 122–23, 125–27
Innis, Mary Q., 117
Innovation, 16
Innsbruck, University of (Austria), 87–89
Inoguchi, Kuniko, 215
Inoguchi, Takashi, 212–15
Inoki, Masamichi, 212
Inquiry, logic of, 214
Institit Français d'Opinion Publique, 159
Institut Auguste Comte (France), 161
Institut belge de Science politique, 95–99
Institut Canadien, 117
Institut des Sciences de l'Action (France), 161
Institut d'Etudes Politiques (France), 154, 156, 166
Institutionalism, 113, 118–19
Institutions and political mechanisms, 49–50
Institut national d'études politiques (Belgium), 95
Instituts d'Etudes Politiques (France), 161, 342
Institut universitaire de sondage d'opinion publique (Belgium), 98
Instrumentalism, theory of, 395
Instrument of Government of 1809 (Sweden), 299, 311–12
Inter-American Development Bank, 109
Interest groups, 50, 53, 309–10, 397–99
Interfaculty Delft en Rotterdam, 227
International Affairs (Japan), 215
International Affairs (UK), 356
International Affairs, Swedish Institute of, 313
International Bibliography of Political Science, 50, 54
International Center for Public Enterprises in Developing Countries, in Ljubljana (Yugoslavia), 403
International Committee for Social Science Documentation, 62

International Committee on Sociology, 266
International Conferences on Participation . . . and Self-Management, 42
International Development Research Center (Canada), 41
International House of Japan, 218
International Institute of Administrative Sciences, 80
International Labor Organization, 313
International law, organization, and behavior, 366
International Law and Diplomacy, Journal of (Japan), 215
International organization, study of, 221
International Peace Research Institute (Norway), 256, 258, 261, 264–65, 269
International Political Science Abstracts, 51, 54
International Political Science Association, 3, 5, 9, 34–35, 37–43, 48, 51, 53, 69–70, 80, 95, 107–9, 111, 169, 194, 224, 239, 255, 266, 293, 324, 328–29, 351–52, 356, 360, 362, 403–4: activities, 36–39; character, 35; formation, 35; founding, 2; growth, 36; location of meetings, 38–39; membership, 37–39; participation in its meetings, 39; representation on governing organs, 38; research committees and study groups, 40; round tables and seminars, 37; topics of sessions and round tables, 40
International Politics and Economics, Institute for (GDR), 181–82
International relations, 2, 208–9, 217, 221, 234–35, 249, 251, 312, 314, 393, 399: study of, 50
International Relations (Japan), 215
International Relations, Institute for (GDR), 182
International School of International Studies (India), 198
International Social Science Council, 43, 109
International Sociological Association, 42
International Spectator, 228, 234
International Studies, Graduate Institute of (Switzerland), 328–29, 331
International Studies Association, 215
International Workers' Movement, Institute of (Belgrade), 402

International Workers' Movement, Scientific Council for (GDR), 182
Inter-University Consortium for Political and Social Research, 364
INUSOP, 97
Iqbal, Mohammad, 275, 284, 288
Iqbal, Mohd, 275, 281–82
Irie, Keishiro, 213
Irish, Marian D., 45, 289, 380
Iriye, Akira, 28, 213
Isberg, Magnus, 306, 310, 316
Ishida, Takeshi, 211–13
Ishii, Yoneo, 213
Ishikawa, Akihiro, 211
Ispahani, M. A. H., 284
ISSC Center (Vienna), 266
Ito, Takashi, 212
Ivanov, S. S., 353
Iveković, Ivan, 409

Jabalpur University (India), 204
Jackson, G. E., 128
Jackson, Robert J., 45, 126, 128, 131
Jackson, W. K., 250, 254–55
Jacobsen, Knut Dahl, 217, 256, 264
Jadavpur University (India), 204
Jaensch, Dean, 80, 84, 419
Jaffré, Jérôme, 161
Jaguaribe, Hélio, 16, 24, 26, 28, 54, 110
Jahoda, 86
Jahoda, Marie, 20, 26
Jakimovski, Ljubomir, 407
James Cook, University of (Australia), 76
Jamia Millia Islamia (India), 204
Jammu, University of (India), 204
Jampol'skaya, C. A., 353
Janković, Branimir M., 410–11
Janković, Dragoslav, 410
Janne, H., 97
Janowitz, Morris, 28, 44
Jansen, Alf-Inge, 265
Jansen, Max, 423
Jansson, Bo, 316, 318
Jansson, Jan-Mogens, 142–43, 145, 151–52
Japan Association of International Law, 215
Japan Association of Public Administration, 215
Japan Association of Southeast Asian Studies, 215
Japan Center for International Exchange, 218
Japan Echo, The, 216
Japanese Annals of International Affairs, 215

Japanese Association of International Relations, 208–9, 212, 215–16
Japanese Association of Theoretical Economics, 215
Japanese Political Science Association, 207–9, 211, 213, 215–16
Japanese Sociological Association, 215
Japanese political science: associational activities, 215–16; associations, 215; attitudes and behavior, 211; East Asian and Southeast Asian studies, 217; evolution since 1945, 207–9; graduate-level teaching, 210; impact of political configurations on, 216–17; intellectual structure, 208; international relations, 217; international relations and comparative politics, 213; introduction, 207; institutions and processes, 211–12; Japanese politics, 217; journals, 215–16; methodological developments, 213–14; the more scientific methodology, 214–15; the more traditional methodology, 213–14; most noteworthy research contributions, 210–11; in 1945, 207; political and diplomatic history, 212–13; present state and future prospects, 217–18; quantitative political analysis, 218; relation with government, 217; research, 211–15; its teaching, 209; theory and philosophy, 211; undergraduate-level teaching, 209–10; and the world of politics, 216–17
Japan Foundation, 207, 218
Japan Institute of International Affairs, 215
Japan Interpreter, The, 216
Japan Peace Research Group, 216
Japan Peace Studies Association, 215
Jarlov, Carsten, 141–42
Jaros, Dean, 380
JASEAR *Southeast Asian Research* (Japan), 215
Javić, L. S., 353
Jawaharlal Nehru University (India), 195, 204
Jayaprakash Narayan Institute of Political Philosophy (India), 205
Jeannin, Pierre, 157
Jefferson, Thomas, 9
Jellinek, Georg, 145, 151
Jennings, Sir Ivor, 81, 114, 281, 356
Jensen, Arthur, 10
Jeppesen, Jens, 141
Jervas, Gunnar, E., 313–14, 326

Jetzschmann, Horst, 183
Jevtić, Bora, 408, 411
Jiji, Tsushinsha, 211
Jimenez de Parga, 68
Jinnah, Quaid-e-Azam Mohammad Ali, 278, 281, 284, 287
Jiwaji University (India), 204
Jobert, B., 167
Jodhpur University (India), 204
Jogan, Drago Božič-Savin, 408
Jóhannsson, Ingi Valur, 190, 192
Johansen, L. Norby, 141
Johansen, Robert, 28
Johansson, Leif, 316
John of Salisbury, 9
Johns Hopkins University, 2, 41, 376
Johnson, Chalmers, 24, 28
Johnson, Harry, 115
Johnson, Karl F., 382
Johnson, Leo, 122
Johnson, Nevil, 363
Joint Committee on the Organization of Congress (US), 375
Joint Program of Studies on Latin American Economic Integration (Brazil), 109
Joint University Council of Social Studies (UK), 356
Joji, Watanuki, 207
Joka, Mile, 409
Jones, Charles, 376
Jónsdóttir, Sigríður, 192
Jónsdóttir, Sigurveig, 190, 192
Jónsdóttir, Thorbjörg, 190, 192
Jonsson, Bo, 303
Jönsson, Christer, 313
Jordana de Pozas, L., 61, 429
Jørgensen, Jørgen, 140
Jouvenel, Bertrand de, 9, 18, 28, 47, 49–51, 54, 68, 157
Jovanov, Neca, 407
Judge, Anthony, 217
Juergensmeyer, M., 203
Julliard, J., 160
Junker, Beat, 335
Junta of Government (Argentina), 70–71
Jürgens, U., 85, 91–92
Juristic approach, 292
Jurrjens, Rudolf Th., 234, 242
Justo Lopez, Mario, 73
Južnić, Stane, 408–9, 411

Kaartvedt, Alf, 217, 264, 269
Kaase, Max, 13, 21, 25
Kägi, Werner, 328
Kahin, George, 275, 281
Kahn, Herman, 9, 18, 28

Kaitken, Hugh, 117
Kakakhel, Nazir, 278
Kalela, Aira, 264
Kalela, Jaakko, 264
Kalman filter, 215
Kaltefleiter, Werner, 171
Kalyani University (India), 204
Kamaraj Madurai University (India), 204
Kamishima, Jiro, 211, 213, 422
Kamiya, Fuji, 213
Kamo, Takehiko, 213
Kandidaty degree, in USSR, 347–48
Kanpur University (India), 204
Kant, Immanuel, 10–11, 19
Kaplan, Abraham, 19, 285–86
Kaplan, Morton, A., 23, 30, 61, 213, 372, 429
Karachi, University of (Pakistan), 276, 279–80, 286
Kardelj, Edvard, 390, 395, 400, 406–9, 411–12
Kariel, Henry S., 45, 373, 378, 380
Karl Marx Party College at the Central Committee of SED (GDR), 180
Karlsson, Örlygur, 190, 192
Karlsson, Stefan, 189, 192
Karnatak University (India), 204
Karstem, Rafael, 144, 150
Kashmir, University of (India), 204
Kastari, Paave, 153
Kastendieck, H., 85, 91–92, 175
Kasturba Institute of Rural Studies (India), 205
Kataoka, Hiromitsu, 212
Kataoka, Tetsuya, 213
Katowice, University of (Poland), 293
Katsuta, Yoshitaro, 211
Katz, Daniel, 142, 259, 261, 273, 285
Katzenstein, Peter J., 22, 28, 129
Kautilya, 276
Kavanagh, Dennis, 363
Kavčič, Bogdan, 407–8
Kawai, Hidekazu, 213
Kawai, Kazuo, 23, 28
Kawata, Tadashi, 213
Kazmi, 289
Keček'jan, S. G., 353
Keirstead, B. S., 129
Kelman, Herbert, 12, 20, 28
Kelsen, Hans, 12, 21, 28, 145
Kelson, R. N., 254–55
Kemper, J. de Bosch, 227
Kennaway, Richard, 251, 255
Kennedy, John F., 375
Kenski, H. C., 380
Kenski, M. C., 380

Keohane, Robert, 23
Kerala, University of (India), 204
Kerala Academy of Politics (India), 205
Kerala Institute of Marxist Studies (India), 205
Kerimov, D. A., 337, 425
Kernig, C. D., 5
Kerver-Garnett, Liz, 227
Ketzerov, N. M., 352
Key, V. O., 12, 20, 28, 50, 370, 381
Key Concepts in Political Science (book series), 53
Khaldun, Ibn-i-, 282–83
Khan, Abdul Hamid, 279
Khan, A. Saleem, 278, 286–89, 423
Khan, Liaquat Ali, 278
Khan, Quaid-e-Azam Mohammad Ali, 278
Khan, Sir Syed Ahmed, 276, 281, 284
Khilafat Movement (Pakistan), 284
Kidrič, Boris, 408
Kiev, University of, 342–43
Kiev Institute for Civil Aviation Engineers, 343
Kiev Institute for Civil Engineering, 343
Kihlberg, Leif, 316
Kildal, N., 269
Kim, Ke Soo, 225–26
Kim, Wha Ryong, 225–26
Kim, Yongjak, 212
King, Anthony, 115, 126, 379
King, Preston, 6, 126, 362–63
Kirchheimer, Otto, 169
Kirkpatrick, Evron M., 377–78
Kirkpatrick, Jeane, 375
Kirkpatrick, Samuel A., 381
Kissinger, Henry, 3, 9, 18, 28, 83, 169, 217, 375
Kjartansson, Helgi Skúli, 192
Kjellberg, Francesco, 217, 259, 262, 264–65, 267, 269
Kjellén, Rudolf, 313
Klason, Lars-Erik, 316
Klassen, D. M. C., 45
Kleerekoper, S., 237
Kleijn, A., 243
Klein, Peter, 183
Klinkers, L. E. M., 236, 244
Klováč, J., 353
Knapp, V., 426
Kneucker, Raoul F., 419
Knorr, Klaus, 9, 18, 28
Knudsen, Harald, 264
Knudsen, Olav, 264
Koch, K., 423

Koenig, 170
Kogekar, S. V., 50, 203
Kogon, Ernst, 170
Kohei Shinsaku, 207
Kohl, Helmut, 174
Kok, W., 241
Kolaja, J., 426
Kolaković, Juraj, 394, 408
Kolberg, Jon Eivind, 217, 265, 269
Kolko, Gabriel, 122
Kołłątaj, Hugo, 297
Komsomol (USSR), 346
Konstantinov, F. V., 353
Kooiman, J., 233, 236, 241–42
Koontz, Harold, 284
Kopelmanns, L., 166
Korean Association of International Relations, 222, 224–25
Korean Association of Public Administration, 222, 224–25
Korean International Relations Review, 225
Korean political science: associations, 226; departments and personnel, 226; influence of political events on, 236; introduction, 219; journals, 226; from 1945 to 1953, 220–21; in 1945, 219–20; from 1954 to 1961, 221–22; from 1962 to the present, 222–25; and politics, 236, 238–39; present state and future prospects, 225; publications, 222, 224
Korean Political Science Association, 221–25
Korean Political Science Review, 224–25
Korean Political Scientists in North America, Association of, 224
Korean Public Administration Review, 225
Korean Unification Center, 224
Korean University, 220
Kornberg, Allan, 124
Kort, Fred, 381
Kosaka, Masataka, 212
Kositsyn, A. P., 337
Kotarbiński, T., 294, 297
Kothari, Rajni, 16, 24, 28, 50
Kottman, R. H. P. W., 236, 244
Kouba, Ernest, 419
Kožarov, Asen, 407
Kramer, H., 91–92
Kranenburg, R., 233, 241
Kranjc, Stane, 410
Kreisky, P., 91
Krejci, Jaroslav, 28
Krešić, Andrija, 406, 408

Krieken, Peter J., 243
Kriesberg, M., 61
Krippendorff, Ekkehart, 172
Krishna, Gopal, 16, 24, 28
Kristan, Ivan, 408
Kristensen, Ole P., 141–42
Kristjánsson, Baldur, 192
Kristjánsson, Svanur, 186, 189, 192
Kroeber, Alfred L., 20
Kroes, P., 243
Kroes, R., 240
Kronvall, Kai, 310
Kuan, John C., 420
Kruger, Joachim, 183
Kruhlak, O. M., 129
Kuhlberg, S., 353
Kuhn, Thomas S., 17, 24, 28, 59, 115, 126, 140, 163, 166, 278
Kuhnle, Stein, 45, 217, 260–61, 266, 269–70
Kuiper, D. Th., 242
Kulesar, K., 426
Kulturni radnik (Yugoslavia), 404
Kumarappa Institute of Gram Swaraj (India), 205
Kumaun University (India), 204
Küng, Hans, 328
Kurin, D., 353
Kurth, James R., 129
Kurtović, Todo, 407
Kušej, Gorazd, 405
Kuyper, A., 227, 231
Kuypers, G., 229–30, 234, 236, 240, 242, 244–45
Kuznecova, S. I., 353
Kvavik, Robert, 217, 263
Kwanry, H. A., 62
Kyogoku, Junichi, 16, 23, 28, 211, 213–16

Labor party (Australia), 83
Labor party (Norway), 263–64
Labour party (NZ), 250, 253
Labour party (UK), 362
Lacan, Jacques, 12, 20, 29, 164
Lachs, M., 294
Lacroix, Bernard, 154, 163
Ladd, Everett C., 45, 368, 378
Ładosz, J., 297
Ladrière, J., 95, 97
Lafer, Celso, 24, 29, 110
Laferrière, Julien, 154
Lafferty, William, 217, 260–61, 263, 266
Lagerroth, Fredrik, 300, 312
Lahore, University of Engineering and Technology at (Pakistan), 276
Lahore Resolution, 284

Lajos, Tomori, 421
Lakatos, Imre, 97, 112, 124
Lalande, Gilles, 129
Lal Bahadur Shastri National Academy of Administration (India), 205
Lalit Narayan Mithila University (India), 204
Lally, J., 255
Lamontagne, Maurice, 117
Lampert, Richard, 24–25
La Nauze, J. A., 83
Lancelot, Alain, 158–61, 167–68
Lanctot, Gustave, 126
Land, L. van der, 229, 232, 235, 240–41, 243
Landau, Martin, 381
Landelius, Torsten, 313
Landqvist, Åke, 319
Landtman, Gunnar, 144, 150
Lane, Jan Erik, 303
Lane, Robert E., 12, 20, 29, 45, 50, 54, 378, 381
Lange, Oskar, 59–60
Langer, T., 298
Langrod, G., 50, 353, 429
Lansing, Marjorie, 25
La Palombara, Joseph, 16, 23, 29, 242
Lapierre, Jean-William, 54, 167
La Plata, Catholic University of (Argentina), 68
La Plata, National University of (Argentina), 67–70
Laponce, Jean, 13, 21, 29, 44, 50, 54, 120, 129, 414
Larsen, Stein Ugelvik, 217, 263
Larsson, Reidar, 304, 308
Lárusson, Erlendur, 190, 192
Lasina, M. V., 353
Laski, Harold, 222–23, 283, 355, 359, 408
Lasswell, Harold D., 12–13, 17, 19–21, 29, 45, 49, 54, 59–60, 114, 119, 222–23, 286, 370, 378, 381
Latent structure analysis, 17
Latham, Earl, 381
Latin American Studies Association, 108
La Trobe, University of (Australia), 77
Laurin-Frenette, Nicole, 122, 126
Lausanne, University of (Switzerland), 331, 334
Laval University (Canada), 117, 120, 127
Lavau, Georges, 50–51, 54, 154, 157–61, 166, 421

Lavigne, P., 353
Lavroff, Dmitri-Georges, 167
Law Concerning the Course of Study of Law (Austria), 89
Law Concerning the Study of Philosophy (Austria), 87
Laxer, Robert, 122, 129
Lazarsfeld, Paul, 13, 21, 29, 86, 134, 140–41, 259, 381
Leacock, Stephen, 116, 126–27
Leader (Pakistan), 279
League of Communists (Yugoslavia), 383, 391, 397
Leal, Victor Nunes, 110
Leca, Jean, 162, 167
Leclercq, Canon, 95, 98
Lederle, J. W., 62
Leemans, A. F., 236, 244
Lefort, Claude, 164
Lefroy, A. H., 126
Leftists, 42
Legendre, Pierre, 164
Legitimacy, 14, 49
Legon, Faustino J., 73
Lehner, F., 175
Lehning, Arthur, 243
Lehtinen, Risto, 152
Leibnitz, Baron von, 14
Leiserson, Avery, 50, 370
Lejst, O. E., 352
Lemelle, Tilden L., 19
Lémieux, Vincent, 114, 120, 125–26, 129, 131
Lemounier, Bolivar, 102, 109–10
Lenin, Vladimir I., 9–11, 19, 29, 49, 129, 135, 171, 282, 342–46, 348, 391, 393, 396, 409
Leningrad, University of, 342–44
Leningrad Shipbuilding Institute, 342
Leninism, 11, 342–44
Léon, V., 353
Leonardi, F., 427
Leoni, B., 427
Lepsius, Rainer M., 21, 29, 171
Lerner, Daniel, 13, 16, 21, 23, 29, 260, 381
Lerner, Michael, 380
Lerotić, Zvonko, 407
Leser, N., 91–92
Lessing, Gotthold E., 10, 19, 29
Letterie, J. W., 235, 243
Levas, C., 96
Lévesque, Père Georges-Henri, 117, 129
Lévesque, René, 117
Leviathan (FRG), 173
Levine, R. A., 306
Levine, S., 250, 254–55

Levinson, Daniel, 12, 20
Levinson, S., 129
Lévi-Strauss, Claude, 12, 20, 29
Levitt, Kari, 113, 122–23, 125, 129
Lévy, Bernard-Henri, 164
Lewin, Leif, 304–6, 310, 312, 315–18, 326
Leyden, University of (Netherlands), 227–28, 232–33
Liberal Democratic party (Japan), 216
Liberalism, 48, 52
Liberal party (Australia), 75, 83
Liberal positivism, 124
Licence degree, in France, 156–57
Licenciat degree, in Sweden, 320, 323, 325
Licenciatura degree, in Argentina, 69–70
Licencié degree, in Belgium, 93
Lieberam, Ekkehard, 183
Liebscher, Gertrud, 183
Liège, State University of (Belgium), 93–94
Liepelt, Klaus, 13, 21
Lifton, Robert J., 9, 12, 20
Lijphart, Arend, 16, 24, 29, 50, 231, 234, 240, 242–45
Linares Quintana, Segundo V., 67–68, 70–71, 73, 419
Lindahl, Göran, 308
Lindahl, Rutger, 424
Lindberg, Leon, 269
Lindblad, Ingemar, 306, 309, 312, 316–17, 326
Lindblom, Charles E., 29, 50, 54
Linde, Claes, 311
Lindeberg, Sven-Ola, 303
Lindman, Sven, 145, 151
Line, Maurice, 44–45, 311
Linguistic Research, Scientific Council, for (GDR), 182
LINK Project, 215
Linköping, University of (Sweden), 320, 325
Lintonen, Raimo, 264
Linz, Juan, 44
Lipschits, L., 232, 234–35, 241, 243
Lipset, Seymour Martin, 10, 13, 15–16, 19, 21, 23, 28, 44–45, 54, 68, 148, 151–52, 217, 260, 266, 378, 381, 425
Lipson, Leslie, 247, 250–51, 254–55
Liska, George, 23, 29
Lisnevskii, E. V., 338–39
Litchfield, Edward, 377
Litoral, University del (Argentina), 68–69
Littunen, Yrjo, 21, 151, 273

Lobkowicz, Nikolaus, 170
Local, Regional, and National Planning, Institute for (Switzerland) 330
Local Authority Administration (NZ), 253
Local government, study of, 50, 53
Local Government Act (NZ), 253
Local Government Officers, National Association of (UK), 356
Local Government Project (Sweden), 322
Local Government Studies, Institute of (UK), 359
Lock, Grahame, 235, 243, 245
Lockard, Duane, 372
Locke, John, 9, 49, 208, 282, 368
Łodz, University of (Poland), 292, 294
Loew, Christoph, 21
Loewenberg, Gerhard, 169
Loewenstein, Karl, 68, 169
Lohse, Lennart, 308, 317
Loi d'orientation (France), 156
Lojkine, J., 163
Lombardi, F., 427
London, University of, 276
London School of Economics and Political Science, 126, 169, 355–56
Łopatka, A., 297–98
López, Vicente Fidel, 71
Lopez Portillo, J., 62
Lorentzen, Jens, 217, 270
Lorenz, Konrad, 10, 19, 29
Lorincz, L., 353
Lorraine Political Science Group (France), 159
Lorwin, Val, 97
Loschak, Danielle, 167
Louniev, A. J., 426
Louvain, Catholic University of (Belgium), 93, 98
Louw, Michael H. H., 60
Loveday, Peter, 419
Lovenduski, Joni, 363, 425
Lowe, Bernd P., 183
Lowell, A. Lawrence, 127, 368, 370, 376
Lowi, Theodore J., 45, 129, 141
Lubbe, Hermann, 13, 21, 29
Lucas Verdu, Pablo, 45, 68, 70, 73, 353
Lucknow, University of (India), 204
Ludz, Peter Christian, 170–71
Luhmann, Niklas, 13, 22, 29, 170, 175
Lukàcz, Georg 11, 20, 29, 129
Lukić, Radomir, 394, 405–6, 408–10, 412

Lumsden, Ian, 122, 124, 131
Lund, Niels, 143
Lund, University of (Sweden), 299–300, 303–6, 308–9, 311–13, 320–21
Lundquist, Lennart J., 303–4, 311
Lunev, A. E., 353
Lussier, Doris, 127
Lutčenko, A., 353
Luxemburg, Rosa, 129
Luykx, T., 97

Maarseveen, H. T. J. F. van, 241
Mabileau, Albert, 158
Macaulay, Lord, 275
McCallum, Douglas, 76, 80, 84
McCloskey, Robert G., 45
McCoy, Charles A., 54, 379, 381
McCulloch, Warren S., 22, 29
Mach, Ernst, 12
Machiavelli, Nicolò, 9–10, 48–49, 208, 235, 288
McGill University (Canada), 120, 126–27
McGowan, Patrick J., 23
McGregor, James P., 379, 381
McIntyre, Sir Laurence, 80
MacIver, Robert M., 22, 29, 116, 127, 222–23
McKay, R. A., 117, 127
MacKay, X. A., 128
McKenzie, Robert T., 44, 115, 126, 359
Mackenzie, W. J. M., 43, 45, 50, 54, 358, 363
Mackerras, Malcolm, 84
MacKinnon, Frank, 128
MacKinnon, James, 124
Mackintosh, John, 361
Mackintosh, W. A., 127–28
McLuhan, Marshall, 117
MacMahon-Ball, William, 75
Macovescu, George, 424
MacPherson, C. B., 45, 48, 50, 114, 117, 122, 125–28, 131
Macquarie University (Australia), 76–77
Macridis, Roy C., 22–23, 26, 29, 50, 166, 275, 281, 381
McRobie, A., 254–55
Maddick, Henry, 54
Madison, James, 10, 13
Madrasa (Pakistan), 289
Madras Chepauk, University of (India), 204
Madras Institute of Development Studies (India), 205
Madsen, Ole Norgaard, 141

Maeda, Hisashi, 213
Maeda, Yasuhiro, 214
Maesen, C. E. van der, 232, 241
Magadh University (India), 204
Magalhaes Godinho, V., 428
Magister Artium degree, in Norway, 257–58
Mahmood, Safdar, 281
Mahon, Riane, 129
Maier, H., 170, 174–75
Mailick, 284
Maine, Henry, 116
Mainichi (Japanese newspaper), 214
Maitrise degree, in France, 156–57
Majunedar, B., 203
Malevski, Denko, 407
Malignon, Jean, 54
Malikova, Bela, 420
Mallory, J. R., 113–14, 117, 121, 125
Man, H. de, 241
Management Studies, Institute of (India), (UK), 205
Manchester, University of, 358
Manitoba, University of (Canada), 126
Mann, Thomas E., 377, 425
Mannari, Hiroshi, 215
Mannheim, Karl, 11, 20, 29, 112, 124
Mannheim, University of (FRG), 50
Mansfield, Harvey, 376
Mansson, Lennart, 311
Mao Tse-Tung, 10, 19, 29, 130, 135, 282
Marathwada University (India), 204
Maravall, J. A., 429
Marburg, University of, (FRG), 173
March, James, 217, 269, 372
March, R. R., 45, 128, 131, 259, 284
Marchard, Jean, 117
Marcuse, Herbert, 11, 19, 29, 52, 114, 122, 135
Markič, Boštjan, 408
Marko, Lolić, 410
Markoja, I., 426
Marković, Živko, 410
Markovits, Andrei, 24, 26, 54
Marksistička misao (Yugoslavia), 404
Marongiu, A., 427
Marradi, A., 428
Marsh, David, 359
Marshall, Joan, 84, 254–55
Marshall, T. H., 54
Martikainen, Tuomo, 148, 151–52
Martin, Roscoe, 370
Martin, Yves, 129
Martins, Luciano, 110

Martinussen, Willy, 217, 261, 273
Martonyi, J., 426
Marusic, Ante, 408
Maruyama, Masao, 16, 23, 29, 208, 211, 213
Marvick, Dwaine, 44, 372
Marx, Karl, 9–11, 19, 29, 49, 74, 112, 116, 124, 129, 135, 138, 148, 163–64, 174, 181, 208, 214, 218, 282, 346, 387, 391, 393, 396, 406, 409
Marx and Engels, Scientific Council for Research on (GDR), 181–82
Marxism, 11, 23, 34, 42–43, 49, 52, 113, 130, 135–36, 141, 146, 158, 163, 171–72, 189, 196, 200, 207–8, 214, 230, 237, 260, 292–94, 301, 304, 306, 334, 342–44, 348–49, 385–87, 390, 394–96, 401–2, 406
Marxism-Leninism, 2, 4, 42, 52, 178, 180–82, 189, 294–95, 337, 341–47, 349
Marxism-Leninism of SED, Institute for (GDR), 181–82
Marxist Centers (Yugoslavia), 402
Marxist-Leninist Cultural Sciences and Art, Scientific Council for (GDR), 180–82
Marxist-Leninist Philosophy, Scientific Council for (GDR), 178, 180, 182
Masato, Ninomiya, 207
Mason, Henry L., 244
Maspero, 42
Massachusetts, University of, 278
Massey University (NZ), 248
Mast, A., 97, 99
Master of Arts degree: in Australia, 78; in Brazil, 100–102, 106, 108; in Finland, 146–147, 150; in the Netherlands, 228; in New Zealand, 248, 349; in Pakistan, 277–82, 285–86, 289; in Poland, 293; in the United States, 368
Master of Economics degree, in Australia, 78
Master of Philosophy degree, in Pakistan, 277–80
Master of Science degree, in Pakistan, 277
Master's degree in International Economic Law, in Brazil, 101
Masud, Asad, 288
Masumi, Junnosuke, 212
Mates, Leo, 411–12
Mathematical analysis, 12
Mathematical models, 215
Mathews, Robin, 122, 124, 129

Mathiot, André, 158
Matić, Milan, 407–8
Matos Mar, José, 24, 26
Matous, Milan, 420
Matrix analysis, 14, 17, 52
Matsubara, Haruo, 211
Matsumoto, Sannosuke, 211, 213
Matsushita, Keiichi, 212
Mavor, James, 126, 127, 128
Mawardi, Al, 275, 283
Maxey, Chester, 283
Max Planck *Gesellschaft* (FRG), 174
Max Planck Institute (FRG), 174
May, William H., 23, 31
May, Association of (Argentina), 71
Mayer, Henry, 80–81, 84
Mayo, Elton, 286
Mayo, Henry, 129
Mayon, Carlos Alberto, 70
Mazrui, Ali, 44, 50, 60
Mead, Margaret, 12, 20, 29, 126
Meadows, Dennis, 24, 30, 52–53
Medici, G., 428
Meerut University (India), 204
Meijer, Hans, 311, 325
Meinecke, Friedrich, 10, 19, 30
Meisel, John, 44, 113–14, 119, 125
Melanson, Phillip H., 381
Melbourne, University of (Australia), 74–75, 77
Mellbourn, Anders, 311
Melzer, Helmut, 183
Mendel, Gregor, 10
Mendes de Almeida, Candido, 16, 24, 30, 44, 110, 414
Mendietta y Nuñez, L., 62
Mendlovitz, Saul, 17, 25, 30
Mendoza Navarro, R., 62
Menting, C. L., 236, 244
Meray, S. L., 430
Mercandante, Paulo, 110
Merkl, Peter, 169, 175, 381
Merle, Marcel, 44, 50, 54–55, 162
Merriam, Charles, 19, 23, 30, 49, 54, 114, 119, 169, 222–23, 370, 381
Merritt, Richard L., 13, 21–24, 26, 30, 54
Merton, Robert K., 13, 21, 30, 112, 125
Mesarovic, Mihejlo, 22, 24, 30, 52–53
Methodological Center of Education in Political Science (Poland), 293
Methodology, 366
Meyer, Poul, 139–43
Meynaud, Jean, 45, 48, 50–51, 53, 55, 68, 95, 157–58, 328, 334–35, 417
Meyriat, Jean, 158, 166, 273

Michalska, A., 298
Michelat, Guy, 161, 168
Michels, Roberto, 49
Michigan, University of, 109, 135
Mickiewicz, Ellen Propper, 30
Middel, Bert, 241
Middendorp, C. P., 232, 241
Midgaard, Knut, 259, 272
Milačić, E., 61
Milburn, Josephine, 81, 84
Miliband, Ralph, 59, 122, 129, 170
Military Political Academy (Poland), 293
Mill, James, 116
Mill, John Stuart, 10–11, 116, 368
Millar, T. B., 80
Miller, J. G., 22, 30
Miller, Warren, 13, 50, 372
Mills, C. Wright, 19, 122
Mills, R. M., 353
Mills, Walter Thomas, 381
Milne, R. S., 50, 80, 250, 254–55
Milner, Henry, 129
Milner, I., 83
Milton Campos Foundation for Research and Political Studies (Brazil), 107
Minas Gerais, Federal University of (Brazil), 100–102, 107
Minesters, Council of (USSR), 347
Mining Institute (USSR), 342
Minnesota, University of, 221, 368
Minville, Edras, 117, 128–29
Mirčev, Dmitar, 408
Mirić, Jovan, 406–7, 410, 412
Mirkoć-Lebl, Divna, 410
Miron, Murray S., 23, 31
MISEREOR Foundation (Germany), 109
M.I.T. (Massachusetts Institute of Technology), 41
Mitani, Taichiro, 212
Mitchell, Austin, 250, 252, 254–55
Mitchell, William C., 151–52, 381
Mitchell College (Australia), 76
Mitkov, Vladimir, 408
Mitre, Bartolomé, 71–73
Miwa, Kimitada, 212
Miyakawa, Takayoshi, 214
Miyake, Ichiro, 207, 211–12, 214
Miyatake, Nobuharu, 215
Miyazato, Seigen, 212
Mjeldheim, Leiv, 265, 269, 272
Moberg, Erik, 315, 326
Model Construction, 14, 259–60
Modrzewski, Andrzej Frycz, 291
Moedano, N. G., 62
Moghul, Nazeer Ahmed, 278
Mohov, N., 353

Mohr, A., 172, 176
Moisseev, 59
Mokken, R. J., 231, 233, 240, 242
Moldovan, D. R., 428
Molen, van der, 234
Molenaar, Bob, 241
Molin, Bjorn, 305, 311
Molitor, A., 97, 99
Molleman, H. A. A., 231–32, 240–41
Mollnau, Karl A., 183
Molnos, A., 60
Momose, Hiroshi, 212
Monash University (Australia), 76–77
Moncton, University of (Canada), 121
Monism, 390
Monnier, L., 61
Monod, Jerome, 22, 30
Montesquieu, 48, 67–68, 70, 154
Montpetit, Edouard, 117, 126–27
Montreal, University of, 117, 126
Moon, Syun Ek, 422
Moore, Barrington, Jr., 30, 84
Moren, Jorolv, 263, 269, 272
Moreno, F. J., 61
Moreno, Mariano, 70
Morgan, Janet, 363
Morgenthau, Hans J., 9, 18, 30, 45, 55, 114, 169, 284, 373, 378, 381
Morin, Claude, 117
Morlan, R. L., 233, 242
Morón, University of (Argentina), 68
Morov, N., 353
Morris, Charles W., 12, 21, 30
Morris, Desmond, 19, 30
Morris-Jones, 275
Morstein Marx, Fritz, 169
Mosca, Gaetano, 12, 20, 30, 49, 114
Moscow, University of, 342–43
Moscow Institute of Aviation, 343
Moscow Institute of Engineering Physics, 345
Moscow Institute of Finance, 343
Moscow Institute of Steel and Alloys, 342
Mounier, J. P., 163, 167
Moynihan, Daniel P., 22, 30, 375
Muchakoji, Kinhide, 30, 214
Mujaju, R., 45, 60
Mukherjee, R. K., 16, 24, 30, 203
Mulaibrahimovic, Halim, 409
Mulik, Mohsin-ul-, 284
Mulk, Viqar-ul-, 284
Mulk Tusi, Nizam ul, 275
Multan, University of (Pakistan), 276, 280, 286
Munari, F., 352
Munk, Knud Jorgen, 143
Münke, S., 428

Munro, W. B., 280
Murakami, Yasusuke, 211–12
Muramatsu, Michio, 212
Murdoch, William W., 30
Murphy, Robert E., 381
Murray, Vera, 129
Murray, Walter C., 126
Musgrave, Alan, 112, 124
Mushakoji Kinhide, 23, 213, 215
Mushi, S. S., 419
Mushkin, A. E., 337, 339
Musio, G., 428
Mussolini, Benito, 10, 19, 30, 288
Mustafa, A. A. al-R, 61
Mutual Economic Assistance, Council for (CEMA), 179
Myklebust, Jan-Peter, 263, 272
Myrdal, Gunnar, 11, 20, 23, 30, 80, 386
Mýrdal, Sigurjon, 193
Myrman, Yngve, 311
Mysore University (India), 204

Nabolz, Hans, 328
Naegele, K. D., 125
Naftalin, Arthur, 375
Nagai, Yonosuke, 207, 213
Nagazumi, Akira, 212
Nagel, Ernest, 12, 21, 30, 112, 124
Nagi, Saad Z., 378
Nagpur University (India), 204
Nagy, I., 427
Nagy, L., 426
Nahlik, S. E., 353
Nakajima, Mineo, 213
Nakamura, Kikuo, 207
Nakamura, Takafusa, 212
Nakazawa, Seiichiro, 213
Nambara, Shigeru, 211
Nannestad, Peter, 141, 143
Napoleoni, C., 428
Narr, Wolf-Dieter, 15, 23, 30, 170–71, 176, 408
Naschold, Frieder, 23–24, 30, 170, 175
Naseer, Sajjad, 278
Naše teme (Yugoslavia), 404
Natale, Alberto A., 73
Natanson, Maurice, 19
National Academy of Law (Argentina), 72
National Assembly (Pakistan), 286, 288
National Congress (Korea), 224–25
National Economy Institute (USSR), 342
National Housing Bank (Brazil), 108
National Institute of Community Development (India), 205

National Institute of Rural Development (India), 205
National party (NZ), 250, 253
National Political Science Fund (Switzerland), 332
National Preservation party (Iceland), 189
National Scientific Research Fund (Switzerland), 332–34
National Socialist party (Norway), 263
National Unity Front (Poland), 294
National University Plan (Korea), 220
National government, study of, 53
Nation building, 15
NATO, 189
Naylor, R. T., 113, 122, 125
Nazism, 374
Nedbailo, P. E., 337–39
Nedev, Ivan, 420
Negri, G., 428
Neill, Robin, 128
Neiman, Peter B., 19, 30
Neisser, H., 91–92
Neo-Fascism, 395
Neo-institutionalism, 121, 123
Neo-Machiavellian political science, 59
Neo-Marxists, 42, 113–15, 121–23, 130, 170–71, 173–75
Neo-Platonic political science, 59
Neo-Thomism, 117, 127
Neuchâtel, University of (Switzerland), 331
Neumann, Franz, 169
Neumann, Sigmund, 169
Newcastle, University of, 76
New Democratic party (Canada), 122
New Economic World Order (Norway), 267
New England, University of (Australia), 76–80
New Left, 11, 52
Newman, A. S., 381
New Perspectives in Political Science (book series), 53
NEWS (US), 376
Newsletter, (NZPSA), 252
New South Wales, University of (Australia), 76–77
New South Wales University of Technology (Australia), 76–77
New Swiss Society, 328
New Zealand, University of, 246–47
New Zealand Institute of International Affairs, 251, 253
New Zealand Institute of Public Administration, 251, 253

New Zealand International Review, 253

New Zealand Journal of Public Administration, 253

New Zealand political science: associational activities, 252–53; associations, 252; evolution since 1945, 247–48; intellectual structure, 247–48; introduction, 246; journals and special publications, 252–53; in 1945, 246–47; political scientists in politics, 253; present state and future prospects, 253–254; relations with government, 253; research, 250, 252; its teaching, 248; and the world of politics, 253

New Zealand Political Studies Association, 252, 255

Ng, Chiautong, 212

NHK Public Opinion Research Institute, 211, 214

Nichols, David, 24, 30

Nie, Norman H., 13, 21–22, 24

Niekirk, A. E. van, 234, 242

Nielsen, Hans Jørgen, 141

Niemi, Richard G., 315, 317

Niezing, J., 240

Nijmegen, Catholic University of, 227–28, 232, 237–38

Nikolaev, V. V., 338–39

Nikolaevsk Shipbuilding Institute (USSR), 343

Nilsson, Clarence, 317

Nilsson, Lars-G., 316

Nilsson, Sten Sparre, 261, 263, 269, 272

Ninčić, Dj., 410, 412

Nishihara, Masashi, 213

Nishimura, Fumio, 213

Nisihin, 211

Nisihira, Sigeki, 212

Noelle-Neumann, Elisabeth, 13, 21, 30

Noguchi, Yukio, 215

Nohlen, 171

Noomen, G. W., 241

Noordzij, G. P., 230, 240

Noponen, Martti, 151

Nord, Lars, 314

Nordbø, Eldrid, 264, 269, 272

Nordenstam, G., 353

Nordic Cooperation Committee on International Politics, 41, 269

Nordic Council, 269, 313

Nordic countries, 148

Nordic Political Science Association, 149, 266, 274, 311–12

Nordland Distriktshøsskole (Norway), 257

North, Robert C., 21, 30

North Bengal University (India), 204

North Eastern Hill University (India), 204

Northeastern National University (Argentina), 68

North East India Council for Social Science Research (India), 205

Northwestern University (US), 214

Norwegian Institute of Foreign Affairs, 256, 258, 264

Norwegian political science: address of association, 268, 273; associational activities, 266–67; associations, 266–67; comparative cross-national research, 265–66; evolution since 1945, 256–57; graduate theses, 258; impact of political events on, 267; institutional infrastructure, 258; institutions of government and processes of policy production, 263–65; intellectual structure, 256–57; introduction, 256, 258; journals, 267; mass reactions and electoral behavior, 260–62; membership of association, 268, 273; models and conceptual frameworks, 258–60; number of graduates, 257; parties, 262–63; present state and future prospects, 268; publications, 274; relations with government, 268; research, 258–66; special publications and other activity, 267; statistics on departments, 274; its teaching, 257–58; and the world of politics, 267–68

Norwegian Political Science Association, 257, 266–67, 273–74

Norwegian Social Science Data Services, 258, 261, 265, 268

Nousiainen, Jaakko, 146, 148, 151, 153

NOVIPE (Netherlands), 109

Novosel, Pavle, 406

Novosibirsk Institute of Electrical Engineering (USSR), 344

Nowak, L., 297

Nozick, Robert, 18, 30

Nuffield College (UK), 356

Nuffield school (Oxford), 175

Nuffield studies, 250, 359

Nun, J., 61

Nurmi, Hannu, 149, 152

Nuschler, 171

Nye, Joseph S., 15, 23, 30

Nyholm, Pekka, 151

Nyman, Elmer, 311

Nyman, Olle, 308, 311

Oberndorfer, D., 176

Oberschall, Anthony, 112, 125

O'Brien, D. C., 381

O'Connor, James, 122

Odense, University of (Denmark), 136, 138, 141

Odmark, Torsten, 316

O'Donnell, Cyril, 284

OECD, 30, 85, 313

Oertlé, Philippe, 424

Oertzen, 174

Offe, 170

Offerdal, Auden, 217, 262, 272

Office national de la recherche et du développement, 95

Ogata, Norio, 215

Ogata, Sadako, 212

Ogawa, Koichi, 207

Ogg, Frederic A., 376

Ohlson, O., 317

Øidne, Gabriel, 261

Ojanen, Jihani, 353

Oka, Yoshisato, 211, 213

Oka, Yoshitake, 212

Okabe, Tatsumi, 213–14

Okamura, Tadao, 214

Oksanen, Matti, 151

Ólafsson, Hannes, 190, 193

Ólafsson, Haraldur, 186, 191

Ólafsson, Haukur, 189, 193

Ólafsson, Stefán P., 190, 193

Ólafsson, Thórir, 190, 193

Oldenburg, University of (FRG), 173

Olguin, F., 62

Oliveira Marinho, Armando de, 419

Oliver, Michael, 120

Ollero, C., 429

Ollman, B., 24, 30

Olsen, Dennis, 129

Olsen, Johan P., 217, 259, 263–64, 269–70, 272

Olson, Mancur, 12–13, 20, 30, 163

Olsson, Claes Olof, 312

Ombudsman, 16

Omori, Wataru, 339

Onishi, Akira, 215

Onogawa, Hidemi, 211

Onulduran, Ersin, 425

Oost-West (Netherlands), 228, 234

Opałek, Kazimierz, 294–95, 297–98

OPEC, 41

Openbare Uitgaven (Netherlands), 228, 236

Opredeljenja (Yugoslavia), 404

Ordinance Concerning Diploma Examinations . . . (Austria), 87

Ori, Kan, 214

Ornauer, H., 269

Ortega y Gassett, José, 23, 30

Ørvik, Nils, 263, 269, 272
Orzechowski, M., 294, 298
Osgood, Charles E., 23, 31
Oslo, University of (Norway), 256–58, 262, 274
Osmania University (India), 204
Osnovin, V. S., 337
Ossowski, S., 297
Østbuy, Helge, 262, 272
Østerud, Øyvind, 259–60, 266, 269–70, 272
Ostróg, Jan, 291
Ostroumov, G. S., 337
Ostrowski, K., 298
Otago University College (NZ), 246–48, 251
Otake, Hideo, 212
Ottawa, University of (Canada), 121
Otto Suhr-Institute (Berlin), 169
Overacker, Louise, 81, 84
Oxford City Council, 361
Oxford University, 75, 84, 113, 116, 127, 247, 277, 355–56
Oyen, Else, 265, 272

Padilla, Alberto G., 71–73
Painchaud, Paul, 420
Pakistan Administrative College, Journal of the, 287
Pakistan political science: associational activities, 286; curriculum, 280–81, 283–85; impact of political events on, 286, 288; interest in, 285; introduction, 275–76; journals, 286; methodological developments, 286; in 1947, 277–78; political scientists in politics, 288; present state and future prospects, 288–89; relations with government, 288; its structure, 280–81, 283–85; university postgraduate studies, 277; and the world of politics, 286, 288
Paligorić, Ljubomir, 409
Palmberg, Maj, 306
Palmer, G. W. R., 254
Palmer, Norman D., 275, 284
Palonen, Kari, 151–52
Pálsdóttir, Katrin, 190, 193
Panikkar, K. M., 203
Panitch, Leo, 113–14, 122, 125, 129
Pannenborg, Charles, O., 243
Parekh, B. C., 126
Parent, E., 127
Pareto, Vilfredo, 10, 12, 19, 31, 148
Paris, University of, 156
Paris commune, 391
Park, Julian, 127
Parker, Robert S., 75
Parkes, D. N., 31

Parkinson, C. Northcote, 23, 31
Parliament: in Australia, 74–75, 83; in Denmark, 139, 141; in Finland, 148; in the Netherlands, 232–33, 238; in New Zealand, 250; in Norway, 259, 262–64, 267–68; in Sweden, 310–11; in Switzerland, 329; in the United Kingdom, 357, 359, 361; in the United States, 375
Parliamentary Affairs (UK), 360
Parliamentary democracy, 49
Parmentier, Guillaume, 421
Parry, Geraint, 425
Parsons, Talcott, 22, 31, 125, 260
Parti ouvrier (Belgium), 96
Parti socialiste belge (Belgium), 96
Partridge, Percy H., 75–76, 78
Pascal, Blaise, 14
Pašić, Najdan, 386, 406–12
Pasierb, B., 294
Pasquino, G., 428
Passigli, Stefano, 428
Pastusiak, L., 295, 298
Patna University (India), 204
Patterson, J. W., 381
Patterson, Samuel C., 142, 241
Paulsen, David Warren, 382
Pavlović, Vukašin, 407, 410
Payne, James, 372
Paz, Pedro, 23, 31
Pažanin, Ante, 406, 412
Peabody, Robert, 376
Peace Research, 17, 52
Peace Research, Journal of (Norway), 259, 269
Peace Research, Study Center for (Netherlands), 235
Peace Research in Japan, 216
Peace Research Institute (Netherlands), 235
Peace Studies (Japan), 215
Pearson, Lester, 120
Peck, S. R., 129
Pečujlić, Miroslav, 406, 412
Pedersen, Leif, 142
Pedersen, Mogens N., 141–43
Pedersen, Ole Karup, 142–43
Pedrero, Enrique Gonzalez, 422
Pejanović, Obrad, 406
Pelinka, A., 91–92
Pelletier, Rejean, 129
Peltason, Jack, 372
Pena, Demetrio, 71
Pena, Félix, 24, 29
Penniman, Howard, 82, 84, 254–55
Pennock, J. Roland, 81, 381
Pennsylvania State University, 84
People's Alliance (Iceland), 189
People's Daily, 214

People's Open University (Pakistan), 277–78
People's party (Pakistan), 288
Perales, L., 429
Percheron, Annick, 162
Perin, F., 95, 97, 99
Perkins, John A., 284
Perttsik, V. A., 337, 339
Peshawar, Edwards College for Boys in (Pakistan), 285
Peshawar, Frontier College for Women in (Pakistan), 285
Peshawar, Islamia College in (Pakistan), 285, 289
Peshawar, Jinnah College for Women in (Pakistan), 285
Peshawar, University of (Pakistan), 276, 278–79, 285–89
Pestel, Eduard, 24, 30, 52
Peteri, Z., 427
Petersen, Nikolaj, 141, 143
Peterson, Carl Gunnar, 310
Peterson, Harry, 316
Petersson, Hans F., 313
Petersson, Knut, 316
Petersson, Olof, 309
Petković, Ranko, 411
Petras, J., 125
Petrella, R., 44, 269
Petrič, Ernest, 407
Petrinović, Ivo, 409
Petrović, Blazo M., 409–10
Pettee, George S., 24, 31
Pettersen, Per Arnt, 262, 265, 269, 272
Petzold-Pernia, Hermann, 425
Peyrefitte, Alain, 164
Pfabigan, A., 91–92
Pfaff, D., 353
Pfiffner, J. M., 284
Pfotenhauer, D., 45, 176
Philippart, André, 4, 36, 44–45, 55, 417, 419
Philosophers, political, 52
Piaget, Jean, 12, 20, 31
Pijl, Kees van der, 243
Pikwer, Birgitta, 325
Pimenta De Moraes, Martha, 419
Pinard, Maurice, 114, 125–26
Piotte, Jean-Marc, 122
Pirzada, S. S., 284
Piskotin, M. I., 338
Pitts, Jesse R., 125
Plamenatz, John, 359
Planning and Economic Accounting, Scientific Council for Problems of Improving of (GDR), 179, 182
Plato, 9, 17, 48, 167, 235, 282–83, 368

Platt, John R., 10, 19, 31
Playford, John, 379, 381
Playford, Sir Thomas, 74
Pleschberger, Werner, 419
Plijter, R. C., 242
Pluralism, 52, 389–91, 407
Pobihushchy, S. I., 129
Podunavac, Milan, 412
Poelj, G. A. van, 235, 243
Poesland, P. G., 60
Pogledi (Yugoslavia), 404
Polaschek, R. J., 254–55
Polder, W. K., 243
Polec, X., 55
Polhøgda Foundation (Norway), 256, 264
Policy and Politics (UK), 360
Policy research, 10, 12–13, 236, 249, 252, 264–65, 294, 303, 312, 366
Policy Studies Institute (UK), 362
Polin, Raymond, 11, 20, 31
Polish Academy of Sciences, 293, 295–97
Polish Institute of International Affairs, 294–96
Polish political science: associational activities, 294–95; associations, 294–95; evolution since 1949, 292–93; impact of political events on, 295–96; intellectual structure, 292–93; introduction, 291; journals, 295; methodological developments, 294; most noteworthy contributions, 293–94; from 1945 to 1949, 291–92; political scientists in politics, 296; present state and future prospects, 296–97; relations with government, 296; research, 293–94; special publications, 295; its teaching, 293; and the world of politics, 295–96
Polish Political Science Association, 293–97
Polish Round Table, 295
Polish United Workers party, 295
Politburo (USSR), 144
Politica (UK), 356
Politica, 99
Political Economy Network (Canada), 42
Political Economy of Socialism, Scientific Council for the (GDR), 179, 182
Political power, 49
Political Quarterly (UK), 356
Political Review (Brazil), 107
Political Science (Brazil), 106
Political Science (Korea), 222

Political Science (NZ), 252
Political Science, Institute of (Berlin), 170–72
Political Science, Institute of (Munich), 172
Political Science, Institute of (Tübingen), 171
Political Science, Journal of (Netherlands), 228
Political Science, Journal of (NZ), 247
Political Science, Journal of (Pakistan), 279
Political Science Bibliography (Switzerland), 334
Political Science Department Notes (Brazil), 100
Political Science Quarterly (US), 368
Political Science Review (Brazil), 101, 106
Political Science Reviews (Poland), 295
Political Science Society (NZ), 247
Political Science Year Book (Switzerland), 330, 334
Political Studies (UK), 355, 360
Political Studies Association (UK), 35, 355–56, 359, 361–63
Political Studies Monthly (NZ), 253
Political attitudes, 50, 250–51
Political communication, 17
Political culture, 213, 251
Political development, 16–17, 52, 393
Political economy approach, 113, 118–19, 122–23, 127, 249
Political finance, 50
Political historians, 49
Political history, 208, 247, 299
Political innovation, 14
Political interaction, 17
Political knowledge, 50
Political leadership, 50
Political models, 51–52
Political modernization, 51
Political participation, 17
Political parties, 50, 250, 263–64, 310, 396
Political philosophy, 208, 247, 249, 299–300, 397
Political process, 303
Political relations, 2
Political science: in Afghanistan, 3; in Africa, 3, 60; in Ancient Greece, 2; antecedents, 2; in Asian countries, 60; in Australia, 2; in Austria, 4, 6; its basis, 47; in Belgium, 4–5, 35, 53; in Bulgaria, 426; in Canada, 2, 4, 35, 38; in Caribbean, 3, 61;

causes of uncertainty, 2–5; in Central America, 3; changes in regard to methods, 17; character, 1; in Chile, 61; in China, 3; in Colombia, 61; in Communist countries, 426; concept and outlines, 47; concern for cognition, 10; concern for institutions, 10; concern for interplay, 10; concern for justice, 9; concern for large-scale trends, 10; concern for legitimacy, 10; concern for power, 9–10; concern for procedures, 10; concern for stability, 10; concern for systems, 10; in Congo, 61; in Costa Rica, 61; as culture bound, 4; cures for its uncertainty, 5; in Czechoslovakia, 426; in Denmark, 2, 5, 300; definition, 1, 5, 52–53; designation, 1; in developing countries, 56–57, 61, 123; development, 2; its distinctiveness, 5; in Eastern Europe, 3; in Egypt, 61; in Eire, 3, 5; in Ethiopia, 61; in Europe, 3, 327; in Federal Republic of Germany, 2, 4–5, 52, 85, 87, 90, 230; in Finland, 4–5; first generation, 48–50; in France, 2, 5, 35, 52, 113, 124, 148, 230; in German Democratic Republic, 2; in Germany, 38, 145; growth of, 9, 18; in Hungary, 426–27; in Iceland, 2, 5–6, 140; identity crisis, 1–2, 52–53; its image, 3–4; in India, 35, 38, 52, 111; international contacts outside IPSA, 41–43; international development, 34–38; its internationalization, 43; in Iran, 3; In Israel, 3; in Italy, 5, 427–28; in Japan, 4, 38, 220; in Korea, 4; in Latin America, 58, 61, 65, 68, 113; in Lebanon, 3, 62; in Luxemburg, 3; main orientations, 47–48; in Mexico, 62; in the Middle East, 3, 62; in Morocco, 3; multiple paternity, 2; national associations, 3; new centers of attention, 10–17; in the Netherlands, 5; in North America, 3; in Norway, 5, 300; objectives for study, 56–57; its opportunity, 5; in Pakistan, 4; in Paraguay, 62; in the Philippines, 62; pluralism in, 4; in Poland, 35; as "political studies," 1; polymorphic orientation of, 51; in Portugal, 3, 428; as "rainbow science," 4; retarded development, 2–3; role of UNESCO, 34–36; in Rumania, 428–29; search for meth-

odology, 58–60; second generation, 50–51; in Senegal, 62; in South America, 3; in Southeast Asia, 3; in Spain, 5, 68; in Sweden, 4–5; in Switzerland, 4–5; symptoms of uncertainty, 1–2; in Thailand, 429; third generation, 51–52; traditional foci, 9–10; in Turkey, 3, 429–30; in the United Kingdom, 1, 4–5, 35, 38, 113, 116, 207, 246; in the United States, 1–4, 35, 38, 40–41, 43, 52, 85, 87, 89, 111, 116, 118–19, 145–46, 170–73, 175, 207–8, 210, 220, 222–23, 230, 235, 246, 300, 303, 327–28, 331, 333, 359; university teaching of, 3; in Uruguay, 430; in the U.S.S.R., 2, 4, 6; in Venezuela, 430; ways of tradition, 48–50; in Western Europe, 5–6, 116, 123, 173–74; its youth, 2, 34–35; in Yugoslavia, 2, 4, 35
Political simulation, 17
Political socialization, 17
Political sociology, 146, 148, 150, 249
Political stability, instability, and change, 366
Political Studies, Council for (India), 205
Political theory, 235, 293, 304, 366, 392–93
Political thought, history of, 393
Politicka misae (Yugoslavia), 404
Politicological studies, 2
Politicologue, 47
Politics (Australia), 80–82, 252
Politics, science of, 2
Politics, theory of, 2
Politics as Rational Action Project (Sweden), 303
Politiikka (Finland), 150, 295
Politik (NZ), 253
Politique (France), 160
Politische Vierteljahresschrift (FRG), 173
Politologen (Sweden), 324–25
Pollock, James K., 46, 50, 414
Polsby, Nelson W., 32, 376
Polyarchy, study of, 52
Polyethnic and multilingual societies, study of, 50
POLS newsletter (NZ), 254
Pontifical Catholic University (Argentina), 68
Poona University (India), 204
Popkin, Samuel, 17, 31

Popper, Karl R., 12, 20, 31, 112, 124, 146, 149, 164, 170, 174, 373, 381
Porter, Alex, 363
Porter, John, 114, 123, 125–26
Portus, Garnet V., 74
Posada, Victor Manuel Orlando Adolfo, 67–68
Positivist social science, 120
Post-behavioralism, 230
Pot, C. W. van der, 240
Pototschnig, M., 428
Pouvoirs, 160, 163
Powell, David, 6, 44, 46, 55, 353, 426
Powell, G. Bingham, Jr., 53, 275
Power, idea of, 49
Poznán, University of (Poland), 292–94
Prado, Caio, Jr., 110
Praska (Yugoslavia), 404
Pratt, Larry, 122, 129
Précis Dalloz (French book series), 167
Précis Domat (French book series), 167
Pregled (Yugoslavia), 404
Preiswerk, Roy, 327, 330
Prélot, Marcel, 49, 68, 157, 161
Presidential system, 49
Press and Public Relations Association, 205
Presser, J., 237
Pressman, Jeffrey L., 22, 31
Presthus, Robert, 126, 284
Preston, Richard, 124, 129
Preuves (France), 160
Pribičević, Branko, 408–9, 411
Prifold, Cora, 378, 381
Priklmajer-Tomanović, Zorica, 411
Princeton University (US), 41
Pritchett, Herman, 370, 372
Probabilistic approach, 14
Probleme des Klassenkampfes (FRG), 173
Problems of National Councils (Poland), 293, 295
Problemy Rad Narodowych (Poland), 293
Professor Periaswamy-Thayammal Institute . . . (India), 205
Progressive party (Iceland), 189
Project (France), 160
Project 87 (US), 377
Pross, A. Paul, 125, 128
Protestantism, 48
Proudhon, 49
Proust, Marcel, 47

PS (APSA newsletter), 376–79
Psychology, 12
Public administration, 50, 221, 236, 250, 257, 264, 311, 366, 400
Public Administration (UK), 356
Public Administration, Institute of (India), 205
Public Administration, Institute of (NZ), 247
Public Administration Clearing House, 61
Public Sector (NZ), 253
Publications on Political Science in Japan, 216, 218
Public law, 2
Public Law and Political Science, Institute of (Brazil), 101, 106
Puhovski, Žarko, 406
Pulišelić, Stjepan, 409
Punjab, University of (Pakistan), 204, 276–80, 286–89
Punjabi University (Pakistan), 204
Pusić, Eugen, 411
Putnam, Robert, 25, 31
Putten, J. van, 231, 240–41
Pye, Lucien, 16, 23, 31, 260, 285, 306, 372, 378, 381

Quaide-Azam University (Pakistan), 276–77
Quarterly Review of Theoretical Economic Studies (Japan), 215
Quebec, University of, at Montreal, 130
Queensland, University of (Australia), 74–77
Queen's University (Canada), 126
Quermonne, Jean-Louis, 50
Quilitzsch, Siegmar, 183
Qureshi, Ishtiaq Hussain, 281, 284, 286–87
Qureshi, Saleem, 284

Raalte, E. van, 241
Rabindra Bharati University (India), 204
Rabisankar University (India), 204
Racz, Miklos, 244
Radenović, Predrag, 409
Radovanović, Svetoslav, 409
Rahmaninova, E. A., 353
Rai, H., 203
Rajasthan, University of (India), 198, 202, 204
Rajasthen Institute of Social Science Research (India), 205
Rajkiewicz, A., 294, 298
Raksasataya, A., 429

Ramachandran, J., 421
Ramirez, M., 429
Ramirez Jimenez, Manuel, 424
Ramström, Dick, 302, 315, 326
Ranchi University (India), 204
Randall, V., 425
Ranger, Jean, 161
Ranney, Austin, 25, 45, 50, 372, 376–78, 381
Ratala, Onni, 147, 151
Rapoport, Anatol, 12, 17, 20, 25, 31, 52, 55, 59
Rasmussen, Erik, 132–33, 140–43
Rathore, L. S., 421
Rational order and spirit of justice, 48–49
Ratković, Radomir, 405, 412
Ratković, Radoslav, 406, 409, 411
Rawls, John, 9, 13, 18, 31
Real, Alberto Ramon, 70
Rechtskundige Weekblad, 98–99
Redder, K. W., 141
Redelbach, A., 298
Redman, Eric, 22, 31
Regional government, study of, 53
Regional state, 49
Reich, Richard, 335
Reid, Gordon S., 76
Reid, H. G., 381
Reinhold, Otto, 183
Relations Internationales, 159
Religion, study of, 50
Rémond, René, 50, 158, 168
Renner, 85–86
Renouvin, Pierre, 158, 162, 166
Rens, Ivo, 98
Representation, theories of, 393
Republican party (US), 375
Research areas, minor, 190
Research [Committee] on Political Relations in the National Economy (Poland), 295
Research Council (Norway), 261
Research on Youth Problems, Scientific Advisory Committee for (GDR), 182
Resnick, Philip, 122, 129
Res Publica (Belgium), 96, 99, 295
Reuber, G. L., 128
Revesz, L., 61
Review of the Institute of Philosophy and Human Sciences (Brazil), 100–101, 107
Revue de l'Institut de sociologi de . . . Bruxelles (Belgium), 98–99
Revue d'études constitutionnelles et politiques (France), 160
Revue du Droit public et de la Science Politique (France), 166

Revue française d'administration publique, 159
Revue française de Science Politique, 159, 167
Revue Française de Sociologie, 159, 167
Revue générale belge, 98–99
Revue nouvelle (Belgium), 99
Revue Politique et Parlementaire (France), 160
Reyes Heroles, J., 62
Reynarsson, Bjarni, 193
Rhee, Sang-Woo, 422
Rhee, Syngman, 221–23
Rhodes, R.A.W., 363
Riaz, Syed Hassan, 281
Riazvi, Hasan Askari, 284
Ribičič, Ciril, 408
Ricardo, David, 116
Rice, Stuart A., 381
Rickman, John, 20, 31
Ricknell, Lars, 309
Ridley, F. F., 125, 363
Riedi, Rupert, 10, 19, 31
Rieselbach, Leroy N., 22, 31
Riggs, Fred, 51, 372
Rijpperda Wierdsma, J. V., 239, 245
Riker, William H., 381
Ringeling, A. B., 236, 244
Ringer, Fritz, 150
Rio de Janeiro, Catholic University of, 101
Rio de Janeiro, Federal University of, 100–101, 107
Rio de Janeiro, University Institute of Research of, 100, 102, 106, 108
Rio de Janeiro National Institute of Political Science, 106
Rio dos Sinos, University of (Brazil), 107
Rio Grande do Sul, Federal University of (Brazil), 101–2, 107
Rio Research Center (Brazil), 41
Rist, R. C., 45
Rittberger, V., 172
Ritter, Gerhard, 9, 18, 31
Rizman, Rudi, 407
Rizvi, Hasan Askari, 287
Roberts, Nigel S., 254–55
Roberts, Stephen, 44–45
Robinson, A. D., 233, 241, 254–55
Robinson, James, 372
Robinson, T. W., 354
Robson, William A., 44, 46, 50, 356, 362, 414
Rockefeller, R. C., 61
Röder, Karl-Heinz, 183, 421
Rodin, Davor, 406
Rodolfo Orlandi, Hector, 73

Roe, R. A., 243
Roepke, W., 12, 20, 31
Rogaland Distriktschøgskole (Norway), 257
Rogers, E. B., 128
Rogger, H., 354
Rogow, Arnold A., 381
Rohilkhand University (India), 204
Rokkan, Stein, 5, 10, 13, 15, 19, 21, 31, 43, 45–46, 50, 54–55, 134, 141–43, 148, 152, 185, 217, 242, 256, 259–63, 266, 269–70, 272–73
Rolbiecki, W., 297
Röling, B. V. A., 235, 243
Romero, Cesar E., 70, 73
Roness, Paul G., 423
Ronge, 170
Roosevelt, Franklin D., 235
Roper Center (US), 364
Rosario, National University of (Argentina), 68
Rosas, Quiroga, 71
Rose, Richard, 31, 44, 46, 358–59, 363
Rosen, Paul L., 381
Rosenau, James, 372
Rosenstock, Eure, 24, 31
Rosenthal, E. I. J., 275, 289–90
Rosenthal, U., 230, 232, 235–36, 240–41, 243–45
Roskilde, University of (Denmark), 136
Rossi, P. H., 378
Roter, Zdenko, 409
Rotstein, Abe, 122
Rousseau, Jean-Jacques, 9, 11, 49, 67–68, 70, 154, 208, 282, 368
Rowell-Sirois Commission (Canada), 117, 120, 123, 129
Royal Commission on Bilingualism and Biculturalism (Canada), 120, 123, 129
Royal Commission (UK), 361
Royal Institute of International Affairs (UK), 80, 362
Royal Institute of Public Administration (UK), 79–80, 362
Royal Military College (Australia), 76–77, 84
Royama, Masamichi, 211
Rozin, V. P., 354
Rozsa, G., 427
Rubenstein, Robert, 378
Rudebeck, Lars, 308, 316, 326
Ruf, Werner K., 16, 23, 31
Ruffieux, Roland, 46, 334–35
Ruge, Mari Holmboe, 264, 273

Ruin, Olof, 46, 304–6, 308–9, 311, 317, 326
Ruiter, G. van, 241
Ruller, H. van, 236, 244
Runciman, W. G., 285
Runnstron, Cecilia, 424
Rupnik, Janko, 411
Rus, Vojan, 406
Rush, Michael, 285
Rusk, Jerrold G., 142, 241
Russell, Bertrand, 12, 80, 288
Russett, Bruce M., 13, 20–22, 31
Russian Communist League of Youth, 343
Rustow, Dankwart, 16, 23, 32, 308, 316
Ruutu, Yrjö, 144–45, 151
Rybicki, Z., 294–95, 298
Ryerson, Stanley, 122, 129
Ryszka, F., 298

Saavedra, Cornelia, 70
Sabine, George, 235, 283
Sadiković, Ćazim, 408
Saeter, Martin, 264, 273
Sætren, Harald, 263, 269–70, 274
Sagan, Carl, 10, 19, 31
Saglie, Tor, 274
Šahović, Milan, 410
Saint Augustine, 9
Saint-Gall, University of (Switzerland), 331, 334
Saint-Gall Graduate School of Economic and Social Sciences (Switzerland), 331
Saint-Simon, 49
Saito, Makoto, 212
Saito, Takashi, 212
Sakakibara, Eisuke, 215
Sakamoto, Yoshikazu, 213
Salis, Jean-Rodolphe de, 328, 335
Salvador, Universidad del (Argentina), 68
Salzburg, University of (Austria), 88–89, 91
Sambalpur University (India), 204
Samsong Cultural Foundation (Korea), 224
Sanchez Agesta, L., 68, 429
Sanchez Sarto, M., 62
Sanchez Viamonte, Carlos, 70, 73
Sandberg, H. W., 243
Sande, Terje, 261–62, 265, 269, 273
Sandor, Lakos, 421
Sani, G., 428
San Juan, National University of (Argentina), 68
Sankiaho, Risto, 147–48, 151

Santa Catarina Labor Foundation (Brazil), 109
Santa Fé, Catholic University of (Argentina), 68
Santamaria Ossorio, Julian, 424
São Paulo, Pontifical Catholic University of (Brazil), 100–102
São Paulo, School of Sociology and Politics of (Brazil), 100
São Paulo, University of (Brazil), 101
Sarajevo Faculty of Political Sciences (Yugoslavia), 384, 400–402
Sardar, Riffat, 288
Sardar Patel University (India), 204
SAREC (Sweden), 109
Särlvik, Bo, 303, 309
Sarmiento, Domingo Faustino, 71–72
Sartori, Giovanni, 44, 51, 68, 428
Sartre, Jean-Paul, 160
Sasaki, Takeshi, 211
Saskatchewan, University of (Canada), 118, 126
Sato, Seizaburo, 212, 339
Sauerberg, Steen, 141
Saugar, University of (India), 204
Saurasthra University (India), 204
Sauvy, Alfred, 158
Savaford, Nevy, 20
Savci, Bahri, 425
Savičević, Desanka, 409
Savova, E., 426
Savremenot (Yugoslavia), 404
Sawer, Geoffrey, 81–82, 84
Scalai, A., 269
Scalapino, Robert, 21, 31
Scaling, 17
Scandinavian Institute of African Studies, 308
Scandinavian Political Studies, 138, 143, 149–50, 173, 258, 267, 274, 305–6, 309, 311, 320
Scaramozzino, P., 428
Schad, Susanne P., 112, 125
Schaff, Adam, 44–45, 48, 297
Schaffer, B. B., 76
Schaper, W. A., 368
Scharpf, Fritz W., 15, 23, 31, 171, 174–75
Scheer, G., 91–92
Schelling, Thomas, 114
Schemeil, Y., 167
Schendelen, M.P.C.M. van, 229, 232, 235, 240–41, 243–45
Scheuch, Erwin, 13, 44, 170, 269
Schilling, Dora, 424
Schindler, Dietrich, 335
Schlichting, L.G.A., 227, 230
Schlozman, Kay Leham, 31
Schmid, Gerhard, 424

Schmidt, E., 91, 171
Schmidt, Max, 183
Schmitt, Carl, 171
Schmitter, P. C., 135, 141
Schmoller, Gustav, 144
Schneider, H., 91–92
Schneider, Wolfgang, 183
Schokking, Jacqueline, 232, 241
Scholten, G. H., 232, 235–36, 240–41, 243–45
Schoneburg, Karl-Heinz, 183
Schrenk-Notzing, C., 175
Schubert, Glendon, 273, 372
Schultz, Richard, 129
Schulze, Gerhard, 184
Schuman, Frederick L., 9, 18, 31
Schumpeter, Joseph, 12, 20, 31, 408
Schurmann, Franz, 24, 31
Schüssler, Gerhard, 184
Schütz, Alfred, 11, 19, 31
Schütz, Klaus, 174
Schwartz, D. C., 381
Schwartz, Mildred, 120, 126, 129
Schwartzenberg, Roger-Gérard, 55
Schwartzman, Simon, 24, 31
Schweigler, Gebhard L., 23, 31
Sciat, Loretta Makasiar, 423
Science and Technology, National Council on (Brazil), 108
Science Center (Berlin), 41, 175
Science of History, Council for the (GDR), 178, 181–82
Science of the state, 2
Sciences of State and Law, Council for (GDR), 179, 182
Scientific and Technological Development, National Council for (Brazil), 108
Scohy-Goethals, Michele E., 44, 46
Scott, F. R., 117
Scott, K. J., 250, 254–55
Scott, R., 77, 84
Sedlacek, Margrit, 419
Seigneur, Philippe, 96
Seip, Jens Arup, 269, 273
Seki, Hiroharu, 212–14
Senate (US), 375
Senghaas, Dieter, 15, 23, 31–32, 170, 172
Seoul National University (Korea), 220–21
Seppanen, Paavo, 151
SETUPS (US), 368–69
Seurin, Jean-Louis, 158
Sfez, L., 168
Shabad, B. A., 338
Shah, Mahmud Ali, 279
Shakhnazarov, Georgii, 352, 435
Shannon, Claude E., 14, 22, 32

Sharabi, H. B., 275
Sharif, M. M., 275
Sharkansky, Ira, 55
Sharma, S. K., 203
Sharp, Walter, 44
Sharpe, L. J., 361, 363, 425
Sharma, B. V., 421
Shatz, Marshall S., 32
Shaw, George Bernard, 287
Shepard, George W., 19, 32
Sherwani, H. K., 289
Sherwood, 284
Shils, Edward, 112, 125, 275, 285
Shindo, Eiichi, 212
Shinohara, Hajime, 212
Shiratori, Rei, 213–14
Shivaji University (India), 204
Shocket, Frances, 382
Shortt, Adam, 116, 118, 126–28
Shoup, Paul, 6, 44, 55, 353, 426
Shue, Henry, 32
Siber, Ivan, 303, 411
Sicinski, A., 269
Sidjanski, D., 46
Sidney, 284
Siegel, Mark A., 375
Siegerist, E., 236, 244
Siegfried, André, 48, 50, 148, 154, 159, 161, 166, 249
Siffin, William J., 379, 381
Sigmund, Paul E., 32
Sigmundsdóttir, Bergthóra, 190, 193
Sills, David, L., 5, 55, 378, 381
Silveira, Onesimo, 316
Simeon, Richard, 114, 125, 129
Simon, Alois, 97
Simon, Herbert A., 114, 259, 284, 370, 372, 381
Simon, M., 168
Simulation, 52
"Simulmatic" method, 17
Sinclair, Elsa, 19
Sind, University of (Pakistan), 278–80, 286–87, 289
Sindler, Allen, 372
Singer, J. David, 15, 23, 32, 372
Sinha, A. N., Institute of Social Studies (India), 205
Sinkkonen, Sirkka, 152
Sirinelli, Jean, 157
Sirsikar, V. M., 16, 24, 32
Sisakjan, N. M., 354
Siune, Karen, 142
Sivak, A. F., 354
Sizoo, J., 235, 243
Sjöblom, Gunnar, 305–6, 315, 326
Sjöstedt, Gunnar, 313
Skelton, O. D., 116, 126–27, 131

Skilling, Gordon, 354
Skjelsbæk, Kjell, 264, 273
Sköld, Lars, 311
Skopje Sociological and Political-Legal Research Institute (Yugoslavia), 402
Slavin, V., 354
Slomp, J.F.W., 234, 242
Sluimers, L.E.L., 243
Smailagić, Nerkez, 408
Smaller European Democracies project, 185, 187, 190
Smiers, Joost, 244
Smiley, Donald, 121, 124, 126, 129, 131
Smiljković, Radoš, 406, 409–10, 412
Smirnov, Stanislav, 6
Smirnov, William, 425
Smit, C., 234, 235, 242, 244
Smith, Adam, 23, 116
Smith, Barbara Leigh, 382
Smith, David, 16, 23
Smith, David E., 128
Smith, David G., 382
Smith, Denis, 124
Smith, Edward Munroe, 5, 382
Smith, Geoffrey, 32
Smith, H. A., 128
Smith, Lannes Bruce, 51
Smith, T. B., 251, 254–55
Smoker, Paul, 21, 29, 54
Snellen, I. Th., 236, 244
Snyder, Richard C., 22, 32, 372
Soares, Galaucio Ary Dillon, 32
Sobolewska, B., 298
Sobolewski, M., 294, 298
Social administration, 2
Social and Cultural Research, Council for (India), 205
Social and Political Sciences, School of (Switzerland), 328, 331
Social and Political Studies (Brazil), 107
Social Catholicism, 115, 117
Social Credit party (Canada), 114
Social Darwinism, 10
Social Democratic party (Germany), 173–74
Social Democratic party (Iceland), 189
Social Democratic party (Sweden), 300, 310
Social Development, Council for (India), 205
Socialism, 11, 36, 42, 48–49, 383–84, 386–87, 389–96, 402, 405
Socialisme (Belgium), 98–99

Socialism in the World (Yugoslavia), 404
Socialist Alliance of Working People (Yugoslavia), 390, 397–98
Socialist Economic Integration, Scientific Council for Problems of (GDR), 179, 182
Socialist Industrial Management, Scientific Council for Problems of (GDR), 179, 182
Social Policy and Demography, Scientific Council for Problems of (GDR), 180
Socialist self-management (Yugoslavia), 389
Socialist Thought and Practice (Yugoslavia), 404
Socialist Unity party (GDR), 179
Socialistische Standpunten (Belgium), 98–99
Socialization, political, 51
Social Research, Institute for (Norway, 256–60
Social Research, Institute of (Denmark), 141
Social Science Graduate Programs, National Association of (Brazil), 109
Social Science Research, Swedish Council of, 301–2, 322
Social Science Research Council (UK), 357–58
Social Science Research Council (US), 142, 370
Social Science Review (Brazil), 107
Social Sciences, Academy of (Poland), 294
Social Sciences, Institute for, of the Central Committee of the SED (GDR), 178, 180, 182
Social Sciences, Institute for, of SED (GDR), 180–182
Social Sciences, Institute of (Yugoslavia), 383, 402
Social Security Administration (Norway), 265
Social self-management (Yugoslavia), 384, 387, 389–93, 396, 398, 405
Social Studies, Institute of (India), 205
Société canadienne de Science politique, 113, 121
Socijalizam (Yugoslavia), 404
Socio-Economic Council (Netherlands), 236
Sociological approach, 292
Sociological Research, Scientific Council for (GDR), 180, 182

Sociological Review (Japan), 215
Sociologie du Travail (France), 159
Sociologie politique (France), 160
Sociology, Institute of, in Ljubljana (Yugoslavia), 402
Söder, Gunter, 184
Söderberg, Olle, 309, 317
Söderfelt, Björn, 306, 316
Sodré, Nelson Werneck, 110
Sokol, Oleg Mandić-Smiljko, 409
Sokol, S., 406
Sola Pool, Ithiel de, 13, 16–17, 21, 24, 32, 370, 378–79, 381
Solari, A. E., 430
Sollie, Finn, 264, 273
Solon, 9, 48
Solvang, Bernt Krohn, 274, 423
Solzhenitsyn, Alexander, 164
Soma, Masao, 212, 214
Somit, Albert, 46, 55, 128, 172, 368, 378–79, 382
Somjee, A. H., 16, 24, 32, 128
Sondages (France), 159
Songgok Foundation (Korea), 224
Sontheimer, K., 175–76
Sorauf, Frank J., 382
Sörbon, Dag, 316, 318
Sorensen, Ole Aagaard, 143
Sorenson, Carsten Lehmann, 142–43
Sorgenicht, Klaus, 184
Sorkin, M., 55
Southeast Asian Studies (Japan), 215
Southern Political Science Association (US), 108
South Gujrat University (India), 204
Sovereignty, national, 16; and legitimacy, 49
Soviet International Law Association, 351
Soviet political science: advocates of socialist political science, 338; associational activities, 351–52; association's publications, 351; proposals for improvement, 336–38; recent trends, 336; separating social management, 337–38; theorists of state and law, 337; varying its content, 338–39
Soviet Political Science Association, 351–52
Soviet professionals: training of, 341; traits of, 341
Soviet social science: Brezhnev comments, 341; consequences, 346; its importance, 345; importance of improvement, 347; improvement of teachers, 347–48; Lenin comments, 343; number of teachers, 347; opportunities, 345–46; requirements for improvement, 343–45; research, 348–50; role of departments, 342–43; role of higher education, 341–42; shortcomings of departments, 342, 346; special courses, 278–80, 342; tasks defined by CPSU, 340; its teachers, 347; its teachings, 341; textbooks, 342; theoretical heritage, 342
Soviet Sociological Association, 351
Soviet Studies (UK), 361
Soviet Studies, Institue for (FRG), 175
Sozialistische Politik (FRG), 173
Spadaro, R. N., 46
Špadijer, Balša, 408
Spann, R. N., 46, 76, 78, 81, 84
Spencer, Herbert, 10, 116
Spengler, Oswald, 10, 19, 32
Spinner, H., 175–76
Spiro, Herbert, 169
Spragens, T. A., 382
Spreafico, A., 428
Sreemati Nathi-Bai Damodar Thackersey Women's University (India), 205
Srivastava, G. P., 203
Sri Venkateswara University (India), 205
Staatslehre, 209
Staatswissenschaft, 2, 220
Staden, A. van, 234, 243
Stadener, Sam, 317
Ståhl, Michael, 316
Stahlberg, Krister, 152
Staley, A. A., 83
Stalin, Joseph, 10, 19, 32, 383
Stålvant, Carl-Einar, 318
Stambuck, Vladimir, 409
Stammer, Otto, 44, 142, 170–71
Stamokap school [of Marxism], 136
Stamovčić, V., 406
Stanford University (US), 41
Stanič, Gojko, 410
Stanisław of Skarbimierz, 291
Stanyer, Jeffrey, 260
Starnovsky, B., 426
Starosciak, J., 61
Stassen, J. L., 235, 243
Staszic, Stanisław, 291
State and Law, Institute of (Poland), 293
State and law, theory of, 2, 229, 384, 387, 393
State Institute of Community Development . . . (India), 205
State Legislative Service program (US), 375
State science, 2
State Services, Royal Commission on (NZ), 251
Statistics and Mathematics, Institute of (Japan), 214
Statsvetenskapliga Förbundet (Sweden), 324–25
Statsvetenskaplig Tidskrift (Sweden), 311–12
Statsviteren (Norway), 267, 274
Stauffer, Pierre-André, 335
Stava, Per, 265, 273
Stavenhagen, R., 62
Steele, James, 122, 124, 129
Steering capabilities, 15
Stefanov, N. K., 354
Steffani, 171
Steffen, 174
Stehouwer, Jan, 142
Stein, Michael, 124–25, 128
Steinbruner, John, 22, 32, 55
Steinfels, Peter, 32
Stenelo, Lars-G., 313–14
Stengers, J., 97
Steperski, J., 297
Stephens, D., 84
Stephens, Jerome, 126
Sternberger, Dolf, 170–71
Stevens, Bertram, 75
Stevenson, Garth, 122, 129
Stjernquist, Nils, 310–11
Stobbe, 174
Stochastic processes, 14, 52
Stockholm, University of, 299–300, 303–4, 306, 309, 311, 313, 320, 322
Stoetzel, Antoine, 21–22, 60
Stoetzel, Jean, 13, 20, 26, 32, 158
Stoicoiu, V., 428
Stojanović, Radoslav, 410–12
Stojković, Momir, 410
Stokes, Donald K., 13, 21, 26, 359, 372
Stokman, F. N., 231, 233, 235, 240, 242–43
Stone, Philip J., 24, 32
Stoppino, M., 428
Storing, Herbert, 265, 373, 378, 382
Stouffer, Samuel, 13, 21, 29
Stout, Sir Robert, 247
Strand, Torodd, 265–66, 273
Strategic Studies, Institute of (UK), 362
Strathclyde, University of (UK), 357
Strauss, Leo, 11, 19, 32, 169–70, 373, 378

Stretton, Hugh, 74, 382
Strobl, Majda, 408
Strömberg, Lars, 311
Structuralism, 12
Studies in Political Science (Poland), 295
"Study of Congress" (US), 376
Study of Parliament Group (UK), 359
Study of the Distribution of Power (Norway), 258, 264, 267
Study-of-the-Japanese survey, 214
Stuurman, S., 240, 243, 245
Subhas School of Social and Political Studies (India), 205
Sučurlija, Živko, 407, 409
Sudbury, University of (Canada), 121
Sufin, Z., 298
Sukagami, Nobuo, 212
Sukmyong Women's College (Korea), 220
Sundberg, Per, 311
Sunkel, Osvaldo, 23, 32
Superintendence for the Development of the Northeast (Brazil), 109
"SUP-Le politique," 160
Surkin, M., 46
Survey (Yugoslavia), 404
Survey research, 13, 17, 18, 214, 260-61, 266
Survey Research Center (University of Michigan, US), 41, 135, 250, 364, 372
Susiluoto, Ilmari, 151-52, 354
Šuvar, Stipe, 407-8
Suys, J., 235, 237, 239, 243
Suzman, Helen, 80
Sveinsson, Jón Rúnar, 190, 193
Svendsen, Bo Ander, 142
Svenson, Palle, 142-43
Sveveborg, Jan-Olof, 309
Swann, A. de, 234, 242
Swedish Broadcasting Corporation, 302, 309
Swedish political science: administration, 311; analysis of arguments, 304-6; association, 324-25; background, 299-302; careers of graduates, 324; domestic network of contacts, 301; effects on society, 314-15; empirical theory, 304-6; funding, 301-2; general features of research, 302-4; intellectual tradition, 299-300; interest organization, 309-10; international contacts, 300-301; international politics, 312-14; local and regional politics, 306-8; mass media, 309; national politics, 308, 311; normative theory, 304; number of graduate students, 322-23; number of students, 321; parliament and government, 310-11; political parties, 310; relations with society, 302; research, 304; its teaching, 320-24; teaching staff, 321-22; topics of dissertations, 323; voters, 309
Swedish Political Science Association, 325
Swedish School of Economics, 144
Swedish Universities, Office of the Chancellor of, 302, 315
Sweezy, Paul, 129
Swiss political science: its amplitude, 332-33; associational activities, 328, 330; association members, 328; association's aims, 329; association's publications, 330; its birth, 327-28; creation of association, 328; its development, 328, 330; its institutionalization, 330; in 1959, 330-31; in the 1960s, 331; its orientation, 331-32; its pioneers, 328; at present, 331; research, 331-33; or sciences, 327-28; superfluous science, 327; its teaching, 334; and the world of politics, 333-34
Swiss Political Science Association, 327-30, 334
Swiss Society for Human Sciences, 330
Swiss Society of Psychology, 330
Swiss Society of Sociology, 330
Swiss Society of Statistics and Economics, 330
Swiss Society of the Humanities, 332
Sydney, University of (Australia), 74-77
Syed, Khalid bin, 281, 284
Symonides, J., 294
System characteristics, 10, 14-16
System performance, 10
Systems, theory of, 14
Systems analysis, 14
Systems theory, 14
System transformation, 16-17
Szacka, B., 297
Szalai, A., 46
Szamel, L., 427
Szigeti, J., 427
Szlapczynski, J., 176

Tadić, Bojana, 409, 411
Takabatake, Michitoshi, 212, 214-15, 422
Takahara, Yasuhiko, 22, 30
Takane, Masaaki, 212, 215
Talos, Emmerich, 91-92, 419
Tamiz ud-din, Maulvi, 286
Tammes, A.J.P., 234, 242
Tampere, University of (Finland), 144
Tampere Peace Research Institute (Finland), 149
Tanaka, Yasumasa, 207, 211, 214
Tanenhaus, Joseph, 46, 55, 128, 172, 368, 378-79, 382
Tani, Akira, 215
Taniuchi, Akira, 212-13
Tännsjö, Torbjörn, 317
Tanović, Arif, 406, 412
Tarkiainen, Tuttu, 151
Tarschys, Daniel, 304, 308, 312
Tašković, Dragan, 407
Tasmania, University of (Australia), 74-75, 77
Tata Institute of Social Science (India), 205
Tatz, Colin M., 76
Taylor, Charles L., 13, 21-22, 24, 32
Taylor, K. W., 127, 131
Teaching Politics (UK), 360
Teeple, Gary, 113, 122, 125
Technical Schools, Institute for (GDR), 180
Techno-Economic Studies, Institute for (India), 205
Teljo, Jussi, 144-46, 151
Temps Modernes, Les (France), 160
Teorija in praksa (Yugoslavia), 404
Textor, Robert, 13, 21, 25, 53
Thakurdas, F., 46, 203
Thaysen, 171
Theen, Rolf H. W., 6, 46, 354
Theimer, 235
Thémis (French book series), 166-67
Theorists, 209
Thibaudet, A., 154
Thies, Wallace, J., 32
Third World countries, 16, 56; cultural dependency of, 58; economic dependency of, 56-57; internal development of, 57
Thomas, L. V., 62
Thomas, Senator, 375
Thomassen, J.J.A., 232, 241
Thompson, Arthur, 318
Thompson, Kenneth W., 32
Thorbecke, J. R., 227
Thorgrimsdóttir, Rangheiour, 190, 193
Thorkelsson, Guðmundur Birkir, 189, 193
Thórlindsson, Thórólfur, 186
Thormann, M., 46
Thorp, Alan, 124, 129

Thoveron, 97
Thrift, N. J., 31
Thunell, Lars, 318
Tibor, Halay, 421
Tibor, Polgar, 427
Tidsskrift for samfunnsforskning (Norway), 267
Tiger, Lionel, 10, 19, 32
Tinbergen, Nikolaas, 10, 19, 32
Tingsten, Herbert, 300, 303–5
Tinker, I., 382
Tito, Josip Broz, 395, 407–9
Titograd Socioeconomic Research Institute (Yugoslavia), 402
Tlustý, V., 353
Tobisson, Lars F., 308
Tocqueville, Aléxis de, 34, 48, 71, 154, 368
Togeby, Lisa, 142
Tointet, M. F., 162
Tokuda, Noriyuki, 213
Tokyo, University of (Japan), 212
Tokyo University of Foreign Studies (Japan), 216
Tomić, Stojan, 406, 412, 425
Tominaga, Kenichi, 215
Tominaga, Yukio, 213
Tomita, Akira, 212
Tomita, Nobuo, 212
Tomsk, University of (USSR), 342
Topornin, B., 354
Torgvisen, Ulf, 269
Tornudd, Klaus, 152
Toronto, University of (Canada), 116–18, 122, 124, 126–27
Torsvik, Per, 262, 273
Touchard, Jean, 5, 49, 157, 235
Toulmin, Stephen E., 112, 124
Touraine, Alain, 164
Tower, John, 375
Townsley, W. A., 75
Toynbee, Arnold, 10, 19, 32, 80
Tozi, Gjoko, 407
Traditionalists, 208, 230
Transactie (Netherlands), 228
Trasnea, O., 428
Tremblay, Maurice, 126–27
Tremblay Commission (Canada), 120, 123, 129
Trent, John E., 6, 46, 51, 53, 124, 129, 417
Tribal Research Bureau (India), 205
Triepel, Heinrich, 23, 32
Trobe University (Australia), 76
Troclet, L. E., 97
Tromsø, University of (Norway), 257–58, 274
Truman, David, 50, 370, 382

Truman, Harry, 375
Tsuji, Kiyoaki, 212
Tsujimura, Akira, 214
Tucumán, University of (Argentina), 68
Tudyka, Kurt P., 229, 234, 240, 242–43
Tufte, Edward B., 382
Tullock, Gordon, 12, 20, 26, 52, 382
Tunc, André, 158
Tunc, Suzanne, 158
Tung, Ko-Chih, 309, 317, 325
Turku, University of (Finland), 146
Turner, John E., 380
Tusi, Nizam ul Mulk, 275, 283
Twente University of Technology (Netherlands), 227, 233
Tyagi, A. R., 203

Ucakar, Karl, 91–92, 419
Uchiyama, Hideo, 213
Udaipur, University of (India), 205
Uddman, Paula, 310
Ulam, Adam, 23, 25
Ullah, Shah Wali, 275, 282, 288
Umeå, University of, 301, 303, 308–9, 313, 320–22
Umemoto, Takao, 215
Underhill, Frank, 117, 127
UNESCO, 2–3, 6, 34–36, 46, 48, 61, 67–69, 81, 108–9, 286, 328, 335, 356; conference of 1948, 1, 3
Union of Political Science Associations (Yugoslavia), 403–4
Union of Socialist Youth (Yugoslavia), 397
Unitary state, 49
United Australian party, 75
United Nations, 18, 35, 49, 140, 142, 221, 235, 313, 375
United Peasants' party (Poland), 294
United Socialist party (Iceland), 189
United States institutions, processes, and behavior, 366
United States political science: academic base, 367; advancing the profession, 377; associational activities, 376; association's publications, 376–77; association's structure, 377; behavioralism *regnant,* 370–72; behavioral revolution in, 368, 370; challenges to behavioralism, 372–74; characteristics, 370; data accumulation, 364; degree production, 367; doctoral dissertation fields, 367; early history, 368; efforts at improvement, 368–69;

empirical theory in, 365, 372; explanations of success, 371–72; focus on individual, 371; growth, 364, 368, 370; impact, 371–72; impact of natural sciences, 364, 368; importance of scholarship, 368; intellectual structure, 365–67; introduction, 364; methodological developments, 364–65; normative theory in, 365–66; outside activist criticism, 374; outside intellectual criticism, 373; political scientists in politics, 375; and political world, 375–76; problems, 368; programs and services to members, 377; research, 369–74; self-criticism, 373; since 1945, 365–74; subfields, 366–67; its teaching, 367–69; use of psychology and statistics, 371–72
Universities, Association of (India), 205
University Act of 1970 (Denmark), 135–36
University education, in Pakistan, 276–77
University Foundation of Brazilia, 101, 107
University Grants Commission (India), 196
University Grants Commission (Pakistan), 277
University Grants Committee (UK), 356
University Teachers Union (Sweden), 325
Uno, Kimio, 215
Uotila, Jaakko, 150, 153
Uppsala, University of (Sweden), 299–300, 302–4, 306, 309–13, 320–21, 325
Uppsala School, 145
Uprimny, Leopoldo, 70, 73
Urals, University of the (USSR), 342
Urals Polytechnical Institute (USSR), 343
Urbain, R., 99
Uribe Villegas, O., 429
Urwin, Derek, 266, 270, 273
U.S. Military Government (in Korea), 220
USSR Philosophical Society, 351
Usui, Hisakazu, 214
Utkal University (India), 205
Utrecht, University of (Netherlands), 227
Uusitalo, Hannu, 152–53

Vacancy chain analysis, 14
Valdimarsson, Kristján, 189, 193
Valen, Henry, 142–43, 259–63, 266, 270, 272–73
Valinder, Torbjörn, 309, 311, 424
Valkenburgh, P., 229–30, 234, 240, 243, 245
Valles, A. de, 428
Valsecchi, Franco, 422
Van Dyke, Vernon, 68, 284–85, 372, 382
Vanhanen, Tatu, 152
Van Hassel, Hugo, 94, 419
Van Impe, Herman, 96
Van Loon, Rick, 121, 126, 129
Vanress, 284
Varma, S. P., 203
Vasilev, Mito-Hadži, 406
Vasović, Vučina, 408, 411–12
Vas-Zoltan, P., 427
Vayrynen, Raimo, 149, 152
Veblen, Thorstein, 128
Vedel, Georges, 50, 154, 157, 161
Vedia y Mitre, Mariano de, 73
Vedung, Evert, 303, 306, 312, 315, 326
Vegleris, Phedon, 48, 421
Veld, R. J. in't, 230, 240, 243
Velinsky, V., 28
VENEVOLENTIA Foundation (Italy), 109
Venkatarangaiya, M., 203
Verba, Sidney, 13, 15, 21–25, 31–32, 50, 55, 214, 266, 275, 372
Veredy, K., 427
Verhaegen, B., 61, 95
Verhoef, J., 242
Verkade, W., 232, 241
Verney, Douglas, 129
Verstehende Soziologie, 11
Verton, P. C., 242
Vervaeck, S., 96
Veszi, Beda, 427
Vianna, Francisco J. Oliviera, 110
Vico, Giambattista, 10, 19
Victoria University College (NZ), 247–48, 251–53, 349
Vidaković, Zoran, 408
Vidal, E., 428
Vidart Campos, Germán J., 65, 70, 73
Vidya Bhawan Rural Institute (India), 205
Vienna, University of (Austria), 87–89
Vienna Center for the Coordination of Research and Documentation in the Social Sciences, 41
Viet, 266

Vietnam, 18
Viken, A., 269
Vikram University (India), 205
Vilhjálmsdóttir, Guorún Sigriður, 189–90, 193
Villadsen, Søren, 142
Villafane, Benjamin, 71
Vilmar, F., 172
Vincent, J. M., 163
Visva Bharati University (India), 205
Vito, F., 428
Vlekke, V.J.M., 234, 242
Vloemans, A., 235, 243
Vocational Training Assistance Foundation (Korea), 224
Voegelin, Eric, 86, 169–70, 382
Vogel, 174–75
Vogt, Walter, 184, 193
Voisé, W., 297
Volkov, Iu. E., 339
Voluntary Agencies for Rural Development, Association of (India), 205
Vondeling, A., 241
Voronezh University (USSR), 344
Vos, H. de, 243
Vranicki, Predrag, 409
Vratuša, Antor, 407, 411
Vućo, Nikola, 409
Vujičić, Radislav, 406, 408
Vukadinović, Radovan, 399, 410–12
Vuković, Ilija, 410
Vuzfilm Studio (USSR), 344
Vyshinsky, A. Ja., 354

Waage, Kristin, 190, 192–93
Wach, Joachim, 19, 32
Waddington, C. H., 10, 19, 32
Wagner, Ingo, 183
Waheed us-zaman, 287
Wahlbäck, Krister, 312
Waikato, University of (NZ), 247–48, 349
Waldahl, Ragnar, 261, 273
Waldenberg, M., 294, 298
Waldo, Dwight, 46, 382
Walker, Jack L., 379, 382
Wall, Roger, 313
Wallas, Graham, 368
Wallensteen, Peter, 313
Waller, D. J., 275
Wallerstein, Immanuel, 122
Wallin, Gunnar, 307, 311
Walter, Oliver, 382
Waltmans, H.J.G., 232, 241
Ward, Norman, 113, 121, 125–26, 128
Ward, Robert E., 16, 23, 32, 275, 281, 372

War of Independence (India/Pakistan), 275
Warsaw, University of (Poland), 292–94
Wasby, Stephen L., 382
Watanabe, Akio, 213–14
Watanuki, Joji, 207, 211–16, 339
Watkins, M. H., 113, 122, 125, 127
Watkins Report (Canada), 122
Watson, J. R., 428
Watson, James, 22, 33
Weaver, Warren, 22, 32
Webb, Beatrice, 355
Webb, Keith, 190, 192
Webb, Lester C., 75, 254
Webb, Sidney, 355
Weber, M., 428
Weber, Max, 10–12, 19, 33, 49, 148, 163, 170
Weber, Werner, 171
Weede, E., 172
Weffort, Francisco Correa, 110
Weibel, Ernest, 424
Weibull, Lennart, 309, 312, 317
Weichelt, Wolfgang, 184
Weil, Eric, 157
Weimar Constitution, 178
Weiner, Myron, 23, 33, 242
Weissberg, H. F., 315
Weizsacjer, 174
Welan, M., 91–92
Welch, Claude E., 285
Weldon, James, 11
Wemegah, Monica, 327
Wennås, Olof, 311
Wertheim, W. F., 242
Wesołowski, W., 298
Westerhult, Bo, 311
Westermarck, Edward, 144
Western Australia, University of, 74, 76–77
West European Politics (UK), 361
Westerståhl, Jorgen, 303, 306–7, 309–10, 315–17, 326, 424
Westin, Alan, 372
West Virginia, University of (US), 84
Wettergren, Anders, 306, 310, 316, 326
Wewerka, W., 338
Wheare, Kenneth C., 74–75
Whitaker, Reginald, 129
White, Harrison C., 14, 22, 33
White, Leonard D., 46, 284, 370
White, R. K., 354
Whitlam, E. G., 83
Whittington, Michael, 126, 129
Wiatr, E., 337, 339

Wiatr, Jerzy, 44, 46, 50, 293–95, 297–98
Wibble, Jan, 310
Wiberg, H., 269
Wicha, B., 91–92
Wickleus, Jan Åse, 310
Widder, H., 91–92
Widerszpil, Stanisław, 183, 297–98
Wiener, Norbert, 14, 22, 33
Wieslander, Hans, 303
Wigny, P., 97
Wiklund, Claes, 312, 314, 318
Wilcox, Wayne, 284
Wildavsky, Aaron B., 22, 359
Wildenmann, Rudolf, 5, 13, 21–22, 33, 50, 170–71
Wilder, E., 354
Wilensky, Harold L., 23, 33
Wilhelmy von Wolff, M., 61
Willequet, J., 96
Williams, John R., 84
Williams, Philip L., 359
Willoughby, W. F., 368
Willoughby, W. W., 368, 376
Wilson, Harold, 361–62
Wilson, James, 33
Wilson, V. Seymour, 121, 125, 128, 420
Wilson, Woodrow, 10, 74, 127, 368, 370, 373, 376, 378, 382
Windhager, F., 91–92
Winter, Søren, 141
Wirth, Louis, 125
Wiseman, H. V., 275, 284
Wissenschaft und Politik Foundation (FRG), 174–75
Witrock, Björn, 303, 306, 310, 316, 326
Włodkowic, Paweł, 291
Wojtasik, L., 298
Wołczew, W., 298
Wolfe, Alan, 46, 54–55, 382
Wolfsohn, Hugo A., 76
Wolin, Sheldon, 17, 25, 33, 52, 55, 126, 373, 378
Wollongong, University of (Australia), 76
Women, study of, 50
"Women in Socialist Society," Scientific Advisory Committee (GDR), 182

Wood, Ellen, 124, 131
Wood, F.L.W., 254–55
Wood, G. A., 423
Wood, Neil, 124, 131
Wood, Robert, 375
Woodall, Jean, 425
Woodward, Peter, 363
Woronitzin, S., 354
Worre, Torben, 141
Wriggins, Howard, 284
Wright, Quincy, 17, 24, 33, 46, 48, 370, 382, 414
Wrocław, University of (Poland), 293
Wu, Teh-Yao, 60
Wyller, Thomas, 256
Wynar, Lubomyr R., 55

Xavier Institute of Social Services (India), 205
Xifra Heras, Jorge, 68, 70, 73, 429

Yakushiji, Taizo, 215
Yale Data Center (US), 364
Yale University (US), 41, 259
Yamamoto, Mitsuru, 213
Yanaga, Chitoshi, 23, 33
Yanarella, E. J., 381
Yano, Toru, 213
Yasuda, Saburo, 215
Ycaza Tigerino, J., 429
Yi dynasty (Korea), 219
Yokoyama Shin, 213
Yonsei University (Japan), 220
Yoshinobu, Yamomoto, 207, 215
Young, Oran R., 22, 33, 55, 59–60, 285, 382
Young, Roland, 378, 382
Young, Walter D., 420
Youth, study of, 50
Yugoslavian political science: associations, 403–4; association's publications, 403–4; class and national dimension of politics, 388–89; concept of politics and political science, 384–87; contemporary political ideas, 395; definition of politics, 384–85; its differentiation and integration, 384, 386; fields, 392–400; history of political theories, 394–95; institutionalized, 383–84, 400–402; interest groups, 397–98; interests and politics, 387–88; international relations, 398–400; introduction, 383; major foci of attention, 387–92; monism and pluralism, 389–92; political parties and sociopolitical organizations, 396–97; political theory, 392–94; relation to Marxism, 386–87; relation to political philosophy, 384; relation to political sociology, 385; research institutionalized, 402–3; results, 404; socialism, 391–92; theory and problems of the state, 395–96; in World War II, 383–84
Yushin Reforms (Korea), 222, 225

Zagreb Faculty of Political Science (Yugoslavia), 384, 400–401
Zagreb Institute for Developing Countries (Yugoslavia), 403
Zakrzewski, W., 297
Zapf, Wolfgang, 13, 21, 27, 33, 171
Zawadzki, S., 50, 293, 298, 303
Zecević, Miodrag, 410
Zeckhauser, Richard, 13
Zeisel, 86
Zeitschrift für Parlamentsfragen (FRG), 171
Zeitschrift für Politik (FRG), 173
Zetterholm, Steffan, 420
Zeuner, 171
Ziegler, J., 50
Zielinsky, 59
Zimmerman, I., 62
Zinnes, Dina A., 376, 425
Zivs, S. L., 352
Znaderin, Lars, 316
Zorbas, A., 61
Zor'kin, V. D., 354
Zrmanovski, Kiro, 407
Žubrinić, Dušan, 409
Zupanov, Josip, 408
Zurich, University of (Switzerland), 331, 334
Zuzanek, Jiri, 33
Zvorikine, A., 354
Zvorykin, A. A., 354
Zychowski, M., 297

CONTRIBUTORS

Juan R. Aguirre Lanari, Agregar, Titular Professor of Constitutional Law at the University of Buenos Aires; former Federal Senator; Secretary, Argentine Political Science Assn.; Argentine ambassador to Venezuela.

Erik Allardt, Research Professor in Social Science, University of Helsinki; Board Chairman, Finnish Research Institute on Peace and Conflict, 1977-78; Chairman, Finnish Political Science Assn., 1971-74; Editor, *Scandinavian Political Studies,* 1977-78; Chairman, Committee on Political Sociology, International Political Science Assn., and International Studies Assn., 1979-.

William G. Andrews, Professor of Political Science, Department Chairman, 1967-71, Dean, 1970-79, State University College at Brockport; SUNY Faculty Exchange Scholar.

Raul Bejar Navarro, National School of Professional Studies, National Autonomous University of Mexico.

Klaus von Beyme, Professor of Political Science, University of Heidelberg; Rector, University of Tübingen, 1971; President, German Political Science Assn., 1973-75; Vice-President, International Political Science Assn., 1973-79; Editor, *German Political Studies* yearbook.

Adolf Bibič, Professor and Chairman of Political Science, Edvard Kardelj University; Editor in Chief, *Teorija in praksa* monthly; Presidency Member, Union of Political Science Assns. of Yugoslavia; Executive Committee Member, International Political Science Assn., since 1976.

German J. Bidart Campos, Titular Professor of Constitutional Law and Political Law at the University of Buenos Aires; member, National Academy of Law and Social Science.

Francisco Casanova Alvarez, National School of Professional Studies, National Autonomous University of Mexico.

Themistocles Brandão Cavalcanti, Emeritus Professor, Federal University of Rio de Janeiro; Director, Institute of Public Law and Political Science, Getulio Vargas Foundation; Retired Judge, Brazilian Supreme Court; President, Brazilian Political Science Assn.; former Executive Committee Member, International Political Science Assn. (Professor Cavalcanti died in March 1980.)

V. E. Chirkin, holder, degree of Juridical Science; Vice-President, Soviet Political Science Assn., 1978-.

Karl W. Deutsch, Stanfield Professor of International Peace, Harvard University; Director, International Institute for Comparative Social Research, Science Center, West Berlin; President, American Political Science Assn., 1969-70; President, 1976-79, Executive Committee member, 1979-, International Political Science Assn.

V. Eliutin, USSR Minister of Higher and Secondary Education.

Nils Elvander, Professor of Political Science, 1967-, University of Uppsala; Editorial Board Member, *Scandinavian Political Studies;* Chairman, Scandinavian Political Science Assn., 1978-81.

Pierre Favre, Professor of Political Science, University of Clermont-Ferrand and C.N.R.S. (National Foundation of Political Sciences).

Jorg Franke, staff member, National Committee of Political Science, and of the Institute for the Theory of State and Law, Academy of Science of the German Democratic Republic.

Daniel Frei, Professor of Political Science, University of Zurich, Director, Swiss Institute of International Studies; former editor, *Annuaire Suisse de Science Politique;* Executive Director, 1974-75, President, Swiss Political Science Assn.; Executive Committee Member, International Political Science Assn.

Øystein Gaasholt, Associate Professor, Institute of Political Science, University of Aarhus.

Alfredo N. Galletti, former Titular Professor of Constitutional History, University of La Plata.

Peter Gerlich, Professor, Dean, Faculty of Economic and Social Sciences, University of Vienna; President, Austrian Political Science Assn., 1975-78.

Ray Goldstein, Senior Lecturer in Political Science, Victoria University of Wellington; National Coordinator, 1975-76, Executive Secretary, 1976-79, New Zealand Political Science Assn.; former Editor, *Political Science;* Council Member, International Political Science Assn., 1979-.

Ólafur Ragnar Grimsson, Lecturer, University of Iceland.

John Halligan, Postdoctoral Fellow, Urban Research Unit, The Australian National University; Foundation Executive Member and Editor of New Zealand Political Studies Assn. newsletter.

Jack Hayward, Professor of Politics, University of Hull; Chairman, 1975–77, Vice-President, 1977–79, President, 1979, Political Studies Assn. of the United Kingdom; Council Member, since 1976, Executive Committee Member, since 1979, International Political Science Assn.

Andries Hoogerwerf, Professor of Policy Studies, University of Technology Twente at Enschede; Chairman, Netherlands Foundation for Research in Politics and Public Administration; Delegate, Council Member of International Political Science Assn., 1973.

Takashi Inoguchi, Associate Professor of Political Science, University of Tokyo; Visiting Professor, Graduate Institute of International Studies, Geneva, Switzerland, 1977–78.

Lian Karp S, National School of Professional Studies, National Autonomous University of Mexico.

A. Saleem Khan, Professor of Political Science, University of Peshawar; President, All-Paskistan Political Science Assn.

Ke-soo Kim, Professor of Political Science, Hankuk University of Foreign Studies; President, Korean Political Science Assn., 1977–79.

Evron Kirkpatrick, Professional Lecturer, Georgetown University; Executive Secretary, American Political Science Assn., 1954–81; President, the American Peace Society, since 1969; Council Member, International Political Science Assn., 1955–67.

Stein Kuhnle, University Lecturer, University of Bergen; Board Member, Norwegian Political Science Assn., 1975–76, Editor of its newsletter *Statsviteren;* Board Member, Nordic Political Science Assn., 1975–76.

Segundo V. Linares Quintana, Agregar former Titular Professor of Political Science and Constitutional Law at the Universities of Buenos Aires and La Plata; President, Argentine Political Science Assn., since 1957; member, Argentine National Academy of Science and the National Academy of Moral and Political Sciences; Vice-President, National Academy of Law and Social Science.

Mario Justo Lopez, Agregar Titular Professor of Political Law, University of Buenos Aires; Member, Argentine National Academy of Science and National Academy of Law and Social Science.

P. C. Mathur, Member, Department of Political Science, University of Rajasthan, Jaipur.

Peter Nannestad, Associate Professor, Institute of Political Science, University of Aarhus.

Iqbal Narain, Member, Department of Political Science, University of Rajasthan, Jaipur.

Kazimierz Opałek, Professor, Institute of Political Science, Director of the Institute, 1969–75, Dean of the Law School, 1954–58, Vice-President, 1962–64, University of Krakow; President, Polish Political Science Assn., 1973–76; Executive Committee Member, International Political Science Assn., since 1973.

Hector Rodolfo Orlandi, Titular Professor of Political Law at the Universities of Buenos Aires and La Plata; Treasurer, Argentine Political Science Association.

André Philippart, Professor, State Institute of Social Studies; Research Fellow, Institute of Sociology, Free University of Brussels; Director, Political Science Institute (Belgium); Director, Scientific Research Administration in the Belgian National Education Ministry; General Secretary, International Political Science Association, 1967–76.

Lidice Aparecida Pontes Maduro, Coordinator of Research, Institute of Public Law and Political Science, Getulio Vargas Foundation.

Karl-Heinz Röder, Professor of Law; Vice-President, National Committee for Political Science of the German Democratic Republic; Deputy-Director, Institute for the Theory of State and Law, Academy of Science of the German Democratic Republic; Member, Editorial Board, *State and Law.*

Olof Ruin, Lars Hierta Professor of Government, Dean, Social Science Faculty, University of Stockholm; Deputy Chancellor of the Swedish Universities, 1978–79; President, Swedish Political Science Association, 1973–76; Editor, *Scandinavian Political Studies,* 1969–70; Executive Committee Member, European Consortium for Political Research, 1976–.

William V. Smirnov, General Secretary, Soviet Political Science Association, since 1977.

Graëme Starr, Senior Lecturer, University of New England, former Research Director, Liberal Party of Australia.

Michael Stein, Professor of Political Science, Department Chairman, 1980–83, McMaster University, Hamilton.

Emmerich Talos, Assistant, Institute for Political Science, University of Vienna; Editor, *Österreichische Zeitschrift für Politik wissenschaft,* since 1975; Treasurer, Austrian Political Science Association, 1975–78.

Colin Tatz, Professor of Politics, University of New England; former President, Australasian Political Studies Association; Council and Executive Member, Australian Institute of Aboriginal Studies.

John E. Trent, Professor, University of Ottawa; Executive Director, Sosicl Science Federation of Canada; General Secretary, International Political Science Association, 1976–.

Karl Ucakar, Assistant, Institute for Political Science, University of Vienna; Editor, *Osterreichische Zeitschrift für Politik wissenschaft,* since 1975; Treasurer, Austrian Political Science Association, 1973–74.

Monica Wemegah, Researcher, United Nations University, Tokyo; Executive Secretary, 1974–77, Executive Committee Member, since 1977, Swiss Political Science Association.

About the Editor

WILLIAM G. ANDREWS is Professor of Political Science at the State University of New York at Brockport and S.U.N.Y. Faculty Exchange Scholar. Among his earlier publications are *Constitutions and Constitutionalism, European Political Institutions, The Politics of International Crises,* and *The Fifth Republic at Twenty*.